TENTH EDITION

Sensation and Perception

E. Bruce Goldstein
University of Pittsburgh
University of Arizona

and

James R. Brockmole
University of Notre Dame

CENGAGE
Learning·

Australia • Brazil • Mexico • Singapore • United Kingdom • United States

CENGAGE
Learning®

Sensation and Perception, **Tenth Edition**
E. Bruce Goldstein and James R. Brockmole

Product Director: Jon-David Hague

Product Manager: Timothy Matray

Content Developer: Shannon LeMay-Finn

Media Developer: Kyra Kane

Product Assistant: Adrienne McCrory

Marketing Manager: Melissa Larmon

Content Project Manager: Michelle Clark

Art Director: Vernon Boes

Manufacturing Planner: Karen Hunt

Production Service: Jill Traut, MPS Limited

Photo and Text Researcher: Lumina Datamatics

Copy Editor: Margaret Tropp

Illustrator: MPS Limited

Text Designer: Ellen Pettengell

Cover Designer: Denise Davidson

Cover Image: Buddy Mays/Encyclopedia/Corbis

Compositor: MPS Limited

For product information and technology assistance, contact us at
Cengage Learning Customer & Sales Support, 1-800-354-9706

For permission to use material from this text or product,
submit all requests online at **www.cengage.com/permissions**
Further permissions questions can be e-mailed to
permissionrequest@cengage.com

Library of Congress Control Number: 2015951380

Student Edition:
ISBN: 978-1-305-58029-9

Loose-leaf Edition:
ISBN: 978-1-305-67404-2

Cengage Learning
20 Channel Center Street
Boston, MA 02210
USA

Cengage Learning is a leading provider of customized learning solutions with employees residing in nearly 40 different countries and sales in more than 125 countries around the world. Find your local representative at **www.cengage.com**

Cengage Learning products are represented in Canada by Nelson Education, Ltd.

To learn more about Cengage Learning Solutions, visit **www.cengage.com**

Purchase any of our products at your local college store or at our preferred online store **www.cengagebrain.com**

Printed in Canada
Print Number: 01   Print Year: 2016

To Barbara: It's been a long and winding road, but we made it all the way to the 10th edition! Thank you for your unwavering love and support through all of the editions of this book.

I also dedicate this book to the editors I have had along the way, especially Ken King, who convinced me to write the book in 1976, and also those that followed: Marianne Taflinger, Jaime Perkins, and Tim Matray. Thank you all, for believing in my book and supporting its creation.

Finally, I dedicate this book to the memory of Anne Draus (1952–2014) of Scratchgravel Publishing Services, whose caring about books was evident as she shepherded many previous editions of this book from manuscript to finished book. But Anne was more than a production service. She was a warm, caring person, who is greatly missed.

Bruce Goldstein

To Jessica, for her smile, laughter, hugs, and secret-recipe spaghetti sauce.

James Brockmole

About the Authors

E. BRUCE GOLDSTEIN is Associate Professor Emeritus of Psychology at the University of Pittsburgh and Adjunct Professor of Psychology at the University of Arizona. He has received the Chancellor's Distinguished Teaching Award from the University of Pittsburgh for his classroom teaching and textbook writing. He received his bachelor's degree in chemical engineering from Tufts University and his PhD in experimental psychology from Brown University; he was a postdoctoral fellow in the Biology Department at Harvard University before joining the faculty at the University of Pittsburgh. Bruce has published papers on a wide variety of topics, including retinal and cortical physiology, visual attention, and the perception of pictures. He is the author of *Cognitive Psychology: Connecting Mind, Research, and Everyday Experience*, 4th Edition (Cengage, 2015), and the editor of the *Blackwell Handbook of Perception* (Blackwell, 2001) and the two-volume *Sage Encyclopedia of Perception* (Sage, 2010).

JAMES R. BROCKMOLE is Associate Professor of Psychology at the University of Notre Dame. He received his bachelor's degrees in psychology and sociology from Notre Dame and his master's and doctoral degrees in cognitive psychology at the University of Illinois at Urbana-Champaign. He was a postdoctoral research associate at Michigan State University before joining the faculty in the School of Philosophy, Psychology, and Language Sciences at the University of Edinburgh. He returned to Notre Dame in 2009 to teach and conduct research at his alma mater. Jim's research focuses on the representation of visual information in the mind and brain, the allocation and control of visual attention, and the many interactions between perception, memory, and action. He edited *The Visual World in Memory* (Psychology Press, 2008) and *Binding*, a special issue of *Visual Cognition* (Psychology Press, 2009), and has served as the associate editor of the journals *Attention, Perception, & Psychophysics* (Springer/Psychonomic Society) and the *Journal of Experimental Psychology: Human Perception and Performance* (American Psychological Association).

Brief Contents

1 Introduction to Perception 3

2 The Beginnings of the Perceptual Process 21

3 Neural Processing 49

4 Cortical Organization 73

5 Perceiving Objects and Scenes 93

6 Visual Attention 125

7 Taking Action 149

8 Perceiving Motion 171

9 Perceiving Color 195

10 Perceiving Depth and Size 227

11 Hearing 259

12 Hearing II: Location and Organization 289

13 Speech Perception 317

14 The Cutaneous Senses 337

15 The Chemical Senses 361

APPENDIX

A Methods of Adjustment and Constant Stimuli 384
B The Difference Threshold 385
C Magnitude Estimation and the Power Function 386
D The Signal Detection Approach 388

Glossary 394
References 413
Name Index 438
Subject Index 445

Contents

CHAPTER 1

Introduction to Perception   3

Why Read This Book?   4
The Perceptual Process   5
But What About "Sensation"?   5
Distal and Proximal Stimuli (Steps 1 and 2)   6
Receptor Processes (Step 3)   7
Neural Processing (Step 4)   7
Behavioral Responses (Steps 5–7)   8
Knowledge   9
DEMONSTRATION | Perceiving a Picture   9
Studying the Perceptual Process   10
The Two "Stimulus" Relationships (A and B)   11
The Physiology–Perception Relationship (C)   12
Cognitive Influences on Perception   12
TEST YOURSELF 1.1   13
Measuring Perception   13
Gustav Fechner Introduces Methods to Measure Thresholds   13
METHOD | Method of Limits   14
Five Questions About the Perceptual World   15
METHOD | Magnitude Estimation   15
Something to Consider: Why Is the Difference Between Physical and Perceptual Important?   17
TEST YOURSELF 1.2   18
THINK ABOUT IT   19
KEY TERMS   19

CHAPTER 2

The Beginning of the Perceptual Process   21

Starting at the Beginning   21
Light, the Eye, and the Visual Receptors   22
Light: The Stimulus for Vision   22
The Eye   22
DEMONSTRATION | Becoming Aware of the Blind Spot   24
DEMONSTRATION | Filling In the Blind Spot   25
Focusing Light Onto the Receptors   25
DEMONSTRATION | Becoming Aware of What Is in Focus   26
Receptors and Perception   27
Transforming Light Energy Into Electrical Energy   27
Adapting to the Dark   28
METHOD | Measuring the Dark Adaptation Curve   28
Spectral Sensitivity   31
METHOD | Measuring a Spectral Sensitivity Curve   31
TEST YOURSELF 2.1   33
Electrical Signals in Neurons   33
Recording Electrical Signals in Neurons   34
METHOD | The Setup for Recording From a Single Neuron   34
Basic Properties of Action Potentials   34
Chemical Basis of Action Potentials   36
Transmitting Information Across a Gap   37
Neural Convergence and Perception   39
Convergence Causes the Rods to Be More Sensitive Than the Cones   39
Lack of Convergence Causes the Cones to Have Better Acuity Than the Rods   41
DEMONSTRATION | Foveal Versus Peripheral Acuity   41
Something to Consider: Early Events Are Powerful   42
Developmental Dimension: Infant Visual Acuity   43

METHOD | Preferential Looking   44
TEST YOURSELF 2.2   45
THINK ABOUT IT   46
KEY TERMS   47

CHAPTER 3

Neural Processing   49

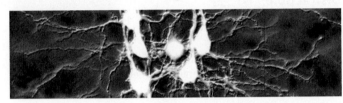

Inhibitory Processes in the Retina   50
Lateral Inhibition in the *Limulus*   50
Using Lateral Inhibition to Explain Perception   51
Problems with the Lateral Inhibition Explanations of the Chevreul Illusion and the Hermann Grid   54
TEST YOURSELF 3.1   55

Processing From Retina to Visual Cortex and Beyond   55
Responding of Single Fibers in the Optic Nerve   56
Hubel and Wiesel's Rationale for Studying Receptive Fields   58
METHOD | Presenting Stimuli to Determine Receptive Fields   58
Receptive Fields of Neurons in the Visual Cortex   60

Do Feature Detectors Play a Role in Perception?   62
Selective Adaptation   62
METHOD | Psychophysical Measurement of the Effect of Selective Adaptation to Orientation   62
Selective Rearing   63

Higher-Level Neurons   65

Sensory Coding   65
Something to Consider: "Flexible" Receptive Fields   68
TEST YOURSELF 3.2   69
THINK ABOUT IT   70
KEY TERMS   70

CHAPTER 4

Cortical Organization   73

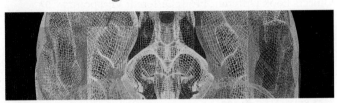

Spatial Organization in the Visual Cortex   74
The Neural Map on the Striate Cortex (Area V1)   74
METHOD | Brain Imaging   75
DEMONSTRATION | Cortical Magnification of Your Finger   76
The Cortex Is Organized in Columns   76
How Do Orientation-Sensitive Neurons Respond to a Scene?   78
TEST YOURSELF 4.1   79

Pathways for What, Where, and How   79
Streams for Information About What and Where   79
METHOD | Brain Ablation   79
Streams for Information About What and How   81
METHOD | Double Dissociations in Neuropsychology   81

Modularity   83
Face Neurons in the Monkey's IT Cortex   83
The Fusiform Face Area in Humans   83
Areas for Places and Bodies in Humans   84

Distributed Representation   84
Two Experiments That Demonstrate Distributed Representation   84
Distributed Representation of Multidimensional Stimuli   86

Where Perception Meets Memory   86
Something to Consider: The Mind–Body Problem   88
Developmental Dimension: Experience and Neural Responding   89
Experiences Can Shape Neural Firing   89
The Expertise Hypothesis   89
TEST YOURSELF 4.2   90
THINK ABOUT IT   90
KEY TERMS   91

CHAPTER 5

Perceiving Objects and Scenes 93

DEMONSTRATION | Perceptual Puzzles in a Scene 93

Why Is It So Difficult to Design a Perceiving Machine? 96
The Stimulus on the Receptors Is Ambiguous 96
Objects Can Be Hidden or Blurred 97
Objects Look Different From Different Viewpoints 97

Perceptual Organization 98
The Gestalt Approach to Perceptual Grouping 98
Gestalt Principles of Perceptual Organization 100
Perceptual Segregation 102
DEMONSTRATION | Finding Faces in a Landscape 105
TEST YOURSELF 5.1 106

Perceiving Scenes and Objects in Scenes 106
Perceiving the Gist of a Scene 107
METHOD | Using a Mask to Achieve Brief Stimulus Presentations 107
Regularities in the Environment: Information for Perceiving 108
DEMONSTRATION | Visualizing Scenes and Objects 109
The Role of Inference in Perception 111
TEST YOURSELF 5.2 112

Connecting Neural Activity and Object/Scene Perception 113
Brain Responses to Perceiving Faces and Places 113
Spotlight on the Parahippocampal Place Area 113
Neural Mind Reading 114
METHOD | Neural Mind Reading 114
Something to Consider: Are Faces Special? 116

Developmental Dimension: Infant Face Perception 119
TEST YOURSELF 5.3 120
THINK ABOUT IT 120
KEY TERMS 122

CHAPTER 6

Visual Attention 125

Scanning a Scene 126
DEMONSTRATION | Looking for a Face in the Crowd 126

What Directs Our Attention? 127
Visual Salience 127
DEMONSTRATION | Attentional Capture 127
Cognitive Factors 128

What Are the Benefits of Attention? 130
Attention Speeds Responding 130
METHOD | Precueing 130
Attention Can Influence Appearance 132
Attention Can Influence Physiological Responding 133
TEST YOURSELF 6.1 135

Attention and Experiencing a Coherent World 136
Why Is Binding Necessary? 136
Feature Integration Theory 136
DEMONSTRATION | Searching for Conjunctions 138

What Happens When We Don't Attend? 138
Inattentional Blindness 138
Change Blindness 139
DEMONSTRATION | Change Detection 139
Is Attention Necessary for Perceiving Scenes? 140

Distraction 141
Distraction and Task Characteristics 141
Attention and Perceptual Load 142
Something to Consider: Distracted Driving 143

Developmental Dimension: Attention and Perceptual Completion 144
METHOD | Habituation 145
TEST YOURSELF 6.2 146
THINK ABOUT IT 147
KEY TERMS 147

CHAPTER 7

Taking Action 149

The Ecological Approach to Perception 149
The Moving Observer Creates Information in the Environment 150
Self-Produced Information 151
The Senses Do Not Work in Isolation 152
DEMONSTRATION | Keeping Your Balance 152

Staying on Course: Walking and Driving 153
Walking 153
Driving a Car 154

Wayfinding 155
The Importance of Landmarks 155
The Brain's "GPS" 157
Individual Differences in Wayfinding 159
TEST YOURSELF 7.1 160

Acting on Objects 160
Affordances: What Objects Are Used For 160
The Physiology of Reaching and Grasping 161
Observing Other People's Actions 163
Mirroring Others' Actions in the Brain 163
Predicting People's Intentions 164
Something to Consider: Action-Based Accounts of Perception 166
Developmental Dimension: Imitating Actions 167
TEST YOURSELF 7.2 168
THINK ABOUT IT 169
KEY TERMS 169

CHAPTER 8

Perceiving Motion 171

Functions of Motion Perception 171
Motion Provides Information About Objects 171
Motion Attracts Attention 173
Motion Helps Us Understand Events in Our Environment 173
Life Without Motion Perception 174
Studying Motion Perception 174
When Do We Perceive Motion? 174
Comparing Real and Apparent Motion 175
What We Want to Explain 176
Motion Perception: Information in the Environment 176
Motion Perception: Retina/Eye Information 177
The Reichardt Detector 178
Corollary Discharge Theory 179
DEMONSTRATION | Eliminating the Image Displacement Signal With an Afterimage 180
DEMONSTRATION | Seeing Motion by Pushing on Your Eyelid 180
TEST YOURSELF 8.1 182
Motion Perception and the Brain 182
The Movement Area of the Brain 182
Effects of Lesioning, Deactivating, and Stimulating 183
METHOD | Transcranial Magnetic Stimulation (TMS) 183
METHOD | Microstimulation 184
Motion from a Single Neuron's Point of View 184
DEMONSTRATION | Movement of a Bar Across an Aperture 185
Motion and the Human Body 186
Apparent Motion of the Body 186
Motion of Point-Light Walkers 187

Something to Consider: Motion Responses to Still Pictures 189
Developmental Dimension: Biological Motion Perception in Newborns 191
TEST YOURSELF 8.2 192
THINK ABOUT IT 192
KEY TERMS 193

CHAPTER 9

Perceiving Color 195

Functions of Color Perception 196
Color and Light 196
Reflectance and Transmission 197
Color Mixing 198
Perceptual Dimensions of Color 200
TEST YOURSELF 9.1 201
The Trichromatic Theory of Color Vision 201
Color-Matching Evidence for Trichromatic Theory 202
METHOD | Color Matching 202
Physiological Evidence for Trichromatic Theory 203
Are Three Receptor Mechanisms Necessary for Color Vision? 204
Opponent-Process Theory of Color Vision 206
Hering's Phenomenological Evidence for Opponent-Process Theory 206
Hurvich and Jameson's Psychophysical Measurements of the Opponent Mechanisms 207
DEMONSTRATION | Afterimages 207
METHOD | Hue Cancellation 207
Physiological Evidence for Opponent-Process Theory 209
How Opponent Responding Can Be Created by Three Types of Receptors 209
Color in the Cortex 210
Is There a Single Color Center in the Cortex? 210
Types of Opponent Neurons in the Cortex 211
Color Deficiency 212
Monochromatism 212
Dichromatism 212
TEST YOURSELF 9.2 213
Color in a Dynamic World 214
Color Constancy 214
DEMONSTRATION | Adapting to Red 215
DEMONSTRATION | Color and the Surroundings 216
Lightness Constancy 217
DEMONSTRATION | The Penumbra and Lightness Perception 219

DEMONSTRATION | Perceiving Lightness at a Corner **219**

Something to Consider: Color Is a Creation of the Nervous System **219**

Developmental Dimension: Infant Color Vision **222**

TEST YOURSELF 9.3 **223**

THINK ABOUT IT **223**

KEY TERMS **224**

CHAPTER 10

Perceiving Depth and Size 227

Perceiving Depth **227**

Oculomotor Cues **228**

DEMONSTRATION | Feelings in Your Eyes **229**

Monocular Cues **229**

Pictorial Cues **229**

Motion-Produced Cues **232**

DEMONSTRATION | Deletion and Accretion **233**

Binocular Depth Information **233**

DEMONSTRATION | Two Eyes: Two Viewpoints **233**

Seeing Depth With Two Eyes **234**

Binocular Disparity **235**

Disparity (Geometrical) Creates Stereopsis (Perceptual) **239**

The Correspondence Problem **240**

The Physiology of Binocular Depth Perception **242**

TEST YOURSELF 10.1 **243**

Perceiving Size **243**

The Holway and Boring Experiment **244**

Size Constancy **246**

DEMONSTRATION | Perceiving Size at a Distance **247**

DEMONSTRATION | Size–Distance Scaling and Emmert's Law **247**

Illusions of Depth and Size **248**

The Müller-Lyer Illusion **248**

DEMONSTRATION | The Müller-Lyer Illusion With Books **250**

The Ponzo Illusion **250**

The Ames Room **251**

The Moon Illusion **252**

Something to Consider: Depth Information Across Species **253**

Developmental Dimension: Infant Depth Perception **254**

Binocular Disparity **254**

Pictorial Cues **255**

METHOD | Preferential Reaching **256**

TEST YOURSELF 10.2 **256**

THINK ABOUT IT **257**

KEY TERMS **257**

CHAPTER 11

Hearing 259

The Perceptual Process for Hearing **260**

Physical Aspects of Sound **260**

Sound as Pressure Changes **260**

Pure Tones **261**

METHOD | Using Decibels to Shrink Large Ranges of Pressures **262**

Complex Tones and Frequency Spectra **263**

Perceptual Aspects of Sound **264**

Thresholds and Loudness **264**

Pitch **266**

Timbre **267**

TEST YOURSELF 11.1 **267**

From Pressure Changes to Electricity **268**

The Outer Ear **268**

The Middle Ear **268**

The Inner Ear **269**

How Frequency Is Represented in the Auditory Nerve **272**

Békésy Discovers How the Basilar Membrane Vibrates **272**

The Cochlea Functions as a Filter **273**

METHOD | Neural Frequency Tuning Curves **274**

Returning to the Outer Hair Cells: The Cochlear Amplifier **274**

TEST YOURSELF 11.2 **276**

The Physiology of Pitch Perception **276**

Place and Pitch **276**

Temporal Information and Pitch **277**

Place and Pitch (Again) **277**

Problems Remaining to Be Solved **278**

The Pathway to the Brain **278**

Pitch and the Brain **279**

Hearing Loss **281**

Presbycusis **281**

Noise-Induced Hearing Loss **282**

Hidden Hearing Loss **282**

Something to Consider: Cochlear Implants **283**

Developmental Dimension: Infant Hearing **284**

Thresholds and the Audibility Curve **284**

Recognizing Their Mother's Voice **284**

TEST YOURSELF 11.3 **285**

THINK ABOUT IT **285**

KEY TERMS **285**

CHAPTER 12

Hearing II: Location and Organization 289

Location

Auditory Localization 290
Binaural Cues for Sound Localization 290
Monaural Cue for Localization 292
The Physiology of Auditory Localization 294
The Jeffress Neural Coincidence Model 294
Broad ITD Tuning Curves in Mammals 295
Cortical Mechanisms of Localization 296
Hearing Inside Rooms 298
Perceiving Two Sounds That Reach the Ears at Different Times 299
Architectural Acoustics 299
TEST YOURSELF 12.1 301

Organization

The Auditory Scene: Separating Sound Sources 301
Location 302
Onset Time 302
Timbre and Pitch 302
Auditory Continuity 304
Experience 304
Musical Organization: Melody 304
What Is Melody? 305
Phrases 305
Grouping 305
Tonality 306
METHOD | Event-Related Potential in Language 307
Expectation 308
Musical Organization: Rhythm 309
What Is Rhythm? 309
The Beat 309
Meter 310
METHOD | Head-Turning Preference Procedure 310
Something to Consider: Connections Between Hearing and Vision 312
Hearing and Vision: Perceptions 312
Hearing and Vision: Physiology 312
TEST YOURSELF 12.2 314
THINK ABOUT IT 314
KEY TERMS 315

CHAPTER 13

Speech Perception 317

The Speech Stimulus 317
The Acoustic Signal 318
Basic Units of Speech 319
The Variability of the Acoustic Signal 320
Variability From Context 320
Variability From Different Speakers 321
Perceiving Phonemes 322
Categorical Perception 322
Information Provided by the Face 322
Information From Our Knowledge of Language 324
TEST YOURSELF 13.1 324
Perceiving Words and Sentences 325
Perceiving Words in Sentences 325
DEMONSTRATION | Perceiving Degraded Sentences 325
Perceiving Breaks Between Sequences of Words 325
DEMONSTRATION | Organizing Strings of Sounds 326
Perceiving Degraded Speech 327
Speech Perception and the Brain 328
Something to Consider: Speech Perception and Action 331
Developmental Dimension: Infant Speech Perception 332
The Categorical Perception of Phonemes 332
Learning the Sounds of a Language 333
TEST YOURSELF 13.2 334
THINK ABOUT IT 334
KEY TERMS 335

CHAPTER 14

The Cutaneous Senses 337

Perception by the Skin and Hands

Overview of the Cutaneous System 338
The Skin 338
Mechanoreceptors 338
Pathways From Skin to Cortex 340
The Somatosensory Cortex 340

The Plasticity of Cortical Body Maps 342

Perceiving Details 342

METHOD | Measuring Tactile Acuity 343

Receptor Mechanisms for Tactile Acuity 343

DEMONSTRATION | Comparing Two-Point
Thresholds 344

Cortical Mechanisms for Tactile Acuity 344

Perceiving Vibration and Texture 344

Vibration of the Skin 345

Surface Texture 345

DEMONSTRATION | Perceiving Texture With
a Pen 347

Perceiving Objects 347

DEMONSTRATION | Identifying Objects 347

Identifying Objects by Haptic Exploration 348

The Cortical Physiology of Tactile Object Perception 348

TEST YOURSELF 14.1 351

Pain Perception

The Gate Control Model of Pain 351

Top-Down Processes 353

Expectation 353

Attention 353

Emotions 354

The Brain and Pain 354

Brain Areas 355

Chemicals and the Brain 355

Observing Pain in Others 357

Something to Consider: Social Pain and Physical
Pain 357

TEST YOURSELF 14.2 358

THINK ABOUT IT 359

KEY TERMS 359

CHAPTER 15

The Chemical Senses 361

Taste 362

Taste Quality 362

Basic Taste Qualities 362

Connections Between Taste Quality and a Substance's
Effect 362

The Neural Code for Taste Quality 363

Structure of the Taste System 363

Population Coding 364

Specificity Coding 365

Individual Differences in Taste 367

TEST YOURSELF 15.1 368

Olfaction and Flavor

The Functions of Olfaction 368

Olfactory Abilities 369

Detecting Odors 369

METHOD | Measuring the Detection Threshold 369

Discriminating Between Odors 370

Identifying Odors 370

DEMONSTRATION | Naming and Odor
Identification 370

Individual Differences in Olfaction 370

Analyzing Odorants: The Mucosa and Olfactory Bulb 371

The Puzzle of Olfactory Quality 371

The Olfactory Mucosa 372

How Olfactory Receptor Neurons Respond
to Odorants 373

METHOD | Calcium Imaging 373

The Search for Order in the Olfactory Bulb 374

METHOD | Optical Imaging 374

METHOD | The 2-Deoxyglucose Technique 375

Representing Odors in the Cortex 375

How Odorants Are Represented in the
Piriform Cortex 376

How Odor Objects Are Represented 376

TEST YOURSELF 15.2 378

The Perception of Flavor 378

DEMONSTRATION | "Tasting" With and Without
the Nose 378

Taste and Olfaction Meet in the Mouth
and Nose 378

Taste and Olfaction Meet in the Nervous System 379

Flavor Is Influenced by Cognitive Factors 380

Flavor Is Influenced by Food Intake: Sensory-Specific
Satiety 380

Something to Consider: The *Proust* Effect: Memories, Emotions,
and Smell 381

Developmental Dimension: Infant Chemical Sensitivity 382

TEST YOURSELF 15.3 383

THINK ABOUT IT 383

KEY TERMS 383

APPENDIX

A Methods of Adjustment
and Constant Stimuli 384

B The Difference Threshold 385

C Magnitude Estimation and the
Power Function 386

D   The Signal Detection
    Approach   388
A Signal Detection Experiment   388
The Basic Experiment   389
Payoffs   389
What Does the ROC Curve Tell Us?   390
Signal Detection Theory   391
Signal and Noise   391

Probability Distributions   391
The Criterion   391
The Effect of Sensitivity on the ROC Curve   392

Glossary   394

References   413

Name Index   438

Subject Index   445

Demonstrations

Perceiving a Picture   9

Becoming Aware of the Blind Spot   24

Filling In the Blind Spot   25

Becoming Aware of What Is in Focus   26

Foveal Versus Peripheral Acuity   41

Cortical Magnification of Your Finger   76

Perceptual Puzzles in a Scene   93

Finding Faces in a Landscape   105

Visualizing Scenes and Objects   109

Looking for a Face in the Crowd   126

Attentional Capture   127

Searching for Conjunctions   138

Change Detection   139

Keeping Your Balance   152

Eliminating the Image Displacement Signal With an Afterimage   180

Seeing Motion by Pushing on Your Eyelid   180

Movement of a Bar Across an Aperture   185

Afterimages   207

Adapting to Red   215

Color and the Surroundings   216

The Penumbra and Lightness Perception   219

Perceiving Lightness at a Corner   219

Feelings in Your Eyes   229

Deletion and Accretion   233

Two Eyes: Two Viewpoints   233

Perceiving Size at a Distance   247

Size–Distance Scaling and Emmert's Law   247

The Müller-Lyer Illusion With Books   250

Perceiving Degraded Sentences   325

Organizing Strings of Sounds   326

Comparing Two-Point Thresholds   344

Perceiving Texture With a Pen   347

Identifying Objects   347

Naming and Odor Identification   370

"Tasting" With and Without the Nose   378

Methods

Method of Limits   14

Magnitude Estimation   15

Measuring the Dark Adaptation Curve   28

Measuring a Spectral Sensitivity Curve   31

The Setup for Recording From a Single Neuron   34

Preferential Looking   44

Presenting Stimuli to Determine Receptive Fields   58

Psychophysical Measurement of the Effect of Selective
    Adaptation to Orientation   62

Brain Imaging   75

Brain Ablation   79

Double Dissociations in Neuropsychology   81

Using a Mask to Achieve Brief Stimulus Presentations   107

Neural Mind Reading   114

Precueing   130

Habituation   145

Transcranial Magnetic Stimulation (TMS)   183

Microstimulation   184

Color Matching   202

Hue Cancellation   207

Preferential Reaching   256

Using Decibels to Shrink Large Ranges of Pressures   262

Neural Frequency Tuning Curves   274

Event-Related Potential in Language   307

Head-Turning Preference Procedure   310

Measuring Tactile Acuity   343

Measuring the Detection Threshold   369

Calcium Imaging   373

Optical Imaging   374

The 2-Deoxyglucose Technique   375

Preface

by Bruce Goldstein

When I first began working on this book in 1976, Hubel and Wiesel were studying feature detectors in the striate cortex and were five years away from receiving their Nobel Prize; one of the hottest new discoveries in perception was that the response properties of neurons in young kittens could be influenced by experience; and little was known about the mechanisms responsible for odor perception. Today, specialized areas in the visual cortex have been mapped using brain imaging; neurons have been identified throughout the cortex that respond to complex visual stimuli; and researchers are exploring not only the mechanisms for perceiving objects but also mechanisms linking our perception of objects to how we physically interact with them. Additionally, the idea that experience can shape both perception and neural responding has been widely embraced and expanded beyond young kittens to include adult humans, and genetic methods and neural recording have revealed specialized olfactory receptors and cortical mechanisms of smell and taste.

But some things haven't changed. Teachers still stand in front of classrooms to teach students about perception, and students still read textbooks that reinforce what they are learning in the classroom. Another thing that hasn't changed is that teachers prefer texts that are easy for students to read, that present both classic studies and up-to-date research, and that present both the facts of perception and overarching themes and principles.

When I began teaching perception, I looked at the textbooks that were available and was disappointed, because none of them seemed to be written for students. They presented "the facts," but not in a way that seemed very interesting or inviting. I therefore wrote the first edition of *Sensation and Perception*, which came out in 1980, with the idea of involving students in their study of perception by presenting the material as a story. The story is a fascinating one, because it is a narrative of one discovery following from another, a scientific "whodunit" in which the goal is to uncover the hidden mechanisms responsible for our ability to perceive.

Though my goal in writing this book has been to tell a story, this is, after all, a textbook designed for teaching. So in addition to presenting the story of perceptual research, this book also contains a number of features, most of which appeared in the ninth edition, that are designed to highlight specific material and to help students learn.

Features

- **Demonstrations.** *Demonstrations* have been a popular feature of this book for many editions. They are integrated into the flow of the text and are easy enough to be carried out with little trouble, thereby maximizing the probability that students will do them. See list on page xiv.

- **Methods.** It is important not only to present the facts of perception, but also to make students aware of how these facts were obtained. Highlighted *Methods* sections, which are integrated into the ongoing discussion, emphasize the importance of methods, and the highlighting makes it easier to refer back to them when referenced later in the book. See list on page xv.

- **Something to Consider.** This end-of-chapter feature offers the opportunity to consider especially interesting phenomena and new findings. Some examples: Why Is the Difference Between Physical and Perceptual Important? (Chapter 1); Distracted Driving (Chapter 6); Connections Between Hearing and Vision (Chapter 12); The Proust Effect (Chapter 15).

- **Developmental Dimensions**. The *Developmental Dimension* feature, which was introduced in the ninth edition, has proven to be popular and so has been continued and slightly expanded in this edition. This feature, which appears at the end of chapters, focuses on perception in infants and young children.

- **Test Yourself.** *Test Yourself* questions appear in the middle and at the end of each chapter. These questions are broad enough that students have to unpack the questions themselves, thereby making students more active participants in their studying.

- **Think About It.** The *Think About It* section at the end of each chapter poses questions that require students to apply what they have learned and that take them beyond the material in the chapter.

- **Full-Color Illustrations.** Perception, of all subjects, should be illustrated in color, so I was especially pleased when in 2007 the seventh edition became "full-color." What pleases me about the illustrations is not only how beautiful the color looks, but how well it serves pedagogy. There are more than 500 figures in this edition, including 85 new to this edition.

- **MindTap** for Sensation and Perception engages and empowers students to produce their best work—consistently. For those courses that include MindTap, the textbook is supplemented with videos, activities, apps, and much more. MindTap creates a unique learning path that fosters increased comprehension and efficiency.

For students:

- MindTap delivers real-world relevance with activities and assignments that help students build critical thinking and analytic skills that will transfer to other courses and their professional lives.
- MindTap helps students stay organized and efficient with a single destination that reflects what's important to the instructor, along with the tools students need to master the content.
- MindTap empowers and motivates students with information that shows where they stand at all times—both individually and compared to the highest performers in class.

Additionally, for instructors, MindTap allows you to:

- Control what content students see and when they see it with a learning path that can be used as is, or matched to your syllabus exactly.
- Create a unique learning path of relevant readings, multimedia, and activities that move students up the learning taxonomy from basic knowledge and comprehension to analysis, application, and critical thinking.
- Integrate your own content into the MindTap Reader, using your own documents or pulling from sources like RSS feeds, YouTube videos, websites, Google Docs, and more.
- Use powerful analytics and reports that provide a snapshot of class progress, time in course, engagement, and completion.

In addition to the benefits of the platform, MindTap for Sensation and Perception includes:

- **Exploration.** The MindTap *Exploration* feature enables students to view experimental stimuli, perceptual demonstrations, and short film clips about the research being discussed. These features have been updated in this edition, and new items have been added to the labs carried over from the ninth edition. Most of these items have been generously provided by researchers in vision, hearing, and perceptual development.

Changes in This Edition

This edition offers many improvements in organization, designed to make the text read more smoothly and flow more logically. In addition, each chapter has been updated to highlight new advances in the field, supported by over 190 new references. Here are a few examples of new material that has been added in this edition.

Perceptual Principles (Chapters 1–4)

- New discussion emphasizing the difference between physical and perceptual
- New research that questions the lateral inhibition explanation of the Chevreul and Hermann grid illusions (Geier & Hudach, 2010)
- Distributed mapping of visual categories across the cortex (Huth et al., 2012)

Visual Qualities (Chapters 5–10: Object and Scene; Attention, Action, Motion, Color, Depth, and Size)

- Bayesian inference and object perception (Geisler, 2011; Tanenbaum et al., 2011)
- Lateralization of FFA response to faces (Meng et al., 2012)
- Parahippocampal Place Area responds to sense of 3D space (Mullally & Maguire, 2011)
- Attention synchronizes neural activity in the cortex (Baldauf & Desimone, 2014; Bosman et al., 2012)
- Distracted driving (Hickman & Hanowski, 2012; Strayer et al., 2013)
- 2014 Nobel Prize research on the brain's GPS (O'Keefe, Moser and Moser's research; Moser, 2014)
- Revised description of Reichardt motion detectors
- Expanded discussion of Newton's color experiments and history of trichromatic and opponent-process theories
- Discussion of crossed and uncrossed disparity

Hearing (Chapters 11–12: Pitch, Location, Organization)

- Physiology of pitch perception updated to reflect shift in thinking from Bekesy place theory to filtering action of basilar membrane, and emphasis on temporal factors
- Pitch perception of resolved and unresolved harmonics (Oxenham, 2013)
- Localization of pitch in auditory cortex (Norman-Haignere et al., 2013)
- Hidden hearing loss (Kujawa & Liberman, 2009; Plack et al., 2014)
- New section on music perception, emphasizing rhythm, musical organization, and motor response to music (Chen et al., 2008; Grahn & Rowe, 2009; Krumhansl, 1985; Patel et al., 1996)

Speech (Chapter 13)

- Perceiving degraded speech (Davis et al., 2005)
- Cortical response to phonemes and phonetic features (Mesgarani et al., 2014)
- Link between speech production and perception in the cortex (Silbert et al., 2014)
- Social gating hypothesis of infant speech perception (Kuhl, 2014)

The Skin Senses (Chapter 14)

- Response of SA1 and PC fibers to coarse and fine textures (Weber et al., 2013)
- Effect of expectation on pain reduction by drugs (Bingel et al., 2011)

- Comparing social pain and physical pain (Eisenberger, 2014; Woo et al., 2014)

The Chemical Senses (Chapter 15)

- Social effects of anosmia (Croy et al., 2013)
- Revised estimate of the number of odors that can be discriminated (Bashid et al., 2014)
- Diffuse representation of odorants in piriform cortex (Omanski et al., 2014)

A Note on the Creation of This Edition

I wrote the first nine editions of this book myself, but with the addition of James Brockmole of the University of Notre Dame, this edition became a team effort. Taking the ninth edition as the starting point, I revised Chapters 1–5 and 11–15, and Jim revised Chapters 6–10. Having Jim revise these chapters had a number of benefits. First, he brought new ideas to the material, which are reflected in changes such as updating the description of the Reichardt motion detector, adding historical highlights about Newton, Helmholtz, and Hering to the discussion of color vision, and creating a number of new *Developmental Dimensions*. Second, the process of revising all of the chapters was collaborative. We read and commented on each other's chapters and made suggestions about new material to add and old material that needed to be omitted. A third collaborator, who was crucial to the success of this project, was my longtime developmental editor, Shannon LeMay-Finn, who made sure we explained things clearly and in the same style throughout the book. The goal was to create a book that instructors would easily recognize because of its similarity to the previous editions, but that also contains new research and reflects changing trends in the field.

Acknowledgments

It is a pleasure to acknowledge the following people who worked tirelessly to turn the manuscript into an actual book. Without these people, this book would not exist, and both Jim and I are grateful to all of them.

- Tim Matray, editor, for providing resources to support the book, and, most important, for your willingness to listen to my concerns and to provide advice and support regarding various situations that came up as I was writing the book.
- Shannon LeMay-Finn, developmental editor extraordinaire, who has spoiled me with her attention to details, and with queries and suggestions that often amazed me. Many of the details of this edition of the book owe their existence to Shannon's perceptive feedback. Also thank you, Shannon, for your humor, for your appreciation of my humor, and for becoming interested in perception.
- Jill Traut of MPS Limited Production Services, for taking care of the amazing number of details involved

in turning my manuscript into a book. Thank you, Jill, not only for taking care of details, but for your flexibility and your willingness to take care of all of those "special requests" that I made during the production process.
- Vernon Boes, art guru, who directed the design for the book. Thanks, Vernon, for our continuing relationship, and the great design and cover.
- Ellen Pettengell for the elegant design and Denise Davidson for the striking cover.
- Peggy Tropp, for her expert and creative copyediting.
- Kyra Kane, associate content developer, for helping initiate the process involved in obtaining new interactions for MindTap.
- Mary Noel for making MindTap for Sensation and Perception happen.
- Brittani Morgan and Deanna Ettinger for their relentless quests for permissions.
- Michelle Clark, senior content project manager, who coordinated all of the elements of the book during production and made sure everything happened when it was supposed to so the book would get to the printer on time.
- Joshua Taylor, associate content vendor services manager, for coordinating the Instructor's Manual, Test Bank, and PowerPoint slides.

In addition to the help I received from all of these people on the editorial and production side, I also received a great deal of help from perception researchers. One of the things I have learned in my years of writing is that other people's advice is crucial. The field of perception is a broad one, and I rely heavily on the advice of experts in specific areas to alert me to emerging new research and to check the content for accuracy. The following is a list of "expert reviewers." Some checked entire chapters for accuracy and completeness (indicated by *) and others checked portions of chapters that related directly to their research.

Chapter 3

Karl Gegenfurtner
Giessen University, Germany

János Geier
Stereo Vision Ltd., Budapest, Hungary

Chapter 6

Conrado Bosman
University of Amsterdam

* Michael Dodd
University of Nebraska

Pascal Fries
Ernst Strüngmann Institute for Neuroscience, Frankfurt

Chapter 7

* Rob McIntosh
University of Edinburgh

Chapter 8

* Duje Tadin
University of Rochester

Chapter 9

* Hannah Smithson
University of Oxford

Chapter 10

* Julie Harris
University of St. Andrews

Chapter 11

Nancy Kanwisher
Massachusetts Institute of Technology

Sam Norman-Haignere
Massachusetts Institute of Technology

* Andrew Oxenham
University of Minnesota

Christopher Plack
University of Manchester

William Yost
Arizona State University

Chapter 12

Flavio Chamis
Composer/Conductor

Matthew Davis
Medical Research Council, Cambridge

Diana Deutsch
University of California, San Diego

* Jessica Grahn
University of Western Ontario

Stefan Koelsch
Freie Universität Berlin

* Elizabeth Hellmuth Margulis
University of Arkansas

Stephen McAdams
McGill University

Robert Zatorre
McGill University

Chapter 13

Edward Chang
University of California, San Francisco

Uri Hasson
Princeton University

Chapter 14

Naomi Eisenberger
University of California, Los Angeles

Tor Wager
University of Colorado

Chapter 15

Marion Frank
University of Connecticut

Donald Wilson
New York University

I also thank the following people who donated photographs and research records for illustrations that are new to this edition.

Coronado Bosman
Radbond University, Nijmegen

Matt Cashore
University of Notre Dame

Edward Chang
University of California, San Francisco

Naomi Eisenberger
University of California, Los Angeles

János Geier
Stereo Vision Ltd., Budapest

Hirac Gurden
University of Paris, Orsay

Uri Hasson
Princeton University

Alex Huth
University of Prague

Ewald Hering
University of California, Berkeley

George L. Malcolm
George Washington University

Sam Norman-Haignere
Massachusetts Institute of Technology

Andrew Oxenham
University of Minnesota

Sarah Shomstein
George Washington University

Pawan Sinha
Massachusetts Institute of Technology

I also thank Michael Hout of the University of New Mexico for tracking down many new demonstrations for the Exploration feature of MindTap, and the many researchers who contributed the demonstrations. These researchers are credited in the online Exploration feature.

Perception is a miracle. Somehow, the markings on this page become a sidewalk, stone walls, and a quaint ivy-covered house. Even more miraculous is that if you were standing in the real scene, the flat image on the back of your eye would be transformed into three-dimensional space that you could walk through. This book explains how this miracle occurs.

CHAPTER 1

Introduction
to Perception

CHAPTER CONTENTS

Why Read This Book?

The Perceptual Process
But What About "Sensation"?
Distal and Proximal Stimuli (Steps 1 and 2)
Receptor Processes (Step 3)
Neural Processing (Step 4)
Behavioral Responses (Steps 5–7)
Knowledge

Studying the Perceptual Process
The Two "Stimulus" Relationships (A and B)
The Physiology–Perception Relationship (C)
Cognitive Influences on Perception

Measuring Perception
Gustav Fechner Introduces Methods to Measure Thresholds

Five Questions About the Perceptual World

SOMETHING TO CONSIDER: Why Is the Difference Between Physical and Perceptual Important?

THINK ABOUT IT

Some Questions We Will Consider:

- Why should you read this book? (p. 4)
- What is the sequence of steps from looking at a stimulus like a tree to perceiving the tree? (p. 5)
- What is the difference between perceiving something and recognizing it? (p. 8)
- How do perceptual psychologists go about measuring the varied ways that we perceive the environment. (p. 13)

magine that you have been given the following hypothetical science project.

Project: Design a device that can *locate*, *describe*, and *identify* all objects in the environment, including their distance from the device and their relationships to each other. In addition, make the device capable of traveling from one point to another, avoiding obstacles along the way.

Extra credit: Make the device capable of having *conscious experience*, such as what *people* experience when they look out at a scene.

Warning: This project, should you decide to accept it, is extremely difficult. It has not yet been solved by the best computer scientists, even though they have access to the world's most powerful computers.

Hint: Humans and animals have solved these problems in a number of elegant ways. They use (1) two spherical sensors called "eyes," which contain a light-sensitive chemical, to sense light; (2) two detectors on the sides of the head, called "ears," which are fitted with tiny vibrating hairs to sense pressure changes in the air; (3) small pressure detectors of various shapes imbedded under the skin to sense stimuli on the skin; and (4) two types of chemical detectors to detect gases that are inhaled and solids and liquids that are ingested.

Additional note: Designing the detectors is just the first step in creating the system. An information processing system is also needed. In the case of the human, this information processing system is a "computer" called the brain, with 100 billion active units and interconnections so complex that they have still not been completely deciphered. Although the detectors are an important part of the project, the design of the computer is crucial, because the information that is picked up by the detectors needs to be analyzed. Note that the operation of the human system is still not completely understood and that the best scientific minds in the world have made little progress with the extra credit part of the problem. Focus on the main problem first, and leave conscious experience until later.

The "science project" just described is about **perception**—conscious experience that results from stimulation of the senses. Our goal in this book is to understand how humans and animals perceive, starting with the detectors—the eyes, ears, skin receptors, and receptors in the nose and mouth—and then moving on to the computer—the brain. We want to understand how we sense things in the environment and interact with them. The paradox we face is that although we still don't understand perception, perceiving is something that occurs almost effortlessly. In most situations, we simply open our eyes and see what is around us, listen and hear sounds, eat and taste, without expending any particular effort.

Because of the ease with which we perceive, many people see perception as something that "just happens" and don't see the feats achieved by our senses as complex or amazing. "After all," the skeptic might say, "for vision, a picture of the environment is focused on the back of my eye, and that picture provides all the information my brain needs to duplicate the environment in my consciousness." But the idea that perception is not very complex is exactly what misled computer scientists in the 1950s and 1960s to propose that it would take only about a decade or so to create "perceiving machines" that could negotiate the environment with humanlike ease. That prediction, made half a century ago, has yet to come true, even though a computer defeated the world chess champion in 1997 and defeated two *Jeopardy!* champions in 2010. From a computer's point of view, perceiving a scene is more difficult than playing world championship chess or accessing vast amounts of knowledge to answer quiz questions. In this chapter, we will consider a few practical reasons for studying perception, how perception occurs in a sequence of steps, and how to measure perception.

Why Read This Book?

The most obvious answer to the question "Why read this book?" is that it is required reading for a course you are taking. Thus, it is probably an important thing to do if you want to get a good grade. But beyond that, there are a number of other reasons for reading this book. For one thing, it will provide you with information that may be helpful in other courses and perhaps even your future career. If you plan to go to graduate school to become a researcher or teacher in perception or a related area, this book will provide you with a solid background to build on. In fact, many of the research studies you will read about were carried out by researchers who read earlier editions of this book when they were undergraduates.

The material in this book is also relevant to future studies in medicine or related fields, because much of our discussion is about how the body operates. Medical applications that depend on an understanding of perception include devices to restore perception to people who have lost vision or hearing and treatments for pain. Other applications include robotic vehicles that can find their way through unfamiliar environments, face recognition systems that can identify people as they pass through airport security, speech recognition systems that can understand what someone is saying, and highway signs that are visible to drivers under a variety of conditions.

But reasons to study perception extend beyond the possibility of useful applications. Studying perception can help you become more aware of the nature of your own perceptual experiences. Many of the everyday experiences that you take for granted—such as tasting food, looking at a painting in a museum, or listening to someone talking—can be appreciated at a deeper level by considering questions such as "Why do I lose my sense of taste when I have a cold?" "How do artists create an impression of depth in a picture?" and "Why does an unfamiliar language sound as if it is one continuous stream of sound, without breaks between words?" This book will not only answer these questions but will answer other questions that you may not have thought of, such as "Why don't I see colors at dusk?" and "How come the scene around me doesn't appear to move as I walk through it?" Thus, even if you aren't planning to become a physician or a robotic vehicle designer, you will come away from reading this book with a heightened appreciation of both the complexity and the beauty of the mechanisms responsible for your perceptual experiences, and perhaps even with an enhanced awareness of the world around you.

Because perception is something you experience constantly, knowing about how it works is interesting in its own right. To appreciate why, consider what you are experiencing right now. If you touch the page of this book, or look out at what's around you, you might get the feeling that you are perceiving exactly what is "out there" in the environment. After all, touching this page puts you in direct contact with it, and it seems likely that what you are seeing is what is actually there. But one of the things you will learn as you study perception is that everything you see, hear, taste, feel, or smell is the result of the activity in your nervous system and your knowledge gained from past experience.

Think about what this means. There are things out there that you want to see, hear, taste, smell, and feel. But the only way to achieve this is by activating *sensory receptors* in your body designed to respond to light energy, sound energy, chemical stimuli, and pressure on the skin. When you run your fingers over the pages of this book, you feel the page and its texture because the pressure and movement are activating small receptors just below the skin. Thus, whatever you are feeling depends on the activation of these receptors. If the receptors weren't there, you would feel nothing, or if they had different properties, you might feel something different from what you feel now. This idea that *perception depends on the properties of the sensory receptors* is one of the themes of this book.

A few years ago, I received an email from a student (not one of my own, but from another university) who was using an earlier edition of this book.[1] In her email, "Jenny" made a

---

[1]Who is "I"? In various places in the book you will see first-person references such as this one ("I received an email") or others, like "a student in *my* class," or "*I* tell my students," or "*I* had an interesting experience." Because this book has two authors, you may wonder who *I* or *my* is. The answer is that, unless otherwise noted, it is author B. G., because most of the first-person references in this edition are carried over from the 9th edition, which was written by B. G.

number of comments about the book, but the one that struck me as being particularly relevant to the question "Why read this book?" is the following: "By reading your book, I got to know the fascinating processes that take place every second in my brain, that are doing things I don't even think about." Your reasons for reading this book may turn out to be totally different from Jenny's, but hopefully you will find out some things that will be useful, or fascinating, or both.

The Perceptual Process

Perception happens at the end of what can be described, with apologies to the Beatles, as a long and winding road (McCartney, 1970). This road begins outside of you, with stimuli in the environment—trees, buildings, birds chirping, smells in the air—and ends with the behavioral responses of perceiving, recognizing, and taking action. We picture this journey from stimuli to responses by the seven steps in **Figure 1.1**, called the **perceptual process**. The process begins with a stimulus in the environment (a tree in this example) and ends with the conscious experiences of perceiving the tree, recognizing the tree, and taking action with respect to the tree.

Because this process is involved in everything we will be describing in this book, it is important to note that Figure 1.1 is a simplified version of what happens. First, many things happen within each "box." For example, "neural processing,"

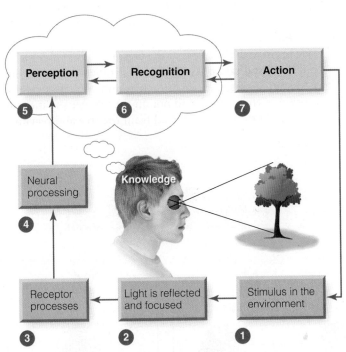

Figure 1.1 The perceptual process. These seven steps, plus "knowledge" inside the person's brain, summarize the major events that occur between the time a person looks at the stimulus in the environment (the tree in this example) and perceives the tree, recognizes it, and takes action toward it. Figures 1.3–1.6 describe the steps in the perceptual process in more detail.

involves understanding not only how cells called neurons work, but how they interact with each other and how they operate within different areas of the brain. Another reason we say the series of boxes in Figure 1.1 is simplified is that steps in the perceptual process do not always unfold in a one-follows-the-other order. For example, research has shown that perception ("I see something") and recognition (That's a tree") may not always happen one after another, but could happen at the same time, or even in reverse order (Gibson & Peterson, 1994). And when perception or recognition leads to action ("Let's have a closer look at the tree"), that action could change perception and recognition ("Looking closer shows that what I thought was an oak tree turns out to be a maple tree"). This is why there are reverse arrows between perception, recognition, and action. In addition, there is an arrow from "action" back to the stimulus. This turns the perceptual process into a "cycle" in which taking action, for example, walking toward the tree, changes the observer's view of the tree.

Even though the process is simplified, Figure 1.1 provides a good way to think about how perception occurs and introduces some important principles that will guide our discussion of perception throughout this book. In the first part of this chapter, we will briefly describe each stage of the process; in the second part, we will consider ways of measuring the relationship between stimuli and perception.

But What About "Sensation"?

Before we begin describing the stages of the perceptual process, let's consider something that may have occurred to you: Why is Figure 1.1 called the *perceptual* process, when the title of this book is *Sensation and Perception*? To answer this question, let's consider the terms *sensation* and *perception*. When a distinction is made between *sensation* and *perception*, **sensation** is often identified as involving simple "elementary" processes that occur right at the beginning of a sensory system, as when light stimulates receptors in the eye. In contrast, *perception* is identified with complex processes that involve higher-order mechanisms such as interpretation and memory that involve activity in the brain. It is therefore often stated, especially in introductory psychology textbooks, that *sensation* involves detecting elementary properties of a stimulus (Carlson, 2010), and perception involves the higher brain functions involved in interpreting events and objects (Myers, 2004).

Keeping this distinction in mind, let's consider the displays in **Figure 1.2**. **Figure 1.2a** is extremely simple—a single dot. Let's for the moment assume that this simplicity means that there is no interpretation or higher-order processes, so sensation is involved. Looking at **Figure 1.2b**, with three dots, we might now think that we are dealing with perception, because we interpret the three dots as creating a triangle. Going even further, we can say that **Figure 1.2c**, which is made up of many dots, is a "house." Surely this must be perception because it involves many dots and our past experience with houses. But let's return to Figure 1.2a, which we called a dot. As it turns out, even a stimulus this simple can be seen in more than one

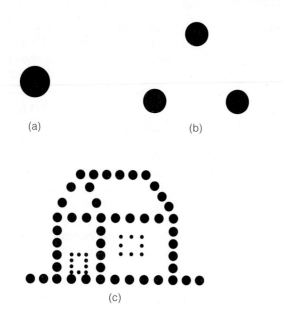

(a)　　　　　　　　　　(b)

(c)

Figure 1.2 (a) One dot, (b) a triangle, (c) a house. What do these stimuli tell us about sensations and perceptions? See text for discussion.

way. Is this a black dot on a white background or a hole in a piece of white paper? Now that interpretation is involved, does our experience with Figure 1.2a become *perception*?

This example illustrates that deciding what is *sensation* and what is *perception* is not always obvious. As we will see in this book, there are experiences that depend heavily on processes that occur right at the beginning of a sensory system, in the sensory receptors or nearby, and there are other experiences that depend on interpretation and past experiences, using information stored in the brain. But this book takes the position that calling some processes *sensation* and others *perception* doesn't add anything to our understanding of how our sensory experiences are created, so the term *perception* is used almost exclusively throughout this book.

Perhaps the main reason not to use the term *sensation* is that, with the exception of papers on the history of perception research (Gilchrist, 2012), the term *sensation* appears only rarely in modern research papers (for example, papers on the sense of taste occasionally refer to taste *sensations*), whereas the term *perception* is extremely common. Despite the fact that introductory psychology books may distinguish between sensation and perception, modern perception researchers don't make this distinction.

So why is this book called *Sensation and Perception*? Blame history. Sensation was discussed in the early history of perceptual psychology, and courses and textbooks followed suit by including *sensation* in their titles. But while researchers eventually stopped using the term *sensation*, the titles of the courses and books remained the same. So sensations are historically important (we will discuss this briefly in Chapter 5), but as far as we are concerned, everything that involves understanding how we experience the world through our senses comes under the heading of perception. With that bit of terminology out of the way, we are now ready to consider Steps 1 and 2 of the perceptual process, by accompanying someone who is observing a tree in a field.

Distal and Proximal Stimuli (Steps 1 and 2)

There are stimuli within the body that produce internal pain and enable us to sense the positions of our body and limbs. But for the purposes of this discussion, we will focus on stimuli that exist "out there" in the environment, and we will consider what happens to stimuli in the first two steps of the perceptual process in which stimuli in the environment reach receptors in the eye (**Figure 1.3**).

We begin with the tree that the person is observing, which we call the **distal stimulus** (Step 1). It is called distal because it is "distant"—out there in the environment. The person's perception of the tree is based not on the tree getting into his eye (ouch!), but on light reflected from the tree and reaching

Figure 1.3 Steps 1 and 2 of the perceptual process. Step 1: Information about the tree (the *distal stimulus*) is carried by light. Step 2: The light is transformed when it is reflected from the tree, when it travels through the atmosphere, and when it is focused by the eye's optical system. The result is the *proximal stimulus*, the image of the tree on the retina, which is a representation of the tree.

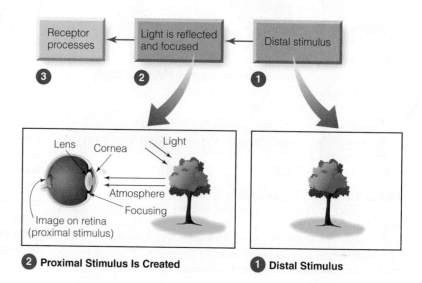

the visual receptors (Step 2). The reflection of light from the tree introduces one of the central principles of perception, the **principle of transformation**, which states that *stimuli and responses created by stimuli are transformed, or changed, between the distal stimulus and perception.*

The first transformation occurs when light hits the tree and is then reflected from the tree to the person's eyes. The nature of the reflected light depends on properties of the light energy hitting the tree (is it the midday sun, light on an overcast day, or a spotlight illuminating the tree from below?), properties of the tree (its textures, shape, the fraction of light hitting it that it reflects), and properties of the atmosphere through which the light is transmitted (is the air clear, dusty, or foggy?).

When this reflected light enters the eye, it is transformed as it is focused by the eye's optical system, which is the *cornea* at the front of the eye and the *lens* directly behind it. If these optics are working properly, they form a sharp image of the tree on the *receptors* of the person's *retina*, a 0.4-mm-thick network of nerve cells that covers the back of the eye and that contains the receptors for vision. This image on the retina is the **proximal stimulus**, so called because it is "in proximity" to the receptors (Step 2). If the eye's optics are not working properly, this proximal stimulus—the image that reaches the retina—may be blurred.

The fact that an image of the tree is focused on the retina introduces another principle of perception, the **principle of representation**, which states that *everything a person perceives is based not on direct contact with stimuli but on representations of stimuli that are formed on the receptors and the resulting activity in the person's nervous system.*

The distinction between the distal stimulus (Step 1) and the proximal stimulus (Step 2) illustrates both transformation and representation. The distal stimulus (the tree) is *transformed* into the proximal stimulus, and this image *represents* the tree in the person's eyes. But this transformation from "tree" to "image of the tree on the retina" is just the first in a series of transformations. The next transformation occurs within the receptors at the back of the eye.

Receptor Processes (Step 3)

Sensory receptors are cells specialized to respond to environmental energy, with each sensory system's receptors specialized to respond to a specific type of energy. Visual receptors respond to light, auditory receptors to pressure changes in the air, touch receptors to pressure transmitted through the skin, and smell and taste receptors to chemicals entering the nose and mouth. When the visual receptors that line the back of the eye receive the light reflected from the tree, they do two things: (1) They transform environmental energy into electrical energy; and (2) they shape perception by the way they respond to different properties of stimuli (**Figure 1.4**).

Visual receptors transform light energy into electrical energy because they contain a light-sensitive chemical called **visual pigment**, which reacts to light. The transformation of one form of energy (light energy in this example) to another form (electrical energy) is called **transduction**. Another

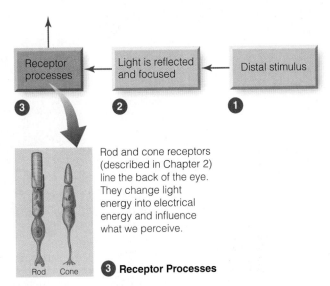

Rod and cone receptors (described in Chapter 2) line the back of the eye. They change light energy into electrical energy and influence what we perceive.

3 Receptor Processes

Rod   Cone

Figure 1.4 Step 3 of the perceptual process. *Receptor processes* include transduction (the transformation of light energy into electrical energy) and the shaping of perception by the properties of visual pigments in the receptor's outer segments. The end result is an electrical representation of the tree.

example of transduction occurs when you touch the "withdrawal" button or icon on an ATM. The pressure exerted by your finger is transduced into electrical energy, which causes a device that uses mechanical energy to dispense your money out of the machine.

Transduction by the visual pigments is crucial for perception, because without it information about the representation of the tree formed on the retina would not reach the brain and perception would not occur. In addition, the visual pigments shape perception in two ways: (1) The ability to see dim light depends on having a high concentration of light-sensitive pigment in the receptors; and (2) there are different types of pigments, which respond best to light in different parts of the visible spectrum. Some pigments respond better to light in the blue-green part of the spectrum; others respond better to the yellow-red part of the spectrum. We will describe both transduction and how the properties of the different pigments influence perception in Chapter 2.

Neural Processing (Step 4)

Once transduction occurs, the tree becomes represented by electrical signals in thousands of visual receptors. But what happens to these signals? As we will see in Chapter 2, they travel through a vast interconnected network of neurons that (1) *transmit* signals from the receptors, through the retina, to the brain, and then within the brain; and (2) *change* (or *process*) these signals as they are transmitted. These changes occur because of interactions between neurons as the signal travels from the receptors to the brain. Because of this processing, some signals become reduced or are prevented from getting through, and others are amplified so they arrive at the brain with added strength. This processing then continues as signals travel to various places in the brain.

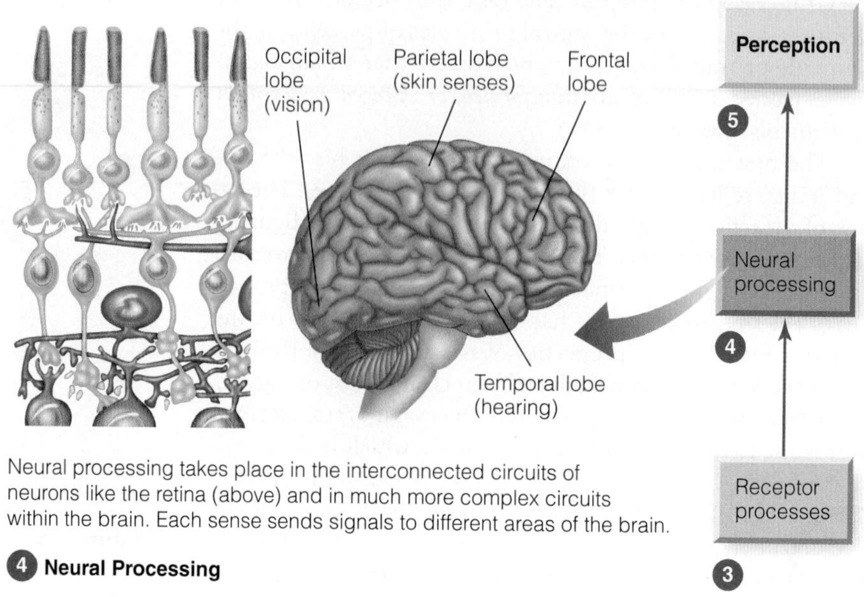

Figure 1.5 Step 4 of the perceptual process. *Neural processing* involves interactions between the electrical signals traveling in networks of neurons early in the system, in the retina; later, on the pathway to the brain; and finally, within the brain.

Occipital lobe (vision)   Parietal lobe (skin senses)   Frontal lobe

Temporal lobe (hearing)

Perception

5

Neural processing

4

Receptor processes

3

Neural processing takes place in the interconnected circuits of neurons like the retina (above) and in much more complex circuits within the brain. Each sense sends signals to different areas of the brain.

4 **Neural Processing**

The changes in these signals that occur as they are transmitted through this maze of neurons is called **neural processing** (**Figure 1.5**). Processing will be described in more detail in Chapters 2 and 3. For now, the main point is that processing continues the process of transformation that began when looking at the tree created an image of the tree inside the eye, which was then changed into electrical signals in the visual receptors. A similar process occurs for other senses as well. For example, sound energy (pressure change in the air) is transformed into electrical signals inside the ear and is transmitted out of the ear along the auditory nerve, then through a series of structures on the way to the brain.

Electrical signals from each sense arrive at the **primary receiving area** for that sense in the cerebral cortex of the brain (as shown in Figure 1.5). The **cerebral cortex** is a 2-mm-thick layer that contains the machinery for creating perceptions, as well as other functions, such as language, memory, and thinking. The primary receiving area for vision occupies most of the **occipital lobe**; the area for hearing is located in part of the **temporal lobe**; and the area for the skin senses—touch, temperature, and pain—is located in an area in the **parietal lobe**. As we study each sense in detail, we will see that once signals reach the primary receiving areas, they are then transmitted to many other structures in the brain. For example, the **frontal lobe** receives signals from all of the senses, and it plays an important role in perceptions that involve the coordination of information received through two or more senses.

The sequence of transformations that occurs between the receptors and the brain, and then within the brain, means that the pattern of electrical signals in the brain is changed compared to the electrical signals that left the receptors. It is important to note, however, that although these signals have changed, they still represent the tree. In fact, the changes that occur as the signals are transmitted and processed are crucial for achieving the next step in the perceptual process, the *behavioral responses.*

Behavioral Responses (Steps 5–7)

Finally, after all that reflection, focusing, transduction, transmission, and processing, we reach the behavioral responses (**Figure 1.6**). This transformation is perhaps the most miraculous of all, because *electrical signals* (Step 4) are transformed into *conscious experience*: The person *perceives* the tree (Step 5) and *recognizes* it (Step 6). We can distinguish between *perception*, which is conscious awareness of the tree, and *recognition*, which is placing an object in a category, such as "tree," that gives it meaning, by considering the case of Dr. P., a patient described by neurologist Oliver Sacks (1985) in the title story of his book *The Man Who Mistook His Wife for a Hat.*

Dr. P., a well-known musician and music teacher, first noticed a problem when he began having trouble recognizing his students visually, although he could immediately identify them by the sound of their voices. But when Dr. P. began misperceiving common objects, for example addressing a parking meter as if it were a person or expecting a carved knob on a piece of furniture to engage him in conversation, it became clear that his problem was more serious than just a little forgetfulness. Was he blind, or perhaps crazy? It was clear from an eye examination that he could see well, and by many other criteria it was obvious that he was not crazy.

Dr. P.'s problem was eventually diagnosed as **visual form agnosia**—an inability to recognize objects—that was caused by a brain tumor. He perceived the parts of objects but couldn't identify the whole object, so when Sacks showed him a glove, Dr. P. described it as "a continuous surface unfolded on itself. It appears to have five outpouchings, if this is the word." When Sacks asked him what it was, Dr. P. hypothesized that it was "a container of some sort. It could be a change purse, for example, for coins of five sizes." The normally easy process of object recognition had, for Dr. P., been derailed by his brain tumor.

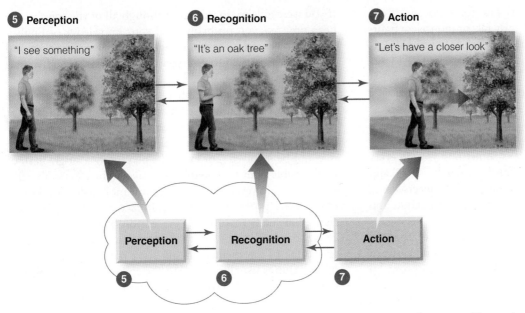

5 Perception

"I see something"

6 Recognition

"It's an oak tree"

7 Action

"Let's have a closer look"

Perception → Recognition → Action

5 **6** **7**

Figure 1.6 Steps 5–7 of the perceptual process. The behavioral responses: *perception, recognition,* and *action.*

He could perceive the object and recognize parts of it, but he couldn't perceptually assemble the parts in a way that would enable him to recognize the object as a whole. Cases such as this show that it is important to distinguish between perception and recognition.

The final behavioral response is **action** (Step 7), which involves motor activities. For example, the person might decide to walk toward the tree, have a picnic under it, or climb it. Even if he doesn't decide to interact directly with the tree, he is taking action when he moves his eyes and head to look at different parts of the tree, even if he is standing in one place.

Some researchers see action as an important outcome of the perceptual process because of its importance for survival. David Milner and Melvyn Goodale (1995) propose that early in the evolution of animals, the major goal of visual processing was not to create a conscious perception or "picture" of the environment but to help the animal control navigation, catch prey, avoid obstacles, and detect predators—all crucial functions for the animal's survival.

The fact that perception often leads to action—whether it be an animal's increasing its vigilance when it hears a twig snap in the forest or a person's deciding to interact with an object or just look more closely at something that looks interesting—means that perception is a continuously changing process. For example, the image of the tree on the back of the eye changes every time the person moves his body or his eyes relative to the tree, and this change creates new representations and a new series of transformations. Thus, although we can describe the perceptual process as a series of steps that "begins" with the distal stimulus and "ends" with perception, recognition, and action, the overall process is dynamic and continually changing.

Knowledge

Our diagram of the perceptual process includes one more factor: *knowledge.* **Knowledge** is any information that the perceiver brings to a situation. Knowledge is placed inside the person's brain in Figure 1.1 because it can affect a number of the steps in the perceptual process. Knowledge that a person brings to a situation can be information acquired years ago or, as in the following demonstration, information just recently acquired.

DEMONSTRATION | Perceiving a Picture

After looking at the drawing in **Figure 1.7**, close your eyes, turn to page 11, and open and shut your eyes rapidly to briefly expose the picture in **Figure 1.11**. Decide what the picture is; then open your eyes and read the explanation below it. Do this now, before reading further.

Figure 1.7 See "Demonstration: Perceiving a Picture" for instructions. (Adapted from Bugelski & Alampay, 1961)

Did you identify Figure 1.11 as a rat (or a mouse)? If you did, you were influenced by the clearly rat- or mouselike figure you observed initially. But people who first observe Figure 1.14 (page 13) instead of Figure 1.7 usually identify Figure 1.11 as a man. (Try this on someone else.) This demonstration, which is called the **rat–man demonstration**, shows how recently acquired knowledge ("that pattern is a rat") can influence perception.

An example of how knowledge acquired years ago can influence the perceptual process is your ability to **categorize**—to place objects into categories. This is something you do every time you name an object. "Tree," "bird," "branch," "car," and everything else you can name are examples of objects being placed into categories that you learned as a young child and that have become part of your knowledge base.

Another way to describe the effect of information that the perceiver brings to the situation is by distinguishing between bottom-up processing and top-down processing. **Bottom-up processing** (also called **data-based processing**) is processing that is based on the stimuli reaching the receptors. These stimuli provide the starting point for perception because, with the exception of unusual situations such as drug-induced perceptions or "seeing stars" from a bump to the head, perception involves activation of the receptors. The woman sees the moth on the tree in **Figure 1.8** because of processes triggered by the moth's image on her retina. The image is the "incoming data" that is the basis of bottom-up processing.

Top-down processing (also called **knowledge-based processing**) refers to processing that is based on knowledge. When the woman labels what she is seeing as a "moth" or perhaps a particular kind of moth, she is accessing what she has learned about moths. Knowledge such as this isn't always involved in perception, but as we will see, it often is—sometimes without our even being aware of it.

To experience top-down processing in action, try reading the following sentence:

M*RY H*D * L*TTL* L*MB

If you were able to do this, even though all of the vowels have been omitted, you probably used your knowledge of English words, how words are strung together to form sentences, and your familiarity with the nursery rhyme to create the sentence (Denes & Pinson, 1993).

Students often ask whether top-down processing is always involved in perception. The answer to this question is that it is "very often" involved. There are some situations, typically involving very simple stimuli, in which top-down processing may not be involved. For example, perceiving a single flash of easily visible light is probably not affected by a person's prior experience. However, as stimuli become more complex, the role of top-down processing increases. In fact, a person's past experience is usually involved in perception of real-world scenes, even though in most cases the person is unaware of this influence. One of the themes of this book is that our knowledge of how things usually appear in the environment can play an important role in determining what we perceive.

Studying the Perceptual Process

The goal of perceptual research is to understand each of the steps in the perceptual process that lead from the stimulus to the behavioral responses of perception, recognition, and action. (For simplicity, we will use the term *perception* to stand for all of these behavioral outcomes in the discussion that follows.) One way the perceptual process has been studied is by determining the following three relationships, shown in **Figure 1.9**:

- Relationship A: The stimulus–perception relationship
- Relationship B: The stimulus–physiological relationship
- Relationship C: The physiology–perception relationship

To illustrate how these relationships have been measured in actual experiments, we consider how researchers have studied a

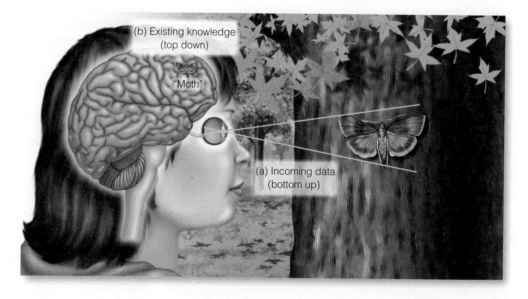

Figure 1.8 Perception is determined by an interaction between bottom-up processing, which starts with the image on the receptors, and top-down processing, which brings the observer's knowledge into play. In this example, (a) the image of the moth on the woman's retina initiates bottom-up processing; and (b) her prior knowledge of moths contributes to top-down processing.

(b) Existing knowledge (top down)

"Moth"

(a) Incoming data (bottom up)

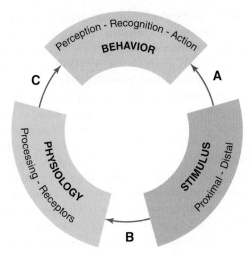

Figure 1.9 Simplified perceptual process showing the three relationships described in the text. The three boxes represent the three major components of the seven-step perceptual process: Stimuli (Steps 1 and 2); Physiology (Steps 3 and 4); and the three Behavioral responses (Steps 5–7). The three relationships that are usually measured to study the perceptual process are (A) the stimulus–perception relationship; (B) the stimulus–physiology relationship; and (C) the physiology–perception relationship.

Figure 1.10 Measuring grating acuity. The finest line width at which a subject can perceive the bars in a black-and-white grating stimulus is that subject's grating acuity. Stimuli with different line widths are presented one at a time, and the subject indicates the grating's orientation until the lines are so close together that the subject can no longer indicate the orientation.

phenomenon called the oblique effect. The **oblique effect** is that people see vertical or horizontal lines better than lines oriented obliquely (at any orientation other than vertical or horizontal). We will first consider how the oblique effect has been studied, by measuring relationships A and B, which both involve stimuli.

The Two "Stimulus" Relationships (A and B)

The stimulus is involved in two relationships, one behavioral (Arrow A in Figure 1.9, from the stimulus to behavioral responses), the other physiological (Arrow B, from the stimulus to physiological responses). Relationship A, the first stimulus relationship, is the **stimulus–perception relationship**, which relates stimuli (Steps 1 and 2 in Figure 1.1) to behavioral responses (Steps 5–7). This was the main relationship measured during the first 100 years of the scientific study of perception, before physiological methods became widely available.

To illustrate this relationship, let's consider an experiment that measures the oblique effect. The oblique effect has been demonstrated by presenting black and white striped stimuli called gratings, and measuring **grating acuity**, the smallest width of lines that subjects can detect. One way to measure grating acuity is to ask subjects to indicate the grating's orientation and testing with thinner and thinner lines. Eventually, the lines are so thin that they can't be seen, and the area inside the circle looks uniform, so subjects can no longer indicate the grating's orientation. The smallest line-width at which the subject can still indicate the correct orientation is the grating acuity (**Figure 1.10**). When grating acuity is determined for different orientations, the acuity is best for gratings oriented vertically or horizontally (Appelle, 1972). This is a behavioral demonstration of the oblique effect.

The second stimulus relationship (Arrow B in Figure 1.9) is the **stimulus–physiology relationship**, the relationship between stimuli (Steps 1–2) and physiological responses (Steps 3–4). David Coppola and coworkers (1998) measured the oblique effect physiologically by presenting lines with different orientations (**Figure 1.12a**) to ferrets. When they measured the ferret's brain activity using a technique called *optical brain imaging* that measures activity over a large area of the ferret's visual cortex, they found that horizontal or vertical orientations caused larger brain responses than oblique orientations (**Figure 1.12b**).[2] This is a physiological demonstration of the oblique effect.

Figure 1.11 Did you see a "rat" or a "man"? Looking at the more ratlike picture in Figure 1.7 increased the chances that you would see this one as a rat. But if you had first seen the man version (Figure 1.14), you would have been more likely to perceive this figure as a man. (Adapted from Bugelski & Alampay, 1961)

[2]Because a great deal of physiological research has been done on animals, students often express concerns about how these animals are treated. All animal research in the United States follows strict guidelines for the care of animals established by organizations such as the American Psychological Association and the Society for Neuroscience. The central tenet of these guidelines is that every effort should be made to ensure that animals are not subjected to pain or distress. Research on animals has provided essential information for developing aids for people with sensory disabilities such as blindness and deafness and for helping develop techniques to ease severe pain.

(a) **Stimuli:** vertical, horizontal, slanted

(b) **Brain response:** Bigger to vertical and horizontal orientations

Miroslav Hlavko/Shutterstock.com

Figure 1.12 Coppola and coworkers (1998) measured the relationship between bar orientation (stimuli) and brain activity (physiology) in ferrets. Verticals and horizontals generated the greatest brain activity.

Note that even though the stimulus–perception experiment was carried out on humans and the stimulus–physiology experiment was carried out on ferrets, the results are similar. Horizontal and vertical orientations result in better acuity (Relationship A) and larger physiological responses (Relationship B) than oblique orientations. When behavioral and physiological responses to stimuli are similar like this, researchers often infer relationship C, between physiological responding and perception, which in this case would be the association between greater physiological responses to horizontals and verticals and better perception of horizontals and verticals. But in some cases, researchers have measured the physiology–perception relationship directly.

The Physiology–Perception Relationship (C)

The **physiology–perception relationship** relates physiological responses (Steps 3–4 in Figure 1.1) and behavioral responses (Steps 5–7) (Arrow C in Figure 1.9). Christopher Furmanski and Stephen Engel (2000) determined this relationship for different line orientations by measuring the brain response and behavioral sensitivity in the same subjects. The behavioral measurements were made by decreasing the intensity difference between light and dark bars of a grating until the subject could no longer detect the grating's orientation. Subjects were able to detect the horizontal (90°) and vertical (0°) orientations at smaller light–dark differences than for the oblique orientations (45° and 135°). This

means that subjects were more sensitive to the horizontal and vertical orientations (**Figure 1.13a**). The physiological measurements were made using a technique called functional magnetic resonance imaging (fMRI), which we will describe in Chapter 4 (see page 75). These measurements showed larger brain responses to vertical or horizontal gratings than to oblique gratings (**Figure 1.13b**).

The results of this experiment, therefore, are consistent with the results of the other two experiments, which both demonstrated the oblique effect. The beauty of this experiment is that the behavioral and physiological responses were measured in the same subjects. The reason for the visual system's preference for horizontal and vertical orientations, which has to do with the prevalence of verticals and horizontals in the environment, will be discussed in Chapter 5.

Cognitive Influences on Perception

As we study perception measuring the three relationships in Figure 1.9, we will also be concerned with how the knowledge, memories, and expectations that people bring to a situation influence their perceptions. These factors, which we have

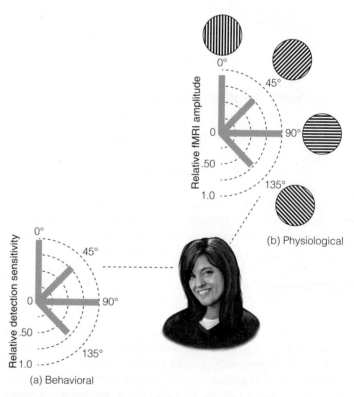

Figure 1.13 Furmanski and Engel (2000) made both behavioral and physiological measurements of subjects' response to oriented gratings. (a) Bars indicate sensitivity to gratings of different orientations. Sensitivity is highest to the vertical (0 degree) and horizontal (90 degree) orientations; (b) Bars indicate fMRI amplitude to different orientations. Amplitudes were greater to the 0- and 90-degree orientations.

described as the starting place for top-down processing, are called **cognitive influences on perception**. These cognitive influences were represented by the word "knowledge" inside the person's brain in the perceptual cycle in Figure 1.1. Researchers study cognitive influences by measuring how knowledge and other factors, such as memories and expectations, affect all of the relationships in Figure 1.9.

For example, consider the rat–man demonstration. If we were to measure the stimulus–perception relationship by showing just Figure 1.11 to a number of people, we would probably find that some people see a rat and some people see a man. But when we add some "knowledge" by first presenting the more rat-like picture in Figure 1.7, most people see Figure 1.11 as a "rat" or "mouse." Thus, in this example, knowledge has affected the stimulus–perception relationship. As we will see throughout this book, these cognitive influences affect perception not only for demonstrations like rat–man, in which knowledge is presented just before testing the subject, but also for other perceptual phenomena, in which knowledge has been accumulated over a long period of time.

One of the things that becomes apparent when we step back and look at the three relationships is that each one provides information about different aspects of the perceptual process. An important message of this book is that to truly understand perception, we have to study it by measuring both behavioral (A) and physiological (B and C) relationships. Only by considering both behavior and physiology together can we create a complete picture of the mechanisms responsible for perception.

TEST YOURSELF 1.1

1. What are some reasons for studying perception?

2. Describe the process of perception as a series of seven steps, beginning with the distal stimulus and culminating in the behavioral responses of perceiving, recognizing, and acting.

3. What is the role of higher-level or "cognitive" processes in perception? Be sure you understand the difference between bottom-up and top-down processing.

4. What does it mean to say that perception can be studied by measuring three relationships? Give an example of how the oblique effect was studied by measuring each relationship.

Measuring Perception

So far we've pictured the perceptual process as having a number of steps (Figure 1.1), and we've demonstrated how we can study the process by studying three different relationships (Figure 1.9). But what, exactly, do we *measure* to determine these relationships? In this section we will describe a number of different ways to measure behavioral responses. We will describe physiological methods in the chapters that follow.

What is measured in an experiment looking at the relationship between stimuli and behavior? The grating acuity experiment described on page 11 (Figure 1.10) measured the threshold for seeing fine lines, where the *threshold* is the smallest line width that can be detected. **Thresholds** measure the limits of sensory systems; they are measures of minimums—the smallest line-width that can be detected, the smallest amount of light energy we can see, the smallest amount of sound energy we can hear, the smallest concentration of a chemical we can taste or smell. Thresholds have an important place in the history of perceptual psychology, and of psychology in general, so let's consider them in more detail before describing other ways of measuring perception. As we will now see, the importance of being able to accurately measure thresholds was recognized very early in the history of the scientific study of the senses.

Gustav Fechner Introduces Methods to Measure Thresholds

Gustav Fechner (1801–1887), professor of physics at the University of Leipzig, had wide-ranging interests, having published papers on electricity, mathematics, color perception, aesthetics (the judgment of art and beauty), the mind, the soul, and the nature of consciousness. But of all his accomplishments, the most significant one was providing a new way to study the mind.

Fechner's thinking about the mind must be viewed against the backdrop of how people thought about the mind in the mid-1800s. Prevailing thought at that time was that it was impossible to study the mind. The mind and the body were thought to be totally separate from one another. People saw the body as physical and therefore something that could be seen, measured, and studied, whereas the mind was considered not physical and was therefore invisible and something that couldn't be measured and studied. Another reason proposed to support the idea that the mind couldn't be studied was the assertion that it is impossible for the mind to study itself.

Against this backdrop of skepticism regarding the possibility of studying the mind, Fechner, who had been thinking about this problem for many years, had an insight, the story goes, while lying in bed on the morning of October 22, 1850. His insight was that the mind and body should not be thought of as totally separate from one another but as two

Figure 1.14 Man version of the rat–man stimulus. (Adapted from Bugelski & Alampay, 1961)

sides of a single reality (Wozniak, 1999). Most important, Fechner proposed that the mind could be studied by measuring the relationship between changes in physical stimulation (the body part of the relationship) and a person's experience (the mind part). This proposal was based on the observation that as physical stimulation is increased—for example, by increasing the *intensity* of a light—the person's perception of the *brightness* of the light also increases.

Ten years after having his insight about the mind, Fechner (1860/1966) published his masterpiece, *Elements of Psychophysics*, in which he coined the term **psychophysics**—the study of the relation between mental (psycho) and physical (physics)—and proposed a number of methods for measuring this relationship. One of the major contributions of *Elements of Psychophysics* was the proposal of three methods for measuring the threshold. One of these methods, called the **method of limits**, is described in the Methods section below.

Every so often we will introduce a new method by describing it in a "Method" section. Students are sometimes tempted to skip these sections because they think the content is unimportant. However, you should resist this temptation because these methods are essential tools for the study of perception. These "Method" sections are often related to experiments described immediately afterward and also provide the background for understanding experiments that are described later in the book.

METHOD | Method of Limits

In the **method of limits**, the experimenter presents stimuli in either ascending order (intensity is increased) or descending order (intensity is decreased), as shown in **Figure 1.15**, which indicates the results of an experiment that measures a person's threshold for hearing a tone.

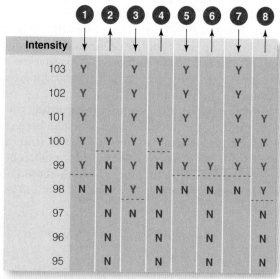

Figure 1.15 The results of an experiment to determine the threshold using the method of limits. The dashed lines indicate the crossover point for each sequence of stimuli. The threshold—the average of the crossover values—is 98.5 in this experiment.

On the first series of trials, the experimenter begins by presenting a tone with an intensity we will call 103, and the observer indicates by a "yes" response that he hears the tone. This response is indicated by a Y at an intensity of 103 in the far left column of the table. The experimenter then presents another tone, at a lower intensity, and the observer responds to this tone. This procedure continues, with the observer making a judgment at each intensity until he responds "no," he did not hear the tone. This change from "yes" to "no," indicated by the dashed line, is the *crossover point*, and the threshold for this series is taken as the mean between 99 and 98, or 98.5. The next series of trials begins below the observer's threshold, so that he says "no" on the first trial (intensity 95), and continues until he says "yes" (when the intensity reaches 100). Notice that the crossover point when starting below the threshold is slightly different. Because the crossover points may vary slightly, this procedure is repeated a number of times, starting above the threshold half the time and starting below the threshold half the time. The threshold is then determined by calculating the average of all of the crossover points.

The method of limits takes into account the variability of human perception by averaging the results of a number of trials. Fechner's other two methods, *adjustment* and *constant stimuli*, which are described in Appendix A (page 384), also do this. Taken together, these methods, which are called the **classical psychophysical methods**, opened the way for the founding of scientific psychology by providing methods to measure an aspect of the mind. Because of the impact of Fechner's ideas, October 22, the date Fechner awoke with his insight that led to the founding of psychophysics, is known among psychophysical researchers as "Fechner Day." Add that date to your calendar if you're looking for another holiday to celebrate!

The example used to illustrate the method of limits involves measuring the **absolute threshold**—the smallest stimulus level that can just be detected. Another type of threshold is the **difference threshold**—the smallest *difference* between two stimuli that enables us to tell the difference between them. In *Elements of Psychophysics*, Fechner not only proposed his psychophysical methods but also described the work of Ernst Weber (1795–1878), a physiologist who, a few years before the publication of Fechner's book, measured the difference threshold for different senses. See Appendix B (page 385) for more details about difference thresholds.

Fechner's and Weber's methods not only made it possible to measure the ability to detect stimuli but also made it possible to determine *mechanisms* responsible for experiences. For example, consider what happens when you enter a dark place and then stay there for a while. At first you may not be able to see much (**Figure 1.16a**), but eventually your vision gets better and you are able to see light and objects that were invisible before (**Figure 1.16b**). This improved vision occurs because your threshold for seeing light is becoming smaller and smaller as you stay in the dark.

(a)   (b)

© Bruce Goldstein

Figure 1.16 (a) How a dark scene might be perceived when seen just after being in the light. (b) How the scene would be perceived after spending 10 to 15 minutes adapting to the dark. The improvement in perception after spending some time in the dark reflects a decrease in the threshold for seeing light.

By measuring how a person's threshold changes moment by moment, we can determine a function called the *dark adaptation curve* that shows how the threshold becomes smaller as the person spends more time in the dark. Thus, measuring thresholds takes us beyond simply saying that "we see better when we spend time in the dark" to providing a quantitative description of what is happening from moment to moment as a person's ability to see improves. In Chapter 2, we will show how measuring the dark adaptation curve has enabled researchers to determine the physiological mechanisms that cause our vision to improve in the dark, and later in the book we will describe other experiments in which measuring thresholds has helped uncover other perceptual mechanisms.

As significant as the methods for measuring thresholds are, we know that perception includes far more than just what happens at threshold. To understand the richness of experience, we need to be able to measure other aspects of sensory experience in addition to thresholds. We will describe some of the ways perceptual researchers measure sensory experience above threshold by considering five questions about the perceptual world and the techniques used to answer these questions.

Five Questions About the Perceptual World

We begin with a question about stimuli that are easy to detect because they are above threshold.

Question 1: What Is the Perceptual Magnitude of a Stimulus? Technique: Magnitude Estimation

Things are big and small (an elephant; a bug), loud and soft (rock music; a whisper); intense and just perceptible (sunlight;

a dim star), overpowering and faint (heavy pollution; a faint smell). Fechner was not only interested in measuring thresholds using the classical psychophysical methods; he was also interested in determining the relationship between physical stimuli (like rock music and a whisper) and the perception of their magnitude (like perceiving one to be *loud* and the other *soft*). Fechner created a mathematical formula relating physical stimuli and perception; modern psychologists have modified Fechner's equation based on a method not available in Fechner's time called **magnitude estimation** (Stevens, 1957, 1961).

METHOD | Magnitude Estimation

The procedure for a magnitude estimation experiment is relatively simple: The experimenter first presents a "standard" stimulus to the subject (let's say a light of moderate intensity) and assigns it a value of, say, 10. The subject then sees lights of different intensities, and is asked to assign a number to each of these lights that is proportional to the brightness of the original light. This number for "brightness" is the **perceived magnitude** of the stimulus. If the light appears twice as bright as the standard, it gets a rating of 20; half as bright, a 5; and so on. Thus, the subject assigns a brightness to each light intensity.

The results of experiments using magnitude estimation to measure brightness are discussed further in the "Something to Consider" section at the end of this chapter, and the mathematical formulas relating physical intensity and perceptual magnitude are discussed in Appendix C (p. 386).

Question 2: What Is the Identity of the Stimulus? Technique: Recognition Testing
When you name things, you are categorizing them (see page 10). The process of

Figure 1.17 A stimulus like those used in an experiment in which subjects are asked to recognize a rapidly flashed scene. Subjects can often recognize general properties of a rapidly flashed scene, such as "houses near water and a boat," but need more time to perceive the details.

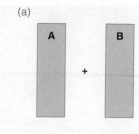

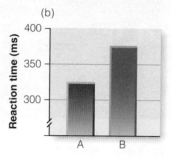

Figure 1.18 (a) A reaction time experiment in which the subject is told to look at the + sign, but pay attention to the location at A, and to push a button as quickly as possible when a dark target flashes anywhere on the display. (b) Reaction times in milliseconds, which indicates that reaction time was faster when the target was flashed at A, where the subject was attending, than when it was flashed at B, where the subject was not attending. (Data from Egly et al., 1994)

categorizing, which is called **recognition**, is measured in many different types of perceptual experiments. One application is testing the ability of people with brain damage. As we saw earlier in this chapter, Dr. P's brain damage led him to have trouble recognizing common objects, like a glove. The recognition ability of people with brain damage is tested by asking them to name objects or pictures of objects.

Recognition is also used to assess the perceptual abilities of people without brain damage. In Chapter 5 we will describe experiments that show that people can identify rapidly flashed pictures ("It's a docking area for boats lined with houses"), although seeing all of the details requires more time (**Figure 1.17**).

Recognition is not only visual; it can also include hearing ("that's a car revving its engine"), touch (identifying an object by scanning it with your fingers), taste ("mmm, chocolate"), and smell ("that's a rose"). Because recognizing objects is so crucial for our survival, many perception researchers have shifted their emphasis from asking "What do you see?" (perception) to asking "What is that called?" (recognition).

Question 3: How Quickly Can I React to It? Technique: Reaction Time

The speed with which we react to something can be determined by measuring **reaction time**—the time between presentation of a stimulus and the person's reaction to it. An example of a reaction time experiment is to ask subjects to keep their eyes fixed on the + in the display in **Figure 1.18a** and pay attention to location A on the left rectangle. Because the subject is *looking at* the + but *paying attention to* the top of the left rectangle, this task resembles what happens when you are looking in one direction but are paying attention to something off to the side.

While directing attention to the top of the left rectangle, the subject's task was to push a button as quickly as possible when a dark target flashed anywhere on the display. The results, shown in **Figure 1.18b**, indicate that the subject responded more quickly when the target was flashed at A, where he or she was directing attention, compared to B, off to the side (Egly et al., 1994). These findings are relevant to a topic we will discuss in Chapter 7: How does talking on a cell phone while driving affect the ability to drive?

Question 4: How Can I Describe What Is Out There? Technique: Phenomenological Report

Look around. Describe what you see. You could name the objects you recognize, or you could describe the pattern of lights and darks and colors, or how things are arranged in space, or that two objects appear to be the same or different sizes or colors. Describing what is out there is called **phenomenological report**. For example, do you see a vase or two faces in **Figure 1.19a**? We will see in Chapter 5 that displays like this are used to study how people perceive objects in front of backgrounds.

Another exercise in phenomenal reporting is to describe what you see in **Figure 1.19b**, which is called the **Hermann grid**. People often report that there are dark spots in the white areas at the intersections, but when they look directly at an intersection, the spot vanishes. (Try it!) We will discuss this interesting illusion in Chapter 3.

Phenomenological reports are important because they define the perceptual phenomena we want to explain and once a phenomenon is identified, we can then study it using other methods. For example, once a display like the Hermann grid is

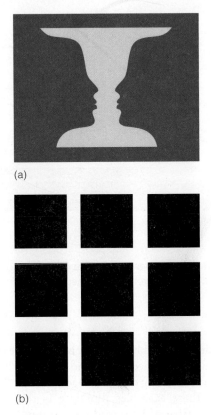

(a)

(b)

Figure 1.19 (a) Vase–face stimulus used to demonstrate how people perceive objects in front of a background. (b) Hermann grid. Notice the dark spots at the intersections of the white "corridors." These spots occur even though the corridors are the same white all over.

identified, we can then do experiments using other methods to determine why the spots are occurring.

Question 5: How Can I Interact With It? Technique: Physical Tasks and Judgments All of the other questions have focused on different ways of measuring what we perceive. This last question is concerned not with perception but with actions that follow perception. Many perceptual researchers believe that one of the primary functions of perception is to enable us to take action within our environment. Look at it this way: Morg the caveman sees a dangerous tiger in the woods. He could stand there and marvel at the beauty of its fur, or the power of its legs, but if he doesn't take action by either hiding or getting away and the tiger sees him, his days of perceiving will be over. On a less dramatic level, we need to be able to see a saltshaker and then accurately reach across the table to pick it up, or navigate from one place on campus to another to get to class. Research on perception and action, which we will describe in Chapter 7, has subjects carry out tasks that involve both perception and action, such as reaching for a target, navigating through a maze, or driving a car, under different conditions.

Physical tasks have also been studied by having people make judgments about tasks before they actually carry them out. For example, we will see in Chapter 7 that people judge a box to be heavier if they think they will be lifting it than when they think someone will be helping them.

The examples above provide a hint as to the wide range of methods that are used in perception research. This book discusses research using the methods described above, plus others as well. Although we won't describe the details of the methods used in every experiment we consider, we will highlight the most important methods in "Methods" sections like the ones on the method of limits and on magnitude estimation in this chapter. Additionally, many physiological methods will be described in Methods sections in the chapters that follow. What will emerge as you read this book is a story in which important roles are played by both behavioral and physiological methods, which combine to create a more complete understanding of perception than is possible using either type of method alone.

SOMETHING TO CONSIDER:
Why Is the Difference Between Physical and Perceptual Important?

One of the most crucial distinctions in the study of perception is the distinction between *physical* and *perceptual*. To illustrate the difference, consider the two situations in **Figure 1.20**. In (a), the light from one light bulb with a physical intensity of 10 is focused into a person's eye. In (b), the light from two light bulbs, with a total intensity of 20, is focused into the person's eye. All of this so far has been *physical*. If we were to measure the intensities of the lights with a light meter we would find that the person receives twice as much light in (b) as in (a).

But what does the person *perceive*? Perception of the light is measured not by determining the intensity but by

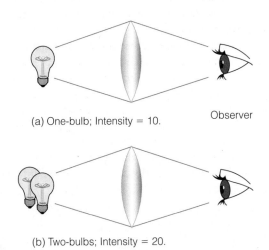

(a) One-bulb; Intensity = 10.   Observer

(b) Two-bulbs; Intensity = 20.

Figure 1.20 A subject (indicated by the eye) is viewing lights with different physical intensities. The two lights at (b) have twice the physical intensity as the single light at (a). However, when the subject is asked to judge brightness, which is a perceptual judgment, the light at (b) is judged to be only about 20 or 30 percent brighter than the light at (a).

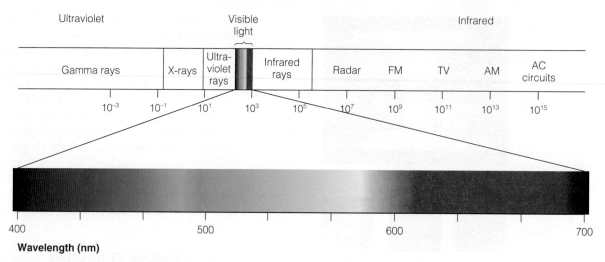

Ultraviolet   Visible light   Infrared

| Gamma rays | X-rays | Ultra-violet rays | | Infrared rays | Radar | FM | TV | AM | AC circuits |

10^{-3} 10^{-1} 10^{1} 10^{3} 10^{5} 10^{7} 10^{9} 10^{11} 10^{13} 10^{15}

400   500   600   700

Wavelength (nm)

Figure 1.21 The electromagnetic spectrum, shown on top, stretches from gamma rays to AC circuits. The visible spectrum, shown exploded below, accounts for only a small part of the electromagnetic spectrum. We are blind to energy outside of the visible spectrum.

determining *perceived brightness* using a method such as magnitude estimation (see page 15). What happens to brightness when we double the intensity from (a) to (b)? The answer is that (b) will appear brighter than (a), but not twice as bright. If the brightness is judged to be 10 for light (a), the brightness of light (b) will be judged to be about 12 or 13 (Stevens, 1962; also see Appendix C, page 386). Thus, there is not a one-to-one relationship between the physical intensity of the light and our perceptual response to the light.

Another example of the distinction between physical and perceptual is the Hermann grid in Figure 1.19b, because while the white corridors are all exactly the same white, people perceive dark spots at the intersections. Physical and perceptual are clearly not the same in this situation.

The Hermann grid creates an "illusory perception" in which we perceive dark spots that aren't physically present. But sometimes we fail to perceive stimuli that *are* physically present. Consider, for example the **electromagnetic spectrum** in **Figure 1.21**. The electromagnetic spectrum is a band of energy ranging from gamma rays at the short-wave end of the spectrum to AM radio and AC circuits at the long-wave end. But we see just the small band of energy called visible light, sandwiched between the ultraviolet and infrared energy bands. We are blind to ultraviolet and shorter wavelengths (although hummingbirds can see ultraviolet wavelengths that are invisible to us). We also can't see at the high end of the spectrum, in the infrared and

above, which is probably a good thing—imagine the visual clutter we would experience if we could see all of those cell phone conversations carrying their messages through the air!

What these examples illustrate is that what physical measuring instruments record and what we perceive are two different things. Ludy Benjamin, in his book *A History of Psychology* (1997), makes this point when he observes that "If changes in physical stimuli always resulted in similar changes in perception of those stimuli . . . there would be no need for psychology; human perception could be wholly explained by the laws of the discipline of physics" (p. 120). But perception is psychology, not physics, and perceptual responses are not necessarily the same as the responses of physical measuring devices. We will, therefore, be careful, throughout this book, to distinguish between physical stimuli and the perceptual responses to these stimuli.

TEST YOURSELF 1.2

1. What was Fechner's contribution to psychology?
2. Describe the five questions that can be asked about the world out there and the measurement techniques that are used to answer them.
3. Why is it important to distinguish between physical and perceptual?

THINK ABOUT IT

1. This chapter argues that although perception seems simple, it is actually extremely complex when we consider "behind the scenes" activities that are not obvious as a person is experiencing perception. Cite an example of a similar situation from your own experience, in which an "outcome" that might seem as though it was achieved easily actually involved a complicated process that most people are unaware of.

2. Describe a situation in which you initially thought you saw or heard something but then realized that your initial perception was in error. What was the role of bottom-up and top-down processing in this example of first having an incorrect perception and then realizing what was actually there?

KEY TERMS

Absolute threshold (p. 14)
Action (p. 9)
Bottom-up processing (p. 10)
Categorize (p. 10)
Cerebral cortex (p. 8)
Classical psychophysical methods (p. 14)
Cognitive influences on perception (p. 13)
Difference threshold (p. 14)
Distal stimulus (p. 6)
Electromagnetic spectrum (p. 18)
Frontal lobe (p. 8)
Grating acuity (p. 11)
Hermann grid (p. 16)
Knowledge (p. 9)
Magnitude estimation (p. 15)

Method of limits (p. 14)
Neural processing (p. 8)
Oblique effect (p. 11)
Occipital lobe (p. 8)
Parietal lobe (p. 8)
Perceived magnitude (p. 15)
Perception (p. 4)
Perceptual process (p. 5)
Phenomenological report (p. 16)
Physiology–perception relationship (p. 12)
Primary receiving area (p. 8)
Principle of representation (p. 7)
Principle of transformation (p. 7)
Proximal stimulus (p. 7)

Psychophysics (p. 14)
Rat–man demonstration (p. 10)
Reaction time (p. 16)
Recognition (p. 16)
Sensation (p. 5)
Sensory receptors (p. 7)
Stimulus–perception relationship (p. 11)
Stimulus–physiology relationship (p. 11)
Temporal lobe (p. 8)
Thresholds (p. 13)
Top-down processing (knowledge-based processing) (p. 10)
Transduction (p. 7)
Visual form agnosia (p. 8)
Visual pigment (p. 7)

One message of this book is that your experience is created by properties of your perceptual system. This chapter starts at the beginning of the process and shows how visual experience depends on whether you are seeing with cone receptors or with rod receptors. Cone vision creates a sharp full-color experience, whereas rod vision creates a less sharp black-and-white experience.

CHAPTER 2

The Beginning of the Perceptual Process

CHAPTER CONTENTS

Starting at the Beginning

Light, the Eye, and the Visual Receptors
Light: The Stimulus for Vision
The Eye

Focusing Light Onto the Receptors

Receptors and Perception
Transforming Light Energy Into Electrical Energy

Adapting to the Dark
Spectral Sensitivity

Electrical Signals in Neurons
Recording Electrical Signals in Neurons
Basic Properties of Action Potentials
Chemical Basis of Action Potentials
Transmitting Information Across a Gap

Neural Convergence and Perception

Convergence Causes the Rods to Be More Sensitive Than the Cones
Lack of Convergence Causes the Cones to Have Better Acuity Than the Rods

SOMETHING TO CONSIDER: Early Events Are Powerful

DEVELOPMENTAL DIMENSION: Infant Visual Acuity

THINK ABOUT IT

Some Questions We Will Consider:

- How does the focusing system at the front of our eye affect our perception? (p. 25)
- How do chemicals in the eye called visual pigments affect our perception? (p. 30)
- How can the way neurons are "wired up" affect perception? (p. 39)

How does a tree become a perception of a tree? One way to answer this question is to refer back to the perceptual process shown in Figure 1.1: Information about the tree (*distal stimulus*) is carried in light reflected from the tree and into the eye. When this light reaches the receptors in the retina, creating the *proximal stimulus*, it becomes transformed into electrical signals that contain information about the tree, which are transmitted to the brain, where eventually these electrical signals become transformed into a *perception* of the tree.

In this chapter we will focus on the beginning of the perceptual process. Although we will use visual examples to describe the initial processes of the perceptual process, many of the principles we will be describing hold for the other senses as well. Just as the person from Chapter 1 sees the tree because light is reflected from it into his eyes, he hears the rustle of its branches because sound energy in the form of pressure changes in the air enters his ears. In both cases, stimuli trigger a process that ends up with perception occurring as a result of activity in the brain. Similar events occur for feeling the texture of the tree's bark, smelling its blossoms, and tasting its fruit. By the time you finish this book, you will see that although there are numerous differences between the senses, they all operate according to similar principles.

Starting at the Beginning

The idea that perception starts at the beginning of the perceptual process may sound obvious. But as we will see, there is enough going on right at the beginning of the perceptual process to fill a whole chapter and more, and most of what goes on can affect perception. So, the first step in understanding perception is to take a close look at the processes that begin, in the case of vision, with light reflected from an object into the eye.

Figure 2.1 shows the first four steps of the visual process, which starts on the right and moves to the left to match the perceptual process in Figure 1.1. Following the sequence of the physical events in the process, shown in black along the bottom of the figure, we begin with Step 1, the distal stimulus (the tree); then move to Step 2, in which light is reflected from the tree and enters the eye to create the proximal stimulus on

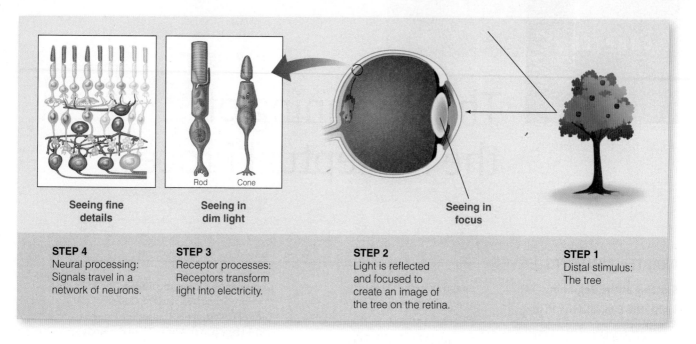

Seeing fine details	**Seeing in dim light**	**Seeing in focus**	

STEP 4	**STEP 3**	**STEP 2**	**STEP 1**
Neural processing: Signals travel in a network of neurons.	Receptor processes: Receptors transform light into electricity.	Light is reflected and focused to create an image of the tree on the retina.	Distal stimulus: The tree

Figure 2.1 Chapter preview. This chapter will describe the first three steps of the perceptual process for vision and will introduce Step 4. Physical processes are indicated in black; the perceptual outcomes of these processes are indicated in blue.

the visual receptors; then to Step 3, in which receptors transform light into electrical signals; and finally to Step 4, in which electrical signals are "processed" as they travel through a network of neurons. Our goal in this chapter is to show how these physical events influence the following aspects of perception, shown in blue in Figure 2.1: (1) seeing in focus, (2) seeing in dim light, and (3) seeing fine details. We begin by describing light, the eye, and the receptors in the retina that line the back of the eye.

Light, the Eye, and the Visual Receptors

The ability to see a tree, or any other object, depends on light being reflected from that object into the eye.

Light: The Stimulus for Vision

Vision is based on visible light, which is a band of energy within the electromagnetic spectrum. The electromagnetic spectrum is a continuum of electromagnetic energy that is produced by electric charges and is radiated as waves (see Figure 1.21, page 18). The energy in this spectrum can be described by its **wavelength**—the distance between the peaks of the electromagnetic waves. The wavelengths in the electromagnetic spectrum range from extremely short-wavelength gamma rays (wavelength = about 10^{-12} meters, or one ten-billionth of a meter) to long-wavelength radio waves (wavelength = about 10^4 meters, or 10,000 meters).

Visible light, the energy within the electromagnetic spectrum that humans can perceive, has wavelengths ranging from about 400 to 700 nanometers (nm), where 1 nanometer = 10^{-9} meters, which means that the longest visible wavelengths are slightly less than one-thousandth of a millimeter long. For humans and some other animals, the wavelength of visible light is associated with the different colors of the spectrum, with short wavelengths appearing blue, middle wavelengths green, and long wavelengths yellow, orange, and red.

The Eye

The **eyes** contain the receptors for vision. The first eyes, which appeared back in the Cambrian period (570–500 million years ago), were eyespots on primitive animals such as flatworms that could distinguish light from dark but couldn't detect features of the environment. Detecting an object's details didn't become possible until more sophisticated eyes evolved to include optical systems that could produce images and therefore provide information about shapes and details of objects and the arrangement of objects within scenes (Fernald, 2006).

Light reflected from objects in the environment enters the eye through the **pupil** and is focused by the **cornea** and **lens** to form sharp images of the objects on the **retina**, the network of neurons that covers the back of the eye and that contains the receptors for vision (**Figure 2.2a**). There are two types of visual receptors, **rods** and **cones**, so called because of the rod- and cone-shaped **outer segments** (**Figure 2.3**). The outer segments are the part of the receptor that contains light-sensitive

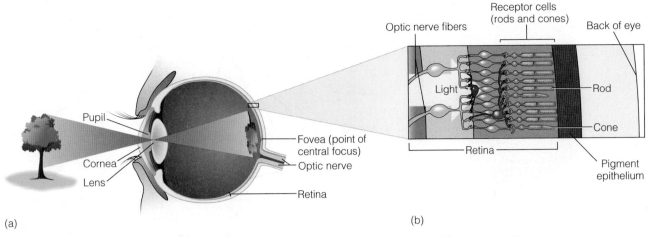

Figure 2.2 An image of the tree is focused on the retina, which lines the back of the eye. The close-up of the retina on the right shows the receptors and other neurons that make up the retina.

chemicals called **visual pigments** that react to light and trigger electrical signals. Signals from the receptors flow through the network of neurons that make up the retina (**Figure 2.2b**) and emerge from the back of the eye in the **optic nerve**, which contains a million optic nerve fibers that conduct signals toward the brain.

The rod and cone receptors not only have different shapes, they are also distributed differently across the retina. From **Figure 2.4**, which indicates the rod and cone distributions, we can conclude the following:

1. One small area, the **fovea**, contains only cones. When we look directly at an object, the object's image falls on the fovea.
2. The **peripheral retina**, which includes all of the retina outside of the fovea, contains both rods and cones. It is important to note that although the fovea has *only* cones, there are also many cones in the peripheral retina.

The fovea is so small (about the size of this "o") that it contains only about 1 percent, or 50,000, of the 6 million cones in the retina (Tyler, 1997a, 1997b).

3. The peripheral retina contains many more rods than cones because there are about 120 million rods and only 6 million cones in the retina.

One way to appreciate the fact that the rods and cones are distributed differently in the retina is by considering what happens when functioning receptors are missing from one area of the retina. A condition called **macular degeneration**, which is most common in older people, destroys the cone-rich fovea and a small area that surrounds it. (*Macula* is a term usually associated with medical practice that includes the fovea plus a small area surrounding the fovea.) This creates a blind region in central vision, so when a person looks directly at something, he or she loses sight of it (**Figure 2.5a**).

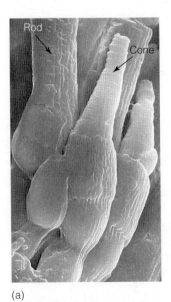

(a)

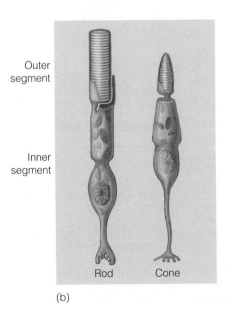

(b)

Figure 2.3 (a) Scanning electromicrograph of the rod and cone receptors in the retina, showing the rod-shaped and cone-shaped receptor outer segments. (b) Rod and cone receptors, showing the inner and outer segments. The outer segments contain the light-sensitive visual pigment. (From Lewis et al., 1969)

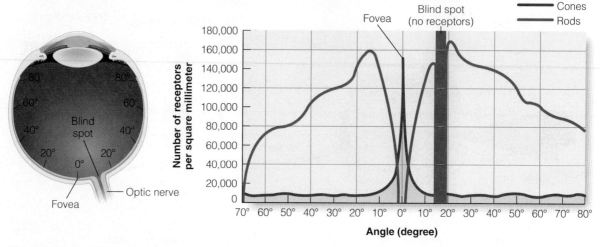

Figure 2.4 The distribution of rods and cones in the retina. The eye on the left indicates locations in degrees relative to the fovea. These locations are repeated along the bottom of the chart on the right. The vertical brown bar near 20 degrees indicates the place on the retina where there are no receptors because this is where the ganglion cells leave the eye to form the optic nerve. (Adapted from Lindsay & Norman, 1977)

(a) (b)

Figure 2.5 (a) In a condition called macular degeneration, the fovea and surrounding area degenerate, so the person cannot see whatever he or she is looking at. (b) In retinitis pigmentosa, the peripheral retina initially degenerates and causes loss of vision in the periphery. The resulting condition is sometimes called "tunnel vision."

Another condition, called **retinitis pigmentosa**, is a degeneration of the retina that is passed from one generation to the next (although not always affecting everyone in a family). This condition first attacks the peripheral rod receptors and results in poor vision in the peripheral visual field (**Figure 2.5b**). Eventually, in severe cases, the foveal cone receptors are also attacked, resulting in complete blindness.

Before leaving the rod–cone distribution shown in Figure 2.4, note that there is one area in the retina, indicated by the vertical brown bar, where there are no receptors. **Figure 2.6** shows a close-up of the place where this occurs, which is where the nerve fibers that make up the optic nerve leave the eye. Because of the absence of receptors, this place is called the **blind spot**. Although you are not normally aware

of the blind spot, you can become aware of it by doing the following demonstration.

DEMONSTRATION | Becoming Aware of the Blind Spot

Place the book (or your electronic device if you are reading the ebook) on your desk. Close your right eye, and position yourself above the book/device so that the cross in **Figure 2.7** is aligned with your left eye. Be sure the book page is flat and, while looking at the cross, slowly move closer. As you move closer, be sure not to move your eye from the cross, but at the same time keep noticing the circle off to the side. At some point, around 3 to 9 inches from the book/device, the circle should disappear. When this happens, the image of the circle is falling on your blind spot.

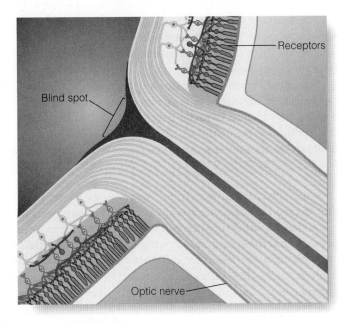

Figure 2.6 There are no receptors at the place where the optic nerve leaves the eye. This enables the receptor's ganglion cell fibers to flow into the optic nerve. The absence of receptors in this area creates the blind spot.

Figure 2.7 Blind spot demonstration.

Why aren't we usually aware of the blind spot? One reason is that the blind spot is located off to the side of our visual field, where objects are not in sharp focus. Because of this and because we don't know exactly where to look for it (as opposed to the demonstration, in which we are focusing our attention on the circle), the blind spot is hard to detect.

But the most important reason that we don't see the blind spot is that some mechanism in the brain "fills in" the place where the image disappears (Churchland & Ramachandran, 1996). The next demonstration illustrates an important property of this filling-in process.

DEMONSTRATION | Filling In the Blind Spot

Close your right eye and, with the cross in **Figure 2.8** lined up with your left eye, move toward the "wheel". When the center of the wheel falls on your blind spot, notice how the spokes of the wheel fill in the hole (Ramachandran, 1992).

These demonstrations show that the brain does not fill in the area served by the blind spot with "nothing"; rather, it creates a perception that matches the surrounding pattern—the white page in the first demonstration, and the spokes of the wheel in the second one. This "filling in" is a preview of one of the themes of the book: how the brain creates a coherent perception of our world. For now, however, we return to the beginning of the perceptual process, as light reflected from objects in the environment is focused onto the receptors.

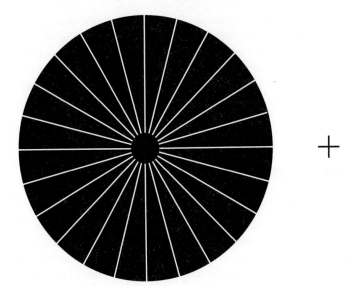

Figure 2.8 View the pattern as described in the text, and observe what happens when the center of the wheel falls on your blind spot. (Adapted from Ramachandran, 1992)

Focusing Light Onto the Receptors

Light reflected from an object into the eye is focused onto the retina by a two-element optical system: the cornea and the lens. The cornea, the transparent covering of the front of the eye, accounts for about 80 percent of the eye's focusing power, but like the lenses in eyeglasses, it is fixed in place so it can't adjust its focus. The lens, which supplies the remaining 20 percent of the eye's focusing power, can change its shape to adjust the eye's focus for objects located at different distances. This change in shape is achieved by the action of *ciliary muscles*, which increase the focusing power of the lens (its ability to bend light) by increasing its curvature (compare **Figure 2.9b** and **Figure 2.9c**).

We can understand why the eye needs to adjust its focus by first considering what happens when the eye is relaxed and a person with normal (20/20) vision views a small object that is far away. If the object is located more than about 20 feet away, the light rays that reach the eye are essentially parallel (**Figure 2.9a**), and the cornea–lens combination brings these parallel rays to a focus on the retina at point A. But if the object moves closer to the eye, the light rays reflected from this object enter the eye at more of an angle, and this pushes the focus point back so if the back of the eye weren't there, light would be focused at point B (**Figure 2.9b**). Because the light is stopped by the back of the eye before it reaches point B, the image on the retina is out of focus. If things remained in this state, the person would see the object as blurred.

The adjustable lens, which controls a process called *accommodation*, comes to the rescue to help prevent blurring. **Accommodation** is the change in the lens's shape that occurs when the ciliary muscles at the front of the eye tighten and increase the curvature of the lens so that it gets thicker (**Figure 2.9c**). This increased curvature increases the bending of the light rays passing through the lens so the focus point is pulled back to A to create a sharp image on the retina. This means that as you look around at different objects, your eye is constantly adjusting its focus by accommodating, especially for nearby objects. The following demonstration shows that this is necessary because everything is not in focus at once.

DEMONSTRATION | Becoming Aware of What Is in Focus

Accommodation occurs unconsciously, so you are usually unaware that the lens is constantly changing its focusing power to let you see clearly at different distances. This unconscious focusing process works so efficiently that most people assume that everything, near and far, is always in focus. You can demonstrate that this is not so by holding a pen or a pencil, point up, at arm's length, closing one eye, and looking past the pencil at

an object that is at least 20 feet away. As you stay focused on the faraway object, notice the pencil point without actually looking at it (be sure to stay focused on the far object). The point will probably appear slightly blurred.

Then slowly move the pencil toward you while still looking at the far object. Notice that as the pencil moves closer, the point becomes more blurred. When the pencil is about 12 inches away, shift your focus to the pencil point. This shift in focus causes the pencil point to appear sharp, but the far object is now out of focus.

When you changed focus from far away to the nearby pencil point during this demonstration, you were changing your accommodation. Either near objects or far objects can be in focus, but not both at the same time. Accommodation, therefore, makes it possible to adjust vision for different distances. However, as people get older, their ability to accommodate decreases due to hardening of the lens and weakening of the ciliary muscles, and

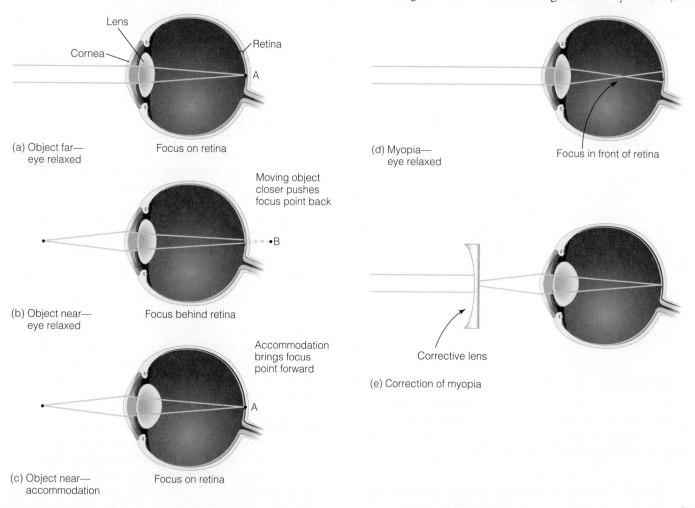

Figure 2.9 Focusing of light rays by the eye. (a) Rays of light coming from a small light source that is more than 20 feet away are approximately parallel. The focus point for parallel light is at A on the retina. (b) Moving an object closer to the relaxed eye pushes the focus point back. Here the focus point is at B, but light is stopped by the back of the eye, so the image on the retina is out of focus. (c) Accommodation of the eye (indicated by the fatter lens) increases the focusing power of the lens and brings the focus point for a near object back to A on the retina, so it is in focus. This accommodation is caused by the action of the ciliary muscles, which are not shown. (d) In the myopic (nearsighted) eye, parallel rays from a distant spot of light are brought to a focus in front of the retina, so distant objects appear blurred. (e) A corrective lens bends light so it is focused on the retina.

so they become unable to accommodate enough to see objects, or read, at close range. This loss of the ability to accommodate, called **presbyopia** (for "old eye"), can be dealt with by wearing reading glasses, which brings near objects into focus by replacing the focusing power that can no longer be provided by the lens.

Another problem that can be solved by a corrective lens is **myopia**, or **nearsightedness**, an inability to see distant objects clearly. The reason for this difficulty, which affects more than 70 million Americans, is illustrated in **Figure 2.9d**. Myopia occurs when the optical system brings parallel rays of light into focus at a point in front of the retina, so the image that reaches the retina is blurred. This problem can be caused by either of two factors: (1) **refractive myopia**, in which the cornea and/or the lens bends the light too much, or (2) **axial myopia**, in which the eyeball is too long. Either way, images of faraway objects are not focused sharply, so objects look blurred. Corrective lenses can solve this problem, as shown in **Figure 2.9e**.

Finally, people with **hyperopia**, or **farsightedness**, can see distant objects clearly but have trouble seeing nearby objects because the focus point for parallel rays of light is located behind the retina, usually because the eyeball is too short. Young people can bring the image forward onto the retina by accommodating. However, older people, who have difficulty accommodating, often use corrective lenses that bring the focus point forward onto the retina.

Focusing an image clearly onto the retina is the initial step in the process of vision, but although a sharp image on the retina is essential for clear vision, we do not see the image on the retina. Vision occurs not in the retina but in the brain. Before the brain can create vision, the light on the retina must activate the visual receptors in the retina.

Receptors and Perception

Light entering visual receptors triggers electrical signals when the light is absorbed by light-sensitive *visual pigment* molecules in the receptors. This step is crucial for vision because it creates electrical signals that eventually signal the properties of the distal stimulus to the brain. But the importance of these visual pigments extends beyond triggering electrical signals. Visual pigments also shape our perceptions by determining our ability to see dim lights and our ability to see light in different parts of the visual spectrum. In this section, we first describe transduction, and then how the receptors shape perception.

Transforming Light Energy Into Electrical Energy

Transduction is the transformation of one form of energy into another form of energy (see Chapter 1, page 7). Visual transduction occurs in the rod and cone receptors, which transform light into electricity. The starting point for understanding how the rods and cones create electricity are the millions of molecules of a light-sensitive visual pigment that are contained in the outer segments of the receptors (Figure 2.3). Visual pigments have two parts: a long protein called *opsin* and a much smaller light-sensitive component called *retinal*. **Figure 2.10a** shows a model of a retinal molecule attached to opsin (Wald, 1968). Note that only a small part of the opsin is shown here; it is actually hundreds of times longer than the retinal.

Despite its small size compared to the opsin, retinal is the crucial part of the visual pigment molecule, because when the retinal and opsin are combined, the resulting molecule absorbs visible light. When the retinal part of the visual pigment molecule absorbs light, the retinal changes its shape, from being bent, as shown in Figure 2.10a, to straight, as shown in **Figure 2.10b**. This change of shape, called **isomerization**, creates a chemical chain reaction, illustrated in **Figure 2.11**, that activates thousands of charged molecules to create electrical signals in receptors.

What is important about the chain reaction that follows isomerization is that it amplifies the effect of isomerization. Isomerizing one visual pigment molecule triggers a chain of chemical reactions that releases as many as a million charged molecules, which leads to activation of the receptor (Baylor, 1992; Hamer et al., 2005).

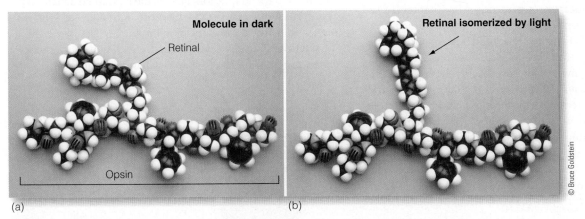

(a)　　　　　　　　　　　　　　　　　(b)

Figure 2.10 Model of a visual pigment molecule. The horizontal part of the model shows a tiny portion of the huge opsin molecule near where the retinal is attached. The smaller molecule on top of the opsin is the light-sensitive retinal. (a) The retinal molecule's shape before it absorbs light. (b) The retinal molecule's shape after it absorbs light. This change in shape, which is called isomerization, triggers a sequence of reactions that culminates in generation of an electrical response in the receptor.

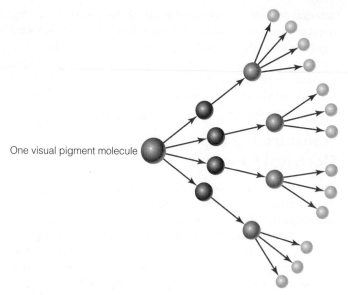

One visual pigment molecule

Figure 2.11 This sequence symbolizes the chain reaction that is triggered when a single visual pigment molecule is isomerized by absorption of a single photon of light. In the actual sequence of events, each visual pigment molecule activates hundreds more molecules, which, in turn, each activate about a thousand molecules. Isomerization of just one visual pigment molecule activates about a million other molecules, which activates the receptor.

Visual pigments not only create electrical signals in the receptors, they also shape specific aspects of our perceptions. Next, we will demonstrate how properties of the pigments influence perception. We do this by comparing the perceptions caused by the rod and cone receptors. As we will see, the visual pigments in these two types of receptors influence two aspects of visual perception: (1) how we adjust to darkness, and (2) how well we see light in different parts of the spectrum.

Adapting to the Dark

When we discussed measuring perception in Chapter 1, we noted that when a person goes from a lighted environment to a dark place, it may be difficult to see at first, but that after some time in the dark, the person becomes able to make out lights and objects that were invisible before (Figure 1.16, page 15). This process of increasing sensitivity in the dark, called **dark adaptation**, is measured by determining a **dark adaptation curve**. In this section we will show how the rod and cone receptors control an important aspect of vision: the ability of the visual system to adjust to dim levels of illumination. We will describe how the dark adaptation curve is measured, and how the increase in sensitivity that occurs in the dark has been linked to properties of the rod and cone visual pigments.

Measuring the Dark Adaptation Curve The study of dark adaptation begins with measuring the dark adaptation curve, which is the function relating sensitivity to light to time in the dark, beginning when the lights are extinguished.

METHOD | Measuring the Dark Adaptation Curve

The first step in measuring a dark adaption curve is to have the subject look at a small fixation point while paying attention to a flashing test light that is off to the side (**Figure 2.12**). Because the subject is looking directly at the fixation point, its image falls on the fovea, so the image of the test light falls on the peripheral retina, which contains both rods and cones. While still in the light, the subject turns a knob that adjusts the intensity of the flashing light until it can just barely be seen. This threshold for seeing the light, the minimum amount of energy necessary to just barely see the light, is then converted to *sensitivity*. Because sensitivity = 1/threshold, this means that a *high threshold* corresponds to *low sensitivity*. The sensitivity measured in the light is called the **light-adapted sensitivity**, because it is measured while the eyes are adapted to the light. Because the room (or adapting) lights are on, the intensity of the flashing test light has to be high to be seen. At the beginning of the experiment, then, the threshold is high and the sensitivity is low.

Once the light-adapted sensitivity to the flashing test light is determined, the adapting light is extinguished so the subject is in the dark. The subject continues adjusting the intensity of the flashing light so he or she can just barely see it, tracking the increase in sensitivity that occurs in the dark. As the subject becomes more sensitive to the light, he or she must decrease the light's intensity to keep it just barely visible. The result, shown as the red curve in **Figure 2.13**, is a dark adaptation curve.

The dark adaptation curve shows that as adaptation proceeds, the subject becomes more sensitive to the light. Note that higher sensitivity is at the bottom of this graph, so movement of the dark adaptation curve downward means that the subject's sensitivity is increasing. The red dark adaptation curve indicates that the subject's sensitivity increases in two phases. It increases rapidly for the first 3 to 4 minutes after the light is extinguished and then levels off. At about 7 to 10 minutes, it begins increasing again and continues to do so until the subject has been in the dark for about 20 or 30 minutes (Figure 2.13). The sensitivity at the end of dark adaptation, labeled **dark-adapted sensitivity**, is about 100,000 times greater than the light-adapted sensitivity measured before dark adaptation began.

Dark adaptation was involved in a 2007 episode of the *Mythbusters* program on the Discovery Channel, which was devoted

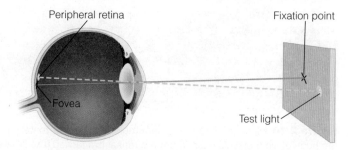

Peripheral retina

Fixation point

Fovea

Test light

Figure 2.12 Viewing conditions for a dark adaptation experiment. In this example, the image of the fixation point falls on the fovea, and the image of the test light falls on the peripheral retina.

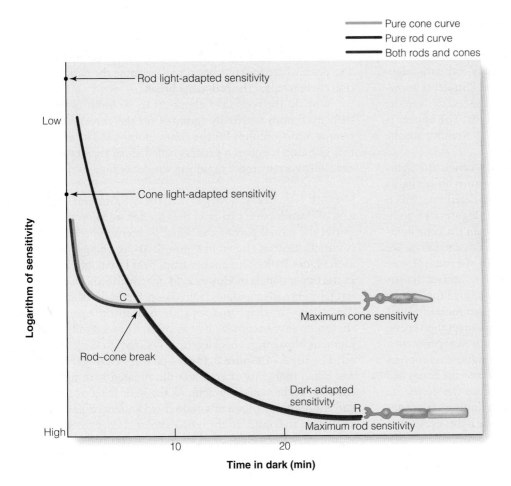

Pure cone curve
Pure rod curve
Both rods and cones

Figure 2.13 Three dark adaptation curves. The red line is the two-stage dark adaptation curve, with an initial cone branch and a later rod branch, which occurs when the test light is in the peripheral retina, as shown in Figure 2.12. The green line is the cone adaptation curve, which occurs when the test light falls on the fovea. The purple curve is the rod adaptation curve measured in a rod monochromat. Note that the downward movement of these curves represents an *increase* in sensitivity. The curves actually begin at the points indicating "light-adapted sensitivity," but there is a slight delay between the time the lights are turned off and when measurement of the curves begins.

to investigating myths about pirates. One of the myths was that pirates wore eye patches to preserve night vision in one eye so that when they went from the bright light outside to the darkness below decks, removing the patch would enable them to see. To determine whether this would work, the Mythbusters carried out some tasks in a dark room just after both of their eyes had been in the light and did some different tasks with an eye that had previously been covered with a patch for 30 minutes. It isn't surprising that they completed the tasks much more rapidly when using the eye that had been patched. Anyone who has taken a course on sensation and perception could have told the Mythbusters that the eye patch would work because keeping an eye in the dark triggers the process of dark adaptation, which causes the eye to increase its sensitivity in the dark.

Whether pirates actually used patches to help them see below decks remains an unproven hypothesis. One argument against the idea that pirates wore eye patches to keep their sensitivity high is that patching one eye causes a decrease in depth perception, which might be a serious disadvantage when the pirate is working on deck. We will discuss why two eyes are important for depth perception in Chapter 10.

Although the Mythbusters showed that dark adapting one eye made it easier to see with that eye in the dark, we have a more specific goal. We are interested in showing that the first part of the dark adaptation curve is caused by the cones and the second part is caused by the rods. We will do this by running two additional dark adaptation experiments, one measuring adaptation of the cones and another measuring adaptation of the rods.

Measuring Cone Adaptation The reason the red curve in Figure 2.13 has two phases is that the flashing test light fell on the peripheral retina, which contains both rods and cones. To measure dark adaptation of the cones alone, we have to ensure that the image of the test light falls only on cones. We achieve this by having the subject look directly at the test light so its image falls on the all-cone fovea, and by making the test light small enough so that its entire image falls within the fovea. The dark adaptation curve determined by this procedure is indicated by the green line in Figure 2.13. This curve, which measures only the activity of the cones, matches the initial phase of our original dark adaptation curve but does not include the second phase. Does this mean that the second part of the curve is due to the rods? We can show that the answer to this question is "yes" by doing another experiment.

Measuring Rod Adaptation We know that the green curve in Figure 2.13 is due only to cone adaptation because our test light was focused on the all-cone fovea. Because the cones are more sensitive to light at the beginning of dark adaptation, they control our vision during the early stages of adaptation, so we can't see what the rods are doing. In order to reveal how the sensitivity of the rods is changing at the very beginning of dark adaptation, we need to measure dark adaptation in a person who has no cones. Such people, who have no cones because of a rare genetic defect, are called **rod monochromats**. Their all-rod retinas provide a way for us to study rod dark adaptation without interference from the cones. (Students sometimes wonder why we can't simply present the test flash to the peripheral retina, which contains mostly rods. The answer is that there are enough cones in the periphery to influence the beginning of the dark adaptation curve.)

Because the rod monochromat has no cones, the light-adapted sensitivity we measure just before we turn off the lights is determined by the rods. The sensitivity we determine, which is labeled "rod light-adapted sensitivity" in Figure 2.13, indicates that the rods are much less sensitive than the cone light-adapted sensitivity we measured in our original experiment. We can also see that once dark adaptation begins, the rods increase their sensitivity, as indicated by the purple curve, and reach their final dark-adapted level in about 25 minutes (Rushton, 1961). The end of this rod adaptation measured in our monochromat matches the second part of the two-stage dark adaptation curve.

Based on the results of our dark adaptation experiments, we can summarize the process of dark adaptation. As soon as the light is extinguished, the sensitivity of *both* the cones *and* the rods begins increasing. However, because the cones are much more sensitive than the rods at the beginning of dark adaptation, we see with our cones right after the lights are turned out. One way to think about this is that the cones have "center stage" at the beginning of dark adaptation, while the rods are working "behind the scenes." However, after about 3 to 5 minutes in the dark, the cones have reached their maximum sensitivity, as indicated by the leveling off of the dark adaptation curve. Meanwhile, the rods are still adapting, behind the scenes, and by about 7 minutes in the dark, the rods' sensitivity

finally catches up to the cones'. The rods then become more sensitive than the cones, and rod adaptation, indicated by the second branch of the dark adaptation curve, becomes visible. The place where the rods begin to determine the dark adaptation curve is called the **rod–cone break**.

Why do the rods take about 20 to 30 minutes to reach their maximum sensitivity (point R on the curve) compared to only 3 to 4 minutes for the cones (point C)? The answer to this question involves a process called *visual pigment regeneration*, which occurs more rapidly in the cones than in the rods.

Visual Pigment Regeneration From our description of transduction earlier in the chapter, we know that light causes the retinal part of the visual pigment molecule, which is initially bent as shown in Figure 2.10a, to change its shape as in Figure 2.10b. This change from bent to straight is shown in the upper panels of **Figure 2.14**, which also shows how the retinal eventually separates from the *opsin* part of the molecule. This change in shape and separation from the opsin causes the molecule to become lighter in color, a process called **visual pigment bleaching**. This bleaching is shown in the lower panels of Figure 2.14. **Figure 2.14a** is a picture of a frog retina that was taken moments after it was illuminated with light. The red color is the visual pigment. As the light remains on, more and more of the pigment's retinal is isomerized and breaks away from the opsin, so the retina's color changes as shown in **Figures 2.14b** and **2.14c**.

When the pigments are in their lighter bleached state, they are no longer useful for vision. In order to do their job of changing light energy into electrical energy, the retinal needs to return to its bent shape and become reattached to the opsin. This process of reforming the visual pigment molecule is called **visual pigment regeneration**.

Figure 2.14 A frog retina was dissected from the eye in the dark and then exposed to light. The top row shows how the relationship between retinal and opsin changes after the retinal absorbs light. Only a small part of the opsin molecule is shown. The photographs in the bottom row show how the color of the retina changes after it is exposed to light. (a) This picture of the retina was taken just after the light was turned on. The dark red color is caused by the high concentration of visual pigment in the receptors that are still in the unbleached state. (b, c) After the retinal isomerizes, the retinal and opsin break apart, and the retina becomes bleached, as indicated by the lighter color.

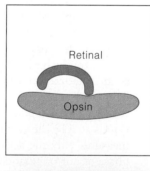
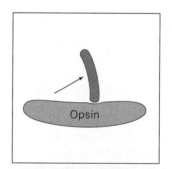
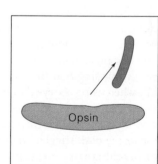
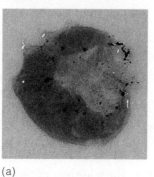
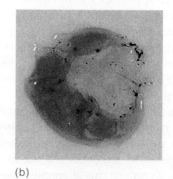
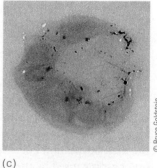

(a)   (b)   (c)

© Bruce Goldstein

When you are in the light, as you are now as you read this book, some of your visual pigment molecules are isomerizing and bleaching, as shown in Figure 2.14, while at the same time, others are regenerating. This means that in most normal light levels, your eye always contains some bleached visual pigment and some intact visual pigment. When you turn out the lights, the bleached visual pigment continues to regenerate, but there is no more isomerization, so eventually the concentration of regenerated pigment builds up so your retina contains only intact visual pigment molecules.

This increase in visual pigment concentration that occurs as the pigment regenerates in the dark is responsible for the increase in sensitivity we measure during dark adaptation. This relationship between pigment concentration and sensitivity was demonstrated by William Rushton (1961), who devised a procedure to measure the regeneration of visual pigment in humans by measuring the darkening of the retina that occurs during dark adaptation. (Think of this as Figure 2.14 proceeding from right to left.)

Rushton's measurements showed that cone pigment takes 6 minutes to regenerate completely, whereas rod pigment takes more than 30 minutes. When he compared the course of pigment regeneration to the dark adaptation curve, he found that the rate of cone dark adaptation matched the rate of cone pigment regeneration and the rate of rod dark adaptation matched the rate of rod pigment regeneration. These results demonstrated two important connections between perception and physiology:

1. Our sensitivity to light depends on the concentration of a chemical—the visual pigment.
2. The speed at which our sensitivity increases in the dark depends on a chemical reaction—the regeneration of the visual pigment.

What happens to vision if something prevents visual pigments from regenerating? This is what occurs when a person's retina becomes detached from the *pigment epithelium* (see Figure 2.2b), a layer that contains enzymes necessary for pigment regeneration. This condition, called **detached retina**, can occur as a result of traumatic injuries of the eye or head, as when a baseball player is hit in the eye by a line drive. When this occurs, the bleached pigment's separated retinal and opsin can no longer be recombined, and the person becomes blind in the area of the visual field served by the separated area of the retina. This condition is permanent unless the detached area of retina is reattached, which can be accomplished by laser surgery.

Spectral Sensitivity

Our discussion of rods and cones has emphasized how they control our vision as we adapt to darkness. Rods and cones also differ in the way they respond to light in different parts of the *visible spectrum* (Figure 1.21, page 18). The differences in the rod and cone responses to the spectrum have been studied by measuring the **spectral sensitivity** of rod vision and cone vision, where spectral sensitivity is the eye's sensitivity to light as a function of the light's wavelength. Spectral sensitivity is

measured by determining the **spectral sensitivity curve**—the relationship between wavelength and sensitivity.

Spectral Sensitivity Curves The following is the psychophysical method used to measure a spectral sensitivity curve.

METHOD | Measuring a Spectral Sensitivity Curve

To measure sensitivity to light at each wavelength across the spectrum, we present one wavelength at a time and measure the subject's sensitivity to each wavelength. Light of a single wavelength, called **monochromatic light**, can be created by using special filters or a device called a *spectrometer*. To determine a person's spectral sensitivity, we determine the person's threshold for seeing monochromatic lights across the spectrum using one of the psychophysical methods for measuring threshold described in Chapter 1 (p. 14) and Appendix A (p. 384). The threshold is usually not measured at *every* wavelength, but at regular intervals. Thus, we might measure the threshold first at 400 nm, then at 410 nm, and so on. The result is the curve in **Figure 2.15a**, which shows that the threshold is higher at short

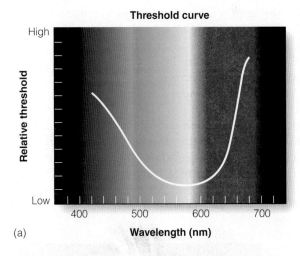

(a)

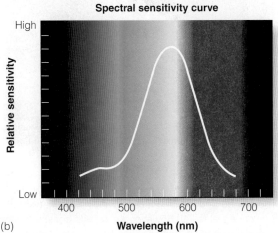

(b)

Figure 2.15 (a) The threshold for seeing a light as a function of wavelength. (b) Relative sensitivity as a function of wavelength—the *spectral sensitivity curve.* (Adapted from Wald, 1964)

and long wavelengths and lower in the middle of the spectrum; that is, less light is needed to see wavelengths in the middle of the spectrum than to see wavelengths at either the short- or long-wavelength end of the spectrum.

The ability to see wavelengths across the spectrum is often plotted not in terms of *threshold* versus wavelength, as in Figure 2.15a, but in terms of *sensitivity* versus wavelength. Using the equation, sensitivity = 1/threshold, we can convert the threshold curve in Figure 2.15a into the curve in **Figure 2.15b**, which is called the *spectral sensitivity curve*.

We measure the **cone spectral sensitivity** curve by having a subject look directly at a test light so that it stimulates only the cones in the fovea. We measure the **rod spectral sensitivity curve** by measuring sensitivity after the eye is dark adapted (so the rods control vision because they are the most sensitive receptors) and presenting test flashes in the peripheral retina, off to the side of the fixation point.

The cone and rod spectral sensitivity curves in **Figure 2.16** show that the rods are more sensitive to short-wavelength light than are the cones, with the rods being most sensitive to light of 500 nm and the cones being most sensitive to light of 560 nm. This difference in the sensitivity of cones and rods to different wavelengths means that as vision shifts from the cones in the light-adapted eye to the rods after the eye has become dark adapted, our vision shifts to become relatively more sensitive to short-wavelength light—that is, light nearer the blue and green end of the spectrum.

You may have noticed an effect of this shift to short-wavelength sensitivity if you have observed how green foliage seems to stand out more near dusk. This enhanced perception of short wavelengths during dark adaptation is called the **Purkinje** (Pur-kin'-jee) **shift** after Johann Purkinje, who described this effect in 1825. You can experience this shift in color sensitivity during dark adaptation by closing one eye for

Figure 2.17 Flowers for demonstrating the Purkinje shift. See text for explanation.

5 to 10 minutes so it dark adapts, then switching back and forth between your eyes and noticing how the blue flower in **Figure 2.17** is brighter compared to the red flower in your dark-adapted eye.

Rod- and Cone-Pigment Absorption Spectra Just as we can trace the difference in the rate of rod and cone dark adaptation to a property of the visual pigments (the cone pigment regenerates faster than the rod pigment), we can trace the difference in the rod and cone spectral sensitivity curves to the rod and cone pigment *absorption spectra*. A pigment's **absorption spectrum** is a plot of the amount of light absorbed versus the wavelength of the light. The absorption spectra of the rod and cone pigments are shown in **Figure 2.18**. The rod pigment absorbs best at 500 nm, the blue-green area of the spectrum.

There are three absorption spectra for the cones because there are three different cone pigments, each contained in its own receptor. The short-wavelength pigment (S) absorbs light best at about 419 nm; the medium-wavelength pigment (M) absorbs light best at about 531 nm; and the long-wavelength pigment (L) absorbs light best at about 558 nm. We will have more to say about the three cone pigments in Chapter 9, because they are the basis of our ability to see colors.

The absorption of the rod visual pigment closely matches the rod spectral sensitivity curve (Figure 2.18), and the short-, medium-, and long-wavelength cone pigments add together to result in a psychophysical spectral sensitivity curve that peaks at 560 nm. Because there are fewer short-wavelength receptors and therefore much less of the short-wavelength pigment, the cone spectral sensitivity curve is determined mainly by the medium- and long-wavelength pigments (Bowmaker & Dartnall, 1980; Stiles, 1953).

It is clear from the evidence we have presented that the increase in sensitivity that occurs in the dark (dark adaptation) and the sensitivity to different wavelengths across the spectrum (spectral sensitivity) are determined by the properties of the rod and cone visual pigments. Thus, even though perception—the conscious experience that results from stimulation of the senses—does not occur in the eye, our experience is definitely affected by what happens there.

We have now traveled through the first three steps in the perceptual process. The tree (Step 1) reflects light, which is

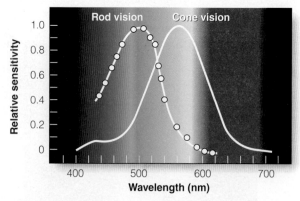

Figure 2.16 Spectral sensitivity curves for rod vision (left) and cone vision (right). The maximum sensitivities of these two curves have been set equal to 1.0. However, the relative sensitivities of the rods and the cones depend on the conditions of adaptation: The cones are more sensitive in the light, and the rods are more sensitive in the dark. The circles plotted on top of the rod curve are the absorption spectrum of the rod visual pigment. (From Wald & Brown, 1958)

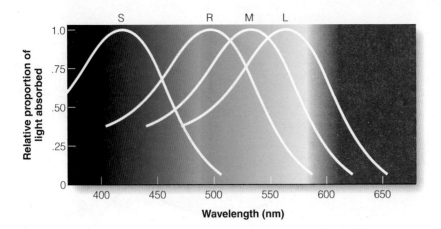

Figure 2.18 Absorption spectra of the rod pigment (R), and the short- (S), medium- (M), and long-wavelength (L) cone pigments. (Based on Dartnall, Bowmaker, & Mollon, 1983)

focused onto the retina by the eye's optical system (Step 2). The visual receptors shape perception as they transform light energy into electrical energy (Step 3). We are now ready to move to Step 4, the transmission and processing of electrical signals. But before we can begin describing electrical signals and what happens to them on their journey from receptors to the brain, we need to spend a few pages describing these electrical signals.

TEST YOURSELF 2.1

1. Describe light, the structure of the eye, and the rod and cone receptors. How are the rods and cones distributed across the retina?

2. How does moving an object closer to the eye affect how light reflected from the object is focused on the retina?

3. How does the eye adjust the focusing of light by accommodation? Describe the following conditions that can cause problems in focusing: presbyopia, myopia, hyperopia. How are these problems solved through either accommodation or corrective lenses?

4. Where on the retina does a researcher need to present a stimulus to test dark adaptation of the cones? How is this related to the distribution of the rods and cones on the retina? How can the adaptation of cones be measured without any interference from the rods? How can adaptation of the rods be measured without any interference from the cones?

5. Describe how rod and cone sensitivity changes starting when the lights are turned off and how this change in sensitivity continues for 20 to 30 minutes in the dark. When do the rods begin adapting? When do the rods become more sensitive than the cones?

6. What happens to visual pigment molecules when they (a) absorb light and (b) regenerate? What is the connection between visual pigment regeneration and dark adaptation?

7. What is spectral sensitivity? How is a cone spectral sensitivity curve determined? A rod spectral sensitivity curve?

8. What is a pigment absorption spectrum? How do rod and cone pigment absorption spectra compare, and what is their relationship to rod and cone spectral sensitivity?

Electrical Signals in Neurons

Electrical signals occur in structures called **neurons**, like the ones shown in **Figure 2.19**. The key components of neurons, shown in the neuron on the right in Figure 2.19, are the **cell body**, which contains mechanisms to keep the cell alive; **dendrites**, which branch out from the cell body to receive electrical signals from other neurons; and the **axon**, or **nerve fiber**,

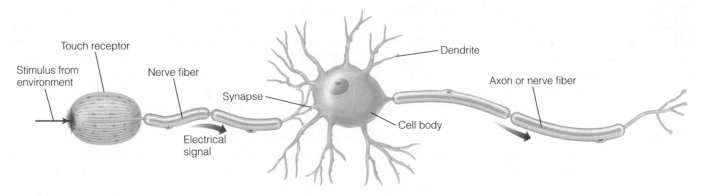

Figure 2.19 The neuron on the right consists of a cell body, dendrites, and an axon, or nerve fiber. The neuron on the left that receives stimuli from the environment has a receptor in place of the cell body.

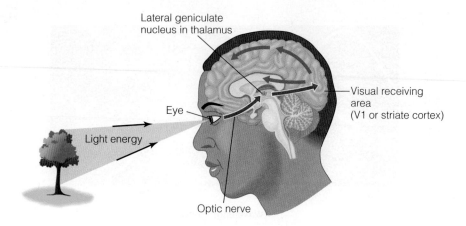

Figure 2.20 Side view of the visual system showing the three major sites along the primary visual pathway: the eye, the lateral geniculate nucleus, and the visual receiving area, which is also called the striate cortex or Area V1.

which is filled with fluid that conducts electrical signals. There are variations on this basic neuron structure: Some neurons have long axons; others have short axons or none at all. Especially important for perception are *sensory receptors*, which are neurons specialized to respond to environmental stimuli. In Figure 2.19, the receptor on the left responds to touch stimuli.

Individual neurons do not, of course, exist in isolation. There are hundreds of millions of neurons in the nervous system and, as we will see, each neuron is connected to many other neurons. In the case of vision, each eye contains more than 100 million receptors, each of which transmits signals to neurons within the retina. These signals are transmitted out of the back of the eye in the optic nerve to a group of neurons called the *lateral geniculate nucleus* and then to the *visual receiving area* in the cortex (**Figure 2.20**). All along this pathway from eye to cortex, and then within the cortex, individual neurons are transmitting messages about the tree.

One of the most important ways of studying how the tree is represented by electrical signals is to record signals from single neurons. We can appreciate the importance of being able to record from single neurons by considering the following analogy: You walk into a large room in which hundreds of people are talking about a political speech they have just heard. There is a great deal of noise and commotion in the room as people react to the speech. Based on hearing this "crowd noise," all you can say about what is going on is that the speech seems to have generated a great deal of excitement. To get more specific information about the speech, you need to listen to what individual people are saying.

Just as listening to individual people provides valuable information about what is happening in a large crowd, recording from single neurons provides valuable information about what is happening in the nervous system. Recording from single neurons is like listening to individual voices. It is important to record from as many neurons as possible, of course, because just as individual people may have different opinions about the speech, different neurons may respond differently to a particular stimulus or situation.

The ability to record electrical signals from individual neurons ushered in the modern era of brain research, and in the 1950s and 1960s, development of sophisticated electronics and the availability of computers made possible more detailed analysis of how neurons function.

Recording Electrical Signals in Neurons

Electrical signals are recorded from the axons (or nerve fibers) of neurons using small electrodes to pick up the signals.

METHOD | The Setup for Recording From a Single Neuron

Figure 2.21a shows a typical setup used for recording from a single neuron. There are two electrodes: a *recording electrode*, shown with its recording tip inside the neuron,[1] and a *reference electrode*, located some distance away so it is not affected by the electrical signals. These two electrodes are connected to a meter that records the difference in charge between the tips of the two electrodes. This difference is displayed on a computer screen, like the one shown in **Figure 2.22**, which shows electrical signals being recorded from a neuron in a laboratory setting.

When the axon, or nerve fiber, is at rest, the difference in the electrical potential between the tips of the two electrodes is –70 millivolts (mV, where a millivolt is 1/1,000 of a volt), as shown on the right in Figure 2.21a. This means that the inside of the axon is 70 mV more negative than the outside. This value, which stays the same as long as there are no signals in the neuron, is called the **resting potential**.

Figure 2.21b shows what happens when the neuron's receptor is stimulated so that a signal is transmitted down the axon. As the signal passes the recording electrode, the charge inside the axon rises to +40 millivolts compared to the outside. As the signal continues past the electrode, the charge inside the fiber reverses course and starts becoming negative again (**Figure 2.21c**), until it returns to the resting level (**Figure 2.21d**). This signal, which is called the **action potential**, lasts about 1 millisecond (1/1,000 second).

Basic Properties of Action Potentials

An important property of the action potential is that it is a **propagated response**—once the response is triggered, it

[1]In practice, most recordings are achieved with the tip of the electrode positioned just outside the neuron because it is technically difficult to insert electrodes into the neuron, especially if it is small. However, if the electrode tip is close enough to the neuron, the electrode can pick up the signals generated by the neuron.

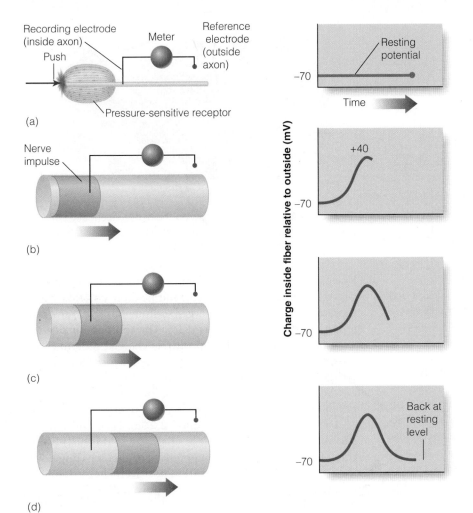

Recording electrode (inside axon)

Push

Meter

Reference electrode (outside axon)

Pressure-sensitive receptor

(a)

Nerve impulse

(b)

(c)

(d)

Charge inside fiber relative to outside (mV)

Resting potential

−70

Time

+40

−70

−70

Back at resting level

−70

Figure 2.21 (a) When a nerve fiber is at rest, there is a difference in charge of −70 mV between the inside and the outside of the fiber. This difference, which is measured by the meter indicated by the blue circle, is displayed on the right. (b) As the nerve impulse, indicated by the red band, passes the electrode, the inside of the fiber near the electrode becomes more positive. This positivity is the rising phase of the action potential. (c) As the nerve impulse moves past the electrode, the charge inside the fiber becomes more negative. This is the falling phase of the action potential. (d) Eventually the neuron returns to its resting state.

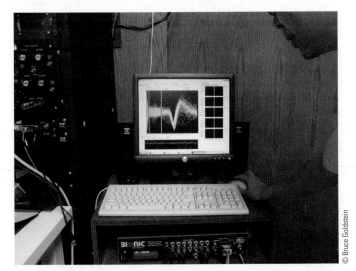

© Bruce Goldstein

Figure 2.22 Electrical signals being displayed on a computer screen, in an experiment in which responses are being recorded from a single neuron. The signal on the screen shows the difference in voltage between two electrodes as a function of time. In this example, many signals are superimposed on one another, creating a thick white tracing. (Photographed in Tai Sing Lee's laboratory at Carnegie Mellon University)

travels all the way down the axon without decreasing in size. This means that if we were to move our recording electrode in Figure 2.21 to a position nearer the end of the axon, the electrical response would take longer to reach the electrode, but it would still be the same size (increasing from −70 to +40 mV) when it got there. This is an extremely important property of the action potential because it enables neurons to transmit signals over long distances.

Another property is that the action potential remains the same size no matter how intense the stimulus is. We can demonstrate this by determining how the neuron fires to different stimulus intensities. **Figure 2.23** shows what happens when we do this. Each action potential appears as a sharp spike in these records because we have compressed the time scale to display a number of action potentials.

The three records in Figure 2.23 represent the axon's response to three intensities of pushing on the skin. **Figure 2.23a** shows how the axon responds to gentle stimulation applied to the skin, and **Figures 2.23b** and **2.23c** show how the response changes as the pressure is increased. Comparing these three records leads to an important conclusion: Changing the stimulus intensity does not affect the *size* of the action potentials but does affect the *rate* of firing.

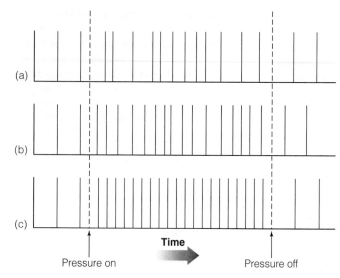

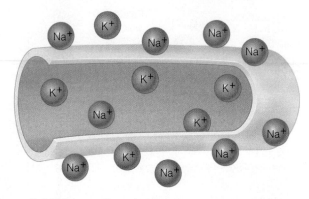

Figure 2.24 A nerve fiber, showing the high concentration of sodium outside the fiber and potassium inside the fiber. Other ions, such as negatively charged chlorine, are not shown.

Figure 2.23 Response of a nerve fiber to (a) soft, (b) medium, and (c) strong stimulation. Increasing the stimulus strength increases both the *rate* and the *regularity* of nerve firing in this fiber, but has no effect on the *size* of the action potentials.

Although increasing the stimulus intensity can increase the rate of firing, there is an upper limit to the number of nerve impulses per second that can be conducted down an axon. This limit occurs because of a property of the axon called the **refractory period**—the interval between the time one nerve impulse occurs and the next one can be generated in the axon. Because the refractory period for most neurons is about 1 ms, the upper limit of a neuron's firing rate is about 500 to 800 impulses per second.

Another important property of action potentials is illustrated by the beginning of each of the records in Figure 2.23. Notice that a few action potentials are occurring even before the pressure stimulus is applied. Action potentials that occur in the absence of stimuli from the environment are called **spontaneous activity**. This spontaneous activity establishes a baseline level of firing for the neuron. The presence of stimulation usually causes an increase in activity above this spontaneous level, but under some conditions, which we will describe shortly, it can cause firing to decrease below the spontaneous level.

Chemical Basis of Action Potentials

What causes these rapid changes in charge that travel down the axon? Because this is a traveling electrical charge, we might be tempted to equate it to the electrical signals that are conducted along electrical power lines or the wires used for household appliances. But action potentials create electricity not in the dry environment of metal wires, but in the wet environment of the body.

The key to understanding the "wet" electrical signals transmitted by neurons is understanding the components of the neuron's liquid environment. Neurons are bathed in a liquid solution rich in **ions**, molecules that carry an electrical charge (**Figure 2.24**). Ions are created when molecules gain or

lose electrons, as happens when compounds are dissolved in water. For example, adding table salt (sodium chloride, NaCl) to water creates positively charged sodium ions (Na^+) and negatively charged chlorine ions (Cl^-). The solution outside the axon of a neuron is rich in positively charged sodium (Na^+) ions, whereas the solution inside the axon is rich in positively charged potassium (K^+) ions.

You can understand how these ions result in the action potential by imagining yourself just outside an axon next to a recording electrode (**Figure 2.25a**). (You will have to shrink yourself down to a very small size to do this!) Everything is quiet until an action potential begins traveling down the axon. As it approaches, you see positively charged sodium ions (Na^+) rushing into the axon (**Figure 2.25b**). This occurs because channels in the membrane have opened to allow Na^+ to flow across the membrane. This opening of sodium channels represents an increase in the membrane's **permeability** to sodium, where permeability refers to the ease with which a molecule can pass through the membrane. In this case, permeability is selective, which means that the fiber is highly permeable to one specific type of molecule (Na^+ in this case), but not to others. The inflow of positively charged sodium causes an increase in the positive charge inside the axon from the resting potential of -70 mV until it reaches the peak of the action potential of $+40$ mV. This increase in potential from -70 mV to $+40$ mv is the **rising phase of the action potential** (Figure 2.25b).

Continuing your vigil, you notice that once the charge inside the neuron reaches $+40$ mV, the sodium channels close (the membrane becomes impermeable to sodium), and potassium channels open (the membrane becomes selectively permeable to potassium). Positively charged potassium rushes out of the axon, causing the charge inside the axon to become more negative. This increase in negativity from $+40$ mV back to -70 mV is the **falling phase of the action potential** (**Figure 2.25c**). Once the potential has returned to the -70 mV resting level, the K+ flow stops (**Figure 2.25d**).

After reading this description of ion flow, students often ask why the sodium-in, potassium-out flow that occurs during the action potential doesn't cause sodium to build up inside the axon, and potassium to build up outside. The answer is

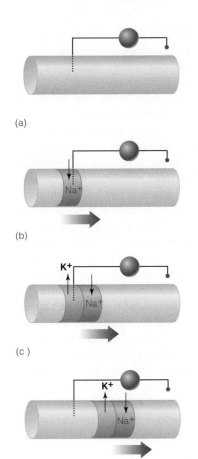

(a)

(b)

(c)

(d)

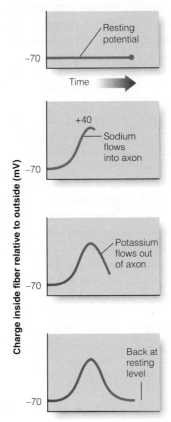

Resting
potential

Time

+40
Sodium
flows
into axon

−70

Potassium
flows out
of axon

−70

Back at
resting
level

−70

Charge inside fiber relative to outside (mV)

Figure 2.25 How the flow of sodium and potassium creates the action potential. (a) When the fiber is at rest, there is no flow of ions, and the record indicates the −70 mV resting potential. (b) Ion flow occurs when an action potential travels down the fiber. Initially, positively charged sodium (Na^+) flows into the axon, causing the inside of the neuron to become more positive (rising phase of the action potential). (c) Later, positively charged potassium (K^+) flows out of the axon, causing the inside of the axon to become more negative (falling phase of the action potential). (d) When the action potential has passed the electrode, the charge returns to the resting level.

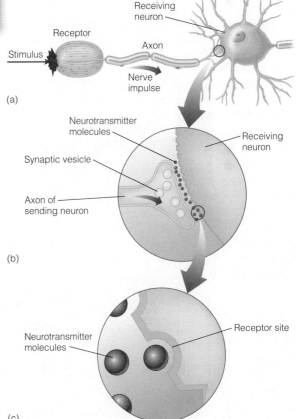

Figure 2.26 Synaptic transmission from one neuron to another. (a) A signal traveling down the axon of a neuron reaches the synapse at the end of the axon. (b) The nerve impulse causes the release of neurotransmitter molecules from the synaptic vesicles of the sending neuron. (c) The neurotransmitters fit into receptor sites that are shaped like the transmitter and cause a voltage change in the receiving neuron.

that a mechanism called the *sodium-potassium pump* keeps this buildup from happening by continuously pumping sodium out and potassium into the fiber.

Transmitting Information Across a Gap

We have seen that action potentials caused by sodium and potassium flow travel down the axon without decreasing in size. But what happens when the action potential reaches the end of the axon? How is the action potential's message transmitted to other neurons? The problem is that there is a very small space between neurons, known as a **synapse** (**Figure 2.26**). The discovery of the synapse raised the question of how the electrical signals generated by one neuron are transmitted across the space separating the neurons. As we will see, the answer lies in a remarkable chemical process that involves molecules called *neurotransmitters*.

Early in the 1900s, it was discovered that when action potentials reach the end of a neuron, they trigger the release of chemicals called **neurotransmitters** that are stored in structures called *synaptic vesicles* in the sending neuron (**Figure 2.26b**). The neurotransmitter molecules flow into the synapse to small areas on the receiving neuron called receptor sites that are sensitive to specific neurotransmitters (**Figure 2.26c**). These receptor sites exist in a variety of shapes that match the shapes of particular neurotransmitter molecules. When a neurotransmitter makes contact with a receptor site matching its shape, it activates the receptor site and triggers a voltage change in the receiving neuron. A neurotransmitter is like a key that fits a specific lock. It has an effect on the receiving neuron only when its shape matches that of the receptor site.

Thus, when an electrical signal reaches the synapse, it triggers a chemical process that causes a new electrical signal in the receiving neuron. The nature of this signal depends on both the type of transmitter that is released and the nature of the receptor sites in the receiving neuron. Two types of responses can occur at these receptor sites, *excitatory* and *inhibitory*. An **excitatory response** occurs when the inside of the neuron becomes more positive, a process called **depolarization**. **Figure 2.27a** shows this effect. Notice, however, that this response is much smaller than the positive action potential. To generate an action potential, enough excitation must occur to increase depolarization to the level indicated by the dashed line. Once depolarization reaches that level, an action potential is triggered (**Figure 2.27b**). Depolarization is an excitatory response because it causes the charge to change in the direction that triggers an action potential.

An **inhibitory response** occurs when the inside of the neuron becomes more negative, a process called **hyperpolarization**.

Figure 2.27c shows this effect. Hyperpolarization is an inhibitory response because it causes the charge inside the axon to move away from the level of depolarization, indicated by the dashed line, needed to generate an action potential.

We can summarize this description of the effects of excitation and inhibition as follows: Excitation increases the chances that a neuron will generate action potentials and is associated with increasing rates of nerve firing. Inhibition decreases the chances that a neuron will generate action potentials and is associated with lowering rates of nerve firing. Since a typical neuron receives both excitation and inhibition, the response of the neuron is determined by the interplay of excitation and inhibition, as illustrated in **Figure 2.28**. In **Figure 2.28a**, excitation (E) is much stronger than inhibition (I), so the neuron's firing rate is high. However, as inhibition becomes stronger and excitation becomes weaker, the neuron's firing decreases, until in **Figure 2.28e**, inhibition has eliminated the neuron's spontaneous activity and has decreased firing to zero.

Why does inhibition exist? If one of the functions of a neuron is to transmit its information to other neurons, what would be the point of decreasing or eliminating firing in the next neuron? The answer to this question is that the function of neurons is not only to transmit information but also to *process* it, and, as we will see in Chapter 3, both excitation and inhibition are involved in this processing.

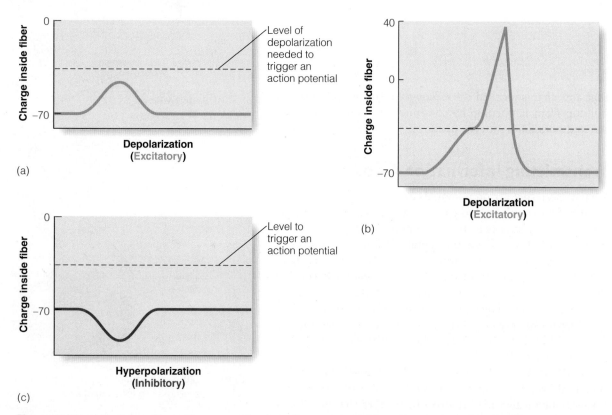

Figure 2.27 (a) Excitatory transmitters cause depolarization, an increased positive charge inside the neuron. (b) When the level of depolarization reaches threshold, indicated by the dashed line, an action potential is triggered. (c) Inhibitory transmitters cause hyperpolarization, an increased negative charge inside the axon.

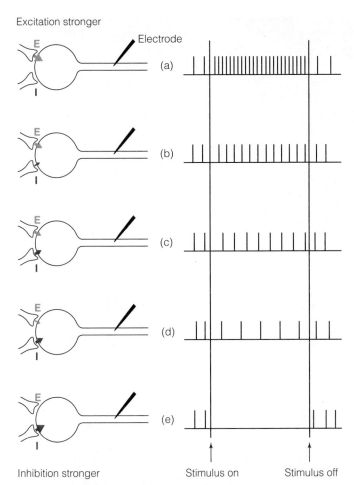

Figure 2.28 Effect of excitatory (E) and inhibitory (I) input on the firing rate of a neuron. The amount of excitatory and inhibitory input to the neuron is indicated by the size of the arrows at the synapse. The responses recorded by the electrode are indicated by the records on the right. The firing that occurs before the stimulus is presented is spontaneous activity. In (a), the neuron receives only excitatory transmitter, which causes the neuron to fire. In (b) to (e), the amount of excitatory transmitter decreases while the amount of inhibitory transmitter increases. As inhibition becomes stronger relative to excitation, firing rate decreases, until eventually the firing rate becomes zero.

Neural Convergence and Perception

Now, with some background about neurons and the electrical signals in neurons, we are ready to look for more connections between physiology and perception. Step 4 in the perceptual process, the transmission and processing of electrical signals, is the topic of Chapters 3 and 4. But we introduce neural processing in this chapter by returning to the rods and cones and showing how perception is related to the way they are "wired up" in the retina.

Figure 2.29a is a cross section of a monkey retina that has been stained to reveal the retina's layered structure. **Figure 2.29b** shows the five types of neurons that make up

these layers and that create **neural circuits**—interconnected groups of neurons—within the retina. Signals generated in the receptors (R) travel to the **bipolar cells** (B) and then to the **ganglion cells** (G). The receptors and bipolar cells do not have long axons, but the ganglion cells have axons like the neurons in Figure 2.19. These axons transmit signals out of the retina in the optic nerve (see Figure 2.6).

In addition to the receptors, bipolar cells, and ganglion cells, there are two other types of neurons that connect neurons across the retina: **horizontal cells** and **amacrine cells**. Signals can travel between receptors through the horizontal cells, and between bipolar cells and between ganglion cells through the amacrine cells. We will return to the horizontal and amacrine cells in Chapter 3. For now we will focus on the direct pathway from the receptors to the ganglion cells. We focus specifically on the property of **neural convergence** (or just **convergence** for short).

Convergence occurs when a number of neurons synapse onto a single neuron. A great deal of convergence occurs in the retina because each eye has 126 million receptors but only 1 million ganglion cells. Thus, on the average, each ganglion cell receives signals from 126 receptors. We can show how convergence can affect perception by returning to the rods and cones. An important difference between rods and cones is that the signals from the rods converge more than do the signals from the cones. We can appreciate this difference by noting that there are 120 million rods in the retina, but only 6 million cones. Thus, on the average, about 120 rods send their signals to one ganglion cell, but only about 6 cones send signals to a single ganglion cell.

This difference between rod and cone convergence becomes even greater when we consider the cones in the fovea. (Remember that the fovea is the small area that contains only cones.) Many of these foveal cones have "private lines" to ganglion cells, so that each ganglion cell receives signals from only one cone, with no convergence. The greater convergence of the rods compared to the cones translates into two differences in perception: (1) the rods result in better sensitivity than the cones, and (2) the cones result in better detail vision than the rods.

Convergence Causes the Rods to Be More Sensitive Than the Cones

In the dark-adapted eye, rod vision is more sensitive than cone vision (see "dark-adapted sensitivity" in the dark adaptation curve of Figure 2.13). This is why in dim light conditions we use our rods to detect faint stimuli. A demonstration of this effect, which has long been known to astronomers and amateur stargazers, is that some very dim stars are difficult to detect when looked at directly (because the star's image falls on the cones in the fovea), but these same stars can often be seen when they are located off to the side of where the person is looking (because then the star's image falls on the rod-rich peripheral retina). One reason for this greater sensitivity of rods, compared to cones, is that it takes less light to generate a response from an individual rod receptor than from an individual cone receptor (Barlow & Mollon, 1982; Baylor, 1992). But there is another reason as well: The rods have greater convergence than the cones.

Figure 2.29 (a) Cross section of a monkey retina, which has been stained to show the various layers. Light is coming from the bottom. The purple circles are cell bodies of the receptors, bipolar cells, and ganglion cells. (b) Cross section of the primate retina showing the five major cell types and their interconnections: receptors (R), bipolar cells (B), ganglion cells (G), horizontal cells (H), and amacrine cells (A). Signals from the three highlighted rods on the right reach the highlighted ganglion cell. This is an example of convergence. (Based on Dowling & Boycott, 1966)

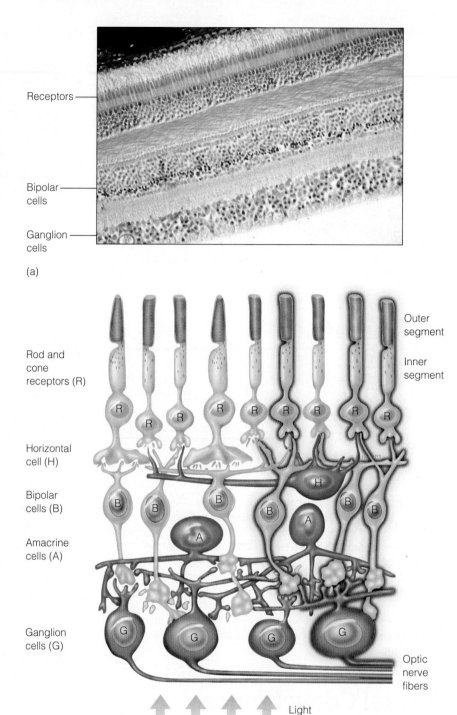

Receptors

Bipolar cells

Ganglion cells

(a)

Rod and cone receptors (R)

Outer segment

Inner segment

Horizontal cell (H)

Bipolar cells (B)

Amacrine cells (A)

Ganglion cells (G)

Optic nerve fibers

Light rays

(b)

Keeping this basic principle in mind, we can see how the difference in rod and cone convergence translates into differences in the maximum sensitivities of the rods and the cones. In the two circuits in **Figure 2.30**, five rod receptors converge onto one ganglion cell and five cone receptors each send signals onto their own ganglion cells. We have left out the bipolar, horizontal, and amacrine cells in these circuits for simplicity, but our conclusions will not be affected by these omissions.

For the purposes of our discussion, we will assume that we can present small spots of light to individual rods and cones. We will also make the following additional assumptions:

1. *One unit of light intensity* causes the release of *one unit of excitatory transmitter*, which causes *one unit of excitation* in the ganglion cell.
2. The ganglion cell fires when it receives 10 units of excitation.
3. When the ganglion cell fires, the light is perceived.

When we present spots of light with an intensity of 1 to each receptor, the rod ganglion cell receives 5 units of excitation,

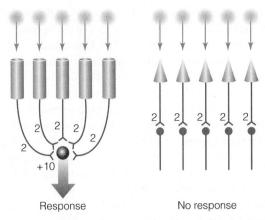

Figure 2.30 The wiring of the rods (left) and the cones (right). The yellow dot and arrow above each receptor represents a "spot" of light that stimulates the receptor. The numbers represent the number of response units generated by the rods and the cones in response to a spot intensity of 2.

1 from each of the 5 rod receptors. In contrast, each cone ganglion cell receives 1 unit of excitation, 1 from each cone receptor. Thus, when intensity = 1, the rod ganglion cell receives more excitation than the cone ganglion cells because of convergence, but not enough to cause it to fire. If, however, we increase the intensity to 2, as shown in the figure, the rod ganglion cell receives 2 units of excitation from each of its 5 receptors, for a total of 10 units of excitation. This causes the ganglion cell to fire, and the light is perceived. Meanwhile, at the same intensity, the cones' ganglion cells are each receiving only 2 units of excitation. For the cones' ganglion cells to fire, we must increase the intensity to 10.

The operation of these circuits demonstrates how the rods' high sensitivity compared to the cones' is caused by the rods' greater convergence. Many rods sum their responses by feeding into the same ganglion cell, but only one or a few cones send their responses to any one ganglion cell. The fact that rod and cone sensitivity is determined not by individual receptors but by groups of receptors converging onto other neurons means that when we describe "rod vision" and "cone vision" we are actually referring to the way *groups* of rods and cones participate in determining our perceptions.

Lack of Convergence Causes the Cones to Have Better Acuity Than the Rods

While rod vision is more sensitive than cone vision because the rods have *more* convergence, the cones have better **visual acuity** because they have *less* convergence. Acuity refers to the ability to see details; thus, being able to see very small letters on an eye chart in the optometrist's or ophthalmologist's office translates into high acuity. (Also, remember grating acuity from Chapter 1, page 11).

One way to appreciate the high acuity of the cones is to think about the last time you were looking for one thing that was hidden among many other things. This could be searching for your cell phone on the clutter of your desk or locating a friend's face in a crowd. To find what you are looking for, you usually need to move your eyes from one place to another. When you move your eyes to look at different things in this way, what you are doing

is scanning with your cone-rich fovea (remember that when you look directly at something, its image falls on the fovea). This is necessary because your visual acuity is highest in the fovea; objects that are imaged on the peripheral retina are not seen as clearly.

DEMONSTRATION | Foveal Versus Peripheral Acuity

D I H C N R L A Z I F W N S M Q P Z K D X

You can demonstrate that foveal vision is superior to peripheral vision for seeing details by looking at the X on the right and, without moving your eyes, seeing how many letters you can identify to the left. If you do this without cheating (resist the urge to look to the left!), you will find that although you can read the letters right next to the X, which are imaged on or near the fovea, it is difficult to read letters that are further off to the side, which are imaged on the peripheral retina.

This demonstration shows that acuity is better in the fovea than in the periphery. Because you were light adapted, the comparison in this demonstration was between the foveal cones, which are tightly packed, and the peripheral cones, which are more widely spaced. Comparing the foveal cones to the rods results in even greater differences in acuity. We can make this comparison by noting how acuity changes during dark adaptation.

The picture of the bookcase in **Figure 2.31** simulates the change in acuity that occurs during dark adaptation. The

Figure 2.31 Simulation of the change from colorful sharp perception to colorless fuzzy perception that occurs during the shift from cone vision to rod vision during dark adaptation. The top shelf simulates cone vision; the bottom shelf, rod vision.

books on the top shelf represent the details we see when viewing the books in the light, when our cones are controlling vision. The books on the middle shelf represent how we might perceive the details midway through the process of dark adaptation, when the rods are beginning to determine our vision, and the books on the bottom shelf represent the poor detail vision of the rods. The poor detail vision of the rods is why it is difficult to read in dim illumination. (Also note that color has disappeared. We will describe why this occurs in Chapter 9.)

We can understand how differences in rod and cone wiring explain the cones' greater acuity by returning to our rod and cone neural circuits. First consider the rod circuit in **Figure 2.32a**. When we present two spots of light next to each other, as on the left, the rod's signals cause the ganglion cell to fire. When we separate the two spots, as on the right, the two separated rods feed into the same ganglion cell and cause it to fire. In both cases, the ganglion cell fires. Thus, firing of the ganglion cell provides no information about whether there are two spots close together or two separated spots.

We now consider the cones in **Figure 2.32b**, each of which synapses on its own ganglion cell. When we present a light that

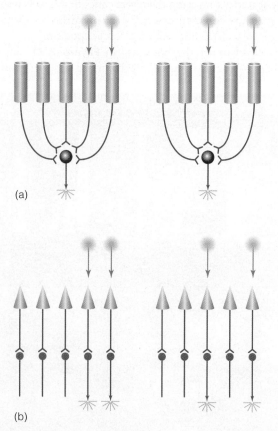

(a)

(b)

Figure 2.32 How the wiring of the rods and cones determines detail vision. (a) Rod neural circuits. On the left, stimulating two neighboring rods causes the ganglion cell to fire. On the right, stimulating two separated rods causes the same effect. (b) Cone neural circuits. On the left, stimulating two neighboring cones causes two neighboring ganglion cells to fire. On the right, stimulating two separated cones causes two separated ganglion cells to fire. This firing of two neurons, with a space between them, indicates that two spots of light have been presented to the cones.

stimulates two neighboring cones, as on the left, two adjacent ganglion cells fire. But when we separate the spots, as on the right, two separate ganglion cells fire. This separation between two firing cells provides information that there are two separate spots of light. Thus, the cones' lack of convergence causes cone vision to have higher acuity than rod vision.

Convergence is therefore a double-edged sword. High convergence results in high sensitivity but poor acuity (the rods). Low convergence results in low sensitivity but high acuity (cones). The way the rods and cones are wired up in the retina, therefore, influences what we perceive. In Chapter 3 we will provide more examples of how neural wiring can influence perception, and we will show how the addition of inhibition adds another dimension to neural processing.

SOMETHING TO CONSIDER:
Early Events Are Powerful

In 1990, a rocket blasted off from Cape Canaveral to place the Hubble space telescope into earth orbit. The telescope's mission was to provide high-resolution images from its vantage point above the interference of the earth's atmosphere. But it took only a few days of data collection to realize that something was wrong. Images of stars and galaxies that should have been extremely sharp were blurred (**Figure 2.33a**). The cause of the problem, it turned out, was that the telescope's lens was ground to the wrong curvature. Although a few of the planned observations were possible, the telescope's mission was severely compromised. Three years later, the problem was solved when a corrective lens was fitted over the original one. The new Hubble, with its "eyeglasses," could now see stars as sharp points (**Figure 2.33b**).

This diversion to outer space emphasizes that what happens early in a system can have a large, often crucial, effect on the outcome. No matter how sophisticated Hubble's electronic computer and processing programs were, the distorted image caused by the faulty lens had fatal effects on the quality of the telescope's image. Similarly, if problems in the eye's focusing system deliver degraded images to the retina, no amount of processing by the brain can create sharp perception.

What we see is also determined by the energy that can enter the eye and can activate the receptors. Although there is a huge range of electromagnetic energy in the environment, the visual pigments in the receptors limit our sensitivity by absorbing only a narrow range of wavelengths. One way to think about the effect of pigments is that they act like filters, only making available for vision the wavelengths they absorb. Thus, at night, when we are perceiving with our rods, we see only wavelengths between about 420 and 580 nm, with the best sensitivity at 500 nm. However, in daylight, when we are perceiving with our cones, we become more sensitive to longer wavelengths, as the best sensitivity shifts to 560 nm.

This idea of visual pigments as limiting our range of seeing is dramatically illustrated by the honeybee, which, as we

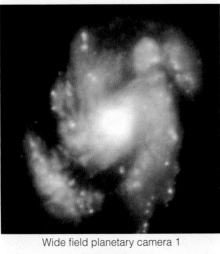

Wide field planetary camera 1

(a)   **Before**

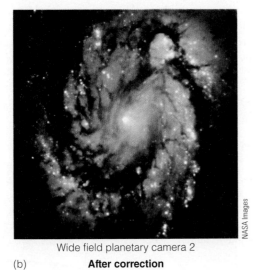

Wide field planetary camera 2

(b)   **After correction**

NASA Images

Figure 2.33 (a) Image of a galaxy taken by the Hubble telescope before the lens was corrected. (b) The same galaxy after the lens was corrected.

(a)

(b)

Bjørn Rørslett

Figure 2.34 (a) A black-and-white photograph of a flower as seen by a human. (b) The same flower, showing markings that become visible to sensors that can detect ultraviolet light. Although we don't know exactly what honeybees see, their short-wavelength cone pigment makes it possible for them to sense these markings.

will see in the chapter on color vision, has a visual pigment that absorbs light all the way down to 300 nm (see Figure 9.43, page 221). This very-short-wavelength pigment enables the honeybee to perceive ultraviolet wavelengths that are invisible to us, so the honeybee can see markings on flowers that reflect ultraviolet light (**Figure 2.34**). Thus, as we noted earlier in this chapter, although perception does not *occur* in the eye, what we see is affected by what happens there. Similar effects occur in the other senses as well. Damage to the receptors in the ear is the main cause of hearing loss (Chapter 11, page 281); differences in the number of "bitter" receptors on people's tongues can cause two people to have different taste experiences to the same substance (Chapter 15, page 368).

DEVELOPMENTAL DIMENSION Infant Visual Acuity

Some chapters in this book will include "Developmental Dimensions," such as this one, which describe perceptual capacities of infants and young children that are related to material in the chapter.

One of the challenges of determining infant capacities is that infants can't respond by saying "yes, I perceive it" or "no, I don't perceive it" in reaction to a stimulus. But this difficulty has not stopped developmental psychologists from devising clever ways to determine what infants or young children are perceiving. One method that has been used to measure infant visual acuity is the **preferential looking (PL) technique.**

The key to measuring infant perception is to pose the correct question. To understand what we mean by this, let's consider how we might determine infants' *visual acuity*, their ability to see details. To test adults, we can ask them to read the letters or symbols on an eye chart. But to test infant acuity, we have to ask another question and use another procedure. A question that works for infants is "Can you tell the difference between the stimulus on the left and the one on the right?" The way infants answer this question is by looking more at one of the stimuli.

In the preferential looking (PL) technique, two stimuli like the ones the infant is observing in **Figure 2.35** are presented, and the experimenter watches the infant's eyes to determine where the infant is looking. In order to guard against bias, the experimenter does not know which stimulus is being presented on the left or right. If the infant looks at one stimulus more than the other, the experimenter concludes that he or she can tell the difference between them.

The reason preferential looking works is that infants have *spontaneous looking preferences*; that is, they prefer to look at certain types of stimuli. For example, infants choose to look at objects with contours over ones that are homogeneous (Fantz et al., 1962). Thus, when we present a grating stimulus (alternating white and black bars like the one shown in Figure 2.35) with large bars on one side, and a gray field that reflects the same total amount of light that the grating would reflect on the other side (again, like the one shown in Figure 2.35), the infant can easily see the bars and therefore looks at the side with the bars more than the side with the gray field. If the infant looks preferentially at the side with the bars when the bars are switched randomly from side to side on different trials, he or she is telling the experimenter "I see the grating."

But decreasing the size of the bars makes it more difficult for the infant to tell the difference between the grating and gray stimulus. Eventually, the infant begins to look equally at each display, which tells the experimenter that very fine lines and the gray field are indiscriminable. Therefore, we can measure the infant's acuity by determining the narrowest stripe width that results in looking more at the grating stimulus.

How well can infants see details? The red curve in **Figure 2.36** shows acuity over the first year of life measured with the preferential looking technique, in which infants are tested with gratings, as in Figure 2.35. The blue curve indicates acuity determined by measuring an electrical signal called the **visual evoked potential** (VEP), which is recorded by disc electrodes placed on the infant's head over the visual cortex. For this technique, researchers alternate a gray field with a grating or checkerboard pattern. If the stripes or checks are large enough to be detected by the visual system, the visual cortex generates an electrical response called the *visual evoked potential*.

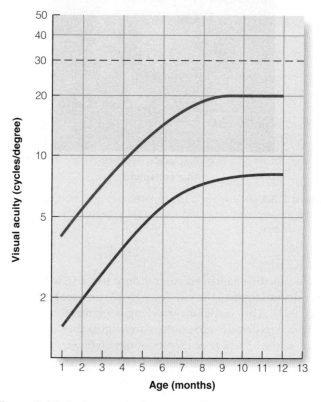

Figure 2.36 Acuity over the first year of life, measured by the visual evoked potential technique (top curve) and the preferential looking technique (bottom curve). The vertical axis indicates the fineness, in cycles per degree, of a grating stimulus that the infant can detect. One cycle per degree corresponds to one pair of black and white lines on a circle the size of a penny viewed from a distance of about a meter. Higher numbers indicate the ability to detect finer lines on the penny-sized circle. The dashed line is adult acuity (20/20 vision). (VEP curve adapted from Norcia & Tyler, 1985; PL curve adapted from Gwiazda et al., 1980, and Mayer et al., 1995)

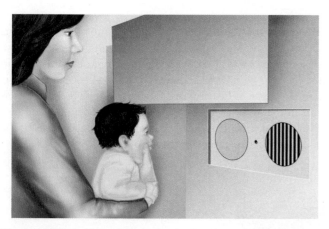

Figure 2.35 An infant being tested using the preferential looking technique. The mother holds the infant in front of the display, which consists of a grating on the right and a homogeneous gray field on the left. The grating and the gray field have the same average light intensity. An experimenter, who does not know which side the grating is on in any given trial, looks through the peephole between the grating and the gray field and judges whether the infant is looking to the left or to the right.

If, however, the stripes are too fine to be detected by the visual system, no response is generated. Thus, the VEP provides an objective measure of the visual system's ability to detect details.

The VEP usually indicates better acuity than does preferential looking, but both techniques indicate that visual acuity is poorly developed at birth (about 20/400 to 20/600 at 1 month). (The expression 20/400 means that the infant must view a stimulus from 20 feet to see the same thing that an adult with normal vision can see from 400 feet.) Acuity increases rapidly over the first 6 to 9 months (Banks & Salapatek, 1978; Dobson & Teller, 1978; Harris et al., 1976; Salapatek et al., 1976). This rapid improvement of acuity is followed by a leveling-off period, and full adult acuity is not reached until sometime after 1 year of age.

From our discussion of how adult rod and cone visual acuity depends on the wiring of the rods and cones, it would make sense to consider the possibility that infants' low acuity might be traced to the development of their receptors. If we look at the newborn's retina, we find that this is the case. Although the rod-dominated peripheral retina appears adultlike in the newborn, the all-cone fovea contains widely spaced and very poorly developed cone receptors (Abramov et al., 1982).

Figure 2.37a compares the shapes of newborn and adult foveal cones. Remember from our discussion of transduction that the visual pigments are contained in the receptor's outer segments. These outer segments sit on top of the other part of the receptor, the inner segment. The newborn's cones have fat inner segments and very small outer segments, whereas the adult's inner and outer segments are larger and are about the same diameter (Banks & Bennett, 1988; Yuodelis & Hendrickson, 1986). These differences in shape and size have a number of consequences. The small size of the outer segment means that the newborn's cones contain less visual pigment and therefore do not absorb light as effectively as adult cones. In addition,

the fat inner segment creates the coarse receptor lattice shown in **Figure 2.37b**, with large spaces between the outer segments. In contrast, when the adult cones have become thin, they can become packed closely together to create a fine lattice that is well suited to detecting small details. Martin Banks and Patrick Bennett (1988) calculated that the cone receptors' outer segments effectively cover 68 percent of the adult fovea but only 2 percent of the newborn fovea. This means that most of the light entering the newborn's fovea is lost in the spaces between the cones and is therefore not useful for vision.

Thus, adults have good acuity because the cones have low convergence compared to the rods and the receptors in the fovea are packed closely together. In contrast, the infant's poor acuity can be traced to the fact that the infant's cones are spaced far apart. Another reason for the infant's poor acuity is that the visual area of the brain is poorly developed at birth, with fewer neurons and synapses than in the adult cortex. The rapid increase in acuity that occurs over the first 6 to 9 months of life can thus be traced to the fact that during that time, more neurons and synapses are being added to the cortex, and the infant's cones are becoming more densely packed.

1. Describe the basic structure of a neuron.
2. Describe how to record electrical signals from a neuron.
3. What are some of the basic properties of action potentials?
4. Describe what happens when an action potential travels along an axon. In your description, indicate how the charge inside the fiber changes, and how that is related to the flow of chemicals across the cell membrane.

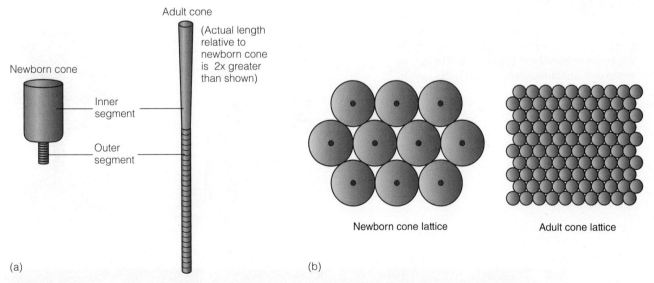

(a)

(b)

Figure 2.37 (a) Idealized shapes of newborn and adult foveal cones. (Real cones are not so perfectly straight and cylindrical.) Foveal cones are much narrower and longer than the cones elsewhere in the retina, so these look different from the one shown in Figure 2.3. (b) Receptor lattices for newborn and adult foveal cones. The newborn cone outer segments, indicated by the red circles, are widely spaced because of the fat inner segments. In contrast, the adult cones, with their slender inner segments, are packed closely together. (Adapted from Banks & Bennett, 1988)

5. How are electrical signals transmitted from one neuron to another? Be sure you understand the difference between excitatory and inhibitory responses.

6. What is convergence, and how can the differences in the convergence of rods and cones explain (a) the rods' greater sensitivity in the dark and (b) the cones' better detail vision?

7. What does it mean to say that early events are powerful shapers of perception? Give examples.

8. What is the young infant's visual acuity, and how does it change over the first year of life? What is the reason for (a) low acuity at birth and (b) the increase in acuity over the first 6 to 9 months?

THINK ABOUT IT

1. Ellen is looking at a tree. She sees the tree because light is reflected from the tree into her eyes, as shown in **Figure 2.38**. One way to describe this is to say that information about the tree is contained in the light. Meanwhile, Roger is off to the side, looking straight ahead. He doesn't see the tree because he is looking away from it. He is however, looking right at the space through which the light that is carrying information from the tree to Ellen is passing. But Roger doesn't see any of this information. Why does this occur? (Hint #1: Consider the idea that "objects make light visible." Hint #2: Outer space contains a great deal of light, but it looks dark, except where there are objects.)

2. In the demonstration "Becoming Aware of What Is in Focus" on page 26, you saw that we see things clearly only when we are looking directly at them so that their image falls on the cone-rich fovea. But consider the common observation that the things we aren't looking at do not appear "fuzzy," that the entire scene appears "sharp" or "in focus." How can this be, in light of the results of the demonstration?

3. Here's an exercise you can do to get more in touch with the process of dark adaptation: Find a dark place where you can make some observations as you adapt to the dark.

A closet is a good place to do this because you can regulate the intensity of light inside the closet by opening or closing the door. The idea is to create an environment in which there is dim light (no light at all, as in a darkroom with the safelight out, is too dark). Take this book into the closet, opened to this page. Close the closet door all the way so it is very dark, and then open the door slowly until you can just barely make out the white circle on the far left in **Figure 2.39** but can't see the others or can see them only as being very dim. As you sit in the dark, become aware that your sensitivity is increasing by noting how the circles to the right in the figure slowly become visible over a period of about 20 minutes. Also note that once a circle becomes visible, it gets easier to see as time passes. If you stare directly at the circles, they may fade, so move your eyes around every so often. Also, the circles will be easier to see if you look slightly above them.

4. Because the long axons of neurons look like electrical wires, and both neurons and electrical wires conduct electricity, it is tempting to equate the two. Compare the functioning of axons and electrical wires in terms of their structure and the nature of the electrical signals they conduct.

Figure 2.38 Ellen sees the tree because light is reflected from the tree into her eyes. Roger doesn't see the tree because he is not looking at it, but he is looking directly across the space where light from the tree is reflected into Ellen's eyes. Why isn't he aware of the information contained in this light?

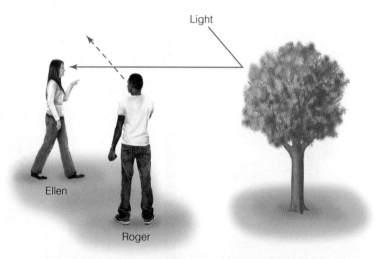

Figure 2.39 Dark adaptation test circles.

KEY TERMS

Absorption spectrum (p. 32)
Accommodation (p. 25)
Action potential (p. 34)
Amacrine cells (p. 39)
Axial myopia (p. 27)
Axon (p. 33)
Bipolar cells (p. 39)
Blind spot (p. 24)
Cell body (p. 33)
Cones (p. 22)
Cone spectral sensitivity (p. 32)
Convergence (p. 39)
Cornea (p. 22)
Dark-adapted sensitivity (p. 28)
Dark adaptation curve (p. 28)
Dark adaptation (p. 28)
Dendrites (p. 33)
Depolarization (p. 38)
Detached retina (p. 31)
Excitatory response (p. 38)
Eyes (p. 22)
Falling phase of the action
    potential (p. 36)
Farsightedness (p. 27)
Fovea (p. 23)

Ganglion cells (p. 39)
Horizontal cells (p. 39)
Hyperopia (p. 27)
Hyperpolarization (p. 38)
Inhibitory response (p. 38)
Ions (p. 36)
Isomerization (p. 27)
Lens (p. 22)
Light-adapted sensitivity (p. 28)
Macular degeneration (p. 23)
Monochromatic light (p. 31)
Myopia (p. 27)
Nearsightedness (p. 27)
Nerve fiber (p. 33)
Neural circuits (p. 39)
Neural convergence (p. 39)
Neurons (p. 33)
Neurotransmitters (p. 37)
Optic nerve (p. 23)
Outer segments (p. 22)
Peripheral retina (p. 23)
Permeability (p. 36)
Preferential looking technique (p. 43)
Presbyopia (p. 27)
Propagated response (p. 34)

Pupil (p. 22)
Purkinje shift (p. 32)
Receptor sites (p. 38)
Refractive myopia (p. 27)
Refractory period (p. 36)
Resting potential (p. 34)
Retina (p. 22)
Retinitis pigmentosa (p. 24)
Rising phase of the action potential (p. 36)
Rod monochromats (p. 30)
Rods (p. 22)
Rod spectral sensitivity curve (p. 32)
Rod–cone break (p. 30)
Spectral sensitivity curve (p. 31)
Spectral sensitivity (p. 31)
Spontaneous activity (p. 36)
Synapse (p. 37)
Transduction (p. 27)
Visible light (p. 22)
Visual acuity (p. 41)
Visual evoked potential (p. 44)
Visual pigment bleaching (p. 30)
Visual pigment regeneration (p. 30)
Visual pigments (p. 23)
Wavelength (p. 22)

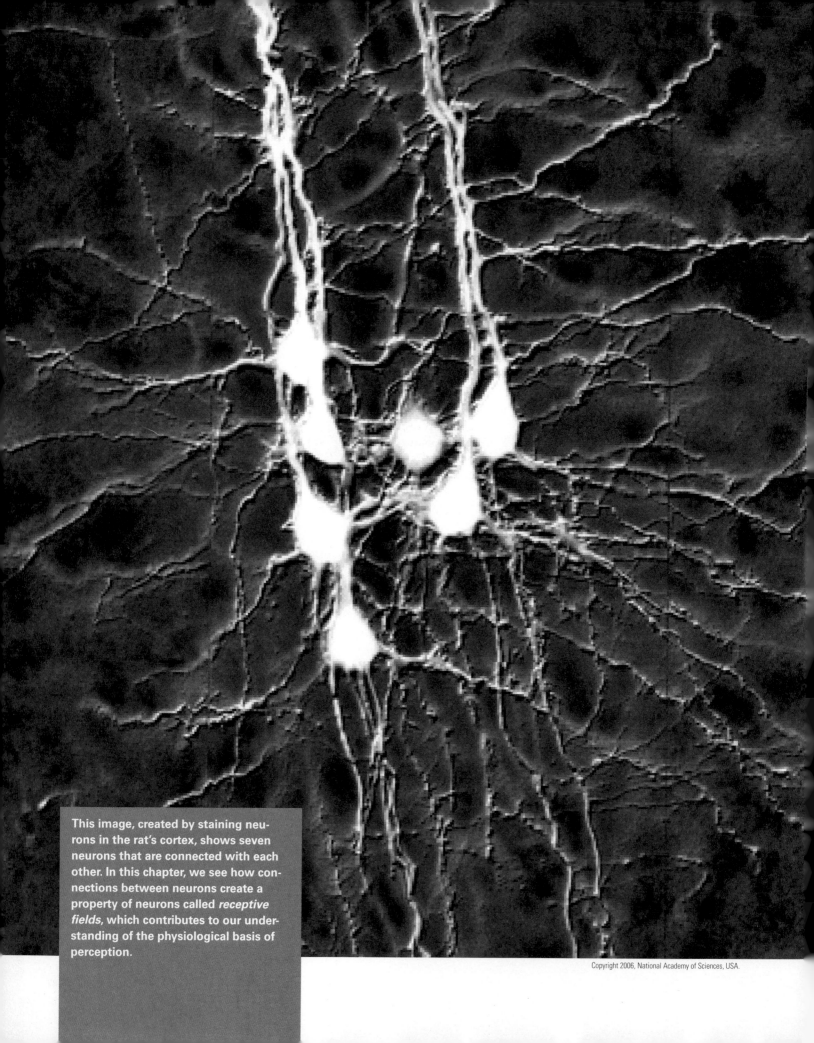

This image, created by staining neurons in the rat's cortex, shows seven neurons that are connected with each other. In this chapter, we see how connections between neurons create a property of neurons called *receptive fields*, which contributes to our understanding of the physiological basis of perception.

CHAPTER 3

Neural Processing

CHAPTER CONTENTS

Inhibitory Processes in the Retina
Lateral Inhibition in the *Limulus*
Using Lateral Inhibition to Explain Perception
Problems with the Lateral Inhibition Explanations of the Chevreul Illusion and the Hermann Grid

Processing From Retina to Visual Cortex and Beyond
Responding of Single Fibers in the Optic Nerve

Hubel and Wiesel's Rationale for Studying Receptive Fields
Receptive Fields of Neurons in the Visual Cortex

Do Feature Detectors Play a Role in Perception?
Selective Adaptation
Selective Rearing

Higher-Level Neurons
Sensory Coding

SOMETHING TO CONSIDER: "Flexible" Receptive Fields

THINK ABOUT IT

Some Questions We Will Consider:

- How do both excitation and inhibition determine how a neuron fires to different types of stimuli? (pp. 56, 60)

- How can making perceptual observations tell us about the connection between neural firing and perception? (p. 62)

- How do the responses of neurons change as we move higher in the visual system? (p. 65)

- How are objects in the environment represented by the firing of neurons in the cortex? (p. 66)

Two cars start at the same place and drive to the same destination. Car A takes an express highway, stopping only briefly for gas. Car B takes the "scenic" route—back roads that go through the countryside and small towns, stopping a number of times along the way to see some sights and meet some people. Each of Car B's stops can influence its route, depending on the information its driver receives. Stopping at a small-town general store, the driver of Car B hears about a detour up the road, so he changes his route accordingly. Meanwhile, Car A is speeding directly to its destination.

The way electrical signals travel through the nervous system is more like Car B's journey. The pathway from receptors to brain is not a nonstop expressway. Every signal leaving a receptor travels through a complex network of interconnected neurons, often meeting, and being affected by, other signals along the way.

What is gained by taking a complex, indirect route? If the goal were just to send a signal to the brain that a particular receptor had been stimulated, then the straight-through method would work. But the purpose of electrical signals in the nervous system goes beyond signaling that a receptor was stimulated. The information that reaches the brain and then continues its journey within the brain is much richer than this. There are neurons in the brain that respond to slanted lines, faces, bodies, and movement in a specific direction. These neurons didn't achieve these properties by receiving signals through a straight-line transmission system from receptors to brain. They achieve these properties by *neural processing*—the interaction of the signals of many neurons (see page 7).

This chapter and the next describe the relationship between neural processing and perception. We begin by going back to the retina, where, at the end of Chapter 2, we introduced neural processing by showing how differences in neural convergence of the rods and cones affect sensitivity and detail vision. We now move from the receptors into the wiring of other neurons in the retina and introduce a process called *lateral inhibition*, which is an important processing mechanism that occurs throughout the visual system and in other sensory systems as well. We will then describe how neurons fire in the optic nerve, the lateral geniculate nucleus, and the cortex. At each of these places, we will show how the responses of single neurons provide information for the perception of object features and the recognition of objects. Finally, we will describe the connection between the responding of groups of neurons and the recognizing of objects.

Inhibitory Processes in the Retina

Remember from our discussion of rods and cones that perception can be affected by neural convergence—more convergence (rods) results in greater sensitivity, and less convergence (cones) is associated with better detail vision. We also introduced inhibition in Chapter 2, and described how inhibition can decrease nerve firing. We now consider what happens when both convergence and inhibition are present. We begin answering that question by considering **lateral inhibition**—inhibition that is transmitted *across* the retina. The pioneering work on lateral inhibition was carried out on a primitive animal called the *Limulus*, more familiarly known as the horseshoe crab (**Figure 3.1**).

Lateral Inhibition in the *Limulus*

In an experiment that is now considered a classic, Keffer Hartline, Henry Wagner, and Floyd Ratliff (1956) used the *Limulus* to demonstrate how lateral inhibition can affect the response of neurons in a circuit. They chose the *Limulus* because the structure of its eye makes it possible to stimulate individual receptors. The *Limulus* eye is made up of hundreds of tiny structures called **ommatidia**, and each ommatidium has a small lens on the eye's surface that is located directly over a single receptor. Each lens and receptor is roughly the diameter of a

pencil point (very large compared to human receptors), so it is possible to illuminate and record from a single receptor without illuminating its neighboring receptors.

When Hartline and coworkers recorded from the nerve fiber of receptor A, as shown in **Figure 3.2,** they found that illumination of that receptor caused a large response (**Figure 3.2a**). But when they added illumination to the three nearby receptors at B, the response of receptor A decreased (**Figure 3.2b**). They also found that further increasing the illumination of B decreased A's response even more (**Figure 3.2c**). Thus, illumination of the neighboring receptors at B inhibited the firing caused by stimulation of receptor A. This decrease in the firing of receptor A is caused by lateral inhibition that is transmitted from B to A across the *Limulus*'s eye by the fibers of the *lateral plexus*, shown in Figure 3.2. Just as the lateral plexus transmits signals laterally in the *Limulus*, the horizontal and amacrine cells (see Figure 2.29, page 40) transmit signals across the human retina.

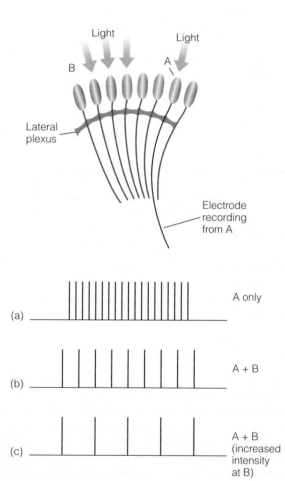

Figure 3.2 A demonstration of lateral inhibition in the *Limulus*. The records show the response recorded by the electrode in the nerve fiber of receptor A: (a) when only receptor A is stimulated; (b) when receptor A and the receptors at B are stimulated together; (c) when A and B are stimulated, with B stimulated at an increased intensity. (Adapted from Ratliff, 1965, Figure 3.25, p. 107)

Figure 3.1 A *Limulus*, or horseshoe crab. Its large eyes are made up of hundreds of ommatidia, each containing a single receptor.

Using Lateral Inhibition to Explain Perception

One of the goals of perception research is to demonstrate links between neural activity and perception. If you were reading an earlier edition of this book, you would, at this point, read about just such a demonstration. Lateral inhibition, transmitted in horizontal and amacrine cells, you would be told, can explain a number of situations in which our perception of light and dark differs from the actual physical situation. But in this edition, that story, which has been featured in textbooks and research papers for many decades, has changed.

Students often, upon hearing that things have changed, wonder why we just don't describe what we know now, rather than describing what we thought we knew then. But as you will see, the "backstory"—describing what led up to our present ideas—has something to teach us both about how lateral inhibition operates and about how science progresses from one idea to another. We will first describe two perceptual illusions that involve the perception of light and dark, along with the lateral inhibition explanations of each one. We then describe how some simple perceptual demonstrations called into question the explanation based on lateral inhibition.

The Lateral Inhibition Explanation of the Chevreul (Staircase) Illusion

The French chemist Michel-Eugene Chevreul (1789–1889) did research on the organic chemistry of fats, which led to improvements in the formulation of soap and in the development of a new improved type of candle. But our interest in Chevreul begins with his appointment as director of dyes in the Gobelin tapestry works, which led to his interest in how placing colors side by side could alter their appearance.

One of the outcomes of his work was the Chevreul illusion, shown in **Figure 3.3a**, which shows four gray rectangles placed side by side, ranging from light on the left to dark on the right. **Figure 3.3b** shows an important feature of these rectangles by plotting the light intensity that would be measured by a light meter scanning the middle two rectangles along the line from A to D. Notice that the light intensity remains the same across the entire distance between A and B, then at the border the intensity drops to a lower level and remains the same between C and D.

You may notice, looking back at Figure 3.3a, that although the *intensity* is the same from A to B, and then from C to D, the *perception* of lightness is not. At the border between B and C there is a lightening at B to the left of the border and a darkening at C to the right of the border. The perceived light and dark bands at the borders, which are not present in the actual physical stimuli, constitute the **Chevreul illusion**. This is also called the **staircase illusion** because of the steplike pattern of intensities in the display. **Figure 3.3c** plots this perceptual effect for the middle two rectangles. The upward bump in perceived lightness at B represents the slight increase in lightness we see at B, and the downward bump at C represents the slight decrease in lightness we see at C.

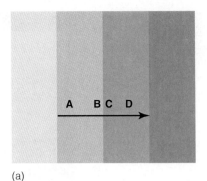

(a)

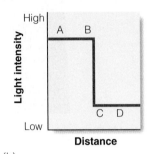

(b)

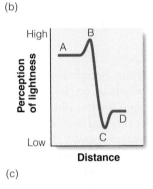

(c)

Figure 3.3 The Chevreul illusion. Look at the borders between light and dark. (a) Just to the left of the border, near B, a faint light band can be perceived, and just to the right at C, a faint dark band can be perceived. (b) The physical intensity distribution of the light, as measured with a light meter. Because the intensity plot looks like a step in a staircase, this illusion is also called the staircase illusion. (c) A plot showing the perceptual effect described in (a). The bump in the curve at B indicates the light band, and the dip in the curve at C indicates the dark band. The bumps that represent our perception of the bands are not present in the physical intensity distribution.

Illusory light and dark bars at borders also occur in the environment, especially in shadows. You might notice this if there are shadows nearby, or see if you can find light and dark bars in **Figure 3.4**. This figure shows a fuzzy shadow border between light and dark, rather than the sharp border in the Chevreul staircase display. Light and dark bands created at fuzzy borders are called **Mach bands**, after German physicist Ernst Mach (1836–1916). The same mechanism is thought to be responsible for the Mach and Chevreul effects.

By using the circuit in **Figure 3.5**, we can show how the light and dark bands of both the Chevreul and Mach band illusions were originally explained by lateral inhibition (Ratliff, 1965). Each of the six receptors in this circuit sends signals to bipolar cells, and each bipolar cell sends lateral inhibition to

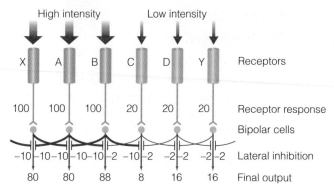

Figure 3.5 Circuit to explain the Chevreul effect based on lateral inhibition. Each bipolar cell sends inhibition to its neighbors. If we know the initial output of each receptor and the amount of lateral inhibition, we can calculate the final output of each bipolar cell.

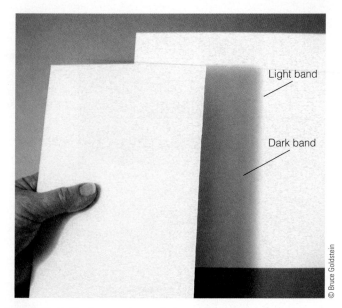

Figure 3.4 Shadow-casting technique for observing illusory bands in shadows. Illuminate a light-colored surface with a lamp and cast a shadow with a piece of paper. When the transition from light to dark is gradual, rather than a step as in the Chevreul illusion, the bands are called *Mach bands*.

its neighbors on both sides. Receptors A and B correspond to A and B in Figure 3.3, which are on the light side of the border and receive the same high level of illumination. Receptors C and D are on the darker side and receive the same level of dimmer illumination. Receptors X and Y have been added to this circuit for the purposes of this calculation so that A and D will receive inhibition from both sides.

Let's assume that receptors X, A, and B generate responses of 100, whereas C, D, and Y generate responses of 20, as shown in Figure 3.5. X, A, and B result in an initial response of 100 in their bipolar cells, and C, D, and Y cause an initial response of 20 in their bipolar cells. If perception were determined only by these responses, we would see a bright rectangle on the left with equal intensity across its width (corresponding to response = 100) and a dimmer rectangle on the right with equal intensity across its width (corresponding to response = 20). But to take lateral inhibition into account, we do the following calculation (**Figure 3.6**).

1. Start with the initial response of each bipolar cell: 100 for X, A, and B; 20 for C, D, and Y.
2. Determine the amount of inhibition that each bipolar cell sends to its neighbor on each side. We will assume that the amount of inhibition each cell sends to the cells on either side is equal to one-tenth of that cell's initial response. Thus, cells X, A, and B send 100 × 0.1 = 10 units of inhibition to their neighbors on each side, and cells C, D, and Y send 20 × 0.1 = 2 units of inhibition to their neighbors on each side.
3. Determine the output of each cell by starting with its initial response and subtracting the amount of inhibition received from the left and from the right. This output is indicated by the "Final output" in Figures 3.5 and 3.6.

Bipolar	Initial Response	Inhibition From Left	Inhibition From Right	Total Inhibition	Final Output
X	100	10	10	20	80
A	100	10	10	20	80
B	100	10	2	12	88 (bright band)
C	20	10	2	12	8 (dark band)
D	20	2	2	4	16
Y	20	2	2	4	16

Figure 3.6 Table for determining the final output of the bipolar cells in Figure 3.5, by starting with the initial response and subtracting inhibition coming from the left and right.

Plotting the numbers in the final output results in the graph in **Figure 3.7**, which is similar to the one in Figure 3.3c, which represents the increase in the perception of lightness on the light side of the border at C and a decrease in the perception of lightness on the dark side at D. Because this calculation of lateral inhibition creates a neural pattern that looks like the illusory light and dark bands we perceive, lateral inhibition became the generally accepted explanation for the Chevreul and Mach effects.

The Lateral Inhibition Explanation of the Hermann Grid Illusion The Hermann grid, shown in **Figure 3.8**, creates another perceptual phenomenon that was originally explained by lateral inhibition. Notice the ghostlike gray images at the intersections of the white "corridors." You can prove that these gray spots are not physically present by noticing that they are reduced or vanish when you look directly at an intersection or, better yet, when you cover two rows of black squares with white paper.

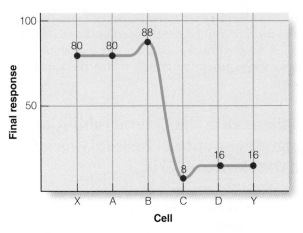

Figure 3.7 A plot showing the final receptor output calculated for the circuit in Figure 3.5. The bump at B and the dip at C correspond to the light and dark bands, respectively, of the Chevreul illusion.

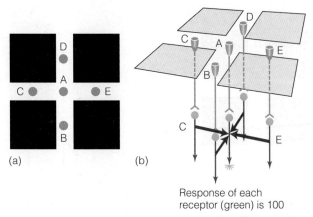

Response of each receptor (green) is 100

Figure 3.9 (a) Four squares of the Hermann grid, showing five of the receptors under the pattern. Receptor A is located at the intersection, and B, C, D, and E have a black square on either side. (b) Perspective view of the grid and five receptors, showing how the receptors (green) connect to bipolar cells (blue). The response of each of the five receptors is 100. The initial response of the bipolar cells matches the response of the receptors. Lateral inhibition travels to bipolar cell A along the red pathways.

Figures 3.9 through 3.12 show how the dark spots at the intersections can be explained by lateral inhibition. **Figure 3.9a** shows four squares of the grid, imaged on the surface of the retina. The green circles are receptors. **Figure 3.9b** is a perspective view of the grid, showing the receptors (in green) and the bipolar cells (in blue) that receive signals from the receptors. Because the receptors are all illuminated by the white of the "corridors," each receives the same illumination and generates the same response. For this example, we assume the response of each receptor is 100.

Our goal is to determine the response associated with receptor A, which is at the intersection of the crossroads, where the dark spot appears. Because perception is determined not by the response of the receptors, but by the response of neurons farther down the system, let's assume, as we did for the Chevreul illusion, that the perception of lightness is determined by the output of the bipolar cells. We focus our attention on the bipolar cells in **Figure 3.10** and assume that the *initial response* of each bipolar cell is the same as the response

of the receptor associated with it. Thus, bipolar cells A, B, C, D, and E would initially each have a response of 100.

Just as we did for the Chevreul illusion, we assume that the final response of each bipolar cell is determined by starting with its initial response and subtracting any decrease caused by lateral inhibition. Focusing on bipolar cell A, which receives signals from the receptor at the intersection, we will assume that the amount of lateral inhibition sent by neurons B, C, D, and E to bipolar cell A is one-tenth the neuron's initial response. Thus, each bipolar cell sends $100 \times 0.1 = 10$ units of inhibition to bipolar cell A (red arrows), and the total lateral inhibition sent to A is $10 + 10 + 10 + 10 = 40$. This means that the final response of bipolar cell A is Initial Response (100) − Inhibition (40) = 60.

We now look at **Figure 3.11** and focus our attention on receptor D, which is not located at the intersection of the corridors. In this example, receptors A, D, and G receive white light

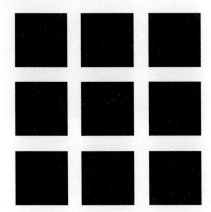

Figure 3.8 The Hermann grid. Notice the gray "ghost images" at the intersections of the white areas, which decrease or vanish when you look directly at an intersection.

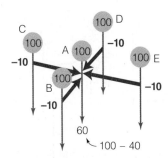

Figure 3.10 The bipolar cells from the circuit in Figure 3.9. Each bipolar cell has an initial response of 100. Bipolar cells B, C, D, and E each send 10 units of inhibition to bipolar cell A, as indicated by the red arrows. Because the total inhibition is 40, the final response of bipolar A is 60.

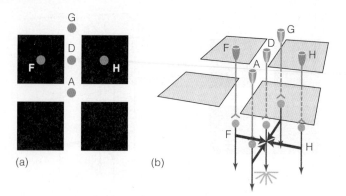

(a)   (b)

Figure 3.11 (a) Four squares of the Hermann grid, as in Figure 3.8, but now focusing on receptor D, which is flanked by two black squares. Receptor D is surrounded by receptors A, F, G, and H. Notice that receptors F and H are located under the two black squares, so they receive less light than the other receptors. (b) Perspective view of the grid and five receptors, showing how the receptors (green) connect to bipolar cells (blue). The response of receptors A and G is 100, and the response of F and H is 20. Lateral inhibition travels to bipolar cell D along the red pathways.

from the corridor, so they will have an initial response of 100. But receptors F and H are illuminated by the black part of the grid, so their response is lower, let's say 20.

Focusing on the bipolars in **Figure 3.12**, we make the same assumption as before that the initial response of the bipolars matches the response received from the receptors. The red arrows show that A and G each send $100 \times 0.1 = 10$ units of inhibition and that F and H each send $20 \times 0.1 = 2$ units of inhibition. Thus, the total inhibition sent to D is $10 + 10 + 2 + 2 = 24$, and bipolar cell D's final response is, therefore, $(100) - (24) = 76$.

Comparing the final responses of A and D enables us to make a prediction about perception: Because the response of 60 associated with receptor A (at the intersection) is smaller than the response of 76 associated with receptor D (in the corridor between the black squares), the intersection should appear darker than the corridor. This is exactly what happens—we perceive gray images at the intersections. Although the *initial*

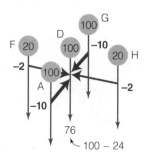

Figure 3.12 The bipolar cells from the circuit in Figure 3.11. Bipolar cells A and G have an initial response of 100, and F and H have an initial response of 20. Bipolar cells A and G each send 10 units of inhibition to bipolar cell D; bipolar cells F and H each send 2 units of inhibition to D. The total inhibition is 24, so the final response of bipolar cell D is 76.

responses of bipolar cells A and D are the same, their *final* responses are different, *because D receives less lateral inhibition than A*. Just as for the Chevreul illusion, lateral inhibition appears to explain why perception doesn't match the actual physical stimulus.

Problems with the Lateral Inhibition Explanations of the Chevreul Illusion and the Hermann Grid

As logical as the explanations above are (and a perfect way for textbook authors to demonstrate how perception is influenced by neural responding), some recent demonstrations have questioned the lateral inhibition explanations. We first return to the Chevreul illusion.

Chevreul Illusion First, consider **Figure 3.13**, which shows two "staircase" displays used to create the Chevreul illusion superimposed on a background called a *luminance ramp*, because the intensity changes smoothly, like an inclined ramp, from light to dark (Geier & Hudak, 2011). These two staircase displays are physically identical, except the dark rectangle is on the left for the top one and on the right for the bottom one. It is obvious, however, that these two displays look very different. There is only a trace of the Chevreul bands in the top display, but they are greatly enhanced in the bottom display. This occurs because of the background, which progresses from light on the left to dark on the right. The Chevreul effect is decreased

Figure 3.13 Two Chevreul staircase patterns that are physically identical, but the one on top has the light rectangle on the right and the one on the bottom has the light rectangle on the left. The patterns look different because they are placed on a luminance ramp that progresses from light on the left to dark on the right. The Chevreul effect is enhanced for the bottom pattern because the light to dark pattern of the Chevreul staircase progresses in the same direction as the luminance ramp. (From Geier & Hudak, 2011)

when the dark to light progression of the staircase pattern is opposite to the luminance ramp (top), but is enhanced if the pattern progresses in the same direction as the ramp (bottom).

What is important about the difference between our perception of the top and bottom displays is that the background ramp should have no effect on lateral inhibition between one rectangle and the next. The fact that our perception has changed even though lateral inhibition has remained the same calls into question the lateral inhibition explanation of the effect.

Hermann Grid **Figure 3.14** provides another example of how a perceptual demonstration can cause problems for an explanation based on lateral inhibition (Geier et al., 2008; Schiller & Carvey, 2005). The top display is the usual Hermann grid, with illusory dark spots at the intersections. However, when the grid's usual straight lines are made curvy, as in the bottom display, the dark spots at the intersections vanish! But making the lines curvy should have little or no effect on lateral inhibition. So just as for the Chevreul illusion, a simple perceptual display has called into question an explanation that has been accepted for many years.

Of course, the next question is, what is the mechanism responsible for these effects? A number of alternatives have been proposed involving interactions between neurons that are more complex than the simple lateral inhibition calculations, but these explanation are unproven, so further research will be needed to determine exactly what is going on (Geier et al., 2008; Geier & Hudak, 2011; Schiller & Carvey, 2005).

Let's consider what we have learned by examining the Chevreul illusion and the Hermann grid. We first saw how physiological explanations based on lateral inhibition were proposed based on (1) *physiological demonstrations* of how lateral inhibition affects neural responding in the *Limulus*; and (2) *calculations* showing how lateral inhibition could affect firing in neural circuits. The lateral inhibition explanation therefore provides a good example of how a physiological mechanism for perception was inferred from what we knew about physiological responding and neural circuits.

But as logical as this link between lateral inhibition and perception was, the perceptual displays in Figures 3.13 and 3.14 have called this link into question. Sometimes explanations have to be modified based on additional evidence, and in this case a physiological explanation is being modified based on perceptual results. Perceptual evidence can, therefore, sometimes provide information about physiology. We will encounter another example of perceptual evidence providing information about physiology later in this chapter when we discuss research on the role of feature detectors in perception, where feature detectors are neurons that respond to features such as lines with specific orientations.

Although a simple explanation based on lateral inhibition may not be adequate to explain the Chevreul and Hermann grid effects, this doesn't mean that lateral inhibition doesn't play an important role in determining our perceptions. Lateral inhibition is present throughout sensory systems, both at the beginning of neural processing, near the receptors, and further up the sensory pathways, in the brain. In the next section, we will see how lateral inhibition helps explain how individual neurons respond to patterns of light and dark.

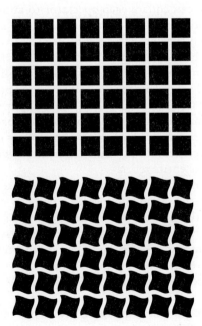

Figure 3.14 Top: The Hermann grid display from Figure 3.8, but with more squares. Bottom: The Hermann grid with curved lines. Changing the lines from straight to curved eliminates the illusory dark spots at the intersections. (From Geier et al., 2008)

TEST YOURSELF 3.1

1. Describe the experiment that demonstrated the effect of lateral inhibition in the *Limulus*.

2. What is the Chevreul illusion? What does it illustrate about the difference between physical and perceptual?

3. How was lateral inhibition used to explain the Chevreul illusion? Be sure you understand the calculations used in conjunction with the circuit in Figure 3.5.

4. What is the Hermann grid, and how was the lateral inhibition explanation used to explain it?

5. What perceptual evidence has been presented that resulted in the conclusion that the Chevreul and Hermann grid illusions can't be accounted for by a simple explanation based on lateral inhibition?

Processing From Retina to Visual Cortex and Beyond

To continue our discussion of neural processing, we will now begin a journey through the visual system that starts with neurons transmitting nerve impulses out of the retina in the optic nerve and then follows these signals as they travel to the visual areas of the brain and beyond.

Responding of Single Fibers in the Optic Nerve

Figure 3.15 shows the optic nerve leaving the back of the eye, with the cross section showing that the nerve is made up of many individual nerve fibers traveling together. These fibers are the axons of the retinal ganglion cells (also see Figure 2.6, page 25). Our story about how neural processing occurs in the visual system begins with H. Keffer Hartline, whose work on lateral inhibition in the *Limulus* and the research we are now going to describe earned him the Nobel Prize in Physiology and Medicine in 1967.

Before beginning his research on the *Limulus*, Hartline (1938, 1940) did research using the opened eyecup of a frog (**Figure 3.16**). He isolated a single fiber in the optic nerve by teasing apart the optic nerve near where it leaves the eye. While recording from this teased-out fiber, Hartline illuminated different areas of the retina and found that the fiber he was recording from responded only when a small area of the retina was illuminated. He called the area that caused the neuron to fire the nerve fiber's **receptive field** (**Figure 3.16a**), which he defined as "the region of the retina that must receive illumination in order to obtain a response in any given fiber" (Hartline, 1938, p. 410).

Hartline went on to emphasize that a neuron's receptive field covers a much greater area than a single rod or cone receptor. The fact that a neuron's receptive field covers hundreds or even thousands of receptors means that the fiber is receiving converging signals from all of these receptors. Finally, Hartline noted that the receptive fields of many different nerve fibers overlap (**Figure 3.16b**). This means that

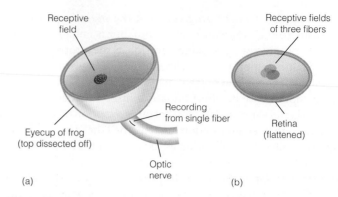

(a)   (b)

Figure 3.16 (a) Hartline's experiment in which he presented stimuli to the retina by dissecting a frog's eye and removing the top to create an "eyecup." He then presented light to the retina to determine which area of a frog's retina caused firing in one of the fibers in the optic nerve. This area is called the *receptive field* of that optic nerve fiber. (b) Receptive fields of three optic nerve fibers. These receptive fields overlap, so stimulating at a particular point on the retina will generally activate a number of fibers in the optic nerve.

shining light on a particular point on the retina activates many ganglion cell fibers.

One way to think about receptive fields is to imagine a football field and a grandstand full of spectators, each with a pair of binoculars trained on one small area of the field. Each spectator is monitoring what is happening in his or her own small area, and all of the spectators together are monitoring the entire field. Since there are so many spectators, some of the areas they are observing will wholly or partially overlap.

To relate this football field analogy to Hartline's receptive fields, we can equate each spectator to an optic nerve fiber, the football field to the retina, and the small areas viewed by each spectator to receptive fields. Imagine each optic nerve fiber is like one of our spectators. Just as each spectator monitors a small area of the football field, but collectively all spectators take in information about what is happening on the entire football field, each optic nerve fiber monitors a small area of retina. However, because there are many optic nerve fibers, just as there are many spectators, all of them together take in information about what is happening over the entire retina.

Researchers following Hartline's lead recorded from optic nerve fibers in the cat and discovered a property of receptive fields that Hartline had not observed in the frog. The cat receptive fields, it turns out, are arranged in a **center-surround organization**, in which the area in the "center" of the receptive field responds differently to light than the area in the "surround" of the receptive field (Barlow et al., 1957; Hubel & Wiesel, 1965; Kuffler, 1953).

For the receptive field in **Figure 3.17a**, presenting a spot of light to the center increases firing, so it is called the **excitatory area** of the receptive field. In contrast, stimulation of the surround causes a decrease in firing, so it is called the **inhibitory area** of the receptive field. This receptive field is called an

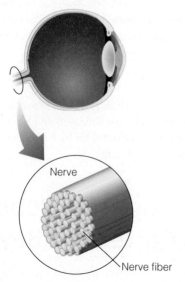

Figure 3.15 The optic nerve, which leaves the back of the eye, contains about one million optic nerve fibers in the human.

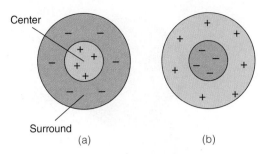

Figure 3.17 Center-surround receptive fields: (a) excitatory center, inhibitory surround; (b) inhibitory center, excitatory surround.

excitatory-center, inhibitory-surround receptive field. The receptive field in **Figure 3.17b**, which responds with inhibition when the center is stimulated and excitation when the surround is stimulated, is an **inhibitory-center, excitatory-surround receptive field.**

The discovery that receptive fields can have oppositely responding areas made it necessary to modify Hartline's definition of receptive field to "the retinal region over which a cell in the visual system can be influenced (excited or inhibited) by light" (Hubel & Wiesel, 1961). The word *influenced* and reference to excitation and inhibition make it clear that *any* change in firing—either an increase or a decrease—needs to be taken into account in determining a neuron's receptive field.

The discovery of **center-surround receptive fields** was also important because it showed that neural processing could result in neurons that respond best to specific patterns of illumination. This is illustrated by an effect called **center-surround antagonism,** illustrated in **Figure 3.18.** A small spot of light presented to the excitatory center of the receptive field causes a small increase in the rate of nerve firing (a); increasing the light's size so that it covers the entire center of the receptive field increases the cell's response, as shown in (b).

Center-surround antagonism comes into play when the spot of light becomes large enough that it begins to cover the inhibitory area, as in (c) and (d). Stimulation of the inhibitory surround counteracts the center's excitatory response, causing a decrease in the neuron's firing rate. Thus, because of center-surround antagonism, this neuron responds best to a spot of light that is the size of the excitatory center of the receptive field.

We can explain center-surround receptive fields and center-surround antagonism in terms of neural processing by describing the operation of a *neural circuit* that involves both convergence and lateral inhibition. **Figure 3.19** shows a neural circuit consisting of seven receptors. These neurons, working together, and with the aid of lateral inhibition, help create the excitatory-center, inhibitory-surround receptive field of neuron B.

Receptors 1 and 2 synapse on neuron A; receptors 3, 4, and 5 synapse on neuron B; and receptors 6 and 7 synapse on neuron C. All of these synapses are excitatory, as indicated by the Ys and + signs. Additionally, neurons A and C synapse on neuron B, with both of these synapses being inhibitory, as indicated by the vertical lines and − signs. Let's now consider how stimulating these receptors will affect the firing of B. Stimulating receptors 3, 4, and 5 causes B's firing to increase because their synapses with B are excitatory. This is what we would expect, because receptors 3, 4, and 5 are located in the excitatory center of the receptive field.

Now consider what happens when we also stimulate receptors 1 and 2. These receptors connect to A with excitatory synapses, so illuminating these receptors causes A's firing to increase. A's signal then travels to neuron B, but because its synapse onto B is inhibitory, this signal causes B's firing to decrease. This is what we would expect, because receptors 1 and 2 are located in the inhibitory surround of the receptive field. The same thing happens when we illuminate receptors 6 and 7, which are also located in the inhibitory surround. Thus, stimulating anywhere in the center (green area) causes B's firing to increase. Stimulating anywhere in the surround (red area) causes B's firing to decrease.

It is easy to see that neuron B would respond poorly when all of the receptors are illuminated simultaneously, because the

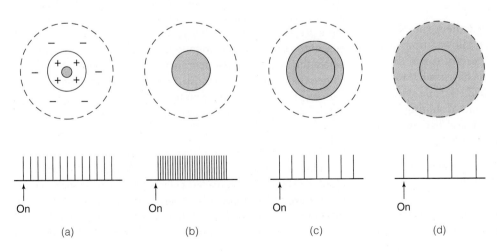

Figure 3.18 Response of an excitatory-center, inhibitory-surround receptive field as stimulus size is increased. Shading indicates the area stimulated with light. The response to the stimulus is indicated below each receptive field. (a) Small response to a small dot in the excitatory center. (b) Increased response when the whole excitatory area is stimulated. (c) Response begins to decrease when the size of the spot is increased so that it stimulates part of the inhibitory surround; this illustrates center-surround antagonism. (d) Covering all of the inhibitory surround decreases the response further.

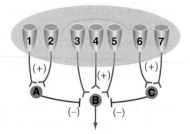

Figure 3.19 A seven-receptor neural circuit underlying a center-surround receptive field. Receptors 3, 4, and 5 are in the excitatory center, and receptors 1, 2, 6, and 7 are in the inhibitory surround.

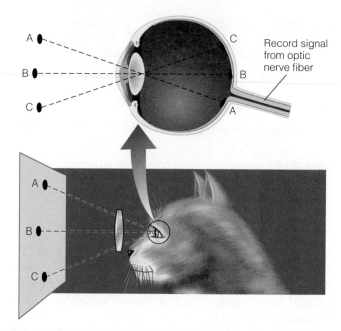

Figure 3.20 Recording electrical signals from a fiber in the optic nerve of an anesthetized cat. Each point on the screen corresponds to a point on the cat's retina.

excitation from 3, 4, and 5 and the inhibition from A and C would counteract each other, causing center-surround antagonism. Although an actual ganglion cell neuron receives signals from many more than seven receptors, and the wiring diagram is much more complex than shown in our example, the basic principle described here operates. Center-surround receptive fields are created by the interplay between excitation and inhibition.

Research on receptive fields ushered in a new era of research on neural processing because researchers realized that they could follow the effects of processing through different levels of the visual system by determining which patterns of light are most effective in generating a response in neurons at each level. This was the strategy adopted by David Hubel and Thorsten Wiesel, whose research extended the study of receptive fields into the cortex.

Hubel and Wiesel's Rationale for Studying Receptive Fields

Hubel and Wiesel (1965) state their tactic for understanding vision as follows:

> One approach ... is to stimulate the retina with patterns of light while recording from single cells or fibers at various points along the visual pathway. For each cell, the optimum stimulus can be determined, and one can note the characteristics common to cells at each level in the visual pathway, and compare a given level with the next. (Hubel & Wiesel, 1965, p. 229)

Hubel and Wiesel's research, which earned them the Nobel Prize in Physiology and Medicine in 1981, showed how neurons at higher levels of the visual system become tuned to respond best to more and more specific kinds of stimuli (Hubel, 1982). To do this, Hubel and Wiesel modified Hartline's procedure for presenting light to the retina. Instead of shining light directly into the animal's eye, Hubel and Wiesel had animals look at a screen on which they projected stimuli.

METHOD | Presenting Stimuli to Determine Receptive Fields

A neuron's receptive field is determined by presenting a stimulus, such as a spot of light, to different places on the retina to determine which areas result in no response, an excitatory response, or an inhibitory response. Hubel and Wiesel projected stimuli onto a screen (**Figure 3.20**). The animal, usually a cat or monkey, was anesthetized and looked at the screen, its eyes focused with glasses so that whatever was presented on the screen would be in focus on the back of the eye.

Because the cat's eye remains stationary, each point on the screen corresponds to a point on the cat's retina. Thus, a stimulus at point A on the screen creates an image on point A on the retina, B creates an image on B, and C on C. There are many advantages to projecting an image on a screen. Stimuli are easier to control compared to projecting light directly into the eye (especially for moving stimuli); they are sharper; and it is easier to present complex stimuli such as faces or scenes.

An important thing to remember about receptive fields, which is always true no matter what method is used, is that *the receptive field is always on the receptor surface.* The receptor surface is the retina in our examples, but as we will see later, there are also receptive fields in the touch system on the surface of the skin. It is also important to note that it doesn't matter where the *neuron* is—the neuron can be in the retina, the visual cortex, the cortex serving touch, or elsewhere in the brain, but the receptive field is always on the receptor surface, because that is where the stimuli are *received.*

To follow Hubel and Wiesel's approach, in which they recorded from single neurons at various points along the visual pathway, we need to consider where signals travel from the retina. **Figure 3.21a** repeats the overall view of the visual system from Figure 2.20, which shows how signals leaving the eye in the optic nerve travel to the **lateral geniculate nucleus (LGN)** and

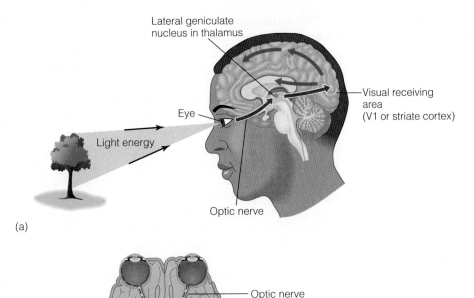

Lateral geniculate
nucleus in thalamus

Visual receiving
area
(V1 or striate cortex)

Eye

Light energy

Optic nerve

(a)

Optic nerve

Optic chiasm

Lateral geniculate nucleus

Superior colliculus

Visual cortex

(b)

Figure 3.21 (a) Side view of the visual system, showing the major sites along the primary visual pathway where processing takes place: the eye, the optic nerve, the lateral geniculate nucleus, and the visual receiving area of the cortex. (b) Visual system seen from underneath the brain, showing the superior colliculus, which receives some of the signals from the eye. The optic chiasm is the place where some of the fibers from each eye cross over to the other side of the brain, so they reach the opposite hemisphere of the visual cortex.

then from the LGN to the *occipital lobe* of the cerebral cortex, the 2- to 4-mm-thick covering of the brain that plays a central role in determining perception and cognition (Fischl & Anders, 2000). The occipital lobe is the **visual receiving area**—the place where signals from the retina and LGN first reach the cortex (Figure 1.5, page 8). Viewing the underside of the brain in **Figure 3.21b** shows the pathway from eye to cortex, plus the **superior colliculus**, which receives some signals from the eye. This structure plays an important role in controlling movements of the eyes.

The visual receiving area is also called the **striate cortex**, because it has a striped appearance when viewed in cross section, or **area V1** to indicate that it is the first visual area in the cortex. As indicated by the blue arrows in Figure 3.21a, signals also travel to other places in the cortex, but for now we focus on the pathway from the eye to the LGN to the visual cortex because this pathway was the staging ground for Hubel and Wiesel's pioneering experiments.

Hubel and Wiesel showed that optic nerve fibers have center-surround receptive fields and that neurons in the LGN also had center-surround receptive fields (Hubel & Wiesel, 1961). The fact that little change occurred in receptive fields when moving from the optic nerve fibers to neurons in the LGN made researchers wonder about the function of the LGN. Something must be going on there, because the LGN receives 90 percent of the optic nerve fibers that leave the eye (the other 10 percent travel to the superior colliculus) and it is a complex structure containing millions of neurons.

One proposal of LGN function is based on the observation that the signal sent from the LGN to the cortex is smaller than the input the LGN receives from the retina (**Figure 3.22**). This decrease in the signal leaving the LGN has led to the suggestion that one of the purposes of the LGN is to regulate neural information as it flows from the retina to the cortex (Casagrande & Norton, 1991; Humphrey & Saul, 1994).

Another important characteristic of the LGN is that it receives more signals from the cortex than from the retina (Sherman & Koch, 1986; Wilson et al., 1984). This "backward" flow of information, called *feedback*, could also be involved in

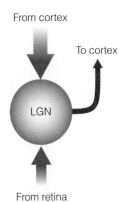

From cortex

To cortex

LGN

From retina

Figure 3.22 Information flow into and out of the LGN. The sizes of the arrows indicate the sizes of the signals.

regulation of information flow, the idea being that the information the LGN receives back from the brain may play a role in determining which information is sent up to the brain. As we will see later in the book, there is good evidence for the role of feedback in perception (Gilbert & Li, 2013). For now, we will continue our journey up the visual pathway, traveling from the LGN to V1, the visual receiving area.

Receptive Fields of Neurons in the Visual Cortex

Hubel and Wiesel's initial research on cortical neurons focused on the striate cortex (area V1) because this is where signals first arrive in the cortex. By flashing spots of light on different places in the retina, Hubel and Wiesel (1959) found cells in the striate cortex with receptive fields that, like center-surround receptive fields of neurons in the retina and LGN, have excitatory and inhibitory areas. However, these areas are arranged side by side rather than in the center-surround configuration (**Figure 3.23a**). Cells with these side-by-side receptive fields are called **simple cortical cells**.

We can tell from the layout of the excitatory and inhibitory areas of the simple cell shown in Figure 3.23a that a cell with this receptive field would respond best to vertical bars. As shown in **Figure 3.23b**, a vertical bar that illuminates only the excitatory area causes high firing, but as the bar is tilted so the inhibitory area is illuminated, firing decreases (**Figure 3.23c**).

The relationship between orientation and firing is indicated by a neuron's **orientation tuning curve**, which is determined by measuring the responses of a simple cortical cell to bars with different orientations. The tuning curve in **Figure 3.23d** shows that the cell responds with 25 nerve impulses per second to a vertically oriented bar and that the cell's response decreases as the bar is tilted away from the vertical and begins stimulating inhibitory areas of the neuron's receptive field. Notice that a bar tilted 20 degrees from the vertical elicits only a small response. This particular simple cell responds best to a bar with a vertical orientation, but there are other simple cells that respond to other orientations, so there are neurons that respond to all of the orientations that exist in the environment.

Although Hubel and Wiesel were able to use small spots of light to map the receptive fields of simple cortical cells like the one in Figure 3.23, they found that many of the cells they encountered in the striate cortex and nearby visual areas did not respond to small spots of light. In his Nobel lecture, Hubel describes how he and Wiesel were becoming increasingly frustrated in their attempts to get these cortical neurons to fire, when something startling happened: As they inserted a glass slide containing a spot stimulus into their slide projector,[1]

[1]A slide projector is a device that, until the advent of digital technology, was the method of choice for projecting images onto a screen. Slides were inserted into the projector and the images on the slides were projected onto the screen. Although slides and slide projectors have been replaced by digital imaging devices, it is still possible to purchase slide projectors on the Internet; however, the popular Kodachrome slide film used to shoot family vacation pictures was discontinued in 2009.

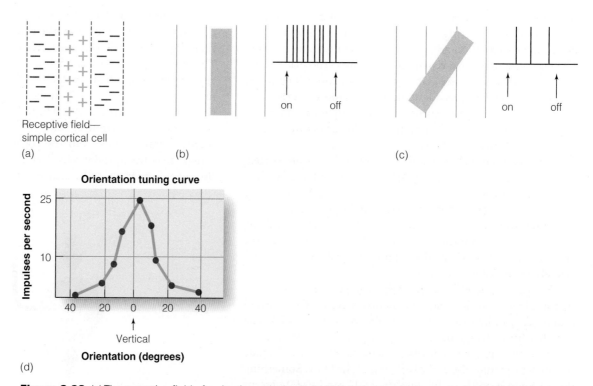

Figure 3.23 (a) The receptive field of a simple cortical cell. (b) This cell responds best to a vertical bar of light that covers the excitatory area of the receptive field. (c) The response decreases as the bar is tilted so that it also covers the inhibitory area. (d) Orientation tuning curve of a simple cortical cell for a neuron that responds best to a vertical bar (orientation = 0).

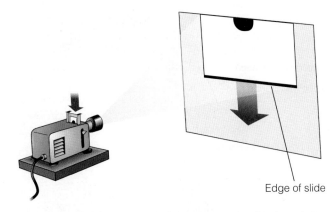

Figure 3.24 When Hubel and Wiesel dropped a slide into their slide projector, the image of the edge of the slide moving down unexpectedly triggered activity in a cortical neuron.

Edge of slide

a cortical neuron "went off like a machine gun" (Hubel, 1982). The neuron, as it turned out, was responding not to the spot at the center of the slide that Hubel and Wiesel had planned to use as a stimulus, but to the image of the slide's edge moving downward on the screen as the slide dropped into the projector (**Figure 3.24**). Upon realizing this, Hubel and Wiesel changed their stimuli from small spots to moving lines and were then able to find cells that responded to oriented moving bars. As with simple cells, a particular neuron had a preferred orientation.

Hubel and Wiesel (1965) discovered that many cortical neurons respond best to moving barlike stimuli with specific orientations. **Complex cells**, like simple cells, respond best to bars of a particular orientation. However, unlike simple cells, which respond to small spots of light or to stationary stimuli, most complex cells respond only when a correctly oriented bar of light moves across the entire receptive field. Further, many complex cells respond best to a particular direction of movement (**Figure 3.25a**). Because these neurons don't respond to stationary flashes of light, their receptive fields are indicated not by pluses and minuses but by outlining the area that, when stimulated, elicits a response in the neuron.

Another type of cell, called **end-stopped cells**, fire to moving lines of a specific length or to moving corners or angles. **Figure 3.25b** shows a light corner stimulus that is being moved up and down across the retina. The records to the right indicate that the neuron responds best to a medium-sized corner that is moving upward.

Hubel and Wiesel's finding that some neurons in the cortex respond only to oriented lines and others respond best to corners was an extremely important discovery because it extended the idea first proposed in connection with center-surround receptive fields that neurons respond to some patterns of light and not to others. This makes sense because the purpose of the visual system is to enable us to perceive objects in the environment, and many objects can be at least crudely represented by simple shapes and lines of various orientations. Thus, Hubel and Wiesel's discovery that neurons respond selectively to oriented lines and stimuli with specific lengths was an important step toward determining how neurons respond to more complex objects.

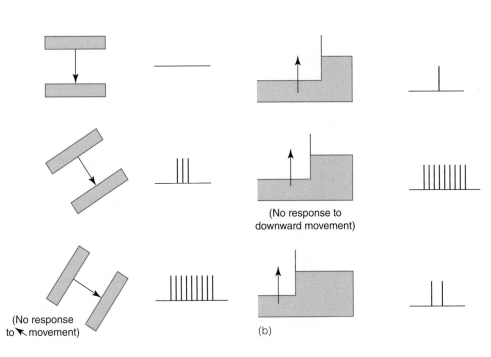

Figure 3.25 (a) Response of a complex cell recorded from the visual cortex of the cat. The stimulus bar is moved back and forth across the receptive field. This cell fires best when the bar is positioned with a specific orientation and is moved from left to right. (b) Response of an end-stopped cell recorded from the visual cortex of the cat. The stimulus is indicated by the light area on the left. This cell responds best to a medium-sized corner that is moving up.

Table 3.1 Properties of Neurons in the Optic Nerve, LGN, and Cortex

TYPE OF CELL	CHARACTERISTICS OF RECEPTIVE FIELD
Optic nerve fiber (ganglion cell)	Center-surround receptive field. Responds best to small spots, but will also respond to other stimuli.
Lateral geniculate	Center-surround receptive fields very similar to the receptive field of a ganglion cell.
Simple cortical	Excitatory and inhibitory areas arranged side by side. Responds best to bars of a particular orientation.
Complex cortical	Responds best to movement of a correctly oriented bar across the receptive field. Many cells respond best to a particular direction of movement.
End-stopped cortical	Responds to corners, angles, or bars of a particular length moving in a particular direction.

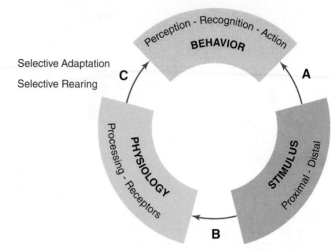

Figure 3.26 Three-part version of the perceptual process, repeated from Figure 1.11, showing the three basic relationships: (A) stimulus–perception, (B) stimulus–physiology, and (C) physiology–perception. "Selective Adaptation" and "Selective Rearing" refer to experiments described in the text that were designed to measure relationship C.

Table 3.1, which summarizes the properties of the neurons we have described so far, illustrates an important fact about neurons in the visual system: As we travel farther from the retina, neurons fire to more complex stimuli. Retinal ganglion cells respond best to spots of light, whereas cortical end-stopped cells respond best to bars of a certain length that are moving in a particular direction. Because simple, complex, and end-stopped cells fire in response to specific features of the stimulus, such as orientation or direction of movement, they have been called **feature detectors**.

Do Feature Detectors Play a Role in Perception?

Neural processing endows neurons with properties that make them feature detectors that respond best to a specific type of stimulus. When researchers show that neurons respond to oriented lines, they are measuring relationship B: the *stimulus–physiology relationship* (**Figure 3.26**). But just measuring this relationship does not prove that these neurons have anything to do with the perception of oriented lines. To demonstrate a link between physiology and perception, it is necessary to measure relationship C: the *physiology–perception relationship*. One way this has been accomplished is by using a psychophysical procedure called *selective adaptation*.

Selective Adaptation

When we view a stimulus with a specific property, neurons tuned to that property fire. The idea behind **selective adaptation** is that this firing causes neurons to eventually

become fatigued, or adapt. This adaptation causes two physiological effects: (1) the neuron's firing rate decreases, and (2) the neuron fires less when that stimulus is immediately presented again. According to this idea, presenting a vertical line causes neurons that respond to vertical lines to respond, but as these presentations continue, these neurons eventually begin to fire less to vertical lines. Adaptation is *selective* because only the neurons that were responding to verticals or near-verticals adapt, and neurons that were not firing do not adapt.

METHod | Psychophysical Measurement of the Effect of Selective Adaptation to Orientation

Measuring the effect of selective adaptation to orientation involves the following three steps:

1. Measure a person's *contrast threshold* to gratings with a number of different orientations (**Figure 3.27a**). A grating's **contrast threshold** is the minimum intensity difference between two adjacent bars that can just be detected. The contrast threshold for seeing a grating is measured by changing the intensity difference between the light and dark bars until the bars can just barely be seen. For example, it is easy to see the four gratings on the left of **Figure 3.28**, because the difference in intensity between the bars is above threshold. However, there is only a small intensity difference between the bars of the grating on the far right, so it is close to the contrast threshold. The intensity difference at which the bars can just barely be seen is the contrast threshold.

2. Adapt the person to one orientation by having the person view a high-contrast *adapting stimulus* for a minute or two.

(a) Measure contrast threshold at a number of orientations.

(b) Adapt to a high-contrast grating.

(c) Remeasure contrast thresholds for same orientations as above.

Figure 3.27 Procedure for carrying out a selective adaptation experiment. See text for details.

Figure 3.28 The contrast threshold for a grating is the minimum difference in intensity at which the observer can just make out the bars. The grating on the left is far above the contrast threshold. The ones in the middle have less contrast but are still above threshold. The grating on the far right is near the contrast threshold. (From Womelsdorf et al., 2006)

In this example, the *adapting stimulus* is a vertical grating (**Figure 3.27b**).

3. Remeasure the contrast threshold of all the test stimuli presented in step 1 (**Figure 3.27c**).

The rationale behind this procedure is that if the adaptation to the high-contrast grating in step 2 decreases the functioning of neurons that determine the perception of verticals, this should cause an increase in contrast threshold so it is more difficult to see low-contrast vertical gratings. In other words, adapting vertical feature detectors should make it is necessary to increase the difference between the black and white vertical bars in order to see them. **Figure 3.29a** shows that this is exactly what happens. The peak of the contrast threshold curve, which indicates that a large increase in the difference between the bars was needed to see the bars, occurs at the vertical adapting orientation.

The important result of this experiment is that our psychophysical curve shows that adaptation selectively affects only some orientations, just as neurons selectively respond to only some orientations. In fact, comparing the psychophysically determined selective adaptation curve (Figure 3.29a) to the orientation tuning curve for a simple cortical neuron (**Figure 3.29b**) reveals that they are very similar. (The psychophysical curve is slightly wider because the adapting stimulus affects some neurons that respond to orientations near the adapting orientation.)

The near match between the orientation selectivity of neurons and the perceptual effect of selective adaptation supports the idea that orientation detectors play a role in perception. The selective adaptation experiment is measuring how a physiological effect (adapting the feature detectors that respond to a specific orientation) causes a perceptual result (decrease in sensitivity to that orientation). This evidence that feature detectors have something to do with perception means that when you look at a complex scene, such as a city street or a crowded shopping mall, feature detectors that are firing to the orientations in the scene are helping to construct your perception of the scene.

Selective Rearing

Further evidence that feature detectors are involved in perception is provided by selective rearing experiments. The idea behind **selective rearing** is that if an animal is reared in an environment that contains only certain types of stimuli, then neurons that respond to these stimuli will become more prevalent.

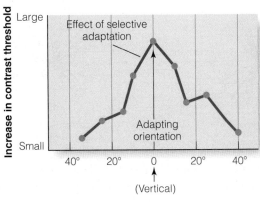

(a)

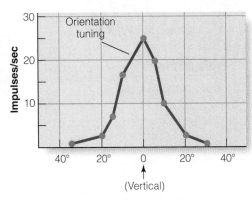

(b)

Figure 3.29 (a) Results of a psychophysical selective adaptation experiment. This graph shows that the person's adaptation to the vertical grating causes a large decrease in her ability to detect the vertical grating when it is presented again but has less effect on gratings that are tilted to either side of the vertical. (b) Orientation tuning curve of the simple cortical neuron from Figure 3.23.

This follows from a phenomenon called **neural plasticity** or **experience-dependent plasticity**—the idea that the response properties of neurons can be shaped by perceptual experience. According to this idea, rearing an animal in an environment that contains only vertical lines should result in the animal's visual system having neurons that respond predominantly to verticals.

This result may seem to contradict the results of the selective adaptation experiment just described, in which exposure to verticals *decreases* the response to verticals. However, adaptation is a short-term effect. Presenting the adapting orientation for a few minutes decreases responding to that orientation. In contrast, selective rearing is a longer-term effect. Presenting the rearing orientation over a period of days or even weeks keeps the neurons that respond to that orientation active. Meanwhile, neurons that respond to orientations that aren't present are not active, so they lose their ability to respond to those orientations.

One way to describe the results of selective rearing experiments is "Use it or lose it." This effect was demonstrated in a classic experiment by Colin Blakemore and Grahame Cooper (1970) in which they placed kittens in striped tubes like the one in **Figure 3.30a**, so that each kitten was exposed to only one orientation, either vertical or horizontal. The kittens were kept in the dark from birth to 2 weeks of age, at which time they were placed in the tube for 5 hours a day; the rest of the time they remained in the dark. Because the kittens sat on a Plexiglas platform, and the tube extended both above and below them, there were no visible corners or edges in their environment other than the stripes on the sides of the tube. The

kittens wore cones around their head to prevent them from seeing vertical stripes as oblique or horizontal stripes by tilting their heads; however, according to Blakemore and Cooper, "The kittens did not seem upset by the monotony of their surroundings and they sat for long periods inspecting the walls of the tube" (p. 477).

When the kittens' behavior was tested after 5 months of selective rearing, they seemed blind to the orientations that they hadn't seen in the tube. For example, a kitten that was reared in an environment of vertical stripes would pay attention to a vertical rod but ignore a horizontal rod. Following behavioral testing, Blakemore and Cooper recorded from cells in the visual cortex and determined the stimulus orientation that caused the largest response from each cell.

Figure 3.30b shows the results of this experiment. Each line indicates the orientation preferred by a single neuron in the cat's cortex. This cat, which was reared in a vertical environment, has many neurons that respond best to vertical or near-vertical stimuli, but none that respond to horizontal stimuli. The horizontally responding neurons were apparently lost because they hadn't been used. The opposite result occurred for the horizontally reared cats. The parallel between the orientation selectivity of neurons in the cat's cortex and the cat's behavioral response to the same orientation provides more evidence that feature detectors are involved in the perception of orientation. This connection between feature detectors and perception was one of the major discoveries of vision research in the 1960s and 1970s.

Related to this result is the oblique effect discussed in Chapter 1 (page 11)—the fact that people perceive vertical and

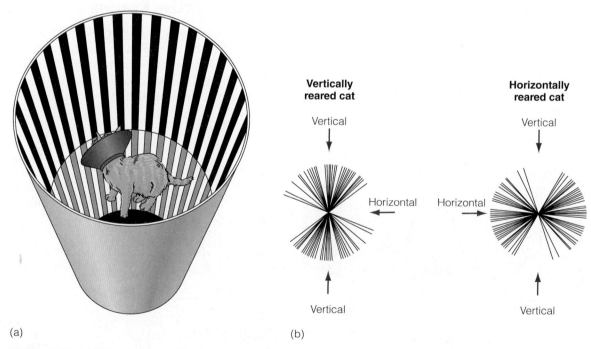

(a)   (b)

Figure 3.30 (a) Striped tube used in Blakemore and Cooper's (1970) selective rearing experiments. (b) Distribution of optimal orientations for 72 cells from a cat reared in an environment of vertical stripes, on the left, and for 52 cells from a cat reared in an environment of horizontal stripes, on the right. (Blakemore & Cooper, 1970)

horizontal lines better than slanted lines. What is important about the oblique effect is not only that people see horizontals and verticals better, but that the brain's response to detecting horizontals and verticals is larger than when detecting slanted lines (Figure 1.13, page 12). Possibly, just as the orientation selectivity of the kitten's neurons matched its horizontal or vertical environment, the response of human neurons reflects the fact that horizontals and verticals are more common than slanted lines in our environment (Coppola et al., 1998).

Higher-Level Neurons

The idea that perception can be explained in terms of feature detectors that respond to straight lines or corners was popular in the 1970s because, as anyone who has played with building blocks or Legos knows, many objects can be created from rectangular shapes. Objects could, according to this idea, be represented by the firing of feature detectors that responded to these rectangular shapes that make up the objects.

But the idea that perception was based solely on what might be called "stick-figure physiology" was not to last. Although researchers continued to study feature detectors in the striate cortex and nearby areas, vision researchers were beginning to pay attention to brain areas far outside of the striate cortex in order to answer the question of how complex stimuli are represented by the firing of neurons in the brain. One answer to this question began to emerge in the laboratory of Charles Gross, who decided that the **inferotemporal (IT) cortex** in the temporal lobe was ripe for study (**Figure 3.31a**). He based this decision on research that showed that removing parts of the IT cortex in monkeys affected the monkeys' ability to tell the difference between different objects (Gross, 1972).

Gross's experiments, in which he recorded from single neurons in the monkey's IT cortex, required a great deal of endurance by the experimenters, because the experiments typically lasted 3 or 4 days. In these experiments, Gross's research team presented a variety of different stimuli to anesthetized monkeys. Using the projection screen procedure, they presented lines, squares, and circles. Some stimuli were light, and some dark. The dark stimuli were created by placing cardboard cutouts against the transparent projection screen.

The discovery that neurons in the IT cortex respond to complex stimuli came a few days into one of their experiments, when they found a neuron that refused to respond to any of the standard stimuli like oriented lines or circles or squares. Nothing worked, until one of the experimenters pointed at something in the room, casting a shadow of his hand on the screen. When this hand shadow caused a burst of firing, the experimenters knew they were on to something and began testing

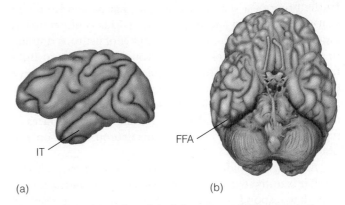

(a)   (b)

Figure 3.31 (a) Location of the inferotemporal (IT) cortex in the monkey. (b) Location of the fusiform face area (FFA) in the human, just under the temporal lobe. Both of these areas are rich in neurons that respond to faces.

the neuron to see what kinds of stimuli caused it to respond. They used a variety of stimuli, including cutouts of a monkey's hand. After a great deal of testing, they determined that this neuron responded to a handlike shape with fingers pointing up (**Figure 3.32**) (Rocha-Miranda, 2011; also see Gross, 2002, 2008). After expanding the types of stimuli presented, they also found some neurons that responded best to faces.

Finding neurons that responded to real-life objects like hands and faces was a revolutionary result. Apparently, neural processing that occurred beyond the initial receiving areas studied by Hubel and Wiesel had created neurons that responded best to very specific types of stimuli. But sometimes revolutionary results aren't accepted immediately, and Gross's results were largely ignored when they were published in 1969 and 1972 (Gross et al., 1969, 1972). Finally, in the 1980s, other experimenters began recording from neurons in the IT cortex of the monkey that responded to faces and other complex objects (Rolls, 1981; Perrett et al., 1982), and in the 1990s, researchers discovered an area on the underside of the temporal lobe of the human cortex that was named the *fusiform face area* because it responded strongly to faces (Kanwisher et al., 1997; McCarthy et al., 1997) (**Figure 3.31b**). We will see in the chapters that follow that neurons that respond to complex real-world stimuli are now considered the norm in vision research.

Sensory Coding

The problem of neural representation for the senses has been called the problem of **sensory coding**, where the sensory code refers to how neurons represent various characteristics of the environment. The idea that an object could be represented

Figure 3.32 Some of the shapes used by Gross and coworkers (1972) to study the responses of neurons in the monkey's inferotemporal cortex. The shapes are arranged in order of their ability to cause the neuron to fire, from none (1) to little (2 and 3) to maximum (6). (From Gross, Rocha-Miranda, & Bender, 1972)

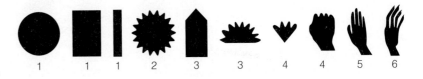

1   1   1   2   3   3   4   4   5   6

by the firing of a specialized neuron that responds only to that object is called **specificity coding**. This is illustrated in **Figure 3.33**, which shows how a number of neurons respond to three different faces. Only neuron #4 responds to Bill's face, only #9 responds to Mary's face, and only #6 responds to Raphael's face. Also note that the neuron specialized to respond only to Bill, which we can call a "Bill neuron," does not respond to Mary or Raphael. In addition, other faces or types of objects would not affect this neuron. It fires only to Bill's face.

Although the idea of specificity coding is straightforward, it is unlikely to be correct. Even though there are neurons that respond to faces, these neurons usually respond to a number of different faces (not just Bill's). There are just too many different faces and other objects (and colors, tastes, smells, and sounds) in the world to have a separate neuron dedicated to each one. An alternative to the idea of specificity coding is that a number of neurons are involved in representing an object.

Population coding is the representation of a particular object by the pattern of firing of a large number of neurons. According to this idea, Bill's face might be represented by the pattern of firing shown in **Figure 3.34a**, Mary's face by a different pattern (**Figure 3.34b**), and Raphael's face by another pattern (**Figure 3.34c**). An advantage of population coding is that a large number of stimuli can be represented, because large groups of neurons can create a huge number of different patterns. There is good evidence for population coding in the senses and for other cognitive functions as well. But for some functions, a large number of neurons isn't necessary. Sparse coding occurs when small groups of neurons are involved.

Sparse coding occurs when a particular object is represented by a pattern of firing of only a small group of neurons, with the majority of neurons remaining silent. As shown in **Figure 3.35a**, sparse coding would represent Bill's face by the pattern of firing of a few neurons (neurons 2, 3, 4, and 7). Mary's face would be signaled by the pattern of firing of a few different neurons (neurons 4, 6, and 7; **Figure 3.35b**), but possibly with some overlap with the neurons representing Bill, and Raphael's face would have yet another pattern (neurons 1, 2, and 4; **Figure 3.35c**). Notice that a particular neuron can respond to more than one stimulus. For example, neuron #4 responds to all three faces, although most strongly to Mary's.

Neurons that respond to very specific stimuli were discovered when recording from the temporal lobe of patients undergoing brain surgery for epilepsy. (Stimulating and recording from neurons is a common procedure before and during brain surgery, because it makes it possible to determine the exact layout of a particular person's brain.) **Figure 3.36** shows the records for a neuron that responded to pictures of the actor Steve Carell and not to other people's faces (Quiroga et al., 2008). However, the researchers who discovered this neuron (as well as

Figure 3.33 Specificity coding, in which each face causes a different neuron to fire. Firing of neuron 4 signals "Bill"; neuron 9 signals "Mary"; neuron 6 signals "Raphael."

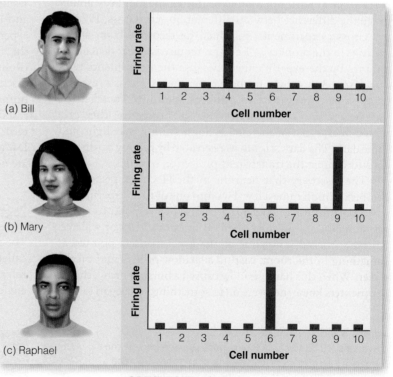

SPECIFICITY CODING

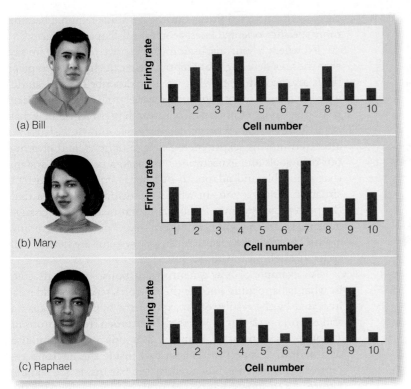

POPULATION CODING

Figure 3.34 Population coding, in which the face's identity is indicated by the pattern of firing of a large number of neurons.

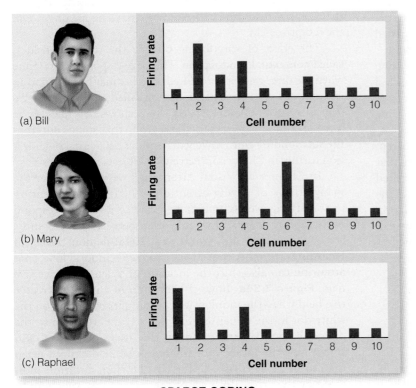

SPARSE CODING

Figure 3.35 Sparse coding, which is like population coding because a face's identity is indicated by the pattern of firing of a number of neurons. However, sparse coding involves fewer neurons than population coding. Thus, the pattern created by neurons 2, 3, 4 and 7 signals "Bill"; the pattern created by 4, 6 and 7 signals "Mary"; the pattern created by 1, 2 and 4 signals "Raphael."

Figure 3.36 Records from a neuron in the temporal lobe that responded to different pictures of Steve Carell similar to the ones shown here (top records) but which did not respond to pictures of other well-known people (bottom records). (From Quiroga et al., 2008)

Photos: Frederick M. Brown/Getty Images; AP Images/Invision for Fox Searchlight/Todd Williamson; Photos 12/Alamy; JStone/Shutterstock.com; Young Nova/Shutterstock.com; s_bukley/Shutterstock.com

other neurons that responded to other people) point out that they had only 30 minutes to record from these neurons and that if more time were available, it is likely that they would have found other faces that would cause this neuron to fire. Given the likelihood that even these special neurons are likely to fire to more than one stimulus, Quiroga and coworkers suggested that their neurons are probably an example of sparse coding.

There is also other evidence that the code for representing objects in the visual system, tones in the auditory system, and odors in the olfactory system may involve a pattern of activity across a relatively small number of neurons, as sparse coding suggests (Olshausen & Field, 2004).

Returning to the question about how neural firing can represent various features in the environment, we can state that part of the answer is that features or objects are represented by the pattern of firing of groups of neurons. Sometimes the groups are small (sparse coding), sometimes large (population coding). But this is just the beginning of the answer. As we will see in the next chapter, another part of the answer involves considering how neurons in sensory systems are organized.

SOMETHING TO CONSIDER:

"Flexible" Receptive Fields

We introduced the idea of a neuron's receptive field by defining the receptive field as the area of the retina that, when stimulated, influences the firing of the neuron. Later, as we worked our way to higher levels of the visual system, the receptive field was still the area that affected firing, but the stimulus required became more specific—oriented lines, geometrical shapes, and faces.

Nowhere in our discussion of receptive fields did we say that the area defining the receptive field can change. Receptive fields are, according to what we have described so far, static, wired-in properties of neurons. However, one of the themes of this book—and of a great deal of research in perception—is that because we exist in an ever-changing environment, because we are often moving, experiencing new situations, and creating our own goals and expectations, we need a perceptual system that is flexible and adapts to our needs and to the current situation. This section—in which we introduce the idea that the perceptual system is flexible and that neurons can change depending on changing conditions—is a "preview of coming events," because the idea that sensory systems are flexible will recur throughout the book.

An example of how a neuron's response can be affected by what is happening outside the neuron's receptive field is illustrated by the results of an experiment by Mitesh Kapadia and coworkers (2000), in which they recorded from neurons in a monkey's visual cortex. **Figure 3.37a** indicates the response of a neuron to a vertical bar located inside the neuron's receptive field, which is indicated by the bar inside the square. **Figure 3.37b** shows that two vertical bars located outside the neuron's receptive field cause little change in the neuron's response. But **Figure 3.37c** shows what happens when the "outside the receptive field" bars are presented along with the "inside the field" bar. There is a large increase in firing! Thus, although our definition of a neuron's receptive field as *the area of retina which, when stimulated, influences the neuron's firing*, is still correct, we can now see that the response to stimulation *within* the receptive field can be affected by what's happening *outside* the receptive field.

The effect of stimulating outside the receptive field is called **contextual modulation**. The large response that occurs when the three lines are presented together may be related to an example of a perceptual phenomenon called *perceptual organization*, illustrated in **Figure 3.37d**, which shows how lines of the same orientation are perceived as a group that stands out from the surrounding clutter. We will consider perceptual organization further in Chapter 5, "Perceiving Objects and Scenes."

In Chapter 6, "Visual Attention," we will consider the many effects of paying attention. When we pay attention to something, we become more aware of it, we can respond more rapidly to it, and we may even perceive it differently. Theo Womelsdorf and coworkers (2006) demonstrated, in recordings from neurons in the monkey temporal lobe, that attention can also shift the location of a neuron's receptive field. **Figure 3.38a** shows the location of a neuron's receptive field when the monkey was keeping its eyes fixed on the white dot in the upper left but was paying attention to the diamond location indicated by the arrow. **Figure 3.38b** shows how the location of the receptive field shifted when the monkey's attention shifted to the circle location indicated by the arrow. In both of these examples, yellow indicates the area of the retina that, when stimulated, causes the greatest response.

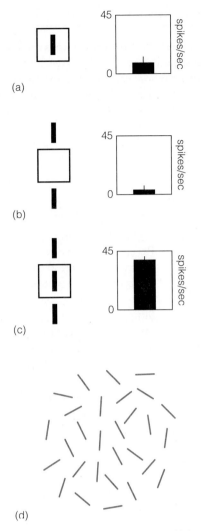

(a)

(b)

(c)

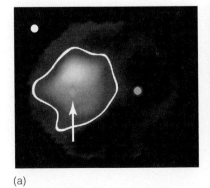

(d)

Figure 3.37 A neuron in the monkey's temporal lobe responds (a) with a small response to a vertical bar flashed inside the receptive field (indicated by the square); (b) with little or no response to two vertical bars presented outside the receptive field; (c) with a large response when the three bars are presented together. This enhanced response caused by stimuli presented outside the receptive field is called *contextual modulation*. (d) A pattern in which the three aligned lines stand out. (a–c from Kapadia et al., 2000)

This shifting of the receptive field, depending on where the monkey is attending, is an amazing result because it means that attention is changing the organization of part of the visual system. Receptive fields, it turns out, aren't fixed in place but can change in response to where the monkey is paying attention. This concentrates neural processing power at the place that is important to the monkey at that moment. As we continue exploring how the nervous system creates our perceptions, we will encounter other examples of how the flexibility of our nervous system helps us function within our ever-changing environment.

TEST YOURSELF 3.2

1. What is a receptive field? What did Hartline's research indicate about receptive fields?

2. What are the characteristics of the receptive fields of a cat's optic nerve and LGN neurons? What new properties were associated with the discovery of these receptive fields? How did these properties require that the definition of receptive field be changed?

3. What function has been suggested for the LGN?

4. Describe the characteristics of simple, complex, and end-stopped cells in the cortex. Why have these cells been called feature detectors?

5. How has the psychophysical procedure of selective adaptation been used to demonstrate a link between feature detectors and the perception of orientation? Be sure you understand the rationale behind a selective adaptation experiment and also how we can draw conclusions about physiology from the results of this psychophysical procedure.

6. How has the procedure of selective rearing been used to demonstrate a link between feature detectors and perception? Be sure you understand the concept of neural plasticity.

7. Describe Gross's experiments on neurons in the inferotemporal cortex of the monkey. Why do you think his results were initially ignored?

8. What is the sensory code? Describe specificity, population, and sparse coding. Which type of coding is most likely to operate in sensory systems?

9. Describe the two experiments that demonstrated the "flexibility" of receptive fields.

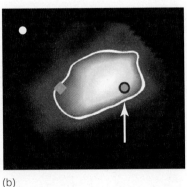

(a)   (b)

Figure 3.38 Receptive field maps on the retina determined when a monkey was looking at the fixation spot (white) but paying attention to locations indicated by the arrows: (a) the diamond or (b) the circle. The arrows were not included in the display seen by the monkey. The yellow areas are areas of the receptive field that generate the largest response. Notice that the receptive field map shifts to the right when the monkey shifts its attention from the diamond to the circle. (From Womelsdorf et al., 2006)

Something to Consider: "Flexible" Receptive Fields   **69**

THINK ABOUT IT

1. Look for shadows, both inside and outside, and see if you can see Mach bands at the borders of the shadows. Remember that Mach bands are easier to see when the border of a shadow is slightly fuzzy. Mach bands are not actually present in the pattern of light and dark, so you need to be sure that the bands are not really in the light but are created by your nervous system. How can you accomplish this? (p. 52)

2. Cell A responds best to vertical lines moving to the right. Cell B responds best to 45-degree lines moving to the right. Both of these cells have an excitatory synapse with cell C. How will cell C fire to vertical lines? To 45-degree lines? What if the synapse between B and C is inhibitory? (p. 60)

KEY TERMS

Area V1 (p. 59)
Center-surround antagonism (p. 57)
Center-surround organization (p. 56)
Center-surround receptive field (p. 57)
Chevreul illusion (p. 51)
Complex cells (p. 61)
Contextual modulation (p. 68)
Contrast threshold (p. 62)
End-stopped cell (p. 61)
Excitatory area (p. 56)
Excitatory-center, inhibitory-surround receptive field (p. 56)

Experience-dependent plasticity (p. 64)
Feature detectors (p. 62)
Inferotemporal (IT) cortex (p. 65)
Inhibitory area (p. 56)
Inhibitory-center, excitatory-surround receptive field (p. 57)
Lateral geniculate nucleus (LGN) (p. 58)
Lateral inhibition (p. 50)
Mach bands (p. 51)
Neural plasticity (p. 64)
Ommatidia (p. 50)
Orientation tuning curve (p. 60)

Population coding (p. 66)
Receptive field (p. 56)
Selective adaptation (p. 62)
Selective rearing (p. 63)
Sensory coding (p. 65)
Simple cortical cell (p. 60)
Sparse coding (p. 66)
Specificity coding (p. 66)
Staircase illusion (p. 51)
Striate cortex (p. 59)
Superior colliculus (p. 59)
Visual receiving area (p. 59)

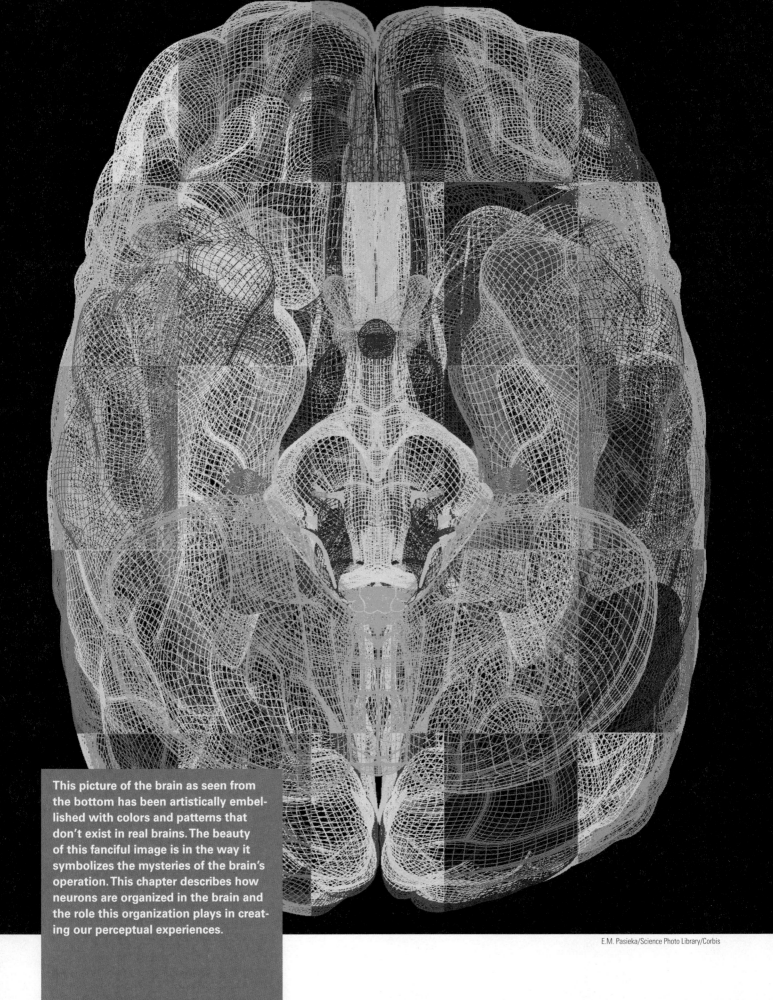

This picture of the brain as seen from the bottom has been artistically embellished with colors and patterns that don't exist in real brains. The beauty of this fanciful image is in the way it symbolizes the mysteries of the brain's operation. This chapter describes how neurons are organized in the brain and the role this organization plays in creating our perceptual experiences.

CHAPTER 4

Cortical Organization

CHAPTER CONTENTS

Spatial Organization in the Visual Cortex

The Neural Map on the Striate Cortex (Area V1)

The Cortex Is Organized in Columns

How Do Orientation-Selective Neurons Respond to a Scene?

Pathways for What, Where, and How

Streams for Information About What and Where

Streams for Information About What and How

Modularity

Face Neurons in the Monkey's IT Cortex

The Fusiform Face Area in Humans

Areas for Places and Bodies in Humans

Distributed Representation

Two Experiments That Demonstrate Distributed Representation

Distributed Representation of Multidimensional Stimuli

Where Perception Meets Memory

SOMETHING TO CONSIDER: The Mind–Body Problem

DEVELOPMENTAL DIMENSION: Experience and Neural Responding

THINK ABOUT IT

Some Questions We Will Consider:

■ Do electrical signals that represent objects at different places in a scene go to different places in the brain? (p. 74)

■ How can brain damage affect a person's perception? (p. 81)

■ Are there separate brain areas that determine our perception of different qualities? (pp. 83, 84)

O rganization is important. We need to "get organized." Companies have an organizational chart. Organizing information in a file cabinet or in your computer makes it easier to access information when you need it. Organizing information in your mind can help you study more effectively for an exam.

The need for organization is especially important in the visual system because of the tasks the visual system faces. One task is to process information about various characteristics of objects, such as size, shape, orientation, color, movement, and location in space. Another task is to process information about different types of objects such as trees, faces, people, furniture, and animals.

This chapter, which describes how information about objects and actions is organized in the visual system, is the culmination

of the discussion we began in Chapter 2. Let's recap what we know so far. Chapter 2 started at the beginning of the visual system—in the eye—and described how perception is affected by the eye's focusing system and by properties of the rod and cone receptors. We saw how dark adaptation, the increase in sensitivity that occurs as we spend time in the dark, can be explained by a chemical process (pigment regeneration), and how visual sensitivity and detail vision can be explained by considering how the receptors are connected to other neurons (convergence).

By the end of Chapter 2 we had introduced electrical signals, but they were still within the retina. Chapter 3 took these signals beyond the retina by describing the receptive fields of neurons in the retina that form the optic nerve, in the lateral geniculate nucleus, in the visual receiving area in the occipital lobe, and in the temporal lobe. This research on receptive fields showed that (1) the response properties of an individual neuron are determined by inputs from many other neurons (Figure 3.19, page 58) and (2) neurons at higher levels of the visual system respond to more complex stimuli. For example, optic nerve neurons respond to spots of light (Figure 3.16, page 56), neurons in the visual cortex respond to oriented bars (Figure 3.23, page 60), and neurons in the temporal cortex respond to complex shapes and faces (Figure 3.36, page 68).

The fact that neurons in different places in the visual system respond best to specific stimuli is evidence that the visual system is organized. As we will now see, there is evidence that the visual system is organized in a number of ways. We begin by considering **spatial organization**—how different locations in the environment and on the retina are represented by activity at specific locations in the visual cortex.

Spatial Organization in the Visual Cortex

When we look out at a scene, things are organized across our visual field. There's a house on the left, a tree next to the house, and a car parked in the driveway on the other side of the house. This organization of objects in visual space becomes transformed into organization in the eye, when an image of the scene is created on the retina. It is easy to appreciate spatial organization at the level of the retinal image because this image is essentially a picture of the scene. But once the house, the tree, and the car have been transformed into electrical signals, the signals created by each object then become organized in the form of "neural maps," so that objects that create images near each other on the retina are represented by neural signals that are near each other in the cortex.

The Neural Map on the Striate Cortex (Area V1)

To begin describing neural maps, let's describe how points in the retinal image are represented *spatially* in the striate cortex (area V1). We determine this by stimulating various places on the retina and noting where neurons fire in the cortex. **Figure 4.1** shows a man looking at a tree so that points A, B, C, and D on the tree stimulate points A, B, C, and D on his retina. Moving to the cortex, the image at point A on the retina causes neurons at point A to fire in the cortex. The image at point B causes neurons at point B to fire, and so on. This example shows how points on the retinal image cause activity in the cortex.

This example also shows that locations on the cortex correspond to locations on the retina. This electronic map of the retina on the cortex is called a **retinotopic map**. This organized spatial map means that two points that are close together on an object and on the retina will activate neurons that are close together in the brain (Silver & Kastner, 2009).

But let's look at this retinotopic map a little more closely, because it has a very interesting property that is relevant to perception. Although points A, B, C, and D in the cortex correspond to points A, B, C, and D on the retina, you might notice something about the *spacing* of these locations. Considering the retina, we note that the man is looking at the leaves at the top of the tree, so points A and B are both near the fovea and the images of points C and D at the bottom of the trunk are in the peripheral retina. But although A and B and C and D are the same distance apart on the retina, the spacing is not the same on the cortex. A and B are farther apart on the cortex than C

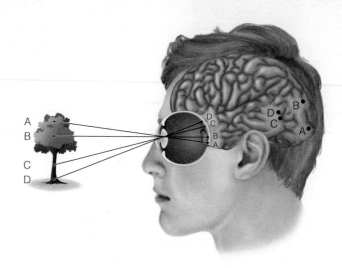

Figure 4.1 A person looking at a tree, showing how points A, B, C, and D are imaged on the retina and where these retinal activations cause activity in the brain. Although the distances between A and B and between C and D are about the same on the retina, the distance between A and B is much greater on the cortex. This is an example of cortical magnification, in which more space is devoted to areas of the retina near the fovea.

and D. What this means is that electrical signals associated with the part of the tree near where the person is looking are allotted more space on the cortex than signals associated with parts of the tree that are located off to the side—in the periphery. In other words, the representation on the cortex is distorted, with more space being allotted to locations near the fovea than to locations in the peripheral retina. Even though the fovea accounts for only 0.01 percent of the retina's area, signals from the fovea account for 8 to 10 percent of the retinotopic map on the cortex (Van Essen & Anderson, 1995). This apportioning of a large area on the cortex to the small fovea is called **cortical magnification**. The size of this magnification, which is called the **cortical magnification factor**, is depicted in **Figure 4.2**.

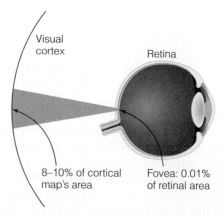

Figure 4.2 The magnification factor in the visual system. The small area of the fovea is represented by a large area on the visual cortex.

Cortical magnification has been determined in the human cortex using a technique called **brain imaging**, which makes it possible to create pictures of the brain's activity. We will describe the procedure of brain imaging and how this procedure has been used to measure the cortical magnification factor in humans.

METHOD | Brain Imaging

In the 1980s, a technique called **magnetic resonance imaging (MRI)** made it possible to create images of structures within the brain. Since then, MRI has become a standard technique for detecting tumors and other brain abnormalities. While this technique is excellent for revealing brain structures, it doesn't indicate neural activity. Another technique, **functional magnetic resonance imaging (fMRI)**, has enabled researchers to determine how various types of cognition activate different areas of the brain.

Functional magnetic resonance imaging takes advantage of the fact that blood flow increases in areas of the brain that are activated. The measurement of blood flow is based on the fact that hemoglobin, which carries oxygen in the blood, contains a ferrous (iron) molecule and therefore has magnetic properties. If a magnetic field is presented to the brain, the hemoglobin molecules line up, like tiny magnets. Areas of the brain that are more active consume more oxygen, so the hemoglobin molecules lose some of the oxygen they are transporting, which makes them more magnetic and increases their response to the magnetic field. The fMRI apparatus determines the relative activity of various areas of the brain by detecting changes in the magnetic response of the hemoglobin.

The setup for an fMRI experiment is shown in **Figure 4.3a**, with the person's head in the scanner. As a person engages in a task, such as perceiving an image, the activity of the brain is recorded. For the purposes of measurement, the brain is divided into voxels, which are small cube-shaped areas of the brain about 2 or 3 mm on a side. Voxels are not brain structures but are simply small units of analysis created by the fMRI scanner. One way to think about voxels is that they are like the small square pixels that make up digital photographs or the image on your computer screen, but because the brain is three-dimensional, voxels are small cubes rather than small squares. **Figure 4.3b** shows the results of an fMRI scan. Increases or decreases in brain activity associated with cognitive activity are indicated by colors, with specific colors indicating the amount of activation.

It bears emphasizing that these colored areas do not appear as the brain is being scanned. They are determined by a calculation in which brain activity that occurred during the cognitive task is compared to baseline activity that was recorded prior to the task. The results of this calculation, which indicate increases or decreases in activity in specific areas of the brain, are then converted into colored displays like the one in Figure 4.3b.

Robert Dougherty and coworkers (2003) used brain imaging to demonstrate cortical magnification in the human visual cortex. **Figure 4.4a** shows the stimulus display viewed by the observer, who was in an fMRI scanner. The observer looked directly at the center of the screen, so the dot at the center fell on the fovea. During the experiment, stimulus light was presented in two places: (1) near the center (red area), which illuminated a small area near the fovea; and (2) farther from the center (blue area), which illuminated an area in the peripheral retina. The areas of the brain activated by these two stimuli are indicated in **Figure 4.4b**. This activation illustrates cortical magnification because stimulation of the small area near the fovea activated a greater area on the cortex (red) than stimulation of the larger area in the periphery (blue). (Also see Wandell, 2011.)

The large representation of the fovea in the cortex is also illustrated in **Figure 4.5**, which shows the space that would be allotted to words on a page (Wandell et al., 2009). Notice that the letter "a," which is near where the person is looking (red arrow), is represented by a much larger area in the cortex than letters that are far from where the person is looking. The extra cortical space allotted to letters and words at which the person is looking provides the extra neural processing needed to accomplish tasks such as reading that require high visual acuity (Azzopardi & Cowey, 1993).

What cortical magnification means when you look at a scene is that information about the part of the scene you

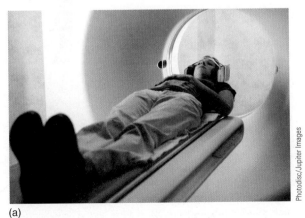

(a)

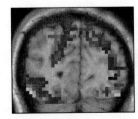

Percent Activation

−1 0 +1 +2

(b)

Figure 4.3 (a) A person in a brain scanner. (b) fMRI record. Each small square represents a voxel, and the colors indicate whether brain activity increased or decreased in the each voxel. Red and yellow indicate increases in brain activity; blue and green indicate decreases.

(Part b from Ishai et al., 2000)

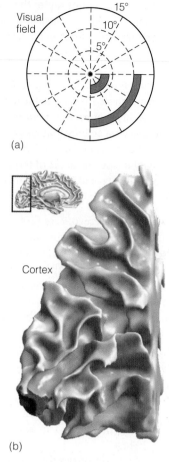

(a)

Visual field 15° 10° 5°

Cortex

(b)

Figure 4.4 (a) Red and blue areas show the extent of stimuli that were presented while a person was in an fMRI scanner. (b) Red and blue indicate areas of the brain activated by the stimulation in (a). (From Dougherty et al., 2003)

are looking at takes up a larger space on your cortex than an area of equal size that is off to the side. Another way to appreciate the magnification factor is to do the following demonstration.

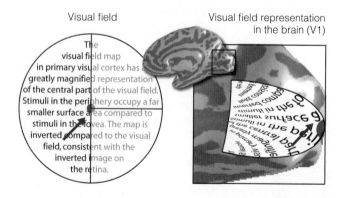

Visual field

Visual field representation in the brain (V1)

The visual field map in primary visual cortex has a greatly magnified representation of the central part of the visual field. Stimuli in the periphery occupy a far smaller surface area compared to stimuli in the fovea. The map is inverted compared to the visual field, consistent with the inverted image on the retina.

Figure 4.5 Demonstration of the magnification factor. A person looks at the red spot on the text on the left. The area of brain activated by each letter of the text is shown on the right. The arrows point to the letter *a* in the text on the left, and the area in the brain activated by the *a* on the right. (Based on Wandell et al., 2009)

Hold your left hand at arm's length, holding your index finger up. As you look at your finger, hold your right hand at arm's length, about a foot to the right of your finger and positioned so the back of your hand is facing you. When you have done this, your left index finger (which you are still looking at) activates an area of cortex as large as the area activated by your whole right hand.

An important thing to note about this demonstration is that even though the image of your finger on the fovea takes up about the same space on the cortex as the image of your hand on the peripheral retina, you do not perceive your finger as being as *large* as your hand. Instead, you see the *details* of your finger far better than you can see details on your hand. That more space on the cortex translates into better detail vision rather than larger size is an example of the fact that what we perceive doesn't exactly match the "picture" in the brain. We will return to this idea shortly.

The Cortex Is Organized in Columns

We determined the retinotopic map on the brain by measuring activity near the surface of the cortex. We are now going to consider what is happening below the surface by looking at the results of experiments in which a recording electrode was lowered into the cortex.

Location and Orientation Columns Hubel and Wiesel (1965) carried out a series of experiments in which they recorded from neurons they encountered as they lowered electrodes into the cortex. When they positioned an electrode perpendicular to the surface of a cat's cortex, they found that every neuron they encountered had its receptive field at about the same location on the retina. Their results are shown in **Figure 4.6a**, which

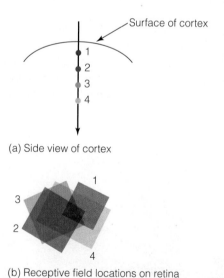

Surface of cortex

1
2
3
4

(a) Side view of cortex

1
3
2
4

(b) Receptive field locations on retina

Figure 4.6 Location column. When an electrode penetrates the cortex perpendicularly, the receptive fields of the neurons encountered along this track overlap. The receptive field recorded at each numbered position along the electrode track (a) is indicated by a correspondingly numbered square (b).

shows four neurons along the electrode track, and **Figure 4.6b**, which shows that these neurons' receptive fields are all located at about the same place on the retina. From this result, Hubel and Wiesel concluded that the striate cortex is organized into **location columns** that are perpendicular to the surface of the cortex, so that all of the neurons within a location column have their receptive fields at the same location on the retina.

As Hubel and Wiesel lowered their electrodes along perpendicular tracks, they noted not only that the neurons along this track had receptive fields with the same *location* on the retina, but that these neurons all preferred stimuli with the same *orientation*. Thus, all cells encountered along the electrode track at A in **Figure 4.7** fired the most to horizontal lines, whereas all those along electrode track B fired the most to lines oriented at about 45 degrees. Based on this result, Hubel and Wiesel concluded that the cortex is also organized into **orientation columns**, with each column containing cells that respond best to a particular orientation.

Hubel and Wiesel also showed that adjacent orientation columns have cells with slightly different preferred orientations. When they moved an electrode through the cortex obliquely (not perpendicular to the surface), so that the electrode cut across orientation columns, they found that the neurons' preferred orientations changed in an orderly fashion, so a column of cells that respond best to 90 degrees is right next to the column of cells that respond best to 85 degrees (**Figure 4.8**). Hubel and Wiesel also found that as they moved their electrode 1 millimeter across the cortex, their electrode passed through orientation columns that represented the entire range of orientations. Interestingly enough, this 1-mm dimension is the size of one location column.

One Location Column: Many Orientation Columns This 1-mm dimension for location columns means that one location column is large enough to contain orientation columns that cover all possible orientations. Thus, the location column shown in **Figure 4.9** serves one location on the

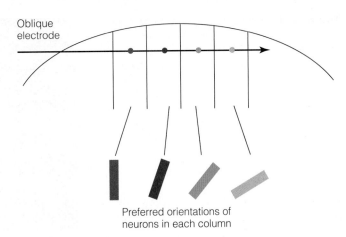

Figure 4.8 If an electrode is inserted obliquely into the cortex, it crosses a sequence of orientation columns. The preferred orientation of neurons in each column, indicated by the bars, changes in an orderly way as the electrode crosses the columns. The distance the electrode is advanced is exaggerated in this illustration.

retina (all the neurons in the column have their receptive fields at about the same place on the retina) *and* contains neurons that respond to all possible orientations.

Think about what this means. Neurons in that location column receive signals from a particular location on the retina, which corresponds to a small area in the visual field. Because this location column contains some neurons that respond to each orientation, any oriented object that falls within the location column's area on the retina will cause some of the neurons in this location column to fire.

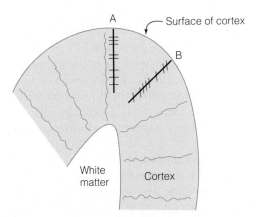

Figure 4.7 Orientation columns. All of the cortical neurons encountered along track A respond best to horizontal bars (indicated by the red lines cutting across the electrode track). All of the neurons along track B respond best to bars oriented at 45 degrees.

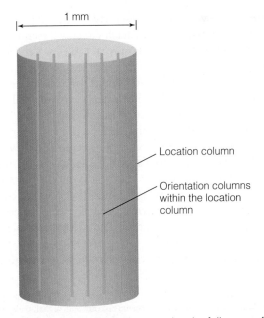

Figure 4.9 A location column that contains the full range of orientation columns. A column such as this, which Hubel and Wiesel called a *hypercolumn*, receives information about all possible orientations that fall within a small area of the retina.

Figure 4.10 (a) A scene from the Pennsylvania woods. (b) Focusing in on part of a tree trunk. A, B, and C represent the parts of the tree trunk that fall on receptive fields in three areas of the retina.

(a)

(b)

© Bruce Goldstein

A location column with all of its orientation columns was called a **hypercolumn** by Hubel and Wiesel. A hypercolumn receives information about all possible orientations that fall within a small area of the retina; it is therefore well suited for processing information from a small area in the visual field.[1]

How Do Orientation-Sensitive Neurons Respond to a Scene?

Determining how the millions of neurons in the cortex respond when we look at a scene such as the one in **Figure 4.10a** is an ambitious undertaking. We will simplify the task by focusing on one small part of the scene—the tree trunk in **Figure 4.10b**. We focus specifically on the part of the trunk shown passing through the three circles, A, B, and C.

Figure 4.11a shows how the image of this part of the tree trunk is imaged on the retina. Each circle represents the area served by a location column. **Figure 4.11b** shows the location columns in the cortex. Remember that each of these location columns contains a complete set of orientation columns (Figure 4.9). This means that the vertical tree trunk will activate neurons in the 90-degree orientation columns in each location column, as indicated by the orange areas in each column.

Thus, the continuous tree trunk is represented by the firing of neurons sensitive to a specific orientation in a number of separate columns in the cortex. Although it may be a bit surprising that the tree is represented by separate columns in the cortex, it simply confirms a property of our perceptual system that we mentioned earlier: The cortical representation of a stimulus does not have to *resemble* the stimulus; it just has to contain information that *represents* the stimulus. The

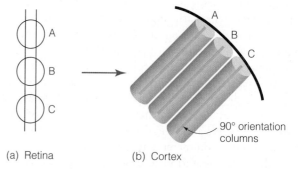

(a) Retina   (b) Cortex

Figure 4.11 (a) Receptive fields A, B, and C, located on the retina, for the three sections of the tree trunk from Figure 4.10b. The neurons associated with each of these receptive fields are in different location columns. (b) Three location columns in the cortex. Neurons that fire to the tree trunk's orientation are within the orange areas of the location column.

representation of the tree in the visual cortex is contained in the firings of neurons in separate cortical columns. At some point in the cortex, the information in these separated columns must be combined to create our perception of the tree.

Before leaving our description of how objects are represented by neural activity in the cortex, let's return to our scene (**Figure 4.12**). Each circle or ellipse in the scene represents an area that sends information to one location column. Working together, these columns cover the entire visual field, an effect called **tiling**. Just as a wall can be covered by adjacent tiles, the visual field is served by adjacent (and often overlapping) location columns (Nassi & Callaway, 2009). (Does this sound familiar? Remember the football field analogy for optic nerve fiber receptive fields on page 56 of Chapter 3, in which each spectator was observing a small area of the field. In that example, the spectators were *tiling* the football field.)

The idea that each part of a scene is represented by activity in many location columns means that a scene containing many objects is represented in the striate cortex by an amazingly complex pattern of firing. Just imagine the process we

---

[1] In addition to location and orientation columns, Hubel and Wiesel also described *ocular dominance columns*. Most neurons respond better to one eye than to the other. This preferential response to one eye is called *ocular dominance*, and neurons with the same ocular dominance are organized into ocular dominance columns in the cortex. This means that each neuron encountered along a perpendicular electrode track responds best to either the left eye or the right eye. There are two ocular dominance columns within each hypercolumn, one for the left eye and one for the right.

Figure 4.12 The yellow circles and ellipses superimposed on the forest scene each represent an area that sends information to one location column in the cortex. There are actually many more columns than shown here, and they overlap, so that they cover the entire scene. The way these location columns cover the entire scene is called *tiling*.

described for the three small areas on the tree trunk multiplied by hundreds or thousands. Of course, this representation in the striate cortex is only the first step in representing the tree. As we will now see, signals from the striate cortex travel to a number of other places in the cortex for further processing.

TEST YOURSELF 4.1

1. How is the retina mapped onto the striate cortex? What is cortical magnification, and what function does it serve?

2. Describe the technique of brain imaging. How has it been used to determine the retinotopic map in humans? How do the results of the brain imaging experiment provide evidence for cortical magnification in the human cortex?

3. Describe location columns and orientation columns. What do we mean when we say that location columns and orientation columns are "combined"? What is a hypercolumn?

4. How do orientation-sensitive neurons respond to a scene? Start by describing how a tree trunk is represented in the cortex and then expand your view to the whole forest scene.

5. What does it mean to say that the cortical representation of a scene does not have to resemble the scene but just has to contain information that represents the scene?

Pathways for What, Where, and How

As we continue our consideration of organization, we will see that there are a number of ways that neurons are organized in terms of their function. One type of functional organization

occurs when neurons that serve similar functions are connected together into "streams" or pathways. Some of the first research on these pathways was carried out by Leslie Ungerleider and Mortimer Mishkin, who presented evidence for two streams serving different functions that transmit information from the striate cortex to other areas of the brain.

Streams for Information About What and Where

Ungerleider and Mishkin (1982) used a technique called *ablation* (also called *lesioning*) to better understand the functional organization of the brain. **Ablation** refers to the destruction or removal of tissue in the nervous system.

METHOD | **Brain Ablation**

The goal of a brain ablation experiment is to determine the function of a particular area of the brain. First, an animal's ability to carry out a specific task is determined by behavioral testing. Most ablation experiments have used monkeys because of the similarity of their visual system to that of humans and because monkeys can be trained in ways that enable researchers to determine perceptual capacities such as acuity, color vision, depth perception, and object perception (Mishkin et al., 1983).

Once the animal's performance on a task has been measured, a particular area of the brain is ablated (removed or destroyed), either by surgery or by injecting a chemical that destroys tissue near the place where it is injected. Ideally, one particular area is removed and the rest of the brain remains intact. After ablation, the monkey is retested to determine how performance has been affected by the ablation.

Ungerleider and Mishkin presented monkeys with two tasks: (1) an object discrimination problem and (2) a landmark discrimination problem. In the **object discrimination problem**, a monkey was shown one object, such as a rectangular solid, and was then presented with a two-choice task like the one shown in **Figure 4.13a**, which included the "target" object (the rectangular solid) and another stimulus, such as the triangular solid. If the monkey pushed aside the target object, it received the food reward that was hidden in a well under the object. The **landmark discrimination problem** is shown in **Figure 4.13b**. Here, the monkey's task was to remove the cover of the food well that was closest to the tall cylinder.

In the ablation part of the experiment, part of the temporal lobe was removed in some monkeys. After ablation, behavioral testing showed that the object discrimination problem was very difficult for these monkeys. This result indicates that the pathway that reaches the temporal lobes is responsible for determining an object's *identity*. Ungerleider and Mishkin therefore called the pathway leading from the striate cortex to the temporal lobe the *what* pathway (**Figure 4.14**).

Other monkeys had their parietal lobes removed, and they had difficulty solving the landmark discrimination problem. This result indicates that the pathway that leads to the

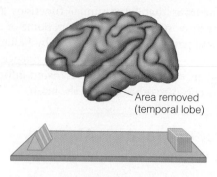

Area removed
(temporal lobe)

(a) Object discrimination

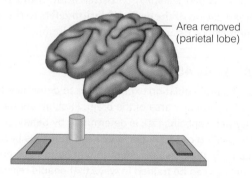

Area removed
(parietal lobe)

(b) Landmark discrimination

Figure 4.13 The two types of discrimination tasks used by Ungerleider and Mishkin. (a) Object discrimination: Pick the correct shape. Lesioning the temporal lobe (shaded area) makes this task difficult. (b) Landmark discrimination: Pick the food well closer to the cylinder. Lesioning the parietal lobe makes this task difficult. (From Mishkin et al., 1983)

parietal lobe is responsible for determining an object's *location*. Ungerleider and Mishkin therefore called the pathway leading from the striate cortex to the parietal lobe the *where* **pathway** (Figure 4.14).

The *what* and *where* pathways are also called the **ventral pathway** (what) and the **dorsal pathway** (where), because the

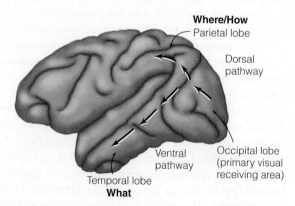

Where/How
Parietal lobe

Dorsal
pathway

Occipital lobe
(primary visual
receiving area)

Ventral
pathway

Temporal lobe
What

Figure 4.14 The monkey cortex, showing the *what*, or ventral, pathway from the occipital lobe to the temporal lobe, and the *where*, or dorsal, pathway from the occipital lobe to the parietal lobe. The *where* pathway is also called the *how* pathway. (From Mishkin et al., 1983)

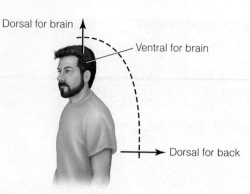

Dorsal for brain

Ventral for brain

Dorsal for back

Figure 4.15 *Dorsal* refers to the back surface of an organism. In upright standing animals such as humans, dorsal refers to the back of the body *and* to the top of the head, as indicated by the arrows and the curved dashed line. Ventral is the opposite of dorsal.

lower part of the brain, where the temporal lobe is located, is the ventral part of the brain, and the upper part of the brain, where the parietal lobe is located, is the dorsal part of the brain. The term *dorsal* refers to the back or the upper surface of an organism; thus, the dorsal fin of a shark or dolphin is the fin on the back that sticks out of the water. **Figure 4.15** shows that for upright, walking animals such as humans, the dorsal part of the brain is the top of the brain. (Picture a person with a dorsal fin sticking out of the top of his or her head!) *Ventral* is the opposite of dorsal; hence it refers to the lower part of the brain.

The discovery of two pathways in the cortex—one for identifying objects (what) and one for locating objects (where)—led some researchers to look back at the retina and the lateral geniculate nucleus (LGN). Using the techniques of both recording from neurons and ablation, they found that properties of the ventral and dorsal streams are established by two different types of ganglion cells in the retina, which transmit signals to different layers of the LGN (Schiller et al., 1990). Thus, the cortical ventral and dorsal streams can actually be traced back to the retina and LGN.

Although there is good evidence that the ventral and dorsal pathways serve different functions, it is important to note that (1) the pathways are not totally separated but have connections between them and (2) signals flow not only "up" the pathway toward the parietal and temporal lobes but "back" as well (Gilbert & Li, 2013; Merigan & Maunsell, 1993; Ungerleider & Haxby, 1994). It makes sense that there would be communication between the pathways because in our everyday behavior we need to both identify and locate objects, and we routinely coordinate these two activities every time we identify something ("there's a pen") and notice where it is ("it's over there, next to the computer"). Thus, there are two distinct pathways, but some information is shared between them. The "backward" flow of information, called *feedback*, provides information from higher centers that can influence the signals flowing into the system (Gilbert & Li, 2013). This feedback is one of the mechanisms behind top-down processing, introduced in Chapter 1 (page 10).

Streams for Information About What and How

Although the idea of ventral and dorsal streams has been generally accepted, David Milner and Melvyn Goodale (1995; see also Goodale & Humphrey, 1998, 2001) have suggested that the dorsal stream does more than just indicate where an object is. Milner and Goodale propose that the dorsal stream is for taking action, such as picking up an object. Taking this action would involve knowing the location of the object, consistent with the idea of *where*, but it goes beyond *where* to involve a physical interaction with the object. Thus, reaching to pick up a pen involves information about the pen's location *plus* information about how a person should move his or her hand toward the pen. According to this idea, the dorsal stream provides information about *how* to direct action with regard to a stimulus.

Evidence supporting the idea that the dorsal stream is involved in how to direct action is provided by the discovery of neurons in the parietal cortex that respond (1) when a monkey looks at an object and (2) when it reaches toward the object (Sakata et al., 1992; also see Taira et al., 1990). But the most dramatic evidence supporting the idea of a dorsal *how* or *action* stream comes from **neuropsychology**—the study of the behavioral effects of brain damage in humans.

METHOD | Double Dissociations in Neuropsychology

One of the basic principles of neuropsychology is that we can understand the effects of brain damage by determining **double dissociations**, which involve two people: In one person, damage to one area of the brain causes function A to be absent while function B is present; in the other person, damage to another area of the brain causes function B to be absent while function A is present.

Ungerleider and Mishkin's monkeys provide an example of a double dissociation. The monkey with damage to the temporal lobe was unable to discriminate objects (function A) but had the ability to solve the landmark problem (function B). The monkey with damage to the parietal lobe was unable to solve the landmark problem (function B) but was able to discriminate objects (function A). These two findings, taken together, are an example of a double dissociation. The fact that object discrimination and the landmark task can be disrupted separately and in opposite ways means that these two functions operate independently of one another.

An example of a double dissociation in humans is provided by two hypothetical patients. Alice, who has suffered damage to her temporal lobe, has difficulty naming objects but has no trouble indicating where they are located (**Table 4.1a**). Bert, who has parietal lobe damage, has the opposite problem—he can identify objects but can't tell exactly where they are located (**Table 4.1b**). The cases of Alice and Bert, taken together, represent a double dissociation and enable us to conclude that recognizing objects and locating objects operate independently of each other.

The Behavior of Patient D.F. Milner and Goodale (1995) used the method of determining double dissociations to study D.F., a 34-year-old woman who suffered damage to

Table 4.1 A Double Dissociation

	NAMING OBJECTS	DETERMINING OBJECT'S LOCATION
(a) ALICE: Temporal lobe damage (ventral stream)	NO	YES
(b) BERT: Parietal lobe damage (dorsal stream)	YES	NO

© Cengage Learning 2014

her ventral pathway from carbon monoxide poisoning caused by a gas leak in her home. One result of her brain damage was that D.F. was not able to match the orientation of a card held in her hand to different orientations of a slot. This is shown in the left circle in **Figure 4.16a**, which indicates D.F.'s attempts to match the orientation of a vertical slot. Perfect matching performance would be indicated by a vertical line for each trial, but D.F.'s responses are widely scattered. The right circle shows the accurate performance of the normal controls.

Because D.F. had trouble orienting a card to match the orientation of the slot, it would seem reasonable that she would also have trouble *placing* the card through the slot, because to do this she would have to turn the card so that it was lined up with the slot. But when D.F. was asked to "mail" the card through the slot, she could do it! Even though D.F. could not turn the card to match the slot's orientation, once she started moving the card toward the slot, she was able to rotate it to match the orientation of the slot (**Figure 4.16b**). Thus, D.F. performed poorly in the *static orientation-matching task* but did well as soon as *action* was involved (Murphy et al., 1996). Milner and Goodale interpreted D.F.'s behavior as showing that there

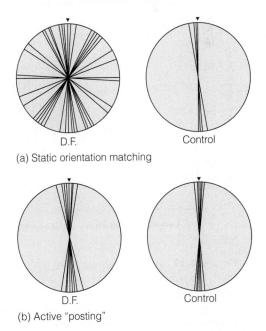

(a) Static orientation matching

(b) Active "posting"

Figure 4.16 Performance of D.F. and a person without brain damage on two tasks: (a) judging the orientation of a slot and (b) placing a card through the slot. Vertical lines indicate perfect matching performance. (Milner & Goodale, 1995)

is one mechanism for judging orientation and another for co-ordinating vision and action (Goodale, 2014).

These results for D.F. are part of a double dissociation because there are other patients whose symptoms are the opposite of D.F.'s. These people can judge visual orientation, but they can't accomplish the task that combines vision and action. As we would expect, whereas D.F.'s ventral stream is damaged, these other people have damage to their dorsal streams.

Based on these results, Milner and Goodale suggested that the ventral pathway should still be called the *what* pathway, as Ungerleider and Mishkin suggested, but that a better description of the dorsal pathway would be the *how* pathway, or the **action pathway**, because it determines *how* a person carries out an *action*. As sometimes occurs in science, not everyone uses the same terms. Thus, some researchers call the dorsal stream the *where* pathway, and some call it the *how* or *action* pathway.

The Behavior of People Without Brain Damage

In our normal daily behavior, we aren't aware of two visual processing streams, one for *what* and the other for *how*, because they work together seamlessly as we perceive objects and take actions toward them. Cases like that of D.F., in which one stream is damaged, reveal the existence of these two streams. But what about people without damaged brains? Psychophysical experiments that measure how people perceive and react to visual illusions have demonstrated the dissociation between perception and action that was evident for D.F.

Figure 4.17a shows the stimulus used by Tzvi Ganel and coworkers (2008) in an experiment designed to demonstrate a separation of perception and action in non-brain-damaged subjects. This stimulus creates a visual illusion: Line 1 is actually longer than line 2 (see **Figure 4.17b**), but line 2 *appears* longer.

Ganel and coworkers presented subjects with two tasks: (1) a *length estimation task* in which they were asked to indicate how they perceived the lines' length by spreading their thumb and index finger, as shown in **Figure 4.17c**; and (2) a *grasping task* in which they were asked to reach toward the lines and grasp each line by its ends. Sensors on the subjects' fingers measured the separation between the fingers as the subjects grasped the lines. These two tasks were chosen because they

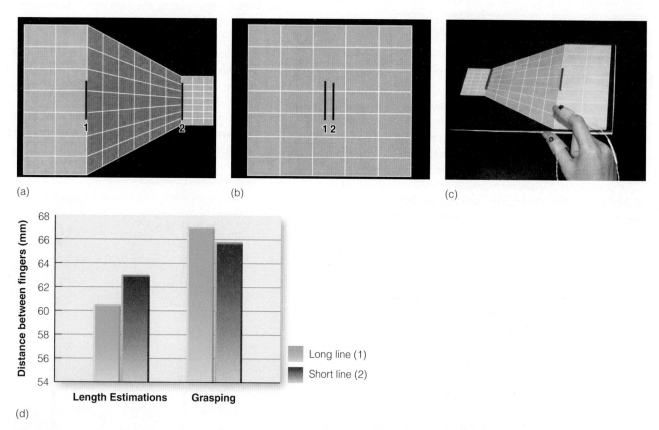

(a)　　　　　　　　(b)　　　　　　　　(c)

(d)

Figure 4.17 (a) The size illusion used by Ganel and coworkers (2008) in which line 2 looks longer than line 1. The numbers were not present in the display seen by the subjects. (b) The two vertical lines from (a), showing that line 2 is actually shorter than line 1. (c) Subjects in the experiment adjusted the space between their fingers either to estimate the length of the lines (length estimation task) or to reach toward the lines to grasp them (grasping task). The distance between the fingers is measured by sensors on the fingers. (d) Results of the length estimation and grasping tasks in the Ganel et al. experiment. The length estimation task indicates the illusion, because the shorter line (line 2) was judged to be longer. In the grasping task, subjects separated their fingers more for the longer line (line 1), which was consistent with the physical lengths of the lines. (From Ganel et al., 2008)

depend on different processing streams. The length estimation task involves the ventral or *what* stream. The grasping task involves the dorsal or *where/how* stream.

The results of this experiment, shown in **Figure 4.17d**, indicate that in the length estimation task, subjects judged line 1 (the longer line) as looking shorter than line 2, but in the grasping task, they separated their fingers farther apart for line 1 to match its longer length. Thus, the illusion works for perception (the length estimation task), but not for action (the grasping task). These results support the idea that perception and action are served by different mechanisms. An idea about functional organization that originated with observations of patients with brain damage is therefore supported by the performance of subjects without brain damage.

Modularity

The idea that there are pathways that serve different functions leads us to **modularity**, the idea that specific areas of the cortex are specialized to respond to specific types of stimuli. Areas that are specialized to specific types of stimuli areas are called **modules** for processing information about these stimuli. For example, there is a great deal of evidence for an area that is rich in neurons that respond to faces.

Face Neurons in the Monkey's IT Cortex

When Edmund Rolls and Martin Tovee (1995) measured the response of neurons in the monkey's inferotemporal (IT) cortex (see Figure 3.31, page 65), they found many neurons that responded best to faces. **Figure 4.18** shows the results for a neuron that responded to faces but hardly at all to other types of stimuli.

What is particularly significant about such "face neurons" is that there are areas in the monkey temporal lobe that are particularly rich in these neurons. Doris Tsao and coworkers (2006) presented 96 images of faces, bodies, fruits, gadgets, hands, and scrambled patterns to two monkeys while recording from cortical neurons inside this face area. They classified neurons as "face selective" if they responded at least twice as strongly to faces as to nonfaces. Using this criterion, they found that 97 percent of the cells were face selective. The high level of face selectivity within this area is illustrated in **Figure 4.19**, which shows the average response for both monkeys to each of the 96 objects. The response to the 16 faces, on the left, is far greater than the response to any of the other objects.

The Fusiform Face Area in Humans

Brain imaging (see Method, page 75) has been used to identify areas of the human brain that contain neurons that respond best to faces. In one of these experiments, Nancy Kanwisher and coworkers (1997) used fMRI to determine brain activity in response to pictures of faces and other objects, such as household objects, houses, and hands. When they subtracted the response to the other objects from the response to the faces, Kanwisher and

Figure 4.18 Size of response of a neuron in the monkey's IT cortex that responds to face stimuli but not to nonface stimuli. (Based on data from Rolls & Tovee, 1995)

coworkers found that activity remained in an area they called the **fusiform face area (FFA)**, which is located in the fusiform gyrus on the underside of the brain directly below the IT cortex (see Figure 3.31, page 65). This area is roughly equivalent to the face areas in the temporal cortex of the monkey. Kanwisher's results, plus the results of many other experiments, have shown that the FFA is specialized to respond to faces (Kanwisher, 2010).

Additional evidence of an area specialized for the perception of faces is that damage to the temporal lobe causes **prosopagnosia**—difficulty recognizing the faces of familiar people. Even very familiar faces are affected, so people with prosopagnosia

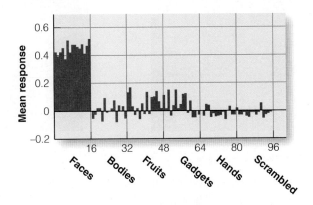

Figure 4.19 Results of the Tsao et al. (2006) experiment in which activity of neurons in the monkey's temporal lobe was recorded in response to faces, other objects, and a scrambled stimulus. (From Tsao et al., 2006)

may not be able to recognize close friends or family members—or even their own reflection in the mirror—although they can easily identify such people as soon as they hear them speak (Burton et al., 1991; Hecaen & Angelerques, 1962; Parkin, 1996).

Areas for Places and Bodies in Humans

In addition to the FFA, which contains neurons that are activated by faces, two other specialized areas in the temporal cortex have been identified. The **parahippocampal place area (PPA)** is activated by pictures depicting indoor and outdoor scenes like those shown in **Figure 4.20a** (Aguirre et al., 1998; Epstein et al., 1999; Epstein & Kanwisher, 1998). Apparently what is important for this area is information about spatial layout, because increased activation occurs both to empty rooms and to rooms that are completely furnished (Kanwisher, 2003). The other specialized area, the **extrastriate body area (EBA)**, is activated by pictures of bodies and parts of bodies (but not by faces), as shown in **Figure 4.20b** (Downing et al., 2001; Grill-Spector & Weiner, 2014).

The three areas we have described—the FFA, PPA, and EBA—all fit our definition of module as an area specialized for processing information about a specific type of stimulus. But there is also evidence that neural representation also involves activity that is spread across the brain (Behrmann & Plaut, 2013).

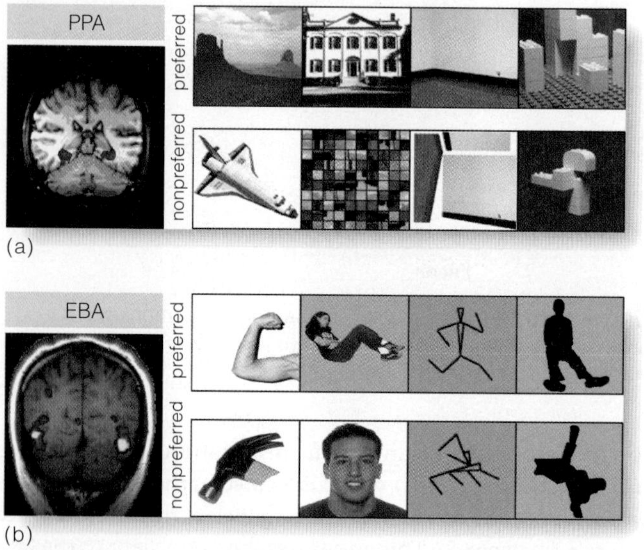

Figure 4.20 (a) The parahippocampal place area (PPA) is activated by places (top row) but not by other stimuli (bottom row). (b) The extrastriate body area (EBA) is activated by bodies (top) but not by other stimuli (bottom). (Kanwisher, 2003)

Distributed Representation

Distributed representation occurs when a stimulus causes neural activity in a number of different areas of the brain, so the activity is *distributed* across the brain.

Two Experiments That Demonstrate Distributed Representation

The results of an fMRI experiment on humans that demonstrates distributed representation are shown in **Figure 4.21**. **Figure 4.21a** shows that the *maximum* activity for houses, faces, and chairs occurs in separate areas in the cortex. This finding is consistent with the idea that there are areas specialized for specific stimuli. If, however, we show *all* of the activity for each type of stimulus, we see that houses, faces, and chairs also cause activity over a wide area of the cortex (**Figure 4.21b**) (Cohen & Tong, 2001; Ishai et al., 1999, 2000; Riesenhuber & Poggio, 2000, 2002). This finding illustrates distributed representation because each type of stimulus causes activity in a number of areas.

Further evidence for distributed representation is provided by an fMRI experiment by Alex Huth and coworkers

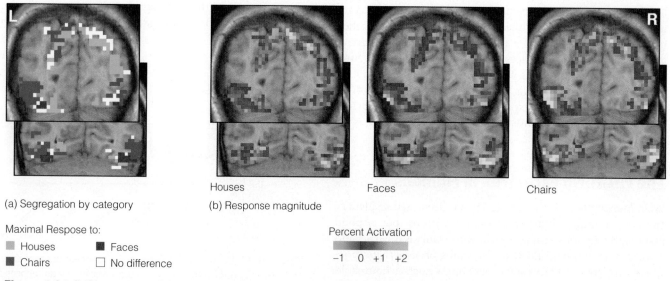

(a) Segregation by category

(b) Response magnitude

Houses   Faces   Chairs

Maximal Respose to:
- Houses
- Chairs
- Faces
- No difference

Percent Activation
−1   0   +1   +2

Figure 4.21 fMRI responses of the human brain to various types of stimuli: (a) areas that were most strongly activated by houses, faces, and chairs; (b) all areas activated by each type of stimulus. (From Ishai et al., 2000)

Movie Clip	Labels	Movie Clip	Labels
	butte.n desert.n sky.n cloud.n brush.n		city.n expressway.n skyscraper.n traffic.n sky.n
	woman.n talk.v gesticulate.v book.n		bison.n walk.v grass.n stream.n

Figure 4.22 Four frames from the movies viewed by subjects in Huth et al.'s (2012) experiment. The words on the right indicate categories that appear in the frames (n = noun; v = verb). (From A. G. Huth et al., A continuous semantic space describes the representation of thousands of object and action categories across the human brain, Neuron, 76, 1210–1224, Figure S1, Supplemental materials, 2012)

(2012) in which subjects viewed 2 hours of film clips while in a brain scanner. To analyze how individual voxels were activated by different objects and actions in the films, Huth created a list of 1,705 different objects and action categories and determined which categories were present in each film scene.

Figure 4.22 shows four scenes and the categories (labels) associated with them. By determining how individual voxels were activated by each scene and then analyzing his results using a complex statistical procedure, Huth was able to determine what kinds of stimuli each voxel responded to. For example, one voxel responded well when streets, buildings, roads, interiors, and vehicles were present.

Figure 4.23 shows the types of stimuli that cause voxels across the surface of the brain to respond. Objects and actions

similar to each other are located near each other in the brain. The reason there are two areas for humans and two for animals is that each area represents different features related to humans or animals. For example, the area labeled "human" at the bottom of the brain (which is actually on the underside of the brain) corresponds to the fusiform face area, which responds to all aspects of faces. The human area higher on the brain responds specifically to facial expressions. The area that responds to buildings is close to the parahippocampal place area (PPA), which was first identified by using still pictures like the ones in Figure 4.20.

The results in Figure 4.23 present an interesting paradox. On one hand, the results confirm the earlier research that identified specific areas of the brain responsible for the perception

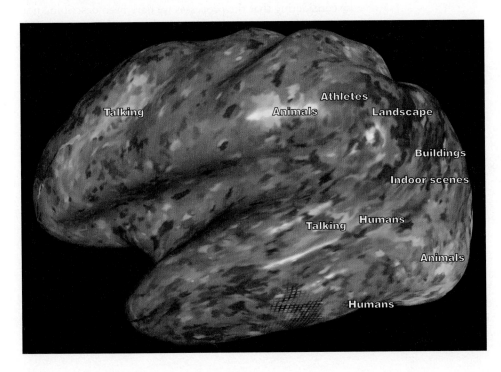

Figure 4.23 The results of Huth et al.'s (2012) experiment, showing locations on the brain where the indicated categories are most likely to activate the brain. Colors indicate areas that respond similarly. For example, both areas marked "Animals" are yellow. (Courtesy of Alex Huth)

of specific types of stimuli, such as faces, places, and bodies. On the other hand, these new results reveal a map that stretches over a large area of the cortex. What this means is that even though some stimuli activate specialized areas, the wide variety of stimuli we encounter in the environment causes activity that is distributed across a wide area of the cortex.

Distributed Representation of Multidimensional Stimuli

We've seen that faces activate the FFA, which has been called a module for faces, and that faces also activate other areas as well, which is evidence for distributed representation. But we can take this idea of distributed representation of faces a step further by realizing that our experience with faces goes beyond identifying an object as a face ("that's a face"). We can also respond to the following additional aspects of faces: (1) emotional aspects ("she is smiling, so she is probably happy," "looking at his face makes me happy"); (2) where someone is looking ("she's looking at me"); (3) how parts of the face move ("I can understand him better by watching his lips move"); (4) how attractive a face is ("he has a handsome face"); and (5) whether

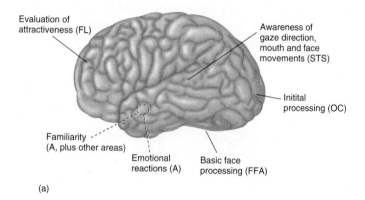

Evaluation of attractiveness (FL)

Awareness of gaze direction, mouth and face movements (STS)

Initital processing (OC)

Familiarity (A, plus other areas)

Emotional reactions (A)

Basic face processing (FFA)

(a)

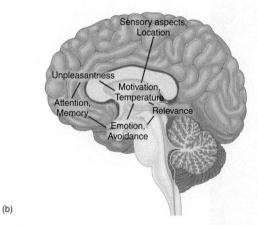

Sensory aspects, Location

Unpleasantness

Motivation, Temperature

Attention, Memory

Relevance

Emotion, Avoidance

(b)

Figure 4.24 (a) Areas of the brain that are activated by different aspects of faces. OC = occipital cortex; FFA = fusiform face area; A = amygdala; FC = frontal lobe; STS = superior temporal sulcus. The dashed line for the amygdala indicates that it is located inside the brain, below the cortex. (b) Areas that are involved in the perception of pain. Each area serves a different aspect of pain perception.

Table 4.2 Brain Areas Activated by Different Aspects of Faces

AREA OF BRAIN	FUNCTION
Occipital cortex (OC)	Initial processing
Fusiform face area (FFA)	Basic face processing
Amygdala (A)	Emotional reactions (face expressions and observer's emotional reactions)
	Familiarity (familiar faces cause more activation in amygdala and other areas associated with emotions)
Frontal lobe (FL)	Evaluation of attractiveness
Superior temporal sulcus (STS)	Gaze direction Mouth movements General face movements

Based on Calder et al., 2007; Gobbini & Haxby, 2007; Grill-Spector et al., 2004; Ishai et al., 2004; Natu & O'Toole, 2011; Pitcher et al., 2011; Puce et al., 1998; Winston et al., 2007.

the face is familiar ("I remember her from somewhere"). What this means is that faces are multidimensional—they cause many different reactions, and, as shown in **Figure 4.24a** and **Table 4.2**, these different reactions are associated with activity in many different places in the brain.

But faces aren't the only multidimensional stimulus. When we consider pain in Chapter 14, we will see that pain has sensory components ("it's throbbing") and emotional aspects ("it's unpleasant"). These dimensions of pain activate a number of structures throughout the brain **(Figure 4.24b)**. Thus, pain presents another example of how a single stimulus can cause widespread activity.

We can take this idea of widespread activity a step further by considering that the processes we have been describing not only create perceptions, but they also provide information that is stored in our memory so we can remember perceptual experiences later. This link between perception and memory has been studied in a number of recent experiments that have measured responding in single neurons in the human **hippocampus**, an area associated with forming and storing memories.

Where Perception Meets Memory

Some of the signals leaving the IT cortex reach structures in the medial temporal lobe (MTL), such as the parahippocampal cortex, the entorhinal cortex, and the hippocampus **(Figure 4.25a)**. These MTL structures are extremely important for memory. The classic demonstration of the importance of one of the structures in the MTL, the hippocampus, is the case of H.M., who had his hippocampus on both sides of his brain removed in an attempt to eliminate epileptic seizures that had not responded to other treatments (Scoville & Milner, 1957).

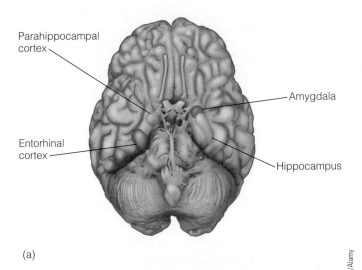

(a)

Halle Berry

(b)

Figure 4.25 (a) Location of the hippocampus and some of the other structures that were studied by Quiroga and coworkers (2005). (b) Some of the stimuli that caused a neuron in the hippocampus to fire.

The operation eliminated H.M.'s seizures, but it also eliminated his ability to store experiences in his memory. Thus, when H.M. experienced something, such as a visit from his doctor, he was unable to remember the experience, so the next time the doctor appeared, H.M. had no memory of having seen him. H.M.'s unfortunate situation occurred because in 1953, the surgeons did not realize that the hippocampus is crucial for the formation of long-term memories. Once they realized the devastating effects of removing the hippocampus on both sides of the brain, H.M.'s operation was never repeated.

The connection between the hippocampus and vision was demonstrated in the experiments by R. Quian Quiroga and coworkers (2005, 2008) that we introduced in Chapter 3 (page 66). These experiments showed that there are neurons in the hippocampus that respond to faces of specific people, like Steve Carell (see Figure 3.36, page 68), and also to specific buildings such as the Eiffel Tower or the Sydney Opera House. Let's now look at these experiments in more detail.

Quiroga recorded from eight patients with epilepsy who, in preparation for surgery, had electrodes implanted in their hippocampus or other areas in the medial temporal lobe to help localize precisely where their seizures originated. Patients saw a number of different views of specific individuals and objects plus pictures of other things, such as faces, buildings, and animals. Not surprisingly, a number of neurons responded to some of these stimuli. What was surprising, however, was that some neurons responded to a number of different views of just one person or building, or to a number of ways of representing that person or building. For example, one neuron responded to pictures of the actresses Jennifer Aniston and Lisa Kudrow, who both starred in the TV series *Friends*, but did not respond to faces of other famous people, nonfamous people, landmarks, animals, or other objects. As we noted in Chapter 3, another neuron responded to pictures of actor Steve Carell. Still another neuron responded to photographs of Halle Berry, to drawings of her, to pictures of her dressed as Catwoman from *Batman*, and also to seeing the words "Halle Berry" (**Figure 4.25b**).

The role of these neurons in memory is supported by the way they respond to many different views of the stimulus, different modes of depiction, and even words signifying the stimulus. These neurons are not responding to visual features of the pictures, but to *concepts*—"Jennifer Aniston," "Halle Berry," "Sydney Opera House"—that the stimuli represent. We can guess, for example, that the reason the neuron that responded to Jennifer Aniston also responded to Lisa Kudrow was that both appeared on the *Friends* TV series. The response of these MTL neurons to visual stimuli appears to depend, therefore, on a particular person's past experiences. Thus, if a football fan had a neuron that responded to seeing a picture of Russell Wilson of the Seattle Seahawks, it wouldn't be surprising if that neuron also responded to Aaron Rogers of the Green Bay Packers.

Although the hippocampus neurons studied by Quiroga respond when a person sees a picture of a particular person or building, Quiroga points out that these neurons are not responsible for recognizing objects. Patient H.M. for example, who had no hippocampus, could still recognize objects. He just couldn't remember them later. Thus, just because a hippocampus neuron responds to a visual stimulus doesn't mean it is responsible for seeing. What it is responsible for is remembering.

The link between these MTL neurons that respond to visual stimuli and memories has received additional support from the results of an experiment by Hagan Gelbard-Sagiv and coworkers (2008). These researchers had epilepsy patients view a series of 5- to 10-second video clips a number of times while recording from neurons in the MTL. The clips showed famous people, landmarks, and nonfamous people and animals engaged in various actions. As the person was viewing the clips, some neurons responded better to certain clips. For example, a neuron in one of the patients responded best to a clip from *The Simpsons* TV program.

The firing to specific video clips is similar to what Quiroga found for viewing still pictures. However, this experiment went a step further by asking the patients to think back to any of the film clips they had seen while the experimenter continued to record from the MTL neurons. One result is shown in **Figure 4.26**, which indicates the response of the neuron that fired to *The Simpsons*. The patient's description of what he was remembering is shown at the bottom of the figure. First the patient remembered "something about New York," then "the Hollywood sign." The neuron responds weakly or not at all to those two memories. However, remembering *The Simpsons* causes a large response, which continues as the person continues remembering the episode (indicated by the laughter).

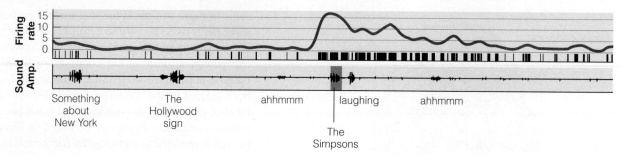

Figure 4.26 Activity of a neuron in the MTL of an epilepsy patient as he remembered the things indicated below the record. A response occurs when the person remembered *The Simpsons* TV program. Earlier, this neuron had been shown to respond to viewing a video clip of *The Simpsons*. (From Gelbard-Sagiv et al., 2008)

Results such as this support the idea that the neurons in the MTL that respond to *perceiving* specific objects or events may also be involved in *remembering* these objects and events. Moran Cerf and coworkers (2010) have provided another demonstration of how thoughts can influence the firing of neurons.

SOMETHING TO CONSIDER:
The Mind–Body Problem

The main goal of our discussion so far has been to explore the electrical signals that are the link between the environment and our perception of the environment. The idea that nerve impulses can represent things in the environment is what is behind the following statement, written by Bernita Rabinovitz, a student in my class.

> A human perceives a stimulus (a sound, a taste, etc.). This is explained by the electrical impulses sent to the brain. This is so incomprehensible, so amazing. How can one electrical impulse be perceived as the taste of a sour lemon, another impulse as a jumble of brilliant blues and greens and reds, and still another as bitter, cold wind? Can our whole complex range of sensations be explained by just the electrical impulses stimulating the brain? How can all of these varied and very concrete sensations—the ranges of perceptions of heat and cold, colors, sounds, fragrances and tastes—be merely and so abstractly explained by differing electrical impulses?

When Bernita asks how hot and cold, colors, sounds, fragrances and tastes can be explained by electrical impulses, she is asking about the **mind-body problem**: How do physical processes like nerve impulses (the body part of the problem) become transformed into the richness of perceptual experience (the mind part of the problem)?

We can appreciate what the mind–body problem involves by looking back at the research we have described in this book, which has demonstrated many connections between electrical signals in the nervous system and what we perceive. We know that when we look out at a scene, countless neurons are firing—some to features of objects, like oriented lines (Figure 3.23, page 60), and others to entire objects, like faces or bodies (Figures 4.18, 4.20). We also know that neural activity caused by objects in our environment is spread over a large area of the cortex (Figure 4.23) and that numerous areas are associated with perceiving the multidimensional aspects of faces and pain (Figure 4.24).

You may think that all of these connections between electrical signals and perception provide a solution to the mind–body problem. This is not, however, the case, because as impressive as these connections are, they are all just *correlations*—demonstrations of *relationships* between neural firing and perception (**Figure 4.27a**). But the mind–body problem goes

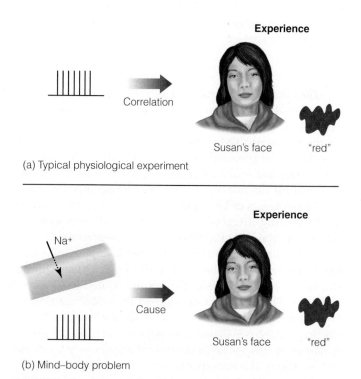

(a) Typical physiological experiment

(b) Mind–body problem

Figure 4.27 (a) This illustrates the situation for most of the physiological experiments we will be describing in this book, which determine *correlations* between physiological responding such as nerve firing and experiences such as perceiving "Susan's face" or "red." (b) Solving the mind–body problem requires going beyond demonstrating correlations to determine how ion flow or nerve firing *causes* the experiences of "Susan's face" or the color "red."

beyond asking how physiological responses *correlate* with perception. It asks how physiological processes *cause* our experience. Think about what this means. The mind–body problem is asking how the flow of sodium and potassium ions across membranes that creates nerve impulses becomes *transformed* into the experience we have when we see a friend's face or when we experience the color of a red rose (**Figure 4.27b**). Just showing that a neuron *fires* to a face or the color red doesn't answer the question of how the firing *creates* the experience of seeing a face or perceiving the color red.

Thus, the physiological research we have been describing in this book, although extremely important for understanding the physiological mechanisms responsible for perception, does not provide a solution to the mind–body problem. Researchers (Baars, 2001; Crick & Koch, 2003) and philosophers (Block, 2009) may discuss the mind–body problem, but when researchers step into the laboratory, their efforts are devoted to doing experiments like the ones we have discussed so far, which search for correlations between physiological responses and experience.

DEVELOPMENTAL DIMENSION Experience and Neural Responding

What is the role of experience in creating neurons that respond best to specific stimuli? There is evidence, which we will be describing in later Developmental Dimensions, that some perceptual capacities, such as the ability to perceive movement, light–dark contrasts, faces, depth, tastes, and smells, are present at or near birth, although not at adult levels. Other capacities, such as color perception, depth that can be seen with one eye, and visual attention, emerge slightly later, as a child develops. Over time, these capacities improve—some rapidly, such as visual acuity, which reaches near adult levels by 9 months of age (Figure 2.36, page 44), and some over a longer time, such as recognizing faces, which continues developing into adolescence (Grill-Spector et al., 2008; Sherf et al., 2007).

Experiences Can Shape Neural Firing

What causes improvement in recognizing faces over time? Biological maturation is clearly involved, as we saw when we described the connection between improvement of visual acuity and the development of the rod and cone receptors. On a longer time scale, there is evidence that some aspects of face recognition depend on the emergence of the fusiform face area (FFA), which is not fully developed until adolescence (Grill-Spector et al., 2008).

In addition to biological maturation, experience in perceiving the environment also plays a role in perceptual development. One line of evidence supporting the role of experience is the research on *experience-dependent plasticity* that we described in Chapter 3. Blakemore and Cooper's (1970) experiments, in which they reared kittens in striped tubes, showed that these kittens' visual systems were shaped by the environment in which they were raised, so kittens reared seeing only vertical stripes had neurons that responded only to vertical or near vertical orientations.

Humans aren't usually reared in deprived environments, but we do grow up in an environment in which many features occur regularly, and these repeating features of the environment can influence how our visual system develops and, therefore, how we perceive. One example of this, which we described in Chapter 1, is the oblique effect: people perceive horizontal and vertical orientations more easily than other orientations

(page 11). There is evidence that horizontals and verticals occur more frequently in the environment than slanted orientations and that there are more cortical neurons that respond to horizontal and vertical orientations. There is, therefore, a link between stimuli that typically occur in the environment, neurons that prefer these stimuli, and our ability to perceive these stimuli.

The Expertise Hypothesis

The fact that experience with the environment can shape the nervous system is the basis of the **expertise hypothesis**, which proposes that our proficiency in perceiving certain things can be explained by changes in the brain caused by long exposure, practice, or training (Bukach et al., 2006; Gauthier et al., 1999). Isabel Gauthier and coworkers (1999) demonstrated an expertise effect by using fMRI to determine the level of activity in the fusiform face area (FFA) in response to faces and to objects called Greebles—families of computer-generated "beings" that all have the same basic configuration but differ in the shapes of their parts (**Figure 4.28a**). Initially, the observers were shown both human faces and Greebles. The results for this part of the

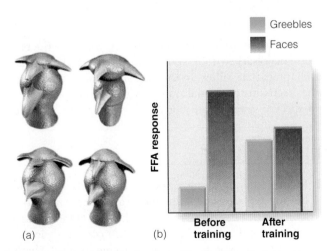

Figure 4.28 (a) Greeble stimuli used by Gauthier. Participants were trained to name each different Greeble. (b) Brain responses to Greebles and faces before and after Greeble training. (From Gauthier et al., 1999)

experiment, shown by the left pair of bars in **Figure 4.28b**, indicate that the FFA neurons responded poorly to the Greebles but well to the faces.

The participants were then trained in "Greeble recognition" for 7 hours over a 4-day period. After the training sessions, participants had become "Greeble experts," as indicated by their ability to rapidly identify many different Greebles by the names they had learned during the training. The right pair of bars in Figure 4.28b shows how becoming a Greeble expert affected the neural response in the participants' FFA. After the training, the FFA neurons responded about as well to Greebles as to faces.

This result shows that the FFA area of the cortex responds not just to faces but to other complex objects as well, and that the objects that the neurons respond to can be established by experience with those objects. In fact, Gauthier has also shown that neurons in the FFA of people who are experts in recognizing cars or birds respond well not only to human faces but to cars (for the car experts) and to birds (for the bird experts; Gauthier et al., 2000). Recently, another study showed that viewing the positions of chess pieces on a chess board causes a larger activation of the FFA in chess experts than in nonexperts (Bilalić et al., 2011). Results such as these have led many researchers to suggest that that the reason the FFA responds well to faces is because we are all "face experts."

It is important to note that although there is good evidence that experience can influence the types of stimuli to which a neuron responds, the role of experience in establishing the FFA as a module for faces is controversial. Some researchers agree with Gauthier that experience is important for establishing the FFA as a module for faces (Bukach et al., 2006); others argue that the FFA's role as a face area is based largely on built-in wiring that doesn't depend on experience (Kanwisher, 2010).

Whatever the outcome of this ongoing debate about the FFA, there is no question that properties of neurons are influenced by our experience with stimuli in the environment. This experience, which "tunes" our perceptual system to respond best to what is usually present in the environment, is likely to play a role in determining the improvements in perception that occur from infancy into adulthood.

Now that you have finished this chapter, you have the background necessary to understand the physiological material in the chapters that follow. In the next six chapters we will continue discussing the visual system, with each chapter devoted to a specific visual quality or process. Chapter 5 continues

our discussion of how we perceive objects. We will still be concerned with faces, but our main focus will be on objects in general, as well as how we perceive multiple objects that are organized to create scenes. One thing you will notice as you read the next chapter is that you won't encounter the word *neuron* until two-thirds of the way through the chapter. One of the messages of Chapter 5 is that a large amount of research in perception occurs at the behavioral level, measuring the relationship between stimuli and perception. Of course, we never get away from neurons, because physiology is part of the story. But when neurons reappear, you will be ready for them!

TEST YOURSELF 4.2

1. How has ablation been used to demonstrate the existence of the ventral and dorsal processing streams? What is the function of these streams?

2. How has neuropsychology been used to show that one of the functions of the dorsal stream is to process information about coordinating vision and action? How do the results of a behavioral experiment support the idea of two primary streams in people without brain damage?

3. What is the evidence that there are modules for faces, places, and bodies? What is the evidence that stimuli like faces and places also activate a wide area of the cortex?

4. Describe Huth's experiment, in which he measured brain activity as people watched film clips. How are Huth's results related to the idea of distributed representation? How are the results also consistent with the idea of modules?

5. What does it mean to say that our experience of stimuli is multimodal? How is the multimodal nature of experience related to the idea of distributed representation?

6. Describe the connection between vision and memory, as illustrated by experiments that recorded from neurons in the MTL and hippocampus. Describe both the experiments using still pictures and the one using film clips.

7. Describe the possible role of experience-dependent plasticity in determining how neurons and brain areas respond to (a) horizontal, vertical, and slanted lines and (b) Greebles.

8. What is the mind–body problem? Why do we say that demonstrating connections between nerve firing and a particular stimulus like a face or a color does not solve the mind–body problem?

THINK ABOUT IT

1. Ralph is hiking along a trail in the woods. The trail is bumpy in places, and Ralph has to avoid tripping on occasional rocks, tree roots, or ruts in the trail. Nonetheless, he is able to walk along the trail without constantly looking down to see exactly where he is placing his feet. That's a good thing because Ralph enjoys looking out at the woods to see whether he can spot interesting birds or animals.

How can you relate this description of Ralph's behavior to the operation of the dorsal and ventral streams in the visual system? (p. 80)

2. Although most neurons in the striate cortex respond to stimulation of small areas of the retina, many neurons in the temporal lobe respond to areas that represent as much

as half of the visual field. What do you think the function of such neurons is?

3. We have seen that the neural firing associated with an object in the environment does not necessarily look like, or resemble, the object. Can you think of situations that you encounter in everyday life in which objects or ideas are represented by things that do not exactly resemble those objects or ideas?

4. We described faces and pain as being "multidimensional." Can you think of ways that other objects or experiences are multidimensional? If you can, what does that say about the neural representation of these objects or experiences?

KEY TERMS

Ablation (p. 79)
Action pathway (p. 82)
Brain imaging (p. 75)
Cortical magnification (p. 74)
Cortical magnification factor (p. 74)
Distributed representation (p. 84)
Dorsal pathway (p. 80)
Double dissociations (p. 81)
Expertise hypothesis (p. 89)
Extrastriate body area (EBA) (p. 84)
Functional magnetic resonance imaging (fMRI) (p. 75)

Fusiform face area (FFA) (p. 83)
Hippocampus (p. 86)
How pathway (p. 82)
Hypercolumn (p. 78)
Landmark discrimination problem (p. 79)
Location columns (p. 77)
Magnetic resonance imaging (MRI) (p. 75)
Mind–body problem (p. 88)
Modularity (p. 83)
Modules (p. 83)

Neuropsychology (p. 81)
Object discrimination problem (p. 79)
Orientation columns (p. 77)
Parahippocampal place area (PPA) (p. 84)
Prosopagnosia (p. 83)
Retinotopic map (p. 74)
Spatial organization (p. 74)
Tiling (p. 78)
Ventral pathway (p. 80)
What pathway (p. 79)
Where pathway (p. 80)

Scenes in the environment are made up of many smaller components, such as the houses clustered together to create the hillside town of Manarola, Italy, or the many things that you might see looking down a city street. In this chapter, we consider how we see individual objects as well as larger scenes that are created by many objects.

CHAPTER 5

Perceiving Objects and Scenes

CHAPTER CONTENTS

Why Is It So Difficult to Design a Perceiving Machine?
The Stimulus on the Receptors Is Ambiguous
Objects Can Be Hidden or Blurred
Objects Look Different From Different Viewpoints

Perceptual Organization
The Gestalt Approach to Perceptual Grouping
Gestalt Principles of Perceptual Organization

Perceptual Segregation
Perceiving Scenes and Objects in Scenes
Perceiving the Gist of a Scene
Regularities in the Environment: Information for Perceiving
The Role of Inference in Perception
Connecting Neural Activity and Object/Scene Perception
Brain Responses to Perceiving Faces and Places

Spotlight on the Parahippocampal Place Area
Neural Mind Reading
SOMETHING TO CONSIDER: **Are Faces Special?**
DEVELOPMENTAL DIMENSION: **Infant Face Perception**
THINK ABOUT IT

Some Questions We Will Consider:

- Why are even the most sophisticated computers unable to match a person's ability to perceive objects? (p. 94)
- Why do some perceptual psychologists say "The whole differs from the sum of its parts"? (p. 99)
- Can we tell what people are perceiving by monitoring their brain activity? (p. 114)
- Why are faces special compared to other objects like cars or houses? (p. 116)
- How do infants perceive faces? (p. 119)

S itting in the upper deck in PNC Park, home of the Pittsburgh Pirates, Roger looks out over the city (**Figure 5.1**). He sees a group of about 10 buildings on the left and can easily tell one building from another. Looking straight ahead, he sees a small building in front of a larger one, and has no trouble telling that they are two separate buildings. Looking down toward the river, he notices a horizontal yellow band above the right field bleachers. It is obvious to him that this is not part of the ballpark but is located across the river.

All of Roger's perceptions come naturally to him and require little effort. But when we look closely at the scene, it becomes apparent that the scene poses many "puzzles." The following demonstration points out a few of them.

DEMONSTRATION | Perceptual Puzzles in a Scene

The questions below refer to the areas labeled in Figure 5.1. Your task is to answer each question and indicate the reasoning behind each answer:

- What is the dark area at A?
- Are the surfaces at B and C facing in the same or different directions?
- Are areas B and C on the same or on different buildings?
- Does the building at D extend behind the one at A?

Although it may have been easy to answer the questions, it was probably somewhat more challenging to indicate what your "reasoning" was. For example, how did you know the dark area at A is a shadow? It could be a dark-colored building that is in front of a light-colored building. Or on what basis might you have decided that building D extends behind building A? It could, after all, simply end right were A begins. We could ask similar questions about everything in this scene because, as we will see, a particular pattern of shapes can be created by a large number of objects.

Figure 5.1 It is easy to tell that there are a number of different buildings on the left and that straight ahead there is a low rectangular building in front of a taller building. It is also possible to tell that the horizontal yellow band above the bleachers is across the river. These perceptions are easy for humans but would be quite difficult for a computer vision system. The letters on the left indicate areas referred to in the Demonstration on page 93.

One of the messages of this chapter is that we need to go beyond the pattern of illumination that a scene creates on the retina to determine what is "out there." One way to appreciate the importance of this "going beyond" process is to consider how difficult it has been to program even the most powerful computers to accomplish perceptual tasks that humans achieve with ease.

Consider, for example, the robotic vehicles that were designed to compete in the Urban Challenge race on November 3, 2007, in Victorville, California. This race, which was sponsored by the Defense Advanced Research Project Agency (DARPA), required that vehicles drive for 55 miles through a course that resembled city streets, with other moving vehicles, traffic signals, and signs. The vehicles had to accomplish this feat on their own, with human involvement limited to entering global positioning coordinates of the course's layout into the vehicle's guidance system. Vehicles had to stay on course and avoid unpredictable traffic without any human

intervention, based only on the operation of onboard computer systems.

The winner of the race, a vehicle from Carnegie Mellon University, succeeded in staying on course and avoiding other cars while maintaining an average speed of 14 miles per hour. Vehicles from Stanford, Virginia Tech, MIT, Cornell, and the University of Pennsylvania also successfully completed the course, out of a total of 11 teams that qualified for the final race.

The ability of driverless cars to navigate through an environment, especially one that contains moving obstacles, is extremely impressive. Continued development of robotic vehicles has resulted in the Google driverless car, which has logged nearly a million miles of driving and is being developed as an alternative to today's driver-operated vehicles. While these driverless vehicles are able to sense things to be avoided, they can't recognize the large number of different objects that humans identify with little effort. For example, even though a driverless car might be able to avoid an obstacle in the middle

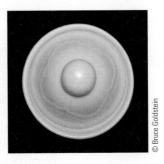

Figure 5.2 Even computer vision programs that can recognize objects fairly accurately make mistakes, such as confusing objects that have similar shapes. In this example, the lens cover and the top of the teapot are erroneously classified as a "tennis ball." (Based on Simonyan et al., 2012)

of the road, it can't tell whether the obstacle is a pile of rocks, a bush, or a dog.

In addition to driverless cars, computer vision research has also focused on designing artificial vision systems that can make fine-grained judgments, such as recognizing specific species of animals and plants (Yang et al., 2012). However, performance of these systems is still below what humans routinely achieve. For example, programs have been developed that can tell the difference between cats and dogs with about 90 percent accuracy and can identify different breeds of cats and dogs with about 60 percent accuracy (Parkhi et al., 2012). This is a difficult task for computers, involving complex programs and a great deal of training on thousands of different images. One of the problems facing many of the current computer programs is that even though they may be able to identify some objects, they often make errors that a human would never make, such as mistaking a camera lens cover or the top of a teapot for a tennis ball (Simonyan et al., 2012; see **Figure 5.2**).

One type of object that has received a tremendous amount of attention from computer vision researchers is faces, in an effort to develop computer surveillance systems that can recognize faces. With large amounts of research invested in computer face recognition systems, new programs have been developed that can determine, as well as humans can, whether two faces that are seen straight on, as in **Figures 5.3a** and **5.3b**, are the same or different people (O'Toole, 2007; O'Toole et al., 2007; Simonyan et al., 2012; Yang, 2009). However, when one of the faces is seen at an angle, as in **Figure 5.3c**, humans still outperform computers.

Finally, computer vision systems specifically designed to determine the corners of a room, where the walls meet, and the location of furniture within the room are able to achieve these tasks crudely for some photographs, as in **Figure 5.4a**, but they often make large errors, as in **Figure 5.4b** (Del Pero et al., 2011, 2012). Although the location and extent of the bed in Figure 5.4b may be obvious to a person, it isn't so obvious to a computer, even though the computer program was specifically designed to detect objects (like the bed) that are defined by straight lines. Even if it could find the borders of the bed, determining the identity of other objects in the room is far beyond the capabilities of this state-of-the-art program.

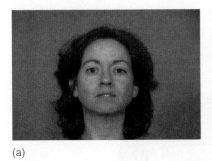
(a)

(b)

(c)

Figure 5.3 A computer or a person can determine whether the two straight-on views in (a) and (b) are the same person, but the person outperforms the computer when comparing a straight-on view to a face at an angle, as in (c). (From O'Toole et al., 2005)

(a)

(b)

Figure 5.4 (a) The red lines represent the attempt of a computer vision program to determine the corners of the room—the places where the wall, ceiling, and floor meet. In this example, the computer does a fairly good job. (b) In another example for the same computer vision program, the green and blue lines indicate that the program identified other straight-line contours in the room inaccurately. (From L. Del Pero, J. Guan, E. Brau, J. Schlecht, & K. Barnard, Sampling Bedrooms, IEEE Computer Society Conference on Computer Vision And Pattern Recognition [CVPR], pp. 2009-2016, 2011. Reproduced by permission.)

Why Is It So Difficult to Design a Perceiving Machine?

We will now describe a few of the problems involved in designing a "perceiving machine." Remember that the point of these problems is that although they pose difficulties for computers, humans solve them easily.

The Stimulus on the Receptors Is Ambiguous

When you look at a page of a book, the image cast by the borders of the page on your retina is ambiguous. It may seem strange to say that, because (1) the rectangular shape of the page is obvious, and (2) once we know the page's shape and its distance from the eye, determining its image on the retina is a simple geometry problem, which, as shown in **Figure 5.5**, can be solved by extending "rays" from the red corners of the page into the eye.

But the perceptual system is not concerned with determining an object's image on the retina. It *starts* with the image on the retina, and its job is to determine the object "out there" that created the image. The task of determining the object responsible for a particular image on the retina is called the **inverse projection problem**, because it involves starting with the retinal image and extending rays *out* from the eye. When we do this, as shown by extending the lines in Figure 5.5, we see that the retinal image created by the rectangular page could have been created by a number of other objects, including a tilted trapezoid, a much larger rectangle, and an infinite number of other objects located at different distances. When we consider that a particular image on the retina can be created by many different objects in the environment, it is easy to see why we say that the image on the retina is ambiguous.

The ambiguity of the image on the retina is also illustrated by **Figure 5.6a**, which, when viewed from one specific location, creates a circular image on the retina and appears to be a circle of rocks. However, moving to another viewpoint reveals that the rocks aren't arranged in a circle after all (**Figure 5.6b**). Thus, just as a rectangular image on the retina can be created by trapezoids and other nonrectangular objects, a circular image on the retina can be created by objects that aren't circular.

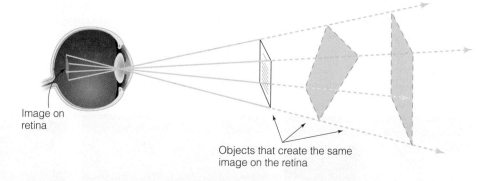

Figure 5.5 The projection of the book (red object) onto the retina can be determined by extending rays (solid lines) from the corners of the book into the eye. The principle behind the inverse projection problem is illustrated by extending rays out from the eye past the book (dashed lines). When we do this, we can see that the image created by the book can be created by an infinite number of objects, among them the tilted trapezoid and the large rectangle shown here. This is why we say that the image on the retina is ambiguous.

Image on retina

Objects that create the same image on the retina

(a)

(b)

Thomas Macaulay

Figure 5.6 An environmental sculpture by Thomas Macaulay. (a) When viewed from the exact right vantage point (the second-floor balcony of the Blackhawk Mountain School of Art, Black Hawk, Colorado), the stones appear to be arranged in a circle. (b) Viewing the stones from the ground floor reveals a truer indication of their configuration. (Courtesy of Thomas Macaulay, Blackhawk Mountain School of Art, Blackhawk, CO)

The "environmental rock sculpture" in Figure 5.6 is designed to fool us by creating a special condition (viewing from a specific place) that results in an erroneous perception. Most of the time, erroneous perceptions like this don't occur; the visual system solves the inverse projection problem and determines which object out of all the possible objects is responsible for a particular image on the retina. However, as easy as this is for the human perceptual system, solving the inverse projection problem poses serious challenges to computer vision systems.

Objects Can Be Hidden or Blurred

Sometimes objects are hidden or blurred. For example, look for the pencil and eyeglasses in **Figure 5.7** before reading further. Although it might take a little searching, people can find the pencil in the foreground and the glasses frame sticking out from behind the computer, next to the picture, even though only a small portion of these objects is visible. People can also easily identify the book, scissors, and paper, even though they are partially hidden by other objects.

This problem of hidden objects occurs anytime one object obscures part of another object. This occurs frequently in the environment, but people easily understand that the part of an object that is covered continues to exist, and they are able to use their knowledge of the environment to determine what is likely to be present.

People are also able to recognize objects that are not in sharp focus, such as the faces in **Figure 5.8**. See how many of these people you can identify, and then consult the answers on page 121. Despite the degraded nature of these images, people can often identify most of them, whereas computers perform poorly on this task (Sinha, 2002).

Objects Look Different From Different Viewpoints

Another problem facing any perceiving machine is that objects are often viewed from different angles. This means that the images of objects are continually changing, depending on the angle from which they are viewed. Thus, although humans

Figure 5.7 A portion of the mess on the author's desk. Can you locate the hidden pencil (easy) and the author's glasses (hard)?

Figure 5.8 Who are these people? See page 121 for the answers.
s_bukley/ Shutterstock.com; Featureflash/Shutterstock.com; Soeren Stache/dpa picture alliance archive/Alamy; peter muhly/alamy; s_bukley/ Shutterstock.com; Joe Seer/Shutterstock.com; DFree/Shutterstock.com

continue to perceive the object in **Figure 5.9** as the same chair viewed from different angles, this isn't so obvious to a computer. The ability to recognize an object seen from different viewpoints is called **viewpoint invariance**. We've already seen that viewpoint invariance enables people to tell whether faces seen from different angles are the same person (refer back to Figure 5.3), but this task is difficult for computers.

The difficulties facing any perceiving machine illustrate that the process of perception is more complex than it seems (something you already knew from the perceptual process in Figure 1.1, page 5, and the physiological material in Chapters 2–4). But how do humans overcome these complexities? We begin answering this question by considering *perceptual organization*.

(a)   (b)   (c)

Figure 5.9 Your ability to recognize each of these views as being of the same chair is an example of viewpoint invariance.

Perceptual Organization

Perceptual organization is the process by which elements in the environment become perceptually grouped to create our perception of objects. During this process, incoming stimulation is organized into coherent units such as objects. The process of perceptual organization involves two components: *grouping* and *segregation* (**Figure 5.10**; Peterson & Kimchi, 2013). **Grouping** is the process by which visual events are "put together" into units or objects. Thus, when Roger sees each building in Pittsburgh as an individual unit, he has grouped the visual elements in the scene to create each building. If you can perceive the Dalmatian dog in **Figure 5.11**, you have perceptually grouped some of the dark areas to form a Dalmatian, with the other dark areas being seen as shadows on the ground.

The process of grouping works in conjunction with **segregation**, which is the process of separating one area or object from another. Thus, seeing two buildings in Figure 5.10 as separate from one another, with borders indicating where one building ends and the other begins, involves segregation.

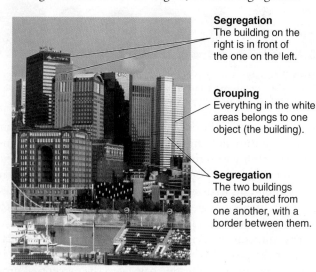

Segregation
The building on the right is in front of the one on the left.

Grouping
Everything in the white areas belongs to one object (the building).

Segregation
The two buildings are separated from one another, with a border between them.

Figure 5.10 Examples of grouping and segregation in a city scene. © Bruce Goldstein

Figure 5.11 Some black and white shapes that become perceptually organized into a Dalmatian. See page 121 for an outline of the Dalmatian.

The Gestalt Approach to Perceptual Grouping

What causes some elements to become grouped so they are part of one object? Answers to this question were provided in the early 1900s by the **Gestalt psychologists**—where *Gestalt*, roughly translated, means *configuration*. "How," asked the Gestalt psychologists, "are configurations formed from smaller elements?"

Structuralism We can understand the Gestalt approach by first considering an approach that came before Gestalt psychology, called *structuralism*, which was proposed by Wilhelm Wundt, who established the first laboratory of scientific psychology at the University of Leipzig in 1879. **Structuralism** distinguished between *sensations*—elementary processes that occur in response to stimulation of the senses—and *perceptions*, more complex conscious experiences such as our awareness of objects. The structuralists saw sensations as analogous to the atoms of chemistry. Just as atoms combine to create complex molecular structures, sensations combine to create complex perceptions. Sensations might be linked to very simple experiences, such as seeing a single flash of light, but perception accounts for the vast majority of our sensory experiences. For example, when you look at **Figure 5.12**, you perceive a face, but

Figure 5.12 According to structuralism, a number of sensations (represented by the dots) add up to create our perception of the face.

according to structuralists the starting point would be many sensations, which are indicated by the small dots.

The Gestalt psychologists rejected the idea that perceptions were formed by "adding up" sensations. We can appreciate why the Gestalt psychologists rejected this idea by considering the experience of psychologist Max Wertheimer, who was on vacation taking a train ride through Germany in 1911 (Boring, 1942). When he got off the train to stretch his legs at Frankfurt, he bought a toy stroboscope from a vendor who was selling toys on the train platform. The stroboscope, a mechanical device that created an illusion of movement by rapidly alternating two slightly different pictures, caused Wertheimer to wonder how the structuralist idea that experience is created from sensations could explain the illusion of movement he observed.

Apparent Movement **Figure 5.13** diagrams the principle behind the illusion of movement created by the stroboscope, which is called **apparent movement** because although movement is perceived, nothing is actually moving. The three components that create apparent movement (in this case, using flashing lights) are shown in Figure 5.13: (1) One light flashes (**Figure 5.13a**); (2) there is a period of darkness, lasting a fraction of a second (**Figure 5.13b**); and (3) the second image flashes (**Figure 5.13c**). Physically, then, there are two images flashing separated by a period of darkness. But we don't see the darkness because our perceptual system adds something during the period of darkness—the perception of an image moving through the space between the flashing lights (**Figure 5.13d**). Modern examples of apparent movement are electronic signs like the one in **Figure 5.14**, which display

Figure 5.14 The stock ticker in Times Square, New York. The letters and numbers that appear to be moving smoothly across the screen are created by hundreds of small lights that are flashing on and off.

moving advertisements or news headlines and movies. The perception of movement in these displays is so compelling that it is difficult to imagine that they are made up of stationary lights flashing on and off (for the news headlines) or still images flashed one after another (for the movies).

Wertheimer drew two conclusions from the phenomenon of apparent movement. His first conclusion was that apparent movement can't be explained by sensations, because there is nothing in the dark space between the flashing lights. His second conclusion became one of the basic principles of Gestalt psychology: *The whole is different than the sum of its parts*, because the perceptual system creates the perception of movement where there actually is none. This idea, that the whole is different than the sum of its parts, became the battle cry of the Gestalt psychologists. "Wholes" were in; "sensations" were out (see page 5 for more on sensations).

Illusory Contours Another demonstration that argues against sensations and for the idea that the whole is different than the sum of its parts is shown in **Figure 5.15**. This demonstration involves circles with a "mouth" cut out, which resemble "Pac Man" figures from the classic video game introduced in the 1980s. We begin with the Pac Men in **Figure 5.15a**. You may see an edge running between the "mouths" of the Pac Men, but if you cover up one of them, the edge vanishes. This single edge becomes part of a triangle when we add the third Pac Man, in **Figure 5.15b**. The three Pac Men have created the perception of a triangle, which becomes more obvious by adding lines, as shown in **Figure 5.15c**. The edges that create the triangle are called **illusory contours** because there are actually no physical edges present. Sensations can't explain illusory contours, because there aren't any sensations along the contours. The idea that the whole is different than the sum of its parts led the Gestalt psychologists to propose a number of *principles of perceptual organization* to explain the way elements are grouped together to create larger objects.

(a) One light flashes

(b) Darkness

(c) The second light flashes

(d) Flash—dark—flash

Figure 5.13 The conditions for creating apparent movement. (a) One light flashes, followed by (b) a short period of darkness, followed by (c) another light flashing in a different position. The resulting perception, symbolized in (d), is a light moving from left to right. Movement is seen between the two lights even though there is only darkness in the space between them. (© Cengage Learning 2014)

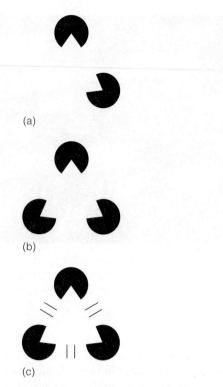

(a)

(b)

(c)

Figure 5.15 The illusory contours clearly visible in (b) and (c) cannot be caused by sensations, because there is only white there.

Gestalt Principles of Perceptual Organization

Having questioned the idea that perceptions are created by adding up sensations, the Gestalt psychologists proposed that perception depends on a number of **principles of perceptual organization**, which determine how elements in a scene become grouped together. The starting points for the principles of organization are things that usually occur in the environment. Consider, for example, how you perceive the rope in **Figure 5.16a**. Although there are many places where one strand is overlapped by another strand, you probably perceive the rope not as a number of separate pieces but as a continuous strand, as illustrated by the highlighted segment of rope in **Figure 5.16b**. The Gestalt psychologists, being keen observers of perception, used this kind of observation to formulate the *principle of good continuation*.

Figure 5.16 (a) Rope on the beach. (b) Good continuation helps us perceive the rope as a single strand.

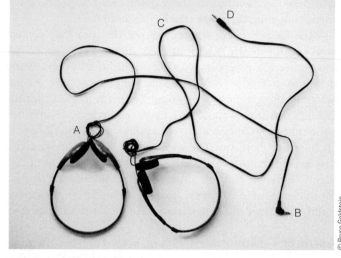

Figure 5.17 Good continuation helps us perceive two separate wires, even though they overlap.

Good Continuation The **principle of good continuation** states the following: *Points that, when connected, result in straight or smoothly curving lines are seen as belonging together, and the lines tend to be seen in such a way as to follow the smoothest path.* The wire starting at A in **Figure 5.17** flowing smoothly to B is an example of lines following the smoothest path. The path from A does not go to C or D because those paths would violate good continuation by making sharp turns. The principle of good continuation also states that *objects that are partially covered by other objects are seen as continuing behind the covering object.* The rope in Figure 5.16 illustrates how covered objects are seen as continuing behind the object that covers them.

Pragnanz *Pragnanz*, roughly translated from the German, means "good figure." The **principle of pragnanz**, also called the **principle of good figure** or the **principle of simplicity** states: *Every stimulus pattern is seen in such a way that the resulting structure is as simple as possible.* The familiar Olympic symbol in **Figure 5.18a** is an example of the principle of simplicity at work. We see this display as five circles and not as a larger number of more complicated shapes such as the ones in the "exploded view" of the Olympic symbol in **Figure 5.18b**.

(a)

(b)

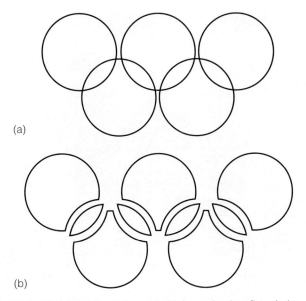

(a)

(b)

Figure 5.18 (a) The Olympic symbol is perceived as five circles, not as the nine shapes in (b).

The principle of good continuation also contributes to perceiving the five circles. Can you see why this is so?

Similarity Most people perceive **Figure 5.19a** as either horizontal rows of circles, vertical columns of circles, or a square filled with evenly spaced dots. But when we change the color of some of the columns, as in **Figure 5.19b**, most people perceive vertical columns of circles. This perception illustrates the **principle of similarity**: *Similar things appear to be grouped together.* This law causes circles of the same color to be grouped together. A striking example of grouping by similarity of color is shown in **Figure 5.20**. Grouping can also occur because of similarity of shape, size, or orientation.

Grouping also occurs for auditory stimuli. For example, notes that have similar pitches and that follow each other closely in time can become perceptually grouped to form a melody. We will consider this and other auditory grouping effects when we describe organizational processes in hearing in Chapter 12.

Proximity (Nearness) Our perception of **Figure 5.21** as three groups of candles illustrates the **principle of proximity**, or **nearness**: *Things that are near each other appear to be grouped together.*

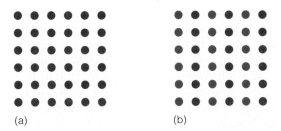

(a)   (b)

Figure 5.19 (a) These dots are perceived as horizontal rows or vertical columns or both. (b) These dots are perceived as vertical columns.

Wilma Hurskainen

Figure 5.20 This photograph, *Waves*, by Wilma Hurskainen, was taken at the exact moment that the front of the white water aligned with the white area on the woman's clothing. Similarity of color causes grouping; differently colored areas of the dress are perceptually grouped with the same colors in the scene. Also notice how the front edge of the water creates grouping by good continuation across the woman's dress.

© Bruce Goldstein

Figure 5.21 The candles are grouped by proximity to create three separate groups. Can you identify additional Gestalt principles in the patterns on the menorah?

Common Fate According to the **principle of common fate**, *things that are moving in the same direction appear to be grouped together.* Thus, when you see a flock of hundreds of birds all flying together, you tend to see the flock as a unit; if some of the birds start flying in another direction, this creates a new unit. Note that common fate can work even if the objects in a group are dissimilar. The key to common fate is that a group of objects are moving in the same direction.

The principles we have just described were proposed by the Gestalt psychologists in the early 1900s. The following additional principles have been proposed by modern perceptual psychologists.

Common Region **Figure 5.22a** illustrates the **principle of common region**: *Elements that are within the same region of space appear to be grouped together.* Even though the circles inside the ovals are farther apart than the circles that are next to each other in neighboring ovals, we see the circles inside the ovals as belonging together. This occurs because each oval is seen as a separate region of space (Palmer, 1992; Palmer & Rock, 1994). Notice that in this example, common region overpowers proximity, because proximity would predict that the nearby circles would be perceived together. But even though the circles that are in different regions are close to each other in space, they do not group with each other, as they did in Figure 5.21.

Uniform Connectedness According to the **principle of uniform connectedness**, *a connected region of the same visual properties, such as lightness, color, texture, or motion, is perceived as a single unit* (Palmer & Rock, 1994). For example, in **Figure 5.22b**, the connected circles are perceived as grouped together, just as they were when they were in the same region in Figure 5.22a. Again, connectedness overpowers proximity.

The Gestalt principles we have described predict what we will perceive, based on what usually happens in the environment. Many of my students react to this idea by saying that the Gestalt principles therefore aren't anything special, because all they are doing is describing the obvious things we see every day. When they say this, I remind them that the reason we perceive scenes like the city buildings in Figure 5.1 or the scene in **Figure 5.23** so easily is that we use observations about commonly occurring properties of the environment to organize the scene. Thus, we assume, without even thinking about it, that the men's legs in Figure 5.23 extend behind the gray boards, because generally in the environment when two visible parts of an object (like the men's legs) have the same color and are

Figure 5.23 A usual occurrence in the environment: Objects (the men's legs) are partially hidden by another object (the gray boards). In this example, the men's legs continue in a straight line and are the same color above and below the boards, so it is highly likely that they continue behind the boards.

"lined up," they belong to the same object and extend behind whatever is blocking it.

People don't usually think about how we perceive situations like this as being based on assumptions, but that is, in fact, what is happening. The reason the "assumption" seems so obvious is that we have had so much experience with things like this in the environment. That the "assumption" is actually almost a "sure thing" may cause us to take the Gestalt principles for granted and label them as "obvious." But the reality is that the Gestalt principles are nothing less than the basic operating characteristics of our visual system that determine how our perceptual system organizes elements of the environment into larger units.

Perceptual Segregation

The Gestalt psychologists were also interested in determining characteristics of the environment responsible for **perceptual segregation**—the perceptual separation of one object from another, as occurred when you saw the buildings in Figure 5.1 as separate from one another. One approach to studying perceptual segregation is to consider the problem of **figure–ground segregation**. When we see a separate object, it is usually seen as a **figure** that stands out from its background, which is called the **ground**. For example, sitting at your desk, you would probably see a book or papers on your desk as figure and the surface of your desk as ground, or stepping back from the desk, you might see the desk as figure and the wall behind it as ground. The Gestalt psychologists were interested in determining the

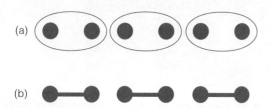

Figure 5.22 Grouping by (a) common region and (b) uniform connectedness.

properties of the figure and the ground and what causes us to perceive one area as figure and the other as ground.

Properties of Figure and Ground One way the Gestalt psychologists studied the properties of figure and ground was by considering patterns like the one in **Figure 5.24**, which was introduced by Danish psychologist Edgar Rubin in 1915. This pattern is an example of **reversible figure–ground** because it can be perceived alternately either as two dark blue faces looking at each other, in front of a gray background, or as a gray vase on a dark blue background. Some of the properties of the figure and ground are:

- The figure is more "thinglike" and more memorable than the ground. Thus, when you see the vase as figure, it appears as an object that can be remembered later. However, when you see the same light area as ground, it does not appear to be an object but is just "background" and is therefore not particularly memorable.
- The figure is seen as being in front of the ground. Thus, when the vase is seen as figure, it appears to be in front of the dark background (**Figure 5.25a**), and when the faces are seen as figure, they are on top of the light background (**Figure 5.25b**).

Figure 5.24 A version of Rubin's reversible face–vase figure.

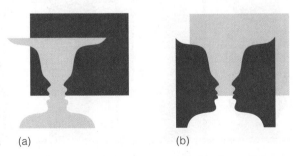

(a) (b)

Figure 5.25 (a) When the vase is perceived as figure, it is seen in front of a homogeneous dark background. (b) When the faces are seen as figure, they are seen in front of a homogeneous light background.

- Near the borders it shares with the figure, the ground is seen as unformed material, without a specific shape, and seems to extend behind the figure. This is not to say that grounds lack shape entirely. Grounds are often shaped by borders distant from those they share with the figure; for instance, the backgrounds in Figure 5.25 are square.
- The border separating the figure from the ground appears to belong to the figure. Consider, for example, the Rubin face–vase in Figure 5.24. When the two faces are seen as figure, the border separating the blue faces from the grey background belongs to the faces. This property of the border belonging to one area is called **border ownership**. When perception shifts so the vase is perceived as figure, border ownership shifts as well, so now the border belongs to the vase.

Image-Based Factors That Determine Which Area Is Figure The Gestalt psychologists specified a number of factors within the image that determine which areas are perceived as figure. This idea that information *within the image* determines perception is similar to the approach the Gestalt psychologists took to grouping, in which their principles all referred to how properties of the image determined which elements were seen as being grouped together.

One image-based factor proposed by the Gestalt psychologists was that areas lower in the field of view are more likely to be perceived as figure (Ehrenstein, 1930; Koffka, 1935). This idea was confirmed experimentally years later by Shaun Vecera and coworkers (2002), who flashed stimuli like the ones in **Figure 5.26a** for 150 milliseconds (ms) and determined which area was seen as figure, the red area or the green area. The

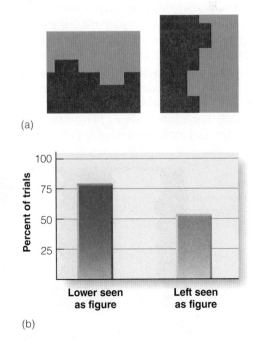

(a)

(b)

Figure 5.26 (a) Stimuli from the Vecera et al. (2002) experiment. (b) Percentage of trials on which lower or left areas were seen as figure.

Figure 5.27 The field, in the bottom half of the visual field, is seen as figure. The sky, in the upper half of the visual field, is seen as ground.

results, shown in **Figure 5.26b**, indicate that for the upper–lower displays, observers were more likely to perceive the lower area as figure, but for the left–right displays, they showed only a small preference for the left region. From this result, Vecera concluded that there is no left–right preference for determining figure, but there is a definite preference for seeing objects lower in the display as figure. The conclusion from this experiment, that the lower region of a display tends to be seen as figure, makes sense when we consider a scene like the one in **Figure 5.27**, in which the lower part of the scene is figure and the sky is ground. What is significant about this scene is that it is typical of scenes we perceive every day. In our normal experience, the "figure" is much more likely to be below the horizon.

Another Gestalt proposal was that figures are more likely to be perceived on the convex side of borders (borders that bulge outward) (Kanizsa & Gerbino, 1976). Mary Peterson and Elizabeth Salvagio (2008) demonstrated this by presenting

displays like the one in **Figure 5.28a** and asking observers to indicate whether the red square was "on" or "off" a perceived figure. Thus, if they perceived the dark area in this example as being a figure, they would say "on." If they perceived the dark area as ground, they would say "off." The result, in agreement with the Gestalt proposal, was that convex regions, like the dark regions in Figure 5.28a, were perceived as figure 89 percent of the time.

But Peterson and Salvagio went beyond simply confirming the Gestalt proposals by also presenting displays like the ones in **Figures 5.28b** and **5.28c**, which had fewer components. Doing this greatly decreased the likelihood that convex displays would be seen as figure, with the black convex region in the two-component display (Figure 5.28b) being seen as figure only 58 percent of the time. What this result means, according to Peterson and Salvagio, is that to understand how segregation occurs we need to go beyond simply identifying factors

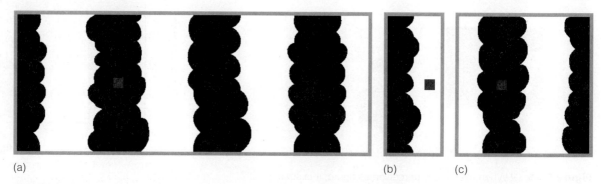

(a) (b) (c)

Figure 5.28 Stimuli from Peterson and Salvagio's (2008) experiment: (a) 8-component display; (b) 2-component display; (c) 4-component display. The red squares appeared on different areas on different trials. The subject's task was to judge whether the area the red square was on was "figure" or "ground."

like convexity. Apparently, segregation is determined not by just what is happening at a single border but by what is happening in the wider scene. This makes sense when we consider that perception generally occurs in scenes that extend over a wide area. We will return to this idea later in the chapter when we consider how we perceive scenes.

The Role of Perceptual Principles and Experience in Determining Which Area Is Figure The Gestalt psychologists' emphasis on perceptual principles led them to minimize the role of a person's past experiences in determining perception. They believed that although perception can be affected by experience, built-in principles can override experience. The Gestalt psychologist Max Wertheimer (1912) provided the following example to illustrate how built-in principles could override experience: Most people recognize the display in **Figure 5.29a** as a "W" sitting on top of an "M," largely because of our past experiences with those two letters. However, when the letters are arranged as in **Figure 5.29b**, most people see two uprights plus a pattern in between them. The uprights, which are created by the principle of good continuation, are the dominant perception and override the effects of past experience with *W*s or *M*s.

The Gestalt idea that past experience and the meanings of stimuli (like the *W* and *M*) play a minor role in perceptual organization is also illustrated by the Gestalt proposal that one of the first things that occurs in the perceptual process is the segregation of figure from ground. They contended that the figure must stand out from the ground before it can be recognized. In other words, the figure has to be separated from the ground before we can assign a meaning to the figure.

But Bradley Gibson and Mary Peterson (1994) did an experiment that argued against this idea by showing that figure–ground formation can be affected by the meaningfulness of a stimulus. They demonstrated this by presenting a display like the one in **Figure 5.30a**, which can be perceived in two ways: (1) a standing woman (the black part of the display) or (2) a less meaningful shape (the white part of the display). When they presented stimuli such as this for a fraction of a second and asked observers which region seemed to be the figure, they

(a)   (b)

Figure 5.30 Gibson and Peterson's (1994) stimulus. (a) The black area is more likely to be seen as figure because it is meaningful. (b) This effect does not occur when meaningfulness is decreased by turning the picture upside down.

found that observers were more likely to say that the meaningful part of the display (the woman, in this example) was the figure.

Why were the observers more likely to perceive the woman? One possibility is that they recognized that the black area was a familiar object. In fact, when Gibson and Peterson turned the display upside down, as in **Figure 5.30b**, so that it was more difficult to recognize the black area as a woman, subjects were less likely to see that area as being the figure. The fact that meaningfulness can influence the assignment of an area as figure means that the process of recognition must be occurring either before or at the same time as the figure is being separated from the ground (Peterson, 1994, 2001).

Gibson and Peterson were studying rapid processes that operate on a time scale of fractions of a second to determine figure and ground. The next demonstration illustrates how meaning can influence perceptual organization on a longer time scale, when it is initially difficult to perceive figures hidden in the scene.

DEMONSTRATION | Finding Faces in a Landscape

Consider the picture in **Figure 5.31**. At first glance, this scene appears to contain a person and two horses plus trees, rocks, and water. On closer inspection, however, you can see some faces in the trees in the background, and if you look more closely, you can see that a number of faces are formed by various groups of rocks. See if you can find all 13 faces hidden in this picture.

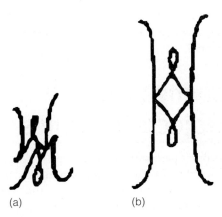

(a)   (b)

Figure 5.29 (a) *W* on top of *M*. (b) When combined, a new pattern emerges, overriding the meaningful letters. (From Wertheimer, 1912)

Figure 5.31 *The Forest Has Eyes* by Bev Doolittle (1984). Can you find 13 faces in this picture? See page 121 for the answer.

Some people find it difficult to perceive the faces at first, but then suddenly they succeed. The change in perception from "rocks in a stream" or "trees in a forest" to "faces" occurs because of our familiarity with faces. The two shapes that you at first perceive as two separate rocks in the stream become perceptually grouped together to create the left and right eyes of a face. The remarkable thing about how meaning influences perception in this situation is that once you perceive a particular grouping of rocks as a face, it is often difficult *not* to perceive them in this way—they have become permanently organized into a face. This is similar to the process we observed for the Dalmatian on page 98. Once we see the Dalmatian, it is difficult not to perceive it.

So far, the principles and research we have been describing have focused largely on how our perception of individual objects depends on organizing principles and principles that determine which parts of a display will be seen as figure and which will be seen as ground. If you look back at the illustrations in this section, you will notice that most of them are simple displays designed to illustrate a specific principle of perceptual organization. But to truly understand perception as it occurs in the environment, we need to expand our view to consider not just individual objects but more complex scenes as well, which is the subject of the next section.

TEST YOURSELF 5.1

1. What are some of the problems that make object perception difficult for computers but not for humans?

2. What is structuralism, and why did the Gestalt psychologists propose an alternative to this way of explaining perception?

3. How did the Gestalt psychologists explain perceptual organization?

4. How did the Gestalt psychologists describe figure–ground segregation? What are some basic properties of figure and ground?

5. What image-based properties of a stimulus tend to favor perceiving an area as "figure"? Be sure you understand Vecera's experiment that showed that the lower region of a display tends to be perceived as figure, and why Peterson and Salvagio stated that to understand how segregation occurs we have to consider what is happening in the wider scene.

6. Describe the Gestalt ideas about the role of meaning and past experience in determining figure–ground segregation.

7. Describe Gibson and Peterson's experiment that showed that meaning can play a role in figure–ground segregation.

8. What does the Bev Doolittle scene in Figure 5.31 demonstrate?

Perceiving Scenes and Objects in Scenes

Our discussion of perceptual organization and figure–ground perception described how perception is influenced by characteristics such as good continuation, similarity, and nearness; position (higher or lower) in the visual field; and shape (convexity) of borders. But at the end of this discussion, we also noted that the *meaning* of a stimulus can affect both figure–ground formation (Gibson and Peterson's experiment) and our perception of objects in a scene (the "Finding Faces" demonstration). Meaning now takes center stage in our discussion, as we describe modern research on how observers perceive objects and scenes.

A **scene** is a view of a real-world environment that contains (1) background elements and (2) multiple objects that are organized in a meaningful way relative to each other and the background (Epstein, 2005; Henderson & Hollingworth, 1999). One way of distinguishing between objects and scenes is that objects are compact and are *acted upon*, whereas scenes are extended in space and are *acted within*. For example, if we are walking down the street and mail a letter, we would be *acting upon* the mailbox (an object) and *acting within* the street (the scene).

Perceiving the Gist of a Scene

Perceiving scenes presents a paradox. On one hand, scenes are often large and complex. However, despite this size and complexity, you can identify important properties of most scenes after viewing them for only a fraction of a second. This general description of the type of scene is called the **gist of a scene**. An example of your ability to rapidly perceive the gist of a scene is the way you can rapidly flip from one TV channel to another, yet still grasp the meaning of each picture as it flashes by—a car chase, quiz contestants, or an outdoor scene with mountains—even though you may be seeing each picture for a second or less and so may not be able to identify specific objects. When you do this, you are perceiving the gist of each scene (Oliva & Torralba, 2006).

Exactly how long does it take to perceive the gist of a scene? Mary Potter (1976) showed observers a target picture and then asked them to indicate whether they saw that picture as they viewed a sequence of 16 rapidly presented pictures. Her observers could do this with almost 100 percent accuracy even when the pictures were flashed for only 250 ms (ms = milliseconds; 250 ms = 1/4 second). Even when the target picture was only specified by a written description, such as "girl clapping," observers achieved an accuracy of almost 90 percent (**Figure 5.32**).

Another approach to determining how rapidly people can perceive scenes was used by Li Fei-Fei and coworkers (2007), who presented pictures of scenes for exposures ranging from 27 ms to 500 ms and asked observers to write a description of what they saw. This method of determining the observer's response is a nice example of the phenomenological report, described in Chapter 1 (page 16). Fei-Fei used a procedure called *masking* to be sure the observers saw the pictures for exactly the desired duration.

METHOD | Using a Mask to Achieve Brief Stimulus Presentations

What if we want to present a stimulus that is visible for only 100 ms? Although you might think that the way to do this would be to flash a stimulus for 100 ms, this won't work because of a phenomenon called **persistence of vision**—the perception of a visual stimulus continues for about 250 ms (1/4 second) after the stimulus is extinguished. Thus, a picture that is presented for 100 ms will be *perceived* as lasting about 350 ms. But the persistence of vision can be eliminated by presenting a **visual masking stimulus**, usually a random pattern that covers the original stimulus, so if a picture is flashed for 100 ms followed immediately by a masking stimulus, the picture is visible for just 100 ms. A masking stimulus is therefore often presented immediately after a test stimulus to stop the persistence of vision from increasing the duration of the test stimulus.

Typical results of Fei-Fei's experiment are shown in **Figure 5.33**. At brief durations, observers saw only light and dark areas of the pictures. By 67 ms they could identify some large objects (a person, a table), and when the duration was increased to 500 ms (half a second) they were able to identify smaller objects and details (the boy, the laptop). For a picture of an ornate 1800s living room, observers were able to identify the picture as a room in a house at 67 ms and to identify details, such as chairs and portraits, at 500 ms. Thus, the overall gist of the scene is perceived first, followed by perception of details and smaller objects within the scene.

Figure 5.32 Procedure for Potter's (1976) experiment. She first presented either a target photograph or, as shown here, a description, and then rapidly presented 16 pictures for 250 ms each. The observer's task was to indicate whether the target picture had been presented. In this example, only 3 of the 16 pictures are shown, with the target picture being the second one presented. On some trials, the target picture was not included in the series of 16 pictures.

Alice O'Donnell

27 ms   Looked like something black in the center with four straight
         lines coming out of it against a white background.
         (Subject: AM)

40 ms   The first thing I could recognize was a dark splotch in
         the middle. It may have been rectangular-shaped, with a
         curved top... but that's just a guess.
         (Subject: KM)

67 ms   A person, I think, sitting down or crouching. Facing the left
         side of the picture. We see their profile mostly. They were
         at a table or where some object was in front of them (to
         their left side in the picture).
         (Subject: EC)

500 ms   This looks like a father or somebody helping a little boy.
         The man had something in his hands, like a LCD screen or
         a laptop. They looked like they were standing in a cubicle.
         (Subject: WC)

Figure 5.33 Observer's description of a photograph presented in Fei-Fei's (2007) experiment. Viewing durations are indicated on the left. (From Fei-Fei et al., 2007)

What enables observers to perceive the gist of a scene so rapidly? Aude Oliva and Antonio Torralba (2001, 2006) propose that observers use information called **global image features**, which can be perceived rapidly and are associated with specific types of scenes. Some of the global image features proposed by Oliva and Torralba are:

- *Degree of naturalness*. Natural scenes, such as the ocean and forest in **Figure 5.34**, have textured zones and undulating contours. Man-made scenes, such as the street, are dominated by straight lines and horizontals and verticals.
- *Degree of openness*. Open scenes, such as the ocean, often have a visible horizon line and contain few objects. The street scene is also open, although not as much as the ocean scene. The forest is an example of a scene with a low degree of openness.
- *Degree of roughness*. Smooth scenes (low roughness) like the ocean contain fewer small elements. Scenes with high roughness like the forest contain many small elements and are more complex.

- *Degree of expansion*. The convergence of parallel lines, like what you see when you look down railroad tracks that appear to vanish in the distance, or in the street scene in Figure 5.34, indicates a high degree of expansion. This feature is especially dependent on the observer's viewpoint. For example, in the street scene, looking directly at the side of a building would result in low expansion.
- *Color*. Some scenes have characteristic colors, like the ocean scene (blue) and the forest (green and brown). (Castelhano & Henderson, 2008a; Goffaux et al., 2005)

Global image features are *holistic* and *rapidly perceived*. They are properties of the scene as a whole and do not depend on time-consuming processes such as perceiving small details, recognizing individual objects, or separating one object from another. Another property of global image features is that they contain information about a scene's structure and spatial layout. For example, the degree of openness and the degree of expansion refer directly to characteristics of a scene's layout; naturalness also provides layout information that comes from knowing whether a scene is from nature or contains human-made structures.

Global image properties not only help explain how we can perceive the gist of scenes based on features that can be seen in brief exposures, they also illustrate the following general property of perception: Our past experiences in perceiving properties of the environment play a role in determining our perceptions. We learn, for example, that blue is associated with open sky, that landscapes are often green and smooth, and that verticals and horizontals are associated with buildings. Characteristics of the environment such as this, which occur frequently, are called **regularities in the environment**. We will now describe these regularities in more detail.

Regularities in the Environment: Information for Perceiving

Modern perceptual psychologists have introduced the idea that perception is influenced by two types of regularities: *physical regularities* and *semantic regularities*.

Physical Regularities Physical regularities are regularly occurring physical properties of the environment. For example, there are more vertical and horizontal orientations in the environment than oblique (angled) orientations. This occurs in human-made environments (for example, buildings contain many horizontals and verticals) and also in natural

Figure 5.34 Three scenes that have different global image properties. See text for description.

Aude Oliva

Figure 5.35 In these two scenes from nature, horizontal and vertical orientations are more common than oblique orientations. These scenes are special examples, picked because the large proportion of verticals. However, randomly selected photos of natural scenes also contain more horizontal and vertical orientations than oblique orientations. This also occurs for human-made buildings and objects.

environments (trees and plants are more likely to be vertical or horizontal than slanted) (Coppola et al., 1998) (**Figure 5.35**). It is, therefore, no coincidence that people can perceive horizontals and verticals more easily than other orientations— the oblique effect we introduced in Chapter 1 (see page 11) (Appelle, 1972; Campbell et al., 1966; Orban et al., 1984). Another example of a physical regularity is that when one object partially covers another one, the contour of the partially covered object "comes out the other side," as occurs for the rope in Figure 5.16.

Yet another example is provided by the pictures in **Figure 5.36**. **Figure 5.36a** shows indentations created by people walking in the sand. But when we turn this picture upside down, as in **Figure 5.36b**, the indentations in the sand become rounded mounds. Our perception in these two situations has been explained by the **light-from-above assumption**: we usually assume that light is coming from above, because light in the environment, including the sun and most artificial light, usually comes from above (Kleffner & Ramachandran, 1992). **Figure 5.36c** shows how light coming from above and to the left illuminates an indentation, leaving a shadow on the left.

Figure 5.36d shows how the same light illuminates a bump, leaving a shadow on the right. Our perception of illuminated shapes is influenced by how they are shaded, combined with the brain's assumption that light is coming from above.

One of the reasons humans are able to perceive and recognize objects and scenes so much better than computer-guided robots is that our perceptual system is adapted to respond to physical characteristics of our environment, such as the orientation of objects and the direction of light. But this adaptation goes beyond physical characteristics. It also occurs because we have learned about what types of objects typically occur in specific types of scenes.

Semantic Regularities In language, *semantics* refers to the meanings of words or sentences. Applied to perceiving scenes, semantics refers to the meaning of a scene. This meaning is often related to what happens within a scene. For example, food preparation, cooking, and perhaps eating occur in a kitchen; waiting around, buying tickets, checking luggage, and going through security checkpoints happen in airports. **Semantic regularities** are the characteristics associated with activities that are common in different types of scenes.

One way to demonstrate that people are aware of semantic regularities is simply to ask them to imagine a particular type of scene or object, as in the following demonstration.

DEMONSTRATION | Visualizing Scenes and Objects

Your task in this demonstration is simple. Close your eyes and then visualize or simply think about the following scenes and objects:

1. An office
2. The clothing section of a department store
3. A microscope
4. A lion

Most people who have grown up in modern society have little trouble visualizing an office or the clothing section of a department store. What is important about this ability, for our purposes, is that part of this visualization involves details within these scenes. Most people see an office as having a desk with a computer on it, bookshelves, and a chair. The department store scene may contain racks of clothes, a changing room, and perhaps a cash register.

What did you see when you visualized the microscope or the lion? Many people report seeing not just a single object, but an object within a setting. Perhaps you perceived the microscope sitting on a lab bench or in a laboratory, and the lion in a forest or on a savannah or in a zoo. The point of this demonstration is that our visualizations contain information based on our knowledge of different kinds of scenes. This knowledge of what a given scene typically contains is called a **scene schema**.

An example of how a scene schema can influence perception is an experiment by Stephen Palmer (1975), which used

Figure 5.36 (a) Indentations made by people walking in the sand. (b) Turning the picture upside down turns indentations into rounded mounds. (c) How light from above and to the left illuminates an indentation, causing a shadow on the left. (d) The same light illuminating a bump causes a shadow on the right.

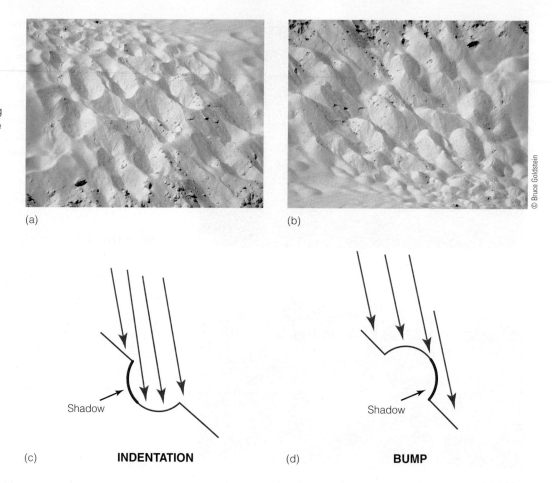

(a)

(b)

© Bruce Goldstein

(c) **INDENTATION**

(d) **BUMP**

Shadow

Shadow

stimuli like the picture in **Figure 5.37**. Palmer first presented a context scene such as the one on the left and then briefly flashed one of the target pictures on the right. When Palmer asked observers to identify the object in the target picture, they correctly identified an object like the loaf of bread (which is appropriate to the kitchen scene) 80 percent of the time, but correctly identified the mailbox or the drum (two objects that don't fit into the scene) only 40 percent of the time. Apparently,

Palmer's observers were using their knowledge about kitchens to help them perceive the briefly flashed loaf of bread.

The effect of semantic regularities is also illustrated in **Figure 5.38**, which is called "the multiple personalities of a blob" (Oliva & Torralba, 2007). The blob (a) is perceived as different objects depending on its orientation and the context within which it is seen. It appears to be an object on a table in (b), a shoe on a person bending down in (c), and a car and

Figure 5.37 Stimuli used in Palmer's (1975) experiment. The scene at the left is presented first, and the observer is then asked to identify one of the objects on the right.

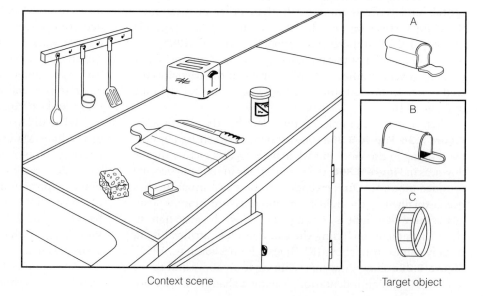

Context scene

Target object

A

B

C

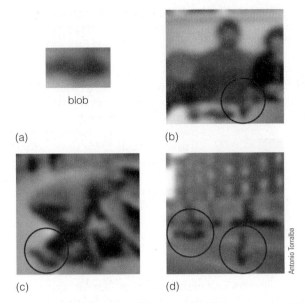

blob

(a)

(b)

(c)

(d)

Antonio Torralba

Figure 5.38 "Multiple personalities of a blob." What we expect to see in different contexts influences our interpretation of the identity of the "blob" inside the circles. (From Oliva & Torralba, 2007)

a person crossing the street in (d), even though it is the same shape in all of the pictures.

Although people make use of regularities in the environment to help them perceive, they are often unaware of the specific information they are using. This aspect of perception is similar to what occurs when we use language. Even though people easily string words together to create sentences in conversations, they may not know the rules of grammar that specify how these words are being combined. Similarly, we easily use our knowledge of regularities in the environment to help us perceive, even though we may not be able to identify the specific information we are using.

The Role of Inference in Perception

People use their knowledge of physical and semantic regularities such as the ones we have been describing to *infer* what is present in a scene. The idea that perception involves inference is nothing new; it was introduced in the 18th century by Hermann von Helmholtz (1866/1911), who proposed the *theory of unconscious inference*.

Helmholtz's Theory of Unconscious Inference
Helmholtz made many discoveries in physiology and physics, developed the ophthalmoscope (the device that an optometrist or ophthalmologist uses to look into your eyes), and proposed theories of object perception, color vision, and hearing. One of Helmholtz's contributions to perception was based on his realization that the image on the retina is ambiguous. We have seen that retinal ambiguity means that a particular pattern of stimulation on the retina can be caused by many different possible objects in the environment (see Figure 5.5). For example, what does the pattern of stimulation in **Figure 5.39a** represent? For most people, this pattern results in perception

of a blue rectangle in front of a red rectangle, as shown in **Figure 5.39b**. But as **Figure 5.39c** indicates, this display could have been caused by a six-sided red shape positioned in front of, behind, or right next to the blue rectangle.

Helmholtz's question was, "How does the perceptual system 'decide' that this pattern on the retina was created by overlapping rectangles?" His answer was the **likelihood principle**, which states that we perceive the object that is *most likely* to have caused the pattern of stimuli we have received. This judgment of what is most likely occurs, according to Helmholtz, by a process called **unconscious inference**, in which our perceptions are the result of unconscious assumptions, or inferences, that we make about the environment. Thus, we *infer* that it is likely that Figure 5.39a is a rectangle covering another rectangle because of experiences we have had with similar situations in the past.

Helmholtz's description of the process of perception resembles the process involved in solving a problem. For perception, the problem is to determine which object caused a particular pattern of stimulation, and this problem is solved by a process in which the perceptual system uses the observer's knowledge of the environment to infer what the object might be.

The idea that inference is important for perception has recurred throughout the history of perception research in various forms, from Helmholtz to the idea that regularities of the environment help determine perception to, most recently, a modern idea called Bayesian inference.

Bayesian Inference Two of the ideas we have described—(1) Helmholtz's idea that we resolve the ambiguity of the retinal image by inferring what is most likely, given the situation, and (2) the idea that regularities in the environment provide information we can use to resolve ambiguities—are the starting point for an approach to object perception called *Bayesian inference* (Geisler, 2008, 2011; Kersten et al., 2004; Yuille & Kersten, 2006).

Bayesian inference was named after Thomas Bayes (1701–1761), who proposed that our estimate of the probability of an outcome is determined by two factors: (1) the **prior probability**, or simply the **prior**, which is our initial estimate of the probability of an outcome, and (2) the extent to which the available evidence is consistent with the outcome. This second factor is called the **likelihood** of the outcome.

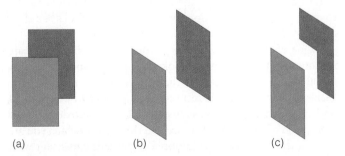

(a)

(b)

(c)

Figure 5.39 The display in (a) is usually interpreted as being (b) a blue rectangle in front of a red rectangle. It could, however, be (c) a blue rectangle and an appropriately positioned six-sided red figure.

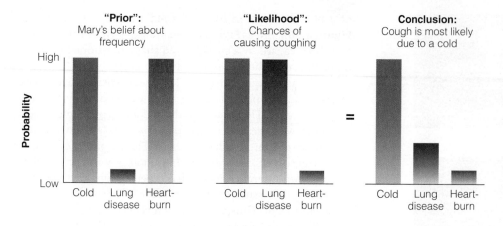

Figure 5.40 These graphs present hypothetical probabilities, to illustrate the principle behind Bayesian inference. (a) Maria's beliefs about the relative frequency of having a cold, lung disease, and heartburn. These beliefs are her *priors*. (b) Further data indicate that colds and lung disease are associated with coughing, but heartburn is not. These data contribute to the *likelihood*. (c) Taking the priors and likelihood together results in the conclusion that Charles's cough is probably due to a cold.

To illustrate Bayesian inference, let's first consider **Figure 5.40a**, which shows Maria's *priors* for three types of health problems. Maria believes that having a cold or heartburn is likely to occur, but having lung disease is unlikely. With these priors in her head (along with lots of other beliefs about health-related matters), Maria notices that her friend Charles has a bad cough. She guesses that three possible causes could be a cold, heartburn, or lung disease. Looking further into possible causes, she does some research and finds that coughing is often associated with having either a cold or lung disease, but isn't associated with heartburn (**Figure 5.40b**). This additional information, which is the *likelihood*, is combined with Maria's *prior* to produce the conclusion that Charles probably has a cold (**Figure 5.40c**) (Tenenbaum et al., 2011). In practice, Bayesian inference involves a mathematical procedure in which the prior is multiplied by the likelihood to determine the probability of the outcome. Thus, people start with a prior, then use additional evidence to update the prior and reach a conclusion (Wolpert & Ghahramani, 2009).

Applying this idea to object perception, let's return to the inverse projection problem from Figure 5.5. Remember that the inverse projection problem occurs because a huge number of possible objects could be associated with a particular image on the retina. So the problem is how to determine what is "out there" that is causing a particular retinal image. Luckily, we don't have to rely only on the retinal image, because we come to most perceptual situations with prior probabilities based on our past experiences.

One of the *priors* you have in your head is that books are rectangular. Thus, when you look at a book on your desk, your initial belief is that it is likely that the book is rectangular. The *likelihood* that the book is rectangular is provided by additional evidence such as the book's retinal image, combined with your perception of the book's distance and the angle at which you are viewing the book. If this additional evidence is consistent with your prior that the book is rectangular, the likelihood is high and the perception "rectangular" is strengthened. Further testing by changing your viewing angle and distance can further strengthen the conclusion that the shape is a rectangle. Note that you aren't

necessarily conscious of this testing process—it occurs automatically and rapidly. The important point about this process is that while the retinal image is still the starting point for perceiving the shape of the book, adding the person's prior beliefs reduces the possible shapes that could be causing that image.

What Bayesian inference does is to restate Helmholtz's idea that we perceive what is most likely to have created the stimulation we have received in terms of probabilities. It isn't always easy to specify these probabilities, particularly when considering complex perceptions. However, because Bayesian inference provides a specific procedure for determining what might be out there, researchers have used it to develop computer vision systems that can apply knowledge about the environment to more accurately translate the pattern of stimulation on their sensors into conclusions about the environment (also see Goldreich & Tong, 2013, for an example of how Bayesian inference has been applied to tactile perception).

TEST YOURSELF 5.2

1. What is a "scene," and how is it different from an "object"?
2. What is the evidence that we can perceive the gist of a scene very rapidly? What information helps us identify the gist?
3. What are regularities in the environment? Give examples of physical regularities, and discuss how these regularities are related to the Gestalt laws of organization.
4. What are semantic regularities? How do semantic regularities affect our perception of objects within scenes? What is the relation between semantic regularities and the scene schema?
5. Describe Helmholtz's theory of unconscious inference. What does this have to say about inference and perception?
6. Describe Bayesian inference. Be sure you understand the "sickness" example in Figure 5.40 and how Bayesian inference can be applied to object perception.
7. What is the relation between Helmholtz's idea of unconscious inference and Bayesian inference?

Connecting Neural Activity and Object/Scene Perception

We look around. We see objects arranged in space, which creates a scene. So far in our discussion of objects and scenes, we have focused on how perception is determined by aspects of *stimuli*. In fact, the words *neuron* and *brain* haven't appeared even once! We now consider the neural side of object and scene perception by continuing our discussion from Chapter 4 of how different types of perceptions are associated with specific areas in the brain. Figures 4.19 and 4.20 (pages 83, 84) showed how faces, places, and bodies have been linked to the fusiform face area (FFA), parahippocampal place area (PPA), and extrastriate body area (EBA). In addition, Figure 4.23 (page 85) showed how objects are also represented over a large area of the brain. We take up from this starting point by considering an experiment that demonstrates a connection between perceiving faces and places and activity in the FFA and PPA.

Brain Responses to Perceiving Faces and Places

We've seen that *looking at* a face or place causes activity in the FFA or PPA. But is there any evidence that *perceiving* a face or place is associated with activity in these areas? That evidence has been provided by a technique in which different images are presented to the left and right eyes.

In normal everyday perception, our two eyes receive slightly different images because the eyes are in two slightly different locations. These two images, however, are similar enough that the brain can combine them into a single perception. But if the two eyes receive totally different images, the brain can't combine the two images and a condition called **binocular rivalry** occurs, in which the observer perceives either the left-eye image or the right-eye image, but not both at the same time.[1]

Frank Tong and coworkers (1998) used binocular rivalry to connect perception and neural responding by presenting a picture of a person's face to one eye and a picture of a house to the other eye and having observers view the pictures through colored glasses, as shown in **Figure 5.41**. The colored glasses caused the face to be presented to the left eye and the house to the right eye. Because each eye received a different image, binocular rivalry occurred, so while the images remained the same on the retina, observers perceived just the face or just the house, and these perceptions alternated back and forth every few seconds.

The subjects pushed one button when they perceived the house and another button when they perceived the face, while

[1] This all-or-none effect of rivalry, in which one image is seen at a time (the house or the face), occurs most reliably when the image presented to each eye covers a small area of the visual field. When larger images are presented, observers sometimes see parts of the two images at the same time. In the experiment described here, observers generally saw either the house or the face, alternating back and forth.

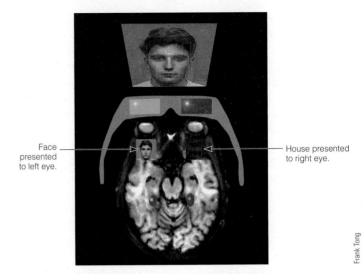

Frank Tong

Figure 5.41 Observers in Tong et al.'s (1998) experiment viewed the overlapping red house and green face through red–green glasses, so the house image was presented to the right eye and the face image to the left eye. Because of binocular rivalry, the observers' perception alternated back and forth between the face and the house. When the observers perceived the house, activity occurred in the parahippocampal place area (PPA) in the left and right hemispheres (red ellipses). When observers perceived the face, activity occurred in the fusiform face area (FFA) in the left hemisphere (green ellipse). (From Tong et al., 1998)

Tong used fMRI to measure activity in the subject's parahippocampal place area (PPA) and fusiform face area (FFA). When observers were perceiving the house, activity increased in the PPA (and decreased in the FFA); when they were perceiving the face, activity increased in the FFA (and decreased in the PPA). Even though the images on the retina remained the same throughout the experiment, activity in the brain changed depending on what the person was experiencing. This experiment and others like it generated a great deal of excitement among brain researchers because they measured brain activation and perception simultaneously and demonstrated a dynamic relationship between perception and brain activity in which changes in perception and changes in brain activity mirrored each other.

Spotlight on the Parahippocampal Place Area

When Tong's subjects perceived the house, their parahippocampal place area (PPA) became active. We saw in Chapter 4 that this area was named the "place area" by Epstein and Kanwisher (1998) because it responded to pictures of buildings, furnished rooms, and empty rooms. Some researchers have, however, asked whether the PPA really is a "place" area, as the name implies. Some of these researchers prefer the term *parahippocampal cortex (PHC)*, which identifies the location of the area in the brain without making a statement about its function.

One hypothesis for what the PPA/PHC does is Russell Epstein's (2008) **spatial layout hypothesis**, which proposes that the PPA/PHC responds to the *surface geometry* or *geometric layout* of a scene. This proposal is based partially on the fact that scenes cause larger responses than buildings. But Epstein doesn't think buildings are totally irrelevant, because the response to buildings is larger than for objects in general. Epstein explains this by stating that buildings are "partial scenes" that are associated with space, and concludes that the function of the PPA/PHC is to respond to qualities of objects that are relevant to *navigation through a scene* or *locating a place* (also see Troiani et al., 2014). When we discuss navigation through scenes in more detail in Chapter 7, we will consider more evidence linking the PPA/PHC to navigation and will see that other nearby brain areas are also involved in navigation.

But are "scenes" or "places" necessary for activation of the PPA/PHC? Sinead Mullally and Eleanor Maguire (2011) propose that the PPA/PHC is activated by any stimulus that results in a sense of three-dimensional space, even if there is no scene. They determined the connection between three-dimensional space and PPA/PHC activity by creating a list of 399 everyday objects that are typically found within an indoor environment and having subjects rate each object as "space defining" or "space ambiguous." *Space defining (SD) objects* are ones that, when seen or imagined in isolation, evoke a strong sense of surrounding space. *Space ambiguous (SA) objects* do not have this quality. Examples of SD objects are "a large oak bed" and "an antique rocking horse." Examples of SA objects are "a large cardboard box" and "a small white fan heater." Subjects were asked to imagine the objects while their brain activity was measured in an fMRI scanner. The results indicated that SD objects caused more activity in the PPA/PHC than SA objects. Thus, the PPA/PHC is activated not only by full scenes but by objects that create a sense of surroundings.

In another experiment, Peter Zeidman and coworkers (including Mullally and Maguire) (2012) showed that the PPA/PHC is activated by patterns like the foreground of the scene in Figure 5.27, which create an impression of three-dimensional space but contain no objects. These experiments support the idea that the PPA/PHC responds to the sense of 3-D space, no matter how that space is created.

Other researchers have emphasized other things. Aminoff and coworkers (2013) emphasize contextual relations—how related objects are organized in space, such as items that belong in a kitchen—as important for PPA/PHC responding. Others have presented evidence that the PPA/PHC is subdivided into different areas that may have different functions (Baldassano et al., 2013). Although discussion of the function of the PPA/PHC is continuing among researchers, we can conclude that it is important for perceiving space, whether the space is defined by single objects or the more extensive areas associated with scenes.

Neural Mind Reading

We've presented numerous examples of experiments in which stimuli—like houses, scenes, and faces—are presented and the brain response is measured. Some researchers have reversed the process, measuring the person's brain response and determining the stimuli that generated that response. They achieve this using a procedure we will call *neural mind reading*.

METHOD | Neural Mind Reading

Neural mind reading refers to using a neural response, usually brain activation measured by fMRI, to determine what a person is perceiving or thinking. As we saw in Chapter 4 (page 75), fMRI measures the activity in *voxels*, which are small cube-shaped volumes in the brain about 2 or 3 mm on a side. The pattern of voxels activated depends on the task and the nature of the stimulus being perceived. For example, **Figure 5.42a** shows eight voxels that are activated by a slanted black-and-white grating stimulus. Viewing a different orientation activates another pattern of voxels.

Figure 5.43 illustrates the basic procedure for neural mind reading. First, the relationship between orientation and the voxel pattern is determined by measuring the brain's response to a number of orientations (**Figure 5.43a**). Then these data are used to create a "decoder" program that can determine orientation based on the voxel activation pattern (**Figure 5.43b**). Finally, the decoder is tested by measuring brain activation as a person is looking at different orientations, as before, but this time using the decoder to predict the orientation the person is

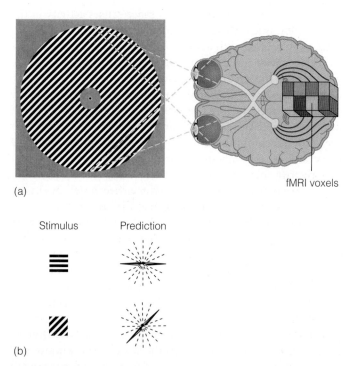

Figure 5.42 (a) Viewing an oriented grating like the one on the left causes a pattern of activation of voxels. The cubes in the brain represent the response of eight voxels. The differences in shading represent the pattern of activation of the orientation being viewed (b) Results of Kamitani and Tong's (2005) experiment for two orientations. The gratings are the stimuli presented to the observer. The line is the orientation predicted by the decoder. The decoder was able to accurately predict the orientations of all eight of the gratings tested.

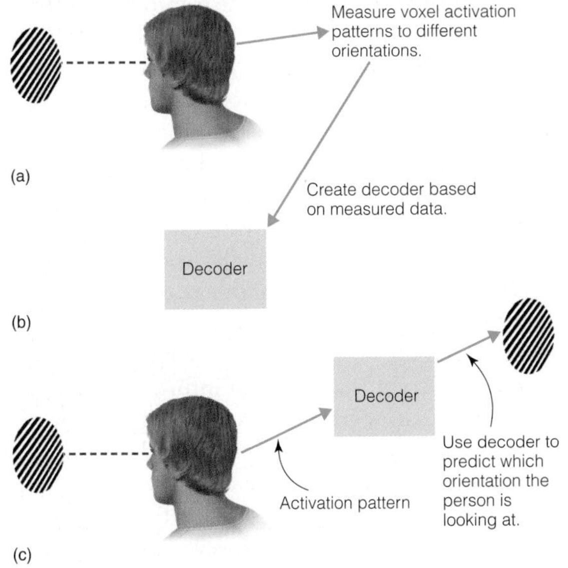
Measure voxel activation patterns to different orientations.
(a)
Create decoder based on measured data.
Decoder
(b)
Decoder
Use decoder to predict which orientation the person is looking at.
Activation pattern
(c)

Figure 5.43 Principle behind neural mind reading. (a) As the subject looks at different orientations, fMRI is used to determine voxel activation patterns for each orientation. (b) A decoder is created based on the voxel patterns collected in (a). (c) As a subject looks at an orientation, the decoder analyzes the voxel pattern recorded from the subject's visual cortex. Based on this voxel pattern, the decoder predicts the orientation that the subject is observing.

perceiving (**Figure 5.43c**). If this works, it should be possible to predict what orientation a person is looking at based on his or her brain activation alone.

When Yukiyasu Kamitani and Frank Tong (2005) used the procedure above, they were able to predict, based on the pattern of activity of 400 voxels in the visual cortex, the orientations of eight different gratings that a person was observing (**Figure 5.42b)**.

Creating a decoder that can determine from brain activity what orientation a person is perceiving was an impressive achievement. But what about complex stimuli like scenes in the environment? Expanding our stimulus set from eight grating orientations to every possible scene in the environment is quite a jump! But recent work toward creating such a "scene decoder" has had some success.

Thomas Naselaris and coworkers (2009) created a brain-reading device by developing two methods for analyzing the patterns of voxel activation recorded from visual areas of an observer's brain. The first method, called **structural encoding**, is based on the relationship between voxel activation and structural characteristics of a scene, such as lines, contrasts, shapes, and textures. Just as Kamitani and Tong's orientation decoder was calibrated by determining the voxel activation patterns generated by eight different orientations, Naselaris's structural decoder was calibrated by presenting a large number of images, like the ones in **Figure 5.44**, and determining how voxels responded to specific features of each scene, such as line orientation, detail, and the position of the image. These data

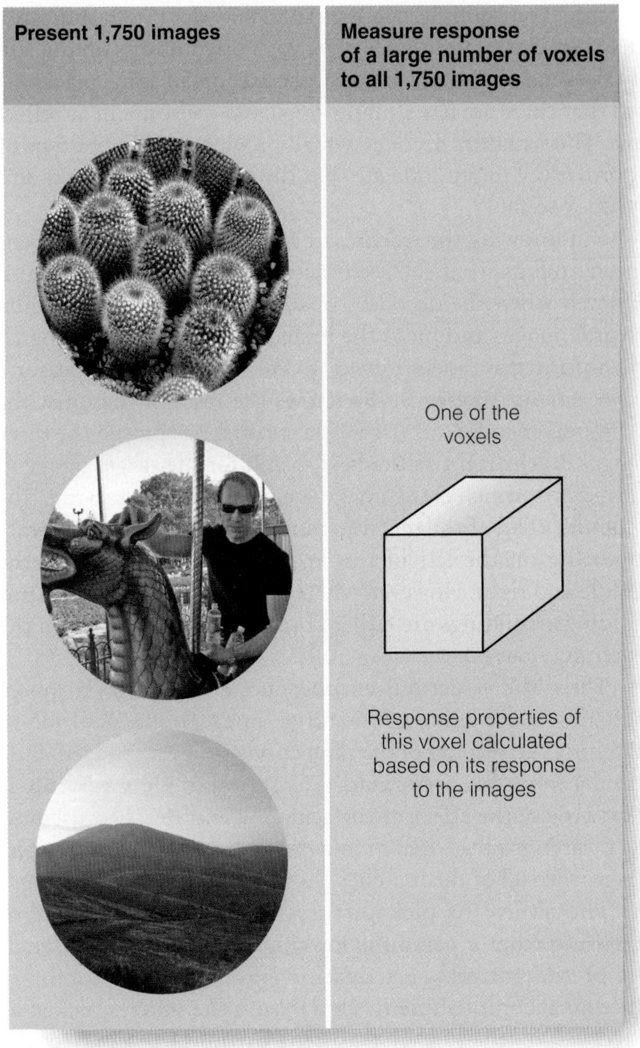
Present 1,750 images
Measure response of a large number of voxels to all 1,750 images
One of the voxels
Response properties of this voxel calculated based on its response to the images

© Bruce Goldstein

Figure 5.44 Calibration of Naselaris's structural decoder. Natural images are presented to a subject, and the way a large number of voxels respond to the features contained in each image is determined. Just three of the images and one voxel are shown here.

were used to calibrate the structural encoder so it could use patterns of voxel responses to predict the features of the image that the subject was viewing.

The second method for analyzing patterns of voxel activation, called **semantic encoding**, is based on the relationship between voxel activation and the *meaning* or *category* of a scene. The semantic encoder is calibrated by measuring the pattern of voxel activation to a large number of images that have previously been classified into categories such as "crowd," "portrait," "vehicle," and "outdoor." From this calibration, the relationship between the pattern of voxel activation and image category is determined. This semantic decoder then uses the pattern of voxel responses to make predictions about the type of scene the subject is viewing.

The information provided by the structural decoder and by the semantic decoder provides a clue to what the subject is seeing. For example, the structural encoder might indicate that there are straight lines of various orientations on the left of the scene, that there are curved contours in some places and that there are few straight or curved contours in another area. The semantic decoder, which provides a different type of information, might indicate that the subject is looking at an outdoor scene.

But knowing the features of a scene and the type of scene doesn't tell us what the scene actually looks like. This step is achieved when the decoder consults a database of 6 million natural images and picks the images that most closely match the information determined from analyzing the person's brain activity. **Figure 5.45a** shows the results when just the structural encoder was used. The encoder has picked the three images on the right as the best match for the target image in the red box, which is the image the person was observing. The structure of all of the matching images is similar, with objects appearing on the left of the image and open spaces in the middle and right. However, whereas the target image contains buildings, buildings are either absent or difficult to see in the matching images.

Thus, the structural encoder alone does a good job of matching the *structure* of the target image, but a poor job of matching the *meaning* of the target image. Adding the semantic encoder improves performance, as shown in **Figure 5.45b**. It is easy to see the effect of the semantic encoder, because now the meanings of the match images are much closer to the test image, with all of the matches showing the sides of buildings.

The ability to pick pictures that come this close to matching what a person is looking at, based only on analysis of the pattern of activation of the person's brain, is quite an accomplishment. One reason the images picked as matches are not exactly the same as the target is that the target images are not contained in the 6-million-picture database of images from which the encoder selected. Eventually, according to Naselaris, much larger image databases will result in matches that are much closer to the target. Accuracy will also increase as we learn more about how the neural activity of various areas of the brain represents the characteristics of environmental scenes.

Of course, the ultimate decoder won't need to compare its output to huge image databases. It will just analyze the voxel activation patterns and recreate the image of the scene. Presently, there is only one "decoder" that has achieved this, and that is your own brain! (Although it is worth noting that your brain does make use of a "database" of information about the environment, as we know from the role of regularities of the environment in perceiving scenes.) Achieving this ultimate decoder in the laboratory falls into the category of the "science project" described at the beginning of this book (see page 3) and is still far from being achieved. However, the decoders that presently exist are amazing achievements, which only recently might have been classified as "science fiction."

SOMETHING TO CONSIDER:
Are Faces Special?

Having described perceptual organization and how we perceive objects and scenes, we now focus on one specific type of object: faces. Why should faces get their own section? The answer to this question is, as the title of this section implies, that there is something special about faces. A number of things lead to this conclusion. First, faces are pervasive in the environment. Unless you avoid people, faces are everywhere. But what makes them special is that they are important sources of information. Faces establish a person's identity, which is important for social interactions (who is the person who just said hello to me?) and for security surveillance (checking people as they pass through airport security). Faces also provide information about a person's mood and where the person is looking, and can elicit evaluative judgments (the person seems unfriendly, the person is attractive, and so on).

Faces are also special because, as we've discussed in previous chapters, there are neurons that respond selectively to faces, and there are specialized places in the brain, such as the fusiform face area (FFA), that are rich in these neurons. Recently, Ming Meng and coworkers (2012) found that the FFA on the left and right sides of the brain appear to have different functions. This discovery made use of people's tendency to see faces in stimuli ranging from the rocks in Figure 5.31, to craters on the moon, to Jesus's face on a tortilla (Google "Jesus face on tortilla" for examples).

Meng and coworkers collected many images of non-face stimuli that resembled faces (**Figure 5.46a**), as well as images of real faces (**Figure 5.46b**). When they measured the FFA response to these stimuli, they found that the response of the left FFA depended on how closely the stimulus *resembled* a face, so increasing face likeness, as occurs from left to right

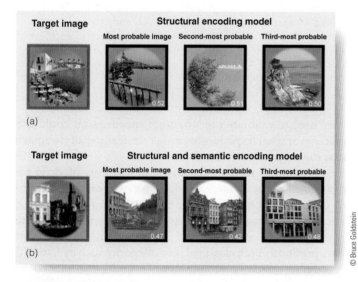

© Bruce Goldstein

Figure 5.45 (a) The subject viewed the image in the red square. The structural decoder picked the other three images as the best match from the database of 6 million images. (b) Another image viewed by the subject and the three images picked by structural and semantic decoders as the best matches from the database. (From Naselaris et al., 2009)

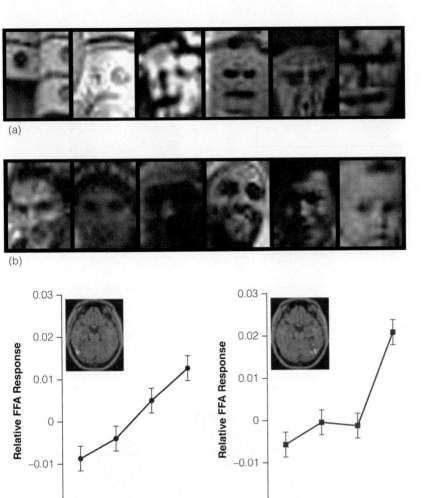

Figure 5.46 Stimuli for the Meng et al. (2012) experiment: (a) Non-face stimuli that resembled faces, ordered with the most face-like stimuli on the right. (b) Face stimuli. (c) Response of left FFA to non-face and face stimuli. NF_0 = no resemblance to face; NF_L = low resemblance; NF_H = high resemblance: F = Real faces. Response increases as stimuli become more face-like. (d) Response of right FFA to non-face and face stimuli. Response remains low for all non-face stimuli, but jumps to a higher level for the real face stimuli.

(The Royal Society Publishing)

in Figure 5.46a, caused increased response in the left FFA (**Figure 5.46c**). But the right FFA didn't respond to these non-face stimuli, no matter how closely they resembled a face. The right FFA only responded to the *real* faces (**Figure 5.46d**). Thus, the left FFA responds to how closely a stimulus *resembles* a face, and the right FFA responds to whether a stimulus actually *is* a face. Faces, therefore, have an area that responds *yes* or *no* to the question "Is this a face?"

Another special thing about faces is that when people are asked to look as rapidly as possible at a picture of either a face, an animal, or a vehicle, faces elicit the fastest eye movements, occurring within 138 ms, compared to 170 ms for animals and 188 ms for vehicles (Crouzet et al., 2010). Results such as these have led to the suggestion that faces have special status that allows them to be processed more efficiently and faster than other classes of objects (Crouzet et al., 2010; Farah et al., 1998).

One research finding that had been repeated many times is that inverting a picture of a face (turning it upside down) makes it more difficult to identify the face or to tell if two inverted faces are the same or different (Busigny & Rossion, 2010). Similar effects occur for other objects, such as cars, but the effect is much smaller (**Figure 5.47**).

Because inverting a face makes it more difficult to process configurational information—the relationship between features such as the eyes, nose, and mouth—the inversion effect has been interpreted as providing evidence that faces are processed holistically (Freire et al., 2000). Thus, while all faces contain the same basic features—two eyes, a nose, and a mouth—our ability to distinguish thousands of different faces seems to be based on our ability to detect the configuration of these features—how they are arranged relative to each other on the face.

But features are not totally irrelevant. Changing a photograph of a face into a negative image, as in **Figure 5.48**, makes it much more difficult to recognize; changing only the eyes back to positive greatly increases the ability to recognize the face (Gilad et al., 2009). This suggests that eyes are an important cue for facial recognition and may explain why it is difficult to recognize someone who is wearing a mask that covers just the eyes.

Finally, although the existence of areas of the brain that respond specifically to faces provides evidence for specialized modules in the brain, faces provide evidence for distributed processing as well, because there are areas throughout the brain that processes information associated with faces.

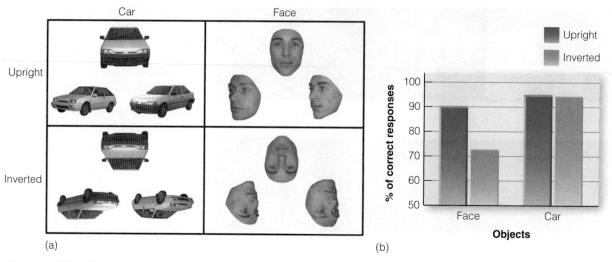

Figure 5.47 (a) Stimuli from Busigny and Rossion's (2010) experiment in which subjects were presented with a front view of a car or a face and were asked to pick the three-quarter view that was the same car or face. For example, the car on the right in the upper panel is the same car as the one shown in front-view above. (b) Performance for upright cars and faces (blue bars) and inverted cars and faces (orange bars). Notice that inverting the cars has little or no effect on performance but that inverting faces causes performance to decrease from 89 percent to 73 percent. (From Busigny & Rossion, 2010)

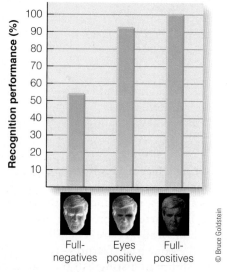

Figure 5.48 Ability to recognize faces of well-known people who were familiar to the subjects. Each type of image (negative and negative with eyes changed to positive) was shown to different groups of subjects, followed by the full-positive image. The subjects' task was to identify the face (Newt Gingrich in this example). Changing just the eyes in the negative image to positive causes a large increase in performance. (From Gilad et al., 2009)

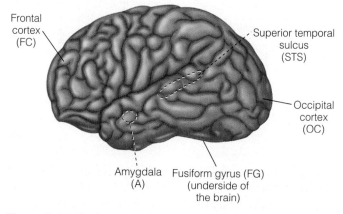

Figure 5.49 The human brain, showing some of the areas involved in perceiving faces. See text for the function of each area. Note that the labels indicate a general area of cortex but not the overall extent of an area. Also, the fusiform face area (FFA) is located in the fusiform gyrus, and the amygdala is located deep inside the cortex, approximately under the area indicated here.

The list below indicates some of these areas and what they do (see **Figure 5.49**):

- *Occipital cortex*: Initial processing of face information
- *Fusiform face area (FFA)*: Identification of faces (Grill-Spector et al., 2004)
- *Amygdala*: Emotional aspects of faces; reactions to facial expressions (Gobbini & Haxby, 2007; Ishai et al., 2004)

- *Superior temporal sulcus*: Evaluation of where a person is looking (Calder et al., 2007; Puce et al., 1998)
- *Frontal cortex*: Evaluation of a face's attractiveness (Winston et al., 2007)

Initial processing of faces occurs in the occipital cortex, which sends signals to the fusiform gyrus, where visual information concerned with identification of the face is processed (Grill-Spector et al., 2004). Emotional aspects of the face, including facial expression and the observer's emotional reaction to the face, are reflected in activation of the amygdala, which is located deep within the brain (Gobbini & Haxby, 2007; Ishai et al., 2004). Evaluation of where a person is looking is linked to activity in the superior temporal sulcus; this area is also involved in perceiving movements of a person's mouth as the person speaks (Calder et al., 2007; Puce et al., 1998) and general movement of faces (Pitcher et al., 2011). Evaluation of a face's attractiveness is linked to activity in the frontal area of the brain (Winston et al., 2007), and the pattern of activation across many areas of the brain differs in familiar faces compared to unfamiliar faces, with familiar faces causing more activation in areas associated with emotions (Natu & O'Toole, 2011). Faces, it appears, are special both because of the role they play in our environment and because of the widespread activity they trigger in the brain (also see page 86).

(also see page 86).

DEVELOPMENTAL DIMENSION Infant Face Perception

What do newborns and young infants see? In the Developmental Dimension in Chapter 2 (page 43), we saw that infants have poor detail vision compared to adults but that the ability to see details increases rapidly over the first year of life. We should not conclude from young infants' poor detail vision, however, that they can see nothing at all. At very close distances, a young infant can detect some gross features, as indicated in **Figure 5.50**, which simulates how infants perceive a face from a distance of about 2 feet. At birth, the contrast perceived between light and dark areas is so low that it is difficult to determine it is a face, but it is possible to see very high contrast areas. By 8 weeks, however, the infant's ability to perceive the contrast between light and dark perception has improved so that the image looks clearly facelike. By 3 to 4 months, infants can tell the difference between faces that look happy and those that show surprise, anger, or are neutral (LaBarbera et al., 1976; Young-Browne et al., 1977) and can also tell the difference between a cat and a dog (Eimas & Quinn, 1994).

Human faces are among the most important stimuli in an infant's environment. As a newborn or young infant stares up from the crib, numerous faces of interested adults appear in the infant's field of view. The face that the infant sees most frequently is usually the mother's, and there is evidence that young infants can recognize their mother's face shortly after they are born.

Using preferential looking in which 2-day-old infants were given a choice between their mother's face and a stranger's, Ian Bushnell and coworkers (1989) found that newborns looked at the mother about 63 percent of the time. This result is above the 50 percent chance level, so Bushnell concluded that the 2-day-olds could recognize their mother's face.

To determine what information the infants might be using to recognize the mother's face, Olivier Pascalis and coworkers (1995) showed that when the mother and the stranger wore pink scarves that covered their hairline, the preference for the mother disappeared. The high-contrast border between the mother's dark hairline and light forehead apparently provide important information about the mother's physical characteristics that infants use to recognize the mother (see Bartrip et al., 2001, for another experiment that shows this).

In an experiment that tested newborns within an hour after they were born, John Morton and Mark Johnson (1991) presented stimuli (see bottom of **Figure 5.51**) to the newborns and then moved the stimuli to the left and right.

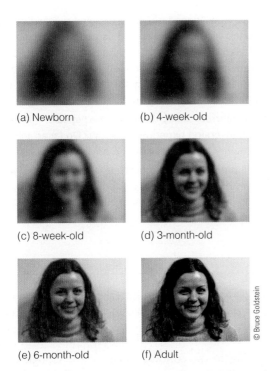

(a) Newborn   (b) 4-week-old

(c) 8-week-old   (d) 3-month-old

(e) 6-month-old   (f) Adult

© Bruce Goldstein

Figure 5.50 Simulations of perceptions of a mother located 124 inches from an observer, as seen by newborns and various ages. (Simulations courtesy of Alex Wade)

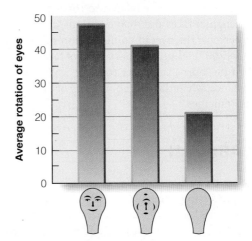

Figure 5.51 The magnitude of infants' eye movements in response to movement of each stimulus. The average rotation of the infants' eyes was greater for the facelike stimulus than for the scrambled-face stimulus or the blank stimulus. (Adapted from Morton & Johnson, 1991)

As they did this, they videotaped the infant's face. Later, scorers who were unaware of which stimulus had been presented viewed the tapes and noted whether the infant turned its head or eyes to follow the moving stimulus. The results in the graph in Figure 5.51 show that the newborns looked at the moving face more than at the other moving stimuli, which led Morton and Johnson to propose that infants are born with some information about the structure of faces.

But there is also evidence for a role of experience in infant face perception. Ian Bushnell (2001) observed newborns over the first 3 days of life to determine whether there was a relationship between their looking behavior and the amount of time they were with their mother. He found that at 3 days of age, when the infants were given a choice between looking at a stranger's face or their mother's face, the infants who had been exposed to their mother longer were more likely to prefer her over the stranger. The two infants with the lowest exposure to the mother (an average of 1.5 hours) divided their looking evenly between the mother and stranger, but the two infants with the longest exposure (an average of 7.5 hours) looked at the mother 68 percent of the time. Analyzing the results from all of the infants led Bushnell to conclude that face perception emerges very rapidly after birth, but that experience in looking at faces does have an effect.

Although the infant's ability to recognize faces develops rapidly over the first few months, these impressive gains are only a starting point, because even though 3- to 4-month-old infants can recognize some facial expressions, their ability to identify faces doesn't reach adult levels until adolescence or early adulthood (Mondlach et al., 2003, 2004; Grill-Spector et al., 2008).

One reason for this prolonged course of the development of face perception can be traced to physiology. **Figure 5.52** shows that the fusiform face area (FFA), indicated by red, is small in an 8-year-old child compared to the FFA in an adult (Golarai et al., 2007; Grill-Spector et al., 2008). In contrast, the parahippocampal place area (PPA), indicated by green, is similar in the 8-year-old child and the adult.

It has been suggested that this slow development of the specialized face area may be related to the maturation of the ability to recognize faces and their emotions, and especially the ability to perceive the overall configuration of facial features (Scherf et al., 2007). Thus, the specialness of faces extends from birth, when newborns can react to some aspects of faces, to late adolescence, when the true complexity of our responses to faces finally emerges.

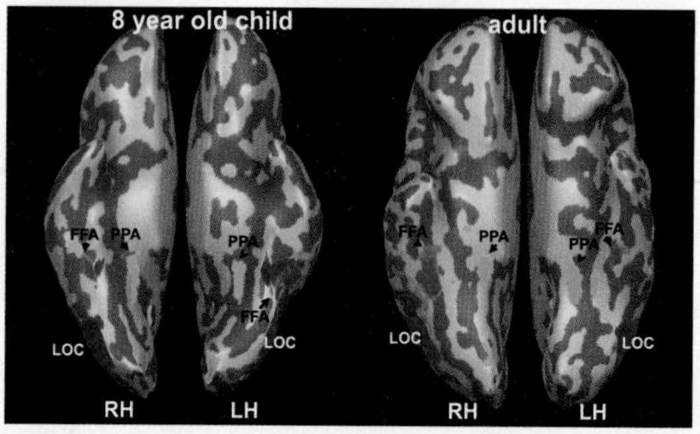

Figure 5.52 Face (red), place (green), and object (blue) selective activations for one representative 8-year-old and one representative adult. The place and object areas are well developed in the child, but the face area is small compared to the adult. (From Grill-Spector et al., 2008)

TEST YOURSELF 5.3

1. Describe Tong's experiment in which he presented a picture of a house to one eye and a picture of a face to the other eye. What did the results indicate?

2. What is the spatial layout hypothesis? How does this idea differ from Epstein and Kanwisher's proposal that the PPA is important for "place"?

3. How does Epstein explain the fact that buildings cause a larger PPA/PHC response than objects? What function does he assign to the PPA/PHC?

4. Describe Mullally and Maguire's (2011) experiment on space defining objects.

5. What is the general conclusion about the function of the PPA/PHC?

6. Describe how "decoders" have enabled researchers to use the brain's response, measured using fMRI, to predict what orientation or what picture a person is looking at. Be sure you understand Kamitani and Tong's (2005) orientation experiment and Naselaris et al.'s (2009) experiment that used both semantic and structural encoding.

7. Why is it correct to say that faces are "special"? What do the face inversion experiments show? Do faces activate the brain mainly in one place or in many different places?

8. What is the evidence that newborns and young infants can perceive faces? What is the evidence that perceiving the full complexity of faces does not occur until late adolescence or adulthood?

THINK ABOUT IT

1. Consider this situation: We saw in Chapter 1 that top-down processing occurs when perception is affected by the observer's knowledge and expectations. Of course, this knowledge is stored in neurons and groups of neurons in the brain. In this chapter, we saw that there are neurons that have become tuned to respond to specific characteristics of the environment. We could therefore say that some knowledge of the environment is built into these neurons. Thus, if a particular perception occurs because of the firing of these tuned neurons, does this qualify as top-down processing?

2. Reacting to the announcement of the Google driverless car (p. 94), Harry says, "Well, we've finally shown that computers can perceive as well as people." How would you respond to this statement?

3. Biological evolution caused our perceptual system to be tuned to the Stone Age world in which we evolved. Given this fact, how well do we handle activities like downhill skiing or driving, which are very recent additions to our behavioral repertoire?

4. Vecera showed that regions in the lower part of a stimulus are more likely to be perceived as figure (p. 103). How does this result relate to the idea that our visual system is tuned to regularities in the environment?

5. When you first look at **Figure 5.53**, do you notice anything funny about the walkers' legs? Do they initially appear tangled? What is it about this picture that makes the legs appear to be perceptually organized in that way? Can you relate your perception to any of the laws of perceptual organization? To cognitive processes based on assumptions or past experience? (pp. 100, 108)

Answers for Figure 5.8

Will Smith, Taylor Swift, Barak Obama, Hillary Clinton, Jackie Chan, Ben Affleck, Oprah Winfrey

Charles Feil

Figure 5.53 Is there something wrong with these people's legs? (Or is it just a problem in perception?)

Figure 5.54 The Dalmatian in Figure 5.11.

Figure 5.55 The faces in Figure 5.31. [The Forest Has Eyes by Bev Doolittle (1984)]

KEY TERMS

Apparent movement (p. 99)
Bayesian inference (p. 111)
Binocular rivalry (p. 113)
Border ownership (p. 103)
Figure (p. 102)
Figure–ground segregation (p. 102)
Gestalt psychologist (p. 98)
Gist of a scene (p. 107)
Global image features (p. 108)
Ground (p. 102)
Grouping (p. 98)
Illusory contour (p. 99)
Inverse projection problem (p. 96)
Light-from-above assumption (p. 109)
Likelihood principle (Helmholtz) (p. 111)

Neural mind reading (p. 114)
Perceptual organization (p. 98)
Perceptual segregation (p. 102)
Persistence of vision (p. 107)
Physical regularities (p. 108)
Principle of common fate (p. 102)
Principle of common region (p. 102)
Principle of good continuation (p. 100)
Principle of good figure (p. 100)
Principle of pragnanz (p. 100)
Principle of proximity (nearness) (p. 101)
Principle of similarity (p. 101)
Principle of simplicity (p. 100)
Principle of uniform connectedness
   (p. 102)

Principles of perceptual organization
   (p. 100)
Regularities in the environment (p. 108)
Reversible figure–ground (p. 103)
Scene (p. 107)
Scene schema (p. 109)
Segregation (p. 98)
Semantic encoding (p. 115)
Semantic regularities (p. 109)
Spatial layout hypothesis (p. 114)
Structural encoding (p. 115)
Structuralism (p. 98)
Unconscious inference (p. 111)
Viewpoint invariance (p. 97)
Visual masking stimulus (p. 107)

Where we direct our attention is affected by *salience*: physical characteristics of a scene that make certain things stand out. In this scene our attention is drawn to the tree because of its isolation and color. In this chapter we consider what attracts our attention, how attending enhances perception, and the consequences of not attending.

Charles Feil

CHAPTER 6

Visual Attention

CHAPTER CONTENTS

Scanning a Scene

What Directs Our Attention?
Visual Salience
Cognitiv e Factors

**What Are the Benefits
of Attention?**
Attention Speeds Responding
Attention Can Influence Appearance
Attention Can Influence Physiological
Responding

**Attention and Experiencing
a Coherent World**
Why Is Binding Necessary?
Feature Integration Theory

**What Happens When We Don't
Attend?**
Inattentional Blindness
Change Blindness
Is Attention Necessary for Perceiving
Scenes?

Distraction
Distraction and Task Characteristics
Attention and Perceptual Load

SOMETHING TO CONSIDER: Distracted
Driving

DEVELOPMENTAL DIMENSION:
Attention and Perceptual Completion

THINK ABOUT IT

Some Questions We Will Consider:

■ Why do we pay attention to some parts of a scene but not to others? (p. 127)

■ Does paying attention to an object change its appearance? (p. 132)

■ Do we have to pay attention to something to perceive it? (p. 138)

■ How does distraction affect driving? (p. 143)

We have come a long way from Chapter 1, when we described light entering the eye at the very beginning of the perceptual process. By Chapter 4, we had reached areas in the cortex that are specialized for perceiving faces, places, and bodies and explored the role of networks in determining perception. Chapter 5 continued where Chapter 4 left off by considering objects and scenes and by introducing the idea that perception is an active process that involves making inferences based on knowledge gained from a lifetime of experiencing the environment.

This chapter continues our journey into "real world" perception by focusing on the idea that we don't just passively sit there as stimuli create images of objects or scenes in our eyes. Instead, we direct our attention toward specific objects or locations within a scene and ignore other objects or locations. This process of focusing on specific objects while ignoring others is the process of **attention**. We will see, however, that attention is far more than just "looking around" at things. The act of attending not only brings an object into view; it enhances the processing of that object and therefore our perception of the object.

The effects of attention on perception were described in the 19th century by William James (1842–1910), the first professor of psychology at Harvard. James relied not on the results of experiments but rather on his own personal observations when making statements such as the following description of attention, from his 1890 textbook *Principles of Psychology*:

> Millions of items . . . are present to my senses which never properly enter my experience. Why? Because they have no interest for me. My experience is what I agree to attend to. . . . Everyone knows what attention is. It is the taking possession by the mind, in clear and vivid form, of one out of what seem several simultaneously possible objects or trains of thought. . . . It implies withdrawal from some things in order to deal effectively with others.

Thus, according to James, we focus on some things to the exclusion of others. As you walk down the street, the things you pay attention to—a classmate you recognize, the "Don't Walk" sign at a busy intersection, the fact that just about everyone except you seems to be carrying an umbrella—stand out more than many other things in the environment. The reason you are paying attention to those things is that saying hello to your friend, not crossing the street against the light, and your concern that it might rain later in the day are all important to you.

But there is also another reason for paying attention to some things and ignoring others. Your perceptual system has a limited capacity for processing information (Chun et al., 2011). Thus, to prevent overloading the system and therefore not processing anything well, the visual system, in James's words, "withdraws from some things in order to deal more effectively with others." One of the mechanisms for selecting certain things in the visual environment for enhanced processing is **visual scanning**—looking from one place to another. This scanning is necessary because there is only one place on the retina—the cone-rich fovea—that creates good detail vision.

Scanning a Scene

The following demonstration illustrates the importance of scanning for finding specific objects in a cluttered scene.

DEMONSTRATION | Looking for a Face in the Crowd

Your task in this demonstration is to find Jennifer Hudson and Robin Thicke in the group of people in **Figure 6.1**. Notice how long it takes to accomplish this task.

Unless you were lucky and just happened to look at Jennifer Hudson or Robin Thicke immediately, you probably had to scan the scene, checking each face in turn, before finding them. What you were doing is aiming your fovea at one face after another.

Each time you briefly paused on one face you were making a **fixation**. Fixations provide us with the opportunity to focus on a particular person (or object) so that we can recognize him or her (or it). When you moved your eyes to observe another face, you made a **saccadic eye movement**—a rapid jerky movement from one fixation to the next. These eye movements allow us to shift our attention and focus to other people and objects in a scene.

It isn't surprising that you were moving your eyes from one place to another, because you were consciously looking for particular targets (Hudson and Thicke). But it may surprise you to know that even when you are freely viewing an object or scene without searching for a target, you move your eyes about three times per second, and more than 200,000 times each day. This rapid scanning is shown in **Figure 6.2**, which is a pattern of fixations (dots) separated by saccadic eye movements (lines) that occurred as a subject viewed a picture of the Trevi Fountain in Rome, Italy, for only 5 seconds.

Scanning involves **overt attention**—attention that involves looking directly at the attended object. Although we often look directly at the objects of our attention, objects can also be attended even when they are not fixated. **Covert attention** is attention without looking. Covert attention enables you to monitor the actions of that interesting man or woman sitting near you in class without staring. It is also an important part of many sports. Consider, for example, a basketball player who looks to the right but then suddenly throws a dead-on pass to a teammate he was covertly attending to off to the left.

We are constantly shifting our overt and covert attention to monitor what is going on in our environment. Throughout this chapter, we will consider both forms of attention. In the next section, we consider what determines where we attend.

Figure 6.1 Where is Jennifer Hudson? Where is Robin Thicke?

Kevin Mazur/WireImage/Getty Images

Figure 6.2 Scan path of a person freely viewing a picture. Fixations are indicated by the yellow dots and saccadic eye movements by the red lines. Notice that this person looked preferentially at areas of the picture such as the statues but ignored areas such as the water, rocks, and buildings.

One answer to that question, as suggested by James, is that we attend to what interests us. But, as we will now see, there are also other factors that determine where we attend.

What Directs Our Attention?

Where we direct our attention can be caused by an involuntary process, in which stimuli that stand out capture our attention, and by voluntary processes, in which attention is guided by our goals and intentions (Anderson et al., 2011). We first consider attention that is determined by stimuli that stand out because of their physical properties.

Visual Salience

Some things in the world draw our attention because they stand out against their backgrounds. For example, the man in the red shirt in **Figure 6.3** is conspicuous because his shirt's color starkly contrasts with the whites and pale blues worn by everyone else in the scene. Scene regions that are markedly different from their surroundings, whether in color, contrast, movement, or orientation, are said to have **visual salience**. Visually salient objects can attract attention, as you will see in the following demonstration.

DEMONSTRATION | Attentional Capture

Each shape in **Figure 6.4** at the top of the next page contains a vertical or horizontal line. Turn the page and determine the orientation of the line inside the green circle before reading further.

It probably wasn't too difficult to find the green circle and to determine that it contains a horizontal line. But did you look at the red diamond first? Most people do. The question is, why

Figure 6.3 The red shirt is visually salient because it is bright and contrasts with its surroundings.

would they do so? You were asked to find a green circle, and the red diamond is neither green nor a circle. Regardless, people attend to the red diamond because it is highly salient, and salient items attract people's attention (Theeuwes, 1992). Researchers use the term **attentional capture** to describe situations like this, in which properties of a stimulus grab attention, seemingly against a person's will. Even though attentional capture can distract us from what we want to be doing, it is an important means of directing attention. Conspicuous stimuli like sudden movement or loud sounds can capture our attention to warn us of something dangerous like an animal or object moving rapidly toward us.

To investigate how visual salience influences attention in scenes that do not contain a single salient object, researchers have developed an approach in which they analyze characteristics

Figure 6.4. An example of attentional capture: When subjects are instructed to find the green circle, they often look at the red diamond first. (Adapted from Theeuwes, J. (1992). Perceptual selectivity for color and form. *Perception & Psychophysics, 51,* 599-606. Figure 1, p. 601)

(a) Visual scene

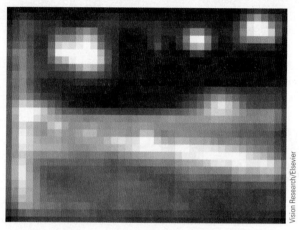

(b) Saliency map

Figure 6.5 (a) A visual scene. (b) Saliency map of the scene determined by analyzing the color, contrast, and orientations in the scene. Lighter areas indicate greater salience. (Adapted from Parkhurst et al., 2002)

such as color, orientation, and intensity at each location in a scene and combine these values to create a **saliency map** of the scene. A saliency map reveals which regions are visually different from the rest of the scene (Itti & Koch, 2000; Parkhurst et al., 2002; Torralba et al., 2006). **Figure 6.5** shows a scene (a) and its saliency map (b) as determined by Derrick Parkhurst and coworkers (2002). Regions of greater visual salience are denoted by brighter regions in the saliency map. Notice how the surf in **Figure 6.5a** is indicated as particularly salient in **Figure 6.5b**. This is because the surf constitutes an abrupt change in color, brightness, and texture relative to the sky, beach, and ocean. The clouds in the sky and the island on the horizon are also salient for similar reasons. When Parkhurst calculated saliency maps for a number of pictures and then measured observers' fixations as they observed the pictures, he found that the first few fixations were more likely to occur on high-saliency areas. After the first few fixations, however, scanning begins to be influenced by cognitive processes that depend on cognitive factors related to an observer's knowledge, goals, interests, and expectations. As we will see in the next section, these cognitive factors are influenced by the observer's past experiences in observing the environment.

Cognitive Factors

Our discussion of visual salience has indicated that shifts of attention can be a reaction to the visual properties of the stimulus. But what about William James's claim (page 125) that our experience is what we agree to attend to? Next, we consider three major determinants of attention that depend on the observer.

Scene Schemas Attention is influenced by *scene schemas*—an observer's knowledge about what is contained in typical scenes (see Chapter 5, page 109). Thus, when Melissa Võ and John Henderson (2009) showed observers pictures like the ones in **Figure 6.6**, observers looked longer at the printer in **Figure 6.6a**

than the pot in **Figure 6.6b** because a printer is less likely to be found in a kitchen. The fact that people look longer at things that seem out of place in a scene means that attention is being affected by their knowledge of what is usually found in the scene.

Another example of how cognitive factors based on knowledge of the environment influence scanning is an experiment by Hiroyuki Shinoda and coworkers (2001) in which they measured subjects' fixations and tested their ability to detect traffic signs as they drove through a computer-generated environment in a driving simulator. They found that the subjects were more likely to detect stop signs positioned at intersections than those positioned in the middle of a block, and that 45 percent of the subjects' fixations occurred close to intersections. In this example, the subjects used their knowledge of regularities in the environment (stop signs are usually at corners) to determine when and where to look for stop signs. You can probably think of many situations in which your knowledge about specific types of scenes might influence where you look. You probably know a lot, for example, about kitchens, college campuses, automobile instrument panels, and shopping malls, and your knowledge about where things

Vision Research/Elsevier

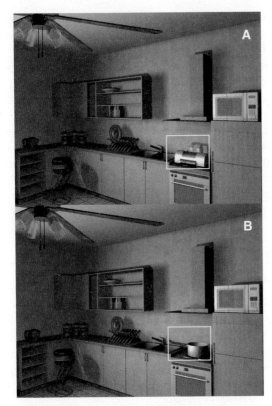

Figure 6.6 Stimuli used by Võ and Henderson (2009). Subjects spent more time looking at (a) the printer than at (b) the pot, shown inside the yellow rectangles (which were not visible to the subjects).

are usually found in these scenes can help guide your attention through each scene (Bar, 2004; Brockmole & Võ, 2010).

Observer Interests and Goals We can also show that where we look isn't determined only by saliency by checking the eye movements of the subject looking at the fountain in Figure 6.2. Notice that this person never looked at the bright blue water, even though it is very salient due to its brightness, color, and position near the front of the scene. Nor did this person look at the rocks, columns, windows, or several other prominent architectural features. Instead, this person focused on aspects of the fountain that might be more interesting, such as the statues. It is likely that the *meaning* of the statues has attracted this particular person's attention. It is important to note, however, that just because this person spent most of his or her time looking at the statues doesn't mean everyone would. Just as there are large variations between people, there are variations in how people scan scenes (Castelhano & Henderson, 2008b; Noton & Stark, 1971). Thus, another person, who might be interested in the architecture of the buildings, might look less at the statues and more at the building's windows and columns.

Attention can also be influenced by a person's goals. In a classic demonstration, Alfred Yarbus (1967) recorded subjects' eye movements while they viewed Ilya Repin's painting *An Unexpected Visitor* (**Figure 6.7a**). The eye movement records in Figure 6.6 b-d show how subjects looked at the picture when told to determine the ages of the people (**Figure 6.7b**), remember the clothes worn by the people (**Figure 6.7c**), or

(a) Unexpected, 1884-88 (oil on canvas), Repin, Ilya Efimovich (1844-1930)/Tretyakov Gallery, Moscow, Russia/Bridgeman Images; Lucs-kho; (b)-(d) James R. Brockmole

(a)

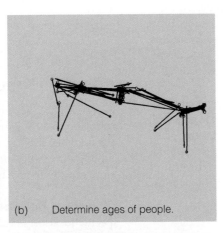

(b) Determine ages of people.

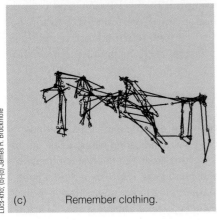

(c) Remember clothing.

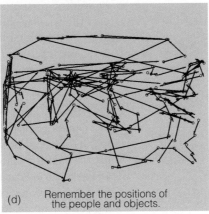

(d) Remember the positions of the people and objects.

Figure 6.7 Yarbus (1967) asked subjects to view the painting in (a) and recorded their eye movements while they had to (b) estimate the ages of the people, (c) remember the clothes worn by the people, or (d) remember the positions of all the people and objects in the room. The figure shows data collected by James Brockmole using Yarbus' original procedures combined with modern eye tracking technology. Results show that subjects' eye movements are strongly influenced by the task.

remember the positions of the people and objects in the room (**Figure 6.7d**). It is clear that the patterns of eye movements depended on the task subjects were given. Eye movements were concentrated on faces when the task was to determine ages, on bodies when the task was to remember clothing, and were more evenly distributed across the painting when the task was to remember the positions of all the people and objects.

More recent work has shown that people's intentions and goals can actually be decoded from their eye movements (Borji & Itti, 2014). For example, John Henderson and coworkers (2013) recorded the eye movements of subjects who either searched for a specific object in a scene or who tried to memorize the entire scene for a later test. After the experiment, the researchers were able to correctly guess the subjects' task on each trial simply by examining their eye movements. Clearly, as people's intentions and tasks change, they will change how they focus their attention on a scene.

Task-Related Knowledge Our goal in viewing scenes is not simply to perceive and understand objects and their arrangements—it is to prepare us for action (a topic we will consider in the next chapter). Our example in which subjects drove through a computer-generated environment looking for stop signs demonstrates this point. Instead of looking at pictures of stationary scenes, subjects were interacting with the environment. This kind of situation, in which people are shifting their attention from one place to another as they are doing things, occurs when people are moving through the environment, as in the driving example, and also when people are carrying out specific tasks.

Some researchers have focused, therefore, on determining where people look as they are carrying out tasks. Because most tasks require attention to different places as the task unfolds, it isn't surprising that the timing of when people look at specific places is determined by the sequence of actions involved in the task. Consider, for example, the pattern of eye movements in **Figure 6.8**, measured as a person was making a peanut butter sandwich. The process of making the sandwich begins with the movement of a slice of bread from the bag to the plate. Notice that this operation is accompanied by an eye movement from the bag to the plate. The person then looks at the peanut butter jar just before lifting the jar and looks at the top just

before removing it. Attention then shifts to the knife, which is picked up and used to scoop the peanut butter and spread it on the bread (Land & Hayhoe, 2001).

The key finding of these measurements is that the person's eye movements were determined primarily by the task. The person rarely fixated on objects or areas that were irrelevant to the task, and eye movements and fixations were closely linked to the action the person was about to take. Furthermore, the eye movement usually preceded a motor action by a fraction of a second, as when the person first fixated on the peanut butter jar and then reached over to pick it up. This is an example of the "just in time" strategy—eye movements occur just before we need the information they will provide (Hayhoe & Ballard, 2005; Tatler et al., 2011).

What Are the Benefits of Attention?

Having discussed some of the factors that determine where we attend, we now consider the consequences of attention. What happens when we attend to objects? The answer to this question may seem obvious: When we attend to something, we become aware of it. The benefits of attention, however, extend beyond creating awareness.

Remember William James's statement that attending to an object enables us to "deal effectively" with it? In line with that statement, researchers have found that attention enhances our response to objects (we respond faster to things that are located where we are attending), perception of objects (attention can make it easier to see an object), and physiological responding (attention can enhance the neural response to objects).

Attention Speeds Responding

We often pay attention to specific locations, as when paying attention to what is happening in the road directly in front of our car when driving. Paying attention informs us about what is happening at a location, and also enables us to respond more rapidly to anything that happens in that location.

Speeding Responding to Locations Attention to a specific location is called **spatial attention**. In a classic series of studies on spatial attention, Michael Posner and coworkers (1978) asked whether paying attention to a location improves a person's ability to respond to stimuli presented there. To answer this question, Posner used the **precueing** procedure shown in Figure 6.9.

METHOD | Precueing

The general principle behind a precueing experiment is to determine whether presenting a cue indicating where a test stimulus will appear enhances the processing of the test stimulus. The subjects in Posner and coworkers' (1978) experiment kept their eyes stationary throughout the experiment, always looking at the + in the display in Figure 6.9. They first saw an arrow

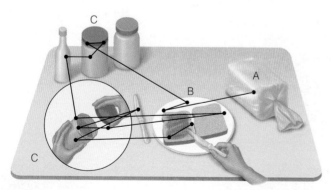

Figure 6.8 Sequence of fixations of a person making a peanut butter sandwich. The first fixation is on the loaf of bread. (From Land & Hayhoe, 2001)

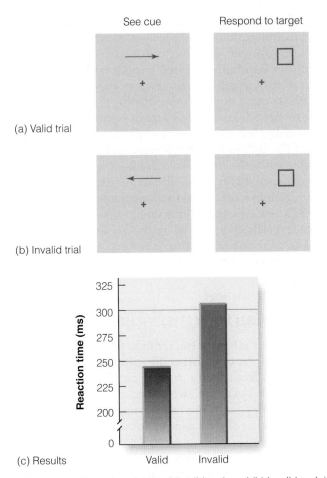

See cue | Respond to target

(a) Valid trial

(b) Invalid trial

(c) Results

Figure 6.9 Procedure for the (a) valid task and (b) invalid task in Posner and coworkers' (1978) precueing experiment. See text for details. (c) The results of the experiment. The average reaction time was 245 ms for valid trials but 305 ms for invalid trials.

cue (as shown in the left panels) indicating on which side of the target a stimulus was likely to appear. In **Figure 6.9a**, the arrow cue indicates that subjects should focus their attention to the right. (Remember, they do this without moving their eyes, so this is an example of covert attention.) The subjects' task was to press a key as rapidly as possible when a target square was presented off to the side (as shown in the right panel). The trial shown in Figure 6.9a is a *valid trial* because the square appears on the side indicated by the arrow cue. The location indicated by the arrow cue was valid 80 percent of the time, but 20 percent of the trials were invalid; that is, the arrow cue indicated that the target was going to be presented on one side but it actually appeared on the other side, as shown in **Figure 6.9b**. For this *invalid trial*, the arrow cue indicates that the subject should attend to the left, but the target is presented on the right.

The results of this experiment, shown in **Figure 6.9c**, indicate that subjects reacted more rapidly on valid trials than on invalid trials. Posner interpreted this result as showing that information processing is more effective *at the place where attention is directed*. This result and others like it gave rise to the idea

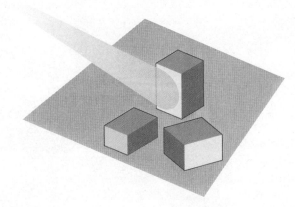

Figure 6.10 Spatial attention can be compared to a spotlight that scans a scene.

that attention operates like a spotlight or zoom lens that improves processing when directed toward a particular location (**Figure 6.10**; Marino & Scholl, 2005).

Speeding Responding to Objects In addition to attending to locations, we can also attend to specific objects in the environment. You see a person you know in a crowd and focus your attention on that person. You are looking at a table of items for sale at a flea market and focus your attention on one object after another. We will now consider some experiments that show (1) that attention can enhance our response to objects and (2) that when attention is directed to one part of an object, the enhancing effect of that attention spreads to other parts of the object.

Consider, for example, the experiment diagrammed in **Figure 6.11** (Egly et al., 1994). As subjects kept their eyes on the +, one end of the rectangle was briefly highlighted (**Figure 6.11a**). This was the cue signal that indicated where a target, a dark square (**Figure 6.11b**), would probably appear. In this example, the cue indicates that the target is likely to appear in position A, at the upper part of the right rectangle. (The letters used to illustrate positions in our description did not appear in the actual experiment.)

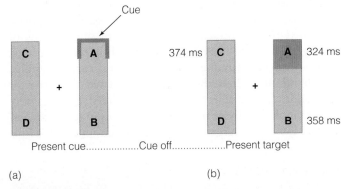

Figure 6.11 In Egley and coworkers' (1994) experiment, (a) a cue signal appears at one place on the display, then the cue is turned off and (b) a target is flashed at one of four possible locations, A, B, C, or D. Numbers are reaction times in ms for positions A, B, and C, when the cue appeared at position A.

Malcolm, G. L., & Shomstein, S. 2015. Object-based attention in real-world scenes. *Journal of Experimental Psychology: General, 144*, 257–263.

Figure 6.12 A stimulus used by Malcolm and Shomstein (2015). In the experiment the apple was presented first, followed by one of the light bulbs.

The subjects' task was to press a button when the target was presented anywhere on the display. The numbers indicate their average reaction times, in milliseconds, for three target locations when the cue signal had been presented at A. Not surprisingly, subjects responded most rapidly when the target was presented at A, where the cue had been presented. However, the most interesting result is that subjects responded more rapidly when the target was presented at B (reaction time = 358 ms) than when the target was presented at C (reaction time = 374 ms). Why does this occur? It can't be because B is closer to A than C, because B and C are exactly the same distance from A. Rather, B's advantage occurs because it is located *within the object* that was receiving the subject's attention. Attending at A, where the cue was presented, causes the maximum effect at A, but the effect of this attention spread throughout the object so some enhancement occurred at B as well. The faster responding that occurs when enhancement spreads within an object is called the **same-object advantage** (Marino & Scholl, 2005).

The same-object advantage also occurs in real-world scenes. George L. Malcolm and Sarah Shomstein (2015) demonstrated this by presenting subjects with photographs of scenes like the one in **Figure 6.12**, which initially appeared without the cue stimulus (the apple) or the target stimulus (the lightbulbs). After the subject had viewed the scene for 3 seconds, the cue object (the apple) appeared. Subjects were told to look directly at the apple as soon as it appeared, and then to look at the target (a lightbulb), which appeared 317 ms

after they had fixated the apple. Their task was to indicate, by pressing the correct button as rapidly as possible, whether the letter on the lightbulb was a *T* or an *L*.

Only one lightbulb appeared on each trial, and the key variable in this experiment is where it appeared. The target either appeared on the same object as the apple (on the arm of the right chair for the scene in Figure 6.12), or on a different object (on the arm of the left chair). Based on the results of the Egly experiment (Figure 6.11), you can probably guess what the result was: Subjects responded more rapidly when the target lightbulb was presented on the same object (826 ms reaction time) than when it was on the other object (872 ms), even though the targets were both the same distance from the apple. Based on this result, Malcolm and Shomstein concluded that when a person fixates on a location on an object, the entire object is selected for attentional processing.

Attention Can Influence Appearance

Does the fact that attention can result in faster reaction times show that attention can change the *appearance* of an object? Not necessarily. It is possible that the target stimulus always appears identical, but attention enhances the observer's ability to press the button quickly. To answer the question of whether attention affects an object's appearance, we need to do an experiment that measures the *perceptual response* to a stimulus rather than the *speed of responding* to the stimulus.

A study by Marissa Carrasco and coworkers (2004) was designed to measure the perceptual response to grating stimuli with alternating light and dark bars, like the ones in **Figure 6.13c**. She was interested in determining whether attention affected the perceived contrast between the bars, where *perceived contrast* refers to how different the light and dark bars appear. Carrasco's hypothesis was that attention would cause an *increase* in the perceived contrast of the gratings.

The procedure for Carrasco's experiment, shown in **Figure 6.13,** was as follows: (a) Subjects were instructed to keep their eyes fixed on the small fixation dot at all times; (b) a cue stimulus was flashed for 67 ms either on the left or on the right. Subjects were told that this cue had no relation to the stimuli that followed it; (c) a pair of gratings was flashed for 40 ms. The gratings were tilted in different directions (one to the left and one to the right).

The contrast between the bars of the gratings was randomly varied from trial to trial, so sometimes the contrast of the right grating was higher, sometimes the contrast of the left grating was higher, and sometimes the two gratings were identical. The subjects' task was to indicate on each trial whether

Figure 6.13 Procedure for Carrasco and coworkers' (2004) experiment. See text for explanation.

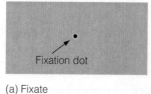

(a) Fixate

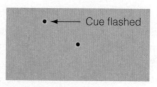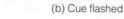

(b) Cue flashed

(c) Stimuli presented

the grating stimulus with the greatest contrast was tilted to the left or to the right. Thus, the subject first decided which grating had a higher contrast, and then indicated the orientation of that grating. Carrasco had subjects indicate orientation, rather than directly reporting how they perceived the gratings' contrast, to reduce the chances they might be influenced by any expectation they might have that attention might enhance the grating's perceived contrast.

Carrasco found that when two gratings were different, the attention-capturing dot had no effect. However, when two gratings were physically identical, subjects were more likely to report the orientation of the one that was on the same side as the flashed cue. Thus, when the two gratings were the same, the one that received attention appeared to have more contrast (see also Liu et al., 2009).

In addition to perceived contrast, a variety of other perceptual characteristics are affected by attention. For example, attended objects are perceived to be bigger, faster, and more richly colored (Anton-Erxleben et al., 2007; Fuller & Carrasco, 2006; Turatto et al., 2007). Thus, more than 100 years after William James suggested that attention makes an object "clear and vivid," researchers have provided experimental evidence that attention does, in fact, enhance the appearance of an object. (Also see Carrasco, 2011; Carrasco et al., 2006.)

From the experiments we have described, it is clear that attention can affect both how a person *responds* to a stimulus and how a person *perceives* a stimulus. It should be no surprise that these effects of attention are accompanied by changes in physiological responding.

Attention Can Influence Physiological Responding

In Chapter 3 (page 68), we described an experiment that showed that attention can cause a monkey's receptive field to shift toward the place where attention is directed (see Figure 3.38, page 69; Womelsdorf et al., 2006). A large number of experiments have shown that attention affects other aspects of physiological responding in a variety of ways. We begin by considering evidence that attention increases the neural response to an attended item.

Attention to Objects Increases Activity in Specific Areas of the Brain In an experiment by Kathleen O'Craven and coworkers (1999), subjects saw a face and a house superimposed (**Figure 6.14a**). You may remember the experiment by Tong and coworkers in which a picture of a house was presented to one eye and a picture of a face was presented to the other eye (see Figure 5.41, page 113). In Tong's experiment, presenting different images to each eye created binocular rivalry, so perception alternated between the two images. When the face was perceived, activation increased in the fusiform face area (FFA). When the house was perceived, activation increased in the parahippocampal place area (PPA).

In O'Craven's experiment, the superimposed face and house stimuli were presented to both eyes, so there was no binocular rivalry. Instead of letting rivalry select the image that is visible, O'Craven asked subjects to direct their attention to one stimulus or the other. For each pair, one of the stimuli was stationary and the other was moving slightly back and forth. When looking at a pair, subjects were told to attend to either the moving or stationary house, the moving or stationary face, or the direction of movement. As they were doing this, activity in their FFA, PPA, and MT/MST (an area specialized for movement that we will discuss in Chapter 8) was measured.

The results for when subjects attended to the house or the face show that attending to the moving or stationary *face* caused enhanced activity in the FFA (**Figure 6.14b**) and attending to the moving or stationary *house* caused enhanced activity in the PPA (**Figure 6.14c**). In addition, attending to the movement caused activity in the movement areas, MT/MST, for both moving face and moving house stimuli. Thus, attention to different types of objects influences the activity in areas of the brain that process information about that type of object (see also Çukur et al., 2013).

Attention to Locations Increases Activity in Specific Areas of the Brain What happens in the brain when people shift their attention to different locations while keeping their eyes stationary? Ritobrato Datta and Edgar DeYoe (2009; see also Chiu & Yantis, 2009) answered this question by measuring how brain activity changed when covert

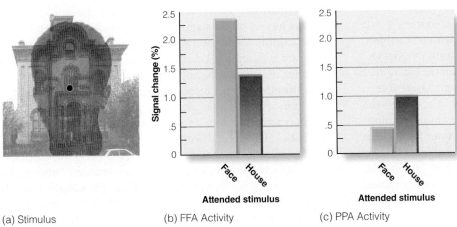

(a) Stimulus   (b) FFA Activity   (c) PPA Activity

Figure 6.14 (a) Superimposed face and house stimulus used in O'Craven and coworkers' (1999) experiment. (b) FFA activation when the subject attended to the face or the house. (c) PPA activation for attention to the face or the house. (Based on data from O'Craven et al., 1999)

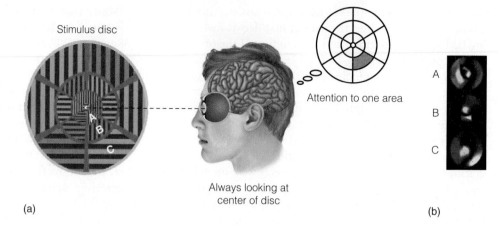

Figure 6.15 (a) Subjects in Datta and DeYoe's (2009) experiment directed their attention to different areas of this circular display while keeping their eyes fixed on the center of the display. (b) Activation of the brain that occurred when the subjects attended to the areas indicated by the letters on the stimulus disc. The center of each circle is the place on the brain that corresponds to the center of the stimulus. The yellow "hot spot" is the area of the brain that is maximally activated by attention. (Datta & DeYoe, 2009)

Stimulus disc

Always looking at center of disc

Attention to one area

(a)

(b)

attention was focused on different locations. They measured brain activity using fMRI as subjects kept their eyes fixed on the center of the stimulus shown in **Figure 6.15a** and shifted their attention to different locations within the display. Because the eyes did not move, the visual image on the retina did not change. Nevertheless, they found that patterns of activity within the visual cortex changed depending on where a subject was directing his or her attention.

The colors in the circles in **Figure 6.15b** indicate the area of brain that was activated when a subject directed his attention to the locations indicated by the letters on the stimulus in Figure 6.15a. Notice that the yellow "hot spot," which is the place of greatest activation, is near the center when the subject is paying attention to area A, near where he is looking. But as he shifts his attention to areas B and C, while keeping his eyes stationary, the increase in brain activity moves out from the center.

By collecting brain activation data for all of the locations on the stimulus, Datta and DeYoe created "attention maps" that show how directing attention to a specific area of space activates a specific area of the brain. These attention maps are like the retinotopic map we described in Chapter 4 (see Figure 4.1, page 74), in which presenting objects at different locations on the retina activates different locations on the brain. However, in Datta and DeYoe's experiment, brain activation is changing not because images are appearing at different places on the retina, but because the subject is directing his or her mind to different places in the visual field.

What makes this experiment even more interesting is that after attention maps were determined for a particular subject, that subject was told to direct his or her attention to a "secret" place, unknown to the experimenters. Based on the location of the resulting yellow "hot spot," the experimenters were able to predict, with 100 percent accuracy, the "secret" place where the subject was attending. This is similar to the "mind reading" experiment we described on page 114 of Chapter 5, in which brain activity caused by an oriented line was analyzed to determine what orientation the person was seeing (see Figure 5.43, page 115). In the attention experiments, brain activity caused by *where the person was attending* was analyzed to determine where the person was directing his or her mind!

Attention Synchronizes Neural Activity Between Areas of the Brain We've described fMRI experiments that show that paying attention to an object or to a location causes an increase in activation in specific areas of the brain. Other research, recording from single neurons, shows that paying attention to a stimulus causes an increase in firing in neurons that are activated by that stimulus (Colby et al., 1995). But attention has another physiological effect, which may be just as important as these increases in activity.

Attention also causes changes in the *relationship* between activity in different areas of the brain (Fries, 2005). A recent experiment by Conrado Bosman and coworkers (2012) demonstrated this by recording a response called the **local field potential (LFP)** from the monkey's cortex. Local field potentials, recorded from small disc electrodes placed on the surface of the brain, reflect electrical signals from thousands of neurons near the electrode.

Bosman presented a monkey that was looking at a fixation dot with two stimuli (see "Stimuli" in **Figure 6.16a**) and recorded from three locations in the monkey's brain: locations A and B in area V1, in the occipital cortex, and location C in area V4, in the temporal cortex (see "Recording Sites"). The arrows indicate that both A and B send signals to C. Bosman found that stimulus 1 caused an LFP response at location A in the cortex, and also at location C (because A sends signals to C). Stimulus 2 caused responses at locations B and C.

Bosman then asked what happens when the monkey, while keeping its eyes on the fixation dot, directs its attention to one of the stimuli. The answer might surprise you, because paying attention to stimulus 1 caused little change in the size of the response recorded at A, and shifting attention to stimulus 2 had little effect on the responses recorded at B. The reason for this "non-effect" is that attention generally has only a small effect on activity in area V1, where A and B are located (Buffalo et al., 2011; Luck et al., 1997).

The effect of attention, it turns out, isn't on the *size* of the responses recorded from V1, but on the *relationship* between the responses recorded from V1 and V4. **Figure 6.16b** shows LFPs recorded from A (in V1) and from C (in V4) when the monkey wasn't paying attention to stimulus 1. Notice that there is little

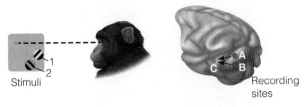

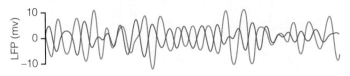

(a) Stimuli, monkey, and recording sites

(b) LFPs for sites A and C. No attention to stimulus 1

(c) LFPs for sites A and C. Attention to stimulus 1

Figure 6.16 In the Bosman et al. (2012) experiment (a) the monkey kept eyes fixed on the blue dot and paid attention to either stimulus 1, which caused LFP responding in A and C, or stimulus 2, which caused LFP responding in B and C. (b) LFP responses recorded from sites A (red) and C (green) when monkey was not attending to stimulus 1. (c) LFP responses recorded from A and C when monkey was attending to stimulus 1. Notice that the responses are more synchronized in (c). (Figure courtesy of Pascal Fries and Conrado Bosman)

relationship between the two responses. **Figure 6.16c** shows what happened when the monkey directed its attention to stimulus 1. Notice that the responses at A and C have become synchronized with each other—the hills and valleys in the signals recorded from A and C occur at about the same time.

Bosman used a statistical procedure to determine a measure called *coherence*, which indicates the degree to which two signals are synchronized. The results of these calculations, shown in **Figure 6.17**, indicate that when the monkey was paying attention to stimulus 1, there was synchronization between the LFPs recorded from A and C (red bar in **Figure 6.17a**). However, when the monkey shifted its attention to stimulus

2, the synchronization between A and C vanished and was replaced by synchronization between B and C (blue bar in **Figure 6.17b**).

Attention, therefore, enhances the communication between neurons in areas V1 and V4, by causing these neurons to fire with similar patterns. This effect is often referred to as "communication through coherence" (Fries, 2005). Similar synchronization also occurs between neurons higher up in the visual system, so attention causes physiological effects that spread throughout the visual system (Baldauf & Desimone, 2014). One of the central questions facing researchers is exactly how these far-reaching physiological effects are translated into the behavioral effects associated with attention (Baldauf & Desimone, 2014; Brunet et al., 2015; Womelsdorf et al., 2007).

TEST YOURSELF 6.1

1. What are the two main points that William James makes about attention? (Hint: what it is and what it does.) What are two reasons for paying attention to some things and ignoring others?

2. What does the demonstration that involved finding Jennifer Hudson and Robin Thicke tell us about attention and scanning?

3. What are fixations? Saccadic eye movements? Overt attention? How is overt attention measured? What is covert attention?

4. Describe the following factors that determine where we look: visual salience, scene schemas, observer goals, and task-related knowledge. Describe the examples or experiments that illustrate each factor.

5. What is spatial attention? Describe Posner's experiment on the speeding of responses to locations. Be sure you understand the precueing procedure, covert attention, and what Posner's results demonstrated.

6. Describe Egly's experiment and Malcolm and Shomstein's experiment on speeding response to objects. What is the same-object advantage?

7. Describe Carrasco's experiment that showed an object's appearance can be changed by attention. Why did Carrasco have subjects report the *orientations* of the gratings rather than the *contrast* of the gratings?

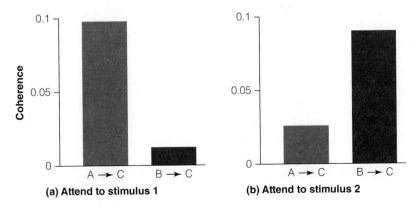

(a) Attend to stimulus 1

(b) Attend to stimulus 2

Figure 6.17 Coherence, which is a measure of synchronization, between A and C (red bar) and between B and C (blue bar): (a) when the monkey is attending to stimulus 1; (b) when attending to stimulus 2. (Based on data in Bosman, et al., 2012)

8. Describe O'Craven's experiment that showed how attention to faces or houses affects responding of areas specialized to respond to faces or houses.

9. Describe Datta and DeYoe's experiment on how attending to different locations activates the brain. What is an attention map? What was the point of the "secret place" experiment? Compare this experiment to the "mind reading" experiments described at the end of Chapter 5.

10. Describe Bosman's experiment that demonstrated that attention synchronizes responding in different areas of the brain.

Attention and Experiencing a Coherent World

We have seen that attention is an important determinant of what we perceive. Attention brings things to our awareness and can enhance our ability to perceive and to respond. We now consider yet another function of attention, one that is not obvious from our everyday experience. This function of attention is to help create **binding**, which is the process by which visual features—such as color, form, motion, and location—are combined to create our perception of a coherent object.

Why Is Binding Necessary?

We can appreciate why binding is necessary by remembering our discussion of modularity in Chapter 4, when we saw that separated areas of the brain are specialized for the perception of different qualities. In Chapter 4 we focused on the inferotemporal (IT) cortex, which is associated with perceiving forms. But there are also areas associated with motion, location, and color located at different places in the cortex.

Thus, when the person in **Figure 6.18** observes a red ball roll by, cells sensitive to the ball's shape fire in his IT cortex, cells sensitive to movement fire in his middle temporal cortex, and cells sensitive to color fire in other areas. But even though the ball's shape, movement, and color cause firing in different areas of the person's cortex, he doesn't perceive the ball as separated shape, movement, and color perceptions. He experiences an integrated perception of a "rolling red ball," with all of its features bound together in a coherent whole. The question of how an object's individual features become bound together, called the **binding problem**, is one of the most challenging research questions in perception, and several solutions to the problem have been proposed (see Feldman, 2013; Holcombe, 2009; Treisman, 1999). We will focus on *feature integration theory*, originally proposed by Anne Treisman (Treisman & Gelade, 1980; Treisman, 1986, 1988, 1999) and subsequently refined by others (e.g., Quinlan, 2003; Wolfe, 1994). Treisman's theory has proved to be one of the most influential approaches to understanding not just how the binding problem may be solved, but also how visual attention works.

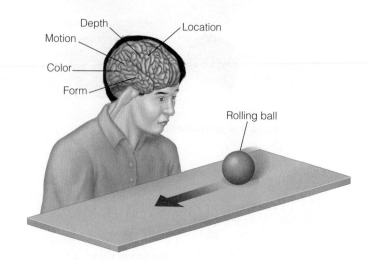

Figure 6.18 Any stimulus, even one as simple as a rolling ball, activates a number of different areas of the cortex. Binding is the process by which these separated signals are combined to create a unified perception.

Feature Integration Theory

Feature integration theory (FIT) tackles the question of how we perceive individual features as parts of the same object. We will begin by describing the theory's claims, and then we will review the empirical evidence supporting them.

According to FIT, the first step in object processing is the **preattentive stage** (the first box in the flow diagram in **Figure 6.19**). As its name implies, the preattentive stage occurs *before* we focus attention on an object. Because attention is not involved, researchers argue that this stage is automatic, unconscious, and effortless. In this stage, the features of objects are analyzed independently in separate areas of the brain and are not yet associated with a specific object. For example, during the preattentive stage, the visual system of the man observing the rolling red ball in Figure 6.18 would process the qualities of redness (color), roundness (form), and rightward movement (motion) separately. These independent features are then combined in a second stage of processing, called the **focused attention stage** (Figure 6.19). When the man in Figure 6.18 focuses his attention on the object in front of him, the independent features derived in the preattentive stage become linked together so that he becomes consciously aware of a red ball rolling to the right.

In this two-stage process, you can think of visual features as components of a "visual alphabet." At the very beginning

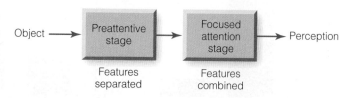

Figure 6.19 Flow diagram of Treisman's (1988) feature integration theory.

of the process, perceptions of each of these components exist independently of one another, just as the letter tiles in a game of Scrabble exist as individual units when the tiles are scattered at the beginning of the game. However, just as the individual Scrabble tiles are combined to form words, the individual features combine to form perceptions of whole objects.

The idea that an object is automatically broken into features may seem counterintuitive because we always see whole objects, not objects that have been divided into individual features. The reason we aren't aware of this process of feature analysis is that it occurs early in the perceptual process, before we have become conscious of the object. Thus, when you see this book, you are conscious of its rectangular shape, but you are not aware that before you saw this rectangular shape, your perceptual system analyzed the book in terms of individual features such as lines with different orientations.

FIT and Divided Attention Having described the claims of FIT, we now turn to the evidence supporting the theory. We begin with **divided attention** tasks, in which subjects are given multiple tasks to complete at once.

To provide initial perceptual evidence for FIT, Anne Treisman and Hilary Schmidt (1982) did an ingenious experiment to show that early in the perceptual process, features may exist independently of one another. Treisman and Schmidt's display consisted of four objects flanked by two black numbers (**Figure 6.20**). They flashed this display onto a screen for one-fifth of a second, followed by a random-dot masking field designed to eliminate any residual perception that might remain after the stimuli were turned off. Subjects were told to report the black numbers first and then to report what they saw at each of the four locations where the shapes had been. Thus, subjects had to divide their attention across two tasks: identifying numbers and identifying shapes. As you have no doubt experienced yourself, doing two things at once is often difficult, as our attention has to be split across more than one task. By dividing subjects' attention, Treisman and Schmidt reduced their ability to focus attention on the shapes.

Figure 6.20 Stimuli for Treisman and Schmidt's (1982) experiment. When subjects first attended to the black numbers and then to the other objects, some illusory conjunctions, such as "green triangle," occurred.

So what did subjects report seeing? Interestingly, on about one-fifth of the trials, subjects reported seeing objects that were made up of a combination of features from two different stimuli. For example, after being presented with the display in Figure 6.20, in which the small triangle is red and the small circle is green, they might report seeing a small red circle and a small green triangle. These combinations of features from different stimuli are called **illusory conjunctions**. Illusory conjunctions can occur even if the stimuli differ greatly in shape and size. For example, a small blue circle and a large green square might be seen as a large blue square and a small green circle. Illusory conjunctions also occur outside the world of shapes. For example, when a person sees words like "toothpaste" and "headache," they sometimes erroneously remember seeing "toothache."

According to FIT, these illusory conjunctions occur because the divided attention task reduces subjects' ability to focus their attention on the shapes, and this allows independent visual features to be combined incorrectly. In contrast, when Treisman and Schmidt instructed subjects to ignore the black numbers and focus all of their attention on the four shapes, illusory conjunctions were eliminated and all of the shapes were paired with their correct colors.

Perhaps you are thinking that the illusory conjunction effects just described are all rather subtle. After all, most of the time subjects correctly reported the shapes shown to them, even in the very controlled laboratory settings designed to elicit mistakes. Remember, however, that Treisman's task reduced subjects' ability to focus their attention on the shapes, but it did not eliminate it. Larger binding failures can be observed in patients with neurological disorders that severely hamper their ability to focus attention. As evidence of this, we describe the case of R.M.

R.M. is a patient who had parietal lobe damage that resulted in a condition called **Balint's syndrome**. A crucial characteristic of Balint's syndrome is an inability to focus and shift attention when multiple objects are present in a scene. According to feature integration theory, an inability to focus attention would make it difficult for R.M. to combine features correctly, and this is exactly what happened. When R.M. was presented with two different letters of different colors, such as a red T and a blue O, he reported illusory conjunctions such as "blue T" on 23 percent of the trials, *even when he was able to view the letters for as long as 10 seconds* (Friedman-Hill et al., 1995; Robertson et al., 1997). Clearly, the case of R.M. illustrates how a breakdown in the ability to attend can severely affect the ability to correctly combine the features of objects.

FIT and Visual Search Another approach to studying the role of attention in binding has used specialized types of visual search tasks. **Visual search** is something we do anytime we look for an object among a number of other objects, such as looking for Jennifer Hudson or Robin Thicke in a group of musicians or trying to find Waldo in a *Where's Waldo?* picture (Handford, 1997). A type of visual search called a **conjunction search** has been particularly useful in studying binding.

DEMONSTRATION | Searching for Conjunctions

We can understand what a conjunction search is by first describing another type of search called a feature search. Before reading further, find the horizontal line in **Figure 6.21a**. This is a feature search because you could find the target by looking for a single feature—"horizontal." Now find the horizontal green line in **Figure 6.21b**. This is a conjunction search because you had to search for a combination (or conjunction) of two or more features in the same stimulus—"horizontal" and "green." In Figure 6.19b, you couldn't focus just on horizontal because there are horizontal red lines and you couldn't focus just on green because there are vertical green lines. You had to look for the *conjunction* of horizontal and green.

Conjunction searches are useful for studying binding because finding the target in a conjunction search involves scanning a display in order to focus attention at a specific location. To test the idea that attention to a location is required for a conjunction search, a number of researchers have tested the Balint's patient R.M. and have found that he cannot find the target when a conjunction search is required (Robertson et al., 1997). This is what we would expect because of R.M's difficulty in focusing attention. R.M. can, however, find targets when only a feature search is required, as in Figure 6.21a, because attention at a location is not required for this kind of search. Feature integration theory therefore considers attention to be an essential component of the mechanism that creates our perception of objects from a number of different features.

FIT and Top-Down Control The feature integration approach involves mostly bottom-up processing because knowledge is usually not involved. In some situations, however,

Figure 6.22 Stimuli used to show that top-down processing can reduce illusory conjunctions. (Treisman & Schmidt, 1982)

top-down, or cognitive, processing can come into play. For example, when Treisman and Schmidt (1982) did an illusory conjunction experiment using stimuli such as the ones in **Figure 6.22** and asked subjects to identify the objects, the usual illusory conjunctions occurred; the orange triangle, for example, would sometimes be perceived to be black. However, when she told subjects that they were being shown a carrot, a lake, and a tire, illusory conjunctions were less likely to occur, and subjects were more likely to perceive the triangular "carrot" as being orange. In this situation, the subjects' knowledge of the usual colors of objects influenced their ability to correctly combine the features of each object. In our everyday experience, in which we often perceive familiar objects, top-down processing combines with feature analysis to help us perceive things accurately.

What Happens When We Don't Attend?

We have seen that paying attention affects both responding to stimuli and perceiving them. But what happens when we don't pay attention? One idea is that you don't perceive things you aren't attending to. After all, if you're looking at something over to the left, you're not going to see something else that is far to the right. But research has shown not only that we miss things that are out of our field of view, but that not attending can cause us to miss things even if we are looking directly at them. One example of this is a phenomenon called **inattentional blindness**.

Inattentional Blindness

In 1998, Arien Mack and Irvin Rock published a book titled *Inattentional Blindness*, in which they described experiments that showed that subjects can be unaware of clearly visible stimuli if they aren't directing their attention to them. In an experiment based on one of Mack and Rock's experiments, Ula Cartwright-Finch and Nilli Lavie (2007) presented the cross stimulus shown in **Figure 6.23**. The cross was presented for five trials, and the subjects' task was to indicate which arm of the briefly flashed cross was longer, the horizontal or the vertical. This is a difficult task because the cross was flashed rapidly, the arms were just slightly different in length, and the arm that was longer changed from trial to trial. On the sixth trial, a small outline of a square was added to the display (**Figure 6.23b**). Immediately after the sixth trial, subjects were asked whether they noticed if anything had appeared on the

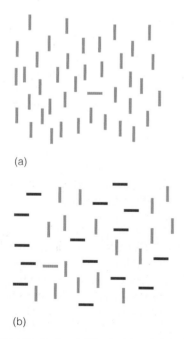

(a)

(b)

Figure 6.21 Find the horizontal line in (a) and then the green horizontal line in (b). Which task took longer?

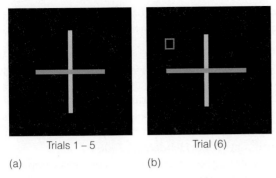

Trials 1 – 5   Trial (6)

(a)   (b)

Figure 6.23 Inattentional blindness experiment. (a) The cross display is presented for five trials. One arm of the cross is slightly longer on each trial. The subject's task is to indicate which arm (horizontal or vertical) is longer. (b) On the sixth trial, the subjects carry out the same task, but a small square is included in the display. After the sixth trial, subjects are asked if they saw anything different than before. (From Cartwright-Finch & Lavie, 2007; Lavie, 2010)

screen that they had not seen before. Out of 20 subjects, only 2 reported that they had seen the square. In other words, most of the subjects were "blind" to the small square, even though it was located right next to the cross.

This demonstration of inattentional blindness used a rapidly flashed geometric test stimulus. But similar effects occur for more naturalistic stimuli that are visible for longer periods of time. For example, imagine looking at a display in a department store window. When you focus your attention on the display, you probably fail to notice the reflections on the surface of the window. Shift your attention to the reflections, and you become less aware of the display inside the window.

The idea that attention can affect perception of overlapping scenes was tested in an experiment by Daniel Simons and Christopher Chabris (1999), who created a 75-second film that showed two "teams" of three players each. One team, dressed in white, was passing a basketball around, and the other was "guarding" that team by following them around and putting their arms up as in a basketball game (**Figure 6.24**). Subjects

were told to count the number of passes, a task that focused their attention on the team wearing white. After about 45 seconds, one of two events occurred. Either a woman carrying an umbrella or a person in a gorilla suit walked through the "game," an event that took 5 seconds.

After seeing the video, subjects were asked whether they saw anything unusual happen or whether they saw anything other than the six players. Nearly half of the observers—46 percent—failed to report that they saw the woman or the gorilla. This experiment demonstrated that when people are attending to one sequence of events, they can fail to notice another event, even when it is right in front of them (also see Goldstein & Fink, 1981; Neisser & Becklen, 1975).

Change Blindness

Following in the footsteps of inattentional blindness experiments, researchers developed another way to demonstrate how a lack of attention can affect perception. Instead of presenting several stimuli at the same time, they first presented one picture, then another slightly different picture. To appreciate how this works, try the following demonstration.

DEMONSTRATION | Change Detection

When you are finished reading these instructions, look at the picture in **Figure 6.25** for just a moment, and then turn the page and see whether you can determine what is different in **Figure 6.27**. Do this now.

Were you able to see what was different in the second picture? People often have trouble detecting the change even though it is obvious when you know where to look. (See the bottom of page 147 for a hint and then try again.) Ronald Rensink and coworkers (1997) did a similar experiment in which they presented one picture, followed by a blank field, followed by the same picture but with an item missing, followed

Figure 6.24 Frame from Simons and Chabris's (1999) experiment.

Figure 6.25 Stimulus for change-blindness demonstration. See text.

by a blank field, followed by the original picture, and so on. The pictures were alternated in this way until observers were able to determine what was different about them. Rensink found that the pictures had to be alternated back and forth a number of times before the difference was detected. This difficulty in detecting changes in scenes is called **change blindness** (Rensink, 2002).

The frequency with which change blindness occurs can be startling. For example, in one study (Grimes, 1996), 100% of observers failed to detect a one-fourth increase in the size of a building, 92% failed to detect a one-third reduction in a flock of birds, 58% failed to detect a change in a model's swimsuit from bright pink to bright green, 50% failed to notice that two cowboys had exchanged their heads, and 25% failed to notice a 180-degree rotation of Cinderella's Castle at Disneyland! If you find this hard to believe, you can reflect upon your own ability to detect changes while watching movies. Change blindness occurs regularly in popular films, in which some aspect of the scene, which should remain the same, changes from one shot to the next. Have you ever noticed that, in the *Wizard of Oz* (1939), Dorothy's (Judy Garland's) hair changes length many times from short to long and back again? Were you surprised while watching *Pretty Woman* (1990) when Vivian (Julia Roberts) began to reach for a croissant for breakfast that suddenly turned into a pancake? Were you confused watching a scene in *Harry Potter and the Sorcerer's Stone* (2001) when Harry (Daniel Radcliffe) suddenly changed where he was sitting during a conversation in the Great Hall? These changes in films, called **continuity errors**, have been well documented on the Internet (search for "continuity errors in movies").

One important conclusion that we can draw from demonstrations of change blindness is that our experience of a coherent world is sometimes a false reality. A lot can happen right before our eyes that completely escapes our awareness. The importance of attention (or lack of it) in noticing changes to objects and scenes has been established by showing that we can detect changes better in some situations than in others. For example, changes to objects that we typically attend to—those that are meaningful to us, that are surprising, or that are

important to our tasks and goals—are detected more quickly than changes to mundane or irrelevant objects:

- Smokers detect changes to smoking-related objects (e.g., lighters) better than changes to other household objects (Yaxley & Zwaan, 2005).
- Changes to objects appearing in odd locations (such as a printer in a kitchen, see Figure 6.6) are detected faster than changes to objects in their typical environments (Hollingworth & Henderson, 2000).
- When sorting blocks according to color in a computer-based task, sudden changes to task-relevant features (i.e., a block's color) are detected better than changes to task-irrelevant features such as a block's height (Droll et al., 2005).

Is Attention Necessary for Perceiving Scenes?

Inattentional blindness, change blindness, and a host of other experiments show that people can miss things that they aren't attending to, even when these events occur right before their eyes. But does the fact that attention is important for perception mean that it is always necessary? We will now consider two sets of experiments: one that concludes attention is not necessary for perceiving objects and another that comes to the opposite conclusion.

Evidence That Perception Can Occur Without Attention One reason it seems reasonable to suppose that attention may not be necessary for perceiving scenes is that people can identify the type of scene in a picture (like "forest," "seashore," or "classroom") after seeing the picture for less than a quarter of a second (Bronfman et al., 2014; Van Rullen & Thorpe, 2001). Fei Fei Li and coworkers (2002) took this as their starting point for an experiment using the **dual-task procedure**, in which subjects are required to carry out simultaneously a *central task* that demands attention and a *peripheral task* that involves making a decision about the contents of a scene.

Li's subjects looked at the + on a fixation screen (**Figure 6.26a**) and then saw the central stimulus, an array of

Figure 6.26 (a–c) Procedure for Li and coworkers' (2002) experiment. See text for details. (d) Results of the experiment. Performance is the percent correct when carrying out the central task compared to the percent correct when not carrying out the central task. Performance drops only slightly for the scene, but drops to near chance for the colored-disc task. (Li et al., 2002)

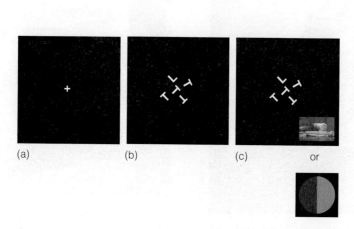

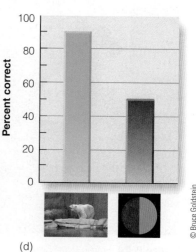

(d)

Figure 6.27 Stimulus for change-blindness demonstration. See text.

© Bruce Goldstein

five letters (**Figure 6.26b**). On some trials, all of the letters were the same; on other trials, one of the letters was different from the other four. The letters were followed immediately by the peripheral stimulus—either a disc that was half green and half red or a picture of a scene—flashed for 27 ms at a random position on the edge of the screen (**Figure 6.26c**).

The subjects' central task was to indicate if all of the letters in the central stimulus were the same, and their peripheral task was to indicate whether the scene contained an animal (for the picture) or whether the colored discs were red–green or green–red (for the discs). Even though subjects had to keep their attention focused on the letters in the middle in order to carry out the central letter task, their performance was 90 percent on the peripheral picture task, but only 50 percent on the peripheral colored-disc task (**Figure 6.26d**). Thus, performance on the colored discs was reduced to chance levels by the central task but stayed high for the pictures. Li concluded from this result that properties of scenes can be perceived with little or no attention (see also Tsuchiya & Koch, 2009). Similar conclusions have been drawn regarding perceiving faces, because people can determine the identity and gender of faces in the near-absence of attention (Reddy et al., 2004, 2006).

Evidence That Perception Requires Attention

The suggestion that object, face, and scene perception could occur in the absence of attention was surprising to many vision scientists and, as often occurs when a new discovery is made, other researchers worked to verify the conclusions. For example, Michael Cohen and coworkers (2011) wondered if Li's central letter task did not distract attention enough. To test this idea, Cohen created a letter–number task in which a series of letters and numbers were rapidly flashed (for example, G, N, W, 4, A, Y, 5, T) and subjects indicated how many numbers they saw. While they were doing this central task, subjects indicated if a picture flashed rapidly off to the side contained an animal or a vehicle. When the peripheral animal–vehicle task was presented alone, without the central task, subjects were correct

89 percent of the time. However, their performance dropped to 63 percent when their attention was distracted by the central letter–number task. From this result, Cohen concluded that "the perception of natural scenes does require attention" (p. 1170). Several other researchers, using a variety of methods, have come to the same conclusion (Cohen et al., 2012; Evans & Treisman, 2005; Mack & Clarke, 2012; Slagter et al., 2010; Walker et al., 2008). Proponents of the idea that perception is possible without attention might note, however, that even though performance on a range of tasks drops when attention is distracted from the scene, it typically remains above chance. Perhaps, then, there are some aspects of scene perception that require attention and some that don't.

The debate as to whether attention is required for perception will undoubtedly continue as further research is conducted. In fact, we raised this discussion, in part, to make the point that vision scientists don't have all the answers yet. There is still a great deal about perception that we do not understand, a fact we will continue to highlight through this book. For now, however, it is safe to conclude that attention is a fundamental component of perception, even if it might not always be necessary.

Distraction

Earlier in the chapter we noted that stimuli that are highly salient, such as a rapid movement or a loud noise, can capture our attention and possibly warn us of a dangerous situation that we want to avoid (see page 127). But sometimes when unattended stimuli attract our attention, they simply distract us from something we are doing. For example, a colorful pop-up ad for a dating service that suddenly appears on your computer screen might interfere with your search for a recently received email in your inbox; or an eye-catching billboard along the side of the highway might distract your attention from the traffic on the road in front of you (Forster & Lavie, 2008).

Stimuli that don't provide information relevant to the task at hand are **task-irrelevant stimuli**. Examples such as the computer pop-up or the billboard are *distracting* task-irrelevant stimuli, which can potentially decrease our performance of a task. It isn't surprising that the amount of distraction depends on properties of the distracting stimulus, with highly salient stimuli being more likely to cause distraction. However, the effect of a potentially distracting stimulus also depends on the characteristics of the task.

Distraction and Task Characteristics

The idea that the effect of an unattended stimulus depends on the nature of the task was suggested by Nilli Lavie (1995, 2005, 2010), who showed, in a number of experiments, that if the task is easy, then task-irrelevant stimuli have an effect on performance, but if the task is hard, task-irrelevant stimuli have little or no effect on performance.

An experiment by Sophie Forster and Lavie (2008) illustrates this result. The subjects' task was to respond as quickly

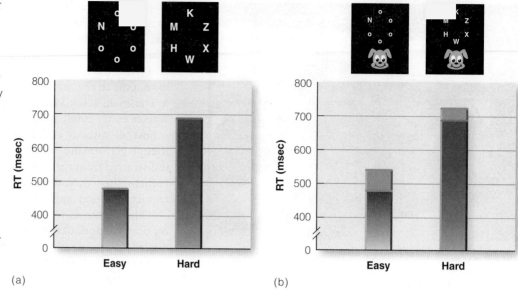

Figure 6.28 The task in Forster and Lavie's (2008) experiment was to indicate the identity of a target (X or N) in displays like the ones shown above as quickly as possible. (a) The reaction time for the easy condition like the display on the left, in which the target is accompanied by small o's, is faster than the reaction time for the hard condition, in which the target is accompanied by other letters. (b) Flashing a distracting cartoon character off to the side increases the reaction time for the easy task but has less effect for the hard task. The increase for each task is indicated by the blue extensions of the bars.

as possible when they identified a target, either X or N, in displays like the ones in **Figure 6.28a**. Subjects pressed one key if they saw the X and another key if they saw the N. This task is easy for displays like the one on the left in which the target is surrounded by just one type of letter, like the o's. However, the task becomes harder when the target is surrounded by different letters, as in the display on the right. This difference is reflected in the reaction times, with the hard task resulting in slower reaction times than the easy task. When a task-irrelevant stimulus is flashed off to the side, like the cartoon character in the displays in **Figure 6.28b**, responding slows for the easy task but is affected only slightly for the hard task (see also Biggs et al., 2012).

Attention and Perceptual Load

Lavie explains results such as the ones in Figure 6.28b in terms of her **load theory of attention**, which involves two key concepts: *perceptual capacity* and *perceptual load* (Lavie, 2005, 2010). **Perceptual capacity** refers to the idea that a person has a certain capacity that can be used for carrying out perceptual tasks. **Perceptual load** is the amount of a person's perceptual capacity needed to carry out a particular perceptual task. Some tasks, especially easy, well-practiced ones, have low perceptual loads; these **low-load tasks** use up only a small amount of the person's perceptual capacity. Other tasks, those that are difficult and perhaps not as well practiced, are **high-load tasks** and use more of a person's perceptual capacity. Lavie proposes that the amount of perceptual capacity that remains as a person is carrying out a task determines how susceptible the person is to being distracted by task-irrelevant stimuli.

This idea is illustrated in **Figure 6.29**. The circle in this figure represents a person's total perceptual capacity, and the shading represents the portion that is used up by a task. In

Figure 6.29a, only part of the person's resources are being used by a low-load task, leaving resources available for processing other stimuli that may be present, as was the case for the "easy" or low-load task in Forster and Lavie's experiment (Figure 6.28).

Figure 6.29b shows a situation in which all or most of a person's perceptual capacity is being used by a high-load task, such as the hard task in the experiment. When this occurs, no resources remain to process other stimuli, so irrelevant stimuli can't be processed and they have little effect on performance of the task.

One way to understand the idea that load is important is to think about situations in which you have been totally

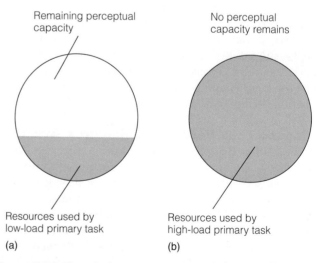

Figure 6.29 The rationale for the idea that (a) low-load tasks that use few cognitive resources may leave resources available for processing unattended task-irrelevant stimuli, whereas (b) high-load tasks that use all of a person's cognitive resources don't leave any resources to process unattended task-irrelevant stimuli.

focused on something because it is either extremely interesting or difficult to carry out. Saying that such a situation demands your full attention is another way of saying that you are using all of your perceptual capacity and therefore are less likely to be distracted by task-irrelevant stimuli.

We can also apply Lavie's load theory to the phenomenon of inattentional blindness described earlier. Remember that when subjects had to decide which line in a display like Figure 6.23 was longer, only 10 percent of the subjects were aware of the small square presented near the cross. In terms of load theory, the difficult length estimation task was a high-load task that used up most of a person's perceptual capacity, so there were few resources left to detect the small unattended stimulus. However, when the task was turned into a low-load task by asking subjects to indicate which arm of the cross was green (horizontal or vertical), then 55 percent of the subjects reported seeing the unattended object (Cartwright-Finch & Lavie, 2007; Lavie, 2010).

SOMETHING TO CONSIDER:
Distracted Driving

Driving is a task that demands constant attention. Not paying attention because of drowsiness or involvement in other tasks can have disastrous consequences. The seriousness of driver inattention was verified by a research project called the 100-Car Naturalistic Driving Study (Dingus et al., 2006). In this study, video recorders in 100 vehicles created records of both what the drivers were doing and the view out the front and rear windows. These recordings documented 82 crashes and 771 near crashes in more than 2 million miles of driving. In 80 percent of the crashes and 67 percent of the near crashes, the driver was inattentive in some way 3 seconds beforehand. One man kept glancing down and to the right, apparently sorting through papers in a stop-and-go driving situation, until he slammed into an SUV. A woman eating a hamburger dropped her head below the dashboard just before she hit the car in front of her. One of the most distracting activities was pushing buttons on a cell phone or similar device. More than 22 percent of near crashes involved that kind of distraction.

In a laboratory experiment on the distracting effects of cell phones, David Strayer and William Johnston (2001) gave subjects a simulated driving task that required them to apply the brakes as quickly as possible in response to a red light. Doing this task while talking on a cell phone caused subjects to miss twice as many of the red lights as when they weren't talking on the phone (**Figure 6.30a**) and also increased the time it took them to apply the brakes (**Figure 6.30b**). Perhaps the most important finding of this experiment is that this decrease in performance occurred when subjects used either handheld or hands-free cell phones.

Taking into account results such as these, plus many other experiments on the effect of cell phones on driving, Strayer and

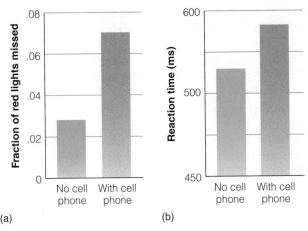

(a)   (b)

Figure 6.30 Results of Strayer and Johnston's (2001) cell phone experiment. When subjects were talking on a cell phone, they (a) missed more red lights and (b) took longer to apply the brakes.

coworkers (2013) concluded that talking on the phone uses mental resources that would otherwise be used for driving the car (also see Haigney & Westerman, 2001; Lamble et al., 1999; Spence & Read, 2003; Violanti, 1998). This idea that the problem posed by cell phone use during driving is related to the use of mental resources is an important one. The problem isn't driving with one hand. It is driving with fewer mental resources available to focus on driving.

Students often react to results such as this by asking what the difference is between talking on a hands-free cell phone and having a conversation with a passenger in the car. There is, in fact, some evidence that having a conversation with a passenger can have an adverse effect on driving, especially if the passenger isn't paying attention to current driving conditions (Strayer et al., 2013). But one way to appreciate the difference between talking on a cell phone and what often happens when talking to a passenger is to imagine the situation in which you place a call to your friend's cell phone. Your friend answers and you start talking. As far as you are concerned, you are just having a phone conversation. But unbeknownst to you, the person you called is driving and is in the process of negotiating his way through heavy traffic, or is perhaps reacting to a car that has just cut in front of him, traveling 70 miles per hour on the highway. The question to ask yourself is, would you be having the same conversation if you were a passenger sitting next to the driver? As a passenger, you would be aware of the traffic situation and would be able to react by pausing the conversation or perhaps warning the driver of upcoming hazards (sometimes called "backseat driving"!). It is also relevant to consider the social demands of phone conversations. Because it is generally considered poor form to suddenly stop talking or to pause for long periods on the phone, the person talking on the phone while driving might continue talking even when driving is becoming challenging.

An interesting phenomenon related to cell phone use is revealed by the results of a 2008 survey by Nationwide Mutual Insurance, which found that even though an overwhelming majority of people who talk on cell phones while driving consider themselves safe drivers, 45 percent of them reported that they had been hit or nearly hit by another driver talking on a cell phone. Thus, people identify talking on cell phones while driving as risky, but they think others are dangerous, not themselves (Nationwide Insurance, 2008).

Another idea about cell phones and driving that people sometimes express goes like this: "If I have the mental resources for driving and have some left over for a cell phone, what's wrong with doing both?" The answer to this question is that no matter how many years you have been driving without incident while talking on the phone, talking on the phone (and definitely texting!) may be using more of your mental resources than you realize. But most important, sometimes things happen suddenly while driving that require all of a person's mental resources *immediately*. With more people beginning to send text messages while driving, a study by the Virginia Tech Transportation Institute found that truck drivers who text while driving are 23 times more likely to cause a crash or near crash than truckers who are not texting (Hickman & Hanowski, 2012; Olson et al., 2009). Because of results like these, most states now have laws against texting while driving.

The main message here is that anything that distracts attention can degrade driving performance. And cell phones aren't the only attention-grabbing device found in cars. A 2004 article in the *New York Times* titled "Hi, I'm Your Car. Don't Let Me Distract You" notes that many cars have distraction-producing devices such as GPS systems and menu screens for computer controls (Peters, 2004). In the decade since that article appeared, the number of distracting devices available for cars has greatly increased. For example, voice-activated apps are available that enable drivers to make movie or dinner reservations, send and receive texts or emails, and make postings on social media. While this sounds like fun, it is important to note that a recent study from the AAA Foundation for Traffic Safety titled *Measuring Cognitive Distraction in the Automobile* found voice-activated activities to be more distracting, and therefore potentially more dangerous, than either hands-on or

Figure 6.31 Two bike riders in Amsterdam, using their phones while riding. Notice that the one on the right is not only holding his phone in his right hand, but has a cigarette between the fingers of his left hand. Bikers in Amsterdam share the road with cars and many other bikers. Cell phone use is illegal while driving a car in the Netherlands, but is not regulated for bike riders.

hands-free cell phones. The study concludes that "just because a new technology does not take the eyes off the road does not make it safe to be used while the vehicle is in motion" (Strayer et al., 2013).

As a postscript to this discussion of cell phones and driving, it is worth noting that using cell phones while traveling is not limited to automobiles. In cities where bikes are prevalent it is not uncommon to see riders using cell phones, as in **Figure 6.31**, which shows two of the many bikers in Amsterdam who are somehow managing to talk or read messages on their phones while negotiating their way through traffic. There are no statistics to indicate whether cell phone use while biking has affected accidents, but their use poses the question of whether effects might occur that are similar to what happens when cell phones are used during driving. What do you think?

DEVELOPMENTAL DIMENSION Attention and Perceptual Completion

Although newborns have limited visual acuity (see "Developmental Dimension: Infant Visual Acuity" in Chapter 2, page 43), they show by their looking behavior that they prefer to look at some objects more than others. They look more at contours and high contrasts, and exhibit a preference for faces (see "Developmental Dimension: Infant Face Perception" in Chapter 5, page 119). However, many attentional processes don't begin to emerge until after 3 months of age, and the full development of processes such as scanning the details of scenes continues well unto childhood and early adolescence (Amso, 2010).

Our concern here is not to survey the research on the development of attention but to consider a possible link between the early emergence of attentional processes and **perceptual completion**—the perception of an object as extending behind occluding objects, such as the horizontal boards that partially block the view of the three men in Figure 5.23 (see page 102). (This is also referred to as achieving *object unity*.)

When adults look at a scene like the one in Figure 5.23, they perceive the men's bodies as continuing behind the boards on which they are leaning. But would a young infant perceive the upper, middle, and lower parts of the men's bodies as separate units or as parts of single objects that continue behind the boards? Research on this question has used the *habituation procedure*, which is based on the following fact about infant looking behavior: When given a choice between a familiar stimulus and a novel one, an infant is more likely to look at the novel one (Fagan, 1976; Slater et al., 1984).

METHOD | Habituation

Because infants are more likely to look at a novel stimulus, we can create a preference for one stimulus over another by familiarizing the infant with one stimulus but not with the other. For this technique, which is called habituation, one stimulus is presented to the infant repeatedly, and the infant's looking time is measured on each presentation (**Figure 6.32**). As the infant becomes more familiar with the stimulus, he or she habituates to it, looking less and less on each trial, as indicated by the green circles in Figure 6.32.

Once the infant has habituated to this stimulus, we determine whether the infant can tell the difference between it and another stimulus by presenting a new stimulus. In Figure 6.32, the new stimulus is presented on the eighth trial. If the infant can tell the difference between the habituation stimulus and the new stimulus, he or she will exhibit dishabituation—an increase in looking time when the stimulus is changed, as shown by the open red circles. If, however, the infant cannot tell the difference between the two stimuli, he or she will continue to habituate to the new stimulus (because it will not be perceived as novel), as indicated by the open blue squares. Remember that the occurrence of dishabituation means that the second stimulus appears different to the infant from the habituation stimulus.

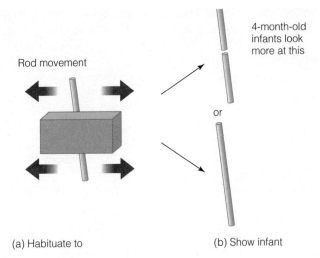

Figure 6.33 (a) Stimuli used in the habituation phase of the Kelman and Spelke (1983) experiment. A rod moves back and forth behind rectangular occluder. (b) Stimuli that are presented in the dishabituation phase of the experiment.

Habituation has been used to study the development of perceptual completion by presenting stimuli like the one in **Figure 6.33a**, which is a rod moving back and forth behind a rectangular occluder. Adults perceive the gray bars as part of a single rod that extends behind the rectangle. To determine how 4-month-old infants perceive this display, Philip Kellman and Elizabeth Spelke (1983) first habituated the infants to the rod moving back and forth behind a block, so the infants looked less and less at this stimulus. They then presented either two separated moving rods (top stimulus in **Figure 6.33b**) or a single longer moving rod (bottom stimulus in Figure 6.32b).

Remember that the principle of habituation is that after habituation to a stimulus, the infant looks longer at a new stimulus that is perceived as *different* from the habituation stimulus. Thus, looking longer at the *separated bars* on top would indicate that the infants perceived the display in Figure 6.32a as a *single bar* moving behind the rectangle. Kellman and Spelke obtained this result, and concluded that the infants had perceived a single rod moving behind the rectangle and therefore are capable of perceptual completion. This result did not occur, however, when the infant was habituated to a stationary rod and rectangle display. Thus, movement helped the 4-month-old infants infer that the bar extended behind the block.

If 4-month-olds perceive a moving object as continuing behind an occluding stimulus, can younger infants do this as well? When Alan Slater and coworkers (1990) repeated Kellman and Spelke's experiment with newborns, they found that when the newborns saw the moving rod during habituation and were then given the choice between the segmented or single rod, they looked more at the single rod. This suggests that they saw the moving rods as two separate units and not as a single rod extending behind the occluder. Apparently

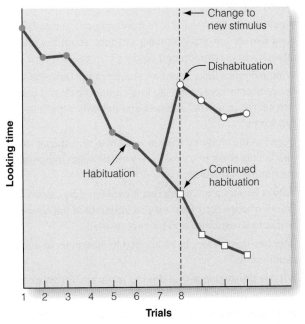

Figure 6.32 Possible results of a habituation experiment. See text for details.

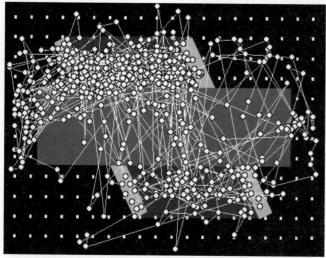

(a) Infants who perceived rod as continuing behind the occluder

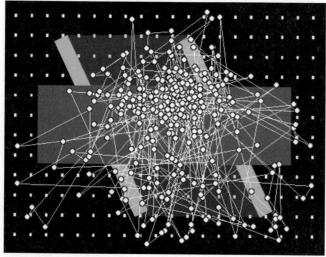

(b) Infants who did not perceive rod as continuing

Figure 6.34 How infants looked at a display during habituation, in which a rod moved back and forth behind a rectangular occluder. (a) Fixations for an infant who perceived the moving rod as a single object (a "perceiver"). (b) Fixations for an infant who did not perceive the moving rod as a single object (a "nonperceiver"). (From Johnson, Slemmer, & Amso, 2004)

newborns do *not* make the inference that 4-month-olds make about the moving display.

Thus, the capacity demonstrated at 4 months does not exist (or can't be measured using this particular procedure) at birth. But when does it appear? Scott Johnson and Richard Aslin (1995) helped determine the answer when they tested 2-month-olds and obtained results for some of the infants that were similar to those for the 4-month-olds. Apparently, the ability to use movement as a way to organize the perceptual world develops rapidly over the first few months of life.

To connect performance on perceptual completion tasks and attention, Johnson and coworkers (2004) first determined that at the age of 3 months, some infants perceived the moving

rod as continuing behind the occluder and some did not. They labeled the infants who demonstrated perceptual completion *perceivers* and those who did not, *nonperceivers*. They then determined the eye fixation patterns for the two groups. **Figure 6.34** shows eye fixation records measured during habituation for a perceiver (**Figure 6.34a**) and a nonperceiver (**Figure 6.34b**). The two rods in each figure indicate the left- and right-most positions of the moving rod.

Notice that the perceiver fixated mainly on the rod, whereas the nonperceiver fixated on the rectangular occluder. Eye movement records also showed that, as a group, perceivers made more horizontal eye movements than nonperceivers. The perceivers, therefore, tended to look at the rod and follow its movement, whereas the nonperceivers looked more at the stationary occluder and other parts of the display that were not related to perceiving the rod as extending behind the occluder. Based on these results and others, Johnson and coworkers (2008) concluded that the infants' ability to achieve perceptual completion is closely linked to the development of scanning patterns that enable them to actively explore the display and pick up the information necessary to infer that the two separated rods are actually one. Not surprisingly, there is a connection between how infants attend and what they perceive.

TEST YOURSELF 6.2

1. Describe the following two situations that illustrate how not attending can result in not perceiving: (1) inattentional blindness and (2) change detection.

2. Describe Li's experiment that shows that under certain conditions we can perceive qualities of things that we are not attending. How does the situation in Li's experiment differ from the situation in the change blindness experiments?

3. What are the two stages in feature integration theory? What does feature integration theory propose about the role of attention in perception and binding?

4. What evidence links attention and binding? Describe evidence that involves both illusory conjunctions and conjunction search in normal subjects and patients with Balint's syndrome.

5. Describe the study by Forster and Lavie that shows that the distracting effect of a task-irrelevant stimulus depends on the nature of the task.

6. How is Forster and Lavie's result explained by Lavie's load theory of attention? Be sure you understand the concepts of perceptual resources and perceptual load.

7. How has load theory been applied to inattentional blindness experiments?

8. What is the evidence that driving while talking on a cell phone or while texting is a bad idea?

9. What is perceptual completion? Describe the experiment that demonstrates the existence of perceptual completion in infants. What is the role of attention in determining perceptual completion?

THINK ABOUT IT

1. If salience is determined by characteristics of a scene such as contrast, color, and orientation, why might it be correct to say that paying attention to an object can increase its salience? (p. 127)

2. How is the idea of regularities of the environment that we introduced in Chapter 5 (see page 108) related to the cognitive factors that determine where people look? (p. 128)

3. Can you think of situations from your experience that are similar to the change detection experiments in that you missed seeing an object that became easy to see once you knew it was there? What do you think was behind your initial failure to see this object? (p. 139)

4. In describing the habituation procedure, it was stated that when given a choice between a familiar stimulus and a novel one, an infant is more likely to look at the novel one. But in the "Developmental Dimension" in Chapter 5, we saw that young infants tend to look more at a mother's face than at a stranger's face. Why do you think this would occur if infants usually tend to prefer looking at novel objects? (p. 145)

Hint for change detection demonstration on page 139: Pay attention to the sign near the lower left portion of the picture.

KEY TERMS

Attention p. 125
Attentional capture p. 127
Balint's syndrome p. 137
Binding p. 136
Binding problem p. 136
Change blindness p. 140
Conjunction search p. 137
Continuity errors p. 140
Covert attention p. 126
Dishabituation p. 145
Divided attention p. 137
Dual-task procedure p. 140
Feature integration theory (FIT) p. 136

Feature search p. 138
Fixation p. 126
Focused attention stage p. 136
Habituation p. 145
High-load tasks p. 142
Illusory conjunctions p. 137
Inattentional blindness p. 138
Load theory of attention p. 142
Local field potential (LFP) p. 134
Low-load tasks p. 142
Overt attention p. 126
Perceptual capacity p. 142
Perceptual completion p. 144

Perceptual load p. 142
Preattentive stage p. 136
precueing p. 130
Saccadic eye movement p. 126
Saliency map p. 128
Same-object advantage p. 132
Spatial attention p. 130
Task-irrelevant stimuli p. 141
Visual salience p. 127
Visual scanning p. 126
Visual search p. 137

How did Andrew McCutcheon time his jump so his glove met up with the ball at exactly the right moment? As we see in this chapter, the answer involves connections between perception and action that holds not just for spectacular athletic feats but also for everyday actions such as walking across campus or reaching across a table to pick up a cup of coffee.

CHAPTER 7

Taking Action

CHAPTER CONTENTS

**The Ecological Approach
to Perception**
The Moving Observer Creates
    Information in the Environment
Self-Produced Information
The Senses Do Not Work in Isolation
**Staying on Course: Walking
and Driving**
Walking
Driving a Car

Wayfinding
The Importance of Landmarks
The Brain's "GPS"
Individual Differences in
    Wayfinding
Acting on Objects
Affordances: What Objects Are
    Used For
The Physiology of Reaching
    and Grasping

Observing Other People's Actions
Mirroring Others' Actions in
    the Brain
Predicting People's Intentions
SOMETHING TO CONSIDER: Action-Based
Accounts of Perception
DEVELOPMENTAL DIMENSION: Imitating
Actions
THINK ABOUT IT

Some Questions We Will Consider:

- What is the connection between perceiving and moving through the environment? (p. 150)
- What is the connection between somersaulting and vision? (p. 151)
- How do neurons in the brain respond when a person performs an action and when the person watches someone else carry out the same action? (p. 163)

Serena straps on her helmet for a fast, thrilling, and perhaps dangerous ride. As a rider for the Speedy Delivery Package Service, her mission is to deliver two packages strapped to the back of her bicycle to an address 30 blocks uptown. Once on her bike, she weaves through traffic, staying alert to cars, trucks, pedestrians, and potholes. Seeing a break in traffic, she reaches down to grab her water bottle for a quick drink before the next obstacle. As she replaces the water bottle, she downshifts and keeps a wary eye on the pedestrian ahead who looks as though he might step off the curb at any moment.

During her ride, Serena must use her perception both of the world around her and of her own body to monitor what is happening in the environment, to stay on course, to remain balanced and steady on her bike, to reach for her water bottle, and to avoid the pedestrian who does, as she predicted, step off the curb just as she is approaching. This chapter considers the ways in which perceptual processes such as these are involved in being *physically active* in the world. As we explain how Serena is able to stay on course, grab her water bottle, or predict what is going to happen ahead, we will be describing how perception and action interact. We will see, in this chapter, that we need to consider action to understand perception.

The Ecological Approach to Perception

Through most of the 20th century, the dominant way perception research was carried out was by having stationary observers look at static stimuli in a laboratory situation. However, in the 1970s and 1980s, one group of psychologists, led by J. J. Gibson, argued that this traditional way of studying perception lacked **ecological validity**. An ecologically valid experiment matches its stimuli, conditions, and procedures to those present in the natural world. Placing subjects in small testing rooms to look at simple stimuli doesn't accomplish this goal because such experiments ignore what a person perceives when he or she performs natural, real-world, tasks like walking through a hallway, riding a bike through the street, or landing an airplane on a runway. Perception, Gibson argued, evolved so that we can move within, and act upon, the world; therefore, he thought, a better approach was to study perception in situations where people move through and interact with the environment. Because Gibson's approach focused on perception in natural contexts, it is called the **ecological approach to perception** (Gibson, 1950, 1962, 1979). A major goal of the ecological approach is to determine how movement creates perceptual information that both guides further movement and helps observers perceive the environment.

The Moving Observer Creates Information in the Environment

To understand what it means to say that movement creates perceptual information, imagine that you are driving down an empty street. No other cars or people are visible, so everything around you—buildings, trees, traffic signals—is stationary. Even though the objects around you aren't moving, your movement *relative to the objects* causes you to see the houses and trees moving past when you look out of the side window. And when you look at the road ahead, you see the road moving toward you. As your car hurtles forward when crossing a bridge, everything around you—the sides and top of the bridge, the road below—moves past you in a direction opposite to the direction you are moving (**Figure 7.1**).

Optic Flow The movement described above, in which movement of an observer creates movement of objects and the scene relative to the observer, is called **optic flow**. Optic flow has two important characteristics:

Figure 7.1 The side and top of the bridge and the road below appear to move toward a car that is moving forward. This movement is called *optic flow*.

© Bruce Goldstein

Figure 7.2 Optic flow created by an airplane coming in for a landing. The focus of expansion (FOE), indicated by the small red dot, is the place where the plane will touch down on the runway. (From Gibson, 1950)

1. Optic flow is more rapid near the moving observer, as shown in Figure 7.1 by longer arrows indicating more rapid flow. The different speed of flow—fast near the observer and slower farther away—is called the **gradient of flow**. The gradient of flow provides information about how fast the observer is moving. According to Gibson, the observer uses the information provided by the gradient of flow to determine his or her speed of movement.

2. There is no flow at the destination toward which the observer is moving. The absence of flow at the destination point is called the **focus of expansion (FOE)**. In Figure 7.1 the FOE, marked by the small white dot, is at the end of the bridge; it indicates where the car will end up if its course is not changed. Another example is in **Figure 7.2**, which shows optic flow lines for an airplane coming in for a landing. The FOE here (small red dot) indicates the place where the plane will touch down on the runway if it maintains its present course.

Research on whether people use optic flow information has asked observers to make judgments regarding where they are heading based on computer-generated displays of moving dots that create optic flow stimuli. The observer's task is to judge, based on optic flow stimuli, where he or she would be heading relative to a reference point. Examples of these stimuli are depicted in **Figures 7.3a** and **7.3b**. In each figure, the lines represent the movement trajectories of individual dots. Longer lines indicate faster movement (as in Figure 7.1). Depending on the trajectory and speed of the dots, different flow patterns can be created. The flow in Figure 7.3a indicates movement directly toward the vertical line on the horizon; the flow in Figure 7.3b indicates movement to the right of the vertical line. Observers viewing stimuli such as this can judge where they are heading relative to the vertical line to within about 0.5 to 1 degree (Warren, 1995, 2004; also see Fortenbaugh et al., 2006; Li et al., 2006).

Invariant Information Another important concept of the ecological approach is the idea of **invariant information**—

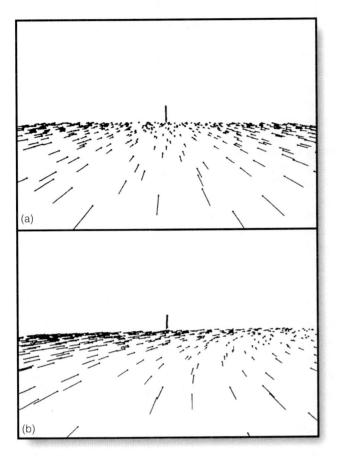

Figure 7.3 (a) Optic flow generated by a person moving straight ahead toward the vertical line on the horizon. The lengths of the lines indicate the person's speed. (b) Optic flow generated by a person moving in a curved path that is headed to the right of the vertical line. (From Warren, 1995)

information that remains constant regardless of what the observer is doing or how the observer is moving. Optic flow provides invariant information because the same flow information is present each time the observer is moving through the environment in a particular way. For example, the FOE always occurs at the point toward which the observer is moving. If an observer changes direction, the FOE shifts to a new location, but the FOE is still there. Thus, even when specific aspects of a scene change, optic flow and the FOE continue to provide information about how fast a person is moving and where he or she is heading. When we consider depth perception in Chapter 10, we will see that Gibson proposed other sources of invariant information that indicate an object's size and its distance from the observer.

Self-Produced Information

Another important concept within the ecological approach is **self-produced information**: When a person makes a movement, that movement creates information, and this information, in turn, is used to guide further movement (**Figure 7.4**).

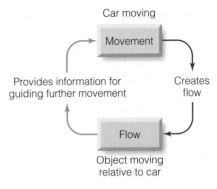

Figure 7.4 The relationship between movement and flow is reciprocal, with movement causing flow and flow guiding movement. This is the basic principle behind much of our interaction with the environment.

For example, when a person is driving down the street, movement of the car provides optic flow information, and the observer then uses this flow information to help steer the car. A different example of a movement that creates information that is then used to guide further movement is provided by somersaulting.

We can appreciate the problem facing a gymnast who wants to execute an airborne backward somersault (or backflip) by realizing that, within 600 ms, the gymnast must execute the somersault and then end in exactly the correct body configuration precisely at the moment that he or she hits the ground (**Figure 7.5**). One way this could be accomplished is to learn to run a predetermined sequence of motions within a specific period of time. In this case, performance should be the same with eyes open or closed. However, Benoit Bardy and Makel Laurent (1998) found that expert gymnasts performed somersaults more poorly with their eyes closed. Films showed that when their eyes were open, the gymnasts appeared to be making in-the-air corrections to their trajectory. For example, a gymnast who initiated the extension of his or her body a little too late compensated by performing the rest of the movement more rapidly.

Figure 7.5 "Snapshots" of a somersault, or backflip, starting on the left and finishing on the right. (From Bardy & Laurent, 1998)

An especially interesting result of Bardy & Laurent's study was that closing the eyes did not affect the performance of novice somersaulters as much as it affected the performance of experts. Apparently, experts learn to coordinate their movements with their perceptions, a skill that novices have not yet learned. Therefore, when the novices closed their eyes, the loss of visual information had less of an effect than it did for the experts. Thus, somersaulting, like driving a car or piloting an airplane, involves using information created by movement to guide further movement.

The Senses Do Not Work in Isolation

Another of Gibson's ideas was that the senses do not work in isolation. He felt that rather than considering vision, hearing, touch, smell, and taste as separated senses, we should consider how each one provides information for the same behaviors. One example of how a behavior originally thought to be the exclusive responsibility of one sense is also served by another one is the sense of balance.

Your ability to stand up straight, and to keep your balance while standing still or walking, depends on systems that enable you to sense the movement and position of your body relative to gravity. These systems include the vestibular canals of your inner ear and receptors in the joints and muscles. However, Gibson (and others) noted that information provided by vision also plays a role in keeping our balance, a fact we can use to emphasize the way the senses work together. One way to illustrate the role of vision in balance is to consider what happens when visual information isn't available, as in the following demonstration.

DEMONSTRATION | Keeping Your Balance

Keeping your balance is something you probably take for granted. Stand up. Raise one foot from the ground and stay balanced on the other. Then close your eyes and notice what happens.

Did staying balanced become more difficult when you closed your eyes? This occurs because vision provides a frame of reference that helps the muscles constantly make adjustments to help maintain balance. (See Aartolahti et al., 2013; Hallemans et al., 2010; Lord & Menz, 2000, for some experiments that show other ways in which poor vision affects balance, posture, and mobility.)

The importance of a visual frame of reference for balance has also been examined by considering what happens to a person when his or her visual and vestibular senses provide conflicting information regarding posture. For example, David Lee and Eric Aronson (1974) placed 13- to 16-month-old toddlers in a "swinging room" (**Figure 7.6**). In this room, the floor was stationary, but the walls and ceiling could swing toward and away from the toddler. **Figure 7.6a** shows the room swaying toward the toddler. This movement

of the wall creates the optic flow pattern on the right. Notice that this pattern is similar to the optic flow that occurs when moving forward, as when driving across the bridge in Figure 7.1.

The optic flow pattern that the toddler observes creates the impression that he or she is swaying forward. After all, the only natural circumstance in which the entire world suddenly moves toward you is a situation in which you are moving (or falling) forward. This perception causes the toddler to sway back to compensate (**Figure 7.6b**). When the room moves back, as in **Figure 7.6c**, the optic flow pattern creates the impression of swaying backward, so the toddler sways forward to compensate. In Lee and Aronson's experiment, although a few of the toddlers were unaffected by the sway, 26 percent swayed, 23 percent staggered, and 33 percent fell down, even though the floor remained stationary throughout the entire experiment!

Even adults, who have more extensive practice standing up and maintaining their balance than toddlers who have only recently begun to walk, were affected by the swinging room. Lee describes their behavior as follows: "oscillating the experimental room through as little as 6 mm caused adult subjects to sway approximately in phase with this movement. The subjects were like puppets visually hooked to their surroundings and were unaware of the real cause of their disturbance" (p. 173). Adults who didn't brace themselves could, like the toddlers, be knocked over by their perception of the moving room. The swinging room experiments are not alone in showing that vision can override the traditional sources of balance information provided by the inner ear and the receptors in the muscles and joints (see also Fox, 1990, and Stoffregen et al., 1999, for more evidence that optic flow information can influence posture while standing still; and Warren et al., 1996, for evidence that flow is involved in maintaining posture while walking).

Gibson's emphasis on (1) studying the acting observer, (2) identifying invariant information in the environment that observers use for perception, and (3) considering the senses as working together was revolutionary for its time. But even though perception researchers were aware of Gibson's ideas, most research continued in the traditional way—testing stationary subjects looking at stimuli in laboratory settings. Of course, there is nothing wrong with testing stationary observers in the laboratory, and much of the research described in this book takes this approach. However, Gibson's idea that perception should also be studied as it is often experienced, by observers who are moving and in more naturalistic settings, finally began to take hold in the 1980s, and today perception in naturalistic settings is one of the major themes of perception research.

The remainder of this chapter focuses on research that considers the following ways that perception and action occur together in the environment: (1) walking or driving through the environment; (2) finding one's way from one location to another; (3) reaching out and grasping objects; and (4) watching other people take action.

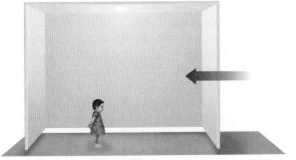

(a) Room swings toward person.   Floor remains stationary

(b) Person sways back to compensate.

(c) When room swings away, person sways forward to compensate.

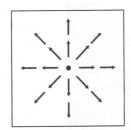

Flow when wall
is moving
toward person

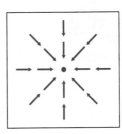

Flow when wall
is moving
away from person

Figure 7.6 Lee and Aronson's swinging room. (a) Moving the room toward the observer creates an optic flow pattern associated with moving forward, so (b) the observer sways backward to compensate. (c) As the room moves away from the observer, flow corresponds to moving backward, so the person leans forward to compensate and may even lose his or her balance. (From Bardy & Laurent, 1998)

Staying on Course: Walking and Driving

Following in Gibson's footsteps, a number of researchers have considered the types of information that people use when they are walking or driving. As we will see, perceptual information we have already discussed such as optic flow is important, but other sources of information come into play as well.

Walking

How does a person stay on course as he or she is walking toward a specific location? We have already discussed how optic flow can provide invariant information regarding a person's

trajectory and speed, but other information seems to be used as well. For example, various strategies can play a role in maintaining one's heading. One is the **visual direction strategy**, in which observers keep their body pointed toward a target. If they go off course, the target will drift to the left or right (**Figure 7.7**). When this happens, the walker can correct course by realigning his or her body with the target (Fajen & Warren, 2003; Rushton et al., 1998).

Another indication that optic flow information is not always necessary for navigation is that we can find our way even when flow information is minimal, such as at night or in a snowstorm (Harris & Rogers, 1999). Jack Loomis and co-workers (1992; Philbeck et al., 1997) have demonstrated this by eliminating optic flow altogether, using a "blind walking" procedure in which people observe a target object located up to 12 meters away, then walk to the target with their eyes closed (red line in **Figure 7.8**).

Figure 7.7 (a) As long as a person is moving toward the tree, it remains in the center of the person's field of view. (b) When the person walks off course, the tree drifts to the side. (c) When the person corrects the course, the tree moves back to the center of the field of view, until (d) the person arrives at the tree.

© Bruce Goldstein

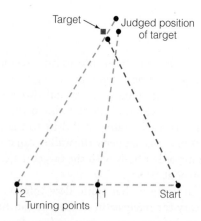

Figure 7.8 A "blind walking" experiment (Philbeck et al., 1997). Red line: Subjects closed their eyes, walked toward a target 6 meters away, and stopped when they thought they had reached it. Green line: With closed eyes, subjects began walking in the wrong direction. Blue lines: Keeping their eyes closed, subjects turned at point 1 or point 2 and continued walking until they thought they had reached the target.

These experiments show that people are able to walk directly toward the target and stop within a fraction of a meter of it. In fact, people can do this even when they are asked to walk off in the wrong direction first and then make a turn and walk to the target, all while keeping their eyes closed. The green lines in Figure 7.8 show the paths taken when a person first walked to the left and then was told to turn either at turning point 1 or 2 and walk to a target that was 6 meters away (blue lines). The fact that the person generally stopped close to the target shows that we are able to navigate short distances accurately in the absence of any visual stimulation at all (also see Sun et al., 2004). Subjects in the blind walking experiment accomplished this feat by mentally combining knowledge of their own movements (e.g., muscle movements can give the walker a sense of his or her speed as well as shifts in direction) with their memory for the position of the target throughout their walk. The process by which people and animals keep track of their position within a surrounding environment while they move is called **spatial updating** (see Wang, 2003).

Just because people can walk toward objects and locations without optic flow information does not mean that they don't use such information to help them when it is available. In fact, studies have shown that optic flow does provide important information about direction and speed when walking (Durgin & Gigone, 2007) and that this information can be combined with the visual direction strategy and spatial updating processes to guide walking behaviors (Turano et al., 2005; Warren et al., 2001).

Driving a Car

Another common activity that requires people to keep track of their movement through the environment is driving. To study information people use to stay on course when driving, Michael Land and David Lee (1994) fitted an automobile in the United Kingdom with instruments to record the angle of the steering wheel and the car's speed, and measured where the driver was looking with a video eye tracker. As we noted earlier, according to Gibson, the focus of expansion (FOE) provides information about the place toward which a moving observer is headed. However, Land and Lee found that although drivers look straight ahead while driving, they tend to look at a spot closer to the front of the car rather than directly at the FOE (**Figure 7.9a**). Because drivers don't look at the FOE, which would be farther down the road, Land and Lee suggested that drivers, like walkers, probably take advantage of information in addition to optic flow to determine the direction they are heading.

One way Land and Lee studied what information drivers use to maintain their heading was to record what drivers look at as they are negotiating a curve. This task is particularly well suited for detecting information and strategies beyond optic flow because the driver's destination, and hence the FOE, keeps changing as the car rounds the curve, making

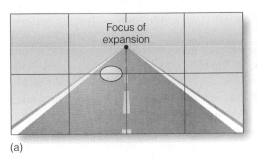
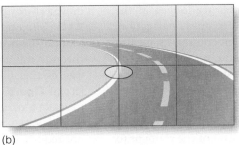

(a) (b)

Figure 7.9 Results of Land and Lee's (1994) experiment. Because this study was conducted in the United Kingdom, subjects were driving on the left side of the road. The ellipses indicate the place where the drivers were most likely to look while driving down (a) a straight road and (b) a curve to the left.

the FOE a poor indicator of how the car should be steered. Land and Lee found that when going around a curve, drivers don't look directly at the road, but instead look at the tangent point of the curve on the side of the road, as shown in **Figure 7.9b**. This allows drivers to constantly note the position of the car relative to the lines at the side of the road. By maintaining a constant distance between the car and the lines on the road, a driver can keep the car headed in the right direction (see Kandel et al., 2009; Land & Horwood, 1995; Rushton & Salvucci, 2001; Wann & Land, 2000; Wilkie & Wann, 2003).

Wayfinding

In the last section, we considered information in the immediate environment that helps walkers and drivers stay on course as they walk toward a goal or drive along a road. But we often travel to more distant destinations that aren't visible from our starting point, such as when we walk across campus from one class to another or drive to a destination several miles away. This kind of navigation, in which we take a route that usually involves making turns, is called **wayfinding**.

Our ability to get from one place to another may seem simple, especially for routes we have traveled many times. But just as there is nothing simple about perception, there is nothing simple about wayfinding. It is a complex process that involves perceiving objects in the environment, remembering objects and their relation to the overall scene, and knowing when to turn and in what direction.

The Importance of Landmarks

One important source of information for wayfinding is landmarks—objects on the route that serve as cues to indicate where to turn. Sahar Hamid and coworkers (2010) studied how subjects used landmarks as they learned to navigate through a mazelike environment displayed on a computer screen in which pictures of common objects served as landmarks. Subjects first navigated through the maze until they learned its layout (training phase) and then were told to travel from one location in the maze to another (testing phase). During both the training and testing phases, subjects'

eye movements were measured using a head-mounted eye tracker like the one used in the experiment described in Chapter 6 in which eye movements were measured as a subject made a peanut butter and jelly sandwich (see page 130). This maze contained both *decision-point landmarks*—objects at corners where the subject had to decide which direction to turn—and *non-decision-point landmarks*—objects located in the middle of corridors that provided no critical information about how to navigate.

The eye-tracking measurements showed that subjects spent more time looking at decision-point landmarks than non-decision-point landmarks, probably because the decision-point landmarks were more important for navigating the maze. In fact, when maze performance was tested with half of the landmarks removed, removing landmarks that had been viewed less (which were likely to be in the middle of the corridors) had little effect on performance (**Figure 7.10a**). However, removing landmarks that observers had looked at longer caused a substantial drop in performance (**Figure 7.10b**).

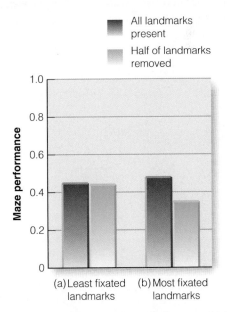

Figure 7.10 Effect of removing landmarks on maze performance. Red = all landmarks are present; blue = half have been removed. (a) Removing half of the least fixated landmarks has no effect on performance. (b) Removing half of the most fixated landmarks causes a decrease in performance. (From Hamid et al., 2010)

It makes sense that landmarks that are looked at the most would be the ones that are used to guide navigation, and it isn't surprising that decision-point landmarks are also more likely to be remembered. This better memory for decision-point landmarks was demonstrated by Jared Miller and Laura Carlson (2011), who asked subjects to learn a walking route through a simulated museum filled with exhibits that was displayed on a computer screen. When subjects were then asked either to create a written description of the route or to draw a map, including as many exhibits as possible, exhibits located at decision-points were included more often than exhibits located at non-decision points. Thus decision-point landmarks are more likely to be *reproduced* later. They are also more likely to be *recognized*, as indicated by a study in which subjects learned a walking route through the University of Pennsylvania campus. Afterward, subjects were more likely to recognize pictures of buildings that were located at decision points than those located in the middle of a block (Schinazi & Epstein, 2010).

The studies we have described have measured eye movements, maze performance, and memory, all of which are behaviors related to landmarks. But what is happening in the brain? To find out, Gabriele Janzen and Miranda van Turennout (2004) had subjects study a film sequence that moved through a computer-simulated museum (**Figure 7.11**). Subjects were told they needed to learn their way around the museum well enough to be able to guide a tour through it. Objects ("exhibits") were located along the hallway of this museum. Decision-point objects, like the object in **Figure 7.11a**, marked places where it was necessary to make a turn. Non-decision-point objects, like the one in **Figure 7.11b**, were located at places where a decision was not required.

After studying the museum's layout in the film, subjects were given a recognition test while in an fMRI scanner. They saw objects that had been in the hallway and some objects they had never seen. Their brain activation was measured in the scanner as they indicated whether they remembered seeing each object. **Figure 7.11c** indicates activity in an area of the brain known to be associated with navigation called the parahippocampal gyrus (see Figure 4.25a, page 87). The left pair of bars indicates that for objects that the subjects remembered, activation was greater for decision-point objects than for non-decision-point objects. Thus, decision-point landmarks are not only more likely to be recognized than non-decision-point landmarks, they also generate greater levels of brain activity. A more interesting result, indicated by the right pair of bars, was that the advantage for decision-point objects

Figure 7.11 (a & b) Two locations in the "virtual museum" viewed by Janzen and van Turennout's (2004) observers. (c) Brain activation during the recognition test for objects that had been located at decision points (red bars) and non-decision points (blue bars). Notice that brain activation was greater for decision-point objects even if they weren't remembered. (Adapted from Janzen & van Turennout, 2004)

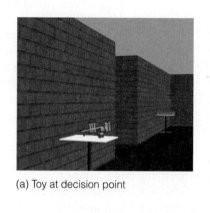

(a) Toy at decision point

(b) Toy at non-decision point

Non-decision points

Decision points

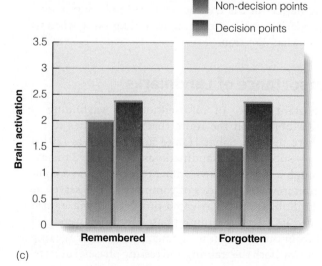

(c)

also occurred for objects that were not remembered during the recognition test.

Janzen and van Turennout concluded that the brain automatically distinguishes objects that are used as landmarks to guide navigation. The brain therefore responds not just to the object but also to how relevant that object is for guiding navigation. This means that the next time you are trying to find your way along a route that you have traveled before but aren't totally confident about, activity in your parahippocampal gyrus may automatically be "highlighting" landmarks that indicate when you should continue going straight, turn right, or turn left, even when you may not remember having seen these landmarks before (see also Janzen, 2006; Janzen et al., 2008).

The link between a person's ability to recognize landmarks and his or her wayfinding ability has also been shown in patients suffering from **topographical agnosia**, a condition defined by an inability to recognize landmarks in real-world environments. It is commonly associated with the loss of brain tissue in the parahippocampal gyrus. To see how this problem with landmark recognition is associated with wayfinding, Constant Rainville and coworkers (2005) conducted an experiment with F.G., a 71-year-old man who was severely impaired in his ability to recognize both famous landmarks (e.g., the Eiffel Tower) and landmarks in his hometown where, at the time of the study, he had lived for 30 years. The researchers first led F.G. along a 2 km route through an unfamiliar city and then asked him to walk the route on his own. F.G. struggled when it was his turn to reproduce the route: Out of the 21 decision points along the route, F.G. turned the correct direction only 10 times, a rate not different from chance. In contrast, members of a control group turned the correct direction an average of 18.8 times. Clearly, F.G.'s inability to recognize landmarks was strongly associated with a problem in wayfinding, a result we might have expected given the importance of landmarks highlighted in the fMRI studies on neurologically normal subjects described above.

Interestingly, when the researchers asked F.G. to navigate around his hometown, he did so quite well. However, it was not because he used landmarks. Instead, he used street signs and printed building names to help him keep track of his location within a "mental map" that he could use to find his way around. You may not think of wayfinding as involving a map, especially for routes that are very familiar, but physiological research shows that there are neurons in the brain that map the environment.

The Brain's "GPS"

In the 1930s and 1940s, Edward Tolman was studying how rats learned to run through mazes to find rewards. In one of his experiments, Tolman (1938) placed a rat in a maze like the one in **Figure 7.12**. Initially, the rat explored the maze, running up and down each of the alleys (**Figure 7.12a**). After this initial period of exploration, the rat was placed at A and food was placed at B, and the rat quickly learned to turn right at the intersection to obtain the food (**Figure 7.12b**). According to simple learning theories of the time, rewarding the rat with food every time it turns right should strengthen the "turn right" response, and so increase the chances that the rat will turn right to obtain food in future.

However, when Tolman (after taking precautions to be sure the rat couldn't determine the location of the food based on smell) placed the rat at C, something interesting happened. The rat turned *left* at the intersection to reach the food at B (**Figure 7.12c**). This result is important because it shows that the rat did not merely learn a sequence of moves to a get to the food during training. Instead, the rat had created a **cognitive map** of the spatial layout of the maze, and was able to use this map to locate the food (Tolman, 1948).

More than 30 years after Tolman's experiments, British researcher John O'Keefe was working to identify the brain

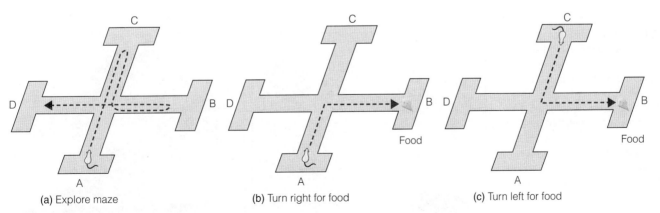

(a) Explore maze   (b) Turn right for food   (c) Turn left for food

Figure 7.12 Maze used by Tolman. (a) The rat initially explores the maze. (b) The rat learns to turn right to obtain the food at B when it starts at A. (c) When placed at C, the rat turns left to reach the food at B. In this experiment, precautions were taken to prevent the rat from knowing where the food was based on cues such as smell.

mechanisms that give rise to cognitive maps (O'Keefe & Dostrovsky, 1971; O'Keefe & Nadel, 1978). Using rats as his subjects, O'Keefe recorded the activity of individual neurons in the hippocampus, an area important for creating memories, which we introduced in Chapter 4 (page 86; Figure 4.25a). Every time one of the hippocampal neurons fired, O'Keefe noted the rat's location in the box. When O'Keefe plotted these positions along the rat's walking path, he found something rather amazing. The individual neurons he recorded from each fired when the rat was in a specific place within the box, and different cells preferred different locations.

A record similar to those determined by O'Keefe is shown in **Figure 7.13a**. The gray lines depict the path taken by a rat as it wandered around a recording box. Overlaid on top of this path are the locations where four different neurons fired. Each neuron is denoted by a different color. So, in this example, the "purple neuron" only fired when the animal was in the upper right portion of the box, and the "red neuron" only fired when the rat was in the lower left corner. By identifying neurons such as these, O'Keefe discovered that the activity of individual neurons within the hippocampus can code an animal's position within the environment. These neurons have come to be called **place cells** because they only fire when an animal is in a certain place in the environment. The area of the environment within which a place cell fires is called its **place field**.

The discovery of place cells was an important first step in determining how the brain's "GPS system" works. Subsequent research has identified other types of cells that further aid in the coding of cognitive maps and an animal's location within them. For example, May-Britt Moser and Edvard Moser and their students (Fyhn et al., 2008; Hafting et al., 2005) discovered **grid cells** in a brain area near the hippocampus called the entorhinal cortex (see Figure 4.25a, page 87). As with place cells, the firing rate of a grid cell depends on the animal's position in the environment. Unlike place cells, however, grid cells have multiple place fields that

are arranged in regular, gridlike patterns like the three types of grid cells (denoted by orange, blue, and green dots) shown in **Figure 7.13b**. The hexagonal pattern for the orange grid cells is indicated by the black line.

The exact functions of grid cells are still being investigated (Moser, Moser, et al., 2014; Moser, Roudi, et al., 2014), but because of their spatial regularity, they are likely able to provide information about the direction of movement. For example, movement along the pink arrow would lead to responses in the "orange cell," then the "blue cell," and then the "green cell." Movement in other directions would result in different patterns of firing across grid cells. As a result, grid cells may be able to code distance and direction information as an animal moves.

It is likely that place cells and grid cells work together, because they are connected with each other, perhaps as closely as by a single synapse. In addition to place and grid cells, there are also **head direction cells** that fire depending on the direction an animal is facing (Taube, 2007) and **border cells** that fire when an animal is near the edge of the environment (Solstad et al., 2008). There is much left to learn about these cells and their interconnections, but these discoveries are already recognized as being so important that John O'Keefe, May-Britt Moser, and Edvard Moser were jointly awarded the 2014 Nobel Prize in Physiology or Medicine for their discovery of place and grid cells.

What makes these place and grid cells especially important is that recent experiments suggest that similar cells may also exist in humans. Determining whether humans have cells similar to the ones discovered in rats poses the challenge of recording electrical signals as a subject explores the environment. This challenge was met by Joshua Jacobs and coworkers (2013), who found neurons in humans similar to the rat grid cells by recording from single neurons in patients, like those described in Chapter 4 (page 87), who were being prepared for surgery to treat severe epilepsy. The patients were confined to their beds, and so couldn't navigate, but were fitted with a virtual reality device that enabled them to navigate through a virtual environment (much like a

Figure 7.13 A record similar to those O'Keefe produced by recording from neurons in a rat's hippocampus as it walked inside a box. (a) The path taken by a rat in a box is outlined in gray. The positions within the box where four places cells fired are highlighted by red, blue, purple, and green dots. (b) The positions within the box where three grid cells fired are denoted by orange, blue, and green dots. See text for details.

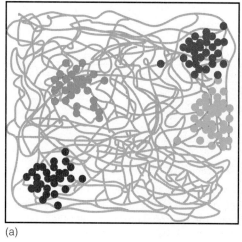
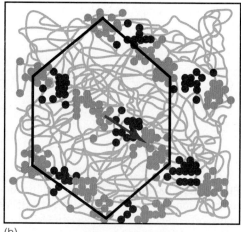

(a) (b)

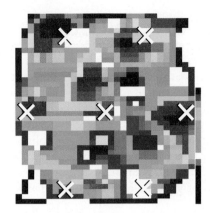

Figure 7.14 Colors indicate firing of a neuron in a subject's entorhinal cortex at locations in the area that the subject was visiting in the virtual environment. Red indicates the locations associated with a high firing rate. Note that they are arranged in a hexagonal layout, similar to what was observed in earlier experiments on rats. (From Jacobs et al., 2013)

three-dimensional computer game) as they searched for hidden targets.

Figure 7.14 shows the results for a neuron in one patient's entorhinal cortex (see Figure 4.25a, page 87). The red areas, which indicate high firing frequency, form a grid pattern, shown by X's, similar to what occurs in the rat. Although the human patterns are "noisier" than the rats', the results from 10 different patients led Jacobs to conclude that these neurons, like the rat grid cells, help humans create maps of the environment. Cells similar to rat place cells have also been discovered in humans (Ekstrom et al., 2003). So the next time you have to navigate along a route, give credit both to your knowledge of landmarks and to neurons that are signaling where you are and where you are going.

Individual Differences in Wayfinding

Do you (or does someone you know) have a particularly difficult time learning your way around new cities or unfamiliar buildings? Or do you know someone who is a whiz at finding their way around? Just as different people have different mental abilities, wayfinding ability varies from one individual to another. One difference in wayfinding can be traced to experience. People who have practiced getting from one place to another in a particular environment are often good at finding their way. It isn't that surprising that experience within a particular environment can lead to better wayfinding. But this obvious conclusion becomes more interesting when we look at the physiological consequences of this experience.

Eleanor Maguire and coworkers (2006) studied the effect of wayfinding practice on the brain by studying two groups of subjects: (1) London bus drivers, who have learned specific routes through the city, and (2) London taxi drivers, who have to travel to many different places throughout the city. **Figure 7.15a**

shows the results of an experiment in which bus drivers and taxi drivers were asked to identify pictures of London landmarks. Taxi drivers scored higher than bus drivers, as we might expect from their more widespread exposure to London. When the bus and taxi drivers' brains were then scanned, Maguire found that the taxi drivers' hippocampus was larger, as shown in **Figure 7.15b**.

This result is similar to the results of the experience-dependent plasticity experiments described in Chapter 3 (page 64). Remember that kittens reared in an environment of vertical stripes had more neurons in their cortex that responded to vertical stripes (see Figure 3.30, page 64). Similarly, taxi drivers who have extensive experience navigating have a larger hippocampus. Importantly, drivers with the largest hippocampi were the ones with the most years of experience. This final result provides strong support for experience-dependent plasticity (more experience translates to a larger hippocampus) and rules out the possibility that it is simply that people with a larger hippocampus are more likely to become taxi drivers than bus drivers.

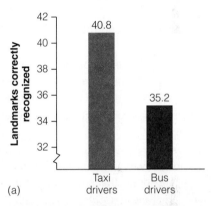

(a)

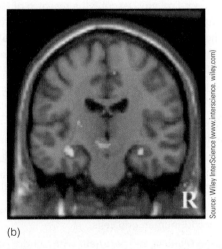

(b)

Figure 7.15 (a) Performance on a landmark test by London taxi drivers and bus drivers. A perfect score is 48. (b) Cross section of the brain. Yellow indicates greater hippocampus volume in London taxi drivers compared to London bus drivers, as determined by magnetic resonance imaging. (From Maguire, Wollett, & Spiers, 2006)

When taken together, the important message of all of these studies is that wayfinding is multifaceted. It depends on numerous sources of information and is distributed throughout many structures in the brain. This isn't surprising when we consider that wayfinding involves seeing and recognizing objects along a route (perception), paying attention to specific objects (attention), using information stored from past trips through the environment (memory), and combining all this information to create maps that help us relate what we are perceiving to where we are now and where we need to go next.

TEST YOURSELF 7.1

1. What two factors does the ecological approach to perception emphasize?

2. What is optic flow? What are two characteristics of optic flow? Describe the experiment that considered whether people can use optic flow to determine their heading.

3. What is invariant information? How is invariance related to optic flow?

4. What is observer-produced information? Describe its role in somersaulting and why there is a difference between novices and experts when they close their eyes.

5. Describe the swinging room experiments. What principles do they illustrate?

6. What does research on walking and driving a car tell us about how optic flow may (or may not) be used in navigation? What are some other sources of information for navigation?

7. What is wayfinding? Describe the research of Hamid (looking at landmarks) Miller and Carlson (reproducing landmarks), and the University of Pennsylvania study (recognizing landmarks) that investigated the role of landmarks in wayfinding.

8. What do the brain-scanning experiments of Janzen and van Turennout indicate about brain activity and landmarks?

9. What did Tolman's rat maze experiment demonstrate?

10. Describe the rat experiments that discovered place cells and grid cells. How might these cells, plus head direction and border cells, help rats navigate?

11. Describe Jacobs and coworkers' experiment that provided evidence for human grid cells.

12. Describe Maguire's experiment with London taxi drivers and bus drivers. What did her results reveal about the physiology of individual differences in wayfinding?

13. What does it mean to say that wayfinding is "multifaceted?" How does wayfinding reveal interactions between perception, attention, memory, and action?

Acting on Objects

So far, we have been describing how we move around in the environment—but we also *interact* with objects in an environment. One of the major actions we take is reaching to pick something up, as Serena did on her bike ride when she reached down to grab her water bottle. Reaching and grasping are directed toward specific objects, to accomplish specific goals. We reach for and grasp a doorknob to open a door; we reach for a hammer to pound a nail. An important concept relevant to this kind of goal-directed action is *affordances*, which we describe next.

Affordances: What Objects Are Used For

Remember that Gibson's ecological approach involves identifying the connections between perceptual information in the environment and the performance of various actions. Earlier in the chapter we described the connection between the perception of optic flow and actions ranging from maintaining balance to landing airplanes. Another type of information that connects perception and action is Gibson's concept of **affordances**—information that indicates how an object can be used. In Gibson's words, "The affordances of the environment are what it *offers* the animal, what it *provides for* or *furnishes*" (1979, p. 127). A chair, or anything that is sit-on-able, affords sitting; an object of the right size and shape to be grabbed by a person's hand affords grasping; and so on.

What this means is that perception of an object includes not only its physical properties, such as shape, size, color, and orientation, that enable us to recognize the object, but also information about how the object is or could be used. For example, when you look at a cup, you might see that it is "a round white coffee cup, about 5 inches high, with a handle," but your perceptual system would also respond with information indicating that it "can be picked up," "can be filled with liquid," or even "can be thrown." Affordances thus go beyond simply recognizing the cup; they guide our interactions with it. Another way of saying this is that "potential for action" is part of our perception of an object.

One way that affordances have been studied is by looking at the behavior of people with brain damage. Glyn Humphreys and Jane Riddoch (2001) studied affordances by testing patient M.P., who had damage to his temporal lobe that impaired his ability to name objects. M.P. was given a cue, either (1) the name of an object ("cup") or (2) an indication of the object's function ("an item you could drink from"). He was then shown 10 different objects and was told to press a key as soon as he found an object that matched the cue. M.P. identified the object more accurately and rapidly when given the cue that referred to the object's function. Humphreys and Riddoch concluded from this result that M.P. was using his knowledge of an object's affordances to help him find it.

(a) Perceive cup   (b) Reach for cup   (c) Grasp cup

Figure 7.16 Picking up a cup of coffee: (a) perceiving and recognizing the cup, (b) reaching for it, and (c) grasping and picking it up. This action involves coordination between perceiving and action that is carried out by two separate streams in the brain, as described in the text.

Although M.P. wasn't reaching for these objects, it is likely that he would be able to use the information about an object's function to help him take action with respect to the object. In line with this idea, there are other patients with temporal lobe damage who cannot name objects, or even describe how they can be used, but who can pick them up and use them nonetheless.

The Physiology of Reaching and Grasping

An important breakthrough in studying the physiology of reaching and grasping came with the discovery of the ventral (*what*) and dorsal (*where/how/action*) pathways described in Chapter 4 (see Figure 4.14, page 80).

The Dorsal and Ventral Pathways Remember that D.F., who had damage to her ventral pathway, had difficulty recognizing objects or judging their orientation, but she could "mail" an object by placing it through an oriented opening. The idea that there is one processing stream for perceiving objects and another for acting on them helps us understand what is happening when Serena, sitting at a coffee shop after her bike ride, reaches for her cup of coffee (**Figure 7.16**). First she identifies the coffee cup among the flowers and other objects on the table (ventral pathway). Once the coffee cup is perceived, she reaches for it, taking into account its location on the table (dorsal pathway). As she reaches, avoiding the flowers, she positions her hand and fingers to grasp the cup (dorsal), taking into account her perception of the cup's handle (ventral). She then lifts the cup with just the right amount of force (dorsal), taking into account her estimate of how heavy it is based on her perception of its fullness (ventral).

Thus, reaching for and picking up the cup involves continually perceiving the position of the cup, shaping her hand and fingers relative to the cup, and calibrating her actions in order to accurately grasp the cup and pick it up without spilling any coffee (Goodale, 2011). Even a seemingly simple action like picking up a coffee cup involves a number of areas of the brain, which coordinate their activity to create perceptions and behaviors.

The Parietal Reach Region One of the most important areas of the brain for reaching and grasping is the parietal lobe. The areas in the monkey and human parietal cortex that are involved in reaching for objects have been called the **parietal reach region (PRR) (Figure 7.17)**. This region contains neurons that control not only reaching but also grasping (Connelly et al., 2003; Vingerhoets, 2014). Evidence suggests that there are a number of different parietal reach regions in the human parietal lobe (Filimon et al., 2009).

Recording from single neurons in a monkey's parietal lobe has revealed neurons in an area next to the parietal reach region that respond to specific types of hand grips. The procedure for the monkey hand grip experiment, which was carried out by Patrizia Fattori and coworkers (2010), is shown in

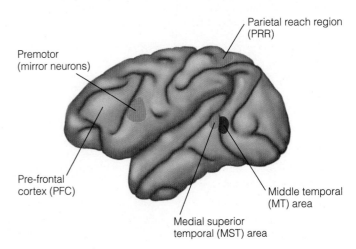

Figure 7.17 Monkey cortex showing location of the parietal reach region (PRR) and the area of premotor cortex where mirror neurons were found. Areas MT, MST, and PFC are discussed in Chapter 8.

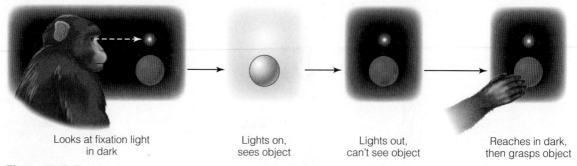

| Looks at fixation light in dark | Lights on, sees object | Lights out, can't see object | Reaches in dark, then grasps object |

Figure 7.18 The monkey's task in Fattori and coworkers' (2010) experiment. The monkey always looked at the small light above the sphere. The monkey sees the object to be grasped when the lights go on, then reaches for and grasps the object once the lights go off and the fixation light changes color. (From Fattori et al., 2010)

Figure 7.18: (1) The monkey observed a small fixation light in the dark; (2) lights were turned on for half a second to reveal the object to be grasped; (3) the lights went out and then, after a brief pause, the fixation light changed color, signaling that the monkey should reach for the object.

The key part of this sequence occurred when the monkey reached for the object in the dark. The monkey knew what the object was from seeing it when the lights were on (a round ball in this example), so when it reached for the object in the dark, it adjusted its grip to match the object. A number of different objects were used, as shown in **Figure 7.19a**, each of which required a different grip.

The key result of the experiment is that there are neurons that respond best to specific grips. For example, neuron A (**Figure 7.19b**) responds best to "whole-hand prehension," whereas neuron B (**Figure 7.19c**) responds best to "advanced precision grip." There are also neurons, like C (**Figure 7.19d**), that respond to a number of different grips. Remember that when these neurons were firing, the monkey was reaching for the object in the dark, so the firing did not reflect visual perception but rather the monkey's actions.

In a follow-up experiment on the same monkeys, Fattori and coworkers (2012) discovered neurons that responded not only when a monkey was preparing to grasp a specific object,

Figure 7.19 Results of Fattori and coworkers' (2010) experiment showing how three different neurons respond to reaching and grasping of four different objects. (a) Four objects. The type of grasping movement associated with each object is indicated above the object. (b) Response of neuron A to grasping each object. This neuron responds best to whole-hand prehension. (c) Response of neuron B, which responds best to advanced precision grip. (d) Response of neuron C, which responds to all four types of grasping.

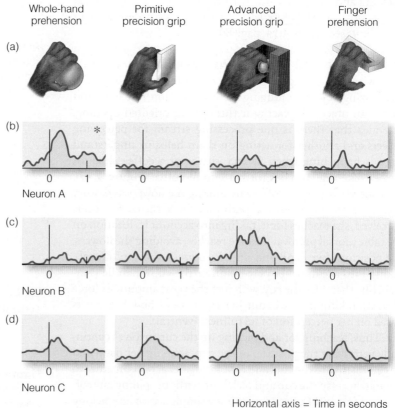

Horizontal axis = Time in seconds
Vertical axis = Rate of nerve firing

but also when the monkey *viewed* that specific object. An example of this type of neuron, which Fattori calls **visuomotor grip cells**, is a neuron that initially responds when the monkey sees a specific object and then also responds as the monkey is forming its hand to grasp the same object. This type of neuron is therefore involved in both perception (identifying the object and/or its affordances by seeing) and action (reaching for the object and gripping it with the hand).

Observing Other People's Actions

We not only take action ourselves, but we regularly watch other people take action. This "watching others act" is most obvious when we watch other people's actions on TV or in a movie, but it also occurs any time we are around someone else who is doing something. One of the most exciting outcomes of research studying the link between perception and action was the discovery of neurons in the premotor cortex (Figure 7.17) called *mirror neurons.*

Mirroring Others' Actions in the Brain

In the early 1990s, a research team led by Giacomo Rizzolatti was investigating how neurons in the monkey's premotor cortex fired as the monkey performed actions like picking up a toy or a piece of food. Their goal was to determine how neurons fired as the monkey carried out specific actions. But as sometimes happens in science, they observed something they didn't expect. When one of the experimenters picked up a piece of food while the monkey was watching, neurons in the monkey's cortex fired. What was so unexpected was that the neurons that fired to observing the experimenter pick up the food were the same ones that had fired earlier when the monkey had itself picked up the food (Gallese et al., 1996).

This initial observation, followed by many additional experiments, led to the discovery of **mirror neurons**—neurons that respond both when a monkey observes someone else grasping an object such as food on a tray (**Figure 7.20a**) and when the monkey itself grasps the food (**Figure 7.20b**; Rizzolatti et al., 2006). They are called mirror neurons because the neuron's response to watching the experimenter grasp an object is similar to the response that would occur if the monkey were performing the same action. Just looking at the food causes no response, and watching the experimenter grasp the food with a pair of pliers, as in **Figure 7.20c**, causes only a small response (Gallese et al., 1996; Rizzolatti et al., 2000). This last result indicates that mirror neurons can be specialized to respond to only one type of action, such as grasping or placing an object somewhere.

Simply finding a neuron that responds when an animal observes a particular action doesn't tell us why the neuron is firing, however. For example, we could ask if the mirror neurons in Rizzolatti's study were responding to the anticipation of receiving food rather than to the experimenter's specific actions. It turns out that this cannot be a reasonable explanation because the type of object made little difference. The neurons responded just as well when the monkey observed the experimenter pick up an object that was not food.

But could the mirror neurons simply be responding to the pattern of motion? The fact that the neuron does not respond when watching the experimenter pick up the food with pliers argues against this idea. Further evidence that mirror neurons are doing more than just responding to a particular pattern of motion is the discovery of neurons that respond to sounds that are *associated with* actions. These neurons in the premotor cortex, called **audiovisual mirror neurons**, respond when a monkey performs a hand action *and* when it hears the sound associated with this action (Kohler et al., 2002). For example, the results in **Figure 7.21** show the response of a neuron that fires (a) when the monkey sees and hears the experimenter break a peanut, (b) when the monkey just sees the experimenter break the peanut, (c) when the monkey just hears the sound of the breaking peanut, and (d) when the *monkey* breaks the peanut. What this means is that just *hearing* a peanut breaking or just *seeing* a peanut being broken causes activity that is also associated with the perceiver's *action* of breaking a peanut. These neurons are responding, therefore, to what is "happening"—breaking a peanut—rather than to a specific pattern of movement.

At this point you might be asking whether mirror neurons are also present in the human brain. After all, we've only been talking about monkey brains so far. Some research with humans does indeed suggest that our brains also contain mirror

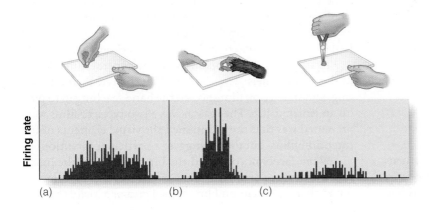

(a)   (b)   (c)

Figure 7.20 Response of a mirror neuron. (a) Response to watching the experimenter grasp food on the tray. (b) Response when the monkey grasps the food. (c) Response to watching the experimenter pick up food with a pair of pliers. (From Rizzolatti et al., 2000)

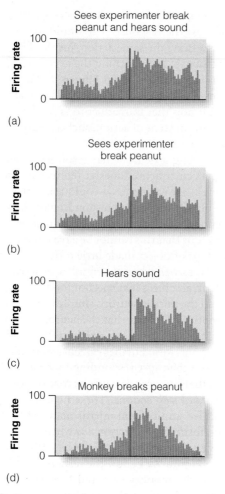

(a)

Sees experimenter break
peanut and hears sound

(b)

Sees experimenter
break peanut

(c)

Hears sound

(d)

Monkey breaks peanut

Figure 7.21 Response of an audiovisual mirror neuron to four different stimuli. (From Kohler et al., 2002)

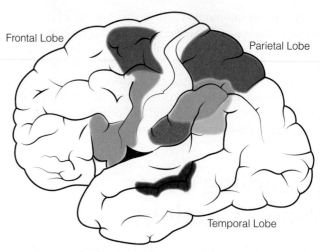

Figure 7.22 Cortical areas in the human brain associated with the mirror neuron system. Colors indicate the type of actions processed in each region: turquoise, movements directed toward objects; purple, reaching movements; orange, tool use; green, movements not directed toward objects; blue, upper limb movements. (Adapted from Cattaneo & Rizzolatti, 2009)

neurons. For example, researchers using electrodes to record the brain activity in people with epilepsy in order to determine which part of their brains was generating their seizures have recorded activity from neurons with the same mirror properties as those identified in monkeys (Mukamel et al., 2010). Additional work using fMRI in neurologically normal individuals has further suggested that these neurons are distributed throughout the frontal, parietal, and temporal lobes (**Figure 7.22**) in a network that has been broadly called the **mirror neuron system** (Caspers et al., 2010; Cattaneo & Rizzolatti, 2009; Grosbras et al., 2012; Molenberghs et al., 2012). However, a great deal more research is needed to determine if and how this mirror neuron system supports perception and action in humans. In the next section, we highlight some of the work that seems promising in identifying the role mirror neurons play in human perception and performance.

Predicting People's Intentions

Some researchers have proposed that there are mirror neurons that respond not just to *what* is happening but to *why* something is happening, or more specifically, to the *intention*

behind what is happening. To understand what this means, let's return to Serena in the coffee shop. As we see her reach for her coffee cup, we might wonder why she is reaching for it. One obvious answer is that she intends to drink some coffee, although if we notice that the cup is empty, we might instead decide that she is going to take the cup back to the counter to get a refill, or if we know that she never drinks more than one cup, we might decide that she is going to place the cup in the used cup bin. Thus, there are a number of different intentions that may be associated with the same action.

What is the evidence that the response of mirror neurons can be influenced by different intentions? Mario Iacoboni and coworkers (2005) provided this evidence in an experiment in which they measured subjects' brain activity as they watched short film clips represented by the stills in **Figure 7.23**. Stills for the two Intention films, on the right, show a hand reaching in to pick up a cup, but there is an important difference between the two scenes. In the top panel, the table is neatly set up, the food is untouched, and the cup is full of tea. In the bottom panel, the table is a mess, the food has been eaten, and the cup appears to be empty. Iacoboni hypothesized that viewing the top film would lead the viewer to infer that the person picking up the cup intended to drink from it and viewing the bottom film would lead the viewer to infer that the person was cleaning up.

Iacoboni's subjects also viewed the control films shown in the other panels. The Context film showed the table setting, and the Action film showed the hand reaching in to pick up an isolated cup. The reason these two types of films were presented was that they contained the visual elements of the Intention films, but didn't suggest a particular intention.

When Iacoboni compared the brain activity in the Intention films to the activity in the Context and Action films, he found that the Intention films caused greater activity than the

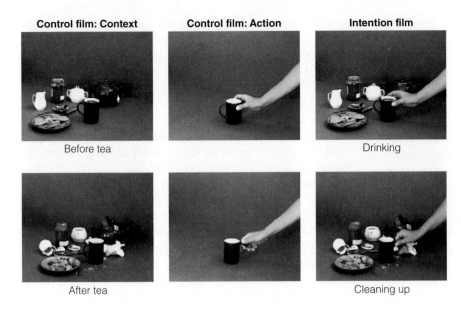

Control film: Context   Control film: Action   Intention film

Before tea

After tea

Drinking

Cleaning up

Figure 7.23 Images from the Context, Action, and Intention film clips viewed by Iacoboni and coworkers' (2005) subjects. Each column corresponds to one of the experimental conditions. In the Context condition, there were two clips: before tea (everything in its place) and after tea (a mess). In the Action condition, the two types of grips (whole hand and using the handle) were shown an equal number of times. In the Intention condition, the "drinking" context was the same as "before tea" but with the hand added. The "cleaning up" context corresponded to "after tea." The two types of hand grips (whole hand and using the handle) were shown an equal number of times during the "drinking" and "cleaning" clips. (From Iacoboni et al., 2005)

control films in areas of the brain known to have mirror neuron properties. **Figure 7.24** shows that the amount of activity was least in the Action condition, was higher for the Cleaning Up condition, and was highest for the Drinking condition. Based on the increased activity for the two Intention conditions, Iacoboni concluded that the mirror neuron area is involved with understanding the intentions behind the actions shown in the films. He reasoned that if the mirror neurons were just signaling the action of picking up the cup, then a similar response would occur regardless of whether a context surrounding the cup was present. Mirror neurons, according to Iacoboni, code the "why" of actions and respond differently to different intentions.

If mirror neurons do, in fact, signal intentions, how do they do it? One possibility is that the response of these neurons is determined by the chain of motor activities that could be *expected* to happen in a particular context (Fogassi et al., 2005;

Gallese, 2007). For example, when a person picks up a cup with the intention of drinking, the next expected actions would be to bring the cup to the mouth and then to drink some coffee or tea. However, if the intention is to clean up, the expected action might be to carry the cup over to the sink. According to this idea, mirror neurons that respond to different intentions are responding to the action that is happening *plus* the sequence of actions that is most likely to follow, given the context.

The exact functions of mirror neurons in humans are still being actively researched (Caggiano et al., 2009; de Lange et al., 2008; Gazzola et al., 2007; Kilner, 2011). In addition to proposing that mirror neurons signal what is happening as well as the intentions behind various actions, researchers have also proposed that mirror neurons help us understand (1) communications based on facial expressions (Buccino et al., 2004; Ferrari et al., 2003); (2) emotional expressions (Dapretto et al., 2006); (3) gestures used while speaking (Gallese, 2007); (4) the meanings of sentences (Gallese, 2007); and (5) differences between ourselves and others (Uddin et al., 2007). As might be expected from this list, it has also been proposed that mirror neurons play an important role in guiding social interactions (Rizzolatti & Sinigaglia, 2010; Yoshida et al., 2011).

As with any newly discovered phenomenon, the function of mirror neurons is a topic of debate among researchers. Some researchers propose that mirror neurons play important roles in human behavior (as noted above), and others take a more cautious view (Cook et al., 2014; Hickock, 2009). Consider that when feature detectors that respond to oriented moving lines were discovered in the 1960s, some researchers proposed that these feature detectors could explain how we perceive objects. With the information available at the time, this was a reasonable proposal. However, later, when neurons that respond to faces, places, and bodies were discovered, researchers revised their initial proposals to take these new findings into account. In all likelihood, a similar process will occur for mirror neurons. Some of the proposed functions will be confirmed, but others may need to be revised.

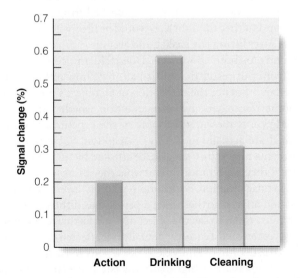

Figure 7.24 Iacoboni and coworkers' (2005) results, showing the brain response for the Action, Drinking, and Cleaning conditions.

SOMETHING TO CONSIDER:
Action-Based Accounts of Perception

The traditional approach to perception has focused on how the environment is *represented* in the nervous system and in the perceiver's mind. According to this idea, the purpose of visual perception is to create a representation in the mind of whatever we are looking at. Thus, if you look at a scene and see buildings, trees, grass, and some people, your perception of the buildings, trees, grass, and people is representing what is "out there," and so accomplishes vision's purpose of representing the environment.

But as you might have suspected after reading this chapter, many researchers believe that the purpose of vision is not to create a representation of what is out there but to guide our actions (Brockmole et al., 2013; Goodale, 2014; Witt, 2011a). We can appreciate the reasoning behind this idea by imagining a situation in which action is important for survival. Consider a monkey foraging for food in the forest. The monkey's color perception enables it to see some orange fruit that stands out against green leaves. The monkey reaches for the fruit and eats it. Of course, seeing (and perhaps smelling) the fruit is crucial, because it makes the monkey aware that the fruit is present. But the second step—reaching for the fruit—is just as important, because the monkey can't live on visual experiences alone. It has to reach for and grab the fruit in order to survive.

The idea that action is crucial for survival has been described by Melvyn Goodale (2011) as follows: "Many researchers now understand that brains evolved not to enable us to think, but to enable us to move and interact with the world. Ultimately, all thinking (and by extension, all perception) is in the service of action" (p. 1583). According to this idea, perception may provide valuable information about the environment, but taking a step beyond perception and acting on this information enables us to survive so we can perceive another day (Milner & Goodale, 2006). While there may be situations in which we take enjoyment in simply perceiving an object or scene—such looking at paintings in an art gallery or looking out at a misty lake in the morning—the vast majority of our experience involves two intertwined processes: *perceiving* an object or scene and *taking action* toward the objects or within the scene.

The idea that the purpose of perception is to enable us to interact with the environment has been taken a step farther by researchers who have turned the equation around from "action depends on perception" to "perception depends on action." The **action-specific perception hypothesis** (Witt, 2011a) states that people perceive their environment in terms of their ability to act on it. This hypothesis has been largely based on the results of experiments involving sports. For example, Jessica Witt and Dennis Proffitt (2005) presented a series of circles to softball players just after they had finished a game, and asked them to pick the circle that best corresponded to the size of a softball. When they compared the players' estimates to their batting averages from the just-completed game, they found that batters who hit well perceived the ball to be bigger than batters who were less successful.

Other experiments have shown that tennis players who have recently won report that the net is lower (Witt & Sugovic, 2010) and subjects who were most successful at kicking football field goals estimated the goal posts to be farther apart (Witt & Dorsch, 2009). The field goal experiment is especially interesting because the effect occurred only after they had attempted 10 field goals. Before they began, the estimates of the poor kickers and the good kickers were the same.

These sports examples all involved making judgments after doing either well or poorly. This supports the idea that perception can be affected by performance. What about situations in which the person hasn't carried out any action but has an expectation about how difficult it would be to perform that action? For example, what if people who were physically fit and people who were not physically fit were asked to estimate distances? To answer this question, Jessica Witt and her colleagues (2009) asked people with chronic back and/or leg pain to estimate their distance from various objects placed in a long hallway. Compared to people without pain, the chronic pain group consistently overestimated their distance from objects. The reason for this, according to Witt, is that over time people's general fitness level affects their perception of how difficult it will be to carry out various sorts of physical activity, and this in turn affects their perception of the activity. Thus, people with pain that makes walking difficult will perceive an object as being farther away, even if they are just looking at the object (see also Proffitt, 2006; Sugovic & Witt, 2013).

The idea that the expected difficulty of carrying out an action can influence a person's judgment of an object's properties was also studied by Adam Doerrfeld and coworkers (2012), who asked subjects to estimate the weight of a basket of golf balls before and after lifting the basket. Subjects made this estimate under two conditions: (1) solo, in which the subject expected that he or she would be lifting the basket alone, and (2) joint, in which the subject expected that he or she would be lifting the basket with another person. The actual weight of the basket of golf balls was 20 pounds. Before lifting the basket, the subjects, on average, estimated that the basket weighed 21 pounds if they thought they would be lifting it alone, and 17.5 pounds if they thought they would be lifting it with another person. After lifting the basket, the average estimate was about 20 pounds for both conditions. Doerrfeld and coworkers conclude from this result that anticipation of how difficult a task will be can influence the perception of an object's properties.

Some researchers, however, question whether the perceptual judgments measured in some of the experiments we have described are actually measuring perception. Subjects in these experiments might, they suggest, be affected by "judgment bias," caused by their expectations about what they think would happen in a particular situation. For example, subjects' *expectation* that objects could appear further when a person has difficulty walking, might cause them to say the object appears farther, even though their *perception* of distance was actually not affected (Durgin et al., 2009, 2012; Loomis & Philbeck, 2008; Woods et al., 2009).

This explanation highlights a basic problem in measuring perception in general: Our measurement of perception is based on people's responses, and there is no guarantee that these responses accurately reflect what a person is perceiving. Thus, as pointed out above, there may be some instances in which subjects' responses reflect not what they are perceiving, but what they think they should be perceiving. For this reason, researchers have tried very hard to conduct experiments in which the effects of action have been demonstrated even when there are no obvious expectations or task demands (Witt, 2011a, 2011b; Witt et al., 2010). A reasonable conclusion, taking a large number of experiments into account, is that in some experiments subjects' judgments may be affected by their expectations, but in other experiments their judgments may reflect a real relationship between their ability to act and their perception.

The results of the experiments demonstrating a relationship between ability to act and perception are consistent with J. J. Gibson's idea of affordances, described earlier (page 160).

Affordances, according to Gibson, are an object's "possibilities for action." Thus, perception of a particular object is determined both by what the object looks like and by the way we might interact with it (Witt & Riley, 2014).

This brings us to the following statement by J. J. Gibson, from his final book, *The Ecological Approach to Perception* (1979): "Perceiving is an achievement of the individual, not an appearance in the theater of his consciousness. It is a keeping-in-touch with the world, an experiencing of things, rather than a having of experiences" (p. 239). This statement did not lead to much research when it was proposed, but years later many researchers have embraced the idea that perception is not just "an appearance in the theater of consciousness," but is the first step toward taking action in the environment. In addition, some researchers have gone a step further and suggested that action, or the potential for action, may affect perception.

DEVELOPMENTAL DIMENSION Imitating Actions

Throughout this chapter, we have discussed many ways in which humans use perception to support action. We have seen how perceptual information such as optic flow is used to maintain balance, to perform a somersault, to walk toward an object, and even to land an airplane. We have discussed how the perception of landmarks is used to support wayfinding. We have even seen how the brain is able to integrate perception and action through the dorsal and ventral pathways, the parietal reach region, and the mirror neuron system. Clearly, humans are "built to act," and perception is an important component in the production of successful actions in the world. One way researchers have investigated the link between perception and action has been to determine how infants and young children learn to imitate the actions of others (Meltzoff et al., 2013).

The capacity to imitate the actions of others seems to be present from birth. In a classic demonstration of this, Andrew Meltzoff and Keith Moore (1977) showed that a group of infants aged 12 to 17 days imitate the facial expressions of an adult model (**Figure 7.25**). Imitating facial expressions may seem simple, but doing so reveals rather complex mental processing on the part of the infant. In order to imitate an adult's facial expressions, the infant must have the ability to see, the ability to control his or her facial muscles, *and* the mental ability to transform what is seen visually into an action that can be performed nonvisually (i.e., we can't see our own faces). This transformation is not simply the result of an automatic perception-to-action conversion process, however. Instead, it is purposeful and goal-oriented: children (and adults) imitate others because doing so teaches them how to perform and complete new tasks.

But infants don't always imitate exactly what they see other people doing. As they get older, they become able to use the information picked up from observing others' actions to create new, original actions. An example of how this occurs is provided by another experiment by Meltzoff (1995), who randomly assigned

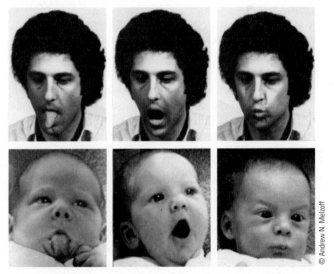

Figure 7.25 Newborn infants imitating facial expressions made by an adult. (From Meltzoff & Moore, 1977)

18-month-olds to one of three groups. Each group was shown five toys (**Figure 7.26a**). Children in the *successful demonstration group* watched an adult play with each toy. The adult modeled five target actions: pulling a barbell apart, placing a stick in the opening of a box, hanging a nylon loop on a peg, placing beads inside a jar, and placing a square cutout over a post.

Children in the *unsuccessful demonstration group* watched an adult attempt but fail to complete the target activities. The adult's hand slipped off the barbell before pulling it apart, missed the aperture with the stick, dropped the loop next to the peg so that it fell on the table, dropped the beads just to the left or right of the jar, and misaligned the square cutout so that the post never went through the hole. Children in the *control group* did not observe any demonstration. They were simply given the toys to play with.

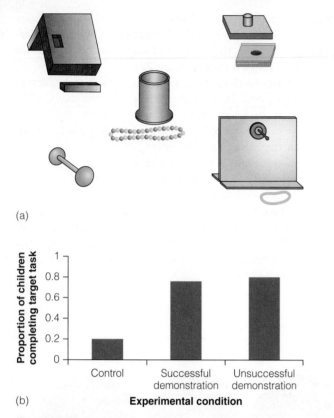

(a)

(b)

Experimental condition

Proportion of children completing target task (y-axis: 0, 0.2, 0.4, 0.6, 0.8, 1)

Control — Successful demonstration — Unsuccessful demonstration

Figure 7.26 (a) The toys used in Meltzoff's (1995) experiment were (starting top left) a box and stick toy, square and post, cylinder and beads, dumbbell, and a prong and loop toy. See text for description of the task associated with each toy. (b) Results of the experiment, showing the proportion of 18-month-olds in each experimental group that successfully completed the target actions. The key result is that the 18-month-olds who witnessed the adult unsuccessfully perform the action performed as well as those who saw the adult successfully perform the action. (Adapted from Meltzoff, 1995)

Meltzoff wanted to know how often the children in each group successfully completed the target actions. As you can see in **Figure 7.26b**, children in the control group successfully completed 24 percent of the target actions. In contrast, children in the successful interaction group completed the actions 78 percent of the time. This makes sense, because these children saw the adult complete the actions. But what about the children in the unsuccessful demonstration group? Rather than imitating the unsuccessful actions, these children successfully performed the target actions just as often as the children in the successful demonstration group. Children in the unsuccessful demonstration group pulled the barbell apart, placed the stick in the hole, hung the loop on the peg, placed the beads in the jar, and placed the cutout on the post even though they had never observed the adult complete these actions. This means that the children did not imitate the actions that they saw, but instead imitated the actions that they thought the adult was trying to complete.

Thus, as children get older, they go beyond rote imitation of the actions they see. They start to take into account not only what they see, but also other things they are observing and what they have learned about the world. Many experiments

have shown that when infants and young children see someone do something, they don't automatically imitate the action, but regulate their response based on what is happening in the environment. For example, Betty Repacholi and Meltzoff (2007) had 18-month-olds observe an adult carry out various actions that made noise, such as squashing a plastic cup, which made a popping or scraping noise. Another person, called the *emoter*, was in the room along with the child and the adult. The emoter commented on the adult's actions. In the anger condition, she made an unpleasant face and negative statements, like "that's annoying," after the adult carried out an action. In the neutral condition, the emoter's facial expression was neutral, and she said neutral or positive things, like "that's interesting."

The question was, would the child imitate the adult's actions when given an opportunity? The answer depended on whether the emoter was angry or neutral toward the adult actor. Children were less likely to imitate the adult actor when the emoter was angry. Experiments like this, plus many others (see Meltzoff et al., 2013), show that at an early age infants begin using top-down information (see Chapter 1, p. 10), based on the situation they are in, to determine whether and how often they should imitate others. This use of top-down information is exactly what adults do when they predict other people's intentions (page 164) and perceive the environment in terms of their ability to act on it (page 166). The link between perception and action begins early and continues developing into adulthood.

TEST YOURSELF 7.2

1. What is an affordance? Describe the results of the experiments on patient M.P. that illustrates the operation of affordances.

2. How does the idea of *what* (ventral) and *how* (dorsal) streams help us describe an action such as reaching for a coffee cup?

3. What is the parietal reach region? Describe Fattori's experiments on "grasping neurons."

4. What are mirror neurons? What is the evidence that mirror neurons aren't just responding to a specific pattern of motion?

5. Describe Iacoboni's experiment that suggested there are mirror neurons that respond to intentions.

6. What is a possible mechanism that might be involved in mirror neurons that respond to intentions?

7. What are some of the proposed functions of mirror neurons? What is the scientific status of these proposals?

8. Describe the action-based account of perception. In your discussion, indicate (a) why some researchers think the brain evolved to enable us to take action and (b) how experiments have demonstrated a link between perception and "ability to act."

9. How did Meltzoff and Moore demonstrate imitation in 12- to 17-day-old infants?

10. Describe experiments that show that infants don't always imitate exactly what they see other people doing. How do the results of these experiments relate to adult behaviors related to perception and action?

THINK ABOUT IT

1. Can you identify specific environmental information that you use to help you carry out actions in the environment? This question is often particularly relevant to athletes.

2. It is a common observation that people tend to slow down as they are driving through long tunnels. Explain the possible role of optic flow in this situation. (p. 150)

3. We have seen that gymnasts appear to take visual information into account as they are in the act of executing a somersault. In the sport of synchronized diving, two people execute a dive simultaneously from two side-by-side diving boards. They are judged based on how well they execute the dive and how well the two divers are synchronized with each other. What environmental stimuli do you think synchronized divers need to take into account in order to be successful? (p. 151)

4. If mirror neurons do signal intentions, what does that say about the role of top-down and bottom-up processing in determining the response of mirror neurons? (p. 163)

5. How do you think the response of your mirror neurons might be affected by how well you know a person whose actions you were observing? (p. 163)

6. How does your experience in interacting with the environment (climbing hills, playing sports) correspond or not correspond to the findings of the "potential for action" experiments described in the Something to Consider section? (p. 166)

KEY TERMS

Action-specific perception hypothesis (p. 166)
Affordances (p. 160)
Audiovisual mirror neurons (p. 163)
Border cells (p. 158)
Cognitive map (p. 157)
Ecological approach to perception (p. 150)
Ecological validity (p. 149)
Focus of expansion (FOE). (p. 150)

Gradient of flow (p. 150)
Grid cells (p. 158)
Head direction cells (p. 158)
Invariant information (p. 150)
Landmarks (p. 155)
Mirror neurons (p. 163)
Mirror neuron system (p. 164)
Optic flow (p. 150)
Parietal reach region (PRR) (p. 161)

Place cells (p. 158)
Place field (p. 158)
Self-produced information (p. 151)
Spatial updating (p. 154)
Topographical agnosia (p. 157)
Visual direction strategy (p. 153)
Visuomotor grip cells (p. 163)
Wayfinding (p. 155)

We perceive motion when an image, such as the one created by these flying birds, moves across our retina. But we also see these birds as moving if we follow them with our eyes, so their image remains stationary on our retina. This chapter explores cognitive and physiological mechanisms that enable us to perceive movement under a variety of conditions.

CHAPTER 8

Perceiving Motion

CHAPTER CONTENTS

Functions of Motion Perception

Motion Provides Information About
    Objects

Motion Attracts Attention

Motion Helps Us Understand Events
    in Our Environment

Life Without Motion Perception

Studying Motion Perception

When Do We Perceive Motion?

Comparing Real and Apparent Motion

What We Want to Explain

**Motion Perception: Information
in the Environment**

**Motion Perception: Retina/
Eye Information**

The Reichardt Detector

Corollary Discharge Theory

Motion Perception and the Brain

The Movement Area of the Brain

Effect of Lesioning, Deactivating,
    and Stimulating

Motion From a Single Neuron's Point
    of View

Motion and the Human Body

Apparent Motion of the Body

Motion of Point-Light Walkers

SOMETHING TO CONSIDER: **Motion
Responses to Still Pictures**

DEVELOPMENTAL DIMENSION: **Motion
Preferences Among Newborn Babies**

THINK ABOUT IT

Some Questions We Will Consider:

- Why do some animals freeze in place when they sense danger? (p. 171)

- How do films create movement from still pictures? (p. 174)

- When we scan or walk through a room, the image of the room moves across the retina, but we perceive the room and the objects in it as remaining stationary. Why does this occur? (p. 179)

W e are constantly taking action, either dramatically—as in Serena's bike ride in Chapter 7 (page 149)—or routinely, as in reaching for a coffee cup or walking across a room. Whatever form action takes, it involves motion, and one of the things that makes the study of motion perception both fascinating and challenging is that we are not simply passive observers of the motion of others—we are often moving ourselves. Thus, we perceive motion when we are stationary, as when we are watching other people cross the street (**Figure 8.1a**), and we also perceive motion when we ourselves are moving, as might happen when playing basketball (**Figure 8.1b**). We will see in this chapter that both the "simple" case of a stationary observer perceiving motion and the more complicated case of a moving observer perceiving motion involve complex "behind-the-scenes" mechanisms.

Functions of Motion Perception

Motion perception has a number of different functions, ranging from helping us perceive things such as the shapes of objects to providing us with updates about what is happening. Perhaps most important of all, especially for animals, the perception of motion is intimately linked to survival.

Motion Provides Information About Objects

Motion is an important aspect of object recognition because it reveals information about objects that might otherwise be difficult to discern. Look at **Figure 8.2**. How easy is it to spot the animal in each picture? When remaining stationary, as they are in these photographs, each animal is difficult to find because its color, shape, and patterning are similar to those found in the surrounding environment. However, even a perfectly camouflaged animal is revealed by motion. Movement perceptually organizes all the elements of the animal (think back to our discussion of common fate in Chapter 5, page 102), and results in a single figure that is separated from the background. A hungry leopard therefore moves very slowly while stalking an

(a)

(b)

Figure 8.1 Motion perception occurs (a) when a stationary observer perceives moving stimuli, such as this couple crossing the street, and (b) when a moving observer, like this basketball player, perceives moving stimuli, such as the other players on the court.

antelope, and a frightened field mouse will freeze in the hope that stillness will make it more difficult for a hawk to see it against the surrounding landscape.

You might say that camouflaged animals seem like a special case of motion being important for object recognition because most of the objects we see in the world are not intentionally hidden. But if you remember our discussion from Chapter 5 (page 97) about how even clearly visible objects may be ambiguous, you can appreciate how motion of an object can reveal characteristics that might not be obvious

from a single, stationary view (**Figure 8.3a**). Movement of an observer around an object can have a similar effect: viewing the "horse" in **Figure 8.3b** from different perspectives reveals that its shape is not exactly what you may have expected based on your initial view. Thus, our own motion relative to objects is constantly adding to the information we have about those objects, and, most relevant to this chapter, we receive similar information when objects move relative to us. Observers perceive shapes more rapidly and accurately when an object is moving (Wexler et al., 2001).

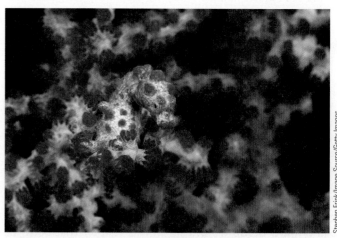

(a)

(b)

Figure 8.2 Even perfectly camouflaged animals like this (a) leaf-tail gecko and (b) pygmy sea horse would be instantly revealed by their movement.

(a)

(b)

Figure 8.3 (a) The shape and features of this car are revealed as different aspects of it become visible as it moves. (b) Moving around this "horse" reveals its true shape.

© Bruce Goldstein

Motion Attracts Attention

Movement also plays an important role in animal survival because motion attracts attention. You may have experienced this yourself in several ways. For example, as you try to find your friend among a sea of faces in the stadium, you realize you have no idea where to look. But suddenly you see a person waving and recognize that it is your friend. Alternatively, you may be reading a book (perhaps this one!) under your favorite tree on the quad when a stray baseball flies in your general direction. Without thinking, your natural response is to look up from your book and quickly move out of the ball's path. These are examples of *attentional capture*, discussed in Chapter 6 (page 127), in which our attention is automatically drawn to salient objects. Motion is a very salient aspect of the environment, so it attracts our attention (Franconeri & Simons, 2003). Combining attentional capture with our earlier discussion of the effects of motion on object recognition, we can see that not only is a still animal more likely to maintain its camouflage, it is also less likely to be noticed because freezing in place eliminates the attention-attracting effects of movement.

Motion Helps Us Understand Events in Our Environment

As you walk through a shopping mall, looking at the displays in the store windows, you are also observing other actions—a group of people engaged in an animated conversation, a salesperson rearranging piles of clothing and then walking over to the cash register to help a customer, people in a crowded restaurant captivated by a climactic moment in a basketball game.

Much of what you observe involves information provided by motion. The gestures of the people in the group indicate the intensity of their conversation; the motions of the salesperson indicate what she is doing, and changes in her motion indicate when she has shifted to a new task; and motion indicates, even in the absence of sound, that something important is happening in the game (Zacks, 2004; Zacks & Swallow, 2007).

A particularly compelling demonstration of motion's power to indicate what is happening was provided by Fritz Heider and Marianne Simmel (1944), who showed a 2½-minute animated film to subjects and asked them to describe what was happening in the movie. The movie consisted of a "house" and three "characters"—a small circle, a small triangle, and a large triangle. These three geometric objects moved around both inside and outside the house, and sometimes interacted with each other (**Figure 8.4**). Although the characters were geometric objects, the subjects created stories to explain the objects' actions, often giving them humanlike characteristics and personalities. For example, one account described the small triangle and circle as a couple who were trying to be alone in the house when the big triangle ("a bully") entered the house and interrupted them. The small triangle didn't appreciate this intrusion and attacked the big triangle. In other studies, researchers have shown how such simple motion displays can evoke interpretations of desire, coaxing, chasing, fighting, mocking, fearfulness, and seduction (Abell et al., 2000; Barrett et al., 2005; Castelli et al., 2000; Csibra, 2008; Gao et al., 2009). Who would have thought the world of geometric objects could be so exciting?

Returning to the world of people, let's consider the role motion plays in understanding the events that might take place within a campus coffee shop. For example, you might observe a man enter the shop, stop at the counter, have a brief conversation with the barista, who in turn leaves and returns with coffee in a paper cup. The customer pushes down on the lid to make sure it is secure, pays for the coffee, drops a tip into the tip jar, turns around, and walks out the door. This short description, which represents only a small fraction of what is happening in the coffee shop, is a sequence of events unfolding in time. Just as we can segment a static scene into individual objects, we can segment ongoing behavior into a sequence of events, where an **event** is defined as a segment of time at a particular location that is perceived by observers to have a beginning and an end (Zacks & Tversky, 2001; Zacks et al., 2009). In our coffee shop scenario, placing an order with the coffee

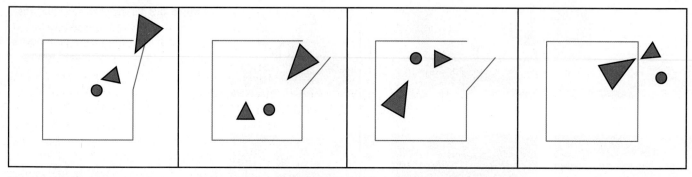

Figure 8.4 Still images from a film like one used by Heider and Simmel (1944). The objects moved in various ways, going in and out of the "house" and sometimes interacting with each other. The nature of the movements led subjects to make up stories that often described the objects as having feelings, motivations, and personalities.

barista is an event, reaching out to accept the cup of coffee is an event, dropping change in the tip jar is an event, and so on. The point in time when each of these events ends and the next one begins is called an **event boundary**.

The connection of events to motion perception becomes obvious when we consider that events almost always involve motion, and that changes in the nature of motion are often associated with event boundaries. One pattern of motion occurs when placing the order, another when reaching out for the coffee cup, and so on. Jeffrey Zacks and coworkers (2009) have measured the connection between events and motion perception by having subjects watch films of common activities such as paying bills or washing dishes and asking them to press a button when they believe one unit of meaningful activity ends and another begins (Newtson & Engquist, 1976; Zacks et al., 2001). When Zacks compared event boundaries to the actor's body movements measured with a motion tracking system, he found that event boundaries were more likely to occur when there was a change in the speed or acceleration of the actor's hands. From the results of this and other experiments, Zacks concluded that the perception of movement plays an important role in separating activities into meaningful events.

This brings us back to our example at the beginning of this section, in which we described the motions of a salesperson in a clothing store and noted that the person's motions indicated not only what she was doing (rearranging clothes) but also indicated when a new task began (helping a customer). Events, which are often defined by motion, follow one after the other to create our understanding of what is happening.

Life Without Motion Perception

Perhaps the most dramatic way to illustrate the importance of motion perception to daily life (and survival) comes from case studies of individuals who, through disease or trauma, suffer from damage to parts of the brain responsible for perceiving and understanding movement. When this happens, a person is said to suffer from a condition called **akinetopsia** or "motion blindness," where motion is either very difficult or impossible to perceive. The most famous and well-studied case

of akinetopsia is that of a 43-year-old woman known as L.M. (Zihl et al., 1983, 1991). Without the ability to perceive motion following a stroke, L.M. was unable to successfully complete activities as simple as pouring a cup of tea. As she put it, "the fluid appeared to be frozen, like a glacier," and without the ability to perceive the tea rising in the cup, she had trouble knowing when to stop pouring. Her condition caused other, more serious problems as well. It was difficult for her to follow dialogue because she couldn't see the motions of a speaker's face and mouth, and people suddenly appeared or disappeared because she couldn't see them approaching or leaving. Crossing the street presented serious problems because at first a car might seem far away, but then suddenly, without warning, it would appear very near. Thus, her disability was not just a social inconvenience but enough of a threat to the woman's well-being that she rarely ventured outside into the world of moving—and sometimes dangerous—objects.

Studying Motion Perception

To describe how motion perception is studied, the first question we will consider is: When do we perceive motion?

When Do We Perceive Motion?

The answer to this question may seem obvious: We perceive motion when something moves across our field of view. Actual motion of an object is called **real motion**. Perceiving a car driving by, people walking, or a bug scurrying across a tabletop are all examples of the perception of real motion.

The perception of motion can also be produced by stimuli that are not moving. Perception of motion when there actually is none is called **illusory motion**. The most famous, and best studied, type of illusory motion is called **apparent motion**. We introduced apparent motion in Chapter 5 when we told the story of Max Wertheimer's observation that when two stimuli in slightly different locations are alternated with the correct timing, an observer perceives one stimulus moving back and forth smoothly between the two locations (**Figure 8.5a;** also see Figure 5.13, page 99). This perception is called apparent

(a)　　　Flash　　　　　Dark　　　　　Flash

(b)

© Bruce Goldstein

Figure 8.5 Apparent motion (a) between two lights when they are rapidly flashed one after the other; (b) on a moving sign. Our perception of words moving across a lighted display is so compelling that it is often difficult to realize that signs like this are simply lights flashing on an off.

motion because there is no actual (or real) motion between the stimuli. This is the basis for the motion we perceive in movies, on television, and in moving signs that are used for advertising and entertainment (**Figure 8.5b**).

Induced motion occurs when motion of one object (usually a large one) causes a nearby stationary object (usually smaller) to appear to move. For example, the moon usually appears stationary in the sky. However, if clouds are moving past the moon on a windy night, the moon may appear to be racing through the clouds. In this case, movement of the larger object (clouds covering a large area) makes the smaller, but actually stationary, moon appear to be moving.

Motion aftereffects occur when viewing a moving stimulus causes a stationary stimulus to appear to move (Glasser et al., 2011). One example of a motion aftereffect is the **waterfall illusion** (Addams, 1834) (**Figure 8.6**). If you look at a waterfall for 30 to 60 seconds (be sure it fills up only part of your field of view) and then look off to the side at part of the scene that is stationary, you will see everything you are looking at—rocks, trees, grass—appears to move upward for a few seconds. If you're short on waterfalls, next time you are at the cinema, you may be able to induce this illusion by carefully watching the rolling credits at the end of the movie (you should sit toward the rear of the theater).

Dennis Barnes/Britain On View/Getty Images

Figure 8.6 An image of the Falls of Foyers near Loch Ness in Scotland where Robert Addams (1834) first experienced the waterfall illusion. Looking at the downward motion of the waterfall for 30 to 60 seconds can cause a person to then perceive stationary objects such as the rocks and trees that are off to the side as moving upward.

Researchers studying motion perception have investigated all the types of perceived motion described above—and a number of others as well (Blaser & Sperling, 2008; Cavanaugh, 2011). Our purpose, however, is not to understand every type of motion perception but to understand some of the principles governing motion perception in general. To do this, we will focus on real and apparent motion.

Comparing Real and Apparent Motion

For many years, researchers treated the apparent motion created by flashing stationary objects or pictures and the real motion created by actual motion through space as though they were separate phenomena, governed by different mechanisms. However, there is ample evidence that these two types of motion have much in common. For example, Axel Larsen and coworkers (2006) presented three types of displays to a person in an fMRI scanner: (1) a *control condition*, in which

Figure 8.7 Three conditions in Larsen's (2006) experiment: (a) control condition, in which two squares in slightly different positions were flashed simultaneously; (b) real motion, in which a small square moved back and forth; (c) apparent motion, in which squares were flashed one after another so that they appeared to move back and forth. Stimuli are shown on top and the resulting brain activation is shown below. In (c), the brain is activated in the space that represents the area between the two dots, where movement was perceived but no stimulus was present. (From Larsen et al., 2006)

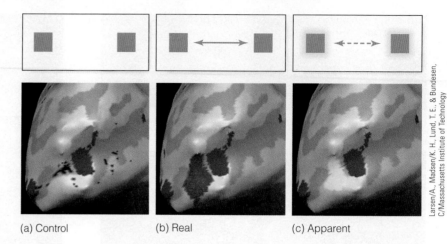

Larsen/A., Madsen/K. H., Lund, T. E., & Bundesen, C/Massachusetts Institute of Technology

(a) Control   (b) Real   (c) Apparent

two squares in slightly different positions were flashed simultaneously (**Figure 8.7a**); (2) a *real motion display*, in which a small square moved back and forth (**Figure 8.7b**); and (3) an *apparent motion display*, in which squares were flashed one after another so that they appeared to move back and forth (**Figure 8.7c**).

Larsen's results are shown below the dot displays. The blue-colored area in Figure 8.7a is the area of visual cortex activated by the control squares, which are perceived as two squares simultaneously flashing on and off with no motion between them. Each square activates a separate area of the cortex. In Figure 8.7b, the red indicates the area of cortex activated by real movement of the square. In Figure 8.7c, the yellow indicates the area of cortex activated by the apparent motion display. Notice that the activation associated with apparent motion is similar to the activation for the real motion display. Two flashed squares that result in apparent motion activate the area of brain representing the space between the positions of the flashing squares even though no stimulus was presented there.

Because of the similarities between the neural responses to real and apparent motion, researchers study both types of motion together and concentrate on discovering general mechanisms that apply to both. In this chapter, we will follow this approach as we look for general mechanisms of motion perception.

What We Want to Explain

Our goal is to understand how we perceive things that are moving. At first this may seem like an easy problem. For example, **Figure 8.8a** shows what Maria sees when she looks straight ahead as Jeremy walks by. Because she doesn't move her eyes, Jeremy's image sweeps across her retina. Explaining motion perception in this case seems straightforward because as Jeremy's image moves across Maria's retina, it stimulates a series of receptors one after another, and this stimulation signals Jeremy's motion.

Figure 8.8b shows what Maria sees when she follows Jeremy's motion with her eyes. In this case, Jeremy's image

(a) Jeremy walks past Maria; Maria's eyes are stationary (creates local disturbance in optic array)

(b) Jeremy walks past Maria; Maria follows him with her eyes (creates local disturbance in optic array)

(c) Scans scene by moving her eyes from left to right (creates global optic flow)

Figure 8.8 Three motion situations. (a) Maria is stationary and looks straight ahead as Jeremy walks past. (b) Maria follows Jeremy's movement with her eyes. (c) Maria scans the room by moving her eyes to the right. (The optic array and optic flow are described in the next section.)

remains stationary on Maria's retinas as he walks by. This adds an interesting complication to explaining motion perception, because although Jeremy's image remains stationary on her retina, Maria perceives Jeremy as moving. This means that

Table 8.1 Conditions for Perceiving and Not Perceiving Motion Depicted in Figure 8.8

	SITUATION	OBJECT	EYES	IMAGE ON OBSERVER'S RETINA	OBJECT MOVEMENT PERCEIVED?
1	Look straight as an object moves past	Moves	Stationary	Moves	YES
2	Follow a moving object with eyes	Moves	Move	Stationary	YES
3	Look around the room	Stationary	Move	Moves	NO

motion perception can't be explained just by the motion of an image across the retina.

Let's consider what happens if Jeremy isn't present, and Maria scans the room by moving her eyes from left to right. When Maria does this, the images of the walls and objects in the room move to the left across her retina (**Figure 8.8c**), but Maria doesn't see the room or its contents as moving. In this case, there is motion across the retina but no perception that objects are moving. This is another example of why we can't simply consider what is happening on the retina. **Table 8.1** summarizes the three situations in Figure 8.8.

In the sections that follow, we will consider a number of different approaches to explaining motion perception, with the goal being to explain each of the situations in Figure 8.8 and Table 8.1. We begin by considering an approach that focuses on how information in the environment signals motion.

Motion Perception: Information in the Environment

From the three situations in Figure 8.8, we saw that motion perception can't be explained by considering only what is happening on the retina. A solution to this problem was suggested by J. J. Gibson, who founded the ecological approach to perception. In Chapter 7 we noted that Gibson's approach (1950, 1966, 1979) involves looking for information in the environment that is useful for perception (see page 149). This information for perception, according to Gibson, is located not on the retina but "out there" in the environment. He thought about information in the environment in terms of the **optic array**—the structure created by the surfaces, textures, and contours of the environment—and he focused on how movement of the observer causes changes in the optic array. Let's see how this works by returning to Jeremy and Maria in Figure 8.8.

In Figure 8.8a, when Jeremy walks across Maria's field of view, portions of the optic array become covered as he walks by and then are uncovered as he moves on. This result is called a **local disturbance in the optic array**. This local disturbance in the optic array occurs when Jeremy moves relative to the environment, covering and uncovering the stationary background. According to Gibson, this local disturbance in the optic array provides information that Jeremy is moving relative to the environment.

In Figure 8.8b, Maria follows Jeremy with her eyes. Remember that Gibson doesn't care what is happening on the retina. Even though Jeremy's image is stationary on the retina, the same local disturbance information that was available when Maria was keeping her eyes still—Jeremy covering and uncovering parts of the array—remains available when she is moving her eyes, and this local disturbance information indicates that Jeremy is moving.

However, when Maria scans the scene in Figure 8.8c, something different happens: As her eyes move across the scene from left to right, everything around her—the walls, the window, the trash can, the clock, and the furniture—moves to the left of her field of view. A similar situation would occur if Maria were to walk through the scene. The fact that everything moves at once in response to movement of the observer's eyes or body is called **global optic flow**; this signals that the environment is stationary and that the observer is moving, either by moving her body or by scanning with her eyes, as in this example. Thus, according to Gibson, motion is perceived when one part of the visual scene moves relative to the rest of scene, and no motion is perceived when the entire field moves, or remains stationary. While this is a reasonable explanation for motion perception, we will see in the next section that we also need to consider other sources of information to fully understand how we perceive motion in the environment.

Motion Perception: Retina/Eye Information

Gibson's approach focuses on information that is "out there" in the environment. Another approach to explaining the various movement situations in Figure 8.8 is to consider the neural signals that travel from the eye to the brain. One such approach was a neural circuit proposed by Werner Reichardt (1969), which has come to be called the *Reichardt detector*.

The Reichardt Detector

A simplified version of the **Reichardt detector**, shown in **Figure 8.9**, can be used to explain the situation in Figure 8.8a, in which Jeremy walks across Maria's visual field, as she keeps her eyes steady. This circuit consists of two neurons, A and B, which send their signals to an **output unit** which compares the signals it receives from neurons A and B. The key to the operation of this circuit is the **delay unit** that slows down the signals from A as they travel toward the output unit. In addition, the output unit has an important property: It multiplies the responses from A and B to create the movement signal that results in the perception of motion (Borst, 2007).

Let's now consider how this circuit responds as Jeremy, whose position is indicated by the red dot, moves from left to right. **Figure 8.9a** shows that Jeremy, approaching from the left, first activates neuron A. This is represented by the "spikes" shown in record 1. This response starts traveling toward the output unit, but is slowed by the delay unit. During this delay, Jeremy continues moving and stimulates neuron B (**Figure 8.9b**), which also sends a signal down to the output unit (record 2). If the timing is right, the delayed signal from A (record 3) reaches the output unit just when the signal

from B (record 2) arrives. Because the output unit multiples the responses from A and B, a large movement signal results (record 4). Thus, when Jeremy moves from left to right at the right speed, a movement signal occurs and Maria perceives Jeremy's movement.

An important property of the circuit diagrammed in Figure 8.9 is that it creates a movement signal in response to movement from left to right, but does not create a signal for movement from right to left. We can see why this is so by considering what happens when Jeremy walks from right to left. Approaching from the right (**Figure 8.9c**), Jeremy first activates neuron B, which sends its signals directly to the output unit (record 5). Jeremy continues moving and activates neuron A (**Figure 8.9d**), which generates a signal (record 6). At this point, the response from B has become smaller because it is no longer being stimulated (record 7), and by the time the response from A passes through the delay unit and reaches the output unit, the response from B has dropped to zero (**Figure 8.9e**). When the output unit multiplies the delayed signal from neuron A (record 8) and the zero signal from neuron B, the result is zero, so no movement signal is generated.

More complicated versions of this circuit, which have been discovered in amphibians, rodents, primates, and humans

Figure 8.9 The Reichardt detector. Neurons A and B are stimulated when an object (the red dot) enters its receptive field. Activation is indicated by green, and by the numbered spike records. Panels (a) and (b) show activity within the detector as an object moves from left to right at two different points in time. The signals from neurons A and B meet at the output unit, and motion is perceived. Panels (c), (d), and (e) show activity within the same detector when an object moves from right to left at two points in time. In this case, the signals from A and B do not meet at the output unit, so no motion is perceived. See text for details.

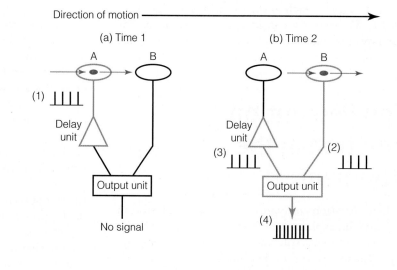

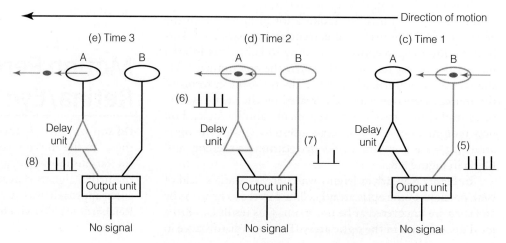

(Borst & Egelhaaf, 1989), create directionally sensitive neurons, which fire only to a particular direction of motion. The visual system contains many circuits like this, each tuned to a different direction of motion; working together, they can create signals that indicate the direction of movement across the visual field, as in Figure 8.8a.

Besides enabling us to determine the direction of motion, the Reichardt detector provides an additional benefit: it lets us determine speed (Meso & Zanker, 2009). To see why this is so, think back to the purpose of the delay unit. The delay is meant to ensure that activity from neuron A and neuron B arrive at the output unit at the same time. The duration of the delay is therefore crucial. If the signal from neuron A is not delayed long enough, it will arrive at the output unit before neuron B is stimulated. As a result, no motion will be detected (the signal from neuron B would be 0 when A arrives). If the duration of the delay is too long, the signal from neuron B will arrive at the output before the signal from neuron A (so the signal from A will be zero), and no motion will be detected. So, what is too short, too long, and just right? It depends on the speed of the moving object. Detectors that include a short delay will be selective for fast movement while detectors that include a long delay will be selective for slow movement.

Corollary Discharge Theory

Although Reichardt detectors might seem to have solved the problem of how neural responses signal movement, these detectors only work for situations such as Figure 8.8a, in which movement sweeps across an observer's stationary eyes. In order to explain situations like those in Figure 8.8b (when Maria moves her eyes to follow Jeremy's movements) and Figure 8.8c (when Maria scans the room), we need to take into account not only how the image is moving on the retina but also how the eye is moving. **Corollary discharge theory** takes eye movements into account. The first step in understanding corollary discharge theory is to consider how neural signals associated with the retina and with the eye muscles are related to the three situations in Figure 8.8 and Table 8.1.

Signals From the Retina and the Eye Muscles

Corollary discharge theory explains motion perception by taking into account the following signals, which are generated by movement of a stimulus on the retina and by movement of the eyes.

1. An **image displacement signal (IDS)** (**Figure 8.10a**) occurs when an image moves across receptors in the retina, as when Jeremy walks across Maria's field of view while she stares straight ahead.
2. A **motor signal (MS)** (**Figure 8.10b**) occurs when a signal is sent from the brain to the eye muscles. This signal occurs when Maria moves her eyes to follow Jeremy as he walks across the room.
3. A **corollary discharge signal (CDS)** is a copy of the motor signal that, instead of going to the eye muscles, is sent to a different place in the brain (Figure 8.10b). This is

analogous to using the "cc" (copy) function when sending an email message. The email goes to the person it is addressed to, and a copy of the email is simultaneously sent to someone else at another address.

Now that we have introduced these signals, we can see a solution to our problem by asking what situations 1 and 2, in which the object is perceived to move, have in common. We can answer that question by focusing on the two signals that are transmitted toward the brain: the image displacement signal (IDS) and the corollary discharge signal (CDS). In situation 1, when Maria keeps her eyes stationary and Jeremy's image moves across her retina, only an IDS occurs. In situation 2, in which Maria moves her eyes to follow Jeremy, so his image doesn't move across her retina, only a CDS occurs. So perhaps the solution is this: When only one type of signal, either the IDS or the CDS, is sent to the brain, motion is perceived. But if both signals occur, as happens in situation 3, when an observer scans the room as in Figure 8.8c, then no motion is perceived. This solution is, in fact, the basis of corollary discharge theory.

According to corollary discharge theory, the brain contains a structure or mechanism called the **comparator** that receives both the IDS and the CDS. The operation of the

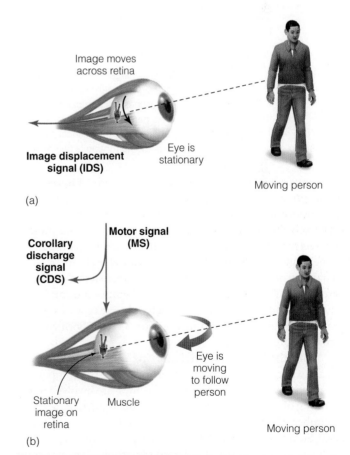

(a)

(b)

Figure 8.10 (a) When the image of an object moves across the retina, movement of the image across the retina creates an image displacement signal (IDS). (b) When a motor signal (MS) to move the eyes is sent to the eye muscles, so the eye can follow a moving object, there is a corollary discharge signal (CDS), which splits off from the motor signal.

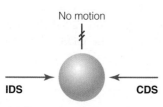

Perceive motion

IDS →

(a) Eye is stationary; stimulus is moving.

Perceive motion

CDS ←

(b) Eye follows moving stimulus.

No motion

IDS → ← **CDS**

(c) Eye moves across stationary scene.

Figure 8.11 According to the corollary discharge model, (a) when the IDS reaches the comparator alone, a signal is sent to the brain and motion is perceived; (b) when the CDS reaches the comparator alone, a signal is sent to the brain and motion is perceived; (c) if both a CDS and an IDS reach the comparator simultaneously, they cancel each other, so no signals are sent to the brain and no motion is perceived.

comparator is governed by the rules illustrated in **Figure 8.11**. If just one type of signal reaches the comparator—either the IDS (**Figure 8.11a**) or the CDS (**Figure 8.11b**)—it relays a message to the brain that "movement has occurred," and motion is perceived. If both the CDS and IDS reach the comparator at the same time (**Figure 8.11c**), they cancel each other, so no signal is sent to the area of the brain responsible for motion perception. This handles our problem, because motion is perceived in situations 1 and 2, in which only one type of signal is present, but isn't perceived in situation 3, when both types of signal are present.

While the IDS clearly originates in the retina, students often ask where the CDS comes from and where the comparator is located. Because several parts of the brain are involved in the planning of eye movements, the CDS probably originates from a number of different places in the brain (Sommer & Crapse, 2010; Sommer & Wurtz, 2008). Similarly, the comparator most likely involves a number of different structures. The important thing for our purposes is that corollary discharge theory proposes that the visual system takes into account both information about stimulation of the receptors and information about movement of the eyes. And although we can't pinpoint exactly where the CDS and comparator are located, there is evidence

Eye moves

Bleached patch stays stationary

(a)   (b)

Figure 8.12 Afterimage demonstration. (a) Stimulus to stare at. (b) When the eye moves, the image on the retina (the bleached area indicated by the red oval) remains stationary, but a CDS is sent to the comparator, so the afterimage appears to move.

that supports the theory. Here is some of the behavioral and physiological evidence.

Behavioral Evidence for Corollary Discharge Theory The next two demonstrations create a perception of motion even though there is no motion across the retina.

DEMONSTRATION | Eliminating the Image Displacement Signal With an Afterimage

Look at the center of the red circle in **Figure 8.12a** for about 60 seconds. Then look at a homogeneous surface such as your desk and observe what happens to the circle's afterimage, which appears on the surface (blink to make it come back if it fades), as you look around. Notice that the afterimage moves in synchrony with your eye motions.

Why does the afterimage appear to move when you move your eyes? The answer cannot be that an image is moving across your retina because the circle's image always remains at the same place on the retina. (The circle's image on the retina has created a small area of bleached visual pigment, which remains in the same place no matter where the eye is looking.) (**Figure 8.12b**) Without motion of the stimulus across the retina, there is no image displacement signal. However, the motor signals sent to move your eyes are creating a corollary discharge signal, which reaches the comparator alone, so the afterimage appears to move (Figure 8.11b).

DEMONSTRATION | Seeing Motion by Pushing on Your Eyelid

Pick a point in the environment and keep looking at it while *very gently* pushing back and forth on the side of your eyelid, as shown in **Figure 8.13**. As you do this, you will see the scene move.

Why do you see motion when you push on your eyeball? Lawrence Stark and Bruce Bridgeman (1983) did an

Figure 8.13 Why is this woman smiling? Because when she pushes on her eyelid, while keeping her eye fixed on one place, she sees the world jiggle.

experiment in which they instructed observers to keep looking at a particular point while pushing on their eyelid. Because the observers were paying strict attention to the instructions ("Keep looking at that point!"), the push on their eyelid didn't cause their eyes to move. This lack of movement occurred because the observer's eye muscles were pushing back against the force of the finger to keep the eye in place. According to corollary discharge theory, the motor signal sent to the eye muscles to hold the eye in place created a corollary discharge signal, which reached the comparator alone, as in Figure 8.11b, so Stark and Bridgeman's observers saw the scene move (also see Bridgeman & Stark, 1991; Ilg et al., 1989). ("Think About It" question 3, on page 192, is related to this explanation.)

These demonstrations support the central idea proposed by corollary discharge theory that there is a signal (the corollary discharge) that indicates when the observer moves, or tries to move, his or her eyes. When the theory was first proposed, there was little physiological evidence to support it, but now there is a great deal of physiological evidence for the theory.

Physiological Evidence for Corollary Discharge Theory In both of our demonstrations, there was a corollary discharge signal but no image displacement signal. What would happen if there were *no* corollary discharge signal but there *was* an image displacement signal? That is apparently what happened to R.W., a 35-year-old man who experienced vertigo (dizziness) anytime he moved his eyes or experienced motion when he looked out the window of a moving car.

A brain scan revealed that R.W. had lesions in an area of his cortex called the medial superior temporal (MST) area (see Figure 7.17, page 161), which plays an important role in the control of eye movements. Behavioral testing of R.W. also revealed that as he moved his eyes, the stationary environment

appeared to move with a velocity that matched the velocity with which he was moving his eyes (Haarmeier et al., 1997). Thus, when he moved his eyes to the left, there was an IDS, because images were moving across his retina to the right but the damage to his brain had apparently eliminated the CDS. Because only the IDS reached the comparator, R.W. saw motion when there actually was none.

Other physiological evidence for the theory comes from experiments that involve recording from neurons in the monkey cortex. **Figure 8.14** shows the response recorded from a motion-sensitive neuron in a monkey's extrastriate cortex. This neuron responds strongly when the monkey looks steadily at the fixation point (FP) as a moving bar (B) sweeps across the neuron's receptive field (RF) (**Figure 8.14a**). But what if the monkey moves its eyes to follow a moving fixation point so its eyes sweep across a stationary bar (**Figure 8.14b**)? In this case, the bar's image will sweep across the neuron's receptive field, just as it did in Figure 8.14a. Even though the bar is sweeping across the receptive field, just as before, the neuron doesn't fire (Galletti & Fattori, 2003).

This neuron is called a **real-motion neuron** because it responds only when the stimulus moves and doesn't respond when the eye moves, even though the stimulus on the retina—a bar sweeping across the cell's receptive field—is the same in both situations. This real-motion neuron must be receiving information like the corollary discharge signal, which tells the neuron when the eye is moving. Real-motion neurons have also been observed in many other areas of the cortex (Battaglini et al., 1996; Robinson & Wurtz, 1976), and more recent research has begun to determine where the corollary discharge signal is acting in the brain (Sommer & Wurtz, 2006; Wang et al., 2007).

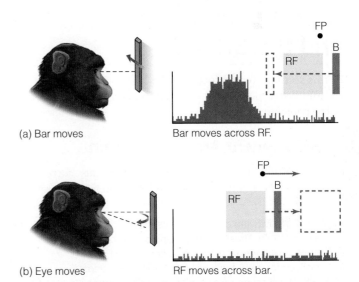

Figure 8.14 Responses of a real-motion neuron in extrastriate cortex of a monkey. In both cases, a bar (B) sweeps across the neuron's receptive field (RF) as the monkey looks at a fixation point (FP). (a) The neuron fires when the bar moves to the left across the receptive field. (b) The neuron doesn't fire when the eye moves to the right even though this causes the bar to move across the receptive field. (Adapted from Galletti & Fattori, 2003)

1. Describe four different functions of motion perception.

2. What is an event? What is the evidence that motion helps determine the location of event boundaries? What is the relation between events and our ability to predict what is going to happen next?

3. Describe four different situations that can result in motion perception. Which of these situations involves real motion, and which involve illusions of motion?

4. What is the evidence for similar neural responding to real motion and apparent motion?

5. Describe Gibson's ecological approach to motion perception. What is the advantage of this approach? (Give a specific example of how the ecological approach can explain the situations in Figure 8.8).

6. Describe the operation of the neural circuit that creates the Reichardt detector. Be sure you understand why the circuit leads to firing to movement in one direction, but no firing to movement in the opposite direction. Also explain how a detector circuit can be created that fires to a specific speed of motion.

7. Describe the corollary discharge model. In your description, indicate (1) what the model is designed to explain; (2) the three types of signals—image displacement signal, motor signal, corollary discharge signal; and (3) when these signals do and do not cause motion perception when reaching the comparator.

8. Describe behavioral and physiological evidence that supports the corollary discharge model.

Motion Perception and the Brain

In this section, we will focus on the brain, and specifically on the middle temporal (MT) area, which plays an important role in the perception of motion.

The Movement Area of the Brain

The perception of motion begins in the striate cortex, the region of the occipital lobe where information from the retinas first reaches the cortex (Figure 3.21, page 59). It is here that Hubel and Wiesel (1959, 1965) discovered neurons called complex cells that respond to bars that move in a specific direction (see Figure 3.25, page 61). While the striate cortex is therefore important for motion perception, it is only the first in a series of brain regions that are involved. Another area that contains many directionally sensitive cells is the middle temporal (MT) area (see Figure 7.17, p. 161). Evidence that the MT cortex is specialized for processing information about motion comes from experiments that have used moving dot displays in which the direction of motion of individual dots can be varied.

Figure 8.15a represents a display in which all of the dots are moving in random directions. William Newsome and coworkers (1995) used the term **coherence** to indicate the degree to which the dots move in the same direction. When the dots are all moving in random directions, coherence is 0 percent. **Figure 8.15b** represents a coherence of 50 percent, as indicated by the darkened dots, which means that at any point in time half of the dots are moving in the same direction. **Figure 8.15c** represents 100 percent coherence, which means that all of the dots are moving in the same direction.

Newsome and coworkers used these moving dot stimuli to determine the relationship between (1) a monkey's ability to judge the direction in which dots were moving and (2) the response of a neuron in the monkey's MT cortex. They found that as the dots' coherence increased, two things happened: (1) the monkey judged the direction of motion more accurately, and (2) the MT neuron fired more rapidly. The monkey's behavior and the firing of the MT neurons were so closely related that the researchers could predict one from the other. For example, when the dots' coherence was 0.8 percent, the monkey was not able to judge the direction of the dots' motion and the neuron's response did not differ appreciably from its baseline firing rate. But at a coherence of 12.8 percent—so, out of 200 moving dots, about 25 were moving in the same direction—the monkey judged the direction of the dots that were moving together correctly on virtually every trial, and the MT neuron always fired faster than its baseline rate.

Newsome's experiment demonstrates a relationship between the monkey's perception of motion and neural firing in its MT cortex. What is especially striking about Newsome's experiment is that he measured perception and neural activity in the same monkeys. Returning to the perceptual process introduced in Chapter 1 (Figure 1.11, page 11), which is shown in **Figure 8.16**, we can appreciate that what Newsome has done is to measure relationship C: the physiology–perception relationship.

Figure 8.15 Moving dot displays used by Britten and coworkers (1992). These pictures represent moving dot displays that were created by a computer. Each dot survives for a brief interval (20–30 microseconds), after which it disappears and is replaced by another randomly placed dot. Coherence is the percentage of dots moving in the same direction at any point in time. (a) Coherence = 0 percent. (b) Coherence = 50 percent. (c) Coherence = 100 percent. (Adapted from Britten et al., 1992)

No correlation
Coherence = 0

50% correlation
Coherence = 50%

100% correlation
Coherence = 100%

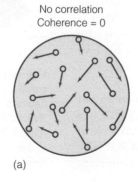

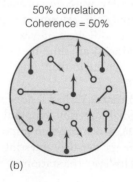

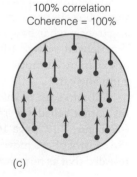

(a)　　　　　(b)　　　　　(c)

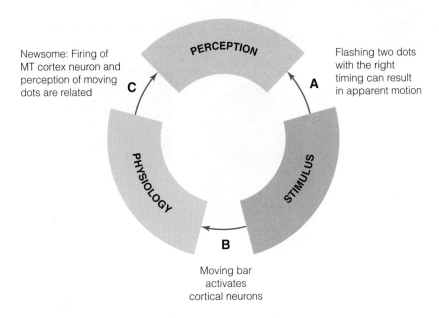

Newsome: Firing of MT cortex neuron and perception of moving dots are related

PERCEPTION

C

A

Flashing two dots with the right timing can result in apparent motion

PHYSIOLOGY

STIMULUS

B

Moving bar activates cortical neurons

Figure 8.16 The perceptual process from Chapter 1 (page 11). Newsome measured relationship C: the physiology–perception relationship, by simultaneously recording from neurons and measuring the monkey's behavioral response. Other research we have discussed has measured relationship A: the stimulus–perception relationship (for example, when flashing two dots creates apparent motion) and relationship B: the stimulus–physiology relationship (for example, when a moving bar causes a cortical neuron to fire).

This measurement of physiology and perception in the same organism completes our perceptual process circle, which also includes relationship A: stimulus–perception—the connection between how stimuli are moving and what we perceive; and relationship B: stimulus–physiology—the connection between how stimuli are moving and neural firing. While all three relationships are important for understanding motion perception, Newsome's demonstration is notable because of the difficulty of simultaneously measuring perception and physiology. In the next section, we will see how this relationship has been demonstrated by showing how perception is affected both by (1) lesioning (destroying) or (2) deactivating some or all of the MT cortex and by (3) electrically stimulating neurons in the MT cortex.

Effects of Lesioning, Deactivating, and Stimulating

A monkey with an intact MT cortex can begin detecting the direction dots are moving when coherence is as low as 1 to 2 percent. However, after the MT is lesioned, the coherence must be 10 to 20 percent before monkeys can begin detecting the direction of motion (Newsome & Paré, 1988; also see Movshon & Newsome, 1992; Newsome et al., 1995; Pasternak & Merigan, 1994). Further evidence linking the firing of MT neurons to perception of the direction of motion has been derived from experiments on human subjects using a method called **transcranial magnetic stimulation (TMS)** that temporarily disrupts the normal functioning of neurons.

METHOD | Transcranial Magnetic Stimulation (TMS)

One way to investigate whether an area of the brain is involved in determining a particular function is to remove that part of the brain, as Newsome did in his studies of the MT cortex in monkeys. Of course, we cannot purposely remove a portion of a person's brain, but it is possible to temporarily disrupt the functioning of a particular area by applying a strong magnetic

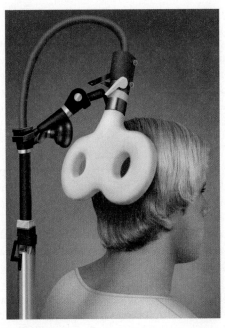

Figure 8.17 TMS coil positioned to present a magnetic field to the back of a person's head.

field using a stimulating coil placed over the person's skull (**Figure 8.17**). A series of electromagnetic pulses presented to a particular area of the brain for a few seconds interferes with brain functioning in that area for seconds or minutes. If a particular behavior is disrupted by the pulses, researchers conclude that the disrupted area of the brain is involved in that behavior.

When researchers applied TMS to the MT cortex, participants had difficulty determining the direction in which a random pattern of dots was moving (Beckers & Homberg, 1992). Although the effect was temporary, these subjects experienced a form of akinetopsia much like patient L.M., discussed earlier in this chapter.

The link between the MT cortex and motion perception has been studied not only by disrupting normal neural activity, but also by stimulating neurons in the MT cortex using a technique called *microstimulation*.

METHOD | Microstimulation

Microstimulation is achieved by lowering a small wire electrode into the cortex and passing a weak electrical charge through the tip of the electrode. This weak shock stimulates neurons that are near the electrode tip and causes them to fire, just as they would if they were being stimulated by chemical neurotransmitters released from other neurons. Thus, after locating neurons that normally respond to certain stimuli using methods such as single neuron recording (page 34), microstimulation techniques can be used to stimulate those neurons even when these stimuli are absent from the animal's field of view.

Kenneth Britten and coworkers (1992) used this procedure in an experiment in which a monkey was looking at dots moving in a particular direction while indicating the direction of motion it was perceiving. For example, **Figure 8.18a** shows that, under normal conditions, as a monkey observed dots moving to the right, it reported that the dots were indeed moving to the right. **Figure 8.18b**, however, shows how the monkey responded when the researchers stimulated neurons that are activated by downward motion. Instead of perceiving rightward motion, the monkey began responding as though the dots were moving downward and to the right. The fact that stimulating the MT neurons shifted the monkey's perception of the direction of movement provides more evidence linking MT neurons and motion perception.

In addition to the MT cortex, another area highly involved in motion perception is the nearby medial superior temporal (MST) area. In describing patient R.W. above (see page 181), we noted that the MST area is involved in eye movements, so it is particularly important in localizing a moving object in space. For example, a monkey's ability to reach for a moving object is adversely affected by both microstimulation and lesioning of the MST cortex (Ilg, 2008). Because motion plays a role in many processes, including object recognition, attentional selection, and the interpretation of events, it isn't surprising that aspects of motion activate many areas of the brain (Fischer et al., 2012; Gilaie-Dotan et al., 2013; Kourtzi et al., 2008; Murray et al., 2003; Rao et al., 2004; Williams et al., 2003).

Motion From a Single Neuron's Point of View

Having looked at the cortical areas specialized for perceiving motion, we will now look at a close-up of how motion perception is served by the firing of single neurons within the cortex (specifically area MT). The obvious answer to the question of how the firing of neurons can signal the direction in which an

(a) No stimulation

(b) Stimulation

Figure 8.18 (a) A monkey judges the motion of dots moving horizontally to the right. (b) When a column of neurons that are activated by downward motion is stimulated, the monkey judges the same motion as being downward and to the right.

object is moving is that as an image of the object sweeps across the retina, it activates directionally selective neurons that respond to movement in a specific direction (see Figure 3.25, page 61).

Although this appears to be a straightforward solution to signaling the direction an object is moving, it turns out that the response of individual directionally selective neurons does not provide sufficient information to indicate the direction of movement. We can understand why this is so by considering how a directionally selective neuron would respond to movement of a vertically oriented pole like the one being carried by the woman in **Figure 8.19a**.

We are going to focus on the pole, which is essentially a vertical bar. The ellipse represents the area of the receptive field of a neuron in the cortex that responds when a vertical bar moves to the right across the neuron's receptive field. Figure 8.19a shows the pole entering the receptive field on the left. As the pole moves to the right, it moves across the receptive field in the direction indicated by the red arrow, and the neuron fires.

(a)   (b)

Figure 8.19 The aperture problem. (a) The pole's overall motion is horizontally to the right (blue arrows). The ellipse represents the area in an observer's field of view that corresponds to the receptive field of a cortical neuron on the observer's retina. The pole's motion across the receptive field is also horizontal to the right (red arrows). (b) In this situation, the pole's overall motion is up and to the right (blue arrows). However, the pole's motion across the receptive field is horizontal to the right (red arrows), as in (a). Thus, the receptive field "sees" the same motion for motion that is horizontal and motion that is up and to the right.

But what happens if the woman climbs some steps? **Figure 8.19b** shows that as she walks up the steps, she and the pole are now moving up and to the right (blue arrows). We know this because we can see the woman and the flag moving up. But the neuron, which only sees movement through the narrow view of its receptive field, only receives information about the rightward movement (red arrows). You can demonstrate this for yourself by doing the following demonstration.

DEMONSTRATION | Movement of a Bar Across an Aperture

Make a small aperture, about 1 inch in diameter, by creating a circle with the fingers of your left hand, as shown in **Figure 8.20** (or you can create a circle by cutting a hole in a piece of paper). Then orient a pencil vertically, and move the pencil from left to right behind the circle, as shown by the blue arrows in **Figure 8.20a**. As you do this, focus on the direction that the *front edge* of the pencil appears to be moving across the aperture. Now, again holding the pencil vertically, position the pencil below the circle, as shown in **Figure 8.20b**, and move it up behind the aperture at a 45-degree angle (being careful to keep its orientation vertical). Again, notice the direction in which the *front edge* of the pencil appears to be moving across the aperture.

If you were able to focus only on what was happening inside the aperture, you probably noticed that the direction that the front edge of the pencil was moving appeared the same

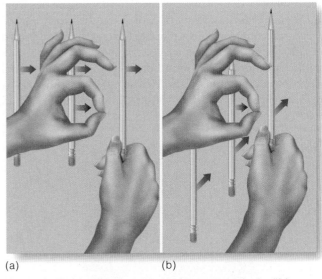

(a)   (b)

Figure 8.20 Moving a pencil behind an aperture in the "Movement of a Bar Across an Aperture" demonstration. See text for details.

whether the pencil was moving (a) horizontally to the right or (b) up and to the right. In both cases, the front edge of the pencil moves across the aperture horizontally, as indicated by the red arrow. Another way to state this is that the movement of an edge across an aperture occurs *perpendicular to the direction in which the edge is oriented*. Because the pencil in our demonstration was oriented vertically, motion through the aperture was horizontal.

Because the motion of the edge was the same in both situations, a single directionally selective neuron would fire similarly in (a) and (b), so based just on the activity of this neuron, it isn't possible to tell whether the pencil is moving horizontally to the right or upward at an angle. The fact that viewing only a small portion of a larger stimulus can result in misleading information about the direction in which the stimulus is moving is called the **aperture problem**.

Solving the Aperture Problem There are at least two solutions to the aperture problem (Bruno & Bertamini, 2015). The first was highlighted by one of my students who tried the pencil demonstration in Figure 8.20. He noticed that when he followed the directions for the demonstration, the edge of the pencil did appear to be moving horizontally across the aperture, whether the pencil was moving horizontally or up at an angle. However, he noted that when he moved the pencil so that he could see its tip moving through the aperture, as in **Figure 8.21**, he could tell that the pencil was moving up. Thus, a neuron could use information about the end of a moving object (such as the tip of the pencil) to determine its direction of motion. As it turns out, neurons that could signal this information, because they respond to the ends of moving objects, have been found in the striate cortex (Pack et al., 2003).

The second solution is to pool, or combine, responses from a number of neurons. Evidence for pooling comes from studies in which the activity of neurons in the monkey's MT cortex are recorded while the monkey looks at moving oriented lines like the pole or our pencil. For example, Christopher Pack and Richard Born (2001) found that the MT neurons' initial response to the stimulus, about 70 msec after the stimulus was presented, was determined by the orientation of the bar. Thus,

the neurons responded in the same way to a vertical bar moving horizontally to the right and a vertical bar moving up and to the right (red arrows in Figure 8.19). However, 140 msec after presentation of the moving bars, the neurons began responding to the *actual* direction in which the bars were moving (blue arrows in Figure 8.19). Apparently, MT neurons receive signals from a number of neurons in the striate cortex and then combine these signals to determine the actual direction of motion.

What all of this means is that the "simple" situation of an object moving across the visual field as an observer looks straight ahead is not so simple because of the aperture problem. The visual system apparently solves this problem (1) by using information from neurons in the striate cortex that respond to the movement of the ends of objects and (2) by using information from neurons in the MT cortex that pool the responses of a number of directionally selective neurons (also see Rust et al., 2006; Smith et al., 2005; Zhang & Britten, 2006).

Motion and the Human Body

Experiments using dots and lines as stimuli have taught us a great deal about the mechanisms of motion perception, but what about the more complex stimuli created by moving humans and animals that are so prevalent in our environment? We will now consider two examples of the ways in which researchers have studied how we perceive movement of the human body.

Apparent Motion of the Body

Earlier in this chapter we described *apparent motion* as the perception of motion that occurs when two stimuli that are in slightly different locations are presented one after the other. Even though these stimuli are stationary, movement is perceived back and forth between them if they are alternated with the correct timing. Generally, this movement follows a principle called the **shortest path constraint**—apparent movement tends to occur along the shortest path between two stimuli.

Maggie Shiffrar and Jennifer Freyd (1990, 1993) had observers view photographs like the ones in **Figure 8.22a**, with the photographs alternating rapidly. Notice that in the first picture, the woman's hand is in front of her head, and in the second, it is behind her head. According to the shortest path constraint, motion should be perceived in a straight line between the hands in the alternating photos, which means observers would see the woman's hand as moving through her head, as shown in **Figure 8.22b**. This is, in fact, exactly what happens when the pictures are alternated very rapidly (five or more times a second), even though motion through the head is physically impossible.

While the straight-line motion of the hand through the head is an interesting result, the most important result

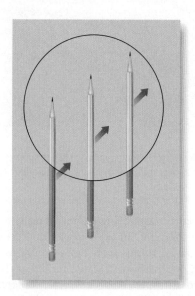

Figure 8.21 The circle represents a neuron's receptive field. When the pencil is moved up and to the right, as shown, movement of the tip of the pencil provides information indicating that the pencil is moving up and to the right.

Apparent motion stimulus (pictures alternate)

(a)

Two possible perceptions (as seen from above)

Path through head

Path around head

(b)   (c)

Figure 8.22 The two pictures in (a) are photographs similar to those used in Shiffrar and Freyd's (1993) experiment. The pictures were alternated either rapidly or more slowly. (b) When alternated rapidly, observers perceived the hand as moving through the head. (c) When alternated more slowly, the hand was seen as moving around the head.

occurred when the rate of alternation was slowed. When the pictures were alternated less than five times per second, observers began perceiving the motion shown in **Figure 8.22c**: the hand appeared to move around the woman's head. These results are interesting for two reasons: (1) They show that the visual system needs time to process information in order to perceive the movement of complex meaningful stimuli. (2) They suggest that there may be something special about the meaning of the stimulus—in this case, the human body—that influences the way movement is perceived. To test the idea that the human body is special, Shiffrar and coworkers showed that when objects such as boards are used as stimuli, the likelihood of perceiving movement along the longer path does not increase at lower rates of alternation, as it does for pictures of humans (Chatterjee et al., 1996).

What is happening in the cortex when observers view apparent motion generated by pictures like the ones in Figure 8.22? To find out, Jennifer Stevens and coworkers (2000) measured brain activation using brain imaging. They found that both movement through the head and movement around the head activated areas in the parietal cortex associated with movement. However, when the observers saw movement as occurring around the head, the motor cortex was activated as well. Thus, the motor cortex is activated when the perceived movements are humanly possible but isn't activated when the perceived movements are not possible. This connection between the brain area associated with perceiving movement and the motor area reflects the close connection between perception and taking action that we discussed in Chapter 7.

Motion of Point-Light Walkers

Another approach to studying motion of the human body involves stimuli called **point-light walkers** that are created by placing small lights on people's joints and then filming the patterns created by these lights when people walk and carry out other actions in the dark (Johansson, 1973, 1975; **Figure 8.23**).

Perceptual Organization At the beginning of the chapter, we discussed how movement can cause individual elements to become perceptually organized. Similarly, motion creates organization for point-light walkers. When the person wearing the lights is stationary, the lights look like a meaningless pattern. However, as soon as the person starts walking, with arms and legs swinging back and forth and feet moving in flattened arcs, first one leaving the ground and touching down, and then the other, the motions of the lights is immediately perceived as being caused by a walking person. This self-produced motion of a person or other living organism is called **biological motion**.

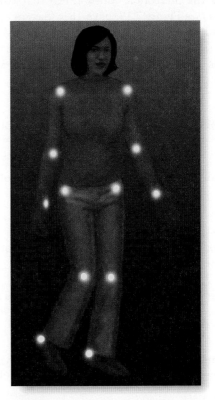

Figure 8.23 A point-light walker is created by placing lights on a person and having the person walk in the dark so only the lights can be seen.

Motion and the Human Body

One reason we are particularly good at perceptually organizing the complex motion of an array of moving dots into the perception of a walking person is that we see biological motion all the time. Every time you see a person walking, running, or behaving in any way that involves movement, you are seeing biological motion.

Brain Mechanisms Our ability to easily perceive biological motion in moving points of light led some researchers to suspect that there may be a specific area in the brain that responds to biological motion, just as there are areas such as the extrastriate body area (EBA) and fusiform face area (FFA) that are specialized to respond to bodies and faces, respectively (see pages 83–84).

Emily Grossman and Randolph Blake (2001) provided evidence supporting the idea of a specialized area in the brain for biological motion by measuring observers' brain activity as they viewed the moving dots created by a point-light walker (**Figure 8.24a**) and as they viewed dots that moved similarly to the point-light walker dots, but were scrambled so they did not result in the impression of a person walking (**Figure 8.24b**). They found that a small area in the superior temporal sulcus (STS; see Figure 5.49, page 118) was more active when viewing biological motion than viewing scrambled motion in all eight of their observers. In later experiments, researchers determined that other brain areas are also involved in the perception of biological motion. For example, both the FFA (Grossman & Blake, 2002) and the portions of the prefrontal cortex (PFC) that contain mirror neurons (see Figure 7.17, page 161) (Saygin et al., 2004) are activated more by biological motion than by scrambled motion. Based on these results, researchers have concluded that there is a network of areas that together are specialized

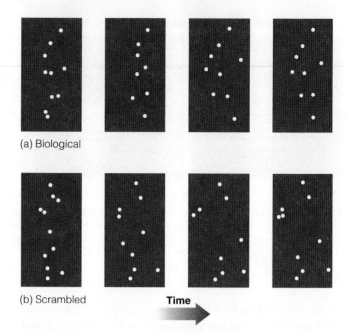

(a) Biological

(b) Scrambled   **Time**

Figure 8.24 Frames from the stimuli used by Grossman and Blake (2001). (a) Sequence from the point-light walker stimulus. (b) Sequence from the scrambled point-light stimulus.

for the perception of biological motion (also see Grosbras et al., 2012; Grossman et al., 2000; Pelphrey et al., 2003, 2005; Saygin, 2007, 2012). See **Table 8.2** for a summary of the structures involved in motion perception that we have discussed in this chapter.

One of the principles we have discussed in this book is that just showing that a structure responds to a specific type of stimulus does not prove that the structure is involved in *perceiving* that stimulus. Earlier in the chapter we described

Table 8.2 Brain Regions Involved in the Perception of Motion

BRAIN REGION	FUNCTIONS RELATED TO MOTION	EXAMPLE
Striate Cortex (V1)	Direction of motion across small receptive fields	
Middle Temporal Area (MT)	Direction and speed of object motion	
Medial Superior Temporal Area (MST)	Processing optic flow; locating moving objects; reaching for moving objects	
Superior Temporal Sulcus (STS)	Perception of motion related to animals and people (biological motion)	

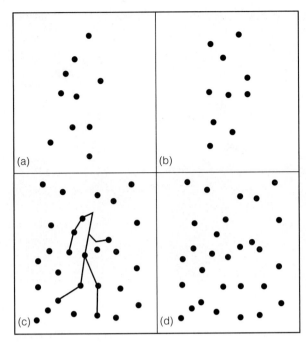

Figure 8.25 (a) Biological motion stimulus. (b) Scrambled stimulus. (c) Biological motion stimulus with noise added. The dots corresponding to the walker are indicated by lines (which were not seen by the observer). (d) How the stimulus appeared to the observer. (From Grossman et al., 2005)

how Newsome used a number of different methods to show that the MT cortex is specialized for the perception of motion (page 182). In addition to showing that the MT cortex is *activated* by motion, he also showed that *perception* of motion is decreased by lesioning the MT cortex and is influenced by stimulating neurons in the MT cortex. Directly linking brain processes and perception enabled Newsome to conclude that the MT cortex is important for the perception of motion.

Just as Newsome showed that disrupting operation of the MT cortex decreases a monkey's ability to perceive the direction of moving dots, Emily Grossman and coworkers (2005) showed that using transcranial magnetic stimulation (TMS) to disrupt the operation of the STS in humans decreases the ability to perceive biological motion (see "Method: Transcranial Magnetic Stimulation," page 183).

The observers in Grossman's (2005) experiment viewed point-light stimuli for activities such as walking, kicking, and throwing (**Figure 8.25a**), and they also viewed scrambled point-light displays (**Figure 8.25b**). Their task was to determine whether a display was biological motion or scrambled motion. This is normally an extremely easy task, but Grossman made it more difficult by adding extra dots to create "noise" (**Figures 8.25c** and **8.25d**). The amount of noise was adjusted for each observer so that they could distinguish between biological and scrambled motion with 71 percent accuracy.

The key result of this experiment was that presenting transcranial magnetic stimulation to the area of the STS that

is activated by biological motion caused a significant decrease in the observers' ability to perceive biological motion. Such magnetic stimulation of other motion-sensitive areas, such as the MT cortex, had no effect on the perception of biological motion. From this result, Grossman concluded that normal functioning of the "biological motion" area, STS, is necessary for perceiving biological motion. This conclusion is also supported by studies showing that people who have suffered damage to this area have trouble perceiving biological motion (Battelli et al., 2003). The ability to discriminate biological motion from randomly moving dots has also been shown to be adversely affected when transcranial magnetic stimulation is applied to other regions involved in the perception of biological motion, such as the prefrontal cortex (van Kemenade et al., 2012). What all of this means is that biological motion is more than just "motion"; it is a special type of motion that is served by specialized areas of the brain.

SOMETHING TO CONSIDER:

Motion Responses to Still Pictures

Throughout this chapter we have considered real and apparent motion. Consider, however, the picture in **Figure 8.26**. Most people perceive this picture as a "freeze frame" of an action—skiing—that involves motion. It is not hard to imagine the person moving to a different location immediately after this picture was taken. A situation such as this, in which a still picture depicts an action involving motion, is called **implied motion**. Despite the lack of any real or apparent motion, a variety of experiments have shown that the perception of implied motion depends on many of the mechanisms we introduced in this chapter.

Jennifer Freyd (1983) conducted an experiment involving implied motion by briefly showing observers pictures that depicted a situation involving motion, such as a person

Figure 8.26 A picture that creates implied motion.

Figure 8.27 Stimuli like those used by Freyd (1983). See text for details.

(a) First picture   (b) Forward in time   (c) Backward in time

jumping off a low wall (**Figure 8.27a**). Freyd predicted that subjects looking at this picture would "unfreeze" the implied motion depicted in the picture and anticipate the motion that was about to happen. If this occurred, observers might "remember" the picture as depicting a situation that occurred slightly later in time. For the picture of the person jumping off the wall, that would mean the observers might remember the person as being closer to the ground (as in **Figure 8.27b**) than he was in the initial picture.

To test this idea, Freyd showed subjects a picture of a person in midair, like Figure 8.27a, and then after a pause, she showed her observers either (1) the same picture; (2) a picture slightly forward in time (the person who had jumped off the wall was closer to the ground, as in Figure 8.27b); or (3) a picture slightly backward in time (the person was farther from the ground, as in **Figure 8.27c**). The observers' task was to indicate, as quickly as possible, whether the second picture was the same as or different from the first picture.

When Freyd compared the time it took for subjects to decide if the "time-forward" and "time-backward" pictures were different from the first picture they had seen, she found that subjects took longer to decide if the time-forward picture was the same or different. She concluded from this that the time-forward judgment was more difficult because her subjects had anticipated the downward motion that was about to happen and so confused the time-forward picture with what they had actually seen.

The idea that the motion depicted in a picture tends to continue in the observer's mind is called **representational momentum** (David & Senior, 2000; Freyd, 1983). Representational momentum is an example of experience influencing perception because it depends on our knowledge of the way situations involving motion typically unfold.

If implied motion causes an object to continue moving in a person's mind, then it would seem reasonable that this continued motion might be reflected by activity in the brain.

When Zoe Kourtzi and Nancy Kanwisher (2000) measured the fMRI response in the MT and MST cortex to pictures like the ones in **Figure 8.28**, they found that the area of the brain that responds to actual motion also responds to *pictures* of motion, and that implied-motion (IM) pictures caused a greater response than no-implied-motion (no-IM) pictures, at rest (R) pictures, or house (H) pictures. Thus, activity occurs in the brain that corresponds to the continued motion that implied-motion pictures create in a person's mind (also see Lorteije et al., 2006; Senior et al., 2000).

Building on the idea that the brain responds to implied motion, Jonathan Winawer and coworkers (2008) wondered whether still pictures that implied motion, like the one in Figure 8.26, would elicit a motion aftereffect (MAE) (see page 175). To test this, they conducted a psychophysical

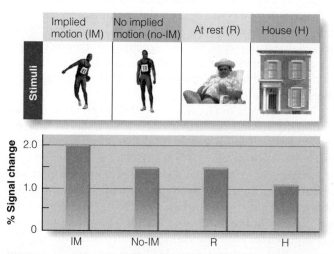

Figure 8.28 Examples of pictures used by Kourtzi and Kanwisher (2000) to depict implied motion (IM), no implied motion (no-IM), "at rest" (R), and a house (H). The height of the bar below each picture indicates the average fMRI response of the MT cortex to that type of picture. (From Kourtzi & Kanwisher, 2000)

experiment in which they asked whether viewing still pictures showing implied motion in a particular direction can cause a motion aftereffect (MAE) in the opposite direction. We described one type of motion aftereffect at the beginning of the chapter by noting that after viewing the downward movement of a waterfall, nearby stationary objects appear to move upward. There is evidence that this occurs because prolonged viewing of the waterfall's downward motion decreases the activity of neurons that respond to downward motion, so more upward motion neuronal activity remains (Barlow & Hill, 1963; Mather et al., 1998).

To determine whether implied motion stimuli would have the same effect, Winawer had his subjects observe a series of pictures showing implied motion. For a particular trial, subjects saw either a series of pictures that all showed movement to the right or a series of pictures that all showed movement to the left. After adapting to this series of pictures for 60 seconds, the subjects' task was to indicate the direction of movement of arrays of moving dots like the ones we described earlier (see Figure 8.15).

The key result of this experiment was that before observing the implied-motion stimuli subjects were equally likely to perceive dot stimuli with zero coherence (all the dots moving in random directions) as moving to the left or to the right. However, after viewing photographs showing rightward implied motion, subjects were more likely to see the dots as moving to the left. After viewing leftward implied motion, subjects were more likely to see the dots as moving to the right. Because this is the same result that would occur for adapting to real movement to the left or right, Winawer concluded that viewing implied motion in pictures decreases the activity of neurons selective to that direction of motion.

DEVELOPMENTAL DIMENSION Biological Motion Perception in Newborns

Many accounts of biological motion perception argue that our own experiences with people and animals are critical for developing the ability to perceive biological motion. Evidence for this claim comes, in part, from developmental studies that have shown that a child's ability to recognize biological motion in point-light displays improves as he or she gets older (Freire et al., 2006; Hadad et al., 2011). In fact, some studies suggest that adultlike levels of performance on point-light tasks is not achieved until early adolescence (Hadad et al., 2011). But even though it may take years to reach adult levels of performance, some research suggests that the ability to distinguish biological from nonbiological motion may be present at birth.

One line of evidence suggesting that the perception of biological motion may not depend on visual experience comes from animal studies. For example, Giorgio Vallortigara and his coworkers (2005) examined the preferences of newly hatched chicks for different types of motion. The chicks used in these experiments hatched in a dark room and were tested when they were only 2 hours old. Thus, these animals had no prior visual experiences. In the experiment, the chicks were placed in the middle of a long

platform (**Figure 8.29a**). Then, two point-light motion displays were presented, one at each end of the platform. At one end, the point-lights moved randomly while at the other end the motion of the point-lights resembled a walking adult hen (**Figure 8.29b**). Over the course of a 6-minute trial, the chicks were free to move along the platform naturally. Results showed that the chicks preferred to approach the biological motion display and spent the majority of their time on the end of the platform near the biological motion. This indicates that the chicks were able to identify—and, in fact, preferred—the biological motion displays despite not having had any prior visual experience. In order for this to happen, Vallortigara argued, chicks must possess perceptual mechanisms tuned to biological motion prior to hatching.

Intrigued by Vallortigara's experiments with newly hatched chicks, Francesca Simion and her coworkers (2008) wondered whether similar biological motion detector mechanisms might also be present in newborn humans. To find out, the researchers conducted a version of the chick study with 1- and 2-day-old newborns using the preferential looking procedure (see Chapter 2, page 44).

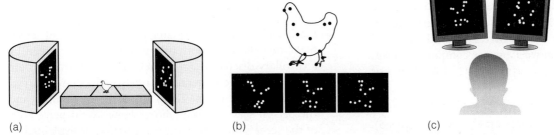

(a) (b) (c)

Figure 8.29 (a) The testing apparatus used by Vallortigara et al. (2005) to measure chicks' reactions to biological motion stimuli. Stimuli were shown on the monitors at each end of a platform. A chick's preference for one stimulus over the other is revealed by the amount of time the chick spends at each end of the platform. (b) Top: placement of point-lights on an adult hen. Bottom: three still images from an animated movie depicting a walking hen. (c) The testing apparatus used by Simion et al. (2008) to measure newborn reactions to biological motion. The newborn's preference for one stimulus over the other was revealed by the amount of time the newborn spent looking at each stimulus.

Simion conducted her experiment in the maternity ward of a hospital with full-term newborns. Infants in the study sat on an adult's lap while they were shown two movies simultaneously on side-by-side computer monitors (**Figure 8.29c**). On one screen, infants saw 14 point-lights moving in random directions. On the other screen, they were shown a movie where the 14 moving point-lights depicted the same walking hen used by Vallortigara in his experiment with chicks. Simion used the hen-walking animation because she could not ethically deprive the newborns of any visual experience prior to their participation in her study. So, the newborns may have obtained some *very* limited experience with human motion prior to the experiment, but it was very unlikely that they had seen any hens wandering about the hospital.

The researchers wanted to know if these newborns, like newly hatched chicks, would prefer the biological motion display to the random point-light display. They therefore compared the amount of time the infants spent looking at each movie. They discovered that the infants spent 58 percent of their time looking at the point-light hen, which was statistically greater than the time spent looking at the random point-light display. Thus, Simion and her colleagues concluded that, like chicks, humans are born with an ability to detect biological motion.

From their results, both Vallortigara and Simion argued that the ability to perceive biological motion occurs independent of experience. Perhaps perceptual mechanisms exist across many vertebrate animals that are specifically tuned to motion that is characteristic of locomotion. Evolutionarily, there may be important reasons for such mechanisms to be present, at least rudimentarily, early in life. For example, distinguishing biological from nonbiological motion may underlie processes by which animals distinguish living creatures from other objects. Even though it may take years of experience to fully develop the ability to perceive biological motion, having some

ability to do so very early in life might facilitate survival by, for example, helping animals detect predators.

TEST YOURSELF **8.2**

1. What is the evidence that the MT cortex is specialized for processing movement? Describe the series of experiments that used moving dots as stimuli and (a) recorded from neurons in the MT cortex, (b) lesioned the MT cortex, and (c) stimulated neurons in the MT cortex. What do the results of these experiments enable us to conclude about the role of the MT cortex in motion perception?

2. Describe the aperture problem—why the response of individual directionally selective neurons does not provide sufficient information to indicate the direction of motion. Also describe two ways that the brain might solve the aperture problem.

3. What is biological motion, and how has it been studied using point-light displays?

4. Describe experiments on apparent motion of a person's arm. How do the results differ for slow and fast presentations of the stimuli? How is the brain activated by slow and fast presentations?

5. Describe the experiments that have shown that an area in the STS is specialized for perceiving biological motion.

6. What is implied motion? Representational momentum? Describe behavioral evidence demonstrating representational momentum, physiological experiments that investigated how the brain responds to implied motion stimuli, and the experiment that used photographs to generate a motion aftereffect.

7. Describe how experiments with young animals and infants have been used to determine the origins of biological motion perception.

THINK ABOUT IT

1. We described the role of the Reichardt detector in the perception of real motion that occurs when we see things that are physically moving, such as cars on the road and people on the sidewalk. Explain how the detector illustrated in Figure 8.9 could also be used to detect the kinds of apparent motion on TV, in movies, on our computer screens, and in electronic displays such as those in Las Vegas or Times Square.

2. In the present chapter, we have described a number of principles that also hold for object perception (Chapter 5). Find examples from Chapter 5 of the following (page numbers are for this chapter):
   - There are neurons that are specialized to respond to specific stimuli. (p. 178)
   - More complex stimuli are processed in higher areas of the cortex. (pp. 182, 188)

   - Experience can affect perception. (pp. 188, 189)
   - There are parallels between physiology and perception. (pp. 183, 187, 190)

3. Stark and Bridgeman explained the perception of movement that occurs when pushing gently on the eyelid by a corollary discharge signal generated when muscles are pushing back to counteract the push on the side of the eye. What if the push on the eyelid causes the eye to move, and the person sees the scene move? How would perception of the scene's movement in this situation be explained by corollary discharge theory?

4. We described how the representational momentum effect shows how knowledge can affect perception. Why could we also say that representational momentum illustrates an interaction between perception and memory?

KEY TERMS

Akinetopsia (p. 174)
Aperture problem (p. 186)
Apparent motion (p. 174)
Biological motion (p. 187)
Coherence (p. 182)
Comparator (p. 179)
Corollary discharge signal (CDS) (p. 179)
Corollary discharge theory (p. 179)
Delay unit (p. 178)
Event boundary (p. 174)

Event (p. 173)
Global optic flow (p. 177)
Illusory motion (p. 174)
Image displacement signal (IDS) (p. 179)
Implied motion (p. 189)
Induced motion (p. 175)
Local disturbance in the optic array (p. 177)
Motion aftereffects (p. 175)
Motor signal (MS) (p. 179)

Optic array (p. 177)
Output unit (p. 178)
Point-light walkers (p. 187)
Real motion (p. 174)
Real-motion neuron (p. 181)
Reichardt detector (p. 178)
Representational momentum (p. 190)
Shortest path constraint (p. 186)
Transcranial magnetic stimulation (TMS) (p. 183)
Waterfall illusion (p. 175)

Each object in this picture of a Tucson doorway has a color, but as we see in this chapter, the color isn't in the objects themselves but is created by physiological mechanisms that begin in the retina and culminate in the brain.

CHAPTER 9

Perceiving Color

CHAPTER CONTENTS

Functions of Color Perception

Color and Light

Reflectance and Transmission

Color Mixing

Perceptual Dimensions of Color

The Trichromatic Theory of Color Vision

Color-Matching Evidence for Trichromatic Theory

Physiological Evidence for Trichromatic Theory

Are Three Receptor Mechanisms Necessary for Color Vision?

Opponent-Process Theory of Color Vision

Hering's Phenomenological Evidence for Opponent-Process Theory

Hurvich and Jameson's Psychophysical Measurements of the Opponent Mechanisms

Physiological Evidence for Opponent-Process Theory

How Opponent Responding Can Be Created by Three Types of Receptors

Color in the Cortex

Is There a Single Color Center in the Cortex?

Types of Opponent Neurons in the Cortex

Color Deficiency

Monochromatism

Dichromatism

Color in a Dynamic World

Color Constancy

Lightness Constancy

SOMETHING TO CONSIDER: Color Is a Creation of the Nervous System

DEVELOPMENTAL DIMENSION: Infant Color Vision

THINK ABOUT IT

Some Questions We Will Consider:

- Why does mixing yellow and blue paints create green? (p. 198)
- Why do colors look the same indoors and outdoors? (p. 214)
- Does everyone perceive color the same way? (pp. 212, 219)

Color is one of the most obvious and pervasive qualities in our environment. We interact with it every time we note the color of a traffic light, choose clothes that are color coordinated, or appreciate the colors of a painting. We pick favorite colors (blue is the most favored; Terwogt & Hoeksma, 1994), we associate colors with emotions (we turn purple with rage, red with embarrassment, green with envy, and feel blue; Terwogt & Hoeksma, 1994; Valdez & Mehribian, 1994), and we imbue colors with special meanings (for example, in many cultures red signifies danger; purple, royalty; green, ecology). But for all of our involvement with color, we sometimes take it for granted, and—just as with our other perceptual abilities—we may not fully appreciate color unless we lose our ability to experience it. The depth of this loss is illustrated by the case of Mr. I., a painter who became color blind at the age of 65 after suffering a concussion in an automobile accident.

In March 1986, the neurologist Oliver Sacks received an anguished letter from Mr. I., who, identifying himself as a "rather successful artist," described how, ever since he had been involved in an automobile accident, he had lost his ability to experience colors. He exclaimed with some anguish, "My dog is gray. Tomato juice is black. Color TV is a hodgepodge. . . ." In the days following his accident, Mr. I. became more and more depressed. His studio, normally awash with the brilliant colors of his abstract paintings, appeared drab to him, and his paintings, meaningless. Food, now gray, became difficult for him to look at while eating; and sunsets, once seen as rays of red, had become streaks of black against the sky (Sacks, 1995).

Mr. I.'s color blindness, a condition called **cerebral achromatopsia**, was caused by cortical injury after a lifetime of experiencing color, whereas most cases of total color blindness or of color deficiency (partial color blindness, which we'll discuss in more detail later in this chapter) occur at birth because of the genetic absence of one or more types of cone receptors. Most people who are born partially color blind are not disturbed by their decreased color perception compared to "normal," because they have never experienced color as a person with normal color vision does. However, some of their reports, such as the darkening of reds, are similar to Mr. I.'s. People with total color blindness often echo Mr. I.'s complaint that it is sometimes difficult to distinguish one object from another, as when his brown dog, which he could easily see silhouetted against a light-colored road, became very difficult to perceive when seen against irregular foliage.

Eventually, Mr. I. overcame his strong psychological reaction and began creating striking black-and-white pictures. But his account of his color-blind experiences provides an impressive testament to the central place of color in our everyday lives. (See Heywood et al., 1991; Nordby, 1990; Young et al., 1980; Zeki, 1990, for additional descriptions of cases of complete color blindness.) Besides adding beauty to our lives, color has other functions as well.

Functions of Color Perception

Color serves important signaling functions, both natural and contrived by humans. The natural and human-made world provides many color signals that help us identify and classify things: we know a banana is ripe when it has turned yellow, and we know to stop when the traffic light turns red.

In addition to its signaling function, color helps facilitate perceptual organization (Smithson, 2016), the processes discussed in Chapter 5 by which similar elements become grouped together and objects are segregated from their backgrounds (see Figures 5.19, 5.20, and 5.23 on pages 101–102).

Color's role in perceptual organization is crucial to the survival of many species. Consider, for example, a monkey foraging for fruit in the forest or jungle. A monkey with good color vision easily detects red fruit against a green background (**Figure 9.1a**), but a color-blind monkey would find it more difficult to find the fruit (**Figure 9.1b**). Color vision thus enhances the contrast of objects that, if they didn't appear colored, would be more difficult to perceive.

This link between good color vision and the ability to detect colored food has led to the proposal that monkey and human color vision may have evolved for the express purpose of detecting fruit (Mollon, 1989, 1997; Sumner & Mollon, 2000; Walls, 1942). This suggestion sounds reasonable when we consider the difficulty that color-blind humans have when confronted with the seemingly simple task of picking berries.

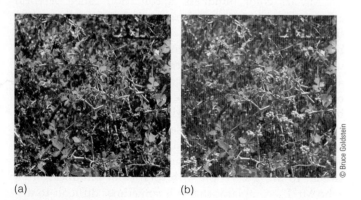

© Bruce Goldstein

(a)　　　　　　　　(b)

Figure 9.1 (a) Red berries in green foliage. (b) These berries become more difficult to detect without color vision.

Figure 9.2 Subjects in Tanaka and Presnell's (1999) experiment were able to recognize appropriately colored objects like the fruits on the left more rapidly than inappropriately colored objects like the fruits on the right.

Knut Nordby (1990), a totally color-blind vision scientist who sees the world in shades of gray, has described his own experience: "Picking berries has always been a big problem. I often have to grope around among the leaves with my fingers, feeling for the berries by their shape" (p. 308).

Our ability to perceive color not only helps us detect objects that might otherwise be obscured by their surroundings, it also helps us recognize and identify things we can see easily. James Tanaka and Lynn Presnell (1999) demonstrated this by asking observers to identify objects like the ones in **Figure 9.2**, which appeared either in their normal colors, like the yellow banana, or in inappropriate colors, like the purple banana. The result was that observers recognized the appropriately colored objects more rapidly and accurately. Thus, knowing the colors of familiar objects helps us recognize these objects (Oliva & Schyns, 2000; Tanaka et al., 2001). Expanding our view beyond single objects, color also helps us recognize natural scenes (Gegenfurtner & Rieger, 2000) and rapidly perceive the gist of scenes (Castelhano & Henderson, 2008) (see page 107).

In the discussion that follows, we will consider how our nervous system creates our perception of color. We begin by considering the relationship between color and light, and will then consider two theories of color vision.

Color and Light

For much of his career, Isaac Newton (1642–1727) studied the properties of light and color. One of his most famous experiments is diagrammed in **Figure 9.3a** (Newton, 1704). First, Newton made a hole in a window shade, which let a beam of sunlight enter the room. When he placed Prism 1 in its path, the beam of white-appearing light was split into the components of the visual spectrum shown in **Figure 9.3b**. Why did this happen? At the time, many people thought that prisms (which were common novelties) *added* color to light. Newton, however, thought that white light was a mixture of differently colored lights and that the prism separated the white light into its individual components. To support this hypothesis, Newton next placed a board in the path of the differently colored beams. Holes in the board allowed only particular beams to pass through while the rest were blocked. Each beam that passed through the board then went through a second prism, shown as Prisms 2, 3, and 4, for the red, yellow, and blue rays of light.

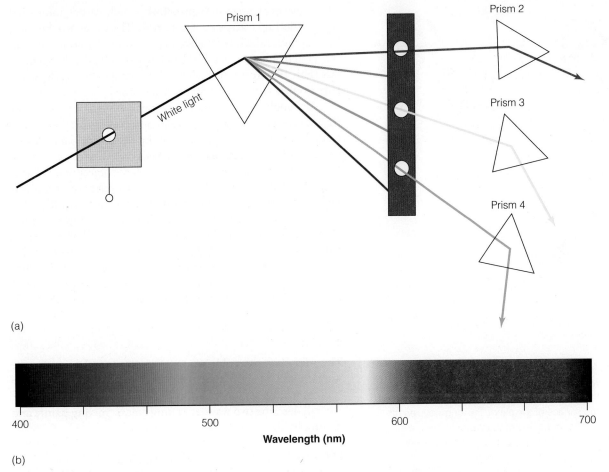

(a)

Wavelength (nm)

(b)

Figure 9.3 (a) Diagram of Newton's prism experiment. Light entered through a hole in the window shade and then passed through the prism. The colors of the spectrum were then separated by passing them through holes in a board. Each color of the spectrum then passed through a second prism. Different colors were bent by different amounts. (b) The visible spectrum.

Newton noticed two important things about the light that passed through the second prism. First, the second prism did not change the color appearance of any light that passed through it. For example, a red beam continued to look red after it passed through the second prism. To Newton, this meant that unlike white light, the individual colors of the spectrum are not mixtures of other colors. Second, the degree to which beams from each part of the spectrum were "bent" by the second prism was different. Red beams were bent only a little, yellow beams were bent a bit more, and violet beams were bent the most. From this observation, Newton concluded that light in each part of the spectrum is defined by different physical properties and that these physical differences give rise to our perception of different colors.

Throughout his career, Newton was embroiled in debate with other scientists regarding what the physical differences were between differently colored lights. Newton thought that prisms separated differently colored light particles while others thought the prism separated light into differently colored waves. Clarity on these matters would come in the 19th century when scientists conclusively showed that the colors of the spectrum are associated with different wavelengths of

light (Figure 9.3b). Wavelengths from about 400 to 450 nm appear violet; 450 to 490 nm, blue; 500 to 575 nm, green; 575 to 590 nm, yellow; 590 to 620 nm, orange; and 620 to 700 nm, red. Thus, our perception of color depends critically on the wavelengths of light that enter our eyes.

Reflectance and Transmission

The colors of *light* in the spectrum are related to their wavelengths, but what about the colors of *objects*? The colors of objects are largely determined by the wavelengths of light that are *reflected* from the objects into our eyes. **Chromatic colors**, such as blue, green, and red, occur when some wavelengths are reflected more than others, a process called **selective reflection**. The sheet of paper illustrated in **Figure 9.4a** reflects long wavelengths of light and absorbs short and medium wavelengths. As a result, only the long wavelengths reach our eyes, and the paper appears red. **Achromatic colors**, such as white, gray, and black, occur when light is reflected equally across the spectrum. Because the sheet of paper in **Figure 9.4b** reflects all wavelengths of light, it appears white.

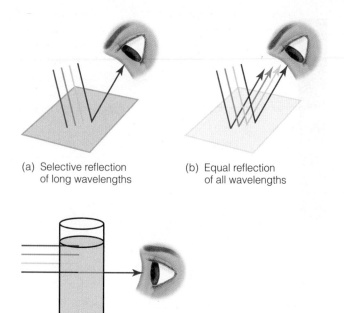

(a) Selective reflection of long wavelengths

(b) Equal reflection of all wavelengths

(c) Selective transmission of long wavelengths

Figure 9.4 (a) White light contains all of the wavelengths of the spectrum. A beam of white light is symbolized here by showing beams with wavelengths associated with blue, green, yellow, and red. When white light hits the surface of the paper, the long-wavelength light is selectively reflected and the rest of the wavelengths are absorbed. We therefore perceive the paper as looking red. (b) When all of the wavelengths are reflected equally, we see white. (c) In this example of selective transmission, the long-wavelength light is transmitted and the other wavelengths are absorbed by the liquid.

Individual objects don't usually reflect a single wavelength of light, however. **Figure 9.5a** shows **reflectance curves** that plot the percentage of light reflected from lettuce and tomatoes at each wavelength in the visible spectrum. Notice that both vegetables reflect a range of wavelengths, but each selectively reflects more light in one part of the spectrum. Tomatoes predominantly reflect long wavelengths of light into our eyes, whereas lettuce principally reflects medium wavelengths. As a result, tomatoes appear red whereas lettuce appears green. You can also contrast the reflectance curves for the lettuce and tomato with the curves for the achromatic (black, gray, and

white) pieces of paper in **Figure 9.5b**, which are flat, indicating equal reflectance across the spectrum. The difference between black, gray, and white is related to the overall amount of light reflected from an object. The black paper in Figure 9.5b reflects less than 10 percent of the light that hits it, whereas the white paper reflects more than 80 percent of the light.

Although most colors in the environment are created by the way objects selectively reflect some wavelengths, the color of things that are transparent, such as liquids, plastics, and glass, is created by **selective transmission**. Selective transmission means that only some wavelengths *pass through* the object or substance (**Figure 9.4c**). For example, cranberry juice selectively transmits long-wavelength light and appears red, whereas limeade selectively transmits medium-wavelength light and appears green. **Transmission curves**—plots of the percentage of light transmitted at each wavelength—look similar to the reflectance curves in Figure 9.5, but with percent transmission plotted on the vertical axis. Table 9.1 indicates the relationship between the wavelengths reflected or transmitted and the color perceived.

Color Mixing

The idea that the color we perceive depends largely on the wavelengths of light that reach our eyes provides a way to explain what happens when we mix different colors together. We will describe two ways of mixing colors: mixing paints and mixing lights.

Mixing Paints In kindergarten you learned that mixing yellow and blue paints results in green. Why is this so? Consider

Table 9.1 Relationship Between Predominant Wavelengths Reflected and Color Perceived

WAVELENGTHS REFLECTED OR TRANSMITTED	PERCEIVED COLOR
Short	Blue
Medium	Green
Long and medium	Yellow
Long	Red
Long, medium, and short	White

Figure 9.5 Reflectance curves for (a) lettuce and tomatoes (adapted from Williamson & Cummins, 1983) and (b) white, gray, and black paper (adapted from Clulow, 1972).

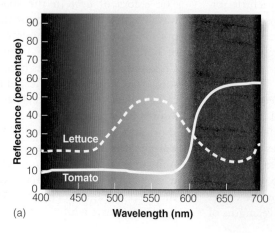

(a)

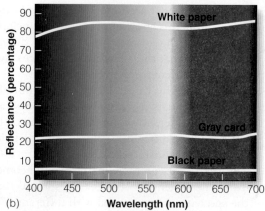

(b)

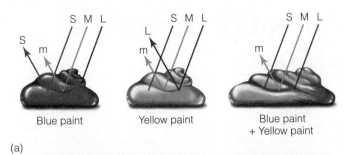

(a)

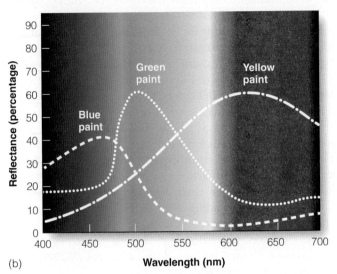

(b)

Figure 9.6 Color mixing with paint. Mixing blue paint and yellow paint creates a paint that appears green. This is subtractive color mixture.

the blobs of paint in **Figure 9.6a**. The blue blob absorbs long-wavelength light and reflects some short-wavelength light and some medium-wavelength light (see the reflectance curve for "blue paint" in **Figure 9.6b**). The yellow blob absorbs short-wavelength light and reflects some medium- and long-wavelength light (see the reflectance curve for "yellow paint" in Figure 9.6b).

The key to understanding what happens when colored paints are mixed together is that when mixed, *both paints still absorb the same wavelengths they absorbed when alone, so the only wavelengths reflected are those that are reflected by both paints in common.* Because medium wavelengths are the only ones reflected by both paints in common, a mixture of blue and yellow paints appears green (Table 9.2). Because the blue and yellow blobs

subtract all of the wavelengths except some that are associated with green, mixing paints is called a **subtractive color mixture**.

The reason that mixing blue and yellow paints results in green is that both paints reflect some light in the green part of the spectrum (notice that the overlap between the blue and yellow paint curves in Figure 9.6b coincides with the peak of the reflectance curve for green paint). If our blue paint had reflected only short wavelengths and our yellow paint had reflected only medium and long wavelengths, these paints would reflect no color in common, so mixing them would result in little or no reflection across the spectrum, and the mixture would appear black. Like objects, however, most paints reflect a band of wavelengths. If paints didn't reflect a range of wavelengths, then many of the color-mixing effects of paints that we take for granted would not occur.

Mixing Lights Let's now think about what would happen if we mix together blue and yellow lights. If a light that appears blue is projected onto a white surface and a light that appears yellow is projected on top of the blue light, the area where the lights are superimposed is perceived as *white* (**Figure 9.7**). Given your lifelong knowledge that yellow and blue make green, and our discussion of paints above, this

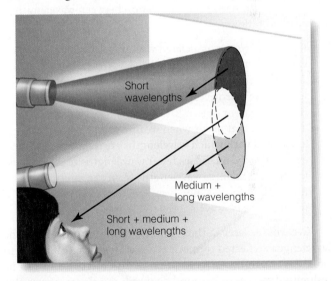

Figure 9.7 Color mixing with light. Superimposing a blue light and a yellow light creates the perception of white in the area of overlap. This is additive color mixing.

Table 9.2 Mixing Blue and Yellow Paints (Subtractive Color Mixture)

Parts of the spectrum that are absorbed and reflected by blue and yellow paint. Wavelengths that are reflected from the mixture are highlighted. Light that is usually seen as green is the only light that is reflected in common by both paints.

	WAVELENGTHS		
	SHORT	MEDIUM	LONG
Blob of blue paint	Reflects all	Reflects some	Absorbs all
Blob of yellow paint	Absorbs all	Reflects some	Reflects some
Mixture of blue and yellow blobs	Absorbs all	Reflects some	Absorbs all

result may surprise you. But you can understand why this occurs by considering the wavelengths that are reflected into the eye by a mixture of blue and yellow lights. Because the two spots of light are projected onto a white surface, which reflects all wavelengths, all of the wavelengths that hit the surface are reflected into an observer's eyes (see the reflectance curve for white paper in Figure 9.4). The blue spot consists of a band of short wavelengths, so when it is projected alone, the short-wavelength light is reflected into the observer's eyes (Table 9.3). Similarly, the yellow spot consists of medium and long wavelengths, so when presented alone, these wavelengths are reflected into the observer's eyes.

The key to understanding what happens when colored lights are superimposed is that *all of the light that is reflected from the surface by each light when alone is also reflected when the lights are superimposed.* Thus, where the two spots are superimposed, the light from the blue spot and the light from the yellow spot are both reflected into the observer's eye. The added-together light therefore contains short, medium, and long wavelengths, which results in the perception of white. Because mixing lights involves adding up the wavelengths of each light in the mixture, mixing lights is called an **additive color mixture.**

We can summarize the connection between wavelength and color as follows:

- Colors of *light* are associated with wavelengths in the visible spectrum.
- The colors of *objects* are associated with which wavelengths are *reflected* (for opaque objects) or *transmitted* (for transparent objects).
- The colors that occur when we mix colors are also associated with which wavelengths are reflected into the eye. Mixing *paints* causes fewer wavelengths to be reflected (each paint *subtracts* wavelengths from the mixture); mixing *lights* causes more wavelengths to be reflected (each light *adds* wavelengths to the mixture).

We will see later in the chapter that things other than the wavelengths reflected into our eye can influence color perception. For example, our perception of an object's color can be influenced by the background on which the object is seen. But for now our main focus is on the connection between wavelength and color.

Perceptual Dimensions of Color

Isaac Newton described the visible spectrum (Figure 9.3b) in his experiments in terms of seven colors: red, orange, yellow, green, blue, indigo, and violet. His use of seven color terms probably had more to do with mysticism than science, however, as he wanted to harmonize the visible spectrum (7 colors) with musical scales (7 notes) (Mollon, 2003b). Modern vision scientists tend to exclude indigo from the list of **spectral colors** because humans actually have a difficult time distinguishing it from blue and violet. There are also many **nonspectral colors**—colors that do not appear in the spectrum because they are mixtures of other colors, such as magenta (a mixture of blue and red). Ultimately, the number of colors we can differentiate is enormous: If you've ever decided to paint your bedroom wall, you will have discovered a dizzying number of color choices in the paint department of your local home improvement store. In fact, major paint manufacturers have thousands of colors in their catalogs, and your computer monitor can display millions of different colors. Although estimates of how many colors humans can discriminate vary widely, a conservative estimate is that we can tell the difference between about 2 million different colors (Nickerson & Newhall, 1943; Pointer & Attridge, 1998).

How can we perceive millions of colors when we can describe the visible spectrum in terms of only six or seven colors? The answer is that there are three perceptual dimensions of color, which together can create the large number of colors we can perceive. We previously called colors like blue, green, and red *chromatic colors.* Another term for these colors is **hues. Figure 9.8** shows a number of color patches, which we would describe as all having a red hue. What makes these colors appear different is their variation in the other two dimensions of color, *saturation* and *value.*

Saturation is determined by the amount of white that has been added to a particular hue. Moving from left to right in Figure 9.8, progressively more white has been added to each color patch and, as a result, saturation decreases. When hues become **desaturated,** they can take on a faded or washed-out appearance. For example, color patch A in Figure 9.8 appears to be a deep and vivid red, but color patch B appears to be a

Table 9.3 Mixing Blue and Yellow Lights (Additive Color Mixture)

Parts of the spectrum that are reflected from a white surface for blue and yellow spots of light projected onto the surface. Wavelengths that are reflected from the mixture are highlighted.

| | WAVELENGTHS | | |
	SHORT	MEDIUM	LONG
Spot of blue light	Reflected	No Reflection	No Reflection
Spot of yellow light	No Reflection	Reflected	Reflected
Overlapping blue and yellow spots	**Reflected**	**Reflected**	**Reflected**

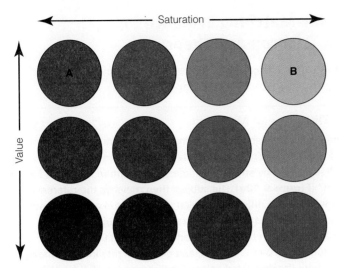

Figure 9.8 These 12 color patches have the same hue (red). Saturation decreases from left to right. Brightness decreases from top to bottom.

desaturated muted pink. **Value** refers to the light-to-dark dimension of color. Moving down the columns in Figure 9.8, value decreases as the colors become darker.

Another useful way to illustrate the relationship among hue, saturation, and value is to arrange colors systematically within a three-dimensional color space called a **color solid**. There are a number of different color solids, but we will focus on one example. **Figure 9.9a** depicts a cylindrical color solid called the **HSV color solid**, because its three dimensions are *Hue, Saturation*, and *Value*.

Different hues are arranged around the circumference of the cylinder with perceptually similar hues placed next to each other. Notice, in fact, that the order of the hues around the cylinder matches the order of the colors in the visible spectrum shown in Figure 9.3b. Saturation is depicted by placing more saturated colors toward the outer edge of the cylinder and more desaturated colors toward the center. Value is represented by the cylinder's height, with lighter colors at the top and darker colors at the bottom. The color solid therefore creates a coordinate system in which our perception of any color can be defined by hue, saturation, and value.

Arranging colors geometrically not only shows how hue, saturation, and value are related, it also allows us to determine how differently colored lights will combine to produce new colors. For example, the color that would result from mixing

yellow and blue light can be determined by drawing a line that connects the yellow and blue hues (**Figure 9.9b**). Any mixture of these two hues will fall on this line, with the exact location depending on the amount of each light added to the mixture. If we add some blue light to the yellow (75 percent yellow, 25 percent blue), the yellow light becomes less saturated. If we add even more blue light, so the blue and yellow lights are mixed equally (50 percent yellow, 50 percent blue) the resulting color will fall on the midpoint of our line (aha, it's white, just as we noted in Figure 9.7!). Thus, the color solid illustrates both the multitude of different colors we perceive and the way different colors interact.

TEST YOURSELF 9.1

1. Describe the case of Mr. I. What does it illustrate about color perception?

2. What are the various functions of color vision?

3. What physical characteristic of light is most closely associated with color perception? How is this demonstrated by differences in reflection and transmission of light of different objects?

4. Describe subtractive and additive color mixing. How can the results of these two types of color mixing be related to the wavelengths that are reflected into an observer's eyes?

5. What are spectral colors? Nonspectral colors? How many different colors can humans discriminate?

6. What are hue, saturation, and value? What is the HSV color solid? How can it be used to predict the results of mixing lights?

The Trichromatic Theory of Color Vision

How does the visual system create our perception of different colors? We will answer this question by describing two different theories of color vision, both of which were proposed in the 19th century: *trichromatic theory* and *opponent-process theory*.

We begin by discussing trichromatic theory, which brings us back to Isaac Newton's prism experiment (Figure 9.3). When Newton separated white light into its components to

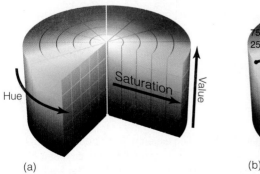

(a)

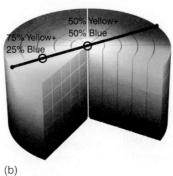

(b)

Figure 9.9 (a) An example of a color solid. (b) The result of mixing two colored lights will fall on a line connecting the hues that are mixed.

reveal the visible spectrum, he argued that each component of the spectrum must stimulate the retina differently in order for us to perceive color. He proposed that "rays of Light in falling upon the bottom of the Eye excite vibrations in the …retina.… Which vibrations, being propagated along the solid fibres of the optick Nerves into the Brain, cause the sense of seeing" (Newton, 1704). We know now that electrical signals, not "vibrations," are what is transmitted down the optic nerve to the brain, but Newton was on the right track in proposing that activity associated with different lights gives rise to the perceptions of different colors.

About 100 years later, the British physicist Thomas Young (1773–1829), starting with Newton's proposed vibrations, suggested that Newton's idea of a link between each size of vibration and each color won't work, because a particular place on the retina can't be capable of the large range of vibrations required. His exact words were: "Now, as it is almost impossible to conceive of each sensitive point on the retina to contain an infinite number of particles, each capable of vibrating in perfect unison with every possible undulation, it becomes necessary to suppose the number limited, for instance, to the three principal colors, red, yellow, and blue" (Young, 1802).

The actual quote from Young is included here because it is so important. It is this proposal—that color vision is based on *three* principal colors—that marks the birth of what is today called the **trichromatic theory of vision**, which in modern terminology states that color vision depends on the activity of three different receptor mechanisms. At the time it was proposed, however, Young's theory was little more than an insightful idea that, if correct, would provide an elegant solution to the puzzle of color perception. Young had little interest in conducting experiments to test his ideas, however, and never published any research to support his theory (Gurney, 1831; Mollon, 2003a; Peacock, 1855). Thus, it was left to James Clerk Maxwell (1831–1879) and Hermann von Helmholtz (whose proposal of unconscious inference we discussed in Chapter 5) to provide the needed experimental evidence for trichromatic theory (Helmholtz, 1860; Maxwell, 1855). Although Maxwell conducted his experiments before Helmholtz, Helmholtz's name became attached to Young's idea of three receptors, and trichromatic theory became known as the **Young-Helmholtz theory**. That trichromatic theory became known as the Young-Helmholtz theory rather than the Young-Maxwell theory has been attributed to Helmholtz's prestige in the scientific community and to the popularity of his *Handbook of Physiology* (1860), in which he described the idea of three receptor mechanisms (Heesen, 2015; Sherman, 1981).

Even though Maxwell was denied "naming rights" for his discoveries in color vision, if it is any consolation to him, a 1999 poll of leading physicists named him the third greatest physicist of all time, behind only Newton and Einstein, for his work in electromagnetism (Durrani & Rogers, 1999). It is also Maxwell's critical color-matching experiments that we will describe in detail in the next section as we begin to consider the evidence for trichromatic theory.

Color-Matching Evidence for Trichromatic Theory

Trichromatic theory was supported by the results of a psychophysical procedure called **color matching**.

METHOD | Color Matching

The procedure used in a color-matching experiment is shown in **Figure 9.10**. The experimenter presents a reference color that is created by shining a single wavelength of light on a "test field" (**Figure 9.10a**). The subject then matches the reference color by mixing different wavelengths of light in a "comparison field" (**Figure 9.10b**). In this example, the subject is shown a 500-nm light in the test field and then asked to adjust the amounts of 420-nm, 560-nm, and 640-nm lights in a comparison field until the perceived color of the comparison field matches the perceived color of test field.

The key finding from Maxwell's color-matching experiments was that any reference color could be matched provided

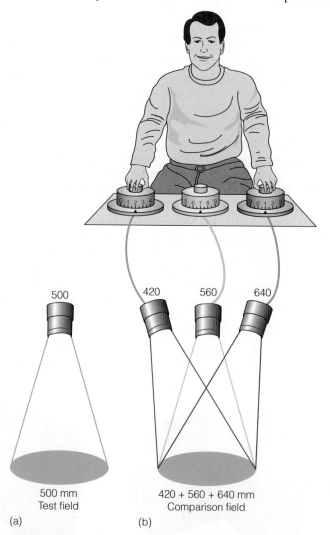

500

420   560   640

500 mm
Test field

420 + 560 + 640 mm
Comparison field

(a)   (b)

Figure 9.10 In a color-matching experiment, the observer adjusts the amount of three wavelengths in one field (right) so that it matches the color of the single wavelength in the other field (left).

that subjects were able to adjust the proportions of *three* wavelengths in the comparison field. Two wavelengths allowed subjects to match some, but not all, reference colors, and subjects never needed four wavelengths to match any reference color.

Based on the finding that people with normal color vision need at least three wavelengths to match any other wavelength, Maxwell reasoned that color vision depends on three receptor mechanisms, each with different spectral sensitivities. (Remember from Chapter 2 that spectral sensitivity indicates the sensitivity to wavelengths in the visible spectrum, as shown in Figure 2.15 on page 31.) According to trichromatic theory, light of a particular wavelength stimulates each receptor mechanism to different degrees, and the pattern of activity in the three mechanisms results in the perception of a color. Each wavelength is therefore represented in the nervous system by its own pattern of activity in the three receptor mechanisms.

Physiological Evidence for Trichromatic Theory

One of the amazing things about trichromatic theory is that it proposed physiological mechanisms for color vision based on psychophysical results, long before techniques were available to make the necessary physiological measurements. What is even more amazing is that the mechanism it proposed turned out to be generally correct, although it was necessary to wait nearly 100 years before the physiological results became available. That confirmation came with the discovery of three different types of cone pigments in the retina.

Cone Pigments Physiological researchers who were working to identify the receptor mechanisms proposed by trichromatic theory asked the following question: Are there three mechanisms, and if so, what are their physiological properties? This question was answered in the 1960s, when researchers were able to determine that there were three different cone pigments: the short-wavelength pigment (S), with maximum absorption at 419-nm; the middle-wavelength pigment (M), with maximum absorption at 531-nm; and the long-wavelength pigment (L), with maximum absorption at 558-nm (S, M, and L in **Figure 9.11**) (Brown & Wald, 1964; Dartnall et al., 1983; Schnapf et al., 1987). As you may recall from Chapter 2

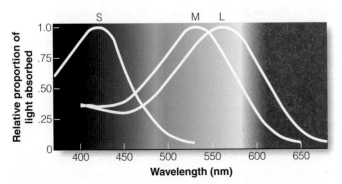

Figure 9.11 Absorption spectra of the three cone pigments.
(From Dartnall et al., 1983)

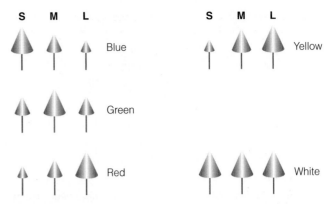

Figure 9.12 Patterns of firing of the three types of cones to different colors. The size of the cone symbolizes the size of the receptor's response.

(page 27), all visual pigments are made up of a large protein component called *opsin* and a small light-sensitive component called *retinal*. Differences in the structure of the long opsin part of the pigments are responsible for the three different absorption spectra (Nathans et al., 1986). (See Chapter 2, page 32, to review pigments and absorption spectra.)

Cone Responding and Color Perception If color perception is based on the pattern of activity of these three cone receptor mechanisms, we should be able to determine which colors will be perceived if we know the response of each of the receptor mechanisms. **Figure 9.12** shows the relationship between the responses of the three kinds of receptors and our perception of color. In this figure, the responses in the S, M, and L receptors are indicated by the drawn size of the receptors. For example, blue is signaled by a large response in the S receptor, a smaller response in the M receptor, and an even smaller response in the L receptor. Yellow is signaled by a very small response in the S receptor and large responses in the M and L receptors. White is signaled by equal activity in all the receptors.

Thinking of wavelengths as causing certain patterns of receptor responding helps us predict which colors should result when we combine lights of different colors. We have already seen that combining equal amounts of blue and yellow lights on a white background results in white. The patterns of receptor activity in Figure 9.12 show that blue light causes high activity in the S receptor and that yellow light causes high activity in the M and L receptors. Thus, combining both lights should stimulate all three receptors equally, which is associated with the perception of white.

Now that we know that our perception of colors is determined by the pattern of activity in different kinds of receptors, we can explain the physiological basis behind the color-matching results that led to the proposal of trichromatic theory. Remember that in a color-matching experiment, a wavelength in one field is matched by adjusting the proportions of three different wavelengths in another field (Figure 9.10). This result is interesting because the lights in the two fields are physically different (they contain different wavelengths) but they are perceptually identical (they look the same). This situation, in

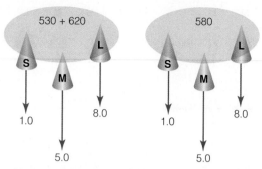

Figure 9.13 Principle behind metamerism. The proportions of 530-nm and 620-nm lights in the field on the left have been adjusted so that the mixture appears identical to the 580-nm light in the field on the right. The numbers indicate the responses of the short-, medium-, and long-wavelength receptors. There is no difference in the responses of the two sets of receptors, so the two fields are perceptually indistinguishable.

which two physically different stimuli are perceptually identical, is called **metamerism**, and the two identical fields in a color-matching experiment are called **metamers**.

The reason metamers look alike is that they both result in the same pattern of response in the three cone receptors. For example, when the proportions of a 620-nm red light and a 530-nm green light are adjusted so the mixture matches the color of a 580-nm light, which looks yellow, the two mixed wavelengths create the same pattern of activity in the cone receptors as the single 580-nm light (**Figure 9.13**). The 530-nm green light causes a large response in the M receptor, and the 620-nm red light causes a large response in the L receptor. Together, they result in a large response in the M and L receptors and a much smaller response in the S receptor. This is the pattern for yellow and is the same as the pattern generated by the 580-nm light. Thus, even though the lights in these two fields are *physically different*, the two lights result in identical patterns of physiological responses so they are identical as far as the brain is concerned and they are therefore perceived as being the same.

Are Three Receptor Mechanisms Necessary for Color Vision?

According to trichromatic theory, a light's wavelength is signaled by the pattern of activity of *three* receptor mechanisms. But do we need three different mechanisms to see colors? Let's first consider why color vision does not occur in individuals who have just one receptor type (so they have only one pigment).

Vision With One Receptor Type We can understand why color vision is not possible in a person with just one receptor type by considering how a person with just one pigment would perceive two lights, one 480 nm and one 600 nm (**Figure 9.14a**), which a person with normal color vision sees as blue and orange, respectively. The absorption spectrum for the single pigment, shown in **Figure 9.14b**, indicates that the pigment absorbs 10 percent of 480-nm light and 5 percent of 600-nm light.

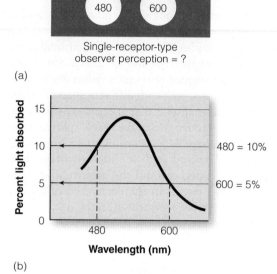

Figure 9.14 (a) Two fields, 480 nm on the left and 600 nm on the right. (b) Absorption spectrum of a visual pigment that absorbs 10 percent of 480-nm light and 5 percent of 600-nm light.

To discuss what happens when our one-pigment observer looks at the two lights, we have to return to our description of visual pigments in Chapter 2 (see page 27). Remember that when light is absorbed by the *retinal* part of the visual pigment molecule, the retinal changes shape, a process called *isomerization*. (Although we will usually specify light in terms of its wavelength, light can also be described as consisting of small packets of energy called *photons*, with one photon being the smallest possible packet of light energy.) The visual pigment molecule isomerizes when the molecule absorbs one photon of light. This isomerization activates the molecule and triggers the process that activates the visual receptor and leads to seeing the light.

If the intensity of each light is adjusted so 1,000 photons of each light enters our one-pigment observer's eyes, we can see from **Figure 9.15a** that the 480-nm light isomerizes $1,000 \times 0.10 = 100$ visual pigment molecules and the 600-nm light isomerizes $1,000 \times 0.05 = 50$ molecules. Because the 480-nm light isomerizes twice as many visual pigment molecules as the 600-nm light, it will cause a larger response in the receptor, resulting in perception of a brighter light. But if we increase the intensity of the 600-nm light to 2,000 photons, as shown in **Figure 9.15b**, then this light will also isomerize 100 visual pigment molecules.

When the 1,000 photon 480-nm light and the 2,000 photon 600-nm light both isomerize the same number of molecules, the result will be that the two spots of light will appear identical. The fact that the wavelengths of light are different doesn't matter, because of the **principle of univariance**, which states that once a photon of light is absorbed by a visual pigment molecule, the identity of the light's wavelength is lost. An isomerization is an isomerization no matter what wavelength caused it. Univariance means that the receptor does not know the *wavelength* of light it has absorbed, only the *total amount* it has absorbed. Thus, by adjusting the intensities of the two

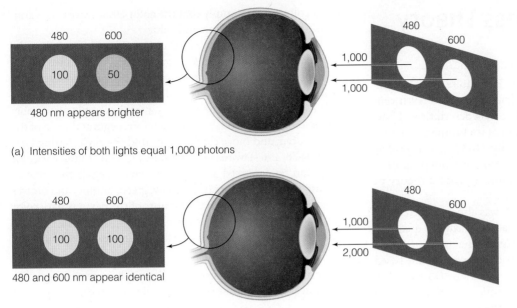

(a) Intensities of both lights equal 1,000 photons

(b) 600-nm light increased to 2,000 photons

Figure 9.15 Calculation of how many molecules of the visual pigment in Figure 9.14 are isomerized (a) when the intensity of both is 1,000 photons. In this case, the 480-nm light isomerizes 100 molecules and the 600-nm light isomerizes 50 molecules, so the 480-nm light would look brighter. (b) When the intensity of the 600-nm light is increased to 2,000, both wavelengths isomerize the same number of molecules, so the two wavelengths are perceived as identical.

lights, we can cause the single pigment to result in identical responses, so the lights will appear the same even though their wavelengths are different.

What this means is that a person with only one visual pigment can match any wavelength in the spectrum by adjusting the *intensity* of any other wavelength, and sees all of the wavelengths as shades of gray. Thus, adjusting the intensity appropriately can make the 480-nm and 600-nm lights (or any other wavelengths) look identical.

How can the nervous system tell the difference between the two wavelengths, no matter what the light intensity? The answer is to add a second pigment, which we describe next.

Vision With Two Receptor Types Let's consider what happens when we add a second pigment, with an absorption spectrum shown by the dashed curve in **Figure 9.16**. This pigment absorbs more 600-nm light than 480-nm light, so the intensity in Figure 9.15b that caused pigment 1 to generate the same response to the two wavelengths would cause pigment 2 to generate a much larger response to the 600-nm light. Thus, the responses created by both pigments together could indicate a difference between the two different wavelengths.

Another way to look at this two-pigment situation is to consider the *ratios* of responses of the two pigments to the two wavelengths. From Figure 9.16 we can see that the 480-nm light causes a large response from pigment 1 and a smaller response from pigment 2, and that the 600-nm light causes a larger response in pigment 2 and a smaller response in pigment 1. These ratios remain the same no matter what the light intensities. The ratio of the response of pigment 1 to pigment 2 is always 10 to 2 for the 480-nm light and 5 to 10 for the 600-nm light. Thus, the visual system can use ratio information such as this to identify the wavelength of any light. This same constancy of the ratio information also occurs when there are three pigments, which is the basis of trichromatic

theory's proposal that color perception depends on the *pattern of activity* in three receptor mechanisms.

When we consider color deficiencies later in this chapter, we will see that there are people with just one type of pigment, called **monochromats**, who see in shades of gray. There are also people with just two types of cone pigment, called **dichromats**, who see chromatic colors, just as our calculations predict, but they confuse some colors that people with three visual pigments, who are called **trichromats**, can distinguish. The addition of a third pigment, although not necessary for creating color vision, provides additional ratios that allow additional discriminations of wavelength across the visual spectrum.

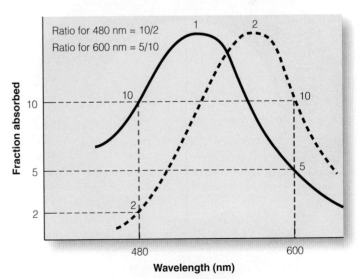

Figure 9.16 Adding a second pigment (dashed curve) to the one in Figure 9.14. Now the 480-nm and 600-nm lights can be identified by the ratio of response in the two pigments. The ratio for the 480-nm light is 10/2. The ratio for the 600-nm light is 5/10. These ratios occur no matter what the intensity of the light.

Opponent-Process Theory of Color Vision

Trichromatic theory, championed by Helmholtz and Maxwell, two of the most highly respected scientists of the 19th century, was thought by many to be the correct description of how color vision works. But the reputation of trichromatic theory's proponents didn't stop Ewald Hering (1834–1918), professor of physiology at the University of Prague, from proposing an alternative theory called the **opponent-process theory of color vision** (Turner, 1993, 1994).

Hering's theory (1878, 1905, 1964) was also proposed based on behavioral observations, but instead of Maxwell's quantitative psychophysical color-matching experiments that supported trichromatic theory, opponent-process theory was initially based on the results of phenomenological observations (see page 16). Based on these phenomenological observations, Hering proposed that color vision is caused by opposing physiological responses generated by blue and yellow, red and green, and black and white.

Hering's Phenomenological Evidence for Opponent-Process Theory

Hering's ideas about opponent colors were based on people's color experiences when looking at a *color circle* like the one in **Figure 9.17**. A **color circle** arranges perceptually similar colors next to each other around its perimeter just like the color solid depicted in Figure 9.9. The difference between a color circle

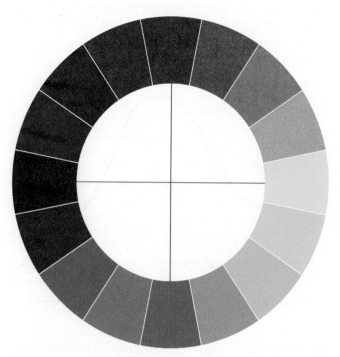

Figure 9.17 A color circle. Colors on the left all appear yellowish, colors on the right appear bluish, colors on the top appear greenish, and colors on the bottom appear reddish. Lines connect opponent colors.

and a color solid is simply that the color circle leaves out variations in a hue's saturation and value.

When looking at the color circle, Hering noted that the colors all seem to fall into four groups that are defined by the amount of yellowness, blueness, greenness, and redness in each group. It is instructive to consider how Hering described the whole color circle, because it offers a vivid example of the phenomenological method. We will, therefore, begin at the top of the circle, at red, and move clockwise around the circle, letting Hering's (1878, 1964) words be our guide. The trip around the color circle can be described as a journey, which begins with one of **Hering's primary colors** (red, yellow, green, or blue) and evolves into different colors as small amounts of the next primary color are added. Hering describes the changes in color that occur as small amounts of yellow are added to the red primary as follows:

> increasing more yellowish ... passing through orange and gold yellow, we reach a yellow with no remaining trace of the redness that was so obvious in the orange.

Hering describes the next color changes, which occur as amounts of green are added to the yellow, as the following progression:

> sulfur yellow ... canary yellow .... sap green, ... and we finally reach a green that is free of yellow.

Moving around the circle, by adding blue to the green:

> green colors ... tend into blue (sea green) ... blueness become continuously stronger and the greenness continuously weakens (sea blue), until we reach a blue that no longer shows any greenness.

Almost there! Adding red to the blue takes us back to the starting point:

> after this blue comes blue of increasing redness ..... (blue violet, red violet, purple red), until the last trace of blueness vanishes in a true red. (Hering, 1964, p. 42)

Hering's description is revealing, both because it illustrates his phenomenological descriptions, and also because it set the stage for his idea that color vision can be explained based on pairs of opposing colors. Looking back at the color circle, Hering observed that it can be divided into an upper portion where the colors possess some amount of redness, a lower portion where the colors have some amount of greenness, a left portion where the colors seem to contain varying degrees of blueness, and a right portion where the colors have more or less yellowness. What's important to realize, according to Hering, is that while we can see yellowish reds (upper right) and yellowish greens (lower right), and we can see bluish greens (lower left) and bluish reds (upper left), there is no color anywhere in the circle that appears to be both yellowish and bluish, or any color that appears to be a combination of red and green. In fact, we can't even imagine what a bluish yellow or reddish green would even look like. (Try it!) Thus, Hering proposed that our color experience is built from four primary chromatic colors that are arranged into two opponent pairs: yellow–blue and red–green. In addition to these chromatic colors, Hering also considered black and white to be an opponent achromatic pair.

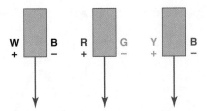

Figure 9.18 The three opponent mechanisms proposed by Hering.

The basic idea underlying Hering's theory is shown in **Figure 9.18**. He proposed three mechanisms, each of which responds in opposite ways to different intensities or wavelengths of light. The White (+) Black (−) mechanism responds positively to white light and negatively to the absence of light. The Red (+) Green (−) mechanism responds positively to red and negatively to green, and the Yellow (+) Blue (−) mechanism responds positively to yellow and negatively to blue. Thus, the more white a light appears, the less black it also appears; the more red a light appears, the less green it appears; the more yellow a light appears, the less blue it appears.

Ingenious as Hering's opponent-mechanism proposal was, the theory wasn't widely accepted, for three reasons: (1) its main competition, trichromatic theory, was championed by Helmholtz, who had great prestige in the scientific community; (2) Hering's phenomenological descriptions, using terms such as "canary yellow," "sap green," and "sea blue," could not compete with Maxwell's quantitative color mixing data; and (3) there was no neural mechanism known at that time that could respond in opposite ways.

The poor acceptance of opponent-process theory extended into the 20th century. For example, a standard reference book, *Light, Color and Vision*, authored by eminent color researcher Yves LeGrand (1957), devotes 25 pages to trichromatic theory but less than a page to opponent-process theory (also see LeGrand, 1959). But this lack of acceptance of opponent-process theory was about to change because of two developments that occurred in the late 1950s: (1) psychophysical experiments by Leo Hurvich and Dorthea Jameson (1957) that provided quantitative measurements of the strengths of each of the opponent mechanisms; and (2) physiological demonstrations of opponent neural responses in the retina and lateral geniculate nucleus.

Hurvich and Jameson's Psychophysical Measurements of the Opponent Mechanisms

In 1957, Hurvich and Jameson published a paper titled "An Opponent-Process Theory of Color Vision." In this paper, they noted Hering's proposal of the opponent-process theory and made a number of observations of their own to support the idea of opponency. For example, they noted that in cases of color deficiency (which we will discuss below), colors tend to drop out in pairs, so people lose the ability to perceive blue and yellow or to perceive red and green. They also noted the phenomenon of complementary afterimages, which you can experience for yourself by doing the following demonstration.

Figure 9.19 Display for afterimage demonstration.

DEMONSTRATION | Afterimages

Look at the center of **Figure 9.19** for 30 seconds. Then look at a white surface and observe the afterimages on the white background. Note the position of the different colors.

In the afterimage demonstration, red and green switch places and blue and yellow switch places. Thus, looking at red causes a green afterimage, looking at blue causes a yellow afterimage, and so on. These afterimages, which are called **complementary afterimages** because the afterimage is the color on the opposite side of the color circle, were taken by Hurvich and Jameson as supporting opponent-process theory.

But the purpose of Hurvich and Jameson's paper was to go beyond evidence such as Hering's color circle and complementary afterimages to provide quantitative measurements of the strengths of the Blue–Yellow and Red–Green components of the opponent mechanism. Let's first consider how they used a method called **hue cancellation** to determine the strength of the blue mechanism, beginning at 430 nm.

METHOD | Hue Cancellation

The blue mechanism obviously has substantial strength at 430 nm, because 430-nm light looks violet (reddish blue). Hurvich and Jameson reasoned that because yellow is the opposite of blue and therefore cancels it, they could determine the amount of blueness in a 430-nm light by determining how much yellow needs to be added to cancel all perception of "blueness." Once this is determined for the 430-nm light, the measurement is repeated for 440 nm and so on, across the spectrum, until reaching the wavelength where there is no blueness. Similarly, hue cancellation can be used to determine the strength of the yellow mechanism by determining how much blue needs to be added to cancel yellowness at each wavelength. For red and green, the strength of the red mechanism is determined by measuring how much green needs to be added to cancel the perception of redness, and the strength of

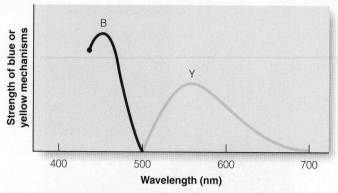

Figure 9.20 Strength of the blue opponent mechanism (blue curve) and yellow mechanism (yellow curve) across the spectrum, as measured by the hue cancellation technique. The blue dot indicates the strength of the blue mechanism at 430 nm. Note that at no wavelength do blue and yellow occur together and that at 500 nm the strengths of both mechanisms are zero, indicating that a 500-nm light (which appears green) contains no traces of blue or yellow. (From Hurvich & Jameson, 1957)

the green mechanism is determined by measuring how much red needs to be added to cancel the perception of greenness.

When Hurvich and Jameson applied the hue cancellation procedure to the 430-nm light, adding more and more yellow caused the light to eventually lose all of its blueness. After measuring how much yellow it took to eliminate all blueness at 430 nm (indicated by the blue dot in **Figure 9.20**), Hurvich and Jameson made similar measurements at other wavelengths and obtained the blue curve in Figure 9.20, which shows that the strength of the blue mechanism reaches a maximum at 440 nm and then decreases, until at 500 nm its strength is zero. This means that 500-nm light, which looks green, does not appear blue at all.

Hurvich and Jameson then determined the strength of the yellow mechanism by increasing the wavelength of the test light above 500 nm and adding blue to these wavelengths until it eliminated all perception of yellowness. The result is the yellow curve in Figure 9.20. The yellow mechanism responds to lights between 500 and 700 nm, with its maximum response at about 550 nm.

Figure 9.21 shows the results of similar experiments in which Hurvich and Jameson measured the strengths of the red and green mechanisms. The results for the red mechanism, which show considerable strength not only at long wavelengths (where we would expect it) but also at short wavelengths, far from the red end of the spectrum, might seem surprising. The red mechanism's strength at short wavelengths becomes less surprising, however, if we remember that short-wavelength light looks violet, which is a reddish blue. The curve for the green mechanism indicates that this mechanism responds to wavelengths between about 490 nm and 580 nm, with its maximum response at about 525 nm.

Figure 9.22 plots the results of Figures 9.20 and 9.21 on the same graph. In this figure, the blue and green curves have been inverted to emphasize that blue (plotted as negative in the figure) opposes yellow (plotted as positive) and that green (negative) opposes red (positive). These curves could just as

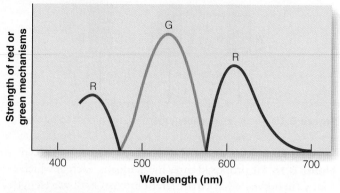

Figure 9.21 Strength of the red and green mechanisms across the spectrum. Note that at no wavelength do red and green occur together and that at 475 nm and 580 nm the strengths of both mechanisms are zero, indicating that neither a 475-nm light nor a 580-nm light contains any traces of red or green. (From Hurvich & Jameson, 1957)

well be reversed, with blue and green positive and red and yellow negative. Additionally, we can use the curves in Figure 9.22 to determine the amount of each color present at any wavelength in the spectrum. For example, these curves show that at 450 nm, both the blue and red mechanisms are activated (hence we see violet, or a bluish red) and at 600 nm both the red and yellow mechanisms are activated (hence we see orange, or a reddish yellow). Notice, just as Hering would have predicted, there is no color in the spectrum that simultaneously activates the yellow and blue mechanisms, nor is there any color that activates both the red and green mechanisms.

Hurvich and Jameson's (1957) hue cancellation experiments were an important step toward acceptance of opponent-process theory because they went beyond Hering's phenomenological observations by providing quantitative

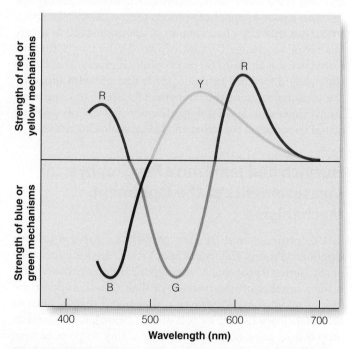

Figure 9.22 The curves of Figures 9.20 and 9.21 plotted together, with the blue and green curves inverted to indicate the opponent nature of the blue–yellow and red–green pairs. (From Hurvich & Jameson, 1957)

measurements of the strengths of the opponent mechanisms. Even more crucial for the acceptance of opponent-process theory, however, was the discovery of **opponent neurons** in the retina and lateral geniculate nucleus that responded with an excitatory response to light from one part of the spectrum and with an inhibitory response to light from another part (DeValois, 1960; Svaetichin, 1956).

Physiological Evidence for Opponent-Process Theory

In an early paper that reported opponent neurons in the lateral geniculate nucleus of the monkey, Russell DeValois (1960) recorded from neurons that responded with an excitatory response to light from one part of the spectrum and with an inhibitory response to light from another part (also see Svaetichin, 1956). For example, the left column of **Figure 9.23** shows records for a neuron DeValois and Jacobs (1968) called a +B −Y neuron because it increased firing, above the spontaneous level, to wavelengths perceived as blue and decreased firing to wavelengths perceived as yellow. The right column shows records for a +R −G neuron that increases firing to wavelengths perceived as red and decreases firing to wavelengths perceived as green. Later papers on opponent neurons have called +B −Y neurons +S −ML because, as we will see in the next section, +B corresponds to firing of the short-wavelength cone, and −Y to combined activity of the medium- and long-wavelength cones. Similarly, +R −G are now called +L −M neurons.

The discovery of opponent neurons provided physiological evidence for opponent-process theory. As we will see now, the opponent responses of opponent-process theory can be created by the three different cone pigments of trichromatic theory.

How Opponent Responding Can Be Created by Three Types of Receptors

When trichromatic and opponent-process theories were first proposed in the 1800s, they were seen as competitors. The idea

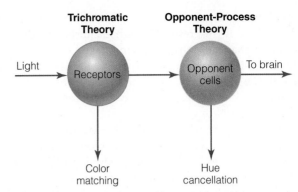

Figure 9.24 Our experience of color is shaped by physiological mechanisms both in the receptors and in opponent neurons.

at that time was that one or the other was correct, but not both. When physiological evidence was later obtained for both theories, perception researchers realized that both theories were correct. How could this be? The answer is that each theory describes neural processes that take place in different parts of the visual system. Specifically, trichromatic theory describes processes that take place in the receptors in the retina, whereas opponent-process theory describes processing that takes place within opponent neurons within the lateral geniculate nucleus. This is diagrammed in **Figure 9.24**.

The circuits in **Figure 9.25** show how these processes work together. In **Figure 9.25a**, the L-cone sends excitatory input to a bipolar cell (see Chapter 2, page 39), whereas the M-cone

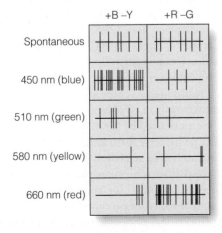

Figure 9.23 Characteristics of +B −Y and +R −G opponent cells in the monkey's lateral geniculate nucleus.

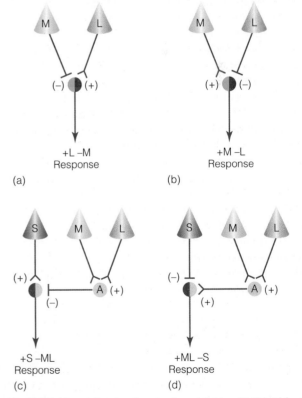

Figure 9.25 Neural circuits showing how (a) +L −M, (b) +M −L, (c) +S −ML, and (d) +ML −S mechanisms can be created by excitatory and inhibitory inputs from the three types of cone receptors.

sends inhibitory input to the cell. This creates an +L −M (or +R −G) cell that responds with excitation to the long wavelengths that cause the L-cone to fire and with inhibition to the medium wavelengths that cause the M-cone to fire. **Figure 9.25b** shows how excitatory input from the M-cone and inhibitory input from the L-cone creates an +M −L (or +G −R) cell.

Figure 9.25c shows that the +S −ML (or +B −Y) cell also receives inputs from the cones. It receives an excitatory input from the S cone and an inhibitory input from cell A, which sums the inputs from the M and L cones. This arrangement makes sense if we remember that we perceive yellow when both the M and the L receptors are stimulated. Thus, cell A, which receives inputs from both of these receptors, causes the "yellow" response of the +S −ML mechanism. **Figure 9.25d** shows the connections among neurons forming the +ML −S (or +Y −B) cell.

Although these diagrams are greatly simplified, they illustrate the basic principles of the neural circuitry for color coding in the retina. (See DeValois & DeValois, 1993; Solomon & Lennie, 2007, for examples of more complex neural circuits that have been proposed to explain opponent responding.) The important thing about these circuits is that their responses are determined both by the wavelengths to which the receptors respond best and by the arrangement of inhibitory and excitatory synapses. Processing in these circuits therefore takes place in two stages: First, the receptors respond with different patterns to different wavelengths (trichromatic theory); then, later, neurons integrate the inhibitory and excitatory signals from the receptors (opponent-process theory).

This description of opponent neurons brings us back to the idea that the signals for color that are sent to the brain indicate the *difference* in responding of pairs of cones. We can understand how this works at a neural level by looking at **Figure 9.26**, which shows how a +L −M neuron receiving excitation from the L-cone and inhibition from the M-cone responds to 500-nm and 600-nm lights. **Figure 9.26a** shows that the 500-nm light results in an inhibitory signal of −80 and an excitatory signal of +50, so the response of the +L −M neuron would be −30. **Figure 9.26b** shows that the 600-nm light results in an inhibitory signal of −25 and an excitatory signal of +75, so the response of the +L −M neuron would be +50. This "difference information" is the type of information sent by the opponent neurons to the brain.

The trichromatic "ratio information" and opponent "difference information" for wavelength originate in the receptors and neural connections in the retina. But what happens to all this information when it reaches the cortex?

Color in the Cortex

What are the cortical mechanisms of color perception? We will consider a number of facets of this question: (1) Is there a single "color center" in the cortex? (2) What is the relation between color and form? (3) What types of opponent neurons are found in the cortex, and what is their function?

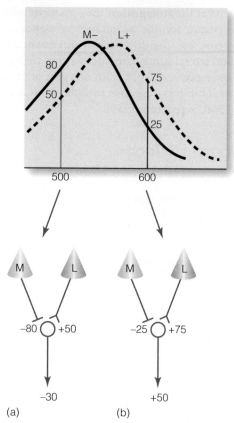

Figure 9.26 How opponent neurons determine the difference between the receptor responses to different wavelengths. (a) The response of the +L −M neuron to a 500-nm light is negative because the M receptor results in an inhibitory response that is larger than receptor L's excitatory response. This means the action of the 500-nm light on this neuron will cause a decrease in any ongoing activity. (b) The response to a 600-nm light is positive, so this wavelength causes an increase in the response of this neuron.

Is There a Single Color Center in the Cortex?

Is there one area in the cortex specialized for processing information about color? If there is such an area, that would make color similar to faces, bodies, and places, which can claim the fusiform face area (FFA), extrastriate body area (ESB), and parahippocampal place area (PPA) as specialized processing areas (see Chapter 4, pages 83–84). The idea of an area specialized for color was put forth by Semir Zeki (1983a, 1983b, 1990) based on (1) his finding that many neurons in a visual area called V4 responded to color and (2) the phenomenon of cerebral achromatopsia, a condition caused by damage to the brain like that experienced by Mr. I. (page 195), which spares a person's ability to perceive form and motion but causes a person to lose the ability to see color. The fact that the damage that typically results in achromatopsia is near or identical to areas identified as human color areas supports the idea of a specialized module for color perception.

However, additional evidence has led many researchers to reject the idea of a "color center" in favor of the idea that color processing is distributed across a number of different cortical areas that process information about color and about other types of information as well. One result that has led to this conclusion is that opponent neurons have been found in many areas of the cortex, including the primary visual receiving area, V1; the inferotemporal cortex (IT), which is associated with form perception; and V4, which was originally proposed as the color center (Engel, 2005; Harada et al., 2009; Johnson et al., 2008; Shapley & Hawken, 2011; Tanigawa et al., 2010; Tootell et al., 2004).

The studies cited above all involved recording from single neurons in the monkey cortex. There is also evidence for areas in the human cortex that respond both to color and to other visual qualities. Cristiana Cavina-Pratesi and coworkers (2010) demonstrated this by showing pictures of irregular objects resembling furry balls (**Figure 9.27a**) to subjects while their brain activity was being measured in an fMRI scanner. The subjects' task was to press a button to indicate whether two objects presented one after the other were the same or different. In different blocks of trials, subjects were told to make their same/different judgments based on either color, shape, or texture. The brain scans, shown in **Figure 9.27b**, located areas indicated by yellow that responded to shape, texture, and color. In addition, there were areas that responded selectively to color (indicated by green), areas that responded selectively to shape (red), and areas that responded selectively to texture (blue). The important result for our purposes is the large yellow area that indicates how responding to color can occur in areas that respond to other visual qualities as well. In addition, a survey of the effects of brain damage on color perception has shown that when brain damage causes achromatopsia (color blindness),

it causes other effects as well, including prosopagnosia—the inability to recognize faces (Bouvier & Engel, 2006).

Types of Opponent Neurons in the Cortex

Regardless of whether there is a "color center" in the cortex, there is no doubt that there are neurons in many areas that respond in an opponent way—increasing firing to wavelengths in one region of the spectrum and decreasing firing to neurons in another region. Two types of opponent neurons in the cortex are **single-opponent neurons** and **double-opponent neurons**.

The receptive field of a single-opponent neuron is shown in **Figure 9.28a**. This +M −L neuron increases firing to medium wavelengths presented to the center of the receptive field and decreases firing to long wavelengths presented to the surround. Most double-opponent neurons have receptive fields like the one in **Figure 9.28b**, with side-by-side regions, like the simple cortical cells we described in Chapter 3 (see page 60). The neuron with the receptive field in Figure 9.28b responds best to a medium-wavelength vertical bar presented to the left side of the receptive field and to a long-wavelength vertical bar presented to the right side of the receptive field. It has been suggested that single-opponent cells are important for perceiving the color within regions, and double-opponent cells are important for perceiving boundaries between different colors (Johnson et al., 2008).

Neurons with side-by-side receptive fields have been used to provide evidence for a connection between color and form. These neurons can fire to oriented bars even when the intensity of the side-by-side bars is adjusted so they appear equally bright. In other words, these cells fire when the bar's form is determined only by differences in color. Evidence such as this has been used to support the idea of a close bridge between the processing of color and the processing of form in the cortex (Friedman et al., 2003; Johnson et al., 2008). Thus, when you look out at a colorful scene, the colors you see are not only "filling in" the objects and areas in the scene but may also be helping define the edges and shapes of these objects and areas.

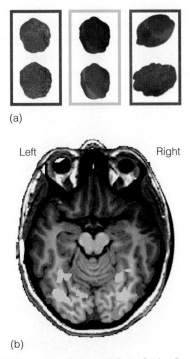

(a)

Left   Right

(b)

Figure 9.27 (a) Stimuli and (b) results from Cavina-Pratesi and coworkers (2010). Green areas selectively responded to color, red areas selectively responded to shape, blue areas selectively responded to texture, and yellow areas responded to all three features.

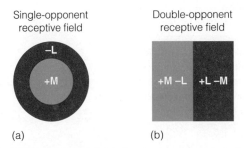

Single-opponent receptive field   Double-opponent receptive field

−L

+M

+M −L +L −M

(a)   (b)

Figure 9.28 (a) Receptive field of a single-opponent cortical neuron. This +M −L neuron has a center-surround receptive field. Its firing increases when a medium-wavelength light is presented to the center area of the receptive field and decreases when a long-wavelength light is presented to the surrounding area. (b) Receptive field of a double-opponent cortical neuron. This neuron increases firing when a vertical medium-wavelength bar is presented to the left side of the receptive field and when a vertical long-wavelength bar is presented to the right side of the receptive field.

Color Deficiency

When we discussed whether three receptor mechanisms are responsible for vision (page 204), we saw that someone with only one receptor mechanism would not be able to perceive different colors, but that a person with two types would be able to perceive some colors. We now consider real-life examples of these situations.

Monochromatism

Monochromatism is a rare form of color blindness that is usually hereditary and occurs in only about 10 people out of 1 million (LeGrand, 1957). Monochromats usually have no functioning cones; therefore, their vision has the characteristics of rod vision in both dim and bright lights. Monochromats see only in shades of lightness (white, gray, and black); they can therefore be called **color blind** (as opposed to dichromats, who see some chromatic colors and therefore are called *color deficient*). A person with normal color vision can experience what it is like to be a monochromat by sitting in the dark for several minutes. When dark adaptation is complete (see page 28), vision is controlled by the rods, which causes the world to appear in shades of gray. Like our one-pigment observer from Figure 9.14, monochromats can match any wavelength in the spectrum by adjusting the intensity of any other wavelength. Thus, a monochromat needs only one wavelength to match any color in the spectrum. In addition to a loss of color vision, people with hereditary monochromatism have poor visual acuity and are so sensitive to bright lights that they often must protect their eyes with dark glasses during the day. The rod system is not designed to function in bright light and so becomes overloaded in strong illumination, creating a perception of glare.

Dichromatism

People with **dichromatism** are missing one of the three cone pigments and hence experience some colors. However, they cannot distinguish as many colors as can trichromats. A dichromat,

like our two-pigment observer in Figure 9.15, needs only two wavelengths to match any other wavelength in the spectrum. Thus, one way to determine the presence of color deficiency is by using the color-matching procedure to determine the minimum number of wavelengths needed to match any other wavelength in the spectrum. Another way to diagnose color deficiency is by a color vision test that uses stimuli called **Ishihara plates**. An example plate is shown in **Figure 9.29a**. In this example, people with normal color vision see the number "74," but people with a form of red–green color deficiency might see something like the depiction in **Figure 9.29b**, in which the "74" is not visible.

Once we have determined that a person's vision is color deficient, we are still left with the question: What colors does a person with color deficiency see? Students sometimes suggest that we can answer this question by pointing to objects of various colors and asking a color deficient person what he sees (most color deficient people are male; see below). This method does not really tell us what the person perceives, however, because a color deficient person may say "red" when we point to a strawberry simply because he has learned that people call strawberries "red." It is quite likely that the color deficient person's experience of "red" is very different from the experience of the person without color deficiency. For all we know, he may be having an experience similar to what a person without deficient color vision would call "yellow."

To determine what a dichromat perceives, we need to locate a **unilateral dichromat**—a person with trichromatic vision in one eye and dichromatic vision in the other. Both of the unilateral dichromat's eyes are connected to the same brain, so this person can look at a color with his dichromatic eye and then determine which color it corresponds to in his trichromatic eye. Although unilateral dichromats are extremely rare, the few who have been tested have helped us determine the nature of a dichromat's color experience (Alpern et al., 1983; Graham et al., 1961; Sloan & Wollach, 1948). Let's now look at the three kinds of dichromats and the nature of their color experience.

There are three major forms of dichromatism: *protanopia*, *deuteranopia*, and *tritanopia*. The two most common kinds,

Figure 9.29 (a) An example of an Ishihara plate for testing color deficiency. A person with normal color vision sees a "74" when the plate is viewed under standardized illumination. (b) The same Ishihara plate as perceived by a person with a form of red–green color deficiency.

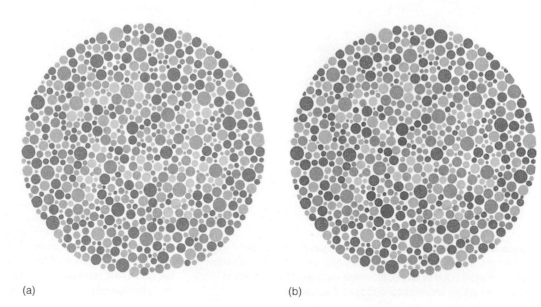

(a)

(b)

protanopia and deuteranopia, are inherited through a gene located on the X chromosome (Nathans et al., 1986). Males (XY) have only one X chromosome, so a defect in the visual pigment gene on this chromosome causes color deficiency. Females (XX), on the other hand, with their two X chromosomes, are less likely to become color deficient because only one normal gene is required for normal color vision. These forms of color vision are therefore called sex-linked because women can carry the gene for color deficiency without being color deficient themselves. Thus, many more males than females are dichromats.

As we describe what the three types of dichromats perceive, we use as our reference points **Figures 9.30a** and **9.31a**, which show how a trichromat perceives a bunch of colored paper flowers and the visible spectrum, respectively.

- **Protanopia** affects 1 percent of males and 0.02 percent of females and results in the perception of colors shown in **Figure 9.30b**. A protanope is missing the long-wavelength pigment. As a result, a protanope perceives short-wavelength light as blue, and as the wavelength is increased, the blue becomes less and less saturated until, at 492 nm, the protanope perceives gray (**Figure 9.31b**). The wavelength at which the protanope perceives gray is called the **neutral point**. At wavelengths above the neutral point, the protanope perceives yellow, which becomes less intense at the long wavelength end of the spectrum.
- **Deuteranopia** affects about 1 percent of males and 0.01 percent of females and results in the perception of color in **Figure 9.30c**. A deuteranope is missing the medium-wavelength pigment. A deuteranope perceives blue at short wavelengths, sees yellow at long wavelengths, and has a neutral point at about 498 nm (**Figure 9.31c**) (Boynton, 1979).

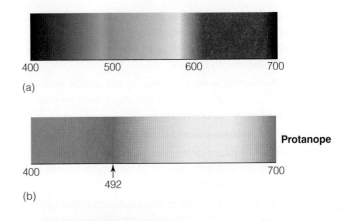

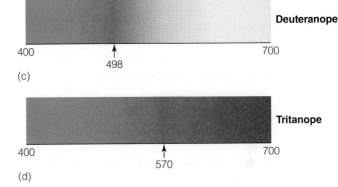

(a)

(b)   Protanope

(c)   Deuteranope

(d)   Tritanope

Figure 9.31 How the visible spectrum appears to (a) trichromats; (b) protanopes; (c) deuteranopes; and (d) tritanopes. The number indicates the wavelength of the neutral point. (Spectra courtesy of Jay Neitz and John Carroll)

- **Tritanopia** is very rare, affecting only about 0.002 percent of males and 0.001 percent of females. A tritanope is missing the short-wavelength pigment. A tritanope sees colors as in **Figure 9.30d** and sees the spectrum as in **Figure 9.31d**—blue at short wavelengths, red at long wavelengths, and a neutral point at 570 nm (Alpern et al., 1983).

In addition to monochromatism and dichromatism, there is one other prominent type of color deficiency called **anomalous trichromatism**. An anomalous trichromat needs three wavelengths to match any wavelength, just as a normal trichromat does. However, the anomalous trichromat mixes these wavelengths in different proportions from a trichromat, and an anomalous trichromat is not as good as a trichromat at discriminating between wavelengths that are close together.

(a)   (b)

(c)   (d)

Figure 9.30 How colored paper flowers appear to (a) trichromats; (b) protanopes; (c) deuteranopes; and (d) tritanopes.

© Bruce Goldstein; color processing courtesy of Jay Neitz and John Caroll

TEST YOURSELF 9.2

1. Describe trichromatic theory and the experiments on which it was based. How is this theory based on the results of color-matching experiments?
2. Describe how trichromatic theory is based on cone pigments and how the wavelengths are indicated by the activity of cones.
3. What are metamers and how can our perception of metamers be explained by the activity of the cones?

4. Why is color vision possible when there are only two different pigments but not possible when there is just one pigment? What is the effect on color vision of having three pigments rather than just two?

5. Describe Hering's phenomenological observations involving the color circle and the opponent-process theory he proposed based on these observations.

6. Why wasn't opponent-process theory initially accepted?

7. Describe the hue cancellation procedure used by Hurvich and Jameson. How did the results of their experiments support opponent-process theory?

8. Describe modern physiological evidence supporting opponent-process theory. How can opponent responding be created by three types of receptors?

9. What is the evidence for and against the idea of a specialized "color center" in the cortex?

10. Describe the opponent neurons in the cortex, including their receptive fields and possible functions.

11. What is monochromatism? Why do we say that a person with monochromatism is color blind?

12. What is dichromatism? Why do we say people with dichromatism are color deficient?

13. How can we determine what a dichromat perceives at different wavelengths?

14. What are the three types of dichromatism? Describe the experience associated with each type.

Color in a Dynamic World

Throughout a normal day, we view objects under many different lighting conditions: morning sunlight, afternoon sunlight, indoors under incandescent light, indoors under fluorescent light, and so forth. So far in this chapter, we have only linked our perception of color to the light that is reflected from objects. What happens when the light shining on an object changes? In this section, we will think about the relationship between color perception and the light that is available in the environment.

Color Constancy

It is midday, with the sun high in the sky, and as you are walking to class you notice a classmate who is wearing a green sweater. Then, as you are sitting in class a few minutes later, you again notice the same green sweater. The fact that the sweater appears green both outdoors under sunlight illumination and indoors under artificial illumination may not seem particularly remarkable. After all, the sweater *is* green, isn't it? However, when we consider the interaction between illumination and the properties of the sweater, we can appreciate that your perception of the sweater as green, both outside and inside, represents a remarkable achievement of the visual system. This achievement is called **color constancy**—we perceive the colors of objects as being relatively constant even under changing illumination.

We can appreciate why color constancy is an impressive achievement by considering the interaction between illumination, such as sunlight or lightbulbs, and the reflection properties of an object, such as the green sweater. First, let's consider the illumination. **Figure 9.32a** shows the wavelengths of sunlight and the wavelengths emitted from incandescent (the "old style" tungsten bulbs that are being phased out) and newer light-emitting diode (LED) lightbulbs. Sunlight contains approximately equal amounts of energy at all wavelengths, which is a characteristic of white light. The incandescent bulb, however, contains much more energy at long wavelengths (which is why they look slightly yellow), whereas LED bulbs emit light at substantially shorter wavelengths (which is why they look slightly blue).

Now consider the interaction between the wavelengths produced by the illumination and the wavelengths reflected from the green sweater. The reflectance curve of the sweater is indicated in **Figure 9.32b**. It reflects mostly medium-wavelength light, as we would expect of something that is green.

The actual light that is reflected from the sweater depends both on its reflectance curve and on the illumination that

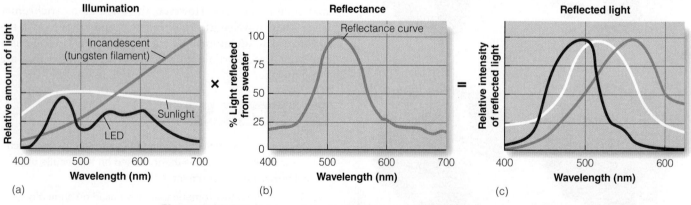

Figure 9.32 Determining what wavelengths are reflected from the green sweater under different illuminations. Light reflected from the sweater is determined by multiplying (a) the illumination of sunlight, incandescent, and LED lightbulbs times (b) the sweater's reflectance. The result is (c) the light reflected from the sweater. The maximum of each of the curves in (c) has been set at the same level to make the wavelength distributions easier to compare.

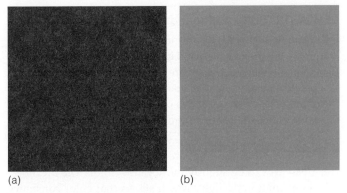

(a)   (b)

Figure 9.33 (a) Red adapting field for "Adapting to Red" demonstration. (b) Green adapting field for "Color and the Surroundings" demonstration (page 216).

DEMONSTRATION | Adapting to Red

Illuminate **Figure 9.33a** with a bright light from your desk lamp; then, with your left eye near the page and your right eye closed, look at the field with your left eye for about 30 to 45 seconds. Then look at various colored objects in your environment, first with your left eye and then with your right.

reaches the sweater and is then reflected from it. To determine the wavelengths that are actually reflected from the sweater, we multiply the sweater's reflectance curve at each wavelength by the amount of illumination at each wavelength. The result of this calculation is shown in **Figure 9.32c**, which shows that light reflected from the sweater includes relatively more long-wavelength light when it is illuminated by incandescent light (the orange line in Figure 9.32c) than when it is illuminated by light from a LED bulb (the blue line in Figure 9.32c). The fact that we still see the sweater as green even though the wavelength composition of the reflected light differs under different illuminations is color constancy. Without color constancy, the color we see would depend on how the sweater was being illuminated (Delahunt & Brainard, 2004; Olkkonen et al., 2010).

Why does a green sweater look green even when viewed under different illuminations? The answer to this question involves a number of different mechanisms (Smithson, 2005). We begin by considering how the eye's sensitivity is affected by the color of the illumination of the overall scene, a process called *chromatic adaptation*.

Chromatic Adaptation The following demonstration highlights one possible mechanism for color constancy.

This demonstration shows that color perception can be changed by **chromatic adaptation**—prolonged exposure to chromatic color. Adaptation to the red light selectively reduces the sensitivity of your long-wavelength cone pigment, which decreases your sensitivity to red light and causes you to see the reds and oranges viewed with your left (adapted) eye as less saturated and bright than those viewed with the right eye.

The idea that chromatic adaptation is responsible for color constancy has been tested in an experiment by Keiji Uchikawa and coworkers (1989). Observers viewed isolated patches of colored paper under three different conditions (**Figure 9.34**): (a) *baseline*—paper and observer illuminated by white light; (b) *observer not adapted*—paper illuminated by red light, observer by white (the observer is not chromatically adapted); and (c) *observer adapted to red*—both paper and observer illuminated by red light (the observer is chromatically adapted).

The results from these three conditions are shown above each condition. In the *baseline* condition, a green paper is perceived as green. In the *observer not adapted* condition, the observer perceives the paper's color as being shifted toward the red. Color constancy does not occur in this condition because the observer is not adapted to the red light that is illuminating the paper. But in the *observer adapted to red* condition, perception is shifted only slightly to the red, so it appears more yellowish. Thus, the chromatic adaptation has created **partial color constancy**—the perception of the object is shifted after adaptation, but not as much as when there was no adaptation. This means that the eye can adjust its sensitivity to different wavelengths to keep color perception approximately constant as illumination changes.

Perception: Paper is green   **Perception:** Paper shifted toward red   **Perception:** Paper shifted only slightly toward red so it appears more yellowish

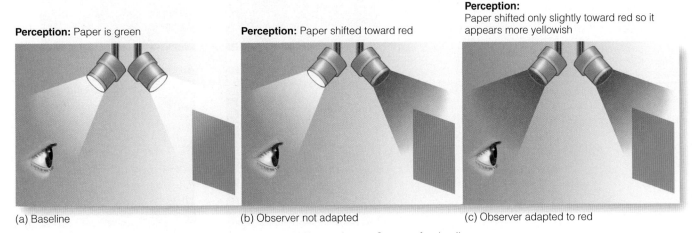

(a) Baseline   (b) Observer not adapted   (c) Observer adapted to red

Figure 9.34 The three conditions in Uchikawa et al.'s (1989) experiment. See text for details.

This principle operates when you walk into a room illuminated with yellowish tungsten light. The eye adapts to the long-wavelength-rich light, which decreases your eye's sensitivity to long wavelengths. This decreased sensitivity causes the long-wavelength light reflected from objects to have less effect than before adaptation, and this compensates for the greater amount of long-wavelength tungsten light that is reflected from everything in the room. Because of this adaptation, the yellowish tungsten illumination has only a small effect on your perception of color.

A similar effect also occurs in environmental scenes, which can have different dominant colors in different seasons. For example, the same scene can be "lush" in summer, with a lot of green (**Figure 9.35a**) and "arid" in winter, with more yellows (**Figure 9.35b**). Based on calculations taking into account how this "greenness" and "yellowness" would affect the cone receptors, Michael Webster (2011) determined that adaptation to the green in the lush scene would decrease the perception of green in that scene (**Figure 9.35c**), and adaptation to the yellow of the arid scene would decrease the perception of yellow in the arid scene (**Figure 9.35d**). Thus, adaptation "tones down" the dominant colors in a scene, so if we compare the *perceived* color of the lush and arid scenes in (c) and (d), we see that the colors are more similar than before the chromatic adaptation. This adaptation also causes novel colors to stand out, so yellow becomes more obvious in the lush scene and the green stands out in the arid scene.

The Effect of the Surroundings An object's perceived color is affected not only by the observer's state of adaptation but also by the object's surroundings, as shown by the following demonstration.

When the surroundings are masked, most people perceive the green area to be slightly more yellow under the incandescent light than in daylight, which shows that color constancy breaks down when an object is seen in isolation. A number of investigators have shown that color constancy works best when an object is surrounded by objects of many different colors, a situation that often occurs when viewing objects in the environment (Foster, 2011; Land, 1983, 1986; Land & McCann, 1971).

The surroundings help us achieve color constancy because the visual system—in ways that are still not completely understood—uses the information provided by the way objects in a scene are illuminated to estimate the characteristics of the illumination and to make appropriate corrections. (For some theories about exactly how the presence of the surroundings enhances color constancy, see Brainard & Wandell, 1986; Land, 1983, 1986; Pokorny et al., 1991.)

Memory and Color Another thing that helps achieve color constancy is our knowledge about the usual colors of objects in the environment. This effect on perception of prior knowledge of the typical colors of objects is called **memory color**. Research has shown that because people know the

Figure 9.35 How chromatic adaptation to the dominant colors of the environment can influence perception of the colors of a scene. The dominant color of the scene in (a) is green. Looking at this scene causes adaptation to green and decreases the perception of green in the scene, as shown in (c). The dominant color of the arid scene in (b) is yellow. Adapting to this scene causes a decreased perception of yellow in the scene, as shown in (d).

Lush environment   Arid environment

(a)   (b)

(c)   (d)

After adapting to lush scenes   After adapting to arid scenes

© Bruce Goldstein

colors of familiar objects, like a red stop sign or a green tree, they judge these familiar objects as having richer, more saturated colors than unfamiliar objects that reflect the same wavelengths (Ratner & McCarthy, 1990).

Thorsten Hansen and coworkers (2006) demonstrated an effect of memory color by presenting observers with pictures of fruits with characteristic colors, such as lemons, oranges, and bananas, against a gray background. Observers also viewed a spot of light against the same gray background. When the intensity and wavelength of the spot of light were adjusted so the spot was physically the same as the background, observers reported that the spot appeared the same gray as the background. But when the intensity and wavelength of the fruits were set to be physically the same as the background, observers reported that the fruits appeared slightly colored. For example, a banana that was physically the same as the gray background appeared slightly yellowish, and an orange looked slightly orange. This led Hansen to conclude that the observer's knowledge of the fruit's characteristic colors actually changed the colors they were experiencing. The effect of memory on our experience of color is a small one, but nonetheless may make a contribution to our ability to accurately perceive the colors of familiar objects under different illuminations.

Lightness Constancy

Just as we perceive chromatic colors like red and green as remaining relatively constant even when the illumination changes, we also perceive achromatic colors—white, gray, and black—as remaining about the same when the illumination changes. Imagine, for example, a black Labrador retriever lying on a living room rug illuminated by a lightbulb. A small percentage of the light that hits the retriever's coat is reflected, and we see it as black. But when the retriever runs outside into the much brighter sunlight, its coat still appears black. Even though more light is reflected in the sunlight, the perception of the shade of achromatic color (white, gray, and black), which we call **lightness**, remains the same. The fact that we see whites, grays, and blacks as staying about the same shade under different illuminations is called **lightness constancy**.

The visual system's problem is that the intensity of light reaching the eye from an object depends on two things: (1) the illumination—the *total amount of light* that is striking the object's

surface—and (2) the object's **reflectance**—the *proportion of this light* that the object reflects into our eyes. When lightness constancy occurs, our perception of lightness is determined not by the *intensity of the illumination* hitting an object, but by the object's *reflectance*. Objects that look black reflect less than 10 percent of the light. Objects that look gray reflect about 10 to 70 percent of the light (depending on the shade of gray); and objects that look white, like the pages of a book, reflect 80 to 95 percent of the light. Thus, our perception of an object's lightness is related not to the *amount* of light that is reflected from the object, which can change depending on the illumination, but to the *percentage* of light reflected from the object, which remains the same no matter what the illumination.

You can appreciate the existence of lightness constancy by imagining a checkerboard, like the one in **Figure 9.36**, illuminated by room light. Let's assume that the white squares have a reflectance of 90 percent, and the black squares have a reflectance of 9 percent. If the illumination inside the room is 100 units, the white squares reflect 90 units and the black squares reflect 9 units (**Figure 9.36a**). Now, if we take the checkerboard outside into bright sunlight, where the illumination is 10,000 units, the white squares reflect 9,000 units of light and the black squares reflect 900 units (**Figure 9.36b**). But even though the black squares when outside reflect much more light than the white squares did when the checkerboard was inside, the black squares still look black. Your perception is determined by the reflectance, not the amount of light reflected. What is responsible for lightness constancy? There are a number of possible explanations.

The Ratio Principle One observation about our perception of lightness is that when an object is illuminated evenly—that is, when the illumination is the same over the whole object, as in our checkerboard example—then lightness is determined by the *ratio* of reflectance of the object to the reflectance of surrounding objects. According to the **ratio principle**, as long as this ratio remains the same, the perceived lightness will remain the same (Jacobson & Gilchrist, 1988; Wallach, 1963). For example, consider one of the black squares in the checkerboard. The ratio of a black square to the surrounding white squares is 9/90 = 0.10 under low illuminations and 900/9,000 = 0.10 under high illuminations. Because the ratio of the reflectances is the same, our perception of the lightness remains the same.

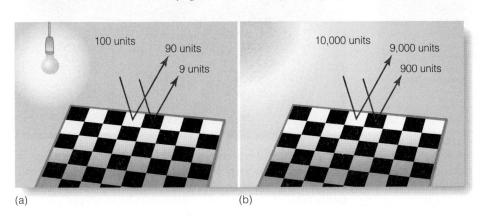

(a) (b)

Figure 9.36 A black-and-white checkerboard illuminated by (a) tungsten light and (b) sunlight.

The ratio principle works well for flat, evenly illuminated objects like our checkerboard. However, things get more complicated in three-dimensional scenes, which are usually illuminated unevenly.

Lightness Perception Under Uneven Illumination

If you look around, you will probably notice that the illumination is not even over the entire scene, as was the case for our two-dimensional checkerboard. The illumination in three-dimensional scenes is usually uneven because of shadows cast by one object onto another or because one part of an object faces the light and another part faces away from the light. For example, in **Figure 9.37**, in which a shadow is cast across a wall, we need to determine whether the changes in appearance we see across the wall are due to differences in the properties of different parts of the wall or to differences in the way the wall is illuminated.

The problem for the perceptual system is that it has to somehow take the uneven illumination into account. One way to state this problem is that the perceptual system needs to distinguish between *reflectance edges* and *illumination edges*. A **reflectance edge** is an edge where the reflectance of two surfaces changes. The border between areas *a* and *c* in Figure 9.37 is a reflectance edge because the two surfaces are made of different materials that reflect different amounts of light. An **illumination edge** is an edge where the lighting changes. The border between *a* and *b* is an illumination edge because area *a* is receiving more light than area *b*, which is in shadow.

Some explanations for how the visual system distinguishes between these two types of edges have been proposed (see Adelson, 1999; Gilchrist, 1994; Gilchrist et al., 1999, for details). The basic idea behind these explanations is that the perceptual system uses a number of sources of information to take illumination into account.

The Information in Shadows

In order for lightness constancy to work, the visual system needs to be able to take the uneven illumination created by shadows into account. It must determine that this change in illumination caused by a shadow is due to an illumination edge and not to a reflectance edge. Obviously, the visual system usually succeeds in doing this because although the light intensity is reduced by shadows, you don't usually see shadowed areas as gray or black. For example, in the case of the wall in **Figure 9.38**, you assume that the shadowed and unshadowed areas are bricks with the same lightness but that less light falls on some areas than on others because of the shadow cast by the tree.

How does the visual system know that the change in intensity caused by the shadow is an illumination edge and not a reflectance edge? One thing the visual system may take into account is the shadow's meaningful shape. In this particular example, we know that the shadow was cast by a tree, so we know it is the illumination that is changing, not the color of the bricks on the wall. Another clue is provided by the nature of the shadow's contour, as illustrated by the following demonstration.

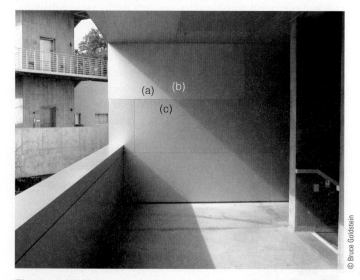

Figure 9.37 This unevenly illuminated wall contains both reflectance edges (between *a* and *c*) and illumination edges (between *a* and *b*). The perceptual system must distinguish between these two types of edges to accurately perceive the actual properties of the wall, and other parts of the scene as well.

Figure 9.38 In this photo, you assume that the shadowed and unshadowed areas are bricks with the same lightness but that less light falls on some areas than on others because of the shadow cast by the tree.

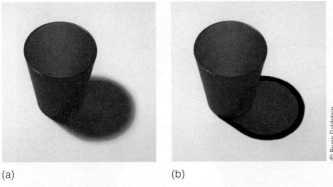

(a)   (b)

Figure 9.39 (a) A cup and its shadow. (b) The same cup and shadow with the penumbra covered by a black border.

© Bruce Goldstein

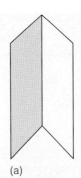
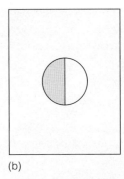

(a)   (b)

Figure 9.40 Viewing a shaded corner. (a) Illuminate the card so one side is illuminated and the other is in shadow. (b) View the card through a small hole so the two sides of the corner are visible, as shown.

DEMONSTRATION | The Penumbra and Lightness Perception

Place an object, such as a cup, on a white piece of paper on your desk. Then illuminate the cup at an angle with your desk lamp and adjust the lamp's position to produce a shadow with a slightly fuzzy border, as in **Figure 9.39a**. (Generally, moving the lamp closer to the cup makes the border get fuzzier.) The fuzzy border at the edge of the shadow is called the shadow's **penumbra**. Now take a marker and draw a thick line, as shown in Figure 9.39b, so you can no longer see the penumbra. What happens to your perception of the shadowed area inside the black line?

Covering the penumbra causes most people to perceive a change in the appearance of the shadowed area. Apparently, the penumbra provides information to the visual system that the dark area next to the cup is a shadow, so the edge between the shadow and the paper is an illumination edge. However, masking off the penumbra eliminates that information, so the area covered by the shadow is seen as a change in reflectance. In this demonstration, lightness constancy occurs when the penumbra is present but does not occur when it is masked.

The Orientation of Surfaces The following demonstration provides an example of how information about the orientation of a surface affects our perception of lightness.

DEMONSTRATION | Perceiving Lightness at a Corner

Stand a folded index card on end so that it resembles the outside corner of a room, and illuminate it so that one side is illuminated and the other is in shadow. When you look at the corner, you can easily tell that both sides of the corner are made of the same white material but that the nonilluminated side is shadowed (**Figure 9.40a**). In other words, you perceive the edge between the illuminated and shadowed "walls" as an illumination edge.

Now create a hole in another card and, with the hole a few inches from the corner of the folded card, view the corner with one eye about a foot from the hole (**Figure 9.40b**). If, when

viewing the corner through the hole, you perceive the corner as a flat surface, your perception of the left and right surfaces will change.

In this demonstration, the illumination edge you perceived at first became transformed into an erroneous perception of a reflectance edge, so you saw the shadowed white paper as being gray paper. The erroneous perception occurs because viewing the shaded corner through a small hole eliminated information about the conditions of illumination and the orientation of the corner. In order for lightness constancy to occur, it is important that the visual system have adequate information about the conditions of illumination. Without this information, lightness constancy can break down and a shadow can be seen as a darkly pigmented area.

Figure 9.41a provides another example of a possible confusion between perceiving an area as being "in shadow" or perceiving it as being made of "dark material." This photograph of the statue of St. Mary was taken at night in the Grotto of Our Lady of Lourdes at the University of Notre Dame. Observing the statue at night, it is unclear whether the dark area above Mary's arms is colored blue, like the sash, or whether it is simply in shadow. The lighting seems to indicate a shadow, but the almost perfect color match between that area and the sash suggests blue material. The statue is perched on a high ledge, so it isn't easy to tell. But **Figure 9.41b**, taken in daylight, reveals that the dark area was, in fact, a shadow. Mystery solved! As with color perception, sometimes we are fooled by conditions of illumination or by ambiguous information, but most of the time we perceive lightness accurately.

SOMETHING TO CONSIDER:

Color Is a Creation of the Nervous System

Our discussion so far has been dominated by the idea that there is a connection between wavelength and color. This idea is most strongly demonstrated by the visual spectrum in which each

Figure 9.41 A statue of St. Mary illuminated at night from below on the left. The same statue during the day on the right.

wavelength is associated with a specific color (**Figure 9.42a**). But this connection between wavelength and color can be misleading, because it might lead you to believe that wavelengths are colored—450-nm light is blue, 520-nm light is green, and

so on. As it turns out, however, wavelengths are completely colorless. This is demonstrated by considering what happens to our perception of color under dim illumination, as happens at dusk. As illumination decreases, we dark adapt and our vision

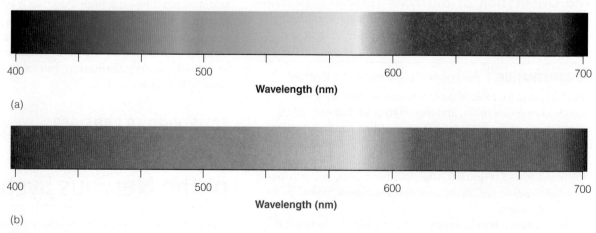

Figure 9.42 (a) Visible spectrum in color. (b) Spectrum as perceived at low intensities, when only the rod receptors are controlling vision.

shifts to the rods (page 30). This causes hues such as blue, green, and red to become less distinct and eventually disappear altogether, until the spectrum, once lushly colored, becomes a series of different shades of gray (**Figure 9.42b**). This effect of dark adaptation illustrates that the nervous system constructs color from wavelengths through the action of the cones.

The idea that color is *not* a property of wavelengths was asserted by Isaac Newton in his *Optiks* (1704):

> For the rays to speak properly are not coloured. In them there is nothing else than a certain power and disposition to stir up a Sensation of this or that Colour.... so Colours in the Object are nothing but a Disposition to reflect this or that sort of Rays more copiously than the rest....

Newton's idea is that the colors we see in response to different wavelengths are not contained in the rays of light themselves, but that the rays "stir up a sensation of this or that color." Stating this idea in modern-day physiological terms, we would say that light rays are simply energy, so there is nothing intrinsically "blue" about short wavelengths or "red" about long wavelengths, and that we perceive color because of the way our nervous system responds to this energy.

We can appreciate the role of the nervous system in creating color experience by considering not only what happens when vision shifts from cone to rod receptors but also the fact that people like Mr. I., the artist who lost his ability to see color in a car accident, see no colors, even though they are receiving the same stimuli as people with normal color vision. Also, many animals perceive either no color or a greatly reduced palette of colors compared to humans, and others sense a wider range of colors than humans, depending on the nature of their visual systems.

For example, **Figure 9.43** shows the absorption spectra of a honeybee's visual pigments. The pigment that absorbs short-wavelength light enables the honeybee to see short wavelengths that can't be detected by humans (Menzel & Backhaus, 1989; Menzel et al., 1986). What "color" do you think bees perceive at 350 nm, which you can't see? You might be tempted to say

"blue" because humans see blue at the short-wavelength end of the spectrum, but you really have no way of knowing what the honeybee is seeing, because, as Newton stated, "The Rays . . . are not coloured." There is no color in the wavelengths; it is the bee's nervous system that creates the bee's experience of color. For all we know, the honeybee's experience of color at short wavelengths is quite different from ours, and may also be different for wavelengths in the middle of the spectrum that humans and honeybees can both see.

The idea that the nervous system is responsible for the quality of our experience also holds for other senses. For example, we will see in Chapter 11 that our experience of hearing is caused by pressure changes in the air. But why do we perceive slow pressure changes as low pitches (like the sound of a tuba) and rapid pressure changes as high pitches (like a piccolo)? Is there anything intrinsically "high-pitched" about rapid pressure changes (**Figure 9.44a**)? Or consider the sense of taste. We perceive some substances as "bitter" and others as "sweet," but where is the "bitterness" or "sweetness" in the molecular structure of the substances that enter the mouth? Again, the answer is that these perceptions are not in the molecular structures. They are created by the action of the molecular structures on the nervous system (**Figure 9.44b**).

One of the themes of this book has been that our experience is filtered through our nervous system, so the properties of the nervous system can affect what we experience. We know,

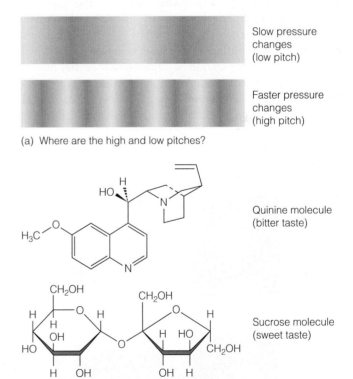

(a) Where are the high and low pitches?

Slow pressure changes (low pitch)

Faster pressure changes (high pitch)

Quinine molecule (bitter taste)

Sucrose molecule (sweet taste)

(b) Where are the bitter and sweet tastes?

Figure 9.44 (a) Low and high pitches are associated with slow and fast pressure waves, but pressure waves don't have "pitch." The pitch is created by how the auditory system responds to the pressure waves. (b) Molecules don't have taste. The nervous system creates different tastes in response to the action of the molecules on the taste system.

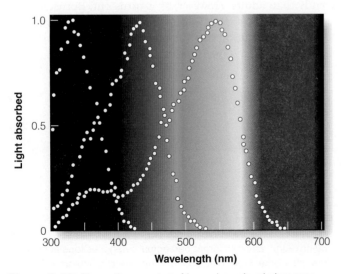

Figure 9.43 Absorption spectra of honeybee visual pigments.

for example, that our ability to detect dim lights and fine details is affected by the way the rod and cone receptors converge onto other neurons in the retina (see Chapter 2, page 39). The idea we have introduced here is that our perceptual experience is not only *shaped* by the nervous system, as in the example of rod and cone vision, but—in cases such as color vision, hearing, taste, and smell—the very essence of our experience is *created* by the nervous system.

We know that our perception of color is determined by the action of three different types of cone receptors (Figure 9.10). Because the cones are poorly developed at birth, we can guess that the newborn would not have good color vision. However, research has shown that color vision develops early and that appreciable color vision is present within the first 3 to 4 months of life.

One of the challenges in determining whether infants have color vision is that perception of a light stimulus can vary on at least two dimensions: (1) its chromatic color and (2) its brightness. Thus, if we present the red and yellow patches in **Figure 9.45** to a color-deficient person and ask him whether he can tell the difference between them, he might say yes, because the yellow patch looks brighter than the red one.

You can make this observation, if you don't have access to a color-deficient person, by using a "color-blind" black-and-white photocopier as your "observer." Photocopies of the red and yellow patches (**Figure 9.45b**) show that the color-blind photocopier can distinguish between the two patches because the red patch is darker than the yellow one. This means that when stimuli with different wavelengths are used to test color vision, their intensity should be adjusted so that they have the same brightness. For example, for the stimuli in Figure 9.45, it would be necessary to make the red patch lighter and the yellow patch darker. The experiment we will now describe has done this.

Marc Bornstein, William Kessen, and Sally Weiskopf (1976) assessed the color vision of 4-month-old infants by determining whether they perceived the same color categories in the spectrum as adults. People with normal trichromatic vision see the spectrum as a sequence of color categories, starting with blue at the short-wavelength end, followed by green, yellow, orange, and red, with fairly abrupt transitions between one color and the next (see the spectrum in Figure 9.42).

Bornstein and coworkers used the method of habituation, described in Chapter 6 (see page 145). They habituated infants to a 510-nm light—a wavelength that appears green to an adult with normal color vision (**Figure 9.46**)—by presenting the light a number of times and measuring how long the infant looked at it (**Figure 9.47**). The decrease in looking time (green dots) indicates that habituation is occurring.

After trial 15 of habituation, a 480-nm light (Figure 9.46) is presented. This wavelength appears blue to an adult observer and is therefore in a different category than the 510-nm light for adults. The infants' increase in looking time, called dishabituation, indicates that the perception caused by the 480-nm light is also in a different category for the infants. However, when this procedure is repeated, first presenting the 510-nm light and then a 540-nm light (which is also perceived as green by adults and so is in the same category; see Figure 9.46), dishabituation does not occur, indicating that the 540-nm light is in the same category for the infants. From this result and the results of other experiments, Bornstein concluded that 4-month-old infants categorize colors the same way adult trichromats do.

Bornstein and coworkers dealt with the problem of equating brightness by setting the intensity at each wavelength so each stimulus looked equally bright to adults. This is not an ideal procedure because infants may perceive brightness differently than adults. However, as it turns out, Bornstein's result appears to be correct, because later research has confirmed Bornstein's conclusion that young infants have color vision (see Franklin & Davies, 2004; Hamer et al., 1982; Varner et al., 1985).

(a)

(b)

Figure 9.45 (a) Two color patches. (b) The same two patches as "seen" by a photocopy machine.

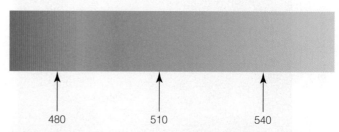

480   510   540

Figure 9.46 Three wavelengths (indicated by arrows) used in Bornstein, Kessen, and Weiskopf's (1976) experiment. The 510- and 480-nm lights are in different perceptual categories (one appears green, the other blue to adults), but the 510- and 540-nm lights are in the same perceptual category (both appear green to adults).

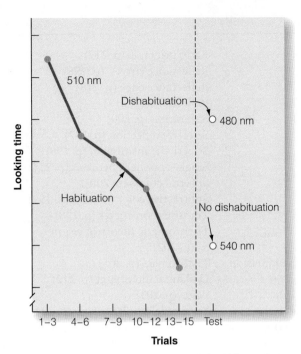

Figure 9.47 Results of the Bornstein et al. (1976) experiment. Looking time decreases over the first 15 trials as the infant habituates to repeated presentations of a 510-nm stimulus. Looking times for presentation of 480-nm and 540-nm stimuli presented on trial 16 are indicated by the dots on the right.

As with all research in which we are drawing conclusions about how things appear to subjects, it is important to realize that research that indicates that infants categorize colors in the same way as adults doesn't tell us how those colors appear to the infants (Dannemiller, 2009). Just as it is not possible to know whether two adults who call a light "red" are having exactly the same experience, it is also not possible to know exactly what the infants are experiencing when their looking behavior indicates that they can tell the difference between two wavelengths. In addition, there is evidence that color vision continues to develop into the teenage years (Teller, 1997). It is safe to say, however, that the foundations of trichromatic vision are present at about 4 months of age.

TEST YOURSELF 9.3

1. What is color constancy? Describe three factors that help us achieve color constancy.
2. What is lightness constancy? Describe the factors that are responsible for lightness constancy. Under what condition might lightness constancy break down?
3. What does it mean to say that color is created by the nervous system?
4. Describe Bornstein's experiment that showed that infants categorize colors in the same way as adults. What does this result tell us about what the infants are experiencing?

THINK ABOUT IT

1. A person with normal color vision is called a trichromat. This person needs to mix three wavelengths to match all other wavelengths and has three cone pigments. A person who is color deficient is called a dichromat. This person needs only two wavelengths to match all other wavelengths and has only two operational cone pigments. A tetrachromat needs four wavelengths to match all other wavelengths and has four cone pigments. If a tetrachromat were to meet a trichromat, would the tetrachromat think that the trichromat was color deficient? How would the tetrachromat's color vision be "better than" the trichromat's? (p. 202)

2. When we discussed color deficiency, we noted the difficulty in determining the nature of a color-deficient person's color experience. Discuss how this is related to the idea that color experience is a creation of our nervous system. (pp. 212, 221)

3. When you walk from outdoors, which is illuminated by sunlight, to an indoor space that is illuminated by tungsten or LED bulbs, your perception of colors remains fairly constant. But under some illuminations, such as sodium-vapor lights that sometimes illuminate highways or parking lots, colors do seem to change. Why do you think color constancy would hold under some illuminations but not others? (p. 214)

4. **Figure 9.48** shows two displays (Knill & Kersten, 1991). The display in (b) was created by changing the top and bottom of the display in (a), while keeping the intensity distributions across the centers of the displays constant. (You can convince yourself that this is true by masking off the top and bottom of the displays.) But even though the intensities are the same, the display in (a) looks like a dark surface on the left and a light surface on the right, whereas the display in (b) looks like two curved cylinders with a slight shadow on the left one. How would you explain this, based on what we know about the causes of lightness constancy? (p. 217)

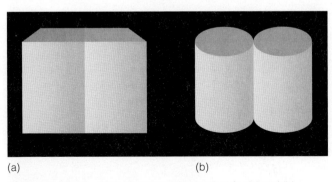

(a)   (b)

Figure 9.48 The light distribution is identical for (a) and (b), although it appears to be different. (Figure courtesy of David Knill and Daniel Kersten)

KEY TERMS

Achromatic colors (p. 197)
Additive color mixture (p. 200)
Anomalous trichromatism (p. 213)
Cerebral achromatopsia (p. 195)
Chromatic adaptation (p. 215)
Chromatic colors (p. 197)
Color blind (p. 212)
Color circle (p. 206)
Color constancy (p. 214)
Color matching (p. 202)
Color solid (p. 201)
Complementary afterimages (p. 207)
Desaturated (p. 200)
Dichromatism (p. 212)
Dichromats (p. 205)
Double-opponent neurons (p. 211)
Hering's primary colors (p. 206)
HSV color solid (p. 201)

Hue cancellation (p. 207)
Hues (p. 200)
Illumination edge (p. 218)
Ishihara plates (p. 212)
Lightness constancy (p. 217)
Lightness (p. 217)
Memory color (p. 216)
Metamerism (p. 204)
Metamers (p. 204)
Monochromatism (p. 212)
Monochromats (p. 205)
Nonspectral colors (p. 200)
Opponent neurons (p. 209)
Opponent-process theory of color vision
   (p. 206)
Partial color constancy (p. 215)
Penumbra (p. 219)
Principle of univariance (p. 204)

Ratio principle (p. 217)
Reflectance curves (p. 198)
Reflectance edge (p. 218)
Reflectance (p. 217)
Saturation (p. 200)
Selective reflection (p. 197)
Selective transmission (p. 198)
Single-opponent neurons (p. 211)
Spectral colors (p. 200)
Subtractive color mixture (p. 199)
Transmission curves (p. 198)
Trichromatic theory of vision
   (p. 202)
Trichromats (p. 205)
Unilateral dichromat (p. 212)
Value (p. 201)
Young-Helmholtz theory (p. 202)

Most rubber duckies are small, but this one, floating in the Allegheny River in Pittsburgh, is huge. In this chapter, we see that our perception of an object's size is influenced by our perception of its distance from us. We begin by considering the many things that create depth perception, and then describe the connection between perceiving depth and perceiving size.

CHAPTER 10

Perceiving Depth and Size

CHAPTER CONTENTS

Perceiving Depth

Oculomotor Cues

Monocular Cues
Pictorial Cues
Motion-Produced Cues

Binocular Depth Information
Seeing Depth With Two Eyes
Binocular Disparity
Disparity (Geometrical) Creates
    Stereopsis (Perceptual)
The Correspondence Problem

The Physiology of Binocular Depth Perception

Perceiving Size
The Holway and Boring Experiment
Size Constancy

Illusions of Depth and Size
The Müller-Lyer Illusion
The Ponzo Illusion
The Ames Room
The Moon Illusion

SOMETHING TO CONSIDER: Depth
Information Across Species

DEVELOPMENTAL DIMENSION: Infant
Depth Perception
Binocular Disparity
Pictorial Cues

THINK ABOUT IT

Some Questions We Will Consider:

- How can we perceive depth in a scene based on the two-dimensional image on the retina? (p. 227)

- Why do we see depth better with two eyes than with one eye? (p. 235)

- Why don't people appear to shrink in size when they walk away? (p. 246)

Our final chapter on vision focuses on the perception of depth and size. At first, you might think that depth and size are separate issues in perception, but they are in fact closely related. To see why, let's consider **Figure 10.1a**. What do you see in this image? Most people see what appears to be a very small man standing on a chair. This is, however, an illusion created by a misperception of the man's distance from the camera. Although the man appears to be standing on a chair that is next to the woman, he is actually standing on a platform located next to the black curtain (**Figure 10.1b**). The illusion that the man is standing on a chair is created by lining up the camera so a structure located across from the woman lines up with the platform, to create the perception of a chair. Showing the woman apparently pouring into the man's glass enhances the misperception of the man's distance,

and our incorrect perception of his depth leads to an incorrect perception of his size.

The illusion in Figure 10.1 was specifically created to trick your brain into misperceiving the man's depth and size, but why don't we confuse a short man who is close by and a tall man who is far away in our everyday perception of the world? We will answer this question by describing the many ways we use different sources of optical and environmental information to help us accurately determine the depth and size of objects in our everyday environments.

Perceiving Depth

You can easily tell that the page you are reading is about 12 to 18 inches away and, when you look up at the scene around you, that other objects are located at distances ranging from your nose (very close!) to across the room, down the street, or even as far as the horizon, depending on where you are. What's amazing about this ability to see the distances of objects in a three-dimensional environment is that your perception of these objects, and the scene as a whole, is based on the two-dimensional image on your retina.

We can appreciate the problem of perceiving three-dimensional depth based on the two-dimensional information on the retina by considering two points on the scene in

Figure 10.1 (a) Misperception of the man's depth leads to an incorrect perception of his size. (b) When the illusion of the "chair" is removed, the man's actual depth can be determined, and he appears to be taller.

(a)

(b)

Dr. Peter Thompson

Figure 10.2a. Light is reflected from point T on the tree and from point H on the house onto points T′ and H′ on the retina at the back of the eye. Looking just at these points on the flat surface of the retina (**Figure 10.2b**), we have no way of knowing how far the light has traveled to reach each point. For all we know, the light stimulating either point on the retina could have come from 1 foot away or from a distant star. Clearly, we need to expand our view beyond single points on the retina to determine where objects are located in space.

When we expand our view from two isolated points to the entire retinal image, we increase the amount of information available to us because now we can see the images of the house and the tree. However, because this image is two-dimensional, we still need to explain how we get from the flat image on the retina to the three-dimensional perception of the scene.

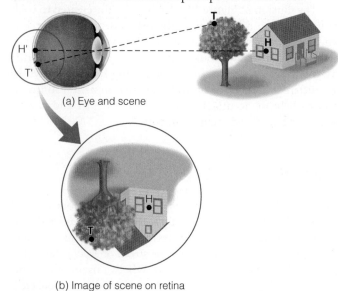

(a) Eye and scene

(b) Image of scene on retina

Figure 10.2 (a) In the scene, the house is farther away than the tree, but images of points H on the house and T on the tree fall on points H′ and T′ on the two-dimensional surface of the retina on the back of the eye. (b) These two points on the retinal image, considered by themselves, do not tell us the distances of the house and the tree.

One way researchers have approached this problem is by the **cue approach to depth perception**, which focuses on identifying information in the retinal image that is correlated with depth in the scene. For example, when one object partially covers another object, as the tree in the foreground in Figure 10.2a covers part of the house, the object that is partially covered must be farther than the object that is covering it. This situation, called **occlusion**, is a cue that one object is in front of another. According to cue theory, we learn the connection between this cue and depth through our previous experience with the environment. After this learning has occurred, the association between particular cues and depth becomes automatic, and when these depth cues are present, we experience the world in three dimensions. A number of different types of cues that signal depth in a scene have been identified. We can divide these cues into three major groups:

1. *Oculomotor.* Cues based on our ability to sense the position of our eyes and the tension in our eye muscles.
2. *Monocular.* Cues based on the visual information available within one eye.
3. *Binocular.* Cues that depend on visual information within both eyes.

Oculomotor Cues

The **oculomotor cues** are created by (1) convergence, the inward movement of the eyes that occurs when we look at nearby objects, and (2) accommodation, the change in the shape of the lens that occurs when we focus on objects at various distances. The idea behind these cues is that we can *feel* the inward movement of the eyes that occurs when the eyes converge to look at nearby objects, and we feel the tightening of eye muscles that change the shape of the lens to focus on a nearby object. You can experience the feelings in your eyes associated with convergence and accommodation by doing the following demonstration.

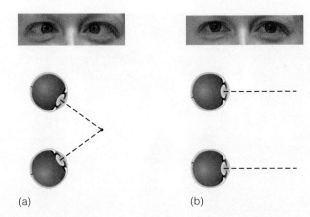

Figure 10.3 (a) Convergence of the eyes occurs when a person looks at something that is very close. (b) The eyes look straight ahead when the person observes something that is far away.

DEMONSTRATION | **Feelings in Your Eyes**

Look at your finger as you hold it at arm's length. Then, as you slowly move your finger toward your nose, notice how you feel your eyes looking inward and become aware of the increasing tension inside your eyes.

The feelings you experience as you move your finger closer are caused by (1) the change in convergence angle as your eye muscles cause your eyes to look inward, as in **Figure 10.3a**, and (2) the change in the shape of the lens as the eye accommodates to focus on a near object (see Figure 2.9, page 26). If you move your finger farther away, the lens flattens, and your eyes move away from the nose until they are both looking straight ahead, as in **Figure 10.3b**. Convergence and accommodation indicate when an object is close; they are useful up to a distance of about arm's length, with convergence being the more effective of the two (Cutting & Vishton, 1995; Mon-Williams & Tresilian, 1999; Tresilian et al., 1999).

Monocular Cues

Monocular cues work with only one eye. They include *accommodation*, which we have described under oculomotor cues; *pictorial cues*, which are sources of depth information in a two-dimensional picture; and *movement-based cues*, which are sources of depth information created by movement.

Pictorial Cues

Pictorial cues are sources of depth information that can be depicted in a picture, such as the illustrations in this book or an image on the retina (Goldstein, 2001).

Occlusion We have already described the depth cue of occlusion. Occlusion occurs when one object hides or partially hides another from view. The partially hidden object is seen as being farther away, so the mountains in **Figure 10.4** are perceived as being farther away than the cactus and the hill. Note that occlusion does not provide precise information about an object's distance. It simply indicates that the object that is partially covered is farther away than another object, but from occlusion alone we can't tell how much farther.

Relative Height In the photograph of the scene in **Figure 10.4a**, some objects are near the bottom of the frame and others nearer the top. The height in the frame of the photo corresponds to the height in our field of view, and objects that are higher in the field of view are usually farther away. This is illustrated in **Figure 10.4b**, in which dashed lines 1, 2, and 3 have been added under the front motorcycle, the rear motorcycle, and one of the telephone poles. Notice that dashed lines higher in the picture are under objects that are farther away. You can demonstrate this by looking out at a scene and placing your finger at the places where objects contact the ground. When you do this, you will notice that your finger is higher for farther

(a)

(b)

© Bruce Goldstein

Figure 10.4 (a) A scene in Tucson, Arizona, containing a number of depth cues: occlusion (the cactus on the right occludes the hill, which occludes the mountain); relative height (the far motorcycle is higher in the field of view than the closer one); relative size (the far motorcycle and telephone pole are smaller than the near ones); and perspective convergence (the sides of the road converge in the distance). (b) 1, 2, and 3 indicate the increasing height in the field of view of the bases of the motorcycles and the far telephone pole, which reveals that being higher in the field of view causes objects on the ground to appear farther away; 4 and 5 reveal that being *lower* in the field of view causes objects in the *sky* to appear farther away, so cloud 5 appears farther from the viewer than cloud 4.

objects. According to the cue of **relative height**, objects with their bases closer to the horizon are usually seen as being more distant. This means that being *higher* in the field of view causes objects on the *ground* to appear farther away (see lines 1, 2, and 3 in Figure 10.4b), whereas being *lower* in the field of view causes objects in the *sky* to appear farther away (see lines 4 and 5).

Familiar and Relative Size We use the cue of **familiar size** when we judge distance based on our prior knowledge of the sizes of objects. We can apply this idea to the coins in **Figure 10.5a**. If you are influenced by your knowledge of the actual size of dimes, quarters, and half-dollars (**Figure 10.5b**), you might say that the dime is closer than the quarter. An experiment by William Epstein (1965) shows that under certain conditions, our knowledge of an object's size influences our perception of that object's distance (see also McIntosh & Lashley, 2008). The stimuli in Epstein's experiment were equal-sized photographs of a dime, a quarter, and a half-dollar (Figure 10.5a), which were positioned the same distance from an observer. By placing these photographs in a darkened room, illuminating them with a spot of light, and having subjects view them with one eye, Epstein created the illusion that these pictures were real coins.

When the observers judged the distance of each of the coin photographs, they estimated that the dime was closest, the quarter was farther than the dime, and the half-dollar was the farthest of all. Thus, the observers' judgments were influenced by their knowledge of the sizes of these coins. This result does not occur, however, when observers view the scene with both eyes, because, as we will see when we discuss binocular (two-eyed) vision, the use of two eyes provides information indicating the coins are at the same distance. The cue of familiar size is therefore most effective when other information about depth is absent (see also Coltheart, 1970; Schiffman, 1967).

A depth cue related to familiar size is **relative size**. According to the cue of relative size, when two objects are known to be of equal physical size, the one that is farther away will take up less of your field of view than the one that is closer. For example, knowing (or assuming) that the two telephone poles, or the

(a)

(b)

Figure 10.5 (a) Drawings of coins similar to the photographs used in Epstein's (1965) familiar-size experiment. Each coin was depicted as being the same size as the quarter. (b) The actual relative sizes of a dime, quarter, and half-dollar.

Figure 10.6 Pietro Perugino, *Christ Handing the Keys to St. Peter* (Sistine Chapel). The convergence of lines on the plaza illustrates perspective convergence. The sizes of the people in the foreground and middle ground illustrate relative size.

two motorcycles, in Figure 10.4 are about the same size, we can determine which pole, or motorcycle, is closer than the other.

Perspective Convergence When you look down parallel railroad tracks that appear to converge in the distance, you are experiencing **perspective convergence**. This cue was often used by Renaissance artists to add to the impression of depth in their paintings, as in Pietro Perugino's painting in **Figure 10.6**. Notice that in addition to the perspective convergence provide by the lines on the plaza, Perugino has included people in the middle ground, further enhancing the perception of depth through the cue of relative size. Figure 10.4 illustrates both perspective convergence (the road) and relative size (the motorcycles) in our Tucson mountain scene.

Atmospheric Perspective **Atmospheric perspective** occurs because the farther away an object is, the more air and particles (dust, water droplets, airborne pollution) we have to look through, so that distant objects appear less sharp than nearer objects and often have a slight blue tint. **Figure 10.7** illustrates atmospheric perspective. The details in the foreground are

Figure 10.7 A scene on the coast of Maine showing the effect of atmospheric perspective.

sharp and well defined, but details become less and less visible as we look farther into the distance.

The reason that farther objects look bluer is related to the reason the sky appears blue. Sunlight contains a distribution of all of the wavelengths in the spectrum, but the atmosphere preferentially scatters short-wavelength light, which appears blue. This scattered light gives the sky its blue tint and also creates a veil of scattered light between us and objects we are looking at, although the blueness becomes obvious only when we are looking through a large distance or when there are more particles in the atmosphere to scatter the light.

If, instead of viewing this cliff along the coast of Maine, you were standing on the moon, where there is no atmosphere and hence no atmospheric perspective, far craters would not look blue and would look just as clear as near ones. But on Earth, there is atmospheric perspective, with the exact amount depending on the nature of the atmosphere.

Texture Gradient When several similar objects are equally spaced throughout a scene, like the marathon runners in **Figure 10.8**, they produce a perception of texture when viewed in depth, with farther elements seen as being spaced more closely. Our perception of the resulting change in texture is called a **texture gradient**. Notice, for example, that the runners appear to be more closely packed as distance increases. The increasing density of textural elements as distance increases enhances the perception of depth.

Shadows Shadows—decreases in light intensity caused by the blockage of light—can provide information regarding the locations of these objects. Consider, for example, **Figure 10.9a**, which shows seven spheres and a checkerboard. In this picture, the location of the spheres relative to the checkerboard is unclear. They could be resting on the surface of the checkerboard or floating above it. But adding shadows, as shown in **Figure 10.9b**, makes the spheres' locations clearer—the ones on the left are resting on the checkerboard, and the ones on the right are floating above it. This illustrates how shadows can help determine the location of objects (Mamassian, 2004; Mamassian et al., 1998).

(a)

(b)

Figure 10.9 (a) Where are the spheres located in relation to the checkerboard? (b) Adding shadows makes their location clearer. (Courtesy of Pascal Mamassian)

Shadows also enhance the three-dimensionality of objects. For example, shadows make the circles in Figure 10.9 appear spherical and help define some of the contours in the mountains in **Figure 10.10**, which appear three-dimensional in the early morning when there are shadows (**Figure 10.10a**), but

(a)

(b)

© Bruce Goldstein

Figure 10.10 (a) Early morning shadows emphasize the mountain's contours. (b) When the sun is overhead, the shadows vanish and it becomes more difficult to see the mountain's contours.

Vismar Ravagnani/Getty Images

Figure 10.8 Texture gradient created by marathon runners. The increasing fineness of texture as distance increases enhances the perception of depth.

Figure 10.11 One eye moving past (a) a nearby tree; (b) a faraway house. Because the tree is closer, its image moves farther across the retina than the image of the house.

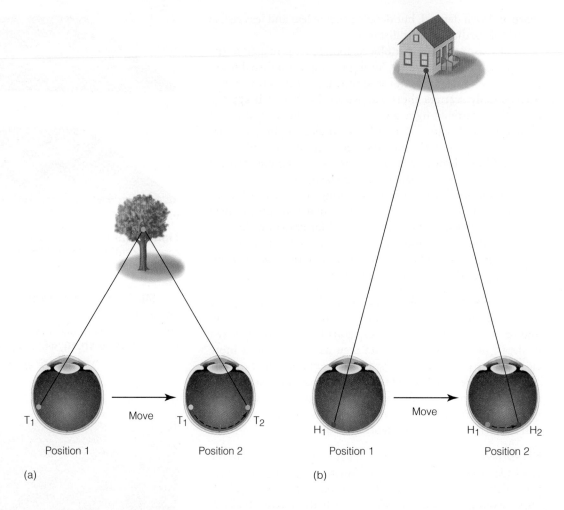

Position 1   Position 2   Position 1   Position 2

(a)   (b)

flat in the middle of the day when the sun is directly overhead and there are no shadows (**Figure 10.10b**).

Motion-Produced Cues

All of the cues we have described so far work if the observer is stationary. But once we start moving, new cues emerge that further enhance our perception of depth. We will describe two motion-produced cues: (1) *motion parallax* and (2) *deletion* and *accretion*.

Motion Parallax Motion parallax occurs when, as we move, nearby objects appear to glide rapidly past us, but more distant objects appear to move more slowly. Thus, when you look out the side window of a moving car or train, nearby objects appear to speed by in a blur, whereas objects that are farther away may appear to be moving only slightly.[1] We can understand why motion parallax occurs by noting how the image of a near object (the tree in **Figure 10.11a**) and a far object (the house in **Figure 10.11b**) move across the retina as an eye moves from position 1 to position 2 without rotating.

First let's consider the tree: Figure 10.11a shows one eye that moves from 1 to 2, so the tree's image moves all the way across the retina from T1 to T2, as indicated by the dashed arrow. Figure 10.11b shows that the house's image moves a shorter distance, from H1 to H2. Because the image of the tree travels a larger distance across the retina than the house, in the same amount of time, it appears to move more rapidly.

Motion parallax is one of the most important sources of depth information for many animals. For example, before jumping out toward an object such as prey, locusts move their heads from side to side to generate motion parallax signals that indicate the distance of their target (Wallace, 1959). By artificially manipulating environmental information in a way that alters the motion parallax signals obtained by a locust, researchers can "trick" the animal into either jumping short of, or beyond, their intended target (Sobel, 1990). The information provided by motion parallax has also been used to enable human-designed mechanical robots to determine how far they are from obstacles as they navigate through the environment (Srinivasan & Venkatesh, 1997). Motion parallax is also widely used to create an impression of depth in cartoons and video games.

Deletion and Accretion As an observer moves sideways, some things become covered, and others become uncovered. Try the following demonstration.

[1]If, when looking out the window, you keep your eyes fixed on one object, objects farther and closer than the object you are looking at appear to move in opposite directions.

Figure 10.12 Position of the hands for the "Deletion and Accretion" demonstration. See text for explanation.

Table 10.1a Cues That Indicate Relative Depth

DEPTH CUE	0–2 METERS	2–20 METERS	ABOVE 20 METERS
Occlusion	√	√	√
Deletion & accretion		√	√
Relative height		√	√
Atmospheric perspective			√

Table 10.1b Cues That Contribute to Determination of Actual Depth

DEPTH CUE	0–2 METERS	2–20 METERS	ABOVE 20 METERS
Relative size	√	√	√
Texture gradients		√	√
Motion parallax	√	√	
Accommodation	√		
Convergence	√		

DEMONSTRATION | Deletion and Accretion

Close one eye. Position your hands as shown in **Figure 10.12**, so your right hand is at arm's length and your left hand at about half that distance, just to the left of the right hand. Then as you look at your right hand, move your head sideways to the left, being sure to keep your hands still. As you move your head, your left hand appears to cover your right hand. This covering of the farther right hand is **deletion**. If you then move your head back to the right, the nearer hand moves back and uncovers the right hand. This uncovering of the far hand is **accretion**. Deletion and accretion occur all the time as we move through the environment and create information that the object or surface being covered and uncovered is farther away (Kaplan, 1969).

Integrating Monocular Depth Cues Our discussion so far has described a number of the monocular cues that contribute to our perception of depth. But it is important to understand that each of these cues gives us "best guess" information regarding object depth and that each cue can, by itself, be uninformative in certain situations. For example, relative height is most useful when we can see where objects touch the ground, shadow is most useful if the scene is illuminated at an angle, familiar size is most useful if we have prior knowledge of the objects' sizes, and so forth. Furthermore, as shown in **Table 10.1**, monocular depth cues work over different distances: some only at close range (accommodation, convergence); some at close and medium ranges (motion parallax, deletion and accretion); some at long range (atmospheric perspective, relative height, texture gradients); and some at the whole range of depth perception (occlusion, relative size; Cutting & Vishton, 1995). Thus, for a nearby object, we don't look for atmospheric perspective but instead rely more on convergence, occlusion, or relative size information. Additionally, some depth cues only provide information on relative depth (**Table 10.1a**) while others can contribute to a more precise determination of actual depth (**Table 10.1b**). No depth cue is perfect. No depth cue is applicable to every situation. But by combining different depth cues when they are available, we can achieve a reasonable interpretation of depth.

Binocular Depth Information

The power of monocular cues to signal depth is plain to see when you close one eye. When you do so, you can still tell what is near and what is far away. However, closing one eye removes some of the information that your brain uses to compute the depth of objects. Two-eyed depth perception involves mechanisms that take into account differences in the images formed on the left and right eyes. The following demonstration illustrates these differences.

DEMONSTRATION | Two Eyes: Two Viewpoints

Close your right eye. Hold a finger on your left hand at arm's length. Position a right-hand finger about a foot away, so it covers the other finger. Then open the right eye and close the left. When you switch eyes, how does the position of your front finger change relative to the rear finger?

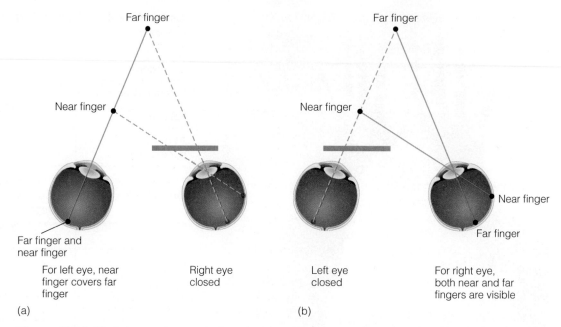

Far finger

Near finger

Near finger

Far finger

Near finger

Far finger

Far finger and near finger

For left eye, near finger covers far finger

Right eye closed

Left eye closed

For right eye, both near and far fingers are visible

(a)

(b)

Figure 10.13 Black dots on the eyes indicate locations of images on the retina when (a) only the left eye is open. (b) only the right eye is open.

When you switched from looking with your left eye to your right, you probably noticed that the front finger appeared to move to the left relative to the far finger. **Figure 10.13** diagrams what happened on your retinas. The green line in **Figure 10.13a** shows that when the left eye was open, the images of the near and far fingers were lined up with the same place on the retina. This occurred because you were looking directly at both objects, so both images would fall on the foveas of the left eye. The green lines in **Figure 10.13b** show that when the right eye was open, the image of the far finger still fell on the fovea because you were looking at it, but the image of the near finger was now off to the side.

Whereas the fingers were lined up relative to the left eye, the right eye "looks around" the near finger, so the far finger becomes visible. These different viewpoints for the two eyes is the basis of **stereoscopic depth perception**—depth perception created by input from both eyes. Before describing these mechanisms, we will consider what it means to say that stereoscopic depth perception is qualitatively different from monocular depth perception.

Seeing Depth With Two Eyes

One way to appreciate the qualitative difference between monocular depth perception and stereoscopic depth perception is to consider the story of Susan Barry, a neuroscientist at Mt. Holyoke College. Her story—first described by neurologist Oliver Sacks, who dubbed her "Stereo Sue" (Sacks, 2006, 2010), and then in her own book, *Fixing My Gaze* (Barry, 2011)—begins with Susan's childhood eye problems. She was cross-eyed, so when she looked at something with one eye, the other eye would be looking somewhere else. For most people, both eyes aim at the same place and work in coordination with each other, but in Susan's case, the input was uncoordinated.

Situations such as this, along with a condition called "walleye" in which the eyes look outward, are forms of **strabismus**, or misalignment of the eyes. When this occurs, the visual system suppresses vision in one of the eyes to avoid double vision, so the person sees the world with only one eye at a time.

Susan had a number of operations as a child that made it more difficult to detect her strabismus, but her vision was still dominated by one eye. Although her perception of depth was only achieved through monocular cues, she was able to get along quite well. She could drive, play softball, and do most of the things people with stereoscopic vision can do. For example, she describes her vision in a college classroom as follows:

> I looked around. The classroom didn't seem entirely flat to me. I knew that the student sitting in front of me was located between me and the blackboard because the student blocked my view of the blackboard. When I looked outside the classroom window, I knew which trees were located further away because they looked smaller than the closer ones. (Barry, 2011, Chapter 1)

Although Susan could use these monocular cues to perceive depth, her knowledge of the neuroscience literature and various other experiences she describes in her book led her to realize that she was still seeing with one eye despite her childhood operations. She therefore consulted an optometrist, who confirmed her one-eyed vision and assigned eye exercises designed to improve the coordination between her two eyes. These exercises enabled Susan to coordinate her eyes, and one day after leaving the optometrist's office, she had her first experience with stereoscopic depth perception, which she describes as follows:

> I got into my car, sat down in the driver's seat, placed the key in the ignition, and glanced at the

steering wheel. It was an ordinary steering wheel against an ordinary dashboard, but it took on a whole new dimension that day. The steering wheel was floating in its own space, with a palpable volume of empty space between the wheel and the dashboard. I closed one eye and the steering wheel looked "normal" again; that is, it lay flat just in front of the dashboard. I reopened the closed eye, and the steering wheel floated before me. (Barry, 2011, Chapter 6)

From that point on, Susan had many more experiences that astounded her, much as someone who had never experienced stereoscopic vision might react if they could put on 3-D movie glasses and suddenly begin seeing in stereoscopic three dimensions. It is important to note that Susan didn't suddenly gain stereovision equivalent to that experienced by a person with stereoscopic vision from birth. Her stereovision occurred first for nearby objects and then, as her training progressed, was extended to farther distances. But what she did experience dramatically illustrates the richness that stereoscopic vision adds to the experience of depth perception.

The added experience of depth created by stereoscopic depth perception is also illustrated by the difference between standard movies and 3-D movies. Standard movies, which project images on a flat screen, create a perception of depth based on monocular depth cues like occlusion, relative height, shadows, and motion parallax. Three-dimensional movies add stereoscopic depth perception. This is achieved by using two cameras placed side by side. Like each of your eyes, each camera receives a slightly different view of the scene (**Figures 10.14a** and **10.14b**). These two images are then overlaid on the movie screen (**Figure 10.14c**).

When you put your 3-D glasses on, the lenses separate the two overlapping images so that each eye only receives one of the images. This image separation can be achieved in several ways, but the most common method in movie theaters today uses polarized light—light waves that vibrate in only one orientation. One image is polarized so its vibration is vertical and the other is polarized so its vibration is horizontal. The glasses you wear have polarized lenses that let only vertically polarized light into one eye and horizontally polarized light into the other eye. Thus, sending these two different views to two different eyes duplicates what happens in the real 3-D world, and suddenly some objects appear to be recessed behind the screen while others appear to jut far out in front of it.

Binocular Disparity

Binocular disparity, the difference in the images on the left and right retinas, is the basis of stereoscopic vision. We now look more closely at the information on the left and right retinas that the brain uses to create an impression of depth.

Corresponding Retinal Points We begin by introducing **corresponding retinal points**—points on the retina that would overlap if the eyes were superimposed on each other (**Figure 10.15**). We can illustrate corresponding points

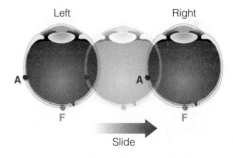

Figure 10.15 Corresponding points on the two retinas. To determine corresponding points, imagine that the left eye is slid on top of the right eye. F indicates the fovea, where the image of an object occurs when an observer looks directly at the object, and A is a point in the peripheral retina. Images on the fovea always fall on corresponding points. Notice that the A's, which also fall on corresponding points, are the same distance from the fovea in the left and right eyes.

(a) Left camera

(b) Right camera

(c) Overlay of camera images

© Bruce Goldstein

Figure 10.14 (a) and (b) 3-D movies are filmed using two side-by-side cameras so that each camera records a slightly different view of the scene. (c) The images are then projected onto the same 2-D surface. Without 3-D glasses, both images are visible to both eyes. 3-D glasses separate the images so that one is only seen by the left eye and the other is only seen by the right eye. When the left and right eyes receive these different images, stereoscopic depth perception occurs.

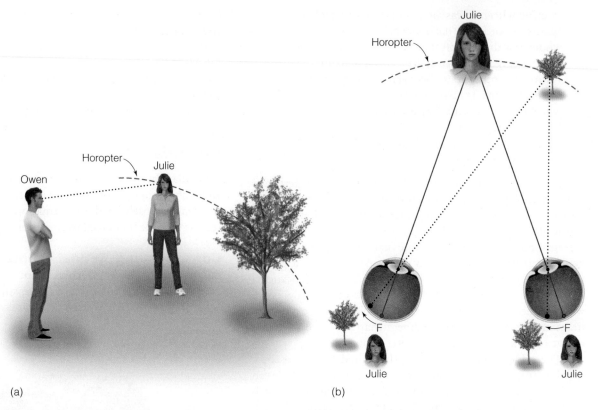

Figure 10.16 (a) Owen is looking at Julie's face, with a tree off to the side. (b) Owen's eyes, showing where the images of Julie and the tree fall on each eye. Julie's images fall on the fovea, so they are on corresponding points. The arrows indicate that the tree's images are located the same distances from the fovea in the two eyes, so they are also on corresponding points. The dashed line in (a) and (b) is the horopter. The images of objects that are on the horopter fall on corresponding points.

by considering what Owen sees in **Figure 10.16a**, when he is looking directly at Julie. **Figure 10.16b** shows where Julie's images are located on Owen's retinas. Because Owen is looking directly at Julie, her images fall on Owen's foveas in both eyes, indicated by the green dots. The two foveas are corresponding points, so Julie's images fall on corresponding points.

In addition, the images of other objects also fall on corresponding points. Consider, for example, the tree in Figure 10.16b. The tree's images are on the same place relative to the foveas—to the left and at the same distance (indicated by the arrows). This means that the tree's images are on corresponding points. (If you were to slide the eyes on top of each other, Julie's images would overlap, and the tree's images would overlap.) Thus, whatever a person is looking at directly (like Julie) falls on corresponding points, and some other objects (like the tree) fall on corresponding points as well. Julie, the tree, and any other objects that fall on corresponding points are located on a surface called the **horopter**. The blue dashed curves in Figures 10.16a and 10.16b show part of the horopter.

Noncorresponding Points and Absolute Disparity The images of objects that are *not* on the horopter fall on **noncorresponding points**. This is illustrated in

Figure 10.17a, which shows Julie again, with her images on corresponding points, and a new character, Bill, who is located in front of the horopter. Because Bill is not on the horopter, his image falls on noncorresponding points in each retina. The degree to which Bill's image *deviates* from falling on corresponding points is called **absolute disparity**. The amount of absolute disparity, called the **angle of disparity**, is indicated by the blue arrow in Figure 10.17a; it is the angle between the corresponding point on the right eye for the left-eye image of Bill (large blue dot) and the actual location of the image on the right eye. **Figure 10.17b** shows that binocular disparity also occurs when objects are behind the horopter (farther away than a fixated object).

Although objects appearing in front of the horopter (Figure 10.17a) and behind the horopter (Figure 10.17b) both result in retinal disparity, the disparity is somewhat different in the two situations. To understand this difference, let's think about what each eye sees individually in Figures 10.17a and 10.17b.

The pictures at the bottom of Figure 10.17a show what the left and right eyes see when Bill is in front of Julie. In this situation, the left eye sees Bill to Julie's right, while the right eye sees Bill to Julie's left. This pattern of disparity where the left eye sees an object (e.g., Bill) to the right of the observer's fixation

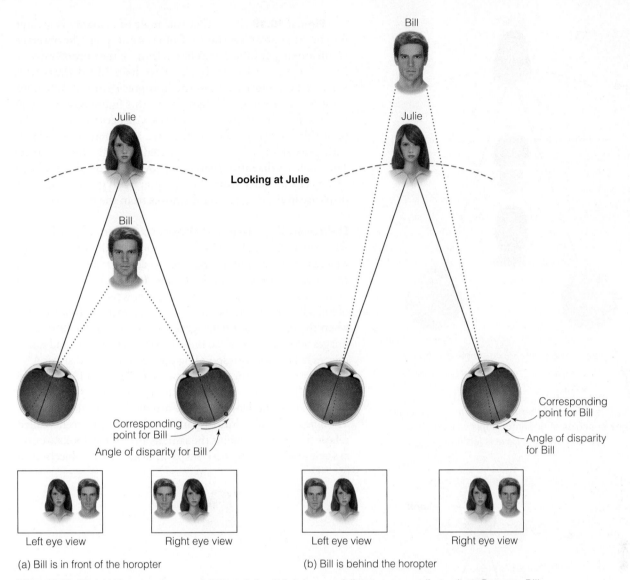

Looking at Julie

Corresponding
point for Bill

Angle of disparity for Bill

Corresponding
point for Bill

Angle of disparity
for Bill

Left eye view   Right eye view   Left eye view   Right eye view

(a) Bill is in front of the horopter   (b) Bill is behind the horopter

Figure 10.17 (a) When an observer looks at Julie, Julie's images fall on corresponding points. Because Bill is in front of the horopter, his images fall on noncorresponding points. The angle of disparity, indicated by the blue arrow, is determined by measuring the angle between where the corresponding point for Bill's image would be located (large blue dot) and where Bill's image is actually located. (b) Disparity is also created when Bill is behind the horopter. The pictures at the bottom of the figure illustrate how the positions of Julie and Bill are seen by each eye.

point (e.g., Julie) and the right eye sees that same object to the left of the fixation point is called **crossed disparity** (you can remember this by thinking about the fact that you would need to "cross" your eyes in order to fixate Bill). Crossed disparity occurs whenever an object is closer to the observer than where the observer is looking.

Now let's consider what happens when an object is behind the horopter. The pictures at the bottom of Figure 10.17b show what each eye sees when Bill is behind Julie. This time, the left eye sees Bill to Julie's left and the right eye sees Bill is to Julie's right. This pattern of disparity where the left eye sees an object to the left of the observer's fixation point and the right eyes sees that same object to the right of the fixation point is called **uncrossed disparity** (in order to fixate on Bill you would

need to "uncross" your eyes). Uncrossed disparity occurs whenever an object is behind the horopter. Thus, by determining whether an object produces crossed or uncrossed disparity, the visual system can determine whether that object is in front of or behind a person's point of fixation.

Absolute Disparity Indicates Distance From the Horopter Determining whether absolute disparity is crossed or uncrossed indicates whether an object is in front of or behind the horopter. This is of course important information to have, but it provides only part of the story. To perceive depth accurately, we also need to know the distance between an object and the horopter. This information is provided by the amount of disparity associated with an object.

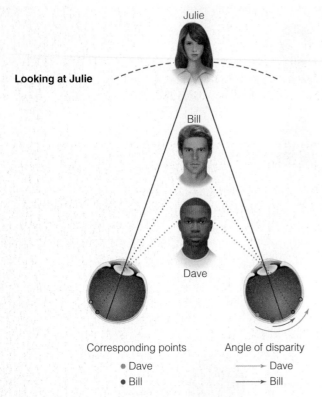

Looking at Julie

Julie

Bill

Dave

Corresponding points Angle of disparity
- Dave   ——→ Dave
- Bill   ———→ Bill

Figure 10.18 Objects that are farther away from the horopter are associated with greater angles of disparity. In this case, both Dave and Bill are in front of the horopter, but Dave is farther from the horopter than Bill.

Figure 10.18 shows that the angle of disparity is greater for objects at greater distances from the horopter. The observer is still looking at Julie, and Bill is in front of the horopter where he was in Figure 10.17a, but now we have added Dave, who is located even farther from the horopter than Bill. When we compare Dave's angle of disparity in this figure (green arrow) to Bill's (blue arrow), we see that Dave's disparity is greater. The same thing happens for objects farther away than the horopter, with greater distance also associated with greater disparity. The angle of disparity therefore provides information about an object's distance from the horopter, with greater angles of disparity indicating greater distances from the horopter.

Relative Disparity Is Related to Objects' Positions Relative to Each Other Let's now consider what happens when the observer shifts his gaze from one object to another. When the observer is looking at Julie (**Figure 10.19a**), Julie's images fall on the observer's foveas (so Julie's disparity is zero), but the images of Bill fall on noncorresponding points (so there is disparity). But when the observer shifts his gaze to Bill (**Figure 10.19b**), Bill's images fall on the foveas (so Bill's disparity is now zero) and Julie's images fall on noncorresponding points (so there is disparity).

If we compare the two situations in Figure 10.19, we notice that the difference in absolute disparities between Julie and Bill (indicated by the lengths of the arrows) is the same in both. The *difference* in absolute disparities of objects in a scene, called **relative disparity**, remains the same as an observer looks around a scene. Relative disparity helps indicate where objects in a

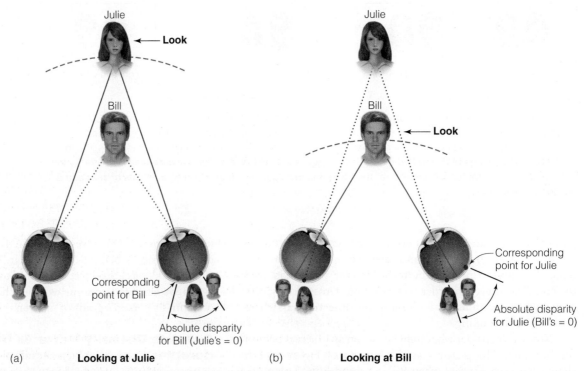

Julie

Look

Bill

Corresponding point for Bill

Absolute disparity for Bill (Julie's = 0)

(a)   **Looking at Julie**

Julie

Bill

Look

Corresponding point for Julie

Absolute disparity for Julie (Bill's = 0)

(b)   **Looking at Bill**

Figure 10.19 Absolute disparities change when an observer's gaze shifts from one place to another. (a) When the observer looks at Julie, the disparity of her images is zero. Bill's angle of disparity is indicated by the arrow. (b) When the observer looks at Bill, the disparity of Bill's images becomes zero. Julie's angle of disparity is indicated by the arrow. Because one of the disparities in each pair is zero, the arrows indicate the *difference in disparity* between the Julie's and Bill's images. Note, that the difference in disparity is the same in (a) and (b). This means that the *relative disparity* of Julie and Bill remains the same as the observer looks at different places.

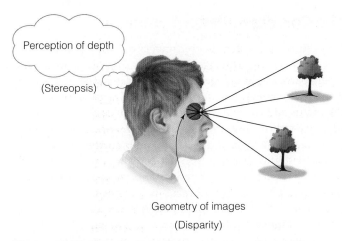

Perception of depth

(Stereopsis)

Geometry of images

(Disparity)

Figure 10.20 Disparity is related to geometry—the locations of images on the retina. Stereopsis is related to perception—the experience of depth created by disparity.

scene are located relative to one another. As we will see, there is evidence that both absolute and relative disparity information is represented by neural activity in the visual system.

Disparity (Geometrical) Creates Stereopsis (Perceptual)

We have seen that both absolute and relative disparity information contained in the images on the retinas provides information indicating an object's relative distance from where the observer is looking. Notice, however, that our description of disparity has focused on *geometry*—looking at where objects' images fall on the retina—but has not mentioned *perception*, the observer's experience of an object's depth or its relation to other objects in the environment (**Figure 10.20**). We consider the relationship between disparity and what observers perceive by introducing **stereopsis**—the impression of depth that results from information provided by binocular disparity.

In order to demonstrate that disparity creates stereopsis, we need to isolate disparity information from other depth cues, such as occlusion and relative height, because these other cues can also contribute to our perception of depth. In order to show that disparity alone can result in depth perception, Bela Julesz (1971) created a stimulus called the *random-dot stereogram*, which contains no pictorial cues. By creating stereoscopic images of random-dot patterns, Julesz showed that observers can perceive depth in displays that contain no depth information other than disparity. Two such random-dot patterns, which together constitute a **random-dot stereogram**, are shown in **Figure 10.21**. These patterns were constructed by first generating two identical random-dot patterns on a computer and then shifting a square-shaped section of the dots one or more units to the side.

In the stereogram in **Figure 10.21a**, a section of dots from the pattern on the left has been shifted one unit to the right to form the pattern on the right. This shift is too subtle to be seen in the dot patterns, but we can understand how it is accomplished by looking at the diagrams below the dot patterns (**Figure 10.21b**). In these diagrams, the black dots are

(a)

Figure 10.21 (a) A random-dot stereogram. (b) The principle for constructing the stereogram. See text for explanation.

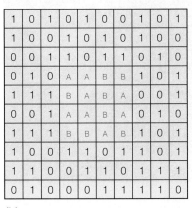

(b)

indicated by 0's, A's, and X's and the white dots by 1's, B's, and Y's. The A's and B's indicate the square-shaped section where the shift is made in the pattern. Notice that the A's and B's are shifted one unit to the right in the right-hand pattern. The X's and Y's indicate areas uncovered by the shift that must be filled in with new black dots and white dots to complete the pattern.

As you look at Figure 10.21a in the book, information from both the left and right image travel to both your left and right eyes and it is difficult, if not impossible, to tell that the dots have been shifted. The visual system can, however, detect a difference between these images if we separate the visual information on the page so that the left image is only seen by the left eye and the right image is only seen by the right eye. With two side-by-side images (rather than slightly overlapping as in Figure 10.14c) this separation is accomplished by using a device called a **stereoscope** (**Figure 10.22**) that uses two lenses to focus the left image on the left eye and the right image on the right eye. When viewed in this way, the disparity created by the shifted section results in perception of a small square floating above the background. Because binocular disparity is the only depth information present in these stereograms, disparity alone must be causing the perception of depth.

Psychophysical experiments, particularly those using Julesz's random-dot stereograms, show that retinal disparity creates a perception of depth. But before we can fully understand the mechanisms responsible for depth perception, we must answer one more question: How does the visual system match the parts of the images in the left and right eyes that correspond to one another? This is called the **correspondence problem**, and as we will see, it has still not been fully explained.

The Correspondence Problem

Let's return to the stereoscopic images of Figure 10.14c. When we view this image through 3-D glasses (page 235), we see different parts of the image at different depths because of the disparity between images on the left and right retinas. Thus, the cactus and the window appear to be at different distances when viewed through the stereoscope because they create different amounts of disparity. But in order for the visual system to calculate this disparity, it must compare the images of the cactus on the left and right retinas and the images of the window on the left and right retinas.

To see why this comparison poses a problem, let's take a look at **Figure 10.23**, which shows how the light reflected from two different configurations of objects would fall on the left and right retinas. Notice that points 1–4 on the left retina in **Figure 10.23a** are the same as those in the left retina of **Figure 10.23b**. The same is true for points 5–8 on the right retina in each figure. This means that the information on each retina is exactly the same in Figures 10.23a and 10.23b, even though the configuration of objects in the world is very different. We can tell the two configurations apart, however, if we compare the information available *across* the retinas. In Figure 10.23a, object A stimulates points 1 and 5, but in Figure 10.23b, object A stimulates points 1 and 6 (objects B and C also stimulate different retinal points in each configuration). But how do we know when points 1 and 5 are stimulated by the same object (Figure 10.23a) or by different objects (Figure 10.23b)? How does the visual system match up the images in the two eyes with the objects out in the world?

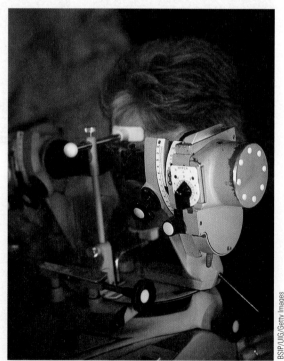

Figure 10.22 Examples of (a) antique and (b) modern stereoscopes.

(a)

(b)

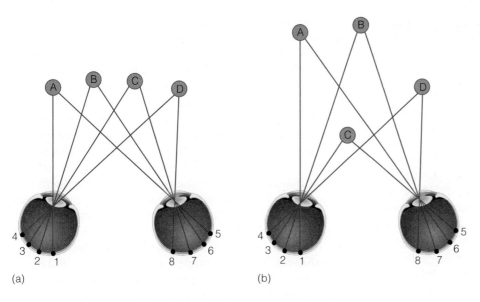

Figure 10.23 Two possible configurations of objects that stimulate the same points on the left and right retinas. How can the visual system tell the two configurations of objects apart? One possibility is shown in Figure 10.24.

A possible answer to this question is that the visual system may match the images on the left and right retinas on the basis of the specific features of the objects. This is shown in **Figures 10.24a** and **10.24b**. In this case, each object is a different color. We can use this color information to match the objects in each retina. In Figure 10.24a, we know that object A falls on points 1 and 5 because the same color information is provided to each point. Similarly, in Figure 10.24b, we can use color to determine that object A falls upon points 1 and 6. Explained in this way, the solution seems simple: Most things in the world are quite discriminable from one another, so it is easy to match an image on the left retina with the image of the same thing on the right retina. Returning to our more "real-world" example in Figure 10.14, the upper-left windowpane that falls on the left retina could be matched with the upper-left pane on the right retina, and so on. But what about images in which matching similar points would be extremely difficult, as with Julesz's random-dot stereogram?

You can appreciate the problem involved in matching similar parts of a stereogram by trying to match up the points in the left and right images of the stereogram in Figure 10.21a. Most people find this to be an extremely difficult task, involving switching their gaze back and forth between the two pictures and comparing small areas of the pictures one after another. But even though matching similar features on a random-dot stereogram is much more difficult and time-consuming than matching features in the real world, the visual system somehow matches similar parts of the two stereogram images, calculates their disparities, and creates a perception of depth.

From the random-dot stereogram example, it is clear that the visual system accomplishes something rather amazing when it solves the correspondence problem. Researchers in fields as diverse as psychology, neuroscience, mathematics, and engineering have put forth a number of specific proposals, all too complex to discuss here, that seek to explain how the visual system fully solves the correspondence problem (Blake & Wilson, 1991; Carrasco, 2012; Kaiser et al., 2013; Marr & Poggio, 1979; Menz & Freeman, 2003; Ohzawa, 1998; Ringbach, 2003; Tanabe et al., 2011). Despite these efforts, however, a totally satisfactory solution to the correspondence problem has yet to be proposed.

Figure 10.24 One way the visual system can match the images on the two retinas is on the basis of features of the objects. In this example, adding color to the objects in Figure 10.23 makes it possible to tell which points on the retina go with which objects.

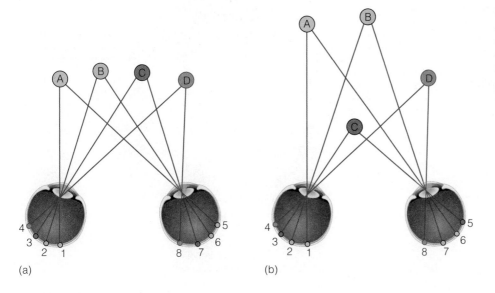

The Physiology of Binocular Depth Perception

The idea that binocular disparity provides information about the positions of objects in space implies that there should be neurons that signal different amounts of disparity, and indeed there are. Fittingly, they are called **binocular depth cells** or **disparity-selective cells**. Research beginning in the 1960s and 1970s first revealed neurons that respond to absolute disparity (Barlow et al., 1967; Hubel & Wiesel, 1970). These cells respond best when stimuli presented to the left and right eyes create a specific amount of absolute disparity (Hubel et al., 2015; Uka & DeAngelis, 2003). **Figure 10.25** shows a **disparity tuning curve** for one of these neurons. This particular neuron responds best when the left and right eyes are stimulated to create an absolute disparity of about 1 degree.

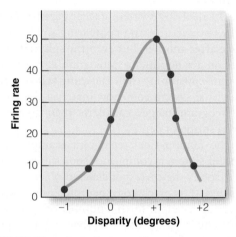

Figure 10.25 Disparity tuning curve for a neuron sensitive to absolute disparity. This curve indicates the neural response that occurs when stimuli presented to the left and right eyes create different amounts of disparity.

Neurons sensitive to absolute disparity first appear in V1 (primary visual cortex, see page 59), which is the first place in the brain where information from both eyes converges (Bakin et al., 2000; Cumming & DeAngelis, 2001; Poggio et al., 1988). After V1, cells that respond to absolute disparity are primarily found in brain regions making up the dorsal (*where/how*) visual pathway (see Figure 4.14) (Backus et al., 2001; Hubel et al., 2015; Neri, 2005). These cells likely play a key role in determining depth information important for performing actions such as reaching and grasping. Further research has shown that there are also neurons in the visual system that respond to relative disparity (Neri, 2005; Parker, 2007; Umeda et al., 2007). These neurons are primarily located in brain regions along the ventral (*what*) visual pathway (Anzai et al., 2011; Neri et al., 2004), where they provide depth information that can be used to support shape perception and object recognition. Apparently, depth perception involves a number of stages of processing, beginning in the primary visual cortex and extending to many different areas in both the ventral and dorsal streams.

The relationship between binocular disparity and the firing of binocular depth cells is an example of the stimulus–physiology relationship in the diagram of the perceptual process in **Figure 10.26** (relationship B). This diagram, which we introduced in Chapter 1 (see Figure 1.11, page 11) and repeated in Chapter 8 (see Figure 8.16, page 183), also depicts two other relationships. The stimulus–perception relationship (A) is the relationship between binocular disparity and the perception of depth. The final relationship, between physiology and perception (C), involves demonstrating a connection between disparity-selective neurons and depth perception. This has been achieved in a number of ways.

An early demonstration of a connection between binocular neurons and perception involved the selective rearing procedure we described in our discussion of the relationship between feature detectors and perception in Chapter 3 (see page 62). Applying this procedure to depth perception,

Figure 10.26 The three relationships in the perceptual process, as applied to binocular disparity. We have described experiments relating disparity to perception (A) and relating disparity to physiological responding (B). The final step is to determine the relationship between physiological responses to disparity and perception (C). This has been studied by selective rearing, which eliminates disparity-selective neurons, and by microstimulation, which activates disparity-selective neurons.

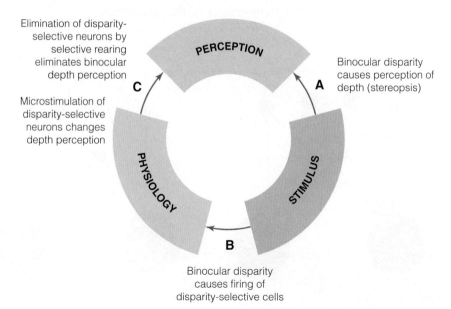

Elimination of disparity-selective neurons by selective rearing eliminates binocular depth perception

Microstimulation of disparity-selective neurons changes depth perception

Binocular disparity causes perception of depth (stereopsis)

PERCEPTION

C

A

PHYSIOLOGY

STIMULUS

B

Binocular disparity causes firing of disparity-selective cells

Randolph Blake and Helmut Hirsch (1975) reared cats so that their vision was alternated between the left and right eyes every other day during the first 6 months of their lives. After this 6-month period of presenting stimuli to just one eye at a time, Blake and Hirsch recorded from neurons in the cat's cortex and found that (1) these cats had few binocular neurons and (2) they were not able to use binocular disparity to perceive depth. Thus, eliminating binocular neurons eliminates stereopsis and confirms what everyone suspected all along—that disparity-selective neurons are responsible for stereopsis (also see Olson & Freeman, 1980).

Another technique that has been used to demonstrate a link between neural activity and depth perception is microstimulation, a procedure in which a small electrode is inserted into the cortex and an electrical charge is passed through the electrode to activate the neurons near the electrode (Cohen & Newsome, 2004) (see Method: Microstimulation in Chapter 8, page 184). In Chapter 8, we described research that showed that stimulating neurons that respond best to specific directions of movement shifts a monkey's perception of moving dots toward that direction of movement. Gregory DeAngelis and coworkers (1998) demonstrated the same effect for depth perception by training monkeys to indicate the depth created by presenting images with different absolute disparities. Presumably, the monkey perceived depth because the disparate images on the monkey's retinas activated disparity-selective neurons in the cortex. But what would happen if microstimulation were used to activate a different group of disparity-selective neurons?

Neurons that are sensitive to the same disparities tend to be organized in clusters, so stimulating one of these clusters activates a group of neurons that respond best to a specific disparity (Hubel et al., 2015). When DeAngelis and coworkers stimulated neurons that were tuned to a disparity different from what was indicated by the images on the retina, the monkey shifted its depth judgment toward the disparity signaled by the stimulated neurons (**Figure 10.27**). The results of the selective rearing and the microstimulation experiments indicate that binocular

depth cells are a physiological mechanism responsible for depth perception, thus providing the physiology–perception relationship of the perceptual process in Figure 10.26.

TEST YOURSELF 10.1

1. What is the basic problem of depth perception, and how does the cue approach deal with this problem?
2. What monocular cues provide information about depth in the environment?
3. What do comparing the experience of "Stereo Sue" and the experience of viewing 3-D and 2-D movies tell us about what binocular vision adds to our perception of depth?
4. What is binocular disparity? What is the difference between crossed and uncrossed disparity? What is the difference between absolute disparity and relative disparity? How are absolute and relative disparity related to the depths of objects in a scene?
5. What is stereopsis? What is the evidence that disparity creates stereopsis?
6. What does perception of depth from a random-dot stereogram demonstrate?
7. What is the correspondence problem? Has this problem been solved?
8. Describe each of the relationships in the perceptual process of Figure 10.26, and provide examples for each relationship that has been determined by psychophysical and physiological research on depth perception.

Perceiving Size

Now that we have described our perception of depth, we will turn our attention to the perception of size. As we noted at the start of this chapter, our perception of size is related to our perception of depth, but this is a point worth repeating. Consider, for example, the following story based on an actual incident at an Antarctic research facility where a helicopter pilot was flying through whiteout weather conditions:

> As Frank pilots his helicopter across the Antarctic wastes, blinding light, reflected down from thick cloud cover above and up from the pure white blanket of snow below, makes it difficult to see the horizon, details on the surface of the snow, or even up from down. He is aware of the danger because he has known pilots dealing with similar conditions who flew at full power directly into the ice. He thinks he can make out a vehicle on the snow far below, and he drops a smoke grenade to check his altitude. To his horror, the grenade falls only three feet before hitting the ground. Realizing that what he thought was a truck was actually a small box, Frank pulls back on the controls and soars up, his face drenched in sweat, as he comprehends how close he just came to becoming another whiteout fatality.

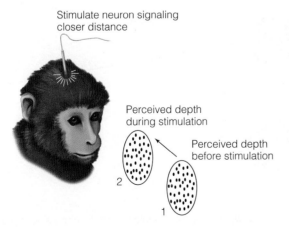

Stimulate neuron signaling closer distance

Perceived depth during stimulation

Perceived depth before stimulation

2

1

Figure 10.27 While the monkey was observing a random-dot stereogram, DeAngelis and coworkers (1998) stimulated neurons in the monkey's cortex that were sensitive to a particular amount of disparity. This stimulation shifted the monkey's perception of the depth of the field of dots from position 1 to position 2.

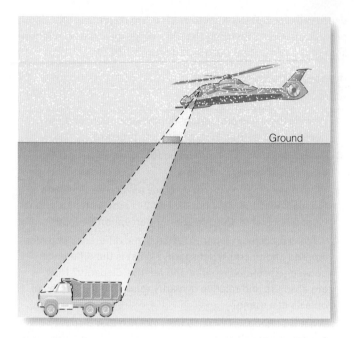

Figure 10.28 When a helicopter pilot loses the ability to perceive distance because of a "whiteout," a small box that is close can be mistaken for a truck that is far away.

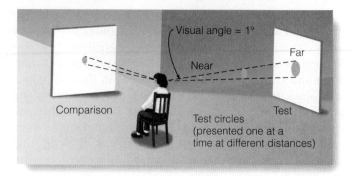

Figure 10.29 Setup of Holway and Boring's (1941) experiment. The observer changes the diameter of the comparison circle in the left corridor to match his or her perception of the size of test circles presented in the right corridor. Each test circle has a visual angle of 1 degree and is presented separately. This diagram is not drawn to scale. The actual distance of the far test circle was 100 feet.

This account illustrates that our ability to perceive an object's size can sometimes be drastically affected by our ability to perceive the object's distance. A small box seen close up can, in the absence of accurate information about its distance, be misperceived as a large truck seen from far away (**Figure 10.28**). The idea that we can misperceive size when accurate depth information is not present was demonstrated in a classic experiment by A. H. Holway and Edwin Boring (1941).

The Holway and Boring Experiment

Observers in Holway and Boring's experiment sat at the intersection of two hallways and saw a luminous *test circle* when looking down the right hallway and a luminous *comparison circle* when looking down the left hallway (**Figure 10.29**). The comparison circle was always 10 feet from the observer, but the test circles were presented at distances ranging from 10 feet to 120 feet. An important property of the fixed-in-place comparison circle was that its size could be adjusted. The observer's task on each trial was to adjust the diameter of the comparison circle in the left corridor to match his or her perception of the sizes of the various test circles presented in the right corridor.

An important feature of the test stimuli in the right corridor was that they all cast exactly the same-sized image on the retina. We can understand how this was accomplished by introducing the concept of *visual angle*.

What Is Visual Angle? Visual angle is the angle of an object relative to the observer's eye. **Figure 10.30a** shows how we determine the visual angle of a stimulus (a person, in this example) by extending lines from the person to the lens of the observer's eye. The angle between the lines is the visual angle. Notice that the

visual angle depends both on the size of the stimulus and on its distance from the observer; when the person moves closer, as in **Figure 10.30b**, the visual angle becomes larger.

The visual angle tells us how large the object will be on the back of the eye. There are 360 degrees around the entire circumference of the eyeball, so an object with a visual angle of 1 degree would take up 1/360 of this circumference—about 0.3 mm in an average-sized adult eye. One way to get a feel for visual angle is to fully extend your arm and look at your thumb, as the woman in **Figure 10.31** is doing. The approximate visual angle of the *width* of the thumb at arm's length is 2 degrees. Thus, an object that is exactly covered by the thumb held at arm's length, such as the phone in Figure 10.31, has a visual angle of approximately 2 degrees.

This "thumb technique" provides a way to determine the approximate visual angle of any object in the environment. It also illustrates an important property of visual angle: A small object that is near (like the thumb) and a larger object that is far (like the phone) can have the same visual angle.

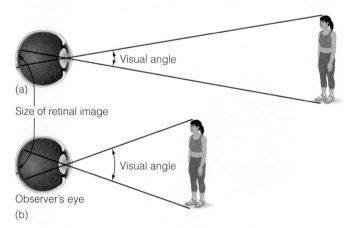

Figure 10.30 (a) The visual angle depends on the size of the stimulus (the woman in this example) and its distance from the observer. (b) When the woman moves closer to the observer, both the visual angle and the size of the image on the retina increase. This example shows that halving the distance between the stimulus and the observer doubles the size of the image on the retina.

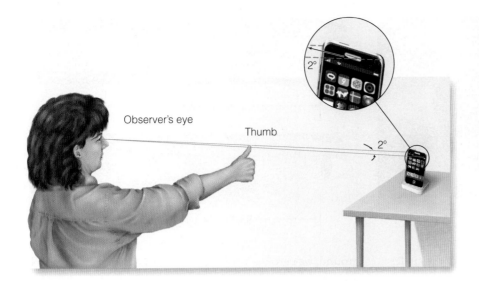

A good example of this is illustrated in **Figure 10.32**, which shows a photograph taken by one of our students. To take this picture, the student adjusted the distance between her fingers so that the Eiffel Tower just fit between them. When she did this, the space between her fingers, which were about a foot away, had the same visual angle as the Eiffel Tower, which was hundreds of yards (meters) away.

How Holway and Boring Tested Size Perception in a Hallway

The idea that objects with different sizes can have the same visual angle was used in the creation of the test circles in Holway and Boring's experiment. As shown in Figure 10.29, small circles that were positioned close to the observer and larger circles that were positioned farther away all had visual angles of 1 degree. Because objects with the same visual angle create the same-sized image on the retina, all of the test circles had the same-sized image on the observers' retinas, no matter where in the hallway they were located.

In the first part of Holway and Boring's experiment, many depth cues were available, including binocular disparity, motion parallax, and shading, so the observer could easily judge the distance of the test circles. The results, plotted in **Figure 10.33**, show that when the observers viewed a large test circle that was located far away (far circle in Figure 10.29), they made the comparison circle large (point F in Figure 10.33); when they viewed a small test circle that was located nearby (near circle in Figure 10.29), they made the comparison circle small (point N in Figure 10.33). Thus, when good depth cues

Figure 10.32 The visual angle between the two fingers is the same as the visual angle of the Eiffel Tower.

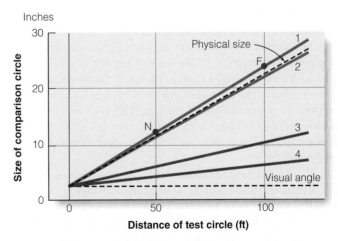

Figure 10.33 Results of Holway and Boring's experiment. The dashed line marked *physical size* is the result that would be expected if the observers adjusted the diameter of the comparison circle to match the actual diameter of each test circle. The line marked *visual angle* is the result that would be expected if the observers adjusted the diameter of the comparison circle to match the visual angle of each test circle.

Figure 10.34 The moon's disk almost exactly covers the sun during an eclipse because the sun and the moon have the same visual angles.

Eclipse of the sun

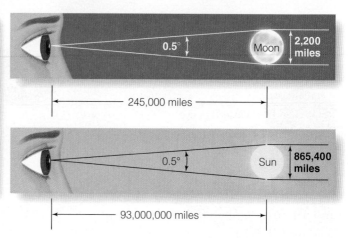

were present, the observer's judgments of the size of the circles matched the physical sizes of the circles.

Holway and Boring then determined how eliminating depth information would affect the observer's judgments of size. They did this by having the observer view the test circles with one eye, which eliminated binocular disparity (line 2 in Figure 10.33); then by having the observer view the test circles through a peephole, which eliminated motion parallax (line 3); and finally by adding drapes to the hallway to eliminate shadows and reflections (line 4). Each time some depth information was eliminated, the observer's judgments of the sizes of the test circles became less accurate. When all depth information was eliminated, the observer's perception of size was determined not by the actual size of the test circles but by the relative sizes of the circle's images on the observer's retinas.

Because all of the test circles in Holway and Boring's experiment had the same retinal size, eliminating depth information caused them to be perceived as being about the same size. Thus, the results of this experiment indicate that size estimation is based on the actual sizes of objects when there is good depth information (blue lines), but that size estimation is strongly influenced by the object's visual angle when depth information is eliminated (red lines).

An example of size perception that is determined by visual angle is our perception of the sizes of the sun and the moon, which, by cosmic coincidence, have the same visual angle. The fact that they have identical visual angles becomes most obvious during an eclipse of the sun. Although we can see the flaming corona of the sun surrounding the moon, as shown in **Figure 10.34**, the moon's disk almost exactly covers the disk of the sun.

If we calculate the visual angles of the sun and the moon, the result is 0.5 degrees for both. As you can see in Figure 10.34, the moon is small (diameter 2,200 miles) but close (245,000 miles from Earth), whereas the sun is large (diameter 865,400 miles) but far away (93 million miles from Earth). Even though these two celestial bodies are vastly different in size, we perceive them to be the same size because, as we are unable to perceive their distance, we base our judgment on their visual angles.

In yet another example, we perceive objects viewed from a high-flying airplane as very small. Because we have no way of accurately estimating the distance from the airplane to the

ground, we perceive size based on objects' visual angles, which are very small because we are so high up.

Size Constancy

One of the most obvious features of the scene in **Figure 10.35**, on the campus of the University of Arizona, is that looking down the row of palm trees, each more distant tree becomes smaller in the picture. If you were standing on campus observing this scene, the more distant trees would appear to take up less of your field of view, as in the picture, but at the same time you would not perceive the farther tree as shorter than the near trees. Even though the far trees take up less of your field of view (or to put it another way, have a smaller *visual angle*), they appear constant in size. The fact that our perception of an object's size is relatively constant even when we view the object from different distances is called **size constancy**.

To introduce the idea of size constancy to our perception classes, we ask someone in the front row to estimate our heights when we are standing about 3 feet away. Their guess is usually accurate, around 5 feet 9 inches for BG and 6 feet 2 inches for JB. We then take one large step back so we are now twice as far

Figure 10.35 All of the palm trees appear to be the same size when viewed in the environment, even though the farther ones have a smaller visual angle.

away and ask the person to estimate our heights again. It probably doesn't surprise you that the second estimate of our heights is about the same as the first. The point of this demonstration is that even though our images on our students' retinas become half as large when we double our distance (compare Figures 10.30a and 10.30b), we do not appear to shrink to about 3 feet tall, but still appear to be our normal size. The following demonstration illustrates size constancy in another way.

DEMONSTRATION | Perceiving Size at a Distance

Hold a quarter between the fingertips of each hand so you can see the faces of both coins. Hold one coin about a foot from you and the other at arm's length. Observe the coins with both of your eyes open and note their sizes. Under these conditions, most people perceive the near and far coins as being approximately the same size. Now close one eye, and holding the coins so they appear side-by-side, notice how your perception of the size of the far coin changes so that it now appears smaller than the near coin. This demonstrates how size constancy is decreased under conditions of poor depth information.

Although students often propose that size constancy works because we are familiar with the sizes of objects, research has shown that observers can accurately estimate the sizes of unfamiliar objects viewed at different distances (Haber & Levin, 2001).

Size Constancy as a Calculation The link between size constancy and depth perception has led to the proposal that size constancy is based on a mechanism called **size-distance scaling** that takes an object's distance into account (Gregory, 1966). Size-distance scaling operates according to the equation

$$S = K(R \times D)$$

where S is the object's perceived size, K is a constant, R is the size of the retinal image, and D is the perceived distance of the object. (Since we are mainly interested in R and D, and K is a scaling factor that is always the same, we will omit K in the rest of our discussion).

According to the size–distance equation, as a person walks away from you, the size of the person's image on your retina (R) gets smaller, but your perception of the person's distance (D) gets larger. These two changes balance each other, and the net result is that you perceive the person's size (S) as staying the same.

DEMONSTRATION | Size–Distance Scaling and Emmert's Law

You can demonstrate size–distance scaling to yourself by looking back at Figure 8.12a in Chapter 8 (page 180). Look at the center of the circle for about 60 seconds. Then look at the white space to the side of the circle. If you blink, you should see the circle's afterimage floating in front of the page. Before the afterimage fades, also look at a wall far across the room. You should see that the size of the afterimage depends on where you look. If you look at a distant surface, such as the far wall of the room,

you see a large afterimage that appears to be far away. If you look at a near surface, such as a piece of paper, you see a small afterimage that appears to be close.

Figure 10.36 illustrates the principle underlying the effect you just experienced, which was first described in 1881 by Emil Emmert (1844–1911). Staring at the circle bleached a small circular area of visual pigment on your retina. This bleached area of the retina determined the retinal size of the afterimage and remained constant no matter where you were looking.

The perceived size of the afterimage, as shown in Figure 10.36, is determined by the distance of the surface against which the afterimage is viewed. This relationship between the apparent distance of an afterimage and its perceived size is known as **Emmert's law**: The farther away an afterimage appears, the larger it will seem. This result follows from our size-distance scaling equation, $S = R \times D$. The size of the bleached area of pigment on the retina (R) always stays the same, so that increasing the afterimage's distance (D) increases the magnitude of $R \times D$. We therefore perceive the size of the afterimage (S) as larger when it is viewed against the far wall.

The size-distance scaling effect demonstrated by the afterimage demonstration is working constantly when we look at objects in the environment, with the visual system taking both an object's size in the field of view (which determines retinal size) and its distance into account to determine our perception of its size. This process, which happens without any effort on our part, helps us perceive a stable environment. Just think of how confusing it would be if objects appeared to shrink or expand just because we happened to be viewing them from different distances. Luckily, because of size constancy, this doesn't happen.

Other Information for Size Perception Although we have been stressing the link between size constancy and depth perception and how size-distance scaling works, other sources of information in the environment also help us achieve

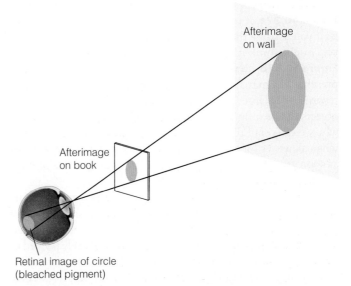

Figure 10.36 The principle behind the observation that the size of an afterimage increases as the afterimage is viewed against more distant surfaces.

(a)

(b)

Figure 10.37 (a) The size of the chair is ambiguous until (b) a person is standing next to it.

size constancy. One source of information for size perception is relative size. We often use the sizes of familiar objects as a yardstick to judge the size of other objects. **Figure 10.37** shows two views of Henry Bruce's sculpture *The Giant's Chair*. In **Figure 10.37a**, it is difficult to determine how large the chair is; if you assume that the camera is positioned on the ground, you might think it looks to be a nice normal size for a chair. **Figure 10.37b**, however, leads us to a different conclusion. The presence of a man next to the chair indicates that the chair is extraordinarily large. This idea that our perception of the sizes of objects can be influenced by the sizes of nearby objects explains why we often fail to appreciate how tall basketball players are, when all we see for comparison are other basketball players. But as soon as a person of average height stands next to one of these players, the player's true height becomes evident.

Another source of information for size perception is the relationship between objects and texture information on the ground. We saw that a texture gradient occurs when elements that are equally spaced in a scene appear to be more closely packed as distance increases (Figure 10.8). **Figure 10.38** shows two cylinders sitting on a texture gradient formed by a cobblestone road. Even if we have trouble perceiving the depth of the near and far cylinders, we can tell that they are the same size because their bases both cover the same portion of a paving stone.

Figure 10.38 Two cylinders resting on a texture gradient. The fact that the bases of both cylinders cover the same number of units on the gradient indicates that the bases of the two cylinders are the same size.

Illusions of Depth and Size

Visual illusions fascinate people because they demonstrate how our visual system can be "tricked" into seeing inaccurately (Bach & Poloschek, 2006). We have already described a number of types of illusions. Illusions of lightness include the Chevreul illusion (page 51) and Mach bands (page 51), in which small changes in lightness are seen near a border even though no changes are present in the physical pattern of light; and the Hermann grid (page 52), in which small gray spots are seen that aren't there in the light. Attentional effects include change blindness (page 139), in which two alternating scenes appear similar even though there are differences between them. Illusions of motion are those in which stationary stimuli are perceived as moving (page 175).

We will now describe some illusions of size—situations that lead us to misperceive the size of an object. We will see that some of these illusions can be explained by the connection between the perception of size and the perception of depth. We will also see that some of the most familiar illusions have yet to be fully explained. A good example of this situation is the *Müller-Lyer illusion*.

The Müller-Lyer Illusion

In the **Müller-Lyer illusion**, the right vertical line in **Figure 10.39** appears to be longer than the left vertical line, even though they are both exactly the same length (measure them). A number of different explanations have been proposed to explain this illusion. An influential early explanation involves size–distance scaling.

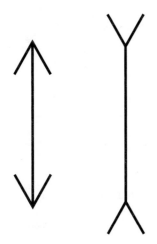

Figure 10.39 The Müller-Lyer illusion. Both lines are actually the same length.

Misapplied Size Constancy Scaling

Why does the Müller-Lyer display cause a misperception of size? Richard Gregory (1966) explains the illusion on the basis of a mechanism he calls **misapplied size constancy scaling**. He points out that size constancy normally helps us maintain a stable perception of objects by taking distance into account (as expressed in the size–distance scaling equation). Thus, size constancy scaling causes a 6-foot-tall person to appear 6 feet tall no matter what his distance. Gregory proposes, however, that the very mechanisms that help us maintain stable perceptions in the three-dimensional world sometimes create illusions when applied to objects drawn on a two-dimensional surface.

We can see how misapplied size constancy scaling works by comparing the left and right lines in Figure 10.39 to the left and right lines that have been superimposed on the corners in **Figure 10.40**. Both lines are the same size, but according to Gregory the lines appear to be at different distances because the fins on the right line in Figure 10.40 make this line look like part of an inside corner of a room, and the fins on the left line make this line look like part of a corner viewed from outside. Because inside corners appear to "recede" and outside corners "jut out," our size–distance scaling mechanism treats the inside corner as if it is farther away, so the term D in the equation $S = R \times D$ is larger and this line therefore appears longer. (Remember that the retinal sizes, R, of the two lines are the same, so perceived size, S, is determined by the perceived distance, D.)

At this point, you could say that although the Müller-Lyer figures may remind Gregory of inside and outside corners, they don't look that way to you (or at least they didn't until Gregory told you to see them that way). But according to Gregory, it is not necessary that you be consciously aware that these lines can represent three-dimensional structures; your perceptual system unconsciously takes the depth information contained in the Müller-Lyer figures into account, and your size–distance scaling mechanism adjusts the perceived sizes of the lines accordingly.

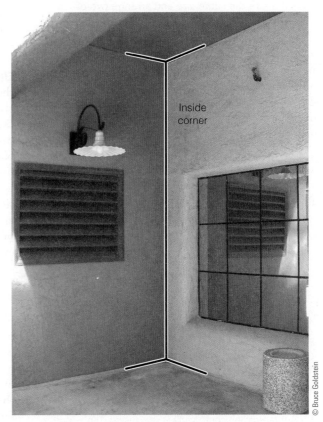

Figure 10.40 According to Gregory (1966), the Müller-Lyer line on the left corresponds to an outside corner, and the line on the right corresponds to an inside corner. Note that the two vertical lines are the same length (measure them!).

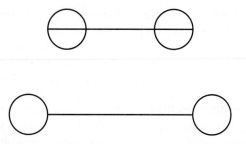

Figure 10.41 The "dumbbell"' version of the Müller-Lyer illusion. As in the original Müller-Lyer illusion, the two straight lines are actually the same length.

Gregory's theory of visual illusions has not, however, gone unchallenged. For example, figures like the dumbbells in **Figure 10.41**, which contain no obvious perspective or depth, still result in an illusion. And Patricia DeLucia and Julian Hochberg (1985, 1986, 1991; Hochberg, 1987) have shown that the Müller-Lyer illusion occurs for a three-dimensional display like the one in **Figure 10.42**. In this display, the distance between corners B and C appears to be greater than the distance between A and B, even though they are the same and it is obvious that the spaces between the two sets of fins are not at different depths. You can experience this effect for yourself by doing the following demonstration.

DEMONSTRATION | The Müller-Lyer Illusion With Books

Pick three books that are the same size and arrange two of them with their corners making a 90-degree angle and standing in positions A and B, as shown in Figure 10.42. Then, without using a ruler, position the third book at position C, so that distance x appears to be equal to distance y. Check your placement, looking down at the books from the top and from other angles as well. When you are satisfied that distances x and y appear about equal, measure the distances with a ruler. How do they compare?

If you set distance y so that it was smaller than distance x, this is exactly the result you would expect from the two-dimensional Müller-Lyer illusion, in which the distance between the outward-facing fins appears enlarged compared to the distance between the inward-facing fins. You can also

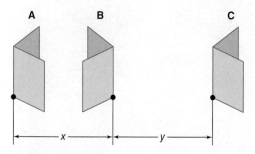

Figure 10.42 A three-dimensional Müller-Lyer illusion. The 2-foot-high wooden "fins" stand on the floor. Although the distances x and y are the same, distance y appears larger, just as in the two-dimensional Müller-Lyer illusion.

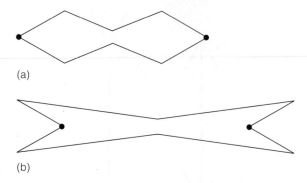

(a)

(b)

Figure 10.43 An alternate version of the Müller-Lyer illusion. We perceive that the distance between the dots in (a) is less than the distance in (b), even though the distances are the same. (From Day, 1989)

duplicate the illusion shown in Figure 10.42 with your books by using your ruler to make distances x and y equal. Then, notice how the distances actually appear. The fact that we can create the Müller-Lyer illusion by using three-dimensional stimuli such as these, along with demonstrations like the dumbbell in Figure 10.41, is difficult for Gregory's theory to explain.

Conflicting Cues Theory R. H. Day (1989, 1990) has proposed the **conflicting cues theory**, which states that our perception of line length depends on two cues: (1) the actual length of the vertical lines, and (2) the overall length of the figure. According to Day, these two conflicting cues are integrated to form a compromise perception of length. Because the overall length of the figure with outward-oriented fins is greater (Figure 10.39), the vertical line appears longer.

Another version of the Müller-Lyer illusion, shown in **Figure 10.43**, results in the perception that the space between the dots is greater in the lower figure than in the upper figure, even though the distances are actually the same. According to Day's conflicting cues theory, the space in the lower figure appears greater because the overall extent of the figure is greater. Notice that conflicting cues theory can also be applied to the dumbbell display in Figure 10.41. Thus, although Gregory believes that depth information is involved in determining illusions, Day rejects this idea and proposes that cues for length are what is important. Let's now look at some more examples of illusions and the mechanisms that have been proposed to explain them.

The Ponzo Illusion

In the **Ponzo** (or railroad track) **illusion**, shown in **Figure 10.44**, both animals are the same size on the page, and so have the same visual angle, but the one on top appears longer. According to Gregory's misapplied scaling explanation, the top animal appears bigger because of depth information provided by the converging railroad tracks that make the top animal appear farther away. Thus, just as in the Müller-Lyer illusion, the scaling mechanism corrects for this apparently increased depth (even though there really isn't any, because the illusion is on a flat page), and we perceive the top animal to be larger. (Also see

Figure 10.44 The Ponzo (or railroad track) illusion. The two animals are the same length on the page (measure them), but the far one appears larger.

Prinzmetal et al., 2001, and Shimamura & Prinzmetal, 1999, for another explanation of the Ponzo illusion.)

The Ames Room

The **Ames room** causes two people of equal size to appear very different in size (Ittelson, 1952). In **Figure 10.45a**, you can see that the woman on the left looks much taller than the man on the right. In **Figure 10.45b**, the man and woman change sides and the illusion is reversed. This time, the man appears much larger than the woman. This perception occurs even though both people are actually about the same height. The reason for this erroneous perception of size lies in the construction of the room. The shapes of the wall and the windows at the rear of the room make it look like a normal rectangular room when viewed from a particular observation point; however, as shown in the diagram in **Figure 10.46**, the Ames room is actually shaped so that the right corner of the room is almost twice as far from the observer as the left corner.

What's happening in the Ames room? The construction of the room causes the woman on the left to have a much smaller visual angle than the one on the right. We think that we are looking into a normal rectangular room at two people who appear to be at the same distance, so we perceive the one with the smaller visual angle as shorter. We can understand why this occurs by returning to our size–distance scaling equation, $S = R \times D$. Because the *perceived* distance (D) is the same for the two women, but the size of the retinal image (R) is smaller for the woman on the left, her perceived size (S) is smaller.

(a)

(b)

Figure 10.45 The Ames room. Although both people are about the same height, (a) the woman appears taller or (b) the man appears taller because of the distorted shape of the room.

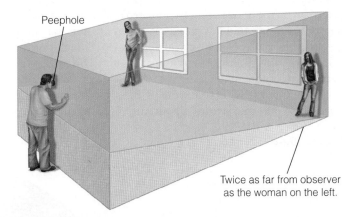

Peephole

Twice as far from observer as the woman on the left.

Figure 10.46 The Ames room, showing its true shape. The person on the right is actually almost twice as far away from the observer as the person on the left; however, when the room is viewed through the peephole, this difference in distance is not seen. In order for the room to look normal when viewed through the peephole, it is necessary to enlarge the right side of the room.

Figure 10.47 An artist's conception of the how the moon is perceived when it is on the horizon and when it is high in the sky. Note that the visual angle of the horizon moon is depicted as larger than the visual angle of the moon high in the sky. This is because the picture is simulating the illusion. In the environment, the visual angles of the two moons are the same.

Another explanation for the Ames room is based not on size–distance scaling but on relative size. The relative size explanation states that our perception of the size of the two people is determined by how they fill the distance between the bottom and top of the room. Because the person on the left fills the entire space and the person on the right occupies only a little of it, we perceive the person on the left as taller (Sedgwick, 2001).

The Moon Illusion

You may have noticed that when the moon is on the horizon, it appears much larger than when it is higher in the sky. This enlargement of the horizon moon compared to the elevated moon, shown in **Figure 10.47**, is called the **moon illusion**. When we discuss this in class, we first explain that visual angles of the horizon moon and elevated moon are the same. This must be so because the moon's physical size (2,200 miles in diameter) stays the same (obviously) and it remains the same distance from Earth (245,000 miles) throughout the night; therefore, the

moon's visual angle must be constant. (If you are still skeptical, photograph the horizon moon and the elevated moon with a digital camera. When you compare the two images, you will find that the diameters in the resulting two pictures are identical. Or you can view the moon through a quarter-inch-diameter hole held at about arm's length. For most people, the moon just fits inside this hole, wherever it is in the sky.)

Once students are convinced that the moon's visual angle remains the same throughout the night, we ask why they think the moon appears larger on the horizon. One common response is "When the moon is on the horizon, it appears closer, and that is why it appears larger." When we ask why it appears closer, we often receive the explanation "Because it appears larger." But saying "It appears larger because it appears closer, and it appears closer because it appears larger" is clearly a case of circular reasoning that doesn't really explain the moon illusion.

One explanation that isn't circular is called the **apparent distance theory**. This theory does take distance into account, but in a way opposite to our hypothetical student's explanation. According to apparent distance theory, the moon on the horizon appears more distant because it is viewed across the filled space of the terrain, which contains depth information; but when the moon is higher in the sky, it appears less distant because it is viewed through empty space, which contains little depth information.

The idea that the horizon is perceived as farther away than the sky overhead is supported by the fact that when people estimate the distance to the horizon and the distance to the sky directly overhead, they report that the horizon appears to be farther away. That is, the heavens appear "flattened" (**Figure 10.48**).

The key to the moon illusion, according to apparent distance theory, is that the horizon moon and the elevated moon have the same visual angle, but because the horizon moon is seen against the horizon, which appears farther than the zenith sky, it appears larger. This follows from the size–distance scaling equation, $S = R \times D$. Retinal size, R, is the same for both locations of the moon (remember that the visual angle is always the same no matter where the moon appears in the sky), so the moon that appears farther away will appear larger. This is the principle we invoked in the Emmert's law demonstration to explain why an afterimage appears larger if it is viewed against a faraway surface.

Just as the near and far afterimages in the Emmert's law demonstration have the same visual angles, so do the horizon and elevated moons. The afterimage that appears on the far

Figure 10.48 When observers are asked to consider the sky as a surface and to compare the distance to the horizon (H) with the distance to the top of the sky on a clear moonless night, they usually say that the horizon appears farther away. This results in the "flattened heavens" shown here.

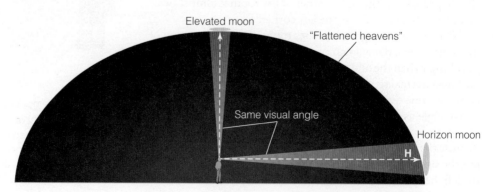

Elevated moon

"Flattened heavens"

Same visual angle

Horizon moon

H

wall simulates the horizon moon; the circle appears farther away, so your size–distance scaling mechanism makes it appear larger. The afterimage that is viewed on a close surface simulates the elevated moon; the circle appears closer, so your scaling mechanism makes it appear smaller (King & Gruber, 1962).

Lloyd Kaufman and Irvin Rock (1962a, 1962b) have done a number of experiments that support the apparent distance theory. In one of their experiments, they showed that when the horizon moon was viewed over the terrain, which made it seem farther away, it appeared 1.3 times larger than the elevated moon; however, when the terrain was masked off so that the horizon moon was viewed through a hole in a sheet of cardboard, the illusion vanished (Kaufman & Rock, 1962a, 1962b; Rock & Kaufman, 1962).

Some researchers, however, are skeptical of the apparent distance theory. They question the idea that the horizon moon appears farther, as shown in the flattened heavens effect in Figure 10.48, because some observers see the horizon moon as floating in space in front of the sky (Plug & Ross, 1994).

Another theory of the moon illusion is the **angular size contrast theory**, which states that the moon appears smaller when it is surrounded by larger objects. Thus, when the moon is elevated, the large expanse of sky surrounding it makes it appear smaller. However, when the moon is on the horizon, less sky surrounds it, so it appears larger (Baird et al., 1990).

Even though scientists have been proposing theories to explain the moon illusion for hundreds of years, there is still no agreement on an explanation (Hershenson, 1989). Apparently a number of factors are involved, in addition to the ones we have considered here, including atmospheric perspective (looking through haze on the horizon can increase size perception), color (redness increases perceived size), and oculomotor factors (convergence of the eyes, which tends to occur when we look toward the horizon and can cause an increase in perceived size; Plug & Ross, 1994). Just as many different sources of depth information work together to create our impression of depth, many different factors may work together to create the moon illusion, and perhaps the other illusions as well.

SOMETHING TO CONSIDER:
Depth Information Across Species

Humans make use of a number of different sources of depth information in the environment. But what about other species? Many animals have excellent depth perception. Cats leap on their prey; monkeys swing from one branch to the next; and a male housefly maintains a constant distance of about 10 cm as it follows a flying female. There is no doubt that many animals are able to judge distances in their environment, but what depth information do they use? Considering the information used by different animals, we find that animals use the entire range of cues described in this chapter. Some animals use many cues, and others rely on just one or two.

To make use of binocular disparity, an animal must have eyes that have overlapping visual fields. Thus, animals such as cats, monkeys, and humans that have **frontal eyes** (**Figure 10.49a**), which result in overlapping fields of view, can use disparity to perceive depth. Animals with **lateral eyes**, such as the rabbit (**Figure 10.49b**), do not have overlapping visual fields and therefore cannot use disparity to perceive depth.

(a)
© Bruce Goldstein

(b)
© Barbara Goldstein

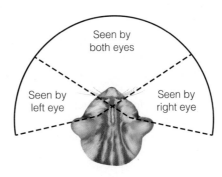

Seen by both eyes

Seen by left eye

Seen by right eye

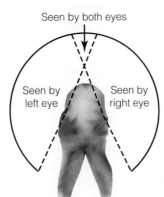

Seen by both eyes

Seen by left eye

Seen by right eye

Figure 10.49 (a) Frontal eyes, such as those of the cat, have overlapping fields of view that provide good stereoscopic depth perception. (b) Lateral eyes, such as those of the rabbit, provide a panoramic view but poorer stereoscopic depth perception.

Note, however, that in sacrificing binocular disparity, animals with lateral eyes gain a wider field of view—something that is extremely important for animals that need to constantly be on the lookout for predators.

The pigeon is an example of an animal with lateral eyes that are placed so that the visual fields of the left and right eyes overlap only in a 35-degree area surrounding the pigeon's beak. This overlapping area, however, happens to be exactly where pieces of grain would be located when the pigeon is pecking at them, and psychophysical experiments have shown that the pigeon does have a small area of binocular depth perception right in front of its beak (McFadden, 1987; McFadden & Wild, 1986).

Movement parallax is probably insects' most important method of judging distance, and they use it in a number of different ways (Collett, 1978; Srinivasan & Venkatesh, 1997). For example, the locust uses a "peering" response—moving its body from side to side to create movement of its head—as it observes potential prey. T. S. Collett (1978) measured a locust's "peering amplitude"—the distance of this side-to-side sway—as it observed prey at different distances, and found that the locust swayed more when targets were farther away. Since more distant objects move less across the retina than nearer objects for a given amount of observer movement, a larger sway would be needed to cause the image of a far object to move the same distance across the retina as the image of a near object. The locust may therefore be judging distance by noting how much sway is needed to cause the image to move a certain distance across its retina (also see Sobel, 1990).

These examples show how depth can be determined from different sources of information in light. But bats, some of which are blind to light, use a form of energy we usually associate with sound to sense depth. Bats sense objects by using a method similar to the sonar system used in World War II to detect underwater objects such as submarines and mines. *Sonar*, which stands for *so*und *na*vigation and *r*anging, works by sending out pulses of sound and using information contained in the echoes of this sound to determine the location of objects. Donald Griffin (1944) coined the term *echolocation* to describe the biological sonar system used by bats to avoid objects in the dark.

Bats emit pulsed sounds that are far above the upper limit of human hearing, and they sense objects' distances by noting the interval between when they send out the pulse and when

(a)   (b)   (c)

Figure 10.50 When a bat sends out its pulses, it receives echoes from a number of objects in the environment. This figure shows the echoes received by the bat from (a) a nearby moth; (b) a tree located about 2 meters away; and (c) a house, located about 4 meters away. The echoes from more distant objects take longer to return. The bat locates the positions of objects in the environment by sensing how long it takes the echoes to return.

they receive the echo (**Figure 10.50**). Since they use sound echoes to sense objects, they can avoid obstacles even when it is totally dark (Suga, 1990). Although we don't have any way of knowing what the bat experiences when these echoes return, we do know that the timing of these echoes provides the information the bat needs to locate objects in its environment. (Also see von der Emde et al., 1998, for a description of how electric fish sense depth based on "electrolocation.") From these examples, we can see that animals use a number of different types of information to determine depth and distance, with the type of information used depending on the animal's specific needs and on its anatomy and physiological makeup.

DEVELOPMENTAL DIMENSION Infant Depth Perception

At what age are infants able to use different kinds of depth information? The answer to this question is that different types of information become operative at different times. Binocular disparity becomes functional early, and pictorial depth cues become functional later.

Binocular Disparity

One requirement for the operation of binocular disparity is that the eyes must be able to **binocularly fixate**, so that the

two eyes are both looking directly at the object and the two foveas are directed to exactly the same place. Newborns have only a rudimentary, imprecise ability to fixate binocularly, especially on objects that are changing in depth (Slater & Findlay, 1975).

Richard Aslin (1977) determined when binocular fixation develops by making some simple observations. He filmed infants' eyes while he moved a target back and forth between 12 cm and 57 cm from the infant. When the infant is directing both eyes at a target, the eyes should diverge (rotate outward) as the target moves away and should converge (rotate inward) as the target moves closer. Aslin's films indicate that although some divergence and convergence do occur in 1- and 2-month-old infants, these eye movements do not reliably direct both eyes toward the target until about 3 months of age.

Although binocular fixation may be present by 3 months of age, this does not guarantee that the infant can use the resulting disparity information to perceive depth. To determine when infants can use this information to perceive depth, Robert Fox and coworkers (1980) presented random-dot stereograms to infants ranging in age from 2 to 6 months (see page 239 to review random-dot stereograms).

The beauty of random-dot stereograms is that the binocular disparity information in the stereograms results in stereopsis. This occurs only (1) if the stereogram is observed with a device that presents one picture to the left eye and the other picture to the right eye and (2) if the observer's visual system can convert this disparity information into the perception of depth. Thus, if we present a random-dot stereogram to an infant whose visual system cannot yet use disparity information, all he or she sees is a random collection of dots.

In Fox's experiment, an infant wearing special viewing glasses was seated in his or her mother's lap in front of a television screen (**Figure 10.51**). The child viewed a random-dot stereogram that appeared, to an observer sensitive to disparity information, as a rectangle-in-depth, moving either to the left or to the right. Fox's premise was that an infant sensitive to disparity will move his or her eyes to follow the moving rectangle. He found that infants younger than about 3 months of age would not follow the rectangle, but that infants between 3 and 6 months of age would follow it. He therefore concluded that the ability to use disparity information to perceive depth emerges sometime between 3½ and

6 months of age. This time for the emergence of binocular depth perception has been confirmed by other research using a variety of different methods (Held et al., 1980; Shimojo et al., 1986; Teller, 1997).

Pictorial Cues

Another type of depth information is provided by pictorial cues. These cues develop later than disparity, presumably because they depend on experience with the environment and the development of cognitive capabilities. In general, infants begin to use pictorial cues such as overlap, familiar size, relative size, shading, linear perspective, and texture gradients sometime between about 4 and 7 months of age (Kavšek et al., 2009; Shuwairi & Johnson, 2013; Yonas et al., 1982). We will describe research on two of these cues: familiar size and cast shadows.

Depth From Familiar Size Granrud, Haake, and Yonas (1985) conducted a two-part experiment to see whether infants can use their knowledge of the sizes of objects to help them perceive depth. In the *familiarization period*, 5- and 7-month-old infants played with a pair of wooden objects for 10 minutes. One of these objects was large (**Figure 10.52a**), and one was small (**Figure 10.52b**). In the *test period*, which occurred about a minute after the familiarization period, objects (c) and (d) were presented at the same distance from the infant. The prediction was that infants sensitive to familiar size would perceive the object at (c) to be closer if they remembered, from the familiarization period, that this shape was smaller than the other one. In other words, if the infant remembered the green object as being small, then seeing it as big in their field of view could lead the infant to think it was the same small object, but located much closer. How can we determine whether an infant perceives one object as closer than another? The most widely used method is observing an infant's reaching behavior.

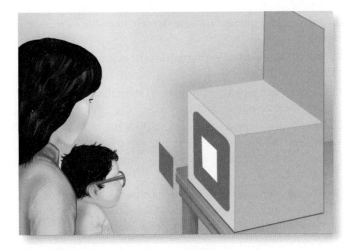

Figure 10.51 The setup used by Fox et al. (1980) to test infants' ability to use binocular disparity information. If the infant can use disparity information to see depth, he or she sees a rectangle moving back and forth in front of the screen. (From Shea et al., 1980)

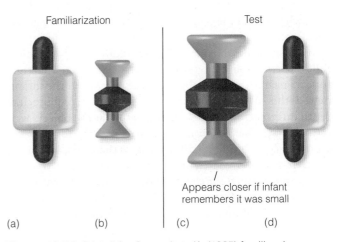

Familiarization　　　　　　　Test

Appears closer if infant remembers it was small

(a)　　　　(b)　　　　(c)　　　　(d)

Figure 10.52 Stimuli for Granrud et al.'s (1985) familiar size experiment. See text for details. (From Granrud et al., 1985)

The preferential reaching procedure is based on observations that infants as young as 2 months old will reach for nearby objects and that 5-month-old infants are extremely likely to reach for an object that is placed within their reach and unlikely to reach for an object that is beyond their reach (Yonas & Hartman, 1993). Infants' sensitivity to depth has therefore been measured by presenting two objects side by side. As with the preferential looking procedure (Chapter 2, page 43), the left–right position of the objects is changed across trials. The ability to perceive depth is inferred when the infant consistently reaches more for the object that contains information indicating it is closer. When a real depth difference is presented, infants use binocular information and reach for the closer object almost 100 percent of the time. To test infants' use of pictorial depth information only, an eye patch is placed on one eye (this eliminates the availability of binocular information, which overrides pictorial depth cues). If infants are sensitive to the pictorial depth information, they reach for the apparently closer object approximately 60 percent of the time.

When Granrud and coworkers presented the objects to infants, 7-month-olds reached for object (c), as would be predicted if they perceived it as being closer than object (d). The 5-month-olds, however, did not reach for object (c), which indicated that these infants did not use familiar size as information for depth. Thus, the ability to use familiar size to perceive depth appears to develop sometime between 5 and 7 months.

This experiment is interesting not only because it indicates when the ability to use familiar size develops, but also because the infant's response in the test phase depends on a cognitive ability—the ability to remember the sizes of the objects that he or she played with in the familiarization phase. The 7-month-old infant's depth response in this situation is therefore based on both what is perceived and what is remembered.

Depth From Cast Shadows We know that shadows provide information indicating an object's position relative to a surface, as occurred in Figure 10.9 (page 231). To determine when this ability is present in infants, Albert Yonas and Carl Granrud (2006) presented 5- and 7-month-old infants with a display like the one in **Figure 10.53**. Adults and older children consistently report that the object on the right appears nearer than the object on the left. When the infants viewed this display monocularly (to eliminate binocular depth information that would indicate that the objects were actually flat), the 5-month-old infants reached for both the right and left objects on 50 percent of the trials, indicating no preference for the right object. However, the 7-month-old infants reached for the right object on 59 percent of the trials. Yonas and Granrud concluded from this result that 7-month-old infants perceive depth information provided by cast shadows.

This finding fits with other research that indicates that sensitivity to pictorial depth cues develops between 5 and

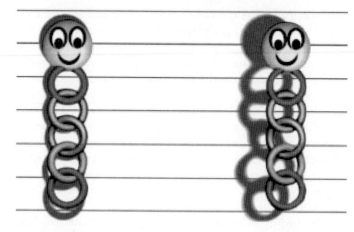

Figure 10.53 Stimuli presented to 7-month-old children in Granrud et al.'s (1985) familiar size experiment: (a) familiarization stimulus; (b) test stimulus.

7 months. But what makes these results especially interesting is that they imply that the infants were able to tell that the dark areas under the toy were shadows and not dark markings on the wall. It is likely that this ability, like the other pictorial depth cues, is based largely on learning from interacting with objects in the environment. In this case, infants need to know something about shadows, including an understanding that most light comes from above (see page 109).

TEST YOURSELF 10.2

1. Describe the Holway and Boring experiment. What do the results of this experiment tell us about how size perception is influenced by depth perception?

2. What are some examples of situations in which our perception of an object's size is determined by the object's visual angle? Under what conditions does this occur?

3. What is size constancy, and under what conditions does it occur?

4. What is size–distance scaling? How does it explain size constancy?

5. Describe two types of information (other than depth) that can influence our perception of size.

6. Describe how illusions of size, such as the Müller-Lyer illusion, the Ponzo illusion, the Ames room, and the moon illusion, can be explained in terms of size–distance scaling.

7. What are some problems with the size–distance scaling explanation of (a) the Müller-Lyer illusion and (b) the moon illusion? What alternative explanations have been proposed?

8. Describe experiments that showed when infants can perceive depth using binocular disparity and using pictorial (monocular) cues. Which develops first? What methods were used?

THINK ABOUT IT

1. One of the triumphs of art is creating the impression of depth on a two-dimensional canvas. Go to a museum or look at pictures in an art book, and identify the depth information that helps increase the perception of depth in these pictures. You may also notice that you perceive less depth in some pictures, especially abstract ones. In fact, some artists purposely create pictures that are perceived as "flat." What steps do these artists have to take to accomplish this? (p. 229)

2. Texture gradients are said to provide information for depth perception because elements in a scene become more densely packed as distance increases. The examples of texture gradients in Figures 10.6 and 10.8 contain regularly spaced elements that extend over large distances. But regularly spaced elements are more the exception than the rule in the environment. Make an informal survey of your environment, both inside and outside, and decide (a) whether texture gradients are present in your environment and (b) if you think the principle behind texture gradients could contribute to the perception of depth even if the texture information in the environment is not as obvious as in the examples in this chapter. (p. 231)

3. How could you determine the contribution of binocular vision to depth perception? One way would be to close one eye and notice how this affects your perception. Try this, and describe any changes you notice. Then devise a way to quantitatively measure the accuracy of depth perception that is possible with two-eyed and one-eyed vision. (p. 235)

KEY TERMS

Absolute disparity (p. 236)
Accretion (p. 233)
Ames room (p. 251)
Angle of disparity (p. 236)
Angular size contrast theory (p. 253)
Apparent distance theory (p. 252)
Atmospheric perspective (p. 230)
Binocular depth cells (p. 242)
Binocular disparity (p. 235)
Binocularly fixate (p. 254)
Conflicting cues theory (p. 250)
Correspondence problem (p. 240)
Corresponding retinal points (p. 235)
Crossed disparity (p. 237)
Cue approach to depth perception (p. 228)
Deletion (p. 233)

Disparity tuning curve (p. 242)
Disparity-selective cells. (p. 242)
Emmert's law (p. 247)
Familiar size (p. 230)
Frontal eyes (p. 253)
Horopter (p. 236)
Illusion (p. 250)
Lateral eyes (p. 253)
Misapplied size constancy scaling (p. 249)
Monocular cues (p. 229)
Moon illusion (p. 252)
Motion parallax (p. 232)
Müller-Lyer illusion (p. 248)
Noncorresponding points (p. 236)
Occlusion (p. 228)
Oculomotor cues (p. 228)

Perspective convergence (p. 230)
Pictorial cues (p. 229)
Ponzo illusion (p. 250)
Random-dot stereogram (p. 239)
Relative disparity (p. 238)
Relative height (p. 230)
Relative size (p. 230)
Size constancy (p. 246)
Size–distance scaling (p. 247)
Stereopsis (p. 239)
Stereoscope (p. 240)
Stereoscopic depth perception (p. 234)
Strabismus (p. 234)
Texture gradient (p. 231)
Uncrossed disparity (p. 237)
Visual angle (p. 244)

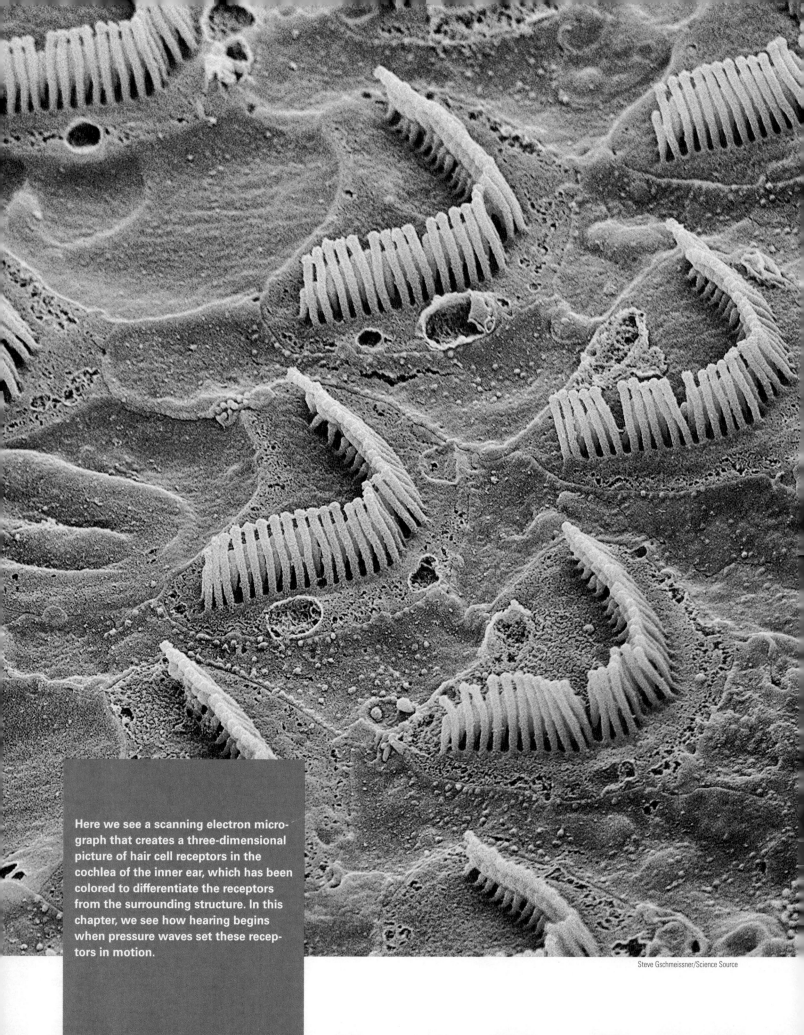

Here we see a scanning electron micrograph that creates a three-dimensional picture of hair cell receptors in the cochlea of the inner ear, which has been colored to differentiate the receptors from the surrounding structure. In this chapter, we see how hearing begins when pressure waves set these receptors in motion.

CHAPTER 11

Hearing

CHAPTER CONTENTS

The Perceptual Process for Hearing

Physical Aspects of Sound
Sound as Pressure Changes
Pure Tones
Complex Tones and Frequency Spectra

Perceptual Aspects of Sound
Thresholds and Loudness
Pitch
Timbre

From Pressure Changes to Electricity
The Outer Ear
The Middle Ear
The Inner Ear

How Frequency Is Represented in the Auditory Nerve
Békésy Discovers How the Basilar Membrane Vibrates
The Cochlea Functions as a Filter
Returning to the Outer Hair Cells: The Cochlear Amplifier

The Physiology of Pitch Perception
Place and Pitch
Temporal Information and Pitch
Place and Pitch (Again)
Problems Remaining to Be Solved
The Pathway to the Brain
Pitch and the Brain

Hearing Loss
Presbycusis
Noise-Induced Hearing Loss
Hidden Hearing Loss

SOMETHING TO CONSIDER: Cochlear Implants

DEVELOPMENTAL DIMENSION: Infant Hearing
Thresholds and the Audibility Curve
Recognizing Their Mother's Voice

THINK ABOUT IT

Some Questions We Will Consider:

- If a tree falls in the forest and no one is there to hear it, is there a sound? (p. 260)

- How do sound vibrations inside the ear lead to the perception of different pitches? (p. 276)

- How can sound damage the auditory receptors? (p. 281)

Jill Robbins, a student in my class, wrote the following about the importance of hearing in her life:

Hearing has an extremely important function in my life. I was born legally blind, so although I can see, my vision is highly impaired and is not correctable. Even though I am not usually shy or embarrassed, sometimes I do not want to call attention to myself and my disability. ... There are many methods that I can use to improve my sight in class, like sitting close to the board or copying from a friend, but sometimes these things are impossible. Then I use my hearing to take notes. ... My hearing is very strong. While I do

not need my hearing to identify people who are very close to me, it is definitely necessary when someone is calling my name from a distance. I can recognize their voice, even if I cannot see them.

Hearing is extremely important to Jill because of her reduced vision. But even people with clear vision depend on hearing more than they may realize. Unlike vision, which depends on light traveling from objects to the eye, sound travels around corners to make us aware of events that otherwise would be invisible. For example, in my office in the psychology department, I hear things that I would be unaware of if I had to rely only on my sense of vision: people talking in the hall; a car passing by on the street below; an ambulance, siren blaring, heading up the hill toward the hospital. If it weren't for hearing, my world at this particular moment would be limited to what I can see in my office and the scene directly outside my window. Although the silence might make it easier to concentrate on writing this book, without hearing I would be unaware of many of the events in my environment.

Our ability to hear events that we can't see serves an important signaling function for both animals and humans.

For an animal living in the forest, the rustle of leaves or the snap of a twig may signal the approach of a predator. For humans, hearing provides signals such as the warning sound of a smoke alarm or an ambulance siren, the distinctive high-pitched cry of a baby who is distressed, or telltale noises that indicate problems in a car engine. Hearing not only informs us about things that are happening that we can't see, but perhaps most important of all, it adds richness to our lives through music and facilitates communication by means of speech.

This chapter is the first of three chapters on hearing. We begin, as we did for vision, by asking some basic questions about the stimulus: How can we describe the pressure changes in the air that is the stimulus for hearing? How is the stimulus measured? What perceptions does it cause? We then describe the anatomy of the ear and how the pressure changes make their way through the structures of the ear in order to stimulate the receptors for hearing.

Once we have established these basic facts about auditory system stimulus and structure, we consider one of the central questions of auditory research: What is the physiological mechanism for our perception of pitch, which is the quality that orders notes on a musical scale, as when we go from low to high pitches by moving from left to right on a piano keyboard? We will see that the search for the physiological mechanism of pitch has led to a number of different theories and that, although we understand a great deal about how the auditory system creates pitch, there are still problems that remain to be solved.

Near the end of this chapter, we complete our description of the structure of the auditory system by describing the pathway from the ear to the auditory cortex. This sets the stage for the next two chapters, in which we will expand our horizons beyond pitch to consider how hearing occurs in the natural environment, which contains many sound sources, and also what mechanisms are responsible for our ability to perceive complex stimuli like music and speech. The starting point for all of this is the perceptual process that we introduced in Chapter 1, which begins with the distal stimulus—the stimulus in the environment.

The Perceptual Process for Hearing

The first step in understanding the perceptual process for hearing is identifying the distal stimulus. The distal stimulus for vision, in our example in Figure 1.1 (page 5), was a tree, which our observer was able to see because light was reflected from the tree into his eyes. Information about the tree, transmitted by the light, then created a representation on the visual receptors.

But what happens when a bird, perched on the tree, sings? The action of the bird's vocal organ is transformed into a sound stimulus—pressure changes in the air. These pressure changes trigger a sequence of events that results in a representation of the bird's song within the ears, the sending of neural signals to the brain, and our eventual perception of the bird's song.

We will see that sound stimuli can be simple repeating pressure changes, like those often used in laboratory research, or more complex pressure changes such as those produced by our singing bird, musical instruments, or a person talking. The properties of these air pressure changes determine our ability to hear and are translated into sound qualities such as soft or loud, low-pitched or high-pitched, mellow or harsh. We begin by describing sound stimuli and their effects.

Physical Aspects of Sound

The first step in understanding hearing is to define what we mean by *sound* and to describe the characteristics of sound. One way to answer the question "What is sound?" is to consider the following question: *If a tree falls in the forest and no one is there to hear it, is there a sound?*

This question is useful because it shows that we can use the word **sound** both as a physical stimulus and as a perceptual response. The answer to the question about the tree depends on which of the following definitions of sound we use.

- Physical definition: Sound is *pressure changes* in the air or other medium.
- Perceptual definition: Sound is the *experience* we have when we hear.

The answer to the question "Is there a sound?" is "yes" if we are using the physical definition, because the falling tree causes pressure changes whether or not someone is there to hear them. The answer to the question is "no" if we are using the perceptual definition, because if no one is in the forest, there will be no experience.

This difference between physical and perceptual is important to be aware of as we discuss hearing in this chapter and the next two (also see page 264). Luckily, it is usually easy to tell from the context in which the terms are used whether "sound" refers to the physical stimulus or to the experience of hearing. For example, "the piercing sound of the trumpet filled the room" refers to the *experience of sound*, but "the sound had a frequency of 1,000 Hz" refers to sound as a *physical stimulus*. In general, we will use the term "sound" or "sound stimulus" to refer to the physical stimulus and "sound perception" to refer to the experience of sound. We begin by describing sound as a physical stimulus.

Sound as Pressure Changes

A sound stimulus occurs when the movements or vibrations of an object cause pressure changes in air, water, or any other elastic medium that can transmit vibrations. Let's begin by considering a loudspeaker, which is really a device for producing vibrations to be transmitted to the surrounding air. People have been known to turn up the volume on their stereos so high that vibrations can be felt through a neighbor's wall, but even at lower levels, the vibrations are there.

The speaker's vibrations affect the surrounding air, as shown in **Figure 11.1a**. When the diaphragm of the speaker

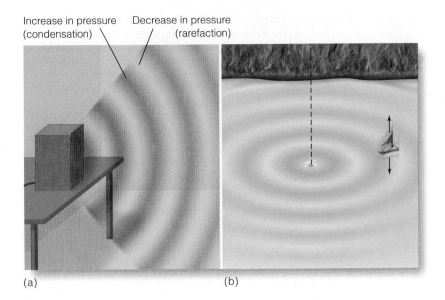

Increase in pressure (condensation) Decrease in pressure (rarefaction)

(a)

(b)

Figure 11.1 (a) The effect of a vibrating speaker diaphragm on the surrounding air. Dark areas represent regions of high air pressure, and light areas represent areas of low air pressure. (b) When a pebble is dropped into still water, the resulting ripples appear to move outward. However, the water is actually moving up and down, as indicated by movement of the boat. A similar situation exists for the sound waves produced by the speaker in (a).

moves out, it pushes the surrounding air molecules together, a process called *condensation*, which causes a slight increase in the density of molecules near the diaphragm. This increased density results in a local increase in the air pressure above atmospheric pressure. When the speaker diaphragm moves back in, air molecules spread out to fill in the increased space, a process called *rarefaction*. The decreased density of air molecules caused by rarefaction causes a slight decrease in air pressure. By repeating this process hundreds or thousands of times a second, the speaker creates a pattern of alternating high- and low-pressure regions in the air, as neighboring air molecules affect each other. This pattern of air pressure changes, which travels through air at 340 meters per second (and through water at 1,500 meters per second), is called a **sound wave**.

You might get the impression from Figure 11.1a that this traveling sound wave causes air to move outward from the speaker into the environment. However, although *air pressure changes* move outward from the speaker, the *air molecules* at each location move back and forth but stay in about the same place. What is transmitted is the pattern of increases and decreases in pressure that eventually reach the listener's ear. What is actually happening is analogous to the ripples created by a pebble dropped into a still pool of water (**Figure 11.1b**). As the ripples move outward from the pebble, the water at any particular place moves up and down. The fact that the water does not move forward becomes obvious when you realize that the ripples would cause a toy boat to bob up and down—not to move outward.

Pure Tones

To describe the pressure changes associated with sound, we will first focus on a simple kind of sound wave called a pure tone. A **pure tone** occurs when changes in air pressure occur in a pattern described by a mathematical function called a *sine wave*, as shown in **Figure 11.2**. Tones with this pattern of pressure changes are occasionally found in the environment. A

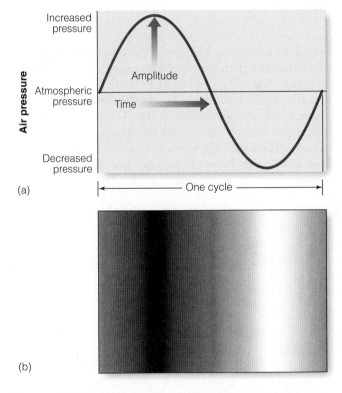

(a)

(b)

Figure 11.2 (a) Plot of sine-wave pressure changes for a pure tone. (b) Pressure changes are indicated, as in Figure 11.1, by darkening (pressure increased relative to atmospheric pressure) and lightening (pressure decreased relative to atmospheric pressure).

person whistling or the high-pitched notes produced by a flute are close to pure tones. Tuning forks, which are designed to vibrate with a sine-wave motion, also produce pure tones. For laboratory studies of hearing, computers generate pure tones that cause a speaker diaphragm to vibrate in and out with a sine-wave motion. This vibration can be described by noting its **frequency**—the number of cycles per second that the pressure changes repeat—and its **amplitude**—the size of the pressure change.

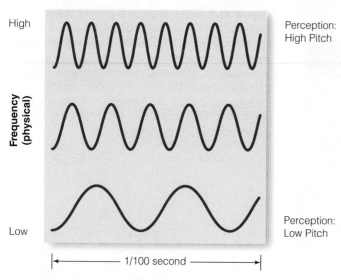

Figure 11.3 Three different frequencies of a pure tone. Higher frequencies are associated with the perception of higher pitches.

Table 11.1 Relative Amplitudes and Decibels for Environmental Sounds

SOUND	RELATIVE AMPLITUDE	DECIBELS (DB)
Barely audible (threshold)	1	0
Leaves rustling	10	20
Quiet residential community	100	40
Average speaking voice	1,000	60
Express subway train	100,000	100
Propeller plane at takeoff	1,000,000	120
Jet engine at takeoff (pain threshold)	10,000,000	140

Sound Frequency Frequency, the number of cycles per second that the change in pressure repeats, is measured in units called **Hertz (Hz)**, in which 1 Hz is 1 cycle per second. Thus, the middle stimulus in **Figure 11.3**, which repeats five times in 1/100 second, would be a 500-Hz tone. As we will see, humans can perceive frequencies ranging from about 20 Hz to about 20,000 Hz. (When we discuss how frequency is perceived, later in the chapter, we will see that higher frequencies are usually associated with higher pitches.)

Sound Amplitude and the Decibel Scale One way to specify a sound's amplitude would be to indicate the difference in pressure between the high and low peaks of the sound wave. **Figure 11.4** shows three pure tones with different amplitudes.

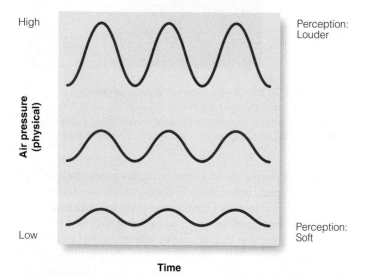

Figure 11.4 Three different amplitudes of a pure tone. Larger amplitude is associated with the perception of greater loudness.

The range of amplitudes we can encounter in the environment is extremely large, as shown in **Table 11.1**, which indicates the relative amplitudes of environmental sounds, ranging from a whisper to a jet taking off. (When we discuss how amplitude is perceived, later in the chapter, we will see that the amplitude of a sound wave is associated with the loudness of a sound.)

We can dramatize how large the range of amplitudes is as follows: If the pressure change plotted in the middle record of Figure 11.4, in which the sine wave representing a near-threshold sound like a whisper is about ½-inch high on the page, then in order to plot the graph for a very loud sound, such as music at a rock concert, you would need to represent the sine wave by a curve several miles high! Because this is somewhat impractical, auditory researchers have devised a unit of sound called the **decibel (dB)**, which converts this large range of sound pressures into a more manageable scale.

METHOD | Using Decibels to Shrink Large Ranges of Pressures

The following equation is used for transforming sound pressure level into decibels:

$$dB = 20 \times \text{logarithm}\ (p/p_0)$$

The key term in this equation is "logarithm." Logarithms are often used in situations in which there are extremely large ranges. One example of a large range can be seen in a classic animated film by Charles Eames (1977) called *Powers of Ten*. The first scene shows a person lying on a picnic blanket on a beach. The camera then zooms out, as if the person were being filmed from a spaceship taking off. The rate of zoom increases by a factor of 10 every 10 seconds, so the "spaceship's" speed and view increase extremely rapidly. From the 10 × 10 meter scene showing the man on the blanket the scene becomes 100 meters on a side, so Lake Michigan becomes visible, and as the camera speeds away at faster and faster rates, it reaches 10,000,000 meters, so the Earth is visible, and eventually 1,000 million million meters near the edge of the Milky Way. (The film actually continues to zoom out, until reaching the outer limits of the Universe. But we will stop here!)

When numbers become this huge, they become difficult to deal with, especially if they need to be plotted on a graph. Logarithms come to the rescue by converting numbers into exponents or powers. The logarithm of a number is the exponent to which the base, which is 10 for *common logarithms*, has to be raised to produce that number.[1] This is illustrated in **Table 11.2**. The logarithm of 10 is 1 because the base, 10, has to be raised to the first power to equal 10. The logarithm of 100 is 2 because 10 has to be raised to the second power to equal 100. The main thing to take away from this table is that multiplying a number by 10 corresponds to an increase of just 1 log unit. A log scale, therefore, converts a huge and unmanageable range of numbers to a smaller range that is easier to deal with. Thus the increase in size from 1 to 1,000 million million that occurs as Charles Eames's spaceship zooms out to the edge of the Milky Way is converted into a more manageable scale of 14 log units. The range of sound pressures encountered in the environment, while not as astronomical as the range in Eames's film, ranges from 1 to 10,000,000, which in powers of 10 is a range of 7 log units.

Let's now return to our equation, dB = 20 × logarithm (p/p_0). According to this equation, decibels are 20 times the logarithm of a ratio of two pressures: p, the pressure of the sound we are considering; and p_0, the reference pressure, usually set at 20 micropascals, which is the pressure near hearing threshold for a 1,000-Hz tone. Let's consider this calculation for two sound pressures.

If the sound pressure, p, is 2,000 micropascals, then

$$dB = 20 × \log(2,000/20) = 20 × \log 100$$

and since the log of 100 is 2,

$$dB = 20 × 2 = 40$$

If we multiply the sound pressure by 10 so p is 20,000 micropascals, then

$$dB = 20 × \log(20,000/20) = 20 × \log 1,000$$

The log of 1,000 is 3, so

$$dB = 20 × 3 = 60$$

Table 11.2 Common Logarithms

NUMBER	POWER OF 10	LOGARITHM
10	10^1	1
100	10^2	2
1,000	10^3	3
10,000	10^4	4

[1]Other bases are used for different applications. For example, logarithms to the base 2, called binary logarithms, are used in computer science.

Notice that multiplying sound pressure by 10 causes an increase of 20 decibels. Thus, looking back at Table 11.1, we can see that when the sound pressure increases from 1 to 10,000,000, the decibels increase only from 0 to 140. This means that we don't have to deal with graphs that are several miles high!

When specifying the sound pressure in decibels, the notation **SPL**, for **sound pressure level**, is added to indicate that decibels were determined using the standard pressure p_0 of 20 micropascals. In referring to the sound pressure of a sound stimulus in decibels, the term **level** or **sound level** is usually used.

Complex Tones and Frequency Spectra

We have been using pure tones to illustrate frequency and amplitude. Pure tones are important because they are the fundamental building blocks of sounds, and pure tones have been used extensively in auditory research. Pure tones are, however, rare in the environment. As noted earlier, sounds in the environment, such as those produced by musical instruments or people speaking, have waveforms that are more complex than the pure tone's sine-wave pattern of pressure changes.

Figure 11.5a shows the pressure changes associated with a complex tone that would be created by a musical instrument. Notice that the waveform repeats (for example, the waveform

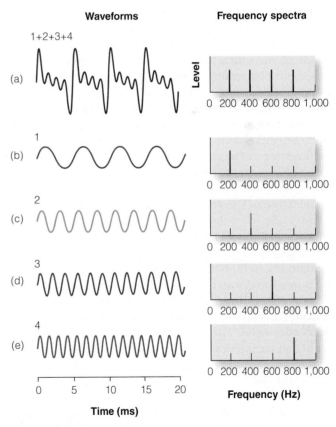

Figure 11.5 Left: Waveforms of (a) a complex periodic sound with a fundamental frequency of 200 Hz; (b) fundamental (first harmonic) = 200 Hz; (c) second harmonic = 400 Hz; (d) third harmonic = 600 Hz; (e) fourth harmonic = 800 Hz. Right: Frequency spectra for each of the tones on the left. (Adapted from Plack, 2005)

in Figure 11.5a repeats four times). This property of repetition means that this complex tone, like a pure tone, is a **periodic tone**. From the time scale at the bottom of the figure, we see that the tone repeats four times in 20 msec. Because 20 msec is 20/1,000 sec = 1/50 sec, this means that the pattern for this tone repeats 200 times per second. That repetition rate is called the **fundamental frequency** of the tone.

Complex tones like the one in Figure 11.5a are made up of a number of pure tone (sine-wave) components added together. Each of these components is called a **harmonic** of the tone. The **first harmonic**, a pure tone with frequency equal to the fundamental frequency, is usually called the **fundamental** of the tone. The fundamental of this tone, shown in **Figure 11.5b**, has a frequency of 200 Hz, which matches the repetition rate of the complex tone.

Higher harmonics are pure tones with frequencies that are *whole-number* (2, 3, 4, etc.) multiples of the fundamental frequency. This means that the second harmonic of our complex tone has a frequency of 200 × 2 = 400 Hz (**Figure 11.5c**), the third harmonic has a frequency of 200 × 3 = 600 Hz (**Figure 11.5d**), and so on. These additional tones are the higher harmonics of the tone. Adding the fundamental and the higher harmonics in Figures 11.5b, c, d, and e results in the waveform of the complex tone (that is, Figure 11.5a).

Another way to represent the harmonic components of a complex tone is by **frequency spectra**, shown on the right of Figure 11.5. Notice that the horizontal axis is *frequency*, not *time*, as is the case for the waveform plot on the left. The position of each line on the horizontal axis indicates the frequency of one of the tone's harmonics, and the height of the line indicates the harmonic's amplitude. Frequency spectra provide a way of indicating a complex tone's fundamental frequency and harmonics that add up to the tone's complex waveform.

Although a repeating sound wave is composed of harmonics with frequencies that are whole-number multiples of the fundamental frequency, not all the harmonics need to be present for the repetition rate to stay the same. **Figure 11.6** shows what happens if we remove the first harmonic of a complex tone. The tone in **Figure 11.6a** is the one from Figure 11.5a, which has a fundamental frequency of 200 Hz. The tone in **Figure 11.6b** is the same tone with the first harmonic (200 Hz) removed, as indicated by the frequency spectrum on the right. Note that removing a harmonic changes the tone's waveform, but that the rate of repetition remains the same. Even though the fundamental is no longer present, the 200-Hz repetition rate corresponds to the frequency of the fundamental. The same effect also occurs when removing higher harmonics. Thus, if the 400-Hz second harmonic is removed, the tone's waveform changes, but the repetition rate is still 200.

You may wonder why the repetition rate remains the same even though the fundamental or higher harmonics have been removed. Looking at the frequency spectra on the right, we can see that the spacing between harmonics equals the repetition rate. When the fundamental is removed, this spacing remains, so there is still information in the waveform indicating the frequency of the fundamental.

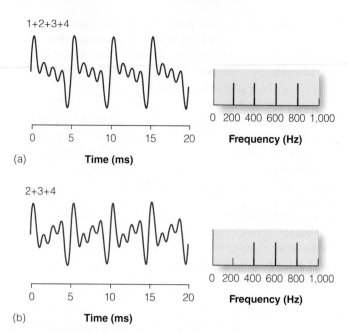

Figure 11.6 (a) The complex tone from Figure 11.5a and its frequency spectrum; (b) the same tone with its first harmonic removed. (Adapted from Plack, 2005)

Perceptual Aspects of Sound

Our discussion so far has been focused on *physical aspects of the sound stimulus*. Everything we have described so far can be measured by a sound meter that registers pressure changes in the air. A person need not be present, as occurs in our example of a tree falling in the forest when no one is there to hear it. But now let's add a person (or an animal) and consider what people actually *hear*. We will consider two perceptual dimensions: (1) *loudness*, which involves differences in the perceived magnitude of a sound, illustrated by the difference between a whisper and a shout; and (2) *pitch*, which involves differences in the low to high quality of sounds, illustrated by what we hear playing notes from left to right on a piano keyboard.

Thresholds and Loudness

We consider loudness by asking the following two questions about sound: "Can you hear it?" and "How loud does it sound?" These two questions come under the heading of thresholds (the smallest amount of sound energy that can just barely be detected) and loudness (the perceived intensity of a sound that ranges from "just audible" to "very loud").

Loudness and Level Loudness is the perceptual quality most closely related to the *level* or *amplitude* of an auditory stimulus, which is expressed in decibels. Thus, decibels are often associated with loudness, as shown in Table 11.1, which indicates that a sound of 0 dB SPL is just barely detectable and 120 dB SPL is extremely loud (and can cause permanent damage to the receptors inside the ear).

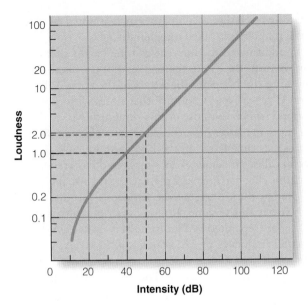

Figure 11.7 Loudness of a 1,000-Hz tone as a function of intensity, determined using magnitude estimation. (Adapted from Gulick et al., 1989)

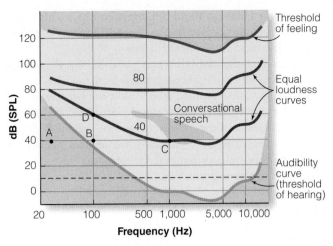

Figure 11.8 The audibility curve and the auditory response area. Hearing occurs in the light green area between the audibility curve (the threshold for hearing) and the upper curve (the threshold for feeling). Tones with combinations of dB and frequency that place them in the light red area below the audibility curve cannot be heard. Tones above the threshold of feeling result in pain. The frequencies between the places where the dashed line at 10 dB crosses the audibility function indicate which frequencies can be heard at 10 dB SPL. (From Fletcher & Munson, 1933)

The relationship between level in decibels (physical) and loudness (perceptual) was determined by S. S. Stevens, using the magnitude estimation procedure (see Chapter 1, page 15; Appendix C, page 386). **Figure 11.7** shows the relationship between decibels and loudness for a 1,000-Hz pure tone. In this experiment, loudness was judged relative to a 40-dB SPL tone, which was assigned a value of 1. Thus, a pure tone that sounds 10 times louder than the 40-dB SPL tone would be judged to have a loudness of 10. The dashed lines indicate that increasing the sound level by 10 dB (from 40 to 50) almost doubles the sound's loudness.

It would be tempting to conclude from Table 11.1 and the curve in Figure 11.7 that "higher decibels" equals greater loudness. But it isn't quite that simple, because thresholds and loudness depend not only on decibels but also on frequency. One way to appreciate the importance of frequency in the perception of loudness is to consider the *audibility curve*.

Thresholds Across the Frequency Range: The Audibility Curve

A basic fact about hearing is that we only hear within a specific range of frequencies. This means that there are some frequencies we can't hear, and that even within the range of frequencies we can hear, some are easier to hear than others. Some frequencies have low thresholds—it takes very little sound pressure change to hear them; other frequencies have high thresholds—large changes in sound pressure are needed to make them heard. This is illustrated by the curve in **Figure 11.8**, called the **audibility curve**. This audibility curve, which indicates the threshold for hearing versus frequency, indicates that we can hear sounds between about 20 Hz and 20,000 Hz and that we are most sensitive (the threshold for hearing is lowest) at frequencies between 2,000 and 4,000 Hz, which happens to be the range of frequencies that is most important for understanding speech.

The light green area above the audibility curve is called the **auditory response area** because we can hear tones that fall

within this area. At intensities below the audibility curve, we can't hear a tone. For example, we wouldn't be able to hear a 30-Hz tone at 40 dB SPL (point A). The upper boundary of the auditory response area is the curve marked "threshold of feeling." Tones with these high amplitudes are the ones we can "feel"; they can become painful and can cause damage to the auditory system. Although humans hear frequencies between about 20 Hz and 20,000 Hz, other animals can hear frequencies outside the range of human hearing. Elephants can hear stimuli below 20 Hz. Above the high end of the human range, dogs can hear frequencies above 40,000 Hz, cats can hear above 50,000 Hz, and the upper range for dolphins extends as high as 150,000 Hz.

But what happens between the audibility curve and the threshold of feeling? To answer this question, we can pick any frequency and select a point, such as point B, that is just slightly above the audibility curve. Because that point is just above threshold, it will sound very soft. However, as we increase the level by moving up the vertical line, the loudness increases (also see Figure 11.7). Thus, each frequency has a threshold or "baseline"—the decibels at which it can just barely be heard, as indicated by the audibility curve—and loudness increases as we increase the level above this baseline.

Another way to understand the relationship between loudness and frequency is by looking at the red **equal loudness curves** in Figure 11.8. These curves indicate the sound levels that create the same perception of loudness at different frequencies. An equal loudness curve is determined by presenting a standard pure tone of one frequency and level and having a listener adjust the level of pure tones with frequencies across the range of hearing to match the loudness of the standard. For example, the curve marked 40 in Figure 11.8 was determined by matching the loudness of frequencies across the range of hearing to the loudness of a 1,000-Hz 40-dB SPL tone (point C). This means that a 100-Hz tone needs to be played at 60 dB (point D) to have the same loudness as the 1,000-Hz tone at 40 dB.

Notice that the audibility curve and the equal loudness curve marked 40 bend up at high and low frequencies, but the equal loudness curve marked 80 is almost flat between 30 and 5,000 Hz, meaning that tones at a level of 80 dB SPL are roughly equally loud between these frequencies. Thus, at threshold, the level can be very different for different frequencies, but at some level above threshold, different frequencies can have a similar loudness at the same decibel level.

Pitch

Pitch, the perceptual quality we describe as "high" or "low," can be defined as *the property of auditory sensation in terms of which sounds may be ordered on a musical scale* (Bendor & Wang, 2005). The idea that pitch is associated with the musical scale is reflected in another definition of pitch, which states that *pitch is that aspect of auditory sensation whose variation is associated with musical melodies* (Plack, 2014). While often associated with music, pitch is also a property of speech (low-pitched or high-pitched voice) and other natural sounds.

Pitch is most closely related to the physical property of fundamental frequency (the repetition rate of the sound waveform). Low fundamental frequencies are associated with low pitches (like the sound of a tuba), and high fundamental frequencies are associated with high pitches (like the sound of a piccolo). However, remember that pitch is a psychological, not a physical, property of sound. So pitch can't be measured in a physical way. For example, it isn't correct to say that a sound has a "pitch of 200 Hz." Instead we say that a particular sound has a low pitch or a high pitch, based on how we *perceive* it.

One way to think about pitch is in terms of a piano keyboard. Hitting a key on the left of the keyboard creates a low-pitched rumbling "bass" tone; moving up the keyboard creates higher and higher pitches, until tones on the far right are high-pitched and might be described as "tinkly." The *physical* property that is related to this low to high perceptual experience is *fundamental frequency*, with the lowest note on the piano having a fundamental frequency of 27.5 Hz and the highest note 4,166 Hz (**Figure 11.9**). The perceptual experience of

increasing pitch that accompanies increases in a tone's fundamental frequency is called **tone height**.

In addition to the increase in tone height that occurs as we move from the low to the high end of the piano keyboard, something else happens: the letters of the notes A, B, C, D, E, F, and G repeat, and we notice that notes with the same letter sound similar. Because of this similarity, we say that notes with the same letter have the same **tone chroma**. Every time we pass the same letter on the keyboard, we have gone up an interval called an **octave**. Tones separated by octaves have the same tone chroma. For example, each of the A's in Figure 11.9, indicated by the arrows, has the same tone chroma.

Notes with the same chroma have fundamental frequencies that are separated by a multiple of two. Thus, A_1 has a fundamental frequency of 27.5 Hz, A_2's is 55 Hz, A_3's is 110 Hz, and so on. This doubling of frequency for each octave results in similar perceptual experiences. Thus, a male with a low-pitched voice and a female with a high-pitched voice can be regarded as singing "in unison," even when their voices are separated by one or more octaves.

While the connection between pitch and fundamental frequency is nicely illustrated by the piano keyboard, there is more to the story than fundamental frequency. If the fundamental or other harmonics of a complex tone are removed, the tone's pitch remains the same, so the two waveforms in Figure 11.6 result in the same pitch. The fact that pitch remains the same, even when the fundamental or other harmonics are removed, is called the **effect of the missing fundamental**. The effect of the missing fundamental has practical consequences. Consider, for example, what happens when you listen to someone talking to you on the telephone. Even though the telephone does not reproduce frequencies below about 300 Hz, you can hear the low pitch of a male voice that corresponds to a 100-Hz fundamental frequency because of the pitch created by the higher harmonics (Truax, 1984).

Another way to illustrate the effect of the missing fundamental is to imagine hearing a long tone created by bowing a violin in a quiet room. We then turn on a noisy air conditioner that creates a loud low-frequency hum. Even though the air conditioner noise may make it difficult to hear the lower harmonics of the violin's tone, the tone's pitch remains the same (Oxenham, 2013).

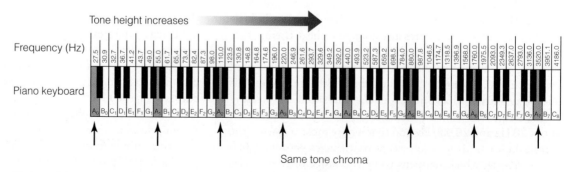

Figure 11.9 A piano keyboard, indicating the frequency associated with each key. Moving up the keyboard to the right increases frequency and tone height. Notes with the same letter, like the A's (arrows), have the same tone chroma.

Timbre

Although removing harmonics does not affect a tone's pitch, another perceptual quality, the tone's **timbre** (pronounced TIM-ber or TAM-ber), does change. Timbre is the quality that distinguishes between two tones that have the same loudness, pitch, and duration, but still sound different. For example, when a flute and an oboe play the same note with the same loudness, we can still tell the difference between these two instruments. We might describe the sound of the flute as *clear* and the sound of the oboe as *reedy*. When two tones have the same loudness, pitch, and duration but sound different, this difference is a difference in timbre.

Timbre is closely related to the harmonic structure of a tone. In **Figure 11.10**, frequency spectra indicate the harmonics of a guitar, a bassoon, and an alto saxophone playing the note G_3 with a fundamental frequency of 196 Hz. Both the relative strengths of the harmonics and the number of harmonics are different in these instruments. For example, the guitar has more high-frequency harmonics than either the bassoon or the alto saxophone. Although the frequencies of the harmonics are always multiples of the fundamental frequency, harmonics may be absent, as is true of some of the high-frequency harmonics of the bassoon and the alto saxophone. It is also easy to notice differences in the timbre of people's voices. When we describe one person's voice as sounding "nasal" and another's as being "mellow," we are referring to the timbres of their voices.

The difference in the harmonics of different instruments is not the only factor that creates the distinctive timbres of musical instruments. Timbre also depends on the time course of a tone's **attack** (the buildup of sound at the beginning of the tone) and of the tone's **decay** (the decrease in sound at the end of the tone). Thus, it is easy to tell the difference between a high note played on a clarinet and the same note played on a flute. It is difficult, however, to distinguish between the same instruments when their tones are recorded and the tone's attack and decay are eliminated by erasing the first and last 1/2 second of each tone's recording (Berger, 1964; also see Risset & Mathews, 1969).

Another way to make it difficult to distinguish one instrument from another is to play an instrument's tone backward. Even though this does not affect the tone's harmonic structure, a piano tone played backward sounds more like an organ than a piano because the tone's original decay has become the attack and the attack has become the decay (Berger, 1964; Erickson, 1975). Thus, timbre depends both on the tone's steady-state harmonic structure and on the time course of the attack and decay of the tone's harmonics.

The sounds we have been considering so far—pure tones and the tones produced by musical instruments—are all **periodic sounds**. That is, the pattern of pressure changes repeats, as in the tone in Figure 11.5a. There are also aperiodic sounds, which have sound waves that do not repeat. Examples of **aperiodic sounds** would be a door slamming shut, people talking, and noises such as the static on a radio not tuned to a station. The sounds produced by these events are more complex than musical tones, but all of these sound stimuli can also be analyzed into a number of simpler frequency components. We will describe how we perceive speech stimuli in Chapter 13. We will focus in this chapter on pure tones and musical tones because these sounds are the ones that have been used in most of the basic research on the operation of the auditory system. In the next section, we will begin considering how the sound stimuli we have been describing are processed by the auditory system so that we can experience sound.

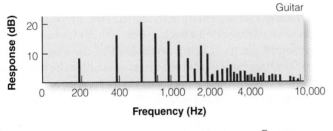

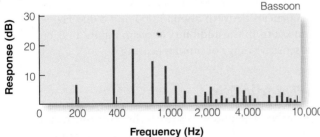

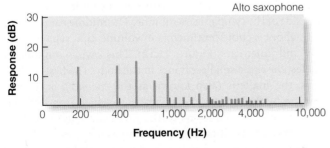

Figure 11.10 Frequency spectra for a guitar, a bassoon, and an alto saxophone playing a tone with a fundamental frequency of 196 Hz. The position of the lines on the horizontal axis indicates the frequencies of the harmonics and their height indicates their intensities. (From Olson, 1967)

TEST YOURSELF 11.1

1. What are some of the functions of sound? Especially note what information sound provides that is not provided by vision.
2. What are two possible definitions of sound? (Remember the tree falling in the forest.)
3. How is the sound stimulus described in terms of pressure changes in the air? What is a pure tone? Sound frequency?
4. What is the amplitude of a sound? Why was the decibel scale developed to measure amplitude? Is decibel "perceptual" or "physical"?
5. What is a complex tone? What are harmonics? Frequency spectra?

6. How does removing one or more harmonics from a complex tone affect the repetition rate of the sound stimulus?

7. What is the relationship between sound level and loudness? Which one is physical, and which one is perceptual?

8. What is the audibility curve, and what does it tell us about the relationship between a tone's physical characteristics (level and frequency) and perceptual characteristics (threshold and loudness)?

9. What is pitch? What physical property is it most closely related to? What are tone height and tone chroma?

10. What is the effect of the missing fundamental?

11. What is timbre? Describe the characteristics of complex tones and how these characteristics determine timbre.

From Pressure Changes to Electricity

Now that we have described the stimuli and their perceptual effects, we are ready to begin describing what happens inside the ear. What we will be describing in this next part of our story is a journey that begins as sound enters the ear and culminates deep inside the ear at the receptors for hearing.

The auditory system accomplishes three basic tasks during this journey. First, it delivers the sound stimulus to the receptors; second, it transduces this stimulus from pressure changes into electrical signals; and third, it processes these electrical signals so they can indicate qualities of the sound source, such as pitch, loudness, timbre, and location.

As we describe this journey, we will follow the sound stimulus through a complex labyrinth on its way to the receptors. But this is not simply a matter of sound moving through one dark tunnel after another. It is a journey in which sound sets structures along the pathway into vibration, with these vibrations being transmitted from one structure to another, starting with the eardrum at the beginning and ending with the vibration of small hairlike parts of the hearing receptors called *cilia* deep within the ear. The ear is divided into three divisions: outer, middle, and inner. We begin with the outer ear.

The Outer Ear

Sound waves first pass through the **outer ear**, which consists of the **pinnae**, the structures that stick out from the sides of the head, and the **auditory canal**, a tubelike recess about 3 cm long in adults (**Figure 11.11**). Although the pinnae are the most obvious part of the ear and help us determine the location of sounds, as we will see in Chapter 12, it is the part of the ear we could most easily do without. Van Gogh did *not* make himself deaf in his left ear when he attacked his pinna with a razor in 1888.

The auditory canal protects the delicate structures of the middle ear from the hazards of the outside world. The auditory canal's 3-cm recess, along with its wax, protects the delicate **tympanic membrane**, or **eardrum**, at the end of the canal and

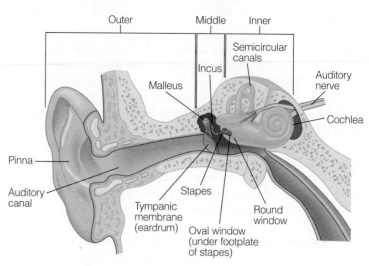

Figure 11.11 The ear, showing its three subdivisions—outer, middle, and inner. (From Lindsay & Norman, 1977)

helps keep this membrane and the structures in the middle ear at a relatively constant temperature.

In addition to its protective function, the auditory canal has another effect: to enhance the intensities of some sounds by means of the physical principle of resonance. **Resonance** occurs in the auditory canal when sound waves that are reflected back from the closed end of the auditory canal interact with sound waves that are entering the canal. This interaction reinforces some of the sound's frequencies, with the frequency that is reinforced the most being determined by the length of the canal. The frequency reinforced the most is called the **resonant frequency** of the canal.

Measurements of the sound pressures inside the ear indicate that the resonance that occurs in the auditory canal has a slight amplifying effect that increases the sound pressure level of frequencies between about 1,000 and 5,000 Hz, which, as we can see from the audibility curve in Figure 11.8, covers the most sensitive range of human hearing.

The Middle Ear

When airborne sound waves reach the tympanic membrane at the end of the auditory canal, they set it into vibration, and this vibration is transmitted to structures in the middle ear, on the other side of the tympanic membrane. The **middle ear** is a small cavity, about 2 cubic centimeters in volume, that separates the outer and inner ears (**Figure 11.12**). This cavity contains the **ossicles**, the three smallest bones in the body. The first of these bones, the **malleus** (also known as the *hammer*), is set into vibration by the tympanic membrane, to which it is attached, and transmits its vibrations to the **incus** (or *anvil*), which, in turn, transmits its vibrations to the **stapes** (or *stirrup*). The stapes then transmits its vibrations to the inner ear by pushing on the membrane covering the **oval window**.

Why are the ossicles necessary? We can answer this question by noting that both the outer ear and middle ear are filled with air, but the inner ear contains a watery liquid that is much

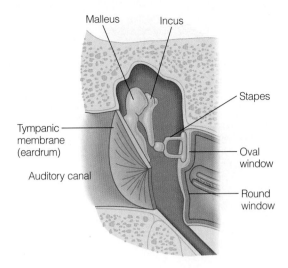

Figure 11.12 The middle ear. The three bones of the middle ear transmit the vibrations of the tympanic membrane to the inner ear.

Figure 11.13 Environments inside the outer, middle, and inner ears. The fact that liquid fills the inner ear poses a problem for the transmission of sound vibrations from the air of the middle ear.

denser than the air (**Figure 11.13**). The mismatch between the low density of the air and the high density of this liquid creates a problem: pressure changes in the air are transmitted poorly to the much denser liquid. This mismatch is illustrated by the difficulty you would have hearing people talking to you if you were underwater and they were above the surface.

If vibrations had to pass directly from the air in the middle ear to the liquid in the inner ear, less than 1 percent of the vibrations would be transmitted (Durrant & Lovrinic, 1977). The ossicles help solve this problem in two ways: (1) by concentrating the vibration of the large tympanic membrane onto the much smaller stapes, which increases the pressure by a factor of about 20 (**Figure 11.14a**); and (2) by being hinged to create a lever action—an effect similar to what happens when a fulcrum is placed under a board, so that pushing down on the long end of the board makes it possible to lift a heavy weight on the short end (**Figure 11.14b**). We can appreciate the effect of the ossicles by noting that in patients whose ossicles have been damaged beyond surgical repair, it is necessary to increase the sound pressure by a factor of 10 to 50 to achieve the same hearing as when the ossicles were functioning (Bess & Humes, 2008).

Not all animals require the concentration of pressure and lever effect provided by the ossicles in the human ear. For example, there is only a small mismatch between the density of water, which transmits sound in a fish's environment, and the liquid inside the fish's ear. Thus, fish have no outer or middle ear.

The middle ear also contains the **middle-ear muscles**, the smallest skeletal muscles in the body. These muscles are

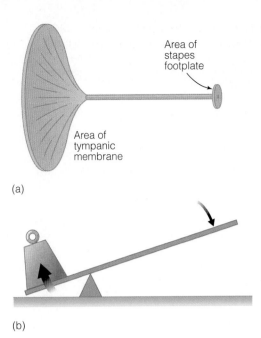

Figure 11.14 (a) A diagrammatic representation of the tympanic membrane and the stapes, showing the difference in size between the two. (b) How lever action can amplify a small force, presented on the right, to lift the large weight on the left. The lever action of the ossicles amplifies the sound vibrations reaching the tympanic inner ear. (From Schubert, 1980)

attached to the ossicles, and at very high sound levels they contract to dampen the ossicles' vibration. This reduces the transmission of low-frequency sounds and helps to prevent intense low-frequency components from interfering with our perception of high frequencies. In particular, contraction of the muscles may prevent our own vocalizations, and sounds from chewing, from interfering with our perception of speech from other people—an important function in a noisy restaurant!

The Inner Ear

We will describe first the structure of the inner ear, and then what happens when structures of the inner ear are set into vibration.

Inner Ear Structure The main structure of the **inner ear** is the liquid-filled **cochlea**, the snaillike structure shown in green in Figure 11.11, and shown partially uncoiled in **Figure 11.15a**. **Figure 11.15b** shows the cochlea completely uncoiled to form a long straight tube. The most obvious feature of the uncoiled cochlea is that the upper half, called the *scala vestibuli*, and the lower half, called the *scala tympani*, are separated by a structure called the **cochlear partition**. This partition extends almost the entire length of the cochlea, from its base near the stapes to its apex at the far end. Note that this diagram is not drawn to scale and so does not show the cochlea's true proportions. In reality, the uncoiled cochlea would be a cylinder 2 mm in diameter and 35 mm long.

Although the cochlear partition is indicated by a thin line in Figure 11.15b, it is actually relatively large and contains the

Figure 11.15 (a) A partially uncoiled cochlea. (b) A fully uncoiled cochlea. The cochlear partition, which is indicated here by a line, actually contains the basilar membrane and the organ of Corti, as shown in Figure 11.16.

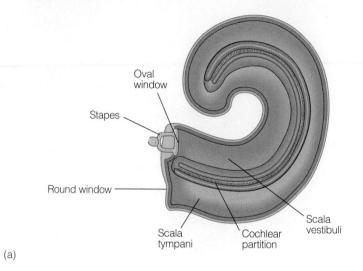

(a)

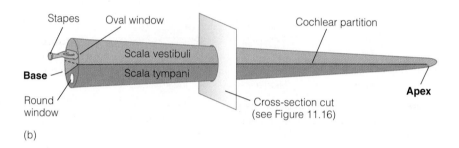

(b)

structures that transform the vibrations inside the cochlea into electricity. We can see the structures within the cochlear partition by taking a cross section cut of the cochlea, as shown in Figure 11.15b, and looking at the cochlea end-on and in cross section, as in **Figure 11.16a**. When we look at the cochlea in this way, we see the **organ of Corti**, which contains the **hair cells**, the receptors for hearing. It is important to remember that Figure 11.16 shows just one place along the organ of Corti, but as shown in Figure 11.15, the cochlear partition, which contains the organ of Corti, extends the entire length of the cochlea. There are, therefore, hair cells from one end of the

cochlea to the other. In addition, there are two membranes, the **basilar membrane** and the **tectorial membrane**, which also extend the length of the cochlea, and which play crucial roles in activating the hair cells.

The hair cells are shown in red in **Figure 11.16b**. **Figure 11.17** shows **cilia**, thin processes that protrude from the tops of the hair cells, which bend in response to pressure changes. The human ear contains one row of **inner hair cells** and about three rows of **outer hair cells**, with about 3,500 inner hair cells and 12,000 outer hair cells. The cilia of the tallest row of outer hair cells are embedded in the tectorial

Figure 11.16 (a) Cross section of the cochlea. (b) Close-up of the organ of Corti, showing how it rests on the basilar membrane. Arrows indicate the motions of the basilar membrane and tectorial membrane that are caused by vibration of the cochlear partition. Although not obvious in this figure, the cilia of the outer hair cells are embedded in the tectorial membrane, but the cilia of the inner hair cells are not.
(Adapted from Denes & Pinson, 1993)

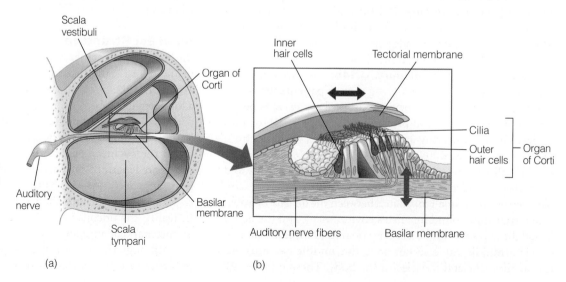

(a)

(b)

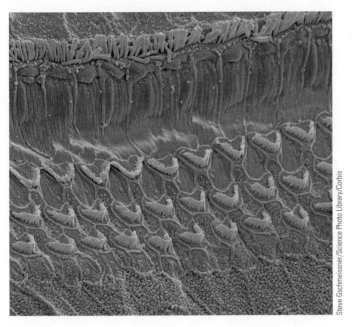

Figure 11.17 Scanning electron micrograph showing inner hair cells (top) and the three rows of outer hair cells (bottom). The hair cells have been colored to stand out.

membrane and the cilia of the rest of the outer hair cells and all of the inner hair cells are not (Moller, 2006).

Vibration Bends the Cilia The scene we have described—the organ of Corti sitting on the basilar membrane, with the tectorial membrane arching over the hair cells—is the staging ground for events that occur when vibration of the stapes in the middle ear sets the oval window into motion. The back and forth motion of the oval window transmits vibrations to the liquid inside the cochlea, which sets the basilar membrane into motion (blue arrow in Figure 11.16b). The up-and-down motion of the basilar membrane has two results: (1) it sets the organ of Corti into an up-and-down vibration, and (2) it causes the tectorial membrane to move back and forth, as shown by the red arrow. These two motions mean that the tectorial membrane slides back and forward just above the hair cells. The movement of the tectorial membrane causes the cilia of the outer hair cells that are embedded in the membrane to bend. The cilia of the other outer hair cells and the inner hair cells also bend, but in response to pressure waves in the liquid surrounding the cilia (Dallos, 1996).

Bending Causes Electrical Signals We have now reached the point in our story where the vibrations that have reached the inner ear become transformed into electrical signals. This is the process of transduction we described for vision in Chapter 2, which occurs when the light-sensitive part of a visual pigment molecule absorbs light, changes shape, and triggers a sequence of chemical reactions that ends up affecting the flow of ions (charged molecules) across the visual receptor membrane. As we describe this process for hearing, we will focus on the inner hair cells, because these are the main receptors responsible for generating signals that are sent to the

cortex in auditory nerve fibers. We will return to the outer hair cells later in the chapter.

Transduction for hearing also involves a sequence of events that creates ion flow. First, the cilia of the hair cells bend in one direction (**Figure 11.18a**). This bending causes structures called **tip links** to stretch, and this opens tiny ion channels in the membrane of the cilia, which function like trapdoors. When the ion channels are open, positively charged potassium ions flow into the cell and an electrical signal results. When the cilia bend in the other direction (**Figure 11.18b**), the tip links slacken, the ion channels close, and ion flow stops. Thus, the back-and-forth bending of the hair cells causes alternating bursts of electrical signals (when the cilia bend in one direction) and no electrical signals (when the cilia bend in the opposite direction). The electrical signals in the hair cells result in the release of neurotransmitters at the synapse separating the inner hair cells from the auditory nerve fibers and cause these auditory nerve fibers to fire.

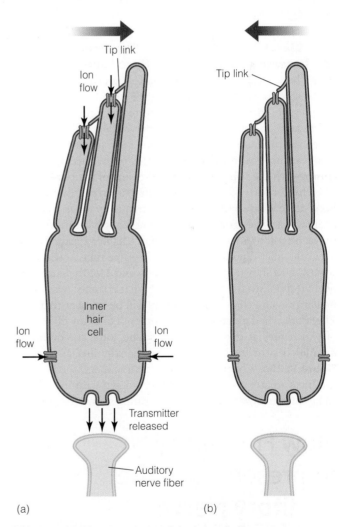

Figure 11.18 How movement of the hair cell cilia causes an electrical change in the hair cell. (a) When the cilia are bent to the right, the tip links are stretched and ion channels are opened. Positively charged potassium ions (K+) enter the cell, causing the interior of the cell to become more positive. (b) When the cilia move to the left, the tip links slacken, and the channels close. (Based on Plack, 2005)

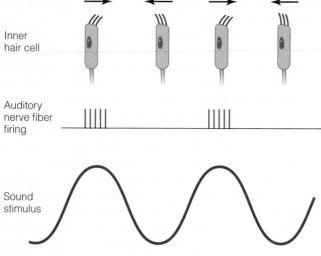

Inner
hair cell

Auditory
nerve fiber
firing

Sound
stimulus

Figure 11.19 How hair cell activation and auditory nerve fiber firing are synchronized with pressure changes of the stimulus. The auditory nerve fiber fires when the cilia are bent to the right. This occurs at the peak of the sine-wave change in pressure.

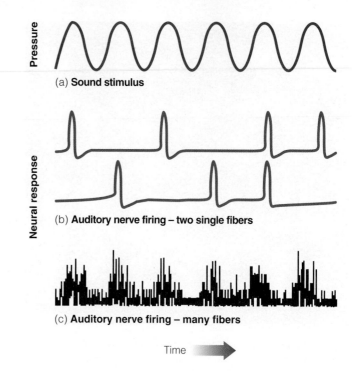

Pressure

(a) **Sound stimulus**

Neural response

(b) **Auditory nerve firing – two single fibers**

(c) **Auditory nerve firing – many fibers**

Time

Figure 11.20 (a) Pressure changes for a 250-Hz tone. (b) Pattern of nerve spikes produced by two separate nerve fibers. Notice that the spikes always occur at the peak of the pressure wave. (c) The combined spikes produced by 500 nerve fibers. Although there is some variability in the single neuron response, the response of the large group of neurons represents the periodicity of the 250-Hz tone. (Based on Plack, 2005)

The Electrical Signals Are Synchronized With the Pressure Changes of a Pure Tone **Figure 11.19**

shows how the bending of the cilia follows the increases and decreases of the pressure of a pure tone sound stimulus. When the pressure increases, the cilia bend to the right, the hair cell is activated, and attached auditory nerve fibers will tend to fire. When the pressure decreases, the cilia bend to the left, and no firing occurs. This means that auditory nerve fibers fire in synchrony with the rising and falling pressure of the pure tone.

This property of firing at the same place in the sound stimulus is called **phase locking**. For high-frequency tones, a nerve fiber may not fire every time the pressure changes because it needs to rest after it fires (see *refractory period*, Chapter 2, page 37). But when the fiber does fire, it fires at the same time in the sound stimulus, as shown in **Figures 11.20a** and **11.20b**. Since many fibers respond to the tone, it is likely that if some "miss" a particular pressure change, other fibers will be firing at that time. Therefore, when we combine the response of many fibers, each of which fires at the peak of the sound wave, the overall firing matches the frequency of the sound stimulus, as shown in **Figure 11.20c**. What this means is that a sound's repetition rate produces a pattern of nerve firing in which the timing of nerve spikes matches the timing of the repeating sound stimulus.

How Frequency Is Represented in the Auditory Nerve

Now that we know how electrical signals are created, the next question is, how do these signals provide information about a tone's frequency? The search for the answer to the question of how frequency is signaled by activity in the auditory nerve has focused on determining how the basilar membrane vibrates

to different frequencies. Pioneering research on this problem was carried out by Georg von Békésy (1899–1972), who won the Nobel Prize in physiology and medicine in 1961 for his research on the physiology of hearing.

Békésy Discovers How the Basilar Membrane Vibrates

Békésy determined how the basilar membrane vibrates to different frequencies by observing the vibration of the basilar membrane. He accomplished this by boring a hole in cochleas taken from animal and human cadavers. He presented different frequencies of sound and observed the membrane's vibration by using a technique similar to that used to create stop-action photographs of high-speed events (Békésy, 1960). When he observed the membrane's position at different points in time, he saw that the basilar membrane's vibration as a **traveling wave**, like the motion that occurs when a person holds the end of a rope and "snaps" it, sending a wave traveling down the rope.

Figure 11.21a shows a perspective view of this traveling wave. **Figure 11.21b** shows side views of the traveling wave caused by a pure tone at three successive moments in time. The solid horizontal line represents the basilar membrane at rest. Curve 1 shows the position of the basilar membrane at one moment during its vibration, and curves 2 and 3 show the positions of the membrane at two later moments. Békésy's

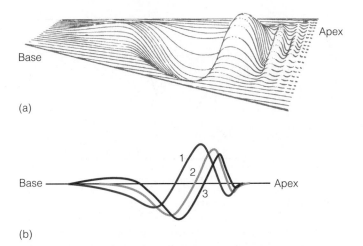

(a)

(b)

Figure 11.21 (a) A traveling wave like the one observed by Békésy. This picture shows what the membrane looks like when the vibration is "frozen" with the wave about two-thirds of the way down the membrane. (b) Side views of the traveling wave caused by a pure tone, showing the position of the membrane at three instants in time as the wave moves from the base to the apex of the cochlear partition. [(a) Adapted from Tonndorf, 1960; (b) Adapted from Békésy, 1960]

measurements showed that most of the membrane vibrates, but that some parts vibrate more than others.

Although the motion takes the form of a traveling wave, the important thing is what happens at particular points along the basilar membrane. If you were at one point on the basilar

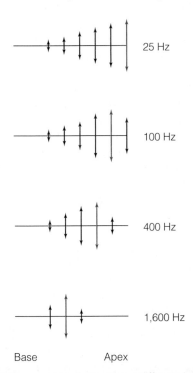

Figure 11.22 The amount of vibration at different locations along the basilar membrane is indicated by the size of the arrows at each location, with the place of maximum vibration indicated in red. When the frequency is 25 Hz, maximum vibration occurs at the apex of the cochlear partition. As the frequency is increased, the location of the maximum vibration moves toward the base of the cochlear partition. (Based on data in Békésy, 1960)

membrane, you would see the membrane vibrating up and down at the frequency of the tone. If you observed the entire membrane, you would see that vibration occurs over a large portion of the membrane but that one place vibrates the most.

Békésy's most important finding was that the place that vibrates the most depends on the frequency of the tone, as shown in **Figure 11.22**. The arrows indicate the extent of the up-and-down displacement of the basilar membrane at different places on the membrane. The red arrows indicate the place where the membrane vibrates the most for each frequency. Notice that as the frequency increases, the place on the membrane that vibrates the most moves from the **apex** at the end of the cochlea toward the **base** at the oval window. Thus, the place of maximum vibration, which is near the apex of the basilar membrane for a 25-Hz tone, has moved to nearer the base for a 1,600-Hz tone. Because the place of maximum vibration depends on frequency, this means that basilar membrane vibration effectively functions as a filter that sorts tones by frequency.

The Cochlea Functions as a Filter

We can appreciate how the cochlea acts like a filter that sorts sound stimuli by frequency by leaving hearing for a moment and considering **Figure 11.23a**, which shows how coffee beans

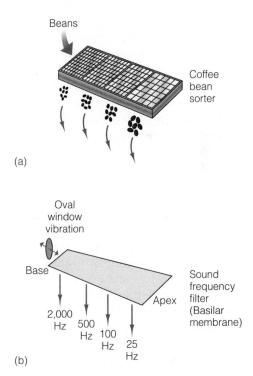

Figure 11.23 Two ways of sorting. (a) Coffee beans of different sizes are deposited at one end of the sieve. By shaking and gravity, the beans travel down the sieve. Smaller coffee beans drop through the small openings at the beginning of the sieve; larger ones drop through the larger openings near the end. (b) Sound vibrations of different frequencies, which occur at the oval window, set the basilar vibration into motion. Higher frequencies cause vibration at the base of the basilar membrane, near the oval window. Low frequencies cause vibrations nearer the apex of the basilar membrane.

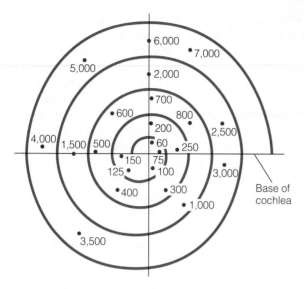

Figure 11.24 Tonotopic map of the guinea pig cochlea. Numbers indicate the location of the maximum electrical response for each frequency. (From Culler et al., 1943)

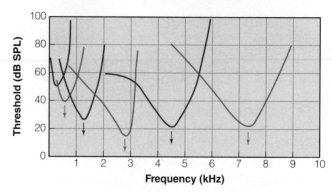

Figure 11.25 Frequency tuning curves of cat auditory nerve fibers. The characteristic frequency of each fiber is indicated by the arrows along the frequency axis. The frequency scale is in kilohertz (kHz), where 1 kHz = 1,000 Hz. Only a small number of curves are shown here. Each of the 3,500 inner hair cells has its own tuning curve, and because each inner hair cell sends signals to about 20 auditory nerve fibers, each frequency is represented by a number of neurons located at that frequency's place along the basilar membrane. (Adapted from Palmer, 1987)

are filtered to sort them by size. Beans with a variety of sizes are deposited at one end of a sieve that contains small holes at the beginning and larger holes toward the far end. The beans travel down the sieve, with smaller beans dropping through the first holes and larger and larger beans dropping through holes farther down the sieve. The sieve, therefore, filters coffee beans by size.

Just as the different sized holes along the length of the sieve separate coffee beans by size, the different places of maximum vibration along the length of the basilar membrane separate sound stimuli by frequency (**Figure 11.23b**). High frequencies cause more vibration near the base end of the cochlea, and low frequencies cause more vibration at the apex of the cochlea. Thus, vibration of the basilar membrane "sorts" or "filters" by frequency so hair cells are activated at different places along the cochlea for different frequencies.

Figure 11.24 shows the results of measurements made by placing electrodes at different positions on the outer surface of a guinea pig's cochlea and stimulating with different frequencies (Culler, 1935; Culler et al., 1943). This "map" of the cochlear illustrates the sorting of frequencies, with high frequencies activating the base of the cochlea and low frequencies activating the apex. This map of frequencies is called a **tonotopic map**.

Another way of demonstrating the connection between frequency and place is to record from single auditory nerve fibers located at different places along the cochlea. Measurement of the response of auditory nerve fibers to frequency is depicted by a fiber's *neural frequency tuning curve*.

METHOD | Neural Frequency Tuning Curves

A neuron's **frequency tuning curve** is determined by presenting pure tones of different frequencies and measuring the sound level necessary to cause the neuron to increase its firing above the baseline or "spontaneous" rate in the absence of sounds. This level is the threshold for that frequency. Plotting the

threshold for each frequency results in frequency tuning curves like the ones in **Figure 11.25**. The arrow under each curve indicates the frequency to which the neuron is most sensitive. This frequency is called the **characteristic frequency** of the particular auditory nerve fiber.

The cochlea's filtering action is reflected by the following three characteristics of tuning curves: (1) the neurons respond best to one frequency; (2) each frequency is associated with nerve fibers located at a specific place along the basilar membrane, with fibers originating near the base of the cochlea having high characteristic frequencies and those originating near the apex having low characteristic frequencies; (3) the curves become wider at higher frequencies.

The second characteristic—the relation between place and characteristic frequency—illustrates the tonotopic map created by cochlear filtering. But the third characteristic—the narrow curves at low frequencies and the broader curves at higher frequencies—adds another dimension to the cochlea's filtering action: The filters are narrow at low frequencies and become broader at high frequencies. What this means is that filtering is more selective at low frequencies than at high frequencies. Thus, while two nearby low frequencies may activate different filters, two nearby high frequencies may activate the same filters. We will see shortly that this difference between the widths of low- and high-frequency filters has implications for our ability to perceive pitch at low and high frequencies.

Returning to the Outer Hair Cells: The Cochlear Amplifier

While Békésy's measurements located the places where specific frequencies caused maximum vibration along the basilar membrane, he also observed that this vibration was spread out over a large portion of the membrane, especially for low-frequency tones. This large spread is puzzling when we consider narrow frequency tuning curves like the ones for low frequencies shown in Figure 11.25, and also because of psychophysical data that shows that listeners can tell the difference between frequencies such as 1,000 and 1,005 Hz, which according to Békésy's measurements would cause almost identical patterns of basilar membrane vibration.

Later researchers realized that one reason for Békésy's broad vibration patterns was that his measurements were carried out on "dead" cochleas that were isolated from animal and human cadavers. When modern researchers used more advanced technology that enabled them to measure vibration in live cochleas, they showed that the pattern of vibration for specific frequencies was much narrower than what Békésy had observed (Khanna & Leonard, 1982; Rhode, 1971, 1974).

But what was responsible for this narrower vibration? In 1983 Hallowell Davis published a paper titled "An Active Process in Cochlear Mechanics," which began with the attention-getting statement: "We are in the midst of a major breakthrough in auditory physiology." He went on to propose a mechanism that he named the **cochlear amplifier**, which explained why neural turning curves were narrower than what would be expected based on Békésy's measurements of basilar membrane vibration.

Davis proposed that the cochlear amplifier was an active mechanical process that took place in the outer hair cells. We can appreciate what this active mechanical process is by describing how the outer hair cells respond to and influence the vibration of the basilar membrane.[2]

The major purpose of outer hair cells is to influence the way the basilar membrane vibrates, and they accomplish this by changing length (Ashmore, 2008; Ashmore et al., 2010). While ion flow in inner hair cells causes an electrical response in auditory nerve fibers, ion flow in outer hair cells causes mechanical changes inside the cell that causes the cell to expand and contract, as shown in **Figure 11.26**. The outer hair cells become elongated when the cilia bend in one direction and contract when they bend in the other direction. This mechanical response of elongation and contraction pushes and pulls on the basilar membrane, which increases the motion of the basilar membrane and sharpens its response to specific frequencies.

The importance of the cochlear amplifier is illustrated by the frequency tuning curves in **Figure 11.27**. The solid blue curve shows the frequency tuning of a cat's auditory nerve fiber with a characteristic frequency of about 8,000 Hz. The dashed red curve shows what happened when the cochlear amplifier was eliminated by destroying the outer hair cells with a chemical that attacked the outer hair cells but left the inner hair cells intact. Whereas originally the fiber had a low threshold at 8,000 Hz, indicated by the arrow, it now takes much higher intensities to get the auditory nerve fiber to respond to 8,000 Hz and nearby frequencies (Fettiplace & Hackney, 2006; Liberman & Dodds, 1984). The conclusion from Figure 11.27

[2]Theodore Gold (1948), who was to become a well-known researcher in cosmology and astronomy, made the original proposal that there is an active process in the cochlea. But it wasn't until many years later that further developments in auditory research led to the proposal of the cochlear amplifier mechanism (see Gold, 1989).

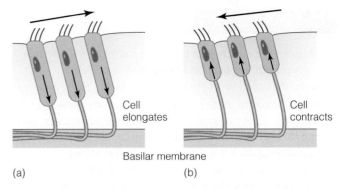

Cell elongates

Cell contracts

Basilar membrane

(a)

(b)

Figure 11.26 The outer hair cell cochlear amplifier mechanism occurs when the cells (a) elongate when cilia bend in one direction and (b) contract when the cilia bend in the other direction. This results in an amplifying effect on the motion of the basilar membrane.

and the results of other experiments is that the cochlear amplifier greatly sharpens the tuning of each place along the cochlea.

All of our descriptions so far have been focused on physical events that occur within the inner ear. Our story has focused on physical processes such as trapdoors opening and ions flowing, nerve firing that is synchronized with the sound stimulus, and how basilar membrane vibrations separate different frequencies along the length of the cochlea. All of this information is crucial for understanding how the ear functions and prepares us for the next section, in which we consider the connection between these physical processes and perception.

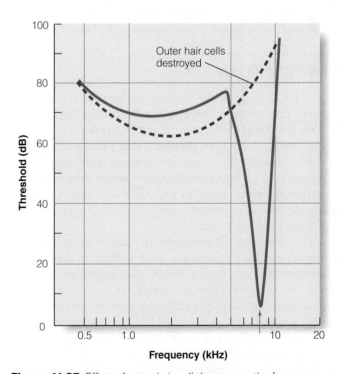

Figure 11.27 Effect of outer hair cell damage on the frequency tuning curve. The solid curve is the frequency tuning curve of a neuron with a characteristic frequency of about 8,000 Hz (arrow). The dashed curve is the frequency tuning curve for the same neuron after the outer hair cells were destroyed by injection of a chemical. (Adapted from Fettiplace & Hackney, 2006)

1. Describe the structure of the ear, focusing on the role that each component plays in transmitting the vibrations that enter the outer ear to the auditory receptors in the inner ear.

2. Focusing on the inner ear, describe (a) what causes the bending of the cilia of the hair cells; (b) what happens when the cilia bend; (c) how phase locking causes the electrical signal to follow the timing of the sound stimulus.

3. Describe Békésy's discovery of how the basilar membrane vibrates. Specifically, what is the relationship between sound frequency and basilar membrane vibration?

4. What does it mean to say that the cochlea acts as a filter? How is this supported by the tonotopic map and by neural frequency tuning curves? What is a neuron's characteristic frequency?

5. What was puzzling about Békésy's measurements of basilar membrane vibration?

6. How do the outer hair cells function as cochlear amplifiers?

The Physiology of Pitch Perception

We are now ready to describe what we know about the relation between physiological events in the auditory system and the perception of pitch. We begin by describing physiological processes in the ear and will then move on to the brain.

Place and Pitch

Our starting point is the connection between a tone's frequency and the perception of pitch. Given that low frequencies are associated with low pitch and higher frequencies with higher pitch, it has been proposed that pitch perception is determined by the firing of neurons that respond best to specific frequencies. This idea follows from Békésy's discovery that specific frequencies cause maximum vibration at specific *places* along the basilar membrane, which creates a tonotopic map like the one in Figure 11.24.

The association of frequency with place led to the following explanation of the physiology of pitch perception: A pure tone causes a peak of activity at a specific place on the basilar membrane. The neurons connected to that place respond strongly to that frequency, as indicated by the auditory nerve fiber frequency tuning curves in Figure 11.25, and this information is carried up the auditory nerve to the brain. The brain identifies which neurons are responding the most and uses this information to determine the pitch. This explanation of the physiology of pitch perception has been called the **place theory**, because it is based on the relation between a sound's frequency and the place along the basilar membrane that is activated.

This explanation is elegant in its simplicity, and it became the standard explanation of the physiology of pitch

in textbooks like this one. Meanwhile, however, auditory researchers were questioning the validity of place theory. One argument against place was based on the effect of the missing fundamental, in which removing the fundamental frequency of a complex tone does not change the tone's pitch (p. 266). Thus, the tone in Figure 11.6a, which has a fundamental frequency of 200 Hz, has the same pitch after the 200 Hz fundamental is removed, as in Figure 11.6b. What this means is that there is no longer peak vibration at the place associated with 200 Hz.

A modified form of place theory explains this result by considering how the basilar membrane vibrates to complex tones. Research that has measured how the basilar membrane vibrates to complex tones shows that the basilar membrane vibrates to each of the tone's harmonics (Hudspeth, 1989). **Figure 11.28a** shows the frequency spectrum of four harmonics of a complex tone with a fundamental frequency of 100 Hz. **Figure 11.28b** shows where the peaks in vibration on the basilar membrane occur in response to this tone; each harmonic causes peak vibration in the place corresponding to its frequency. Eliminating the 100 Hz fundamental would eliminate the peak at 100 Hz, but peaks would remain at 200, 300, and 400, and this pattern of places, spaced 100 Hz apart, provides information that can be used to determine the pitch.

But other research revealed other phenomena that were difficult for even the modified version of place theory to explain. Edward Burns and Neal Viemeister (1974) created a sound stimulus that wasn't associated with vibration of a particular place on the basilar membrane, but which created a perception of pitch. This stimulus was called **amplitude-modulated noise**. **Noise** is a stimulus that contains many random frequencies so it doesn't create a vibration pattern on the basilar membrane that corresponds to a specific frequency. **Amplitude modulation** means that the level (or intensity) of the noise was changed so the loudness of the noise fluctuated rapidly up and down.

Burns and Viemeister found that this noise stimulus resulted in a perception of pitch, which they could change by varying the rate of the up-and-down changes in level. The conclusion from this finding, that pitch can be perceived even in the absence of place information, has been demonstrated in a large number experiments using different types of stimuli (Oxenham, 2013; Yost, 2009).

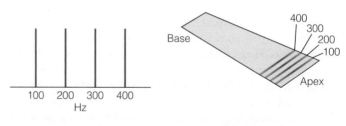

(a) **Frequency spectrum**   (b) **Basilar membrane**

Figure 11.28 (a) Frequency spectrum for a complex tone with fundamental frequency 200 Hz, showing the fundamental and three harmonics. (b) Basilar membrane. The shaded areas indicate approximate locations of peak vibration associated with each harmonic in the complex tone.

Temporal Information and Pitch

If place isn't the answer, what is? One way to answer this question is to look back at Figure 11.6 and note what happens when the 200-Hz fundamental frequency is removed. Notice that although the waveform of the tone changes, the timing, or repetition rate, remains the same. Thus, there is information in the *timing* of a tone stimulus that is associated with the tone's pitch. We also saw that this timing occurs in the neural response to a tone because of phase locking.

When we discussed phase locking on page 272, we saw that because nerve fibers fire at the same time in the sound stimulus, the sound produces a pattern of nerve firing in groups of neurons that matches the frequency of the sound stimulus (Figure 11.20). Thus, the timing of firing of groups of neurons provides information about the fundamental frequency of a complex tone, and this information exists even if the fundamental frequency or other harmonics are absent.

The reason phase locking has been linked to pitch perception is that pitch perception occurs only for frequencies up to about 5,000 Hz, and phase locking also occurs only up to 5,000 Hz. The idea that tones have pitch only for frequencies up to 5,000 Hz may be surprising, especially given that the audibility curve (Figure 11.8) indicates that the range of hearing extends up to 20,000 Hz. However, remember from page 266, that pitch is defined as *that aspect of auditory sensation whose variation is associated with musical melodies* (Plack, Barker, & Hall, 2014). This definition is based on the finding that when tones are strung together to create a melody, we only perceive a melody if the tones are below 5,000 Hz (Attneave & Olson, 1971). It is probably no coincidence that the highest note on an orchestral instrument (the piccolo) is about 4,500 Hz. Melodies played using frequencies above 5,000 Hz sound rather strange. You can tell that something is changing but it doesn't sound musical. So it seems that our sense of musical pitch may be limited to those frequencies that create phase locking.

The existence of phase locking below 5,000 Hz, along with other evidence, has led most researchers to conclude that **temporal coding** is the major mechanism of pitch perception. However, there is more to the story, because place hasn't been counted out entirely, as we will see in the next section.

Place and Pitch (Again)

Even though pitch can occur in the absence of place information, there is evidence that place information can enhance the perception of pitch. We can understand this evidence by returning to our description of how the cochlea acts as a bank of filters that sort out the different frequencies in the sound stimulus. Remember that frequency tuning curves of auditory nerve fibers are narrow at low frequencies and become wider at higher frequencies (Figure 11.25). **Figure 11.29a** is a frequency spectrum showing 18 harmonics of a tone with a fundamental frequency of 440 Hz. **Figure 11.29b** shows the cochlear filter bank. These filters correspond to frequency tuning curves, and like frequency tuning curves, the filters

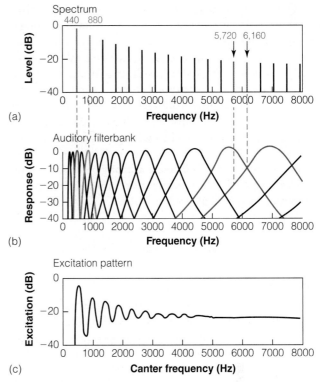

Figure 11.29 (a) Frequency spectrum for the first 18 harmonics for a tone with 440-Hz fundamental frequency. (b) Cochlear filter bank. Note that the filters are narrower at lower frequencies. The red filter is activated by the 440-Hz harmonic; the green one by the 880-Hz harmonic; the blue ones by the 5,720- and 6,160-Hz harmonics. The filters correspond to the frequency tuning curves of cochlear nerve fibers like the ones shown in Figure 11.25. (c) Excitation pattern on the basilar membrane, which shows individual peaks of vibration for the early (resolved) harmonics and no peaks for the later (unresolved) harmonics. (Adapted from Oxenham, 2013)

are very narrow at low frequencies and are wider at high frequencies.

Now let's consider what happens when we present the 440-Hz complex tone. The fundamental (440 Hz) most strongly activates the filter highlighted in red, and the 880-Hz second harmonic most strongly activates the filter highlighted in green. Now let's move up to higher harmonics. The 5,720-Hz 13th harmonic and the 6,160-Hz 14th harmonic both activate the two overlapping filters highlighted in blue. This means that lower harmonics activate separated filters while high harmonics can activate the same filters. Taking the properties of the filter bank into account results in the excitation curve in **Figure 11.29c**, which is essentially a picture of the amplitude of basilar membrane vibration caused by each of the tone's harmonics (Oxenham, 2013).

What stands out about the excitation curve is that the tone's lower harmonics each cause a distinct bump in the excitation curve. Because each of these lower harmonics can be distinguished by a peak, they are called **resolved harmonics**. In contrast, the excitations caused by the higher harmonics create a smooth function that doesn't indicate the individual harmonics. These higher harmonics are called **unresolved harmonics.**

What's important about resolved and unresolved harmonics is that a series of resolved harmonics results in a strong perception of pitch, but unresolved harmonics result in a weak perception of pitch. Thus, a tone with the spectral composition 100, 200, 300, 400, and 500 Hz results in a strong perception of pitch corresponding to the 100-Hz fundamental. However, the smeared out pattern that would be caused by higher harmonics of the 100-Hz fundamental, such as 2,100, 2,200, 2,300, 2,400, and 2,500 Hz, results in a weak perception of pitch corresponding to 100 Hz. The fact that resolved harmonics contain place information and create a strong perception of pitch supports a role for place information in perceiving the pitch represented by these harmonics.

Problems Remaining to Be Solved

You may, at this point, be getting the idea that there is nothing simple about the physiology of pitch perception. The complexity of the problem of pitch perception is highlighted further by research by Andrew Oxenham and coworkers (2011) in which they asked the question: "Can pitch be perceived for frequencies above 5,000 Hz?" (which, remember, is supposed to be the upper frequency limit for perceiving pitch). They answered this question by showing that if a large number of high-frequency harmonics are presented, subjects do, in fact, perceive pitch. For example, when presented with 7,200, 8,400, 9,600, 10,800, and 12,000 Hz, which are harmonics of a tone with 1,200-Hz fundamental frequency, subjects perceived a pitch corresponding to 1,200 Hz, which is the spacing between the harmonics (although the perception of pitch was weaker than the perception to lower harmonics). A particularly interesting aspect of this result is that although each harmonic presented alone did not result in perception of pitch (because they are all above 5,000 Hz), pitch was perceived when a number of harmonics were presented together.

This result raises a number of questions. Is it possible that phase locking occurs above 5,000 Hz? Is it possible that some kind of place mechanism is responsible for the pitch Oxenham's subjects heard? We don't know the answer to these questions because we don't know what the limits of phase locking are in humans. And just to make things even more interesting, it is important to remember that while pitch perception may depend on the information created by vibration of the basilar membrane and by the firing of auditory nerve fibers that are carrying information from the cochlea, pitch perception is not created by the cochlea. It is created by the brain. This parallels the situation in vision. What we see depends on information in the retinal image, but vision is created in the cortex. Because of the importance of the cortex in creating pitch perception, we need to move up the auditory pathway to the cortex. We begin by describing the trip that nerve impulses take as they travel from the auditory nerve to the auditory cortex.

The Pathway to the Brain

Signals generated in the hair cells of the cochlea are transmitted out of the cochlea in nerve fibers of the auditory nerve

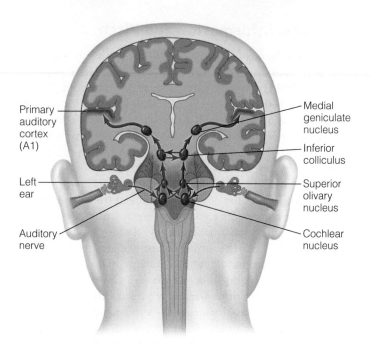

Figure 11.30 Diagram of the auditory pathways. This diagram is greatly simplified, as numerous connections between the structures are not shown. Note that auditory structures are bilateral—they exist on both the left and right sides of the body—and that messages can cross over between the two sides. (Adapted from Wever, 1949)

(refer back to Figure 11.16). The auditory nerve carries the signals generated by the inner hair cells away from the cochlea and toward the auditory receiving area in the cortex, as shown in **Figure 11.30**. Auditory nerve fibers from the cochlea synapse in a sequence of **subcortical structures**—structures below the cerebral cortex. This sequence begins with the **cochlear nucleus** and continues to the **superior olivary nucleus** in the brain stem, the **inferior colliculus** in the midbrain, and the **medial geniculate nucleus** in the thalamus.

From the medial geniculate nucleus, fibers continue to the **primary auditory cortex** (or **auditory receiving area, A1**) in the temporal lobe of the cortex. If you have trouble remembering this sequence of structures, remember the acronym SONIC MG (a very fast sports car), which represents the three structures between the cochlear nucleus and the auditory cortex, as follows: SON = superior olivary nucleus; IC = inferior colliculus; MG = medial geniculate nucleus.

A great deal of processing occurs as signals travel through the subcortical structures along the pathway from the cochlea to the cortex. Processing in the superior olivary nucleus is important for locating sounds because it is here that signals from the left and right ears first meet (indicated by the presence of both red and blue arrows in Figure 11.30). We will discuss how signals from the two ears help us locate sounds in Chapter 12.

Auditory signals arrive at the primary auditory receiving area (A1) in the temporal lobe (**Figure 11.31a**) and then travel to other cortical auditory areas (**Figure 11.31b**): (1) the **core area**, which includes the primary auditory cortex (A1) and some nearby areas; (2) the **belt area**, which surrounds the

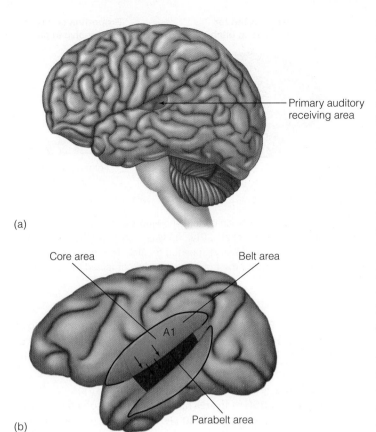

(a)

Core area

Belt area

A1

Parabelt area

(b)

Figure 11.31 (a) The human brain, showing the location of the primary auditory receiving area, A1, which also extends inside the temporal lobe. (b) A monkey brain, in which the temporal lobe has been pulled back to reveal additional auditory areas: the core area, which contains A1; the belt area; and the parabelt area. Signals, indicated by the arrows, travel from core to belt to parabelt. The function of the core, belt, and parabelt areas will be discussed in Chapter 12. (From Kaas et al., 1999)

core, and (3) the **parabelt area** (Kaas et al., 1999; Rauschecker, 1997, 1998).

Pitch and the Brain

Something interesting happens as nerve impulses are traveling up the SONIC MG pathway to the auditory cortex. The temporal information that dominated pitch coding in the cochlea and auditory nerve fibers becomes less important. The main indication of this is that phase locking, which occurred up to about 5,000 Hz in auditory nerve fibers, occurs only up to 100–200 Hz in the auditory cortex (Oxenham, 2013; Wallace et al., 2000). But while phase locking is disappearing as nerve impulses travel toward the cortex, experiments in the marmoset have demonstrated the existence of individual neurons that seem to be responding to pitch, and experiments in humans have located areas in the auditory cortex that also appear to be responding to pitch.

Pitch Neurons in the Marmoset An experiment by Daniel Bendor and Xiaoqin Wang (2005) determined how neurons in an area just outside the auditory cortex of a marmoset (a species of New World monkey) responded to complex tones that differed in their harmonic structure but would be perceived by humans as having the same pitch. When they did this, they found neurons that responded similarly to complex tones with the same fundamental frequency but with different harmonic structures. For example, **Figure 11.32a** shows the frequency spectra for a tone with a fundamental frequency of 182 Hz. In the top record, the tone contains the fundamental frequency and the second and third harmonics; in the second record, harmonics 4–6 are present; and so on, until at the bottom, only harmonics 12–14 are present. Even though these stimuli contain different frequencies (for example, 182, 364, and 546 Hz in the top record; 2,184, 2,366, and 2,548 Hz in the bottom record), they are all perceived by humans as having a pitch corresponding to the 182-Hz fundamental frequency.

The corresponding cortical response records (**Figure 11.32b**) show that these stimuli all caused an increase in firing. To demonstrate that this firing occurred only when information about the 182-Hz fundamental frequency was present, Bendor and Wang showed that the neuron responded well to a 182-Hz tone presented alone, but not to any of the harmonics when they were presented alone. These cortical neurons, therefore, responded only to stimuli associated with the 182-Hz tone, which is associated with a specific pitch. For this reason, Bendor and Wang called these neurons **pitch neurons**.

Pitch Representation in the Human Cortex Research on where pitch is processed in the human cortex has used brain scanning (fMRI) to measure the response to stimuli associated with different pitches. This is not as simple as

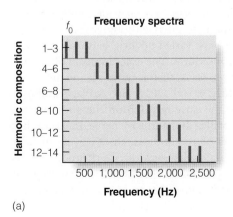

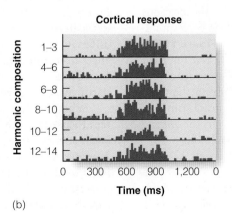

Figure 11.32 Records from a pitch neuron recorded from the auditory cortex of marmoset monkeys. (a) Frequency spectra for tones with a fundamental frequency of 182 Hz. Each tone contains three harmonic components of the 182-Hz fundamental frequency. (b) Response of the neuron to each stimulus. (Adapted from Bendor & Wang, 2005)

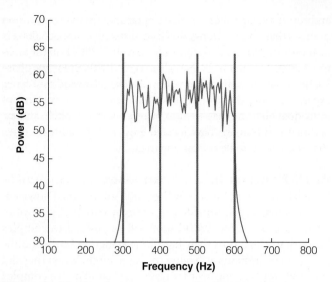

Figure 11.33 Blue: frequency spectra for the 300-, 400-, 500-, and 600-Hz harmonics of a pitch stimulus with fundamental frequency of 100 HZ. Orange: frequency-matched noise, which covers the same range, but without the peaks that produce pitch.

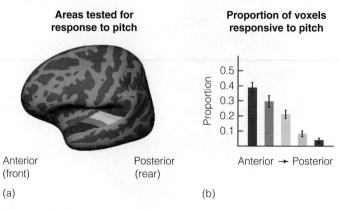

Figure 11.34 (a) Human cortex, showing areas, in color, tested by Norman-Haignere et al. (2013). (b) Graph showing the proportion of voxels in each area that responded to pitch. The more anterior areas (located toward the front of the brain) contained more pitch-responsive voxels.

it may seem, because when a neuron responds to sound, this doesn't necessarily mean it is involved in perceiving pitch. To determine whether areas of the brain are responding to pitch, researchers have looked for brain regions that are more active in response to a pitch-evoking sound, such as a complex tone, than to another sound, such as a band of noise that has similar physical features but does not produce a pitch. By doing this, researchers hope to locate brain regions that respond to pitch, irrespective of other properties of the sound.

A pitch-evoking stimulus and a noise stimulus used in an experiment by Sam Norman-Haignere and coworkers (2013) are shown in **Figure 11.33**. The pitch stimulus, shown in blue, is the 3rd, 4th, 5th, and 6th harmonics of a complex tone with a fundamental frequency of 100 Hz (300, 400, 500, and 600 Hz); the noise, shown in red, consists of a band of frequencies from 300 to 600 Hz. Because the noise stimulus covers the same range as the pitch stimulus, it is called *frequency-matched noise.*

By comparing fMRI responses generated by the pitch-evoking stimulus to the response from the frequency-matched noise, Norman-Haignere located areas in the primary auditory cortex, or core, and some nearby areas, that responded more to the pitch-evoking stimulus (see Figure 11.31b for the locations of core, belt, and parabelt areas in the monkey; corresponding areas exist in humans). The colored areas in **Figure 11.34a** show areas in the human cortex that were tested for their response to pitch. **Figure 11.34b** shows the proportions of fMRI voxels in each area in which the response to the pitch stimulus was greater than the response to the noise stimulus. The areas most responsive to pitch are located in the *anterior auditory cortex*—the area close to the front of the brain.

Evidence supporting the idea that these voxels near the front of the auditory area are responding to pitch was provided by presenting stimuli containing resolved harmonics and stimuli containing unresolved harmonics (see page 277).

For example, **Figure 11.35a** indicates, in red, harmonics 3–6 of a tone with a fundamental frequency of 400 Hz and the calculated excitation pattern associated with these harmonics. The fact that harmonics 3–6 of this tone are resolved is indicated by the peaks in the excitation pattern for each harmonic.

Figure 11.35b indicates harmonics 12–24 of a tone with a fundamental frequency of 100 Hz, with its excitation pattern. That harmonics 12–24 of this tone are unresolved is indicated by the smooth excitation curve, showing no peaks for the harmonics. Although both sets of harmonics span the same range of frequencies, from 1,200 to 2,400 Hz, the stimulus with resolved harmonics caused a large response in the pitch-responsive areas of cortex, whereas the stimulus with unresolved harmonics caused a small response.

Remember from our discussion of resolved and unresolved harmonics on page 277 that resolved harmonics result in a good perception of pitch and unresolved harmonics result in a weak perception of pitch. The fact that resolved harmonics (1) are associated with good pitch perception and (2) cause a large response in the areas that respond best to the pitch stimulus strengthens the conclusion that these areas are actually responding to pitch.

As we indicated at the beginning of this discussion, determining areas of the brain that respond to pitch involves more than just presenting tones and measuring responses. Researchers in many laboratories have identified auditory areas in the human that respond to pitch, although the results from different laboratories have varied slightly because of differences in stimuli and procedures. The exact location of the human pitch-responding areas is, therefore, still being discussed (Griffiths, 2012; Griffiths & Hall, 2012; Hall & Plack, 2009).

Whereas most of the early research on the auditory system focused on the cochlea and auditory nerve, the brain has become a major focus of recent research. We will consider more research on the brain when we describe the mechanisms responsible for locating sounds in space and for the perceptual organization of sound (Chapter 12) and for how we perceive speech (Chapter 13).

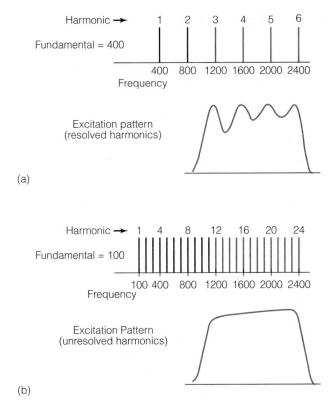

(a)

(b)

Figure 11.35 Examples of stimuli with resolved and unresolved harmonics used by Norman-Hagnere et al. (2013). (a) A stimulus spectrum for a tone with fundamental frequency of 400-Hz has harmonics spaced every 400 Hz. Harmonics 3–6 are indicated in red. The excitation pattern for these harmonics, shown below the spectrum, has peaks, indicating that these harmonics are resolved. (b) A stimulus with a fundamental frequency of 100 Hz has harmonics spaced every 100 Hz. Harmonics 12–24, indicated in red, cover the same range as harmonics 3–6 of the tone with the 400-Hz fundamental frequency shown above. These harmonics create an excitation pattern with no peaks, indicating that these harmonics are unresolved.

Hearing Loss

Out there in the environment, the ears are often bombarded with noises such as crowds of people talking (or yelling, if at a sporting event), construction sounds, and traffic noise. Noises such as these are the most common cause of hearing loss. Hearing loss is usually associated with damage to the outer hair

cells, and recent evidence indicates that damage to auditory nerve fibers may be involved as well. When the outer hair cells are damaged, the response of the basilar membrane becomes similar to the broad response seen for the dead cochleas examined by Békésy; this results in a loss of sensitivity (inability to hear quiet sounds) and a loss of the sharp frequency tuning seen in healthy ears, as shown in Figure 11.27 (Moore, 1995; Plack et al., 2004). The broad tuning makes it harder for hearing-impaired people to separate out sounds—for example, to hear speech sounds in noisy environments.

Inner hair cell damage can also cause a large effect, resulting in a loss of sensitivity. Hearing loss occurs for the frequencies corresponding to the frequencies detected by the damaged inner or outer hair cells. Sometimes inner hair cells are lost over an entire region of the cochlea (a "dead region"), and sensitivity to the frequencies that normally excite that region of the cochlea becomes much reduced.

Of course, you wouldn't want to purposely damage your hair cells, but sometimes we expose ourselves to sounds that over the long term do result in hair cell damage. One of the things that contributes to hair cell damage is living in an industrialized environment, which contains sounds that contribute to a type of hearing loss called *presbycusis*.

Presbycusis

Presbycusis is caused by hair cell damage resulting from the cumulative effects over time of noise exposure, the ingestion of drugs that damage the hair cells, and age-related degeneration. The loss of sensitivity associated with presbycusis, which is greatest at high frequencies, affects males more severely than females. **Figure 11.36** shows the progression of loss as a function of age. Unlike the visual problem of presbyopia (see Chapter 2, page 27), which is an inevitable consequence of aging, presbycusis is largely caused by factors in addition to aging; people in preindustrial cultures, who have not been exposed to the noises that accompany industrialization or to drugs that could damage the ear, often do not experience large decreases in high-frequency hearing in old age. This may be why males, who historically have been exposed to more workplace noise than females, as well as to noises associated with hunting and wartime, experience a greater presbycusis effect.

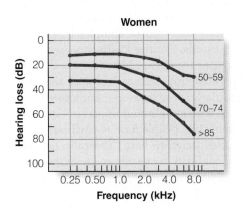

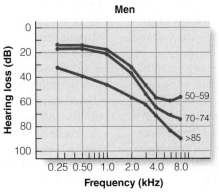

Figure 11.36 Hearing loss in presbycusis as a function of age. All of the curves are plotted relative to the 20-year-old curve, which is taken as the standard. (Adapted from Bunch, 1929)

Although presbycusis may be unavoidable, since most people are exposed over a long period of time to the everyday sounds of our modern environment, there are situations in which people expose their ears to loud sounds that could be avoided. This exposure to particularly loud sounds results in *noise-induced hearing loss*.

Noise-Induced Hearing Loss

Noise-induced hearing loss occurs when loud noises cause degeneration of the hair cells. This degeneration has been observed in examinations of the cochleas of people who have worked in noisy environments and have willed their ear structures to medical research. Damage to the organ of Corti is often observed in these cases. For example, examination of the cochlea of a man who worked in a steel mill indicated that his organ of Corti had collapsed and no receptor cells remained (Miller, 1974). More controlled studies of animals exposed to loud sounds provide further evidence that high-intensity sounds can damage or completely destroy inner hair cells (Liberman & Dodds, 1984).

Because of the danger to hair cells posed by workplace noise, the United States Occupational Safety and Health Agency (OSHA) has mandated that workers not be exposed to sound levels greater than 85 dB for an 8-hour work shift. In addition to workplace noise, however, other sources of intense sound can cause hair cell damage leading to hearing loss.

If you turn up the volume on your portable music player, you are exposing yourself to what hearing professionals call **leisure noise**. Other sources of leisure noise are activities such as recreational gun use, riding motorcycles, playing musical instruments, and working with power tools. A number of studies have demonstrated hearing loss in people who listen to portable music players (Okamoto et al., 2011; Peng et al., 2007), play in rock/pop bands (Schmuziger et al., 2006), use power tools (Dalton et al., 2001), and attend sports events (Hodgetts & Liu, 2006). The amount of hearing loss depends on the level of sound intensity and the duration of exposure. Given the high levels of sound that occur in these activities, such as the levels above 90 dB SPL that can occur for the 3 hours of a hockey game (Hodgetts & Liu, 2006), about 100 dB SPL for music venues such as clubs or concerts (Howgate & Plack, 2011), and levels as high as 90 dB SPL while using power tools in woodworking, it isn't surprising that both temporary and permanent hearing losses are associated with these leisure activities. These findings suggest that it might make sense to use ear protection when in particularly noisy environments and to turn down the volume on your portable music player.

The potential for hearing loss from listening to music at high volume for extended periods of time cannot be overemphasized, because at their highest settings, portable music players reach levels of 100 dB SPL or higher—far above OSHA's recommended maximum of 85 dB. This has led Apple Computer to add a setting their devices that limits the maximum volume, although an informal survey of my students indicates, not surprisingly, that few of them use this feature.

Hidden Hearing Loss

Is it possible to have normal hearing as measured by a standard hearing test, but to have trouble understanding speech in noisy environments? The answer for a large number of people is "yes." People with "normal" hearing who have trouble hearing in noisy environments may be suffering from a recently discovered type of hearing loss called **hidden hearing loss** (Plack, Barker, & Prendergast, 2014). We can understand why this type of hearing loss occurs by considering what the standard hearing test measures.

The standard hearing test involves measuring thresholds for hearing tones across the frequency spectrum. The person sits in a quiet room and is instructed to indicate when he or she hears very faint tones being presented by the tester. The results of this test can be plotted as thresholds covering a range of frequencies—like the audibility curve in Figure 11.8, or as an **audiogram**, like the curves in Figure 11.36, which plot hearing loss versus frequency. "Normal" hearing is indicated by a horizontal function at 0 dB on the audiogram, indicating no deviation from the normal standard. The standard hearing test, along with the audiograms it produces, has been called the gold standard of hearing test function (Kujawa & Liberman, 2009).

One reason for the popularity of this test is that it is thought to indicate hair cell functioning. But for hearing complex sounds like speech, especially under noisy conditions such as at a party or in the noise of city traffic, the auditory nerve fibers that transmit signals from the cochlea are also important. Sharon Kujawa and Charles Liberman (2009) determined the importance of having intact auditory nerve fibers through experiments on the effect of noise on hair cells and auditory nerve fibers in the mouse.

Kujawa and Liberman exposed the mice to a 100-dB SPL noise for 2 hours and then measured their hair cell and auditory nerve functioning using physiological techniques we won't describe here. **Figure 11.37a** shows the results for the hair cells when tested with a 75-dB tone. One day after the noise exposure, hair cell function was decreased below normal (with normal indicated by the dashed line). However, by 8 weeks after the noise exposure, hair cell function had returned almost to normal.

Figure 11.37b shows the response of the auditory nerve fibers to the 75-dB tone. Their function was also decreased right after the noise, but unlike the hair cells, auditory nerve function never returned to normal. The response of nerve fibers to low-level sounds did recover completely, but the response to high-level sounds, like the 75-dB tone, remained below normal. This lack of recovery reflects the fact that the noise exposure had permanently damaged some of the auditory nerve fibers, particularly those that represent information about high sound levels. It is thought that similar effects occur in humans, so that even when people have normal sensitivity to low-level sounds and therefore have "clinically normal" hearing, the damaged auditory nerve fibers are responsible for problems hearing speech in noisy environments (Plack, Barker, & Prendergast, 2014).

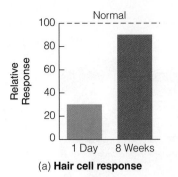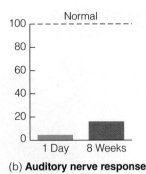

Figure 11.37 (a) Mouse hair cell response, as a percentage of normal, to a 75-dB SPL tone following a 2-hour exposure to a 100-dB SPL tone. The response is greatly decreased compared to normal (indicated by the dashed line) 1 day after the exposure but has increased back to normal by 8 weeks after the exposure. (b) The response of auditory nerve fibers is also decreased 1 day after the exposure but fails to recover at 8 weeks, indicating permanent damage. (Based on data from Kujawa & Liberman, 2009)

What is important about this result is that even though some auditory nerve fibers were permanently damaged, the behavioral thresholds to quiet sounds had returned to normal. Thus, a normal audiogram does not necessarily indicate normal auditory functioning. This is why hearing loss due to nerve fiber damage has been described as "hidden" hearing loss (Schaette & McAlpine, 2011). Hidden hearing loss can be lurking in the background, causing serious problems in day-to-day functioning especially in noisy environments. Further research on hidden hearing loss is focusing on determining what causes it and on developing a test to detect it so this type of hearing loss will no longer be hidden (Plack, Barker, & Prendergast, 2014).

SOMETHING TO CONSIDER:

Cochlear Implants

Békésy's discovery that each place on the basilar membrane is associated with a particular frequency has led to the development of a device called a **cochlear implant**, shown in **Figure 11.38**, which is used to create hearing in people with deafness caused by damage to the hair cells in the cochlea. When the hair cells are damaged, hearing aids are ineffective because the damaged hair cells cannot convert the amplified sound provided by the hearing aid into electrical signals. As shown in Figure 11.38, the cochlear implant consists of (1) a microphone that receives sound signals from the environment; (2) a sound processor that divides the sound received by the microphone into a number of frequency bands; (3) a transmitter that sends these signals to (4) an array of 12–22 electrodes that are implanted along the length of the cochlea. These electrodes stimulate the cochlea at different places along its length, depending on the intensities of the frequencies in the stimuli received by the microphone. This stimulation activates auditory nerve fibers along the cochlea, which send signals toward the brain. The hearing that results enables people to recognize everyday sounds such as horns honking, doors closing, water running, and in some cases, speech.

The development of the cochlear implant is an impressive demonstration of how basic research yields practical benefits. The technology of cochlear implants, which has made it possible to bring deaf adults and children into the world of hearing (Kiefer et al., 1996; Tye-Murray et al., 1995), can be traced directly to the discovery of the tonotopic map along the cochlea.

Figure 11.38 Cochlear implant device. See text for details.

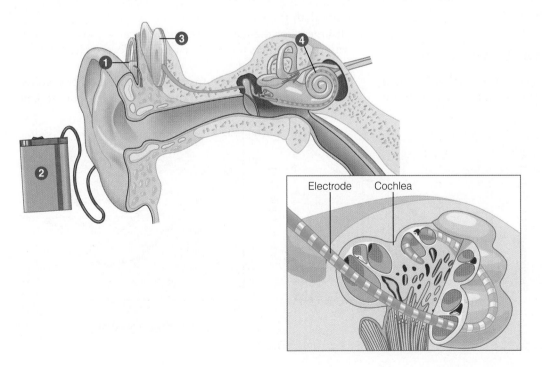

What do newborn infants hear, and how does hearing develop as infants get older? Although some early psychologists believed that newborns were functionally deaf, recent research has shown that newborns do have some auditory capacity and that this capacity improves as the child gets older (Werner & Bargones, 1992).

Thresholds and the Audibility Curve

What do infant audibility curves look like, and how do their thresholds compare to adults'? Lynne Werner Olsho and co-workers (1988) used the following procedure to determine infants' audibility curves: An infant is fitted with earphones and sits on the parent's lap. An observer, sitting out of view of the infant, watches the infant through a window. A light blinks on, indicating that a trial has begun, and a tone is either presented or not. The observer's task is to decide whether the infant heard the tone (Olsho et al., 1987).

How can observers tell whether the infant has heard a tone? They decide by looking for responses such as eye movements, changes in facial expression, a wide-eyed look, a turn of the head, or changes in activity level. These judgments resulted in the curve in **Figure 11.39a** for a 2,000-Hz tone (Olsho et al., 1988). Observers only occasionally indicated that the 3-month-old infants had heard a tone that was presented at low intensity or not at all; observers were more likely to say that the infant had heard the tone when the tone was presented at high intensity. The infant's threshold was determined from this curve, and the results from a number of other frequencies were combined to create audibility functions such as those in **Figure 11.39b**. The curves for 3- and 6-month-olds and adults indicate that infant and adult audibility functions look similar and that by 6 months of age the infant's threshold is within about 10 to 15 dB of the adult threshold.

Recognizing Their Mother's Voice

Another approach to studying hearing in infants has been to show that newborns can identify sounds they have heard

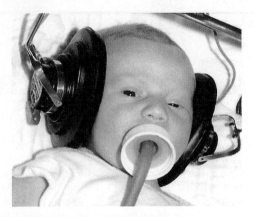

Figure 11.40 This baby, from DeCasper and Fifer's (1980) study, could control whether she heard a recording of her mother's voice or a stranger's voice by the way she sucked on the nipple. (From DeCasper, A. J., & Fifer, W. P. (1980). Of human bonding: Newborns prefer their mothers' voices. *Science*, 208, 1174–1176.)

before. Anthony DeCasper and William Fifer (1980) demonstrated this capacity in newborns by showing that 2-day-old infants will modify their sucking on a nipple in order to hear the sound of their mother's voice. They first observed that infants usually suck on a nipple in bursts separated by pauses. They fitted infants with earphones and let the length of the pause in the infant's sucking determine whether the infant heard a recording of the mother's voice or a recording of a stranger's voice (**Figure 11.40**). For half of the infants, long pauses activated the tape of the mother's voice, and short pauses activated the tape of the stranger's voice. For the other half, these conditions were reversed.

DeCasper and Fifer found that the babies regulated the pauses in their sucking so that they heard their mother's voice more than the stranger's voice. This is a remarkable accomplishment for a 2-day-old, especially because most had been with their mothers for only a few hours between birth and the time they were tested.

Why did the newborns prefer their mother's voice? DeCasper and Fifer suggested that newborns recognized their

Figure 11.39 (a) Data obtained by Olsho et al. (1987), showing the percentage of trials on which the observer indicated that a 3-month-old infant had heard 2,000-Hz tones presented at different intensities. NS indicates no sound. (b) Audibility curves for 3- and 6-month-old infants determined from functions like the one in (a). The curve for 12-month-olds, not shown here, is similar to the curve for 6-month-olds. The adult curve is shown for comparison. (Adapted from Olsho et al., 1988)

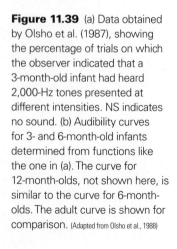
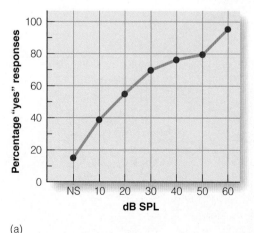

(a)

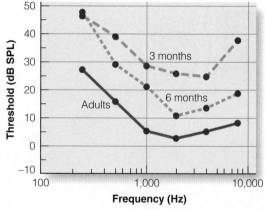

(b)

mother's voice because they had heard the mother talking during development in the womb. This suggestion is supported by the results of another experiment, in which DeCasper and M. J. Spence (1986) had one group of pregnant women read from Dr. Seuss's book *The Cat in the Hat* and another group read the same story with the words *cat* and *hat* replaced with *dog* and *fog*. When the children were born, they regulated the pauses in their sucking in a way that caused them to hear the version of the story their mother had read when they were in the womb. Moon and coworkers (1993) obtained a similar result by showing that 2-day-old infants regulated their sucking to hear a recording of their native language rather than a foreign language (see also DeCasper et al., 1994).

The idea that fetuses become familiar with the sounds they hear in the womb was supported by Barbara Kisilevsky and coworkers (2003), who presented loud (95-dB) recordings of the mother reading a 2-minute passage and a stranger reading a 2-minute passage through a loudspeaker held 10 cm above the abdomen of full-term pregnant women. When they measured the fetus's movement and heart rate as these recordings were being presented, they found that the fetus moved more in response to the mother's voice, and that heart rate increased in response to the mother's voice but decreased in response to the stranger's voice. Kisilevsky concluded from these results that fetal voice processing is influenced by experience, just as the results of earlier experiments had suggested (see also Kisilevsky et al., 2009).

TEST YOURSELF 11.3

1. Describe place theory.
2. How is place theory challenged by the effect of the missing fundamental? How can a modification of place theory explain the effect of the missing fundamental?

3. Describe the Burns and Viemeister experiment, which used amplitude-modulated noise, and its implications for place theory.
4. What is the evidence supporting the idea that pitch perception depends on the timing of auditory nerve firing?
5. What are resolved and unresolved harmonics? What is the connection between resolved harmonics and place theory?
6. What problems do Oxenham et al.'s (2011) experiment pose for understanding the physiology of pitch perception?
7. Describe the pathway that leads from the ear to the brain.
8. Describe the auditory areas in the brain.
9. Describe the experiments that suggest a relationship between the firing of neurons in the auditory cortex and the pitch of complex tones in (a) the marmoset and (b) humans.
10. What is the connection between hair cell damage and hearing loss? Exposure to occupational or leisure noise and hearing loss?
11. What is hidden hearing loss?
12. What is a cochlear implant? Why do we say that it is a practical application that can be traced to discoveries of basic research?
13. Describe the procedures for measuring auditory thresholds in infants. How does the infant's audibility curve compare to the adult curve?
14. Describe experiments that show that newborn infants can recognize their mother's voice, and that this capacity can be traced to the infants' having heard the mother talking during development in the womb.

THINK ABOUT IT

1. We saw that decibels are used to compress the large range of sound pressures in the environment into more manageable numbers. Describe how this same principle is used in the Richter scale to compress the range of earth vibrations from barely perceptible tremors to major earthquakes into a smaller range of numbers.

2. Presbycusis usually begins with loss of high-frequency hearing and gradually involves lower frequencies. From what you know about cochlear function, can you guess why the high frequencies are more vulnerable to damage? (p. 281)

KEY TERMS

Amplitude modulation (p. 276)
Amplitude (p. 261)
Amplitude-modulated noise (p. 276)
Aperiodic sounds (p. 267)
Apex (p. 273)
Attack (p. 267)
Audibility curve (p. 265)
Audiogram (p. 282)
Auditory canal (p. 268)
Auditory receiving area, A1 (p. 278)

Auditory response area (p. 265)
Base (p. 273)
Basilar membrane (p. 270)
Belt area (p. 278)
Characteristic frequency (p. 274)
Cilia (p. 270)
Cochlea (p. 269)
Cochlear amplifier (p. 275)
Cochlear implant (p. 283)
Cochlear nucleus (p. 278)

Cochlear partition (p. 269)
Core area (p. 278)
Decay (p. 267)
Decibel (dB) (p. 262)
Eardrum (p. 268)
Effect of the missing fundamental (p. 266)
Equal loudness curves (p. 265)
First harmonic (p. 264)
Frequency (p. 261)

Frequency spectra (p. 264)
Frequency tuning curve (p. 274)
Fundamental frequency (p. 264)
Fundamental (p. 264)
Hair cells (p. 270)
Harmonic (p. 264)
Hertz (Hz) (p. 262)
Hidden hearing loss (p. 282)
Higher harmonics (p. 264)
Incus (p. 268)
Inferior colliculus (p. 278)
Inner ear (p. 269)
Inner hair cells (p. 270)
Leisure noise (p. 282)
Level (p. 263)
Loudness (p. 264)
Malleus (p. 268)
Medial geniculate nucleus (p. 278)
Middle ear (p. 268)
Middle-ear muscles (p. 269)

Noise (p. 276)
Noise-induced hearing loss (p. 282)
Octave (p. 266)
Organ of Corti (p. 270)
Ossicles (p. 268)
Outer ear (p. 268)
Outer hair cells (p. 270)
Oval window (p. 268)
Parabelt area (p. 279)
Periodic sounds (p. 267)
Periodic tone (p. 264)
Phase locking (p. 272)
Pinnae (p. 268)
Pitch neurons (p. 279)
Pitch (p. 266)
Place theory (p. 276)
Presbycusis (p. 281)
Primary auditory cortex (p. 278)
Pure tone (p. 261)
Resolved harmonics (p. 277)

Resonance (p. 268)
Resonant frequency (p. 268)
Sound level (p. 263)
Sound (p. 260)
Sound pressure level (p. 263)
Sound wave (p. 261)
SPL (p. 263)
Stapes (p. 268)
Subcortical structures (p. 278)
Superior olivary nucleus (p. 278)
Tectorial membrane, (p. 270)
Temporal coding (p. 277)
Timbre (p. 267)
Tip links (p. 271)
Tone chroma (p. 266)
Tone height (p. 266)
Tonotopic map (p. 274)
Traveling wave (p. 272)
Tympanic membrane (p. 268)
Unresolved harmonics (p. 277)

These musicians draw their bows over strings, creating vibrations that result in musical sounds. In this chapter, we consider how we perceive where a sound is coming from, how our perceptions are influenced by the acoustics of a room, how we are able to separate the sounds of different instruments from one another, and how we perceive music as patterns of sound in time.

CHAPTER 12

Hearing II: Location and Organization

CHAPTER CONTENTS

Location

Auditory Localization
Binaural Cues for Sound Localization
Monaural Cue for Localization

The Physiology of Auditory Localization
The Jeffress Neural Coincidence Model
Broad ITD Tuning Curves in Mammals
Cortical Mechanisms of Localization

Hearing Inside Rooms
Perceiving Two Sounds That Reach
   the Ears at Different Times
Architectural Acoustics

Organization

The Auditory Scene: Separating Sound Sources
Location
Onset Time
Timbre and Pitch
Auditory Continuity
Experience

Musical Organization: Melody
What Is Melody?
Phrases
Grouping
Tonality
Expectation

Musical Organization: Rhythm
What Is Rhythm?
The Beat
Meter

SOMETHING TO CONSIDER: Connections Between Hearing and Vision
Hearing and Vision: Perceptions
Hearing and Vision: Physiology

THINK ABOUT IT

Some Questions We Will Consider:

- What makes it possible to tell where a sound is coming from in space? (p. 290)

- Why does music sound better in some concert halls than in others? (p. 298)

- When we are listening to a number of musical instruments playing at the same time, how can we perceptually separate the sounds coming from the different instruments? (p. 301)

- Why do we move to the beat of music? (p. 309)

The last chapter was focused mainly on laboratory studies of pitch, staying mostly within the inner ear, with a short trip to the cortex. This chapter broadens our perception beyond pitch to consider other auditory qualities, most of which depend on higher-order processes. Here are four "scenarios," each of which is relevant to one of the auditory qualities we will discuss.

Scenario 1: Something Suddenly Happens Outside You're walking down the street, lost in thought, although paying enough attention to avoid bumping into oncoming pedestrians. Suddenly, you hear a screech of brakes and a woman screaming. You quickly turn to the right and see that no one was hurt. But how did you know to turn to the right, and where to look? Somehow you could tell where the sound was coming from. This is *auditory localization* (pages 290–298).

Scenario 2: Some Sounds Inside You're inside a deli, which is actually just a small room with a meat counter at one end. You take a number and are waiting your turn as the butcher calls numbers, one by one. Why do you hear each number only once, despite the fact that the sound waves the butcher is producing when he speaks travel two different paths to reach your ears: (1) directly, from his mouth to your ears; and (2) indirectly, bouncing off the walls of the small room to your ears. As you will see, what you hear depends mainly on sound reaching your ears along the first path, a phenomenon called the *precedence effect* (page 299).

Scenario 3: A Conversation With a Friend You're sitting in a noisy coffee shop, talking with a friend. You can hear her, but there are many other sounds as well—other people talking nearby, the screech of the espresso machine, music from a speaker overhead. How you can separate the sounds your friend is speaking from all the other sounds in the room? The ability to separate one stream of sound from another is called *auditory stream segregation* (page 309).

Scenario 4: At a Concert You're at a concert, standing right in front of the stage. The band's first number is one of your favorites, and you're having a hard time standing still. Why do we often have the urge to move to music when we hear it? Music taps into mechanisms beyond those just responsible for hearing sound. One of those mechanisms, as we will see, involves the connection between music and movement (pages 310–311).

This chapter considers these situations in two sections. In the first part of the chapter, *Location*, we consider the mechanisms that enable us to determine where sound is coming from (Scenario 1) and the mechanisms that enable us to not be confused by sound waves that are bouncing off the walls of a room (Scenario 2). In the second part, *Organization*, we consider how we can separate individual sounds when many sounds are occurring simultaneously (Scenario 3). We also consider how the sounds of music are organized to create melodies, and how the beat of music makes us want to move (Scenario 4).

Location

Every sound comes from someplace. This may sound like an obvious statement because, of course, something, with a specific location, must be producing each sound. But while we often pay attention to where visible objects are, because they may be destinations to reach, things to avoid, or scenes to observe, we often pay less attention to where sounds are coming from. But locating sounds, especially ones that might signal danger, can be important for our survival. And even though most sounds don't signal danger, sounds and their locations are constantly structuring our auditory environment. In this section, we describe how you are able to extract information that indicates where a sound came from, and how the brain uses this information to create a neural representation of sounds in space.

Auditory Localization

After reading this sentence, close your eyes for a moment, listen, and notice what sounds you hear and where they are coming from. When I do this right now, sitting in a coffee shop, I hear the beat and vocals of a song coming from a speaker above my head and slightly behind me, a woman talking somewhere in front of me, and the "fizzy" sound of an espresso maker off to the left.

I hear each of the sounds—the music, the talking, and the mechanical fizzing sound as coming from different locations in space. These sounds at different locations create an **auditory space**, which exists all around, wherever there is sound. The locating of sound sources in auditory space is called **auditory localization**. We can appreciate the problem the auditory system faces in determining these locations by comparing the information for location for vision and hearing.

To do this, consider the tweeting bird and the meowing cat in **Figure 12.1**. Visual information for the relative locations of the bird and the cat is contained in the images of the bird and the cat on the surface of the retina. The ear, however, is different. The bird's "tweet, tweet" and the cat's "meow" stimulate the cochlea based on their sound frequencies, and as we saw in Chapter 11, these frequencies cause patterns of nerve firing

that result in our perception of a tone's pitch and timbre. But activation of nerve fibers in the cochlea is based on the tones' frequency components and not on where the tones are coming from. This means that two tones with the same frequency that originate in different locations will activate the same hair cells and nerve fibers in the cochlea. The auditory system must therefore use other information to determine location. The information it uses involves **location cues** that are created by the way sound interacts with the listener's head and ears.

There are two kinds of location cues: *binaural cues*, which depend on both ears, and *monaural cues*, which depend on just one ear. Researchers studying these cues have determined how well people can locate the position of a sound in three dimensions: the **azimuth**, which extends from left to right (**Figure 12.2**); **elevation**, which extends up and down; and the **distance** of the sound source from the listener. In this chapter, we will focus on the azimuth and elevation.

Binaural Cues for Sound Localization

Binaural cues use information reaching both ears to determine the azimuth (left–right position) of sounds. The two binaural cues are *interaural level difference* and *interaural time difference*. Both are based on a comparison of the sound signals reaching the left and right ears. Sounds that are off to the side are louder at one ear than the other and reach one ear before the other.

Interaural Level Difference Interaural level difference (ILD) is based on the difference in the sound pressure level (or just "level") of the sound reaching the two ears. A difference in level between the two ears occurs because the head is a barrier that creates an **acoustic shadow**, reducing the intensity of sounds that reach the far ear. This reduction of intensity at the far ear occurs for high-frequency sounds, as shown in **Figure 12.3a**, but not for low-frequency sounds, as shown in **Figure 12.3b**.

We can understand why an ILD occurs for high frequencies but not for low frequencies by drawing an analogy between sound waves and water waves. Consider, for example, a situation in which small ripples in the water are approaching

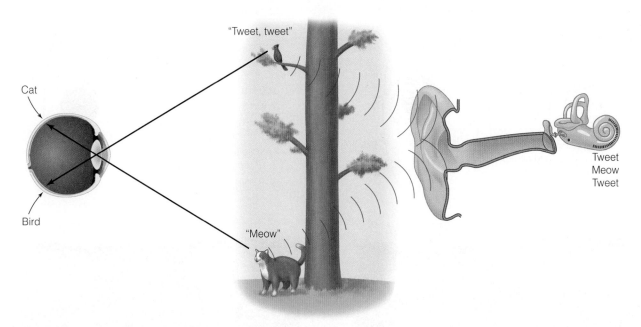

Figure 12.1 Comparing location information for vision and hearing. *Vision:* The bird and the cat, which are located at different places, are imaged on different places on the retina. *Hearing:* The frequencies in the sounds from the bird and cat are spread out over the cochlea, with no regard to the animals' locations.

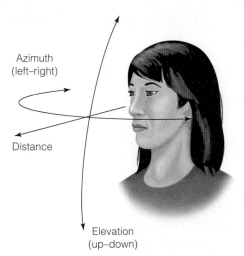

Figure 12.2 The three directions used for studying sound localization: azimuth (left–right), elevation (up–down), and distance.

the boat in **Figure 12.3c**. Because the ripples are small compared to the boat, they bounce off the side of the boat and go no further. Now imagine the same ripples approaching the cattails in **Figure 12.3d**. Because the distance between the ripples is large compared to the stems of the cattails, the ripples are hardly disturbed and continue on their way. These two examples illustrate that an object has a large effect on the wave if it is larger than the distance between the waves (as occurs when short high-frequency sound waves hit the head), but has a small effect if it is smaller than the distance between the waves (as occurs for longer low-frequency sound waves). For this reason, the ILD is an effective cue for location only for high-frequency sounds.

Interaural Time Difference The other binaural cue, **interaural time difference (ITD)**, is the time difference between when a sound reaches the left ear and when it reaches the right ear (**Figure 12.4**). If the source is located directly in front of the listener, at A, the distance to each ear is the same; the sound reaches the left and right ears simultaneously, so the ITD is zero. However, if a source is located off to the side, at B, the sound reaches the right ear before it reaches the left ear. Because the ITD becomes larger as sound sources are located more to the side, the magnitude of the ITD can be used as a cue to determine a sound's location. Behavioral experiments show that ITD is most effective for determining the locations of low-frequency sounds (Wightman & Kistler, 1992). Thus ITD (which works for low frequencies) and ILD (which works for high frequencies) cover the frequency range for hearing. However, because most sounds in the environment contain low-frequency components, ITD is the dominant binaural cue for hearing (Wightman & Kistler, 1992).

The Cone of Confusion While the time and level differences provide information that enables people to judge location along the azimuth coordinate, they provide ambiguous information about the elevation of a sound source. You can understand why this is so by imagining you are extending your hand directly in front of you at arm's length and are holding a sound source. Because the source would be equidistant from your left and right ears, the time and level differences would be zero. If you now imagine moving your hand straight up, increasing the sound source's elevation, the source will still be equidistant from the two ears, so both time and level differences are still zero.

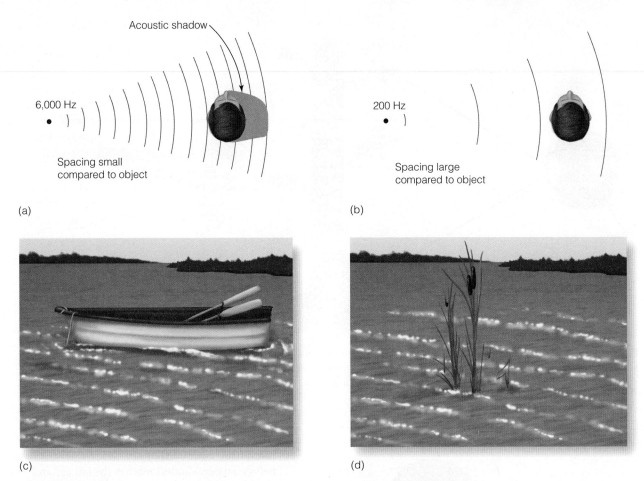

Figure 12.3 Why interaural level difference (ILD) occurs for high frequencies but not for low frequencies. (a) Person listening to a high-frequency sound; (b) person listening to a low-frequency sound. (c) When the spacing between waves is smaller than the size of the object, illustrated here by water ripples that are smaller than the boat, the waves are stopped by the object. This occurs for the high-frequency sound waves in (a) and causes the sound intensity to be lower on the far side of the listener's head. (d) When the spacing between waves is larger than the size of the object, as occurs for the water ripples and the narrow stalks of the cattails, the object does not interfere with the waves. This occurs for the low-frequency sound waves in (b), so the sound intensity on the far side of the head is not affected.

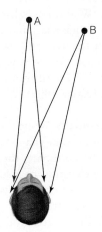

Figure 12.4 The principle behind interaural time difference (ITD). The tone directly in front of the listener, at A, reaches the left and right ears at the same time. However, when the tone is moved to the side, at B, it reaches the listener's right ear before it reaches the left ear.

Because the time and level differences can be the same at a number of different elevations, they cannot reliably indicate the elevation of the sound source. Similar ambiguous information is provided when the sound source is off to the side. These places of ambiguity are illustrated by the **cone of confusion** shown in **Figure 12.5**. All points on the surface of this cone have the same ILD and ITD. For example, points A and B would result in the same ILD and ITD because the distance from A to the left and right ears is the same as the distance from B to the right and left ears. Similar situations occur for other points on the cone, and there are other smaller and larger cones as well. In other words, there are many locations in space where two sounds could result in the same ILD and ITD.

Monaural Cue for Localization

The ambiguous nature of the information provided by the ILD and ITD at different elevations means that another source of information is needed to locate sounds along the elevation

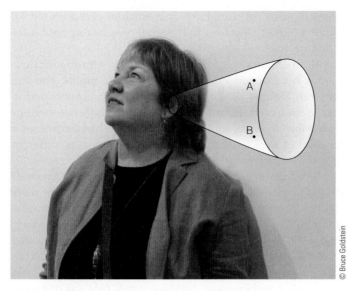

Figure 12.5 The "cone of confusion." There are many pairs of points on this cone that have the same left-ear distance and right-ear distance and so result in the same ITD and ILD. There are also other cones in addition to this one.

coordinate. This information is provided by a **monaural cue**—a cue that depends on information from only one ear.

The primary monaural cue for localization is called a **spectral cue**, because the information for localization is contained in differences in the distribution (or spectrum) of frequencies that reach each ear from different locations. These differences are caused by the fact that before the sound stimulus enters the auditory canal, it is reflected from the head and within the various folds of the pinnae (**Figure 12.6a**). The effect of this interaction with the head and pinnae has been measured by placing small microphones inside a listener's ears

and comparing frequencies from sounds that are coming from different directions.

This effect is illustrated in **Figure 12.6b**, which shows the frequencies picked up by the microphone when a broadband sound (one containing many frequencies) is presented at elevations of 15 degrees above the head and 15 degrees below the head. Sounds coming from these two locations would result in the same ILD and ITD because they are the same distance from the left and right ears, but differences in the way the sounds bounce around within the pinna create different patterns of frequencies for the two locations (King et al., 2001). The importance of the pinnae for determining elevation has been demonstrated by showing that smoothing out the nooks and crannies of the pinnae with molding compound makes it difficult to locate sounds along the elevation coordinate (Gardner & Gardner, 1973).

The idea that localization can be affected by using a mold to change the inside contours of the pinnae was also demonstrated by Paul Hofman and coworkers (1998). They determined how localization changes when the mold is worn for several weeks, and then what happens when the mold is removed. The results for one listener's localization performance measured before the mold was inserted are shown in **Figure 12.7a**. Sounds were presented at positions indicated by the intersections of the black grid. Average localization performance is indicated by the blue grid. The overlap between the two grids indicates that localization was fairly accurate.

After measuring initial performance, Hofman fitted his listeners with molds that altered the shape of the pinnae and therefore changed the spectral cue. **Figure 12.7b** shows that localization performance is poor for the elevation coordinate immediately after the mold is inserted, but locations can still be judged at locations along the azimuth coordinate. This

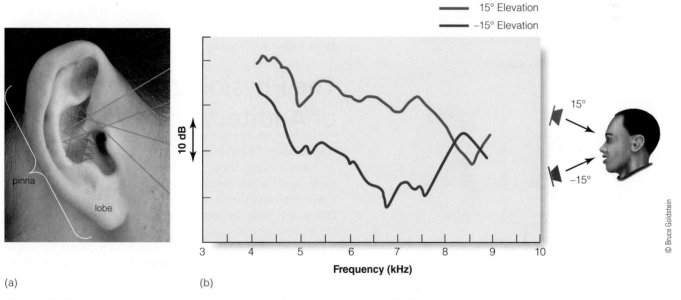

(a)　　　　(b)

Figure 12.6 (a) Pinna showing sound bouncing around in nooks and crannies. (b) Frequency spectra recorded by a small microphone inside the listener's right ear for the same broadband sound coming from two different locations. The difference in the pattern when the sound is 15 degrees above the head (blue curve) and 15 degrees below the head (red curve) is caused by the way different frequencies bounce around within the pinna when entering it from different angles. (Adapted from Plack, 2005; photo by Bruce Goldstein)

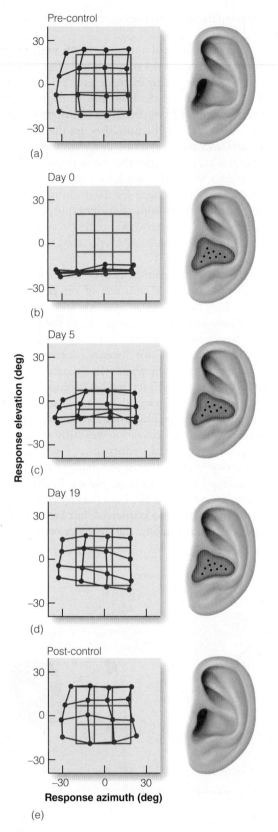

Figure 12.7 How localization changes when a mold is placed in the ear. See text for explanation. (Reprinted from King et al., 2001)

is exactly what we would expect if binaural cues are used for judging azimuth location and spectral cues are responsible for judging elevation locations.

Hofman continued his experiment by retesting localization as his listeners continued to wear the molds. You can see from **Figures 12.7c** and **12.7d** that localization performance improved, until by 19 days localization had become reasonably accurate. Apparently, the person had learned, over a period of weeks, to associate new spectral cues to different directions in space.

What do you think happened when the molds were removed? It would be logical to expect that once adapted to the new set of spectral cues created by the molds, localization performance would suffer when the molds were removed. However, as shown in **Figure 12.7e**, localization remained excellent immediately after removal of the ear molds. Apparently, training with the molds created a new set of correlations between spectral cues and location, but the old correlation was still there as well. One way this could occur is if different sets of neurons were involved in responding to each set of spectral cues, just as separate brain areas are involved in processing different languages in people who speak more than one language (King et al., 2001; Wightman & Kistler, 1998; also see Van Wanrooij & Van Opstal, 2005).

We have seen that each type of cue works best for different frequencies and different coordinates. ILDs and ITDs work for judging azimuth location, with ILD best for high frequencies and ITD for low frequencies. Spectral cues work best for judging elevation, especially at higher frequencies. These cues work together to help us locate sounds. In real-world listening, we also move our heads, which provides additional ILD, ITD, and spectral information that helps minimize the effect of the cone of confusion and helps locate continuous sounds. Vision also plays a role in sound localization, as when you hear talking and see a person making gestures and lip movements that match what you are hearing. Thus, the richness of the environment and our ability to actively search for information help us zero in on a sound's location.

The Physiology of Auditory Localization

Having identified the cues that are associated with where a sound is coming from, we now ask how the information in these cues is represented in the nervous system. Are there neurons in the auditory system that signal ILD or ITD? Because ITD is the most important binaural cue for most listening situations, we will focus on this cue. We begin by describing a neural circuit that was proposed in 1948 by Lloyd Jeffress to show how signals from the left and right ears can be combined to determine the ITD (Vonderschen & Wagner, 2014).

The Jeffress Neural Coincidence Model

The **Jeffress model** of auditory localization proposes that neurons are wired so they each receive signals from the two ears,

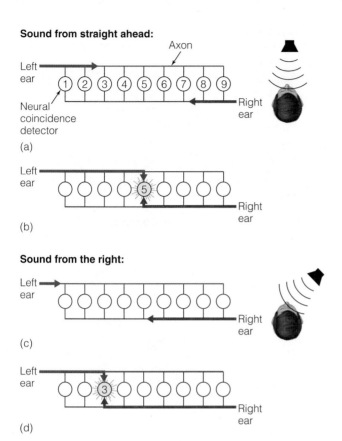

Sound from straight ahead:

(a)

(b)

Sound from the right:

(c)

(d)

Figure 12.8 How the circuit proposed by Jeffress operates. Axons transmit signals from the left ear (blue) and the right ear (red) to neurons, indicated by circles. (a) Sound in front. Signals start in left and right channels simultaneously. (b) Signals meet at neuron 5, causing it to fire. (c) Sound to the right. Signal starts in the right channel first. (d) Signals meet at neuron 3, causing it to fire. (Adapted from Plack, 2005)

as shown in **Figure 12.8**. Signals from the left ear arrive along the blue axon, and signals from the right ear arrive along the red axon.

If the sound source is directly in front of the listener, the sound reaches the left and right ears simultaneously, and signals from the left and right ears start out together, as shown in **Figure 12.8a**. As each signal travels along its axon, it stimulates each neuron in turn. At the beginning of the journey, neurons receive signals from only the left ear (neurons 1, 2, 3) or the right ear (neurons 9, 8, 7), but not both, and they do not fire. But when the signals both reach neuron 5 together, that neuron fires (**Figure 12.8b**). This neuron and the others in this circuit are called **coincidence detectors**, because they only fire when both signals coincide by arriving at the neuron simultaneously. The firing of neuron 5 indicates that ITD = 0.

If the sound comes from the right, as in **Figure 12.8c**, the sound reaches the right ear first, so the ITD is not zero. The signal from the right ear has a head start, as shown in Figure 12.8c, and both signals reach neuron 3 simultaneously (**Figure 12.8d**), so this neuron fires. This neuron, therefore, detects ITDs that occur when the sound is coming from a specific location on the right. The other neurons in the circuit fire to locations corresponding to other ITDs. We can therefore

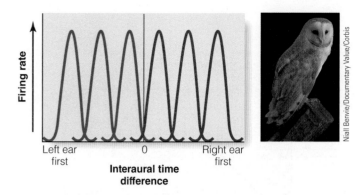

Figure 12.9 ITD tuning curves for six neurons that each respond to a narrow range of ITDs. The neurons on the left respond when sound reaches the left ear first. The ones on the right respond when sound reaches the right ear first. Neurons such as these have been recorded from the barn owl and other animals. However, when we consider mammals, another story emerges, as illustrated in Figure 12.10. (Adapted from McAlpine & Grothe, 2003)

call these coincidence detectors **ITD detectors**, since each one fires best to a particular ITD.

The Jeffress model therefore proposes a circuit that contains a series of ITD detectors, each tuned to respond best to a specific ITD. According to this idea, the ITD will be indicated by which ITD neuron is firing. This has been called a "place code" because ITD is indicated by the place (which neuron) where the activity occurs.

One way to describe the properties of ITD neurons is to measure **ITD tuning curves**, which plot the neuron's firing rate against the ITD. Recording from neurons in the brainstem of the barn owl, which has excellent auditory localization abilities, has revealed narrow tuning curves that respond best to specific ITDs, like the ones in **Figure 12.9** (Carr & Konishi, 1990; McAlpine, 2005). The neurons associated with the curves on the left (blue) fire when the sound reaches the left ear first, and the ones on the right (red) fire when sound reaches the right ear first. These are the tuning curves that are predicted by the Jeffress model, because each neuron responds best to a specific ITD and the response drops off rapidly for other ITDs. The place code proposed by the Jeffress model, with its narrow tuning curves, works for owls and other birds, but the situation is different for mammals.

Broad ITD Tuning Curves in Mammals

The results of research in which ITD tuning curves are recorded from mammals may appear, at first glance, to support the Jeffress model. For example, **Figure 12.10** shows an ITD tuning curve of a neuron in the gerbil's superior olivary nucleus (solid line) (see Figure 11.30, page 278) (Pecka et al., 2008). This curve has a peak in the middle and drops off on either side. However, when we plot the owl curve on the same graph (dashed line), we can see that the gerbil curve is much broader than the owl curve. In fact, the gerbil curve is so broad that it extends far outside the range of ITDs that are actually involved in sound localization, indicated by the light bar (also see Siveke et al., 2006).

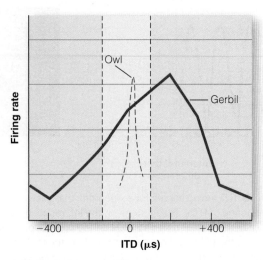

Figure 12.10 Solid curve: ITD tuning curve for a neuron in the gerbil superior olivary nucleus. Dashed curve: ITD tuning curve for a neuron in the barn owl's inferior colliculus. The owl curve appears extremely narrow because of the expanded time scale compared to Figure 12.9. The gerbil curve is broader than the range of ITDs that typically occur in the environment. This range is indicated by the light bar (between the dashed lines).

Because of the broadness of the ITD curves in mammals, it has been proposed that coding for localization is based on broadly tuned neurons like the ones shown in **Figure 12.11a** (Grothe et al., 2010; McAlpine, 2005). According to this idea, there are broadly tuned neurons in the right hemisphere that respond when sound is coming from the left and broadly tuned neurons in the left hemisphere that respond when sound is coming from the right. The location of a sound is indicated by relative responses of these two types of broadly tuned neurons. For example, a sound from the left would cause the pattern of response shown in the left pair of bars in **Figure 12.11b**; a sound located straight ahead, by the middle pair of bars; and a sound to the right, by the far right bars.

This type of coding resembles the population coding we described in Chapter 3, in which information in the nervous system is based on the pattern of neural responding. This is, in fact, how the visual system signals different wavelengths of light, as we saw when we discussed color vision in Chapter 9, in which wavelengths are signaled by the pattern of response of three different cone pigments (Figure 9.12, page 204).

To summarize research on the neural mechanism of binaural localization, we can conclude that it is based on *sharply tuned* neurons for birds and *broadly tuned* neurons for mammals. The code for birds is a *place code* because the ITD is indicated by firing of neurons at a specific place in the nervous system. The code for mammals is a *population code* because the ITD is determined by the firing of many broadly tuned neurons working together. Next, we consider one more piece of the story for mammals, which goes beyond considering how the ITD is coded by neurons to consider how information about localization is organized in the cortex.

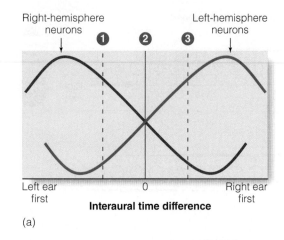

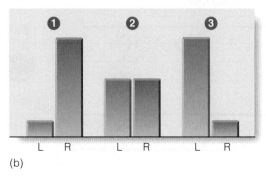

Figure 12.11 (a) ITD tuning curves for broadly tuned neurons like the one shown in Figure 12.10a. The left curve represents the tuning of neurons in the right hemisphere; the right curve is the tuning of neurons in the left hemisphere. (b) Patterns of response of the broadly tuned curves for stimuli coming from the left, in front, and from the right. (Adapted from McAlpine, 2005)

Cortical Mechanisms of Localization

The neural basis of binaural localization begins along the pathway from the cochlea to the brain, in the superior olivary nucleus (remember the acronym SONIC MG, that stands for superior olivary nucleus, inferior colliculus, and medial geniculate; see Figure 11.30, page 278), which is the first place that receives signals from the left and right ears. Although processing for location begins as signals are traveling from the ear to the cortex, we will focus on the cortex, beginning with area A1 (**Figure 12.12**).

Evidence That Area A1 Is Involved in Locating Sound
In a pioneering study, Dewey Neff and coworkers (1956) placed cats about 8 feet away from two food boxes—one about 3 feet to the left, and one about 3 feet to the right. The cats were rewarded with food if they approached the sound of a buzzer located behind one of the boxes. Once the cats learned this localization task, the auditory areas on both sides of the cortex were lesioned (see Method: Brain Ablation, p. 79), and although the cats were then trained for more than 5 months, they were never able to relearn how to localize the sounds. Based on this finding, Neff concluded that an intact auditory cortex is necessary for accurate localization of sounds in space.

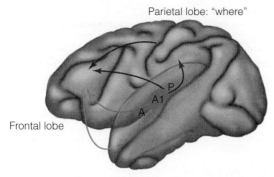

Parietal lobe: "where"

Frontal lobe

Temporal lobe: "what"

Figure 12.12 Auditory pathways in the monkey cortex. Part of area A1 is visible. The core, belt and parabelt areas are not visible because they are hidden within the fold of the temporal lobe. The pathways shown here connect to the anterior and posterior belt areas. A = anterior; P = posterior; green = auditory *what* pathway; red = auditory *where* pathway. (Adapted from Rauschecker & Scott, 2009)

Later studies conducted more than 50 years after Neff's research focused more precisely on area A1. Fernando Nodal and coworkers (2010) showed that lesioning A1 in ferrets decreased, but did not totally eliminate, the ferrets' ability to localize sounds. Another demonstration that A1 is involved in localization was provided by Shveta Malhotra and Stephen Lomber (2007), who showed that deactivating A1 in cats by cooling the cortex results in poor localization (also see Malhotra et al., 2008). These studies of A1 and localization are summarized in **Table 12.1**.

Evidence That the Posterior Belt Area Is Involved in Locating Sound

In Chapter 11, we introduced the core area (which contains area A1), and the belt and parabelt auditory areas, by showing the cortex with the temporal lobe pulled back to reveal these areas, which are hidden within the fold of the temporal lobe (Figure 11.31, page 279). In Figure 12.12, the temporal lobe isn't pulled back, so just A1 and a small area around it are visible. We will be focusing on the **posterior belt area**, which is located toward the back of the cortex, indicated by the *P*, and the **anterior belt area**, which is located toward the front, indicated by the *A*. We first focus on the posterior belt area.

Gregg Recanzone (2000) compared the spatial tuning of neurons in A1 and neurons in the posterior belt. He did this by recording from neurons in the monkey and determining how a neuron responded when a sound source was moved to different locations. He found that neurons in A1 respond when a sound is moved within a specific area of space and don't

respond outside that area. But when Recanzone recorded from neurons in the posterior belt area, he found that these neurons respond to sound within an even smaller area of space, indicating that spatial tuning is better in this area. Thus, neurons in the posterior belt provide more precise information than A1 neurons about the location of sound sources, which suggests that the posterior belt is involved in sound localization.

Additional evidence associating the posterior belt with sound localization is provided by Stephen Lomber and Shveta Malhotra (2008), who showed that temporarily deactivating a cat's posterior auditory areas by cooling the cortex disrupts the cat's ability to localize sounds (**Figure 12.13a**). Cooling the posterior areas does not, however, affect the cat's ability to tell the difference between two sequences of sound presented with different timing patterns. The results of studies on the posterior belt are summarized in **Table 12.2**.

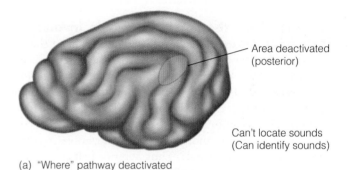

Area deactivated (posterior)

Can't locate sounds (Can identify sounds)

(a) "Where" pathway deactivated

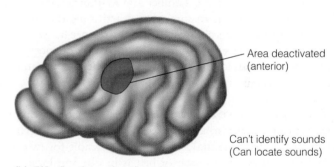

Area deactivated (anterior)

Can't identify sounds (Can locate sounds)

(b) "What" pathway deactivated

Figure 12.13 Results of Lomber and Malhotra's (2008) experiment. (a) When the posterior (*where*) auditory area was deactivated by presenting a cooling probe within the green area, the cat could not locate sounds but could identify sounds. (b) When the anterior (*what*) auditory area of the cat was deactivated by presenting a small cooling probe within the purple area, the cat could not identify sounds but could locate sounds.

Table 12.1 Evidence That A1 Is Involved in Localization

REFERENCE	WHAT DONE	RESULT
Neff et al. (1956)	Cat auditory areas destroyed	Localization ability lost
Nodal et al. (2010)	Ferret A1 destroyed	Localization ability decreased
Malhotra & Lomber (2007)	Cat A1 cooled	Localization ability decreased

Table 12.2 Evidence That the Posterior Belt Is Involved in Localization

REFERENCE	WHAT DONE	RESULT
Recanzone (2000)	Tuning curves of A1 and posterior belt neurons measured	Posterior belt tuning curves are narrower than A1 tuning curves
Lomber & Malhotra (2008)	Cat posterior belt cooled	Localization ability decreased (but ability to tell the difference between two patterns of sound not affected)

Table 12.3 Evidence That the Anterior Belt Is Involved in Perceiving Sound

REFERENCE	WHAT DONE	RESULT
Rauschecker & Tian (2000)	Best stimuli for A1 and anterior belt neurons determined	Anterior belt neurons respond best to more complex sounds
Lomber & Malhotra (2008)	Cat anterior belt cooled	Ability to tell the difference between two patterns of sound decreased (but localization not affected)

Evidence That the Anterior Belt Is Involved in Perceiving Sound Moving toward the front of the cortex, researchers have found evidence that the anterior belt is involved not in localization but in perceiving sound. Josef Rauschecker and Bio Tian (2000) found that while monkey A1 neurons are activated by simple sounds such as pure tones, neurons in the anterior area of the belt respond to more complex sounds, such as monkey calls—vocalizations recorded from monkeys in the jungle. Thus anterior belt neurons are involved in identifying complex sounds.

Returning to the cat, Lomber and Malhotra (2008) used the cooling technique to show that deactivating the anterior belt disrupts the cat's ability to tell the difference between two timing patterns of sound (**Figure 12.13b**) but does not affect the cat's ability to localize sounds. The results of the anterior belt studies are summarized in **Table 12.3**.

***What* and *Where* Auditory Pathways** Considering all of the studies summarized in Tables 12.2 and 12.3, researchers have concluded that the belt area is responsible for two different functions: The posterior belt is involved in localizing sounds, and the anterior belt is involved in perceiving complex sounds and patterns of sound. Additional research, which we won't describe, has shown that these two parts of the belt are the starting points for two auditory pathways, a *what* auditory pathway, which extends from the anterior belt to the temporal lobe and the frontal cortex (green arrows in Figure 12.12), and a *where* auditory pathway, which extends from the posterior belt to the parietal lobe and the frontal cortex (red arrows). The *what* pathway is associated with perceiving sounds and the *where* pathway with locating sounds.

If *what* and *where* pathways sound familiar, it is because we described *what* and *where* pathways for vision in Chapter 4 (see Figure 4.14, page 80). Thus, the idea of pathways serving *what* and *where* functions is a general principle that occurs for both hearing and vision. It is also important to note that although the research we have described is on ferrets, cats, and monkeys, evidence for auditory *what* and *where* auditory functions in human

has been provided by using brain scanning to show that *what* and *where* tasks activate different brain areas in humans (Alain et al., 2001, 2009; De Santis et al., 2007; Wissinger et al., 2001).

We have clearly come a long way from early experiments like Neff's done in the 1950s, which focused on determining the function of large areas of the auditory cortex. In contrast, recent experiments have focused on smaller auditory areas and have also shown how auditory processing extends beyond the auditory areas in the temporal lobe to other areas in the cortex. We will have more to say about auditory pathways when we consider speech perception in Chapter 13.

Hearing Inside Rooms

In this chapter and Chapter 11, we have seen that our perception of sound depends on various properties of the sound, including its frequency, sound level, and location in space. But we have left out the fact that in our normal everyday experience, we hear sounds in a specific setting, such as a small room, a large auditorium, or outdoors. As we consider this aspect of hearing, we will see why we perceive sounds differently when we are outside and inside, and how our perception of sound quality is affected by specific properties of indoor environments.

Figure 12.14 shows how the nature of the sound reaching your ears depends on the environment in which you hear the sound. If you are listening to someone playing a guitar on an outdoor stage, your perception is based mainly on **direct sound**, sound that reaches your ears directly, as shown in **Figure 12.14a**. If, however, you are listening to the same guitar in an auditorium, then your perception is based on direct sound, which reaches your ears directly (path 1), plus **indirect sound** (paths 2, 3, and 4), which reaches your ears after bouncing off the auditorium's walls, ceiling, and floor (**Figure 12.14b**).

The fact that sound can reach our ears directly from where the sound is originating and indirectly from other locations creates a potential problem, because even though the sound *originates* in one place, the sound *reaches the listener* from many directions and

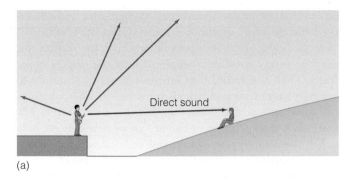

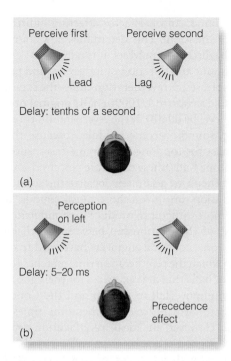

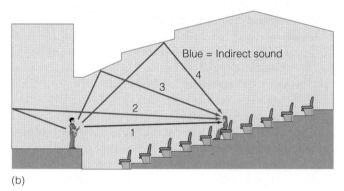

Figure 12.14 (a) When you hear a sound outdoors, sound is radiated in all directions, indicated by the blue arrows, but you hear mainly direct sound, indicated by the red arrow. (b) When you hear a sound inside a room, you hear both direct sound (1) and indirect sound (2, 3, and 4) that is reflected from the walls, floor, and ceiling of the room.

Figure 12.15 (a) When sound is presented first in one speaker and then in the other, with enough time between them, they are heard separately, one after the other. (b) If there is only a short delay between the two sounds, then the sound is perceived to come from the lead speaker only. This is the precedence effect.

at slightly different times. This is the situation that we described in Scenario 2 at the beginning of the chapter, in which some of the sound from the butcher's voice reaches the person directly and some reaches the person after bouncing off the walls. We can understand why we usually perceive just one sound, coming from a single location, in situations such as the concert hall or the deli, by considering the results of research in which listeners were presented with sounds separated by time delays, as would occur when they originate from two different locations.

Perceiving Two Sounds That Reach the Ears at Different Times

Research on sound reflections and the perception of location has usually simplified the problem by having people listen to sounds coming from two loudspeakers separated in space, as shown in **Figure 12.15**. The speaker on the left is the *lead speaker*, and the one on the right is the *lag speaker*. If a sound is presented in the lead speaker followed by a long delay (tenths of a second), and then a sound is presented in the lag speaker, listeners typically hear two separate sounds—one from the left (lead) followed by one from the right (lag). But when the delay between the lead and lag sounds is much shorter, something different happens. Even though the sound is coming from both speakers, listeners hear the sound as coming only from the lead speaker. This situation, in which the sound appears to originate

from the lead speaker, is called the **precedence effect** because we perceive the sound as coming from the source that reaches our ears first (Litovsky et al., 1997, 1999; Wallach et al., 1949). Thus, even though the number called out by the butcher first reaches the listener's ears directly and then is followed a little later by sound arriving along the indirect path, we hear it just once.

The precedence effect governs most of our indoor listening experience. In small rooms, the indirect sounds reflected from the walls have a lower level than the direct sound and reach our ears with delays of about 5 to 10 ms. In larger rooms, like concert halls, the delays are much longer. However, even though our perception of where the sound is coming from is usually determined by the first sound that reaches our ears, the indirect sound, which reaches our ears just slightly later, can affect the *quality* of the sound we hear. The fact that sound quality is determined by both direct and indirect sound is a major concern of the field of architectural acoustics, which is particularly concerned with how to design concert halls.

Architectural Acoustics

Architectural acoustics, the study of how sounds are reflected in rooms, is largely concerned with how indirect sound changes the quality of the sounds we hear in rooms. The major factors affecting indirect sound are the size of the room and the amount of sound absorbed by the walls, ceiling, and floor. If most of the sound is absorbed, then there are few sound reflections and little indirect sound. If most of the sound is reflected, there are many sound reflections and a large amount of indirect sound. Another factor affecting indirect sound is the shape of the room. This determines how sound hits surfaces and the directions in which it is reflected.

The amount and duration of indirect sound produced by a room is expressed as **reverberation time**—the time it takes for the sound to decrease to 1/1000th of its original pressure (or a decrease in level by 60 dB). If the reverberation time of a room is too long, sounds become muddled because the reflected sounds persist for too long. In extreme cases, such as cathedrals with stone walls, these delays are perceived as echoes, and it may be difficult to accurately localize the sound source. If the reverberation time is too short, music sounds "dead," and it becomes more difficult to produce high-intensity sounds.

Because of the relationship between reverberation time and perception, acoustical engineers have tried to design concert halls in which the reverberation time matches the reverberation time of halls that are renowned for their good acoustics, such as Symphony Hall in Boston and the Concertgebouw in Amsterdam, which have reverberation times of about 2.0 seconds. However, an "ideal" reverberation time does not always predict good acoustics. This is illustrated by the problems associated with the design of New York's Philharmonic Hall. When it opened in 1962, Philharmonic Hall had a reverberation time close to the ideal of 2.0 seconds. Even so, the hall was criticized for sounding as though it had a short reverberation time, and musicians in the orchestra complained that they could not hear each other. These criticisms resulted in a series of alterations to the hall, made over many years, until eventually, when none of the alterations proved satisfactory, the entire interior of the hall was destroyed, and in 1992 the hall was completely rebuilt and renamed Avery Fisher Hall. But that's not the end of the story, because even after being rebuilt, the acoustics of Avery Fisher Hall were still not considered adequate. So the hall has been renamed David Geffen Hall, and plans are being made to gut it yet again and rebuild it in 2019.

The experience with Philharmonic Hall, along with new developments in the field of architectural acoustics, has led architectural engineers to consider factors in addition to reverberation time in designing concert halls. Some of these factors have been identified by Leo Beranek (1996), who showed that the following physical measures are associated with how music is perceived in concert halls:

- *Intimacy time:* The time between when sound arrives directly from the stage and when the first reflection arrives. This is related to reverberation but involves just comparing the time between the direct sound and the first reflection, rather than the time it takes for many reflections to die down.
- *Bass ratio:* The ratio of low frequencies to middle frequencies that are reflected from walls and other surfaces.
- *Spaciousness factor:* The fraction of all of the sound received by a listener that is indirect sound.

To determine the optimal values for these physical measures, acoustical engineers measured them in 20 opera houses and 25 symphony halls in 14 countries. By comparing their measurements with ratings of the halls by conductors and music critics, they confirmed that the best concert halls had reverberation times of about 2 seconds, but they found that 1.5 seconds was better for opera houses, with the shorter time being necessary to enable people to hear the singers' voices clearly. They also found that intimacy times of about 20 ms and high bass ratios and spaciousness factors were associated with good acoustics (Glanz, 2000). When these factors have been taken into account in the design of new concert halls, such as the Walt Disney Concert Hall in Los Angeles, the result has been acoustics rivaling the best halls in the world.

In designing Walt Disney Hall, the architects paid attention not only to how the shape, configuration, and materials of the walls and ceiling would affect the acoustics, but also to the absorption properties of the cushions on each of the 2,273 seats. One problem that often occurs in concert halls is that the acoustics depend on the number of people attending a performance, because people's bodies absorb sound. Thus, a hall with good acoustics when full could echo when there are too many empty seats. To deal with this problem, the seat cushions were designed to have the same absorption properties as an "average" person. This means that the hall has the same acoustics when empty or full. This is a great advantage to musicians, who usually rehearse in an empty hall.

Another concert hall with exemplary acoustics is the Leighton Concert Hall in the DeBartolo Performing Arts Center at the University of Notre Dame, which opened in 2004 (**Figure 12.16**). The innovative design of this concert hall features an adjustable acoustic system that makes it possible to adjust the reverberation to between 1.4 and 2.6 seconds. This is achieved by motors that control the position of the canopy over the stage and various panels and banners throughout the hall. These adjustments make it possible to "tune" the hall for different kinds of music, so short reverberation times can be achieved for singing and longer reverberation times for orchestral music.

Having considered how we tell where sounds are coming from, how we can make sense of sounds even when they are bouncing around in rooms, and how characteristics of a room can affect what we hear, we are now ready to take the next step

Figure 12.16 Leighton Concert Hall in the DeBartolo Performing Arts Center at the University of Notre Dame. Reverberation time can be adjusted by changing the position of the panels and banners on the ceiling and draperies on the sides.

in understanding how we make sense of sounds in the environment by considering how we perceptually organize sounds when there are many sound sources.

TEST YOURSELF **12.1**

1. How is auditory space described in terms of three coordinates?
2. What is the basic difference between determining the location of a sound source and determining the location of a visual object?
3. Describe the binaural cues for localization. Indicate the frequencies and directions relative to the listener for which the cues are effective.
4. Describe the monaural cue for localization.
5. What happens to auditory localization when a mold is placed in a person's ear? How well can a person localize sound once he or she has adapted to the mold? What happens when the mold is removed after the person has adapted to it?

6. Describe the Jeffress model, and how neural coding for localization differs for birds and for mammals.
7. Describe how auditory localization is organized in the cortex. What is the evidence that A1 is important for localization? That areas in addition to A1 are involved in localization?
8. Describe the experiments that determined the functions of the anterior and posterior belt areas.
9. What are the *what* and *where* auditory pathways? How are they related to the anterior and posterior belt areas?
10. What is the difference between listening to sound outdoors and indoors? Why does listening indoors create a problem for the auditory system?
11. What is the precedence effect, and what does it do for us perceptually?
12. What are some basic principles of architectural acoustics that have been developed to help design concert halls?
13. Describe some of the techniques used to manipulate the acoustics of some modern concert halls.

Organization

The Auditory Scene: Separating Sound Sources

Our discussion so far has focused on localization—where a sound is coming from. We saw that, in contrast to vision, in which objects at different locations in space create images on different locations on the retina, there is no spatial information on the auditory receptors. Instead, the auditory system uses differences in level and timing between the two ears plus spectral information from sound reflections inside the pinnae to localize sounds. We now add an important complication that occurs constantly in the environment: multiple sources of sound.

At the beginning of the chapter, in Scenario 3, we described two people talking in a noisy coffee shop, with the sounds of music, other people talking, and the espresso machine in the background. The array of sound sources at different locations in the environment is called the **auditory scene**, and the process by which the stimuli produced by each source are separated is called **auditory scene analysis** (Bregman, 1990, 1993; Darwin, 2010; Yost, 2001).

Auditory scene analysis poses a difficult problem because the sounds from different sources are combined into a single acoustic signal, so it is difficult to tell which part of the signal is created by which source just by looking at the waveform of the sound stimulus. We can better understand what we mean when we say that the sounds from different sources are combined into a single acoustic signal by considering the trio in **Figure 12.17**. The guitar, the vocalist, and the keyboard each create their own sound signal, but all of these signals enter the

listener's ear together and so are combined into a single complex waveform. Each of the frequencies in this signal causes the basilar membrane to vibrate, but just as in the case of the bird and the cat in Figure 12.1, in which there was no information on the cochlea for the locations of the two sounds, it isn't obvious what information might be contained in the sound signal to indicate which vibration is created by which sound source.

Listener

Figure 12.17 Each musician produces a sound stimulus, but these signals are combined into one signal, which enters the ear.

How does the auditory system separate each of the frequencies in the "combined" sound signal into information that enables us to hear the guitar, the vocalist, and the keyboard as separate sound sources? In Chapter 5, we posed an analogous question for vision when we asked how the visual system separates elements of a visual scene into separate objects. For vision, we introduced a number of organizing principles, proposed by the Gestalt psychologists and others, that are based on properties of visual stimuli that usually occur in the environment (see page 98). Now, as we turn to the sense of hearing, we will see that a similar situation occurs for auditory stimuli. A number of principles help us perceptually organize elements of an auditory scene, and these principles are based on how sounds are usually organized in the environment. For example, if two sounds start at different times, it is likely that they come from different sources. We will now consider a number of different types of information that are used to analyze auditory scenes.

Location

One way to analyze an auditory scene into its separate components would be to use information about where each source is located. According to this idea, you can separate the sound of the vocalist from the sound of the guitar based on localization cues such as the ILD and ITD. Thus, when two sounds are separated in space, the cue of location helps us separate them perceptually. In addition, when a source moves, it typically follows a continuous path rather than jumping erratically from one place to another. For example, this continuous movement of sound helps us perceive the sound from a passing car as originating from a single source.

But the fact that information other than location is also involved becomes obvious when we consider that we can still separate the different sounds when we hear them through a single loudspeaker (or just one earphone of a portable music player), so that all the sounds are coming from the same location (Litovsky, 2012; Yost, 1997).

Onset Time

As mentioned above, if two sounds start at slightly different times, it is likely that they came from different sources. This occurs often in the environment, because sounds from different sources rarely start at exactly the same time. When sound components do start together, it is likely that they are being created by the same source (Shamma & Micheyl, 2010; Shamma et al., 2011).

Timbre and Pitch

Sounds that have the same timbre or pitch range are often produced by the same source. A flute, for example, doesn't suddenly start sounding like the timbre of a trombone. In fact, the flute and trombone are distinguished not only by their timbres, but also by their pitch ranges. The flute tends to play in a high pitch range, and the trombone in a low one. These distinctions help the listener decide which sounds originate from which source.

Composers made use of grouping by similarity of pitch long before psychologists began studying it. Composers in the Baroque period (1600–1750) knew that when a single instrument plays notes that alternate rapidly between high and low tones, the listener perceives two separate melodies, with the high notes perceived as a single melodic line, and the low notes as another. An excerpt from a composition by J. S. Bach that uses this device is shown in **Figure 12.18**. When this passage is played rapidly, the low notes sound like a single melody, and the high notes sound like another, even though they are played by the same instrument. This separation of different sound sources into perceptually different streams, called *implied polyphony* or *compound melodic line* by musicians, is called **auditory stream segregation** by psychologists (Bregman, 1990; Darwin, 2010; Jones & Yee, 1993; Kondo & Kashino, 2009; Shamma & Micheyl, 2010; Yost & Sheft, 1993).

Albert Bregman and Jeffrey Campbell (1971) demonstrated auditory stream segregation based on pitch by alternating high and low tones, as shown in the sequence in **Figure 12.19**. When the high-pitched tones were slowly alternated with the low-pitched tones, as in **Figure 12.19a**, the tones were heard as part of one stream, one after another: Hi–Lo–Hi–Lo–Hi–Lo, as indicated by the dashed line. But when the tones were alternated very rapidly, the high and low tones became perceptually grouped into two auditory streams; the listener perceived two separate streams of sound, one high-pitched and one low-pitched (**Figure 12.19b**) (see Heise & Miller, 1951; Miller & Heise, 1950, for an early demonstration of auditory stream segregation). This demonstration shows that stream segregation depends not only on pitch but also on the rate at which tones are presented. Thus, returning to the Bach composition, the high and low streams are perceived to be separate if they are played rapidly, but not if they are played slowly.

Figure 12.20 illustrates a demonstration of grouping by similarity of pitch in which two streams of sound are perceived as separated until their pitches become similar. One stream is a series of repeating notes (red), and the other is a scale that goes up (blue) (**Figure 12.20a**). **Figure 12.20b** shows how this

Figure 12.18 Four measures of a composition by J. S. Bach (Choral Prelude on *Jesus Christus unser Heiland*, 1739). When played rapidly, the upper notes become perceptually grouped and the lower notes become perceptually grouped, a phenomenon called *auditory stream segregation*.

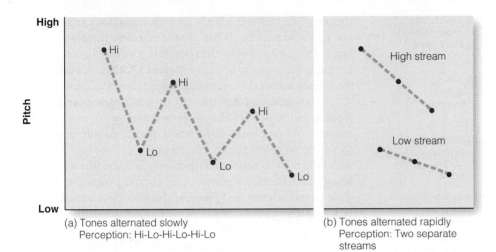

High
Pitch
Low

Hi
Hi
Lo
Lo
Hi
Lo

High stream

Low stream

(a) Tones alternated slowly
    Perception: Hi-Lo-Hi-Lo-Hi-Lo

(b) Tones alternated rapidly
    Perception: Two separate
    streams

Figure 12.19 (a) When high and low tones are alternated slowly, auditory stream segregation does not occur, so the listener perceives alternating high and low tones. (b) Faster alternation results in segregation into high and low streams.

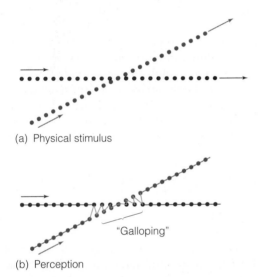

(a) Physical stimulus

"Galloping"

(b) Perception

Figure 12.20 (a) Two sequences of stimuli: a sequence of similar notes (red), and a scale (blue). (b) Perception of these stimuli: Separate streams are perceived when they are far apart in frequency, but the tones appear to jump back and forth between stimuli when the frequencies are in the same range.

stimulus is perceived if the tones are presented fairly rapidly. At first the two streams are separated, so listeners simultaneously perceive the same note repeating and a scale going up. However, when the frequencies of the two stimuli become similar, something interesting happens. Grouping by similarity of pitch occurs, and perception changes to a back-and-forth "galloping" between the tones of the two streams. Then, as the scale continues upward so the frequencies become more separated, the two sequences are again perceived as separated.

Another example of how similarity of pitch causes grouping is an effect called the **scale illusion**, or **melodic channeling**. Diana Deutsch (1975, 1996) demonstrated this effect by presenting two sequences of notes simultaneously through earphones, one to the right ear and one to the left (**Figure 12.21a**). Notice that the notes presented to each ear jump up and down and do not create a scale. However, Deutsch's listeners perceived smooth sequences of notes in each ear, with the higher notes in the right ear and the lower

ones in the left ear (**Figure 12.21b**). Even though each ear received both high and low notes, grouping by similarity of pitch caused listeners to group the higher notes in the right ear (which started with a high note) and the lower notes in the left ear (which started with a low note).

The scale illusion highlights an important property of perceptual grouping. Most of the time, the principles of auditory grouping help us accurately interpret what is happening in the environment. It is most effective to perceive similar sounds as coming from the same source because this is what usually happens in the environment. In Deutsch's experiment, the perceptual system applies the principle of grouping by similarity to the artificial stimuli presented through earphones and makes

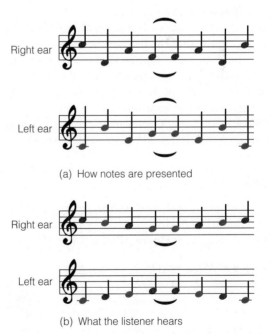

Right ear

Left ear

(a) How notes are presented

Right ear

Left ear

(b) What the listener hears

Figure 12.21 (a) These stimuli were presented to a listener's right ear (red) and left ear (blue) in Deutsch's (1975) scale illusion experiment. Notice how the notes presented to each ear jump up and down. (b) Although the notes in each ear jump up and down, the listener perceives a smooth sequence of notes. This effect is called the scale illusion, or melodic channeling. (From Deutsch, 1975)

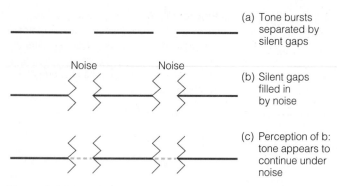

(a) Tone bursts separated by silent gaps

Noise   Noise

(b) Silent gaps filled in by noise

(c) Perception of b: tone appears to continue under noise

Figure 12.22 A demonstration of auditory continuity, using tones.

the mistake of assigning similar pitches to the same ear. But most of the time, when psychologists aren't controlling the stimuli, sounds with similar frequencies tend to be produced by the same sound source, so the auditory system is usually correct in using pitch to determine where sounds are coming from.

Auditory Continuity

Sounds that stay constant or that change smoothly are often produced by the same source. This property of sound leads to a principle that resembles the Gestalt principle of good continuation for vision (see Chapter 5, page 100). Sound stimuli with the same frequency or smoothly changing frequencies are perceived as continuous even when they are interrupted by another stimulus (Deutsch, 1999).

Richard Warren and coworkers (1972) demonstrated auditory continuity by presenting bursts of tone interrupted by gaps of silence (**Figure 12.22a**). Listeners perceived these tones as stopping during the silence. But when Warren filled in the gaps with noise (**Figure 12.22b**), listeners perceived the tone as continuing behind the noise (**Figure 12.22c**). This demonstration is analogous to the demonstration of visual good continuation illustrated by coiled rope in Figure 5.16 (see page 100). Just as the rope is perceived as continuous even when it is covered by another coil of the rope, a tone can be perceived as continuous even though it is interrupted by bursts of noise.

Experience

The effect of past experience on the perceptual grouping of auditory stimuli can be demonstrated by presenting the melody of a familiar song, as in **Figure 12.23a**. These are the notes for

Figure 12.23 "Three Blind Mice." (a) Jumping octave version. (b) Normal version.

the song "Three Blind Mice," but with the notes jumping from one octave to another. When people first hear these notes, they find it difficult to identify the song. But once they have heard the song as it was meant to be played (**Figure 12.23b**), they can follow the melody in the octave-jumping version shown in Figure 12.23a.

This is an example of the operation of a **melody schema**—a representation of a familiar melody that is stored in a person's memory. When people don't know that a melody is present, they have no access to the schema and therefore have nothing with which to compare the unknown melody. But when they know which melody is present, they compare what they hear to their stored schema and perceive the melody (Deutsch, 1999; Dowling & Harwood, 1986).

Each of the principles of auditory grouping that we have described provides information about the number and identity of sources in the auditory environment. But each principle alone is not foolproof, and basing our perceptions on just one principle can lead to error—as in the case of the scale illusion, which is purposely arranged so that similarity of pitch dominates our perception. In most naturalistic situations, we base our perceptions on a number of these cues working together. This is similar to the situation we described for visual perception, in which our perception of objects depends on a number of organizational principles working together, and our perception of depth depends on a number of depth cues working together.

Musical Organization: Melody

Our goal in this chapter has been to consider mechanisms responsible for locating sound and for organizing sound. So far, in considering organization, we've seen that auditory scenes are analyzed into separate sources and streams by using information such as location, onset time, timbre, and pitch. We've used some musical examples (Figures 12.18, 12.21, 12.23), but now we will consider music in more detail.

What does it mean to say that music is organized? **Music** has been described as "organized sound" (Goldman, 1961), which may be true but is perhaps too general for a definition; for example, we might consider the sound of a lawn mower to be "organized" but most people would not consider it to be music. But there is no question that music is organized in a number of ways. We will focus on how the sequences of notes in traditional Western music are organized.

(a)

(b)

One way to appreciate musical organization is by looking at music notation on a page (Figures 12.21, 12.23). Notes are organized vertically so they are high or low on the musical staff. They are organized horizontally as the notes follow one another in time.

Describing organization in terms of how notes are represented by musical notation is a description of *physical organization*. But we are interested in *perceptual organization*: how music is *perceived*. One approach, which focuses on sequences of notes, considers how we perceive melody and harmony and poses questions about organization such as: How are notes perceived as belonging together? What causes some notes to sound as if they don't belong? How are sequences of notes processed as they occur over time? We begin our discussion of musical organization by considering questions such as these, which focus on notes and melody. Then in the next section we will consider how music is organized in time.

What Is Melody?

As you listen to music, you hear a melody. It is the part of music you'd be most likely to sing along with. When you think of "America the Beautiful" and "Hey Jude," different melodies come into your mind. **Melody** is defined as the experience of a sequence of pitches as belonging together (Tan et al., 2010).

When you think of the way notes follow one after another in a song or musical composition, you are thinking about its melody. Remember from Chapter 11 that one definition of pitch was *that aspect of auditory sensation whose variation is associated with musical melodies* (Plack, 2014), and it was noted that when a melody is played using frequencies above 5,000 Hz (where 4,166 Hz is the highest note on the piano), you can tell something is changing, but it doesn't sound musical. So melodies are more than just sequences of notes—they are sequences of notes that belong together and sound musical. We begin by considering how some sequences of notes create phrases, and will then look at how individual notes are organized in melodies.

Phrases

To begin considering melodic organization, try imagining one of your favorite compositions (or, better yet, actually listen to one). As you hear one note following another, can you divide the melody into segments? A common way of subdividing melodies is into short segments called **phrases**, which are similar to phrases in language (Deutsch, 2013a; Sloboda & Gregory, 1980). Consider, for example, the first line of the song in **Figure 12.24**: *Twinkle, twinkle little star, how I wonder what you are*. We can split this sentence into two phrases separated by the comma between *star* and *how*. But if we didn't know the

words and just listened to the music, it is likely that we would divide the melody into the same two phrases.

When people are asked to listen to melodies and indicate the end of one unit and the beginning of the next, they are able to segment the melodies into phrases (Deliege, 1987; Deutsch, 2013a; Frankland & Cohen, 2004). The most powerful cue for the perception of phase boundaries is pauses, with longer intervals separating one phrase from another (Deutsch, 2013a, 2013b; Frankland & Cohen, 2004).

Another cue for phrase perception is the distance between pitches. The interval separating the end of one phrase and the start of another is often larger than the interval separating two notes within a phrase. Pitch differences can be measured in **semitones**, where a semitone is the smallest interval used in Western music—roughly the distance between two notes in a musical scale, such as between C and C#—with 12 semitones in an octave.

David Huron (2006) measured intervals between notes in 4,600 folk songs and found that the average interval within phrases was 2.0 semitones, whereas the average interval between the end of one phrase and the beginning of the next was 2.9 semitones. There is also evidence that longer notes tend to occur at the end of a phrase (Deliege, 1987; Clark & Krumhansl, 1990; Frankland & Cohen, 2004).

Grouping

Returning to your imagined song, focus on the progression of notes. Do they jump wildly from high to low pitches and back again, with large and small gaps between them, or are they closely spaced and seem to follow one from the other? The grouping of notes, first into phrases and then into longer sequences, creates melodies (Deutsch, 2013a). Creating a melody, whether it is "Twinkle, Twinkle, Little Star" or the opening of Beethoven's Fifth Symphony ("Da Da Da Dah..."), involves arranging notes so they form a melodic line in which the notes are perceived as belonging together.

When we described auditory stream segregation earlier in the chapter, we introduced a number of principles such as location, pitch, and timbre that help us group sequences of tones together and create separate streams corresponding to different sources, such as the guitarist, vocalist, and keyboard player in Figure 12.17. Now, rather than considering multiple streams that need to be separated, let's consider a single stream of notes and ask what properties these notes must have in order to create a melody, a process that could be called **auditory stream integration**, to indicate that the emphasis is on integrating notes within a single stream (Micheyl & Oxenham, 2010).

One characteristic that favors grouping notes in Western music is the interval between notes. Small intervals are common

Twin-kle, twin-kle lit-tle star, How I won-der what you are.

Figure 12.24 The first line of "Twinkle, Twinkle, Little Star."

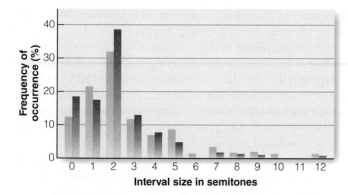

Figure 12.25 Frequency at which intervals occur in a survey of many musical compositions. Green bars: Classical composers and the Beatles. Red bars: ethnic music from a number of different cultures. The most common interval is 1–2 semitones. (From Vos & Troost, 1989)

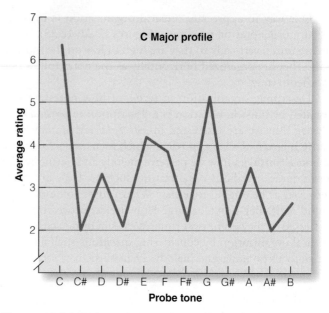

Figure 12.26 Ratings of Krumhansl and Kessler's (1982) probe tone experiment. Ratings indicate how well probe tones fit a scale, with 7 being the best possible fit. See text for details.

in musical sequences, in accordance with the Gestalt principle of proximity we described in Chapter 5 (page 101), which states that elements near each other tend to be perceived as grouped together (Bharucha & Krumhansl, 1983; Divenyi & Hirsh, 1978). Large intervals occur less frequently because large jumps increase the chances that the melodic line will break into separate melodies (Plack, 2014). The prevalence of small intervals is confirmed by the results of a survey of a large number of compositions from different cultures, which shows that the predominant interval is 1–2 semitones (**Figure 12.25**) (Vos & Troost, 1989).

You can check the predominance of small intervals yourself by listening to music while paying attention to the spacing between successive pitches. Generally, you will find that most of the intervals are small. But there are certainly exceptions. Consider, for example, the first two notes of "Over the Rainbow" (*Some–where*), which are separated by an octave (12 semitones), so they are perceptually similar. Generally, after a large jump, the melody turns around to fill in the gap, a phenomenon called **gap fill** (Meyer, 1956; Von Hippel & Huron, 2000).

Finally, certain *trajectories* of notes are commonly found in music. The *arch trajectory*—rise and then fall—is common (see the beginning of "Twinkle, Twinkle, Little Star" in Figure 12.24 for an example of this trajectory). Although there are fewer large changes in pitch than small changes, when large changes do occur they tend to go up (as in the first two notes of "Over the Rainbow"); small changes are likely to descend (Huron, 2006).

Tonality

Another characteristic of melody that helps create organization is **tonality**—organizing pitches around the note associated with the composition's key, which is called the **tonic** (Krumhansl, 1985). For example, C is the tonic for the key of C and its associated scale: C, D, E, F, G, A, B, C. Organizing pitches around a tonic creates a framework within which a listener generates expectations about what might be coming next. One common expectation is that a song that begins with the tonic will end on the tonic. This effect, which is called **return to the tonic**, occurs in "Twinkle, Twinkle, Little Star," which begins and ends on a C.

An example of research on tonality is an experiment by Carol Krumhansl and Edward Kessler (1982), who measured perceptions of tonality by presenting a scale that established a major or minor key and then followed the scale with a probe tone. Listeners assigned a rating of 1–7 to the probe to indicate how well it fit with the scale presented previously (where 7 is the best fit). The results of this experiment, indicated in **Figure 12.26**, indicate that the tonic, C, received the highest rating, followed by E and G, which are the other components of a three-note C-major chord. (Note that the experiment included keys in addition to C; this graph combines the results from all of the keys.) Other notes in the scale, D, F, A, B, received the next highest ratings, and notes not in the scale, like C# and G#, received the lowest ratings. Krumhansl calls these ratings of how notes "fit" a scale the **tonal hierarchy**.

Krumhansl (1985) then considered the possibility that there is a relationship between the tonal hierarchy and the way notes are used in a melody by referring to statistical analyses of the frequency or duration of notes in compositions by composers such as Mozart, Schubert, and Mendelssohn (Hughes, 1977; Knopoff & Hutchinson, 1983; Youngblood, 1958). When she compared these analyses to her tonal hierarchy, she found an average correlation of 0.89. What this match means, says Krumhansl, is that listeners and composers have internalized the statistical properties of music and base their "best fit" ratings on the frequency with which they have heard these tonalities in compositions.

Krumhansl and Kessler's experiment required listeners to rate how well tones fit into a scale. Another approach to tonality is based on the idea of **musical syntax**—"rules" that specify how notes and chords are combined in music. The term **syntax** is associated more with language than with music. Syntax in language refers to grammatical rules that specify correct sentence construction. For example, the sentence *The cats won't eat* follows the rules of syntax, whereas the phrase *The cats won't eating* doesn't follow the rules. We will consider the idea of musical syntax shortly, but first we describe a way syntax has been studied in language using an electrical response called the *event-related potential.*

METHOD | Event-Related Potential in Language

The **event-related potential (ERP)** is recorded with small disc electrodes placed on a person's scalp, as shown in **Figure 12.27a**. Each electrode picks up signals from groups of neurons that fire together. A characteristic of the ERP that makes it useful for studying language (or music) is that it is a rapid response, occurring on a time scale of fractions of a second, as shown in the responses of **Figure 12.27b**. The ERP consists of a number of waves that occur at different delays after a stimulus is presented. The one we are concerned with is called the P600 response, where *P* stands for "positive" and 600 indicates that it occurs about 600 milliseconds after the stimulus is presented. We are interested in the P600 response because it responds to violations of syntax (Kim & Osterhout, 2005;

Osterhout et al., 1997). The two curves in Figure 12.27b illustrate this. The blue curve is the response that occurs after the word *eat* in the sentence "The cats won't eat." The response to this grammatically correct word shows no P600 response. However, the red curve, to the word *eating*, which is grammatically incorrect in the sentence "The cats won't eating," has a large P600 response. This is the brain's way of signaling a violation of syntax.

The reason for introducing the idea that the P600 response indicates violations of syntax in language is that it has been proposed that the ERP can be used in a similar way to determine how the brain responds to violations of musical syntax. One possible violation of musical syntax would be not returning to the tonic (see page 306), because compositions usually return to the tonic and listeners expect this to happen. But what if it doesn't? Try singing the first line of "Twinkle, Twinkle, Little Star," but stop at "you," before the song has returned to the tonic. The effect of pausing just before the end of the phrase, which could be called a violation of musical syntax, is unsettling and has us longing for the final note that will bring us back to the tonic.

Another violation of musical syntax occurs when an unlikely note or chord is inserted that doesn't seem to "fit" in the tonality of the melody. Aniruddh Patel and coworkers (1998) used this type of violation of musical syntax to see if the P600 response occurred in music. Their listeners heard a musical phrase like the one in **Figure 12.28a**, which contained a

(a)

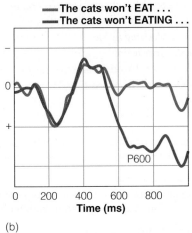

The cats won't EAT . . .
The cats won't EATING . . .

P600

0   200   400   600   800
Time (ms)

(b)

Figure 12.27 (a) A person wearing electrodes for recording the event-related potential (ERP). (b) ERP responses to *eat* (blue curve), which is grammatically correct, and *eating* (red curve), which is not grammatically correct, and so creates a P600 response. Note that positive is down in this record. [(b) From Osterhout, McLaughlin, & Bersick, 1997]

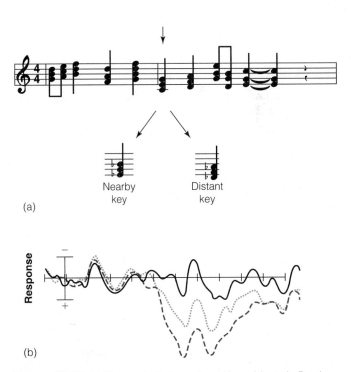

Nearby key   Distant key

(a)

Response

(b)

Figure 12.28 (a) The musical phrase heard by subjects in Patel and coworkers (1998) experiment. The location of the target chord is indicated by the downward pointing arrow. The chord in the music staff is the "In key" chord. The other two chords were inserted in that position for the "Nearby key" and "Distant key" conditions. (b) ERP responses to the target chord: black = In key; green = Near key; red = Far key.

target chord, indicated by the arrow above the music. There were three different targets: (1) an "In key" chord, that fit the piece, shown on the musical staff; (2) a "Nearby key" chord, that didn't fit as well; and (3) a "Distant key" chord that fit even less well. In the first part of the experiment, listeners judged the phrase as acceptable 80 percent of the time when it contained the in-key chord; 49 percent when it contained the nearby-key chord; and 28 percent when it contained the distant-key chord. One way of stating this result is that listeners were judging how "grammatically correct" each version was. This is similar to what Krumhansl was measuring when she asked listeners to indicate how well tones fit into a scale (page 306).

In the second part of the experiment, listeners' ERPs were measured as they heard each of the musical phrases. **Figure 12.28b** shows that there is no P600 response when the phrase contained the in-key chord (black record), but that there are P600 responses for the two other chords, with the bigger response for the more out-of-key chord (red record). Patel concluded from this result that music, like language, has a syntax that influences how we react to it. Other studies following Patel's have also found that electrical responses like P600 occur to violations of musical syntax (Koelsch, 2005; Koelsch et al., 2000; Maess et al., 2001; Vuust et al., 2009).

Looking at the idea of musical syntax in a larger context, we can assume that as we listen to music, we are focusing on the notes we are hearing, while, without thinking about it, we have expectations about what is going to happen next. This occurs not only for music we have heard before, but also for music we are hearing for the first time.

Expectation

While considering phrases and melodies, we have identified a number of characteristics that are associated with music. **Table 12.4** summarizes some properties associated with phrases and melodies. These properties are not absolute—that is, they don't always occur in every phrase or melody. However, taken together they describe things that occur often in music, and thus are similar to the idea of *regularities in the environment*, which we introduced in our discussion of perceiving visual scenes in Chapter 5. When discussing visual scenes, we defined regularities of the environment as *characteristics of the environment that occur frequently*, and we saw that knowledge of these regularities, gained from a lifetime of experience in viewing the environment, can influence our perception of scenes and objects in scenes (see pages 108–111). A similar situation may occur for music, in which listeners use their knowledge of regularities like the ones in Table 12.2 as they perceive musical compositions.

What this means is that much of what we listen to contains no surprises. You can demonstrate your ability to predict what is going to happen by listening to a song, preferably instrumental and not too fast. As you listen, try guessing what notes or phrases are coming next. This is easier for some compositions, such as ones with repeating themes, but even when there isn't repetition, what's coming usually isn't a surprise. What's particularly compelling about this exercise is that it often works even for music you are hearing for the first time. Just as our perception of visual scenes we are seeing for the first time is influenced by our past experiences in perceiving the environment, our perception of music we are hearing for first time can be influenced by our history of listening to music.

Expectations also contribute to becoming actively engaged as we listen to music. We don't merely hear each note as it occurs, we anticipate the note coming after it. Try pausing a familiar song halfway through the chorus: you'll probably continue singing through the remainder of it in your head. This ability to anticipate relies on people's tendency to listen to songs again and again. In a study by Carlos Silva Pereira and coworkers (2011), listeners rated specific pop/rock songs for familiarity and likability. When they listened to the songs while in an fMRI scanner, familiar songs caused activation in areas of the brain associated with emotion, both for songs they liked and songs they didn't like. Pereira interpreted this result as showing that repeated exposure to a song is a crucial factor in determining a listener's emotional response to the song.

The idea of a link between expectation and the response to music has been the basis of proposals that composers can purposely violate a listener's expectations to create emotion, tension, or a dramatic effect. Leonard Meyer suggested this in his book *Emotion and Meaning in Music* (1956), in which he argued that the principal emotional component of music is created by the composer's choreographing of expectation. Later researchers have expanded on this idea (see Huron, 2006; Huron & Margulis, 2010).

Table 12.4 Commonly Occurring Properties of Phrases and Melodies

GROUPING	COMMON CHARACTERISTICS
Phrases	• Large time intervals between end of one phrase and beginning of the next • Large pitch intervals between phrases, compared to within phrases
Melodies	• Melodies contain mostly small pitch intervals • Large pitch changes tend to go up • Smaller pitch changes are likely to go down • Downward pitch change often follows a large upward change • Melodies contain mostly tones that fit the melody's tonality • There is a tendency to return to the tonic at the end of a section of melody

Musical Organization: Rhythm

Another approach to perceptual organization in music is to focus on the time dimension. This involves questions such as: How do notes create rhythm? What is the beat? How come we perceive some beats as accented and others as not? What is the connection between movement and music?

What Is Rhythm?

Can you imagine music without time? Of course not. Music takes time, but more than that, music *structures* time by creating **rhythm**—the time pattern of durations created by notes (Kerman & Tomlinson, 2015; London, 2004; Tan et al., 2010). Although we defined rhythm as the time pattern of durations, what is important is not the durations of notes, but the *inter-onset interval*—the time between the *onset* of each note. This is illustrated in **Figure 12.29**, which shows the first measures of "The Star Spangled Banner." Note onsets are indicated by the blue dots above the music, and the spaces between these dots define the song's rhythm. Because note *onsets* are what defines the rhythm, it is possible that two versions of this song, one in which the notes are played briefly with spaces in between (like notes plucked on a guitar) and another in which the notes are held so the spaces are filled (like a note bowed on a violin), could both have the same rhythm.

Rhythm is, however, only one aspect of musical time. Although rhythms can vary and be irregular, time in music is also subdivided into equally spaced intervals, called the **beat**. The beat, which is what you are tapping to when you tap your feet to music, is indicated in Figure 12.29 by the red arrows. Although the beat is associated with specific notes in this example, the beat marks equally spaced pulses in time, and so occurs even when there are no notes (Grahn, 2009).

The Beat

Every culture has some form of music with a beat (Patel, 2008). The beat can be up front and obvious, as in rock music, or more subtle, as in a quiet lullaby, but it is always there, creating a framework over which the melody creates its rhythmic pattern.

The beat can be likened to the pulse of music, both because of its regularity and because it can result in movement. The link between the beat and movement is expressed not only by behaviors such as tapping or swinging in time to the beat, but also by responses of motor areas in the brain. Jessica Grahn and James Rowe (2009) demonstrated a connection between the beat and a group of subcortical structures at the base of the brain called the *basal ganglia*, which had been associated with movement in previous research. Their subjects listened to "beat" and "non-beat" rhythmic patterns while they were in a brain scanner.

Grahn and Rowe found that the basal ganglia response was greater to the beat stimuli than to the non-beat stimuli. In addition, they calculated neural connectivity between subcortical structures, indicated by red in **Figure 12.30**, and cortical motor areas, indicated by blue, by determining how well the response of one structure can be predicted from the response of a connected structure (Friston et al., 1997). The result of this calculation indicated greater connectivity for the beat condition compared to the non-beat condition.

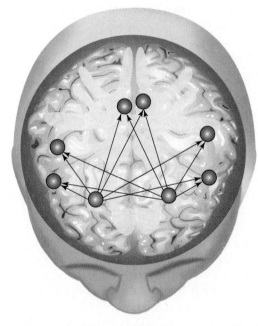

Figure 12.30 Grahn and Rowe (2009) found that connectivity between subcortical structures (red) and cortical motor areas (blue) was increased for the beat condition compared to the non-beat condition.

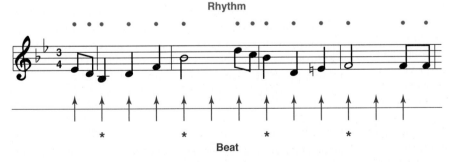

Figure 12.29 First line of "The Star-Spangled Banner." The blue dots indicate note onsets, which define the rhythm. The red arrows indicate the beat. The stars (*) indicate accented beats, which define the meter.

In another experiment, Joyce Chen and coworkers (2008) measured activity in the premotor cortex in three conditions: (1) Tapping: Subjects tapped along with the sequence. (2) Listening with anticipation: Subjects listened to the sequence, but they knew they would be asked to tap to it later. (3) Passive listening: Subjects listened passively to a rhythmic sequence. It isn't surprising that tapping caused the greatest response, because the premotor cortex is involved in creating movements. But a response also occurred in the listening with anticipation condition (70 percent of the response to tapping) and in the passive listening condition (55 percent of the response to tapping), even though subjects were just listening, without moving. Thus, motor areas are activated just by listening to a beat, which, Chen suggests, may partially explain the irresistible urge to tap to the beat when hearing music.

As necessary as the beat is for providing the "pulse" of music, it is important to realize that all beats are not necessarily created equal. Some beats sound more accented than others. The accents in "The Star Spangled Banner," indicated by stars below the arrows in Figure 12.29, create a regular pattern of accented and unaccented beats, which creates *meter*.

Meter

Meter is the organization of beats into bars or measures, with the first beat in each bar often being accented (Lerdahl & Jackendorff, 1983; Plack, 2014; Tan et al., 2013). There are two basic kinds of meter in Western music: *duple meter* in which accents are in multiples of two, such as **12 12 12** or **1234 1234 1234**, like a march; and *triple meter*, in which accents are in groups of three, such as **123 123 123**, as in a waltz.

Metrical structure is typically achieved when musicians accentuate some notes by using a stronger attack or by playing them louder or longer. In doing this, musicians bring an expressiveness to music beyond what is heard by simply playing a string of notes. Thus, although the musical score may be the starting point for a performance, the musicians' *interpretation* of the score is what listeners hear, and the interpretation of which notes are accented can influence the perceived meter of the composition (Ashley, 2002; Palmer, 1997; Sloboda, 2000). But, as we will now see, meter can be created in a series of notes even if there are no accents. Meter can, as it turns out, be created by the listener's mind.

Metrical Structure and the Mind How is metrical structure created by the mind? Even though the ticking of a metronome creates a series of identical beats with regular spacing, it is possible to transform this series of beats into perceptual groups. We can, for example, imagine the beats of a metronome in duple meter (TICK-toc) or, with a small amount of effort, in triple meter (TICK-toc-toc) (Nozaradan et al., 2011).

John Iversen and coworkers (2009) studied the mental creation of meter using magnetoencephalography (MEG) to measure subjects' brain responses as they listened to rhythmic sequences. MEG measures brain responses by recording magnetic fields caused by brain activity. A feature of MEG is that

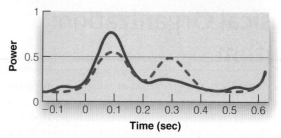

Figure 12.31 Results of the Iversen and coworkers (2009) experiment. Blue: MEG response when imagining the accent on the first note. Red: MEG response when imagining the accent on the second note.

it records brain responses very rapidly, so responses to specific notes in a rhythmic pattern can be determined.

Subjects listened to two-tone sequences and were told to mentally imagine that the beat occurred either on the first note or on the second note of each sequence. **Figure 12.31** shows that the MEG response depended on which beat was accented in the subject's mind. The blue curve indicates a large peak when the imagined beat was on the first note; the red curve indicates a later peak when the imagined beat was on the second note. Thus, our ability to change meter with our mind is reflected directly by activity in the brain.

Metrical Structure and Movement The movement that accompanies music can reflect the metrical structure of the music, as when dancers incorporate the ONE-two-three grouping of a waltz into their footwork. However, the relationship between movement and music also occurs in the opposite direction, when movement influences the perceptual grouping or metrical structure of the beats. Experiments that demonstrate this have been carried out with both adults and infants, so we will describe them together rather than describing the infant research in a separate "Developmental Dimension" section at the end of the chapter.

The idea that how we move may influence our perception of meter was first demonstrated by Jessica Phillips-Silver and Laurel Trainor (2005) in 7-month-old infants. While these infants listened to a regular repeating ambiguous rhythm that had no accents, they were bounced up and down in the arms of the experimenter. These bounces occurred either in a duple pattern (a bounce on every second beat) or in a triple pattern (a bounce on every third beat). After being bounced for 2 minutes, the infants were tested to determine whether this movement caused them to hear the ambiguous pattern in groups of two or in groups of three. The researchers used a head-turning preference procedure to determine whether the infants preferred listening to a pattern that had accents that corresponded to how they had been bounced.

METHOD | Head-Turning Preference Procedure

In the preference technique, an infant sitting on the mother's lap has his or her attention directed to a flashing light illuminating a visual display. When the infant looks at the light, it stays on and the infant hears a repeating sound, which is accented to create either a duple or a triple pattern. The infant hears one of these patterns as long as he or she is looking at the light. When the infant looks away, the sound goes off. This is done for a number of trials, and the infant quickly learns that looking at the light keeps the sound on. Thus the question of whether the infant prefers the duple or triple pattern can be answered by determining which sound the infant listens to longer.

Phillips-Silver and Trainor found that infants listened to the pattern they had been bounced to for an average of 8 seconds but only listened to the other pattern for an average of 6 seconds. The infants therefore preferred the pattern they had been bounced to. To determine whether this effect was due to vision, infants were bounced while blindfolded. (Although the infants loved being bounced, they weren't so thrilled about being blindfolded!) The result, when they were tested later using the head-turning procedure, was the same as when they could see, indicating that vision was not a factor. Also, when the infants just watched the experimenter bounce, the effect didn't occur. Apparently *moving* is the key to influencing metrical grouping.

In another experiment, Phillips-Silver and Trainor (2007) tested adults. In this case, the experimenter didn't hold the subject, but the experimenter and subject held hands and bounced together. After bouncing with the experimenter, the adults were tested by listening to duple and triple patterns and indicated which pattern they had heard while bouncing. On 86 percent of the trials, adults picked the pattern that matched the way they were bounced. As with the infants, this result also occurred when the adults were blindfolded, but not when they just watched the experimenter bounce.

Based on the results of these and other experiments, Phillips-Silver and Trainor concluded that the crucial factor that causes movement to influence the perception of metrical structure is stimulation of the **vestibular system**—the system that is responsible for balance and sensing the position of the body. To check this idea, Trainor and coworkers (2009) had adults listen to the ambiguous series of beats while electrically stimulating their vestibular system in a duple or triple pattern with electrodes placed behind the ear. This caused the subject to feel as if his or her head were moving back and forth, even though it remained stationary. This experiment duplicated the results of the other experiments, with subjects reporting hearing the pattern that matched the metrical grouping created by stimulating the vestibular system on 78 percent of the trials.

Metrical Structure and Language Perception of meter is influenced not only by movement but by longer-term experience—the stress patterns of a person's language. Different languages have different stress patterns, because of the way the languages are constructed. For example, in English, function words like "the," "a," and "to" typically precede content words, as in "the *dog*" or "to *eat*," where *dog* and *eat* are stressed when spoken. In contrast, Japanese speakers place function words after the content words, so "the *book*" in English (with *book* stressed) becomes "*hon ga*" in Japanese (with *hon* stressed). Therefore, the dominant stress pattern in English is *short–long* (*unaccented–accented*), but in Japanese it is *long–short* (*accented–unaccented*).

Comparisons of how native English-speakers and Japanese-speakers perceive metrical grouping supports the idea that the stress patterns in a person's language can influence the person's perception of grouping. John Iversen and Aniruddh Patel (2008) had subjects listen to a sequence of alternating long and short tones (**Figure 12.32a**) and then indicate whether they perceived the tones' grouping as long–short or short–long. The results indicated that English-speakers were more likely to perceive the grouping as short–long (**Figure 12.32b**) and Japanese speakers were more likely to perceive the grouping as long–short (**Figure 12.32c**).

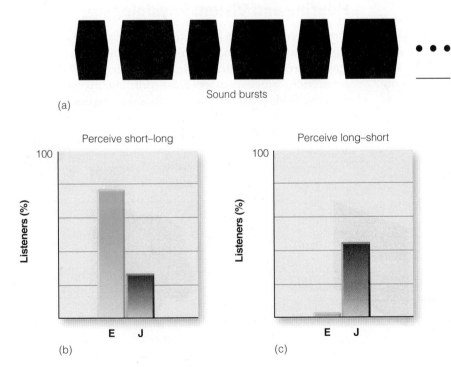

Figure 12.32 Differences between Japanese and American perceptions of meter. (a) Subjects listened to sequences of short and long tones. On half the trials, the first tone was short; on the other half, long. The durations of the tones ranged from about 150 ms to 500 ms (durations varied for different experimental conditions), and the entire sequence repeated for 5 seconds. (b) English-speaking subjects (E) were more likely than Japanese-speaking subjects (J) to perceive the stimulus as short–long. (c) Japanese-speaking subjects were more likely than English-speaking subjects to perceive the stimulus as long–short. (Based on data from Iversen & Patel, 2008)

This result also occurs when comparing 7- to 8-month-old English and Japanese infants (see the head-turning procedure described earlier), but it does not occur for 5- to 6-month-old infants (Yoshida et al., 2010). It has been hypothesized that this shift occurs between about 6 and 8 months because that is when infants are beginning to develop the capacity for language.

SOMETHING TO CONSIDER:

Connections Between Hearing and Vision

The different senses rarely operate in isolation. For hearing, not only is there a connection between perception of musical beat and movement, but there are many examples of connections between hearing and the other senses. We see people's lips move as we listen to them speak; our fingers feel the keys of a piano as we hear the music the fingers are creating; we hear a screeching sound and turn to see a car coming to a sudden stop. All of these combinations of hearing and other senses are examples of **multisensory interactions**. We will focus on interactions between hearing and vision, first perceptually and then physiologically.

Hearing and Vision: Perceptions

One area of multisensory research is concerned with one sense "dominating" the other. If we ask whether vision or hearing is dominant, the answer is "it depends." The **ventriloquism effect**, or **visual capture**, is an example of vision dominating audition. It occurs when sounds coming from one place (the ventriloquist's mouth) appear to come from another place (the dummy's mouth). Movement of the dummy's mouth "captures" the sound (Soto-Faraco et al., 2002, 2004).

Another example of visual capture occurred in movie theaters before the introduction of digital surround sound. An actor's dialogue was produced by a speaker located on one side of the screen but the image of the actor who was talking was located in the center of the screen, many feet away. Despite this separation, moviegoers heard the sound coming from its

seen location (the image at the center of the screen) rather than from where it was actually produced (the speaker to the side of the screen). Sound originating from a location off to the side was captured by vision.

But vision doesn't always win out over hearing. Consider, for example, an amazing effect called the **two-flash illusion**. When a single dot is flashed onto a screen (**Figure 12.33a**), the subject perceives one flash. When a single beep is presented at the same time as the dot, the subject still perceives one flash. However, if the single dot is accompanied by two beeps, the subject sees two flashes, even though the dot was flashed only once (**Figure 12.33b**). The mechanism responsible for this effect is still being researched, but the important finding for our purposes is that sound creates a visual effect (de Haas et al., 2012).

Visual capture and the two-flash illusion, although both impressive examples of auditory–visual interaction, result in perceptions that don't match reality. But sound and vision occur together all the time in real-life situations, and when they do, they often complement each other. For example, when you are having a conversation with someone, you are not only hearing what the person is saying, but you may also be watching his or her lips. Watching people's lip movements makes it easier to understand what they are saying, especially in a noisy environment. This is why theater lighting designers often go to great lengths to be sure that the actors' faces are illuminated, to help the audience understand what they are saying.

Lip movements, whether in everyday conversations or in the theater, provide information about what sounds are being produced. This is the principle behind **speechreading** (sometimes called lipreading), which enables deaf people to determine what people are saying by watching their lip and facial movements.

Hearing and Vision: Physiology

The idea that there are connections between vision and hearing is also reflected in the interconnection of the different sensory areas of the brain (Murray & Spierer, 2011). These connections between sensory areas contribute to coordinated receptive fields (RFs) like the ones shown in **Figure 12.34** for

Figure 12.33 The two-flash illusion. (a) A single dot is flashed on the screen. (b) When the dot is flashed once but is accompanied by two beeps, the subject perceives two flashes.

(a)   (b)

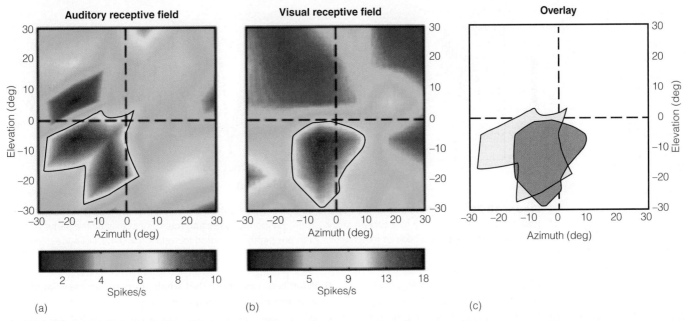

Figure 12.34 Receptive fields of neurons in the monkey's parietal lobe that respond to (a) auditory stimuli that are located in the lower left area of space and (b) visual stimuli presented in the lower left area of the monkey's visual field. (c) Superimposing the two receptive fields indicates that there is a high level of overlap between the auditory and visual fields. [(a) and (b) from Bremmer, 2011]

a neuron in the monkey's parietal lobe that responds to both visual stimuli and sound (Bremmer, 2011; Schlack et al., 2005). This neuron responds when an auditory stimulus is presented in an area that is below eye level and to the left (**Figure 12.34a**) and when a visual stimulus originates from about the same area (**Figure 12.34b**). **Figure 12.34c** shows that there is a great deal of overlap between these two receptive fields.

It is easy to see that neurons such as this would be useful in our multisensory environment. When we hear a sound coming from a specific location in space and also see what is producing the sound—a musician playing or a person talking—the multisensory neurons that fire to both sound and vision help us form a single representation of space that involves both auditory and visual stimuli.

Another example of cross-talk between the senses occurs when the primary receiving area associated with one sense is activated by stimuli that are usually associated with another sense. For example, some blind people use a technique called **echolocation** to locate objects and perceive shapes in the environment. Their technique is similar to the echolocation used by bats and dolphins, which emit high-frequency sounds and use information from the echoes reflected back from objects to sense the shapes and locations of the objects (see Figure 10.50, page 254).

The blind people make a clicking sound with their tongue and mouth and listen for echoes. Skilled echolocators can detect the positions and shapes of objects as they move through the environment. For example, people using echolocation can detect a wall as they walk toward it; more impressively, extremely skilled echolocators can identify objects such as cars, large trashcans, and fire hydrants as they walk along a sidewalk (see www.worldaccessfortheblind.org and Daniel Kish's TED talk "How I Use Sonar to Navigate the World" at www.ted.com).

Lore Thaler and coworkers (2011) had two expert echolocators create their clicking sounds as they stood near objects, and recorded the sounds and resulting echoes with small microphones placed in the ears. The question Thaler and coworkers were interested in is how these sounds would activate the brain. To determine this, they recorded brain activity using fMRI as the expert echolocators and sighted control subjects listened to the recorded sounds that included the echoes. Not surprisingly, they found that the sounds activated the auditory cortex in both the blind and sighted subjects. However, the visual cortex was also strongly activated in the echolocators but was silent in the control subjects.

Apparently, the visual area is activated because the echolocators are having what they describe as "spatial" experiences. In fact, some echolocators lose their awareness of the auditory clicks as they focus on the spatial information the echoes are providing (Kish, 2012). This example of multisensory functioning shows that the response of the brain can be based not just on the type of energy entering the eyes or ears but on the perceptual outcome of that energy. Thus, when sound is used to achieve spatial awareness, the visual cortex becomes involved.

The idea that the brain's response can be based not on the type of energy entering the eyes or ears but on the outcome of the energy is also illustrated in an experiment by Mor Regev and coworkers (2013), who recorded the fMRI response of subjects as they either listened to a 7-minute spoken story or read the words of the story presented at exactly the same rate that the words had been spoken. Not surprisingly, they found that listening to the story activated the auditory receiving area in the temporal lobe and that reading the written version activated the visual receiving area in the occipital lobe. But moving up to the superior temporal gyrus in the temporal lobe, which is

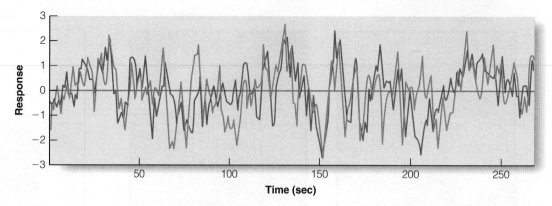

Figure 12.35 fMRI responses of the superior temporal gyrus, which is an area that processes language. Red: Response to listening to a spoken story. Green: Response to reading the story at exactly the same rate as it was told. The responses do not match exactly but are highly correlated (correlation = 0.47). (From Regev et al., 2013)

involved in language processing, they found that the responses from listening and from reading were synchronized in time (**Figure 12.35**). This area of the brain is therefore responding not to "hearing" or "vision," but to the meaning of the messages created by hearing or vision. (The synchronized responding did not occur in a control group that was exposed to unidentifiable scrambled letters or sounds.) In the next chapter, on speech perception, we will venture further into the idea that sound can create meaning, and will describe additional relationships between sound and vision and sound and meaning.

1. What is auditory scene analysis, and why is it a "problem" for the auditory system?

2. What are the basic principles of auditory grouping that help us achieve auditory scene analysis? Be sure you understand the following experiments: Bregman and Campbell (Figure 12.19); "galloping" crossing streams (Figure 12.20); scale illusion (Figure 12.21); auditory continuity (Figure 12.22); and melody schema (Figure 12.23).

3. Describe the ways music is organized, distinguishing between melody, rhythm, beat, and meter.

4. What is melody? How is it related to pitch?

5. What is the evidence that small intervals are associated with grouping that creates melody?

6. What does it mean to say that music can have syntax? How does this relate to syntax in language?

7. Describe the experiment by Patel that related musical syntax and physiological responding.

8. Describe experiments by Grahn and Rowe and by Chen and coworkers that demonstrate a connection between the beat and the response of movement areas in the brain.

9. What does it mean to say that meter can be determined by the mind? Describe the experiment that provides physiological evidence for this idea.

10. Describe the experiments that demonstrate a connection between movement and metrical grouping

11. What is the relationship between language and metrical grouping?

12. Describe the ways that (a) vision "dominates" hearing; (b) hearing dominants vision; (c) sound provides information that influences what we see; (d) vision provides information that influences what we hear.

13. What is the basis of the statement that the brain's response can be based on the *outcome* of the energy stimulating the receptors?

THINK ABOUT IT

1. We can perceive space visually, as we saw in the chapter on depth perception, and through the sense of hearing, as we have described in this chapter. How are these two ways of perceiving space similar and different? (p. 290)

2. How good are the acoustics in your classrooms? Can you hear the professor clearly? Does it matter where you sit? Are you ever distracted by noises from inside or outside the room? (p. 298)

3. How is object recognition in vision like stream segregation in hearing? (p. 302)

4. In the experiments on metrical structure, the stimulus was a steady, accent-free, series of beats, like the sound produced by a metronome. But in most music, specific beats are accented. Determine a number of ways that this accenting is achieved, by listening to a few different kinds of music. (p. 309)

5. What are some situations in which (a) you use one sense in isolation and (b) the combined use of two or more senses is necessary to accomplish a task? (p. 312)

KEY TERMS

Acoustic shadow (p. 290)
Anterior belt area (p. 297)
Architectural acoustics (p. 299)
Auditory localization (p. 290)
Auditory scene analysis (p. 301)
Auditory scene (p. 301)
Auditory space (p. 290)
Auditory stream integration (p. 305)
Auditory stream segregation (p. 302)
Azimuth (p. 290)
Beat (p. 309)
Binaural cues (p. 290)
Coincidence detectors (p. 295)
Cone of confusion (p. 292)
Direct sound (p. 298)
Distance (p. 290)
Echolocation (p. 313)
Elevation (p. 290)
Event-related potential (ERP) (p. 307)

Gap fill (p. 306)
Indirect sound (p. 298)
Interaural level difference (ILD) (p. 290)
Interaural time difference (ITD) (p. 291)
ITD detectors (p. 295)
ITD tuning curves (p. 295)
Jeffress model (p. 294)
Location cues (p. 290)
Melodic channeling (p. 303)
Melody (p. 305)
Melody schema (p. 304)
Meter (p. 310)
Monaural cue (p. 293)
Multisensory interactions (p. 312)
Music (p. 304)
Musical syntax (p. 306)
Phrases (p. 305)
Posterior belt area (p. 297)
Precedence effect (p. 299)

Return to the tonic (p. 306)
Reverberation time (p. 300)
Rhythm (p. 309)
Scale illusion (p. 303)
Semitones (p. 305)
Spectral cue (p. 293)
Speechreading (p. 312)
Syntax (p. 306)
Tonal hierarchy (p. 306)
Tonality (p. 306)
Tonic (p. 306)
Two-flash illusion (p. 312)
Ventriloquism effect (p. 312)
Vestibular system (p. 311)
Visual capture (p. 312)
What auditory pathway (p. 298)
Where auditory pathway (p. 298)

Although this desert scene may be far from your everyday experience, something is happening that is similar to what you experience every day: people are having a conversation. Language is the primary way people communicate, and as we see in this chapter, the starting point for this communication is the ability to perceive the speech sounds that we create when we talk.

CHAPTER 13

Speech Perception

CHAPTER CONTENTS

The Speech Stimulus
The Acoustic Signal
Basic Units of Speech

The Variability of the Acoustic Signal
Variability From Context
Variability From Different Speakers

Perceiving Phonemes
Categorical Perception

Information Provided by the Face
Information From Our Knowledge of Language

Perceiving Words and Sentences
Perceiving Words in Sentences
Perceiving Breaks Between Sequences of Words
Perceiving Degraded Speech

Speech Perception and the Brain

SOMETHING TO CONSIDER: Speech Perception and Action

DEVELOPMENTAL DIMENSION: Infant Speech Perception
The Categorical Perception of Phonemes
Learning the Sounds of a Language

THINK ABOUT IT

Some Questions We Will Consider:

- Can computers perceive speech as well as humans? (p. 317)
- Does each word that we hear have a unique pattern of air pressure changes associated with it? (p. 320)
- Why does an unfamiliar foreign language often sound like a continuous stream of sound, with no breaks between words? (p. 325)
- Are there specific areas in the brain that are responsible for perceiving speech? (p. 328)

Although we perceive speech easily under most conditions, beneath this ease lurks processes as complex as those involved in perceiving the most complicated visual scenes. One way to appreciate this complexity is to consider attempts to use computers to recognize speech. Many companies now use speech recognition systems to provide services such as booking tickets, automated banking, and computer technical support. But if you've ever used one of these systems, it is likely that a friendly computer voice has told you "I can't understand what you said" on more than one occasion.

Computer speech recognition is constantly improving, but it still can't match people's ability to recognize speech. Computers perform well when a person speaks slowly and clearly, when there is no background noise, and when they

are listening for a few predetermined words or phrases. For example, an automated bank teller might say "Tell me what you're asking about: say find balance, recent transactions, mortgage. . . ." However, humans can perceive speech even when confronted with phrases they have never heard and under a wide variety of conditions, including the presence of various background noises, sloppy pronunciation, speakers with different dialects and accents, and the often chaotic give-and-take that routinely occurs when people talk with one another (Huang et al., 2014; Reddy, 1976; Sinha, 2002). This chapter will help you appreciate the complex perceptual problems posed by speech and will describe research that has helped us begin to understand how the human speech perception system has solved some of these problems.

The Speech Stimulus

We began describing sound in Chapter 11 by introducing pure tones—simple sine-wave patterns with different amplitudes and frequencies. We then introduced complex tones consisting of a number of pure tones, called harmonics, with frequencies that are multiples of the tone's fundamental frequency. The sounds of speech increase the complexity one more level. We can still describe speech in terms of frequencies, but a complete description needs to take into account abrupt starts and stops, silences, and noises that occur as speakers form words. It is these words that enable speakers to create meaning by saying words and stringing them together into sentences. These meanings, in turn, influence our perception of the incoming stimuli, so that what we perceive depends not only on the physical sound stimulus but also on cognitive processes that help us interpret what we are hearing. We begin by describing the physical sound stimulus, called the *acoustic signal*.

The Acoustic Signal

Speech sounds are produced by the position or the movement of structures within the vocal apparatus, which produce patterns of pressure changes in the air called the **acoustic stimulus**, or the **acoustic signal**. The acoustic signal for most speech sounds is created by air that is pushed up from the lungs past the vocal cords and into the vocal tract. The sound that is produced depends on the shape of the vocal tract as air is pushed through it. The shape of the vocal tract is altered by moving the **articulators**, which include structures such as the tongue, lips, teeth, jaw, and soft palate (**Figure 13.1**).

Let's first consider the production of vowels. Vowels are produced by vibration of the vocal cords, and the specific sounds of each vowel are created by changing the overall shape of the vocal tract. This change in shape changes the resonant frequency of the vocal tract and produces peaks of pressure at a number of different frequencies (**Figure 13.2**). The frequencies at which these peaks occur are called **formants**.

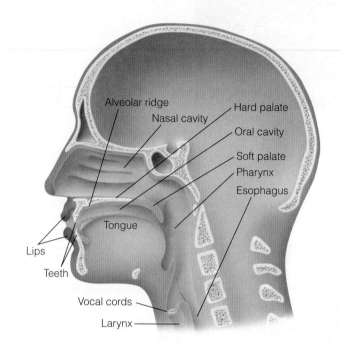

Figure 13.1 The vocal tract includes the nasal and oral cavities and the pharynx, as well as components that move, such as the tongue, lips, and vocal cords.

Each vowel sound has a characteristic series of formants. The first formant has the lowest frequency; the second formant is the next highest; and so on. The formants for the vowel /ae/ (the vowel sound in the word *had*) are shown on a **sound spectrogram** in **Figure 13.3** (speech sounds are

Figure 13.2 Left: the shape of the vocal tract for the vowels /I/ (as in *zip*) and /U/ (as in *put*). Right: the amplitude of the pressure changes produced for each vowel. The peaks in the pressure changes are the *formants*. Each vowel sound has a characteristic pattern of formants that is determined by the shape of the vocal tract for that vowel. (From Denes & Pinson, 1993)

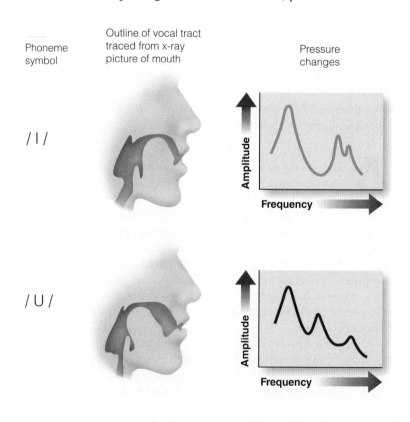

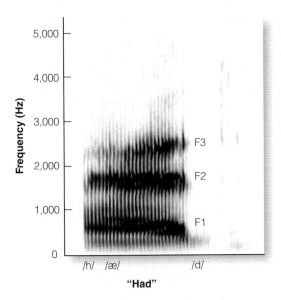

Figure 13.3 Spectrogram of the word *had*. "Time" is on the horizontal axis. The dark horizontal bands are the first (F1), second (F2), and third (F3) formants associated with the sound of the vowel /ae/. Spectrogram courtesy of Kerry Green.

indicated by setting them off with slashes). The sound spectrogram indicates the pattern of frequencies and intensities over time that make up the acoustic signal. Frequency is indicated on the vertical axis and time on the horizontal axis; intensity is indicated by darkness, with darker areas indicating greater intensity. From Figure 13.3, we can see that formants are concentrations of energy at specific frequencies, with the sound /ae/ having formants at 500, 1,700, and 2,500 Hz, which are labeled F1, F2, and F3 in the figure. The vertical lines in the spectrogram are pressure oscillations caused by vibrations of the vocal cord.

Consonants are produced by a constriction, or closing, of the vocal tract. To illustrate how different consonants are produced, let's focus on the sounds /g/, /d/, and /b/. Make these sounds, and notice what your tongue, lips, and teeth are doing. As you produce the sound /d/, you place your tongue against the ridge above your upper teeth (the alveolar ridge of Figure 13.1) and then release a slight rush of air as you move your tongue away from the alveolar ridge (try it). As you produce the sound /b/, you place your two lips together and then release a burst or air.

The way speech sounds are produced is described by the *manner of articulation* and the *place of articulation*. The **manner of articulation** describes how the **articulators**—the mouth, tongue, teeth, and lips—interact when making a speech sound. For example, /b/ is created by blocking the airflow and releasing it quickly. The **place of articulation** describes the locations of the articulation. Notice, for example, how the place of articulation moves from the back to the front of the mouth as you say /g/, /d/, and /b/.

Movements of the tongue, lips, and other articulators create patterns of energy in the acoustic signal that we can observe on the sound spectrogram. For example, the spectrogram for the sentence "Roy read the will," shown in **Figure 13.4**, shows aspects of the signal associated with vowels and consonants. The three horizontal bands marked F1, F2, and F3 are the three formants associated with the /e/ sound of *read*. Rapid shifts in frequency preceding or following formants are called **formant transitions** and are associated with consonants. For example, T2 and T3 in Figure 13.4 are formant transitions associated with the /r/ of *read*.

We have described the physical characteristics of the *acoustic signal*. To understand how this acoustic signal results in *speech perception*, we need to consider the basic units of speech.

Basic Units of Speech

We begin studying speech perception by separating speech sounds into manageable units. What are these units? The flow

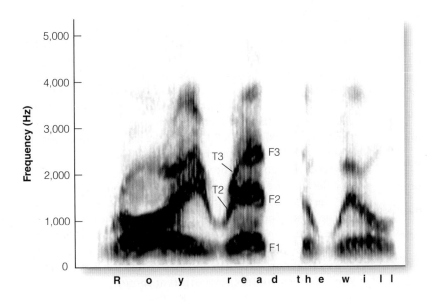

Figure 13.4 Spectrogram of the sentence "Roy read the will," showing formants F1, F2, and F3 and formant transitions T2 and T3. Spectrogram courtesy of Kerry Green.

of a sentence? A particular word? A syllable? The sound of a letter? A sentence is too large a unit for easy analysis, and some letters have no sounds at all. Although there are arguments for the idea that the syllable is the basic unit of speech (Mehler, 1981; Segui, 1984), most speech research has been based on a unit called the **phoneme**. A phoneme is the shortest segment of speech that, if changed, would change the meaning of a word. Consider the word *bit*, which contains the phonemes /b/, /i/, and /t/. We know that /b/, /i/, and /t/ are phonemes because we can change the meaning of the word by changing each phoneme individually. Thus, *bit* becomes *pit* if /b/ is changed to /p/, *bit* becomes *bat* if /i/ is changed to /a/, and *bit* becomes *bid* if /t/ is changed to /d/.

The phonemes of American English, listed in **Table 13.1**, are represented by phonetic symbols that stand for speech sounds. This table shows phonemes for 13 vowel sounds and 24 consonant sounds. Your first reaction to this table may be that there are more vowels than the standard set you learned in grade school (*a, e, i, o, u,* and sometimes *y*). The reason there are more vowels is that some vowels can have more than one pronunciation, so there are more vowel sounds than vowel letters. For example, the vowel *o* sounds different in *boat* and *hot*, and the vowel *e* sounds different in *head* and *heed*. Phonemes, then, refer not to letters but to speech sounds that determine the meaning of what people say.

Because different languages use different sounds, the number of phonemes varies across languages. There are only 13 phonemes in Hawaiian, but as many as 47 have been identified in American English and up to 60 in some African languages. Thus, phonemes are defined in terms of the sounds that are used to create words in a specific language.

It might seem that having identified the phoneme as the basic unit of speech, we could describe speech perception in terms of strings of phonemes. According to this idea, we perceive a series of sounds called phonemes, which create syllables that combine to create words. These syllables and words appear strung together one after another like beads on a string. For example, we perceive the phrase "perception is easy" as the sequence of units "per-sep-shun-iz-ee-zee."

Although perceiving speech may seem to be just a matter of processing a series of discrete sounds that are lined up one after another, the actual situation is much more complex. Rather than following one another, with the signal for one sound ending and then the next beginning, like letters on a page, signals for neighboring sounds overlap one another. A further complication is that the acoustic signal for a particular word can vary greatly depending on whether the speaker is male or female, young or old, speaks rapidly or slowly, or has an accent. This creates a problem called **lack of invariance**, which refers to the fact that there is no simple relationship between a particular phoneme and the acoustic signal. In other words, the acoustic signal for a particular phoneme is variable. We will now describe a number of ways that this variability occurs.

The Variability of the Acoustic Signal

The main problem facing researchers trying to understand speech perception is that there is a variable relationship between the acoustic signal and the sounds we hear. In other words, a particular sound can be associated with a number of different acoustic signals. Let's consider some of the sources of this variability.

Variability From Context

The acoustic signal associated with a phoneme changes depending on its context. For example, look at **Figure 13.5**, which shows spectrograms for the sounds /di/ and /du/. These are smoothed hand-drawn spectrograms that show the two most important characteristics of the sounds: the formants (shown in red) and the formant transitions (shown in blue). Because formants are associated with vowels, we know that the formants at 200 and 2,600 Hz are the acoustic signal for the vowel /i/ in /di/ and that the formants at 200 and 600 Hz are the acoustic signal for the vowel /u/ in /du/.

Because the formants are the acoustic signals for the vowels, the formant transitions that precede the formants must be the signal for the consonant /d/. But notice that the formant transitions for the second (higher-frequency) formants of /di/ and /du/ are different. For /di/, the formant transition starts at about 2,200 Hz and rises to about 2,600 Hz. For /du/, the formant transition starts at about 1,100 Hz and falls

Table 13.1 Major Consonants and Vowels of English and Their Phonetic Symbols

CONSONANTS				VOWELS	
p	pull	s	sip	i	heed
b	bull	z	zip	I	hid
m	man	r	rip	e	bait
w	will	š	should	ɛ	head
f	fill	ž	pleasure	æ	had
v	vet	č	chop	u	who'd
θ	thigh	ǰ	gyp	U	put
ð	that	y	yip	ʌ	but
t	tie	k	kale	o	boat
d	die	g	gale	O	bought
n	near	h	hail	a	hot
l	lear	η	sing	ə	sofa

There are other American English phonemes in addition to those shown here, and specific symbols may vary depending on the source.

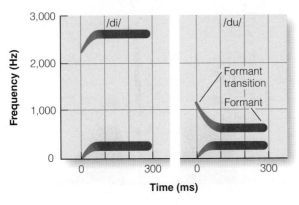

Figure 13.5 Hand-drawn spectrograms for /di/ and /du/. (From Liberman et al., 1967)

to about 600 Hz. Thus, even though we perceive the same /d/ sound in /di/ and /du/, the formant transitions, which are the acoustic signals associated with these sounds, are very different. Thus, the context in which a specific phoneme occurs can influence the acoustic signal that is associated with that phoneme.

This effect of context occurs because of the way speech is produced. Because articulators are constantly moving as we talk, the shape of the vocal tract associated with a particular phoneme is influenced by the sounds that both precede and follow that phoneme. This overlap between the articulation of neighboring phonemes is called **coarticulation**. You can demonstrate coarticulation to yourself by noting how you produce phonemes in different contexts. For example, say *bat* and *boot*. When you say *bat*, your lips are unrounded, but when you say *boot*, your lips are rounded, even during the initial /b/ sound. Thus, even though the /b/ is the same in both words, you articulate each differently. In this example, the articulation of /oo/ in *boot* overlaps the articulation of /b/, causing the lips to be rounded even before the /oo/ sound is actually produced.

The fact that we perceive the sound of a phoneme as the same even though the acoustic signal is changed by coarticulation is an example of *perceptual constancy*. This term may be familiar to you from our observations of constancy phenomena in the sense of vision, such as color constancy (we perceive an object's chromatic color as constant even when the wavelength distribution of the illumination changes, page 214) and size constancy (we perceive an object's size as constant even when the size of its image changes on our retina, page 246). Perceptual constancy in speech perception is similar. We perceive the sound of a particular phoneme as constant even when the phoneme appears in different contexts that change its acoustic signal.

Variability From Different Speakers

People say the same words in a variety of different ways. Some people's voices are high-pitched and some are low-pitched; people speak with various accents; some talk very rapidly and others speak e-x-t-r-e-m-e-l-y s-l-o-w-l-y. These wide variations in speech mean that for different speakers, a particular phoneme or word can have very different acoustic signals. Analysis of how people actually speak has determined that there are 50 different ways to produce the word *the* (Waldrop, 1988).

Speakers also introduce variability through sloppy pronunciation. For example, say the following sentence at the speed you would use in talking to a friend: "This was a best buy." How did you say "best buy"? Did you pronounce the /t/ of best, or did you say "bes buy"? What about "She is a bad girl"? While saying this rapidly, notice whether your tongue hits the top of your mouth as you say the /d/ in bad. Many people omit the /d/ and say "ba girl." Finally, what about "Did you go to the store?" Did you say "did you" or "dijoo"? You have your own ways of producing various words and phonemes, and other people have theirs.

That people do not usually articulate each word individually in conversational speech is reflected in the spectrograms in **Figure 13.6**. The spectrogram in **Figure 13.6a** is for the

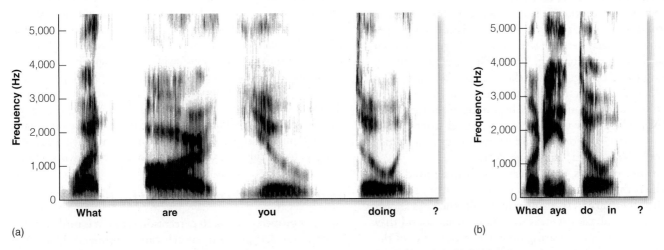

(a)   (b)

Figure 13.6 (a) Spectrogram of "What are you doing?" pronounced slowly and distinctly. (b) Spectrogram of "What are you doing?" as pronounced in conversational speech. Spectrograms courtesy of David Pisoni.

question "What are you doing?" spoken slowly and distinctly; the spectrogram in **Figure 13.6b** is for the same question taken from conversational speech, in which "What are you doing?" becomes "Whad'aya doin'?" This difference shows up clearly in the spectrograms. Although the first and last words (*what* and *doing*) create similar patterns in the two spectrograms, the pauses between words are absent or are much less obvious in the spectrogram of Figure 13.6b, and the middle of this spectrogram is completely changed, with a number of speech sounds missing.

The variability in the acoustic signal caused by coarticulation, different speakers, and sloppy pronunciation creates a problem for the listener, who must somehow transform the information contained in this highly variable acoustic signal into familiar words. In the next section, we will consider some of the ways the speech perception system deals with the variability problem.

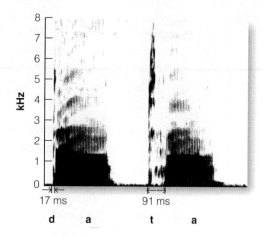

Figure 13.7 Spectrograms for /da/ and /ta/. The voice onset time—the time between the beginning of the sound and the onset of voicing—is indicated at the beginning of the spectrogram for each sound. Spectrogram courtesy of Ron Cole.

Perceiving Phonemes

The speech perception system deals with the variability problem in different ways. We first describe a property of the speech system called *categorical perception* and then consider how information provided by the face and by our knowledge of language helps us perceive speech sounds accurately.

Categorical Perception

Categorical perception occurs when stimuli that exist along a continuum are perceived as divided into discrete categories. For example, consider the visible spectrum (see Figure 1.21, page 18). Starting on the left, at a wavelength of 450 nm, we see blue. As we move toward longer wavelengths, the color remains blue, until suddenly at about 480 nm, we perceive green. Moving along the continuum, we see green all the way to about 570 nm, when the color changes to yellow, then orange, then red. Thus, moving along the entire length of the visible spectrum we encounter just five categories.

Categorical perception in speech occurs in the same way, except the continuum is a property called **voice onset time** (VOT), the time delay between when a sound begins and when the vocal cords begin vibrating. We can illustrate this delay by comparing the spectrograms for the sounds /da/ and /ta/ in **Figure 13.7**. These spectrograms show that the time between the beginning of the sound and the beginning of the vocal cord vibrations (indicated by the presence of vertical stripes in the spectrogram) is 17 ms for /da/ and 91 ms for /ta/. Thus, /da/ has a short VOT, and /ta/ has a long VOT.

By using computers, researchers have created sound stimuli in which the VOT is varied in small steps from short to long. When they vary VOT, using stimuli like the ones shown in Figure 13.7, and ask listeners to indicate what sound they hear, the listeners report hearing only one or the other of the two phonemes, /da/ or /ta/, even though a large number of stimuli with different VOTs are presented.

This result is shown in **Figure 13.8a** (Eimas & Corbit, 1973). At short VOTs, listeners report that they hear /da/, and they continue reporting this even when the VOT is increased. But when the VOT reaches about 35 ms, their perception abruptly changes, so at VOTs above 40 ms, they report hearing /ta/. The VOT when the perception changes from /da/ to /ta/ is called the **phonetic boundary**. The key result of the categorical perception experiment is that even though the VOT is changed continuously across a wide range, the listener perceives only two categories: /da/ on one side of the phonetic boundary and /ta/ on the other side.

Once we have demonstrated categorical perception using this procedure, we can run a *discrimination test*, in which we present two stimuli with different VOTs and ask the listener whether they sound the same or different. When we present two stimuli separated by a VOT of 25 ms that are on the same side of the phonetic boundary, such as stimuli with VOTs of 0 and 25 ms, the listener says they sound the same (**Figure 13.8b**). However, when we present two stimuli that are separated by the same difference in VOT but are on opposite sides of the phonetic boundary, such as stimuli with VOTs of 25 and 50 ms, the listener says they sound different. The fact that all stimuli on the same side of the phonetic boundary are perceived as the same category is an example of perceptual constancy. If this constancy did not exist, we would perceive different sounds every time we changed the VOT. Instead, we experience one sound on each side of the phonetic boundary. This simplifies our perception of phonemes and helps us more easily perceive the wide variety of sounds in our environment.

Information Provided by the Face

Another property of speech perception is that it is **multimodal**; that is, our perception of speech can be influenced by information from a number of different senses. One illustration of how speech perception can be influenced by visual information

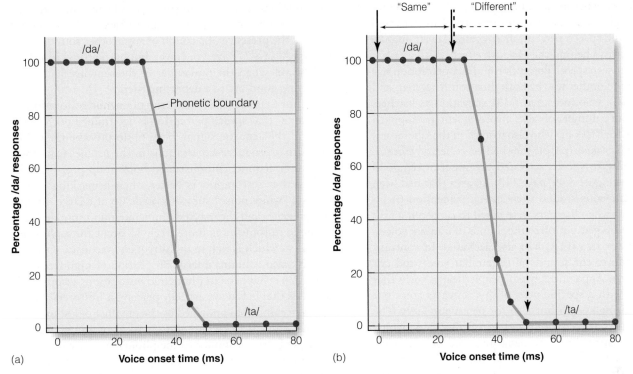

Figure 13.8 (a) The results of a categorical perception experiment indicating a phonetic boundary, with /da/ perceived for VOTs to the left and /ta/ perceived for VOTs to the right. (From Eimas & Corbit, 1973) (b) In the discrimination part of a categorical perception experiment, two stimuli are presented, and the listener indicates whether they are the same or different. The typical result is that two stimuli with VOTs on the same side of the phonetic boundary (VOT = 0 and 25 ms; solid arrows) are judged to be the same, whereas two stimuli on different sides of the phonetic boundary (VOT = 25 ms and 50 ms; dashed arrows) are judged to be different.

Figure 13.9 The McGurk effect. The women is saying /ba-ba/, but her lip movements correspond to /fa-fa/, so the listener reports hearing /fa-fa/.

is shown in **Figure 13.9**. The woman seen in the monitor is saying /ba-ba/, but the woman's lip movements are those that would produce the sounds /fa-fa/. The listener, therefore hears the sound as /fa-fa/ to match the lip movements he is *seeing*, even though the acoustic signal corresponds to /ba-ba/. (Note

that when listener closes his eyes, his perception is no longer be influenced by what he is seeing and he hears /ba-ba/.)

This effect is called the **McGurk effect**, after Harry McGurk, who first described it along with John MacDonald (McGurk & MacDonald, 1976). It illustrates that although auditory information is the major source of information for speech perception, visual information can also exert a strong influence on what we hear (see "Something to Consider: Connections Between Hearing and Vision" in Chapter 12, page 312). This influence of vision on speech perception is called **audiovisual speech perception**. The McGurk effect is one example of audiovisual speech perception. Another example is the way people routinely use information provided by a speaker's lip movements to help understand speech in a noisy environment (also see Sumby & Pollack, 1954).

The link between vision and speech has been shown to have a physiological basis. Gemma Calvert and coworkers (1997) used fMRI to measure brain activity as observers watched a silent videotape of a person making mouth movements for saying numbers. Observers silently repeated the numbers as they watched, so this task was similar to what people do when they read lips. In a control condition, observers watched a static face while silently repeating numbers. A comparison of the brain activity in these two conditions showed that watching the lips move activated an area in the auditory cortex that Calvert had shown in another experiment to be activated when people are perceiving speech. The fact that the same areas are activated for lipreading and speech perception, suggests Calvert, may be a neural mechanism behind the McGurk effect.

The link between speech perception and face perception was demonstrated in another way by Katharina von Kriegstein and coworkers (2005), who measured fMRI activation as listeners were carrying out a number of tasks involving sentences spoken by familiar speakers (people who also worked in the laboratory) and unfamiliar speakers (people they had never heard before).

Just listening to speech activated the superior temporal sulcus (STS; see Figure 5.49, page 118), an area that had been associated in previous studies with speech perception (Belin et al., 2000). But when listeners were asked to carry out a task that involved paying attention to the sounds of familiar voices, the fusiform face area (FFA) was also activated. In contrast, paying attention to the sounds of unfamiliar voices did not activate the FFA. Apparently, when people hear a voice that they associate with a specific person, this activates areas not only for perceiving speech but also for perceiving faces. The link between perceiving speech and perceiving faces, which has been demonstrated in both behavioral and physiological experiments, provides information that helps us deal with the variability of phonemes (for more on the link between observing someone speaking and perceiving speech, see Hall et al., 2005; McGettigan et al., 2012; van Wassenhove et al., 2005).

Information From Our Knowledge of Language

A large amount of research has shown that it is easier to perceive phonemes that appear in a meaningful context. Philip Rubin and coworkers (1976), for example, presented a series of short words, such as *sin*, *bat*, and *leg*, or nonwords, such as *jum*, *baf*, and *teg*, and asked listeners to respond by pressing a key as rapidly as possible whenever they heard a sound that began with /b/. On average, participants took 631 ms to respond to the nonwords and 580 ms to respond to the real words. Thus, when a phoneme was at the beginning of a real word, it was identified about 8 percent faster than when it was at the beginning of a meaningless syllable.

The effect of meaning on the perception of phonemes was demonstrated in another way by Richard Warren (1970), who had participants listen to a recording of the sentence "The state governors met with their respective legislatures convening in the capital city." Warren replaced the first /s/ in "legislatures" with the sound of a cough and told his subjects that they should indicate where in the sentence the cough occurred. None of the participants identified the correct position of the cough, and, even more significantly, none noticed that the /s/ in "legislatures" was missing. This effect, which Warren called the **phonemic restoration effect**, was experienced even by students and staff in the psychology department who knew that the /s/ was missing.

Warren not only demonstrated the phonemic restoration effect but also showed that it can be influenced by the meaning of words following the missing phoneme. For example, the last word of the phrase "There was time to *ave . . ." (where the* indicates the presence of a cough or some other sound) could be "shave," "save," "wave," or "rave," but participants heard the word "wave" when the remainder of the sentence had to do with saying good-bye to a departing friend.

Arthur Samuel (1981) used the phonemic restoration effect to show that speech perception is determined both by the nature of the acoustic signal (bottom-up processing) and by context that produces expectations in the listener (top-down processing). Samuel demonstrated bottom-up processing by showing that restoration is better when a masking sound, such as a "white noise" stimulus made up of a large number of frequencies, and the masked phoneme sound similar. Thus, phonemic restoration is more likely to occur for a phoneme such as /s/, which is rich in high-frequency acoustic energy, if the mask also contains a large proportion of high-frequency energy. What happens in phonemic restoration, according to Samuel, is that before we actually perceive a "restored" sound, its presence must be confirmed by the presence of a sound that is similar to it. If the white-noise mask contains frequencies that make it sound similar to the phoneme we are expecting, phonemic restoration occurs, and we are likely to hear the phoneme. If the mask does not sound similar, phonemic restoration is less likely to occur (Samuel, 1990).

Samuel demonstrated top-down processing by showing that longer words increase the likelihood of the phonemic restoration effect. Apparently, participants used the additional context provided by the long word to help identify the masked phoneme. Further evidence for the importance of context is Samuel's finding that more restoration occurs for a real word such as *prOgress* (where the capital letter indicates the masked phoneme) than for a similar pseudoword such as *crOgress* (Samuel, 1990; also see Samuel, 1997, 2001, for more evidence that top-down processing is involved in phonemic restoration).

TEST YOURSELF 13.1

1. Describe the speech stimulus. Be sure you understand what phonemes are and how the acoustic signal can be displayed using a sound spectrogram to reveal formants and formant transitions.

2. What are two sources of variability that affect the relationship between the acoustic signals and the sounds we hear? Be sure you understand coarticulation.

3. What is categorical perception? Be sure you understand how it is measured and what it illustrates.

4. What is the McGurk effect, and what does it illustrate about how speech perception can be influenced by visual information? What physiological evidence demonstrates a link between visual processing and speech perception?

5. Describe evidence that shows how perceiving phonemes is influenced by the context in which they appear. Describe the phonemic restoration effect and the evidence for both bottom-up and top-down processing in creating this effect.

Perceiving Words and Sentences

Just as perceiving phonemes goes beyond simply processing the acoustic signal, perceiving words depends on a number of factors in addition to the acoustic signal. We begin by showing how placing words in sentences can influence our perception of words. Then we consider how we are able to distinguish words from one another in a sentence, and how we can perceive words even when they are pronounced differently by different speakers.

Perceiving Words in Sentences

One way to illustrate that our perception of words can be enhanced when they occur in a sentence is to show that when words are in a sentence, they can be read even when they are incomplete, as in the following demonstration.

DEMONSTRATION | Perceiving Degraded Sentences

Read the following sentences:

1. M*R* H*D * L*TTL* L*MB I*S FL**C* W*S WH*T* *S SN*W
2. TH* S*N *S N*T SH*N*NGT*D**
3. S*M* W**DS *R* EA*I*RT* U*D*R*T*N*T*A* *T*E*S

Your ability to read the sentences, even though up to half of the letters have been eliminated, was aided by your knowledge of English words, how words are strung together to form sentences, and perhaps in the first example, your familiarity with the nursery rhyme (Denes & Pinson, 1993).

A similar effect of meaningfulness also occurs for spoken words. A classic experiment by George Miller and Steven Isard (1963) demonstrated how meaningfulness makes it easier to perceive spoken words by showing that words are more intelligible when heard in the context of a grammatical sentence than when presented as items in a list of unconnected words. They demonstrated this by creating three kinds of stimuli: (1) normal grammatical sentences, such as *Gadgets simplify work around the house*; (2) anomalous sentences that follow the rules of grammar but make no sense, such as *Gadgets kill passengers from the eyes*; and (3) ungrammatical strings of words, such as *Between gadgets highways passengers the steal*.

Miller and Isard used a technique called **shadowing**, in which they presented these sentences to subjects through earphones and asked them to repeat aloud what they were hearing. The participants reported normal sentences with an accuracy of 89 percent, but their accuracy fell to 79 percent for the anomalous sentences and 56 percent for the ungrammatical strings. The differences among the three types of stimuli became even greater when the listeners heard the stimuli in the presence of a background noise. For example, at a moderately high level of background noise, accuracy was 63 percent for the normal sentences, 22 percent for the anomalous sentences, and only 3 percent for the ungrammatical strings of words. These results tell us that when words are arranged in a meaningful pattern, we can perceive them more easily. But most people don't realize that it is their knowledge of the nature of their language that helps them fill in difficult to hear sounds and words. For example, our knowledge of permissible word structures tells us that ANT, TAN, and NAT are all permissible sequences of letters in English, but that TQN or NQT cannot be English words.

A similar effect of meaning on perception also occurs because our knowledge of the rules of grammar tells us that "There is no time to question" is a permissible English sentence, but "Question, no time there is" is not permissible or, at best, is extremely awkward (unless you are Yoda, who says this in *Star Wars, Episode III: Revenge of the Sith*). Because we mostly encounter meaningful words and grammatically correct sentences, we are continually using our knowledge of what is permissible in our language to help us understand what is being said. This becomes particularly important when listening under less than ideal conditions, such as in a noisy environment or when the speaker's voice quality or accent is difficult to understand, as we will discuss later in the chapter (see also Salasoo & Pisoni, 1985).

Perceiving Breaks Between Sequences of Words

Just as we effortlessly see objects when we look at a visual scene, we usually have little trouble perceiving individual words when conversing with another person. But when we look at the speech signal, we see that the acoustic signal is continuous, with either no physical breaks in the signal or breaks that don't necessarily correspond to the breaks we perceive between words (**Figure 13.10**). The perception of individual words in a conversation is called **speech segmentation**.

The fact that there are often no spaces between words becomes obvious when you listen to someone speaking a foreign language. To someone who is unfamiliar with that language,

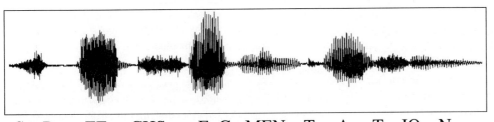

Figure 13.10 Sound energy for the words "speech segmentation." Notice that it is difficult to tell from this record where one word ends and the other begins. Speech signal courtesy of Lisa Sanders.

the words seem to speed by in an unbroken string. However, to a speaker of that language, the words seem separated, just as the words of your native language seem separated to you. We somehow solve the problem of speech segmentation and divide the continuous stream of the acoustic signal into a series of individual words.

The fact that we can perceive individual words in conversational speech, even though there are few breaks in the speech signal, means that our perception of words is not based only on the energy stimulating the receptors. One thing that helps us tell when one word ends and another begins is knowledge of the meanings of words. The link between speech segmentation and meaning is illustrated in the following demonstration.

DEMONSTRATION | Organizing Strings of Sounds

Read the following words: Anna Mary Candy Lights Since Imp Pulp Lay Things. Now that you've read the words, what do they mean?

If you think this is a list of unconnected words beginning with the names of two women, Anna and Mary, you're right; but read this series of words out loud speaking rapidly and ignoring the spaces between the words on the page. When you do this, can you hear a connected sentence that does *not* begin with the names Anna and Mary? (For the answer, see page 334—but don't peek until you've tried reading the words rapidly.)

If you succeeded in creating a new sentence from the series of words, you did so by changing the perceptual organization of the sounds, and this change was achieved by your knowledge of the meaning of the sounds. Just as the perceptual organization of the forest scene in Figure 5.31 (page 106) depended on seeing the rocks as meaningful patterns (faces), your perception of the new sentence depended on knowing the meanings of the sounds you created when you said these words rapidly.

Another example of how meaning and prior knowledge or experience are responsible for organizing sounds into words is provided by these two sentences:

Jamie's mother said, "Be a *big girl* and eat your vegetables."
The thing *Big Earl* loved most in the world was his car.

"Big girl" and "Big Earl" are both pronounced the same way, so hearing them differently depends on the overall meaning of the sentence in which these words appear. This example is similar to the familiar "I scream, you scream, we all scream for ice cream" that many people learn as children. The sound stimuli for "I scream" and "ice cream" are identical, so the different organizations must be achieved by the meaning of the sentence in which these words appear.

While segmentation is aided by knowing the meanings of words and making use of the context in which these words occur, listeners use other information as well to achieve segmentation. As we learn a language, we learn that certain sounds are more likely to follow one another within a word, and other sounds are more likely to be separated by the space between two words. For example, consider the words *pretty baby*. In

English it is likely that *pre* and *ty* will be in the same word (*pretty*) and that *ty* and *ba* will be separated by a space so will be in two different words (pre*ty ba*by). Thus, the space in the phrase *prettybaby* is most likely to be between *pretty* and *baby*.

Psychologists describe the way sounds follow one another in a language in terms of **transitional probabilities**—the chances that one sound will follow another sound. Every language has transitional probabilities for different sounds, and as we learn a language, we not only learn how to say and understand words and sentences, but we also learn about the transitional probabilities in that language. The process of learning about transitional probabilities and about other characteristics of language is called **statistical learning**. Research has shown that infants as young as 8 months of age are capable of statistical learning.

Jennifer Saffran and coworkers (1996) carried out an early experiment that demonstrated statistical learning in young infants. **Figure 13.11a** shows the design of this experiment. During the learning phase of the experiment, the infants heard four nonsense "words" such as *bidaku, padoti, golabu,* and *tupiro*, which were combined in random order to create 2 minutes of continuous sound. An example of part of a string created by combining these words is *bidaku**padoti**golabu**tupiro**padoti**bidaku*.... In this string, every other word is printed in boldface in order to help you pick out the words. However, when the infants heard these strings, all the words were pronounced with the same intonation, and there were no breaks between the words to indicate where one word ended and the next one began.

Because the words were presented in random order and with no spaces between them, the 2-minute string of words the infants heard sounds like a jumble of random sounds. However, there was information within the string of words in the form of transitional probabilities, which the infants could

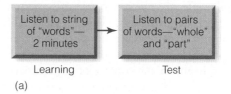

(a)

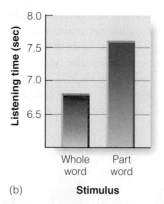

(b) **Stimulus**

Figure 13.11 (a) Design of the experiment by Saffran and coworkers (1996), in which infants listened to a continuous string of nonsense syllables and were then tested to see which sounds they perceived as belonging together. (b) The results, indicating that infants listened longer to the "part-word" stimuli.

potentially use to determine which groups of sounds were words. The transitional probabilities between two syllables that appeared *within* a word was always 1.0. For example, for the word *bidaku*, when /*bi*/ was presented, /*da*/ always followed it. Similarly, when /*da*/ was presented, /*ku*/ always followed it. In other words, these three sounds always occurred together and in the same order, to form the word *bidaku*. However, the transitional probabilities between the *end* of one word and the *beginning* of another was only 0.33. For example, there was a 33 percent chance that the last sound, /*ku*/ from *bidaku*, would be followed by the first sound, /*pa*/, from *padoti*, a 33 percent chance that it would be followed by /*tu*/ from *tupiro*, and a 33 percent chance it would be followed by /*go*/ from *golabu*.

If Saffran's infants were sensitive to transitional probabilities, they would perceive stimuli like *bidaku* or *padoti* as words, because the three syllables in these words are linked by transitional probabilities of 1.0. In contrast, stimuli like *tibida* (the end of *padoti* plus the beginning of *bidaku*) would not be perceived as words, because the transitional probabilities were much smaller.

To determine whether the infants did, in fact, perceive stimuli like *bidaku* and *padoti* as words, the infants were tested by being presented with pairs of three-syllable stimuli. One of the stimuli was a "word" that had been presented before, such as *padoti*. This was the "whole-word" test stimulus. The other stimulus was created from the end of one word and the beginning of another, such as *tibida*. This was the "part-word" test stimulus.

The prediction was that the infants would choose to listen to the part-word test stimuli longer than to the whole-word stimuli. This prediction was based on previous research that showed that infants tend to lose interest in stimuli that are repeated, and so become familiar, but pay more attention to novel stimuli that they haven't experienced before (See Method: Habituation, page 145). Thus, if the infants perceived the whole-word stimuli as words that had been repeated over and over during the 2-minute learning session, they would pay less attention to these familiar stimuli than to the more novel part-word stimuli that they did not perceive as being words.

Saffran measured how long the infants listened to each sound by presenting a blinking light near the speaker where the sound was coming from. When the light attracted the infant's attention, the sound began, and it continued until the infant looked away. Thus, the infants controlled how long they heard each sound by how long they looked at the light.

Figure 13.11b shows that the infants did, as predicted, listen longer to the part-word stimuli. These results are impressive, especially because the infants had never heard the words before, they heard no pauses between words, and they had only listened to the strings of words for 2 minutes. From results such as these, we can conclude that the ability to use transitional probabilities to segment sounds into words begins at an early age.

Perceiving Degraded Speech

One thing you should be convinced of by now is that although the starting point for perceiving speech is the incoming acoustic signal, listeners also use top-down processing, involving their knowledge of meaning and the properties of language, to perceive speech. This additional information helps listeners deal with the variability of speech produced by different speakers. But in our everyday environment, we have to deal with more than just different ways of speaking. We also have to deal with background noise, poor room acoustics, and cell phones under poor reception conditions, all of which prevent a clear acoustic signal from reaching our ears.

How well can we understand speech heard under adverse conditions? Research designed to answer this question has shown that listeners can adapt to adverse conditions by using top-down processing to "decode" the degraded acoustic signal. Matthew Davis and coworkers (2005) tested subjects to determine their ability to perceive speech distorted by a process called *noise vocoding*. **Noise-vocoded speech** is created by dividing the speech signal up into different frequency bands and then adding noise to each band. This process transforms the spectrogram of the original speech stimulus on the left in **Figure 13.12** into the noisy spectrogram on the right. The loss of detail in

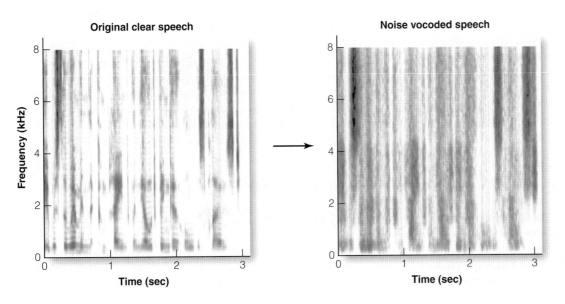

Figure 13.12 How the speech signal was changed for the Davis et al. (2005) noise vocoding experiment. The spectrogram of the original speech stimulus is on the left, and the noise-vocoded version is on the right. See text for details.

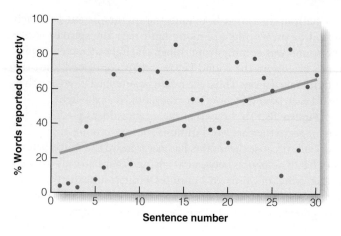

Figure 13.13 Perception of noise-vocoded words correctly identified for a series of 30 different sentences. Each data point is the average performance for the 6 subjects in Davis et al.'s (2005) experiment.

the frequency representation of the noise-vocoded signal transforms clear speech into a harsh noisy whisper.

Subjects in Davis's experiment listened to a vocoded sentence and then wrote down as much of the sentence as they could. This was repeated for a total of 30 sentences. **Figure 13.13** shows the average proportion of words reported correctly by six subjects for each of the 30 sentences. Notice that performance is near zero for the first three sentences, and then increases, until by the 30th sentence, subjects are reporting half or more of the words. (The variability occurs because some vocoded sentences are more difficult to hear than others.) The increase in performance shown in Figure 13.13 is important because all the subjects were doing is listening to one sentence after the other.

What information do listeners use to achieve this clearer understanding? One hint comes from experiments in which subjects first listened to a degraded sentence and wrote down what they heard, as before, and then heard a clear undistorted version of the sentence, followed by the distorted sentence again (hear degraded sentence → hear clear sentence → hear degraded sentence again). Subjects reported that when they listened to the second presentation of the degraded sentence, they heard some words they hadn't heard the first time. Davis calls this ability to hear previously unintelligible words the "pop-out" effect.

The pop-out effect shows that higher-level information such as listeners' knowledge can improve speech perception. But this result becomes even more interesting when we consider that after experiencing the pop-out effect subjects became better at understanding *other* degraded sentences that they were hearing for the first time. Even more interesting, the pop-out effect and later improvement in performance also occurred in a group of subjects who *read* the sentence after hearing the degraded version (hear degraded sentence → read written sentence → hear degraded sentence again). What this means is that it wasn't listening to the clear sound that was important, but knowing the *content* (the speech sounds and words) of what they were hearing that helped with learning.

Thus, this experiment provides another demonstration of how listeners can use information in addition to the acoustic signal to understand speech.

What information can listeners pick up from degraded sentences? One possibility is the temporal pattern—the timing or rhythm of the speech. Robert Shannon and coworkers (1995) used noise-vocoded speech to demonstrate the importance of these slow temporal fluctuations. They showed that when most of the pitch information was eliminated from a speech signal, listeners were still able to recognize speech by focusing on temporal cues such as the rhythm of the sentence.

You can get a feel for the information carried by temporal cues by imagining what speech sounds like when you press your ears to a door and hear only muffled voices. Although hearing-through-the-door speech is difficult to understand, there is information in the rhythm of speaking that can lead to understanding. Much of this information comes from your knowledge of language, learned through years of experience.

One example of learning from experience is the learning of statistical regularities we discussed in connection with Saffran's infant experiments on page 326. We also discussed the idea of learning from experience in Chapter 5, when we described how visual perception is aided by our knowledge of regularities in the environment (page 108). Remember the "multiple personalities of a blob" experiment in which perception of a blob-like shape depended on the type of scene in which it appeared (see Figure 5.38 and page 308 for a similar discussion related to music perception). Demonstrations such as this illustrate how knowledge of what usually happens in the visual environment influences what we see. Similarly, our knowledge of how certain speech sounds usually follow one another can help us learn to perceive words in sentences, even if the individual sounds are distorted.

The ability to determine what is being said, even when sounds are distorted, is something you may have experienced if you have ever listened to someone speaking with a foreign accent that was difficult to understand at first but became easier to understand as you continued to listen. If this has happened to you, it is likely that you were trying to understand what the person were saying—the overall meaning—without focusing on the sounds of individual words. But eventually, listening to determine the overall message results in an increased ability to understand individual words, which in turn makes it easier to understand the overall message. Clearly, transforming "sound" to "meaningful speech" involves a combination of bottom-up processing, based on the incoming acoustic signal, and top-down processing, based on knowledge of meanings and the nature of speech sounds (**Figure 13.14**).

Speech Perception and the Brain

Investigation of the physiological basis for speech perception stretches back to at least the 19th century, but considerable progress has been made only recently in understanding the

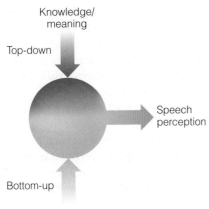

Figure 13.14 Speech perception is the result of top-down processing (based on knowledge and meaning) and bottom-up processing (based on the acoustic signal) working together.

physiological foundations of speech perception and spoken word recognition.

Based on their studies of brain-damaged patients, 19th-century researchers Paul Broca (1824–1880) and Carl Wernicke (1848–1905) showed that damage to specific areas of the brain causes language problems, called **aphasias** (**Figure 13.15**). When Broca tested patients who had suffered strokes that damaged their frontal lobe, in an area that came to be called **Broca's area**, he found that their speech was slow and labored and often had jumbled sentence structure. Here is an example of the speech of a modern patient, who is attempting to describe when he had his stroke, which occurred when he was in a hot tub.

> Alright. . . . Uh . . . stroke and un. . . . I . . . huh tawanna guy. . . . H . . . h . . . hot tub and. . . . And the. . . . Two days when uh. . . . Hos . . . uh. . . . Huh hospital and uh . . . amet . . . am . . . ambulance. (Dick et al., 2001, p. 760)

Patients with this problem—slow, labored, ungrammatical speech caused by damage to Broca's area, are diagnosed as

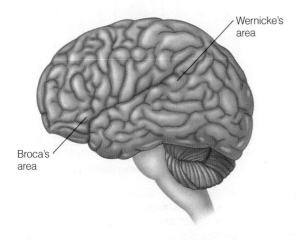

Figure 13.15 Broca's and Wernicke's areas. Broca's area is in the frontal lobe, and Wernicke's is in the temporal lobe.

having **Broca's aphasia**. Later research showed that patients with Broca's aphasia not only have difficulty forming complete sentences, they also have difficulty understanding some types of sentences. Consider, for example, the following two sentences:

> The apple was eaten by the girl.
>
> The boy was pushed by the girl.

Patients with Broca's aphasia have no trouble understanding the first sentence but have difficulty with the second sentence. The problem they have with the second sentence is deciding whether the girl pushed the boy or the boy pushed the girl. While you may think it is obvious that the girl pushed the boy, patients with Broca's aphasia have difficulty processing connecting words such as "was" and "by," and this makes it difficult to determine who was pushed. (Notice what happens to the sentence when these two words are omitted). You can see, however, that the first sentence cannot be interpreted in two ways. It is clear that the girl ate the apple, because it is not possible, outside of an unlikely science fiction scenario, for the apple to eat the girl (Dick et al., 2001; Novick et al., 2005). Taking into account the problems in both producing and understanding speech experienced by Broca's patients, modern researchers have concluded that damage to Broca's area in the frontal lobe causes problems in processing the structure of sentences.

The patients studied by Wernicke, who had damage to an area in their temporal lobe that came to be called **Wernicke's area**, produced speech that was fluent and grammatically correct but tended to be incoherent. Here is a modern example of the speech of a patient with **Wernicke's aphasia**.

> It just suddenly had a feffort and all the feffort had gone with it. It even stepped my horn. They took them from earth you know. They make my favorite nine to severed and now I'm a been habed by the uh stam of fortment of my annulment which is now forever. (Dick et al., 2001, p. 761)

Patients such as this not only produce meaningless speech but are unable to understand speech and writing. While patients with Broca's aphasia have trouble understanding sentences in which meaning depends on word order, as in "The boy was pushed by the girl," Wernicke's patients have more widespread difficulties in understanding and would be unable to understand "The apple was eaten by the girl" as well. In the most extreme form of Wernicke's aphasia, the person has a condition called **word deafness**, in which he or she cannot recognize words, even though the ability to hear pure tones remains intact (Kolb & Whishaw, 2003).

Modern neuropsychological research has gone beyond Broca's and Wernicke's areas through further studies of brain-damaged patients (see Method: Double Dissociations in Neuropsychology, Chapter 4, page 81) and by using brain imaging to locate areas in the brain related to speech. An example of a finding from neuropsychology is that some patients with damage to the parietal lobe have difficulty discriminating between syllables (Blumstein et al., 1977; Damasio & Damasio, 1980). Although we might expect that difficulty in discriminating between syllables would make it difficult to understand words, some patients who have trouble discriminating syllables can still understand words (Micelli et al., 1980). Results such as these illustrate the complex relationship between brain functioning and speech perception.

Measuring brain activity has yielded more straightforward results. For example, Pascal Belin and coworkers (2000) used fMRI to locate a "voice area" in the human superior temporal sulcus (STS; see Figure 5.49) that is activated more by human voices than by other sounds, and Catherine Perrodin and coworkers (2011) recorded from neurons in the monkey's temporal lobe that they called **voice cells** because they responded more strongly to recordings of monkey calls than to calls of other animals or to "non-voice" sounds.

The "voice area" and "voice cells" are located in the temporal lobe, which is part of the *what* processing stream for hearing that we described in Chapter 12 (see page 297). In describing the cortical organization for hearing in Chapter 12, we saw that the *what* pathway is involved in identifying sounds and the *where* pathway is involved in locating sounds (Figure 12.12, page 297). Piggybacking on this dual-stream idea for hearing, researchers have proposed a **dual-stream model of speech perception**. **Figure 13.16** shows one proposed version of this model for the human cortex. Like the dual-stream model for the monkey shown in Figure 12.12, the ventral pathway starts in the anterior (front) part of the auditory cortex and the dorsal pathway starts in the posterior (rear) part of the auditory cortex. The ventral pathway is responsible for recognizing speech, and it has been proposed that the dorsal pathway may be involved in linking the acoustic signal to the movements used to produce speech (Hickock & Poeppel, 2007; Rauschecker, 2011).

More evidence for speech processing in the temporal lobe has been provided by Nima Mesgarani and coworkers (2014), who recorded from electrodes placed directly on the temporal lobe of patients who were undergoing brain surgery for epilepsy. As pointed out in Chapter 3 (page 66), it is standard procedure to record and stimulate from neurons before and during surgery

for epilepsy, in order to determine the functional layout of a particular person's brain. **Figure 13.17a** shows the locations of the electrodes on the temporal lobe. Each dot is an electrode; the darker colored dots indicate locations at which neurons responded most strongly to speech when subjects listened to 500 sentences spoken by 400 different people.

Each column in **Figure 13.17b** shows the results for a single electrode. Red and dark red indicate the neural response for the first 0.4 seconds after the onset of each phoneme, listed on the left. Each of these electrodes records responses to a group of phonemes. For example, electrode 1 responds to /d/, /b/, /g/, /k/, and /t/, and electrode 3 responds to vowels like /a/ and /ae/ (see Table 13.1).

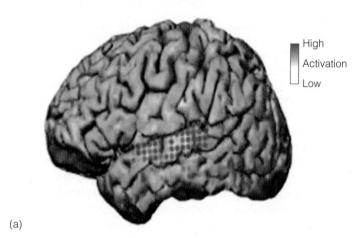

(a)

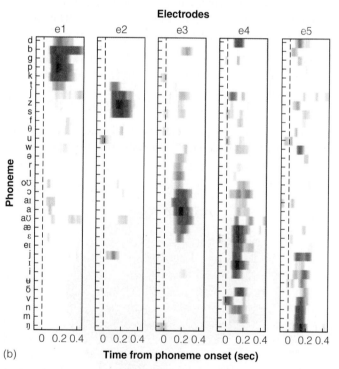

(b)

Figure 13.17 (a) The red dots indicate electrode placements on the temporal lobe for the Mesgarani and coworkers (2014) experiment. Darker dots indicate larger responses to speech sounds. (b) Average neural responses to the phonemes on the left, showing activity in red for five electrodes during the first 0.4 seconds after presentation of the phonemes.

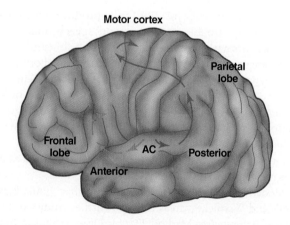

Figure 13.16 Human cortex showing the ventral pathway (green arrows) that is responsible for recognizing speech and the dorsal pathway (red arrows) that links the acoustic signal and motor movements. AC = auditory cortex. The ventral pathway sends signals from the anterior auditory area to the frontal cortex. The dorsal pathway sends signals from the posterior auditory area to the parietal lobe and motor areas. (Adapted from Rauschecker, 2011)

While Mesgarani and coworkers observed electrode responses corresponding to single phonemes, they also found responses corresponding to **phonetic features**, which are cues associated with how a phoneme is produced by the articulators. We have seen that *manner of articulation* describes how the articulators interact while making a speech sound, and *place of articulation* describes the location of articulation (page 319). Mesgarani and coworkers observed responses from some electrodes that were linked to specific phonetic features. For example, one electrode picked up responses to sounds that involved place of articulation in the back of the mouth, such as /g/, and another responded to sounds associated with places near the front, such as /b/.

Thus, neural responses can be linked both to phonemes, which specify specific sounds, and to specific features, which are related to the way these sounds are produced. If we consider the response to a particular phoneme or feature across all electrode positions, we find that each phoneme or feature causes a pattern of activity across the population of feature-selective electrodes. The neural code for phonemes and phonetic features therefore corresponds to population coding, which was described in Chapter 3 (see Figure 3.34, page 67).

What is important about studies such as this one is that they go beyond identifying where speech is processed in the cortex to provide information about how neural responding represents basic units of speech such as phonemes and the phonetic features associated with these phonemes.

SOMETHING TO CONSIDER:
Speech Perception and Action

In Chapter 4, we introduced the idea that visual perception involves both a *what* stream, which is involved in identifying objects, and a *where* or *action* stream, which is involved in locating objects and taking action with respect to objects. The idea that taking action is an important aspect of perception took center stage in Chapter 7, which described the link between visual perception and action.

The link between perception and action also occurs for speech perception. A theory that proposed a link between speech perception and action is the **motor theory of speech perception** (Liberman et al., 1963, 1967). This theory proposed that (1) hearing a particular speech sound activates motor mechanisms controlling the movement of the articulators, such as the tongue and lips, that are responsible for producing sounds; and (2) activation of these motor mechanisms, in turn, activates additional mechanisms that enable us to *perceive* the sound. Thus, the motor theory proposes that activity of motor mechanisms is the first step toward perceiving speech.

When motor theory was first proposed in the 1960s, it was extremely controversial. In the decades that followed, the theory stimulated a large number of experiments, some obtaining results that supported the theory, but many obtaining results that argued against it. It is difficult for motor theory to explain, for example, how people with brain damage that disables their speech motor system can still perceive speech (Lotto et al., 2009), or how young infants can understand speech before they have learned to speak (Eimas et al., 1987). Evidence such as this has led present-day speech researchers to largely reject the idea that our perception of speech is based on the activation of motor mechanisms.

Although the evidence argues against the idea that activation of motor mechanisms is *necessary* for speech perception, there is a great deal of evidence for *links* between motor mechanisms and speech perception. One of the results supporting this idea is the discovery of mirror neurons. In Chapter 7, we saw that mirror neurons in monkeys respond both when the monkey carries out an action and when the monkey sees someone else carry out the action. A type of mirror neuron related to hearing is called *audiovisual mirror neurons*. These neurons fire both when a monkey carries out an action that produces a sound (like breaking a peanut) and when the monkey hears the sound (the sound of a breaking peanut) that results from the action (Kohler et al., 2002; see Chapter 7, page 163). Interestingly, mirror neurons that have been studied in the monkey are found in an area roughly equivalent to Broca's area in humans; for this reason, some researchers have proposed a close link between mirror neurons and language (Arbib, 2001).

But is there any evidence linking *perceiving* speech and *producing* speech in humans? Alessandro D'Ausilio and coworkers (2009) demonstrated a link between production and perception by showing that stimulation of motor areas associated with making sounds like /b/ and /p/, which involve labial articulation (pursing the lips), aids in the perception of these sounds. Similarly, stimulation of a motor area associated with making sounds like /t/ and /d/, which involve dental articulation (the tongue contacting the back of the teeth), aids in perception of these sounds.

The subjects' task in D'Ausilio's experiment was to push a button as quickly as possible to indicate which sound they heard on each trial. In the baseline condition, the subjects carried out this task without any stimulation of their brain. In the stimulation condition, brief pulses of *focal transcranial magnetic stimulation*, which can stimulate a small targeted area of the brain, were presented just before the subject heard the sound, either to the area of the motor cortex responsible for creating labial (lip) articulation or the area creating dental (tongue and teeth) articulation. (See Method: Transcranial Magnetic Stimulation [TMS], Chapter 8, page 183.)

Figure 13.18 shows the sites of stimulation on the motor area of the cortex. Stimulation of the lip area resulted in faster responding to labial phonemes (/b/ and /p/) and stimulation of the tongue area resulted in faster responding to the dental phonemes (/t/ and /d/). Based on these results, D'Ausilio suggested that activity in the motor cortex can influence speech perception.

Our knowledge of the nature of the link between producing and perceiving speech was taken a step further by Lauren Silbert and coworkers (2014), who measured the fMRI response to two 15-minute stories under two conditions: (1) when the person in the scanner was *telling the story* (production condition) and (2) when the person in the scanner was *listening to the story*

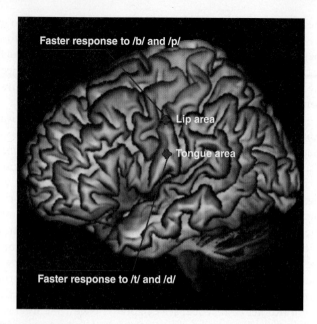

Figure 13.18 Sites of transcranial magnetic stimulation of the motor area for lips and tongue. Stimulation of the lip area increases the speed of responding to /b/ and /p/. Stimulation of the tongue area increases the speed of responding to /t/ and /d/. (From D'Ausilio et al., 2009)

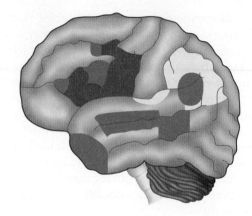

Figure 13.19 Left hemispheres of the cortex, showing areas activated by producing speech (red) and comprehending speech (yellow), and areas that respond to both production and comprehension (blue). The responses to production and comprehension in this area were coupled, which means the time courses of the responses were similar. (From Silbert et al., 2014)

(comprehension condition). One result, shown in **Figure 13.19**, was that the primary motor area (red) responded only when a person was producing speech. This doesn't support the motor theory of speech perception, which states that the motor areas should be responding as a person is comprehending speech.

The most significant result is that many areas, shown in blue in Figure 13.19, respond both when speech is being produced *and* when it is being comprehended. But just because the same brain regions respond during both production and comprehension doesn't necessarily mean that they share

processing mechanisms. It is possible that different kinds of processing could be going on within these regions for these two different tasks. However, the idea that production and comprehension share processing mechanisms is strengthened by Silbert's finding that the brain's response to production and comprehension was "coupled." That is, the time course of the neural responses to these two processes was similar. This result makes it more likely that production and comprehension share mechanisms, and shows that just as action and motor mechanisms play important roles in visual perception, there is a close link between action (production) and perception (comprehension) for speech perception as well (Meister et al., 2007; Wilson & Iacobini, 2006).

DEVELOPMENTAL DIMENSION Infant Speech Perception

We have seen from Saffran's experiments (Figure 13.11) that infants can use speech statistics to achieve speech segmentation. In addition, research has demonstrated categorical perception in 1-month-old infants.

The Categorical Perception of Phonemes

Categorical perception was first reported for adults in 1967 (Liberman et al., 1967). In 1971, Peter Eimas and coworkers began the modern era of research on infant speech perception by using the habituation procedure to show that infants as young as 1 month old perform similarly to adults in categorical perception experiments. The basis of these experiments was the observation that an infant will suck on a nipple in order to hear a series of brief speech sounds, but as the same speech sounds are repeated, the infant's sucking eventually habituates to a low level. By presenting a new stimulus after the rate of sucking had decreased, Eimas determined whether the infant perceived the new stimulus as sounding the same as or different from the old one.

The results of Eimas and coworkers' experiment are shown in **Figure 13.20**. The number of sucking responses when no sound was presented is indicated by the point at B. When a sound with voice onset time (VOT) of 20 ms (sounds like "ba" to an adult) is presented as the infant sucks, the sucking increases to a high level and then begins to decrease. When the VOT is changed to 40 ms (dashed line; sounds like "pa" to an adult), sucking increases, as indicated by the points to the right of the dashed line. This means that the infant perceives a difference between sounds with VOTs of 20 and 40 ms. The center graph, however, shows that changing the VOT from 60 to 80 ms (both sound like "pa" to an adult) has only a small effect on sucking, indicating that the infants perceive little, if any, difference between the two sounds. Finally, the results for a control group (the right graph) show that when the sound is not changed, the number of sucking responses decreases throughout the experiment.

These results show that when the VOT is shifted across the average adult phonetic boundary (left graph), the infants perceive a change in the sound, and when the VOT is shifted

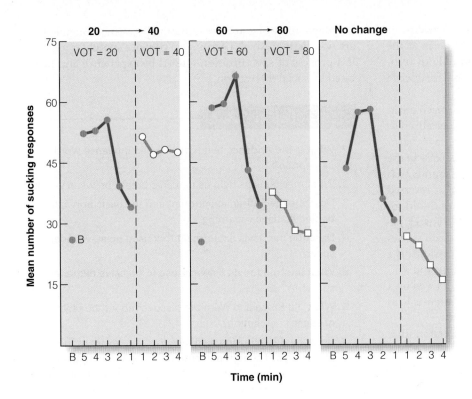

Figure 13.20 Results of a categorical perception experiment on infants using the habituation procedure. In the left panel, VOT is changed from 20 to 40 ms (across the phonetic boundary). In the center panel, VOT is changed from 60 to 80 ms (not across the phonetic boundary). In the right panel, the VOT was not changed. See text for details. (From Eimas et al., 1971)

on the same side of the phonetic boundary (center graph), the infants perceive little or no change in the sound. That infants as young as 1 month old are capable of categorical perception is particularly impressive because these infants have had virtually no experience in producing speech sounds and only limited experience in hearing them. But the story regarding phoneme perception extends beyond the discovery that very young infants can perceive phonemes. As we will see in the next section, the ability to perceive phonemes is affected by the language a child hears during its first year.

Learning the Sounds of a Language

Infants' ability to perceive speech continues to develop as they get older. But what, exactly, is happening as this development occurs? One answer, which considers the evidence that infants are sensitive to statistical regularities in the speech signal (page 326), is that continued exposure to language, from listening to people talking around them, causes infants to learn the properties of the language they are hearing.

But something else very interesting is revealed when comparing very young infants to 12-month-old infants. Patricia Kuhl has described very young infants as "citizens of the world" because young infants in all cultures can tell the difference between sounds that create all of the speech sounds used in the world's languages (Kuhl et al., 2014). However, by the age of 12 months, infants have lost the ability to distinguish between some of these sounds (Kuhl, 2000, 2004; Kuhl et al., 2006). This result is shown in **Figure 13.21**, which plots the ability to discriminate between /ra/ and /la/ in American and Japanese infants. At 6 months, both can tell the difference between these sounds, but by 12 months, the Japanese infants have become worse and the American infants have improved.

Why does this change occur? The answer involves *experience-dependent plasticity*—a change in the brain's ability to respond to specific stimuli that occurs as a result of experience. We introduced experience-dependent plasticity in Chapter

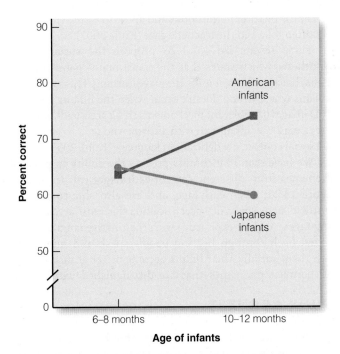

Figure 13.21 The ability of American and Japanese infants to discriminate between the sounds /ra/ and /la/. Performance is about 65 percent for both American and Japanese infants at 6 to 8 months, but then performance becomes different by 10 to 12 months. The performance of the Japanese infants declines, while the performance of the American infants increases. Kuhl (2000) explains this result in terms of experience-dependent plasticity.

3 when we described how raising kittens in an environment consisting entirely of vertical lines causes visual areas of the kitten's brain to contain neurons that respond only to verticals (page 64). Apparently, brain areas responsible for speech perception are similarly shaped by experience.

This "shaping by experience" is a powerful mechanism that transforms the infant's brain so it becomes specialized to discriminate between sounds that occur in the language the infant is hearing. But Kuhl wondered whether the decrease in the ability to discriminate between foreign-language sounds that occurs sometime after 6 months would be halted or reversed by training. Kuhl and coworkers (2003) had 9-month-old infants attend 12 25-minute training sessions over a 4-week period, in which a Mandarin-speaking teacher read them stories in Mandarin and talked to them. During these sessions, the teacher made frequent eye contact with the infants and said their names. After training, the American infants did well on a test of Mandarin sounds, but a control group of infants who didn't receive the training performed more poorly,

Taking this experiment a step further, Kuhl exposed another group of infants to the same training as before, but instead of a live teacher, they saw a DVD presentation of her reading the stories on a video monitor. The performance of these infants was the same as the infants who had received no training in Mandarin. Thus, just observing someone speaking another language on a TV monitor isn't enough. Social interaction, in which a live person interacts with the infant, is also important. This interaction provides interpersonal social cues that attract the infants' attention and motivates learning. In addition, the teachers often look at the pictures in the books and at the toys, and the infants eyes often followed the teacher's gaze (Kuhl, 2007).

These results led Kuhl to propose the **social gating hypothesis**, which states that the social brain "gates" mechanisms that are responsible for language learning. This hypothesis explains why learning doesn't occur when the infants just view DVD images (the relevant mechanisms aren't activated), and suggests a reason why children with autism, who tend to avoid normal social contact, are deficient in language (Kuhl, 2007, 2010).

We have seen that infants possess the ability to perceive phonemes from different categories (categorical perception, Figure 13.20) at an early age, and are also able to perceive contrasts between basic speech sounds that exist across many languages. As their experience with their native language continues, both through hearing people speak and interacting with them socially, their brains become better at discriminating between phonemes that are distinguished within their

language, and worse at discriminating between phonemes that are not distinguished. Learning to perceive speech, it appears, is a process of specialization guided by experience and facilitated by social interaction.

TEST YOURSELF 13.2

1. What is the evidence that meaning can influence word perception?
2. What mechanisms help us perceive breaks between words?
3. Describe the Saffran experiment and the basic principle behind statistical learning.
4. Describe the Davis experiment that used noise-vocoded speech.
5. What information do listeners use to perceive degraded speech?
6. What did Broca and Wernicke discover about the physiology of speech perception?
7. Describe the following evidence that is relevant to the physiology of speech perception: (1) determining the brain's response to speech stimuli; (2) the dual-stream model of speech perception.
8. Describe the Mesgarani experiment. What did it demonstrate about neural responding to phonemes and to phonetic features?
9. What link between perception and motor responding does the motor theory propose? Describe the results of research on mirror neurons and the results of D'Ausilio's transcranial magnetic stimulation experiment. What do these results indicate about the relationship between motor activity and speech perception?
10. How did Silbert and coworkers provide evidence that suggests a close link between speech production and speech comprehension?
11. Describe the experiment that showed that 1-month-old infants are capable of categorical perception.
12. Why does Kuhl call very young infants "citizens of the world"? What happens between 6 and 12 months that takes this title away? Hint: Include experience-dependent plasticity in your answer.
13. Describe how training can slow down or halt the decrease in discrimination ability that occurs after 6 months of age. What is the social gating hypothesis?

THINK ABOUT IT

1. How well can computers recognize speech? You can research this question by getting on the telephone with a computer. Dial a service such as the one that books movie tickets. Then, instead of going out of your way to talk slowly and clearly, try talking in a normal conversational voice (but clearly enough that a human would still understand you), and see whether you can determine the limits of the computer's ability to understand speech. (p. 317)

2. How do you think your perception of speech would be affected if the phenomenon of categorical perception did not exist? (p. 322)

Answer to question on page 326:

An American delights in simple playthings.

KEY TERMS

Acoustic signal (p. 318)
Acoustic stimulus (p. 318)
Aphasias (p. 329)
Articulators (p. 318)
Articulators (p. 319)
Audiovisual speech perception (p. 323)
Broca's aphasia (p. 329)
Broca's area (p. 329)
Categorical perception (p. 322)
Coarticulation (p. 321)
Dual-stream model of speech perception (p. 330)
Formant transitions (p. 319)

Formants (p. 318)
Lack of invariance (p. 320)
Manner of articulation (p. 319)
McGurk effect (p. 323)
Motor theory of speech perception (p. 331)
Multimodal (p. 322)
Noise-vocoded speech (p. 327)
Phoneme (p. 320)
Phonemic restoration effect (p. 324)
Phonetic boundary (p. 322)
Phonetic features (p. 331)
Place of articulation (p. 319)

Shadowing (p. 325)
Social gating hypothesis (p. 334)
Sound spectrogram (p. 318)
Speech segmentation (p. 325)
Statistical learning (p. 326)
Transitional probabilities (p. 326)
Voice cells (p. 330)
Voice onset time (VOT) (p. 322)
Wernicke's aphasia (p. 329)
Wernicke's area (p. 329)
Word deafness (p. 329)

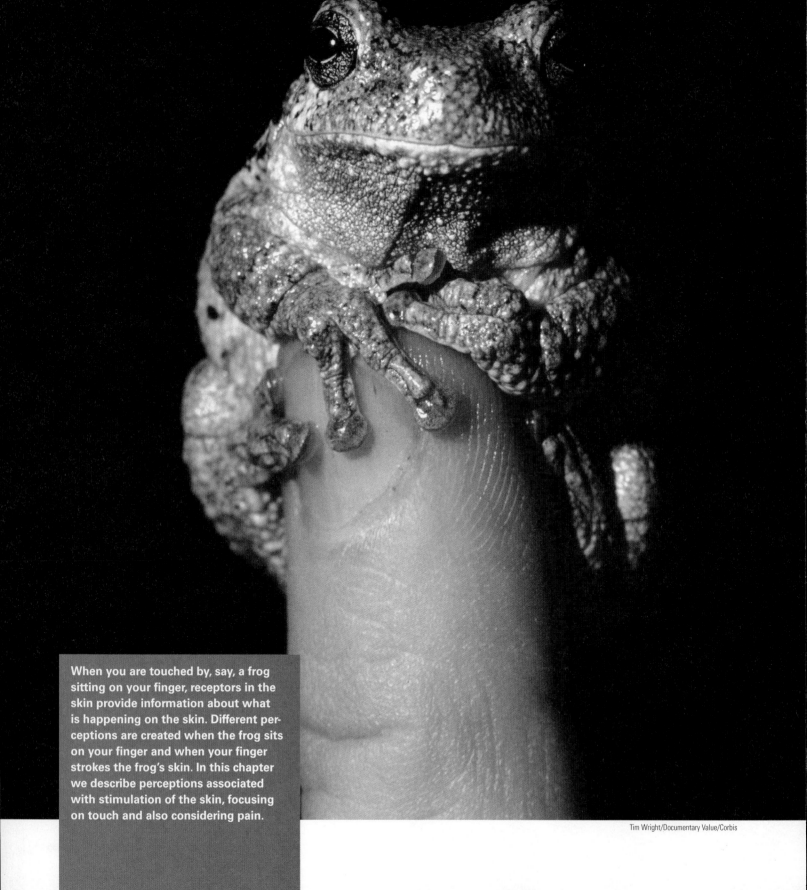

When you are touched by, say, a frog sitting on your finger, receptors in the skin provide information about what is happening on the skin. Different perceptions are created when the frog sits on your finger and when your finger strokes the frog's skin. In this chapter we describe perceptions associated with stimulation of the skin, focusing on touch and also considering pain.

CHAPTER 14

The Cutaneous Senses

CHAPTER CONTENTS

Perception by the Skin and Hands

Overview of the Cutaneous System
The Skin
Mechanoreceptors
Pathways From Skin to Cortex
The Somatosensory Cortex
The Plasticity of Cortical Body Maps

Perceiving Details
Receptor Mechanisms for Tactile Acuity
Cortical Mechanisms for Tactile Acuity

Perceiving Vibration and Texture
Vibration of the Skin
Surface Texture

Perceiving Objects
Identifying Objects by Haptic Exploration
The Cortical Physiology of Tactile Object Perception

Pain Perception

The Gate Control Model of Pain

Top-Down Processes

Expectation
Attention
Emotions

The Brain and Pain
Brain Areas
Chemicals and the Brain

Observing Pain in Others

SOMETHING TO CONSIDER: Social Pain and Physical Pain

THINK ABOUT IT

Some Questions We Will Consider:

- Are there specialized receptors in the skin for sensing different tactile qualities? (p. 338)
- What is the most sensitive part of the body? (p. 342)
- Is it possible to reduce pain with your thoughts? (p. 353)
- How is social pain related to physical pain? (p. 357)

When asked which sense they would choose to lose, if they had to lose either vision, hearing, or touch, some people pick touch. This is understandable given the high value we place on seeing and hearing, but making a decision to lose the sense of touch would be a serious mistake. Although people who are blind or deaf can get along quite well, people with a rare condition that results in losing the ability to feel sensations though the skin often suffer constant bruises, burns, and broken bones in the absence of the warnings provided by touch and pain (Melzack & Wall, 1988; Rollman, 1991; Wall & Melzack, 1994).

But losing the sense of touch does more than increase the chance of injury. It also makes it difficult to interact with the environment because of the loss of feedback from the skin that accompanies many actions. As I type this, I hit my computer keys with just the right amount of force, because I can feel pressure when my fingers hit the keys. Without this feedback, typing and other actions that receive feedback from touch would become much more difficult. Experiments in which subjects have had their hands temporarily anesthetized have shown that the resulting loss of feeling causes them to apply much more force than necessary when carrying out tasks with their fingers and hands (Avenanti et al., 2005; Monzée et al., 2003).

A particularly dramatic case that involved losing the ability to sense with the skin, as well as the closely related ability to sense the movement and positions of the limbs, is that of Ian Waterman, a 17-year-old apprentice butcher, who in May 1971 contracted what at first appeared to be a routine case of the flu (Cole, 1995; Robles-De-La-Torre, 2006). He anticipated returning to work after recovering; however, instead of improving, his condition worsened, with an initial tingling sensation in his limbs becoming a total loss of the ability to feel touch below the neck. Ian's doctors, who were initially baffled by his condition, eventually determined that an autoimmune reaction had destroyed most of the neurons that transmitted signals from his skin, joints, tendons, and muscles to his brain. The loss of the ability to feel skin sensations meant that Ian couldn't feel his body when lying in bed, which resulted in a frightening floating sensation, and he often used inappropriate force when grasping objects—sometimes gripping too tightly, and sometimes dropping objects because he hadn't gripped tightly enough.

As difficult as losing sensations from his skin made Ian's life, destruction of the nerves from his muscles, tendons, and joints caused an even more serious problem. The destruction of these nerves eliminated Ian's ability to sense the position of his arms, legs, and body. This is something we take for granted. When you close your eyes, you can tell where your hands and legs are relative to each other and to your body. But Ian had lost this ability, so even though he could move, because the nerves conducting signals from his brain to his muscles were unaffected, he avoided moving, because not knowing where his limbs were made it difficult to control them.

Eventually, after many years of practice, Ian was able to sit, stand, and even carry out movements and tasks such as writing. Ian was able to do these things not because his sensory nerves had recovered (they remained irreversibly damaged), but because he had learned to use his sense of vision to constantly monitor the positions of his limbs and body. Imagine, for a moment, what it would be like to have to constantly look at your hands, arms, legs, and body, so you could tell where they were and make the necessary muscular adjustments to maintain your posture and carry out actions. Ian described the extreme and constant effort needed to do this as making his life like "running a daily marathon" (Cole, 1995).

Ian's problems were caused by a breakdown of his **somatosensory system**, which includes (1) the **cutaneous senses**, which are responsible for perceptions such as touch and pain that are usually caused by stimulation of the skin; (2) **proprioception**, the ability to sense the position of the body and limbs; and (3) **kinesthesis**, the ability to sense the movement of the body and limbs. In this chapter we will focus on the cutaneous senses, which are important not only for activities like grasping objects and protecting against damage to the skin, but also for motivating sexual activity (another reason picking touch as the sense to lose would be a mistake).

When we recognize that the perceptions we experience through our skin are crucial for carrying out everyday activities, protecting ourselves from injury, and motivating sexual activity, we can see that these perceptions are crucial to our survival and to the survival of our species. In fact, we could make a good case for the idea that perceptions felt through the skin and that enable us to sense the positions and movements of our limbs are more important for survival than those provided by vision and hearing.

Perception by the Skin and Hands

The title of this chapter is "The Cutaneous Senses," and because *cutaneous* refers to the skin, we could take this title to mean that there are a number of different senses associated with the skin. We will simply note that we experience a number of different *qualities* due to stimulation of the skin. Among them are touch, vibration, tickle, and pain. We begin our discussion of the cutaneous senses by first describing the anatomy of the cutaneous system and then focusing on the sense of touch, which enables us to perceive properties of surfaces and objects such as details, vibrations, texture, and shape. In the second half of the chapter, we will focus on the perception of pain.

Overview of the Cutaneous System

In this section we will describe some basic facts about the anatomy and functioning of the various parts of the cutaneous system.

The Skin

M. Comèl (1953) called the skin the "monumental facade of the human body" for good reason. It is the heaviest organ in the human body, and, if not the largest (the surface areas of the gastrointestinal tract and of the alveoli of the lungs exceed the surface area of the skin), it is certainly the most obvious, especially in humans, whose skin is not obscured by fur or large amounts of hair (Montagna & Parakkal, 1974).

In addition to its warning function, the skin also prevents body fluids from escaping and at the same time protects us by keeping bacteria, chemical agents, and dirt from penetrating our bodies. Skin maintains the integrity of what's inside and protects us from what's outside, but it also provides us with information about the various stimuli that contact it. The sun's rays heat our skin, and we feel warmth; a pinprick is painful; and when someone touches us, we experience pressure or other sensations.

Our main experience with the skin is its visible surface, which is actually a layer of tough dead skin cells. (Try sticking a piece of cellophane tape onto your palm and pulling it off. The material that sticks to the tape is dead skin cells.) This layer of dead cells is part of the outer layer of skin, which is called the **epidermis**. Below the epidermis is another layer, called the **dermis** (**Figure 14.1**). Within the skin are **mechanoreceptors**, receptors that respond to mechanical stimulation such as pressure, stretching, and vibration.

Mechanoreceptors

Many of the tactile perceptions that we feel from stimulation of the skin can be traced to mechanoreceptors that are located in the epidermis and the dermis. Two mechanoreceptors, the **Merkel receptor** and the **Meissner corpuscle**, are located close to the surface of the skin, near the epidermis. Because they are located close to the surface, these receptors have small

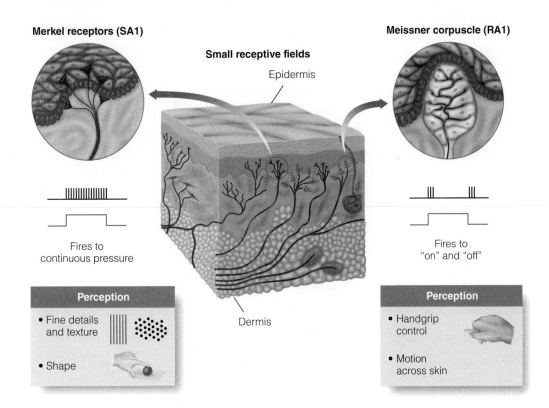

Merkel receptors (SA1)

Meissner corpuscle (RA1)

Small receptive fields

Epidermis

Fires to
continuous pressure

Fires to
"on" and "off"

Perception
• Fine details and texture
• Shape

Perception
• Handgrip control
• Motion across skin

Dermis

Figure 14.1 A cross section of glabrous (without hairs or projections) skin, showing the layers of the skin and the structure, firing properties, and perceptions associated with the Merkel receptor (SA1) and Meissner corpuscle (RA1)—two mechanoreceptors near the surface of the skin.

receptive fields; a **cutaneous receptive field** is the area of skin which, when stimulated, influences the firing of the neuron.

Figure 14.1 shows the structure and firing of these receptors in response to a pressure stimulus that is presented and then removed (blue line). Because the nerve fiber associated with the slowly adapting Merkel receptor fires continuously, as long as the stimulus is on, it is called a **slowly adapting (SA) fiber**. The fibers associated with the Merkel receptor are called **SA1 fibers**. The nerve fiber associated with the rapidly adapting Meissner corpuscle fires only when the stimulus is first applied and when it is removed, and so is called a **rapidly adapting (RA) fiber**. The fibers associated with the Meissner corpuscle are called RA1 fibers. The types of perception associated with

the Merkel receptor/SA1 fiber are details, shape, and texture, and with the Meissner corpuscle/RA1 fiber, controlling handgrip and perceiving motion across the skin.

We can appreciate how the Merkel receptor/SA1 fiber signals information about shape by considering how an object's contour is signaled by the pattern of firing of a large number of mechanoreceptors. This is illustrated by the response profiles in **Figure 14.2**, which indicate how SA1 fibers in the fingertips respond to contact with two different spheres, one with high curvature relative to the fingertip (**Figure 14.2a**) and one that is more gently curved (**Figure 14.2b**). In both cases, the receptors right at the point where the fingers contact the sphere respond the most, and ones farther away fire less, but

Figure 14.2 (a) Response of fibers in the fingertips to touching a high-curvature stimulus. The height of the profile indicates the firing rate at different places across the fingertip. (b) The profile of firing to touching a stimulus with more gentle curvature. (From Goodwin, 1998)

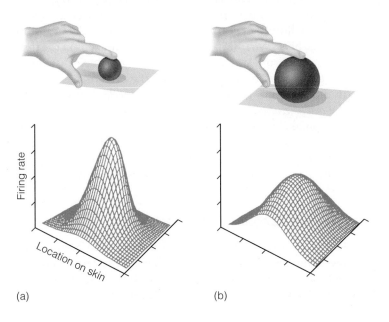

Firing rate

Location on skin

(a)

(b)

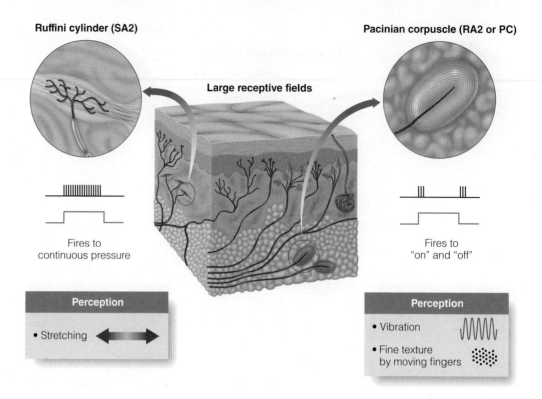

Figure 14.3 A cross section of glabrous skin, showing the structure, firing properties, and perceptions associated with the Ruffini cylinder (SA2) and the Pacinian corpuscle (RA2 or PC)—two mechanoreceptors that are deeper in the skin.

Ruffini cylinder (SA2)

Pacinian corpuscle (RA2 or PC)

Large receptive fields

Fires to continuous pressure

Fires to "on" and "off"

Perception
• Stretching

Perception
• Vibration
• Fine texture by moving fingers

the *pattern* of response is different in the two cases. It is this overall pattern that provides information to the brain about the curvature of the sphere (Goodwin, 1998).

The two other mechanoreceptors, the **Ruffini cylinder (SA2 fiber)** and the **Pacinian corpuscle (RA2 or PC fiber),** are located deeper in the skin (**Figure 14.3**), so they have larger receptive fields. The Ruffini cylinder responds continuously to stimulation, and the Pacinian corpuscle responds when the stimulus is applied and removed. The Ruffini cylinder is associated with perceiving stretching of the skin, the Pacinian corpuscle with sensing rapid vibrations and fine texture.[1]

Our description has associated each receptor/fiber type with specific types of stimulation. However, when we consider how neurons fire when fingers move across natural textures, we will see that the perception of texture often involves the coordinated activity of different types of neurons working together.

Pathways From Skin to Cortex

The receptors for the other senses are localized in one area— the eye (vision), the ear (hearing), the nose (olfaction), and the mouth (taste)—but cutaneous receptors in the skin are distributed over the whole body. This wide distribution, plus the fact that signals must reach the brain before stimulation of the skin can be perceived, creates a travel situation we might call "journey of the long-distance nerve impulses," especially for signals that must travel from the fingertips or toes to the brain.

Signals from all over the body are conducted from the skin to the spinal cord, which consists of 31 segments, each of which

receives signals through a bundle of fibers called the *dorsal root* (**Figure 14.4**). After the signals enter the spinal cord, nerve fibers transmit them to the brain along two major pathways: the **medial lemniscal pathway** and the **spinothalamic pathway.** The lemniscal pathway has large fibers that carry signals related to sensing the positions of the limbs (proprioception) and perceiving touch. These large fibers transmit signals at high speed, which is important for controlling movement and reacting to touch. The spinothalamic pathway consists of smaller fibers that transmit signals related to temperature and pain. The case of Ian Waterman illustrates this separation in function, because although he lost the ability to feel touch and to sense the positions of his limbs (lemniscal pathway), he was still able to sense pain and temperature (spinothalamic pathway).

Fibers from both pathways cross over to the other side of the body during their upward journey to the thalamus. Most of these fibers synapse in the **ventrolateral nucleus** in the thalamus, but some synapse in other thalamic nuclei. (Remember that fibers from the retina and the cochlea also synapse in the thalamus, in the *lateral geniculate nucleus* for vision and the *medial geniculate nucleus* for hearing.) Because the signals in the spinal cord have crossed over to the opposite side of the body, signals originating from the left side of the body reach the thalamus in the right hemisphere of the brain, and signals from the right side of the body reach the left hemisphere.

The Somatosensory Cortex

From the thalamus, signals travel to the **somatosensory receiving area (S1)** in the parietal lobe of the cortex and possibly also to the **secondary somatosensory cortex (S2)** (Rowe et al., 1996; Turman et al., 1998; **Figure 14.5a**). Signals also

[1]Although Michael Paré and coworkers (2002) have reported that there are no Ruffini receptors in the finger pads of monkeys, Ruffini cylinders are still included in most lists of glabrous (nonhairy) skin receptors, so they are included here.

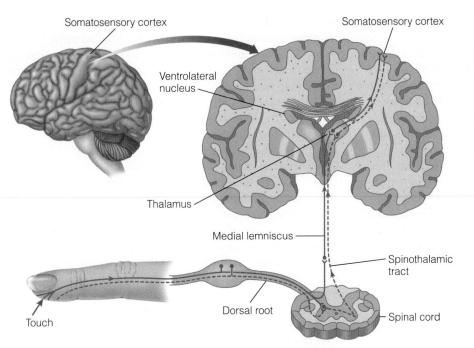

Figure 14.4 The pathway from receptors in the skin to the somatosensory receiving area of the cortex. The fiber carrying signals from a receptor in the finger enters the spinal cord through the dorsal root. The signals then travel up the spinal cord along two pathways: the medial lemniscus and the spinothalamic tract. These pathways synapse in the ventrolateral nucleus of the thalamus and then send signals to the somatosensory cortex in the parietal lobe.

travel between S1 and S2 and from S1 and S2 to additional somatosensory areas.

An important characteristic of the somatosensory cortex is that it is organized into maps that correspond to locations on the body. The existence of a map of the body on S1 was determined in a classic series of investigations carried out by neurosurgeon Wilder Penfield while operating on awake patients who were having brain surgery to relieve symptoms of epilepsy (Penfield &

Rasmussen, 1950). Note that there are no pain receptors in the brain, so the patients cannot feel the surgery.

When Penfield stimulated points on S1 and asked patients to report what they perceived, they reported sensations such as tingling and touch on various parts of their body. Penfield found that stimulating the ventral part of S1 (lower on the parietal lobe) caused sensations on the lips and face, stimulating higher on S1 caused sensations in the hands and fingers,

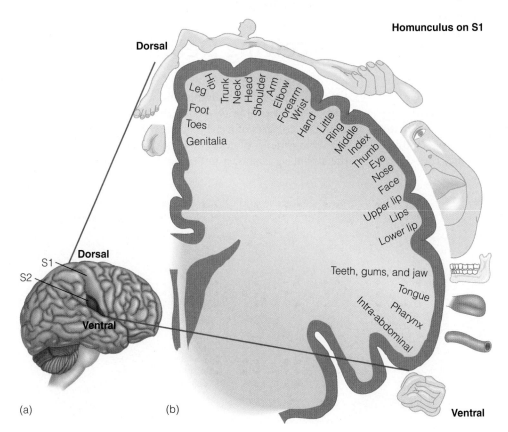

Figure 14.5 (a) The somatosensory cortex in the parietal lobe. The primary somatosensory area, S1 (light purple), receives inputs from the ventrolateral nucleus of the thalamus. The secondary somatosensory area, S2 (dark purple), is partially hidden behind the temporal lobe. (b) The sensory homunculus on the somatosensory cortex. Parts of the body with the highest tactile acuity are represented by larger areas on the cortex. (Adapted from Penfield & Rasmussen, 1950)

and stimulating the dorsal S1 caused sensations in the legs and feet.

The resulting body map, shown in **Figure 14.5b**, is called the **homunculus**, Latin for "little man." The homunculus shows that adjacent areas of the skin project to adjacent areas in the brain, and that some areas on the skin are represented by a disproportionately large area of the brain. The area devoted to the thumb, for example, is as large as the area devoted to the entire forearm. This result is analogous to the magnification factor in vision (see page 74), in which receptors in the fovea, which are responsible for perceiving visual details, are allotted a disproportionate area on the visual cortex. Similarly, parts of the body such as the fingers, which are used to detect details through the sense of touch, are allotted a disproportionate area on the somatosensory cortex (Duncan & Boynton, 2007). A similar body map also occurs in the secondary somatosensory cortex (S2).

This description in terms of S1 and S2 and the homunculus is accurate but simplified. Recent research has shown that S1 is divided into four interconnected areas, each with different functions. For example, the area in S1 involved in perceiving touch is connected to another area that is involved in *haptics* (exploring objects with the hand). In addition, there are a number of homunculi within both S1 and S2 (Keysers et al., 2010). Finally, there are other areas that we will discuss when we consider pain later in the chapter.

The Plasticity of Cortical Body Maps

One of the basic principles of cortical organization is that the cortical representation of a particular function can become larger if that function is used often. We introduced this principle, called *experience-dependent plasticity*, when we described how rearing kittens in a vertical environment caused most of the neurons in their visual cortex to respond best to vertical orientations (see page 64) and how training humans to recognize shapes called Greebles caused the fusiform face area of the cortex to respond more strongly to Greeble stimuli (see page 89).

Most of the early experiments that demonstrated experience-dependent plasticity were carried out in the somatosensory system. In one of these early experiments, William Jenkins and Michael Merzenich (1987) measured the cortical areas devoted to each of a monkey's fingers and then trained monkeys to complete a task that involved the extensive use of a particular location on one fingertip. When they compared the cortical maps of the fingertip measured just before the training to the map measured after 3 months of training, they found that the area representing the stimulated fingertip was greatly expanded after the training. Thus, the cortical area representing part of the fingertip, which is large to begin with, became even larger when the area received a large amount of stimulation.

In most animal experiments, like the one we just described, the effect of plasticity is determined by measuring how special training affects the brain. An experiment that measured this effect in humans determined how training affected the brains of musicians. Consider, for example, players of stringed instruments. A right-handed violin player bows with the right hand and uses the fingers of his or her left hand to finger the strings. One result of this tactile experience is that these musicians have a greater than normal cortical representation for the fingers of their left hand (Elbert et al., 1995). Just as in the monkeys, plasticity created more cortical area for parts of the body that were used more. What this plasticity means is that while we can specify the general area of the cortex that represents a particular part of the body, the exact size of the area representing each part of the body is not totally fixed (Pascual-Leone et al., 2005).

The receptors in the skin make it possible for us to sense different qualities such as small details, vibration, textures of surfaces, the shapes of three-dimensional objects, and potentially damaging stimuli. We will now describe how information for detail, vibration, texture, and object shape are processed by the skin, and then consider pain, which is influenced not only by stimulation of the skin but by other factors as well.

Perceiving Details

One of the most impressive examples of perceiving details with the skin is provided by Braille, the system of raised dots that enables blind people to read with their fingertips. A Braille character consists of a cell made up of one to six dots. Different arrangements of dots and blank spaces represent letters of the alphabet, as shown in **Figure 14.6**; additional characters

Figure 14.6 The Braille alphabet consists of raised dots in a 2 × 3 matrix. The large blue dots indicate the location of the raised dot for each letter. Blind people read these dots by scanning them with their fingertips.

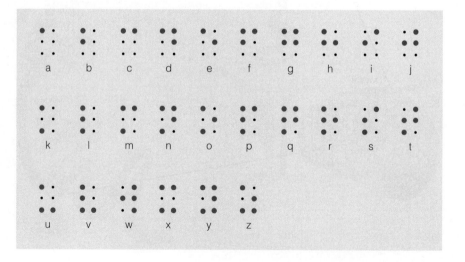

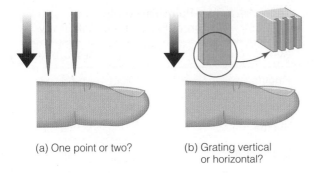

(a) One point or two? (b) Grating vertical or horizontal?

Figure 14.7 Methods for determining tactile acuity: (a) two-point threshold; (b) grating acuity.

represent numbers, punctuation marks, and common speech sounds and words.

Experienced Braille readers can read at a rate of about 100 words per minute, slower than the rate for visual reading, which averages about 250 to 300 words per minute, but impressive nonetheless when we consider that a Braille reader transforms an array of raised dots into information that goes far beyond simply feeling sensations on the skin.

The ability of Braille readers to identify patterns of small raised dots based on the sense of touch depends on tactile detail perception. The first step in describing research on tactile detail perception is to consider how researchers have measured our capacity to detect details of stimuli presented to the skin.

METHOD | Measuring Tactile Acuity

Just as there are a number of different kinds of eye charts for determining a person's visual acuity, there are a number of ways to measure a person's tactile acuity—the ability to detect details on the skin. The classic method of measuring tactile acuity is the **two-point threshold**, the minimum separation between two points on the skin that when stimulated is perceived as two points (**Figure 14.7a**). The two-point threshold is measured by gently touching the skin with two points, such as the points of a drawing compass, and having the person indicate whether he or she feels one point or two.

The two-point threshold was the main measure of acuity in most of the early research on touch. Recently, however, other methods have been introduced. **Grating acuity** is measured by pressing a grooved stimulus like the one in **Figure 14.7b** onto the skin and asking the person to indicate the orientation of the grating. Acuity is measured by determining the narrowest spacing for which orientation can be accurately judged. Finally, acuity can also be measured by pushing raised patterns such as letters onto the skin and determining the smallest sized pattern or letter that can be identified (Cholewaik & Collins, 2003; Craig & Lyle, 2001, 2002).

As we consider the role of both receptor mechanisms and cortical mechanisms in determining tactile acuity, we will see that there are a number of parallels between the cutaneous system and the visual system.

Receptor Mechanisms for Tactile Acuity

The properties of the receptors are one of the things that determine what we experience when the skin is stimulated. We will illustrate this by first focusing on the connection between the Merkel receptor and associated fibers and tactile acuity. We described how SA1 fibers, which are associated with Merkel receptors, respond to a curved shape (Figure 14.2). We now consider how Merkel receptor fibers respond to grooved stimuli.

Figure 14.8a shows how the fiber associated with a Merkel receptor fires in response to a grooved stimulus pushed into the skin. Notice that the firing of the fiber reflects the pattern of the grooved stimuli. This indicates that the firing of the Merkel receptor's fiber signals details (Johnson, 2002; Phillips & Johnson, 1981). For comparison, **Figure 14.8b** shows the firing of the fiber associated with the Pacinian corpuscle. The lack of match between the grooved pattern and the firing indicates that this receptor is not sensitive to the details of patterns that are pushed onto the skin.

It is not surprising that there is a high density of Merkel receptors in the fingertips, because the fingertips are the parts of the body that are most sensitive to details (Vallbo & Johansson, 1978).

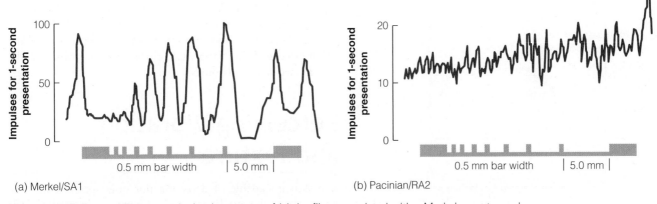

(a) Merkel/SA1 (b) Pacinian/RA2

Figure 14.8 Firing to the grooved stimulus pattern of (a) the fiber associated with a Merkel receptor and (b) the fiber associated with a Pacinian corpuscle receptor. The response to each groove width was recorded during a 1-second indentation for each bar width, so these graphs represent the results for a number of presentations. (Adapted from Phillips & Johnson, 1981)

The relationship between locations on the body and sensitivity to detail has been studied psychophysically by measuring the two-point threshold on different parts of the body. Try this yourself by doing the following demonstration.

DEMONSTRATION | Comparing Two-Point Thresholds

To measure two-point thresholds on different parts of the body, hold two pencils side by side (or better yet, use a drawing compass) so that their points are about 12 mm (0.5 in.) apart; then touch both points simultaneously to the tip of your thumb and determine whether you feel two points. If you feel only one, increase the distance between the pencil points until you feel two; then note the distance between the points. Now move the pencil points to the underside of your forearm. With the points about 12 mm apart (or at the smallest separation you felt as two points on your thumb), touch them to your forearm and note whether you feel one point or two. If you feel only one, how much must you increase the separation before you feel two?

A comparison of grating acuity on different parts of the hand shows that better acuity is associated with less spacing between Merkel receptors (**Figure 14.9**). But receptor spacing can't be the whole story, because although tactile acuity is better on the tip of the index finger than on the tip of the little finger, the spacing between Merkel receptors is the same on all the fingertips. This means that while receptor spacing is part of the answer, the cortex also plays a role in determining tactile acuity (Duncan & Boynton, 2007).

Cortical Mechanisms for Tactile Acuity

Just as there is a parallel between tactile acuity and receptor density, there is also a parallel between tactile acuity and the representation of the body in the brain. **Table 14.1** indicates the two-point threshold measured on different parts of the male body. By comparing these two-point thresholds to how different parts of the body are represented in the brain

Table 14.1 Two-Point Thresholds on Different Parts of the Male Body

PART OF BODY	THRESHOLD (MM)
Fingers	4
Upper lip	8
Big toe	9
Upper arm	46
Back	42
Thigh	44

Source: Data from Weinstein (1968).

(Figure 14.5b), we can see that regions of high acuity, like the fingers and lips, are represented by larger areas on the cortex. As we mentioned earlier, when we described the homunculus, "magnification" of the representation on the brain of parts of the body such as the fingertips parallels the magnification factor in vision (page 74). The map of the body on the brain is enlarged to provide the extra neural processing that enables us to accurately sense fine details with our fingers and other parts of the body.

Another way to demonstrate the connection between cortical mechanisms and acuity is to determine the receptive fields of neurons in different parts of the cortical homunculus. From **Figure 14.10**, which shows the sizes of receptive fields from cortical neurons that receive signals from a monkey's fingers (**Figure 14.10a**), hand (**Figure 14.10b**), and arm (**Figure 14.10c**), we can see that cortical neurons representing parts of the body with better acuity, such as the fingers, have smaller receptive fields. This means that two points that are close together on the fingers might fall on receptive fields that don't overlap (as indicated by the two arrows in Figure 14.10a) and so would cause neurons that are separated in the cortex to fire (**Figure 14.10d**). However, two points with the same separation when applied to the arm are likely to fall on receptive fields that overlap (see arrows in Figure 14.10c) and so could cause neurons that are not separated in the cortex to fire (Figure 14.10d). Thus, the small receptive fields of neurons receiving signals from the fingers translates into more separation on the cortex, which enhances the ability to feel two close-together points on the skin as two separate points.

Perceiving Vibration and Texture

The skin is capable of detecting not only spatial details of objects, but other qualities as well. When you place your hands on mechanical devices that produce vibration, such as a car, a lawnmower, or an electric toothbrush, you can sense these vibrations with your fingers and hands.

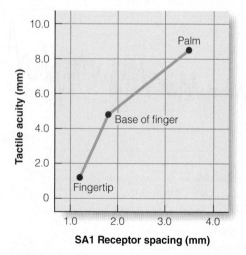

Figure 14.9 Correlation between density of Merkel receptors and tactile acuity. (From Craig & Lyle, 2002)

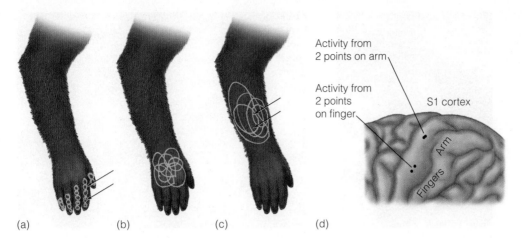

Figure 14.10 Receptive fields of monkey cortical neurons that fire (a) when the fingers are stimulated; (b) when the hand is stimulated; and (c) when the arm is stimulated (Kandel & Jessell, 1991). (d) Stimulation of two nearby points on the finger causes separated activation on the finger area of the cortex, but stimulation of two nearby points on the arm causes overlapping activation in the arm area of the cortex. (From Kandel & Jessell, 1991)

Activity from 2 points on arm

Activity from 2 points on finger

S1 cortex

Arm

Fingers

(a)   (b)   (c)   (d)

Vibration of the Skin

The mechanoreceptor that is primarily responsible for sensing vibration is the Pacinian corpuscle. One piece of evidence linking the Pacinian corpuscle to vibration is that recording from fibers associated with the corpuscle shows that these fibers respond poorly to slow or constant pushing but respond well to high rates of vibration.

Why do the Pacinian corpuscle fibers respond well to rapid vibration? The answer to this question is that the presence of the corpuscle surrounding the nerve fiber determines which pressure stimuli actually reach the fiber. The corpuscle, which consists of a series of layers, like an onion, with fluid between each layer, transmits rapidly repeated pressure, like vibration, to the nerve fiber, as shown in **Figure 14.11a**, but does not transmit continuous pressure, as shown in **Figure 14.11b**. Thus, the corpuscle causes the fiber to receive rapid changes in pressure, but not to receive continuous pressure.

Because the Pacinian corpuscle does not transmit continuous pressure to the fiber, presenting continuous pressure to the corpuscle should cause no response in the fiber. This is exactly what Werner Lowenstein (1960) observed in a classic experiment, in which he showed that when pressure was applied to the corpuscle (at A in **Figure 14.11c**), the fiber responded when the pressure was first applied and when it was removed, but it did not respond to continuous pressure. But when Lowenstein dissected away the corpuscle and applied pressure directly to the fiber (at B in Figure 14.11c), the fiber fired to the continuous pressure. Lowenstein concluded from this result that properties of the corpuscle cause the fiber to respond poorly to continuous stimulation, such as sustained pressure, but to respond well to changes in stimulation that occur at the beginning and end of a pressure stimulus or when stimulation is changing rapidly, as occurs in vibration. As we now consider the perception of surface texture, we will see that vibration plays a role in perceiving fine textures.

Surface Texture

Surface texture is the physical texture of a surface created by peaks and valleys. As can be seen in **Figure 14.12**, visual

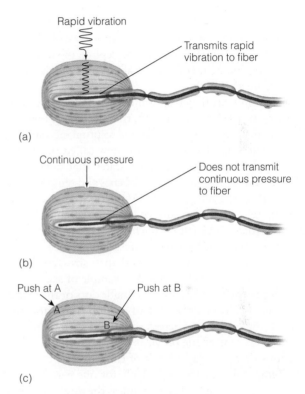

Rapid vibration

Transmits rapid vibration to fiber

(a)

Continuous pressure

Does not transmit continuous pressure to fiber

(b)

Push at A   Push at B

A

B

(c)

Figure 14.11 (a) When a vibrating pressure stimulus is applied to the Pacinian corpuscle, it transmits these pressure vibrations to the nerve fiber. (b) When a continuous pressure stimulus is applied to the Pacinian corpuscle, it does not transmit the continuous pressure to the fiber. (c) Lowenstein determined how the fiber fired to stimulation of the corpuscle (at A) and to direct stimulation of the fiber (at B). (Adapted from Lowenstein, 1960)

inspection can be a poor way of determining surface texture because seeing texture depends on the light–dark pattern determined by the angle of illumination. Thus, although the visually perceived texture of the two sides of the post in Figure 14.12 looks very different, moving the fingers across the two surfaces reveals that their texture is the same.

Touch, which involves direct contact with a surface, therefore provides a more accurate assessment of surface texture than vision. However, this doesn't mean that scanning a

Figure 14.12 The post in (a) is illuminated from the left. The close-up in (b) shows how the visual perception of texture is influenced by illumination. Although the surface on the right side of the pole appears rougher than on the left, the surface textures of the two sides are identical.

(a)   (b)

surface with the fingers always results in an accurate indication of surface texture. As we will see, our perception of surface texture depends on how the surface is scanned and which mechanoreceptors are activated.

Research on texture perception tells an interesting story, extending from 1925 to the present, that illustrates how psychophysics can be used to understand perceptual mechanisms. In 1925, David Katz proposed what is now called the **duplex theory of texture perception**, which states that our perception of texture depends on both spatial cues and temporal cues (Hollins & Risner, 2000; Katz, 1925/1989). **Spatial cues** are provided by relatively large surface elements, such as bumps and grooves, that can be felt both when the skin moves across the surface elements and when it is pressed onto the elements. These cues result in feeling different shapes, sizes, and distributions of these surface elements. An example of spatial cues is perceiving a coarse texture such as Braille dots or the texture you feel when you touch the teeth of a comb. **Temporal cues** occur when the skin moves across a textured surface like fine sandpaper. This type of cue provides information in the form of vibrations that occur as a result of the movement over the surface. Temporal cues are responsible for our perception of fine texture that cannot be detected unless the fingers are moving across the surface.

Although Katz proposed that texture perception is determined by both spatial and temporal cues, research on texture perception has, until recently, focused on spatial cues. However, experiments by Mark Hollins and coworkers (2000, 2001, 2002) show that temporal cues are responsible for our perception of fine textures. Hollins and Ryan Risner (2000) presented evidence for the role of temporal cues by showing that when subjects touched surfaces without moving their fingers and judged "roughness" using the procedure of magnitude estimation (see Chapter 1, page 15; Appendix C, p. 386), they sensed little difference between two fine textures (particle sizes of 10 μm and 100 μm). However, when subjects were allowed to move their fingers across the surface, they could detect the difference between the fine textures. Thus, movement, which generates vibration as the skin scans a surface, makes it possible to sense the roughness of fine surfaces.

Additional evidence for the role of vibration in sensing fine textures was provided by using the selective adaptation procedure we introduced in Chapter 3 (see page 62). This procedure involves presenting a stimulus that adapts a particular type of receptor and then testing to see how inactivation of that receptor by adaptation affects perception. Hollins and coworkers (2001) used this procedure by presenting two adaptation conditions. The first condition was 10-Hz (10 vibrations per second) adaptation, in which the skin was vibrated with a 10-Hz stimulus for 6 minutes. This frequency of adaptation was picked to adapt the Meissner corpuscle, which responds to low frequencies. The second condition was 250-Hz adaptation. This frequency was picked to adapt the Pacinian corpuscle, which responds to high frequencies.

Following each type of adaptation, subjects ran their fingers over two fine textures—a "standard" texture and a "test" texture. The subject's task was to indicate which texture was finer. Because there were two surfaces, chance performance would be 50 percent, as indicated by the dashed line in **Figure 14.13**. The results indicate that subjects could tell the difference between the two textures when they had not been adapted or had received the 10-Hz adaptation. However, after they had been adapted to the 250-Hz vibration, they

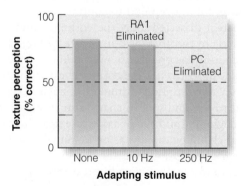

Figure 14.13 Eliminating the action of fibers associated with the Meissner corpuscle by adaptation to a 10-Hz vibration had no effect on perception of a fine texture, but eliminating the action of the Pacinian corpuscle by adapting to a 250-Hz vibration eliminated the ability to sense the fine textures. (Data from Hollins, Bensmaia, & Washburn, 2001)

were unable to tell the difference between two fine textures, as indicated by their chance performance. Thus, adapting the Pacinian corpuscle receptor, which is responsible for perceiving vibration, eliminates the ability to sense fine textures by moving the fingers over a surface. These results and the results of other behavioral experiments (Hollins et al., 2002) support the duplex theory of perception—that the perception of coarse textures is determined by spatial cues and of fine textures by temporal (vibration) cues (also see Weber et al., 2013).

Additional evidence for the role of temporal cues in perceiving texture has been provided by research that shows that vibrations are important for perceiving textures not only when people explore a surface directly with their fingers, but also when they make contact with a surface indirectly, through the use of tools. You can experience this yourself by doing the following demonstration.

DEMONSTRATION | Perceiving Texture With a Pen

Turn your pen over (or cap it) so you can use it as a "probe" (without writing on things). Hold the pen at one end and move the other end over something smooth, such as your desk or a piece of paper. As you do this, notice that you can sense the smoothness of the page, even though you are not directly touching it. Then, try the same thing on a rougher surface, such as a rug, fabric, or concrete.

Your ability to detect differences in texture by running a pen (or some other "tool," such as a stick) over a surface is determined by vibrations transmitted through the tool to your skin (Klatzky et al., 2003). The most remarkable thing about perceiving texture with a tool is that what you perceive is not the vibrations but the texture of the surface, even though you are feeling the surface remotely, with the tip of the tool (Carello & Turvey, 2004).

Perceiving Objects

Imagine that you and a friend are at the seashore. Your friend knows something about shells from the small collection he has accumulated over the years, so as an experiment you decide to determine how well he can identify different types of shells by using his sense of touch alone. When you blindfold your friend and hand him a snail shell and a crab shell, he has no trouble identifying the shells as a snail and a crab. But when you hand him shells of different types of snails that are very similar, he finds that identifying the different types of snails is much more difficult.

Geerat Vermeij, blind at the age of 4 from a childhood eye disease and currently Distinguished Professor of Marine Ecology and Paleoecology at the University of California at Davis, describes his experience when confronted with a similar task. This experience occurred when he was being interviewed by Edgar Boell, who was considering Vermeij's application for graduate study in the biology department at Yale. Boell took

Vermeij to the museum, introduced him to the curator, and handed him a shell. Here is what happened next, as told by Vermeij (1997):

> "Here's something. Do you know what it is?" Boell asked as he handed me a specimen.
>
> My fingers and mind raced. Widely separated ribs parallel to outer lip; large aperture; low spire; glossy; ribs reflected backward. "It's a Harpa," I replied tentatively. "It must be Harpa major." Right so far.
>
> "How about this one?" inquired Boell, as another fine shell changed hands. Smooth, sleek, channeled suture, narrow opening; could be any olive. "It's an olive. I'm pretty sure it's Oliva sayana, the common one from Florida, but they all look alike."
>
> Both men were momentarily speechless. They had planned this little exercise all along to call my bluff. Now that I had passed, Boell had undergone an instant metamorphosis. Beaming with enthusiasm and warmth, he promised me his full support. (pp. 79–80)

Vermeij received his PhD from Yale and is now a world-renowned expert on marine mollusks. His ability to identify objects and their features by touch is an example of **active touch**—touch in which a person actively explores an object, usually with fingers and hands. In contrast, **passive touch** occurs when touch stimuli are applied to the skin, as when two points are pushed onto the skin to determine the two-point threshold. The following demonstration compares the ability to identify objects using active touch and passive touch.

DEMONSTRATION | Identifying Objects

Ask another person to select five or six small objects for you to identify. Close your eyes and have the person place an object in your hand. Your job is to identify the object by touch alone, by moving your fingers and hand over the object. As you do this, be aware of what you are experiencing: your finger and hand movements, the sensations you are feeling, and what you are thinking. Do this for three objects. Then hold out your hand, keeping it still, with fingers outstretched, and let the person move each of the remaining objects around on your hand, moving their surfaces and contours across your skin. Your task is the same as before: to identify the object and to pay attention to what you are experiencing as the object is moved across your hand.

You may have noticed that in the active condition, in which you moved your fingers across the object, you were much more involved in the process and had more control over what parts of the objects you were exposed to. In the active part of the demonstration, you were engaging in **haptic perception**—perception in which three-dimensional objects are explored with the fingers and hand.

Identifying Objects by Haptic Exploration

Haptic perception provides a particularly good example of a situation in which a number of different systems are interacting with each other. As you manipulated the objects in the first part of the demonstration above, you were using three distinct systems to arrive at your goal of identifying the objects: (1) the *sensory system*, which was involved in detecting cutaneous sensations such as touch, temperature, and texture and the movements and positions of your fingers and hands; (2) the *motor system*, which was involved in moving your fingers and hands; and (3) the *cognitive system*, which was involved in thinking about the information provided by the sensory and motor systems.

Haptic perception is an extremely complex process because the sensory, motor, and cognitive systems must all work together. For example, the motor system's control of finger and hand movements is guided by cutaneous feelings in the fingers and the hands, by your sense of the positions of the fingers and hands, and by thought processes that determine what information is needed about the object in order to identify it.

These processes working together create an experience of active touch that is quite different from the experience of passive touch. J. J. Gibson (1962), who championed the importance of movement in perception (see Chapter 7, page 150, and Chapter 8, page 176), compared the experience of active and passive touch by noting that we tend to relate passive touch to the sensation experienced in the skin, whereas we relate active touch to the object being touched. For example, if someone pushes a pointed object into your skin, you might say, "I feel a pricking sensation on my skin"; if, however, you push on the tip of the pointed object yourself, you might say, "I feel a pointed object" (Kruger, 1970). Thus, for passive touch you experience stimulation of the skin, and for active touch you experience the objects you are touching.

Psychophysical research has shown that people can accurately identify most common objects within 1 or 2 seconds (Klatzky et al., 1985). When Susan Lederman and Roberta Klatzky (1987, 1990) observed subjects' hand movements as they made these identifications, they found that people use a number of distinctive movements, which the researchers called **exploratory procedures (EPs)**, and that the types of EPs used depend on the object qualities the subjects are asked to judge.

Figure 14.14 shows four of the EPs observed by Lederman and Klatzky. People tend to use just one or two EPs to determine a particular quality. For example, people use mainly lateral motion and contour following to judge texture, and they use enclosure and contour following to judge exact shape.

The Cortical Physiology of Tactile Object Perception

When we explore objects with our fingers and hands, as described above, we are activating mechanoreceptors that send signals toward the cortex. We now consider what happens when these signals reach the cortex.

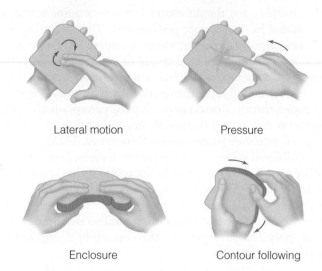

Lateral motion   Pressure

Enclosure   Contour following

Figure 14.14 Some of the exploratory procedures (EPs) observed by Lederman and Klatzky as subjects identified objects. (From Lederman & Klatzky, 1987)

Cortical Neurons Are Specialized
As we move from mechanoreceptor fibers in the fingers toward the brain, we see that neurons become more specialized. This is similar to what occurs in the visual system. Neurons in the ventral posterior nucleus, which is the tactile area of the thalamus, have center-surround receptive fields that are similar to the center-surround receptive fields in the lateral geniculate nucleus, which is the visual area of the thalamus (Mountcastle & Powell, 1959; **Figure 14.15**). In the cortex, we find some neurons with center-surround receptive fields and others that respond to more specialized stimulation of the skin. **Figure 14.16** shows stimuli that cause neurons in the monkey's somatosensory cortex to fire. There are neurons that respond to specific orientations (**Figure 14.16a**) and neurons that respond to movement across the skin in a specified direction (**Figure 14.16b**; Hyvärinen & Poranen, 1978; also see Bensmaia et al., 2008; Pei et al., 2011; Yau et al., 2009).

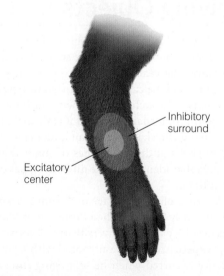

Inhibitory surround

Excitatory center

Figure 14.15 An excitatory-center, inhibitory-surround receptive field of a neuron in a monkey's thalamus.

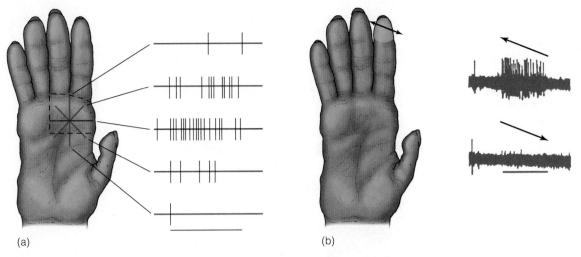

Figure 14.16 Receptive fields of neurons in the monkey's somatosensory cortex. (a) The records to the right of the hand show nerve firing to stimulation of the hand with the orientations shown on the hand. This neuron responds best when a horizontally oriented edge is presented to the monkey's hand. (b) The records on the right indicate nerve firing for movement of a stimulus across the fingertip from right to left (top) and from left to right (bottom). This neuron responds best when a stimulus moves across the fingertip from right to left. (From Hyvärinen & Poranen, 1978)

There are also neurons in the monkey's somatosensory cortex that respond when the monkey grasps a specific object (Sakata & Iwamura, 1978). For example, **Figure 14.17** shows the response of one of these neurons. This neuron responds when the monkey grasps the ruler but does not respond when the monkey grasps a cylinder or a sphere (see also Iwamura, 1998).

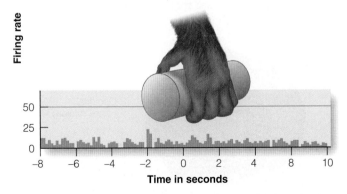

Figure 14.17 The response of a neuron in a monkey's parietal cortex that fires when the monkey grasps a ruler but that does not fire when the monkey grasps a cylinder. The monkey grasps the objects at time = 0. (From Sakata & Iwamura, 1978)

Cortical Responding Is Affected by Attention

Cortical neurons are affected not only by the properties of the object but also by whether the perceiver is paying attention. Steven Hsiao and coworkers (1993, 1996) recorded the response of neurons in areas S1 and S2 to raised letters that were scanned across a monkey's finger. In the tactile-attention condition, the monkey had to perform a task that required focusing its attention on the letters being presented to its fingers. In the visual-attention condition, the monkey had to focus its attention on an unrelated visual stimulus. The results, shown in **Figure 14.18**, show that even though the monkey is receiving exactly the same stimulation on its fingertips in both conditions, the response is larger for the tactile-attention condition. Thus, stimulation of the receptors may trigger a response, but the size of the response can be affected by processes such as attention, thinking, and other actions of the perceiver.

If the idea that events other than stimulation of the receptors can affect perception sounds familiar, it is because similar situations occur in vision (see pages 131, 164) and speech (page 325). A person's active participation makes a difference in

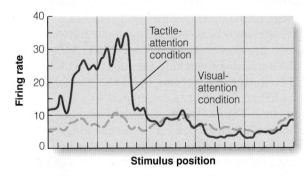

Figure 14.18 Firing rate of a neuron in area S1 of a monkey's cortex to a letter being rolled across the fingertips. The neuron responds only when the monkey is paying attention to the tactile stimulus. (From Hsiao, O'Shaughnessy, & Johnson, 1993)

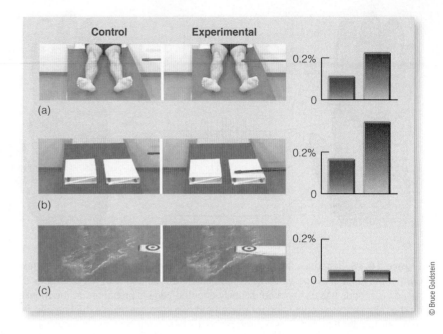

Figure 14.19 Stimuli for the Keysers et al. (2004) experiment. The pictures are stills from control films and experimental films observed by the subjects. (a) Not touching (control) and touching (experimental) legs; (b) not touching and touching object; (c) airplane wing passing over land, no touching. The blue bars are the responses of S2 to the control films. The red bars are the response to the experimental films. (Adapted from Keysers et al., 2004)

Control   Experimental

(a)

(b)

(c)

© Bruce Goldstein

perception, not just by influencing what stimuli stimulate the receptors but by influencing the processing that occurs once the receptors are stimulated. We will see that this is clearly demonstrated for the experience of pain, which is strongly affected by processes in addition to stimulation of the receptors.

Cortical Responding Can Occur While Watching Touching We can take the idea that cortical responding can be influenced by processes other than stimulation of the receptors a step further by considering that cortical areas associated with touch also respond to *observing* touching. Reacting to observing another person's actions is something we considered in Chapter 7 (page 163), when we described mirror neurons in the monkey's premotor cortex, which fire both when the monkey sees someone else grasping an object, such as food, *and* when the monkey itself grasps the food.

Research on the somatosensory system has revealed similar phenomena for touch. Watching someone else being touched activates areas in the somatosensory cortex of the observer that would also be activated in the somatosensory cortex of the person actually being touched. For example, Christian Keysers and coworkers (2004) measured the fMRI response of the cortex while subjects were being touched on the leg and when the subjects viewed movies of other people or objects being touched.

Not surprisingly, stroking the subject's leg activated the two main somatosensory areas, S1 and S2. The interesting result is what happened when the subjects watched films showing touching. **Figure 14.19a** shows the response in area S2 that occurred when the subject viewed the control film when a probe was not touching a person's leg (blue bar) and when the subject viewed the experimental film of a probe touching the leg (red bar). In this condition, the perception of touching increased the activity of S2.

Figure 14.19b shows that the same result occurred when an object—two white binders—was substituted for the person's leg. Thus, perceiving either another person or an object being touched increased activity in S2. Finally, **Figure 14.19c** shows that this result did not occur when subjects viewed two films of an airplane wing, even though the wing passed over the land in the experimental condition. This shows that it was the touch that was important, not the pattern of visual stimulation. Keysers and coworkers conclude from this result that the brain transforms the visual stimulus of touch into an activation of brain areas involved in our own experience of touch (see also Keysers et al., 2010).

Kaspar Meyer and coworkers (2011) obtained a similar result when subjects watched films of another person's hands haptically exploring common objects like a set of keys, a tennis ball, and the leaves of a plant. **Figure 14.20** shows the increase in brain activation caused by watching the touch films compared to just looking at a fixation cross. The red areas show that activation occurred both in the visual cortex and in somatosensory areas associated with touch. Thus, the somatosensory cortex responds to being touched and to observing touch. Near the end of this chapter will see that a similar situation occurs for stimuli associated with pain.

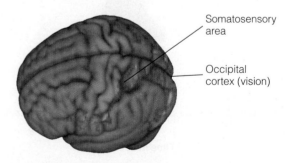

Somatosensory area

Occipital cortex (vision)

Figure 14.20 Brain activation measured by Meyer et al. (2011) caused by observing films of a person's hands haptically exploring objects. Both visual and somatosensory areas are activated. (From Meyer et al., 2011)

1. Describe the four types of mechanoreceptors in the skin, indicating (a) their appearance, (b) where they are located, (c) how they respond to pressure, (d) the sizes of their receptive fields, (e) the type of perception associated with each receptor, and (f) the type of fiber associated with each receptor.

2. Where is the cortical receiving area for touch, and what does the map of the body on the cortical receiving area look like? How can this map be changed by experience?

3. How is tactile acuity measured, and what are the receptor and cortical mechanisms that serve tactile acuity?

4. Which receptor is primarily responsible for the perception of vibration? Describe the experiment that showed that the presence of the receptor structure determines how the fiber fires.

5. What is the duplex theory of texture perception? Describe the series of behavioral experiments that led to the conclusion that vibration is responsible for perceiving fine textures and observations that have been made about the experience of exploring an object with a probe.

6. What processes are involved in identifying objects by haptic exploration?

7. Describe the specialization of cortical areas for touch, how cortical responding to touch is affected by attention, and how cortical responding is affected by watching touching.

Pain Perception

As we mentioned at the beginning of this chapter, pain functions to warn us of potentially damaging situations and therefore helps us avoid or deal with cuts, burns, and broken bones. People born without the ability to feel pain might become aware that they are leaning on a hot stove burner only when they smell burning flesh, or might be unaware of broken bones, infections, or internal injuries—situations that could easily be life-threatening (Watkins & Maier, 2003). The signaling function of pain is reflected in the following definition, from the International Association for the Study of Pain: "Pain is an unpleasant sensory and emotional experience associated with actual or potential tissue damage, or described in terms of such damage" (Merskey, 1991).

Joachim Scholz and Clifford Woolf (2002) distinguish three different types of pain. **Inflammatory pain** is caused by damage to tissue or inflammation of joints or by tumor cells. **Neuropathic pain** is caused by lesions or other damage to the nervous system. Examples of neuropathic pain are carpal tunnel syndrome, which is caused by repetitive tasks such as typing; spinal cord injury; and brain damage due to stroke.

Nociceptive pain is pain caused by activation of receptors in the skin called **nociceptors**, which are specialized to respond to tissue damage or potential damage (Perl, 2007). A number of different kinds of nociceptors respond to different stimuli—heat, chemical, severe pressure, and cold (**Figure 14.21**). We will focus on nociceptive pain. Our discussion will include not only pain that is caused by stimulation of nociceptors in the skin, but also mechanisms that affect the perception of nociceptive pain, and even some examples of pain that can occur when the skin is not stimulated at all.

The Gate Control Model of Pain

We begin our discussion of pain by considering how early researchers thought about pain, and how these early ideas began changing in the 1960s. In the 1950s and early 1960s, pain was explained by the **direct pathway model of pain**. According to

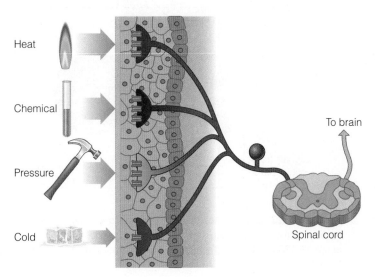

Figure 14.21 Nociceptive pain is created by activation of nociceptors in the skin that respond to different types of stimulation. Signals from the nociceptors are transmitted to the spinal cord and then up the spinal cord in pathways that lead to the brain.

Figure 14.22 The light part of the right arm represents the phantom limb—an extremity that is not physically present, but which the person perceives as existing.

this model, pain occurs when nociceptor receptors in the skin are stimulated and send their signals directly from the skin to the brain (Melzack & Wall, 1965). But in the 1960s, some researchers began noting situations in which pain was affected by factors in addition to stimulation of the skin.

One example was the report by Beecher (1959) that most American soldiers wounded at the Anzio beachhead in World War II "entirely denied pain from their extensive wounds or had so little that they did not want any medication to relieve it" (p. 165). One reason for this was that the soldiers' wounds had a positive aspect: they provided escape from a hazardous battlefield to the safety of a behind-the-lines hospital.

Another example, in which pain occurs without any transmission from receptor to brain, is the phenomena of **phantom limbs**, in which people who have had a limb amputated continue to experience the limb (**Figure 14.22**). This perception is so convincing that amputees have been known to try stepping off a bed onto phantom feet or legs, or to attempt to lift a cup with a phantom hand. For many, the limb moves with the body, swinging while walking. But perhaps most interesting of all, it not uncommon for amputees to experience pain in the phantom limb (Jensen & Nikolajsen, 1999; Katz & Gagliese, 1999; Melzack, 1992; Ramachandran & Hirstein, 1998).

One idea about what causes pain in the phantom limb is that signals are sent from the part of the limb that remains after amputation. However, researchers noted that cutting the nerves that used to transmit signals from the limb to the brain does not eliminate either the phantom limb or the pain and concluded that the pain must originate not in the skin but in the brain. In addition, examples such as not perceiving the pain from serious wounds or perceiving pain when no

signals are being sent to the brain could not be explained by the direct pathway model. This led Ronald Melzak and Patrick Wall (1965, 1983, 1988) to propose the *gate control model* of pain.

The **gate control model** begins with the idea that pain signals enter the spinal cord from the body and are then transmitted from the spinal cord to the brain. In addition, the model proposes that there are additional pathways that influence the signals sent from the spinal cord to the brain. The central idea behind the theory is that signals from these additional pathways can act to open or close a *gate*, located in the spinal cord, which determines the strength of the signal leaving the spinal cord.

Figure 14.23 shows the circuit that Melzack and Wall (1965) proposed. The gate control system consists of cells in the dorsal horn of the spinal cord (**Figure 14.23a**). These cells in the dorsal horn are represented by the red and green circles in the gate control circuit in **Figure 14.23b**. We can understand how this circuit functions by considering how input to the gate control system occurs along three pathways:

- *Nociceptors.* Fibers from nociceptors activate a circuit consisting entirely of excitatory synapses, and therefore send excitatory signals to the **transmission cells**. Excitatory signals from the (+) neurons in the dorsal horn "open the gate" and increase the firing of the transmission cells. Increased activity in the transmission cells results in more pain.
- *Mechanoreceptors.* Fibers from mechanoreceptors carry information about nonpainful tactile stimulation. An example of this type of stimulus would be signals sent from rubbing the skin. When activity in the

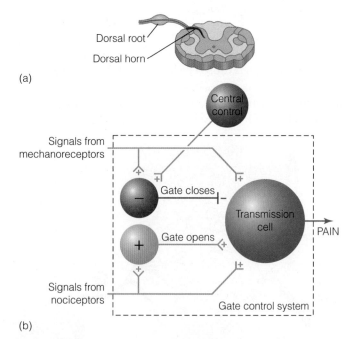

Figure 14.23 (a) Cross section of the spinal cord showing fibers entering through the dorsal root. (b) The circuit proposed by Melzack and Wall (1965, 1988) for their gate control model of pain perception. See text for details.

mechanoreceptors reaches the (−) neurons in the dorsal horn, inhibitory signals sent to the transmission cells "close the gate" and decrease the firing of the transmission cells. This decrease in firing decreases the intensity of pain.

■ *Central control.* These fibers, which contain information related to cognitive functions such as expectation, attention, and distraction, carry signals down from the cortex. As with the mechanoreceptors, activity coming down from the brain also closes the gate, decreases transmission cell activity, and decreases pain.

Since the introduction of the gate control model in 1965, researchers have determined that the neural circuits that control pain are much more complex than what was proposed in the original model (Perl & Kruger, 1996; Sufka & Price, 2002). Nonetheless, the idea proposed by the model—that the perception of pain is determined by a balance between input from nociceptors in the skin and nonnociceptive activity from the skin and the brain—stimulated research that provided a great deal of additional evidence for the idea that the perception of pain is influenced by more than just stimulation of the skin (Fields & Basbaum, 1999; Sufka & Price, 2002; Turk & Flor, 1999; Weissberg, 1999). We will now consider some examples of how cognition can influence the perception of pain.

Top-Down Processes

Modern research has shown that pain can be influenced by what a person expects, how the person directs his or her attention, the type of distracting stimuli that are present, and suggestions made under hypnosis (Rainville et al., 1999; Wiech et al., 2008).

Expectation

In a hospital study in which surgical patients were told what to expect and were instructed to relax to alleviate their pain, the patients requested fewer painkillers following surgery and were sent home 2.7 days earlier than patients who were not provided with this information (Egbert et al., 1964). Studies have also shown that a significant proportion of patients with pathological pain get relief from taking a **placebo**, a pill that they believe contains painkillers but that, in fact, contains no active ingredients (Finniss & Benedetti, 2005; Weisenberg, 1977). This decrease in pain from a substance that has no pharmacological effect is called the **placebo effect**. The key to the placebo effect is that the patient believes that the substance is an effective therapy. This belief leads the patient to expect a reduction in pain, and this reduction does, in fact, occur. Many experiments have shown that expectation is one of the more powerful determinants of the placebo effect (Colloca & Benedetti, 2005).

Ulrike Bingel and coworkers (2011) demonstrated the effect of expectation on painful heat stimulation presented by an

Table 14.2 Effect of Expectation on Pain Ratings

CONDITION	DRUG?	PAIN RATING
Baseline	No	66
No expectation	Yes	55
Positive expectation	Yes	39
Negative expectation	Yes	64

Source: Bingel et al. (2011).

electrode on the calf of a person's leg. The heat was adjusted so the subject reported a pain rating of 70, where 0 corresponds to "no pain," and 100 to "unbearable pain." Subjects then rated the pain under four conditions: (1) *baseline*, in which a saline solution was presented by infusion; (2) *no expectation*, in which the analgesic drug remifentanil was presented, but the subjects thought they were still receiving the saline solution; (3) *positive expectation*, in which the subjects were told that the drug was being presented; and (4) *negative expectation*, in which the subjects were told that the drug was going to be discontinued in order to investigate the possible increase in pain that would occur.

The results, shown in **Table 14.2**, indicate that pain was reduced slightly, from 66 to 55, in the no expectation condition when the drug infusion began, but dropped to 39 in the positive expectation condition, then increased to 64 in the negative expectation condition. The important thing about these results is that after the saline baseline condition, the subject was continuously receiving the same dose of the drug. What was being changed was their expectation, and this change in expectation changed their experience of pain.

The decrease in pain experienced in the positive expectation condition is a placebo effect, in which the positive expectation instructions function as the placebo. Conversely, the negative effect caused by the negative expectation instructions is called a **nocebo effect**, a negative placebo effect (see Tracey, 2010, for a review of placebo and nocebo effects).

This study also measured the subjects' brain activity, and found that the placebo effect was associated with increases in a network of areas associated with pain perception, and the nocebo effect was associated with increases in activity in the hippocampus. A person's expectation, therefore affects both perception and physiological responding.

Attention

When we described perceiving textures by the fingers we saw that the response of cortical neurons can be influenced by attention (Figure 14.18). Similar effects occur for pain perception. Examples of the effect of attention on pain were noted in the 1960s by Melzack and Wall (1965) as they were developing their gate control theory of pain. Here is a recent description of this effect, as reported by a student in my class:

> I remember being around five or six years old, and I was playing Nintendo when my dog ran by and pulled the wire out of the game system. When I got

up to plug the wire back in I stumbled and banged my forehead on the radiator underneath the living room window. I got back up and staggered over to the Nintendo and plugged the controller back into the port, thinking nothing of my little fall. . . . As I resumed playing the game, all of a sudden I felt liquid rolling down my forehead, and reached my hand up to realize it was blood. I turned and looked into the mirror on the closet door to see a gash running down my forehead with blood pouring from it. All of a sudden I screamed out, and the pain hit me. My mom came running in, and took me to the hospital to get stitches. (Ian Kalinowski)

The important message of this description is that Ian's pain occurred not when he was injured but when he *realized* he was injured. One conclusion that we might draw from this example is that one way to decrease pain would be to distract a person's attention from the source of the pain. This technique has been used in hospitals using virtual reality techniques as a tool to distract attention from a painful stimulus. Consider, for example, the case of James Pokorny, who received third-degree burns over 42 percent of his body when the fuel tank of the car he was repairing exploded. While having his bandages changed at the University of Washington Burn Center, he wore a black plastic helmet with a computer monitor inside, on which he saw a virtual world of multicolored three-dimensional graphics. This world placed him in a virtual kitchen that contained a virtual spider, and he was able to chase the spider into the sink so he could grind it up with a virtual garbage disposal (Robbins, 2000).

The point of this "game" was to reduce Pokorny's pain by shifting his attention from the bandages to the virtual reality world. Pokorny reports that "you're concentrating on different things, rather than your pain. The pain level went down significantly." Studies of other patients indicate that burn patients using this virtual reality technique experienced much less pain when their bandages were being changed than patients in a control group who were distracted by playing video games (Hoffman et al., 2000) or who were not distracted at all (Hoffman et al., 2008; also see Buhle et al., 2012).

Emotions

A great deal of evidence shows that pain perception can be influenced by a person's emotional state, with many experiments showing that positive emotions are associated with decreased pain (Bushnell et al., 2013). Two ways this has been demonstrated is by having people look at pictures and having them listen to music.

Looking at Pictures An experiment by Minet deWied and Marinis Verbaten (2001) shows how the content of distracting materials can influence pain perception. The stimuli they used were pictures that had been previously rated as being positive (sports pictures and attractive females), neutral (household objects, nature, and people), or negative (burn victims and accidents). Male subjects looked at the pictures as one of their hands was immersed in cold (2°C; /35.6°F) water. They were told to keep the hand immersed for as long as possible but to withdraw the hand when it began to hurt.

The results indicated that subjects who were looking at the positive pictures kept their hands immersed for an average of 120 seconds, but subjects in the other groups removed their hands more quickly (80 seconds for neutral pictures; 70 seconds for negative pictures). Because the subjects' ratings of the intensity of their pain—made immediately after removing their hands from the water—was the same for all three groups, deWied and Verbaten concluded that the content of the pictures influenced the time it took to reach the same pain level in the three groups. In another experiment, Jaimie Rhudy and coworkers (2005) found that subjects gave lower ratings to pain caused by an electric shock when they were looking at pleasant pictures than when they were looking at unpleasant pictures. They concluded from this result that positive or negative emotions can affect the experience of pain.

Listening to Music Music can have powerful emotional effects, both positive and negative (Altenmüller et al., 2014; Fritz et al., 2009; Koelsch, 2014). While these emotional effects are one of the primary reasons we listen to music, there is also evidence that the positive emotions associated with music can decrease pain. Mathieu Roy and coworkers (2008) measured how music affected the perception of a thermal heat stimulus presented to the forearm by having subjects rate the intensity and unpleasantness of the pain on a scale of 0 (no pain) to 100 (extremely intense or extremely unpleasant). There were three conditions: Silence; Listening to unpleasant music (example: Sonic Youth, *Pendulum Music*); Listening to pleasant music (example: Rossini, *William Tell Overture*).

The results of Roy's experiment for the highest temperature used (48°C/119°F), shown in **Table 14.3**, indicate that listening to unpleasant music didn't affect pain, compared to silence, but that listening to pleasant music decreased both the intensity and the unpleasantness of pain. In fact, the pain relief caused by the pleasant music was comparable to the effects of common analgesic drugs such as ibuprofen.

The Brain and Pain

Research on the physiology of pain has focused on identifying areas of the brain and the chemicals that are involved in pain perception.

Table 14.3 Effect of Pleasant and Unpleasant Music on Pain (Roy et al., 2008)

CONDITION	INTENSITY RATING	UNPLEASANTNESS RATING
Silence	69.7	60.0
Unpleasant music	68.6	60.1
Pleasant music	**57.7**	**47.8**

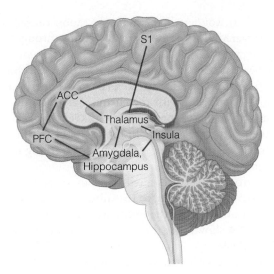

Figure 14.24 The perception of pain is accompanied by activation of a number of different areas of the brain. ACC is the anterior cingulate cortex; PFC is the prefrontal cortex; S1 is the somatosensory cortex. The positions of the structures are approximate, with some, such as the amygdala, hypothalamus, and insula, located deep within the cortex, and others, such as S1 and PFC, located at the surface. Lines indicate connections between the structures.

Brain Areas

A large number of research studies support the idea that the perception of pain is accompanied by activity that is widely distributed throughout the brain. **Figure 14.24** shows a number of the structures that become activated by pain. They include subcortical structures, such as the hypothalamus, the amygdala, and the thalamus, and areas in the cortex, including the somatosensory cortex (S1), the anterior cingulate cortex (ACC), the prefrontal cortex (PFC), the hypothalamus, and the insula (Chapman, 1995; Derbyshire et al., 1997; Price, 2000; Rainville, 2002; Tracey, 2010). Although pain is associated with the overall pattern of firing in the many structures, there is also evidence that certain areas are responsible for specific components of the pain experience.

In the definition of pain on page 351, we stated that pain is "an unpleasant sensory and emotional experience."

This reference to both sensory *and* emotional experience reflects the **multimodal nature of pain**, which is illustrated by how people describe pain. When people describe their pain with words like *throbbing, prickly, hot,* or *dull,* they are referring to the **sensory component of pain**. When they use words like *torturing, annoying, frightful,* or *sickening,* they are referring to the **affective (or emotional) component of pain** (Melzack, 1999).

The sensory and affective components of pain can be distinguished by asking subjects who are experiencing painful stimuli to rate subjective pain intensity (sensory component) and unpleasantness (affective component), as was done in the music study described in the previous section. When R. K. Hofbauer and coworkers (2001) used hypnotic suggestion to increase or decrease these components separately, they found that changes in the sensory component were associated with activity in the somatosensory cortex and changes in the affective component were associated with changes in the anterior cingulate cortex. **Figure 14.25** shows these two areas and some other areas that have been determined from other experiments to be associated with affective (green) and sensory (blue) pain experiences (Eisenberger, 2015). We will return to sensory and affective components when we consider social influences on pain.

Chemicals and the Brain

Another important development in our understanding of the relationship between brain activity and pain perception is the discovery of a link between chemicals called **opioids** and pain perception. This can be traced back to research that began in the 1970s on opiate drugs, such as opium and heroin, which have been used since the dawn of recorded history to reduce pain and induce feelings of euphoria.

By the 1970s, researchers had discovered that opiate drugs act on receptors in the brain that respond to stimulation by molecules with specific structures. The importance of the molecule's structure for exciting these "opiate receptors" explains why injecting a drug called **naloxone** into a person who has overdosed on heroin can almost immediately revive the victim. Because naloxone's structure is similar to heroin's, it attaches

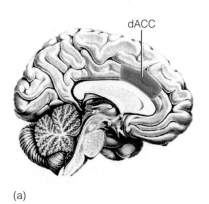

(a)

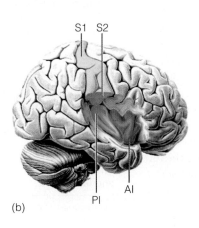

(b)

Figure 14.25 Two views of the brain showing the areas involved in the affective and sensory components of pain. Green = affective component. Blue = sensory component. dACC = dorsal anterior cingulate cortex. S1, S2 = somatosensory areas. PI = posterior insula. AI = anterior insula (Adapted from Eisenberger, 2015, Fig. 1, p. 605)

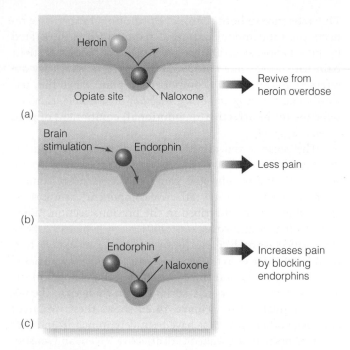

Figure 14.26 (a) Naloxone, which has a structure similar to heroin, reduces the effect of heroin by occupying a receptor site normally stimulated by heroin. (b) Stimulating sites in the brain that cause the release of endorphins can reduce pain by stimulating opiate receptor sites. (c) Naloxone decreases the pain reduction caused by endorphins by keeping the endorphins from reaching the receptor sites.

to the same receptor sites, thereby preventing heroin from binding to those receptors (**Figure 14.26a**).

Why are there opiate receptor sites in the brain? After all, they certainly have been present since long before people started taking heroin. Researchers concluded that there must be naturally occurring substances in the body that act on these sites, and in 1975 neurotransmitters were discovered that act on the same receptors that are activated by opium and heroin. One group of these transmitters is called **endorphins**, for *endogenous* (naturally occurring) *morphine*.

Since the discovery of endorphins, researchers have accumulated a large amount of evidence linking endorphins to pain reduction. For example, pain can be decreased by stimulating sites in the brain that release endorphins (**Figure 14.26b**), and pain can be increased by injecting naloxone, which blocks endorphins from reaching their receptor sites (**Figure 14.26c**).

In addition to decreasing the analgesic effect of endorphins, naloxone also decreases the analgesic effect of placebos (see page 353). This finding, along with other evidence, led to the conclusion that the pain reduction effect of placebos occurs because placebos cause the release of endorphins. As it turns out, there are some situations in which the placebo effect can occur without the release of endorphins, but we will focus on the endorphin-based placebo effect by considering the following question, raised by Fabrizio Benedetti and coworkers (1999): Where are placebo-related endorphins released in the nervous system?

Benedetti wondered whether expectation caused by placebos triggered the release of endorphins throughout the brain, therefore creating a placebo effect for the entire body, or whether expectation caused the release of endorphins only at specific places in the body. To answer this question, Benedetti injected subjects with the chemical *capsaicin* just under the skin at four places on the body: the left hand, the right hand, the left foot, and the right foot. Capsaicin, which is the active component in chili peppers, causes a burning sensation where it is injected.

One group of subjects rated the pain at each part of the body on a scale of 0 (no pain) to 10 (unbearable pain) every minute for 15 minutes after the injection. The "No placebo" row in **Table 14.4** shows that the subjects in this group reported pain at all the locations (ratings between 5.4 and 6.6). Another group of subjects also received the injection, but just before the injections, the experimenter rubbed a cream at one or two of the locations and told subjects that the cream was a potent local anesthetic that would relieve the burning sensation of the capsaicin. The cream was actually a placebo treatment; it had no pain-reducing ingredients.

The second row of Table 14.4 shows that the pain rating for the left hand decreased to 3.0 for a subject who received the cream on the left hand, and the third row shows that the pain ratings for the right and left foot decreased for a subject who received the cream on the right hand and left foot. These results are striking because the placebo effect occurred only where the cream was applied. To demonstrate that this placebo effect was associated with endorphins, Benedetti showed that injecting naloxone abolished the placebo effect.

What this means, according to Benedetti, is that when subjects direct their attention to specific places where they expect pain will be reduced, pathways are activated that release endorphins at specific locations. The mechanism behind endorphin-related analgesia is therefore much more sophisticated than simply chemicals being released into the overall circulation. The mind, as it turns out, can not only reduce pain by causing the release of chemicals, it can literally direct these chemicals to the locations where the pain would be occurring. Research such as this, which links the placebo effect to endorphins, provides a physiological basis for what had previously been described in strictly psychological terms.

Table 14.4 Effect of Placebo Cream on Different Parts of the Body

CONDITION	PAIN RATINGS AT DIFFERENT BODY LOCATIONS			
	LEFT HAND	RIGHT HAND	LEFT FOOT	RIGHT FOOT
No placebo	6.6	5.5	6.0	5.4
Placebo cream on left hand	**3.0**	6.4	5.3	6.0
Placebo cream on right hand and left foot	5.4	**3.0**	**3.8**	6.3

Source: Benedetti et al. (1999).

Observing Pain in Others

How do you feel when you see someone in pain? Do you feel a little pain yourself? Or emotions? A sense of empathy for the person? Or do you turn away because seeing someone in pain can be painful? We have seen that watching someone being touched activates the somatosensory area. We now consider evidence that a similar process occurs for pain, and that responding to someone else in pain reflects **empathy**—the ability to share and vicariously experience someone else's feeling.

Tania Singer and coworkers (2004) demonstrated the connection between brain responses to pain and empathy by bringing romantically involved couples into the laboratory and having the woman, whose brain activity was being measured by an fMRI scanner, either receive shocks herself or watch her male partner receive shocks. The results, shown in **Figure 14.27**, show that a number of brain areas were activated when the woman received the shocks (**Figure 14.27a**), and that some of the same areas were activated when she watched her partner receive shocks (**Figure 14.27b**). The main two areas activated in common were the anterior cingulate cortex (ACC) and the anterior insula (AI), both of which are associated with the affective component of pain (see Figure 14.25).

To show that the brain activity caused by watching their partner was related to empathy, Singer had the women fill out "empathy scales" designed to measure their tendency to empathize with others. As predicted, women with higher empathy scores showed higher activation of their ACC.

In another experiment, Olga Klimecki and coworkers (2014) had subjects undergo training designed to increase their empathy for others and then showed them videos depicting other people experiencing suffering due to injury or natural disasters. Subjects in the empathy-training group showed more empathy and greater activation of the ACC compared to a control group that hadn't received the training *and* greater activation of the ACC. Thus, although the pain associated with watching someone else

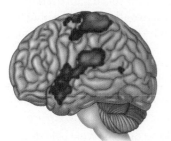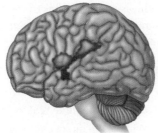

(a) Receive painful stimulation   (b) Watch partner receive painful stimulation

Figure 14.27 Singer and coworkers (2004) used fMRI to determine the areas of the brain activated by (a) receiving painful stimulation and (b) watching another person receive the painful stimulation. Singer proposes that the activation in (b) is related to empathy for the other person. Empathy did not activate the somatosensory cortex but did activate other areas that are activated by pain, such as the insula (tucked between the parietal and temporal lobes) and anterior cingulate cortex (see Figure 14.24, 14.25). (Adapted from Holden, 2004)

experience pain may be caused by stimulation that is very different from physical pain, these two types of pain apparently share some physiological mechanisms. (Also see Avenanti et al., 2005; Lamm et al., 2007; Singer & Klimecki, 2014.)

SOMETHING TO CONSIDER:
Social Pain and Physical Pain

We've seen that a "social" action such as watching someone else experiencing pain can activate areas associated with the affective component of pain. Taking this a step farther, some research suggests that there is a connection between the mechanisms responsible for the pain of social rejection and the mechanisms responsible for physical pain.

The idea that social rejection hurts is well known. When describing emotional responses to negative social experiences, it is common for people to use words associated with physical pain, such as *broken* hearts, *hurt* feelings, or emotional *scars* (Eisenberger, 2012, 2015). In 2003, Naomi Eisenberger and coworkers published a paper titled "Does Rejection Hurt? An fMRI Study of Social Exclusion," which concluded that the dorsal anterior cingulate cortex (dACC; see Figure 14.25) is activated by feelings of social exclusion. They demonstrated this by having subjects participate in a videogame called "Cyberball," in which they were told that they would be playing a ball-tossing game with two other subjects, who were indicated by the two figures at the top of the computer screen, with the subject being indicated by a hand at the bottom of the screen (**Figure 14.28**).

Initially, the two other players included the subject in their ball tossing (**Figure 14.28a**), but then they suddenly excluded the subject and just tossed the ball between themselves (**Figure 14.28b**). This exclusion caused activity in the subject's dACC, as shown in **Figure 14.28c**, and this dACC activity was related to the degree of social distress the subject reported feeling, with greater distress associated with greater dACC activity (**Figure 14.28d**).

Other studies provided more evidence for similar physiological responses to negative social experiences and physical pain. Activation of the dACC and anterior insula (AI) occurred in response to a threat of negative social evaluation (Eisenberger et al., 2011) and when remembering a romantic partner who had recently rejected the person (Kross et al., 2011). Also, taking a pain reliever such as Tylenol not only reduces physical pain but also reduces hurt feelings and dACC and AI activity (DeWall et al., 2010).

Results such as these have led to the **physical-social pain overlap hypothesis**, which proposes that pain resulting from negative social experiences is processed by some of the same neural circuitry that processes physical pain (Eisenberger, 2012, 2015; Eisenberger & Lieberman, 2004). This idea has not gone unchallenged, however. One line of criticism has focused on the idea that activity in the ACC may be reflecting things other than pain. For example, it has been suggested that the ACC may respond to many types of emotional and cognitive

Figure 14.28 The "Cyberball" experiment. (a) The subject is told that the two characters shown on the top of the screen are being controlled by two other subjects. These two characters throw the ball to the subject in the first part of the experiment. (b) In the second part of the experiment, the subject is excluded from the game. (c) Exclusion results in activity in the ACC, shown in orange. (d) Subject's rating of social distress (*y*-axis) is related to ACC activation (*x*-axis). (From Eisenberger & Lieberman, 2004)

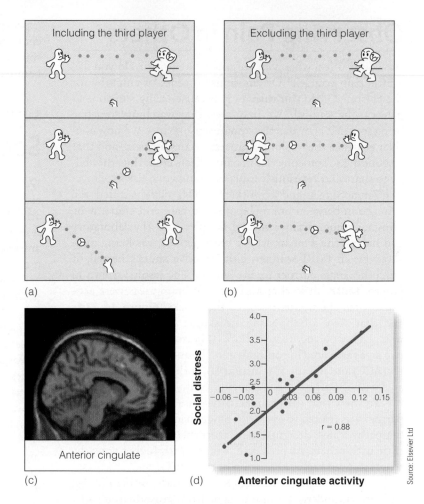

Including the third player

Excluding the third player

(a)   (b)

Anterior cingulate

(c)   (d)   **Anterior cingulate activity**

Social distress

r = 0.88

Source: Elsevier Ltd

tasks, rather than being specialized for pain (Lindquist et al., 2012; Shackman et al., 2011), or that the ACC responds to salience—how much a stimulus stands out from its surroundings (Iannetti et al., 2013).

Another question that has been raised is whether activation of the ACC by both social and physical pain means that the same neural circuits are being activated. To investigate this question, Choong-Wan Woo and coworkers (2014) used a technique called *multivariate pattern analysis* (*MVPA*) to determine the pattern of activation of fMRI voxels caused by social and physical pain. MVPA is analogous to the process described in Chapter 5 for determining the pattern of voxel response to oriented lines (Figures 5.42, 5.43) and images of scenes (Figures 5.44, 5.45), to create computer image decoders for visual stimuli (see page 114). Although MVPA uses different mathematical procedures than those used to create the visual decoders, the goal is the same: to identify patterns of voxels activated by different types of stimuli.

Woo and coworkers found that the voxel pattern generated by recalling social rejection by a romantic partner was different from the pattern generated by painful heat presented to the forearm. Their conclusion is reflected in the title of their paper: "Separate Neural Representations for Physical Pain and Social Rejection."

So which idea is correct? Do social pain and physical pain share neural mechanisms, or are they two separate phenomena

that both use the word "pain"? There is evidence supporting the physical-social pain overlap hypothesis, but there is also evidence that argues against this hypothesis. Because social pain and physical pain are certainly different—it's easy to tell the difference between the feeling of being rejected and the feeling from burning your finger—it is unlikely that mechanisms overlap completely. The physical-social pain overlap hypothesis proposes that there is *some* overlap. But how much is "some"? A little or a lot? Research to answer this question is continuing.

TEST YOURSELF 14.2

1. Describe the three types of pain.

2. What is the direct pathway model of pain? What evidence led researchers to question this model of pain perception?

3. What is the gate control model? Be sure you understand the roles of the nociceptors, mechanoreceptors, and central control.

4. Describe evidence that supports the conclusions that pain is influenced by expectation, attention, and emotion.

5. What does it mean to say that pain is multimodal? Describe the hypnosis experiments that identified areas involved in the sensory component of pain and the emotional component of pain.

6. Describe the role of chemicals in the perception of pain. Be sure you understand how endorphins and naloxone interact at receptor sites, and a possible mechanism that explains why pain is reduced by placebos.

7. Describe the Benedetti et al. (1999) experiment. How did this experiment demonstrate that the placebo's effect can operate on local parts of the body?

8. How is the cortical response to watching someone else experience pain related to empathy?

9. What is the evidence supporting the idea that social and physical pain share some mechanisms? What evidence questions this idea?

THINK ABOUT IT

1. One of the themes in this book is that it is possible to use the results of psychophysical experiments to suggest the operation of physiological mechanisms or to link physiological mechanisms to perception. Cite an example of how psychophysics has been used in this way for each of the senses we have considered so far—vision, hearing, and the cutaneous senses.

2. Some people report situations in which they were injured but didn't feel any pain until they became aware of their injury. How would you explain this kind of situation in terms of top-down and bottom-up processing? How could you relate this situation to the studies we have discussed? (p. 353)

3. Even though the senses of vision and cutaneous perception are different in many ways, there are a number of parallels between them. Cite examples of parallels between vision and cutaneous sensations (touch and pain) for the following: "tuned" receptors, mechanisms of detail perception, receptive fields, plasticity (how changing the environment influences properties of the system), and top-down processing. Also, can you think of situations in which vision and touch interact with one another?

KEY TERMS

Active touch (p. 347)
Affective (p. 355)
Component of pain (p. 355)
Cutaneous receptive field (p. 339)
Cutaneous senses (p. 338)
Dermis (p. 338)
Direct pathway model of pain (p. 351)
Duplex theory of texture perception (p. 346)
Emotional (p. 355)
Empathy (p. 357)
Endorphins (p. 356)
Epidermis (p. 338)
Exploratory procedures (EPs) (p. 348)
Gate control model (p. 352)
Grating acuity (p. 343)
Haptic perception (p. 347)
Homunculus (p. 342)

Inflammatory pain (p. 351)
Kinesthesis (p. 338)
Mechanoreceptors (p. 338)
Medial lemniscal pathway (p. 340)
Meissner corpuscle (p. 338)
Merkel receptor (p. 338)
Multimodal nature of pain (p. 355)
Naloxone (p. 355)
Neuropathic pain (p. 351)
Nocebo effect (p. 353)
Nociceptive pain (p. 351)
Nociceptors (p. 351)
Opioids (p. 355)
Pacinian corpuscle (RA2) (p. 340)
Passive touch (p. 347)
PC fiber (p. 340)
Phantom limbs (p. 352)
Physical-social pain overlap hypothesis (p. 357)
Placebo effect (p. 353)

Placebo (p. 353)
Proprioception (p. 338)
RA1 fibers (p. 339)
Rapidly adapting (RA) fiber (p. 339)
Ruffini cylinder (SA2 fiber) (p. 340)
SA1 fibers (p. 339)
Secondary somatosensory cortex (S2) (p. 340)
Sensory component of pain (p. 355)
Slowly adapting (SA) fiber (p. 339)
Somatosensory receiving area (S1) (p. 340)
Somatosensory system (p. 338)
Spatial cues (p. 346)
Spinothalamic pathway (p. 340)
Surface texture (p. 345)
Temporal cues (p. 346)
Transmission cells (p. 352)
Two-point threshold (p. 343)
Ventrolateral nucleus (p. 340)

This person is enjoying not only the social experience of eating with others but the sensory experiences created by taste and smell. As we see in this chapter, taste stimulates receptors in the tongue, smell stimulates receptors within the nose, and taste and smell work together to create flavor, which is the dominant perception we experience when eating or drinking.

CHAPTER 15

The Chemical Senses

CHAPTER CONTENTS

Taste

Taste Quality
Basic Taste Qualities
Connections Between Taste Quality
and a Substance's Effect

The Neural Code for Taste Quality
Structure of the Taste System
Population Coding
Specificity Coding

Individual Differences in Taste

Olfaction and Flavor

The Functions of Olfaction

Olfactory Abilities
Detecting Odors

Discriminating Between Odors
Identifying Odors
Individual Differences in Olfaction

Analyzing Odorants: The Mucosa and Olfactory Bulb
The Puzzle of Olfactory Quality
The Olfactory Mucosa
How Olfactory Receptor Neurons
Respond to Odorants
The Search for Order in the
Olfactory Bulb

Representing Odors in the Cortex
How Odorants Are Represented in the
Piriform Cortex
How Odor Objects Are Represented

The Perception of Flavor
Taste and Olfaction Meet in the Mouth
and Nose
Taste and Olfaction Meet in the
Nervous System
Flavor Is Influenced by Cognitive
Factors
Flavor Is Influenced by Food Intake:
Sensory-Specific Satiety

SOMETHING TO CONSIDER: The *Proust*
Effect: Memories, Emotions, and Smell

DEVELOPMENTAL DIMENSION: Infant
Chemical Sensitivity

THINK ABOUT IT

Some Questions We Will Consider:

- Are there differences in the way different people experience the taste of food? (p. 367)
- Why is a dog's sense of smell so much better than a human's? (p. 370)
- How do neurons in the cortex combine smell and taste? (p. 379)

We have five senses, but only two that go beyond the boundaries of ourselves. When you look at someone, it's just bouncing light, or when you hear them, it's just sound waves, vibrating air, or touch is just nerve endings tingling. Know what smell is? . . . It's made up of the molecules of what you're smelling. (Kushner, 1993, p. 17)

The character speaking these lines in Tony Kushner's play *Angels in America* probably did not take a course in sensation and perception and so leaves out the fact that vision and hearing are "just nerve endings tingling" as

well. But his point—that smell involves taking molecules into your body—is one of the properties of the chemical senses that distinguishes them from the other senses. Thus, as you drink something, you smell it because molecules in gas form are entering your nose, and you taste it because molecules in liquid form are stimulating your tongue. Smell (which we will refer to as *olfaction*) and taste have been called *molecule detectors* because they endow these gas and liquid molecules with distinctive smells and tastes (Cain, 1988; Kauer, 1987).

Because the stimuli responsible for tasting and smelling are taken into the body, these senses are often seen as "gatekeepers" that (1) identify things that the body needs for survival and that should therefore be consumed and (2) detect things that would be bad for the body and that should therefore be rejected. The gatekeeper function of taste and smell is aided by a large affective, or emotional, component—things that are bad for us often taste or smell unpleasant, and things that are good for us generally taste or smell good. In addition to creating "good" and "bad" affect, smelling an odor associated with a past place or event can trigger memories, which in turn may create emotional reactions.

Because the receptors that serve taste and smell are constantly exposed not only to the chemicals they are designed to sense but also to harmful materials such as bacteria and dirt, they undergo a cycle of birth, development, and death over 5–7 weeks for olfactory receptors and 1–2 weeks for taste receptors. This constant renewal of the receptors, called **neurogenesis**, is unique to these senses. In vision and hearing, the receptors are safely protected inside structures such as the eye and the inner ear, and in the cutaneous senses, under the skin; however, the receptors for taste and smell are relatively unprotected and therefore need to be constantly renewed.

In this chapter, we will consider taste first and then olfaction. We will describe the psychophysics and anatomy of each system and then how different taste and smell qualities are coded in the nervous system. Finally, we consider flavor, which results from the interaction of taste and smell.

Taste

Everyone is familiar with taste. We experience it every time we eat. (Although later in the chapter we will see that what we experience when we eat is actually "flavor," which is a combination of taste and olfaction.) Taste occurs when molecules enter the mouth in solid or liquid form and stimulate taste receptors on the tongue. The perceptions resulting from this stimulation have been described in terms of five basic taste qualities.

Taste Quality

Most taste researchers describe taste quality in terms of five basic taste sensations: salty, sour, sweet, bitter, and umami (which has been described as meaty, brothy, or savory, and is often associated with the flavor-enhancing properties of MSG, monosodium glutamate).

Basic Taste Qualities

Early research that supported the idea of basic tastes showed that people can describe most of their taste experiences in terms of four basic taste qualities (this research was done before umami became the fifth basic taste). In one study, Donald McBurney (1969) presented taste solutions to participants and asked them to make magnitude estimates of the intensity of each of the four taste qualities for each solution (see pages 15 and 386 for descriptions of the magnitude estimation procedure). He found that some substances have a predominant taste and that other substances result in combinations of the four tastes. For example, sodium chloride (salty), hydrochloric acid (sour), sucrose (sweet), and quinine (bitter) are compounds that come the closest to having only one of the four basic tastes. However, the compound potassium chloride (KCl) has substantial salty and bitter components, whereas sodium nitrate ($NaNO_3$) results in a taste consisting of a combination of salty, sour, and bitter (**Figure 15.1**).

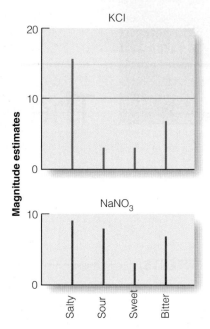

Figure 15.1 The contribution of each of the four basic tastes to the tastes of KCl and $NaNO_3$, determined by the method of magnitude estimation. The height of the line indicates the size of the magnitude estimate for each basic taste. (From McBurney, 1969)

Results such as these have led most researchers to accept the idea of basic tastes. As you will see when we discuss the neural code for taste quality, most of the research on this problem takes the idea of basic tastes as the starting point. (See Erickson, 2000, however, for some arguments against the idea of basic tastes.)

Connections Between Taste Quality and a Substance's Effect

We noted that taste and olfaction can be thought of as "gatekeepers" that help us determine which substances we should consume and which we should avoid. This is especially true for taste because we often use taste to choose which foods to eat and which to avoid (Breslin, 2001).

Taste accomplishes its gatekeeper function by the connection between taste quality and a substance's effect. Thus, sweetness is often associated with compounds that have nutritive or caloric value and that are, therefore, important for sustaining life. Sweet compounds cause an automatic acceptance response and also trigger anticipatory metabolic responses that prepare the gastrointestinal system for processing these substances.

Bitter compounds have the opposite effect—they trigger automatic rejection responses to help the organism avoid harmful substances. Examples of harmful substances that taste bitter are the poisons strychnine, arsenic, and cyanide.

Salty tastes often indicate the presence of sodium. When people are deprived of sodium or lose a great deal of sodium through sweating, they often seek out foods that taste salty in order to replenish the salt their body needs.

Although there are many examples of connections between a substance's taste and its function in the body, this connection is not perfect. People have often made the mistake of eating good-tasting poisonous mushrooms, and there are artificial sweeteners, such as saccharine and sucralose, that have no metabolic value. There are also bitter foods that are not dangerous and do have metabolic value. People can also learn to modify their responses to certain tastes, as when they develop a taste for foods they may have initially found unappealing.

The Neural Code for Taste Quality

One of the central concerns in taste research has been identifying the physiological code for taste quality. We will first describe the structure of the taste system and then describe two proposals regarding how taste quality is coded in this system.

Structure of the Taste System

The process of tasting begins with the tongue (**Figure 15.2a** and **Table 15.1**). The surface of the tongue contains many ridges and valleys caused by the presence of structures called **papillae**, which fall into four categories: (1) filiform papillae, which are shaped like cones and are found over the entire surface of the tongue, giving it its rough appearance; (2) fungiform papillae, which are shaped like mushrooms and are found at the tip and sides of the tongue (see **Figure 15.3**); (3) foliate papillae, which are a series of folds along the back of the tongue on the sides; and (4) circumvallate papillae, which are shaped like flat mounds surrounded by a trench and are found at the back of the tongue.

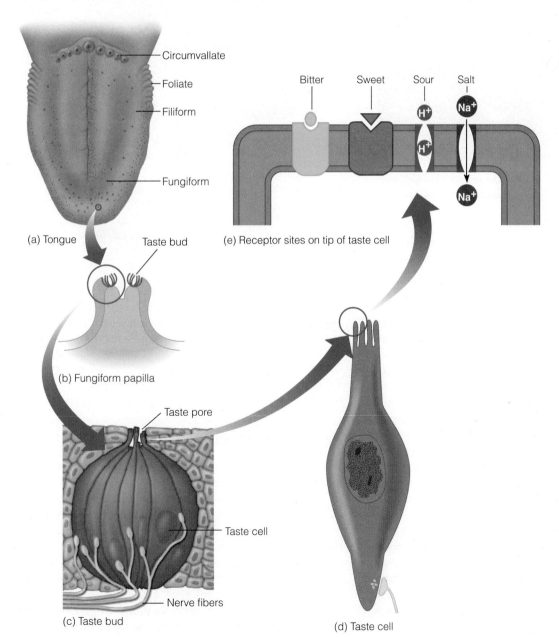

(a) Tongue
- Circumvallate
- Foliate
- Filiform
- Fungiform

(b) Fungiform papilla

Taste bud

(c) Taste bud
- Taste pore
- Taste cell
- Nerve fibers

(d) Taste cell

(e) Receptor sites on tip of taste cell
- Bitter
- Sweet
- Sour — H^+, H^+
- Salt — Na^+, Na^+

Figure 15.2 (a) The tongue, showing the four different types of papillae. (b) A fungiform papilla on the tongue; each papilla contains a number of taste buds. (c) Cross section of a taste bud showing the taste pore where the taste stimulus enters. (d) The taste cell; the tip of the taste cell is positioned just under the pore. (e) Close-up of the membrane at the tip of the taste cell, showing the receptor sites for bitter, sweet, sour, and salty substances. Stimulation of these receptor sites, as described in the text, triggers a number of different reactions within the cell (not shown) that lead to movement of charged molecules across the membrane, which creates an electrical signal in the receptor.

Table 15.1 Structures in the Taste System

STRUCTURE	DESCRIPTION
Tongue	The receptor sheet for taste. Contains papillae and all of the other structures described below.
Papillae	The structures that give the tongue its rough appearance. There are four kinds, each with a different shape.
Taste buds	Contained on the papillae. There are about 10,000 taste buds.
Taste cells	Cells that make up a taste bud. There are a number of cells for each bud, and the tip of each one sticks out into a taste pore. One or more nerve fibers are associated with each cell.
Receptor sites	Sites located on the tips of the taste cells. There are different types of sites for different chemicals. Chemicals contacting the sites cause transduction by affecting ion flow across the membrane of the taste cell.

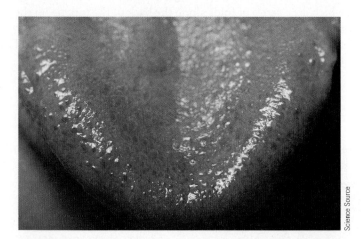

Science Source

Figure 15.3 The surface of the tongue. The red dots are fungiform papillae. Shahbake,M. (2008) PhD Thesis; Anatomical and psychophysical aspects of the development of the sense of taste in humans, University of Western Sydney, pp. 148–153.

All of the papillae except the filiform papillae contain **taste buds** (**Figures 15.2b** and **15.2c**), and the whole tongue contains about 10,000 taste buds (Bartoshuk, 1971). Because the filiform papillae contain no taste buds, stimulation of the central part of the tongue, which contains only these papillae, causes no taste sensations. However, stimulation of the back or perimeter of the tongue results in a broad range of taste sensations.

Each taste bud contains 50 to 100 **taste cells**, which have tips that protrude into the **taste pore** (Figure 15.2c). Transduction occurs when chemicals contact receptor sites located on the tips of these taste cells (**Figure 15.2d** and **15.2e**). Electrical signals generated in the taste cells are transmitted from the tongue in a number of different nerves: (1) the chorda tympani nerve (from taste cells on the front and sides of the tongue); (2) the glossopharyngeal nerve (from the back of the tongue); (3) the vagus nerve (from the mouth and throat); and (4) the superficial petrosal nerve (from the soft palette—the top of the mouth).

The fibers from the tongue, mouth, and throat make connections in the brain stem in the **nucleus of the solitary tract**. From there, signals travel to the thalamus and then to two areas in the frontal lobe that are considered to be the primary taste cortex—the **insula** and the **frontal operculum**—which are partially hidden behind the temporal lobe (**Figure 15.4**; Finger, 1987; Frank & Rabin, 1989).

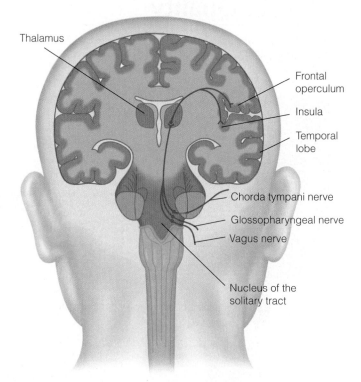

Figure 15.4 The central pathway for taste signals, showing the nucleus of the solitary tract, where nerve fibers from the tongue and the mouth synapse in the medulla at the base of the brain. From the nucleus of the solitary tract, these fibers synapse in the thalamus and then the insula and frontal operculum, which are the cortical areas for taste. (From Frank & Rabin, 1989)

Population Coding

In Chapter 3 we distinguished between two types of coding: *specificity coding*, the idea that quality is signaled by the activity in individual neurons that are tuned to respond to specific qualities; and *population coding*, the idea that quality is signaled by the pattern of activity distributed across many neurons. In that discussion, and in others throughout the book, we have generally favored population coding. The situation for taste, however, is not clear-cut, and there are arguments in favor of both types of coding (Frank et al., 2008).

Let's consider some evidence for population coding. Robert Erickson (1963) conducted one of the first experiments that

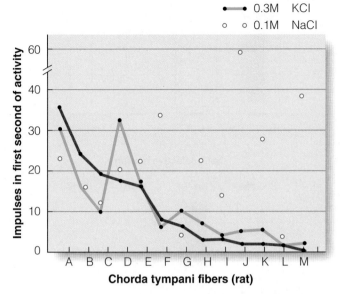

Figure 15.5 Across-fiber patterns of the response of fibers in the rat's chorda tympani nerve to three salts. Each letter on the horizontal axis indicates a different single fiber. (Based on Erickson, 1963)

demonstrated this type of coding by presenting a number of different taste stimuli to a rat's tongue and recording the response of the chorda tympani nerve. **Figure 15.5** shows how 13 nerve fibers responded to ammonium chloride (NH₄Cl), potassium chloride (KCl), and sodium chloride (NaCl). Erickson called these patterns the **across-fiber patterns**, which is another name for population coding. The red and green lines show that the across-fiber patterns for ammonium chloride and potassium chloride are similar to each other but different from the pattern for sodium chloride, indicated by the open circles.

Erickson reasoned that if the rat's perception of taste quality depends on the across-fiber pattern, then two substances with similar patterns should taste similar. Thus, the electrophysiological results would predict that ammonium chloride and potassium chloride should taste similar and that both should taste different from sodium chloride. To test this hypothesis, Erickson shocked rats while they were drinking potassium chloride and then gave them a choice between ammonium chloride and sodium chloride. If potassium chloride and ammonium chloride taste similar, the rats should avoid the ammonium chloride when given a choice. This is exactly what they did. And when the rats were shocked for drinking ammonium chloride, they subsequently avoided the potassium chloride, as predicted by the electrophysiological results.

But what about the perception of taste in humans? When Susan Schiffman and Robert Erickson (1971) asked humans to make similarity judgments between a number of different solutions, they found that substances that were perceived to be similar were related to patterns of firing for these same substances in the rat. Solutions judged more similar psychophysically had similar patterns of firing, as population coding would predict.

Specificity Coding

Most of the evidence for specificity coding comes from research that has recorded neural activity early in the taste system. We begin at the receptors by describing experiments that have revealed receptors for sweet, bitter, and umami.

The evidence supporting the existence of receptors that respond specifically to a particular taste has been obtained by using genetic cloning, which makes it possible to add or eliminate specific receptors in mice. Ken Mueller and coworkers (2005) did a series of experiments using a chemical compound called PTC that tastes bitter to humans but is not bitter to mice. The lack of bitter PTC taste in mice is inferred from the fact that mice do not avoid even high concentrations of PTC in behavioral tests (blue curve in **Figure 15.6**). Because a specific receptor in the family of bitter receptors had been identified as being responsible for the bitter taste of PTC in humans, Mueller decided to see what would happen if he used genetic cloning techniques to create a strain of mice that had this human bitter-PTC receptor. When he did this, the mice with this receptor avoided high concentrations of PTC (red curve in Figure 15.6; see **Table 15.2a**).

In another experiment, Mueller created a strain of mice that *lacked* a bitter receptor that responds to a compound called cyclohexamide (Cyx). Mice normally have this receptor, so they avoid Cyx. But the mice lacking this receptor

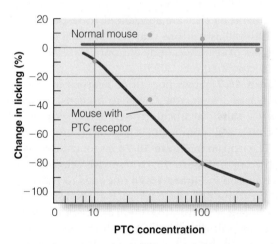

Figure 15.6 Mouse behavioral response to PTC. The blue curve indicates that a normal mouse will consume PTC even in high concentrations. The red curve indicates that a mouse that has a human bitter-PTC receptor avoids PTC, especially at high concentrations. (Adapted from Mueller et al., 2005)

Table 15.2 Results of Mueller's Experiments

CHEMICAL	NORMAL MOUSE	CLONED MOUSE
(a) PTC	No PTC receptor	Has PTC receptor
	Doesn't avoid PTC	Avoids PTC
(b) Cyx	Has Cyx receptor	No Cyx receptor
	Avoids Cyx	Doesn't avoid Cyx

did not avoid Cyx (**Table 15.2b**). In addition, Cyx no longer caused any firing in nerves receiving signals from the tongue. Therefore, when the taste receptor for a substance is eliminated, this is reflected in both nerve firing and the animal's behavior.

It is important to note that in all these experiments, adding or eliminating bitter receptors had no effect on neural firing or behavior to sweet, sour, salty, or umami stimuli. Other research using similar techniques has identified receptors for sugar and umami (Zhao et al., 2003).

The results of these experiments in which adding a receptor makes an animal sensitive to a specific quality and eliminating a receptor makes an animal insensitive to a specific quality have been cited as support for specificity coding—that there are receptors that are specifically tuned to sweet, bitter, and umami tastes. However, not all researchers agree that the picture is so clear-cut. For example, Eugene Delay and coworkers (2006) showed that with different behavioral tests, mice that appeared to have been made insensitive to sugar by eliminating a "sweet" receptor can actually still show a preference for sugar. Based on this result, Delay suggests that perhaps there are a number of different receptors that respond to specific substances like sugar.

Another line of evidence for specificity coding in taste has come from research on how single neurons respond to taste stimuli. Recordings from neurons at the beginning of the taste systems of animals, ranging from rats to monkeys, have revealed neurons that are specialized to respond to specific stimuli, as well as neurons that respond to a number of different types of stimuli (Lundy & Contreras, 1999; Sato et al., 1994; Spector & Travers, 2005).

Figure 15.7 shows how three neurons in the rat taste system respond to sucrose (sweet to humans), sodium chloride (NaCl; salty), hydrochloric acid (HCl; sour in low concentrations), and quinine (QHCl; bitter) (Lundy & Conteras, 1999). The neuron in **Figure 15.7a** responds selectively to sucrose, the one in **Figure 15.7b** responds selectively to NaCl, and the neuron in **Figure 15.7c** responds to NaCl, HCl, and QHCl. Neurons like the ones in Figures 15.7a and 15.7b, which respond selectively to stimuli associated with sweetness (sucrose) and saltiness (NaCl), provide evidence for specificity coding. Neurons have also been found that respond selectively to sour (HCl) and bitter (QHCl) (Spector & Travers, 2005).

Another finding in line with specificity theory is the effect of presenting a substance called **amiloride**, which blocks the flow of sodium into taste receptors. Applying amiloride to the tongue causes a decrease in the responding of neurons in the rat's brainstem (nucleus of the solitary tract) that respond best to salt (**Figure 15.8a**) but has little effect on neurons that respond best to a combination of salty and bitter tastes (**Figure 15.8b**; Scott & Giza, 1990). Thus, eliminating the flow of sodium across the membrane selectively eliminates responding of salt-best neurons but does not affect the response of neurons that respond best to other tastes. As it turns out, the sodium channel that is blocked by amiloride is important for determining saltiness in rats and other animals,

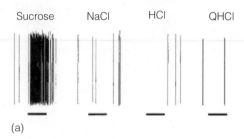

Sucrose-selective neuron

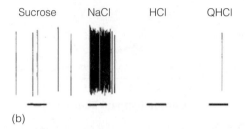

NaCl-selective neuron

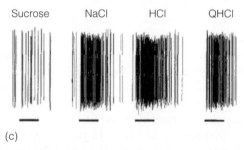

Neuron responds to NaCl, HCl, and QHCl

Figure 15.7 Responses of three neurons recorded from the cell bodies of chorda tympani nerve fibers in the rat. Solutions of sucrose, salt (NaCl), hydrochloric acid (HCl), and quinine hydrochloride (QHCl) were flowed over the rat's tongue for 15 seconds, as indicated by the horizontal lines below the firing records. Vertical lines indicate individual nerve impulses. (a) Neuron responds selectively to sweet stimulus. (b) Neuron responds selectively to salt. (c) Neuron responds to salty, sour, and bitter stimuli. (From Lundy & Contreras, 1999)

but not in humans. More recent research has identified another channel that serves the salty taste in humans (Lyall et al., 2004, 2005).

What does all of this mean? The results of the experiments involving cloning, recording from single neurons, and the effect of amiloride seem to be shifting the balance in the population versus specificity argument toward specificity (Chandrashekar et al., 2006). However, the issue is still not settled. For example, David Smith and Thomas Scott (2003) argue for population coding based on the finding that at more central locations in the taste system, neurons are tuned broadly, with many neurons responding to more than one taste quality. Smith and coworkers (2000) point out that just because there are neurons that respond best to one compound like salty or sour, this doesn't mean that these tastes

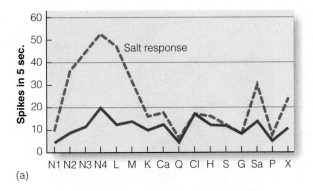

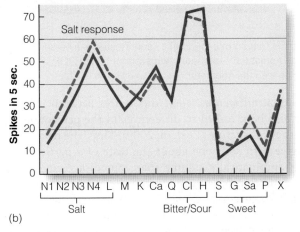

Figure 15.8 The blue dashed lines show how two neurons in the rat's nucleus of the solitary tract respond to a number of different taste stimuli (along the horizontal axis). The neuron in (a) responds strongly to compounds associated with salty tastes. The neuron in (b) responds to a wide range of compounds. The purple lines show how these two neurons fire after the sodium-blocker amiloride is applied to the tongue. This compound inhibits the responses of the neuron that responds to salt (a) but has little effect on neuron (b). (Adapted from Scott & Giza, 1990)

are signaled by just one type of neuron. They illustrate this by drawing an analogy between taste perception and the mechanism for color vision. Even though presenting a long-wavelength light that appears red may cause the highest activation in the long-wavelength cone pigment (see Figure 9.12, page 204), our perception of red still depends on the combined response of both the long- and medium-wavelength pigments. Similarly, salt stimuli may cause high firing in neurons that respond best to salt, but other neurons are probably also involved in creating saltiness.

Because of arguments such as this, some researchers believe that even though there is good evidence for specific taste receptors, population coding is involved in determining taste as well, especially at higher levels of the system. One suggestion is that basic taste qualities might be determined by a specific code, but population coding could determine subtle differences between tastes within a category (Pfaffmann, 1974; Scott & Plata-Salaman, 1991). This would help explain why not all substances in a particular category have the same

taste. For example, the taste of all sweet substances is not identical (Lawless, 2001).

Individual Differences in Taste

The "taste worlds" of humans and animals are not necessarily the same. For example, domestic cats, unlike most mammals, don't prefer the sweetness of sugar, even though they display human-like taste behavior to other compounds, such as avoiding compounds that taste bitter or very sour to humans. Genetic research has shown that this "sweet blindness" occurs because cats lack a functional gene for formation of a sweet receptor and so, lacking a sweet receptor, have no mechanism for detecting sweetness (Li et al., 2005).

This interesting fact about cats has something to tell us about human taste perception, because it turns out that there are genetic differences that affect people's ability to sense the taste of certain substances. One of the best-documented effects involves people's ability to taste the bitter substance phenylthiocarbamide (PTC), which we discussed earlier in connection with Mueller's experiments on specificity coding (see page 365). Linda Bartoshuk (1980) describes the discovery of this PTC effect:

> The different reactions to PTC were discovered accidentally in 1932 by Arthur L. Fox, a chemist working at the E. I. DuPont deNemours Company in Wilmington, Delaware. Fox had prepared some PTC, and when he poured the compound into a bottle, some of the dust escaped into the air. One of his colleagues complained about the bitter taste of the dust, but Fox, much closer to the material, noticed nothing. Albert F. Blakeslee, an eminent geneticist of the era, was quick to pursue this observation. At a meeting of the American Association for the Advancement of Science (AAAS) in 1934, Blakeslee prepared an exhibit that dispensed PTC crystals to 2,500 of the conferees. The results: 28 percent of them described it as tasteless, 66 percent as bitter, and 6 percent as having some other taste. (p. 55)

People who can taste PTC are described as *tasters*, and those who cannot are called *nontasters*. More recently, additional experiments have been done with a substance called 6-*n*-propylthiouracil, or PROP, which has properties similar to those of PTC (Lawless, 1980, 2001). Researchers have found that about one-third of Americans report that PROP is tasteless and two-thirds can taste it.

What causes these differences in people's ability to taste PROP? One reason is that people have different numbers of taste buds on the tongue. Linda Bartoshuk used a technique called **video microscopy** to count the taste buds on people's tongues that contain the receptors for tasting (Bartoshuk & Beauchamp, 1994). The key result of this study was that people

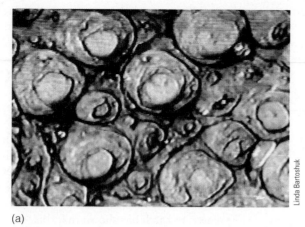
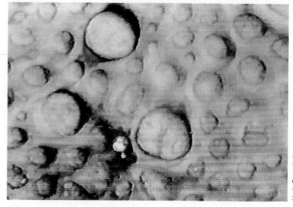

(a)   (b)

Figure 15.9 (a) Video micrograph of the tongue showing the fungiform papillae of a "supertaster"—a person who is very sensitive to the taste of PROP. (b) Papillae of a "nontaster"—someone who cannot taste PROP. The supertaster has both more papillae and more taste buds than the nontaster.

who could taste PROP had higher densities of taste buds than those who couldn't taste it (**Figure 15.9**).

Another factor that determines individual differences in taste, in addition to receptor density, is the presence of specialized receptors. Advances in genetic techniques have made it possible to determine the locations and identities of genes on human chromosomes that are associated with taste and smell receptors. These studies have shown that PROP and PTC tasters have specialized receptors that are absent in nontasters (Bufe et al., 2005; Kim et al., 2003).

What does this mean for everyday taste experience? If PROP tasters also perceived other compounds as being more bitter than nontasters, then certain foods might taste more bitter to the tasters. The evidence on this question, however, has been mixed. Some studies have reported differences between how tasters and nontasters rate the bitterness of other compounds (Bartoshuk, 1979; Hall et al., 1975), and others have not observed this difference (Delwiche et al., 2001b). However, it does appear that people who are especially sensitive to PROP, called *supertasters*, may actually be more sensitive to most bitter substances, as if the amplification in the bitter taste system is turned up for all bitter compounds (Delwiche et al., 2001a).

But the research on PROP nontasters and supertasters has turned out to be just the tip of the iceberg with regard to individual differences. Gene differences between individuals have also been linked to differences in the perception of the sweetness of sucrose (Fushan, 2009). Thus, the next time you disagree with someone about the taste of a particular food, don't automatically assume that your disagreement is simply a reflection of your individual preferences. It may reflect not a difference in *preference* (you *like* sweet things more than John does) but a difference in *experience* (you *experience* more intense sweet tastes than John does) that could be caused by differences in the types and numbers of taste receptors on the tongue or other differences in your taste systems.

1. What is neurogenesis, and what function does it serve?
2. What are the five basic taste qualities?
3. How is taste quality linked to a substance's effect?
4. Describe the anatomy of the taste system, including the receptors and central destinations.
5. What is the evidence for population coding and specificity coding in taste? Is it possible to choose between the two?
6. What kinds of evidence support the idea that different people may have different taste experiences? What mechanisms may be responsible for these differences?

Olfaction and Flavor

Like taste, the sense of smell, or **olfaction**, provides information that can be important for survival, and it also enriches our lives by combining with taste to create flavor.

The Functions of Olfaction

Olfaction provides an alarm system that alerts us to spoiled food, leaking gas, or smoke from a fire. But as important as these signals are to humans, olfaction is even more important in the lives of many other species, because it is often their primary window to the environment (Ache, 1991).

Many animals are **macrosmatic** (having a keen sense of smell that is important to their survival), whereas humans are **microsmatic** (having a less keen sense of smell that is not crucial to their survival). For macrosmatic animals, olfaction provides cues to orient them in space, to mark territory, and to guide them to specific places, other animals, and food sources (Holley, 1991). Olfaction is also extremely important in sexual reproduction because it triggers mating behavior in many species (Doty, 1976; Pfeiffer & Johnston, 1994).

An important aspect of the olfactory world of some animals is the existence of compounds called **pheromones**—molecules that are emitted by members of a species that cause a specific reaction in another individual of the same species (Karlson & Lüscher, 1959; Wyatt, 2010). The term *pheromone*, coined by Peter Karlson and Martin Lüscher, is a combination of two Greek words: *pherein*, to transfer, and *hormon*, to excite. This meaning, "to transfer excitement," is illustrated by many examples of animal behavior—the female silk moth that attracts males from miles away by releasing a chemical bombykol, or the male mouse that releases a pheromone that attracts females and causes aggression in other mice (Novotny et al., 1985).

Whether pheromones exist in humans is a matter of debate (Doty, 2010; Schaal & Porter, 1991; Stern & McClintock, 1998; Wysocki & Preti, 2009), but there is evidence that humans can detect odors related to reproduction. Devendra Singh and Matthew Bronstad (2001) demonstrated a connection between men's ratings of women's body odors and the women's menstrual cycle by showing that men rated the smell of T-shirts that women had worn for three consecutive nights during the ovulatory phase of their menstrual cycle to be more pleasant then the smell of shirts worn during their nonovulatory phase. In another T-shirt experiment, Saul Miller and Jon Maner (2010) showed that when men smelled T-shirts worn by women who were near ovulation, they had higher testosterone levels than when they smelled shirts worn far from ovulation. Olfactory cues can therefore signal a woman's level of reproductive fertility.

Whether these biologically produced olfactory cues actually influence human sexual attraction is unclear. But there is evidence that not having a sense of smell can have social consequences. Ilona Croy and coworkers (2013) found that a group of people who were born without a sense of smell, a condition called **isolated congenital anosmia (ICA)**, reported feeling more socially insecure than people with a sense of smell. Subjects with ICA reported worrying about their own body odor, having problems in interactions with other people, and avoiding eating with others. Men with ICA reported having fewer sexual relationships then men who could smell.

Social relationships aside, people who had experienced smell all their lives and then suffered from **anosmia** due to injury or infection often become acutely aware of the role the sense of smell had played in their lives. One woman who suffered from anosmia and then briefly regained her sense of smell stated, "I always thought I would sacrifice smell to taste if I had to choose between the two, but I suddenly realized how much I had missed. We take it for granted and are unaware that everything smells: people, the air, my house, my skin" (Birnberg, 1988; quoted in Ackerman, 1990, p. 42).

Molly Birnbaum (2011), who lost her sense of smell after being hit by a car while crossing the street, also noted the loss of everyday smells she had taken for granted. She described New York City without smell as "a blank slate without the aroma of car exhaust, hot dogs or coffee" and when she gradually began to regain some ability to smell she reveled in every new odor. "Cucumber!" she writes, "their once common

negligible scent had returned—intoxicating, almost ambrosial. The scent of melon could bring me to tears" (Birnbaum, 2011, p. 110). These descriptions help us realize that olfaction is more important in our lives than most of us realize. Although it may not be essential to our survival, life is often enhanced by our ability to smell and becomes a little more dangerous if we lose the olfactory warning system that can alert us to danger.

Olfactory Abilities

How well can we smell? This question has been answered by investigating how well we detect small concentrations of odorants, by testing our ability to tell one odor from another, and by determining how well we can identify odors.

Detecting Odors

Our sense of smell enables us to detect extremely low concentrations of some odorants. The **detection threshold** for odors is the lowest concentration at which an odorant can be detected.

METHOD | Measuring the Detection Threshold

One way to measure the threshold for detecting an odorant is to present different concentrations of an odorant on different trials. The subjects respond either "yes" (I smell something) or "no" (I don't smell anything) on each trial. However, one problem with this procedure is that it is susceptible to bias. Some people will respond "yes" at the merest hint of a smell, whereas others wait until they are sure they smell something before saying "yes" (see Appendix D, page 388).

The **forced-choice method** avoids this problem by presenting subjects with blocks of two trials—one trial contains a weak odorant and the other, no odorant. The subject's task is to indicate which trial has a stronger smell. This eliminates having to decide whether a smell is present, because the subject knows it is present on one of the trials. Threshold can be determined by measuring the concentration that results in a correct response on 75 percent of the trials (50 percent would be chance performance). When using this procedure, it is important to wait at least 30 seconds between trials to allow for recovery if an odorant was presented on the first trial. The forced-choice procedure generally indicates greater sensitivity than the yes/no procedure (Dalton, 2002).

Table 15.3 lists thresholds for a number of substances. It is notable that there is a very large range of thresholds. T-butyl mercaptan, the odorant that is added to natural gas to warn people of gas leaks, can be detected in very small concentrations of less than 1 part per billion in air. In contrast, to detect the vapors of acetone (the main component of nail polish remover), the concentration must be 15,000 parts per billion, and for the vapor of methanol, the concentration must be 141,000 parts per billion.

Although humans can detect extremely small concentrations of some odorants, they are much less sensitive to odors than many animals. For example, rats are 8 to 50 times more

Table 15.3 Human Odor Detection Thresholds

COMPOUND	ODOR THRESHOLD IN AIR (PARTS PER BILLION)
Methanol	141,000
Acetone	15,000
Formaldehyde	870
Menthol	40
T-butyl mercaptan	0.3

Source: Devos et al., 1990.

sensitive to odors than humans, and dogs are from 300 to 10,000 times more sensitive, depending on the odorant (Laing et al., 1991). But even though humans are unaware of odors that other animals can detect, humans' individual olfactory receptors are as sensitive as any animal's. H. deVries and M. Stuiver (1961) demonstrated this by showing that human olfactory receptors can be excited by the action of just 1 molecule of odorant.

Nothing can be more sensitive than 1 molecule per receptor, so how come humans are less sensitive to odors than dogs? The answer is that humans have far fewer receptors than dogs—only about 10 million receptors, compared to about 1 billion for dogs (Dodd & Squirrell, 1980; Moulton, 1977).

Discriminating Between Odors

Even though humans may not be as sensitive to the small concentrations of odorants that other animals can detect, they do quite well when presented with the task of **odor discrimination**—telling the difference between different odors. One of the challenges of odor discrimination is the vast numbers of odors that are possible, because most natural olfactory stimuli are mixtures of a large number of components. For example, the chemical mixture responsible for the smell of a rose consists of 275 components. What this means is that many different odors can be created by changing some of the components of a mixture, and considering the large number of chemicals and their possible combinations, there are many trillions of possible odors.

Caroline Bushdid and coworkers (2014) tested subjects to determine how many components of a substance they could change before the subjects could detect the difference between two substances. Based on their results, plus an estimate of the number of possible odors, they proposed that humans can discriminate the difference in the smells of more than 1 trillion olfactory stimuli. This is extremely impressive, especially when compared to vision (we can discriminate several million different colors) and hearing (we can discriminate almost half a million different tones).

Identifying Odors

One of the more intriguing facts about odors is that even though humans can *discriminate* more than 1 trillion different odors, they often find it difficult to accurately *identify* specific odors. For example, when people are presented with the

odors of familiar substances such as mint, bananas, and motor oil, they can easily tell the difference between them. However, when they are asked to *identify* the substance associated with the odor, they are successful only about half the time (Engen & Pfaffmann, 1960). J. A. Desor and Gary Beauchamp (1974) found, however, that when they presented participants with the names of the substances at the beginning of the experiment and then reminded them of the correct names when they failed to respond correctly on subsequent trials, they could, after some practice, correctly identify 98 percent of the substances.

One of the amazing things about odor identification is that knowing the correct label for the odor actually seems to transform our perception into that odor. I had this experience a number of years ago when sampling the drink *aquavit* with some friends. Aquavit has a very interesting but difficult to identify smell. Odors such as "anise," "orange," and "lemon" were proposed as we tried to identify its smell, but it wasn't until someone turned the bottle around and read the label on the back that the truth became known: "Aquavit (Water of Life) is the Danish national drink—a delicious, crystal-clear spirit distilled from grain, with a slight taste of caraway." When we heard the word *caraway*, the previous hypotheses of anise, orange, and lemon were transformed into caraway. Thus, when we have trouble identifying odors, this trouble results not from a deficiency in our olfactory system, but from an inability to retrieve the odor's name from our memory (Cain, 1979, 1980).

DEMONSTRATION | Naming and Odor Identification

To demonstrate the effect of naming substances on odor identification, have a friend collect a number of familiar objects for you and, without your looking, try to identify the odors your friend presents. You will find that you can identify some but not others, but when your friend tells you the answers for the ones you were unable to identify correctly, you will wonder how you could have failed to identify such a familiar smell. Don't blame your mistakes on your nose; blame them on your memory.

Individual Differences in Olfaction

We have seen that genetic differences can cause differences in people's experience of taste. This effect of genetics also occurs for smell (Keller et al., 2007; Mainland et al., 2014; Menashe et al., 2003; Pelchat et al., 2011). To take one example, a section of the human chromosome is associated with receptors that are sensitive to the chemical β-ionone, which is often added to foods and beverages to add a pleasant floral note. Individuals sensitive to β-ionone describe paraffin with low concentrations of β-ionone added as "fragrant" or "floral," whereas individuals with less sensitivity to β-ionone describe the same stimulus as "sour," "pungent," or "acid" (Jaeger et al., 2013). This genetically caused variation in sensitivity occurs for many different chemicals, leading to the idea that everyone experiences his or her own unique "flavor world" (McRae et al., 2013).

Another example of individual differences in smell is that the smell of the steroid androsterone, which is derived from testosterone, is described negatively ("sweaty," "urinous") by some people, positively by some people ("sweet," "floral"), and as having no odor by others (Keller et al., 2007). Or consider the fact that after eating asparagus some people's urine takes on a smell that has been described as sulfurous, much like cooked cabbage (Pelchat et al., 2011). Some people, however, can't detect this smell.

Analyzing Odorants: The Mucosa and Olfactory Bulb

We have, so far, been describing the functions of olfaction and the experiences that occur when olfactory stimuli, molecules in the air, enter the nose. We now consider the question of how the olfactory system knows what molecules are entering the nose. The first step toward answering this question is to consider some of the difficulties facing researchers who are searching for connections between molecules and perception.

The Puzzle of Olfactory Quality

Although we know that we can discriminate among a huge number of odors, research to determine the neural mechanisms behind this ability is complicated by difficulties in establishing a system to bring some order to our descriptions of odor quality. Such systems exist for other senses. We can describe visual stimuli in terms of their colors and can relate our perception of color to the physical property of wavelength. We can describe sound stimuli as having different pitches and relate these pitches to the physical property of frequency. Creating a way to organize odors and to relate odors to physical properties of molecules, however, has proven extremely difficult.

One reason for the difficulty is that we lack a specific language for odor quality. For example, when people smell the chemical α-ionone, they usually say that it smells like violets. This description, it turns out, is fairly accurate, but if you compare α-ionone to real violets, they smell different. The perfume industry's solution is to use names such as "woody violet" and "sweet violet" to distinguish between different violet smells, but this hardly solves the problem we face in trying to determine how olfaction works.

Another difficulty in relating odors to molecular properties is that some molecules that have similar structures can smell different (**Figure 15.10a**), and molecules that have very different structures can smell similar (**Figure 15.10b**). But things really become challenging when we consider the kinds of odors we routinely encounter in the environment, which consist of mixtures of many chemicals. Consider, for example, that when you walk into the kitchen and smell freshly brewed coffee, the coffee aroma is created by more than 100 different molecules. Although individual molecules may have their own odors, we don't perceive the odors of individual molecules; we perceive "coffee."

The feat of perceiving "coffee" becomes even more amazing when we consider that odors rarely occur in isolation. Thus, the coffee odor from the kitchen might be accompanied by the smells of bacon and freshly squeezed orange juice. Each of these has its own tens or hundreds of molecules, yet

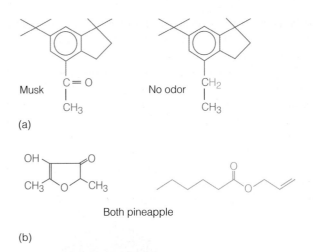

Figure 15.10 (a) Two molecules that have the same structure, but one smells like musk and the other is odorless. (b) Two molecules with different structures but similar odors.

somehow the hundreds of different molecules that are floating around in the kitchen become perceptually organized into smells that refer to three different sources: *coffee*, *bacon*, and *orange juice* (**Figure 15.11**). Sources of odors such as *coffee*, *bacon*, and *orange juice*, as well as nonfood sources such as *rose*,

Figure 15.11 Hundreds of molecules from the coffee, orange juice, and bacon are mixed together in the air, but the person just perceives "coffee," "orange juice," and "bacon." This perception of three odor objects from hundreds of intermixed molecules is a feat of perceptual organization.

dog, and *car exhaust*, are called **odor objects**. Our goal, therefore, is to explain not just how we smell different odor qualities, but how we identify different odor objects.

Perceiving odor objects involves olfactory processing that occurs in two stages. The first stage, which takes place at the beginning of the olfactory system in the *olfactory mucosa* and *olfactory bulb*, involves *analyzing*. In this stage, the olfactory system analyzes the different chemical components of odors and transforms these components into neural activity at specific places in the olfactory bulb (**Figure 15.12**). The second stage, which takes place in the olfactory cortex and beyond, involves *synthesizing*. In this stage, the olfactory system synthesizes the information about chemical components received from the olfactory bulb into representations of odor objects. As we will see, it has been proposed that this synthesis stage involves learning and memory. But let's start at the beginning, when odorant molecules enter the nose and stimulate receptors on the olfactory mucosa.

The Olfactory Mucosa

The **olfactory mucosa** is a dime-sized region located on the roof of the nasal cavity just below the **olfactory bulb** (**Figure 15.12a**). Odorant molecules are carried into the nose in an air stream

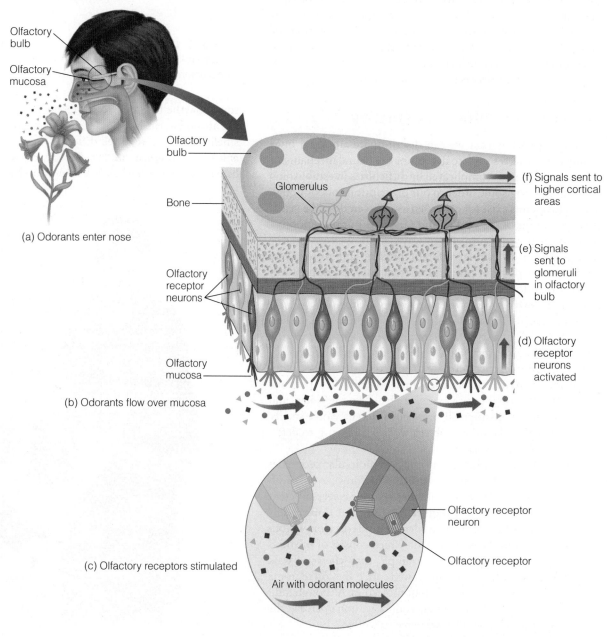

Figure 15.12 The structure of initial structures in the olfactory system. (a) Odorant molecules enter the nose, and then (b) flow over the olfactory mucosa, which contains 350 different types of olfactory receptor neurons (ORNs). (c) Stimulation of receptors in the ORNs (d) activates the ORNs. Three types of ORNs are shown here, indicated by different colors. Each type has its own specialized receptors. (e) Signals from the ORNs are then sent to glomeruli in the olfactory bulb, and then (f) to higher cortical areas.

(blue arrows), which brings these molecules into contact with the mucosa. **Figure 15.12b** shows the **olfactory receptor neurons (ORNs)** that are located in the mucosa (colored parts) and the supporting cells (tan area).

Just as the rod and cone receptors in the retina contain visual pigment molecules that are sensitive to light, the olfactory receptor neurons in the mucosa are dotted with molecules called **olfactory receptors** that are sensitive to chemical odorants (**Figure 15.12c**). One parallel between visual pigments and olfactory receptors is that they are both sensitive to a specific range of stimuli. Each type of visual pigment is sensitive to a band of wavelengths in a particular region of the visible spectrum (see Figure 2.18, page 33), and each type of olfactory receptor is sensitive to a narrow range of odorants.

An important difference between the visual system and the olfactory system is that while there are only four different types of visual pigments (one rod pigment and three cone pigments), there are about 400 different types of olfactory receptors, each sensitive to a particular group of odorants. The discovery that there are 350 to 400 types of olfactory receptors in the human and 1,000 types in the mouse was made by Linda Buck and Richard Axel (1991), who received the 2004 Nobel Prize in Physiology and Medicine for their research on the olfactory system (also see Buck, 2004).

The large number of olfactory receptor types increases the challenges in understanding how olfaction works. One thing that makes things slightly simpler is another parallel with vision: Just as a particular rod or cone receptor contains only one type of visual pigment, a particular olfactory receptor neuron (ORN) contains only one type of olfactory receptor.

How Olfactory Receptor Neurons Respond to Odorants

Figure 15.13a shows the surface of part of the olfactory mucosa. The circles represent ORNs, with two types of ORNs highlighted in red and blue. Remember that there are 400 different types of ORNs in the mucosa in humans. There are about 10,000 of each type of ORN, so the mucosa contains millions of ORNs.

The first step in understanding how we perceive different odorants is to ask how this array of millions of ORNs that blanket the olfactory mucosa respond to different odorants. One way this question has been answered is by using a technique called *calcium imaging*.

METHOD | Calcium Imaging

When an olfactory receptor responds, the concentration of calcium ions (Ca++) increases inside the ORN. One way of measuring this increase in calcium ions is called **calcium imaging**. This involves soaking olfactory neurons in a chemical that causes the ORN to fluoresce with a green glow when exposed to ultraviolet (380 nm) light. This green glow can be used to measure how much Ca++ had entered the neuron because *increasing* Ca++ inside the neuron *decreases* the glow. Thus, measuring the decrease in fluorescence indicates how strongly the ORN is activated.

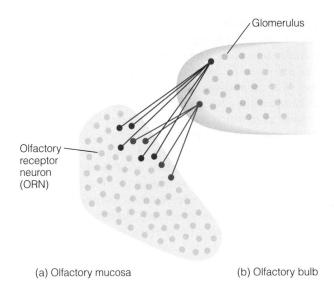

(a) Olfactory mucosa   (b) Olfactory bulb

Figure 15.13 (a) A portion of the olfactory mucosa. The mucosa contains 400 types of ORNs and about 10,000 of each type. The red circles represent 10,000 of one type of ORN, and the blue circles, 10,000 of another type. (b) All ORNs of a particular type send their signals to one or two glomeruli in the olfactory bulb.

Bettina Malnic and coworkers (1999), working in Linda Buck's laboratory, determined the response to a large number of odorants using calcium imaging. The results for a few of her odorants are shown in **Figure 15.14**, which indicates how 10 different ORNs are activated by each odorant. (Remember that each ORN contains only one type of olfactory receptor.)

The response of individual receptors is indicated by the circles in each column. Reading down the columns indicates that each of the receptors, except 19 and 41, respond to some odorants but not to others. The pattern of activation for each odorant, which is indicated by reading across each row, is called the odorant's **recognition profile**. For example, the recognition profile of octanoic acid is weak firing of ORN 79 and strong firing of ORNs 1, 18, 19, 41, 46, 51, and 83, whereas the profile for octanol is strong firing of ORNs 18, 19, 41, and 51.

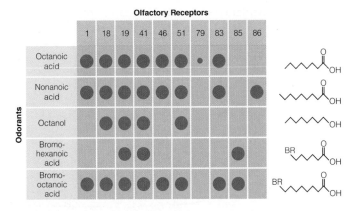

Figure 15.14 Recognition profiles for some odorants. Large dots indicate that the odorant causes a high firing rate for the receptor listed along the top; a small dot indicates a lower firing rate for the receptor. The structures of the compounds are shown on the right. (Adapted from Malnic, Hirono, Sata, & Buck, 1999)

From these profiles, we can see that each odorant causes a different pattern of firing across ORNs. Also, odorants that have similar structures (shown on the right in Figure 15.14), such as octanoic acid and nonanoic acid, often have similar profiles. We can also see, however, that this doesn't always occur (compare the patterns for bromohexanoic acid and bromooctanoic acid, which also have similar structures).

Remember that one of the puzzling facts about odor perception is that some molecules have similar structures but smell different (Figure 15.10a). When Malnic compared such molecules, she found that these molecules had different recognition profiles. For example, octanoic acid and octanol differ only by one oxygen molecule, but the smell of octanol is described as "sweet," "rose," and "fresh," whereas the smell of octanoic acid is described as "rancid," "sour," and "repulsive." This difference in perception is reflected in their different profiles. Although we still can't predict which smells result from specific patterns of response, we do know that when two odorants smell different, they usually have different profiles.

The idea that an odorant's smell can be related to different response profiles is similar to the trichromatic code for color vision that we described in Chapter 9 (see page 202). Remember that each wavelength of light is coded by a different pattern of firing of the three cone receptors, and that a particular cone receptor responds to many wavelengths. The situation for odors is similar—each odorant is coded by a different pattern of firing of ORNs, and a particular ORN responds to many odorants. What's different about olfaction is that there are 350 to 400 different types of ORNs, compared to just three cone receptors for vision.

The Search for Order in the Olfactory Bulb

Activation of receptors in the mucosa causes electrical signals in the ORNs that are distributed across the mucosa. These ORNs send signals to structures called **glomeruli** in the olfactory bulb. **Figure 15.13b** illustrates a basic principle of the relationship between ORNs and glomeruli: All of the 10,000 ORNs of a particular type send their signals to just one or two glomeruli, so each glomerulus collects information about the firing of a particular type of ORN.

We asked how ORNs in the mucosa respond to different odorants, and we now ask the same question for glomeruli in the olfactory bulb. Naoshige Uchida and coworkers (2000) used a technique called *optical imaging* to determine how glomeruli respond to different odorants.

METHOD | Optical Imaging

The technique of **optical imaging** can be used to measure the activity of large areas of the olfactory bulb by measuring how much red light is reflected from the olfactory bulb. The bulb must first be exposed by removing a patch of the skull. Red light is used because when neurons are activated, they consume oxygen from the blood. Blood that contains less oxygen reflects less red light than blood with oxygen, so areas that have been activated reflect less red light and are therefore darker than areas that have not been activated.

The optical imaging procedure involves illuminating the surface of the bulb with red light, measuring how much light is reflected, and then presenting a stimulus and determining which areas of the bulb become slightly darker. These darker areas are the areas that have been activated by the stimulus.

The results of Uchida's optical imaging experiment on the rat are shown in **Figure 15.15**. Each colored area represents the location of clusters of glomeruli in the olfactory bulb that are activated by the chemicals on the right. **Figure 15.15a** shows that each type of carboxylic acid activated a small area, and that there is some overlap between areas. Also notice that as the length of the carbon chain increases, the area of activation moves to the left. **Figure 15.15b** shows that a different group of chemicals—aliphatic alcohols—activates a different location on the olfactory bulb and that the same pattern occurs as before: larger chain lengths activate areas farther to the left.

The finding, using optical imaging, that different odorants activate different areas of the olfactory bulb, has also been demonstrated using a procedure called the *2-deoxyglucose technique*.

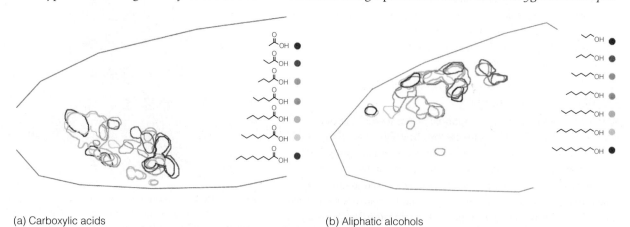

(a) Carboxylic acids

(b) Aliphatic alcohols

Figure 15.15 Areas in the rat olfactory bulb that are activated by various chemicals: (a) a series of carbolic acids; (b) a series of aliphatic alcohols. (Uchida, Takahashi, Tanifuji, & Mori, 2000)

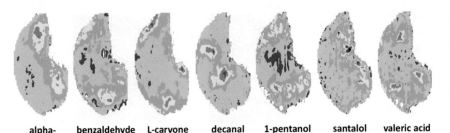

alpha-   benzaldehyde   L-carvone   decanal   1-pentanol   santalol   valeric acid
phellandrene

Figure 15.16 Patterns of activation in the rat olfactory bulb for seven different odorants. Yellow and red areas indicate areas of high activation compared to activation caused by exposure to air. Each odorant causes a distinctive pattern of activation. (Courtesy of Michael Leon)

METHOD | The 2-Deoxyglucose Technique

The **2-deoxyglucose technique** involves injecting a radioactive 2-deoxyglucose (2DG) molecule into an animal and exposing the animal to different chemicals. The radioactive 2DG contains the sugar glucose, which is taken up by active neurons, so by measuring the amount of radioactivity in the various parts of a structure, we can determine which neurons are most activated by the different chemicals.

Patterns of olfactory bulb activation measured for different chemicals using the 2DG technique are shown in **Figure 15.16**, in which areas of high activation are indicated by yellow and red. These results show that different odorants cause distinctive patterns of activation. Results such as this and the result in Figure 15.15 support the idea that there is a map of odorants in the olfactory bulb. This map has been called a **chemotopic map** to signify that it is based on molecular features of odorants such as carbon chain length or functional groups (Johnson & Leon, 2007; Johnson et al., 2010; Murthy, 2011). Some researchers use the terms **odor map** (Restrepo et al., 2009; Soucy et al., 2009; Uchida et al., 2000) or **odotoptic map** (Nikonov et al., 2005) instead of chemotopic map.

The idea that odorants with different properties create a map on the olfactory bulb is similar to the situation we have described for the other senses. There is a retinotopic map for vision, in which locations on the retina are mapped on the visual cortex (page 74); a tonotopic map for hearing, in which frequencies are mapped onto various structures in the auditory system (page 274); and a somatotopic map for the cutaneous senses, in which locations on the body are mapped onto the somatosensory cortex (page 341).

Research on the olfactory map has just begun, however, and much remains to be learned about how odors are represented in the olfactory bulb. Based on what has been discussed so far, it is clear that odorants are at least crudely mapped on the olfactory bulb based on their chemical properties. However, we are far from creating a map based on perception. This map, if it exists, will be a map of different odor experiences arranged on the olfactory bulb (Arzi & Sobel, 2011). But the olfactory bulb represents an early stage of olfactory processing and is not where perception occurs. To understand olfactory perception, we need to follow the output of the olfactory bulb to the olfactory cortex

Representing Odors in the Cortex

To begin our discussion of how odors are represented in the cortex, let's look at where signals are transmitted when they leave the olfactory bulb. **Figure 15.17a** shows the location of

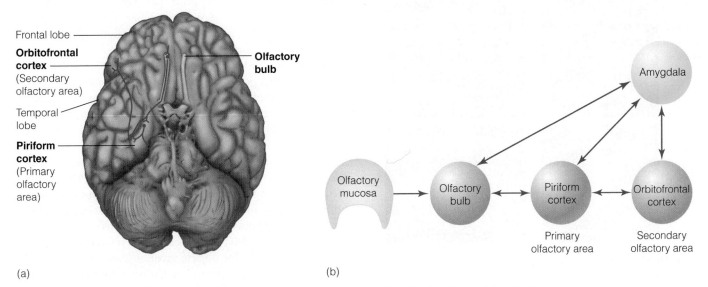

(a)   (b)

Figure 15.17 (a) The underside of the brain, showing the neural pathways for olfaction. On the left side, the temporal lobe has been deflected to expose the olfactory area. (b) Flow diagram of the pathways for olfaction.
[(a) Adapted from Frank & Rabin, 1989. (b) Adapted from Wilson & Stevenson, 2006.]

the two main olfactory areas: (1) the **piriform cortex**, which is the **primary olfactory area**, and (2) the **orbitofrontal cortex**, which is the **secondary olfactory area**. **Figure 15.17b** shows the olfactory system as a flow diagram and adds the **amygdala**, which responds not only to smell but also to faces (Chapter 5, page 118) and pain (Chapter 14, page 355). We begin by considering the piriform cortex.

How Odorants Are Represented in the Piriform Cortex

So far in our journey through the olfactory system, progressing from the olfactory neurons to the olfactory bulb, order has prevailed. Odors that smell different cause different patterns of firing of olfactory receptors (Figure 15.14). Moving to the olfactory bulb, different chemicals cause activity in specific areas, which has led to the proposal of odotopic maps (Figures 15.15 and 15.16).

But when we move up to the piriform cortex (PC), something surprising happens: The map vanishes! Odorants that caused activity in specific locations in the olfactory bulb now cause widespread activity in the PC, and there is overlap between the activity caused by different odorants.

This shift in organization from the olfactory bulb to the PC is illustrated in a study by B. F Osmanski and coworkers (2014), who used a technique called *functional ultrasound imagery*, which, like fMRI, determines brain activation by measuring changes in blood flow. **Figure 15.18a** shows that hexanal and pentyl acetate cause different patterns of activity in the rat olfactory bulb. **Figure 15.18b** shows that hexanal and pentyl acetate cause activity throughout the entire PC.

This widespread activity in the PC has also been demonstrated by recording from single neurons. **Figure 15.19**

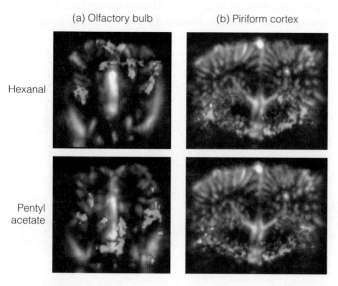

(a) Olfactory bulb   (b) Piriform cortex

Hexanal

Pentyl acetate

Figure 15.18 Response of the rat's (a) olfactory bulb and (b) piriform cortex to hexanal and pentyl acetate, measured by functional ultrasound scanning. The two chemicals create different patterns of activation in the olfactory bulb, but both cause activation throughout the entire piriform cortex. Osmanski et al 2014; Parts of Fig 3B and C, p 180; Parts of Fig 4B and C, p. 181.

(a) Electrode placements   (b) Activation by isoamyl acetate

Figure 15.19 (a) Recording sites used by Rennaker and coworkers (2007) to determine activity of neurons in the piriform cortex of the rat. (b) The pattern of activation caused by isoamyl acetate.

shows the results of an experiment by Robert Rennaker and coworkers (2007), who used multiple electrodes to measure neural responding in the PC. Figure 15.19b shows that isoamyl acetate causes activation across the cortex. Other compounds also cause widespread activity, and there is substantial overlap between the patterns of activity for different compounds.

These results show that the orderly activation pattern in the olfactory bulb no longer exists in the piriform cortex. This occurs because the projection from the olfactory bulb is scattered, so activity associated with a single chemical is spread out over a large area. Things become even more interesting when we ask what the activation pattern might look like for an odor object such as *coffee*.

How Odor Objects Are Represented

We can appreciate how complicated things become for odor objects by imagining what the pattern of activation would be for *coffee*, which contains a hundred different chemical components. Not only will the pattern be very complicated, but if you are smelling a particular odor for the first time, this raises the question of how the olfactory system is able to determine the identity of this "mystery odor" based on the information in this first-time response. Some researchers have answered this question by drawing a parallel between recognizing odors and experiencing memories.

Figure 15.20 indicates what happens when a memory is formed. When a person witnesses an event, a number of neurons are activated (**Figure 15.20a**). At this point, the memory for the event isn't completely formed in the brain; it is fragile and can be easily forgotten or can be disrupted by trauma, such as a blow to the head. But connections begin forming between the neurons that were activated by the event (**Figure 15.20b**), and after these connections are formed (**Figure 15.20c**), the memory is stronger and more resistant to disruption. Formation of stable memories thus involves a process in which linkages are formed between a number of neurons.

Applying this idea to odor perception, it has been proposed that formation of odor objects involves learning, which links together the scattered activations that occur for a particular object. We can see how this works by imagining that you are smelling the odor of a flower for the first time. The odor of this flower, just like the odors of coffee and other substances, is created by a

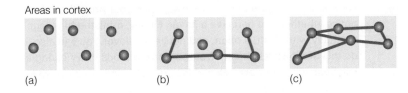

Areas in cortex

(a)   (b)   (c)

Figure 15.20 A model of how memories are formed in the cortex. (a) Initially, incoming information activates a number of areas in the cortex. Tan rectangles are different cortical areas. Red circles are activated areas. (b) As time passes, the neural activity is replayed, which creates connections between activated areas. (c) Eventually, the activated areas for a particular memory are linked, which stabilizes the memory.

large number of chemical compounds (**Figure 15.21a**). These chemical components first activate the olfactory receptors in the mucosa and then create a pattern of activation on the olfactory bulb that is shaped by the chemotopic map. This pattern occurs any time the flower's odor is presented (**Figure 15.21b**). From the research described above, we know that signals from the olfactory bulb are transformed into a scattered pattern of activation in the piriform cortex (**Figure 15.21c**).

Because this is the first time you have ever experienced the flower's odor, the activated neurons aren't associated with each other. This is like the neurons that represent a new memory, which aren't yet linked (see Figure 15.20a). At this point you are likely to have trouble identifying the odor and to confuse it with other odors. But after a number of exposures to the flower, which cause the same activation pattern to occur over and over, neural connections form, and the neurons become associated with each other (**Figure 15.21d**). Once this occurs, a pattern of activation has been created that represents the flower's odor. Thus, just as a stable memory becomes established when neurons become linked, odor objects become formed when experience with an odor causes neurons in the piriform cortex to become linked. According to this idea, when the person in Figure 15.11 walks into the kitchen, the activation caused by the hundreds of molecules in the air become three linked networks of activation in the PC that stand for *coffee*, *orange juice*, and *bacon*.

The idea that learning plays an important role in perceiving odors is supported by research. For example, Donald Wilson (2003) measured the response of neurons in the rat's piriform cortex to two odorants: (1) a *mixture* of isoamyl acetate, which has a banana-like odor, and peppermint and (2) the *component* isoamyl acetate alone. Wilson was interested in how well the rat's neurons could tell the difference between the mixture and the component after the rat had been exposed to the mixture.

Wilson presented the mixture to the rat for either a brief exposure (10 seconds or about 20 sniffs) or a longer exposure (50 seconds or about 100 sniffs) and, after a short pause, measured the response to the *mixture* and to the *component*. Following 10 seconds of sniffing, the piriform neurons responded similarly to the mixture and to the component. However, following 50 seconds of sniffing, the neurons fired more rapidly to the component. Thus, after 100 sniffs of the mixture, the neurons became able to tell the difference between the mixture and the component. Similar experiments measuring responses of neurons in the olfactory bulb did not show this effect.

Wilson concluded from these results that, given enough time, neurons in the piriform cortex can learn to discriminate between different odors, and that this learning may be involved in our ability to tell the difference between different odors in the environment. Numerous other experiments support the idea that a mechanism involving experience and learning is involved in associating patterns of piriform cortex firing with specific odor objects (Choi et al., 2011; Gottfried, 2010; Sosulski et al., 2011; Wilson, 2003; Wilson et al., 2004, 2014; Wilson & Sullivan, 2011).

Before leaving our description of how odor objects are represented in the piriform cortex, it is important to note that not all odor objects require learning. Consider, for example, pheromones that trigger stereotyped behaviors that are necessary for survival of a particular species. These pheromone responses may be determined by a second pathway for olfactory perception that sends signals from the olfactory bulb to the amygdala and does not depend on experience for identifying odors. According to this "dual pathway" idea, odor objects that depend on experience are served by the piriform cortex, and innate responses to chemicals such as pheromones are served by a separate pathway that creates automatic responses to specific odors (Kobayakawa et al., 2007; Sosulski et al., 2011).

For humans, experience is the most important determinant of the formation of odor objects. But we are now going to take yet another step, to consider mechanisms that take us beyond olfaction as simply the experience of "smell." We will now see that olfaction is a crucial component of the convergence of

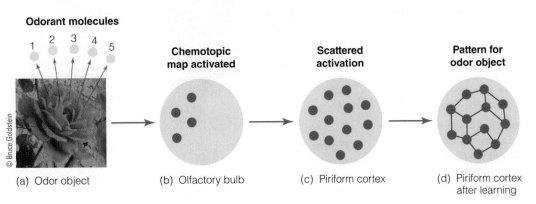

Odorant molecules

1 2 3 4 5

© Bruce Goldstein

(a) Odor object   (b) Olfactory bulb

Chemotopic map activated

Scattered activation

(c) Piriform cortex

Pattern for odor object

(d) Piriform cortex after learning

Figure 15.21 Memory mechanism for forming representations of the flower's odor. See text for details.

taste and olfaction that occurs when we eat, which results in the experience called *flavor*.

1. What are some of the functions of odor perception?

2. What is the difference between detecting odors, discriminating between odors, and identifying odors?

3. How well can people identify odors? What is the role of memory in odor recognition?

4. Describe some genetically determined individual differences in odor perception. What are some of the consequences of losing the ability to smell?

5. Describe the following components of the olfactory system: the olfactory receptors, the olfactory receptor neurons, the olfactory bulb, and the glomeruli. Be sure you understand the relation between olfactory receptors and olfactory receptor neurons, and between olfactory receptor neurons and glomeruli.

6. How do olfactory receptor neurons respond to different odorants, as determined by calcium imaging? What is an odorant's recognition profile?

7. Describe how optical imaging and the 2-deoxyglucose technique have been used to determine a chemotopic map on the olfactory bulb. What is the difference between a chemotopic map and a perceptual map?

8. What are the main structures in the olfactory system past the olfactory bulb?

9. How are odors represented in the piriform cortex? How does this representation differ from the representation in the olfactory bulb?

10. How has formation of the representation of odor objects in the cortex been described as being caused by experience? How is this similar to the process of forming memories?

The Perception of Flavor

What most people refer to as "taste" when describing their experience of food ("That tastes good, Mom") is usually a combination of taste, from stimulation of the receptors in the tongue, and olfaction, from stimulation of the receptors in the olfactory mucosa. This combination, which is called **flavor**, is defined as the overall impression that we experience from the combination of nasal and oral stimulation (Lawless, 2001; Shepherd, 2012). You can demonstrate how smell affects flavor with the following demonstration.

DEMONSTRATION | "Tasting" With and Without the Nose

While pinching your nostrils shut, drink a beverage with a distinctive taste, such as grape juice, cranberry juice, or coffee. Notice both the quality and the intensity of the taste as you are drinking it. (Take just one or two swallows because swallowing with your nostrils closed can cause a buildup of pressure in

your ears.) After one of the swallows, open your nostrils, and notice whether you perceive a flavor. Finally, drink the beverage normally with nostrils open, and notice the flavor. You can also do this demonstration with fruits or cooked foods or try eating a jellybean with your eyes closed (so you can't see its color) while holding your nose.

The reason you may have found it difficult to determine what you were drinking or eating when you were holding your nose is that your experience of flavor depends on a combination of taste and olfaction, and by holding your nose, you eliminated the olfactory component of flavor. This interaction between taste and olfaction occurs at two levels: first in the mouth and nose, and then in the cortex.

Taste and Olfaction Meet in the Mouth and Nose

Chemicals in food or drink cause taste when they activate taste receptors on the tongue. But in addition, food and drink release volatile chemicals that reach the olfactory mucosa by following the **retronasal route**, from the mouth through the **nasal pharynx**, the passage that connects the oral and nasal cavities (**Figure 15.22**). Although pinching the nostrils shut does not close the nasal pharynx, it prevents vapors from reaching the olfactory receptors by eliminating the circulation of air through this channel (Murphy & Cain, 1980).

The fact that olfaction is a crucial component of flavor may be surprising because the flavors of food seem to be

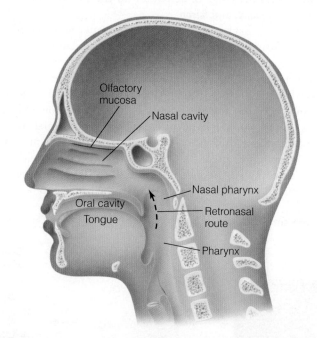

Figure 15.22 Odorant molecules released by food in the oral cavity and pharynx can travel through the nasal pharynx (dashed arrow) to the olfactory mucosa in the nasal cavity. This is the retronasal route to the olfactory receptors.

	Sodium oleate		Ferrous sulfate		MSG	
	Clamped	Open	Clamped	Open	Clamped	Open
Sweet	X		X			
Salty	X				XXXXXXXX	XXXXXXXX
Sour			XX	X	XXX	XXX
Bitter		X	X		XX	X
Soapy	XX	XXXXXXXXX	X	XX		
Metallic		XX	X	XXXXXXXXX		
Sulfurous				X	X	XX
Tasteless	XXXXXXXX		XXXXXX	X		
Other	X	X	X		X	XXX
	(a)		(b)		(c)	

Figure 15.23 How people described the flavors of three different compounds when they tasted them with their nostrils clamped shut and with their nostrils open. Each X represents the judgment of one person. (From Hettinger, Myers, & Frank, 1990)

centered in the mouth. It is only when we keep molecules from reaching the olfactory mucosa that the importance of olfaction is revealed. One reason this localization of flavor occurs is because food and drink stimulate tactile receptors in the mouth, which creates **oral capture**, in which the sensations we experience from both olfactory and taste receptors are referred to the mouth (Small, 2008). Thus, when you "taste" food, you are usually experiencing flavor, and the fact that it is all happening in your mouth is an illusion created by oral capture (Todrank & Bartoshuk, 1991).

The importance of olfaction in the sensing of flavor has been demonstrated experimentally by using both chemical solutions and typical foods. In general, solutions are more difficult to identify when the nostrils are pinched shut (Mozell et al., 1969) and are often judged to be tasteless. For example, **Figure 15.23a** shows that the chemical sodium oleate has a strong soapy flavor when the nostrils are open but is judged tasteless when they are closed. Similarly, ferrous sulfate

(**Figure 15.23b**) normally has a metallic flavor but is judged predominantly tasteless when the nostrils are closed (Hettinger et al., 1990). However, some compounds are not influenced by olfaction. For example, monosodium glutamate (MSG) has about the same flavor whether or not the nose is clamped (**Figure 15.23c**). In this case, the sense of taste predominates.

Taste and Olfaction Meet in the Nervous System

Although taste and olfactory stimuli occur in close proximity in the mouth and nose, our perceptual experience of their combination is created when they interact in the cortex. **Figure 15.24** is the diagram of the olfactory pathway from Figure 15.17b (in blue) with the taste pathway added (in red), showing connections between olfaction and taste (Rolls et al., 2010; Small, 2012). In addition, vision and touch contribute to flavor by sending signals to the amygdala (vision), structures in

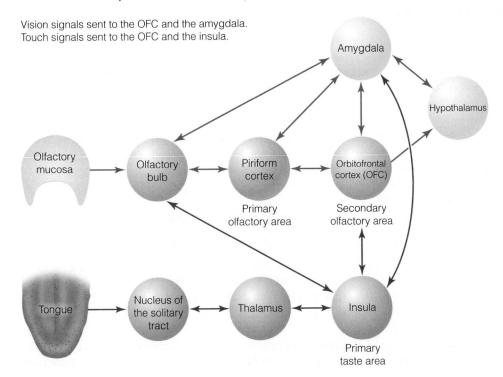

Vision signals sent to the OFC and the amygdala.
Touch signals sent to the OFC and the insula.

Figure 15.24 Flavor is created by interactions among taste, olfaction, vision, and touch. The olfactory pathway (blue) and taste pathway (red) interact as signals are sent between these two pathways. In addition, both taste and olfactory pathways send signals to the orbitofrontal cortex (OFC), signals from touch are sent to the taste pathway and the OFC, and signals from vision are sent to the OFC. Also shown are the amygdala—which is responsible for emotional responses and has many connections to structures in both the taste and olfaction pathways and also receives signals from vision—and the hypothalamus, which is involved in determining hunger.

the taste pathway (touch), and the orbitofrontal cortex (vision and touch).

All of these interactions among taste, olfaction, vision, and touch underscore the multimodal nature of our experience of flavor. Flavor includes not only what we typically call "taste," but also perceptions such as the texture and temperature of food (Verhagen et al., 2004), the color of food (Spence, 2015; Spence et al., 2010), and the sounds of "noisy" foods such as potato chips and carrots that crunch when we eat them (Zampini & Spence, 2010).

Because of this convergence of neurons from different senses, the orbitofrontal cortex contains many **bimodal neurons**, neurons that respond to more than one sense. For example, some bimodal neurons respond to both taste and smell, and others respond to taste and vision. An important property of these bimodal neurons is that they often respond to similar qualities. Thus, a neuron that responds to the taste of sweet fruits would also respond to the smell of these fruits. This means that neurons are tuned to respond to qualities that occur together in the environment. Because of these properties, it has been suggested that the orbitofrontal cortex is a cortical center for detecting flavor and for the perceptual representation of foods (Rolls & Baylis, 1994; Rolls et al., 2010). Other research has shown that the insula, the primary taste cortex, is also involved in the perception of flavor (de Araujo et al., 2012; Veldhuizen et al., 2010).

But flavor isn't a fixed response that is automatically determined by the chemical properties of food. Although the chemicals in a particular food may always activate the same pattern of ORNs in the mucosa, by the time the signals reach the cortex they can be affected by many different factors, including cognitive factors and the amount of a particular food the person has consumed.

Flavor Is Influenced by Cognitive Factors

What you expect can influence both what you experience and neural responding. This was demonstrated by Hilke Plassmann and coworkers (2008) by having subjects in a brain scanner judge the "taste pleasantness" of different samples of wine. Subjects were asked to indicate how much they liked five different wines, which were identified by their price. In reality, there were only three wines; two of them were presented twice, with different price labels. The results, for a wine that was labeled either $10 or $90, are shown in **Figure 15.25**. When the wines are presented without labels, the taste pleasantness judgments are the same (**Figure 15.25a**, left bars), but when tasting is preceded by a price label, the "$90 wine" gets a much higher taste rating than the "$10 wine." In addition to influencing the person's judgments, the labels also influence the response of the orbitofrontal cortex, with the $90 wine causing a much large response (**Figure 15.25b**).

What's happening here is that the response of the orbitofrontal cortex is being determined both by signals that begin with stimulation of the taste and olfactory receptors and by signals created by the person's expectations. In another experiment, subjects rated the same odor as more pleasant when it

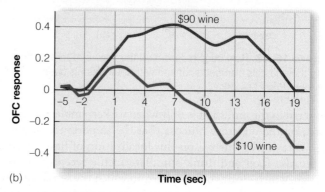

Figure 15.25 Effect of expectation on flavor perception, as indicated by the results of Hilke Plassmann and coworkers' (2008) experiment. (a) The red and blue bars indicate ratings given to two presentations of the same wine (although subjects didn't know they were the same). The two bars on the left indicate ratings when there were no price labels on the wines. The two bars on the right indicate that the subjects gave higher "taste pleasantness" ratings when the wine was labeled $90, compared to when it was labeled $10. (b) Responses of the OFC when tasting the wines labeled $10 and $90. [Part (b) from Plassmann, O'Doherty, Shiv, & Rangel, 2008]

was labeled "cheddar cheese" than when it was called "body odor," and the orbitofrontal cortex response was larger for the cheddar cheese label (de Araujo et al., 2005).

Many other experiments have shown that flavor is influenced by factors in addition to the actual food that is being consumed. The taste of a red frozen strawberry dessert was judged to be 10 percent sweeter and 15 percent more flavorful when it was presented on a white plate compared to on a black plate (Piqueras-Fiszman et al., 2012). The sweetness of café latte was almost doubled when consumed from a blue mug compared to a white mug (van Doorn et al., 2014). And returning to wine, experiments have shown that perception of the flavor of wine can be influenced not only by information about its price but also by the shape of the wine glass (Hummel et al., 2003).

Flavor Is Influenced by Food Intake: Sensory-Specific Satiety

Have you ever experienced the first few forkfuls of a particular food as tasting much better than the last? Food consumed to satiety (when you don't want to eat any more) is often considered less pleasurable than food consumed when hungry.

John O'Doherty and coworkers (2000) showed that both the pleasantness of a food-related odor and the brain's response to the odor can be influenced by satiety. Subjects were tested under two conditions: (1) when hungry and (2) after eating bananas until satiety. Subjects in a brain scanner judged the pleasantness of two food-related odors: banana and vanilla. The pleasantness ratings for both were similar before they had consumed any food. However, after eating bananas until satiety, the pleasantness rating for vanilla decreased slightly (but was still positive), but the rating for banana decreased much more and became negative (**Figure 15.26a**). This larger effect on the odor associated with the food eaten to satiety, called **sensory-specific satiety**, also occurred in the response of the orbitofrontal cortex. The orbitofrontal cortex response decreased for the banana odor but remained the same for the vanilla odor (**Figure 15.26b**). Similar effects also occurred in the amygdala and insula for some (but not all) subjects.

The finding that orbitofrontal cortex activity is related to the pleasantness of an odor or flavor can also be stated in another way: The orbitofrontal cortex is involved in determining the *reward value* of foods. Food is more rewarding when you are hungry and becomes less rewarding as food is consumed, until eventually—at satiety—the reward is gone and eating stops. These changes in the reward value of flavors are important because just as taste and olfaction are important for warning of danger, they are also important for regulating food intake. Also note in Figure 15.24 that the orbitofrontal cortex sends signals to the hypothalamus, where neurons are found that respond to the sight, taste, and smell of food if hunger is present (Rolls et al., 2010).

What we've learned by considering each of the stages of the systems for taste, olfaction, and flavor is that the purpose of the chemical senses extends beyond simply creating experiences of taste, smell, and flavor. Their purpose is to help guide behavior—avoiding potentially harmful substances, seeking out nutrients, and helping control the amount of food consumed.

Does this description of a sense being concerned with behavior sound familiar? You may remember that Chapter 7, "Taking Action," presented a similar message for vision: Although early researchers saw the visual system as being concerned primarily with creating visual experiences, later researchers have argued that the ultimate goal of the visual system is to support taking actions that are necessary for survival (see page 166). The chemical senses have a similar ultimate purpose of guiding and motivating actions required for survival. We eat in order to live, and our experience of flavor helps motivate that eating. (Unfortunately, it should be added, the shutoff mechanisms are sometimes overridden by manufactured foods that are rich in sugar and fat and by other factors, with obesity as an outcome—but that's another story.)

SOMETHING TO CONSIDER:

The *Proust* Effect: Memories, Emotions, and Smell

One of the most famous quotes in literature is Marcel Proust's description of an experience after eating a small lemon cookie called a madeleine:

> The sight of the little madeleine had recalled nothing to my mind before I tasted it … as soon as I had recognized the taste of the piece of madeleine soaked in her decoction of lime-blossom which my aunt used to give me … immediately the old grey house upon the street, where her room was, rose up like a stage set to attach itself to the little pavilion opening on to the garden which had been built out behind it for my parents … and with the house the … square where I used to be sent before lunch, the streets along which I used to run errands, the country roads we took when it was fine. (Marcel Proust, *Remembrance of Things Past*, 1913)

Proust's description of how taste and olfaction unlocked memories he hadn't thought of for years, now called the **Proust effect**, is not an uncommon experience. I once entered a staircase in an old building. It had wooden walls on either side and dusty old rubber treads on each step, but what hit me was the smell, which was the same smell as the staircase I used to climb as a young boy in my grandfather's house. As soon as I smelled that staircase, I experienced memories of that old house and of my grandfather, who had died years before.

So I have experienced the Proust effect, but is there any scientific evidence for its existence? The answer is that a

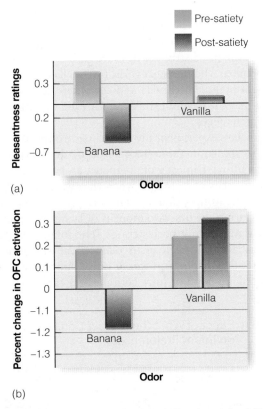

Figure 15.26 Sensory-specific satiety. Results of the O'Doherty et al. (2000) experiment. (a) Pleasantness rating for banana and vanilla odor before eating (blue bars) and after eating bananas to satiety (red bars). (b) Response of the orbitofrontal cortex to banana and vanilla odors before and after eating bananas. (From O'Doherty et al., 2000)

number of experiments have demonstrated a link between odors and specific aspects of memory. Rachel Herz and Jonathan Schooler (2002) had subjects describe a personal memory associated with items like Crayola crayons, Coppertone suntan lotion, and Johnson's baby powder. After describing their memory associated with the objects, subjects were presented with an object either in visual form (a color photograph) or in odor form (smelling the object's odor) and were asked to think about the event they had described and to rate it on a number of scales. The result was that subjects who smelled the odor rated their memories as more emotional than subjects who saw the picture. They also had a stronger feeling than the visual group of "being brought back" to the time the memory occurred (also see Willander & Larsson, 2007).

What's behind this effect? A physiologically based answer for the high emotionality and feeling of "being brought back"

associated with odor-elicited memories is that there are connections from structures involved in both taste and olfaction to the amygdala, which is involved in emotional behavior, and to other structures such as the hippocampus, which is involved in storing memories.

One question raised by this research is whether the emotion associated with the odor-based memories is a perceptual effect that occurs simply because smelling odors activates the amygdala. Or does the effect occur because smelling odors elicits especially emotional memories? There is some evidence that the second explanation is correct (Willander & Larsson, 2007), but more research needs to be done to be sure. Whatever the correct explanation for these effects, it is clear from people's experiences involving odor and memory that there is something special about memories that are associated with odors.

DEVELOPMENTAL DIMENSION Infant Chemical Sensitivity

Do newborn infants perceive odors and tastes? Early researchers, noting that a number of olfactory stimuli elicited responses such as body movements and facial expressions from newborns, concluded that newborns can smell (Kroner, 1881, cited in Peterson & Rainey, 1911). However, some of the stimuli used by these early researchers may have irritated the membranes of the infant's nose, so the infants may have been responding to irritation rather than to smell (Beauchamp et al., 1991; Doty, 1991).

Modern studies using nonirritating stimuli, however, have provided evidence that newborns can smell and can discriminate between different olfactory stimuli. J. E. Steiner (1974, 1979) used nonirritating stimuli to show that infants respond to banana extract or vanilla extract with sucking and facial expressions that are similar to smiles, and they respond to concentrated shrimp odor and an odor resembling rotten eggs with rejection or disgust. Perhaps the most significant odors for the infant originate from the mother, and infants can recognize their mothers through the sense of smell (Porter et al., 1983; Russell, 1976; Schaal, 1986).

Research investigating infants' reactions to taste has included numerous studies showing that newborns can discriminate sweet, sour, and bitter stimuli (Beauchamp et al., 1991). These studies have found that newborns react with different facial expressions to sweet, sour, and bitter stimuli but show little or no response to salty stimuli (Ganchrow, 1995; Ganchrow et al., 1983; Rosenstein & Oster, 1988; Steiner, 1987).

Research studying how newborns and young infants respond to salt indicates that there is a shift toward greater acceptance of salty solutions between birth and 4 to 8 months of age that continues into childhood (Beauchamp et al., 1994). One explanation for this shift is that it reflects the development of receptors sensitive to salt during infancy. But there is also evidence that infants' preferences are shaped by experience that occurs both before birth and during early infancy. For example, infants born to women who reported suffering from

moderate to severe symptoms of morning sickness had significantly higher relative intake of salt solutions at 4 months of age than those whose mothers reported having no more than mild morning sickness (Crystal & Bernstein, 1995, 1998; Lesham, 1998).

Further evidence for the effect of experience before birth is based on the finding that what pregnant women eat can change the smell of the amniotic fluid environment in which the fetus is developing. The amniotic fluid of pregnant women who eat garlic has a stronger or more garlicky smell than the fluid of women who don't eat garlic (Mennella et al., 1995). An experiment by Julie Mennella and coworkers (2001) provides evidence that the flavor of the amniotic fluid can influence an infant's preferences.

Mennella's experiment involved three groups of pregnant women, as shown in **Table 15.4**. Group 1 drank carrot juice during their final trimester of pregnancy and water during the first two months of lactation, when they were breast-feeding their infants. Group 2 drank water during pregnancy and carrot juice during the first two months of lactation, and Group 3 drank water during both periods. The infants' preference for carrot-flavored cereal versus plain cereal was tested four weeks after they had begun eating cereal but before they had experienced any food or juice containing a carrot flavor. The

Table 15.4 Effect of What the Mother Consumes on Infant Preferences

GROUP	LAST TRIMESTER	DURING BREAST FEEDING	INTAKE OF CARROT FLAVOR
1	Carrot juice	Water	0.62
2	Water	Carrot juice	0.57
3	Water	Water	0.51

Note: Intake score above 0.50 indicates preference for carrot-flavored cereal.

results, shown in the right column of Table 15.4, indicate that the infants who had experienced carrot flavor either in utero or in the mother's milk showed a preference for the carrot-flavored cereal (indicated by a score above 0.5), whereas the infants whose mothers had consumed only water showed no preference.

Infant responses to tastes, odors, and flavors are therefore determined both by innate factors and by experience. An important conclusion from the finding that what the mother consumes during pregnancy and lactation influences the odors experienced by the fetus and breast-fed infant is that the first step toward ensuring that young children develop good eating habits is for mothers to eat healthy foods both when pregnant and when nursing. Another conclusion is that infants can become familiar with foods common to a particular culture before they are born (Beauchamp & Mennella, 2009).

1. What is flavor perception? Describe how taste and olfaction meet in the mouth and nose and then later in the nervous system.
2. Describe the experiment that showed how expectations about a wine's taste can influence taste judgments and brain responding.
3. Describe the experiment that demonstrates sensory-specific satiety.
4. What is the Proust effect? Is there any evidence for it?
5. What is the evidence that newborns can detect different taste and smell qualities? Describe the carrot juice experiment and how it demonstrates that what a mother consumes can influence infant taste preferences.

THINK ABOUT IT

1. Consider the kinds of food that you avoid because you don't like the taste. Do these foods have anything in common that might enable you to explain these taste preferences in terms of the activity of specific types of taste receptors? (p. 367)

2. Can you think of situations in which you have encountered a smell that triggered memories about an event or place that you hadn't thought about in years? What do you think might be the mechanism for this type of experience? (p. 381)

KEY TERMS

Across-fiber patterns (p. 365)
Amiloride (p. 366)
Amygdala (p. 376)
Anosmia (p. 369)
Bimodal neurons (p. 380)
Calcium imaging (p. 373)
Chemotopic map (p. 375)
Detection threshold (p. 369)
Flavor (p. 378)
Forced-choice method (p. 369)
Frontal operculum (p. 364)
Glomeruli (p. 374)
Insula (p. 364)
Isolated congenital anosmia (ICA) (p. 369)
Macrosmatic (p. 368)

Microsmatic (p. 368)
Nasal pharynx (p. 378)
Neurogenesis (p. 362)
Nucleus of the solitary tract (p. 364)
Odor discrimination (p. 370)
Odor map (p. 375)
Odor objects (p. 372)
Odotoptic map (p. 375)
Olfaction (p. 368)
Olfactory bulb (p. 372)
Olfactory mucosa (p. 372)
Olfactory receptor neurons (ORNs) (p. 373)
Olfactory receptors (p. 373)
Optical imaging (p. 374)
Oral capture (p. 379)

Orbitofrontal cortex (p. 376)
Papillae (p. 363)
Pheromones (p. 369)
Piriform cortex (p. 376)
Primary olfactory area (p. 376)
Proust effect (p. 381)
Recognition profile (p. 373)
Retronasal route (p. 378)
Secondary olfactory area (p. 376)
Sensory-specific satiety (p. 381)
Taste buds (p. 364)
Taste cells (p. 364)
Taste pore (p. 364)
2-deoxyglucose technique (p. 375)
Video microscopy (p. 367)

Methods of Adjustment and Constant Stimuli

In addition to the method of limits, which we discussed in Chapter 1 (page 14), Fechner proposed two other psychophysical methods: the *method of adjustment* and the *method of constant stimuli*.

As you'll recall from Chapter 1, in the *method of limits*, the experimenter presents stimuli to a subject in either ascending order (intensity is increased) or descending order (intensity is decreased) in order to detect threshold. The **method of adjustment** is similar to the method of limits in that the stimulus intensity is either increased or decreased until the stimulus can just be detected. However, in the method of adjustment, the subject (not the experimenter) adjusts the stimulus intensity continuously until he or she can just barely detect the stimulus. For example, the subject might be told to turn a knob to decrease the intensity of a sound until the sound can no longer be heard, and then to turn the knob back again so the sound is just barely audible. This just barely audible intensity is taken as the threshold. This procedure can be repeated several times and the threshold determined by taking the average setting.

In the **method of constant stimuli**, the experimenter presents five to nine stimuli with different intensities in random order. For example, in a hypothetical experiment designed to determine the threshold for seeing a light, intensities of 150, 160, 170, 180, 190, and 200 are presented one at a time. On each trial, the subject says "yes" or "no" to indicate whether he or she sees the light. The experimenter chooses light intensities so that the lowest intensity is never detected and the highest one is always detected. The intensities in between are detected on some trials and not on others. The result from presenting each intensity many times and determining the percentage of trials on which the light was detected is shown in **Figure A.1**. The threshold is usually defined as the intensity that results in detection on 50 percent of the trials. Applying this definition to the results in Figure A.1 indicates that the threshold is an intensity of 180.

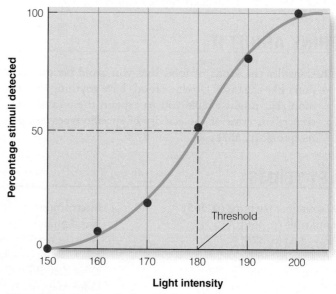

Figure A.1 Results of a hypothetical experiment in which the threshold for seeing a light is measured by the method of constant stimuli. The threshold—the intensity at which the light is seen on half of its presentations—is 180 in this experiment.

The choice among the methods of limits, adjustment, and constant stimuli is usually determined by the degree of accuracy needed and the amount of time available. The method of constant stimuli is the most accurate method because it involves many observations and stimuli are presented in random order, which minimizes how presentation on one trial can affect the subject's judgment of the stimulus presented on the next trial. The disadvantage of this method is that it is time-consuming. The method of adjustment is faster because subjects can determine their threshold in just a few trials by adjusting the intensity themselves.

The Difference Threshold

When Fechner published *Elements of Psychophysics*, he not only described his methods for measuring the absolute threshold but also described the work of Ernst Weber (1795–1878), a physiologist who, a few years before the publication of Fechner's book, measured another type of threshold, the **difference threshold**: the minimum *difference* that must exist *between* two stimuli before we can tell the difference between them. This just detectible difference is the difference threshold (also called DL from the German *Differenze Limen*, which is translated as "difference threshold.")

Measuring instruments, such as an old-fashioned balance scale, can detect very small differences. For example, imagine that a scale is balanced when four 50-penny rolls are placed on each pan. When just one additional penny is placed on one side, the scale succeeds in detecting this very small difference between the two weights. The human sensory system is not as sensitive to weight differences as this type of scale, so a human comparing the weight of 201 pennies to 200 pennies would not be able to tell the difference. The difference threshold for weight is about 2 percent, which means that under ideal conditions, we would have to add 4 pennies to one side before the difference could be detected by the human.

The idea that the difference threshold is a *percentage* of the weights being compared was discovered by Weber, who proposed that the ratio of the DL to the standard is constant. This means that if we doubled the number of pennies to 400, the DL would also double, becoming 8. The ratio DL/Standard for lifting weights is 0.02, which is called the **Weber fraction**, and the fact that the Weber fraction remains the same as the standard is changed is called **Weber's law**. Modern investigators have found that Weber's law is true for most senses, as long as the stimulus intensity is not too close to the absolute threshold (Engen, 1972; Gescheider, 1976).

The Weber fraction remains relatively constant for a particular sense, but each type of sensory judgment has its own Weber fraction. For example, from **Table B.1** we can see that people can detect a 1 percent change in the intensity of an electric shock but that light intensity must be increased by 8 percent before they can detect a difference.

Table B.1 Weber Fractions for a Number of Different Sensory Dimensions

Electric shock	0.01
Lifted weight	0.02
Sound intensity	0.04
Light intensity	0.08
Taste (salty)	0.08

Source: Teghtsoonian (1971).

Magnitude Estimation and the Power Function

The procedure for a magnitude estimation experiment was described in Chapter 1 (page 15). **Figure C.1** shows a graph that plots the results of a magnitude estimation experiment in which subjects assigned numbers to indicate their perception of the brightness of lights. This graph, which presents the average magnitude estimates made by a number of subjects, indicates that doubling the intensity does not necessarily double the perceived brightness. For example, when the intensity is 20, perceived brightness is 28. If we double the intensity to 40, perceived brightness does not double to 56, but instead increases only to 36. This result, in which the increase in perceived magnitude is smaller than the increase in stimulus intensity, is called **response compression**.

Figure C.1 also shows the results of magnitude estimation experiments for the experience caused by an electric shock presented to the finger and for the perception of length of a line. The electric shock curve bends up, indicating that doubling the strength of a shock more than doubles the perceived magnitude of the shock. Increasing the intensity from 20 to 40 increases perception of shock magnitude from 6 to 49. This is called **response expansion**. As intensity is increased, perceptual magnitude increases more than intensity. The curve for estimating line length is straight, with a slope of close to 1.0, meaning that the magnitude of the response almost exactly matches increases in the stimulus, so if the line length is doubled, an observer says it appears to be twice as long.

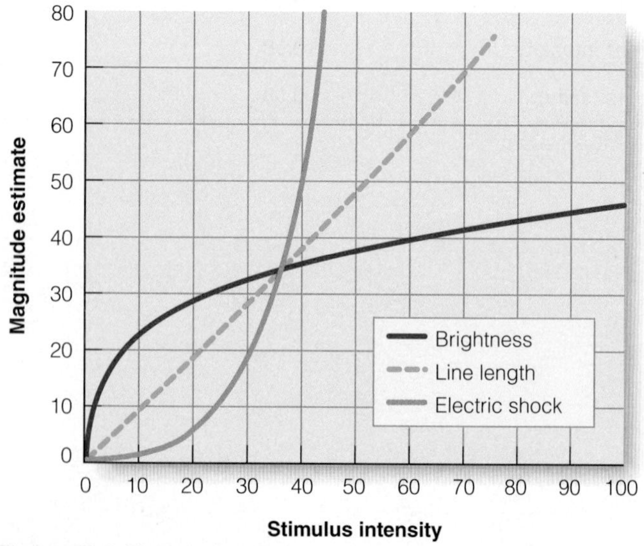

The beauty of the relationships derived from magnitude estimation is that the relationship between the intensity of a stimulus and our perception of its magnitude follows the same general equation for each sense. These functions, which are called **power functions**, are described by the equation $P = KS^n$. Perceived magnitude, P, equals a constant, K, times the stimulus intensity, S, raised to a power, n. This relationship is called **Stevens's power law**.

For example, if the exponent, n, is 2.0 and the constant, K, is 1.0, the perceived magnitude, P, for intensities 10 and 20 would be calculated as follows:

Intensity 10: $P = (1.0) \times (10)^2 = 100$

Intensity 20: $P = (1.0) \times (20)^2 = 400$

In this example, doubling the intensity results in a fourfold increase in perceived magnitude, an example of response expansion.

The exponent of the power function, n, tells us something important about the way perceived magnitude changes as intensity is increased. Exponents less than 1.0 are associated with response compression (as occurs for the brightness of a light), and exponents greater than 1.0 are associated with response expansion (as occurs for sensing shocks).

Response compression and expansion illustrate how the operation of each sense is adapted to how organisms function in their environment. Consider, for example, your experience of brightness. Imagine you are inside reading a book, when you turn to look out the window at a sidewalk bathed in intense sunlight. Your eyes may be receiving thousands of times more light from the sidewalk than from the page of your book, but because of response compression, the sidewalk does not appear thousands

Figure C.1 The relationship between perceived magnitude and stimulus intensity for electric shock, line length, and brightness.
(Adapted from Stevens, 1962)

of times brighter than the page. It does appear brighter, but not so much that you are blinded by the sunlit sidewalk.[1]

[1]Another mechanism that keeps you from being blinded by high-intensity lights is the process of adaptation, which adjusts the eye's sensitivity in response to different light levels (see Chapter 2, page 28).

The opposite situation occurs for electric shock, which has an exponent of 3.5, so small increases in shock intensity cause large increases in pain. This rapid increase in pain associated with response expansion serves to warn us of impending danger, and we therefore tend to withdraw even from weak shocks.

The Signal Detection Approach

In Chapter 1 and Appendix A, we saw that by randomly presenting stimuli of different intensities, we can use the method of constant stimuli to determine a person's threshold—the intensity to which the person reports "I see the light" or "I hear the tone" 50 percent of the time (pages 14, 384). What determines this threshold intensity? Certainly, the physiological workings of the person's eye and visual system are important. But some researchers have pointed out that perhaps other characteristics of the person may also influence the determination of threshold intensity.

To illustrate this idea, let's consider a hypothetical experiment in which we use the method of constant stimuli to measure Lucy's and Cathy's thresholds for seeing a light. We pick five different light intensities, present them in random order, and ask Lucy and Cathy to say "yes" if they see the light and "no" if they don't see it. Lucy thinks about these instructions and decides that she wants to be sure she doesn't miss any presentations of the light. Because Lucy decides to say "yes" if there is even the slightest possibility that she sees the light, we could call her a liberal responder. Cathy, however, is a conservative responder. She wants to be totally sure that she sees the light before saying "yes" and so reports that she sees the light only if she is definitely sure she saw it.

The results of this hypothetical experiment are shown in **Figure D.1**. Lucy gives many more "yes" responses than Cathy does and therefore ends up with a lower threshold. But given what we know about Lucy and Cathy, should we conclude that Lucy's visual system is more sensitive to the lights than Cathy's? It could be that their actual sensitivity to the lights is exactly same, but Lucy's apparently lower threshold occurs because she is more willing than Cathy to report that she sees a light. A way to describe this difference between these two people is that each has a different **response criterion**. Lucy's response criterion is low (she says "yes" if there is the slightest chance a light is present), whereas Cathy's response criterion is high (she says "yes" only when she is sure that she sees the light).

What are the implications of the fact that people may have different response criteria? If we are interested in how one person responds to different stimuli (for example, measuring how a person's threshold varies for different colors of light), then we don't need to take response criterion into account because we are comparing responses within the same person. Response

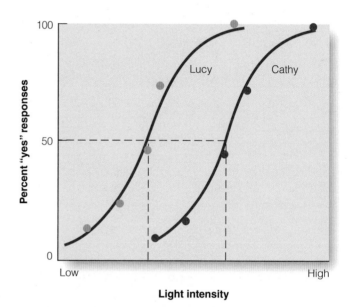

Figure D.1 Data from experiments in which the threshold for seeing a light is determined for Lucy (green points) and Cathy (red points) by means of the method of constant stimuli. These data indicate that Lucy's threshold is lower than Cathy's. But is Lucy really more sensitive to the light than Cathy, or does she just appear to be more sensitive because she is a more liberal responder?

criterion is also not very important if we are testing many people and averaging their responses. However, if we wish to compare two people's responses, their differing response criteria could influence the results. Luckily, an approach called the **signal detection approach** can be used to take differing response criteria into account. We will first describe a signal detection experiment and then describe the theory underlying the experiment.

A Signal Detection Experiment

Remember that in a psychophysical procedure such as the method of constant stimuli (see Appendix A), at least five different stimulus intensities are presented and a stimulus is presented on every trial. In a signal detection experiment studying the detection of tones, we use only a single low-intensity tone that is difficult to hear, and we present this tone on some of the trials and present no tone at all on the rest of the trials.

The Basic Experiment

A signal detection experiment differs from a classical psychophysical experiment in two ways: (1) only one stimulus intensity is presented, and (2) on some of the trials, no stimulus is presented. Let's consider the results of such an experiment, using Lucy as our subject. We present the tone for 100 trials and no tone for 100 trials, mixing the tone and no-tone trials at random. Lucy's results are as follows.

When the tone is presented, Lucy

- Says "yes" on 90 trials. This correct response—saying "yes" when a stimulus is present—is called a **hit** in signal detection terminology.
- Says "no" on 10 trials. This incorrect response—saying "no" when a stimulus is present—is called a **miss**.

When no tone is presented, Lucy

- Says "yes" on 40 trials. This incorrect response—saying "yes" when there is no stimulus—is called a **false alarm**.
- Says "no" on 60 trials. This correct response—saying "no" when there is no stimulus—is called a **correct rejection**.

These results are not very surprising, given that we know Lucy has a low criterion and likes to say "yes" a lot. This gives her a high hit rate of 90 percent but also causes her to say "yes" on many trials when no tone is present, so her 90 percent hit rate is accompanied by a 40 percent false-alarm rate. If we do a similar experiment on Cathy, who has a higher criterion and therefore says "yes" much less often, we find that she has a lower hit rate (say, 60 percent) but also a lower false-alarm rate (say, 10 percent). Note that although Lucy and Cathy say "yes" on numerous trials on which no stimulus is presented, that result would not be predicted by classical threshold theory. Classical theory would say "no stimulus, no response," but that is clearly not the case here. By adding the following new wrinkle to our signal detection experiment, we can obtain another result that would not be predicted by classical threshold theory.

Payoffs

Without changing the tone's intensity at all, we can cause Lucy and Cathy to change their percentages of hits and false alarms. We do this by manipulating each person's motivation by means of **payoffs**. Let's look at how payoffs might influence Cathy's responding. Remember that Cathy is a conservative responder who is hesitant to say "yes." But being clever experimenters, we can make Cathy say "yes'" more frequently by adding some financial inducements to the experiment. We tell Cathy that we are going to reward her for making correct responses and are

going to penalize her for making incorrect responses by using the following payoffs.

Hit:	Win $100
Correct rejection:	Win $10
False alarm:	Lose $10
Miss:	Lose $10

What would you do if you were in Cathy's position? You realize that the way to make money is to say "yes" more. You can lose $10 if a "yes" response results in a false alarm, but this small loss is more than counterbalanced by the $100 you can win for a hit. Although you decide not to say "yes" on every trial—after all, you want to be honest with the experimenter about whether you heard the tone—you decide to stop being so conservative. You decide to change your criterion for saying "yes." The results of this experiment are interesting. Cathy becomes a more liberal responder and says "yes" a lot more, responding with 98 percent hits and 90 percent false alarms.

This result is plotted as data point L (for "liberal" response) in **Figure D.2**, a plot of the percentage of hits versus the percentage of false alarms. The solid curve going through point L is called a **receiver operating characteristic (ROC) curve**. We will see why the ROC curve is important in a moment, but first let's see how we determine the other points on the curve. Doing this is simple: all we have to do is to change the payoffs. We can make Cathy raise her criterion and therefore respond more conservatively by means of the following payoffs.

Hit:	Win $10
Correct rejection:	Win $100
False alarm:	Lose $10
Miss:	Lose $10

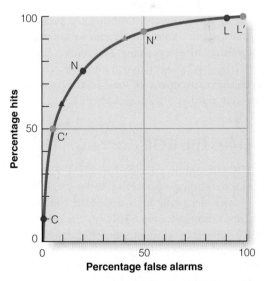

Figure D.2 A receiver operating characteristic (ROC) curve determined by testing Lucy (green data points) and Cathy (red data points) under three different criteria: liberal (L and L'), neutral (N and N'), and conservative (C and C'). The fact that Cathy's and Lucy's data points all fall on this curve means that they have the same sensitivity to the tone. The triangles indicate the results for Lucy and Cathy for an experiment that did not use payoffs.

This schedule of payoffs offers a great inducement to respond conservatively because there is a big reward for saying "no" when no tone is presented. Cathy's criterion is therefore shifted to a much higher level, so Cathy now returns to her conservative ways and says "yes" only when she is quite certain that a tone is presented; otherwise she says "no." The result of this newfound conservatism is a hit rate of only 10 percent and a minuscule false-alarm rate of 1 percent, indicated by point C (for "conservative" response) on the ROC curve. We should note that although Cathy hits on only 10 percent of the trials in which a tone is presented, she scores a phenomenal 99 percent correct rejections on trials in which a tone is not presented. (If there are 100 trials in which no tone is presented, then correct rejections + false alarms = 100. Because there was 1 false alarm, there must be 99 correct rejections.)

Cathy, by this time, is rich and decides to put a down payment on the Miata she's been dreaming about. (So far she's won $8,980 in the first experiment and $9,090 in the second experiment, for a total of $18,070! To be sure you understand how the payoff system works, check this calculation yourself. Remember that the signal was presented on 100 trials and was not presented on 100 trials.) However, we point out that she may need a little extra cash to have a satellite audio system installed in her car, so she agrees to stick around for one more experiment. We now use the following neutral schedule of payoffs.

Hit:	Win $10
Correct rejection:	Win $10
False alarm:	Lose $10
Miss:	Lose $10

With this schedule, we obtain point N (for "neutral") on the ROC curve: 75 percent hits and 20 percent false alarms. Cathy wins $1,100 more and becomes the proud owner of a Miata with a satellite radio system, and we are the proud owners of the world's most expensive ROC curve. (Do not, at this point, go to the psychology department in search of the nearest signal detection experiment. In real life, the payoffs are quite a bit less than in our hypothetical example.)

What Does the ROC Curve Tell Us?

Cathy's ROC curve shows that factors other than sensitivity to the stimulus determine a person's response. Remember that in all of our experiments the intensity of the tone has remained constant. Even though we changed only the person's criterion, we succeeded in drastically changing the person's responses.

Other than demonstrating that people will change how they respond to an unchanging stimulus, what does the ROC curve tell us? Remember, at the beginning of this discussion, we said that a signal detection experiment can tell us whether Cathy and Lucy are equally sensitive to the tone. The beauty of signal detection theory is that the person's sensitivity is indicated by the shape of the ROC curve, so if experiments on two people result in identical ROC curves, their sensitivities must be equal. (This conclusion is not obvious from our discussion

so far. We will explain below why the shape of the ROC curve is related to the person's sensitivity.) If we repeat the above experiments on Lucy, we get the following results (data points L′, N′, and C′ in Figure D.2):

Liberal Payoff
Hits = 99 percent
False alarms = 95 percent

Neutral Payoff
Hits = 92 percent
False alarms = 50 percent

Conservative Payoff
Hits = 50 percent
False alarms = 6 percent

The data points for Lucy's results are shown by the green circles in Figure D.1. Note that although these points are different from Cathy's, they fall on the same ROC curve as do Cathy's. We have also plotted the data points for the first experiments we did on Lucy (open triangle) and Cathy (filled triangle) before we introduced payoffs. These points also fall on the ROC curve.

That Cathy's and Lucy's data both fall on the same ROC curve indicates their equal sensitivity to the tones. This confirms our suspicion that the method of constant stimuli misled us into thinking that Lucy is more sensitive, when the real reason for her apparently greater sensitivity is her lower criterion for saying "yes."

Before we leave our signal detection experiment, it is important to note that signal detection procedures can be used without the elaborate payoffs that we described for Cathy and Lucy. Much briefer procedures, which we will describe shortly, can be used to determine whether differences in the responses of different persons are due to differences in threshold or to differences in response criteria.

What does signal detection theory tell us about functions such as the spectral sensitivity curve (Figure 2.15, page 31) and the audibility curve (Figure 11.8, page 265), which are usually determined using one of the classical psychophysical methods? When the classical methods are used to determine these functions, it is usually assumed that the person's criterion remains constant throughout the experiment, so that the function measured is due not to changes in response criterion but to changes in the wavelength or some other physical property of the stimulus. This is a good assumption because changing the wavelength of the stimulus probably has little or no effect on factors such as motivation, which would shift the person's criterion. Furthermore, experiments such as the one for determining the spectral sensitivity curve usually use highly experienced people who are trained to give stable results. Thus, even though the idea of an "absolute threshold" may not be strictly correct, classical psychophysical experiments run under well-controlled conditions have remained an important tool for measuring the relationship between stimuli and perception.

Signal Detection Theory

We will now discuss the theoretical basis for the signal detection experiments we have just described. Our purpose is to explain the theoretical bases underlying two ideas: (1) the percentage of hits and false alarms depends on a person's criterion, and (2) a person's sensitivity to a stimulus is indicated by the shape of the person's ROC curve. We will begin by describing two key concepts of signal detection theory (SDT): signal and noise. (See Swets, 1964.)

Signal and Noise

The **signal** is the stimulus presented to the person. Thus, in the signal detection experiment we just described, the signal is the tone. The **noise** is all the other stimuli in the environment, and because the signal is usually very faint, noise can sometimes be mistaken for the signal. Seeing what appears to be a flicker of light in a completely dark room is an example of visual noise. Seeing light where there is none is what we have been calling a false alarm, according to signal detection theory. False alarms are caused by the noise. In the experiment we just described, hearing a tone on a trial in which no tone was presented is an example of auditory noise.

Let's now consider a typical signal detection experiment, in which a signal is presented on some trials and no signal is presented on the other trials. Signal detection theory describes this procedure not in terms of presenting a signal or no signal, but in terms of presenting signal plus noise (S + N) or noise (N). That is, the noise is always present, and on some trials, we add a signal. Either condition can result in the perceptual effect of hearing a tone. A false alarm occurs when the person says "yes" on a noise trial, and a hit occurs when the person says "yes" on a signal-plus-noise trial. Now that we have defined signal and noise, we introduce the idea of probability distributions for noise and signal plus noise.

Probability Distributions

Figure D.3 shows two probability distributions. The one on the left represents the probability that a given perceptual effect will be caused by noise (N), and the one on the right represents the probability that a given perceptual effect will be caused by signal plus noise (S + N). The key to understanding these distributions is to realize that the value labeled "Perceptual effect (loudness)" on the horizontal axis is what the person experiences on each trial. Thus, in an experiment in which the person is asked to indicate whether a tone is present, the perceptual effect is the perceived loudness of the tone. Remember that in an SDT experiment the tone always has the same *intensity*. The *loudness* of the tone, however, can vary from trial to trial. The person perceives different loudnesses on different trials, because of either trial-to-trial changes in attention or changes in the state of the person's auditory system.

The probability distributions tell us what the chances are that a given loudness of tone is due to (N) or to (S + N). For

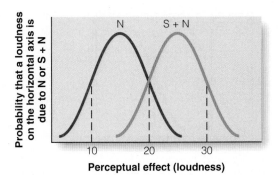

Figure D.3 Probability distributions for noise alone (N, red curve), and for signal plus noise (S + N, green curve). The probability that any given perceptual effect is caused by the noise (no signal is presented) or by the signal plus noise (signal is presented) can be determined by finding the value of the perceptual effect on the horizontal axis and extending a vertical line up from that value. The place where that line intersects the (N) and (S + N) distributions indicates the probability that the perceptual effect was caused by (N) or by (S + N).

example, let's assume that a person hears a tone with a loudness of 10 on one of the trials of a signal detection experiment. By extending a vertical dashed line up from 10 on the "Perceptual effect" axis in Figure D.3, we see that the probability that a loudness of 10 is due to (S + N) is extremely low, because the distribution for (S + N) is essentially zero at this loudness. There is, however, a fairly high probability that a loudness of 10 is due to (N), because the (N) distribution is fairly high at this point.

Let's now assume that, on another trial, the person perceives a loudness of 20. The probability distributions indicate that when the tone's loudness is 20, it is equally probable that this loudness is due to (N) or to (S + N). We can also see from Figure D.3 that a tone with a perceived loudness of 30 would have a high probability of being caused by (S + N) and only a small probability of being caused by (N).

Now that we understand the curves of Figure D.3, we can appreciate the problem confronting the person. On each trial, she has to decide whether no tone (N) was present or whether a tone (S + N) was present. However, the overlap in the probability distributions for (N) and (S + N) means that for some perceptual effects this judgment will be difficult. As we saw before, it is equally probable that a tone with a loudness of 20 is due to (N) or to (S + N). So, on a trial in which the person hears a tone with a loudness of 20, how does she decide whether the signal was presented? According to signal detection theory, the person's decision depends on the location of her criterion.

The Criterion

We can see how the criterion affects the person's response by looking at **Figure D.4**. In this figure, we have labeled three different criteria: liberal (L), neutral (N), and conservative (C). Remember that we can cause people to adopt these different criteria by means of different payoffs. According to signal detection theory, once the person adopts a criterion, he or she

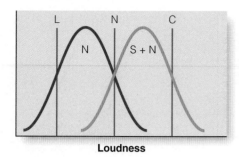

Loudness

Figure D.4 The same probability distributions from Figure D.3, showing three criteria: liberal (L), neutral (N), and conservative (C). When a person adopts a criterion, he or she uses the following decision rule: Respond "yes" ("I detect the stimulus") when the perceptual effect is greater than the criterion, and respond "no" ("I do not detect the stimulus") when the perceptual effect is less than the criterion.

uses the following rule to decide how to respond on a given trial: If the perceptual effect is greater than (to the right of) the criterion, say "Yes, the tone was present"; if the perceptual effect is less than (to the left of) the criterion, say "No, the tone was not present." Let's consider how different criteria influence the person's hits and false alarms.

To determine how the criterion affects the person's hits and false alarms, we will consider what happens when we present (N) and when we present (S + N) under three different criteria.

Liberal Criterion

1. Present (N): Because most of the probability distribution for (N) falls to the right of the criterion, the chances are good that presenting (N) will result in a loudness to the right of the criterion. This means that the probability of saying "yes" when (N) is presented is high; therefore, the probability of a false alarm is high.
2. Present (S + N): Because the entire probability distribution for (S + N) falls to the right of the criterion, the chances are excellent that presenting (S + N) will result in a loudness to the right of the criterion. Thus, the probability of saying "yes" when the signal is presented is high; therefore, the probability of a hit is high. Because criterion L results in high false alarms and high hits, adopting that criterion will result in point L on the ROC curve in **Figure D.5**.

Neutral Criterion

1. Present (N): The person will answer "yes" only rarely when (N) is presented because only a small portion of the (N) distribution falls to the right of the criterion. The false-alarm rate, therefore, will be fairly low.
2. Present (S + N): The person will answer "yes" frequently when (S + N) is presented because most of the (S + N) distribution falls to the right of the criterion. The hit rate, therefore, will be fairly high (but not as high as for the L criterion). Criterion N results in point N on the ROC curve in Figure D.5.

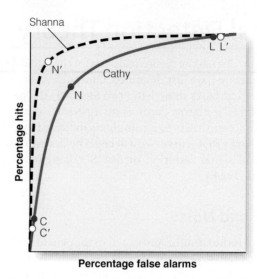

Percentage false alarms

Figure D.5 ROC curves for Cathy (solid curve) and Shanna (dashed curve) determined using liberal (L, L′), neutral (N, N′), and conservative (C, C′) criteria.

Conservative Criterion

1. Present (N): False alarms will be very low because none of the (N) curve falls to the right of the criterion.
2. Present (S + N): Hits will also be low because only a small portion of the (S + N) curve falls to the right of the criterion. Criterion C results in point C on the ROC curve in Figure D.5.

You can see that applying different criteria to the probability distributions generates the solid ROC curve in Figure D.5. But why are these probability distributions necessary? After all, when we described the experiment with Cathy and Lucy, we determined the ROC curve simply by plotting the results of the experiment. The reason the (N) and (S + N) distributions are important is that, according to signal detection theory, the person's sensitivity to a stimulus is indicated by the distance (d′) between the peaks of the (N) and (S + N) distributions, and this distance affects the shape of the ROC curve. We will now consider how the person's sensitivity to a stimulus affects the shape of the ROC curve.

The Effect of Sensitivity on the ROC Curve

We can understand how the person's sensitivity to a stimulus affects the shape of the ROC curve by considering what the probability distributions would look like for Shanna, a person with supersensitive hearing. Shanna's hearing is so good that a tone barely audible to Cathy sounds very loud to Shanna. If presenting (S + N) causes Shanna to hear a loud tone, this means that her (S + N) distribution should be far to the right, as shown in **Figure D.6**. In signal detection terms, we would say that Shanna's high sensitivity is indicated by the large separation (d′) between the (N) and the (S + N) probability distributions. To see how this greater separation between the probability distributions will affect her ROC curve, let's see how she would respond when adopting liberal, neutral, and conservative criteria.

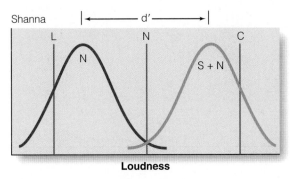

Figure D.6 Probability distributions for Shanna, a person who is extremely sensitive to the signal. The noise distribution (red) remains the same, but the (S + N) distribution (green) is shifted to the right compared to the curves in Figure D.4. Liberal (L), neutral (N), and conservative (C) criteria are shown.

Liberal Criterion

1. Present (N): high false alarms.
2. Present (S + N): high hits.

The liberal criterion, therefore, results in point L′ on the ROC curve of Figure D.5.

Neutral Criterion

1. Present (N): low false alarms. It is important to note that Shanna's false alarms for the neutral criterion will be lower than Cathy's false alarms for the neutral criterion because only a very small portion of Shanna's (N) distribution falls to the right of the criterion, whereas more of Cathy's (N) distribution falls to the right of the neutral criterion (Figure D.4).
2. Present (S + N): high hits.

In this case, Shanna's hits will be higher than Cathy's because almost all of Shanna's (S + N) distribution falls to the right of the neutral criterion, whereas less of Cathy's does (Figure D.4). The neutral criterion, therefore, results in point N′ on the ROC curve in Figure D.5.

Conservative Criterion

1. Present (N): low false alarms.
2. Present (S + N): low hits.

The conservative criterion, therefore, results in point C′ on the ROC curve.

The difference between the two ROC curves in Figure D.5 is obvious because Shanna's curve is more "bowed." But before you conclude that the difference between these two ROC curves has anything to do with where we positioned Shanna's L, N, and C criteria, see whether you can get an ROC curve like Shanna's from the two probability distributions of Figure D.4. You will find that, no matter where you position the criteria, there is no way that you can get a point like point N′ (with very high hits and very low false alarms) from the curves of Figure D.4. In order to achieve very high hits and very low false alarms, the two probability distributions must be spaced far apart, as in Figure D.6.

Thus, increasing the distance (d′) between the (N) and the (S + N) probability distributions changes the shape of the ROC curve. When the person's sensitivity (d′) is high, the ROC curve is more bowed. In practice, d′ can be determined by comparing the experimentally determined ROC curve to standard ROC curves (see Gescheider, 1976), or d′ can be calculated from the proportions of hits and false alarms that occur in an experiment by means of a mathematical procedure we will not discuss here. This mathematical procedure for calculating d′ enables us to determine a person's sensitivity by determining only one data point on an ROC curve, thus using the signal detection procedure without running a large number of trials.

Glossary

The number in parentheses at the end of each entry indicates the chapter in which the term is first used.

Ablation Removal of an area of the brain. This is usually done in experiments on animals to determine the function of a particular area. Also called lesioning. (4)

Absolute disparity *See* **Angle of disparity**. (10)

Absorption spectrum A plot of the amount of light absorbed by a visual pigment versus the wavelength of light. (2)

Accommodation In vision, bringing objects located at different distances into focus by changing the shape of the lens. (2)

Accretion A cue that provides information about the relative depth of two surfaces. Occurs when the farther object is uncovered by the nearer object due to sideways movement of an observer relative to the objects. *See also* **Deletion**. (10)

Achromatic color Color without hue. White, black, and all the grays between these two extremes are achromatic colors. (9)

Acoustic shadow The shadow created by the head that decreases the level of high-frequency sounds on the opposite side of the head. The acoustic shadow is the basis of the localization cue of interaural level difference. (12)

Acoustic signal The pattern of frequencies and intensities of the sound stimulus. (13)

Acoustic stimulus *See* **Acoustic signal**. (13)

Across-fiber patterns The pattern of nerve firing that a stimulus causes across a number of neurons. Also referred to as distributed coding. (15)

Action pathway *See* **Dorsal pathway**. (4)

Action potential Rapid increase in positive charge in a nerve fiber that travels down the fiber. Also called the nerve impulse. (2)

Action-specific perception hypothesis Hypothesis that people perceive their environment in terms of their ability to act on it. (7)

Active touch Touch in which the observer plays an active role in touching and exploring an object, usually with his or her hands. (14)

Additive color mixture *See* **Color mixture, additive**. (9)

Adjustment, method of A psychophysical method in which the experimenter or the observer adjusts the stimulus intensity in a continuous manner until the observer detects the stimulus. (Appendix A)

Affective (emotional) component of pain The emotional experience associated with pain—for example, pain described as *torturing*, *annoying*, *frightful*, or *sickening*. *See also* **Sensory component of pain**. (14)

Affordance The information specified by a stimulus pattern that indicates how the stimulus can be used. An example of an affordance would be seeing a chair as something to sit on or a flight of stairs as something to climb. (7)

Agnosia *See* **Visual form agnosia**. (1)

Akinetopsia A condition in which damage to an area of the cortex involved in motion perception causes blindness to motion. (8)

Amacrine cell A neuron that transmits signals laterally in the retina. Amacrine cells synapse with bipolar cells and ganglion cells. (2)

Ames room A distorted room, first built by Adelbert Ames, that creates an erroneous perception of the sizes of people in the room. The room is constructed so that two people at the far wall of the room appear to stand at the same distance from an observer. In actuality, one of the people is much farther away than the other. (10)

Amiloride A substance that blocks the flow of sodium into taste receptors. (15)

Amplitude In the case of a repeating sound wave, such as the sine wave of a pure tone, amplitude represents the pressure difference between atmospheric pressure and the maximum pressure of the wave. (11)

Amplitude modulation Adjusting the level (or intensity) of a sound stimulus so it fluctuates up and down. (11)

Amplitude-modulated noise A noise sound stimulus that is amplitude modulated. (11)

Amygdala A subcortical structure that is involved in emotional responding and in processing olfactory signals. (15)

Angle of disparity The visual angle between the images of an object on the two retinas. When images of an object fall on corresponding points, the angle of disparity is zero. When images fall on noncorresponding points, the angle of disparity indicates the degree of noncorrespondence. (10)

Angular size contrast theory An explanation of the moon illusion that states that the perceived size of the moon is determined by the sizes of the objects that surround it. According to this idea, the moon appears small when it is surrounded by large objects, such as the expanse of the sky when the moon is overhead. (10)

Anomalous trichromat A person who needs to mix a minimum of three wavelengths to match any other wavelength in the spectrum but mixes these wavelengths in different proportions than a trichromat. (9)

Anosmia Loss of the ability to smell due to injury or infection. (15)

Anterior belt area The front of the posterior belt in the temporal lobe, which is involved in perceiving sound. (12)

Aperiodic sound Sound waves that do not repeat. *See* **Periodic sound**. (11)

Aperture problem Occurs when only a portion of a moving stimulus can be seen, as when the stimulus is viewed through a narrow aperture or through the "field of view" of a neurons' receptive field. This can result in misleading information about the direction in which the stimulus is moving. (8)

Apex (of the cochlea) The end of the cochlea farthest from the middle ear. (11)

Aphasia Difficulties in speaking or understanding speech due to brain damage. (13)

Apparent distance theory An explanation of the moon illusion that is based on the idea that the horizon moon, which is viewed across the filled space of the terrain, should appear farther away than the zenith moon, which is viewed through the empty space of the sky. This theory states that because the horizon and zenith moons have the same visual angle but are perceived to be at different distances, the farther appearing horizon moon should appear larger. (10)

Apparent motion *See* **Apparent movement**. (8)

Apparent movement An illusion of movement that occurs when two objects separated in space are presented rapidly, one after another, separated by a brief time interval. (5)

Architectural acoustics The study of how sounds are reflected in rooms. An important concern of architectural acoustics is how these reflected sounds change the quality of the sounds we hear. (12)

Area V1 The visual receiving area of the brain, called area V1 to indicate that it is the first visual area in the cortex. Also called the striate cortex. (3)

Articulator Structure involved in speech production, such as the tongue, lips, teeth, jaw, and soft palate. (13)

Atmospheric perspective A depth cue. Objects that are farther away look more blurred and bluer than objects that are closer because we look through more air and particles to see them. (10)

Attack The buildup of sound energy that occurs at the beginning of a tone. (11)

Attention The process of focusing on some objects while ignoring others. Attention can enhance the processing of the attended object. (6)

Attentional capture Occurs when stimulus salience causes an involuntary shift of attention. For example, attention can be captured by movement. (6)

Audibility curve A curve that indicates the sound pressure level (SPL) at threshold for frequencies across the audible spectrum. (11)

Audiogram Plot of hearing loss versus frequency. (11)

Audiovisual mirror neuron Neuron that responds to actions that produce sounds. These neurons respond when a monkey performs a hand action *and* when it hears the sound associated with this action. *See also* **Mirror neuron**. (7)

Audiovisual speech perception A perception of speech that is affected by both auditory and visual stimulation, as when a person sees a video of someone making the lip movements for /fa/ while hearing the sound /ba/ and perceives /fa/. Also called the McGurk effect. (13)

Auditory canal The canal through which air vibrations travel from the environment to the tympanic membrane. (11)

Auditory localization The perception of the location of a sound source. (12)

Auditory receiving area (A1) The area of the cortex, located in the temporal lobe, that is the primary receiving area for hearing. (11)

Auditory response area The psychophysically measured area that defines the frequencies and sound pressure levels over which hearing functions. This area extends between the audibility curve and the curve for the threshold of feeling. (11)

Auditory scene The sound environment, which includes the locations and qualities of individual sound sources. (12)

Auditory scene analysis The process by which the sound stimuli produced by different sources in an auditory scene become perceptually organized into sounds at different locations and into separated streams of sound. (12)

Auditory space Perception of where sounds are located in space. Auditory space extends around a listener's head in all directions, existing wherever there is a sound. (12)

Auditory stream segregation The effect that occurs when a series of sounds that differ in pitch or timbre are played so that the tones become perceptually separated into simultaneously occurring independent streams of sound. (12)

Axial myopia Myopia (nearsightedness) in which the eyeball is too long. *See also* **Refractive myopia**. (2)

Axon The part of the neuron that conducts nerve impulses over distances. Also called the nerve fiber. (2)

Azimuth In hearing, specifies locations that vary from left to right relative to the listener. (12)

Balint's syndrome A condition resulting from damage to a person's parietal lobe. One characteristic of this syndrome is an inability to focus attention on individual objects. (6)

Base (of the cochlea) The end of the cochlea nearest the middle ear. (11)

Basilar membrane A membrane that stretches the length of the cochlea and controls the vibration of the cochlear partition. (11)

Bayesian inference A statistical approach to perception in which perception is determined by taking probabilities into account. These probabilities are based on past experiences in perceiving properties of objects and scenes. (5)

Beat In music, equally spaced intervals of time, which occurs even if there are no notes. When you tap your feet to music, you are tapping on the beat. (12)

Belt area Auditory area in the temporal lobe that receives signals from the core area and sends signals to the parabelt area. (12)

Bimodal neuron A neuron that responds to stimuli associated with more than one sense. (15)

Binaural cue Sound localization cue that involves both ears. Interaural time difference and interaural level difference are the primary binaural cues. (12)

Binding The process by which features such as color, form, motion, and location are combined to create our perception of a coherent object. Binding can also occur across senses, as when sound and vision are associated with the same object. (6)

Binding problem The problem of how neural activity in many separated areas in the brain is combined to create a perception of a coherent object. (6)

Binocular depth cell A neuron in the visual cortex that responds best to stimuli that fall on points separated by a specific degree of disparity on the two retinas. Also called a disparity-selective cell. (10)

Binocular disparity Occurs when the retinal images of an object fall on disparate points on the two retinas. (10)

Binocular rivalry A situation in which one image is presented to the left eye, a different image is presented to the right eye, and perception alternates back and forth between the two images. (5)

Binocularly fixate Directing the two foveas to exactly the same spot. (10)

Biological motion Motion produced by biological organisms. Most of the experiments on biological motion have used walking humans with lights attached to their joints and limbs as stimuli. *See also* **Point-light walker**. (8)

Bipolar cell A retinal neuron that receives inputs from the visual receptors and sends signals to the retinal ganglion cells. (2)

Blind spot The small area where the optic nerve leaves the back of the eye. There are no visual receptors in this area, so small images falling directly on the blind spot cannot be seen. (2)

Border cells Neurons that fire when an animal is near the edge of an environment. *See* **Grid cells; Place cells**. (7)

Border ownership When two areas share a border, as occurs in figure–ground displays, the border is usually perceived as belonging to the figure. (5)

Bottom-up processing Processing that is based on the information on the receptors. Also called data-based processing. (1)

Brain imaging Procedures that make it possible to visualize areas of the human brain that are activated by different types of stimuli, tasks, or behaviors. The most common technique used in perception research is functional magnetic resonance imaging (fMRI). (4)

Broca's aphasia Language problems including labored and stilted speech and short sentences, caused by damage to Broca's area in the frontal lobe. (13)

Broca's area An area in the frontal lobe that is important for language perception and production. One effect of damage is difficulty in speaking. (13)

Calcium imaging A method of measuring receptor activity by using fluorescence to measure the concentration of calcium inside the receptor. This technique has been used to measure the activation of olfactory receptor neurons. (15)

Categorical perception In speech perception, perceiving one sound at short voice onset times and another sound at longer voice onset times. The listener perceives only two categories across the whole range of voice onset times. (13)

Categorize Placing objects into categories, such as "tree," "bird," "car." (1)

Cell body The part of a neuron that contains the neuron's metabolic machinery and that receives stimulation from other neurons. (2)

Center-surround antagonism The competition between the center and surround regions of a center-surround receptive field, caused by the fact that one is excitatory and the other is inhibitory. Stimulating center and surround areas simultaneously decreases responding of the neuron, compared to stimulating the excitatory area alone. (3)

Center-surround organization Arrangement of a neuron's receptive fields in which one area is surrounded by another area, like the hole in a donut (corresponding to the center) and the donut (the surround). Stimulation of the center and surround causes opposite responses. *See also* **Excitatory-center, inhibitory-surround receptive field; Inhibitory-center, excitatory-surround receptive field**. (3)

Center-surround receptive field A receptive field that has a center-surround organization. (3)

Cerebral achromatopsia A loss of color vision caused by damage to the cortex. (9)

Cerebral cortex The 2-mm-thick layer that covers the surface of the brain and contains the machinery for creating perception, as well as for other functions, such as language, memory, and thinking. (1)

Change blindness Difficulty in detecting differences between two visual stimuli that are presented one after another, often with a short blank stimulus interposed between them. Also occurs when part of a stimulus is changed very slowly. (6)

Characteristic frequency The frequency at which a neuron in the auditory system has its lowest threshold. (11)

Chemotopic map The pattern of activation in the olfactory system in which chemicals with different properties create a "map" of activation based on these properties. For example, there is evidence that chemicals are mapped in the olfactory bulb based on carbon-chain length. Also called odor map. (15)

Chevreul illusion Occurs when areas of different lightness are positioned adjacent to one another to create a border. The illusion is the perception of a light band on the light side of the border and a dark band on the dark side of the border, even though these bands do not exist in the intensity distribution. (3)

Chromatic adaptation Exposure to light in a specific part of the visible spectrum. This adaptation can cause a decrease in sensitivity to light from the area of the spectrum that was presented during adaptation. (9)

Chromatic color Color with hue, such as blue, yellow, red, or green. (9)

Cilia Fine hairs that protrude from the inner and outer hair cells of the auditory system. Bending the cilia of the inner hair cells leads to transduction. (11)

Classical psychophysical methods The methods of limits, adjustment, and constant stimuli, described by Fechner, that are used for measuring thresholds. (1)

Coarticulation The overlapping articulation that occurs when different phonemes follow one another in speech. Because of these effects, the same phoneme can be articulated differently depending on the context in which it appears. For example, articulation of the /b/ in *boot* is different from articulation of the /b/ in *boat*. (13)

Cochlea The snail-shaped, liquid-filled structure that contains the structures of the inner ear, the most important of which are the basilar membrane, the tectorial membrane, and the hair cells. (11)

Cochlear amplifier Expansion and contraction of the outer hair cells in response to sound sharpens the movement of the basilar membrane to specific frequencies. This amplifying effect plays an important role in determining the frequency selectivity of auditory nerve fibers. (11)

Cochlear implant A device in which electrodes are inserted into the cochlea to create hearing by electrically stimulating the auditory nerve fibers. This device is used to restore hearing in people who have lost their hearing because of damaged hair cells. (11)

Cochlear nucleus The nucleus where nerve fibers from the cochlea first synapse. (11)

Cochlear partition A partition in the cochlea, extending almost its full length, that separates the scala tympani and the scala vestibuli. The organ of Corti, which contains the hair cells, is part of the cochlear partition. (11)

Cognitive influences on perception How the knowledge, memories, and expectations that a person brings to a situation influence his or her perception. (1)

Cognitive map A mental map of the spatial layout of an area of the environment. (7)

Coherence In research on movement perception in which arrays of moving dots are used as stimuli, the degree of correlation between the direction of the moving dots. Zero percent coherence means all of the dots are moving independently; 100 percent coherence means all of the dots are moving in the same direction. (8)

Coincidence detectors Neurons in the Jeffress neural coincidence model, which was proposed to explain how neural firing can provide information regarding the location of a sound source. A neural coincidence detector fires when signals from the left and right ears reach the neuron simultaneously. Different neural coincidence detectors fire to different values of interaural time difference. *See also* **Jeffress model**. (12)

Color blindness A condition in which a person perceives no chromatic color. This can be caused by absent or malfunctioning cone receptors or by cortical damage. (9)

Color circle Perceptually similar colors located next to each other and arranged in a circle. (9)

Color constancy The effect in which the perception of an object's hue remains constant even when the wavelength distribution of the illumination is changed. *Partial color constancy* occurs when our perception of hue changes a little when the illumination changes, though not as much as we might expect from the change in the wavelengths of light reaching the eye. (9)

Color deficiency People with this condition (sometimes incorrectly called color blindness) see fewer colors than people with normal color vision and need to mix fewer wavelengths to match any other wavelength in the spectrum. (9)

Color mixture, additive The creation of colors that occurs when lights of different colors are superimposed. (9)

Color mixture, subtractive The creation of colors that occurs when paints of different colors are mixed together. (9)

Color matching A procedure in which observers are asked to match the color in one field by mixing two or more lights in another field. (9)

Color solid A solid in which colors are arranged in an orderly way based on their hue, saturation, and value. (9)

Common fate, principle of A Gestalt principle of perceptual organization that states that things that are moving in the same direction appear to be grouped together. (5)

Common region, principle of A modern Gestalt principle that states that elements that are within the same region of space appear to be grouped together. (5)

Comparator A structure hypothesized by the corollary discharge theory of movement perception. The corollary discharge signal and the sensory movement signal meet at the comparator to determine whether movement will be perceived. (8)

Complementary afterimage An afterimage that is on the opposite side of the color circle from the inducing color. (9)

Complex cell A neuron in the visual cortex that responds best to moving bars with a particular orientation. (3)

Cone of confusion A surface in the shape of a cone that extends out from the ear. Sounds originating from different locations on this surface all have the same interaural level difference and interaural time difference, so location information provided by these cues is ambiguous. (12)

Cone spectral sensitivity curve A plot of visual sensitivity versus wavelength for cone vision. Often measured by presenting a small spot of light to the fovea, which contains only cones. Can also be measured when the eye is light adapted, so cones are the most sensitive receptors. (2)

Cones Cone-shaped receptors in the retina that are primarily responsible for vision in high levels of illumination and for color vision and detail vision. (2)

Conflicting cues theory A theory of visual illusions proposed by R. H. Day, which states that our perception of line length depends on an integration of the actual line length and the overall figure length. (10)

Conjunction search A visual search task in which it is necessary to search for a combination (or conjunction) of two or more features on the same stimulus to find the target. An example of a conjunction search would be looking for a horizontal green line among vertical green lines and horizontal red lines. (6)

Constant stimuli, method of A psychophysical method in which a number of stimuli with different intensities are presented repeatedly in a random order. (Appendix A)

Contextual modulation Change in response to a stimulus presented within a neuron's receptive field caused by stimulation outside of the receptive field. (3)

Continuity error Mismatch, usually involving spatial position or objects, that occurs from one film shot to another. (6)

Contrast threshold The intensity difference between two areas that can just barely be seen. This is often measured using gratings with alternating light and dark bars. (3)

Convergence (depth cue) *See* **Perspective convergence**. (10)

Convergence (neural) When many neurons synapse onto a single neuron. (2)

Core area The area in the temporal lobe that includes the primary auditory cortex (A1) and some nearby areas. Signals from the core area are transmitted to the belt area of the auditory cortex. (11)

Cornea The transparent focusing element of the eye that is the first structure through which light passes as it enters the eye. The cornea is the eye's major focusing element. (2)

Corollary discharge signal (CDS) A copy of the motor signal that is sent to the eye muscles to cause movement of the eye. The copy is sent to the hypothetical comparator of corollary discharge theory. (8)

Corollary discharge theory The theory that explains motion perception as being determined both by movement of the image on the retina and by signals that indicate movement of the eyes. *See also* **Corollary discharge signal**. (8)

Correct rejection In a signal detection experiment, saying "No, I don't detect a stimulus" on a trial in which the stimulus is not presented (a correct response). (Appendix D)

Correspondence problem The problem faced by the visual system, which must determine which parts of the images in the left and right eyes correspond to one another. Another way of stating the problem is: How does the visual system match up the images in the two eyes? This matching of the images is involved in determining depth perception using the cue of binocular disparity. (10)

Corresponding retinal points The points on each retina that would overlap if one retina were slid on top of the other. Receptors at corresponding points send their signals to the same location in the brain. (10)

Cortical magnification Occurs when a disproportionately large area on the cortex is activated by stimulation of a small area on the receptor surface. One example of cortical magnification is the relatively large area of visual cortex that is activated by stimulation of the fovea. An example in the somatosensory system is the large area of somatosensory cortex activated by stimulation of the lips and fingers. (4)

Cortical magnification factor The size of the cortical magnification effect. (4)

Covert attention Attention without looking. Seeing something "out of the corner of your eye" is an example of covert attention. (6)

Crossed disparity Disparity that occurs when an one object is being fixated, and is therefore on the horopter, and another object is located in front of the horopter, closer to the observer. (10)

Cue approach to depth perception The approach to explaining depth perception that focuses on identifying information in the retinal image that is correlated with depth in the scene. Some of the depth cues that have been identified are overlap, relative height, relative size, atmospheric perspective, convergence, and accommodation. (10)

Cutaneous receptive field Area of skin that, when stimulated, influences the firing of a neuron. (14)

Cutaneous senses The ability to perceive sensations, such as touch and pain, that are based on the stimulation of receptors in the skin. (14)

Dark adaptation Visual adaptation that occurs in the dark, during which the sensitivity to light increases. This increase in sensitivity is associated with regeneration of the rod and cone visual pigments. (2)

Dark adaptation curve The function that traces the time course of the increase in visual sensitivity that occurs during dark adaptation. (2)

Dark-adapted sensitivity The sensitivity of the eye after it has completely adapted to the dark. (2)

Data-based processing Another name for bottom-up processing. Refers to processing that is based on incoming data, as opposed to top-down, or knowledge-based, processing, which is based on prior knowledge. (1)

Decay The decrease in the sound signal that occurs at the end of a tone. (11)

Decibel (dB) A unit that indicates the pressure of a sound stimulus relative to a reference pressure: $dB = 20 \log (p/p_o)$ where p is the pressure of the tone and p_o is the reference pressure. (11)

Delay unit A component of the Reichardt detector proposed to explain how neural firing occurs to different directions of movement. The delay unit delays the transmission of nerve impulses as they travel from the receptors toward the brain. (8)

Deletion A cue that provides information about the relative depth of two surfaces. Deletion occurs when a farther object is covered by a nearer object due to sideways movement of an observer relative to the objects. *See also* **Accretion**. (10)

Dendrites Nerve processes on the cell body that receive stimulation from other neurons. (2)

Depolarization When the inside of a neuron becomes more positive, as occurs during the initial phases of the action potential. Depolarization is often associated with the action of excitatory neurotransmitters. (2)

Dermis The layer of skin below the epidermis. (14)

Desaturated Low saturation in chromatic colors as would occur when white is added to a color. For example, pink is not as saturated as red. (9)

Detached retina A condition in which the retina is detached from the back of the eye. (2)

Detection threshold *See* **Threshold, detection**. (15)

Dichromat A person who has a form of color deficiency. Dichromats can match any wavelength in the spectrum by mixing two other wavelengths. (9)

Difference threshold *See* **Threshold, difference**. (Appendix B)

Direct pathway model of pain The idea that pain occurs when nociceptor receptors in the skin are stimulated and send their signals to the brain. This model does not account for the fact that pain can be affected by other factors in addition to stimulation of the skin. (14)

Direct sound Sound that is transmitted directly from a sound source to the ears. (12)

Dishabituation An increase in responding that occurs when a stimulus is changed. This response is used in testing infants to see whether they can differentiate two stimuli. (6)

Disparity-selective cell *See* **Binocular depth cell**. (10)

Disparity tuning curve A plot of a neuron's response versus the degree of disparity of a visual stimulus. The disparity to which a neuron responds best is an important property of disparity-selective cells, which are also called binocular depth cells. (10)

Distal stimulus The stimulus "out there," in the external environment. (1)

Distance How far a stimulus is from the observer. In hearing, the distance coordinate specifies how far the sound source is from the listener. (12)

Distributed representation Occurs when a stimulus causes neural activity in a number of different areas of the brain, so the activity is distributed across the brain. (4)

Divided attention Occurs when a person divides his or her attention across two or more tasks. (6)

Dorsal pathway Pathway that conducts signals from the striate cortex to the parietal lobe. The dorsal pathway has also been called the *where*, the *how*, or the *action* pathway by different investigators. (4)

Double dissociation In brain damage, when function A is present and function B is absent in one person, and function A is absent and function B is present in another. Presence of a double dissociation means that the two functions involve different mechanisms and operate independently of one another. (4)

Double-opponent neurons Neurons that have receptive fields in which stimulation of one part of the receptive field causes an excitatory response to wavelengths in one area of the spectrum and an inhibitory response to wavelengths in another area of the spectrum, and stimulation of an adjacent part of the receptive field causes the opposite response. An example of double-opponent responding is when the response of one part of a receptive field is $+M-L$ and the response of an adjacent part is $+L-M$. (9)

Dual-stream model of speech perception Model that proposes a ventral stream starting in the temporal lobe that is responsible for recognizing speech, and a dorsal stream starting in the parietal lobe that is responsible for linking the acoustic signal to the movements used to produce speech. (13)

Dual-task procedure An experimental procedure in which subjects are required to carry out simultaneously a central task that demands attention and a peripheral task that involves making a decision about the contents of a scene. (6)

Duplex theory of texture perception The idea that texture perception is determined by both spatial and temporal cues that are detected by two types of receptors. Originally proposed by David Katz and now called the "duplex theory". (14)

Eardrum Another term for the tympanic membrane, the membrane located at the end of the auditory canal that vibrates in response to pressure changes. This vibration is transmitted to the bones of the middle ear. (11)

Echolocation Locating objects by sending out high-frequency pulses and sensing the echo created when these pulses are reflected from objects in the environment. Echolocation is used by bats and dolphins. (12)

Ecological approach to perception This approach focuses on specifying the information in the environment that is used for perception, emphasizing the study of moving observers to determine how their movement results in perceptual information that both creates perception and guides further movement. (7)

Ecological validity An ecologically valid experiment matches its stimuli, conditions, and procedures to those present in the natural world. (7)

Effect of the missing fundamental Removing the fundamental frequency and other lower harmonies from a musical tone does not change the tone's pitch. (11)

Electromagnetic spectrum Continuum of electromagnetic energy that extends from very-short-wavelength gamma rays to long-wavelength radio waves. Visible light is a narrow band within this spectrum. (1)

Elevation In hearing, sound locations that are up and down relative to the listener. (12)

Emmert's law A law stating that the size of an afterimage depends on the distance of the surface against which the afterimage is viewed. The farther away the surface, the larger the afterimage appears. (10)

Empathy The ability to share and vicariously experience what someone else is feeling. (14)

Endorphin Chemical that is naturally produced in the brain and that causes analgesia. (14)

End-stopped cell A cortical neuron that responds best to lines of a specific length that are moving in a particular direction. (3)

Epidermis The outer layers of the skin, including a layer of dead skin cells. (14)

Equal loudness curve A curve that indicates the sound pressure levels that result in a perception of the same loudness at frequencies across the audible spectrum. (11)

Event A segment of time at a particular location that is perceived by observers to have a beginning and an ending. (8)

Event boundary The point in time when one event ends and another begins. (8)

Event-related potential (ERP) The brain's response to a specific event, such as flashing an image or presenting a tone, as measured with small disc electrodes placed on a person's scalp. (12)

Excitatory area Area of a receptive field that is associated with excitation. Stimulation of this area causes an increase in the rate of nerve firing. (3)

Excitatory response The response of a nerve fiber in which the firing rate increases. (2)

Excitatory-center, inhibitory-surround receptive field A center-surround receptive field in which stimulation of the center area causes an excitatory response and stimulation of the surround causes an inhibitory response. (3)

Experience-dependent plasticity A process by which neurons adapt to the specific environment within which a person or animal lives. This is achieved when neurons change their response properties so they become tuned to respond best to stimuli that have been repeatedly experienced in the environment. *See also* **Neural plasticity; Selective rearing**. (3)

Expertise hypothesis The idea that human proficiency in perceiving certain things can be explained by changes in the brain caused by long exposure, practice, or training. (4)

Exploratory procedures (EPs) People's movements of their hands and fingers while they are identifying three-dimensional objects by touch. (14)

Extrastriate body area (EBA) An area of the temporal lobe that is activated by pictures of bodies and parts of bodies. (4)

Eye The eyeball and its contents, which include focusing elements, the retina, and supporting structures. (2)

Falling phase of the action potential In the axon, or nerve fiber, the increase in negativity from +40 mV back to −70 mV (the resting potential level) that occurs during the action potential. This increase in negativity is associated with the flow of positively charged potassium ions (K+) out of the axon. (2)

False alarm In a signal detection experiment, saying "Yes, I detect the stimulus" on a trial in which the stimulus is not presented (an incorrect response). (Appendix D)

Familiar size A depth cue in which judgment of distance is based on knowledge of the sizes of objects. Epstein's coin experiment illustrated the operation of the cue of familiar size by showing that the relative sizes of the coins influenced perception of the coins' distances. (10)

Farsightedness *See* **Hyperopia**. (2)

Feature detector A neuron that responds selectively to a specific feature of the stimulus such as orientation or direction of motion. (3)

Feature integration theory (FIT) A theory proposed by Anne Treisman to explain how an object is broken down into features and how these features are recombined to result in a perception of the object. (6)

Feature search A visual search task in which a person can find a target by searching for only one feature. An example would be looking for a horizontal green line among vertical green lines. (6)

Figure When an object is seen as separate from the background (the "ground"), it is called a figure. *See also* **Figure–ground segregation**. (5)

Figure–ground segregation The perceptual separation of an object from its background. (5)

First harmonic *See* **Fundamental frequency**. (11)

Fixation The brief pause of the eye that occurs between eye movements as a person scans a scene. (6)

Flavor The perception that occurs from the combination of taste and olfaction. (15)

Focus of expansion (FOE) The point in the flow pattern caused by observer movement in which there is no expansion. According to J. J. Gibson, the focus of expansion always remains centered on the observer's destination. (7)

Focused attention stage (of perceptual processing) The stage of processing in feature integration theory in which the features are combined. According to Treisman, this stage requires focused attention. (6)

Forced-choice method Method in which two choices are given, and the subject has to pick one. For example, a subject is presented with a weak odorant on one trial, and no odorant on another trial, and has to pick the trial on which the odorant was presented. (15)

Formant Horizontal band of energy in the speech spectrogram associated with vowels. (13)

Formant transition In the speech stimulus, the rapid shift in frequency that precedes a formant. (13)

Fovea A small area in the human retina that contains only cone receptors. The fovea is located on the line of sight, so that when a person looks at an object, the center of its image falls on the fovea. (2)

Frequency The number of times per second that pressure changes of a sound stimulus repeat. Frequency is measured in Hertz, where 1 Hertz is one cycle per second. (11)

Frequency spectrum A plot that indicates the amplitudes of the various harmonics that make up a complex tone. Each harmonic is indicated by a line that is positioned along the frequency axis, with the height of the line indicating the amplitude of the harmonic. (11)

Frequency tuning curve Curve relating frequency and the threshold intensity for activating an auditory neuron. (11)

Frontal eyes Eyes located in front of the head, so the views of the two eyes overlap. (10)

Frontal lobe Receiving signals from all of the senses, the frontal lobe plays an important role in perceptions that involve the coordination of information received through two or more senses. It also serves functions such as language, thought, memory, and motor functioning. (1)

Frontal operculum cortex An area in the frontal lobe of the cortex that receives signals from the taste system. (15)

Functional magnetic resonance imaging (fMRI) A brain imaging technique that indicates brain activity in awake, behaving organisms. The fMRI response occurs when the response to a magnetic field changes in response to changes in blood flow in the brain. (4)

Fundamental A pure tone with frequency equal to the fundamental frequency of a complex tone. *See also* **Fundamental frequency**. (11)

Fundamental frequency The first harmonic of a complex tone; usually the lowest frequency in the frequency spectrum of a complex tone. The tone's other components, called higher harmonics, have frequencies that are multiples of the fundamental frequency. (11)

Fusiform face area (FFA) An area in the human inferotemporal (IT) cortex that contains neurons that are specialized to respond to faces. (4)

Ganglion cell A neuron in the retina that receives inputs from bipolar and amacrine cells. The axons of the ganglion cells are the nerve fibers that travel out of the eye in the optic nerve. (2)

Gap fill In music, when after a large jump from one note to another, the next notes of the melody turn around, progressing in the opposite direction, to fill the gap. (12)

Gate control model Melzack and Wall's idea that perception of pain is controlled by a neural circuit that takes into account the relative amount of activity in nociceptors, mechanoreceptors, and central signals. This model has been used to explain how pain can be influenced by factors other than stimulation of receptors in the skin. (14)

Gestalt psychology An approach to psychology that developed as a reaction to structuralism. The Gestalt approach proposes principles of perceptual organization and figure–ground segregation and states that "the whole is different than the sum of its parts." (5)

Gist of a scene General description of a scene. People can identify most scenes after viewing them for only a fraction of a second, as when they flip rapidly from one TV channel to another. It takes longer to identify the details within the scene. (5)

Global image features Information that may enable observers to rapidly perceive the gist of a scene. Features associated with specific types of scenes include degree of naturalness, degree of openness, degree of roughness, degree of expansion, and color. (5)

Global optic flow Information for movement that occurs when all elements in a scene move. The perception of global optic flow indicates that it is the observer that is moving and not the scene. (8)

Glomeruli Small structures in the olfactory bulb that receive signals from similar olfactory receptor neurons. One function of each glomerulus is to collect information about a small group of odorants. (15)

Good continuation, principle of A Gestalt principle of perceptual organization that states that points that, when connected, result in straight or smoothly curving lines are seen as belonging together, and that lines tend to be seen in such a way as to follow the smoothest path. (5)

Good figure, principle of *See* **Pragnanz, principle of**. (5)

Gradient of flow In an optic flow pattern, a gradient is created by movement of an observer through the environment. The "gradient" refers to the fact that the optic flow is rapid in the foreground and becomes slower as distance from the observer increases. (7)

Grating acuity (cutaneous) The narrowest spacing of a grooved surface on the skin for which orientation can be accurately judged. *See also* **Two-point threshold**. (14)

Grating acuity (visual) The smallest width of lines for which the orientation of a black and white striped stimulus can be accurately judged. (1)

Grid cells Cells in the entorhinal cortex that fire when an animal is in a particular place in the environment, and which have multiple place fields arranged in a gridlike pattern. (7)

Ground In object perception, the background is called the ground. *See also* **Figure**. (5)

Grouping In perceptual organization, the process by which visual events are "put together" into units or objects. (5)

Habituation Paying less attention when the same stimulus is presented repeatedly. For example, infants look at a stimulus less and less on each successive trial. *See also* **Dishabituation**. (6)

Hair cells Neurons in the cochlea that contain small hairs, or cilia, that are displaced by vibration of the basilar membrane and fluids inside the inner ear. There are two kinds of hair cells: inner and outer. (11)

Hair cells, inner Auditory receptor cells in the inner ear that are primarily responsible for auditory transduction and the perception of pitch. (11)

Hair cells, outer Auditory receptor cells in the inner ear that amplify the response of inner hair cells by amplifying the vibration of the basilar membrane. (11)

Haptic perception The perception of three-dimensional objects by touch. (14)

Harmonics Pure-tone components of a complex tone that have frequencies that are multiples of the fundamental frequency. (11)

Head direction cells Neurons that fire based on which direction an animal is facing. *See also* **Grid cells; Place cells**. (7)

Hering's primary colors The colors red, yellow, green, and blue in the color circle. (9)

Hermann grid A display that results in the illusion of dark areas at the intersection of two white "corridors." This perception can be explained by lateral inhibition. (1)

Hertz (Hz) The unit for designating the frequency of a tone. One Hertz equals one cycle per second. (11)

Hidden hearing loss Hearing loss that occurs at high sound levels, even though the person's thresholds, as indicated by the audiogram, are normal. (11)

Higher harmonics Pure tones with frequencies that are whole-number (2, 3, 4, etc.) multiples of the fundamental frequency. *See also* **Fundamental; Fundamental frequency; Harmonics**. (11)

High-load task Task that involves more processing resources and that therefore uses more of a person's perceptual capacity. (6)

Hippocampus Subcortical structure in the brain that is associated with forming and storing memories. (4)

Hit In a signal detection experiment, saying "Yes, I detect a stimulus" on a trial in which the stimulus is present (a correct response). (Appendix D)

Homunculus Latin for "little man"; refers to the topographic map of the body in the somatosensory cortex. (14)

Horizontal cell A neuron that transmits signals laterally across the retina. Horizontal cells synapse with receptors and bipolar cells. (2)

Horopter An imaginary surface that passes through the point of fixation. Images caused by a visual stimulus on this surface fall on corresponding points on the two retinas. (10)

***How* pathway** *See* **Dorsal pathway**. (4)

HSV color solid A solid in which colors are arranged in an orderly way based on their hue, saturation, and value. (9)

Hue The experience of a chromatic color, such as red, green, yellow, or blue, or combinations of these colors. (9)

Hue cancellation Procedure in which a subject is shown a monochromatic reference light and is asked to remove, or "cancel," the one of the colors in the reference light by adding a second wavelength. This procedure was used by Hurvich and Jameson in their research on opponent-process theory. (9)

Hypercolumn In the striate cortex, unit proposed by Hubel and Wiesel that combines location, orientation, and ocular dominance columns that serve a specific area on the retina. (4)

Hyperopia A condition causing poor vision in which people can see objects that are far away but do not see near objects clearly. Also called farsightedness. (2)

Hyperpolarization When the inside of a neuron becomes more negative. Hyperpolarization is often associated with the action of inhibitory neurotransmitters. (2)

Illumination edge The border between two areas created by different light intensities in the two areas. (9)

Illusory conjunction Illusory combination of features that are perceived when stimuli containing a number of features are presented briefly and under conditions in which focused attention is difficult. For example, presenting a red square and a blue triangle could potentially create the perception of a red triangle. (6)

Illusory contour Contour that is perceived even though it is not present in the physical stimulus. (5)

Illusory motion Perception of motion when there actually is none. *See also* **Apparent motion**. (8)

Image displacement signal (IDS) In corollary discharge theory, the signal that occurs when an image moves across the visual receptors. (8)

Implied motion When a still picture depicts an action that involves motion, so that an observer could potentially extend the action depicted in the picture in his or her mind based on what will most likely happen next. (8)

Inattentional blindness A situation in which a stimulus that is not attended is not perceived, even though the person is looking directly at it. (6)

Incus The second of the three ossicles of the middle ear. It transmits vibrations from the malleus to the stapes. (11)

Indirect sound Sound that reaches a listener's ears after being reflected from a surface such as a room's walls. (12)

Induced motion The illusory movement of one object that is caused by the movement of another object that is nearby. (8)

Inferior colliculus A nucleus in the hearing system along the pathway from the cochlea to the auditory cortex. The inferior colliculus receives inputs from the superior olivary nucleus. (11)

Inferotemporal (IT) cortex An area of the brain outside Area V1 (the striate cortex), involved in object perception and facial recognition. (3)

Inflammatory pain Pain caused by damage to tissues, inflammation of joints, or tumor cells. This damage releases chemicals that create an "inflammatory soup" that activates nociceptors. (14)

Inhibitory area Area of a receptive field that is associated with inhibition. Stimulation of this area causes a decrease in the rate of nerve firing. (3)

Inhibitory response Occurs when a neuron's firing rate decreases due to inhibition from another neuron. (2)

Inhibitory-center, excitatory-surround receptive field A center-surround receptive field in which stimulation of the center

causes an inhibitory response and stimulation of the surround causes an excitatory response. (3)

Inner ear The innermost division of the ear, containing the cochlea and the receptors for hearing. (11)

Inner hair cells *See* **Hair cells, inner**. (11)

Insula An area in the frontal lobe of the cortex that receives signals from the taste system and is also involved in the affective component of the perception of pain. (15)

Interaural level difference (ILD) The difference in the sound pressure (or *level*) between the left and right ears. This difference creates an acoustic shadow for the far ear. The ILD provides a cue for sound localization for high-frequency sounds. (12)

Interaural time difference (ITD) When a sound is positioned closer to one ear than to the other, the sound reaches the close ear slightly before reaching the far ear, so there is a difference in the time of arrival at the two ears. The ITD provides a cue for sound localization. (12)

Invariant information Environmental properties that do not change as the observer moves relative to an object or scene. For example, the spacing, or texture, of the elements in a homogenous texture gradient does not change as the observer moves on the gradient. The texture of the gradient therefore supplies invariant information for depth perception. (7)

Inverse projection problem The idea that a particular image on the retina could have been caused by an infinite number of different objects. This means that the retinal image does not unambiguously specify a stimulus. (5)

Ions Charged molecules. Sodium (Na^+), potassium (K^+), and chlorine (Cl^-) are the main ions found within nerve fibers and in the liquid that surrounds nerve fibers. (2)

Ishihara plate A display of colored dots used to test for the presence of color deficiency. The dots are colored so that people with normal (trichromatic) color vision can perceive numbers in the plate, but people with color deficiency cannot perceive these numbers or perceive different numbers than someone with trichromatic vision. (9)

Isolated congenital anosmia (ICA) A condition in which a person is born without a sense of smell. (15)

Isomerization Change in shape of the *retinal* part of the visual pigment molecule that occurs when the molecule absorbs a quantum of light. Isomerization triggers the enzyme cascade that results in transduction from light energy to electrical energy in the retinal receptors. (2)

ITD detector Interaural time difference detector. Neurons in the Jeffress neural coincidence model that fire when signals reach them from the left and right ears. Each ITD detector is tuned to respond to a specific time delay between the two signals, and so provides information about possible locations of a sound source. (12)

ITD tuning curve A plot of the neuron's firing rate against the ITD (interaural time difference). (12)

Jeffress model The neural mechanism of auditory localization that proposes that neurons are wired to each receive signals from the two ears, so that different neurons fire to different interaural time differences (ITD). (12)

Kinesthesis The sense that enables us to feel the motions and positions of the limbs and body. (14)

Knowledge Any information that the perceiver brings to a situation. *See also* **Top-down processing**. (1)

Lack of invariance In speech perception, refers to the fact that there is no simple relationship between a particular phoneme and the acoustic signal. In other words, the acoustic signal for a particular phoneme is variable. (13)

Landmark Object on a route that serves as a cue to indicate where to turn; a source of information for wayfinding. (7)

Landmark discrimination problem The behavioral task used in Ungerleider and Mishkin's experiment in which they provided evidence for the dorsal, or *where*, visual processing stream. Monkeys were required to respond to a previously indicated location. (4)

Lateral eyes Eyes located on opposite sides of an animal's head, as in the pigeon and the rabbit, so the views of the two eyes do not overlap or overlap only slightly. (10)

Lateral geniculate nucleus (LGN) The nucleus in the thalamus that receives inputs from the optic nerve and, in turn, communicates with the cortical receiving area for vision. (3)

Lateral inhibition Inhibition that is transmitted laterally across a nerve circuit. In the retina, lateral inhibition is transmitted by the horizontal and amacrine cells. (3)

Leisure noise Noise associated with leisure activities such as listening to music, hunting, and woodworking. Exposure to high levels of leisure noise for extended periods can cause hearing loss. (11)

Lens The transparent focusing element of the eye through which light passes after passing through the cornea and the aqueous humor. The lens's change in shape to focus at different distances is called accommodation. (2)

Level Short for sound pressure level or sound level. Indicates the decibels or sound pressure of a sound stimulus. (11)

Light-adapted sensitivity The sensitivity of the eye when in the light-adapted state. Usually taken as the starting point for the dark adaptation curve because it is the sensitivity of the eye just before the lights are turned off. (2)

Light-from-above assumption The assumption that light usually comes from above, which influences our perception of form in some situations. (5)

Lightness The perception of shades ranging from white to gray to black. (9)

Lightness constancy The constancy of our perception of an object's lightness under different intensities of illumination. (9)

Likelihood (Bayes) In Bayesian inference, the extent to which the available evidence is consistent with a particular outcome. (5)

Likelihood principle (Helmholtz) The idea proposed by Helmholtz that we perceive the object that is *most likely* to have caused the pattern of stimuli we have received. (5)

Limits, method of A psychophysical method for measuring threshold in which the experimenter presents sequences of stimuli in ascending and descending order. (1)

Load theory of attention Lavie's proposal that the amount of perceptual capacity that remains as a person is carrying out a task determines how well the person can avoid being distracted by task-irrelevant stimuli. If a person's perceptual load is close to perceptual capacity, the person is less likely to be distracted by task-irrelevant stimuli. *See also* **High-load tasks; Low-load tasks; Perceptual capacity; Perceptual load**. (6)

Local disturbance in the optic array Occurs when one object moves relative to the environment, so that the stationary background is covered and uncovered by the moving object. This local disturbance indicates that the object is moving relative to the environment. (8)

Local field potential (LFP) An electrical response recorded with disc electrodes placed on the surface of the brain, which measures electrical signals from thousands of neurons near the electrode. (6)

Location column A column in the visual cortex that contains neurons with the same receptive field locations on the retina. (4)

Location cues In hearing, characteristics of the sound reaching the listener that provide information regarding the location of a sound source. (12)

Loudness The quality of sound that ranges from soft to loud. For a tone of a particular frequency, loudness usually increases with increasing decibels. (11)

Low-load task A task that uses only a small amount of the person's perceptual capacity. (6)

Macrosmatic Having a keen sense of smell; usually important to an animal's survival. (15)

Macular degeneration A clinical condition that causes degeneration of the macula, an area of the retina that includes the fovea and a small surrounding area. (2)

Magnetic resonance imaging (MRI) Brain scanning technique that makes it possible to create images of structures within the brain. (4)

Magnitude estimation A psychophysical method in which the subject assigns numbers to a stimulus that are proportional to the subjective magnitude of the stimulus. (1)

Malleus The first of the ossicles of the middle ear. Receives vibrations from the tympanic membrane and transmits these vibrations to the incus. (11)

Manner of articulation How a speech sound is produced by interaction of the articulators—the mouth, tongue, and lips—during production of the sound. (13)

McGurk effect *See* **Audiovisual speech perception**. (13)

Mechanoreceptor Receptor that responds to mechanical stimulation of the skin, such as pressure, stretching, or vibration. (14)

Medial geniculate nucleus An auditory nucleus in the thalamus that is part of the pathway from the cochlea to the auditory cortex. The medial geniculate nucleus receives inputs from the inferior colliculus and transmits signals to the auditory cortex. (11)

Medial lemniscal pathway A pathway in the spinal cord that transmits signals from the skin toward the thalamus. (14)

Meissner corpuscle (RA1) A receptor in the skin, associated with RA1 mechanoreceptors. It has been proposed that the Meissner corpuscle is important for perceiving tactile slip and for controlling the force needed to grip objects. (14)

Melodic channeling *See* **Scale illusion**. (12)

Melody The experience of a sequence of pitches as belonging together. Usually refers to the way notes follow one another in a song or musical composition. (12)

Melody schema A representation of a familiar melody that is stored in a person's memory. Existence of a melody schema makes it more likely that the tones associated with a melody will be perceptually grouped. (12)

Memory color The idea that an object's characteristic color influences our perception of that object's color. (9)

Merkel receptor (SA1) A disk-shaped receptor in the skin associated with slowly adapting fibers and the perception of fine details. (14)

Metamerism The situation in which two physically different stimuli are perceptually identical. In vision, this refers to two lights with different wavelength distributions that are perceived as having the same color. (9)

Metamers Two lights that have different wavelength distributions but are perceptually identical. (9)

Meter In music, organization of beats into bars or measures, with the first beat in each bar often being accented. There are two basic kinds of meter in Western music: duple meter, in which accents are in multiples of two, such as 12 12 12 or 1234 1234 1234, like a march; and triple meter, in which accents are in groups of three, such as 123 123 123, as in a waltz. (12)

Method of adjustment *See* **Adjustment, method of**. (Appendix A)

Method of constant stimuli *See* **Constant stimuli, method of**. (Appendix A)

Method of limits *See* **Limits, method of**. (1)

Microsmatic Having a weak sense of smell. This usually occurs in animals, such as humans, in which the sense of smell is not crucial for survival. (15)

Microstimulation A procedure in which a small electrode is inserted into the cortex and an electrical current passed through the electrode activates neurons near the tip of the electrode. This procedure has been used to determine how activating specific groups of neurons affects perception. (8)

Middle ear The small air-filled space between the auditory canal and the cochlea that contains the ossicles. (11)

Middle-ear muscles Muscles attached to the ossicles in the middle ear. The smallest skeletal muscles in the body, they contract in response to very intense sounds and dampen the vibration of the ossicles. (11)

Mind–body problem One of the most famous problems in science: How do physical processes such as nerve impulses or sodium and potassium molecules flowing across membranes (the body part of the problem) become transformed into the richness of perceptual experience (the mind part of the problem)? (4)

Mirror neuron Neuron in the premotor area of the monkey's cortex that responds when the monkey grasps an object and also when the monkey observes someone else (another monkey or the experimenter) grasping the object. There is also evidence for mirror-neuron-like activity in the human brain. *See also* **Audiovisual mirror neuron**. (7)

Mirror neuron system Network of neurons hypothesized to play a role in creating mirror neurons. (7)

Misapplied size constancy scaling A principle, proposed by Richard Gregory, that when mechanisms that help maintain size constancy in the three-dimensional world are applied to two-dimensional pictures, an illusion of size sometimes results. (10)

Miss In a signal detection experiment, saying "No, I don't detect a stimulus" on a trial in which the stimulus is present (an incorrect response). (Appendix D)

Modularity The idea that specific areas of the cortex are specialized to respond to specific types of stimuli. (4)

Module A structure that processes information about a specific behavior or perceptual quality. Often identified as a structure that contains a large proportion of neurons that respond selectively to a particular quality, such as the fusiform face area, which contains many neurons that respond selectively to faces. (4)

Monaural cue Sound localization cue that involves one ear. (12)

Monochromat A person who is completely color-blind and therefore sees everything as black, white, or shades of gray. A monochromat can match any wavelength in the spectrum by adjusting the intensity of any other wavelength. Monochromats generally have only one type of functioning receptors, usually rods. (9)

Monochromatic light Light that contains only a single wavelength. (2)

Monochromatism Rare form of color blindness in which the absence of cone receptors results in perception only of shades of lightness (white, gray, and black), with no chromatic color present. (9)

Monocular cue Depth cue—such as overlap, relative size, relative height, familiar size, linear perspective, movement parallax, and accommodation—that can work when we use only one eye. (10)

Moon illusion An illusion in which the moon appears to be larger when it is on or near the horizon than when it is high in the sky. (10)

Motion aftereffect An illusion that occurs after a person views a moving stimulus and then sees movement in the opposite direction when viewing a stationary stimulus immediately afterward. *See also* **Waterfall illusion**. (8)

Motion parallax A depth cue. As an observer moves, nearby objects appear to move rapidly across the visual field whereas far objects appear to move more slowly. (10)

Motor signal (MS) In corollary discharge theory, the signal that is sent to the eye muscles when the observer moves or tries to move his or her eyes. (8)

Motor theory of speech perception A theory that proposes a close link between how speech is perceived and how it is produced. The idea behind this theory is that when we *hear* a particular speech sound, this activates the motor mechanisms that are responsible for *producing* that sound, and it is the activation of these motor mechanisms that enable us to perceive the sound. (13)

Müller-Lyer illusion An illusion in which two lines of equal length appear to be of different lengths because of the addition of "fins" to the ends of the lines. (10)

Multimodal The involvement of a number of different senses in determining perception. For example, speech perception can be influenced by information from a number of different senses, including audition, vision, and touch. (13)

Multimodal nature of pain The fact that the experience of pain has both sensory and emotional components. (14)

Multisensory interaction Use of a combination of senses. An example for vision and hearing is seeing a person's lips move while listening to the person speak. (12)

Music Sound organized in a way that, in traditional Western music, creates a melody. (12)

Musical syntax Rules that specify how notes and chords are combined in music. (12)

Myopia An inability to see distant objects clearly. Also called nearsightedness. (2)

Naloxone A substance that inhibits the activity of opiates. It is hypothesized that naloxone also inhibits the activity of endorphins and therefore can have an effect on pain perception. (14)

Nasal pharynx A passageway that connects the mouth cavity and the nasal cavity. (15)

Nearsightedness *See* **Myopia**. (2)

Nerve fiber In most sensory neurons, the long part of the neuron that transmits electrical impulses from one point to another. Also called the axon. (2)

Neural circuit A number of neurons that are connected by synapses. (2)

Neural convergence Synapsing of a number of neurons onto one neuron. (2)

Neural mind reading Using a neural response, usually brain activation measured by fMRI, to determine what a person is perceiving or thinking. (5)

Neural plasticity The capacity of the nervous system to change in response to experience. Examples are how early visual experience can change the orientation selectivity of neurons in the visual cortex and how tactile experience can change the sizes of areas in the cortex that represent different parts of the body. *See also* **Experience-dependent plasticity**; **Selective rearing**. (3)

Neural processing Operations that transform electrical signals within a network of neurons or that transform the response of individual neurons. (1)

Neurogenesis The cycle of birth, development, and death of a neuron. This process occurs for the receptors for olfaction and taste. (15)

Neuron The structure that transmits electrical signals in the body. Key components of neurons are the cell body, dendrites, and the axon or nerve fiber. (2)

Neuropathic pain Pain caused by lesions or other damage to the nervous system. (14)

Neuropsychology The study of the behavioral effects of brain damage in humans. (4)

Neurotransmitter A chemical stored in synaptic vesicles that is released in response to a nerve impulse and has an excitatory or inhibitory effect on another neuron. (2)

Nocebo effect A negative placebo effect, characterized by a negative response to negative expectations. (14)

Nociceptive pain This type of pain, which serves as a warning of impending damage to the skin, is caused by activation of receptors in the skin called nociceptors. (14)

Nociceptor A fiber that responds to stimuli that are damaging to the skin. (14)

Noise A sound stimulus that contains many random frequencies. (11)

Noise In signal detector theory, noise is all of the stimuli in the environment other than the signal. (Appendix D)

Noise-induced hearing loss A form of sensorineural hearing loss that occurs when loud noises cause degeneration of the hair cells. (11)

Noise-vocoded speech A procedure in which the speech signal is divided into different frequency bands and then noise is added to each band. (13)

Noncorresponding points Two points, one on each retina, that would not overlap if the retinas were slid onto each other. Also called disparate points. (10)

Nonspectral colors Colors that do not appear in the spectrum because they are mixtures of other colors. An example is magenta, which is a mixture of red and blue. (9)

Nucleus of the solitary tract The nucleus in the brain stem that receives signals from the tongue, the mouth, and the larynx transmitted by the chorda tympani, glossopharyngeal, and vagus nerves. (15)

Object discrimination problem The behavioral task used in Ungerleider and Mishkin's experiment in which they provided evidence for the ventral, or *what*, visual processing stream. Monkeys were required to respond to an object with a particular shape. (4)

Oblique effect Enhanced sensitivity to vertically and horizontally oriented visual stimuli compared to obliquely oriented (slanted) stimuli. This effect has been demonstrated by measuring both perception and neural responding. (1)

Occipital lobe A lobe at the back of the cortex that is the site of the cortical receiving area for vision. (1)

Occlusion Depth cue in which one object hides or partially hides another object from view, causing the hidden object to be perceived as being farther away. A monocular depth cue. (10)

Octave Tones that have frequencies that are binary multiples of each other (2, 4, etc.). For example, an 800-Hz tone is one octave above a 400-Hz tone. (11)

Oculomotor cue Depth cue that depends on our ability to sense the position of our eyes and the tension in our eye muscles. Accommodation and convergence are oculomotor cues. (10)

Odor discrimination Distinguishing the difference between two or more odors. (15)

Odor map. *See* **Chemotopic map.** (15)

Odor object The source of an odor, such as coffee, bacon, a rose, or car exhaust. (15)

Odotoptic map. *See* **Chemotopic map.** (15)

Olfaction The sense of smell. Usually results from stimulation of receptors in the olfactory mucosa. (15)

Olfactory bulb The structure that receives signals directly from the olfactory receptors. The olfactory bulb contains glomeruli, which receive these signals from the receptors. (15)

Olfactory mucosa The region inside the nose that contains the receptors for the sense of smell. (15)

Olfactory receptor A protein string that responds to odor stimuli. (15)

Olfactory receptor neurons (ORNs) Sensory neurons located in the olfactory mucosa that contain the olfactory receptors. (15)

Ommatidium A structure in the eye of the *Limulus* that contains a small lens, located directly over a visual receptor. The *Limulus* eye is made up of hundreds of these ommatidia. The *Limulus* eye has been used for research on lateral inhibition because its receptors are large enough so that stimulation can be applied to individual receptors. (3)

Opioid A chemical such as opium, heroin, and other molecules with related structures that reduce pain and induce feelings of euphoria. (14)

Opponent neuron A neuron that has an excitatory response to wavelengths in one part of the spectrum and an inhibitory response to wavelengths in the other part of the spectrum. (9)

Opponent-process theory of color vision A theory originally proposed by Hering, which claimed that our perception of color is determined by the activity of two opponent mechanisms: a blue-yellow mechanism and a red–green mechanism. The responses to the two colors in each mechanism oppose each other, one being an excitatory response and the other an inhibitory response. In addition, this theory also includes a black–white mechanism, which is concerned with the perception of brightness. *See also* **Opponent neuron.** (9)

Optic array The structured pattern of light created by the presence of objects, surfaces, and textures in the environment. (8)

Optic flow The flow of stimuli in the environment that occurs when an observer moves relative to the environment. Forward movement causes an expanding optic flow, whereas backward movement causes a contracting optic flow. Some researchers use the term *optic flow field* to refer to this flow. (7)

Optic nerve Bundle of nerve fibers that carry impulses from the retina to the lateral geniculate nucleus and other structures. Each optic nerve contains about 1 million ganglion cell fibers. (2)

Optical imaging A technique that has been used to measure the activity of large areas of the olfactory bulb by measuring the intensity of red light reflected from the bulb. (15)

Oral capture The condition in which sensations from both olfaction and taste are perceived as being located in the mouth. (15)

Orbitofrontal cortex An area in the frontal lobe, near the eyes, that receives signals originating in the olfactory receptors. Also known as the secondary olfactory cortex. (15)

Organ of Corti The major structure of the cochlear partition, containing the basilar membrane, the tectorial membrane, and the receptors for hearing. (11)

Orientation column A column in the visual cortex that contains neurons with the same orientation preference. (4)

Orientation tuning curve A function relating the firing rate of a neuron to the orientation of the stimulus. (3)

Ossicles Three small bones in the middle ear that transmit vibrations from the outer to the inner ear. (11)

Outer ear The pinna and the auditory canal. (11)

Outer hair cells *See* **Hair cells, outer**. (11)

Outer segment Part of the rod and cone visual receptors that contains the light-sensitive visual pigment molecules. (2)

Output unit A component of the Reichardt detector that compares signals received from two or more neurons. According to Reichardt's model, activity in the output unit is necessary for motion perception. (8)

Oval window A small, membrane-covered hole in the cochlea that receives vibrations from the stapes. (11)

Overt attention Attention that involves looking directly at the attended object. (6)

Pacinian corpuscle (RA2 or PC) A receptor with a distinctive elliptical shape associated with RA2 mechanoreceptors. It transmits pressure to the nerve fiber inside it only at the beginning or end of a pressure stimulus and is responsible for our perception of vibration and fine textures when moving the fingers over a surface. (14)

Papillae Ridges and valleys on the tongue, some of which contain taste buds. There are four types of papillae: filiform, fungiform, foliate, and circumvallate. (15)

Parabelt area Auditory area in the temporal lobe that receives signals from the belt area. (11)

Parahippocampal place area (PPA) An area in the temporal lobe that is activated by indoor and outdoor scenes. (4)

Parietal lobe A lobe at the top of the cortex that is the site of the cortical receiving area for touch and is the termination point of the dorsal (*where* or *how*) stream for visual processing. (1)

Parietal reach region (PRR) A network of areas in the parietal cortex that contains neurons that are involved in reaching behavior. (7)

Partial color constancy A type of color constancy that occurs when changing an object's illumination causes a change in perception of the object's hue, but less change than would be expected based on the change in the wavelengths of light reaching the eye. Note that in complete color constancy, changing an object's illumination causes no change in the object's hue. (9)

Passive touch A situation in which a person passively receives tactile stimulation. *See also* **Active touch**. (14)

Payoffs A system of rewards and punishments used to influence a participant's motivation in a signal detection experiment. (D)

Perceived magnitude A perceptual measure of stimuli, such as light or sound, that indicates the magnitude of experience. (1)

Perception Conscious sensory experience. (1)

Perceptual capacity The resources a person has for carrying out perceptual tasks. (6)

Perceptual completion The perception of an object as extending behind occluding objects. (6)

Perceptual load The amount of a person's perceptual capacity needed to carry out a particular perceptual task. (6)

Perceptual organization The process by which small elements become perceptually grouped into larger objects. (5)

Perceptual process A sequence of steps leading from the environment to perception of a stimulus, recognition of the stimulus, and action with regard to the stimulus. (1)

Perceptual segregation Perceptual organization in which one object is seen as separate from other objects. (5)

Periodic sound A sound stimulus in which the pattern of pressure changes repeats. (11)

Periodic tone A tone in which the waveform repeats. (11)

Peripheral retina The area of retina outside the fovea. (2)

Permeability A property of a membrane that refers to the ability of molecules to pass through it. If the permeability to a molecule is high, the molecule can easily pass through the membrane. (2)

Persistence of vision A phenomenon in which perception of any stimulus persists for about 250 ms after the stimulus is physically terminated. (5)

Perspective convergence The perception that parallel lines in the distance converge as distance increases. (10)

Phantom limb A person's continued perception of a limb, such as an arm or a leg, even though the limb has been amputated. (14)

Phase locking Firing of auditory neurons in synchrony with the phase of an auditory stimulus. (11)

Phenomenological method Method of determining the relationship between stimuli and perception in which the observer describes what he or she perceives. (1)

Pheromone Chemical signal released by an individual that affects the physiology and behavior of other individuals. (15)

Phoneme The shortest segment of speech that, if changed, changes the meaning of a word. (13)

Phonemic restoration effect An effect that occurs in speech perception when listeners perceive a phoneme in a word even though the acoustic signal of that phoneme is obscured by another sound, such as white noise or a cough. (13)

Phonetic boundary The voice onset time when perception changes from one speech category to another in a categorical perception experiment. (13)

Phonetic feature Cues associated with how a phoneme is produced by the articulators. (13)

Phrase In music, short segments of melodies, similar to phrases in language. (12)

Physical regularities Regularly occurring physical properties of the environment. For example, there are more vertical and horizontal orientations in the environment than oblique (angled) orientations. (5)

Physical-social pain overlap hypothesis Proposal that pain resulting from negative social experiences is processed by some of the same neural circuitry that processes physical pain. (14)

Physiology–perception relationship Relationship between physiological responses and behavioral responses. (1)

Pictorial cue Monocular depth cue, such as overlap, relative height, and relative size, that can be depicted in pictures. (10)

Pinna The part of the ear that is visible on the outside of the head. (11)

Piriform cortex (PC) An area under the temporal lobe that receives signals from glomeruli in the olfactory bulb. Also called the primary olfactory area. (15)

Pitch The quality of sound, ranging from low to high, that is most closely associated with the frequency of a tone. (11)

Pitch neuron A neuron that responds to stimuli associated with a specific pitch. These neurons fire to the pitch of a complex tone even if the first harmonic or other harmonics of the tone are not present. (11)

Place cells Neurons that fire only when an animal is in a certain place in the environment. (7)

Place field Area of the environment within which a place cell fires. (7)

Place of articulation In speech production, the locations of articulation. *See* **Manner of articulation**. (13)

Place theory of hearing The proposal that the frequency of a sound is indicated by the place along the organ of Corti at which nerve firing is highest. Modern place theory is based on Békésy's traveling wave theory of hearing. (11)

Placebo A substance that a person believes will relieve symptoms such as pain but that contains no chemicals that actually act on these symptoms. (14)

Placebo effect A relief from symptoms resulting from a substance that has no pharmacological effect. *See also* **Placebo**. (14)

Point-light walker A biological motion stimulus created by placing lights at a number of places on a person's body and having an observer view the moving-light stimulus that results as the person moves in the dark. (8)

Ponzo illusion An illusion of size in which two objects of equal size that are positioned between two converging lines appear to be different in size. Also called the railroad track illusion. (10)

Population coding Representation of a particular object or quality by the pattern of firing of a large number of neurons. (3)

Posterior belt area Posterior (toward the back of the brain) area of the belt area, which is an area in the temporal lobe involved in auditory processing. (12)

Power function A mathematical function of the form $P = KS^n$, where P is perceived magnitude, K is a constant, S is the stimulus intensity, and n is an exponent. (Appendix C)

Pragnanz, principle of A Gestalt principle of perceptual organization that states that every stimulus pattern is seen in such a way that the resulting structure is as simple as possible. Also called the *principle of good figure* or the *principle of simplicity*. (5)

Preattentive stage (of perceptual processing) An automatic and rapid stage of processing, proposed by Treisman's feature integration theory, during which a stimulus is decomposed into individual features. (6)

Precedence effect When two identical or very similar sounds reach a listener's ears separated by a time interval of less than about 50 to 100 ms, the listener hears the first sound that reaches his or her ears. (12)

Precueing A procedure in which a cue stimulus is presented to direct an observer's attention to a specific location where a test stimulus is likely to be presented. This procedure was used by Posner to show that attention enhances the processing of a stimulus presented at the cued location. (6)

Preferential looking technique A technique used to measure perception in infants. Two stimuli are presented, and the infant's looking behavior is monitored for the amount of time the infant spends viewing each stimulus. (2)

Presbycusis A form of sensorineural hearing loss that occurs as a function of age and is usually associated with a decrease in the ability to hear high frequencies. Since this loss also appears to be related to exposure to environmental sounds, it is also called *sociocusis*. (11)

Presbyopia The inability of the eye to accommodate due to a hardening of the lens and a weakening of the ciliary muscles. It occurs as people get older. (2)

Primary auditory cortex (A1) An area of the temporal lobe that receives signals via nerve fibers from the medial geniculate nucleus in the thalamus. (12)

Primary olfactory area A small area under the temporal lobe that receives signals from glomeruli in the olfactory bulb. Also called the piriform cortex. (15)

Primary receiving area Area of the cerebral cortex that first receives most of the signals initiated by a sense's receptors. For example, the occipital cortex is the site of the primary receiving area for vision, and the temporal lobe is the site of the primary receiving area for hearing. (1)

Principle of common fate *See* **Common fate, principle of**. (5)

Principle of common region *See* **Common region, principle of**. (5)

Principle of good continuation *See* **Good continuation, principle of**. (5)

Principle of good figure *See* **Pragnanz, principle of**. (5)

Principle of pragnanz *See* **Pragnanz, principle of**. (5)

Principle of proximity (nearness) *See* **Proximity, principle of**. (5)

Principle of representation *See* **Representation, principle of**. (1)

Principle of similarity *See* **Similarity, principle of**. (5)

Principle of simplicity *See* **Pragnanz, principle of**. (5)

Principle of transformation *See* **Transformation, principle of**. (1)

Principle of uniform connectedness *See* **Uniform connectedness, principle of**. (5)

Principle of univariance *See* **Univariance, principle of**. (9)

Principles of perceptual organization Principles that describe how elements in a scene become grouped together. Many of these principles were originally proposed by the Gestalt psychologists, but new principles have also been proposed by recent researchers. (5)

Prior probability (or prior) In Bayesian inference, a person's initial estimate of the probability of an outcome. *See also* **Bayesian inference**. (5)

Propagated response A response, such as a nerve impulse, that travels all the way down the nerve fiber without decreasing in amplitude. (2)

Proprioception The sensing of the position of the limbs. (14)

Prosopagnosia A form of visual agnosia in which the person can't recognize faces. (4)

Proust effect The elicitation of memories through taste and olfaction. Named for Marcel Proust, who described how the taste and smell of a tea-soaked madeleine cake unlocked childhood memories. (15)

Proximal stimulus The stimulus on the receptors. In vision, this would be the image on the retina. (1)

Proximity, principle of A Gestalt principle of perceptual organization that states that things that are near to each other appear to be grouped together. Also called the principle of nearness. (5)

Psychophysics Traditionally, the term *psychophysics* refers to quantitative methods for measuring the relationship between properties of the stimulus and the subject's experience. In this book, all methods that are used to determine the relationship between stimuli and perception will be broadly referred to as pychophysical methods. (1)

Pupil The opening through which light reflected from objects in the environment enters the eye. (2)

Pure tone A tone with pressure changes that can be described by a single sine wave. (11)

Purkinje shift The shift from cone spectral sensitivity to rod spectral sensitivity that takes place during dark adaptation. *See also* **Spectral sensitivity**. (2)

RA1 fiber Fiber in the skin associated with Meissner corpuscles that adapts rapidly to stimuli and fires only briefly when a tactile stimulus is presented. (14)

RA2 fiber Fiber in the skin associated with Pacinian corpuscle receptors that is located deeper in the skin than RA1 fibers. (14)

Random-dot stereogram A pair of stereoscopic images made up of random dots. When one section of this pattern is shifted slightly in one direction, the resulting disparity causes the shifted section to appear above or below the rest of the pattern when the patterns are viewed in a stereoscope. (10)

Rapidly adapting (RA) fiber Fiber in the cutaneous system that adapts rapidly to a stimulus and so responds briefly to tactile stimulation. (14)

Ratio principle A principle stating that two areas that reflect different amounts of light will have the same perceived lightness if the ratios of their intensities to the intensities of their surroundings are the same. (9)

Rat–man demonstration The demonstration in which presentation of a "ratlike" or "manlike" picture influences an observer's perception of a second picture, which can be interpreted either as a rat or as a man. This demonstration illustrates an effect of top-down processing on perception. (1)

Reaction time The time between presentation of a stimulus and an observer's or listener's response to the stimulus. Reaction time is often used in experiments as a measure of speed of processing. (1)

Real motion The physical movement of a stimulus. Contrasts with *apparent motion*. (8)

Real-motion neuron Neuron in the monkey's cortex that responds when movement of an image across the retina is caused by movement of a stimulus, but does not respond when movement across the retina is caused by movement of the eyes. (8)

Receiver operating characteristic (ROC) curve A graph in which the results of a signal detection experiment are plotted as the proportion of hits versus the proportion of false alarms for a number of different response criteria. (Appendix D)

Receptive field A neuron's receptive field is the area on the receptor surface (the retina for vision; the skin for touch) that, when stimulated, affects the firing of that neuron. (3)

Receptor site Small area on the postsynaptic neuron that is sensitive to specific neurotransmitters. (2)

Recognition The ability to place an object in a category that gives it meaning—for example, recognizing a particular red object as a tomato. (1)

Recognition profile The pattern of olfactory activation for an odorant, indicating which ORNs (olfactory receptor neurons) are activated by the odorant. (15)

Reflectance The percentage of light reflected from a surface. (9)

Reflectance curve A plot showing the percentage of light reflected from an object versus wavelength. (9)

Reflectance edge An edge between two areas where the reflectance of two surfaces changes. (9)

Refractive myopia Myopia (nearsightedness) in which the cornea and/or the lens bends the light too much. *See also* **Axial myopia**. (2)

Refractory period The time period of about 1/1,000th of a second that a nerve fiber needs to recover from conducting a nerve impulse. No new nerve impulses can be generated in the fiber until the refractory period is over. (2)

Regularities in the environment Characteristics of the environment that occur regularly and in many different situations. (5)

Reichardt detector A neural circuit proposed by Werner Reichardt, in which signals caused by movement of a stimulus across the receptors are processed by a delay unit and an output unit so that signals are generated by movement in one direction but not in the opposite direction. (8)

Relative disparity The difference between two objects' absolute disparities. (10)

Relative height A monocular depth cue. Objects that have bases below the horizon appear to be farther away when they are higher in the field of view. Objects that have bases above the horizon appear to be farther away when they are lower in the field of view. (10)

Relative size A cue for depth perception. When two objects are of equal size, the one that is farther away will take up less of the field of view. (10)

Representation, principle of A principle of perception that everything a person perceives is based not on direct contact with stimuli but on representations of stimuli on the receptors and in the person's nervous system. (1)

Representational momentum Occurs when motion depicted in a still picture continues in an observer's mind. (8)

Resolved harmonics Harmonics in a complex tone that create separated peaks in basilar membrane vibration, and so can be distinguished from one another. Usually lower harmonics of a complex tone. (11)

Resonance A mechanism that enhances the intensity of certain frequencies because of the reflection of sound waves in a closed tube. Resonance in the auditory canal enhances frequencies between about 2,000 and 5,000 Hz. (11)

Resonant frequency The frequency that is most strongly enhanced by resonance. The resonance frequency of a closed tube is determined by the length of the tube. (11)

Response compression The result when doubling the physical intensity of a stimulus less than doubles the subjective magnitude of the stimulus. (Appendix C)

Response criterion In a signal detection experiment, the subjective magnitude of a stimulus above which the participant will indicate that the stimulus is present. (D)

Response expansion The result when doubling the physical intensity of a stimulus more than doubles the subjective magnitude of the stimulus. (Appendix C)

Resting potential The difference in charge between the inside and the outside of the nerve fiber when the fiber is not conducting electrical signals. Most nerve fibers have resting potentials of about –70 mV, which means the inside of the fiber is negative relative to the outside. (2)

Retina A complex network of cells that covers the inside back of the eye. These cells include the receptors, which generate an electrical signal in response to light, as well as the horizontal, bipolar, amacrine, and ganglion cells. (2)

Retinitis pigmentosa A retinal disease that causes a gradual loss of vision, beginning in the peripheral retina. (2)

Retinotopic map A map on a structure in the visual system, such as the lateral geniculate nucleus or the cortex, that indicates locations on the structure that correspond to locations on the retina. In retinotopic maps, locations adjacent to each other on the retina are usually represented by locations that are adjacent to each other on the structure. (4)

Retronasal route The opening from the oral cavity, through the nasal pharynx, into the nasal cavity. This route is the basis for the way smell combines with taste to create flavor. (15)

Return to the tonic Occurs when a song begins with the tonic and ends with the tonic, where the tonic is the pitch associated with a composition's key. (12)

Reverberation time The time it takes for a sound produced in an enclosed space to decrease to 1/1,000th of its original pressure. (12)

Reversible figure–ground A figure–ground pattern that perceptually reverses as it is viewed, so that the figure becomes the ground and the ground becomes the figure. The best-known reversible figure–ground pattern is Rubin's vase–face pattern. (5)

Rhythm In music, the series of changes across time (a mixture of shorter and longer notes) in a temporal pattern. (12)

Rising phase of the action potential In the axon, or nerve fiber, the decrease in negativity from -70 mV to $+40$ mV (the peak action potential level) that occurs during the action potential. This increase is caused by an inflow of Na^+ ions into the axon. (2)

Rod A cylinder-shaped receptor in the retina that is responsible for vision at low levels of illumination. (2)

Rod–cone break The point on the dark adaptation curve at which vision shifts from cone vision to rod vision. (2)

Rod monochromat A person who has a retina in which the only functioning receptors are rods. (3)

Rod spectral sensitivity curve The curve plotting visual sensitivity versus wavelength for rod vision. This function is typically measured when the eye is dark adapted by a test light presented to the peripheral retina. (2)

Ruffini cylinder (SA2) A receptor structure in the skin associated with slowly adapting fibers. It has been proposed that the Ruffini cylinder is involved in perceiving "stretching." (14)

SA1 fiber Fiber in the skin associated with Merkel receptors that adapts slowly to stimulation and so responds continuously as long as a tactile stimulus is applied. (14)

SA2 fiber A slowly adapting fiber in the cutaneous system that is associated with the Ruffini cylinder and is located deeper in the skin than the SA1 fiber. This fiber also responds continuously to a tactile stimulus. (14)

Saccadic eye movement Rapid eye movement between fixations that occurs when scanning a scene. (6)

Saliency map A "map" of a visual display that takes into account characteristics of the display such as color, contrast, and orientation that are associated with capturing attention. (6)

Same-object advantage The faster responding that occurs when enhancement spreads within an object. Faster reaction times occur when a target is located within the object that is receiving the subject's attention, even if the subject is looking at another place within the object. (6)

Saturation (color) The relative amount of whiteness in a chromatic color. The less whiteness a color contains, the more saturated it is. (9)

Scale illusion An illusion that occurs when successive notes of a scale are presented alternately to the left and right ears. Even though each ear receives notes that jump up and down in frequency, smoothly ascending or descending scales are heard in each ear. Also called melodic channeling. (12)

Scene A view of a real-world environment that contains (a) background elements and (b) multiple objects that are organized in a meaningful way relative to each other and the background. (5)

Scene schema An observer's knowledge about what is contained in typical scenes. An observer's attention is affected by knowledge of what is usually found in the scene. (5)

Secondary olfactory area An area in the frontal lobe, near the eyes, that receives signals originating in the olfactory receptors. Also known as the orbitofrontal cortex. (15)

Secondary somatosensory cortex (S2) The area in the parietal lobe next to the primary somatosensory area (S1) that processes neural signals related to touch, temperature, and pain. (14)

Segregation The process of separating one area or object from another. See also **Figure–ground segregation**. (5)

Selective adaptation A procedure in which a person or animal is selectively exposed to one stimulus, and then the effect of this exposure is assessed by testing with a wide range of stimuli. Typically, sensitivity to the exposed stimulus is decreased. (3)

Selective rearing A procedure in which animals are reared in special environments. An example of selective rearing is the experiment in which kittens were reared in an environment of vertical stripes to determine the effect on orientation selectivity of cortical neurons. (3)

Selective reflection When an object reflects some wavelengths of the spectrum more than others. (9)

Selective transmission When some wavelengths pass through visually transparent objects or substances and others do not. Selective transmission is associated with the perception of chromatic color. See also **Selective reflection**. (9)

Self-produced information Generally, environmental information that is produced by actions of the observer. An example is optic flow, which occurs as a result of a person's movement and which, in turn, provides information that can be used to guide that movement. (7)

Semantic encoding A method for analyzing the patterns of voxel activation recorded from visual areas of an observer's brain, based on the relationship between voxel activation and the meaning or category of a scene. (5)

Semantic regularities Characteristics associated with the functions associated with different types of scenes. These characteristics are learned from experience. For example, most people are aware of the kinds of activities and objects that are usually associated with kitchens. (5)

Semitone The smallest interval in Western music—roughly the difference between two notes in a musical scale, such as between C and C#. There are 12 semitones in an octave. (12)

Sensation Often identified with elementary processes that occur at the beginning of a sensory system. See also **Structuralism**. (1)

Sensory coding How neurons represent various characteristics of the environment. See also **Population coding**; **Sparse coding**; **Specificity coding**. (3)

Sensory component of pain Pain perception described with terms such as *throbbing, prickly, hot*, or *dull*. See also **Affective (emotional) component of pain**. (14)

Sensory receptors Cells specialized to respond to environmental energy, with each sensory system's receptors specialized to respond to a specific type of energy. (1)

Sensory-specific satiety The effect on perception of the odor associated with food eaten to satiety (the state of being satiated or "full"). For example, after eating bananas until satiety, the pleasantness rating for vanilla decreased slightly (but was still positive), but the rating for banana odor decreased much more and became negative. (15)

Shadowing Listeners' repetition aloud of what they hear as they are hearing it. (13)

Shortest path constraint In the perception of apparent motion, the principle that apparent movement tends to occur along the shortest path between two stimuli. (8)

Signal The stimulus presented to a participant. A concept in signal detection theory. (Appendix D)

Signal detection approach An approach to detection of stimuli in which subjects' ability to detect stimuli is measured and analyzed in terms of hits and false alarms. This approach can take a subject's criterion into account in determining sensitivity to a stimulus. See also **Correct rejection**; **False alarm**; **Hit**; **Miss**; **Noise**; **Payoffs**; **Receiver operating characteristic (ROC) curve**; **Response criterion**; **Signal**. (Appendix D)

Similarity, principle of A Gestalt principle stating that similar things appear to be grouped together. (5)

Simple cortical cell A neuron in the visual cortex that responds best to bars of a particular orientation. (3)

Simplicity, principle of See **Pragnanz, principle of**. (5)

Single-opponent neuron Neurons that increase firing to long wavelengths presented to the center of the receptive field and decrease firing to short wavelengths presented to the surround (or vice versa). (9)

Size constancy Occurs when the size of an object is perceived to remain the same even when it is viewed from different distances. (10)

Size–distance scaling A hypothesized mechanism that helps maintain size constancy by taking an object's perceived distance into account. According to this mechanism, an object's perceived size, S, is determined by multiplying the size of the retinal image, R, by the object's perceived distance, D. (10)

Slowly adapting (SA) fiber *See* **SA1 fiber; SA2 fiber**. (14)

Social gating hypothesis The hypothesis that the social brain "gates" mechanisms that are responsible for language learning. This hypothesis has been proposed to explain the results of experiments in which infants did learn from interaction with an instructor but did not learn from viewing DVD images. (13)

Somatosensory receiving area (S1) An area in the parietal lobe that receives inputs from the skin and the viscera associated with somatic senses such as touch, temperature, and pain. *See also* **Secondary somatosensory cortex (S2)**. (14)

Somatosensory system The system that includes the cutaneous senses (senses involving the skin), proprioception (the sense of position of the limbs), and kinesthesis (sense of movement of the limbs). (14)

Sound (perceptual) The perceptual experience of hearing. The statement "I hear a sound" is using *sound* in this sense. (11)

Sound (physical) The physical stimulus for hearing. The statement "The sound's level was 10 dB" is using *sound* in this sense. (11)

Sound level The pressure of a sound stimulus, expressed in decibels. *See also* **Sound pressure level (SPL)**. (11)

Sound pressure level (SPL) A designation used to indicate that the reference pressure used for calculating a tone's decibel rating is set at 20 micropascals, near the threshold in the most sensitive frequency range for hearing. (11)

Sound spectrogram A plot showing the pattern of intensities and frequencies of a speech stimulus. (13)

Sound wave Pattern of pressure changes in a medium. Most of the sounds we hear are due to pressure changes in the air, although sound can be transmitted through water and solids as well. (11)

Sparse coding The idea that a particular object is represented by the firing of a relatively small number of neurons. (3)

Spatial attention Attention to a specific location. (6)

Spatial cue In tactile perception, information about the texture of a surface that is determined by the size, shape, and distribution of surface elements such as bumps and grooves. (14)

Spatial layout hypothesis Proposal that the parahippocampal cortex responds to the surface geometry or geometric layout of a scene. (5)

Spatial organization How different locations in the environment and on the receptors are represented in the brain. (4)

Spatial updating Process by which people and animals keep track of their position within a surrounding environment when they move. (7)

Specificity coding Type of neural code in which different perceptions are signaled by activity in specific neurons. *See also* **Distributed coding**. (3)

Spectral colors Colors that appear in the visible spectrum. *See also* **Nonspectral colors**. (9)

Spectral cue In hearing, the distribution of frequencies reaching the ear that are associated with specific locations of a sound. The differences in frequencies are caused by interaction of sound with the listener's head and pinnae. (12)

Spectral sensitivity The sensitivity of visual receptors to different parts of the visible spectrum. *See also* **Spectral sensitivity curve**. (2)

Spectral sensitivity curve The function relating a subject's sensitivity to light to the wavelength of the light. The spectral sensitivity curves for rod and cone vision indicate that the rods and cones are maximally sensitive at 500 nm and 560 nm, respectively. *See also* **Purkinje shift**. (2)

Speech segmentation The process of perceiving individual words from the continuous flow of the speech signal. (13)

Speechreading Process by which deaf people determine what people are saying by observing their lip and facial movements. (12)

Spinothalamic pathway One of the nerve pathways in the spinal cord that conducts nerve impulses from the skin to the somatosensory area of the thalamus. (14)

Spontaneous activity Nerve firing that occurs in the absence of environmental stimulation. (2)

Staircase illusion *See* **Chevreul illusion**. (3)

Stapes The last of the three ossicles in the middle ear. It receives vibrations from the incus and transmits these vibrations to the oval window of the inner ear. (11)

Statistical learning The process of learning about transitional probabilities and other characteristics of the environment. Statistical learning for properties of language has been demonstrated in young infants. (13)

Stereopsis The impression of depth that results from binocular disparity—the difference in the position of images of the same object on the retinas of the two eyes. (10)

Stereoscope A device that presents pictures to the left and the right eyes so that the binocular disparity a person would experience when viewing an actual scene is duplicated. The result is a convincing illusion of depth. (10)

Stereoscopic depth perception The perception of depth that is created by input from both eyes. *See also* **Binocular disparity**. (10)

Stereoscopic vision Two-eyed depth perception involving mechanisms that take into account differences in the images formed on the left and right eyes. (10)

Stevens's power law A law concerning the relationship between the physical intensity of a stimulus and the perception of the subjective magnitude of the stimulus. The law states that $P = KS^n$, where P is perceived magnitude, K is a constant, S is the stimulus intensity, and n is an exponent. (Appendix C)

Stimulus–perception relationship The relationship between stimuli and behavioral responses, where behavioral responses can be perception, recognition, or action. (1)

Stimulus–physiology relationship The relationship between stimuli and physiological responses. (1)

Strabismus Misalignment of the eyes, such as crossed eyes or walleyes (outward looking eyes), in which the visual system suppresses vision in one of the eyes to avoid double vision, so the person sees the world with only one eye at a time. (10)

Striate cortex The visual receiving area of the cortex, located in the occipital lobe. (3)

Structural encoding A method for analyzing the patterns of voxel activation recorded from visual areas of an observer's brain, based on the relationship between voxel activation and structural characteristics of a scene, such as lines, contrasts, shapes, and textures. (5)

Structuralism The approach to psychology, prominent in the late 19th and early 20th centuries, that postulated that perceptions result from the summation of many elementary sensations. The Gestalt approach to perception was, in part, a reaction to structuralism. (5)

Subcortical structure Structure below the cerebral cortex. For example, the superior colliculus is a subcortical structure in the visual system. The cochlear nucleus and superior olivary nucleus are among the subcortical structures in the auditory system. (11)

Subtractive color mixture. *See* **Color mixture, subtractive**. (9)

Superior colliculus An area in the brain that is involved in controlling eye movements and other visual behaviors. This area receives about 10 percent of the ganglion cell fibers that leave the eye in the optic nerve. (3)

Superior olivary nucleus A nucleus along the auditory pathway from the cochlea to the auditory cortex. The superior olivary nucleus receives inputs from the cochlear nucleus. (11)

Surface texture The visual and tactile quality of a physical surface created by peaks and valleys. (14)

Synapse A small space between the end of one neuron (the presynaptic neuron) and the cell body of another neuron (the postsynaptic neuron). (2)

Syntax In language, grammatical rules that specify correct sentence construction. *See also* **Musical syntax**. (12)

Tactile acuity The smallest details that can be detected on the skin. (14)

Task-irrelevant stimulus A stimulus that does not provide information relevant to the task at hand. (6)

Taste bud A structure located within papillae on the tongue that contains the taste cells. (15)

Taste cell Cell located in taste buds that causes the transduction of chemical to electrical energy when chemicals contact receptor sites or channels located at the tip of this cell. (15)

Taste pore An opening in the taste bud through which the tips of taste cells protrude. When chemicals enter a taste pore, they stimulate the taste cells and result in transduction. (15)

Tectorial membrane A membrane that stretches the length of the cochlea and is located directly over the hair cells. Vibrations of the cochlear partition cause the tectorial membrane to bend the hair cells by rubbing against them. (11)

Temporal coding The connection between the frequency of a sound stimulus and the timing of the auditory nerve fiber firing. (11)

Temporal cue In tactile perception, information about the texture of a surface that is provided by the rate of vibrations that occur as we move our fingers across the surface. (14)

Temporal lobe A lobe on the side of the cortex that is the site of the cortical receiving area for hearing and the termination point for the ventral, or *what*, stream for visual processing. A number of areas in the temporal lobe, such as the fusiform face area and the extrastriate body area, serve functions related to perceiving and recognizing objects. (1)

Texture gradient The visual pattern formed by a regularly textured surface that extends away from the observer. This pattern provides information for distance because the elements in a texture gradient appear smaller as distance from the observer increases. (10)

Threshold The minimum stimulus energy necessary for an observer to detect a stimulus. (1)

Tiling The adjacent (and often overlapping) location columns working together to cover the entire visual field (similar to covering a floor with tiles). (4)

Timbre The quality that distinguishes between two tones that sound different even though they have the same loudness, pitch, and duration. Differences in timbre are illustrated by the sounds made by different musical instruments. (11)

Tip links Structures at the tops of the cilia of auditory hair cells, which stretch or slacken as the cilia move, causing ion channels to open or close. (11)

Tonal hierarchy Ratings of how well notes fit in a scale. Notes that sound "right" in a scale would be high in the tonal hierarchy. Notes that don't sound like they fit in a scale are low in the hierarchy. (12)

Tonality Organizing pitches around the note associated with a composition's key. (12)

Tone chroma The perceptual similarity of notes separated by one or more octaves. (11)

Tone height The increase in pitch that occurs as frequency is increased. (11)

Tonic The key of a musical composition. (12)

Tonotopic map An ordered map of frequencies created by the responding of neurons within structures in the auditory system. There is a tonotopic map of neurons along the length of the cochlea, with neurons at the apex responding best to low frequencies and neurons at the base responding best to high frequencies. (11)

Top-down processing Processing that starts with the analysis of high-level information, such as the knowledge a person brings to a situation. Also called knowledge-based processing. Distinguished from bottom-up, or data-based processing, which is based on incoming data. (1)

Topographical agnosia A condition associated with brain damage in which patients are unable to recognize landmarks in real-world environments. (7)

Transcranial magnetic stimulation (TMS) Presenting a strong magnetic field to the head that temporarily disrupts the functioning of a specific area of the brain. (8)

Transduction In the senses, the transformation of environmental energy into electrical energy. For example, the retinal receptors transduce light energy into electrical energy. (1)

Transformation, principle of A principle of perception that stimuli and responses created by stimuli are transformed, or changed, between the environmental stimulus and perception. (1)

Transitional probabilities In language, the chances that one sound will follow another sound. Every language has transitional probabilities for different sounds. Part of learning a language involves learning about the transitional probabilities in that language. (13)

Transmission cell (T-cell) According to gate control theory, the cell that receives + and − inputs from cells in the dorsal horn. T-cell activity determines the perception of pain. (14)

Traveling wave In the auditory system, vibration of the basilar membrane in which the peak of the vibration travels from the base of the membrane to its apex. (11)

Trichromat A person with normal color vision. Trichromats can match any wavelength in the spectrum by mixing three other wavelengths in various proportions. (9)

Trichromatic theory of color vision A theory proposing that our perception of color is determined by the ratio of activity in three receptor mechanisms with different spectral sensitivities. (9)

Tuning curve, frequency *See* **Frequency tuning curve**. (11)

Tuning curve, orientation *See* **Orientation tuning curve**. (3)

2-deoxyglucose technique A procedure that involves injecting a radioactive 2-deoxyglucose (2DG) molecule into an animal and exposing the animal to oriented stimuli. The 2DG is taken up by neurons that respond to the orientation. This procedure is used to visualize orientation columns in the cortex. (15)

Two-flash illusion An illusion that occurs when one flash of light is presented, accompanied by two rapidly presented tones. Presentation of the two tones causes the observer to perceive two flashes of light. (12)

Two-point threshold The smallest separation between two points on the skin that is perceived as two points; a measure of acuity on the skin. *See also* **Grating acuity**. (14)

Tympanic membrane A membrane at the end of the auditory canal that vibrates in response to vibrations of the air and transmits these vibrations to the ossicles in the middle ear. (11)

Unconscious inference The idea proposed by Helmholtz that some of our perceptions are the result of unconscious assumptions that we make about the environment. *See also* **Likelihood principle**. (5)

Uncrossed disparity Disparity that occurs when one object is being fixated, and is therefore on the horoptor, and another object is located behind the horoptor, farther from the observer. (10)

Uniform connectedness, principle of A modern Gestalt principle that states that connected regions of a visual stimulus are perceived as a single unit. (5)

Unilateral dichromat A person who has dichromatic vision in one eye and trichromatic vision in the other eye. People with this condition (which is extremely rare) have been tested to determine what colors a dichromats perceive by asking them to compare the perceptions they experience with their dichromatic eye and their trichromatic eye. (9)

Univariance, principle of Once a photon of light is absorbed by a visual pigment molecule, the identity of the light's wavelength is lost. This means that the receptor does not know the wavelength of the light that is absorbed, only the total amount of light it has absorbed. (9)

Unresolved harmonics Harmonics of a complex tone that can't be distinguished from one another because they are not indicated by separate peaks in the basilar membrane vibration. The higher harmonics of a tone are most likely to be unresolved. (11)

Value The light-to-dark dimension of color. (9)

Ventral pathway Pathway that conducts signals from the striate cortex to the temporal lobe. Also called the *what* pathway because it is involved in recognizing objects. (4)

Ventriloquism effect *See* **Visual capture**. (12)

Ventrolateral nucleus Nucleus in the thalamus that receives signals from the cutaneous system. (14)

Vestibular system The mechanism in the inner ear that is responsible for balance and sensing the position of the body. (12)

Video microscopy A technique that has been used to take pictures of papillae and taste buds on the tongue. (15)

Viewpoint invariance The condition in which object properties don't change when viewed from different angles. Responsible for our ability to recognize objects when viewed from different angles. (5)

Visible light The band of electromagnetic energy that activates the visual system and that, therefore, can be perceived. For humans, visible light has wavelengths between 400 and 700 nanometers. (2)

Visual acuity The ability to resolve small details. (2)

Visual angle The angle of an object relative to an observer's eyes. This angle can be determined by extending two lines from the eye—one to one end of an object and the other to the other end of the object. Because an object's visual angle is always determined relative to an observer, its visual angle changes as the distance between the object and the observer changes. (10)

Visual capture When sound is heard coming from a seen location, even though it is actually originating somewhere else. Also called the ventriloquism effect. (12)

Visual direction strategy A strategy used by moving observers to reach a destination by keeping their body oriented toward the target. (7)

Visual evoked potential An electrical response to visual stimulation recorded by the placement of disk electrodes on the back of the head. This potential reflects the activity of a large population of neurons in the visual cortex. (2)

Visual form agnosia The inability to recognize objects. (1)

Visual masking stimulus A visual pattern that, when presented immediately after a visual stimulus, decreases a person's ability to perceive the stimulus. This stops the persistence of vision and therefore limits the effective duration of the stimulus. (5)

Visual pigment A light-sensitive molecule contained in the rod and cone outer segments. The reaction of this molecule to light results in the generation of an electrical response in the receptors. (1)

Visual pigment bleaching The change in the color of a visual pigment that occurs when visual pigment molecules are isomerized by exposure to light. (2)

Visual pigment regeneration Occurs after the visual pigment's two components—opsin and retinal—have become separated due to the action of light. Regeneration, which occurs in the dark, involves a rejoining of these two components to reform the visual pigment molecule. This process depends on enzymes located in the pigment epithelium. (2)

Visual receiving area The area of the occipital lobe where signals from the retina and LGN first reach the cortex. (3)

Visual salience Characteristics such as bright colors, high contrast, and highly visible orientations that cause stimuli to stand out and therefore attract attention. (6)

Visual scanning Moving the eyes to focus attention on different locations on objects or in scenes. (6)

Visual search A procedure in which a person's task is to find a particular element in a display that contains a number of elements. (6)

Visuomotor grip cell A neuron that initially responds when a specific object is seen and then also responds as a hand grasps the same object. (7)

Voice cells Neurons in the temporal lobe that respond more strongly to same-species voices than to calls of other animals or to "non-voice" sounds. (13)

Voice onset time (VOT) In speech production, the time delay between the beginning of a sound and the beginning of the vibration of the vocal chords. (13)

Waterfall illusion An aftereffect of movement that occurs after viewing a stimulus moving in one direction, such as a waterfall. Viewing the waterfall makes other objects appear to move in the opposite direction. *See also* **Movement aftereffect**. (8)

Wavelength For light energy, the distance between one peak of a light wave and the next peak. (2)

Wayfinding The process of navigating through the environment. Wayfinding involves perceiving objects in the environment, remembering objects and their relation to the overall scene, and knowing when to turn and in what direction. (7)

Weber fraction The ratio of the difference threshold to the value of the standard stimulus in Weber's law. (Appendix B)

Weber's law A law stating that the ratio of the difference threshold (DL) to the value of the stimulus (S) is constant. According to this relationship, doubling the value of a stimulus will cause a doubling of the difference threshold. The ratio DL/S is called the Weber fraction. (Appendix B)

Wernicke's aphasia An inability to comprehend words or arrange sounds into coherent speech, caused by damage to Wernicke's area. (13)

Wernicke's area An area in the temporal lobe involved in speech perception. Damage to this area causes Wernicke's aphasia, which is characterized by difficulty in understanding speech. (13)

***What* pathway** *See* **Ventral pathway**. (4)

***What* pathway, auditory** Pathway that extends from the anterior belt to the front of the temporal lobe and then to the frontal cortex. This pathway is responsible for perceiving complex sounds and patterns of sounds. (12)

***Where* pathway** *See* **Dorsal pathway**. (4)

***Where* pathway, auditory** Pathway that extends from the posterior belt to the parietal lobe and then to the frontal cortex. This pathway is responsible for localizing sounds. (12)

Word deafness Occurs in the most extreme form of Wernicke's aphasia, when a person cannot recognize words, even though the ability to hear pure tones remains intact. (13)

Young-Helmholtz theory *See* **Trichromatic theory of color vision**. (9)

References

Aartolahti, E., Hakkinen, A., & Lonnroos, E. (2013). Relationship between functional vision and balance and mobility performance in community-dwelling older adults. *Aging Clinical and Experimental Research, 25,* 545–552.

Abell, F., Happé, F., & Frith, U. (2000). Do triangles play tricks? Attribution of mental states to animated shapes in normal and abnormal development. *Journal of Cognitive Development, 15,* 1–16.

Abramov, I., Gordon, J., Hendrickson, A., Hainline, L., Dobson, V., & LaBossiere. (1982). The retina of the newborn human infant. *Science, 217,* 265–267.

Ache, B. W. (1991). Phylogeny of smell and taste. In T. V. Getchell, R. L. Doty, L. M. Bartoshuk, & J. B. Snow (Eds.), *Smell and taste in health and disease* (pp. 3–18). New York: Raven Press.

Ackerman, D. (1990). *A natural history of the senses.* New York: Vintage Books.

Addams, R. (1834). An account of a peculiar optical phenomenon seen after having looked at a moving body. *London and Edinburgh Philosophical Magazine and Journal of Science, 5,* 373–374.

Adelson, E. H. (1999). Light perception and lightness illusions. In M. Gazzaniga (Ed.), *The new cognitive neurosciences* (pp. 339–351). Cambridge, MA: MIT Press.

Aguirre, G. K., Zarahn, E., & D'Esposito, M. (1998). An area within human ventral cortex sensitive to "building" stimuli: Evidence and implications. *Neuron, 21,* 373–383.

Alain, C., Arnott, S. R., Hevenor, S., Graham, S., & Grady, C. L. (2001). "What" and "where" in the human auditory system. *Proceedings of the National Academy of Sciences, 98,* 12301–12306.

Alain, C., McDonald, K. L., Kovacevic, N., & McIntosh, A. R. (2009). Spatiotemporal analysis of auditory "what" and "where" working memory. *Cerebral Cortex, 19,* 305–314.

Alpern, M., Kitahara, K., & Krantz, D. H. (1983). Perception of color in unilateral tritanopia. *Journal of Physiology, 335,* 683–697.

Altenmüller, E., Siggel, S., Mohammadi, B., Samii, A., & Münte, T. F. (2014). Play it again Sam: Brain correlates of emotional music recognition. *Frontiers in Psychology, 5,* Article 114, 1–8.

Aminoff, E. M., Kveraga, K., & Bar, M. (2013). The role of the parahippocampal cortex in cognition. *Trends in Cognitive Sciences, 17,* 379–390.

Amso, D. (2010). Perceptual development: Attention. In B. Goldstein (Ed.), *Encyclopedia of perception* (pp. 735–738). Thousand Oaks, CA: Sage.

Anderson, B. A., Laurent, P. A., & Yantis, S. (2011). Value-driven attentional capture. *Proceedings of the National Academy of Sciences, 108,* 10367–10371.

Anton-Erxleben, K., Henrich, C., & Treue, S. (2007). Attention changes perceived size of moving visual patterns. *Journal of Vision, 7*(11), 1–9.

Anzai A., Chowdhury, S. A., & DeAngelis, G. C. (2011). Coding of stereoscopic depth information in visual areas V3 and V3A. *Journal of Neuroscience, 31,* 10270–10282.

Appelle, S. (1972). Perception and discrimination as a function of stimulus orientation: The "oblique effect" in man and animals. *Psychological Bulletin, 78,* 266–278.

Arbib, M. A. (2001). The mirror system hypothesis for the language-ready brain. In A. Cangelosi & D. Parisi (Eds.), *Computational approaches to the evolution of language and communication.* Berlin: Springer-Verlag.

Arzi, A., & Sobel, N. (2011). Olfactory perception as a compass for olfactory and neural maps. *Trends in Cognitive Sciences, 10,* 537–545.

Ashley, R. (2002). Do[n't] change a hair for me: The art of jazz rubato. *Music Perception, 19,* 311–322.

Ashmore, J. (2008). Cochlear outer hair cell motility. *Physiological Review, 88,* 173–210.

Ashmore, J., Avan, P., Brownell, W. E., Dallos, P., Dierkes, K., Fettiplace, R., et al. (2010). The remarkable cochlear amplifier. *Hearing Research, 266,* 1–17.

Aslin, R. N. (1977). Development of binocular fixation in human infants. *Journal of Experimental Child Psychology, 23,* 133–150.

Attneave, F., & Olson, R. K. (1971). Pitch as a medium: A new approach to psychophysical scaling. *American Journal of Psychology, 84,* 147–166.

Avenanti, A., Bueti, D., Galati, G., & Aglioti, S. M. (2005). Transcranial magnetic stimulation highlights the sensorimotor side of empathy for pain. *Nature Neuroscience, 8,* 955–960.

Azzopardi, P., & Cowey, A. (1993). Preferential representation of the fovea in the primary visual cortex. *Nature, 361,* 719–721.

Baars, B. J. (2001). The conscious access hypothesis: Origins and recent evidence. *Trends in Cognitive Sciences, 6,* 47–52.

Bach, M., & Poloschek, C. M. (2006). Optical illusions. *Advances in Clinical Neuroscience and Rehabilitation, 6,* 20–21.

Backus, B. T., Fleet, D. J., Parker, A. J., & Heeger, D. J. (2001). Human cortical activity correlates with stereoscopic depth perception. *Journal of Neurophysiology, 86,* 2054–2068.

Baird, J. C., Wagner, M., & Fuld, K. (1990). A simple but powerful theory of the moon illusion. *Journal of Experimental Psychology: Human Perception and Performance, 16,* 675–677.

Bakin, J. S., Nakayama, K., & Gilbert, C. D. (2000). Visual responses in monkey areas V1 and V2 to three-dimensional surface configurations. *Journal of Neuroscience, 20,* 8188–8198.

Baldassano, C., Beck, D. M., & Fei-Fei, L. (2013). Differential connectivity within the parahippocampal place area. *Neuroimage, 75,* 228–237.

Baldauf, D., & Desimone, R. (2014). Neural mechanisms of object-based attention. *Science, 344,* 424–427.

Banks, M. S., & Bennett, P. J. (1988). Optical and photoreceptor immaturities limit the spatial and chromatic vision of human neonates. *Journal of the Optical Society of America, A5,* 2059–2079.

Banks, M. S., & Salapatek, P. (1978). Acuity and contrast sensitivity in 1-, 2-, and 3-month-old human infants. *Investigative Ophthalmology and Visual Science, 17,* 361–365.

Bar, M. (2004). Visual objects in context. *Nature Reviews Neuroscience, 5,* 617–629.

Bardy, B. G., & Laurent, M. (1998). How is body orientation controlled during somersaulting? *Journal of Experimental Psychology: Human Perception and Performance, 24,* 963–977.

Barlow, H. B., Blakemore, C., & Pettigrew, J. D. (1967). The neural mechanism of binocular depth discrimination. *Journal of Physiology, 193,* 327–342.

Barlow, H. B., Fitzhigh, R., & Kuffler, S. W. (1957). Change of organization in the receptive fields of the cat's retina during dark adaptation. *Journal of Physiology, 137,* 338–354.

Barlow, H. B., & Hill, R. M. (1963). Evidence for a physiological explanation of the waterfall illusion. *Nature, 200,* 1345–1347.

Barlow, H. B., & Mollon, J. D. (Eds.). (1982). *The senses.* Cambridge, UK: Cambridge University Press.

Barrett, H. C., Todd, P. M., Miller, G. F., & Blythe, P. (2005). Accurate judgments of intention from motion alone: A cross-cultural study. *Evolution and Human Behavior, 26,* 313–331.

Barry, S. R. (2011). *Fixing my gaze.* New York: Basic Books.

Bartoshuk, L. M. (1971). The chemical senses: I. Taste. In J. W. Kling & L. A. Riggs (Eds.), *Experimental psychology* (3rd ed.). New York: Holt, Rinehart and Winston.

Bartoshuk, L. M. (1979). Bitter taste of saccharin: Related to the genetic ability to taste the bitter substance propylthioural (PROP). *Science, 205,* 934–935.

Bartoshuk, L. M. (1980, September). Separate worlds of taste. *Psychology Today, 243,* 48–56.

Bartoshuk, L. M., & Beauchamp, G. K. (1994). Chemical senses. *Annual Review of Psychology, 45,* 419–449.

Bartrip, J., Morton, J., & deSchonen, S. (2001). Responses to mother's face in 3-week- to 5-month-old infants. *British Journal of Developmental Psychology, 19,* 219–232.

Battaglini, P. P., Galletti, C., & Fattori, P. (1996). Cortical mechanisms for visual perception of object motion and position in space. *Behavioural Brain Research, 76,* 143–154.

Battelli, L., Cavanagh, P., & Thornton, I. M. (2003). Perception of biological motion in parietal patients. *Neuropsychologia, 41,* 1808–1816.

Baylis, G. C., & Driver, J. (1993). Visual attention and objects: Evidence for hierarchical coding of location. *Journal of Experimental Psychology: Human Perception and Performance, 19,* 451–470.

Baylor, D. (1992). Transduction in retinal photoreceptor cells. In P. Corey & S. D. Roper (Eds.), *Sensory transduction* (pp. 151–174). New York: Rockefeller University Press.

Beauchamp, G. K., Cowart, B. J., Mennella, J. A., & Marsh, R. R. (1994). *Developmental Psychobiology, 27,* 353–365.

Beauchamp, G. K., Cowart, B. J., & Schmidt, H. J. (1991). Development of chemosensory sensitivity and preference. In T. V. Getchell, R. L. Doty, L. M. Bartoshuk, & J. B. Snow (Eds.), *Smell and taste in health and disease* (pp. 405–416). New York: Raven Press.

Beachamp, G. K., & Mennella, J. A. (2009). Early flavor learning and its impact on later feeding behavior. *Journal of Pediatric Gastroenterology and Nutrition, 48,* S25–S30.

Beckers, G., & Homberg, V. (1992). Cerebral visual motion blindness: Transitory akinetopsia induced by transcranial magnetic stimulation of human area V5. *Proceedings of the Royal Society of London B, Biological Sciences, 249,* 173–178.

Beecher, H. K. (1959). *Measurement of subjective responses.* New York: Oxford University Press.

Behrmann, M., & Plaut, D. C. (2013). Distributed circuits, not circumscribed centers, mediate visual recognition. *Trends in Cognitive Sciences, 17,* 210–219.

Békésy, G. von (1960). *Experiments in hearing.* New York: McGraw-Hill.

Belin, P., Zatorre, R. J., Lafaille, P., Ahad, P., & Pike, B. (2000). Voice-selective areas in human auditory cortex. *Nature, 403,* 309–312.

Bendor, D., & Wang, X. (2005). The neuronal representation of pitch in primate auditory cortex. *Nature, 436,* 1161–1165.

Benedetti, F., Arduino, C., & Amanzio, M. (1999). Somatotopic activation of opioid systems by target-directed expectations of analgesia. *Journal of Neuroscience, 19,* 3639–3648.

Benjamin, L. T. (1997). *A history of psychology* (2nd ed.). New York: Mc-Graw Hill.

Bensmaia, S. J., Denchev, P. V., Dammann, J. F. III, Craig, J. C., & Hsiao, S. S. (2008). The representation of stimulus orientation in the early stages of somatosensory processing. *Journal of Neuroscience, 28,* 776–786.

Beranek, L. L. (1996). *Concert and opera halls: How they sound.* Woodbury, NY: Acoustical Society of America.

Berger, K. W. (1964). Some factors in the recognition of timbre. *Journal of the Acoustical Society of America, 36,* 1881–1891.

Bess, F. H., & Humes, L. E. (2008). *Audiology: The fundamentals* (4th ed.). Philadelphia: Lippencott, Williams & Wilkins.

Bharucha, J., & Krumhansl, C. L. (1983). The representation of harmonic structure in music: Hierarchies of stability as a function of context. *Cognition, 13,* 63–102.

Biggs, A. T., Kreager, R. D., Gibson, B. S., Villano, M., & Crowell, C. R. (2012). Semantic and affective salience: The role of meaning and preference in attentional capture and disengagement. *Journal of Experimental Psychology: Human Perception and Performance, 38,* 531–541.

Bilalić, M., Langner, R., Ulrich, R., & Grodd, W. (2011). Many faces of expertise: Fusiform face area in chess experts and novices. *Journal of Neuroscience, 31,* 10206–10214.

Bingel, U., Wanigesekera, V., Wiech, K., Mhuircheartaigh, R. N., Lee, M. C., Ploner, M., et al. (2011). The effect of treatment expectation on drug efficacy: Imaging the analgesic benefit of the opioid Remifentanil. *Science Translational Medicine, 3,* 70ra14.

Birnbaum, M. (2011). *Season to taste.* New York: Harper Collins.

Birnberg, J. R. (1988, March 21). My turn. *Newsweek.*

Blake, R., & Hirsch, H. V. B. (1975). Deficits in binocular depth perception in cats after alternating monocular deprivation. *Science, 190,* 1114–1116.

Blake, R., & Wilson, H. R. (1991). Neural models of stereoscopic vision. *Trends in Neuroscience, 14,* 445–452.

Blakemore, C., & Cooper, G. G. (1970). Development of the brain depends on the visual environment. *Nature, 228,* 477–478.

Blaser, E., & Sperling, G. (2008). When is motion "motion"? *Perception, 37,* 624–627.

Block, N. (2009). Comparing the major theories of consciousness. In M. S. Gazzaniga (Ed.), *The cognitive neurosciences* (4th ed.). Cambridge, MA: MIT Press.

Blumstein, S. E., Baker, E., & Goodglass, H. (1977). Phonological factors in auditory comprehension in aphasia. *Neuropsychologia, 15,* 19–30.

Boring, E. G. (1942). *Sensation and perception in the history of experimental psychology.* New York: Appleton-Century-Crofts.

Borji, A., & Itti, L. (2014). Defending Yarbus: Eye movements reveal observers' task. *Journal of Vision, 14*(3), 1–22.

Bornstein, M. H., Kessen, W., & Weiskopf, S. (1976). Color vision and hue categorization in young human infant. *Journal of Experimental Psychology: Human Perception and Performance, 2,* 115–119.

Borst, A. (2007). Correlation versus gradient type motion detectors: the pros and cons. *Philosophical Transactions of the Royal Society B, 362,* 369–374.

Borst, A., & Egelhaaf, M. (1989). Principles of visual motion detection. *Trends in Neurosciences, 12,* 297–306.

Bosman, C. A., Schoffelen, J.-M., Brunet, N., Oostenveld, R., Bastos, A. M., Womelsdorf, T., et al. (2012). Attention stimulus selection through selective synchronization between monkey visual areas. *Neuron, 75,* 875–888.

Bouvier, S. E., & Engel, S. A. (2006). Behavioral deficits and cortical damage loci in cerebral achromatopsia. *Cerebral Cortex, 16,* 183–191.

Bowmaker, J. K., & Dartnall, H. J. A. (1980). Visual pigments of rods and cones in a human retina. *Journal of Physiology, 298,* 501–511.

Boynton, R. M. (1979). *Human color vision.* New York: Holt, Rinehart and Winston.

Brainard, D. H., & Wandell, B. A. (1986). Analysis of the retinex theory of color vision. *Journal of the Optical Society of America, A3,* 1651–1661.

Bregman, A. S. (1990). *Auditory scene analysis.* Cambridge: MIT Press.

Bregman, A. S. (1993). Auditory scene analysis: Hearing in complex environments. In S. McAdams & E. Bigand (Eds.), *Thinking in sound: The cognitive psychology of human audition* (pp. 10–36). Oxford, UK: Oxford University Press.

Bregman, A. S., & Campbell, J. (1971). Primary auditory stream segregation and perception of order in rapid sequence of tones. *Journal of Experimental Psychology, 89,* 244–249.

Bremmer, F. (2011). Multisensory space: From eye-movements to self-motion. *Journal of Physiology, 589,* 815–823.

Breslin, P. A. S. (2001). Human gustation and flavour. *Flavour and Fragrance Journal, 16,* 439–456.

Bridgeman, B., & Stark, L. (1991). Ocular proprioception and efference copy in registering visual direction. *Vision Research, 31,* 1903–1913.

Britten, K. H., Shadlen, M. N., Newsome, W. T., & Movshon, J. A. (1992). The analysis of visual motion: A comparison of neuronal and psychophysical performance. *Journal of Neuroscience, 12,* 4745–4765.

Brockmole, J. R., Davoli, C. C., Abrams, R. A., & Witt, J. K. (2013). The world within reach: Effects of hand posture and tool-use on visual cognition. *Current Directions in Psychological Science, 22,* 38–44.

Brockmole, J. R., & Vo, M. L.-H. (2010). Semantic memory for contextual regularities within and across scene categories: Evidence from eye movements. *Attention, Perception, & Psychophysics, 72,* 1803–1813.

Bronfman, Z. Z., Brezis, N., Jacobson, H., & Usher, M. (2014). We see more than we can report: "Cost free" color phenomenality outside focal attention. *Psychological Science, 25,* 1394–1403.

Brown, P. K., & Wald, G. (1964). Visual pigments in single rods and cones of the human retina. *Science, 144,* 45–52.

Brunet, N., Bosman, C. A., Roberts, M., Oostenveld, R., Womelsdorf, T., De Weerd, P., et al. (2015). Visual cortical gamma-band activity during free viewing of natural images. *Cerebral Cortex, 25,* 918–926.

Bruno, N., & Bertamini, M. (2015). Perceptual organization and the aperture problem. In J. Wagemans (Ed.), *Oxford handbook of perceptual organization.* Oxford, UK: Oxford University Press.

Buccino, G., Lui, G., Canessa, N., Patteri, I., Lagravinese, G., Benuzzi, F., et al. (2004). Neural circuits involved in the recognition of actions performed by nonconspecifics: An fMRI study. *Journal of Cognitive Neuroscience, 16,* 114–126.

Buck, L. B. (2004). Olfactory receptors and coding in mammals. *Nutrition Reviews, 62,* S184–S188.

Buck, L. B., & Axel, R. (1991). A novel multigene family may encode odorant receptors: A molecular basis for odor recognition. *Cell, 65,* 175–187.

Bufe, B., Breslin, P. A. S., Kuhn, C., Reed, D. R., Tharp, C. D., Slack, J. P., et al. (2005). The molecular basis of individual differences in phenylthiocarbamide and propylthiouracil bitterness perception. *Current Biology, 15,* 322–327.

Buffalo, E. A., Fries, P., Landman, R., Buschman, T. J., & Desimone, R. (2011). Laminar differences in gamma and alpha coherence in the ventral stream. *Proceedings of the National Academy of Sciences, 108,* 11262–11267.

Bugelski, B. R., & Alampay, D. A. (1961). The role of frequency in developing perceptual sets. *Canadian Journal of Psychology, 15,* 205–211.

Buhle, J. T., Stebens, B. L., Friedman, J. J., & Wager, T. D. (2012). Distraction and placebo: Two separate routes to pain control. *Psychological Science, 23,* 246–253.

Bukach, C. M., Gauthier, I., & Tarr, M. J. (2006). Beyond faces and modularity: The power of an expertise framework. *Trends in Cognitive Sciences, 10,* 159–166.

Bunch, C. C. 1929). Age variations in auditory acuity. *Archives of Otolaryngology, 9,* 625–636.

Burns, E. M., & Viemeister, N. F. (1976). Nonspectral pitch. *Journal of the Acoustical Society of America, 60,* 863–869.

Burton, A. M., Young, A. W., Bruce, V., Johnston, R. A., & Ellis, A. W. (1991). Understanding covert recognition. *Cognition, 39,* 129–166.

Bushdid, C., Magnasco, M. O., Vosshall, L. B., & Keller, A. (2014). Humans can discriminate more than 1 trillion olfactory stimuli. *Science, 343,* 1370–1372.

Bushnell, C. M., Ceko, M., & Low, L. A. (2013). Cognitive and emotional control of pain and its disruption in chronic pain. *Nature Reviews Neuroscience, 14,* 502–511.

Bushnell, I. W. R. (2001). Mother's face recognition in newborn infants: Learning and memory. *Infant and Child Development, 10,* 67–74.

Bushnell, I. W. R., Sai, F., & Mullin, J. T. (1989). Neonatal recognition of the mother's face. *British Journal of Developmental Psychology, 7,* 3–15.

Busigny, T., & Rossion, B. (2010). Acquired prosopagnosia abolishes the face inversion effect. *Cortex, 46,* 965–981.

Caggiano, V., Fogassi, L., Rizzolatti, G., Thier, P., & Casile, A. (2009). Mirror neurons differentially encode the peripersonal and extrapersonal space of monkeys. *Science, 324,* 403–406.

Cain, W. S. (1979). To know with the nose: Keys to odor identification. *Science, 203,* 467–470.

Cain, W. S. (1980). *Sensory attributes of cigarette smoking* (Branbury Report: 3. A safe cigarette?, pp. 239–249). Cold Spring Harbor, NY: Cold Spring Harbor Laboratory.

Cain, W. S. (1988). Olfaction. In R. A. Atkinson, R. J. Herrnstein, G. Lindzey, & R. D. Luce (Eds.), *Stevens' handbook of experimental psychology: Vol. 1. Perception and motivation* (Rev. ed., pp. 409–459). New York: Wiley.

Calder, A. J., Beaver, J. D., Winston, J. S., Dolan, R. J., Jenkins, R., Eger, E., et al. (2007). Separate coding of different gaze directions in the superior temporal sulcus and inferior parietal lobule. *Current Biology, 17,* 20–25.

Calvert, G. A., Bullmore, E. T., Brammer, M. J., Campbell, R., Williams, S. C. R., McGuire, P. K., et al. (1997). Activation of auditory cortex during silent lipreading. *Science, 276,* 593–595.

Campbell, F. W., Kulikowski, J. J., & Levinson, J. (1966). The effect of orientation on the visual resolution of gratings. *Journal of Physiology (London), 187,* 427–436.

Carello, C., & Turvey, M. T. (2004). Physics and psychology of the muscle sense. *Current Directions in Psychological Science, 13,* 25–28.

Carlson, N. R. (2010). *Psychology: The science of behavior* (7th ed.). New York: Pearson.

Carr, C. E., & Konishi, M. (1990). A circuit for detection of interaural time differences in the brain stem of the barn owl. *Journal of Neuroscience, 10,* 3227–3246.

Carrasco, M. (2011). Visual attention: The past 25 years. *Vision Research, 51,* 1484–1525.

Carrasco, M. (2012). Multiple partial solutions for the point-to-point correspondence problem in three views. *IEEE International Conference on Intelligent Computer Communication and Processing (ICCP)*, 155–158.

Carrasco, M., Ling, S., & Read, S. (2004). Attention alters appearance. *Nature Neuroscience, 7*, 308–313.

Carrasco, M., Loula, F., & Ho, Y.-X. (2006). How attention enhances spatial resolution: Evidence from selective adaptation to spatial frequency. *Perception and Psychophysics, 68*, 1004–1012.

Cartwright-Finch, U., & Lavie, N. (2007). The role of perceptual load in inattentional blindness. *Cognition, 102*, 321–340.

Casagrande, V. A., & Norton, T. T. (1991). Lateral geniculate nucleus: A review of its physiology and function. In J. R. Coonley-Dillon (Vol. Ed.) & A. G. Leventhal (Ed.), *Vision and visual dysfunction: The neural basis of visual function* (Vol. 4, pp. 41–84). London: Macmillan.

Caspers, S., Ziles, K., Laird, A. R., & Eickoff, S. B. (2010). ALE meta-analysis of action observation and imitation in the human brain. *NeuroImage, 50*, 1148–1167.

Castelhano, M. S., & Henderson, J. M. (2008a). The influence of color on the perception of scene gist. *Journal of Experimental Psychology: Human Perception and Performance, 34*, 660–675.

Castelhano, M. S., & Henderson, J. M. (2008b). Stable individual differences across images in human saccadic eye movements. *Canadian Journal of Psychology, 62*, 1–14.

Castelli, F., Happe, F., Frith, U., & Frith, C. (2000). Movement and mind: A functional imaging study of perception and interpretation of complex intentional movement patterns. *Neuroimage, 12*, 314–325.

Cattaneo, L., & Rizzolatti, G. (2009). The mirror neuron system. *Archives of Neurology, 66*, 557–560.

Cavanagh, P. (2011). Visual cognition. *Visual Research, 51*, 1538–1551.

Cavina-Pratesi, C., Kentridge, R. W., Heywood, C. A., & Milner, A. D. (2010). Separate channels for processing form, texture, and color: Evidence from fMRI adaptation and visual agnosia. *Cerebral Cortex, 20*, 2319–2332.

Cerf, M., Thiruvengadam, N., Mormann, F., Kraskov, A., Quiroga, R. Q., Koch, C., et al. (2010). On-line voluntary control of human temporal lobe neurons. *Nature, 467*, 1104–1108.

Chandrashekar, J., Hoon, M. A., Ryba, N. J. P., & Zuker, C. S. (2006). The receptors and cells for mammalian taste. *Nature, 444*, 288–294.

Chapman, C. R. (1995). The affective dimension of pain: A model. In B. Bromm & J. Desmedt (Eds.), *Pain and the brain: From nociception to cognition: Advances in pain research and therapy* (Vol. 22, pp. 283–301). New York: Raven.

Chatterjee, S. H., Freyd, J., & Shiffrar, M. (1996). Configural processing in the perception of apparent biological motion. *Journal of Experimental Psychology: Human Perception and Performance, 22*, 916–929.

Chen, J. L., Penhune, V. B., & Zatorre, R. J. (2008). Listening to musical rhythms recruits motor regions of the brain. *Cerebral Cortex, 18*, 2844–2854.

Chiu, Y.-C., & Yantis, S. (2009). A domain-independent source of cognitive control for task sets: Shifting spatial attention and switching categorization rules. *Journal of Neuroscience, 29*, 3930–3938.

Choi, G. B., Stettler, D. D., Kallman, B. R., Bhaskar, S. T. Fleischmann, A., & Axel, R. (2011). Driving opposing behaviors with ensembles of piriform neurons. *Cell, 146*, 1004–1015.

Cholewaik, R. W., & Collins, A. A. (2003). Vibrotactile localization on the arm: Effects of place, space, and age. *Perception & Psychophysics, 65*, 1058–1077.

Chun, M. M., Golomb, J. D., & Turk-Browne, N. B. (2011). A taxonomy of external and internal attention. *Annual Review of Psychology, 62*, 73–101.

Churchland, P. S., & Ramachandran, V. S. (1996). Filling in: Why Dennett is wrong. In K. Akins (Ed.), *Perception* (pp. 132–157). Oxford, UK: Oxford University Press.

Clark, E. F., & Krumhansl, C. L. (1990). Perceiving musical time. *Music Perception, 7*, 213–252.

Clulow, F. W. (1972). *Color: Its principles and their applications*. New York: Morgan & Morgan.

Cohen, J. D., & Tong, F. (2001). The face of controversy. *Science, 293*, 2405–2407.

Cohen, M. A., Alvarez, G. A., & Nakayama, K. (2011). Natural-scene perception requires attention. *Psychological Science, 22*, 1165–1172.

Cohen, M. A., Cavanagh, P., Chun, M. M., & Nakayama, K. (2012). The attentional requirements of consciousness. *Trends in Cognitive Sciences, 16*, 411–417.

Cohen, M. R., & Newsome, W. T. (2004). What electrical microstimulation has revealed about the neural basis of cognition. *Current Opinion in Neurobiology, 14*, 169–177.

Colby, C. L., Duhamel, J.-R., & Goldberg, M. E. (1995). Oculocentric spatial representation in parietal cortex. *Cerebral Cortex, 5*, 470–481.

Cole, J. (1995). *Pride and a daily marathon*. Cambridge, MA: MIT Press.

Collett, T. S. (1978). Peering: A locust behavior pattern for obtaining motion parallax information. *Journal of Experimental Biology, 76*, 237–241.

Colloca, L., & Benedetti, F. (2005). Placebos and painkillers: Is mind as real as matter? *Nature Reviews Neuroscience, 6*, 545–552.

Coltheart, M. (1970). The effect of verbal size information upon visual judgments of absolute distance. *Perception and Psychophysics, 9*, 222–223.

Comèl, M. (1953). *Fisiologia normale e patologica della cute umana*. Milan, Italy: Fratelli Treves Editori.

Connolly, J. D., Andersen, R. A., & Goodale, M. A. (2003). fMRI evidence for a "parietal reach region" in the human brain. *Experimental Brain Research, 153*, 140–145.

Cook, R., Bird, G., Catmur, C., Press, C., & Heyes, C. (2014). Mirror neurons: From origin to function. *Behavioral and Brain Sciences, 37*, 177–241.

Coppola, D. M., Purves, H. R., McCoy, A. N., & Purves, D. (1998). The distribution of oriented contours in the real world. *Proceedings of the National Academy of Sciences, 95*, 4002–4006.

Coppola, D. M., White, L. E., Fitzpatrick, D., & Purves, D. (1998). Unequal distribution of cardinal and oblique contours in ferret visual cortex. *Proceedings of the National Academy of Sciences, 95*, 2621–2623.

Craig, J. C., & Lyle, K. B. (2001). A comparison of tactile spatial sensitivity on the palm and fingerpad. *Perception & Psychophysics, 63*, 337–347.

Craig, J. C., & Lyle, K. B. (2002). A correction and a comment on Craig and Lyle (2001). *Perception & Psychophysics, 64*, 504–506.

Crick, F. C., & Koch, C. (2003). A framework for consciousness. *Nature Neuroscience, 6*, 119–127.

Crouzet, S. M., Kirchner, H., & Thorpe, S. J. (2010). Fast saccades toward faces: Face detection in just 100 ms. *Journal of Vision, 10*(4), 1–17.

Croy, I., Bojanowski, V., & Hummel, T. (2013). Men without a sense of smell exhibit a strongly reduced number of sexual relationships, women exhibit reduced partnership security—a reanalysis of previously published data. *Biological Psychology, 92*, 292–294.

Crystal, S. R., & Bernstein, I. L. (1995). Morning sickness: Impact on offspring salt preference. *Appetite, 25*, 231–240.

Crystal, S. R., & Bernstein, I. L. (1998). Infant salt preference and mother's morning sickness. *Appetite, 30*, 297–307.

Csibra, G. (2008). Goal attribution to inanimate agents by 6.5-month-old infants. *Cognition, 107*, 705–717.

Çukur, T., Nishimoto, S., Huth, A. G., & Gallant, J. L. (2013). Attention during natural vision warps semantic representation across the human brain. *Nature Neuroscience, 16*, 763–770.

Culler, E. A. (1935). An experimental study of tonal localization in the cochlea of the guinea pig. *Annals of Otology, Rhinology & Laryngology, 44*, 807.

Culler, E. A., Coakley, J. D., Lowy, K., & Gross, N. (1943). A revised frequency-map of the guinea-pig cochlea. *American Journal of Psychology, 56,* 475–500.

Cumming, B. G., & DeAngelis, G. C. (2001). The physiology of stereopsis. *Annual Review of Neuroscience, 24,* 203–238.

Cutting, J. E., & Vishton, P. M. (1995). Perceiving layout and knowing distances: The integration, relative potency, and contextual use of different information about depth. In W. Epstein & S. Rogers (Eds.), *Handbook of perception and cognition: Perception of space and motion* (pp. 69–117). New York: Academic Press.

Dallos, P. (1996). Overview: Cochlear neurobiology. In P. Dallos, A. N. Popper, & R. R. Fay (Eds.), *The cochlea* (pp. 1–43). New York: Springer.

Dalton, D. S., Cruickshanks, K. J., Wiley, T. L., Klein, B. E. K., Klein, R., & Tweed, T. S. (2001). Association of leisure-time noise exposure and hearing loss. *Audiology, 40,* 1–9.

Dalton, P. (2002). Olfaction. In S. Yantis (Ed.), *Stevens' handbook of experimental psychology: Sensation and perception* (3rd ed., pp. 691–756). New York: Wiley.

Damasio, H., & Damasio, A. R. (1980). The anatomical basis of conduction aphasia. *Brain, 103,* 337–350.

Dannemiller, J. L. (2009). Perceptual development: Color and contrast. E. B. Goldstein (Ed.), *Sage encyclopedia of perception* (pp. 738–742). Thousand Oaks, CA: Sage.

Dapretto, M., Davies, M. S., Pfeifer, J. H., Scott, A. A., Sigman, M., Bookheimer, S. Y., et al. (2006). Understanding emotions in others: Mirror neuron dysfunction in children with autism spectrum disorders. *Nature Neuroscience, 9,* 28–30.

Dartnall, H. J. A., Bowmaker, J. K., & Mollon, J. D. (1983). Human visual pigments: Microspectrophotometric results from the eyes of seven persons. *Proceedings of the Royal Society of London B, 220,* 115–130.

Darwin, C. J. (2010). Auditory scene analysis. In E. B. Goldstein (Ed.), *Sage encyclopedia of perception.* Thousand Oaks, CA: Sage.

Datta, R., & DeYoe, E. A. (2009). I know where you are secretly attending! The topography of human visual attention revealed with fMRI. *Vision Research, 49,* 1037–1044.

D'Ausilio, A., Pulvermuller, F., Salmas, P., Bufalari, I., Begliomini, C., & Fadiga, L. (2009). The motor somatotopy of speech perception. *Current Biology, 19,* 381–385.

David, A. S., & Senior, C. (2000). Implicit motion and the brain. *Trends in Cognitive Sciences, 4,* 293–295.

Davis, H. (1983). An active process in cochlear mechanics. *Hearing Research, 9,* 79–90.

Davis, M. H., Johnsrude, I. S., Hervais-Adelman, A., Taylor, K., & McGettigan, C. (2005). Lexical information drives perceptual learning of distorted speech: Evidence from the comprehension of noise-vocoded sentences. *Journal of Experimental Psychology: General, 134,* 222–241.

Day, R. H. (1989). Natural and artificial cues, perceptual compromise and the basis of veridical and illusory perception. In D. Vickers & P. L. Smith (Eds.), *Human information processing: Measures and mechanisms* (pp. 107–129). North Holland, The Netherlands: Elsevier Science.

Day, R. H. (1990). The Bourdon illusion in haptic space. *Perception and Psychophysics, 47,* 400–404.

de Araujo, I. E., Geha, P., & Small, D. (2012). Orosensory and homeostatic functions of the insular cortex. *Chemical Perception, 5,* 64–79.

de Araujo, I. E., Rolls, E. T., Velazco, M. I., Margot, C., & Cayeux, I. (2005). Cognitive modulation of olfactory processing. *Neuron, 46,* 671–679.

de Haas, B., Kanai, R., Jalkanen, L., & Rees, G. (2012). Grey-matter volume in early human visual cortex predicts proneness to the sound-induced flash illusion. *Proceedings of the Royal Society B, 279,* 4955–4961.

De Lange, F. P., Spronk, M., Willems, R. M., Toni, I., & Bekkering, H. (2008). Complementary systems for understanding action intentions. *Current Biology, 18,* 454–457.

De Santis, L. Clarke, S., & Murray, M. (2007). Automatic and intrinsic auditory "what" and "where" processing in humans revealed by electrical neuroimaging. *Cerebral Cortex, 17,* 9–17.

DeAngelis, G. C., Cumming, B. G., & Newsome, W. T. (1998). Cortical area MT and the perception of stereoscopic depth. *Nature, 394,* 677–680.

DeCasper, A. J., & Fifer, W. P. (1980). Of human bonding: Newborns prefer their mothers' voices. *Science, 208,* 1174–1176.

DeCasper, A. J., & Spence, M. J. (1986). Prenatal maternal speech influences newborns' perception of speech sounds. *Infant Behavior and Development, 9,* 133–150.

DeCasper, A. J., Lecanuet, J.-P., Busnel, M.-C., Deferre-Granier, C., & Maugeais, R. (1994). Fetal reactions to recurrent maternal speech. *Infant Behavior and Development, 17,* 159–164.

Del Pero, L., Bowdish, J., Fried, D., Kermgard, B., Hartley, E., & Barnard, K. (2012). Bayesian geometric modeling of indoor scenes. *IEEE Computer Society Conference on Computer Vision and Pattern Recognition (CVPR),* pp. 2719–2726.

Del Pero, L., Guan, J., Brau, E., Schlecht, J., & Barnard, K. (2011). Sampling bedrooms. *IEEE Computer Society Conference on Computer Vision and Pattern Recognition (CVPR),* pp. 2009–2016.

Delahunt, P. B., & Brainard, D. H. (2004). Does human color constancy incorporate the statistical regularity of natural daylight? *Journal of Vision, 4,* 57–81.

Delay, E. R., Hernandez, N. P., Bromley, K., & Margolskee, R. F. (2006). Sucrose and monosodium glutamate taste thresholds and discrimination ability of T1R3 knockout mics. *Chemical Senses, 31,* 351–357.

Deliege, I. (1987). Grouping conditions in listening to music: An approach to Lerdhal & Jackendoff's grouping preference rules. *Music Perception, 4,* 325–360.

DeLucia, P., & Hochberg, J. (1985). Illusions in the real world and in the mind's eye [Abstract]. *Proceedings of the Eastern Psychological Association, 56,* 38.

DeLucia, P., & Hochberg, J. (1986). Real-world geometrical illusions: Theoretical and practical implications [Abstract]. *Proceedings of the Eastern Psychological Association, 57,* 62.

DeLucia, P., & Hochberg, J. (1991). Geometrical illusions in solid objects under ordinary viewing conditions. *Perception and Psychophysics, 50,* 547–554.

Delwiche, J. F., Buletic, Z., & Breslin, P. A. S. (2001a). Covariation in individuals' sensitivities to bitter compounds: Evidence supporting multiple receptor/transduction mechanisms. *Perception & Psychophysics, 63,* 761–776.

Delwiche, J. F., Buletic, Z., & Breslin, P. A. S. (2001b). Relationship of papillae number to bitter intensity of quinine and PROP within and between individuals. *Physiology and Behavior, 74,* 329–337.

Denes, P. B., & Pinson, E. N. (1993). *The speech chain* (2nd ed.). New York: Freeman.

Derbyshire, S. W. G., Jones, A. K. P., Gyulia, F., Clark, S., Townsend, D., & Firestone, L. L. (1997). Pain processing during three levels of noxious stimulation produces differential patterns of central activity. *Pain, 73,* 431–445.

Desor, J. A., & Beauchamp, G. K. (1974). The human capacity to transmit olfactory information. *Perception and Psychophysics, 13,* 271–275.

Deutsch, D. (1975). Two-channel listening to musical scales. *Journal of the Acoustical Society of America, 57,* 1156–1160.

Deutsch, D. (1996). The perception of auditory patterns. In W. Prinz & B. Bridgeman (Eds.), *Handbook of perception and action* (Vol. 1, pp. 253–296). San Diego, CA: Academic Press.

Deutsch, D. (1999). *The psychology of music* (2nd ed.). San Diego, CA: Academic Press.

Deutsch, D. (2013a). Grouping mechanisms in music. In D. Deutsch (Ed.), *The psychology of music* (3rd ed., pp. 183–248). New York: Elsevier.

Deutsch, D. (2013b). The processing of pitch combinations. In D. Deutsch (Ed.), *The psychology of music* (3rd ed., pp. 249–325). New York: Elsevier.

DeValois, R. L. (1960). Color vision mechanisms in monkey. *Journal of General Physiology, 43*, 115–128.

DeValois, R. L., & DeValois, K. K. (1993). A multistage color model. *Vision Research, 33*, 1053–1065.

DeValois, R. L., & Jacobs, G. H. (1968). Primate color vision. *Science, 162*, 533–540.

Devos, M., Patte, F., Rouault, J., Laffort, P., & Van Gemert, L. J. (Eds.). (1990). *Standardized human olfactory thresholds.* New York: Oxford University Press.

deVries, H., & Stuiver, M. (1961). The absolute sensitivity of the human sense of smell. In W. A. Rosenblith (Ed.), *Sensory communication.* Cambridge, MA: MIT Press.

DeWall, C. N., MacDonald, G., Webster, G. D., Masten, C. L., Baumeister, R. F., Powell, C., et al. (2010). Tylenol reduces social pain: Behavioral and neural evidence. *Psychological Science, 21*, 931–937.

deWied, M., & Verbaten, M. N. (2001). Affective pictures processing, attention, and pain tolerance. *Pain, 90*, 163–172.

Dick, F., Bates, E., Wulfeck, B., Utman, J. A., Dronkers, N., & Gernsbacher, M. A. (2001). Language deficits, localization, and grammar: Evidence for a distributive model of language breakdown in aphasic patients and neurologically intact individuals. *Psychological Review, 108*, 759–788.

Dingus, T. A., Klauer, S. G., Neale, V. L., Petersen, A., Lee, S. E., Sudweeks, J., et al. (2006). *The 100-car naturalistic driving study: Phase II. Results of the 100-car field experiment* (Interim Project Report for DTNH22-00-C-07007, Task Order 6; Report No. DOT HS 810 593). Washington, DC: National Highway Traffic Safety Administration.

Divenyi, P. L., & Hirsh, I. J. (1978). Some figural properties of auditory patterns. *Journal of the Acoustical Society of America, 64*, 1369–1385.

Dobson, V., & Teller, D. (1978). Visual acuity in human infants: Review and comparison of behavioral and electrophysiological studies. *Vision Research, 18*, 1469–1483.

Dodd, G. G., & Squirrell, D. J. (1980). Structure and mechanism in the mammalian olfactory system. *Symposium of the Zoology Society of London, 45*, 35–56.

Doerrfeld, A., Sebanz, N., & Shiffrar, M. (2012). Expecting to lift a box together makes the load look lighter. *Psychological Research, 76*, 467–475.

Doty, R. L. (1991). Olfactory system. In T. V. Getchell, R. L. Doty, L. M. Bartoshuk, & J. B. Snow (Eds.), *Smell and taste in health and disease* (pp. 175–203). New York: Raven Press.

Doty, R. L. (2010). *The great pheromone myth.* Baltimore: Johns Hopkins University Press.

Doty, R. L. (Ed.). (1976). *Mammalian olfaction, reproductive processes and behavior.* New York: Academic Press.

Dougherty, R. F., Koch, V. M., Brewer, A. A., Fischer, B., Modersitzki, J., & Wandell, B. A. (2003). Visual field representations and locations of visual areas V1/2/3 in human visual cortex. *Journal of Vision, 3*, 586–598.

Dowling, J. E., & Boycott, B. B. (1966). Organization of the primate retina. *Proceedings of the Royal Society of London, 166B*, 80–111.

Dowling, W. J., & Harwood, D. L. (1986). *Music cognition.* New York: Academic Press.

Downing, P. E., Jiang, Y., Shuman, M., & Kanwisher, N. (2001). Cortical area selective for visual processing of the human body. *Science, 293*, 2470–2473.

Driver, J., & Baylis, G. C. (1989). Movement and visual attention: The spotlight metaphor breaks down. *Journal of Experimental Psychology: Human Perception and Performance, 15*, 448–456.

Driver, J., & Baylis, G. C. (1998). Attention and visual object segmentation. In R. Parasuraman (Ed.), *The attentive brain* (pp. 299–325). Cambridge, MA: MIT Press.

Droll, J., Hayhoe, M., Triesch, J., & Sullivan, B. (2005). Task demands control acquisition and storage of visual information. *Journal of Experimental Psychology: Human Perception and Performance, 31*, 1416–1438.

Duncan, R. O., & Boynton, G. M. (2007). Tactile hyperacuity thresholds correlate with finger maps in primary somatosensory cortex (S1). *Cerebral Cortex, 17*, 2878–2891.

Durgin, F. H., Baird, J. A., Greenburg, M., Russell, R., Shaughnessy, K., & Waymouth, S. (2009). Who is being deceived? The experimental demands of wearing a backpack. *Psychonomic Bulletin & Review, 16*, 964–969.

Durgin, F. H., & Gigone, K. (2007). Enhanced optic flow speed discrimination while walking: Multisensory tuning of visual coding. *Perception, 36*, 1465–1475.

Durgin, F. H., Klein, B., Spiegel, A., Strawser, C. J., & Williams, M. (2012). The social psychology of perception experiments: Hills, backpacks, glucose and the problem of generalizability. *Journal of Experimental Psychology: Human Perception and Performance, 38*, 1582–1595.

Durrani, M., & Rogers, P. (1999, December). Physics: Past, present, future. *Physics World, 12*(12), 7–13.

Durrant, J., & Lovrinic, J. (1977). *Bases of hearing science.* Baltimore: Williams & Wilkins.

Eames, C. (1977). *Powers of ten.* Pyramid Films.

Egbert, L. D., Battit, G. E., Welch, C. E., & Bartlett, M. D. (1964). Reduction of postoperative pain by encouragement and instruction of patients. *New England Journal of Medicine, 270*, 825–827.

Egly, R., Driver, J., & Rafal, R. D. (1994). Shifting visual attention between objects and locations: Evidence from normal and parietal lesion subjects. *Journal of Experimental Psychology: General, 123*, 161–177.

Ehrenstein, W. (1930). Untersuchungen über Figur-Grund Fragen [Investigations of more figure–ground questions]. *Zeitschrift für Psychologie, 117*, 339–412.

Eimas, P. D., & Corbit, J. D. (1973). Selective adaptation of linguistic feature detectors. *Cognitive Psychology, 4*, 99–109.

Eimas, P. D., Miller, J. L., & Jusczyk, P. W. (1987). On infant speech perception and the acquisition of language. In S. Hamad (Ed.), *Categorical perception.* New York: Cambridge University Press.

Eimas, P. D., & Quinn, P. C. (1994). Studies on the formation of perceptually based basic-level categories in young infants. *Child Development, 65*, 903–917.

Eimas, P. D., Siqueland, E. R., Jusczyk, P., & Vigorito, J. (1971). Speech perception in infants. *Science, 171*, 303–306.

Eisenberger, N. I. (2012). The pain of social disconnection: Examining the shared neural underpinnings of physical and social pain. *Nature Reviews Neuroscience, 13*, 421–434.

Eisenberger, N. I. (2015). Social pain and the brain: Controversies, questions, and where to go from here. *Annual Review of Psychology, 66*, 601–629.

Eisenberger, N. I., Inagaki, T. K., Muscatell, K. A., Haltom, K. E. B., & Leary, M. R. (2011). The neural sociometer: Brain mechanisms underlying state self-esteem. *Journal of Cognitive Neuroscience, 23*, 3448–3455.

Eisenberger, N. I., & Lieberman, M. D. (2004). Why rejection hurts: A common neural alarm system for physical and social pain. *Trends in Cognitive Sciences, 8*, 294–300.

Eisenberger, N. I., Lieberman, M. D., & Williams, K. D. (2003). Does rejection hurt? An fMRI study of social exclusion. *Science, 302*, 290–292.

Ekstrom, A. D., Kahana, M. J., Caplan, J. B., Fields, T. A., Isham, E. A., Newman, E. L. et al. (2003). Cellular networks underlying human spatial navigation. *Nature, 425,* 184–187.

Elbert, T., Pantev, C., Wienbruch, C., Rockstroh, B., & Taub, E. (1995). Increased cortical representation of the fingers of the left hand in string players. *Science, 270,* 305–307.

Emmert, E. (1881). Grossenverhaltnisse der Nachbilder. *Klinische Monatsblätter für Augenheilkunde, 19,* 443–450.

Engel, S. A. (2005). Adaptation of oriented and unoriented color-selective neurons in human visual areas. *Neuron, 45,* 613–623.

Engen, T. (1972). Psychophysics. In J. W. Kling & L. A. Riggs (Eds.), *Experimental psychology* (3rd ed., pp. 1–46). New York: Holt, Rinehart and Winston.

Engen, T., & Pfaffmann, C. (1960). Absolute judgments of odor quality. *Journal of Experimental Psychology, 59,* 214–219.

Epstein, R. A. (2005). The cortical basis of visual scene processing. *Visual Cognition, 12,* 954–978.

Epstein, R. A. (2008). Parahippocampal and retrosplenial contributions to human spatial navigation. *Trends in Cognitive Sciences, 12,* 388–396.

Epstein, R. A., Harris, A., Stanley, D., & Kanwisher, N. (1999). The parahippocampal place area: Recognition, navigation, or encoding? *Neuron, 23,* 115–125.

Epstein, R. A., & Kanwisher, N. (1998). A cortical representation of the local visual environment. *Nature, 392,* 598–601.

Epstein, R. A., & Vass. L. K. (2014). Neural systems for landmark-based wayfinding in humans. *Philosophical Transactions of the Royal Society B, 369,* 20120533.

Epstein, W. (1965). Nonrelational judgments of size and distance. *American Journal of Psychology, 78,* 120–123.

Erickson, R. (1975). *Sound structure in music.* Berkeley: University of California Press.

Erickson, R. P. (1963). Sensory neural patterns and gustation. In Y. Zotterman (Ed.), *Olfaction and taste* (Vol. 1, pp. 205–213). Oxford, UK: Pergamon Press.

Erickson, R. P. (2000). The evolution of neural coding ideas in the chemical senses. *Physiology and Behavior, 69,* 3–13.

Evans, K. K., & Treisman, A. (2005). Perception of objects in natural scenes: Is it really attention free? *Journal of Experimental Psychology: Human Perception and Performance, 31,* 1476–1492.

Fagan, J. F. (1976). Infant's recognition of invariant features of faces. *Child Development, 47,* 627–638.

Fajen, B. R., & Warren, W. H. (2003). Behavioral dynamics of steering, obstacle avoidance and route selection. *Journal of Experimental Psychology: Human Perception and Performance, 29,* 343–362.

Fantz, R. L., Ordy, J. M., & Udelf, M. S. (1962*).* Maturation of pattern vision in infants during the first six months. *Journal of Comparative and Physiological Psychology, 55,* 907–917.

Farah, M. J., Wilson, K. D., Drain H. M., & Tanaka, J. R. (1998). What is "special" about face perception? *Psychological Review, 105,* 482–498.

Fattori, P., Breveglieri, R., Raos, V., Boco, A., & Galletti, C. (2012). Vision for action in the macaque medial posterior parietal cortex. *Journal of Neuroscience, 32,* 3221–3234.

Fattori, P., Raos, V., Breveglieri, R., Bosco, A., Marzocchi, N., & Galleti, C. (2010). The dorsomedial pathway is not just for reaching: Grasping neurons in the medial parieto-occipital cortex of the macaque monkey. *Journal of Neuroscience, 30,* 342–349.

Fechner, G. T. (1966). *Elements of psychophysics.* New York: Holt, Rinehart and Winston. (Original work published 1860)

Fei-Fei, L., Iyer, A., Koch, C., & Perona, P. (2007). What do we perceive in a glance of a real-world scene? *Journal of Vision, 7,* 1–29.

Feldman, J. (2013). The neural binding problem(s). *Cognitive Neurodynamics, 7,* 1–11.

Fernald, R. D. (2006). Casting a genetic light on the evolution of eyes. *Science, 313,* 1914–1918.

Ferrari, P. F., Gallese, V., Rizzolatti, G., & Fogassi, L. (2003). Mirror neurons responding to the observation of ingestive and communicative mouth actions in the monkey ventral premotor cortex. *European Journal of Neuroscience, 15,* 399–402.

Fettiplace, R., & Hackney, C. M. (2006). The sensory and motor roles of auditory hair cells. *Nature Reviews Neuroscience, 7,* 19–29.

Fields, H. L., & Basbaum, A. I. (1999). Central nervous system mechanisms of pain modulation. In P. D. Wall & R. Melzak (Eds.), *Textbook of pain* (pp. 309–328). New York: Churchill Livingstone.

Filimon, F., Nelson, J. D., Huang, R.-S., & Sereno, M. I. (2009). Multiple parietal reach regions in humans: Cortical representations for visual and proprioceptive feedback during on-line reaching. *Journal of Neuroscience, 29,* 2961–2971.

Finger, T. E. (1987). Gustatory nuclei and pathways in the central nervous system. In T. E. Finger & W. L. Silver (Eds.), *Neurobiology of taste and smell* (pp. 331–353). New York: Wiley.

Finniss, D. G., & Benedetti, F. (2005). Mechanisms of the placebo response and their impact on clinical trials and clinical practice. *Pain, 114,* 3–6.

Fischer, E., Bulthoff, H . H., Logothetis, N. K., & Bartels, A. (2012). Visual motion responses in the posterior cingulate sulcus: A comparison to V5/MT and MST. *Cerebral Cortex, 22,* 865–876.

Fischl, G., & Anders, M. D. (2000). Measuring the thickness of the human cerebral cortex from magnetic resonance images. *Proceedings of the National Academy of Sciences, 97,* 11050–11055.

Fletcher, H., & Munson, W. A. (1933). Loudness: Its definition, measurement, and calculation. *Journal of the Acoustical Society of America, 5,* 82–108.

Fogassi, L., Ferrari, P. F., Gesierich, B., Rozzi, S., Chersi, F., & Rizzolatti, G. (2005). Parietal lobe: From action organization to intention understanding. *Science, 302,* 662–667l.

Forster, S., & Lavie, N. (2008). Failures to ignore entirely irrelevant distractors: The role of load. *Journal of Experimental Psychology: Applied, 14,* 73–83.

Fortenbaugh, F. C., Hicks, J. C., Hao, L., & Turano, K. A. (2006). High-speed navigators: Using more than what meets the eye. *Journal of Vision, 6,* 565–579.

Foster, D. H. (2011). Color constancy. *Vision Research, 51,* 674–700.

Fox, C. R. (1990). Some visual influences on human postural equilibrium: Binocular versus monocular fixation. *Perception and Psychophysics, 47,* 409–422.

Fox, R., Aslin, R. N., Shea, S. L., & Dumais, S. T. (1980). Stereopsis in human infants. *Science, 207,* 323–324.

Franconeri, S. L., & Simons, D. J. (2003). Moving and looming stimuli capture attention. *Perception & Psychophysics, 65,* 999–1010.

Frank, M. E., Lundy, R. F., & Contreras, R. J. (2008). Cracking taste codes by tapping into sensory neuron impulse traffic. *Progress in Neurobiology, 86,* 245–263.

Frank, M. E., & Rabin, M. D. (1989). Chemosensory neuroanatomy and physiology. *Ear, Nose and Throat Journal, 68,* 291–292, 295–296.

Frankland, B. W., & Cohen, A. J. (2004). Parsing of melody: Quantification and testing of the local grouping rules of Lerdahl and Jackendoff's *A Generative Theory of Tonal Music. Music Perception, 21,* 499–543.

Franklin, A., & Davies, R. L. (2004). New evidence for infant colour categories. *British Journal of Developmental Psychology, 22,* 349–377.

Freire, A., Lee, K., & Symons, L. A. (2000). The face-inversion effect as a deficit in the encoding of configural information: Direct evidence. *Perception, 29,* 159–170.

Freire, A., Lewis, T. L., Maurer, D., & Blake, R. (2006). The development of sensitivity to biological motion in noise. *Perception, 35*, 647–657.

Freyd, J. (1983). The mental representation of movement when static stimuli are viewed. *Perception & Psychophysics, 33*, 575–581.

Friedman, H. S., Zhou, H., & von der Heydt, R. (2003). The coding of uniform colour figures in monkey visual cortex. *Journal of Physiology, 548*, 593–613.

Friedman-Hill, S. R., Robertson, L. C., & Treisman, A. (1995). Parietal contributions to visual feature binding: Evidence from a patient with bilateral lesions. *Science, 269*, 853–855.

Fries, P. (2005). A mechanism for cognitive dynamics: Neuronal communication through neuronal coherence. *Trends in Cognitive Sciences, 9*, 474–480.

Friston, K. J., Buechel, C., Fink, G. R., Morris, J., Rolls, E., & Dolan, R. J. (1997). Psychophysiological and modulatory interactions in neuroimaging. *Neuroimage, 6*, 218–229.

Fritz, T., Jentschke, S., Gosselin, N., Sammler, D., Peretz, I., Turner, R., et al. (2009). Universal recognition of three basic emotions in music. *Current Biology, 19*, 573–576.

Fuller, S., & Carrasco, M. (2006). Exogenous attention and color perception: Performance and appearance of saturation and hue. *Vision Research, 46*, 4032–4047.

Furmanski, C. S., & Engel, S. A. (2000). An oblique effect in human visual cortex. *Nature Neuroscience, 3*, 535–536.

Fushan, A. A., Simons, C. T., Slack, J. P., Manichalkul, A., & Drayna, D. (2009). Allelic polymorphism within the TAS1R3 promoter is associated with human taste sensitive to sucrose. *Current Biology, 19*, 1288–1293.

Fyhn, M., Hafting, T., Witter, M. P., Moser, E. I., & Moser, M.-B. (2008). Grid cells in mice. *Hippocampus, 18*, 1230–1238.

Gallese, V. (2007). Before and below 'theory of mind': Embodied simulation and the neural correlates of social cognition. *Philosophical Transactions of the Royal Society B, 362*, 659–669.

Gallese, V., Fadiga, L., Fogassi, L., & Rizzolatti, G. (1996). Action recognition in the premotor cortex. *Brain, 119*, 593–609.

Galletti, C., & Fattori, P. (2003). Neuronal mechanisms for detection of motion in the field of view. *Neuropsychologia, 41*, 1717–1727.

Ganchrow, J. R. (1995). Ontogeny of human taste perception. In R. L. Doty (Ed.), *Handbook of olfaction and gustation* (pp. 715–729). New York: Marcel Dekker.

Ganchrow, J. R., Steiner, J. E., & Daher, M. (1983). Neonatal facial expressions in response to different qualities and intensities of gustatory stimuli. *Infant Behavior and Development, 6*, 473–484.

Ganel, T., Tanzer, M., & Goodale, M. A. (2008). A double dissociation between action and perception in the context of visual illusions. *Psychological Science, 19*, 221–225.

Gao, T., Newman, G. E., & Scholl, B. J. (2009). The psychophysics of chasing: A case study in the perception of animacy. *Cognitive Psychology, 59*, 154–179.

Gardner, M. B., & Gardner, R. S. (1973). Problem of localization in the median plane: Effect of pinnae cavity occlusion. *Journal of the Acoustical Society of America, 53*, 400–408.

Gauthier, I., Skudlarski, P., Gore, J. C., & Anderson, A. W. (2000). Expertise for cars and birds recruits brain areas involved in face recognition. *Nature Neuroscience, 3*, 191–197.

Gauthier, I., Tarr, M. J., Anderson, A. W., Skudlarski, P., & Gore, J. C. (1999). Activation of the middle fusiform face area increases with expertise in recognizing novel objects. *Nature Neuroscience, 2*, 568–573.

Gazzola, V., van der Worp, H., Mulder, T., Wicker, B., Rizzolatti, G., & Keysers, C. (2007). Aplasics born without hands mirror the goal of hand actions with their feet. *Current Biology, 17*, 1235–1240.

Gegenfurtner, K. R., & Rieger, J. (2000). Sensory and cognitive contributions of color to the recognition of natural scenes. *Current Biology, 10*, 805–808.

Geier, J., Bernath, L., Hudak, M., & Sera, L. (2008). Straightness as the main factor of the Hermann grid illusion *Perception, 37*, 651–665.

Geier, J., & Hudak, M. (2011). Changing the Chevreul illusion by a background luminance ramp: Lateral inhibition fails at its traditional stronghold—A psychophysical refutation. *PLoS ONE, 6*(10), e26062.

Geisler, W. S. (2008). Visual perception and statistical properties of natural scenes. *Annual Review of Psychology, 59*, 167–192.

Geisler, W. S. (2011). Contributions of ideal observer theory to vision research. *Vision Research, 51*, 771–781.

Gelbard-Sagiv, H., Mukamel, R., Harel, M., Malach, R., & Fried, I. (2008). Internally generated reactivation of single neurons in human hippocampus during free recall. *Science, 322*, 96–101.

Gescheider, G. A. (1976). *Psychophysics: Method and theory.* Hillsdale, NJ: Erlbaum.

Gibson, B. S., & Peterson, M. A. (1994). Does orientation-independent object recognition precede orientation-dependent recognition? Evidence from a cueing paradigm. *Journal of Experimental Psychology: Human Perception and Performance, 20*, 299–316.

Gibson, J. J. (1950). *The perception of the visual world.* Boston: Houghton Mifflin.

Gibson, J. J. (1962). Observations on active touch. *Psychological Review, 69*, 477–491.

Gibson, J. J. (1966). *The senses as perceptual systems.* Boston: Houghton Mifflin.

Gibson, J. J. (1979). The ecological approach to visual perception. Boston: Houghton Mifflin.

Gilad, S., Meng, M., & Sinha, P. (2009). Role of ordinal contrast relationships in face encoding. *Proceedings of the National Academy of Sciences, 106*, 5353–5358.

Gilaie-Dotan, S., Saygin, A. P., Lorenzi, L., Egan, R., Rees, G., & Behrmann, M. (2013). The role of human ventral visual cortex in motion perception. *Brain, 136*, 2784–2798.

Gilbert, C. D., & Li, W. (2013). Top-down influences on visual processing. *Nature Reviews Neuroscience, 14*, 350–363.

Gilchrist, A. L. (2012). Objective and subjective sides of perception. In S. Allred & G. Hatfield (Eds.), *Visual experience: Sensation, cognition and constancy.* New York: Oxford University Press.

Gilchrist, A. L. (Ed.). (1994). *Lightness, brightness, and transparency.* Hillsdale, NJ: Erlbaum.

Gilchrist, A. L., Kossyfidis, C., Bonato, F., Agostini, T., Cataliotti, J., Li, X., et al. (1999). An anchoring theory of lightness perception. *Psychological Review, 106*, 795–834.

Glanz, J. (2000, April 18). Art + physics = beautiful music. *New York Times*, pp. D1–D4.

Glasser, D. M., Tsui, J., Pack, C. C., & Tadin, D. (2011). Perceptual and neural consequences of rapid motion adaptation. *PNAS, 108*, E1080–E1088.

Gobbini, M. I., & Haxby, J. V. (2007). Neural systems for recognition of familiar faces. *Neuropsychologia, 45*, 32–41.

Goffaux, V., Jacques, C., Mauraux, A., Oliva, A., Schynsand, P. G., & Rossion, B. (2005). Diagnostic colours contribute to the early stages of scene categorization: Behavioural and neurophysiological evidence. *Visual Cognition, 12*, 878–892.

Golarai, G., Ghahremani, G., Whitfield-Gabrieli, S., Reiss, A., Eberhardt, J. L., Gabrieli, J. E. E., et al. (2007). Differential development of high-level cortex correlates with category-specific recognition memory. *Nature Neuroscience, 10*, 512–522.

Gold, T. (1948). Hearing. II. The physical basis of the action of the cochlea. *Proceedings of the Royal Society London B, 135*, 492–498.

Gold, T. (1989). Historical background to the proposal, 40 years ago, of an active model for cochlear frequency analysis. In J. P. Wilson & D. T. Kemp (Eds.), *Cochlear mechanisms: Structure, function, and models* (pp. 299–305). New York: Plenum Press.

Goldman, R. F. (1961). Review of records: Varese: Ionisation; Density 21.5; Integrales; Octrndre; Hyperprism; Poeme Electronique. Instrumentalists, cond. Robert Craft. Columbia MS 6146 (stereo). *Musical Quarterly, 47*, 133–134.

Goldreich, D., & Tong, J. (2013). Prediction, postdiction, and perceptual length contraction: A Bayesian low-speed prior captures the cutaneous rabbit and related illusions. *Frontiers in Psychology: Hypothesis and Theory, 4*, Article 221.

Goldstein, E. B. (2001). Pictorial perception and art. In E. B. Goldstein (Ed.), *Blackwell handbook of perception* (pp. 344–378). Oxford, UK: Blackwell.

Goldstein, E. B., & Fink, S. I. (1981). Selective attention in vision: Recognition memory for superimposed line drawings. *Journal of Experimental Psychology: Human Perception and Performance, 7*, 954–967.

Goodale, M. A. (2011). Transforming vision into action. *Vision Research, 51*, 1567–1587.

Goodale, M. A. (2014). How (and why) the visual control of action differs from visual perception. *Proceedings of the Royal Society B, 281*, 20140337.

Goodale, M. A., & Humphrey, G. K. (1998). The objects of action and perception. *Cognition, 67*, 181–207.

Goodale, M. A., & Humphrey, G. K. (2001). Separate visual systems for action and perception. In E. B. Goldstein (Ed.), *Blackwell handbook of perception* (pp. 311–343). Oxford, UK: Blackwell.

Goodwin, A. W. (1998). Extracting the shape of an object from the responses of peripheral nerve fibers. In J. W. Morley (Ed.), *Neural aspects of tactile sensation* (pp. 55–87). New York: Elsevier Science.

Gottfried, J. A. (2010). Central mechanisms of odour object perception. *Nature Reviews Neuroscience, 11*, 628–641.

Graham, C. H., Sperling, H. G., Hsia, Y., & Coulson, A. H. (1961). The determination of some visual functions of a unilaterally color-blind subject: Methods and results. *Journal of Psychology, 51*, 3–32.

Grahn, J. A. (2009). The role of the basal ganglia in beat perception. *Annals of the New York Academy of Sciences, 1169*, 35–45.

Grahn, J. A., & Rowe, J. B. (2009). Feeling the beat: Premotor and striatal interactions in musicians and nonmusicians during beat perception. *Journal of Neuroscience, 29*, 7540–7548.

Granrud, C. E., Haake, R. J., & Yonas, A. (1985). Infants' sensitivity to familiar size: The effect of memory on spatial perception. *Perception and Psychophysics, 37*, 459–466.

Gregory, R. L. (1966). *Eye and brain*. New York: McGraw-Hill.

Griffin, D. R. (1944). Echolocation by blind men and bats. *Science, 100*, 589–590.

Griffiths, T. D. (2012). Cortical mechanisms for pitch perception. *Journal of Neuroscience, 32*, 13333–13334.

Griffiths, T. D., & Hall, D. A. (2012). Mapping pitch representation in neural ensembles with fMRI. *Journal of Neuroscience, 32*, 13343–13347.

Grill-Spector, K., Golarai, G., & Gabrieli, J. (2008). Developmental neuroimaging of the human ventral visual cortex. *Trends in Cognitive Sciences, 12*, 152–162.

Grill-Spector, K., Knouf, N., & Kanwisher, N. (2004). The fusiform face area subserves face perception, not generic within-category identification. *Nature Neuroscience, 7*, 555–562.

Grill-Spector, K., & Weiner, K. S. (2014). The functional architecture of the ventral temporal cortex and its role in categorization. *Nature Reviews Neuroscience, 15*, 536–548.

Grimes, J. A. (1996). On the failure to detect changes in scenes across saccades. In K. Akins (Ed.), *Perception (Vancouver Studies in Cognitive Science)* (pp. 89–110). New York: Oxford University Press.

Grosbras, M. H., Beaton, S., & Eickhoff, S. B. (2012). Brain regions involved in human movement perception: A quantitative voxel-based meta-analysis. *Human Brain Mapping, 33*, 431–454.

Gross, C. G. (1972). Visual functions of inferotemporal cortex. In R. Jung (Ed.), *Handbook of sensory physiology* (Vol. 7, Part 3, pp. 451–482). Berlin: Springer, 1972.

Gross, C. G. (2002). The genealogy of the "grandmother cell." *Neuroscientist, 8*, 512–518.

Gross, C. G. (2008). Single neuron studies of inferior temporal cortex. *Neuropsychologia, 46*, 841–852.

Gross, C. G., Bender, D. B., & Rocha-Miranda, C. E. (1969). Visual receptive fields of neurons in inferotemporal cortex of the monkey. *Science, 166*, 1303–1306.

Gross, C. G., Rocha-Miranda, C. E., & Bender, D. B. (1972). Visual properties of neurons in inferotemporal cortex of the macaque. *Journal of Neurophysiology, 5*, 96–111.

Grossman, E. D., Batelli, L., & Pascual-Leone, A. (2005). Repetitive TMS over posterior STS disrupts perception of biological motion. *Vision Research, 45*, 2847–2853.

Grossman, E. D., & Blake, R. (2001). Brain activity evoked by inverted and imagined biological motion. *Vision Research, 41*, 1475–1482.

Grossman, E. D., & Blake, R. (2002). Brain areas active during visual perception of biological motion. *Neuron, 56*, 1167–1175.

Grossman, E. D., Donnelly, M., Price, R., Pickens, D., Morgan, V., Neighbor, G., et al. (2000). Brain areas involved in perception of biological motion. *Journal of Cognitive Neuroscience, 12*, 711–720.

Grothe, R., Pecka M., & McAlpine, D. (2010). Mechanisms of sound localization in mammals. *Physiological Review, 90*, 983–1012.

Gulick, W. L., Gescheider, G. A., & Frisina, R. D. (1989). *Hearing*. New York: Oxford University Press.

Gurney, H. (1831). *Memoir of the life of Thomas Young, M.D., F.R.S.* London: John & Arthur Arch.

Gwiazda, J., Brill, S., Mohindra, I., & Held, R. (1980). Preferential looking acuity in infants from two to fifty-eight weeks of age. *American Journal of Optometry and Physiological Optics, 57*, 428–432.

Haarmeier, T., Thier, P., Repnow, M., & Petersen, D. (1997). False perception of motion in a patient who cannot compensate for eye movements. *Nature, 389*, 849–852.

Haber, R. N., & Levin, C. A. (2001). The independence of size perception and distance perception. *Perception & Psychophysics, 63*, 1140–1152.

Hadad, B.-S., Maurer, D., & Lewis, T. L. (2011). Long trajectory for the development of sensitivity to global and biological motion. *Developmental Science, 14*, 1330–1339.

Hafting, T., Fyhn, M., Molden, S., Moser, M.-B., & Moser, E. I. (2005). Microstructure of a spatial map in the entorhinal cortex. *Nature, 436*, 801–806.

Haigney, D., & Westerman, S. J. (2001). Mobile (cellular) phone use and driving: A critical review of research methodology. *Ergonomics, 44*, 132–143.

Hall, D. A., Fussell, C., & Summerfield, A. Q. (2005). Reading fluent speech from talking faces: Typical brain networks and individual differences. *Journal of Cognitive Neuroscience, 17*, 939–953.

Hall, D. A., & Plack, C. J. (2009). Pitch processing sites in the human auditory brain. *Cerebral Cortex, 19*, 576–585.

Hall, M. J., Bartoshuk, L. M., Cain, W. S., & Stevens, J. C. (1975). PTC taste blindness and the taste of caffeine. *Nature, 253*, 442–443.

Hallemans, A., Ortibus, E., Meire, F., & Aerts, P. (2010). Low vision affects dynamic stability of gait. *Gait and Posture, 32*, 547–551.

Hamer, R. D., Alexander, K. R., & Teller, D. Y. (1982). Rayleigh discriminations in young human infants. *Vision Research, 22*, 575–587.

Hamer, R. D., Nicholas, S. C., Tranchina, D., Lamb, T. D., & Jarvinen, J. L. P. (2005). Toward a unified model of vertebrate rod phototransduction. *Visual Neuroscience, 22*, 417–436.

Hamid, S. N., Stankiewicz, B., & Hayhoe, M. (2010). Gaze patterns in navigation: Encoding information in large-scale environments. *Journal of Vision, 10*(12), 1–11.

Handford, M. (1997). *Where's Waldo?* Cambridge, MA: Candlewick Press.

Hansen, T., Olkkonen, M., Walter, S., & Gegenfurtner, K. R. (2006). Memory modulates color appearance. *Nature Neuroscience, 9*, 1367–1368.

Harada, T., Goda, N., Ogawa, T., Ito, M., Toyoda, H., Sadato, N., et al. (2009). Distribution of color-selective activity in the monkey inferior temporal cortex revealed by functional magnetic resonance imaging. *European Journal of Neuroscience, 30*, 1960–1970.

Harris, J. M., & Rogers, B. J. (1999). Going against the flow. *Trends in Cognitive Sciences, 3*, 449–450.

Harris, L., Atkinson, J., & Braddick, O. (1976). Visual contrast sensitivity of a 6-month-old infant measured by the evoked potential. *Nature, 246*, 570–571.

Hartline, H. K. (1938). The response of single optic nerve fibers of the vertebrate eye to illumination of the retina. *American Journal of Physiology, 121*, 400–415.

Hartline, H. K. (1940). The receptive fields of optic nerve fibers. *American Journal of Physiology, 130*, 690–699.

Hartline, H. K., Wagner, H. G., & Ratliff, F. (1956). Inhibition in the eye of *Limulus. Journal of General Physiology, 39*, 651–673.

Hayhoe, M., & Ballard, C. (2005). Eye movements in natural behavior. *Trends in Cognitive Sciences, 9*, 188–194.

Hecaen, H., & Angelerques, R. (1962). Agnosia for faces (prosopagnosia). *Archives of Neurology, 7*, 92–100.

Heesen, R. (2015). *The Young-(Helmholtz)-Maxwell theory of color vision.* Unpublished manuscript, Carnegie Mellon University, Pittsburgh, PA.

Heider, F., & Simmel, M. (1944). An experimental study of apparent behavior. *American Journal of Psychology, 13*, 243–259.

Heise, G. A., & Miller, G. A. (1951). An experimental study of auditory patterns. *American Journal of Psychology, 57*, 243–249.

Held, R., Birch, E., & Gwiazda, J. (1980). Stereoacuity of human infants. *Proceedings of the National Academy of Sciences, 77*, 5572–5574.

Helmholtz, H. von. (1860). *Handbuch der physiologischen Optik* (Vol. 2). Leipzig: Voss.

Helmholtz, H. von. (1911). *Treatise on physiological optics* (J. P. Southall, Ed. & Trans.; 3rd ed., Vols. 2 & 3). Rochester, NY: Optical Society of America. (Original work published 1866)

Henderson, J. M., & Hollingworth, A. (1999). High-level scene perception. *Annual Review of Psychology, 50*, 243–271.

Henderson, J. M., Shinkareva, S. V., Wang, J., Luke, S. G., & Olejarczyk, J. (2013). Predicting cognitive state from eye movements. *PLoS ONE, 8*(5): e64937.

Hering, E. (1878). *Zur Lehre vom Lichtsinn.* Vienna: Gerold.

Hering, E. (1905). Grundzüge der Lehre vom Lichtsinn. In *Handbuch der gesamter Augenheilkunde* (Vol. 3, Chap. 13). Berlin.

Hering, E. (1964). *Outlines of a theory of the light sense* (L. M. Hurvich & D. Jameson, Trans.). Cambridge, MA: Harvard University Press.

Hershenson, M. (Ed.). (1989). *The moon illusion.* Hillsdale, NJ: Erlbaum.

Herz, R. S., & Schooler, J. W. (2002). A naturalistic study of autobiographical memories evoked by olfactory and visual cues: Testing the Proustian hypothesis. *American Journal of Psychology, 115*, 21–32.

Hettinger, T. P., Myers, W. E., & Frank, M. E. (1990). Role of olfaction in perception of nontraditional "taste" stimuli. *Chemical Senses, 15*, 755–760.

Heywood, C. A., Cowey, A., & Newcombe, F. (1991). Chromatic discrimination in a cortically colour blind observer. *European Journal of Neuroscience, 3*, 802–812.

Hickman, J. S., & Hanowski, R. J. (2012). An assessment of commercial motor vehicle driver distraction using naturalistic driving data. *Traffic Injury Prevention, 13*, 612–619.

Hickock, G. (2009). Eight problems for the mirror neuron theory of action understanding in monkeys and humans. *Journal of Cognitive Neuroscience, 21*, 1229–1243.

Hickock, G., & Poeppel, D. (2007). The cortical organization of speech processing. *Nature Reviews Neuroscience, 8*, 393–401.

Hochberg, J. E. (1987). Machines should not see as people do, but must know how people see. *Computer Vision, Graphics and Image Processing, 39*, 221–237.

Hodgetts, W. E., & Liu, R. (2006). Can hockey playoffs harm your hearing? *CMAJ, 175*, 1541–1542.

Hofbauer, R. K., Rainville, P., Duncan, G. H., & Bushnell, M. C. (2001). Cortical representation of the sensory dimension of pain. *Journal of Neurophysiology, 86*, 402–411.

Hoffman, H. G., Doctor, J. N., Patterson, D. R., Carrougher, G. J., & Furness, T. A. III (2000). Virtual reality as an adjunctive pain control during burn wound care in adolescent patients. *Pain, 85*, 305–309.

Hoffman, H. G., Patterson, D. R., Seibel, E., Soltani, M., Jewett-Leahy, L., & Sharar, S. R. (2008). Virtual reality pain control during burn wound debridement in the hydrotank. *Clinical Journal of Pain, 24*, 299–304.

Hofman, P. M., Van Riswick, J. G. A., & Van Opstal, A. J. (1998). Relearning sound localization with new ears. *Nature Neuroscience, 1*, 417–421.

Holcombe, A. O. (2009). The binding problem. *Trends in Cognitive Neurosciences, 13*, 216–221.

Holden, C. (2004). Imaging studies show how brain thinks about pain. *Science, 303*, 1131.

Holley, A. (1991). Neural coding of olfactory information. In T. V. Getchell, R. L. Doty, L. M. Bartoshuk, & J. B. Snow (Eds.), *Smell and taste in health and disease* (pp. 329–343). New York: Raven Press.

Hollingworth, A., & Henderson, J. M. (2000). Semantic informativeness mediates the detection of changes in natural scenes. *Visual Cognition, 7*, 213–235.

Hollins, M., Bensmaia, S. J., & Roy, E. A. (2002). Vibrotaction and texture perception. *Behavioural Brain Research, 135*, 51–56.

Hollins, M., Bensmaia, S. J., & Washburn, S. (2001). Vibrotactile adaptation impairs discrimination of fine, but not coarse, textures. *Somatosensory & Motor Research, 18*, 253–262.

Hollins, M., & Risner, S. R. (2000). Evidence for the duplex theory of texture perception. *Perception & Psychophysics, 62*, 695–705.

Holway, A. H., & Boring, E. G. (1941). Determinants of apparent visual size with distance variant. *American Journal of Psychology, 54*, 21–37.

Howgate, S., & Plack, C. J. (2011). A behavioral measure of the cochlear changes underlying temporary threshold shifts. *Hearing Research, 277*, 78–87.

Hsiao, S. S., Johnson, K. O., Twombly, A., & DiCarlo, J. (1996). Form processing and attention effects in the somatosensory system. In O. Franzen, R. Johannson, & L. Terenius (Eds.), *Somesthesis and the neurobiology of the somatosensory cortex* (pp. 229–247). Basel: Biorkhauser Verlag.

Hsiao, S. S., O'Shaughnessy, D. M., & Johnson, K. O. (1993). Effects of selective attention on spatial form processing in monkey primary and secondary somatosensory cortex. *Journal of Neurophysiology, 70*, 444–447.

Huang, X., Baker, J., & Reddy, R. (2014). A historical perspective of speech recognition. *Communications of the ACM, 57*, 94–103.

Hubel, D. H. (1982). Exploration of the primary visual cortex, 1955–1978. *Nature, 299*, 515–524.

Hubel, D. H., & Wiesel, T. N. (1959). Receptive fields of single neurons in the cat's striate cortex. *Journal of Physiology, 148*, 574–591.

Hubel, D. H., & Wiesel, T. N. (1961). Integrative action in the cat's lateral geniculate body. *Journal of Physiology, 155*, 385–398.

Hubel, D. H., & Wiesel, T. N. (1965). Receptive fields and functional architecture in two non-striate visual areas (18 and 19) of the cat. *Journal of Neurophysiology, 28*, 229–289.

Hubel, D. H., & Wiesel, T. N. (1970). Cells sensitive to binocular depth in area 18 of the macaque monkey cortex. *Nature, 225*, 41–42.

Hubel, D. H., Wiesel, T. N., Yeagle, E. M., Lafer-Sousa, R., & Conway, B. R. (2015). Binocular stereoscopy in visual areas V-2, V-3, and V-3a of the macaque monkey. *Cerebral Cortex, 25*, 959–971.

Hughes, M. (1977). A quantitative analysis. In M. Yeston (Ed.), *Readings in Schenker analysis and other approaches* (pp. 144–164). New Haven, CT: Yale University Press.

Hummel, T., Delwihe, J. F., Schmidt, C., & Huttenbrink, K.-B. (2003). Effects of the form of glasses on the perception of wine flavors: A study in untrained subjects. *Appetite, 41*, 197–202.

Humphrey, A. L., & Saul, A. B. (1994). The temporal transformation of retinal signals in the lateral geniculate nucleus of the cat: Implications for cortical function. In D. Minciacchi, M. Molinari, G. Macchi, & E. G. Jones (Eds.), *Thalamic networks for relay and modulation* (pp. 81–89). New York: Pergamon Press.

Humphreys, G. W., & Riddoch, M. J. (2001). Detection by action: Neuropsychological evidence for action-defined templates in search. *Nature Neuroscience, 4*, 84–88.

Huron, D. (2006). *Sweet anticipation: Music and the psychology of expectation.* Cambridge, MA: MIT Press.

Huron, D., & Margulis, E. H. (2011). Music expectancy and thrills. In P. N. Juslin & J. A. Sloboda (Eds.), *Handbook of music and emotion: Theory, research, applications* (pp. 575–604). Oxford, UK: Oxford University Press.

Hurvich, L. M., & Jameson, D. (1957). An opponent-process theory of color vision. *Psychological Review, 64*, 384–404.

Huth, A. G., Nishimoto, S., Vo, A. T., & Gallant, J. L. (2012). A continuous semantic space describes the representation of thousands of objects and action categories across the human brain. *Neuron, 76*, 1210–1224.

Hyvärinin, J., & Poranen, A. (1978). Movement-sensitive and direction and orientation-selective cutaneous receptive fields in the hand area of the postcentral gyrus in monkeys. *Journal of Physiology, 283*, 523–537.

Iacoboni, M., Molnar-Szakacs, I., Gallese, V., Buccino, G., Mazziotta, J. C., & Rizzolatti, G. (2005). Grasping the intentions of others with one's own mirror neuron system. *PLoS Biology, 3*, 529–535.

Iannetti, G. D., Salomons, T. V., Moayedi, M., Mouraux, A., & Davis, K. D. (2013). Beyond metaphor: Contrasting mechanisms of social and physical pain. *Trends in Cognitive Sciences, 17*, 371–378.

Ilg, U. J. (2008). The role of areas MT and MST in coding of visual motion underlying the execution of smooth pursuit. *Vision Research, 48*, 2062–2069.

Ilg, U. J., Bridgeman, B., & Hoffmann, K. P. (1989). Influence of mechanical disturbance on oculomotor behavior. *Vision Research, 29*, 545–551.

Ishai, A., Pessoa, L., Bikle, P. C., & Ungerleider, L. G. (2004). Repetition suppression of faces is modulated by emotion. *Proceedings of the National Academy of Sciences USA, 101*, 9827–9832.

Ishai, A., Ungerleider, L. G., Martin, A., & Haxby, J. V. (2000). The representation of objects in the human occipital and temporal cortex. *Journal of Cognitive Neuroscience, 12*, 35–51.

Ishai, A., Ungerleider, L. G., Martin, A., Schouten, J. L., & Haxby, J. V. (1999). Distributed representation of objects in the human ventral visual pathway. *Proceedings of the National Academy of Sciences USA, 96*, 9379–9384.

Ittelson, W. H. (1952). *The Ames demonstrations in perception.* Princeton, NJ: Princeton University Press.

Itti, L., & Koch C. (2000). A saliency-based search mechanism for overt and covert shifts of visual attention. *Vision Research, 40*, 1489–1506.

Iversen, J. R., & Patel, A. D. (2008). Perception of rhythmic grouping depends on auditory experience. *Journal of the Acoustic Society of America, 124A*, 2263–2271.

Iversen, J. R., Repp, B. H, & Patel, A. D. (2009). Top-down control of rhythm perception modulates early auditory responses. *Annals of the New York Academy of Sciences, 1169*, 58–73.

Iwamura, Y. (1998). Representation of tactile functions in the somatosensory cortex. In J. W. Morley (Ed.), *Neural aspects of tactile sensation* (pp. 195–238). New York: Elsevier Science.

Jacobs, J., Weidman, C. T., Miller, J. F., Solway, A., Burke, J. F., Wei, X.-X., et al. (2013). Direct recordings of grid-like neuronal activity in human spatial navigation. *Nature Neuroscience, 9*, 1188–1190.

Jacobson, A., & Gilchrist, A. (1988). The ratio principle holds over a million-to-one range of illumination. *Perception and Psychophysics, 43*, 1–6.

Jaeger, S. R., McRae, J. F., Bava, C. M., Beresford, M. K., Hunter, D., Jia, Y., et al. (2013). A Mendelian trait for olfactory sensitivity affects odor experience and food selection. *Current Biology, 22*, 1601–1605.

James, W. (1981). *The principles of psychology* (Rev. ed.). Cambridge, MA: Harvard University Press. (Original work published 1890)

Janzen, G. (2006). Memory for object location and route direction in virtual large scale space. *Quarterly Journal of Experimental Psychology, 59*, 493–508.

Janzen, G., Janzen, C., & van Turennout, M. (2008). Memory consolidation of landmarks in good navigators. *Hippocampus, 18*, 40–47.

Janzen, G., & van Turennout, M. (2004). Selective neural representation of objects relevant for navigation. *Nature Neuroscience, 7*, 673–677.

Jeffress, L. A. (1948). A place theory of sound localization. *Journal of Comparative and Physiological Psychology, 41*, 35–39.

Jenkins, W. M., & Merzenich, M. M. (1987). Reorganization of neocortical representations after brain injury: A neurophysiological model of the bases of recovery from stroke. *Progress in Brain Research, 71*, 249–266.

Jensen, T. S., & Nikolajsen, L. (1999). Phantom pain and other phenomena after amputation. In P. D. Wall & R. Melzak (Eds.), *Textbook of pain* (pp. 799–814). New York: Churchill Livingstone.

Johansson, G. (1973). Visual perception of biological motion and a model for its analysis. *Perception & Psychophysics, 14*, 195–204.

Johansson, G. (1975). Visual motion perception. *Scientific American, 232*, 76–89.

Johnson, B. A., & Leon, M. (2007). Chemotopic odorant coding in a mammalian olfactory system. *Journal of Comparative Neurology, 503*, 1–34.

Johnson, B. A., Ong., J., & Michael, L. (2010). Glomerular activity patterns evoked by natural odor objects in the rat olfactory bulb and related to patterns evoked by major odorant components. *Journal of Comparative Neurology, 518*, 1542–1555.

Johnson, E. N., Hawken, M. J., & Shapley, R. (2008). The orientation selectivity of color-responsive neurons in macaque V1. *Journal of Neuroscience, 28*, 8096–8106.

Johnson, K. O. (2002). Neural basis of haptic perception. In H. Pashler & S. Yantis (Eds.), *Steven's handbook of experimental psychology* (3rd ed.): *Vol. 1. Sensation and perception* (pp. 537–583). New York: Wiley.

Johnson, S. P., & Aslin, R. N. (1995). Perception of object unity in 2-month-old infants. *Developmental Psychology, 31*, 739–745.

Johnson, S. P., Davidow, J., Hall-Haro, C., & Frank, M. C. (2008). Development of perceptual completion originates in information acquisition. *Developmental Psychology, 44*, 1214–1224.

Johnson, S. P., Slemmer, J. A., & Amso, D. (2004). Where infants look determines how they see: Eye movement and object perception performance in 3-month-olds. *Infancy, 6*, 185–201.

Jones, M. R., & Yee, W. (1993). Attending to auditory events: The role of temporal organization. In S. McAdams & E. Bigand (Eds.), *Thinking in sound: The cognitive psychology of human audition* (pp. 69–112). Oxford, UK: Oxford University Press.

Julesz, B. (1971). *Foundations of cyclopean perception.* Chicago: University of Chicago Press.

Kaas, J. H., Hackett, T. A., & Tramo, M. J. (1999). Auditory processing in primate cerebral cortex. *Current Opinion in Neurobiology, 9*, 164–170.

Kaiser, A., Schenck, W., & Moller, R. (2013). Solving the correspondence problem in stereo vision by internal simulation. *Adaptive Behavior, 21*, 239–250.

Kamitani, Y., & Tong, F. (2005). Decoding the visual and subjective contents of the human brain. *Nature Neuroscience, 8*, 679–685.

Kandel, E. R., & Jessell, T. M. (1991). Touch. In E. R. Kandel, J. H. Schwartz, & T. M. Jessell (Eds.), *Principles of neural science* (3rd ed., pp. 367–384). New York: Elsevier.

Kandel, F. I., Rotter, A., & Lappe, M. (2009). Driving is smoother and more stable when using the tangent point. *Journal of Vision, 9*(11), 1–11.

Kanizsa, G., & Gerbino, W. (1976). Convexity and symmetry in figure-ground organization. In M. Henle (Ed.), *Vision and artifact* (pp. 25–32). New York: Springer.

Kanwisher, N. (2003). The ventral visual object pathway in humans: Evidence from fMRI. In L. M. Chalupa & J. S. Werner (Eds.), *The visual neurosciences* (pp. 1179–1190). Cambridge, MA: MIT Press.

Kanwisher, N. (2010). Functional specificity in the human brain: A window into the functional architecture of the mind. *Proceedings of the National Academy of Sciences USA, 107*, 11163–11170.

Kanwisher, N., McDermott, J., & Chun, M. M. (1997). The fusiform face area: A module in human extrastriate cortex specialized for face perception. *Journal of Neuroscience, 17*, 4302–4311.

Kapadia, M. K., Westheimer, G., & Gilbert, C. D. (2000). Spatial distribution of contextual interactions in primary visual cortex and in visual perception. *Journal of Neurophsiology, 84*, 2048–2062.

Kaplan, G. (1969). Kinetic disruption of optical texture: The perception of depth at an edge. *Perception and Psychophysics, 6*, 193–198.

Karlson, P., & Lüscher, M. (1959). "Pheromones": A new term for a class of biologically active substances. *Nature, 183*, 55–56.

Katz, D. (1989). *The world of touch.* Trans. L. Kruger. Hillsdale, NJ: Erlbaum. (Original work published 1925)

Katz, J., & Gagliese, L. (1999). Phantom limb pain: A continuing puzzle. In R. J. Gatchel & D. C. Turk (Eds.), *Psychosocial factors in pain* (pp. 284–300). New York: Guilford Press.

Katzner, S., Busse, L., & Treue, S. (2009). Attention to the color of a moving stimulus modulates motion-signal processing in macaque area MT: Evidence for a unified attentional system. *Frontiers in Systems Neuroscience, 3*, 1–8.

Kauer, J. S. (1987). Coding in the olfactory system. In T. E. Finger & W. C. Silver (Eds.), *Neurobiology of taste and smell* (pp. 205–231). New York: Wiley.

Kaufman, L., & Rock, I. (1962a). The moon illusion. *Science, 136*, 953–961.

Kaufman, L., & Rock, I. (1962b). The moon illusion. *Scientific American, 207*, 120–132.

Kavšek, M., Granrud, C. E., & Yonas, A. (2009). Infants' responsiveness to pictorial depth cues in preferential-reaching studies: A meta-analysis. *Infant Behavior and Development, 32*, 245–253.

Keller, A., Zhuang, H., Chi., Q., Vosshall, L. B., & Matsunami, H. (2007). Genetic variation in a human odorant receptor alters odour perception. *Nature, 449*, 468–472.

Kellman, P., & Spelke, E. (1983). Perception of partly occluded objects in infancy. *Cognitive Psychology, 15*, 483–524.

Kerman, J., & Tomlinson, G. (2015). *Listen* (8th ed.). New York: St. Martin's Press.

Kersten, D., Mamassian, P., & Yuille, A. (2004). Object perception as Bayesian inference. *Annual Review of Psychology, 55*, 271–304.

Keysers, C., Kaas, J., & Gazzola, V. (2010). Somatosensation in social perception. *Nature Reviews Neuroscience, 11*, 417–428.

Keysers, C., Wicker, B., Gazzola, V., Anton, J.-L., Fogassi, L., & Gallese, V. (2004). A touching sight: SII/PV activation cueing the observation and experience of touch. *Neuron, 42*, 335–346.

Khanna, S. M., & Leonard, D. G. B. (1982). Basilar membrane tuning in the cat cochlea. *Science, 215*, 305–306.

Kiefer, J., von Ilberg, C., Reimer, B., Knecht, R., Gall, V., Diller, G., et al. (1996). Results of cochlear implantation in patients with severe to profound hearing loss: Implications for the indications. *Audiology, 37*, 382–395.

Kilner, J. (2011). More than on pathway to action understanding. *Trends in Cognitive Sciences, 15*, 352–357.

Kim, A., & Osterhout, L. (2005). The independence of combinatory semantic processing: Evidence from event-related potentials. *Journal of Memory and Language, 52*, 205–255.

Kim, U. K., Jorgenson, E., Coon, H., Leppert, M., Risch, N., & Drayna, D. (2003). Positional cloning of the human quantitative trait locus underlying taste sensitivity to phenylthiocarbamide. *Science, 299*, 1221–1225.

King, A. J., Schnupp, J. W. H., & Doubell, T. P. (2001). The shape of ears to come: Dynamic coding of auditory space. *Trends in Cognitive Sciences, 5*, 261–270.

King, W. L., & Gruber, H. E. (1962). Moon illusion and Emmert's law. *Science, 135*, 1125–1126.

Kish, D. (2012, April 13). *Sound vision: The consciousness of seeing with sound.* Presentation at Toward a Science of Consciousness, Tucson, AZ.

Kisilevsky, B. S., Hains, S. M. J., Brown, C. A., Lee, C. T., Cowperthwaite, B., Stutzman, S. S., et al. (2009). Fetal sensitivity to properties of maternal speech and language. *Infant Behavior and Development, 32*, 59–71.

Kisilevsky, B. S., Hains, S. M. J., Lee, K., Xie, X., Huang, H., Ye, H. H., et al. (2003). Effects of experience on fetal voice recognition. *Psychological Science, 14*, 220–224.

Klatzky, R. L., Lederman, S. J., Hamilton, C., Grindley, M., & Swendsen, R. H. (2003). Feeling textures through a probe: Effects of probe and surface geometry and exploratory factors. *Perception & Psychophysics, 65*, 613–631.

Klatzky, R. L., Lederman, S. J., & Metzger, V. A. (1985). Identifying objects by touch: An "expert system." *Perception and Psychophysics, 37*, 299–302.

Kleffner, D. A., & Ramachandran, V. S. (1992). On the perception of shape from shading. *Perception and Psychophysics, 52*, 18–36.

Klimecki, O. M., Leiberg, S., Ricard, M., & Singer, T. (2014). Differential pattern of functional brain plasticity after compassion and empathy training. *SCAN, 9*, 873–879.

Knill, D. C., & Kersten, D. (1991). Apparent surface curvature affects lightness perception. *Nature, 351*, 228–230.

Knopoff, L., & Hutchinson, W. (1983). Entropy as a measure of style: The influence of sample length. *Journal of Music Theory, 27*, 75–97.

Kobayakawa, K., Kobayakawa, R., Matsumoto, H., Oka, Y., Imai, T., Ikawa, M., et al. (2007). Innate versus learned odour processing in the mouse olfactory bulb. *Nature, 450*, 503–510.

Koelsch, S. (2005). Neural substrates of processing syntax and semantics in music. *Current Opinion in Neurobiology, 15*, 207–212.

Koelsch, S. (2014). Brain correlates of music-evoked emotions. *Nature Reviews Neuroscience, 15*, 170–180.

Koelsch, S., Gunter, T., Friederici, A. D., & Schroger, E. (2000). Brain indices of music processing: "Nonmusicians" are musical. *Journal of Cognitive Neuroscience, 12*, 520–541.

Koffka, K. (1935). *Principles of Gestalt psychology.* New York: Harcourt Brace.

Kohler, E., Keysers, C., Umilta, M. A., Fogassi, L., Gallese, V., & Rizzolatti, G. (2002). Hearing sounds, understanding actions: Action representation in mirror neurons. *Science, 297*, 846–848.

Kolb, N., & Whishaw, I. Q. (2003). *Fundamentals of neuropsychology* (5th ed.). New York: Worth.

Kondo, H. M., & Kashino, M. (2009). Involvement of the thalmocortical loop in the spontaneous switching of percepts in auditory streaming. *Journal of Neuroscience, 29*, 12695–12701.

Kourtzi, Z., & Kanwisher, N. (2000). Activation of human MT/MST by static images with implied motion. *Journal of Cognitive Neuroscience, 12*, 48–55.

Kourtzi, Z., Krekelberg, B., & van Wezel, R. J. A. (2008). Linking form and motion in the primate brain. *Trends in Cognitive Sciences, 12*, 230–236.

Kroner, T. (1881). Über die Sinnesempfindungen der Neugeborenen. *Breslauer aerzliche Zeitschrift.* (Cited in Peterson & Rainey, 1911)

Kross, E., Berman, M. G., Mischel, W., Smith, E. E., & Wager, T. D. (2011). Social rejection shares somatosensory representations with physical pain. *Proceedings for the National Academy of Sciences, 108*, 6270–6275.

Kruger, L. E. (1970). David Katz: Der Aufbau der Tastwelt [The world of touch: A synopsis]. *Perception and Psychophysics, 7*, 337–341.

Krumhansl, C. L. (1985). Perceiving tonal structure in music. *American Scientist, 73*, 371–378.

Krumhansl, C. L., & Kessler, E. J. (1982). Tracing the dynamic changes in perceived tonal organization in a spatial representation of musical keys. *Psychological Review, 89*, 334–368.

Kuffler, S. W. (1953). Discharge patterns and functional organization of mammalian retina. *Journal of Neurophysiology, 16*, 37–68.

Kuhl, P. K. (2000). Language, mind and brain: Experience alters perception. In M. Gazzaniga (Ed.), *The new cognitive neurosciences* (pp. 99–115). Cambridge, MA: MIT Press.

Kuhl, P. K. (2004). Early language acquisition: Cracking the speech code. *Nature Reviews Neuroscience, 5*, 831–843.

Kuhl, P. K. (2007). Is speech learning 'gated' by the social brain? *Developmental Science, 10*, 110–120.

Kuhl, P. K. (2010). Brain mechanisms in early language acquisition. *Neuron, 67*, 713–727.

Kuhl, P. K., Ramirez, R. R., Bosseler, A., Lin, J.-F. L., & Imada, T. (2014). Infants' brain responses to speech suggest Analysis by Synthesis. *Proceedings of the National Academy of Sciences, 111*, 11238–11245.

Kuhl, P. K., Stevens, E., Hayashi, A., Deguchi, T., Kiritani, S., & Iverson, P. (2006). Infants show a facilitation effect for native language phonetic perception between 6 and 12 months. *Developmental Science, 9*, F13–F21.

Kuhl, P. K., Tsao, F.-M., & Liu, H.-M. (2003). Foreign-language experience in infancy: Effects of short-term exposure and social interaction on phonetic learning. *Proceedings of the National Academy of Sciences, 100*, 9096–9101.

Kujawa, S. G., & Liberman, M. C. (2009). Adding insult to injury: Cochlear nerve degeneration after "temporary" noise-induced hearing loss. *Journal of Neuroscience, 45*, 14077–14085.

Kushner, T. (1993). *Angels in America.* New York: Theatre Communications Group.

LaBarbera, J. D., Izard, C. E., Vietze, P., & Parisi, S. A. (1976). Four- and six-month-old infants' visual responses to joy, anger, and neutral expressions. *Child Development, 47*, 535–538.

Laing, D. D., Doty, R. L., & Breipohl, W. (Eds.). (1991). *The human sense of smell.* New York: Springer.

Lamble, D., Kauranen, T., Laakso, M., & Summala, H. (1999). Cognitive load and detection thresholds in car following situations: Safety implications for using mobile (cellular) telephones while driving. *Accident Analysis and Prevention, 31*, 617–623.

Lamm, C., Batson, C. D., & Decdety, J. (2007). The neural substrate of human empathy: Effects of perspective-taking and cognitive appraisal. *Journal of Cognitive Neuroscience, 19*, 42–58.

Land, E. H. (1983). Recent advances in retinex theory and some implications for cortical computations: Color vision and the natural image. *Proceedings of the National Academy of Sciences, USA, 80*, 5163–5169.

Land, E. H. (1986). Recent advances in retinex theory. *Vision Research, 26*, 7–21.

Land, E. H., & McCann, J. J. (1971). Lightness and retinex theory. *Journal of the Optical Society of America, 61*, 1–11.

Land, M. F., & Hayhoe, M. (2001). In what ways do eye movements contribute to everyday activities? *Vision Research, 41*, 3559–3565.

Land, M. F., & Horwood, J. (1995). Which parts of the road guide steering? *Nature, 377*, 339–340.

Land, M. F., & Lee, D. N. (1994). Where we look when we steer. *Nature, 369*, 742–744.

Larsen, A., Madsen, K. H., Lund, T. E., & Bundesen, C. (2006). Images of illusory motion in primary visual cortex. *Journal of Cognitive Neuroscience, 18*, 1174–1180.

Lavie, N. (1995). Perceptual load as a major determinant of the locus of selection in visual attention. *Perception and Psychophysics, 56*, 183–197.

Lavie, N. (2005). Distracted and confused? Selective attention under load. *Trends in Cognitive Sciences, 9*, 75–82.

Lavie, N. (2010). Attention, distraction, and cognitive control under load. *Current Directions in Psychological Science, 19*, 143–148.

Lavie, N., & Driver, J. (1996). On the spatial extent of attention in object-based visual selection. *Perception and Psychophysics, 58*, 1238–1251.

Lawless, H. (1980). A comparison of different methods for assessing sensitivity to the taste of phenylthiocarbamide PTC. *Chemical Senses, 5*, 247–256.

Lawless, H. (2001). Taste. In E. B. Goldstein (Ed.), *Blackwell handbook of perception* (pp. 601–635). Oxford, UK: Blackwell.

Lederman, S. J., & Klatzky, R. L. (1987). Hand movements: A window into haptic object recognition. *Cognitive Psychology, 19*, 342–368.

Lederman, S. J., & Klatzky, R. L. (1990). Haptic classification of common objects: Knowledge-driven exploration. *Cognitive Psychology, 22*, 421–459.

Lee, D. N., & Aronson, E. (1974). Visual proprioceptive control of standing in human infants. *Perception and Psychophysics, 15*, 529–532.

LeGrand, Y. (1957). *Light, color and vision.* London: Chapman & Hall.

LeGrand, Y. (1959). About theories of color vision. *Proceedings of the National Academy of Sciences, 45*, 89–96.

Lerdahl, R., & Jackendoff, R. (1983). *A generative theory of tonal music.* Cambridge, MA: MIT Press.

Lesham, M. (1998). Salt preference in adolescence is predicted by common prenatal and infantile mineral fluid loss. *Physiology & Behavior, 63*, 699–704.

Lewis, E. R., Zeevi, Y. Y., & Werblin, F. S. (1969). Scanning electron microscopy of vertebrate visual receptors. *Brain Research, 15*, 559–562.

Li, F. F., Van Rullen, R., Koch, C., & Perona, P. (2002). Rapid natural scene categorization in the near absence of attention. *Proceedings of the National Academy of Sciences, 99*, 9596–9601.

Li, L., Sweet, B. T., & Stone, L. S. (2006). Humans can perceive heading without visual path information. *Journal of Vision, 6*, 874–881.

Li, X., Li, W., Wang, H., Cao, J., Maehashi, K., Huang, L., et al. (2005). Pseudogenization of a sweet-receptor gene accounts for cats' indifference toward sugar. *PLoS Genetics, 1*(1), e3.

Liberman, A. M., Cooper, F. S., Harris, K. S., & MacNeilage, P. F. (1963). A motor theory of speech perception. *Proceedings of the Symposium* on *Speech Communication Seminar,* Royal Institute of Technology, Stockholm, Paper D3, Volume II.

Liberman, A. M., Cooper, F. S., Shankweiler, D. P., & Studdert-Kennedy, M. (1967). Perception of the speech code. *Psychological Review, 74,* 431–461.

Liberman, M. C., & Dodds, L. W. (1984). Single-neuron labeling and chronic cochlear pathology: III. Stereocilia damage and alterations of threshold tuning curves. *Hearing Research, 16,* 55–74.

Lindquist, K. A., Wager, T. D., Kober, H., Mliss-Moreau, E., & Barrett, L. F. (2012). The brain basis of emotion: A meta-analytic review. *Behavioral and Brain Sciences, 35*(3), 121–143.

Lindsay, P. H., & Norman, D. A. (1977). *Human information processing* (2nd ed.). New York: Academic Press.

Litovsky, R. Y. (2012). Spatial release from masking. *Acoustics Today, 8*(2), 18–25.

Litovsky, R. Y., Colburn, H. S., Yost, W. A., & Guzman, S. J. (1999). The precedence effect. *Journal of the Acoustical Society of America, 106,* 1633–1654.

Litovsky, R. Y., Rakerd, B., Yin, T. C. T., & Hartmann, W. M. (1997). Psychophysical and physiological evidence for a precedence effect in the median saggital plane. *Journal of Neurophysiology, 77,* 2223–2226.

Liu, T., Abrams, J., & Carrasco, M. (2009). Voluntary attention enhances contrast appearance. *Psychological Science, 20,* 354–362.

Lomber, S. G., & Malhotra S. (2008). Double dissociation of "what" and "where" processing in auditory cortex. *Nature Neuroscience, 11,* 601–616.

London, J. (2004). *Hearing in time: Psychological aspects of musical meter.* New York: Oxford University Press.

Loomis, J. M., DaSilva, J. A., Fujita, N., & Fulusima, S. S. (1992). Visual space perception and visually directed action. *Journal of Experimental Psychology: Human Perception and Performance, 18,* 906–921.

Loomis, J. M., & Philbeck, J. W. (2008). Measuring spatial perception with spatial updating and action. In R. L. Klatzky, B. MacWhinney, & M. Behrmann (Eds.), *Embodiment, ego-space, and action* (pp. 1–43). New York: Taylor and Francis.

Lord, S. R., & Menz, H. B. (2000). Visual contributions to postural stability in older adults. *Gerontology, 46,* 306–310.

Lorteije, J. A. M., Kenemans, J. L., Jellema, T., van der Lubbe, R. H. J., de Heer, F., & van Wezel, R. J. A. (2006). Delayed response to animate implied motion n human motion processing areas. *Journal of Cognitive Neuroscience, 18,* 158–168.

Lotto, A. J., Hickok, G. S., & Holt, L. L. (2009). Reflections on mirror neurons and speech perception. *Trends in Cognitive Sciences, 13,* 110–114.

Lowenstein, W. R. (1960). Biological transducers. *Scientific American, 203,* 98–108.

Luck, S. J., Chelazzi, L., Hillyard, S. A., & Desimone, R. (1997). Neural mechanisms of spatial selective attention in areas V1, V2, and V4 of macaque visual cortex. *Journal of Neurophysiology, 77,* 24–42.

Lundy, R. F., Jr., & Contreras, R. J. (1999). Gustatory neuron types in rat geniculate ganglion. *Journal of Neurophysiology, 82,* 2970–2988.

Lyall, V., Heck, G. L., Phan, T.-H. T., Mummalaneni, S., Malik, S. A., Vinnikova, A. K., et al. (2005). Ethanol modulates the VR-1 variant amiloride-insensitive salt taste receptor: I. Effect on TRC volume and Na+ flux. *Journal of General Physiology, 125,* 569–585.

Lyall, V., Heck, G. L., Vinnikova, A. K., Ghosh, S., Phan, T.-H. T., Alam, R. I., et al. (2004). The mammalian amiloride-insensitive non-specific salt taste receptor is a vanilloid receptor-1 variant. *Journal of Physiology, 558,* 147–159.

Mack, A., & Clarke, J. (2012). Gist perception requires attention. *Visual Cognition, 20,* 300–327.

Mack, A., & Rock, I. (1998). *Inattentional blindness.* Cambridge, MA: MIT Press.

Maess, B., Koelsch, S., Gunter, T. C., & Friederici, A. D. (2001). Musical syntax is processed in Broca's area: An MEG study. *Nature Neuroscience, 4,* 540–545.

Maguire, E. A., Wollett, K., & Spiers, H. J. (2006). London taxi drivers and bus drivers: A structural MRI and neuropsychological analysis. *Hippocampus, 16,* 1091–1101.

Mainland, J. D., Keller, A., Li, Y. R., Zhou, T., Trimmer, C., Snyder, L. L., et al. (2014). The missense of smell: Functional variability in the human odorant receptor repertoire. *Nature Neuroscience, 17,* 114–120.

Malcolm, G. L., & Shomstein, S. (2015). Object-based attention in real-world scenes. *Journal of Experimental Psychology: General, 144,* 257–263.

Malhotra, S., & Lomber, S. G. (2007). Sound localization during homo-topic and hererotopic bilateral cooling deactivation of primary and nonprimary auditory cortical areas in the cat. *Journal of Neurophysiology, 97,* 26–43.

Malhotra, S., Stecker, G. C., Middlebrooks, J. C., & Lomber, S. G. (2008). Sound localization deficits during reversible deactivation of primary auditory cortex and/or the dorsal zone. *Journal of Neurophysiology, 99,* 1628–1642.

Malnic, B., Hirono, J., Sata, T., & Buck, L. B. (1999). Combinatorial receptor codes for odors. *Cell, 96,* 713–723.

Mamassian, P. (2004). Impossible shadows and the shadow correspondence problem. *Perception, 33,* 1279–1290.

Mamassian, P., Knill, D., & Kersten, D. (1998). The perception of cast shadows. *Trends in Cognitive Sciences, 2,* 288–295.

Marino, A. C., & Scholl, B. J. (2005). The role of closure in defining the "objects" of object-based attention. *Perception and Psychophysics, 67,* 1140–1149.A

Marr, D., & Poggio, T. (1979). A computation theory of human stereo vision. *Proceedings of the Royal Society of London B: Biological Sciences, 204,* 301–328.

Mather, G., Verstraten, F., & Anstis, S. (1998). *The motion aftereffect: A modern perspective.* Cambridge, MA: MIT Press.

Maxwell, J. C. (1855). Experiments on colour, as perceived by the Eye, with remarks on Colour-Blindness. *Transactions of the Royal Society of Edinburgh, 21,* 275–278.

Mayer, D. L., Beiser, A. S., Warner, A. F., Pratt, E. M., Raye, K. N., & Lang, J. M. (1995). Monocular acuity norms for the Teller Acuity Cards between ages one month and four years. *Investigative Ophthalmology and Visual Science, 36,* 671–685.

McAlpine, D. (2005). Creating a sense of auditory space. *Journal of Physiology, 566,* 21–22.

McAlpine, D., & Grothe, B. (2003). Sound localization and delay lines: Do mammals fit the model? *Trends in Neurosciences, 26,* 347–350.

McBurney, D. H. (1969). Effects of adaptation on human taste function. In C. Pfaffmann (Ed.), *Olfaction and taste* (pp. 407–419). New York: Rockefeller University Press.

McCarthy, G., Puce, A., Gore, J. C., & Allison, T. (1997). Face-specific processing in the human fusiform gyrus. *Journal of Cognitive Neuroscience, 9,* 605–610.

McCartney, P. (1970). *The long and winding road.* Apple Records.

McFadden, S. A. (1987). The binocular depth stereoacuity of the pigeon and its relation to the anatomical resolving power of the eye. *Vision Research, 27,* 1967–1980.

McFadden, S. A., & Wild, J. M. (1986). Binocular depth perception in the pigeon. *Journal of Experimental Analysis of Behavior, 45,* 149–160.

McGettigan, C., Fulkner, A., Altarelli, I., Obleser, J., Baverstock, H., & Scott, S. K. (2012). Speech comprehension aided by multiple modalities: Behavioural and neural interactions. *Neuropsychologia, 50,* 762–776.

McGurk, H., & MacDonald, T. (1976). Hearing lips and seeing voices. *Nature, 264,* 746–748.

McIntosh, R. D., & Lashley, G. (2008). Matching boxes: Familiar size influences action programming. *Neuropsychologica, 46*, 2441–2444.

McRae, J. F., Jaeger, S. R., Bava, C. M., Beresford, M. K., Hunter, D., Jia, Y., et al. (2013). Identification of region associated with variation in sensitivity to food-related odors in the human genome. *Current Biology, 23*, 1596–1600.

Mehler, J. (1981). The role of syllables in speech processing: Infant and adult data. *Transactions of the Royal Society of London, B295*, 333–352.

Meister, I. G., Wilson, S. M., Deblieck, C., Wu, A. D., & Iacoboni, M. (2007). The essential role of premotor cortex in speech perception. *Current Biology, 17*, 1692–1696.

Meltzoff, A. N. (1995). Understanding the intentions of others: Re-enactments of intended acts by 18-month-old children. *Developmental Psychology, 31*, 838–850.

Meltzoff, A. N., & Moore, M. K. (1977). Imitation of facial and manual gestures by human neonates. *Science, 198*, 75–78.

Meltzoff, A. N., Williamson, R. A., & Marshall, P. J. (2013). Developmental perspectives on action science: Lessons from infant imitation and cognitive neuroscience. In W. Prinz, M. Beisert, & A. Herwig (Eds.), *Action science: Foundations of an emerging discipline* (pp. 281–306). Cambridge, MA: MIT Press.

Melzack, R. (1992). Phantom limbs. *Scientific American, 266*, 121–126.

Melzack, R. (1999). From the gate to the neuromatrix. *Pain, Suppl. 6*, S121–S126.

Melzack, R., & Wall, P. D. (1965). Pain mechanisms: A new theory. *Science, 150*, 971–979.

Melzack, R., & Wall, P. D. (1983). *The challenge of pain.* New York: Basic Books.

Melzack, R., & Wall, P. D. (1988). *The challenge of pain* (Rev. ed.). New York: Penguin Books.

Menashe, I., Man, O., Lancet, D., & Gilad, Y. (2003). Different noses for different people. *Nature Genetics, 34*, 143–144.

Meng, M., Cherian, T., Singal, G., & Sinha, P. (2012). Lateralization of face processing in the human brain. *Proceedings of the Royal Society B, 279*, 2052–2061.

Mennella, J. A., Jagnow, C. P., & Beauchamp, G. K. (2001). Prenatal and postnatal flavor learning by human infants. *Pediatrics, 107*(6), 1–6.

Mennella, J. A., Johnson, A., & Beauchamp, G. K. (1995). Garlic ingestion by pregnant women alters the odor of amniotic fluid. *Chemical Senses, 20*, 207–209.

Menz, M. D., & Freeman, R. D. (2003). Stereoscopic depth processing in the visual cortex: A coarse-to-fine mechanism. *Nature Neuroscience, 6*, 59–65.

Menzel, R., & Backhaus, W. (1989). Color vision in honey bees: Phenomena and physiological mechanisms. In D. G. Stavenga & R. C. Hardie (Eds.), *Facets of vision* (pp. 281–297). Berlin: Springer-Verlag.

Menzel, R., Ventura, D. F., Hertel, H., deSouza, J., & Greggers, U. (1986). Spectral sensitivity of photoreceptors in insect compound eyes: Comparison of species and methods. *Journal of Comparative Physiology, 158A*, 165–177.

Merigan, W. H., & Maunsell, J. H. R. (1993). How parallel are the primate visual pathways? *Annual Review of Neuroscience, 16*, 369–402.

Merskey, H. (1991). The definition of pain. *European Journal of Psychiatry, 6*, 153–159.

Mesgarani, N., Cheung, C., Johnson, K., & Chang, E. F. (2014). Phonetic feature encoding in human superior temporal gyrus. *Science, 343*, 1006–1010.

Meso, A. I., & Zanker, J. M. (2009). Speed encoding in correlation motion detectors as a consequence of spatial structure. *Biological Cybernetics, 100*, 361–370.

Meyer, K., Kaplan, J. T., Essex, R., Damasio, H., & Damasio, A. (2011). Seeing touch is correlated with content specific activity in primary somatosensory cortex. *Cerebral Cortex, 21*, 2113–2121.

Meyer, L. B. (1956). *Emotion and meaning in music.* Chicago: University of Chicago Press.

Micelli, G., Gainotti, G., Caltagirone, C., & Masullo, C. (1980). Some aspects of phonological impairment in aphasia. *Brain and Language, 11*, 159–169.

Micheyl, C., & Oxenham, A. J. (2010). Objective and subjective psychophysical measures of auditory stream integration and segregation. *Journal of the Association for Research in Otolaryngology, 11*, 709–724.

Miller, G. A., & Heise, G. A. (1950). The trill threshold. *Journal of the Acoustical Society of America, 22*, 637–683.

Miller, G. A., & Isard, S. (1963). Some perceptual consequences of linguistic rules. *Journal of Verbal Learning and Verbal Behavior, 2*, 212–228.

Miller, J., & Carlson, L. (2011). Selecting landmarks in novel environments. *Psychonomic Bulletin & Review, 18*, 184–191.

Miller, J. D. (1974). Effects of noise on people. *Journal of the Acoustical Society of America, 56*, 729–764.

Miller, S. L., & Maner J. K. (2010). Scent of a woman: Men's testosterone responses to olfactory ovulation cues. *Psychological Science, 21*, 276–283.

Milner, A. D., & Goodale, M. A. (1995). *The visual brain in action.* New York: Oxford University Press.

Mishkin, M., Ungerleider, L. G., & Macko, K. A. (1983). Object vision and spatial vision: Two central pathways. *Trends in Neuroscience, 6*, 414–417.

Molenberghs, P., Hayward, L., Mattingley, J. B., & Cunnington, R. (2012). Activation patterns during action observation are modulated by context in mirror system areas. *NeuroImage, 59*, 608–615.

Moller, A. R. (2006). *Hearing: Anatomy, physiology, and disorders of the auditory system* (2nd ed.). San Diego: Academic Press.

Mollon, J. D. (1989). "Tho' she kneel'd in that place where they grew..."*Journal of Experimental Biology, 146*, 21–38.

Mollon, J. D. (1997). "Tho she kneel'd in that place where they grew …" The uses and origins of primate colour visual information. In A. Byrne & D. R. Hilbert (Eds.), *Readings on color: Vol. 2. The science of color* (pp. 379–396). Cambridge, MA: MIT Press.

Mollon, J. D. (2003a). Introduction: Thomas Young and the trichromatic theory of colour vision. In J. D. Mollon, J. Pokorny, & K. Knoblauch (Eds.), *Normal and defective color vision.* Oxford, UK: Oxford University Press.

Mollon, J. D. (2003b). The origins of modern color science. In S. Shevell (Ed.), *The science of color* (pp. 1–39). Oxford, UK: Elsevier.

Mondloch, C. J., Dobson, K. S., Parsons, J., & Maurer, D. (2004). Why 8-year-olds cannot tell the difference between Steve Martin and Paul Newman: Factors contributing to the slow development of sensitivity to the spacing of facial features. *Journal of Experimental Child Psychology, 89*, 159–181.

Mondloch, C. J., Geldart, S., Maurer, D., & LeGrand, R. (2003). Developmental changes in face processing skills. *Journal of Experimental Child Psychology, 86*, 67–84.

Montagna, W., & Parakkal, P. F. (1974). *The structure and function of skin* (3rd ed.). New York: Academic Press.

Mon-Williams, M., & Tresilian, J. R. (1999). Some recent studies on the extraretinal contribution to distance perception. *Perception, 28*, 167–181.

Monzée, J., Lamarre, Y., & Smith, A. M. (2003). The effects of digital anesthesia on force control using a precision grip. *Journal of Neurophysiology, 89*, 672–683.

Moon, R. J., Cooper, R. P., & Fifer, W. P. (1993). Two-day-olds prefer their native language. *Infant Behavior and Development, 16*, 495–500.

Moore, B. C. J. (1995). *Perceptual consequences of cochlear damage.* Oxford, UK: Oxford University Press.

Morton, J., & Johnson, M. H. (1991). CONSPEC and CONLEARN: A two-process theory of infant face recognition. *Psychological Review, 98*, 164–181.

Moser, E. I., Moser, M.-B., & Roudi, Y. (2014). Network mechanisms of grid cells. *Philosophical Transactions of the Royal Society B, 369*, 20120511.

Moser, E. I., Roudi, Y., Witter, M. P., Kentros, C., Bonhoeffer, T., & Moser, M.-B. (2014). Grid cells and cortical representation. *Nature Reviews Neuroscience, 15*, 466–481.

Moulton, D. G. (1977). Minimum odorant concentrations detectable by the dog and their implications for olfactory receptor sensitivity. In D. Miller-Schwarze & M. M. Mozell (Eds.), *Chemical signals in vertebrates* (pp. 455–464). New York: Plenum Press.

Mountcastle, V. B., & Powell, T. P. S. (1959). Neural mechanisms subserving cutaneous sensibility, with special reference to the role of afferent inhibition in sensory perception and discrimination. *Bulletin of the Johns Hopkins Hospital, 105*, 201–232.

Movshon, J. A., & Newsome, W. T. (1992). Neural foundations of visual motion perception. *Current Directions in Psychological Science, 1*, 35–39.

Mozell, M. M., Smith, B. P., Smith, P. E., Sullivan, R. L., & Swender, P. (1969). Nasal chemoreception in flavor identification. *Archives of Otolaryngology, 90*, 131–137.

Mueller, K. L., Hoon, M. A., Erlenbach, I., Chandrashekar, J., Zuker, C. S., & Ryba, N. J. P. (2005). The receptors and coding logic for bitter taste. *Nature, 434*, 225–229.

Mukamel, R., Ekstrom, A. D., Kaplan, J., Iacoboni, M., & Fried, I. (2010). Single neuron responses in humans during execution and observation of actions. *Current Biology, 20*, 750–756.

Mullally, S. L., & Maguire, E. A. (2011). A new role for the parahippocapal cortex in representing space. *Journal of Neuroscience, 31*, 7441–7449.

Murphy, C., & Cain, W. S. (1980). Taste and olfaction: Independence vs. interaction. *Physiology and Behavior, 24*, 601–606.

Murphy, K. J., Racicot, C. I., & Goodale, M. A. (1996). The use of visuomotor cues as a strategy for making perceptual judgements in a patient with visual form agnosia. *Neuropsychology, 10*, 396–401.

Murray, M. M., & Spierer, L. (2011). Multisensory integration: What you see is where you hear. *Current Biology, 21*, R229–R231.

Murray, S. O., Olshausen, B. A., & Woods, D. L. (2003). Processing shape, motion and three-dimensional shape-from-motion in the human cortex. *Cerebral Cortex, 13*, 508–516.

Murthy, V. N. (2011). Olfactory maps in the brain. *Annual Review of Neuroscience, 34*, 233–258.

Myers, D. G. (2004). *Psychology*. New York: Worth.

Mythbusters. (2007). Episode 71: Pirate special. Program first aired on the Discovery Channel, January 17, 2007.

Naselaris, T., Prenger, R., Kay, K., Oliver, M., & Gallant, J. (2009). Bayesian reconstruction of natural images from human brain activity. *Neuron, 63*, 902–915.

Nassi, J. J., & Callaway, E. M. (2009). Parallel processing strategies of the primate visual system. *Nature Reviews Neuroscience, 10*, 360–372.

Nathans, J., Thomas, D., & Hogness, D. S. (1986). Molecular genetics of human color vision: The genes encoding blue, green, and red pigments. *Science, 232*, 193–202.

Nationwide Insurance. (2008, May). Driving while distracted: Public relations research. www.nationwide.com/pdf/dwd-2008-survey-results.pdf.

Natu, V., & O'Toole, A. J. (2011). The neural processing of familiar and unfamiliar faces: A review and synopsis. *British Journal of Psychology, 102*, 726–747.

Neff, W. D., Fisher, J. F., Diamond, I. T., & Yela, M. (1956). Role of the auditory cortex in discrimination requiring localization of sound in space. *Journal of Neurophysiology, 19*, 500–512.

Neisser, U., & Becklen, R. (1975). Selective looking: Attending to visually specified events. *Cognitive Psychology, 7*, 480–494.

Neri, P. (2005). A stereoscopic look at visual cortex. *Journal of Neurophysiology, 93*, 1823–1826.

Neri, P., Bridge, H., & Heeger D. J. (2004). Stereoscopic processing of absolute and relative disparity in human visual cortex. *Journal of Neurophysiology, 92*, 1880–1891.

Newsome, W. T., & Paré, E. B. (1988). A selective impairment of motion perception following lesions of the middle temporal visual area (MT). *Journal of Neuroscience, 8*, 2201–2211.

Newsome, W. T., Shadlen, M. N., Zohary, E., Britten, K. H., & Movshon, J. A. (1995). Visual motion: Linking neuronal activity to psychophysical performance. In M. S. Gazzaniga (Ed.), *The cognitive neurosciences* (pp. 401–414). Cambridge, MA: MIT Press.

Newton, I. (1704). *Optiks*. London: Smith and Walford.

Newtson, D., & Engquist, G. (1976). The perceptual organization of ongoing behavior. *Journal of Experimental Psychology: General, 130*, 29–58.

Nickerson, D., & Newhall, S. M. (1943). A psychological color solid. *Journal of the Optical Society of America, 33*, 419–421.

Nikonov, A. A., Finger, T. E., & Caprio, J. (2005). Beyond the olfactory bulb: An odotopic map in the forebrain. *Proceedings of the National Academy of Sciences, 102*, 18688–18693.

Nodal, F. R., Kacelnik, O., Bajo, V. M., Bizley, J. K., Moore, D. R., & King, A. J. (2010). Lesions of the auditory cortex impair azimuthal sound localization and its recalibration in ferrets. *Journal of Neurophysiology, 103*, 1209–1225.

Norcia, A. M., & Tyler, C. W. (1985). Spatial frequency sweep VEP: Visual acuity during the first year of life. *Vision Research, 25*, 1399–1408.

Nordby, K. (1990). Vision in a complete achromat: A personal account. In R. F. Hess, L. T. Sharpe, & K. Nordby (Eds.), *Night vision* (pp. 290–315). Cambridge, UK: Cambridge University Press.

Norman-Haignere, S., Kanwisher, N., & McDermott, J. H. (2013). Cortical pitch regions in humans respond primarily to resolved harmonics and are located in specific tonotopic regions of anterior auditory cortex. *Journal of Neuroscience, 33*, 19451–19469.

Noton, D., & Stark, L. W. (1971). Scanpaths in eye movements during pattern perception. *Science, 171*, 308–311.

Novick, J. M., Trueswell, J. C., & Thomson-Schill, S. L. (2005). Cognitive control and parsing: Reexamining the role of Broca's area in sentence comprehension. *Cognitive, Affective and Behavioral Neuroscience, 5*, 263–281.

Novotny, M., Harvey, S., Jemiolo, B., & Alberts, J. (1985). Synthetic pheromones that promote inter-male aggression in mice. *Proceedings of the National Academy of Sciences, 82*, 2059–2061.

Nozaradan, S., Peretz, I., Missal, M., & Mouraux, A. (2011). Tagging the neuronal entrainment to beat and meter. *Journal of Neuroscience, 31*, 10234–10240.

O'Craven, K. M., Downing, P. E., & Kanwisher, N. (1999). fMRI evidence for objects as the units of attentional selection. *Nature, 401*, 584–587.

O'Doherty, J., Rolls, E. T., Francis, S., Bowtell, R., McGlone, F., Kobal, G., et al. (2000). Sensory-specific satiety-related olfactory activation of the human orbitofrontal cortex. *Neuroreport, 11*, 893–897.

O'Keefe, J., & Dostrovsky, J. (1971). The hippocampus as a spatial map. Preliminary evidence from unit activity in the freely-moving rat. *Brain Research, 34*, 171–175.

O'Keefe, J., & Nadel, L. (1978). *The hippocampus as a cognitive map*. Oxford, UK: Clarendon Press.

O'Toole, A. J. (2007). Face recognition algorithms surpass humans matching faces over changes in illumination. *IEE Transactions on Pattern Analysis and Machine Intelligence, 29*, 1642–1646.

O'Toole, A. J., Abdi, H., Jiang, F., & Phillips, P. J. (2007). Fusing face recognition algorithms and humans. *IEEE Transactions on Systems, Man and Cybernetics, 37,* 1149–1155.

O'Toole, A. J., Harms, J., Snow, S. L., Hurst, D. R., Pappas, M. R., & Abdi, H. (2005). A video database of moving faces and people. *IEE Transactions on Pattern Analysis and Machine Intelligence, 27,* 812–816.

Oberman, L. M., Hubbard, E. M., McCleery, J. P., Altschuler, E. L., Ramachandran, V. S., & Pineda, J. (2005). EEG evidence for mirror neuron dysfunction in autism spectrum disorders. *Cognitive Brain Research, 24,* 190–198.

Oberman, L. M., Ramachandran, V. S., & Pineda, J. A. (2008). Modulation of mu suppression in children with autism spectrum disorders in response to familiar or unfamiliar stimuli: The mirror neuron hypothesis. *Neuropsychologia, 46,* 1558–1565.

Ohzawa, I. (1998). Mechanisms of stereoscopic vision: The disparity energy model. *Current Opinion in Neurobiology, 8,* 509–515.

Okamoto, T., Teismann, H., Kakigi, R., & Pantev, C. (2011). Broadened population-level frequency tuning in human auditory cortex of portable music player users. *PLoS ONE, 6*(3): e17022. Doi:10.1371/journal.pone.0017022.

Oliva, A., & Schyns, P. G. (2000). Diagnostic colors mediate scene recognition. *Cognitive Psychology, 41,* 176–210.

Oliva, A., & Torralba, A. (2001). Modeling the shape of the scene: A holistic representation of the spatial envelope. *International Journal of Computer Vision, 42,* 145–175.

Oliva, A., & Torralba, A. (2006). Building the gist of a scene: The role of global image features in recognition. *Progress in Brain Research, 155,* 23–36.

Oliva, A., & Torralba, A. (2007). The role of context in object recognition. *Trends in Cognitive Sciences, 11,* 521–527.

Olkkonen, M., Witzel, C., Hansen, T., & Gegenfurtner, K. R. (2010). Categorical color constancy for real surfaces. *Journal of Vision, 10*(9), 1–22.

Olshausen, B. A., & Field, D. J. (2004). Sparse coding of sensory inputs. *Current Opinion in Neurobiology, 14,* 481–487.

Olsho, L. W., Koch, E. G., Carter, E. A., Halpin, C. F., & Spetner, N. B. (1988). Pure-tone sensitivity of human infants. *Journal of the Acoustical Society of America, 84,* 1316–1324.

Olsho, L. W., Koch, E. G., Halpin, C. F., & Carter, E. A. (1987). An observer-based psychoacoustic procedure for use with young infants. *Developmental Psychology, 23,* 627–640.

Olson, C. R., & Freeman, R. D. (1980). Profile of the sensitive period for monocular deprivation in kittens. *Experimental Brain Research, 39,* 17–21.

Olson, H. (1967). *Music, physics, and engineering* (2nd ed.). New York: Dover.

Olson, R. L., Hanowski, R. J., Hickman, J. S., & Bocanegra, J. (2009). Driver distraction in commercial vehicle operations. U. S. Department of Transportation Report No. FMCSA-RRR-09-042.

Orban, G. A., Vandenbussche, E., & Vogels, R. (1984). Human orientation discrimination tested with long stimuli. *Vision Research, 24,* 121–128.

Osmanski, B. F., Martin, C., Montaldo, G., Laniece, P., Pain, F., Tanter, M., & Gurden, H. (2014). Functional ultrasound imaging reveals different odor-evoked patterns of vascular activity in the main olfactory bulb and the anterior piriform cortex. *Neuroimage, 95,* 176–184.

Osterhout, L., McLaughlin, J., & Bersick, M. (1997). Event-related brain potentials and human language. *Trends in Cognitive Sciences, 1,* 203–209.

Oxenham, A. J. (2013). The perception of musical tones. In D. Deutsch (Ed.), *The psychology of music* (3rd ed., pp. 1–33). New York: Elsevier.

Oxenham, A. J., Micheyl, C., Keebler, M. V., Loper, A., & Santurette, S. (2011). Pitch perception beyond the traditional existence region of pitch. *Proceedings of the National Academy of Sciences, 108,* 7629–7634.

Pack, C. C., & Born, R. T. (2001). Temporal dynamics of a neural solution to the aperture problem in visual area MT of macaque brain. *Nature, 409,* 1040–1042.

Pack, C. C., Livingston, M. S., Duffy, K. R., & Born, R. T. (2003). End-stopping and the aperture problem: Two-dimensional motion signals in macaque V1. *Neuron, 59,* 671–680.

Palmer, A. R. (1987). Physiology of the cochlear nerve and cochlear nucleus. In M. P. Haggard & E. F. Evans (Eds.), *Hearing* (pp. 838–855). Edinburgh: Churchill Livingstone.

Palmer, C. (1997). Music performance. *Annual Review of Psychology, 48,* 115–138.

Palmer, S. E. (1975). The effects of contextual scenes on the identification of objects. *Memory and Cognition, 3,* 519–526.

Palmer, S. E. (1992). Common region: A new principle of perceptual grouping. *Cognitive Psychology, 24,* 436–447.

Palmer, S. E., & Rock, I. (1994). Rethinking perceptual organization: The role of uniform connectedness. *Psychonomic Bulletin and Review, 1,* 29–55.

Paré, M., Smith, A. M., & Rice, F. L. (2002). Distribution and terminal arborizations of cutaneous mechanoreceptors in the glabrous finger pads of the monkey. *Journal of Comparative Neurology, 445,* 347–359.

Parker, A. J. (2007). Binocular depth perception and the cerebral cortex. *Nature Reviews Neuroscience, 8,* 379–391.

Parkhi, O. M., Vedaldi, A., Zisserman, A., & Jawahar, C. V. (2012). Cats and dogs. *Proceedings of the IEEE Conference on Computer Vision and Pattern Recognition (CVPR).*

Parkhurst, D., Law, K., & Niebur, E. (2002). Modeling the role of salience in the allocation of overt visual attention. *Vision Research, 42,* 107–123.

Parkin, A. J. (1996). *Explorations in cognitive neuropsychology.* Oxford, UK: Blackwell.

Pascalis, O., de Schonen, S., Morton, J., Deruelle, C., & Fabre-Grenet, M. (1995). Mother's face recognition by neonates: A replication and an extension. *Infant Behavior and Development, 18,* 79–85.

Pascual-Leone, A., Amedi, A., Fregni, F., & Merabet, L. B. (2005). The plastic human brain cortex. *Annual Review of Neuroscience, 28,* 377–401.

Pasternak, T., & Merigan, E. H. (1994). Motion perception following lesions of the superior temporal sulcus in the monkey. *Cerebral Cortex, 4,* 247–259.

Patel, A. D. (2008). *Music, language, and the brain.* New York: Oxford University Press.

Patel, A. D., Gibson, E., Ratner, J., Besson, M., & Holcomb, P. J. (1998). Processing syntactic relations in language and music: An event-related potential study. *Journal of Cognitive Neuroscience, 10,* 717–733.

Peacock, G. (1855). *Life of Thomas Young MD, FRS.* London: John Murray.

Pecka, M., Bran, A., Behrend, O., & Grothe, B. (2008). Interaural time difference processing in the mammalian medial superior olive: The role of glycinergic inhibition. *Journal of Neuroscience, 28,* 6914–6925.

Pei, Y.-C., Hsiao, S. S., Craig, J. C., & Bensmaia, S. J. (2011). Neural mechanisms of tactile motion integration in somatosensory cortex. *Neuron, 69,* 536–547.

Pelchat, M. L., Bykowski, C., Duke, F. F., & Reed, D. R. (2011). Excretion and perception of a characteristic odor in urine after asparagus ingestion: A psychophysical and genetic study. *Chemical Senses, 36,* 9–17.

Pelphrey, K. A., Mitchell, T, V., McKeown, M, J., Goldstein, J., Allison, T., & McCarthy, G. (2003). Brain activity evoked by the perception of human walking: Controlling for meaningful coherent motion. *Journal of Neuroscience, 23,* 6819–6825.

Pelphrey, K. A., Morris, J., Michelich, C., Allison, T., & McCarthy, G. (2005). Functional anatomy of biological motion perception in posterior temporal cortex: An fMRI study of eye, mouth and hand movements. *Cerebral Cortex, 15,* 1866–1876.

Penfield, W., & Rasmussen, T. (1950). *The cerebral cortex of man.* New York: Macmillan.

Peng, J.-H., Tao, Z.-A., & Huang, Z.-W. (2007). Risk of damage to hearing from personal listening devices in young adults. *Journal of Otolaryngology, 36,* 181–185.

Pereira, C. S., Teixeira, J., Figueiredo, P., Xavier, J., Castro, S. L., & Brattico, E. (2011). Music and emotions in the brain: Familiarity matters. *PLoS One, 6*(11), e27241, 1–9.

Perl, E. R. (2007). Ideas about pain, a historical view. *Nature Reviews Neuroscience, 8,* 71–80.

Perl, E. R., & Kruger, L. (1996). Nociception and pain: Evolution of concepts and observations. In L. Kruger (Ed.), *Pain and touch* (pp. 180–211). San Diego, CA: Academic Press.

Perrett, D. I., Rolls, E. T., & Caan, W. (1982). Visual neurons responsive to faces in the monkey temporal cortex. *Experimental Brain Research, 7,* 329–342.

Perrodin, C., Kayser, C., Logothetis, N. K., & Petkov, C. I. (2011). Voice cells in the primate temporal lobe. *Current Biology, 21,* 1408–1415.

Peters, J. (2004, November 26). "Hi, I'm your car. Don't let me distract you." *New York Times.*

Peterson, F., & Rainey, L. H. (1911). The beginnings of mind in the newborn. *Bulletin of the Lying-In Hospital, 7,* 99–122.

Peterson, M. A. (1994). Object recognition processes can and do operate before figure-ground organization. *Current Directions in Psychological Science, 3,* 105–111.

Peterson, M. A. (2001). Object perception. In E. B. Goldstein (Ed.), *Blackwell handbook of perception* (pp. 168–203). Oxford, UK: Blackwell.

Peterson, M. A., & Kimchi, R. (2013). Perceptual organization in vision. In D. Reisberg (Ed.), *The Oxford handbook of cognitive psychology* (pp. 9–31). New York: Oxford University Press.

Peterson, M. A., & Salvagio, E. (2008). Inhibitory competition in figure-ground perception: Context and convexity. *Journal of Vision, 8*(16), 1–13.

Pfaffmann, C. (1974). Specificity of the sweet receptors of the squirrel monkey. *Chemical Senses, 1,* 61–67.

Pfeiffer, C. A., & Johnston, R. E. (1994). Hormonal and behavioral responses of male hamsters to females and female odors: Roles of olfaction, the vemeronasal system, and sexual experience. *Physiology and Behavior, 55,* 129–138.

Philbeck, J. W., Loomis, J. M., & Beall, A. C. (1997). Visually perceived location is an invariant in the control of action. *Perception & Psychophysics, 59,* 601–612.

Phillips, J. R., & Johnson, K. O. (1981). Tactile spatial resolution: II: Neural representation of bars, edges, and gratings in monkey primary afferent. *Journal of Neurophysiology, 46,* 1177–1191.

Phillips-Silver, J., & Trainor, L. J. (2005). Feeling the beat: Movement influences infant rhythm perception. *Science, 308,* 1430.

Phillips-Silver, J., & Trainor, L. J. (2007). Hearing what the body feels: Auditory encoding of rhythmic movement. *Cognition, 105,* 533–546.

Piqueras-Fiszman, G., Alcaide, J., Roura, E., & Spence, C. (2012). Is it the plate or is it the food? Assessing the influence of the color (black or white) and shape of the plate on the perception of the food placed on it. *Food Quality and Preference, 24,* 205–208.

Pitcher, D., Dilks, D. D., Saxe, R. R., Triantafyllou, C., & Kanwisher, N. (2011). Differential selectivity for dynamic versus static in face-selective cortical regions. *Neuroimage, 56,* 2356–2363.

Plack, C. J. (2005). *The sense of hearing.* New York: Psychology Press.

Plack, C. J. (2014). *The sense of hearing* (2nd ed.). New York: Psychology Press.

Plack, C. J., Barker, D., & Hall, D. A. (2014). Pitch coding and pitch processing in the human brain. *Hearing Research, 307,* 53–64.

Plack, C. J., Barker, D., & Prendergast, G. (2014). Perceptual consequences of "hidden" hearing loss. *Trends in Hearing, 18,* 1–11.

Plack, C. J., Drga, V., & Lopez-Poveda, E. (2004). Inferred basilar-membrane response functions for listeners with mild to moderate sensorineural hearing loss. *Journal of the Acoustical Society of America, 115,* 1684–1695.

Plassmann, H., O'Doherty, J., Shiv, B., & Rangel, A. (2008). Marketing actions can modulate neural representations of experienced pleasantness. *Proceedings of the National Academy of Sciences, 105,* 1050–1054.

Plug, C., & Ross, H. E. (1994). The natural moon illusion: A multifactor account. *Perception, 23,* 321–333.

Poggio, G. F., Gonzalez, F., & Krause, F. (1988). Stereoscopic mechanisms in monkey visual cortex: Binocular correlation and disparity selectivity. *Journal of Neuroscience, 8,* 4531–4550.

Pointer, M. R., & Attridge, G. G. (1998). The number of discernible colours. *Color Research and Application, 23,* 52–54.

Pokorny, J., Shevell, S. K., & Smith, V. C. (1991). Color appearance and color constancy. In P. Gouras (Ed.), *The perception of color: Vol. 6. Vision and visual dysfunction* (pp. 43–61). Boca Raton, FL: CRC Press.

Porter, R. H., Cernoch, J. M., & McLaughlin, F. J. (1983). Maternal recognition of neonates through olfactory cues. *Physiology & Behavior, 30,* 151–154.

Posner, M. I., Nissen, M. J., & Ogden, W. C. (1978). Attended and unattended processing modes: The role of set for spatial location. In H. L. Pick & I. J. Saltzman (Eds.), *Modes of perceiving and processing information.* Hillsdale, NJ: Erlbaum.

Potter, M. C. (1976). Short-term conceptual memory for pictures. *Journal of Experimental Psychology (Human Learning), 2,* 509–522.

Price, D. D. (2000). Psychological and neural mechanisms of the affective dimension of pain. *Science, 288,* 1769–1772.

Prinzmetal, W., Shimamura, A. P., & Mikolinski, M. (2001). The Ponzo illusion and the perception of orientation. *Perception & Psychophysics, 63,* 99–114.

Proffitt, D. R. (2006). Distance perception. *Current Directions in Psychological Science, 15,* 131–135.

Puce, A., Allison, T., Bentin, S., Gore, J. C., & McCarthy, G. (1998). Temporal cortex activation in humans viewing eye and mouth movements. *Journal of Neuroscience, 18,* 2188–2199.

Quinlan, P. (2003). Visual feature integration theory: Past, present, and future. *Psychological Bulletin, 129,* 643–673.

Quiroga, R. Q., Reddy, L., Kreiman, G., Koch, C., & Fried, I. (2005). Invariant visual representation by single neurons in the human brain. *Nature, 435,* 1102–1107.

Quiroga, R. Q., Reddy, L., Kreiman, G., Koch, C., & Fried, I. (2008). Sparse but not "grandmother-cell" coding in the medial temporal lobe. *Trends in Cognitive Sciences, 12,* 87–91.

Rainville, C., Joubert, S., Felician, O., Chabanne, V., Ceccaldi, M., & Peruch, P. (2005). Wayfinding in familiar and unfamiliar environments in a case of progressive topographical agnosia. *Neurocase, 11,* 1–13.

Rainville, P. (2002). Brain mechanisms of pain affect and pain modulation. *Current Opinion in Neurobiology, 12,* 195–204.

Rainville, P., Hofbauer, R. K., Paus, T., Duncan, G. H., Bushnell, M. C., & Price, D. D. (1999). Cerebral mechanisms of hypnotic induction and suggestion. *Journal of Cognitive Neuroscience, 11,* 110–125.

Ramachandran, V. S. (1992, May). Blind spots. *Scientific American,* 86–91.

Ramachandran, V. S., & Hirstein, W. (1998). The perception of phantom limbs. *Brain, 121,* 1603–1630.

Rao, H., Han, S., Jiang, Y., Xue, Y., Gu, H., Cui, Y., et al. (2004). Engagement of the prefrontal cortex in representational momentum: An fMRI study. *Neuroimage, 23,* 98–103.

Ratliff, F. (1965). Mach bands: Quantitative studies on neural networks in the retina. San Francisco: Holden-Day.

Ratner, C., & McCarthy, J. (1990). Ecologically relevant stimuli and color memory. *Journal of General Psychology, 117,* 369–377.

Rauschecker, J. P. (1997). Processing of complex sounds in the auditory cortex of cat, monkey, and man. *Acta Otolaryngol, 532*(Suppl.), 34–38.

Rauschecker, J. P. (1998). Cortical processing of complex sounds. *Current Opinion in Neurobiology, 8,* 516–521.

Rauschecker, J. P. (2011). An expanded role for the dorsal auditory pathway in sensorimotor control and integration. *Hearing Research, 271,* 16–25.

Rauschecker, J. P., & Scott, S. K. (2009). Maps and streams in the auditory cortex: Nonhuman primates illuminate human speech processing. *Nature Neuroscience, 12,* 718–724.

Rauschecker, J. P., & Tian, B. (2000). Mechanisms and streams for processing of "what" and "where" in auditory cortex. *Proceedings of the National Academy of Sciences, USA, 97,* 11800–11806.

Recanzone, G. H. (2000). Spatial processing in the auditory cortex of the macaque monkey. *Proceedings of the National Academy of Sciences, 97,* 11829–11835.

Reddy, L., Reddy, L., & Koch, C. (2006). Face identification in the near-absence of focal attention. *Vision Research, 46,* 2336–2343.

Reddy, L., Wilken, P., & Koch, C. (2004). Face-gender discrimination is possible in the near-absence of attention. *Journal of Vision, 4,* 106–117.

Reddy, S. (1976). Speech recognition by machine: A review. *Proceedings of the IEEE, 64,* 501–531.

Regev, M., Honey, C. J., Simony, E., & Hasson, U. (2013). Selective and invariant neural responses to spoken and written narratives. *Journal of Neuroscience, 33,* 15978–15988.

Reichardt, W. (1969). Movement perception in insects. In W. Reichardt (Ed.), *Processing of optical data by organisms and machines.* New York: Academic Press.

Rennaker, R. L., Chen, C.-F. F., Ruyle, A. M., Sloan, A. M., & Wilson, D. A. (2007). Spatial and temporal distribution of odorant-evoked activity in the piriform cortex. *Journal of Neuroscience, 27,* 1534–1542.

Rensink, R. A. (2002). Change detection. *Annual Review of Psychology, 53,* 245–277.

Rensink, R. A., O'Regan, J. K., & Clark, J. J. (1997). To see or not to see: The need for attention to perceive changes in scenes. *Psychological Science, 8,* 368–373.

Repacholi, B. M., & Meltzoff, A. N. (2007). Emotional eavesdropping: Infants selectively respond to indirect emotional signals. *Child Development, 78,* 503–521.

Restrepo, D., Doucette, W., Whitesell, J. D., McTavish, T. S., & Salcedo, E. (2009). From the top down: Flexible reading of a fragmented odor map. *Trends in Neurosciences, 32,* 525–531.

Rhode, W. S. (1971). Observations of the vibration of the basilar membrane in squirrel monkeys using the Mössbauer technique. *Journal of the Acoustical Society of America, 49*(Suppl.), 1218–1231.

Rhode, W. S. (1974). Measurement of vibration of the basilar membrane in the squirrel monkey. *Annals of Otology, Rhinology & Laryngology, 83,* 619–625.

Rhudy, J. L., Williams, A. E., McCabe, K. M., Thu, M. A. Nguyen, V., & Rambo, P. (2005). Affective modulation of nociception at spinal and supraspinal levels. *Psychophysiology, 42,* 579–587.

Riesenhuber, M., & Poggio, T. (2000). Models of object recognition. *Nature Neuroscience Supplement, 3,* 1199–1204.

Riesenhuber, M., & Poggio, T. (2002). Neural mechanisms of object recognition. *Current Opinion in Neurobiology, 12,* 162–168.

Ringbach, D. L. (2003). Look at the big picture (details will follow). *Nature Neuroscience, 6,* 7–8.

Risset, J. C., & Mathews, M. W. (1969). Analysis of musical instrument tones. *Physics Today, 22,* 23–30.

Rizzolatti, G., Forgassi, L., & Gallese, V. (2000). Cortical mechanisms subserving object grasping and action recognition: A new view on the cortical motor functions. In M. Gazzaniga (Ed.), *The new cognitive neurosciences* (pp. 539–552). Cambridge, MA: MIT Press.

Rizzolatti, G., Fogassi, L., & Gallese, V. (2006, November). Mirrors in the mind. *Scientific American, 295,* 54–61.

Rizzolatti, G., & Sinigaglia, C. (2010). The functional role of the parieto-frontal mirror circuit: Interpretations and misinterpretations. *Nature Reviews Neuroscience, 11,* 264–274.

Robbins, J. (2000, July 4). Virtual reality finds a real place. *New York Times.*

Robertson, L., Treisman, A., Friedman-Hill, S., & Grabowecky, M. (1997). The interaction of spatial and object pathways: Evidence from Balint's syndrome. *Journal of Cognitive Neuroscience, 9,* 295–317.

Robinson, D. L., & Wurtz, R. (1976). Use of an extra-retinal signal by monkey superior colliculus neurons to distinguish real from self-induced stimulus movement. *Journal of Neurophysiology, 39,* 852–870.

Robles-De-La-Torre, G. (2006). The importance of the sense of touch in virtual and real environments. *IEEE Multimedia, 13*(3), pp. 24–30.

Rocha-Miranda, C. (2011). Personal communication.

Rock, I., & Kaufman, L. (1962). The moon illusion: Part 2. *Science, 136,* 1023–1031.

Rollman, G. B. (1991). Pain responsiveness. In M. A. Heller & W. Schiff (Eds.), *The psychology of touch* (pp. 91–114). Hillsdale, NJ: Erlbaum.

Rolls, E. T. (1981). Responses of amygdaloid neurons in the primate. In Y. Ben-Ari (Ed.), *The amygdaloid complex* (pp. 383–393). Amsterdam: Elsevier.

Rolls, E. T., & Baylis, L. L. (1994). Gustatory, olfactory, and visual convergence within the primate orbitofrontal cortex. *Journal of Neuroscience, 14,* 5437–5452.

Rolls, E. T., Critchley, H. D., Verhagen, J. V., & Kadohisa, M. (2010). The representation of information about taste and odor in the orbito-frontal cortex. *Chemical Perception, 3,* 16–33.

Rolls, E. T., & Tovee, M. J. (1995). Sparseness of the neuronal representation of stimuli in the primate temporal visual cortex. *Journal of Neurophysiology, 73,* 713–726.

Rosenstein, D., & Oster, H. (1988). Differential facial responses to four basic tastes in newborns. *Child Development, 59,* 1555–1568.

Rowe, M. J., Turman, A. A., Murray, G. M., & Zhang, H. Q. (1996). Parallel processing in somatosensory areas I and II of the cerebral cortex. In O. Franzen, R. Johansson, & L. Terenius (Eds.), *Somesthesis and the neurobiology of the somatosensory cortex* (pp. 197–212). Basel: Birkhauser Verlag.

Roy, M., Peretz, I., & Rainville, P. (2008). Emotional valence contribute to music-induced analgesia. *Pain, 134,* 140–147.

Rubin, E. (1958). Figure and ground. In D. C. Beardslee & M. Wertheimer (Eds.), *Readings in perception* (pp. 194–203). Princeton, NJ: Van Nostrand. (Original work published 1915)

Rubin, P., Turvey, M. T., & Van Gelder, P. (1976). Initial phonemes are detected faster in spoken words than in spoken nonwords. *Perception & Psychophysics, 19,* 394–398.

Rushton, S. K., & Salvucci, D. D. (2001). An egocentric account of the visual guidance of locomotion. *Trends in Cognitive Sciences, 5,* 6–7.

Rushton, S. K., Harris, J. M., Lloyd, M. R., & Wann, J. P. (1998). Guidance of locomotion on foot uses perceived target location rather than optic flow. *Current Biology, 8,* 1191–1194.

Rushton, W. A. H. (1961). Rhodopsin measurement and dark adaptation in a subject deficient in cone vision. *Journal of Physiology, 156,* 193–205.

Russell, M. J. (1976). Human olfactory communication. *Nature, 260,* 520–522.

Rust, N. C., Mante, V., Simoncelli, E. P., & Movshon, J. A. (2006). How MT cells analyze the motion of visual patterns. *Nature Neuroscience, 9,* 1421–1431.

Sacks, O. (1985). *The man who mistook his wife for a hat.* London: Duckworth.

Sacks, O. (1995). *An anthropologist on Mars.* New York: Vintage.

Sacks, O. (2006, June 19). Stereo Sue. *The New Yorker*, p. 64.

Sacks, O. (2010). *The mind's eye.* New York: Knopf.

Saffran, J. R., Aslin, R. N., & Newport, E. L. (1996). Statistical learning by 8-month-old infants. *Science, 274*, 1926–1928.

Sakata, H., & Iwamura, Y. (1978). Cortical processing of tactile information in the first somatosensory and parietal association areas in the monkey. In G. Gordon (Ed.), *Active touch* (pp. 55–72). Elmsford, NY: Pergamon Press.

Sakata, H., Taira, M., Mine, S., & Murata, A. (1992). Hand-movement-related neurons of the posterior parietal cortex of the monkey: Their role in visual guidance of hand movements. In R. Caminiti, P. B. Johnson, & Y. Burnod (Eds.), *Control of arm movement in space: Neurophysiological and computational approaches* (pp. 185–198). Berlin: Springer-Verlag.

Salapatek, P., Bechtold, A. G., & Bushnell, E. W. (1976). Infant visual acuity as a function of viewing distance. *Child Development, 47*, 860–863.

Salasoo, A., & Pisoni, D. B. (1985). Interaction of knowledge sources in spoken word identification. *Journal of Memory and Language, 24*, 210–231.

Samuel, A. G. (1981). Phonemic restoration: Insights from a new methodology. *Journal of Experimental Psychology: General, 110*, 474–494.

Samuel, A. G. (1990). Using perceptual-restoration effects to explore the architecture of perception. In G. T. M. Altmann (Ed.), *Cognitive models of speech processing* (pp. 295–314). Cambridge, MA: MIT Press.

Samuel, A. G. (1997). Lexical activation produces potent phonemic percepts. *Cognitive Psychology, 32*, 97–127.

Samuel, A. G. (2001). Knowing a word affects the fundamental perception of the sounds within it. *Psychological Science, 12*, 348–351.

Sato, M., Ogawa, H., & Yamashita, S. (1994). Gustatory responsiveness of chorda tympani fibers the cynomolgus monkey. *Chemical Senses, 19*, 381–400.

Saygin, A. P. (2007). Superior temporal and premotor brain areas necessary for biological motion perception. *Brain, 130*, 2452–2461.

Saygin, A. P. (2012). Sensory and motor brain areas supporting biological motion perception: Neuropsychological and neuroimaging studies. In K. Johnson & M. Shiffrar (Eds.), *People watching: Social, perceptual, and neurophysiological studies of body perception* (pp. 369–387). New York: Oxford University Press.

Saygin, A. P., Wilson, S. M., Hagler, D. J., Jr., Bates, E., & Sereno, M. I. (2004). Point-light biological motion perception activates human premotor cortex. *Journal of Neuroscience, 24*, 6181–6188.

Schaal, B. (1986). Presumed olfactory exchanges between mother and neonate in humans. In J. LeCamus & J. Conier (Eds.), *Ethology and psychology* (pp. 101–110). Toulouse, France: Privat-IEC.

Schaal, B., & Porter, R. H. (1991). "Microsmatic humans" revisited: The generation and perception of chemical signals. In P. J. B. Slater, J. S. Rosenblatt, & Colin Beer (Eds.), *Advances in the study of behavior* (Vol. 20, pp. 135–199). San Diego: Academic Press.

Schaette, R., & McAlpine, D. (2011). Tinnitus with a normal audiogram: Physiological evidence for hidden hearing loss and computational model. *Journal of Neuroscience, 31*, 13452–13457.

Scherf, K. S., Behrmann, M., Humphreys, K., & Luna, B. (2007). Visual category-selectivity for faces, places and objects emerges along different developmental trajectories. *Developmental Science, 10*, F15–F30.

Schiffman, H. R. (1967). Size-estimation of familiar objects under informative and reduced conditions of viewing. *American Journal of Psychology, 80*, 229–235.

Schiffman, S. S., & Erickson, R. P. (1971). A psychophysical model for gustatory quality. *Physiology and Behavior, 7*, 617–633.

Schiller, P. H., & Carvey, C. E. (2005). The Hermann grid illusion revisited. *Perception, 34*, 1375–1397.

Schiller, P. H., Logohetis, N. K., & Charles, E. R. (1990). Functions of the colour-opponent and broad-band channels of the visual system. *Nature, 343*, 68–70.

Schinazi, V. R., & Epstein, R. A. (2010). Neural correlates of real-world route learning. *NeuroImage, 53*, 725–735.

Schlack, A., Sterbing-D'Angelo, J., Hartung, K., Hoffmann, K.-P., & Bremmer, F. (2005). Multisensory space representations in the macaque ventral intraparietal area. *Journal of Neuroscience, 25*, 4616–4625.

Schmuziger, N., Patscheke, J., & Probst, R. (2006). Hearing in nonprofessional pop/rock musicians. *Ear & Hearing, 27*, 321–330.

Schnapf, J. L., Kraft, T. W., & Baylor, D. A. (1987). Spectral sensitivity of human cone photoreceptors. *Nature, 325*, 439–441.

Scholz, J., & Woolf, C. J. (2002). Can we conquer pain? *Nature Neuroscience, 5*, 1062–1067.

Schubert, E. D. (1980). *Hearing: Its function and dysfunction.* Wien: Springer-Verlag.

Scott, T. R., & Giza, B. K. (1990). Coding channels in the taste system of the rat. *Science, 249*, 1585–1587.

Scott, T. R., & Plata-Salaman, C. R. (1991). Coding of taste quality. In T. V. Getchell, R. L. Doty, L. M. Bartoshuk, & J. B. Snow (Eds.), *Smell and taste in health and disease* (pp. 345–368). New York: Raven Press.

Scoville, W. B., & Milner, B. (1957). Loss of recent memory after bilateral hippocampus lesions. *Journal of Neurosurgery and Psychiatry, 20*, 11–21.

Sedgwick, H. (2001). Visual space perception. In E. B. Goldstein (Ed.), *Blackwell handbook of perception* (pp. 128–167). Oxford, UK: Blackwell.

Segui, J. (1984). The syllable: A basic perceptual unit in speech processing? In H. Bouma & D. G. Gouwhuis (Eds.), *Attention and performance X* (pp. 165–181). Hillsdale, NJ: Erlbaum.

Senior, C., Barnes, J., Giampietro, V., Simmons, A., Bullmore, E. T., Brammer, M., et al. (2000). The functional neuoroanatomy of implicit-motion perception or "representational momentum." *Current Biology, 10*, 16–22.

Shackman, A. J., Salomons, T. V., Slagter, H. A., Fox, A. S., & Winter, J. J. (2011). The integration of negative affect, pain and cognitive control in the cingulate cortex. *Nature Reviews Neuroscience, 12*, 154–167.

Shahbake, M. (2008). *Anatomical and psychophysical aspects of the development of the sense of taste in humans* (Unpublished doctoral dissertation). University of Western Sydney, New South Wales, Australia.

Shamma, S. A., Elhilali, M., & Micheyl, C. (2011). Temporal coherence and attention in auditory scene analysis. *Trends in Neurosciences, 34*, 114–123.

Shamma, S. A., & Micheyl, C. (2010). Behind the scenes of auditory perception. *Current Opinion in Neurobiology, 20*, 361–366.

Shannon, R. V., Zeng, F.-G., Kamath, V., Wygonski, J., & Ekelid, M. (1995). Speech recognition with primarily temporal cues. *Science, 270*, 303–304.

Shapley, R., & Hawken, M. J. (2011). Color in the cortex: Single- and double-opponent cells. *Vision Research, 51*, 701–707.

Shepherd, G. M. (2012). *Neurogastronomy.* New York: Columbia University Press.

Sherf, K. S., Behrmann, M., Humphreys, K., & Lina, B. (2007). Visual category-selectivity for faces, places and objects emerges along different developmental trajectories. *Developmental Science, 10*, F15–F30.

Sherman, P. D. (1981). *Colour Vision in the Nineteenth Century: The Young-Helmholtz-Maxwell Theory.* Bristol: Adam Hilger.

Sherman, S. M., & Koch, C. (1986). The control of retinogeniculate transmission in the mammalian lateral geniculate nucleus. *Experimental Brain Research, 63*, 1–20.

Shiffrar, M., & Freyd, J. (1990). Apparent motion of the human body. *Psychological Science, 1*, 257–264.

Shiffrar, M., & Freyd, J. (1993). Timing and apparent motion path choice with human body photographs. *Psychological Science, 4,* 379–384.

Shimamura, A. P., & Prinzmetal, W. (1999). The mystery spot illusion and its relation to other visual illusions. *Psychological Science, 10,* 501–507.

Shimojo, S., Bauer, J., O'Connell, K. M., & Held, R. (1986). Pre-stereoptic binocular vision in infants. *Vision Research, 26,* 501–510.

Shinoda, H., Hayhoe, M. M., & Shrivastava, A. (2001). What controls attention in natural environments? *Vision Research, 41,* 3535–3545.

Shuwairi, S. M., & Johnson, S. P. (2013). Oculomotor exploration of impossible figures in early infancy. *Infancy, 18,* 221–232.

Silbert, L. J., Honey, C. J., Simony, E., Poeppel, D., & Hasson, U. (2014). Coupled neural systems underlie the production and comprehension of naturalistic narrative speech. *Proceedings of the National Academy of Sciences, 111,* E4687–E4696.

Silver, M. A., & Kastner, S. (2009). Topographic maps in human frontal and parietal cortex. *Trends in Cognitive Sciences, 13,* 488–495.

Simion, F., Regolin, L., & Bulf, H. (2008). A predisposition for biological motion in the newborn baby. *Proceedings of the National Academy of Sciences, 105,* 809–813.

Simons, D. J., & Chabris, C. F. (1999). Gorillas in our midst: Sustained inattentional blindness for dynamic events. *Perception, 28,* 1059–1074.

Simonyan, K., Aytar, Y., Vedaldi, A., & Zisserman, A. (2012). Presentation at Image Large Scale Visual Recognition Competition (ILSVRC2012).

Singer, T., & Klimecki, O. M. (2014). Empathy and compassion. *Current Biology, 24,* R875–R878.

Singer, T., Seymour, B., O'Doherty, J., Kaube, H., Dolan, R. J., & Frith, C. D. (2004). Empathy for pain involves the affective but not sensory components of pain. *Science, 303,* 1157–1162.

Singh, D., & Bronstad, M. P. (2001). Female body odour is a potential cue to ovulation. *Proceedings of the Royal Society of London B, 268,* 797–801.

Sinha, P. (2002). Recognizing complex patterns. *Nature Neuroscience, 5,* 1093–1097.

Siveke, I., Pecka, M., Seidl, A. H., Baudoux, S., & Grothe, B. (2006). Binaural response properties of low-frequency neurons in the gerbil dorsal nucleus of the lateral lemniscus. *Journal of Neurophysiology, 96,* 1425–1440.

Slagter, H. A., Johnstone, T., Beets, I. A. M., & Davidson, R. J. (2010). Neural competition for conscious representation across time: An fMRI study. *PLoS ONE, 5,* e10556.

Slater, A. M., & Findlay, J. M. (1975). Binocular fixation in the newborn baby. *Journal of Experimental Child Psychology, 20,* 248–273.

Slater, A. M., Morison, V., & Rose, D. (1984). Habituation in the newborn. *Infant Behavior and Development, 7,* 183–200.

Slater, A. M., Morison, V., Somers, M., Mattock, A., Brown, E., & Taylor, D. (1990). Newborn and older infants' perception of partly occluded objects. *Infant Behavior and Development, 13,* 33–49.

Sloan, L. L., & Wollach, L. (1948). A case of unilateral deuteranopia. *Journal of the Optical Society of America, 38,* 502–509.

Sloboda, J. A. (2000). Individual differences in music performance. *Trends in Cognitive Sciences, 4,* 397–403.

Sloboda, J. A., & Gregory, A. H. (1980). The psychological reality of musical segments. *Canadian Journal of Psychology, 34,* 274–280.

Small, D. M. (2008). Flavor and the formation of category-specific processing in olfaction. *Chemical Perception, 1,* 136–146.

Small, D. M. (2012). Flavor is in the brain. *Physiology and Behavior, 107,* 540–552.

Smith, D. V., & Scott, T. R. (2003). Gustatory neural coding. In R. L. Doty (Ed.), *Handbook of olfaction and gustation* (2nd ed.). New York: Marcel Dekker.

Smith, D. V., St. John, S. J., & Boughter, J. D., Jr. (2000). Neuronal cell types and taste quality coding. *Physiology and Behavior, 69,* 77–85.

Smith, M. A., Majaj, N. J., & Movshon, J. A. (2005). Dynamics of motion signaling by neurons in macaque area MT. *Nature Neuroscience, 8,* 220–228.

Smithson, H. E. (2005). Sensory, computational and cognitive components of human colour constancy. *Philosophical Transactions of the Royal Society of London B, Biological Sciences, 360,* 1329–1346.

Smithson, H. E. (2016). Perceptual organization of colour. In J. Wagemans (Ed.), *Oxford handbook of perceptual organization.* Oxford, UK: Oxford University Press.

Sobel, E. C. (1990). The locust's use of motion parallax to measure distance. *Journal of Comparative Physiology A, 167,* 579–588.

Solomon, S. G., & Lennie, P. (2007). The machinery of color vision. *Nature Reviews Neuroscience, 8,* 276–286.

Solstad, T., Boccara, C. N., Kropft, E., Moser, M.-B., & Moser, E. I. (2008). Representation of geometric borders in the entorhinal cortex. *Science, 322,* 1865–1868.

Sommer, M. A., & Crapse, T. B. (2010). Corollary discharge. In E. B. Goldstein (Ed.), *Sage encyclopedia of perception.* Thousand Oaks, CA: Sage.

Sommer, M. A., & Wurtz, R. H. (2006). Influence of the thalamus on spatial visual processing in frontal cortex. *Nature, 444,* 374–377.

Sommer, M. A., & Wurtz, R. H. (2008). Brain circuits for the internal monitoring of movements. *Annual Review of Neuroscience, 31,* 317–338.

Sosulski, D. L., Bloom, M. L., Cutforth, T., Axel, R., & Sandeep, R. D. (2011). Distinct representations of olfactory information in different cortical centres. *Nature, 472,* 213–219.

Soto-Faraco, S., Lyons, J., Gazzaniga, M., Spence, C., & Kingstone, A. (2002). The ventriloquist in motion: Illusory capture of dynamic information across sensory modalities. *Cognitive Brain Research, 14,* 139–146.

Soto-Faraco, S., Spence, C., Lloyd, D., & Kingstone, A. (2004). Moving multisensory research along: Motion perception across sensory modalities. *Current Directions in Psychological Science, 13,* 29–32.

Soucy, E. R., Albenau, D. F., Fantana, A. L., Murthy, V. N., & Meister, M. (2009). Precision and diversity in an odor map on the olfactory bulb. *Nature Neuroscience, 12,* 210–220.

Spector, A. C., & Travers, S. P. (2005). The representation of taste quality in the mammalian nervous system. *Behavioral and Cognitive Neuroscience Reviews, 4,* 143–191.

Spence, C. (2015). Multisensory flavor perception. *Cell, 161,* 24–35.

Spence, C., Levitan, C. A., Shankar, M. U., & Zampini, M. (2010). Does food color influence taste and flavor perception in humans? *Chemical Perception, 3,* 68–84.

Spence, C., & Read, L. (2003). Speech shadowing while driving: On the difficulty of splitting attention between eye and ear. *Psychological Science, 14,* 251–256.

Srinivasan, M. V., & Venkatesh, S. (Eds.). (1997). *From living eyes to seeing machines.* New York: Oxford University Press.

Stark, L., & Bridgeman, B. (1983). Role of corollary discharge in space constancy. *Perception & Psychophysics, 34,* 371–380.

Steiner, J. E. (1974). Innate, discriminative human facial expressions to taste and smell stimulation. *Annals of the New York Academy of Sciences, 237,* 229–233.

Steiner, J. E. (1979). Human facial expressions in response to taste and smell stimulation. *Advances in Child Development and Behavior, 13,* 257–295.

Steiner, J. E. (1987). What the neonate can tell us about umami. In Y. Kawamura & M. R. Kare (Eds.), *Umami: A basic taste* (pp. 97–103). New York: Marcel Dekker.

Stern, K., & McClintock, M. K. (1998). Regulation of ovulation by human pheromones. *Nature, 392,* 177–179.

Stevens, J. A., Fonlupt, P., Shiffrar, M., & Decety, J. (2000). New aspects of motion perception: Selective neural encoding of apparent human movements. *NeuroReport, 111*, 109–115.

Stevens, S. S. (1957). On the psychophysical law. *Psychological Review, 64*, 153–181.

Stevens, S. S. (1961). To honor Fechner and repeal his law. *Science, 133*, 80–86.

Stevens, S. S. (1962). The surprising simplicity of sensory metrics. *American Psychologist, 17*, 29–39.

Stiles, W. S. (1953). Further studies of visual mechanisms by the two-color threshold method. *Coloquio sobre problemas opticos de la vision* (Vol. 1, pp. 65–103). Madrid: Union Internationale de Physique Pure et Appliquée.

Stoffregen, T. A., Smart, J. L., Bardy, B. G., & Pagulayan, R. J. (1999). Postural stabilization of looking. *Journal of Experimental Psychology: Human Perception and Performance, 25*, 1641–1658.

Strayer, D. L., Cooper, J. M., Turrill, J., Coleman, J., Medeiros-Ward, N., & Biondi, F. (2013). *Measuring driver distraction in the automobile*. Washington, DC: AAA Foundation for Traffic Safety.

Strayer, D. L., & Johnston, W. A. (2001). Driven to distraction: Dual-task studies of simulated driving and conversing on a cellular telephone. *Psychological Science, 12*, 462–466.

Sufka, K. J., & Price, D. D. (2002). Gate control theory reconsidered. *Brain and Mind, 3*, 277–290.

Suga, N. (1990, June). Biosonar and neural computation in bats. *Scientific American*, 60–68.

Sugovic, M., & Witt, J. K. (2013). An older view on distance perception: Older adults perceive walkable extents and farther. *Experimental Brain Research, 226*, 383–391.

Sumby, W. H., & Pollack, J. (1954). Visual contributions to speech intelligibility in noise. *Journal of the Acoustical Society of America, 26*, 212–215.

Sumner, P., & Mollon, J. D. (2000). Catarrhine photopigments are optimized for detecting targets against a foliage background. *Journal of Experimental Biology, 23*, 1963–1986.

Sun, H.-J., Campos, J., Young, M., Chan, G. S. W., & Ellard, C. G. (2004). The contributions of static visual cues, nonvisual cues, and optic flow in distance estimation. *Perception, 33*, 49–65.

Svaetichin, G. (1956). Spectral response curves from single cones. *Acta Physiologica Scandinavica Supplementum, 134*, 17–46.

Swets, J. A. (Ed.). (1964). Signal detection and recognition by human observers. New York: Wiley

Taira, M., Mine, S., Georgopoulis, A. P., Murata, A., & Sakata, H. (1990). Parietal cortex neurons of the monkey related to the visual guidance of hand movement. *Experimental Brain Research, 83*, 29–36.

Tan, S.-L., Pfordresher, P., & Harre, R. (2010). *Psychology of music: From sound to significance*. New York: Psychology Press.

Tanabe, S., Haefner, R. M., & Cumming, B. G. (2011). Suppressive mechanisms in monkey V1 help to solve the stereo correspondence problem. *Journal of Neuroscience, 31*, 8295–8305.

Tanaka, J. W., & Presnell, L. M. (1999). Color diagnosticity in object recognition. *Perception & Psychophysics, 61*, 1140–1153.

Tanaka, J. W., Weiskopf, D., & Williams, P. (2001). The role of color in high-level vision. *Trends in Cognitive Sciences, 5*, 211–215.

Tanigawa, H., Lu, H. D., & Roe, A. W. (2010). Functional organization for color and orientation in macaque V4. *Nature Neuroscience, 13*, 1542–1548.

Tatler, B. W., Hayhoe, M. M., Land, M. F., & Ballard, D. H. (2011). Eye guidance in natural vision: Reinterpreting salience. *Journal of Vision, 11*(5): 1–23.

Taube, J. S. (2007). The head-direction signal: Origins and sensory-motor integration. *Annual Review of Neuroscience, 30*, 181–207.

Teghtsoonian, R. (1971). On the exponents in Stevens's Law and the constant in Ekman's Law. *Psychological Review, 78*, 78–80.

Teller, D. Y. (1997). First glances: The vision of infants. *Investigative Ophthalmology and Visual Science, 38*, 2183–2199.

Tenenbaum, J. B., Kemp, C., Griffiths, T. L., & Goodman, N. D. (2011). How to grow a mind: Statistics, structure, and abstraction. *Science, 331*, 1279–1285.

Terwogt, M. M., & Hoeksma, J. B. (1994). Colors and emotions: Preferences and combinations. *Journal of General Psychology, 122*, 5–17.

Thaler, L., Arnott, S. R., & Goodale, M. A. (2011). Neural correlates of natural human echolocation in early and late blind echolocation experts. *PLoS One, 6*(5), e20162 doi:10.1371.journal.pone.0020162.

Theeuwes, J. (1992). Perceptual selectivity for color and form. *Perception & Psychophysics, 51*, 599–606.

Todrank, J., & Bartoshuk, L. M. (1991). A taste illusion: Taste sensation localized by touch. *Physiology and Behavior, 50*, 1027–1031.

Tolman, E. C. (1938). The determinants of behavior at a choice point. *Psychological Review, 45*, 1–41.

Tolman, E. C. (1948). Cognitive maps in rats and men. *Psychological Review, 55*, 189–208.

Tong, F., Nakayama, K., Vaughn, J. T., & Kanwisher, N. (1998). Binocular rivalry and visual awareness in human extrastriate cortex. *Neuron, 21*, 753–759.

Tonndorf, J. (1960). Shearing motion in scalia media of cochlear models. *Journal of the Acoustical Society of America, 32*, 238–244.

Tootell, R. B. H., Nelissen, K., Vanduffel, W., & Orban, G. A. (2004). Search for color 'center(s)' in macaque visual cortex. *Cerebral Cortex, 14*, 353–363.

Torralba, A., Oliva, A., Castelhano, M. S., & Henderson, J. M. (2006). Contextual guidance of eye movements and attention in real-world scenes: The role of global features in object search. *Psychological Review, 113*, 766–786.

Tracey, I. (2010). Getting the pain you expect: Mechanisms of placebo, nocebo and reappraisal effects in humans. *Nature Medicine, 16*, 1277–1283.

Trainor, J. J., Gao, X., Lei, J.-J., Lehtovaara, K., & Harris, L. R. (2009). The primal role of the vestibular system in determining musical rhythm. *Cortex, 45*, 35–43.

Treisman, A. (1986). Features and objects in visual processing. *Scientific American, 255*, 114B–125B.

Treisman, A. (1988). Features and objects: The fourteenth Bartlett memorial lecture. *Quarterly Journal of Experimental Psychology, 40A*, 207–237.

Treisman, A. (1999). Solutions to the binding problem: Progress through controversy and convergence. *Neuron, 24*, 105–110.

Treisman, A., & Gelade, G. (1980). A feature-integration theory of attention. *Cognitive Psychology, 12*, 97–113.

Treisman, A., & Schmidt, H. (1982). Illusory conjunctions in the perception of objects. *Cognitive Psychology, 14*, 107–141.

Tresilian, J., R., Mon-Williams, M., & Kelly, B. (1999). Increasing confidence in vergence as a cue to distance. *Proceedings of the Royal Society of London, 266B*, 39–44.

Troiani, V., Stigliani, A., Smith, M. E., & Epstein, R. A. (2014). Multiple object properties drive scene-selective regions. *Cerebral Cortex, 24*, 883–897.

Truax, B. (1984). *Acoustic communication*. Norwood, NJ: ABLEX.

Tsao, D. Y., Freiwald, W. A., Tootell, R. B., & Livingstone, M. S. (2006). A cortical region consisting entirely of face-selective cells. *Science, 311*, 670–674.

Tsuchiya, N., & Koch, C. (2009). The relationship between consciousness and attention. In S. Lawreys & G. Tononi (Eds.), *The neurology of consciousness* (pp. 63–79). London: Elsevier.

Turano, K. A., Yu, D., Hao, L., & Hicks, J. C. (2005). Optic-flow and egocentric-directions strategies in walking: Central vs peripheral visual field. *Vision Research, 45,* 3117–3132.

Turatto, M., Vescovi, M., & Valsecchi, M. (2007). Attention makes moving objects be perceived to move faster. *Vision Research, 47,* 166–178.

Turk, D. C., & Flor, H. (1999). Chronic pain: A biobehavioral perspective. In R. J. Gatchel & D. C. Turk (Eds.), *Psychosocial factors in pain* (pp. 18–34). New York: Guilford Press.

Turman, A. B., Morley, J. W., & Rowe, M. J. (1998). Functional organization of the somatosensory cortex in the primate. In J. W. Morley (Ed.), *Neural aspects of tactile sensation* (pp. 167–193). New York: Elsevier Science.

Turner, S. R. (1993). Vision studies in Germany: Helmholtz versus Hering. *OSIRIS, 8,* 80–103.

Turner, S. R. (1994). *In the mind's eye: Vision and the Helmholtz-Hering controversy.* Princeton, NJ: Princeton University Press.

Tye-Murray, N., Spencer, L., & Woodworth, G. G. (1995). Acquisition of speech by children who have prolonged cochlear implant experience. *Journal of Speech and Hearing Research, 38,* 327–337.

Tyler, C. W. (1997a). Analysis of human receptor density. In V. Lakshminarayanan (Ed.), *Basic and clinical applications of vision science* (pp. 63–71). Norwell, MA: Kluwer Academic.

Tyler, C. W. (1997b). *Human cone densities: Do you know where all your cones are?* Unpublished manuscript.

Uchida, N., Takahashi, Y. K., Tanifuji, M., & Mori, K. (2000). Odor maps in the mammalian olfactory bulb: Domain organization and odorant structural features. *Nature Neuroscience, 3,* 1035–1043.

Uchikawa, K., Uchikawa, H., & Boynton, R. M. (1989). Partial color constancy of isolated surface colors examined by a color-naming method. *Perception, 18,* 83–91.

Uddin, L. Q., Iacoboni, M., Lange, C., & Keenan, J. P. (2007). The self and social cognition: The role of cortical midline structures and mirror neurons. *Trends in Cognitive Sciences, 11,* 153–157.

Uka, T., & DeAngelis, G. C. (2003). Contribution of middle temporal area to coarse depth discrimination: Comparison of neuronal and psychophysical sensitivity. *Journal of Neuroscience, 23,* 3515–3530.

Umeda, K., Tanabe, S., & Fujita, I. (2007). Representation of stereoscopic depth based on relative disparity in macaque area V4. *Journal of Neurophysiology, 98,* 241–252.

Ungerleider, L. G., & Haxby, J. V. (1994). "What" and "where" in the human brain. *Current Opinion in Neurobiology, 4,* 157–165.

Ungerleider, L. G., & Mishkin, M. (1982). Two cortical visual systems. In D. J. Ingle, M. A. Goodale, & R. J. Mansfield (Eds.), *Analysis of visual behavior* (pp. 549–580). Cambridge, MA: MIT Press.

Valdez, P., & Mehribian, A. (1994). Effect of color on emotions. *Journal of Experimental Psychology: General, 123,* 394–409.

Vallbo, A. B., & Johansson, R. S. (1978). The tactile sensory innervation of the glabrous skin of the human hand. In G. Gordon (Ed.), *Active touch* (pp. 29–54). New York: Oxford University Press.

Vallortigara, G., Regolin, L., & Marconato, F. (2005). Visually inexperienced chicks exhibit spontaneous preference for biological motion patterns. *PLoS Biology, 3,* e208.

Van Doorn, G. H., Wuilemin, D., & Spence, C. (2014). Does the colour of the mug influence the taste of the coffee? *Flavour, 3,* 1–7.

Van Essen, D. C., & Anderson, C. H. (1995). Information processing strategies and pathways in the primate visual system. In S. F. Zornetzer, J. L. Davis, & C. Lau (Eds.), *An introduction to neural and electronic networks* (2nd ed., pp. 45–75). San Diego: Academic Press.

Van Kemenade, B. M., Muggleton, N., Walsh, V., & Saygin, A. P. (2012). Effects of TMS over premotor and superior temporal cortices on biological motion perception. *Journal of Cognitive Neuroscience, 24,* 896–904.

Van Rullen, R., & Thorpe, S. J. (2001). The time course of visual processing: From early perception to decision making. *Journal of Cognitive Neuroscience, 13,* 454–461.

Van Wanrooij, M. M., & Van Opstal, A. J. (2005). Relearning sound localization with a new ear. *Journal of Neuroscience, 25,* 5413–5424.

van Wassenhove, V., Grant, K. W., & Poeppel, D. (2005). Visual speech speeds up the neural processing of auditory speech. *Proceedings of the National Academy of Sciences, 102,* 1181–1186.

Varner, D., Cook, J. E., Schneck, M. E., McDonald, M., & Teller, D. Y. (1985). Tritan discriminations by 1- and 2-month-old human infants. *Vision Research, 25,* 821–831.

Vecera, S. P., Vogel, E. K., & Woodman, G. F. (2002). Lower region: A new cue for figure–ground assignment. *Journal of Experimental Psychology: General, 131,* 194–205.

Veldhuizen, M. G., Nachtigal, D., Teulings, L., Gitelman, D. R., & Small, D. M. (2010). The insular taste cortex contributes to odor quality coding. *Frontiers in Human Neuroscience, 4*(Article 58), 1–11.

Verhagen, J. V., Kadohisa, M., & Rolls, E. T. (2004). Primate insular/opercular taste cortex: Neuronal representations of viscosity, fat texture, grittiness, temperature, and taste of foods. *Journal of Neurophysiology, 92,* 1685–1699.

Vermeij, G. (1997). Privileged hands: A scientific life. New York: Freeman.

Vingerhoets, G. (2014). Contribution of the posterior parietal cortex in reaching, grasping, and using objects and tools. *Frontiers in Psychology, 5,* 151.

Violanti, J. M. (1998). Cellular phones and fatal traffic collisions. *Accident Analysis and Prevention, 28,* 265–270.

Vo, M. L. H., & Henderson, J. M. (2009). Does gravity matter? Effects of semantic and syntactic inconsistencies on the allocation of attention during scene perception. *Journal of Vision, 9*(3), 1–15.

von der Emde, G., Schwarz, S., Gomez, L., Budelli, R., & Grant, K. (1998). Electric fish measure distance in the dark. *Nature, 395,* 890–894.

Von Hippel, P., & Huron, D. (2000). Why do skips precede reversals? The effect of tessitura on melodic structure. *Music Perception, 18,* 59–85.

von Kriegstein, K., Kleinschmidt, A., Sterzer, P., & Giraud, A. L. (2005). Interaction of face and voice areas during speaker recognition. *Journal of Cognitive Neuroscience, 17,* 367–376.

Vonderschen, K., & Wagner, H. (2014). Detecting interaural time differences and remodeling their representation. *Trends in Neurosciences, 37,* 289–300.

Vos, P. G., & Troost, J. M. (1989). Ascending and descending melodic intervals: Statistical findings and their perceptual relevance. *Music Perception, 6,* 383–396.

Vuust, P., Ostergaard, L., Pallesen, K. J., Bailey, C., & Roepstorff, A. (2009). Predictive coding of music: Brain responses to rhythmic incongruity. *Cortex, 45,* 80–92.

Wald, G. (1964). The receptors of human color vision. *Science, 145,* 1007–1017.

Wald, G. (1968). Molecular basis of visual excitation [Nobel lecture]. *Science, 162,* 230–239.

Wald, G., & Brown, P. K. (1958). Human rhodopsin. *Science, 127,* 222–226.

Waldrop, M. M. (1988). A landmark in speech recognition. *Science, 240,* 1615.

Walker, S., Stafford, P., & Davis, G. (2008). Ultra-rapid categorization requires visual attention: Scenes with multiple foreground objects. *Journal of Vision, 8,* 1–12.

Wall, P. D., & Melzack, R. (Eds.). (1994). *Textbook of pain* (3rd ed.). Edinburgh: Churchill Livingstone.

Wallace, G. K. (1959). Visual scanning in the desert locust Schistocerca Gregaria Forskal. *Journal of Experimental Biology, 36,* 512–525.

Wallace, M. N., Rutowski, R. G., Shackleton, T. M., & Palmer, A. R. (2000). Phase-locked responses to pure tones in guinea pig auditory cortex. *Neuroreport, 11,* 3989–3993.

Wallach, H. (1963). The perception of neutral colors. *Scientific American, 208,* 107–116.

Wallach, H., Newman, E. B., & Rosenzweig, M. R. (1949). The precedence effect in sound localization. *American Journal of Psychology, 62,* 315–336.

Walls, G. L. (1942). *The vertebrate eye.* New York: Hafner. (Reprinted in 1967)

Wandell, B. A. (2011). Imaging retinotopic maps in the human brain. *Vision Research, 51,* 718–737.

Wandell, B. A., Dumoulin, S. O., & Brewer, A. A. (2009). Visual areas in humans. In L. Squire (Ed.), *Encyclopedia of neuroscience.* New York: Academic Press.

Wang, R. F. (2003). Spatial representations and spatial updating. In D. E. Irwin & B. H. Ross (Eds.), *The psychology of learning and motivation: Advances in research and theory* (Vol. 42, pp. 109–156). San Diego, CA: Elsevier.

Wang, X., Zhang, M., Cohen, I. S., & Goldberg, M. E. (2007). The proprioceptive representation of eye position in monkey primary somatosensory cortex. *Nature Neuroscience, 10,* 640–646.

Wann, J., & Land, M. (2000). Steering with or without the flow: Is the retrieval of heading necessary? *Trends in Cognitive Science, 4,* 319–324.

Warren, R. M. (1970). Perceptual restoration of missing speech sounds. *Science, 167,* 392–393.

Warren, R. M., Obuseck, C. J., & Acroff, J. M. (1972). Auditory induction of absent sounds. *Science, 176,* 1149.

Warren, W. H. (1995). Self-motion: Visual perception and visual control. In W. Epstein & S. Rogers (Eds.), *Handbook of perception and cognition: Perception of space and motion* (pp. 263–323). New York: Academic Press.

Warren, W. H. (2004). Optic flow. In L. M. Chalupa & J. S. Werner (Eds.), *The visual neurosciences* (pp. 1247–1259). Cambridge, MA: MIT Press.

Warren, W. H., Kay, B. A., & Yilmaz, E. H. (1996). Visual control of posture during walking: Functional specificity. *Journal of Experimental Psychology: Human Perception and Performance, 22,* 818–838.

Warren, W. H., Kay, B. A., Zosh, W. D., Duchon, A. P., & Sahuc, S. (2001). Optic flow is used to control human walking. *Nature Neuroscience, 4,* 213–216.

Watkins, L. R., & Maier, S. F. (2003). Glia: A novel drug discovery target for clinical pain. *Nature Reviews Drug Discovery, 2,* 973–985.

Weber, A. I., Hannes, P. S., Lieber, J. D., Cheng, J.-W., Manfredi, L. R., Dammann, J. F., & Bensmaia, S. J. (2013). Spatial and temporal codes mediate the tactile perception of natural textures. *Proceedings of the National Academy of Sciences, 110,* 17107–17112.

Webster, M. A., (2011). Adaptation and visual coding. *Journal of Vision, 11,* 1–23.

Weinstein, S. (1968). Intensive and extensive aspects of tactile sensitivity as a function of body part, sex, and laterality. In D. R. Kenshalo (Ed.), *The skin senses* (pp. 195–218). Springfield, IL: Thomas.

Weisenberg, M. (1977). Pain and pain control. *Psychological Bulletin, 84,* 1008–1044.

Weissberg, M. (1999). Cognitive aspects of pain. In P. D. Wall & R. Melzak (Eds.), *Textbook of pain* (4th ed., pp. 345–358). New York: Churchill Livingstone.

Werner, L. A., & Bargones, J. Y. (1992). Psychoacoustic development of human infants. In C. Rovee-Collier & L. Lipsett (Eds.), *Advances in infancy research* (Vol. 7, pp. 103–145). Norwood, NJ: Ablex.

Wertheimer, M. (1912). Experimentelle Studien über das Sehen von Beuegung. *Zeitchrift für Psychologie, 61,* 161–265.

Wever, E. G. (1949). *Theory of hearing.* New York: Wiley.

Wexler, M., Panerai, I. L., & Droulez, J. (2001). Self-motion and the perception of stationary objects. *Nature, 409,* 85–88.

Wiech, K., Ploner, M., & Tracey, I. (2008). Neurocognitive aspects of pain perception. *Trends in Cognitive Sciences, 12,* 306–313.

Wightman, F. L., & Kistler, D. J. (1992). The dominant role of low-frequency interaural time differences in sound localization. *Journal of the Acoustical Society of American, 91,* 1648–1661.

Wightman, F. L., & Kistler, D. J. (1998). Of Vulcan ears, human ears and "earprints." *Nature Neuroscience, 1,* 337–339.

Wilkie, R. M., & Wann, J. P. (2003). Eye-movements aid the control of locomotion. *Journal of Vision, 3,* 677–684.

Willander, J., & Larsson, M. (2007). Olfaction and emotion: The case of autobiographical memory. *Memory and Cognition, 35,* 1659–1663.

Williams, J. H. G., Whiten, A., Suddendorf, T., & Perrett, D. I. (2001). Imitation, mirror neurons and autism. *Neuroscience and Biobehavioral Reviews, 25,* 287–295.

Williams, Z. M., Elfar, J. C., Eskandar, E. N., Toth, L. J., & Assad, J. A. (2003). Parietal activity and the perceived direction of ambiguous apparent motion. *Nature Neuroscience, 6,* 616–623.

Williamson, S. J., & Cummins, H. Z. (1983). *Light and color in nature and art.* New York: Wiley.

Wilson, D. A. (2003). Rapid, experience-induced enhancement in odorant discrimination by anterior piriform cortex neurons. *Journal of Neurophysiology, 90,* 65–72.

Wilson, D. A., Best, A. R., & Sullivan, R. M. (2004). Plasticity in the olfactory system: Lessons for the neurobiology of memory. *Neuroscientist, 10,* 513–524.

Wilson, D. A., & Stevenson, R. J. (2006). *Learning to smell.* Baltimore: Johns Hopkins University Press.

Wilson, D. A., & Sullivan, R. M. (2011). Cortical processing of odor objects. *Neuron, 72,* 506–519.

Wilson, D. A., Xu, W., Sadrian, B., Courtiol, E., Cohen, Y., & Barnes, D. C. (2014). Cortical odor processing in health and disease. *Progress in Brain Research, 208,* 275–305.

Wilson, J. R., Friedlander, M. J., & Sherman, M. S. (1984). Ultrastructural morphology of identified X- and Y-cells in the cat's lateral geniculate nucleus. *Proceedings of the Royal Society, 211B,* 411–436.

Wilson, S. M., & Iacobini, M. (2006). Neural responses to non-native phonemes varying in producibility: Evidence for the sensorimotor nature of speech perception. *Neuroimage, 33,* 316–325.

Winawer, J., Huk, A. C., & Boroditsky, L. (2008). A motion aftereffect from still photographs depicting motion. *Psychological Science, 19,* 276–283.

Winston, J. S., O'Doherty, J., Kilner, J. M., Perrett, D. I., & Dolan, R. J. (2007). Brain systems for assessing facial attractiveness. *Neuropsychologia, 45,* 195–206.

Wissinger, C. M., VanMeter, J., Tian, B., Van Lare, J., Pekar, J., & Rauschecker, J. P. (2001). Hierarchical organization of the human auditory cortex revealed by functional magnetic resonance imaging. *Journal of Cognitive Neuroscience, 13,* 1–7.

Witt, J. K. (2011a). Action's effect on perception. *Current Directions in Psychological Science, 20,* 201–206.

Witt, J. K. (2011b). Tool use influences perceived shape and parallelism: Indirect measures of perceived distance. *Journal of Experimental Psychology: Human Perception and Performance, 37,* 1148–1156.

Witt, J. K., & Dorsch, T. (2009). Kicking to bigger uprights: Field goal kicking performance influences perceived size. *Perception, 38,* 1328–1340.

Witt, J. K., Linkenauger, S. A., Bakdash, J. Z., Augustyn, J. A., Cook, A. S., & Proffitt, D. R. (2009). The long road of pain: Chronic pain increases perceived distance. *Experimental Brain Research, 192,* 145–148.

Witt, J. K., & Proffitt, D. R. (2005). See the ball, hit the ball: Apparent ball size is correlated with batting average. *Psychological Science, 16,* 937–938.

Witt, J. K., Proffitt, D. R., & Epstein, W. (2010). When and how are spatial perceptions scaled? *Journal of Experimental Psychology: Human Perception and Performance, 36,* 1153–1160.

Witt, J. K., & Riley, M. A. (2014). Discovering your inner Gibson: Reconciling action-specific and ecological approaches to perception-action. *Psychonomic Bulletin & Review, 21,* 1353–1370.

Witt, J. K., & Sugovic, M. (2010). Performance and ease influence perceived speed. *Perception, 39,* 1341–1353.

Wolfe, J. M. (1994). Guided search 2.0: A revised model of visual search. *Psychonomic Bulletin & Review, 1,* 202–238.

Wolpert, D. M., & Ghahramani, Z. (2004). Bayes rule in perception, action and cognition. In R. L. Gregory (Ed.), *The Oxford companion to the mind* (2nd ed.). New York: Oxford University Press.

Womelsdorf, T., Anton-Erxleben, K., Pieper, F., & Treue, S. (2006). Dynamic shifts of visual receptive fields in cortical area MT by spatial attention. *Nature Neuroscience, 9,* 1156–1160.

Womelsdorf, T., Schoffelen, J.-M., Oostenveld, R., Singer, W., Desimone, R., Engel, A. K., et al. (2007). Modulation of neural interactions through neuronal synchronization. *Science, 316,* 1609–1612.

Woo, C.-W., Koban, L., Kross, E., Lindquist, M. A., Banich, M. T., Ruzic, L., et al. (2014). Separate neural representations for physical pain and social rejection. *Nature Communications, 5,* Article 5380. doi:10.138/ncomms6380.

Woods, A. J., Philbeck, J. W., & Danoff, J. V. (2009). The various perception of distance: An alternative view of how effort affects distance judgments. *Journal of Experimental Psychology: Human Perception and Performance, 35,* 1104–1117.

Wozniak, R. H. (1999). Classics in psychology, 1855–1914: Historical essays. Bristol, UK: Thoemmes Press.

Wyatt, T. D. (2010). Pheromones and signature mixtures: Defining species-wide signals and variable cues for identity in both invertebrates and vertebrates. *Journal of Comparative Physiology A, 196,* 685–700.

Wysocki, C. J., & Preti, G. (2009). *Human pheromones: What's purported, what's supported* (Sense of Smell Institute white paper). New York: Fragrance Foundation.

Yang, M.-H. (2009). Face detection. In S. Z. Li (Ed.), *Encyclopedia of biometrics* (p. 308). New York: Springer.

Yang, S., Bo, L., Want, J., & Shapiro, L. (2012). Unsupervised template learning for fine-grained object recognition. *Neural Information Processing Systems Conference.*

Yarbus, A. L. (1967). *Eye movements and vision.* New York: Plenum Press.

Yau, J. M., Pesupathy, A., Fitzgerald, P. J., Hsiao, S. S., & Connon, C. E. (2009). Analogous intermediate shape coding in vision and touch. *Proceedings of the National Academy of Sciences, 106,* 16457–16462.

Yaxley, R. H., & Zwaan, R. A. (2005). Attentional bias affects change detection. *Psychonomic Bulletin & Review, 12,* 1106–1111.

Yonas, A., & Granrud, C. E. (2006). Infants' perception of depth from cast shadows. *Perception and Psychophysics, 68,* 154–160.

Yonas, A., & Hartman, B. (1993). Perceiving the affordance of contact in four- and five-month old infants. *Child Development, 64,* 298–308.

Yonas, A., Pettersen, L., & Granrud, C. E. (1982). Infant's sensitivity to familiar size as information for distance. *Child Development, 53,* 1285–1290.

Yoshida, K. A., Iversen, J. R., Patel, A. D., Mazuka, R., Nito, H., Gerain, J., et al. (2010). The development of perceptual grouping biases in infancy: A Japanese-English cross-linguistic study. *Cognition, 115,* 356–361.

Yoshida, K., Saito, N., Iriki, A., & Isoda, M. (2011). Representation of others' action by neurons in monkey medial frontal cortex. *Current Biology, 21,* 249–253.

Yost, W. A. (1997). The cocktail party problem: Forty years later. In R. H. Kilkey & T. R. Anderson (Eds.), *Binaural and spatial hearing in real and virtual environments* (pp. 329–347). Hillsdale, NJ: Erlbaum.

Yost, W. A. (2001). Auditory localization and scene perception. In E. B. Goldstein (Ed.), *Blackwell handbook of perception* (pp. 437–468). Oxford, UK: Blackwell.

Yost, W. A. (2009). Pitch perception. *Attention, Perception and Psychophysics, 71,* 1701–1705.

Yost, W. A., & Sheft, S. (1993). Auditory processing. In W. A. Yost, A. N. Popper, & R. R. Fay (Eds.), *Human psychoacoustics* (pp. 193–236). New York: Springer-Verlag.

Young, R. S. L., Fishman, G. A., & Chen, F. (1980). Traumatically acquired color vision defect. *Investigative Ophthalmology and Visual Science, 19,* 545–549.

Young, T. (1802). The Bakerian Lecture: On the theory of light and colours. *Philosophical Transactions of the Royal Society of London, 92,* 12–48.

Youngblood, J. E. (1958). Style as information. *Journal of Music Theory, 2,* 24–35.

Young-Browne, G., Rosenfield, H. M., & Horowitz, F. D. (1977). Infant discrimination of facial expression. *Child Development, 48,* 555–562.

Yuille, A., & Kersten, D. (2006). Vision as Bayesian inference: Analysis by synthesis? *Trends in Cognitive Sciences, 10,* 301–308.

Yuodelis, C., & Hendrickson, A. (1986). A qualitative and quantitative analysis of the human fovea during development. *Vision Research, 26,* 847–855.

Zacks, J. M. (2004). Using movement and intentions to understand simple events. *Cognitive Science, 28,* 979–1008.

Zacks, J. M., Braver, T. S., Sheridan, M. A., Donaldson, D. I., Snyder, A. Z., Ollinger, J. M., et al. (2001). Human brain activity time-locked to perceptual event boundaries. *Nature Neuroscience, 4,* 651–655.

Zacks, J. M., Kumar, S., Abrams, R. A., & Mehta, R. (2009). Using movement and intentions to understand human activity. *Cognition, 112,* 201–206.

Zacks, J. M., & Swallow, K. M. (2007). Event segmentation. *Current Directions in Psychological Science, 16,* 80–84.

Zacks, J. M., & Tversky, B. (2001). Event structure in perception and conception. *Psychological Bulletin, 127,* 3–27.

Zampini, M., & Spence, C. (2010). Assessing the role of sound in the perception of food and drink. *Chemical Perception, 3,* 57–67.

Zeidman, P., Mulally, S. L., Schwarzkopf, S., & Maguire, E. A. (2012). *Neuroreport, 23,* 503–507.

Zeki, S. (1983a). Color coding in the cerebral cortex: The reaction of cells in monkey visual cortex to wavelengths and colours. *Neuroscience, 9,* 741–765.

Zeki, S. (1983b). Color coding in the cerebral cortex: The responses of wavelength-selective and color coded cells in monkey visual cortex to changes in wavelength composition. *Neuroscience, 9,* 767–781.

Zeki, S. (1990). A century of cerebral achromatopsia. *Brain, 113,* 1721–1777.

Zhang, T., & Britten, K. H. (2006). The virtue of simplicity. *Nature Neuroscience, 9,* 1356–1357.

Zhao, G. Q., Zhang, Y., Hoon, M., Chandrashekar, J., Erienbach, I., Ryba, N. J. P., et al. (2003). The receptors for mammalian sweet and umami taste. *Cell, 115,* 255–266.

Zihl, J., von Cramon, D., & Mai, N. (1983). Selective disturbance of movement vision after bilateral brain damage. *Brain, 106,* 313–340.

Zihl, J., von Cramon, D., Mai, N., & Schmid, C. (1991). Disturbance of movement vision after bilateral brain damage. *Brain, 114,* 2235–2252.

Name Index

Aartolahti, E., 152
Abell, F., 173
Abramov, I. 45
Ackerman, D., 369
Addams, R., 175
Aguirre, G. K., 84
Alain, C., 298
Alpern, M., 212
Altenmüller, E., 354
Aminoff, E. M., 114
Amso, D., 144
Anderson, B. A., 127
Anderson, C. H., 74
Angelerques, R., 84
Aniston, J., 87
Anton-Erxleben, K., 133
Anzai, A., 242
Appelle, S., 11, 109
Arbib, M. A., 331
Aronson, E., 152–153
Arzi, A., 375
Ashley, R., 310
Ashmore, J., 275
Aslin, R., 146, 254
Attneave, F., 277
Attridge, G. G., 200
Avenanti, A., 337, 357
Axel, R., 373
Azzopardi, P., 75

Baars, B. J., 89
Bach, M., 248
Bach, J. S., 302
Backhaus, W., 221
Backus, B. T., 242
Baird, J. C., 253
Bakin, J. S., 242
Baldassano, C., 114
Baldauf, D., 135
Ballard, D. H., 130
Banks, M., 45
Bardy, B., 151–152
Bargones, J. Y., 284
Barker, D., 277, 282–283

Barlow, H. B., 191, 242
Barrett, H. C., 173
Barry, S., 234–235
Bartoshuk, L. M., 364, 367–368, 379
Bartrip, J., 119
Basbaum, A. I., 353
Battaglini, P. P., 181
Battelli, L., 189
Bayes, T., 111–112
Baylis, G. C., 380
Beauchamp, G. K., 367, 370, 382–383
Beckers, G., 183
Becklen, R., 139
Beecher, H. K., 352
Behrmann, M., 84
Békésy, G. von, 272–276, 281, 283
Belin, P., 324, 330
Bendor, D., 266, 279
Benedetti, F., 353, 356
Benjamin, L. T., 18
Bennett, P., 45
Bensmaia, S. J., 348
Beranek, L., 300
Berger, K. W., 267
Bernstein, I. L., 382
Berry, H., 87
Bertamini, M., 186
Bess, F. H., 269
Bharucha, J., 306
Bilalić, M., 90
Bingel, U., 353
Birnbaum, M., 369
Birnberg, J. R., 369
Blake, R., 188, 241, 243
Blakemore, C., 64, 89
Blakeslee, A. F., 367
Blaser, E., 175
Block, N., 89
Blumstein, S. E., 329
Boell, E., 347
Boring, E., 99, 244–246
Borji, A., 130
Born, R., 186
Bornstein, M., 222–223

Borst, A., 179
Bosman, C., 134–135
Bouvier, S. E., 211
Bowmaker, J. K., 32
Boynton, R. M., 342, 344
Brainard, D. H., 215–216
Bregman, A., 301–302
Bremmer, F., 313
Breslin, P. A. S., 362
Bridgeman, B., 180–181
Britten, K., 182, 184, 186
Broca, P., 329
Brockmole, J., 129, 166
Bronfman, Z. Z., 140
Bronstad, M., 369
Brown, P. K., 203
Bruce, H., 248
Brunet, N., 135
Bruno, N., 186
Buccino, G., 165
Buck, L., 373
Bufe, B., 368
Buffalo, E. A., 134
Buhle, J. T., 354
Bukach, C. M., 89–90
Burns, E., 276
Burton, A. M., 84
Bushdid, C., 370
Bushnell, C. M., 354
Bushnell, I., 119–120
Busigny, T., 117–118

Caggiano, V., 165
Cain, W. S., 361, 370, 378
Calder, A. J., 118–119
Callaway, E. M., 78
Calvert, G., 323–324
Campbell, F. W., 109
Campbell, J., 302
Carell, S., 66, 68, 87
Carello, C., 347
Carlson, L., 156
Carlson, N. R., 5
Carr, C. E., 295

Carrasco, M., 132–133, 241
Cartwright-Finch, U., 138–139, 143
Carvey, C. E., 55
Casagrande, V. A., 59
Caspers, S., 164
Castelli, F., 173
Castelhano, M. S., 108, 129, 196
Cattaneo, L., 164
Cavanaugh, P., 175
Cavina-Pratesi, C., 211
Cerf, M., 88
Chabris, C., 139
Chandrashekar, J., 366
Chapman, C. R., 355
Chatterjee, S. H., 187
Chen, J., 310
Chevreul, M.-E., 51
Chiu, Y.-C., 133
Choi, G. B., 377
Cholewaik, R. W., 343
Chun, M. M., 126
Churchland, P. S., 25
Clark, E. F., 305
Clarke, J., 141
Cohen, J. D., 84
Cohen, M., 141
Cohen, M .R., 243, 305
Colby, C. L., 134
Cole, J., 337–338
Collett, T. S., 254
Collins, A. A., 343
Colloca, L., 353
Coltheart, M., 230
Comèl, M., 338
Connelly, J. D., 161
Contreras, R. J., 366
Cook, R., 165
Cooper, G., 64, 89
Coppola, D., 11–12, 65, 109
Corbit, J. D., 322–323
Cowey, A., 75
Craig, J. C., 343
Crapse, T. B., 180
Crick, F. C., 89
Crouzet, S. M., 117
Croy, I., 369
Crystal, S. R., 382
Csibra, G., 173
Culler, E. A., 274
Cumming, B. G., 242
Cutting, J. E., 229, 233

Dallos, P., 271
Dalton, D. S., 282
Dalton, P., 369
Damasio, A. R., 329
Damasio, H., 329

Dannemiller, J. L., 223
Dapretto, M., 165
Dartnall, H. J. A., 32, 203
Darwin, C. J., 301–302
Datta, R., 133–134
D'Ausilio, A., 331
David, A. S., 190
Davies, R. L., 222
Davis, H., 275
Davis, M., 327–328
Day, R. H., 250
de Araujo, I. E., 380
de Haas, B., 312
De Lange, F. P., 165
De Santis, L., 298
DeAngelis, G., 242–243
DeCasper, A., 284–285
Del Pero, L., 95
Delahunt, P. B., 215
Delay, E., 366
Deliege, I., 305
DeLucia, P., 250
Delwiche, J. F., 368
Denes, P. B., 10, 325
Derbyshire, S. W. G., 355
Desimone, R., 135
Desor, J. A., 370
Deutsch, D., 303–305
DeValois, K. K., 210
DeValois, R. L., 209–210
deVries, H., 370
DeWall, C. N., 357
deWied, M., 354
DeYoe, E., 133–134
Dick, F., 329
Dingus, T. A., 143
Divenyi, P. L., 306
Dobson, V., 45
Dodd, G. G., 370
Dodds, L. W., 275, 282
Doerrfeld, A., 166
Doolittle, B., 106
Dorsch, T., 166
Dostrovsky, J., 158
Doty, R. L., 369, 382
Dougherty, R., 75
Dowling, J. E., 304
Downing, P. E., 84
Droll, J., 140
Duncan, R. O., 342, 344
Durgin, F. H., 154, 166
Durrani, M., 202
Durrant, J., 269

Egbert, L. D., 353
Egelhaaf, M., 179
Egly, R., 131–132

Ehrenstein, W., 103
Eimas, P. D., 119, 322–323, 331–332
Eisenberger, N., 355, 357
Ekstrom, A. D., 159
Elbert, T., 342
Emmert, E., 247
Engel, S., 12, 211
Engen, T., 370
Engquist, G., 174
Epstein, R. A., 84, 107, 113–114, 156
Epstein, W., 230
Erickson, R., 267
Erickson, R. P., 362, 364–365
Evans, K. K., 141

Fagan, J. F., 145
Fajen, B. R., 153
Farah, M. J., 117
Fattori, P., 161–162
Fechner, G., 13–15
Fei-Fei, L., 107–108
Feldman, J., 136
Ferrari, P. F., 165
Fettiplace, R., 275
Fields, H. L., 353
Fifer, W., 284
Filimon, F., 161
Findlay, J. M., 254
Finger, T. E., 364
Fink, S. I., 139
Finniss, D. G., 353
Fischer, E., 184
Flor, H., 353
Fogassi, L., 165
Forster, S., 141–142
Fortenbaugh, F. C., 150
Foster, D. H., 216
Fox, A. L., 367
Fox, C. R., 152
Fox, R., 255
Franconeri, S. L., 173
Frank, M. E., 364
Frankland, B. W., 305
Franklin, A., 222
Freeman, R. D., 241, 243
Freire, A., 117, 191
Freyd, J., 186–187, 189–190
Friedman, H. S., 211
Friedman-Hill, S. R., 137
Fries, P., 134–135
Friston, K. J., 309
Fritz, T., 354
Fuller, S., 133
Furmanski, C., 12
Fushan, A. A., 368
Fyhn, M., 158

Gagliese, L., 352
Gallese, V., 163, 165
Ganchrow, J. R., 382
Ganel, T., 82
Gao, T., 173
Gardner, M. B., 293
Gardner, R. S., 293
Garland, J., 140
Gauthier, I., 89–90
Gazzola, V., 165
Gegenfurtner, K. R., 196
Geier, J., 54–55
Geisler, W. S., 111
Gelade, G., 136
Gelbard-Sagiv, H., 87
Gerbino, W., 104
Ghahramani, Z., 112
Gibson, B., 5, 105, 107
Gibson, J. J., 149–150, 152, 154, 160, 167,
    177, 348
Gigone, K., 154
Gilad, S., 117
Gilaie-Dotan, S., 184
Gilbert, C. D., 60, 80
Gilchrist, A. L., 6
Gingrich, N., 118
Giza, B. K., 366–367
Glanz, J., 300
Gobbini, M. I., 118
Goffaux, V., 108
Golarai, G., 120
Gold, T., 275
Goldman, R. F., 304
Goldreich, D., 112
Goldstein, E. B., 139
Goodale, M., 9, 81–82, 166
Goodwin, A. W., 340
Gottfried, J. A., 377
Graham, C. H., 212
Grahn, J., 309
Granrud, C., 255–256
Gregory, R., 249–250, 305
Griffin, D., 254
Griffiths, T. D., 280
Grill-Spector, K., 84, 89, 118, 120
Grimes, J. A., 140
Grosbras, M .H., 188
Gross, C., 65
Grossman, E., 188–189
Grothe, R., 296
Gruber, H. E., 253
Gurney, H., 202

Haake, R. J., 255
Haarmeier, T., 181
Hackney, C. M., 275
Hadad, B.-S., 191

Hafting, T., 158
Haigney, D., 143
Hall, D. A., 277, 280, 324
Hall, M. J., 368
Hallemans, A., 152
Hamer, R. D., 222
Hamid, S., 155
Handford, M., 137
Hanowski, R. J., 144
Hansen, T., 217
Harada, T., 211
Harris, J. M., 153
Harris, L., 45
Hartline, K., 50, 56–58
Hartman, B., 256
Harwood, D. L., 304
Hawken, M. J., 211
Haxby, J. V., 80, 118
Hayhoe, M., 130
Hecaen, H., 84
Heesen, R., 202
Heider, F., 173–174
Heise, G. A., 302
Held, R., 255
Helmholtz, H. von, 111–112, 202, 206–207
Henderson, J. M., 107–108, 128–130,
    140, 196
Hendrickson, A., 45
Hering, E., 206–207
Hershenson, M., 253
Herz, R., 382
Hettinger, T. P., 379
Heywood, C. A., 196
Hickman, J. S., 144
Hickock, G., 165, 330
Hill, R. M., 191
Hirsch, H., 243
Hirsh, I. J., 306
Hirstein, W., 352
Hochberg, J., 250
Hodgetts, W. E., 282
Hoeksma, J. B., 195
Hofbauer, R. K., 355
Hoffman, H. G., 354
Hofman, P., 293–294
Holcombe, A. O., 136
Holley, A., 368
Hollingworth, A., 107, 140
Hollins, M., 346–347
Holway, A. H., 244–246
Homberg, V., 183
Horwood, J., 155
Howgate, S., 282
Hsiao, S., 349
Huang, X., 317
Hubel, D., 57–61, 65, 76–78, 182,
    242–243

Hudak, M., 54–55
Hudson, J., 126, 137
Hudspeth, A. J., 276
Hughes, M., 306
Humes, L. E., 269
Hummel, T., 380
Humphrey, A. L., 59, 81
Humphreys, G., 160
Huron, D., 305–306, 308
Hurskainen, W., 101
Hurvich, L., 207–208
Hutchinson, W., 306
Huth, A., 84–85
Hyvärinin, J., 348

Iacobini, M.,332
Iacoboni, M., 164–165
Iannetti, G. D., 358
Isard, S., 325
Ishai, A., 84, 118
Itti, L., 128, 130
Iversen, J., 310
Iwamura, Y., 349

Jackendoff, R., 310
Jacobs, G. H., 209
Jacobs, J., 158–159
Jaeger, S. R., 370
James, W., 125, 127–128, 130, 133
Jameson, D., 207–208
Janzen, G., 156–157
Jeffress, L., 294–296
Jenkins, W., 342
Jensen, T. S., 352
Jessell, T. M., 345
Johansson, G., 187, 343
Johnson, B. A., 375
Johnson, E. N., 211
Johnson, K. O., 343
Johnson, M., 119–120
Johnson, S., 146, 255
Johnston, R. E., 369
Johnston, W., 143
Jones, M. R., 302

Kaas, J. H., 279
Kaiser, A., 241
Kalinowski, I., 354
Kamitani, Y., 115
Kandel, E. R., 155, 345
Kanizsa, G., 104
Kanwisher, N., 65, 83–84, 90, 113, 190
Kapadia, M., 68
Kaplan, G., 233
Karlson, P., 369
Kashino, M., 302
Kastner, S., 74

Katz, D., 346
Katz, J., 352
Kauer, J. S., 361
Kaufman, L., 253
Kavšek, M., 255
Keller, A., 370–371
Kellman, P., 145
Kerman, J., 309
Kersten, D., 111
Kessen, W., 222–223
Kessler, E., 306
Keysers, C., 342, 350
Khanna, S. M., 275
Kiefer, J., 283
Kilner, J., 165
Kim, A., 307, 368
Kimchi, R., 98
King, A. J., 293–294
King, W. L., 253
Kish, D., 313
Kisilevsky, B., 285
Kistler, D. J., 291, 294
Klatzky, R., 347–348
Kleffner, D. A., 109
Klimecki, O., 357
Knopoff, L., 306
Kobayakawa, K., 377
Koch, C., 59, 89, 128, 141
Koelsch, S., 308, 354
Koffka, K., 103
Kohler, E., 163, 331
Kolb, N., 329
Kondo, H. M., 302
Konishi, M., 295
Kourtzi, Z., 184, 190
Kriegstein, K. von, 324
Kroner, T., 382
Kross, E., 357
Kruger, L. E. 348, 353
Krumhansl, C., 305–306, 308
Kudrow, L., 87
Kuhl, P., 333–334
Kujawa, S., 282
Kushner, T., 361

LaBarbera, J. D., 119
Laing, D. D., 370
Lamble, D., 143
Lamm, C., 357
Land, E. H., 216
Land, M. F., 130, 154–155
Larsen, A., 175–176
Larsson, M., 382
Lashley, G., 230
Laurent, M., 151–152
Lavie, N., 138–139, 141–143
Lawless, H., 367, 378

Lederman, S., 348
Lee, D., 152–155
LeGrand, Y., 207, 212
Lennie, P., 210
Leonard, D. G. B., 275, 375
Lerdahl, R., 310
Lesham, M., 382
Li, F. F., 140–141
Li, L., 150
Li, W., 60, 80
Li, X, 367
Liberman, A. M., 275, 282, 331–332
Liberman, C., 282
Lieberman, M. D., 357
Lindquist, K. A., 358
Litovsky, R. Y., 299, 302
Liu, T, 133, 282
Lomber, S., 297–298
London, J., 309
Loomis, J. M., 153, 166
Lord, S. R., 152
Lorteije, J. A. M., 190
Lotto, A. J., 331
Lovrinic, J., 269
Lowenstein, W., 345
Luck, S. J., 134
Lundy, R. F., Jr., 366
Lüscher, M., 369
Lyall, V., 366
Lyle, K. B., 343

Macaulay, T., 96
MacDonald, J., 323
Mach, E., 51
Mack, A., 138, 141
Maess, B., 308
Maguire, E., 114, 159
Maier, S. F., 351
Mainland, J. D., 370
Malcolm, G. L., 132
Malhotra, S., 297–298
Malnic, B., 373–374
Mamassian, P., 231
Maner, J., 369
Margulis, E. H., 308
Marino, A. C., 131–132
Marr, D., 241
Mather, G., 191
Mathews, M. W., 267
Maunsell, J. H. R., 80
Maxwell, J. C., 202–203, 206–207
McAlpine, D., 283, 295–296
McBurney, D., 362
McCann, J. J., 216
McCarthy, G., 65
McCarthy, J., 217
McClintock, M. K., 369

McCutcheon, A., 148
McFadden, S. A., 254
McGettigan, C., 324
McGurk, H., 323
McIntosh, R. D., 230
McRae, J. F., 370
Mehler, J., 320
Mehribian, A., 195
Meister, I. G., 332
Meltzoff, A., 167–168
Melzack, R., 337, 352–353, 355
Menashe, I., 370
Meng, M., 116–117
Mennella, J., 382–383
Menz, H. B., 152
Menz, M. D., 241
Menzel, R., 221
Merigan, W. H., 80, 183
Merskey, H., 351
Merzenich, M., 342
Mesgarani, N., 330–331
Meso, A. I., 179
Meyer, K., 350
Meyer, L. B., 306, 308
Micelli, G., 330
Micheyl, C., 302, 305
Miller, G., 325
Miller, G. A., 302
Miller, J., 156
Miller, J. D., 282
Miller, S., 369
Milner, D., 9, 81–82, 86, 166
Mishkin, M., 79–82
Mollon, J. D., 196, 200, 202
Mondlach, C. J., 120
Montagna, W., 338
Mon-Williams, M., 229
Monzée, J., 337
Moon, R. J., 1993, 285
Moore, B. C. J., 281
Moore, K., 167
Morton, J., 119–120
Moser, E., 158
Moser, M.-B., 158
Moulton, D. G., 370
Mountcastle, V. B., 348
Movshon, J. A., 183
Mozell, M. M., 379
Mueller, K., 365, 367
Mukamel, R., 164
Mullally, S. L., 114
Murphy, C., 378
Murphy, K. J., 81
Murray, M. M., 312
Murray, S. O., 184
Murthy, V. N., 375
Myers, D. G., 5

Nadel, L., 158
Naselaris, T., 115–116
Nassi, J. J., 78
Nathans, J., 203, 213
Natu, V., 119
Neff, D., 296–298
Neisser, U., 139
Neri, P., 242
Newhall, S. M., 200
Newsome, W., 182–183, 189
Newsome, W. T., 243
Newton, I., 196–197, 200–201, 221
Newtson, D., 174
Nickerson, D., 200
Nikolajsen, L., 352
Nikonov, A. A., 375
Nodal, F., 297
Nordby, K., 196
Norman-Haignere, S., 280–281
Norton, T. T., 59
Noton, D., 129
Novick, J. M., 329
Novotny, M., 369
Nozaradan, S., 310

O'Craven, K. M., 133
O'Doherty, J., 380–381
Ohzawa, I., 241
Okamoto, T., 282
O'Keefe, J., 157–158
Oliva, A., 107–108, 110, 196
Olkkonen, M., 215
Olsho, L. W., 284
Olson, C. R., 243
Olson, R. K., 277
Olson, R. L., 144
Orban, G. A., 109
Osmanski, B. F., 376
Oster, H., 382
Osterhout, L., 307
O'Toole, A. J., 95, 119
Oxenham, A. J., 266, 276–279, 305

Pack, C., 186
Palmer, C., 310
Palmer, S. E., 102, 109–110
Parakkal, P. F., 338
Paré, M., 183
Parker, A. J., 242
Parkhi, O. M., 95
Parkhurst, D., 128
Parkin, A. J., 84
Pascalis, O., 119
Pascual-Leone, A., 342
Pasternak, T., 183
Patel, A., 307
Peacock, G., 202

Pei, Y.-C., 348
Pelchat, M. L., 370–371
Pelphrey, K. A., 188
Penfield, W., 341
Peng, J.-H., 282
Pereira, C. S., 308
Perl, E. R., 351, 353
Perrett, D. I., 65
Perrodin, C., 330
Perugino, P., 230
Peters, J., 144
Peterson, F., 382
Peterson, M. A., 5, 98, 104–107
Pfaffmann, C., 367, 370
Pfeiffer, C. J., 369
Philbeck, J. W., 153–154, 166, 208
Phillips, J. R., 343
Phillips-Silver, J., 310–311
Pinson, E. N., 10, 325
Piqueras-Fiszman, G., 380
Pisoni, D., 321, 325
Pitcher, D., 119
Plack, C. J., 277, 280–283, 305, 310
Plassmann, H., 380
Plata-Salaman, C. R., 367
Plaut, D. C., 84
Plug, C., 253
Poeppel, D., 330
Poggio, T., 84, 241–242
Pointer, M. R., 200
Pokorny, J., 216, 354
Pollack, J., 323
Poloschek, C. M., 248
Poranen, A., 348
Porter, R. H., 369, 382
Posner, M., 130–131
Potter, M., 107
Powell, T. P. S., 348
Prendergast, G., 282–283
Presnell, L., 196
Preti, G., 369
Price, D. D., 353, 355
Proffitt, D., 166
Proust, M., 381
Puce, A., 118–119
Purkinje, J., 32

Quinlan, P., 136
Quinn, P. C., 119
Quiroga, R. Q., 66, 68, 87

Rabin, M. D., 364
Rabinovitz, B., 88
Radcliffe, D., 140
Rainey, L. H., 382
Rainville, C., 157
Rainville, P., 353, 355

Ramachandran, V. S., 25, 109, 352
Rao, H., 184
Rasmussen, T., 341
Ratliff, F., 50
Ratner, C., 217
Rauschecker, J. P., 279, 298, 330
Read, S., 143
Recanzone, G., 297
Reddy, L., 141
Reddy, S., 317
Regev, M., 313
Reichardt, W., 177–179
Rennaker, R., 376
Rensink, R., 139–140
Repacholi, B., 168
Repin, I., 129
Restrepo, D., 375
Rhode, W. S., 275
Rhudy, J., 354
Riddoch, J., 160
Rieger, J., 196
Riesenhuber, M., 84
Riley, M. A., 167
Ringbach, D. L., 241
Risner, R., 346
Risner, S. R., 346
Risset, J. C., 267
Rizzolatti, G., 163–165
Robbins, J., 354
Roberts, J., 140
Robertson, L., 137–138
Robinson, D. L., 181
Robles-De-La-Torre, G., 337
Rocha-Miranda, C., 65
Rock, I., 102, 138, 253
Rogers, A., 87
Rogers, B. J., 153
Rogers, P., 202
Rollman, G. B., 337
Rolls, E. T., 65, 83, 379–381
Rosenstein, D., 382
Ross, H. E., 253
Rossion, B., 117–118
Roudi, Y., 158
Rowe, J., 309
Rowe, M. J., 340
Roy, M., 354
Rubin, P., 324
Rushton, S. K., 153, 155
Rushton, W., 31
Russell, M. J., 382
Rust, N. C., 186

Sacks, O., 8, 195, 234
Saffran, J., 326–327, 332
Sakata, H., 81, 349
Salapatek, P., 45

Salasoo, A., 325
Salvagio, E., 104
Salvucci, D., 155
Samuel, A., 324
Sanders, L., 325
Sato, M., 366
Saul, A. B., 59
Saygin, A. P., 188
Schaal, B., 369, 382
Schaette, R., 283
Scherf, K. S., 120
Schiffman, H. R., 230
Schiffman, S., 365
Schiller, P. H., 55, 80
Schinazi, V. R., 156
Schlack, A., 313
Schmidt, H., 137–138
Schmuziger, N., 282
Schnapf, J. L., 203
Scholl, B. J., 131–132
Scholz, J., 351
Schooler, J., 382
Schyns, P. G., 196
Scott, T., 366–367
Scoville, W. B., 86
Segui, J., 320
Senior, C., 190
Shackman, A. J., 358
Shamma, S. A., 302
Shannon, R., 328
Shapley, R., 211
Sheft, S., 302
Shepherd, G. M., 378
Sherf, K.S., 89
Sherman, S. M., 59, 202
Shiffrar, M., 186–187
Shimojo, S., 255
Shinoda, H., 128
Shomstein, S., 132
Shuwairi, S. M., 255
Silbert, L., 331–332
Silver, M. A., 74
Simion, F., 191–192
Simmel, M., 173–174
Simons, D., 139, 173
Simonyan, K., 95
Singer, T., 357
Singh, D., 369
Sinha, P., 97, 317
Sinigaglia, C., 165
Siveke, I., 295
Slagter, H. A., 141
Slater, A. M., 145, 254
Sloan, L. L., 212
Sloboda, J. A., 305, 310
Small, D. M., 379
Smith, D., 366

Smith, M. A., 186
Smithson, H. E., 196, 215
Sobel, E. C., 232, 254, 375
Solomon, S. G., 210
Solstad, T., 158
Sommer, M. A., 180–181
Sosulski, D. L., 377
Soto-Faraco, S., 312
Soucy, E. R., 375
Spector, A. C., 366
Spelke, E., 145
Spence, C., 143, 380
Spence, M. J., 285
Sperling, G., 175
Spierer, L., 312
Squirrell, D. J., 370
Srinivasan, M. V., 232, 254
Stark, L., 129, 180–181
Steiner, J. E., 382
Stern, K., 369
Stevens, S. S., 15
Stevens, J., 187
Stoffregen, T. A., 152
Strayer, D., 143–144
Stuiver, M., 370
Sufka, K. J., 353
Suga, N., 254
Sugovic, M., 166
Sullivan, R. M., 377
Sumby, W. H., 323
Sumner, P., 196
Sun, H.-J., 154
Svaetichin, G., 209
Swallow, K. M., 173

Taira, M., 81
Tan, S. L., 309–310
Tanabe, S., 241
Tanaka, J., 196
Tanigawa, H., 211
Tatler, B. W., 130
Taube, J. S., 158
Teller, D., 45
Teller, D. Y., 223, 255
Tenenbaum, J. B., 112
Terwogt, M. M., 195
Thaler, L., 313
Theeuwes, J., 127
Thicke, R., 126, 137
Thorpe, S. J., 140
Tian, B., 298
Todrank, J., 379
Tolman, E., 157
Tomlinson, G., 309
Tong, F., 112–113, 115, 133
Tong, J., 84
Tootell, R. B. H., 211

Torralba, A., 107–108, 110, 128
Tovee, M., 83
Tracey, I., 353, 355
Trainor, L., 310–311
Travers, S. P., 366
Treisman, A., 136–138, 141
Tresilian, J. R., 229
Troiani, V., 114
Truax, B., 266
Tsao, D., 83
Tsuchiya, N., 141
Turano, K. A., 154
Turatto, M., 133
Turk, D. C., 353
Turman, A. B., 340
Turner, S. R., 4, 206
Turvey, M. T., 347
Tversky, B., 173
Tye-Murray, N., 283

Uchida, N., 374–375
Uchikawa, K., 215
Uddin, L. Q., 165
Uka, T., 242
Umeda, K., 242
Ungerleider, L. G., 79–82

Valdez, P., 195
Vallbo, A. B., 343
Vallortigara, G., 191
van Doorn, G. H., 380
Van Essen, D. C., 74
van Kemenade, B. M., 189
Van Opstal, A. J., 294
Van Rullen, R., 140
Van Turennout, M., 156–157
Van Wanrooij, M. M., 294
van Wassenhove, V., 324
Varner, D., 222
Vecera, S., 103–104
Veldhuizen, M. G., 380
Venkatesh, S., 232, 254
Verbaten, M., 354
Verhagen, J. V., 380
Vermeij, G., 347
Viemeister, N., 276
Vingerhoets, G., 161
Violanti, J. M., 143
Vishton, P. M., 229, 233
Võ, M., 128–129
von der Emde, G., 254
Von Hippel, P., 306
Vonderschen, K., 294
Vuust, P., 308

Wagner, H., 50, 294
Wald, G., 203

Waldrop, M. M., 321
Walker, S., 141
Wall, P. D., 337, 352–353
Wallace, G. K., 232
Wallace, M. N., 279
Wallach, H., 299
Walls, G. L., 196
Wandell, B. A., 75, 216
Wang, X., 181, 266, 279
Wann, J., 155
Warren, R., 304, 324
Warren, W. H., 150,152–154
Waterman, I., 337–338, 340
Watkins, L. R., 351
Weber, A. I., 347
Weber, E., 14
Webster, M., 216
Weiner, K., S., 84
Weisenberg, M., 353
Weiskopf, S., 222–223
Weissberg, M., 353

Werner, L A., 284
Wernicke, C., 329
Wertheimer, M., 99, 105, 174
Westerman, S. J., 143
Wexler, M., 172
Whishaw, I. Q., 329
Wiech, K., 353
Wiesel, T. N., 57–61, 65, 76–78, 182, 242
Wightman, F. L., 291, 294
Wild, J. M., 254
Wilkie, R. M., 155
Willander, J., 382
Williams, Z. M., 184
Wilson, D. A., 332, 377
Wilson, H. R., 241
Wilson, J. R., 59
Wilson, R., 87
Winawer, J., 190
Winston, J. S., 118–119

Wissinger, C. M., 298
Witt, J., 166–167
Wolfe, J. M., 136
Wollach, L., 212
Wolpert, D. M., 112
Womelsdorf, T., 68, 133, 135
Woo, C.-W., 358
Woods, A. J., 166
Woolf, C., 351
Wozniak, R. H., 14
Wundt, W., 98
Wurtz, R., 181
Wurtz, R. H., 180–181
Wyatt, T. D., 369
Wysocki, C. J., 369

Yang, M.-H., 95
Yantis, S., 133
Yarbus, A., 129
Yau, J. M., 348

Yaxley, R. H., 140
Yee, W., 302
Yonas, A., 255–256
Yoshida, K. A., 165
Yost, W. A., 276, 301–302
Young, R. S. L., 196
Young, T., 202
Youngblood, J. E., 306
Young-Browne, G., 119
Yuille, A., 111
Yuodelis, C. 45

Zacks, J. M., 173
Zampini, M., 380
Zanker, J. M., 179
Zeidman, P., 114
Zeki, S., 196, 210
Zhang, T., 186
Zhao, G.Q., 366
Zihl, J., 174
Zwaan, R. A., 140

Subject Index

Ablation, 79
Absolute disparity, 236–239, 242
Absolute threshold, 14
Absorption spectrum, 32
Accommodation, 25–26
    monocular cues and, 229
    oculomotor cues and, 228–229
Accretion, 232–233
Achromatic colors, 197, 217
Achromatopsia, 211
Acoustic shadow, 290
Acoustic signals, 301, 318–322, 324
Acoustic stimulus, 318
Acoustics, 300
Across-fiber patterns, 365
Action, 9, 149–168
    balance and, 152–153
    demonstrations of, 152
    driving, 154–155
    invariant information, 150–151
    moving observer and, 150–151
    objects and, 160–163
    observing other people's actions,
        163–164
    perception and, 150–157, 166–168
    predicting intentions, 164–165
    review questions on, 149, 160, 168–169
    self-produced information, 151–152
    speech perception and, 331
    walking, 153–154
    wayfinding, 155–160
Action pathway, 82
Action potential
    chemical basis of, 36
    falling phase of, 36
    properties of, 34–36
    rising phase of, 36
    transmitting information, 37
Action-specific perception hypothesis,
    166–167

Active touch, 347
Acuity. See Tactile acuity; Visual acuity
Adaptation
    dark, 28–31, 41–42
    selective, 62–63
Adapting stimulus, 62–63
Additive color mixture, 200
Adjustment, 14
Advanced precision grip, 162
Affective component of pain, 355
Affordances, 160–161
Afterimages
    color perception and, 207–208
    demonstrations of, 180
    motion perception and, 180
    size perception and, 252
Aging, presbyopia and, 27, 281
Akinetopsia, 174, 183
Amacrine cells, 39, 50–51
Ambiguity
    retinal image and, 96–97, 111
    sound localization and, 292
Ames room illusion, 251–252
Amiloride, 366
Amplitude, 261–262, 264–265, 276
Amplitude-modulated noise, 276
Amygdala, 86–87, 118, 376–377, 379, 382
Angle of disparity, 236–238
Angular size contrast theory, 253
Animals
    camouflaged, 171–173
    depth perception and, 253–254
    echolocation, 254
    electrolocation, 254
    frontal eyes, 253–254
    lateral eyes, 253–254
    mating behavior, 369
    movement parallax, 254
    olfaction and, 368–370
    sound localization and, 296

Anomalous trichromatism, 213
Anosmia, 369
Anterior auditory cortex, 280
Anterior belt area, 297–298
Anterior cingulate cortex, 357–358
Anterior insula, 357–358
Aperiodic sounds, 267
Aperture problem, 186
Apex of the cochlea, 273
Aphasias, 329
Apparent distance theory, 252–253
Apparent motion/movement, 99,
    174–176, 186–187
Appearance of objects, 132–133
Architectural acoustics, 299–300
Archtrajectory, 306
Area V1 of cortex, 59
Articulators, 318–319
Atmospheric perspective, 230–231
Attack, tone, 267
Attention, 125–146
    appearance and, 132–133
    benefits of, 130–134
    binding and, 136–138
    brain activity and, 133–135
    change detection and, 139–140
    cognition and, 128–130
    demonstrations of, 126–127, 138–139
    directing, 127
    distraction and, 141–144
    divided, 137
    eye movements and, 126–127,
        129–130
    feature integration theory, 136–138
    inattentional blindness, 138–141, 143
    observer interests and goals, 129–130
    pain perception and, 353–354
    perception and, 140–141
    perceptual completion, 144–146
    perceptual load and, 142–143

Attention (*Continued*)
   physiological responding and, 133–135
   response speeds and, 130–133
   review questions on, 135, 146
   scanning process and, 126–127
   scene schemas, 128–129
   spatial, 130–132
   tactile object perception and, 349–350
   task characteristics and, 141–142
   task-related knowledge, 130
   visual salience, 127–129
Attention maps, 134
Attentional capture, 127–128, 173
Audibility curve, 265, 284
Audiogram, 282–283
Audiovisual mirror neurons, 163–164, 331
Audiovisual speech perception, 323
Auditory canal, 268–269
Auditory continuity, 304
Auditory cortex
   anterior, 280
   echolocation and, 313
   effects of damage to, 265, 269
   locating sound and, 296, 298
   pitch perception and, 278–280
Auditory grouping, 302–304
Auditory localization, 289–298, 301–302
   anterior belt area and, 298
   azimuth information for, 290–291, 293–294
   binaural cues for, 290–292, 294
   distance information for, 290–291
   elevation information for, 290–291
   Jeffress model, 294–296
   location cues and, 290
   monaural cues for, 292–294
   physiology of, 294
   posterior belt area and, 297–298
   review questions on, 301
   spectral cues for, 293–294
   vision and, 294
   what pathway, 297–298
   where pathway, 297–298
Auditory nerve, 278
Auditory pathways, 297–298
Auditory receiving area, 278
Auditory response area, 265
Auditory scene, 301
Auditory scene analysis, 301–304
Auditory space, 290

Auditory stream integration, 305–306
Auditory stream segregation, 290, 302–303
Auditory system
   brain diagram of, 278
   causes of damage to, 281–283
   cortical processing and, 278–280, 296–298, 309–310
   frequency represented in, 272–273
   infant development and, 284–285
   phase locking in, 272, 277–279
   place theory of, 276–278
   representing tones, 68
   review questions on, 267–268, 276, 285, 314
   sound separation and, 301–304
   sound stimulus and, 268
   speech perception and, 323
   structure of, 268–275
   See also Hearing
Axial myopia, 27
Axon, 33–36
Azimuth coordinate, 290–291, 293–294

Balance
   senses and, 152
   visual information and, 152–153
Balint's syndrome, 137–138
Basal ganglia, 309
Base of the cochlea, 273
Basilar membrane, 270–272, 276, 283
Bass ratio, 300
Batman (film), 87
Bats, 254
Bayesian inference, 111–112
Beat, 309–310
Behavioral responses, 8–9
Belt area, 278
Bimodal neurons, 380
Binaural cues, 290–291, 294, 296
Binding, 136–138
Binocular cues, 233–239
   3-D images and, 235
   binocular disparity and, 235–241
   corresponding retinal points and, 235–236
   noncorresponding points and, 236–237
   random-dot stereograms, 239–241, 255
   stereopsis and, 239–240
Binocular depth cells, 242–243

Binocular disparity, 235–243, 253–254
Binocular rivalry, 113
Binocularly fixate, 254–255
Biological motion, 187–189, 191–192
Bipolar cells, 39, 52–54
Birds
   sound localization and, 296
   See also Animals
Bitter tastes, 362, 365–367
Blind spots, 24–25
   demonstrations of, 24–25
Blind walking experiment, 153–154
Border cells, 158
Border ownership, 103
Borders, 103–104
Bottom-up processing, 10
Braille, 342–343
Brain
   ablation of, 79
   attention to locations, 133–135
   border cells, 158
   Broca's area, 329
   comparator, 179
   distributed representation, 84–86
   dorsal, 80–83
   experience-dependent plasticity, 333–334
   extrastriate body area (EBA), 84, 188
   face perception and, 113, 116–119
   fusiform face area (FFA), 65, 83–86, 89–90, 113, 116–118, 133, 188, 324
   grid cells, 158
   head direction cells, 158
   hippocampus, 86–87, 382
   inferotemporal (IT) cortex, 65, 83, 86
   medial temporal lobe (MTL), 86–87
   metrical perception and, 310
   middle temporal area, 182–183
   middle temporal (MT) area, 184, 188–190
   mirror neurons, 163–165
   motion perception and, 182–189
   multisensory interactions, 312–314
   navigation and, 156–159
   object perception and, 113–119
   olfaction and, 379
   opioid receptors, 355–356
   pain perception and, 354–356
   parahippocampal place area (PPA), 84, 87, 113–114
   place cells/fields, 158
   primary receiving areas, 8

scene perception and, 114–116
semantic encoding, 115–116
speech perception and, 323–324,
  328–332
structural encoding, 115–116
taste perception and, 364, 379
ventral, 80–83
vision and, 59, 82
voxels, 75
Brain ablation, 79
Brain areas and pathways (figures)
  amygdala, 86–87, 118
  anterior cingulate cortex, 357
  anterior insula, 357
  auditory pathways, 278–279, 297, 309
  Broca's area, 329
  distributed representation, 85–86
  dorsal/ventral, 80
  entorhinal cortex, 87
  extrastriate body area (EBA), 84
  frontal lobes, 86
  fusiform face area (FFA), 65, 86, 113,
    117–118, 120
  hippocampus, 87
  inferotemporal (IT) cortex, 65
  occipital cortex, 86
  olfactory pathway, 375
  pain matrix, 355, 357
  parahippocampal place area (PPA),
    84, 87,
    113, 120
  parietal lobe, 80
  somatosensory, 341, 350
  speech areas, 330, 332
  superior temporal sulcus, 86
  taste pathway, 364
  temporal lobe, 80
  visual system, 34, 59
  voxels, 114
  Wernicke's area, 329
Brain damage
  affordances and, 160–161
  color perception and, 211
  double dissociations, 81–82
  motion perception and, 174, 181, 189
  object perception and, 161
  speech perception and, 329, 331
Brain imaging, 75–76
  attention and, 134
  cortical magnification, 75
  distributed representation, 84–86
  face perception and, 83

magnetic resonance imaging, 75–76
  modularity studies, 83–84
  speech perception and, 329
  wayfinding and, 159
Brightness, 14
Broadly tuned neurons, 296
Broca's aphasia, 329
Broca's area, 329

Calcium imaging, 373
Camouflaged animals, 171–173
Categorical perception, 322, 332–333
Categorizing, 10
Cats, 64, 95, 243, 253, 265, 296–297, 367
Cell body, 33
Cell phones, distraction and, 143–144
Cells
  complex, 61–62
  end-stopped, 61–62
  ganglion, 39–42, 62
  hair, 270–272
  simple cortical, 60, 62
Center-surround antagonism, 57
Center-surround organization, 56
Center-surround receptive fields,
  56–58
Central control fibers, 353
Cerebral achromatopsia, 195
Cerebral cortex, 8
Change blindness, 139–141
Change detection, 139–140
Characteristic frequency, 274
Chemical senses, 359–383
  flavor perception and, 378–383
  olfaction and, 368–383
  overview of, 361–362
  review questions on, 368
  taste perception and, 362–368
Chemotopic map, 375
Chevreul (staircase) illusion, 51–55, 248
Children
  fusiform face area (FFA), 120
  language learning and, 334
  speech perception and, 326
  See also Infants
Chromatic adaptation, 215
Chromatic colors, 197, 200, 217
Cilia, 268, 270–272
Ciliary muscles, 25
Circumvallate papillae, 363
Classical psychophysical methods, 14
Coarticulation, 321

Cochlea, 269–271
  apex of, 273–274
  base of, 273–274
  frequency and, 273–275
  place theory and, 276
  tonotopic maps of, 274
Cochlear amplifier, 274–275
Cochlear implants, 283
Cochlear nucleus, 278
Cochlear partition, 269–270
Code, sensory. See neural code
Cognition
  attention and, 128–130
  flavor perception and, 380
  haptic exploration and, 348
  pain perception and, 353–356
  perception and, 12–13
Cognitive maps, 157–158
Coherence, 135, 182
Coincidence detectors, 295
Color
  achromatic, 197, 217
  chromatic, 197, 200, 217
  mixing, 198–200
  nonspectral, 200
  properties of, 196–197
  saturation of, 200–201
  spectral, 200
  transmission and, 198
  wavelengths and, 220–221
Color blindness, 195–196, 211–213
Color circle, 206
Color constancy, 214–216
  chromatic adaptation and, 215–216
  demonstrations of, 215–216
  effect of surroundings on, 216
  illumination and, 214–217
  memory and, 216–217
  partial, 215–216
Color deficiency
  anomalous trichromatism, 213
  color blindness, 195–196, 211–213
  cortical damage and, 195–196
  dichromatism, 205, 212–213
  monochromatism, 205, 212
  receptor-based, 204–205
  tests for, 212
  trichromats, 205
Color perception, 195–224
  afterimages, 207
  color constancy and, 214–217
  cortex and, 210–211

Color perception (*Continued*)
  deficiency of, 204–205, 211–213
  demonstrations of, 207, 215–216, 219
  effect of surroundings on, 216
  form and, 211
  functions of, 196
  infants and, 222–223
  lightness constancy and, 217–219
  loss or blindness, 195–196, 211–213
  memory and, 216–217
  mixed colors and, 198–200
  nervous system and, 219–222
  opponent-process theory, 201, 206–209
  physiology of, 203–204, 209–210
  reflectance and, 197–198
  review questions on, 201, 213–214, 223
  short wavelength sensitivity, 32
  transmission and, 197–198
  trichromatic theory of, 201–207, 209
  wavelengths and, 196–200, 203–205, 208–210, 213, 220–221
  Young-Helmholtz theory, 202
Color solid, 201
Color-matching experiments, 202, 212
Columnar organization
  hypercolumns, 78
  location columns, 76–78
  ocular dominance columns, 78*n*
  orientation columns, 76–78
Common fate, 102
Common logarithms, 263
Common region, 102
Comparator, 179
Complementary afterimages, 207
Complex cells, 61–62
Complex tones, 263–264
Component of pain, 355
Compound melodic line, 302
Computer vision research, 94–95
Computer vision systems, 94–97, 112
Computers
  face perception and, 95
  object perception and, 94–96
  speech perception and, 317
Concert hall acoustics, 299–300
Condensation, 261
Cone of confusion, 292–293
Cone pigments, 203
Cone spectral sensitivity, 32

Cone vision, 41–42
Cones, 22
  color perception and, 203, 209–210, 212
  dark adaptation and, 28–30
  visual acuity, 41–42
  See also Rod and cone receptors
Conflicting cues theory, 250
Conjunction search, 137–138
Consonants, 319–320
Constancy
  color, 214–217
  lightness, 217–219
  size, 246–250
  speech perception and, 321
Constant stimuli, 14
Context
  meaningfulness and, 324–325
  speech perception and, 320–321, 326
Contextual modulation, 68–69
Continuity errors, 140
Contrast, perceived, 132–133
Contrast threshold, 62–63
Convergence, 39–42
  demonstrations of, 41
  monocular cues and, 230
  oculomotor cues and, 228–229
  perspective, 230
  review questions on, 45–46
Core area, 278
Cornea, 7, 22, 25
Corollary discharge signal (CDS), 179–180
Corollary discharge theory, 179–181
Correlations, 88–89
Correspondence problem, 240–241
Corresponding retinal points, 235–238
Cortex, 210
  anterior cingulate, 357–358
  auditory areas in, 278–280, 296–298, 309–310
  color perception and, 210
  dorsal anterior cingulate, 357
  frontal operculum, 364
  inferotemporal, 65, 83, 86
  maps of the body on, 341–342
  middle temporal area, 182–184, 188–190
  motor area of, 331–332
  occipital, 8, 59, 86, 118
  odor perception and, 375–376
  olfactory, 372

  opponent neurons and, 210–211
  orbitofrontal, 376, 379–381
  pain perception and, 357
  piriform, 376–377
  primary receiving areas, 8
  somatosensory, 340–342, 349
  speech perception and, 329–332
  striate, 59–61, 74, 77–80, 188
  touch perception and, 348–350
  visual, 59–60
Cortical body maps, 341–342
Cortical magnification, 74–75
Cortical magnification factor, 74, 76
Cortical organization, 73–89
  demonstrations of, 76
  hypercolumns, 78
  location columns, 76–78
  magnification factor, 74–76
  orientation columns, 76–78
  retinotopic map, 74
  review questions on, 79, 90–91
Covert attention, 126
Crossed disparity, 237
Cue approach to depth perception, 228
Cutaneous receptive field, 339
Cutaneous senses, 337–359
  cortical body maps and, 341–342
  demonstrations of, 344, 347
  detail perception and, 342–344
  nerve pathways and, 339–341
  object perception and, 347–350
  pain perception and, 351–358
  review questions on, 351, 358–359
  skin receptors and, 338–341
  texture perception and, 344–347
  vibration perception and, 344–345
  See also Touch perception

Dark adaptation, 28–31, 41–42
Dark adaptation curve, 15, 28–31
Dark-adapted sensitivity, 28
Data-based processing, 10
Deactivating, 183
Decay, tone, 267
Decibel (dB), 262–263
Decision-point landmarks, 155–157
Defense Advanced Research Project Agency (DARPA), 94
Degraded speech, 327
Delay units, 178
Deletion, 232–233
Dendrites, 33

Depolarization, 38
Depth cues
 binocular, 233–236
 monocular, 229–234
 oculomotor, 228–229
 pictorial, 229–231
Depth perception, 227–256
 3-D images and, 231–232, 235
 animals and, 253–254
 binocular cues and, 233–241
 binocular disparity and, 253–255
 cast shadows and, 256
 cue approach to, 228
 demonstrations of, 229, 233
 disparity information and, 236–239
 illusions of size and, 248–253
 infants and, 254–256
 monocular cues and, 229–234
 oculomotor cues and, 228–229
 physiology of, 242–243
 pictorial cues and, 255–256
 review questions on, 243, 256–257
 size perception and, 243–253
 stereoscopic, 234–235
Dermis, 338
Desaturated hues, 200–201
Detached retina, 31
Detail perception, touch and, 342–344
Detection
 change, 139–140
 odor perception and, 369–370
Detection threshold, 369–370
Detectors
 feature, 55, 62–65, 108, 115–117
 molecule, 361
Deuteranopia, 212–213
Development of perception
 attention and perceptual completion,
  144–146
 biological motion perception, 191–192
 chemical sensitivity, 382–383
 color vision and, 222–223
 depth perception, 254–256
 experience and, 89–90
 face perception, 119–120
 hearing, 284–285
 imitating actions, 167–168
 speech perception, 332–333
 visual acuity, 43–45
Dichromatism, 205, 212–213
Difference threshold, 14
Direct pathway model of pain, 351–352

Direct sound, 298–299
Discrimination test, 322
Dishabituation, 145
Disparity
 absolute, 236–239
 angle of, 236–238
 crossed, 237
 relative, 238–239
 uncrossed, 237
Disparity tuning curve, 242
Disparity-selective cells, 242–243
Distal stimulus, 6–7, 21, 260
Distance, 290–291
Distracted driving, 143–144
Distraction, 141–144
Distributed processing
 color perception and, 210
 face perception and, 117–119
 olfaction and, 374
 pain perception and, 355
 population coding, 364
 skin receptors and, 340
 wayfinding, 160
Distributed representation, 84–86
Divided attention, 137
Dorsal anterior cingulate cortex, 357
Dorsal pathway, 80–82, 161
Dorsal root, 340
Double dissociations, 81–82
Double-opponent neurons, 211
Driving
 distraction and, 143–144
 environmental information and,
  154–155
Dual-stream model of speech
 perception, 330
Dual-task procedure, 140
Duple meter, 310
Duplex theory of texture perception,
 346–347

Ear
 inner, 269–271
 middle, 268–269
 outer, 268
 structure of, 268–275
 See also Auditory system; Hearing
Eardrum, 268
Echolocation, 254, 313
Ecological approach to perception, 149
 environmental information and,
  150–156

 self-produced information, 151–152
Ecological Approach to Perception, The
 (Gibson), 167
Ecological validity, 149–150
Effect of the missing fundamental,
 266
Electrical energy, 27–28
Electrical signals, 33–34
Electrolocation, 254
Electromagnetic spectrum, 18
Elements of Psychophysics (Fechner), 14
Elevation, 290–291
Emmert's Law, 247
Emoter, 168
Emotional component of pain, 355
Emotions
 facial expressions, 167
 olfaction and, 379, 381–383
 pain perception and, 354–355
Empathy, 357
Endorphins, 356
End-stopped cells, 61–62
Entorhinal cortex, 87
Environment
 indoor, 298–300
 interactions with, 150, 160, 166, 168
 knowledge of, 97, 128
 navigation and, 160
 regularities in the, 108–111
 representing, 166
 spatial updating in, 154
 wayfinding, 155–157
Environmental information
 balance and, 152–153
 driving and, 154–155
 ecological approach to perception
  and, 150–156
 invariant, 151–152
 motion perception and, 173, 177
 optic flow and, 150–151
 self-produced, 151–152
 sound localization and, 291, 294, 296
 walking and, 153–154
Epidermis, 338
Equal loudness curves, 265–266
Event boundary, 174
Event-related potential, 307–308
Events, 173
Excitatory area, 56–57
Excitatory responses, 38–39
Excitatory-center, inhibitory-surround
 receptive field, 57

Expectation
  flavor perception and, 380
  music and, 308
  pain perception and, 353
Experience
  auditory grouping and, 304
  development of perception and, 89–90
  face perception and, 120
  motion perception and, 190–192
  neural processing and, 89–90
  odor perception and, 377, 380
  perceptual organization and, 105–106
  speech perception and, 326–328, 334
Experience-dependent plasticity, 64
  cortical body maps and, 342
  expertise hypothesis and, 89
  speech perception and, 333–334
  touch perception and, 342
  wayfinding and, 159
Expertise hypothesis, 89
Exploratory procedures (EPs), 348
Extrastriate body area (EBA), 84, 188
Eye movements
  attention and, 129–130
  corollary discharge theory and, 179–181
  face perception and, 117, 119
  medial superior temporal area, 184
  perceptual completion and, 146
  scanning a scene, 126–127
Eyes
  accommodation, 25–26
  focusing, 25–27
  frontal, 253–254
  lateral, 253–254
  misalignment of, 234
  parts of, 22–24
  receptors of, 7, 22–27, 34

Face neurons, 83
Face perception
  brain activity and, 113, 116–118
  brain area for, 65, 83–86, 89–90
  computer vision systems, 95
  experience and, 120
  infants and, 119–120
  neural response in, 66–68, 83
  speech perception and, 324
Facial expressions, 167
Falling phase of the action potential, 36
Familiar size, 230
Familiarization period, 255

Feature detectors
  higher-level neurons and, 65
  role in perception, 55, 62–63
  scene perception and, 108, 115–117
  selective rearing and, 64
Feature integration theory (FIT), 136–138
Feature search, 138
Feedback, 59, 80
FFA. See Fusiform face area (FFA)
Figure, 102–106
Figure-ground segregation, 102–106
Filiform papillae, 363–364
First harmonics, 264
Fixation, 126
Flavor perception, 368, 378–381
  brain and, 379–380
  cognition and, 380
  demonstrations of, 378
  expectation and, 380
  infants and, 382–383
  multimodal nature of, 379–380
  olfaction and, 378–379
  review questions on, 383
  sensory-specific satiety and, 380–381
  taste and, 378–380
Focal transcranial magnetic stimulation, 331
Focus of expansion (FOE), 150, 154–155
Focused attention stage, 136
Focusing, visual, 42
  demonstrations of, 26
  problems related to, 26, 42
  process of, 25–27
Foliate papillae, 363
Forced-choice method, 369
Forest Has Eyes, The (Doolittle), 106
Formant transitions, 319
Formants, 318
Fovea, 23, 45, 74–75
Foveal acuity, 41
Frequency
  auditory representation of, 272–273
  characteristic, 274
  interaural level difference, 290–294
  interaural time difference, 291, 293–294
  resonant, 268
  sound, 262
  tone and, 261
Frequency spectra, 263–264, 267

Frequency-matched noise, 280
Friends (television program), 87
Frontal cortex, 118
Frontal eyes, 253–254
Frontal lobe, 8, 86
Frontal operculum, 364
Functional magnetic resonance imaging (fMRI), 12, 75–76, 83–84, 113–115
  See also Brain imaging
Functional ultrasound imagery, 376
Fundamental frequency, 264, 266
Fundamental tone, 264
Fungiform papillae, 363–364
Fusiform face area (FFA), 65, 83–86, 89–90
  attention and, 133
  motion perception and, 188
  object perception and, 113, 116–118
  speech perception and, 324

Ganglion cells, 39–42, 62
Gap fill, 306
Gate control model of pain, 351–353
Geometric layout, 114
Gestalt psychology
  common fate, 102
  common region, 102
  good continuation, 100–101
  perceptual grouping, 98–102
  perceptual segregation, 102–105
  Pragnanz, 100
  proximity (nearness), 101
  similarity, 101
  uniform connectedness, 102
Gist of a scene, 107–108
Global image features, 108
Global optic flow, 177
Glomeruli, 374
Good continuation, 100–101
Google driverless car, 94
Gradient of flow, 150
Grasping, 161–163
Grasping task, 82
Grating acuity, 11–12, 343–344
Grating orientations, 114–115
Greebles, 89–90, 342
Grid cells, 158
Ground, 102–106
Grouping
  auditory, 302–304
  musical, 305–306
  perceptual, 98–102, 303–304

Habituation procedure, 144–146, 222–223
Hair cells, 270–272
Haptic perception, 342, 347–348, 350
Harmonics, 264, 281
Harry Potter and the Sorcerer's Stone (film), 140
Head direction cells, 158
Hearing
  development of, 284–285
  frequency and, 273–275
  importance of, 259–260
  indoor environments and, 298–300
  infants and, 284–285
  loss of, 281–283
  loudness and, 264–266
  metrical perception and, 310–311
  music and, 303–311
  perceptual process for, 260
  pitch and, 266, 276
  place theory of, 276–278
  range of, 262–265, 268
  review questions on, 267–268, 276, 285, 314
  sound localization and, 290–298, 302
  sound separation and, 301–304
  timbre and, 267
  transduction for, 271
  vision and, 312–314
  See also Auditory system; Sound
Hearing impairments
  age-related, 281
  hearing loss, 281–283
  hidden hearing loss, 282–283
  noise-induced, 282
Hereditary monochromatism, 212
Hering's primary colors, 206–207
Hermann grid, 16–18, 52–55, 248
Hidden hearing loss, 282–283
Hidden objects, 97
Higher harmonics, 264
Hippocampus, 86–88, 382
History of Psychology, A (Benjamin), 18
Holway and Boring experiment, 244–245
Homunculus, 342, 344
Honeybees, 42–43
Horizontal cells, 39, 50–51
Horopter, 236–237
How pathway, 80n, 82
HSV color solid, 201
Hubble Telescope, 42–43

Hue cancellation, 207–208
Hues, 200
Hypercolumn, 78
Hyperopia (farsightedness), 27
Hyperpolarization, 38
Hypnotic suggestion, 355
Hypothalamus, 379

Identity, 79
Illumination, 214–219
Illumination edges, 218
Illusions
  apparent movement, 99
  change blindness, 140
  of depth, 248–249
  of lightness, 51–52
  of motion, 175
  perceptual, 51–54
  of size, 248–252
  waterfall, 175
  See also Visual illusions
Illusory conjunctions, 137–138
Illusory contours, 99–100
Illusory motion, 174
Illusory perceptions, 18, 51–54
Image displacement signal (IDS), 179–181
Image-based factors, 103
Implied motion, 189–191
Implied polyphony, 302
Inattentional blindness, 138–141, 143
Inattentional blindness (Mack and Rock), 138
Incus, 268
Indirect sound, 298–300
Infants, 146
  actions and, 167–168
  binocularly fixate, 254–255
  biological motion perception of, 191–192
  categorical perception and, 332–333
  chemical sensitivity, 382–383
  color vision and, 222–223
  depth perception and, 254–256
  development of visual acuity, 43–45
  experience-dependent plasticity, 333–334
  face perception and, 119–120
  familiarization period, 255
  flavor perception and, 382–383
  habituation, 144–146
  hearing and, 284–285

  imitation of facial expressions, 167
  nonperceivers, 146
  perceivers, 146
  pictorial cues and, 255–256
  preferential reaching, 256
  speech perception and, 326–327, 332–334
  statistical learning, 326–327
  taste and, 382–383
  top-down processing, 168
  visual acuity, 43–45
Inference, 111–112
Inferior colliculus, 278–279
Inferotemporal (IT) cortex, 65, 83, 86
Inflammatory pain, 351
Inhibitory area, 56–57
Inhibitory responses, 38–39
Inhibitory-center, excitatory-surround receptive field, 57
Inner ear, 269–271
Inner hair cells, 270
Insula, 364
Intensity, 14
Intentions, predicting, 164–165
Interaural level difference, 290–294
Interaural time difference, 290–294
Inter-onset interval, 309
Intimacy time, 300
Invariance
  invariant information, 150–151
  viewpoint, 97
Invariant information, 150–151
Inverse projection problem, 96
Ions, 36
Ishihara plates, 212
Isolated congenital anosmia (ICA), 369
Isomerization, 27–28, 31, 204
ITD detectors, 295
ITD tuning curves, 295–296

Jeffress model, 294–296

Kinesthesis, 338
Knowledge
  action and, 154
  affordances and, 160
  attention and, 125, 128
  categorizing, 10
  color perception and, 216–217
  motion perception and, 190
  perceptual process and, 9–10
  scene perception and, 109–111

Knowledge (*Continued*)
  speech perception and, 322–329, 331
  task-related, 130
  wayfinding, 159
  See also Cognition; Top-down
    processing
Knowledge-based processing, 10

Lack of invariance, 320
Landmark discrimination problem,
    79–80
Landmarks, 152, 156–157
Language
  aphasias, 329
  event-related potential, 307
  learning the sounds of, 333–334
  metrical structure and, 311–312
  social gating hypothesis and, 334
  syntax, 306–307
  transitional probabilities of, 326–327
Lateral eyes, 253–254
Lateral geniculate nucleus, 34, 58–60,
    62, 80
Lateral inhibition, 49–55, 331
Lateral plexus, 50
Leisure noise, 282
Length estimation task, 82
Lens, 7, 22, 25
Lesioning, 79, 183
Light, 22, 25
  illusions of, 51
  intensity, 51
  mixing colored, 199–200
  perception of, 51
  properties of, 196–197
  reflectance curves, 198
  selective reflection and, 197
  transduction of, 27–28
  transmission curves, 198
Light-adapted sensitivity, 28
Light-from-above assumption, 109
Lightness constancy, 217–219
  demonstrations of, 219
  illumination and, 217–219
  ratio principle, 217–218
  shadows and, 218–219
  surface orientation, 219
Lightness perception, 218–219
Likelihood principle, 111
Limulus (horseshoe crab) experiment, 50,
    55–56
Load theory of attention, 142

Local disturbance in the optic array, 177
Local field potential (LFP), 134
Localizing sound. *See* Auditory
    localization
Location columns, 76–78
Location cues, 290–292, 294, 296, 302
Loudness, 264–265
Low-load tasks, 142
Luminance ramp, 54

Mach bands, 51, 248
Macrosmatic, 368
Macular degeneration, 23–24
Magnetic resonance imaging (MRI),
    75–76
Magnetoencephalography (MEG), 310
Magnification factor
  cortical, 74–76
  homunculus, 342, 344
Magnitude estimation, 15, 18
Malleus, 268
Man Who Mistook His Wife for a Hat, The
    (Sacks), 8
Manner of articulation, 319, 331
Maps
  attention, 134
  chemotopic, 375
  cognitive, 157–158
  cortical body, 341–342
  odor, 375
  odotopic, 375–376
  retinotopic, 74
  saliency, 128
  tonotopic, 274, 283
Masking, 107
McGurk effect, 323–324
Meaning
  context and, 324–325
  phonemes and, 324
  scene perception and, 106–107
  word perception and, 325–326, 328
Measuring perception, 13
  adjustment, 14
  classical psychophysical methods, 14
  constant stimuli, 14
  effect of selective adaptation, 62–63
  method of limits, 14
  thresholds, 13–15
Mechanisms, 14
Mechanoreceptors, 338–340, 348, 352–353
Medial geniculate nucleus, 278–279
Medial lemniscal pathway, 340

Medial superior temporal (MST) area,
    181, 184, 188, 190
Medial temporal lobe (MTL), 86–87
Meissner corpuscle, 338–339, 346
Melodic channeling, 303
Melody, 304–306, 308
Melody schema, 304
Memory
  hippocampus and, 86–87, 382
  olfaction and, 370, 376–377, 381–382
  taste and, 381–382
  vision and, 87–88
Memory color, 216–217
Merkel receptor, 338–339, 343–344
Metamerism, 204
Metamers, 204
Meter, 310–312
Method of limits, 14
Methods feature
  2-deoxyglucose technique, 375
  brain ablation, 79
  brain imaging, 75
  calcium imaging, 373
  color matching, 202
  dark adaptation curve measurement,
    28
  decibels and large ranges of pressures,
    262
  detection threshold measurement, 369
  double dissociations, 81
  event-related potential in language, 307
  habituation, 145
  head-turning preference procedure,
    310–311
  hue cancellation, 207
  magnitude estimation, 15
  masking stimulus, 107
  method of limits, 14
  microstimulation, 184
  neural frequency tuning curves, 274
  neural mind reading, 114
  neuron recording, 34
  optical imaging, 374
  precueing, 130
  preferential looking, 44
  preferential reaching, 256
  receptive fields, 58
  selective adaptation, 62
  spectral sensitivity curve measure-
    ment, 31
  tactile acuity measurement, 343
  transcranial magnetic stimulation, 183

Metrical structure, 310–312
Microsmatic, 368
Microstimulation, 184, 243
Middle ear, 268–269
Middle temporal (MT) area, 182–184, 188–190
Middle-ear muscles, 269
Mind-body problem, 88–89
Mirror neuron system, 164, 167
Mirror neurons, 163–165, 331
Misapplied size constancy scaling, 249–250
Modularity, 83–84
Modules, 83
Molecule detectors, 361
Monaural cues, 290, 292, 294
Monkeys
    attention experiments, 134–135
    brain ablation, 79
    cortical map experiment, 342
    depth perception and, 243, 253
    double dissociations, 81
    face perception experiments, 83
    hand grip experiments, 161–163
    inferotemporal (IT) cortex, 65
    mirror neurons, 163–164, 331
    motion perception experiments, 181–184
    multisensory experiments, 313
    pitch perception experiment, 279–280
    receptive fields and, 58, 69
    sound perception experiments, 297–298
    specificity coding, 366
    tactile object perception in, 344–345, 348–350
    visual cortex and, 68
    voice cells in, 330
Monochromatic light, 31
Monochromatism, 205, 212
Monocular cues, 229–234
    integration of, 233
    motion-produced cues, 232–233
    pictorial cues and, 229–232
Moon illusion, 252–253
Motion
    aftereffects of, 175, 190–191
    apparent, 174–176, 186–187
    attention and, 173
    biological, 187–189, 191–192
    depth cues and, 232–233
    illusory, 174

implied, 189–191
induced, 175
no-implied, 190
real, 174–176
See also Movement
Motion aftereffect, 190–191
Motion blindness, 174
Motion parallax, 232
Motion perception, 171–192
    aftereffects of, 175, 190–191
    aperture problem and, 186
    apparent motion and, 174–176, 186–187
    attention and, 173
    biological motion and, 187–189, 191–192
    brain activity and, 182–186, 188–189
    corollary discharge theory and, 179–181
    demonstrations of, 180–181, 185
    environmental information and, 173, 177
    event perception and, 173–174
    functions of, 171–173
    implied motion and, 189–191
    loss of, 174
    mechanisms for, 176–177
    moving dot experiments on, 182–184
    neural firing and, 178–179, 182–186
    optic array and, 177
    point-light walkers and, 187–188
    real, 174–176
    Reichardt detector and, 177–178
    representational momentum and, 190
    retina/eye information, 177
    review questions on, 182, 192
    shortest path constraint and, 186–187
Motion-produced cues, 232–233
Motor cortex, 331–332
Motor signal (MS), 179
Motor system, 348
Motor theory of speech perception, 331
Movement
    driving, 154–155
    flow and, 151
    focus of expansion, 150
    gradient of flow, 150
    invariant information, 150–151
    music and, 290, 310–311
    optic flow, 150–154
    perception and, 150, 152–153
    relative to the objects, 150

walking, 153–154
wayfinding, 155–160
See also Motion
Movement parallax, 254
Movement-based cues, 229
Moving observer, 150–151
Müller-Lyer illusion, 248–250
Multidimensional stimuli, 86
Multimodal nature
    of flavor perception, 379–380
    of pain, 355
    of speech perception, 322–323
Multisensory interactions, 312–314
Multivariate pattern analysis (MVPA), 358
Music
    acoustics and, 300
    beat, 309–310
    expectation and, 308
    grouping, 305–306
    melody, 304–306
    meter, 310–311
    movement and, 290, 310–311
    organization of, 304–310
    pain perception and, 354
    perception and, 300
    phrases, 305
    pitch perception and, 302–304
    rhythm, 309
    scale illusion, 303
    tonality, 306
Musical syntax, 306–308
Myopia (nearsightedness), 27
Mythbusters (television program), 28–29

Naloxone, 355–356
Nasal pharynx, 378
Navigation
    brain areas for, 157–159
    driving and, 154–155
    environment and, 160
    individual differences in, 159–160
    walking and, 153–154
    wayfinding, 155–157
Nerve fiber, 33–36
Nervous system
    color perception and, 219–222
    olfaction and, 379
    taste perception and, 379
Neural circuits, 39, 42, 57–58
Neural code, 65, 68, 158, 165, 295, 331, 362, 367

Neural convergence. *See* Convergence
Neural frequency tuning curve, 274
Neural maps, 74
Neural mind reading, 114–115
Neural plasticity, 64
Neural point, 213
Neural processing, 7–8
  color coding, 209–211
  contextual modulation, 68–69
  convergence and, 39–42
  correlations, 88–89
  experience and, 89–90
  inferotemporal (IT) cortex, 65
  lateral inhibition and, 49–55
  memory and, 86–88
  orientation columns, 78
  population coding, 66–67
  receptive fields and, 55–60, 62, 68–69
  review questions on, 55
  sensory coding, 65
  sparse coding, 66, 68
  specificity coding, 66–67
Neurogenesis, 362
Neuron, orientation turning curve, 61
Neurons
  action potentials and, 34–36
  audiovisual mirror, 163–164, 331
  bimodal, 380
  binocular, 242–243
  delay units, 178–179
  double-opponent, 211
  electrical signals in, 33–34, 38–39
  face-detecting, 65–68, 83
  higher-level, 65
  ITD tuning curves, 295–296
  mirror, 163–165, 331
  motion perception and, 178–186
  multisensory interactions, 313–314
  opponent, 209–211
  orientation turning curve, 60
  output units, 178–179
  perceptual experience and, 64
  pitch, 279
  properties of, 62
  real-motion, 181
  receptive fields and, 313
  receptor sites, 38
  recording electrical signals, 34–36
  single-opponent, 211
  speech and, 330–331
  transmission between, 37–39
Neuropathic pain, 351

Neuropsychology, 81
Neurotransmitters, 37–38
Newborns. *See* Infants
Nocebo effect, 353
Nociceptive pain, 351
Nociceptors, 351–352
No-implied motion, 190
Noise, 276
  amplitude-modulated, 276
  frequency-matched, 280
  leisure, 282
Noise-induced hearing loss, 282
Noise-vocoded speech, 327–328
Noncorresponding points, 236–237
Non-decision-point landmarks, 155–157
Nonspectral colors, 200
Nontasters, 367–368
Nucleus of the solitary tract, 364

Object discrimination problem, 79–80
Object perception, 92–122
  action and, 160–163
  affordances and, 160–161
  blurred objects, 97
  brain activity and, 113–116, 119
Object perception
  computer vision systems, 94–96
  demonstrations of, 93, 105, 109
  face perception and, 95, 105, 116–120
  focused attention stage, 136
  hidden objects, 97
  inverse projection problem and, 96–97
  machine vision and, 96–97
  perceptual organization and, 97–106
  preattentive stage, 136
  process of, 136–137
  review questions on, 106, 112, 120–121
  scenes and, 106–112
  touch perception and, 347–350
  viewpoint invariance, 97
Object unity, 144
Oblique effect, 11–12
Observing
  action in others, 163–164
  pain in others, 357
  touch in others, 350
Occipital cortex, 8, 59, 86, 118
Occlusion, 228–229
Octave, 266
Ocular dominance, 78*n*
Ocular dominance columns, 78*n*
Oculomotor cues, 228–229

Odor discrimination, 370
Odor map, 375
Odor objects, 372
Odors
  detecting, 370
  identifying, 370–372
  organization of, 371–372, 374–376
  recognition profile of, 373–374
  recognizing, 370, 377
  representing, 376
Odotopic map, 375–376
Olfaction, 361–362, 368–382
  brain and, 375–377, 379–380
  demonstrations of, 370
  detecting odors, 369–370
  flavor perception and, 368, 378–381
  functions of, 369
  genetic differences in, 370–371
  identifying odors, 370–372, 377
  importance of, 368–369
  infant perception of, 382–383
  memory and, 370, 376–377, 381–382
  molecular features and, 371–375
  odor discrimination and, 370
  odor quality and, 371
  receptor neurons for, 370–374,
    376–377
  review questions on, 378
Olfactory bulb, 372–377
Olfactory cortex, 372
Olfactory mucosa, 372–375, 378, 380
Olfactory pathway, 379
Olfactory receptor neurons, 372–374,
  380
Olfactory system, 371–376
  brain and, 375–376
  odor object perception, 372–373
  receptor neurons and, 372–374
  representing odors, 68
Ommatidia, 50
100-Car Naturalistic Driving Study, 143
Onset time, 302, 309
Opioids, 355–356
Opponent neurons, 209–211
Opponent-process theory, 201–202,
  206–209
Opsin, 27, 30, 203
Optic array, 177
Optic flow, 150–154
Optic nerve, 23, 56, 58, 62
Optical brain imaging, 11
  physiological, 12

Optical imaging, 374
Oral capture, 379
Orbitofrontal cortex, 376, 379–381
Organ of Corti, 270–271, 282
Orientation
  contextual modulation, 68
  receptive fields and, 60–61
  selective adaptation and, 62–63
  selective rearing and, 64–65
Orientation columns, 76–78
Orientation turning curve, 60–61, 63
Ossicles, 268–269
Outer ear, 268
Outer hair cells, 270
Outer segments, 22
Output units, 178
Oval window, 268
Overt attention, 126

Pacinian corpuscle, 340, 343, 345
Pain perception, 351–356, 358–359
  affective (emotional) component of,
    355
  attention and, 353–354
  brain and, 354–356
  definition of pain, 351
  direct pathway model of, 351–352
  emotional components of, 354, 357
  empathy and, 357
  endorphins and, 356
  expectation and, 353
  gate control model of, 351–353
  hypnotic suggestion and, 355
  multimodal nature of, 355
  music and, 354
  observing in others, 357
  opioids and, 355–356
  phantom limbs and, 352
  placebo effect and, 353, 356
  review questions on, 358–359
  sensory component of, 355
  social pain, 357–358
  types of, 351
  See also Touch perception
Paint, mixing, 198–200
Papillae, 363–364
Parabelt area, 279
Parahippocampal cortex (PHC), 113–114
Parahippocampal place area (PPA), 84,
  87, 113–114
Parietal lobe, 8
Parietal reach region, 161

Partial color constancy, 215–216
Passive touch, 347
PC fiber, 340
Peering amplitude, 254
Penumbra, 219
Perceived brightness, 18
Perceived contrast, 132–133
Perceived magnitude, 15
Perception
  biological maturation and, 89
  bottom-up processing, 10
  cognitive influence on, 12–13
  convergence and, 39–42
  defined, 5
  demonstrations of, 9
  difference between physical and,
    17–18
  ecological approach to, 149–156
  environmental information and,
    89–90
  experience and, 89–90
  feature detectors and, 62–65
  illusory, 18
  inference in, 111–112
  introduction to, 3–5
  lateral inhibition and, 51–55
  measurement of, 13–18, 62–63
  movement and, 150, 152–153
  performance and, 166
  process of, 5–11
  psychophysical approach to, 13–15
  receptors and, 27
  responses and, 166–167
  reverberation time and, 300
  review questions on, 13, 18–19
  top-down processing, 10
Perceptions, 98–99
Perceptual capacity, 142
Perceptual completion, 144–146
Perceptual constancy, 321
Perceptual grouping, 98–102, 303–304
Perceptual illusions, 51–54
Perceptual load, 142–143
Perceptual organization, 68, 97
  color perception and, 196
  defined, 98
  experience and, 105–106
  Gestalt principles of, 98–105
  grouping, 98–102
  motion perception and, 187–188
  music and, 305
  segregation, 98, 102–105

Perceptual process
  beginning of, 21–22
  dark adaptation and, 28–31
  demonstrations of, 9
  depth perception and, 242
  description of, 6–10
  diagrams of, 5–6, 9, 11, 62
  knowledge and, 9
  light and, 22
  spectral sensitivity, 31–33
  study of, 10–12
  transduction and, 27–28
  visual receptors and, 22–27
Perceptual process (cycle), 11, 183, 242
Perceptual segregation, 102–105
Performance, perception and, 166
Periodic sounds, 267
Periodic tones, 264
Peripheral acuity, 41
Peripheral retina, 23
Peripheral tasks, 140
Permeability, 36
Persistence of vision, 107
Perspective convergence, 230
Phantom limbs, 352
Phase locking, 272, 277–279
Phenomenological reports, 16
Phenylthiocarbamide (PTC), 367–368
Pheromones, 369, 377
Phonemes, 320–321, 324
  categorical perception of, 322, 332–333
  infant perception of, 333–334
  meaning and, 324
  neural response in, 331
  phonetic features, 331
  variability problem and, 320–321
Phonemic restoration effect, 324
Phonetic boundary, 322
Phonetic features, 331
Phonetic symbols, 320
Photons, 204
Phrases, 305, 308
Physical regularities, 108–110
Physical tasks and judgments, 17
Physical-social pain overlap hypothesis,
  357–358
Physiology-perception relationship,
  11–12, 55, 62, 182, 243
  attention and, 133–135
  color perception and, 202–203, 206–207,
  209–210
  depth perception and, 242–243

Physiology-perception relationship
  (Continued)
  differences, 17–18
  hearing and, 294
  physical activity and, 149
  sound and, 260–264
  stimuli and, 11–12, 62
  taste perception and, 363–367
  touch and pain, 351–358
Pictorial cues, 229–232, 255–256
Pigment epithelium, 31
Pinnae, 268, 293
Piriform cortex, 376–377
Pitch
  brain mechanisms determining,
    279–280
  defined, 266, 305
  perception of, 277–278
  place and, 276
  similarity of, 302–304
  temporal information and, 277
Pitch neurons, 279
Place cells, 158
Place codes, 296
Place fields, 158
Place of articulation, 319, 331
Place theory of hearing, 277
  defined, 276
  physiological evidence for, 276
Placebo, 353
Placebo effect, 353, 356
Plasticity. *See* Experience-dependent
    plasticity
Point-light walkers, 187–188
Ponzo illusion, 250–251
Population coding, 66–67, 296, 364–365
Posterior belt area, 297–298
Pragnanz, 100–101
Preattentive stage, 136
Precedence effect, 289, 299
Precueing, 130–132
Preferential looking (PL) technique, 43–44
Preferential reaching, 256
Presbycusis, 281–282
Presbyopia, 27, 281
Pretty Woman (film), 140
Primary auditory cortex, 278
Primary olfactory area, 376
Primary receiving area, 8
Principles
  of common fate, 102
  of common region, 102

of good continuation, 100–101
of good figure, 100
of *Pragnanz*, 100–101
of proximity, 101
of representation, 7
of simplicity, 100–101
of transformation, 7
of uniform connectedness, 102
of uninvariance, 204
Principles of Psychology (James), 125
Propagated responses, 34–35
Proprioception, 338
Prosopagnosia, 83–84
Protanopia, 212–213
Proust effect, 381–382
Proximal stimulus, 7, 21
Proximity (nearness), 101
Psychophysics, 14, 31, 62
Pupil, 22
Pure tones, 261–262
Purkinje shift, 32

RA1 fibers, 339
Random-dot stereograms, 239–241, 255
Rapidly adapting (RA) fibers, 339
Rarefaction, 261
Ratio principle, 217–218
Rat-man demonstration, 9–11, 13
Reaching, 161–163
Reaction time, 16
Real motion, 174–176
Real-motion neuron, 181
Receptive fields, 55–56
  center-surround, 56–58
  excitatory area, 56–57
  flexible, 68–69
  inhibitory area, 56–57
  location columns, 78
  research on, 56, 58–59
  review questions on, 69
  stimuli and, 58
  striate cortex, 60–61
Receptor processes
  bottom-up processing, 10
  description of, 7–8
  diagrams of, 7
  top-down processing, 10
Receptor sites, 363–364
Receptors
  focusing light onto, 25
  olfactory, 362
  opponent responding and, 209–210

perception and, 27
review questions on, 33
rod and cone, 22–24, 28–30
sensory, 4, 7, 34
skin, 338–342, 348–350
taste, 362–366, 368, 379
visual, 22–25
Recognition, 8, 16
  odors and, 370, 373–374, 377
  speech systems for, 317
  spoken word, 329
Recognition profile, 373
Recognition testing, 15–16
Recording electrodes, 34–35
Reference electrodes, 34
Reflectance, 217
Reflectance curves, 198
Reflectance edges, 218
Reflection
  light, 7
  selective, 197
Refractive myopia, 27
Refractory period, 36
Regularities, 128, 308, 328, 222
Regularities in the environment
  light-from-above assumption, 109
  physical, 108–110
  semantic, 109–111
Reichardt detector, 177–179
Relative disparity, 238–239
Relative height, 229–230
Relative size, 230, 252–253
Representational momentum, 190
Resolved harmonics, 277–278
Resonance, 268
Resonant frequency, 268
Resting potential, 34
Retina, 7, 23, 50, 58
  ambiguous stimuli, 96–97
  binocular cues and, 235–241
  motion of stimuli across, 178–180
Retinal, 27, 30, 203–204
Retinitis pigmentosa, 24
Retinotopic map, 74
Retronasal route, 378
Return to the tonic, 306
Reverberation time, 300
Reversible figure-ground, 103
Review questions
  action, 149, 160, 168–169
  attention, 135, 146
  auditory localization, 301

auditory system, 267–268, 276, 285, 314
chemical senses, 368
color perception, 201, 213–214, 223
cutaneous senses, 351, 358–359
depth perception, 243, 256–257
flavor perception, 383
hearing, 267–268, 276, 285, 314
motion perception, 182, 192
neural processing, 55
object perception, 106, 112, 120–121
olfaction, 378
pain perception, 358–359
perception, 13, 18–19
speech perception, 324, 334
taste, 368, 383
touch perception, 351, 358–359
vision, 45–46
Reward value of food, 381
Rhythm, 309
Rising phase of the action potential, 36
Robotic vehicles, 94–95
Rod and cone receptors, 22–24, 28–30, 32
Rod monochromats, 30
Rod spectral sensitivity, 32
Rod vision, 41–42
Rod-cone break, 30
Rods, 22
convergence and, 39–41
dark adaptation and, 28–30
spectral sensitivity and, 31–32
Ruffini cylinder, 340

SA1 fibers, 339
Saccadic eye movement, 126
Salience, 124, 127–129
Saliency maps, 128
Salty tastes, 362, 366, 382
Same-object attention, 132
Saturation, 200–201
Scale illusion, 303
Scene, 107
Scene perception, 106–116
geometric layout of, 114
gist of a scene, 107–108
global image features, 108
meaning and, 106–107
navigation through, 114
regularities in the environment, 108–111
Scene schema, 109–110, 128–129

Secondary olfactory area, 376
Secondary somatosensory cortex (S2), 340–342
Segregation, perceptual, 98, 102–105
Selective adaptation
effects of, 62–63
measurement of, 62
Selective rearing, 63–65
Selective reflection, 197
Selective transmission, 198
Self-produced information, 151–152
Semantic encoding, 115–116
Semantic regularities, 109–111
Semitones, 305
Sensations, 5–6, 98–99
Senses
balance and, 152
primary receiving areas, 8
Sensory coding, 65
Sensory component of pain, 355
Sensory receptors, 4, 7, 34
Sensory system, 348
Sensory-specific satiety, 380–381
Sentence context, 325
Shadow-casting, 52
Shadowing, 325
Shadows
depth cues and, 231–232, 256
lightness constancy and, 218–219
penumbra, 219
three-dimensionality and, 231–232
Sharply tuned neurons, 296
Shortest path constraint, 186–187
Similarity, 101
Simple cortical cells, 60, 62
Simpsons, The (television program), 87
Sine wave, 261
Single-opponent neurons, 211
6-n-propylthiouracil (PROP), 367–368
Size constancy, 246–249
Size perception, 244–253
demonstrations of, 247, 250
depth perception and, 243–253
Holway and Boring experiment on, 244–246
illusions of depth and, 248–253
misapplied size constancy scaling and, 249–250
size constancy and, 246–250
size-distance scaling and, 247
visual angles and, 244–245
Size-distance scaling, 247

Skin
layers of, 338–340
mechanoreceptors in, 338–340, 342, 348, 352–353
nerve pathways from, 339–341
vibration of, 345
Slowly adapting (SA) fibers, 339
Social gating hypothesis, 334
Social interaction, learning and, 334
Social pain, 357–358
Sodium-potassium pump, 37
Somatosensory cortex, 340–342, 349
Somatosensory receiving area (S1), 340–342
Somatosensory system, 338, 350
Sonar, 254
Sound
amplitude of, 261–262, 264–265
aperiodic, 267
definitions of, 260
demonstrations of, 326
direct, 298–299
frequency of, 261–262
indirect, 298–300
language learning and, 333–334
localizing, 290–298, 302
loudness and, 264–266
loudspeakers and, 299
metrical perception and, 310–311
organization of, 326
perceptual aspects of, 264
periodic, 267
physical aspects of, 260–264
pressure changes and, 260–261
pure tones and, 261–262
review questions on, 285
separating sources of, 301–304
Sound amplitude, 262
Sound frequency, 262
Sound level, 263
Sound pressure level, 263
Sound spectrograms, 318–319, 321–322, 325, 327
Sound waves, 261
Sour tastes, 362, 366
Space ambiguous (SA) objects, 114
Space defining (SD) objects, 114
Spaciousness factor, 300
Sparse coding, 66, 68
Spatial attention, 130–132
Spatial cues, 346–347
Spatial layout hypothesis, 114

Spatial organization
   scene perception and, 108, 114
   visual cortex and, 74–75, 77
Spatial updating, 154
Specificity coding, 66–67, 364–366
Spectral colors, 200
Spectral cues, 293–294
Spectral sensitivity, 31–33
Spectral sensitivity curves, 31–32
Spectrometer, 31
Speech perception, 317–334
   acoustic signals and, 318–322, 324
   action and, 331
   audiovisual, 323
   auditory information and, 323
   brain activity and, 323–324, 328–332
   categorical perception and, 322
   degraded speech, 327–328
   demonstrations of, 326
   development of, 326–327, 332–334
   dual-stream model of, 330
   effects of experience on, 326, 328, 334
   face perception and, 324
   infants and, 326–327, 332–334
   motor theory of, 331
   multimodal nature of, 322–323
   perceptual constancy in, 321
   phonemes and, 320–322, 324, 331, 334
   production of speech and, 331–332
   review questions on, 324, 334
   segmentation and, 325–326
   sentence context, 325–328
   social gating hypothesis and, 334
   sound spectograms and, 318–319,
     321–322, 325, 327
   stimulus dimensions of, 317–320
   temporal information and, 328
   units of speech and, 319–320
   variability problem and, 320–322
   vision and, 323
   word perception, 325–327
Speech recognition systems, 317
Speech segmentation, 325–326
Speechreading, 312
Spinothalamic pathway, 340–341
SPL. *See* Sound pressure level
Spontaneous activity, 36
Spontaneous looking preferences, 44
Staircase illusion, 51
Stapes, 268
Static orientation-matching task, 81
Statistical learning, 326–327

Statistical properties, 306, 326, 328, 332, 333
Stereopsis, 239–240, 243
Stereoscope, 240
Stereoscopic depth perception, 234–235
Stimulus
   behavioral, 11–12
   constant stimuli, 14
   description of, 16–17
   diagrams of, 11
   distal, 6–7, 21
   distributed representation, 84–85
   identity of, 15–16
   interacting with, 17
   modules for processing information
     about, 83–84
   multidimensional, 86
   perception and, 113, 132–133
   perceptual magnitude of, 15
   physiological, 11–12
   proximal, 7, 21
   reaction time, 16
   receptive fields and, 58
   speech, 318–319
Stimulus-perception relationship, 11–13,
   62, 183, 242
Stimulus-physiology relationship,
   11–12, 62
Strabismus, 234
Streams, information, 79–81
Striate cortex, 59–61, 74
   hypercolumns, 78
   location columns, 77–79
   motion perception and, 188
   orientation columns, 77
   what pathway, 79
   where pathway, 80
Stroboscope, 99
Structural encoding, 115–116
Structuralism, 98–99
Subcortical structures, 278
Subtractive color mixture, 199
Superior colliculus, 59
Superior olivary nucleus, 278–279
Superior temporal gyrus, 314
Superior temporal sulcus (STS), 86, 118,
   188, 324, 330
Supertasters, 368
Surface geometry, 114
Surface texture, 345–347
Survival, motion perception and, 171, 173

Sweet blindness, 367
Sweet tastes, 362, 366, 368
Swinging room experiment, 152–153
Synapse, 37
Synaptic vesicles, 37
Syntax, 306–307

Tactile acuity, 343
   attention and, 349–350
   cortical mechanisms for, 344, 348–350
   methods of measuring, 343
   receptor mechanisms for, 343–344
Task characteristics, 141–142
Task-irrelevant stimuli, 141
Taste, 361–368
   basic qualities of, 362–363
   demonstrations of, 378
   flavor perception and, 378–380
   genetic differences in, 367–368
   individual differences in, 367–368
   infants and, 382–383
   memory and, 381–382
   neural code for, 363–367
   olfaction and, 378–379
   physiology of, 363–367
   population coding, 364–365, 367
   preference and, 368
   review questions on, 368, 383
   specialized receptors and, 368
   specificity coding, 364–367
Taste buds, 363–364, 367–368
Taste cells, 363–364
Taste pathway, 379–380
Taste pores, 364
Taste quality, 362–363
Tasters, 367–368
Tectorial membrane, 270
Temporal coding, 277
Temporal cues, 346–347
Temporal lobe, 8
Test period, 255
Texture gradient, 231, 248
Texture perception, 344–347
Theory of unconscious inference, 111
Thresholds, 13
   absolute, 14
   audibility curve and, 284
   difference, 14
   frequency, 265–266
   measurement of, 15
   wavelengths and, 31–32
Tiling, 78–79

Timbre, 267, 302
Time, music and, 309
Tip links, 271
Tonal hierarchy, 306
Tonality, 306
Tone chroma, 266
Tone height, 266
Tongue, 363–364
Tonic, 306–307
Tonotopic map, 274, 283
Top-down processing, 10
  illusory conjunctions and, 138
  infants and, 168
  pain perception and, 353
  perception and, 10
  receptor processes, 10
Topographical agnosia, 157
Touch perception, 337–359
  active touch and, 347
  cortical body maps and, 341–342
  cortical mechanisms for, 344–345
  demonstrations of, 344, 347
  detail perception and, 342–344
  haptic exploration and, 347–348
  importance of, 337–338
  measuring acuity of, 343
  nerve pathways for, 339–341
  object perception and, 347–350
  observing in others, 350, 357
  pain perception and, 351–358
  passive touch and, 347
  review questions on, 351, 358–359
  skin receptors and, 338–341
  texture perception and, 344–347
  vibration perception and, 344–345
  See also Cutaneous senses
Trajectories of notes, 306
Transcranial magnetic stimulation
    (TMS), 183, 189, 331–332
Transduction, 7, 27
  auditory, 271
  of light, 27–28
  visual, 27
Transitional probabilities, 326–327
Transmission cells, 352
Transmission curves, 198
Traveling wave, 272–273
Trichromatic theory of color vision,
    201–207, 209
Trichromats, 205
Triple meter, 310
Tritanopia, 212–213

Tuning curves
  disparity, 242
  ITD, 295–296
  neural frequency, 274
2-deoxyglucose technique, 374–375
Two-flash illusion, 312
Two-point thresholds, 343–344
Tympanic membrane, 268–269

U. S. Occupational Safety and Health
    Agency (OSHA), 282
Ultraviolet light, 43
Umami tastes, 362
Unconscious inference, 111
Uncrossed disparity, 237
Unexpected Visitor, An (Repin), 129
Uniform connectedness, 102
Unilateral dichromat, 212
Unresolved harmonics, 277–278, 281

Value, 201
Ventral pathway, 80–82, 161
Ventriloquism effect, 312
Ventrolateral nucleus, 340
Vestibular system, 311
Vibration perception, 344–345
Video microscopy, 367
Viewpoint invariance, 97
Visible light, 22
Visible spectrum, 31, 196–198, 200, 202,
    213, 220
Vision
  attention and, 127–129
  auditory localization and, 294
  balance and, 152–153
  color perception and, 195–224
  dark adaptation and, 28–31
  depth perception and, 227–255
  feature detectors and, 63–65
  hearing and, 312–314
  hippocampus and, 87–88
  motion perception and, 177
  persistence of, 107
  size perception and, 243–253
  speech perception and, 323
  steps in process of, 21–22
  See also Visual system
Visual acuity
  cones and, 41–42
  development of, 43–45
Visual angle, 244–248
Visual attention. See Attention

Visual capture, 312
Visual cortex, 59–60
Visual direction strategy, 153
Visual evoked potential (VEP),
    44–45
Visual form agnosia, 8–9
Visual illusions, 248–249
  Ames room, 251–252
  apparent movement, 99
  Chevreul (staircase) illusion,
    51–55
  Hermann grid, 52, 248
  Mach bands, 51
  moon illusion, 252–253
  Müller-Lyer illusion, 248–250
  Ponzo illusion, 250–251
  waterfall illusion, 175
Visual impairments
  blind spots, 24–25
  color blindness, 195–196, 211–213
  detached retina, 31
  macular degeneration, 24
  retinitis pigmentosa, 24
  strabismus, 234
Visual masking stimulus, 107
Visual pathway, 34
Visual perception
  dark adaptation, 28–31
  demonstrations of, 24–26, 41
  infants and, 43–45
  process of, 21–22
  review questions on, 45–46
  spectral sensitivity, 31–33
Visual pigments, 7, 23
  bleaching of, 30–31
  color perception and, 203–205
  molecules of, 27–28, 31
  regeneration of, 30–31
Visual receiving area, 34, 59
Visual receptors, 22
Visual salience, 127–129
Visual scanning, 127
  covert attention, 126
  fixation, 126
  overt attention, 126
  saccadic eye movements, 126
Visual search, 137
Visual system
  balance and, 152
  color perception and, 201–205, 209,
    214, 216–219, 221
  cortical columns and, 76–78

Visual system (*Continued*)
  diagrams of, 59
  focusing, 25–27
  impairments of, 23–25, 27, 31,
      195–196, 211–213, 234
  magnification factor, 74–76
  motion perception and, 178–180
  receptors of, 7, 22–23, 25–26
  representing objects, 65–68
  spatial organization, 74
  visual pathway, 34
  See also Eyes; Vision
Visual transduction, 27
Visuomotor grip cells, 163
Vocal tract, 318
Voice area, 330
Voice cells, 330
Voice onset time (VOT), 322–323, 332

Vowels, 318, 320
Voxels, 75, 114–115

Walking
  blind experiment in, 153–154
  environmental information and, 153–154
  navigation and, 153–154
Walleye, 234
Waterfall illusion, 175
Wavelengths, 22, 31–32, 197–200,
      203–205, 208–210, 213, 220–221
"Waves" (Hurskainen), 101
Wayfinding
  brain and, 156–159
  environmental information and,
      155–157
  individual differences in, 159–160
  landmarks, 155–157

Wernicke's aphasia, 329
Wernicke's area, 329
What auditory pathway, 297–298
What pathway, 79, 82, 298
Where auditory pathway, 297–298
Where pathway, 80, 82, 298
Whiteout conditions, 243–244
Whole-hand prehension, 162
Wizard of Oz (film), 140
Word deafness, 329
Word perception, 325
  breaks between words, 325–326
  meaningfulness and, 325–326, 328
  noise-vocoded speech, 327–328
  words in sentences, 325–326

Young-Helmholtz theory, 202